S0-BYJ-279

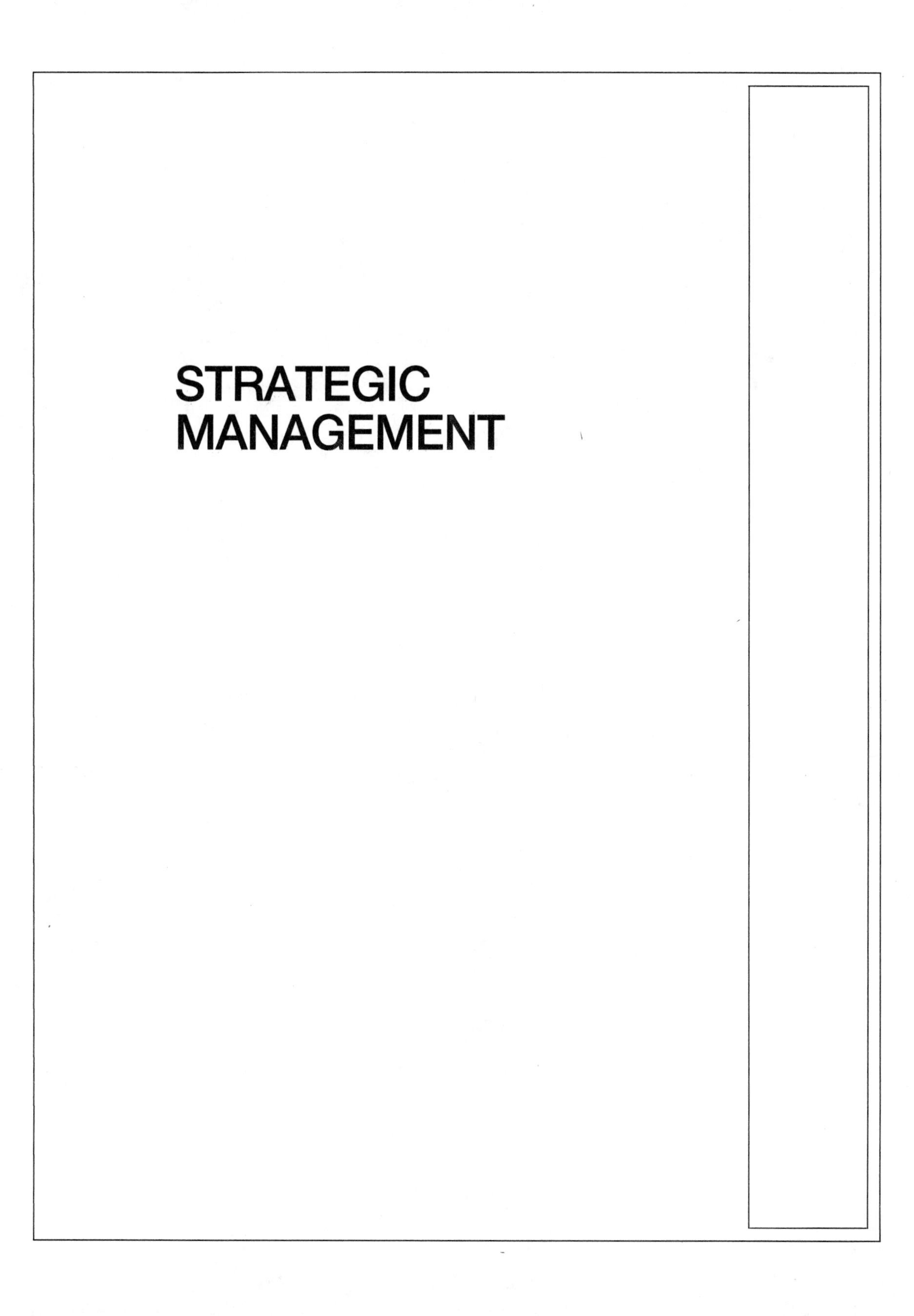

STRATEGIC MANAGEMENT

Second Edition

STRATEGIC MANAGEMENT

Fred R. David
Auburn University

Merrill Publishing Company
A Bell & Howell Information Company
Columbus Toronto London Melbourne

Published by Merrill Publishing Company
A Bell & Howell Information Company
Columbus, Ohio 43216

This book was set in Goudy Old Style and Helvetica.
Administrative Editor: John Stout
Production Coordinator: Anne Daly
Art Coordinator: Jim Hubbard
Cover Designer: Cathy Watterson
Text Designer: Connie Young

Library of Congress Catalog Card Number: 88-63338
International Standard Book Number: 0-675-20938–2
Printed in the United States of America
1 2 3 4 5 6 7 8 9—92 91 90 89

To my family for their love and forbearance
Joy
Forest
Byron
Meredith

Preface

PERSONAL NOTE TO PROFESSORS

Strategic Management (Second Edition) is designed for both undergraduate and graduate courses in business policy and strategic management. This second edition features updated chapters, an updated Cohesion Case, new Experiential Exercises, new cases, and a new section (Part Five) on Case Analysis; ancillaries include an *Instructor's Manual and Test Bank*, and a set of *Transparency Masters*.

Updated Chapters

The second edition places greater emphasis on business ethics, strategy-culture linkages, strategy-production relationships, behavioral aspects of strategic management, bases for gaining competitive and comparative advantage, international strategy issues, and strategy development in small businesses. There is much less repetition and 40 percent new material. Each chapter now begins with Learning Objectives and Notable Quotes and ends with Key Terms and Concepts and Issues for Review and Discussion. Chapters 7 and 8 on strategy implementation have been totally rewritten and reorganized. The information on computer assisted strategic planning (a separate chapter in the first edition) has now been integrated appropriately into other chapters and updated.

Hundreds of new examples in this edition bring strategic management to life and capture the reader's interest. These examples reflect contemporary strategic-management issues, such as takeover mania, leveraged buyouts, middle manager layoffs, information technology, foreign competition, deconglomeration, globalization of industries, and comparative advantage. This edition combines traditional planning concepts with state-of-the-art developments in strategic management, such as the Quantitative Strategic Planning Matrix (QSPM). An improved, comprehensive model of the strategic-management process now appears in all chapters to guide the reader. An average of twenty suggested readings from 1986–1988 are provided at the end of each chapter.

Updated Cohesion Case

This edition features a 1988 Cohesion Case on Ponderosa, an international chain of steakhouse restaurants. Appearing at the end of Chapter 1, the Cohesion Case allows students to apply strategic-management concepts and techniques to a real organization as chapter material is covered in class. This integrative or "cohesive" approach readies students for case analysis. Ponderosa was recently acquired by Asher Edelman in a hostile takeover, so the updated case is especially timely and current.

New Experiential Exercises

Twelve new Experiential Exercises and nineteen improved Experiential Exercises appear in the second edition, the only business policy textbook that currently offers classroom Experiential Exercises centered around leading problems and issues facing owners of businesses and chief executive officers today. Many of the Experiential Exercises apply chapter material to the Cohesion Case. Students have found these exercises to be pertinent, relevant, interesting, challenging, contemporary, and enjoyable.

Instructor's Manual

An *Instructor's Manual* gives answers to the end of chapter discussion questions and answers to all the Experiential Exercises. It also includes a twenty-page glossary that defines all key terms and concepts in the text and more than one thousand true-false, multiple choice, and essay test questions. The *Instructor's Manual* gives alternative course outlines and extensive case teaching notes for all cases in the book. The teacher's notes feature detailed analyses of each case, classroom discussion questions for each case, an internal and external evaluation of each company, an epilogue for each company, and much more helpful information for each case.

Case Analysis

Part Five offers guidelines on how to analyze a business policy case, how to give an oral presentation, and how to prepare a written case analysis. New suggestions for speaking at an effective rate and finding an appropriate tone, managing body language, speaking from notes, constructing visual aids, and answering questions are given. Part Five also includes a list of fifty special "tips for success" in case analysis.

New Cases

Thirty-five *up-to-date cases,* covering a broad spectrum of organizations and environments, are provided in this text. All but one of the cases, Winston Glass Company, are undisguised; students can look up real names and real people in the library. New to this edition are twenty-five current cases on such well known firms as Seagram, BankAmerica, Morton Thiokol, Walt-Disney, PaineWebber, and Sears, Roebuck. Ten cases from the first edition, including Winnebago, Playboy Enterprises, The Limited, Bevell's Hardware, and Super 8 Motels, have been updated. The thirty-five cases include twelve small business cases, twenty-one international strategy cases, thirteen cases on manufacturing firms, and twenty-two cases on service firms. The cases, most written exclusively for this text and targeted to reflect current strategic-management problems and practices, are organized clearly by type of industry.

Paperback Editions Available

For those instructors who desire a text containing only concepts or cases, separate paperback editions of the concepts and case sections of this text are available. *Concepts of Strategic Management* (Second Edition) contains all nine chapters of *Strategic Management* (Second Edition), including the Ponderosa Cohesion Case and Experiential Exercises. *Cases in Strategic Management* (Second Edition) includes all 35 cases as well as a separate section on case analysis.

I invite your suggestions, ideas, comments, or questions about any part of this text or the ancillary materials. Merrill Publishing Company and I are dedicated to providing the very best business policy text on the market and we need your input to achieve this goal.

PERSONAL NOTE TO STUDENTS

Welcome to business policy. This is a challenging and exciting course that will allow you to function as the owner of a business or chief executive officer in many different organizations. Strategic decisions determine the direction and competitive position of an enterprise for a long time. Decisions to expand geographically, to diversify, or to acquire a competitor are examples of strategic decisions. Your major task is business policy will be *to make strategic decisions* and *to justify those decisions through oral and written communication.* You will be called upon in class to demonstrate how your strategic decisions could be successfully implemented.

Strategic decision making occurs in all types and sizes of organizations, from General Motors to a small hardware store. Strategic decisions affect lives and jobs, and even an organization's very survival, so the stakes are high. The primacy of strategic decisions makes this course especially exciting and challenging.

In business policy you can look forward to making strategic decisions both as an individual and as a member of a team. No matter how hard employees work, an organization is in real trouble if strategic decisions are not made effectively. Doing the right things (effectiveness) is much more important than doing things right (efficiency)! For example, the Eastman Kodak Company was an efficient producer of 35-millimeter cameras for decades, but ineffective strategies to shift Kodak's emphasis to disk cameras brought disaster in the 1980s. Disk cameras turned out to be Kodak's Edsel and Kodak's profits declined an average of six percent annually from 1983 to 1987.

Many up-to-date examples and exercises are included in this text to arouse your interest in learning about strategic management. Modern strategic-management concepts are presented that will enable you to formulate, implement, and evaluate strategies in all kinds of profit and nonprofit organizations. You will learn how an organization can gain competitive advantages through information technology. You will also learn how to integrate knowledge acquired in previous business courses.

You will have the opportunity in this course to make actual strategic decisions, perhaps for the first time in your academic career. Do not hesitate to take a stand and defend specific strategies that you determine to be best. The rationale for your strategic decisions will be more important than the actual decision, because no one knows with certainty what the "best strategy" is for a particular organization at a particular time. This fact accents the subjective, contingency nature of the strategic-management process. Use the concepts and techniques presented in this text, coupled with your own intuition and knowledge, to recommend strategies that you can defend as being most appropriate for the organizations that you study.

ACKNOWLEDGMENTS

Many persons have contributed to writing, revising, and improving this text. I would like to thank all my colleagues and friends whose research over the years has shaped our understanding of strategic management. Individuals whose journal articles and books are referenced in this text are listed alphabetically in the Name Index.

I would like to acknowledge the individuals who contributed cases to this edition:

Claire Anderson — Loyola University
Jill Austin — Middle Tennessee State University
Miles Basil — Auburn University
Pat Basil — Auburn University
Charles Boyd — Southwest Missouri State University
James Brunner — The University of Toledo
Mary Coulter — Southwest Missouri State University
Ronald Coulter — Southwest Missouri State University
Robert Crowner — Eastern Michigan University
Tom Davidson — Auburn University
Keith Denton — Southwest Missouri State University
Phil Fisher — University of South Dakota at Vermillion
Elmer Gainok — Northern State College
Fred Haas — Virginia Commonwealth University
Robert Hay — University of Arkansas
Horace Holmes — Mississippi State University
Reatha Holmes — Mississippi State University
William House — University of Arkansas
Dan Kopp — Southwest Missouri State University
Philippe Lindsay — Auburn University
Nancy Marlow — Eastern Illinois University

David McBride	Auburn University
Blane Mooney	Auburn University
Jyoti Prasad	Western Illinois University
Richard Reed	Washington State University
David Rhyne	University of Central Florida
Keith Robbins	George Mason University
Charles Roegiers	University of South Dakota at Vermillion
Lois Shufeldt	Southwest Missouri State University
Ellen Sides	Auburn University
Matthew Sonfield	Hofstra University
Barbara Spencer	Mississippi State University
Charlotte Sutton	Auburn University
Robert Trewatha	Southwest Missouri State University
Richard Ward	Bowling Green State University
Stephanie Weikert	Clemson University
Sharon Wood	Auburn University
Shaker Zahra	George Mason University
Lucretia Zienert	Auburn University

My special thanks go to Dr. Dennis Patzig (James Madison University), Dr. John Champion (University of Florida), Dr. Timothy Stearns (University of Wisconsin), Dr. Francine Newth (Providence College), Dr. Sharon Johnson (Baylor University), and Dr. Richard Wagner (Indiana University) who reviewed the text in manuscript and contributed valuable suggestions and comments.

I would also like to thank my colleagues and friends at Auburn University who provide an excellent academic environment for teaching, research, and writing, especially Dr. James Martin, President of Auburn University; Dr. Bob Niebuhr, Acting Dean of the College of Business; Dr. Achilles Armenakis and Dr. Bill Lloyd, Associate Deans in the College of Business; and Dr. Bill Ledbetter, Acting Chairperson of the Department of Management. In addition, Lucretia Zienert at Auburn helped me immensely in revising this text.

I appreciate the hard work of Merrill employees such as Anne Daly, Dwayne Martin, Susan King, and Jim Hubbard who were involved at various stages of this edition's production.

The persons who sacrificed most for this text are my wife, Joy, and three children, Forest, Byron, and Meredith—the need to meet book deadlines took precedence over vacation many times. To my family and parents, I express love and appreciation for your support and encouragement.

Finally, I want to thank you, the reader. I hope this book will help you formulate, implement, and evaluate strategies for organizations that you become associated with, and I hope you come to share my enthusiasm for the subject area of strategic management.

Fred R. David
Auburn University

Acknowledgments

The author and publisher gratefully acknowledge the following individuals for their valuable comments in responding to an extensive questionnaire about the first edition. Their responses were helpful in shaping the second edition.

Mel Adams; Sol Ahiarah; Carol Ahlvers; Ahmad Ahmadious; William Allen; Kurt Altschul; Claire Anderson; Sonny Ariss

Larry Bailey; R. B. Barton, Jr.; John Beverly; Mary Boehms; Walter Bogumil; Robert Boothe; Weldon Bowling; Steven Bradley; Geoffrey Brooks

Luis Calingo; Filemon Campo-Flores; Alan Carey; Thomas Carey; Donald Caruth; Tommy Cates; John Champion; Robert Cheek; Gordon Chen; James Chester; Jules Cohn; George Cole; Jereng Coleman; Mary Coulter; W. Crittenden; Robert Crowner; Casimir Czarniewicz

Edward Dangler; Robert De Fillippi; Kim DeDee; Bernard Deitzen; Chase De Long; Dale Dickson

George Eddy; Timothy Edlund; Lance Ehuke; Cathy Enz

Richard Fabris; W. Randolph Flynn; Gerald Ford; Fred Fry

E. J. Gainok; Thomas Garsombke; Richard Gendreau; Michael Geringer; Manton Gibbs; Yezdi Godiwalla; James Goes; Martin Gonzalez

Fred Haas; H. Hadji; R. W. Halsac; Claudia Harris; James Hartman; Lindle Hatton; Belmont Haydel; Alan Heffner; Michael Hergert; Frank Hodges; Horace Holmes, Jr.; Henry Houser; George Howick; George Huber; L. P. Huggins

Graham Irwin

Dan Jennings; Laurence Jensen; Sharon Johnson; Raymond Jones; William Judge

Richard Kampf; Marvin Katzman; Lawrence Kellerman; Dale King; Geoffrey King; Michael Koshuta; Carol Kovach; O. J. Krasner; D. E. Kreps

Steven Knickrehm; Rose Knotts

James Lee; Edwin Leonard; Joseph Leonard; Leon Levitt; William Litzinger; Robert Loski; Kenneth Lundahl; John Lyons

Rinado Maestas; Ed Marlow; Thomas Maroney; Michael Matukonis; Lorie Mazzaroppi; James McCollum; Robert McGinty; Richard Merner; Edward Mills; Rick Molz; Debra Moody; William Muhs

Robert Nale; Francine Newth

Vincent Palacino; Dennis Pappas; Gerald Parker; Charles Patton; Robert Pearse; Richard Pesta; Michael Pitts; James Poindexter; Jesus Ponce-de-Leon; Rod Powers

L. D. Redinbaugh; Barbara Redmond; Richard Reed; Keith Robbins; William Roering; Stanley Ross; Daniel Rowledge

Kunal Sadhu; Charles Satterthwaite; Norman Scarborough; Chas Schitiliary; Mel Schnake; Alfred Schoennauer; Paul Sears; Thomas Sharkey; Merrill Kim Sharp; F. B. Simmons; Wayne Smeltz; A. W. Smith; David Smith; Jerald Smith; James Snyder; James Sowers; Squire; Alfred Strandgard

Arus Tajul; Irwin Talbot; Curtis Tate; Brhane Tesfay; Garth Thompson

Robert Vichas; John Joseph Vitton

Kenneth Wadoski; Richard Wagner; Dick Wald; Richard Ward; Walter Warrick; Ira Wessler; Randall White; Tilton Wilcox; Sam Willis; Floyd Willoughby; George Witteried; H. R. Worrell

Betty Yantis; John Yeamans

David Zalewski; Thomas Zimmerer

Contents

Specialty Retailers

Food Retailers

Lodging and Travel

Entertainment

Medical Institutions

MANUFACTURING COMPANIES

Food, Drink, and Glasses

Publishing

[a]Denotes a small business organization
[b]Denotes a nonprofit organization
[c]Denotes an international organization
[d]Updated from first edition of text
[e]New in the second edition of text

PART ONE
OVERVIEW OF STRATEGIC MANAGEMENT

The Strategic-Management Process

NOTABLE QUOTES

If we know where we are and something about how we got there, we might see where we are trending—and if the outcomes which lie naturally in our course are unacceptable, to make timely change.

Abraham Lincoln

Without a strategy, an organization is like a ship without a rudder, going around in circles. It's like a tramp; it has no place to go.

Joel Ross and Michael Kami

When there is no vision, the people perish.

Proverbs 29:18

If business is not based on ethical grounds, it is of no benefit to society, and will, like all other unethical combinations, pass into oblivion.

C. Max Killian

If a man take no thought about what is distant, he will find sorrow near at hand. He who will not worry about what is far off will soon find something worse than worry.

Confucius

It is human nature to make decisions based on emotion, rather than fact. But nothing could be more illogical.

Toshiba Corporation

No business can do everything. Even if it has the money, it will never have enough good people. It has to set priorities. The worst thing to do is a little bit of everything. This makes sure that nothing is being accomplished. It is better to pick the wrong priority than none at all.

Peter Drucker

Information and opportunity combine to make for the most important strategies. But there is a third factor too. That factor is intuition.

Robert Waterman, Jr.

1

OUTLINE

WHAT IS STRATEGIC MANAGEMENT?
KEY TERMS IN STRATEGIC MANAGEMENT
STAGES OF STRATEGIC MANAGEMENT
THE STRATEGIC-MANAGEMENT MODEL
STRATEGIC MANAGEMENT IN SMALL FIRMS
STRATEGIC MANAGEMENT IN NONPROFIT AND GOVERNMENTAL ORGANIZATIONS
STRATEGIC MANAGEMENT IN MULTINATIONAL CORPORATIONS
COMPARING BUSINESS AND MILITARY STRATEGY
INTRODUCING THE COHESION CASE AND EXPERIENTIAL EXERCISES
THE COHESION CASE: PONDEROSA, INC.–1988

Experiential Exercise 1A: Strategy Analysis for Ponderosa
Experiential Exercise 1B: Examining Strategy Articles
Experiential Exercise 1C: Developing a Code of Business Ethics

OBJECTIVES

After studying this chapter, you should be able to

- Describe the strategic-management process.
- Explain the need for integrating analysis with intuition in strategic management.
- Identify and describe key terms in strategic management.
- Discuss the importance of business ethics, social responsibility, and organizational culture to strategic management.
- Describe the nature of strategy formulation, implementation, and evaluation activities.
- Compare and contrast strategic management in small and large companies, domestic and multinational firms, and profit and nonprofit organizations.

This chapter introduces a practical model that provides a basis for studying and applying strategic-management concepts and techniques. It describes basic activities and terms in strategic management and brings those concepts to life with contemporary examples. It explains how the strategic-management process can operate in small businesses, nonprofit organizations, governmental agencies, and multinational firms.

WHAT IS STRATEGIC MANAGEMENT?

Once there were two company presidents who competed in the same industry. These two presidents decided to go on a camping trip to discuss a possible merger. They hiked deep into the woods. Suddenly, they came upon a grizzly bear that rose up on its hind legs and snarled. Almost instantly, the first president began taking off his knapsack and getting out a pair of jogging shoes. The second president said, "Hey, you can't outrun that bear." The first president responded, "Maybe I can't outrun that bear, but I can surely outrun you!" This story captures the notion of strategic management.

Defining Strategic Management

Strategic management can be defined as the art and science of formulating, implementing, and evaluating cross-functional decisions that will enable an organization to achieve its objectives. As the definition implies, strategic management focuses on integrating management, marketing, finance/accounting, production/operations, and research and development aspects of a business to achieve organizational success. Thus the term "strategic management" is used at many colleges and universities as the title for the capstone course in business administration, "business policy," which integrates other functional business courses.

The *strategic-management process* consists of three stages: strategy formulation, strategy implementation, and strategy evaluation. *Strategy formulation* includes identifying an organization's external opportunities and threats, determining internal strengths and weaknesses, establishing a business mission and long-term objectives, generating alternative strategies, and choosing particular strategies to pursue. *Strategy implementation* requires a firm to establish annual objectives, devise policies, motivate employees, and allocate resources so that formulated strategies can be executed; strategy implementation includes developing a strategy-supportive culture, creating an effective organizational structure, redirecting marketing efforts, preparing budgets, and motivating individuals to action. Finally, *strategy evaluation* monitors the results of formulation and implementation and includes measuring individual and organizational performance and taking corrective actions when necessary.

Strategic management focuses on the total enterprise. It looks beyond everyday operations, problems, and crises to focus on an organization's overall growth and development. Strategy concerns the nature of the forest, not of the trees! Strategic management allows an organization to be both proactive and reactive in shaping its own future. That is, strategic management allows organizations to influence and initiate rather than simply respond to changes in the business environment. Strategic management allows organizations to be nimble and adaptive. Due to rapid changes in technologies and market conditions, good strategic management has never been so important as it is today.

Making good strategic decisions is the major responsibility of an organization's owner or chief executive officer. Middle- level and lower-level managers are commonly involved in strategy formulation, implementation, and evaluation activities too. Participation is a key to gaining commitment for needed changes. Business environments are changing so rapidly and are so complex that strategic management is required for the survival of many small, large, profit, and nonprofit organizations. Strategic decisions include determining what new businesses to enter, what businesses to abandon, how to allocate resources, whether to expand operations or to diversify, whether to enter other geographic markets, whether to merge or form a joint venture, and how to avoid a hostile takeover. Peter Drucker says the prime task of strategic management is thinking through the overall mission of a business:

> . . . that is, of asking the question "What is our Business?" This leads to the setting of objectives, the development of strategies, and the making of today's decisions for tomorrow's results. This clearly must be done by a part of the organization that can see the entire business; that can balance objectives and the needs of today against the needs of tomorrow; and that can allocate resources of men and money to key results.[1]

Integrating Intuition and Analysis

The strategic-management process can be described as an objective, systematic approach for making major decisions in an organization. It attempts to organize qualitative and quantitative information in a way that allows effective decisions to be made under conditions of uncertainty. Yet, strategic management is not a pure science that lends itself to a nice, neat, one-two-three approach. *Intuition,* based on past experiences, judgment, and feelings, is essential to making good strategic decisions.

Some managers and owners of businesses profess to have extraordinary abilities for using intuition alone in devising brilliant strategies. For example, Will Durant, who organized General Motors Corporation, was described by Alfred Sloan as "a man who would proceed on a course of action guided solely, as far as I could tell, by some intuitive flash of brilliance. He never felt obliged to make an engineering hunt for the facts. Yet at times he was astoundingly correct in his judgment."[2] Albert Einstein acknowledged the importance of intuition when he said, "I believe in intuition and inspiration. At times I feel certain that I am right while not knowing the reason. Imagination is more important than knowledge, because knowledge is limited, whereas imagination embraces the entire world."[3] Although some organizations today may survive and prosper because they have intuitive geniuses managing them, not many are so fortunate. The majority can benefit from strategic management, which integrates intuition and analysis in decision making.

Choosing an intuitive or analytical approach to decision making is not an either-or proposition. Managers at all levels in an organization should inject their intuition and judgment into strategic-management analyses. Analytical thinking and intuitive thinking complement each other in strategic management. In a sense, the strategic-management process is an attempt to duplicate what goes on in the mind of a brilliant intuitive person who knows the business. A key to successful strategic management is effective integration of intuition and analysis. Intuition or analysis alone is not sufficient, for reasons suggested in this comment:

> The accelerating rate of change today is producing a business world in which customary managerial habits in organizations are increasingly inadequate. Experience was an adequate guide when changes could be made in small increments. But intuitive and experience-based management philosophies are grossly inadequate when decisions are strategic and have major, irreversible consequences.[4]

Adapting to Change

The strategic-management process is based on the belief that organizations should continually monitor internal and external events and trends so that timely changes can be made as needed. The rate and magnitude of changes that affect organizations are increasing. Consider, for example, the rising trade deficit, superconductivity, merger/acquisition mania, hostile takeovers, cellular phones, monoclonal antibodies, fiber optics, junk bond financing, the aging population, taxes on services, *glasnost,* and the Chapter 12 bankruptcy law passed in 1987. To survive in this kind of environment, all sizes and types of firms must be capable of astutely identifying and adapting to changes. Organizations should seek to pursue strategies that capitalize on internal strengths, take advantage of external opportunities, mitigate internal weaknesses, and avoid or mollify the impact of external threats. This is the essence of strategic management!

Small business owners, chief executive officers, presidents, and managers of many profit and nonprofit organizations have concluded that strategic management is vital to success. The imnortance of strategic management to Columbia Gas System Service Corporation and Ogden Corporation is evidenced in Exhibit 1–1. An increasing number of corporations and institutions are using strategic management to make effective decisions. *Planning Review* reports that over 75 percent of all companies now use strategic-management techniques, compared to less than 25 percent in 1979.[5] Organizations that use strategic-management concepts generally outperform organizations that do not on almost all major financial indicators.[6] But strategic management is not a guarantee of success; it can be dysfunctional if conducted haphazardly. The manner in which strategic management is carried out in an organization can be as important as the resultant strategies and plans. This is true because a major aim of the process itself is to achieve understanding and commitment from all managers and employees. The strategic management process can be a vital communication tool, as Waterman suggests in his new book, *The Renewal Factor*:

> I was blown away by the experience of talking with Chief Executive John Akers of IBM and learning how effective and elaborate IBM's strategic-management system was. At IBM, people explained it wasn't just a plan, it was a way of communicating with each other. Strategic management is important because it helps generate information and helps you communicate.[7]

EXHIBIT 1–1 Top managers discuss strategic management in their firms

Columbia Gas System Service Corporation
Headquartered in Wilmington, Delaware, Columbia Gas System's Strategic Plan forms the basis of all other planning activities—marketing plans, capital programs, financial plans, and so forth. Strategic management goes far beyond operational planning that has been traditional throughout Columbia. We are not just looking at projections of how much gas we'll need and where it will come from. The first part of our Strategic Plan is the Mission Statement, which sets the direction for the company. All operating units have their own mission statements, defining their business and their corporate reason for existing. These in turn are followed by long-term objectives which are broad statements of what the company intends to do, followed by annual objectives which for the most part are quantified. (James D. Little, executive vice president of Columbia Gas System, *Columbia Today,* Winter 1985–86, p. 2.)

Ogden Corporation
The best long-run results come from good strategic decisions, which ensure doing the right things (effectiveness), and the combination of design, technology, and automation, which ensure doing things right (efficiency). To predict . . . without the ability to adapt is simply to foresee one's own end! The strategic objectives Ogden has achieved have enabled the adaptation necessary to cope with the changing economic environment for the balance of this century. We are describing a classic example of evolution; in this case, *corporate evolution* [emphasis added]. To survive, both organisms and corporations must adapt to new circumstances. (Ralph Ablon, chairman of the board, Ogden Corporation)

KEY TERMS IN STRATEGIC MANAGEMENT

Before we go any further in discussing the strategic-management process, we should define some key terms.

Strategists

Strategists are the individuals in an organization who are most responsible for the success or failure of that organization. Strategists have many various job titles, such as chief executive officer, president, owner, chairman of the board, executive director, chancellor, dean, or entrepreneur.

Strategists differ as much as organizations themselves, and these differences must be considered in the formulation, implementation, and evaluation of strategies. Strategists differ in their attitudes, values, ethics, willingness to take risks, concern for social responsibility, concern for profitability, concern for short-run versus long-run aims, and management style. Some will not consider some types of strategies due to their personal philosophy. For example, David Wickins, who replaced Colin Chapman as chairman of the board of Lotus, the car manufacturer, says, "Lotus has never been run with the objective of being a profitable company. Colin Chapman was quite simply interested in making cars go fast. I have a different viewpoint."[8]

Some strategists agree with Ralph Nader, who proclaims that organizations have tremendous social obligations. Others exhibit a philosophy more like that of Milton

Friedman, an economist, who maintains that organizations have no obligation to do any more for society than is legally required. Businesses can fulfill social responsibilities best by considering social obligations to be opportunities. The first social responsibility of any business must be to make enough profit to cover the costs of the future, because if this is not achieved, no other social responsibility can be met. Strategists should examine social problems in terms of potential costs and benefits to the firm, and address social issues that could benefit the firm most.

Business Ethics

Business ethics can be defined as conduct or actions within organizations that constitute and support human welfare. Codes of business ethics serve as control mechanisms and symbols in organizations. Newspapers and business magazines daily report legal and moral breaches of ethical conduct by both public and private organizations. Some recent examples are illicit use of inside information by Wall Street manipulators, fraudulent overbilling on Defense Department contracts, bribery of employees, tax fraud, and the sale of top-secret military information to the Soviets. Between 1977 and 1987, the Securities and Exchange Commission brought 137 cases of insider trading of stock to court, compared to only 47 cases in the previous 28 years. The Federal Bureau of Investigation reports that losses from bank fraud, including scams and embezzlements to steal money from banks, thrifts, and other lending institutions, totaled more than $1.1 billion in 1986, up 30 percent from 1985. Bank fraud losses for the entire decade of the 1970s were less than $1.5 billion, but losses are expected to exceed $20 billion for the 1980s.

A new wave of unethical acts and corruption has accented the need for strategists to develop a clear code of business ethics. Policies can then be devised to assure adherence to the code. One reason that strategists' salaries are high relative to those of other individuals in an organization is that they must take the moral risks of the firm. Strategists are responsible for developing, communicating, and enforcing a code of business ethics for their organization. Although primary responsibility for having an effective code of business ethics rests with a firm's strategists, an integral part of the responsibility of all managers is to provide ethics leadership by constant example and demonstration.

Exhibit 1–2 presents fourteen maxims or propositions that enable strategists to deal with the subject of business ethics with confidence. Personal financial gain is an underlying motive for many cases of unethical conduct in organizations. Four common rationalizations explain why individuals sometimes act unethically in ways that jeopardize the strategies of their organization.

1. A belief that the activity is within reasonable ethical and legal limits—that it is not "really" illegal or immoral.
2. A belief that the activity is in the individual's or the corporation's best interests—that the individual would somehow be expected to undertake the activity.
3. A belief that the activity is "safe" because it will never be found out or publicized—the classic crime-and-punishment issue of discovery.
4. A belief that because the activity helps the company, the company will condone it and even protect the persons who engage in it.[9]

EXHIBIT 1–2 Laczniak's fourteen ethical propositions

- Ethical conflicts and choices are inherent in business decision making.
- Proper ethical behavior exists on a plane above the law. The law merely specifies the lowest common denominator of acceptable behavior.
- There is no single satisfactory standard of ethical action agreeable to everyone that a manager can use to make specific operational decisions.
- Managers should be familiar with a wide variety of ethical standards.
- The discussion of business cases or of situations having ethical implications can make managers more ethically sensitive.
- There are diverse and sometimes conflicting determinants of ethical action. These stem primarily from the individual, from the organization, from professional norms, and from the values of society.
- Individual values are the final standard, although not necessarily the determining reason for ethical behavior.
- Consensus regarding what constitutes proper ethical behavior in a decision-making situation diminishes as the level of analysis proceeds from abstract to specific.
- The moral tone of an organization is set by top management.
- The lower the organizational level of a manager, the greater the perceived pressure to act unethically.
- Individual managers perceive themselves as more ethical than their colleagues.
- Effective codes of ethics should contain meaningful and clearly stated provisions, along with enforced sanctions for noncompliance.
- Employees must have a nonpunitive, fail-safe mechanism for reporting ethical abuses in the organization.
- Every organization should appoint a top-level manager or director to be responsible for acting as an ethical advocate in the organization.

Source: Gene Laczniak, "Business Ethics: A Manager's Primer," *Business*, Georgia State University (January-March, 1983): 23–29.

A major responsibility of strategists is to develop and communicate a code of business ethics for their organization. But an integral part of the responsibility of all managers is to provide ethics leadership by constant example and demonstration. Gellerman offers some good advice:

> All managers risk giving too much because of what their companies demand from them. But the same superiors who keep pressing you to do more, or to do it better, or faster, or less expensively, will turn on you should you cross that fuzzy line between right and wrong. They will blame you for exceeding instructions or for ignoring their warnings. The smartest managers already know that the best answer to the question, "How far is too far?" is don't try to find out.[10]

Baxter Travenol Laboratories, IBM, Caterpillar Tractor, and Celanese are firms that have formalized their codes of business conduct. The chief executive officers of these and many other firms have spelled out the ethical standards expected of all their employees. "Trees die from the top," as explained by Drucker:

> A man (or woman) might know too little, perform poorly, lack judgment and ability, and yet not do too much damage as a manager. But if that person lacks in character and integrity—no matter how knowledgeable, how brilliant, how successful—he destroys. He destroys people, the most valuable resource of the enterprise. He destroys spirit. And he destroys performance. This is particularly true of the people at the head of an enterprise. For the spirit of an organization is created from the top. If an organization is great in spirit, it is because the spirit of its top people is great. If it decays, it does so because the top rots; as the proverb has it, "Trees die from the top." No one should ever become a strategist unless he or she is willing to have his character serve as the model for subordinates.[11]

Mission Statements

Another key term is "mission statement." *Mission statements* are "enduring statements of purpose that distinguish one business from other similar firms. A mission statement identifies the scope of a firm's operations in product and market terms."[12] It addresses the basic question that faces all strategists: "What is our Business?" A clear mission statement describes the values and priorities of an organization. Developing a business mission compels strategists to think about the nature and scope of present organizational activities and to assess the potential attractiveness of future markets and activities. A mission statement broadly charts the future direction of an organization.

Recent research suggests that about 60 percent of all organizations have developed a formal mission statement and that high performing firms have more well developed mission statements than low performing firms.[13] The current mission statement of Kraft, Inc., is just one example:

> Kraft's mission is to become the leading food company in the world, not in sheer size but in ways that are more meaningful—quality people, quality products, quality business plans, growth, returns and innovation. Having successfully served the needs of generations of consumers for nearly a century, Kraft has earned the reputation of being the company with "Good Food and Good Food Ideas." We know, however, that our reputation must be nurtured with constant dedication if it is to endure and strengthen. Kraft's heritage is strong; its past achievements impressive. We at Kraft, however, do not view them as indicators of missions completed but of missions yet to be accomplished.[14]

External Opportunities and Threats

Other key terms in our study of strategic management are *external opportunities* and *external threats*. These terms refer to economic, social, political, technological, and competitive trends and events that could significantly benefit or harm an organization in the future. The computer revolution, biotechnology, population shifts, changing work values and attitudes, space technology, and increased competition from foreign companies are examples of opportunities or threats for some companies. These types of changes are creating a different type of consumer and consequently a need for different types of products, services, and strategies. Other external opportunities and threats may include the passage of a new law, the introduction of a new product by a competitor, a national catastrophe, or a technological breakthrough. Opportunities and threats are largely beyond the control of a single organization. A competitor's strength could be a threat. Unrest in the Persian Gulf, rising interest rates, or a new president of the United States could represent an opportunity or threat.

A basic tenet of strategic management calls for firms to formulate strategies to take advantage of external opportunities and to avoid or reduce the impact of external threats. In 1987, for example, the Federal Reserve Board approved of banks expanding into underwriting municipal revenue bonds, commercial paper, and mortgage-backed securities. This new policy represented an external opportunity for many banks. One week after this ruling, Bankers Trust, J. P. Morgan, and Citicorp developed a joint venture to obtain revenue bonds for the Port Authority in New York and New Jersey. Also, a major external threat that faced Burlington Industries (the largest textile company in the United States) in 1987 was the hostile takeover attempt by New York raider Asher Edelman in partnership with the Dominion Textile Company of Canada. Burlington formulated a counterstrategy to buy Dominion. The counterstrategy was intended to disrupt the Edelman-Dominion partnership so Burlington could remain independent.

Internal Strengths and Weaknesses

Internal strengths and *internal weaknesses* are controllable activities within an organization that are performed especially well or poorly. Management, marketing, finance/accounting, production/operations, and research and development activities of a business are areas where internal strengths or weaknesses arise. Successful enterprises pursue strategies that capitalize on internal strengths and mitigate weaknesses. Strengths and weaknesses are determined relative to competitors. "Relative" deficiency or superiority is important information. Also, strengths and weaknesses can be determined by elements of "being rather than performance." For example, a strength may involve ownership of natural resources or a historic reputation for quality. Finally, strengths and weaknesses may be determined relative to a firm's own objectives. For example, high levels of inventory turnover may not be a strength to a firm that seeks never to stock-out.

Organizations are more and more striving to capitalize on internal strengths by adopting a strategic-management approach to decision making. For example, Robert H. Short, chief executive officer of Portland General Corporation, describes his firm's strategy:

> Our strategy now and for the future is shaped by the experience and knowledge gained from almost a century of providing heat, light, and wheel-turning power to the people of Oregon. First and foremost we are an energy company. Indeed, energy is our fundamental strength, and we intend to pursue growth aggressively in this business. To build on our strengths, however, we must mitigate or eliminate our weaknesses. I am proud of the way Portland General is drawing on its strengths to build for another century of success.[15]

An internal weakness which K-Mart Corporation identified in 1987 was its S.S. Kresge and Jupiter five-and-dime stores, which were not nearly as profitable as its K-Mart stores. K-Mart sold 76 Kresge and Jupiter stores to McCrory Corporation, the largest five-and-dime retail chain in the United States. A spokesperson for McCrory said his company bought the Kresge and Jupiter stores because they are located in regions where McCrory had little or no presence. So, for McCrory too, the acquisition strategy was intended to improve upon an internal weakness.

Long-term Objectives

Objectives can be defined as specific results that an organization seeks to achieve in pursuing its basic mission. *Long-term* means more than one year. Objectives are vital to organizational success because they provide direction, aid in evaluation, create synergy, reveal priorities, allow coordination, and provide a basis for effective planning, organizing, motivating, and controlling activities. Objectives should be challenging, measurable, consistent, reasonable, and clear. In a multidivisional firm, objectives should be established for the overall company and for each division.

As an example of long-term objectives, Hardee's Food Systems has a corporate objective to grow 60 percent between 1987 and 1991. This is a challenging objective since the "hamburger industry" is expanding only 4 percent annually. Chairman Jack Laughery of Hardee's expects to acquire an additional one thousand outlets from other companies by 1991 and to add three hundred company-owned and franchised restaurants annually through 1991. Hardee's recently surpassed Wendy's International, the third largest hamburger chain in average restaurant sales and customer traffic. Hardee's stated objectives for 1991 would bring the company close to Burger King, the second company in the industry behind McDonald's.

Strategies

Another key term in the study of strategic management is "strategies." *Strategies* are the means by which long-term objectives will be achieved. Business strategies may include geographic expansion, diversification, acquisition, product development, market penetration, retrenchment, divestiture, liquidation, and joint venture. Strategies being pursued by three different organizations are described in Exhibit 1–3.

Annual Objectives

Annual objectives are short-term milestones that organizations must achieve to reach long-term objectives. Like long-term objectives, annual objectives should be measurable, quantitative, challenging, realistic, consistent, and prioritized. They should be established at the corporate, divisional, and functional level in a large organization. Annual objectives should be stated in terms of management, marketing, finance/accounting, production/operations, and research and development accomplishments. A set of annual objectives is needed for each long-term objective established in an organization. Annual objectives are especially important in strategy implementation, whereas long-term objectives are particularly important in strategy formulation. Annual objectives represent the basis for allocating resources.

The Tribune Company (the nation's fifth largest publisher of newspapers and owner of the Chicago Cubs baseball team) is an example of a firm that has clear annual

EXHIBIT 1–3 Three organizations' strategies

Avon Products, Inc.
Avon acquired Giorgio, Inc. in May, 1987. Giorgio, based in Beverly Hills, California, had $100 million in revenues in 1986—a small amount compared with Avon's $2.9 billion. The importance of this $165 million acquisition goes beyond size. For Avon, the world's largest cosmetics company, this acquisition is the most significant effort yet to broaden its distribution channels from door-to-door sales into retail department stores. (Gaining control over distributors is called *forward integration.*) Avon chairman Hicks B. Waldron says Avon's long-term objective is for retail sales to rise from zero in 1986 to $750 million in 1991, or 20 percent of revenues. Giorgio will be a major factor in that growth. The acquisition gives Avon prime selling space in 710 prestigious stores and a widely recognized brand. Avon expects to boost Giorgio's international sales significantly. Avon's forward integration strategy is also exemplified by a fifty-fifty joint venture with Liz Claiborne, Inc. and the launching of Catherine Deneuve perfume. To implement this strategy, Avon is hiring managers who know the retail cosmetics business, such as Giorgio President Michael Gould.

Atlantic Richfield Company (ARCO)
During the mid-1980s, ARCO began converting its service stations into twenty-four-hour minimarkets called AM/PMs. These stores offer everything from bread and milk to over-the-counter pain remedies and motor oil. By 1990, ARCO plans to have a network of more than one thousand AM/PM stores in place and predicts that revenues from them will surpass $1 billion. (Developing new products or services for present customers is called *horizontal diversification.*) After years of trailing Chevron in West Coast retail sales, ARCO now sells more gas than any of its competitors in the California market. ARCO is currently the nation's sixth-largest oil company.

Otis Group, Inc.
The Otis elevator facility in Bristol, Connecticut is the world's slimmest research and development laboratory. Towering twenty-nine stories, this $20 million structure contains only a lobby and eleven elevators. This laboratory was recently constructed as part of Otis's *product development strategy* to manufacture quieter and faster elevators. The driving force behind Otis's commitment to innovative technology and computerized "smart elevators" is foreign competition. Japanese firms, such as Mitsubishi Corporation, are now selling elevators actively in the United States. Otis wants to protect its 25 percent share of the $10 billion elevator market.

objectives. Stanton Cook, president and chief executive officer of Tribune, emphasizes annual objectives. Tribune strives to have an 18 percent annual return on equity (net income divided by average stockholders' investment) and a 30 percent debt to total capital ratio.

Policies

The final key term to be highlighted here is "policies." *Policies* are the means by which annual objectives will be achieved. Policies include guidelines, rules, and procedures established to support efforts to achieve stated objectives. Policies are guides to decision-making and address repetitive or recurring situations. Policies are most often stated in terms of management, marketing, finance/accounting, production/operations, and research and development activities. Policies can be established at the corporate level and apply to an entire organization, at the divisional level and apply to a single division, or at the functional level and apply to particular operational activities or departments. Policies, like annual objectives, are especially important in strategy implementation because they outline an organization's expectations of its employees and managers. Policies allow consistency and coordination within and between organizational departments.

In 1987, more than 30 percent of corporations in the United States devised policies to restrict employees from smoking on the job. The National Center for Health Promotion estimates that by 1990, more than 80 percent of all American corporations will have "No Smoking" policies. Substantial research suggests that a healthier work force can more effectively and efficiently implement strategies. In 1987, 32 percent of all adults in the United States were smokers, down from a high of 42 percent in 1967. "No Smoking" policies are usually derived from annual objectives that seek to reduce corporate medical costs associated with absenteeism and to provide a healthy workplace.

STAGES OF STRATEGIC MANAGEMENT

Strategy Formulation

Strategy formulation is the process of establishing a business mission, conducting research to determine key internal and external factors, performing analyses to match internal with external factors, establishing long-term objectives, and choosing among alternative strategies. A firm's strategies should capitalize upon strengths, reduce weaknesses, take advantage of external opportunities, and obviate external threats. Sometimes strategy formulation or the strategic-management process is called "strategic planning." The difference between strategic planning and strategic management is that the latter includes strategy implementation and strategy evaluation. In this text, the term "strategy formulation" is used instead of "strategic planning" to reflect the restricted meanings.

Three basic strategy-formulation activities are conducting research, integrating intuition with analysis, and making decisions. Many organizations refer to the research activities as an "external audit" and an "internal audit." Externally, research is required to gather and assimilate the wealth of information published every week about a given firm's industry and markets. This process is sometimes called *environmental scanning*. Internally, research is needed to identify key strengths and weaknesses in the functional areas of business. Key internal factors can be determined in a number of ways that include computing ratios and comparing to industry averages or measuring performance and comparing to past periods. Various types of surveys can also be developed and administered to examine internal factors such as employee morale, production efficiency, advertising effectiveness, and customer loyalty.

Intuition is particularly useful for making decisions in situations of great uncertainty, or little precedent, or highly interrelated variables, or when there is immense pressure to be right, or when it is necessary to choose from several plausible alternatives.[16] These situations affect the nature of strategic management. Since no organization has unlimited resources, strategists must decide which alternative strategies will benefit the firm most. Strategic decisions commit an organization to certain products, markets, resources, and technologies over an extended period of time. They determine long-term competitive advantages. For better or worse, strategic decisions have enduring effects on an organization and have major multifunctional consequences. Strategic decisions are future-oriented. Strategists have the best perspective for understanding the ramifications of formulation decisions and they have the authority to commit the resources necessary for implementation.

Strategy Implementation

Strategy implementation is often called the action stage of strategic management. *Implementing* means mobilizing employees and managers to put formulated strategies into action. Three basic strategy-implementation activities are establishing annual objectives, devising policies, and allocating resources. Often considered to be the most difficult stage in strategic management, strategy implementation requires personal discipline, commitment, and sacrifice. Successful strategy implementation can hinge upon managers' ability to motivate employees, which is more an art than a science. Strategies formulated but not implemented serve no useful purpose.

Interpersonal skills are especially critical for successful strategy implementation. Strategy implementation includes developing strategy-supportive budgets, programs, and cultures, and linking motivation and reward systems to both long-term and annual objectives. These strategy-implementation activities affect all employees and managers in an organization. Every operating department in the organization must decide on answers to the questions, "What must we do to implement our part of the organization's strategy" and "How best can we get the job done?" The challenge of implementation is to stimulate managers and employees throughout an organization to work with pride and enthusiasm towards achieving stated objectives.

Strategy Evaluation

The final stage in strategic management is strategy evaluation. All strategies are subject to future modification because internal and external factors are constantly changing. Three fundamental strategy-evaluation activities are (1) reviewing internal and external factors that are the bases for current strategies, (2) measuring performance, and (3) taking corrective actions. Strategy evaluation is needed because success today is no guarantee of success tomorrow! In fact, success always creates new and different problems. For example, Microsoft Corporation historically dominated the Japanese software market. Sales of Microsoft's MS-DOS in Japan were about $23 million in 1987. However, Lotus Development Corporation recently poured millions of dollars into advertising in Japan. The Japanese version of Lotus 1-2-3 now outsells Microsoft's Multiplan by a five to one margin.

Figure 1–1 depicts a summary of strategic-management stages and activities. Strategy formulation, implementation, and evaluation activities occur at three hierarchical

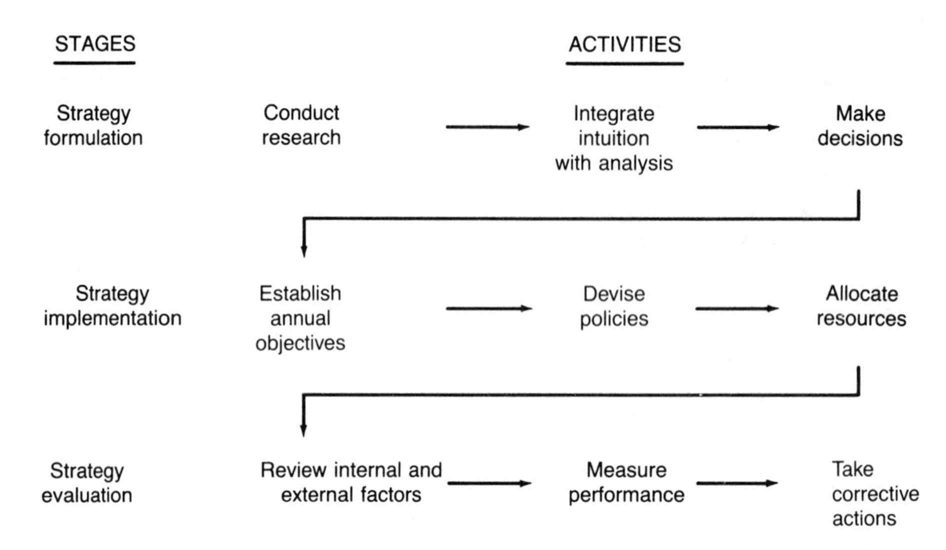

FIGURE 1–1 Stages and activities in the strategic-management process

levels in a large diversified organization: corporate, divisional or strategic business unit, and functional. Figure 1–2 illustrates how strategies formulated at the corporate level are implemented by formulating strategies at the divisional level and how divisional-level strategies are implemented by formulating functional-level strategies; strategy evaluation is essential at all hierarchical levels of an organization. Most small businesses and some large businesses do not have divisions or strategic business units, in which case corporate-level strategies are implemented by formulating functional-level strategies and policies.

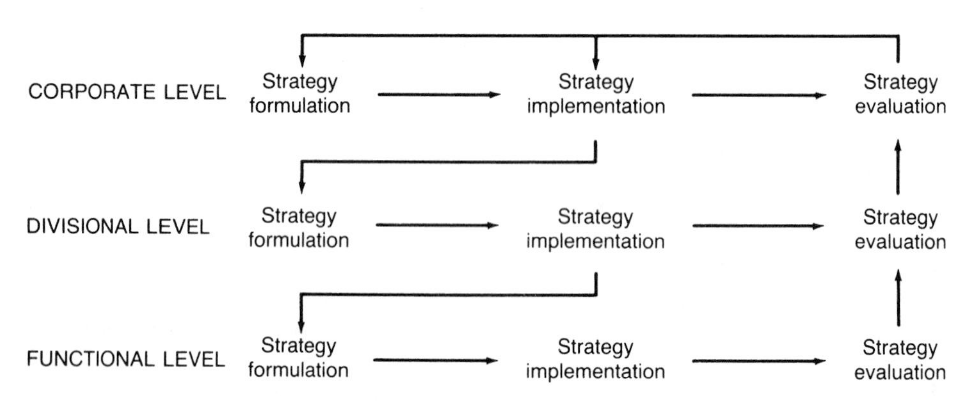

FIGURE 1–2 The strategic-management process at three levels

Source: Adapted from Peter Lorange, *Corporate Planning: An Executive Viewpoint* (Englewood Cliffs, N.J., Prentice-Hall, 1980), 61.

THE STRATEGIC-MANAGEMENT MODEL

The strategic-management process can best be studied and applied using a model. Every model represents some kind of process. The framework illustrated in Figure 1–3 is a comprehensive model of the strategic-management process. This model does not guarantee success, but it does represent a clear and practical approach for formulating, implementing, and evaluating strategies. Relationships among major components of the strategic-management process are shown in the model, which appears in all subsequent chapters with appropriate areas shaded to show the particular focus of each chapter. Identifying an organization's existing mission, objectives, and strategies is the logical starting point for strategic management because a firm's present situation and condition may preclude certain strategies and may even dictate a particular course of action. Every organization has a mission, objectives, and strategy, even if these elements are not consciously designed, written, or communicated. The answer to where an organization is going can be determined largely by where an organization has been!

The strategic-management process is both dynamic and continuous. A change in any one of the major components in the model can necessitate a change in any or all of the other components. For instance, a shift in the economy could represent a major

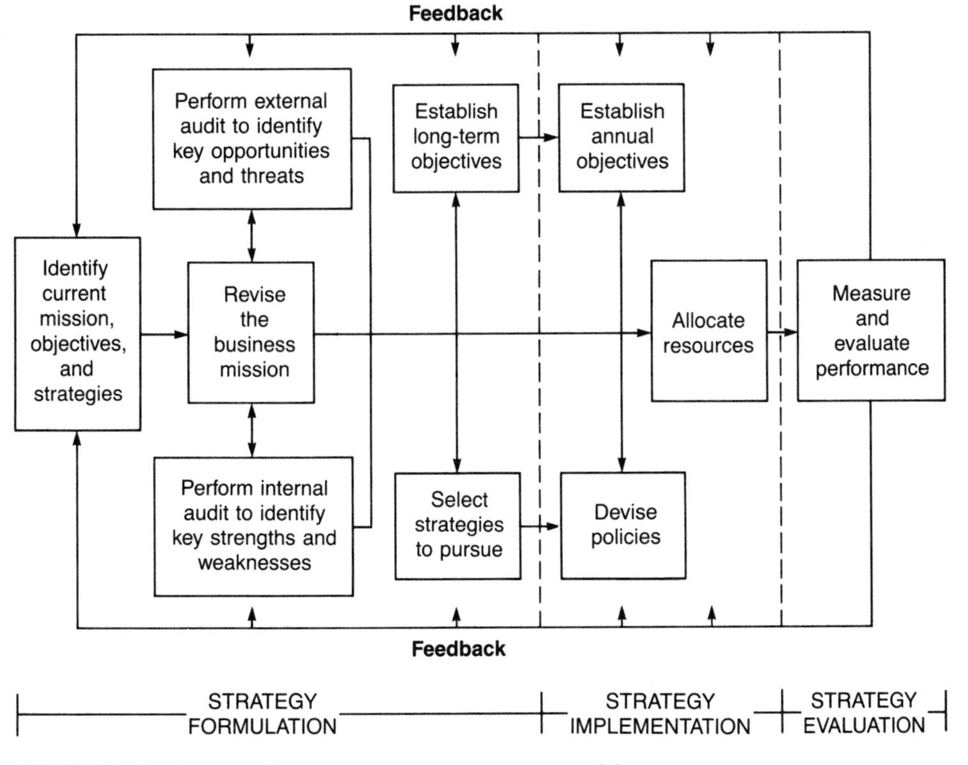

FIGURE 1–3 A comprehensive strategic-management model

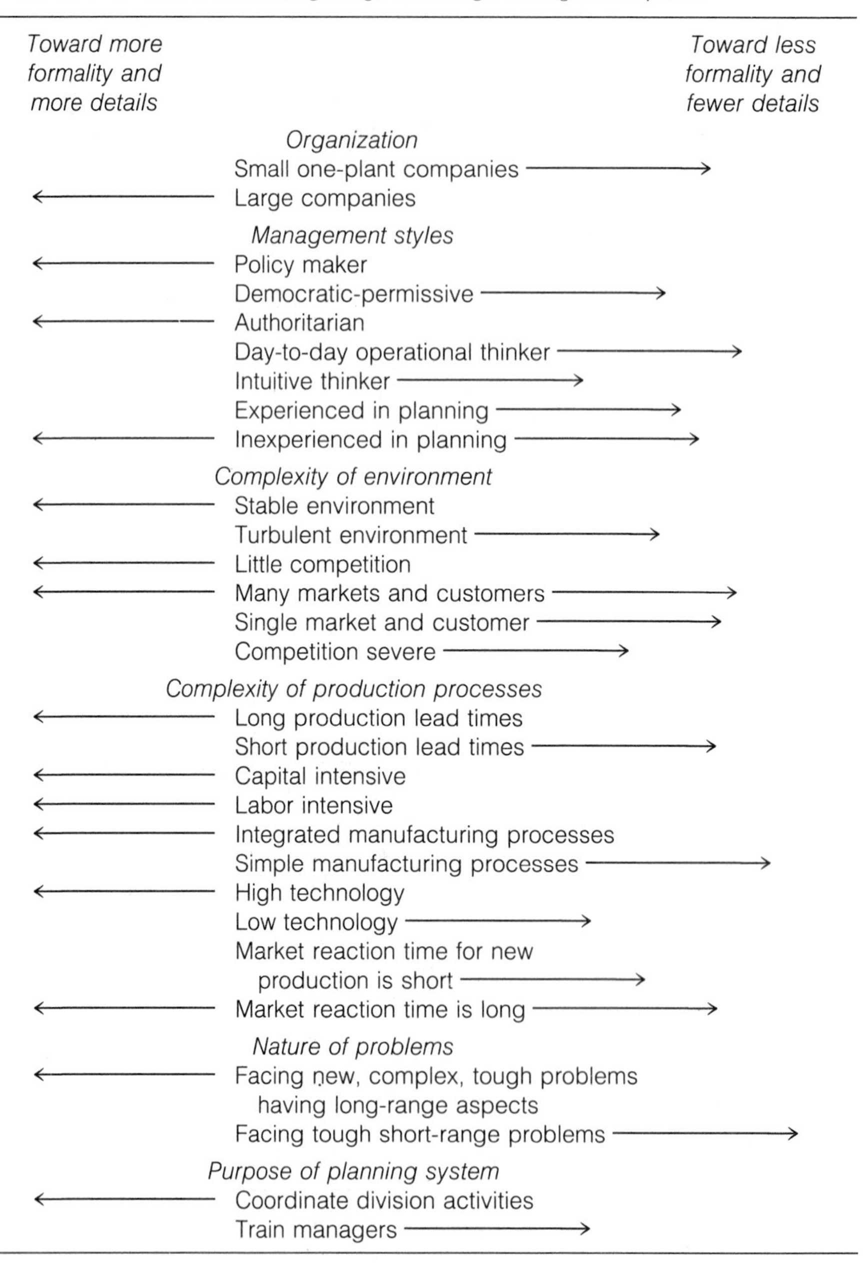

FIGURE 1–4 Forces influencing design of strategic management systems

Source: Reprinted with permission of the Free Press, a Division of Macmillan, Inc., from *Strategic Planning: What Every Manager Must Know* by George A. Steiner (New York: Free Press, 1979), p. 54. Copyright © 1979 by the Free Press.

opportunity and require a change in long-term objectives and strategies; or a failure to obtain annual objectives could require a change in policies; or a major competitor could announce a change in strategy that requires a change in the firm's mission. Therefore, strategy formulation, implementation, and evaluation activities should be performed on a continual basis, not just at the end of the year. The strategic-management process never really ends.

However, the strategic-management process is not cleanly divided and neatly performed in practice as the strategic-management model suggests. Strategists do not go through the process in lockstep fashion. Generally, there is give-and-take among hierarchical levels of an organization. For example, several managers may discuss possible new strategies for performing an external audit or consider new long-term objectives in revising a mission statement. Multidirectional arrows in Figure 1–3 illustrate the importance of good communication and feedback throughout the strategic-management process.

As shown in Figure 1–4, a number of different forces affect the formality of strategic management in organizations. Size of organization is a key factor: smaller firms are less formal in performing strategic-management tasks. Other variables that affect formality are management styles, complexity of environment, complexity of production processes, nature of problems, and purpose of planning system.

STRATEGIC MANAGEMENT IN SMALL FIRMS

Strategic management is vital for large firms' success, but what about small firms? The strategic-management process can benefit small companies, too. From their inception, all organizations have a strategy, even if the strategy just evolves from day-to-day operations. Recent data clearly shows that an ever-increasing number of men and women in the United States are starting their own business. This means more individuals are becoming strategists. During the first half of 1987, 33,055 new retail businesses, 27,278 new service-oriented small businesses, and 16,017 new construction businesses were opened in the United States. The information in Exhibit 1–4 describes additional features of current small businesses.

Numerous magazine and journal articles have focused on applying strategic-management concepts to small businesses.[17] A major conclusion that can be drawn from these articles is that lack of strategic-management knowledge is a serious obstacle for many small business owners. Other problems often encountered in applying strategic-management concepts to small businesses are a lack of sufficient capital to exploit external opportunities and a "day-to-day" cognitive frame of reference. Recent research concludes that strategic management in small firms is more informal than in large firms, but small firms that engage in strategic management outperform those that do not. Strategic management offers significant benefits to both manufacturing and service-oriented small businesses. Across the United States in 1986, 61,601 businesses failed, and most were small businesses. That number fell to 61,236 in 1987, which was the first time in eight years that the annual number of business failures in the United States declined. Business failures include bankruptcies, foreclosures, and court-mandated receiverships.

EXHIBIT 1–4 Small business strategy information

How old are individuals who are starting small businesses?

Age	Percent
20–29	25%
30–39	39%
40–49	24%
50 or over	11%

What sex are individuals who are starting small businesses?

Sex	Percent
Male	77%
Female	22%
No answer	1%

What is the average initial investment of people starting a small business?

Investment	Percent
Under $5,000	17%
$5,000–$9,999	14%
$10,000–$19,999	16%
$20,000–$49,999	25%
$50,000–$99,999	15%
$100,000–$249,999	8%
$250,000 or more	3%

What are the ten fastest growing cities for small business start-ups?

1. Austin, Texas
2. Orlando, Florida
3. Phoenix, Arizona
4. Dallas-Ft. Worth, Texas
5. Tucson, Arizona
6. San Antonio, Texas
7. Raleigh-Durham, North Carolina
8. Manchester-Nashua, New Hampshire
9. Atlanta, Georgia
10. Huntsville, Alabama

What are the ten fastest growing industries for small business start-ups?

Industry	Growth
Amusement and recreation services	12.2%
Masonry, stonework and plastering	11.8%
Credit reporting and collection	11.6%
Outpatient health care	10.8%
Millwork and plywood	10.5%
Medical and dental laboratories	10.1%
Highway and street construction	9.8%
Management and public relations services	8.3%
Painting, paperhanging and decorating	7.4%
Carpentry and flooring	6.6%

Source: Adapted from 1987 research information compiled by the National Federation of Independent Businesses, the Bureau of Labor Statistics, and *Inc. Magazine.*

STRATEGIC MANAGEMENT IN NONPROFIT AND GOVERNMENTAL ORGANIZATIONS

The strategic-management model can be used effectively by nonprofit and governmental organizations as well as private firms. An increasing number of governmental and nonprofit organizations (such as the Boy Scouts, the Red Cross, chambers of commerce, and public utilities) are using strategic management to survive and prosper in the late 1980s and 1990s. Compared to profit firms, nonprofit and governmental organizations often function in a monopolistic environment, produce a product or service that offers little or no measurability of performance, and are totally dependent on outside financing.

Even educational institutions are using the techniques and concepts described in this text more frequently. Richard Cyert, president of Carnegie-Mellon University, says, "I believe we do a far better job of strategic management than any company I know."[18] Population shifts in the United States from the Northeast and Midwest to the Southeast and West are but one factor causing trauma for educational institutions that have not planned for changing enrollments. Ivy League schools in the Northeast are recruiting more heavily in the Southeast and West. This trend represents a significant change in the competitive climate for attracting the best high school graduates each year. Some American colleges are following the lead of British universities that offer degree and certificate programs for would-be "nannies." Brookhaven College in Dallas, for example, gives 500 hours of training in parenting skills plus CPR, defensive driving, and contract negotiation. Colleges and universities are beginning to offer new courses intended to capitalize on the need for increased child care and elderly care in American homes. An excellent book entitled *Academic Strategy* by George Keller focuses on strategic management in colleges and universities.

Medical Organizations

An increasing number of medical organizations in this country are adopting a strategic-management approach to decision making. Medical institutions face severe threats from decreased governmental support and deregulation. Many private and state-supported medical institutions are in financial trouble as a result of traditionally taking a reactive rather than a proactive approach in dealing with their environment. Declining occupancy rates result from an accelerating growth of health maintenance organizations (HMOs), preferred provider organizations (PPOs), urgent care centers, outpatient surgery centers, diagnostic centers, specialized clinics, and group practices represent major threats facing hospitals today.

Current strategies being pursued by many hospitals include creating home health services, establishing nursing homes, and forming rehabilitation centers. In 1986, more than five hundred of the nation's 3,600 obstetric hospitals eliminated the mother-and-baby shuttle approach to delivery and post-partum care. They switched to hotel-like rooms or suites where the mother can stay for most or all of her visit. In 1987 and 1988, an additional 1,300 hospitals plan to begin offering the new service.

A growing number of hospitals are also entering the take-out food business by selling frozen dinners to people with special dietary restrictions. Selling one thousand meals a month, Holyoke Hospital in Massachusetts offers "Just What the Doctor Ordered"—entrees low in sugar, fat, cholesterol, and salt cooked in the hospital kitchen. Two Minnesota hospitals began national distribution of "Nutritious Cuisine" in 1987. NutraCare, Inc. of Newport Beach, California is expanding its line of hospital-marketed meals.

According to Brandon Melton, director of the American Society for Healthcare Human Resources Administration in Chicago, "the human resource director of hospitals has to become much more involved in strategic management for the institution; and he or she has to manage that department in such a way that its annual objectives match perfectly with long-term strategies." Due largely to increasing costs, more and more hospitals are contracting with outside companies to perform services such as providing 24-hour emergency-room and life-support systems. Psicor, Inc. in San Diego, for example, leases equipment and provides technicians for open heart surgery in eighty hospitals across the country. At least one thousand hospitals nationwide have contracted with firms such as Coastal Emergency Services in Durham, N.C. to provide emergency room services.

Government Agencies and Departments

Federal, state, county, and municipal agencies and departments, such as police departments, chambers of commerce, forestry associations, and health departments, meet needs of individuals living in specific geographic areas. Strategists in governmental agencies and departments are responsible for formulating, implementing, and evaluating strategies that use tax payers' dollars in the most cost-effective way to provide services and programs. Strategic-management concepts can enable governmental organizations to be more effective and efficient.

But strategists in governmental organizations operate in a unique environment; they operate with less strategic autonomy than their counterparts in private firms. Public enterprises ordinarily cannot diversify into unrelated businesses or merge with another firm. Governmental strategists usually enjoy little freedom in altering the organization's mission or redirecting objectives. Legislators and politicians often have direct or indirect control over major decisions. Strategic issues get discussed and debated in the media and in legislatures and become politicized.

On the surface, it may seem that strategic management is not applicable to government organizations, but the opposite is in fact the case. A recent article offers the following guidelines for strategic management in government-dependent organizations:

1. Strategies should be negotiated.
2. Outsiders must be involved in the process.
3. Socio-political issues must be adequately addressed.
4. Strategists must play an active and major role.
5. The process must be flexible to avoid bureaucratization.
6. Strategies cannot always be kept confidential.[19]

STRATEGIC MANAGEMENT IN MULTINATIONAL CORPORATIONS

For centuries before Columbus discovered America and surely for centuries to come, businesses have searched and will continue to search for new opportunities beyond their national boundaries. There has never been a more internationalized and economically competitive society than today's. Some domestic industries, such as textiles, semiconductors, and consumer electronics, are in complete disarray as a result of the international challenge. International forces are drawing countries, cultures, and organizations worldwide closer together. Foreign revenue as a percent of total company revenues already exceeds 50 percent in hundreds of American firms, including Exxon, Gillette, Dow Chemical, Citicorp, Colgate-Palmolive, and Texaco. Joint ventures between domestic and foreign firms are becoming the rule rather than the exception.

World trade centers are proliferating in the United States and abroad because of growing interest in foreign trade. In the United States alone, trade centers are now being built in Cedar Rapids, Iowa; Santa Ana, California; Hartford, Connecticut; Pomona, California; Long Beach, California; St. Paul, Minnesota; Toledo, Ohio; and Wichita, Kansas. These new world trade centers offer many specialized services, including helping small businesses in the region break into international trade, housing foreign banks, and including export firms and law offices. Eight of the world's ten largest public companies (in market value) are Japanese, including Nippon Telegraph & Telephone, the largest corporation in the world; among American firms, only IBM and Exxon make the top ten list.

The International Challenge

The strategic-management process in international corporations is conceptually the same as in purely domestic firms. However, competing in international markets makes strategic management far more complex because many more variables and relationships exist. The political, social, technological, economic, and competitive opportunities and threats that face a multinational corporation are almost limitless, and the number and complexity of these factors increase dramatically with the number of products produced and the number of geographic areas served.

More time and effort are required to identify and evaluate key external trends and events in multinational corporations (MNCs). Geographical distance, cultural and national differences, and variations in business practices make communication between domestic headquarters and overseas operations difficult. Strategy implementation can be more difficult because different cultures have different norms, values, and work ethics. In its simplest sense, the international challenge faced by many American businesses is twofold: (1) how to gain and maintain exports to other nations and (2) how to defend domestic markets against imported goods. Few companies can afford to ignore the presence of international competition. Firms that seem insulated and comfortable today may be vulnerable tomorrow. For example, Zenith is now the only major American company producing televisions, and yet it made just two million units in 1986; Japanese firms made eighteen million units and European firms made fifteen million units that year. Zenith's market share dropped from 20.5 percent in 1982 to 14.5 percent in 1987. The company lost $10 million in 1986. Also, four of the top seven manufacturers of semiconductor chips in the world are Japanese or Italian firms, and the largest company, Fujitsu, had 1986 sales of over $300 million.

In 1986, the U.S. ran big trade deficits with its largest trading partners, including a $58 billion deficit with Japan and a $23 billion deficit with Canada; in the same year, the United States had surpluses only with nations that have a low trading volume, such as a $3.48 billion surplus with the Netherlands and a $2.68 billion surplus with Australia. David Garfield, president of Ingersoll-Rand Company, offers three strategy suggestions to make domestic firms more competitive internationally:

1. The best defense is a good offense. Companies need to fight tooth and claw for exports and battle foreign competition on foreign ground wherever possible. This is preferable to competing intensely in domestic markets.

2. Investments that will improve competitive advantage should receive priority attention. Domestic firms should strive to reduce labor costs, lower overhead, compress production cycles, and improve the quality of products and services.
3. Domestic industries and firms need to help one another. They should give preference to U.S. suppliers and distributors; they should encourage one another to take action to improve competitiveness in technology, quality, service, and cost.[20]

Global Interdependence

The European Economic Community (EEC), religions, the Olympics, the World Bank, world trade centers, the Red Cross, conservation efforts, telecommunications, and economic summits all contribute to global interdependencies.[21] America's economy is becoming much less American; a world economy and monetary system is emerging. The American trade deficit skyrocketed to more than $150 billion in 1987, compared to a trade surplus in 1981 of $6 billion. Greater interdependence exists among national economies today than ever before. This interdependence presents enormous opportunities as well as severe economic, political, and social threats to virtually all organizations.

Corporations in every corner of the globe are today taking advantage of the opportunity to share in the benefits of worldwide economic development. Yet markets are shifting so rapidly in tastes, trends, prices, and new products that firms must work continually to stay abreast of changes. Innovative communication and transport systems are accelerating the transfer of technology and shifts in the nature and location of production systems, and are reducing the response time to changing market conditions. Immense strategic risks and potential benefits result from these types of changes. For example, the 50 percent drop in the value of the dollar against the Japanese yen, the Swiss franc, and the German mark in 1987 greatly benefited pharmaceutical and automobile companies in the United States, but greatly hurt petroleum and footwear companies. A low value of the dollar represents a major opportunity for exporting businesses but a major threat for domestic companies that rely on imported goods.

Along with the high degree of global economic interdependence that affects MNCs, *economic nationalism* also has a pronounced effect as evidenced by governments playing a larger role in world commerce than ever before. Governments help their own industries get an upper hand in international competition and restrict the opportunities open to foreign competitors. Globalization of industries is on the rise for many reasons, including a worldwide trend towards similar consumption patterns, the emergence of global buyers and sellers, and the integrated transmission of voice data and video signals.

Given the rapid trend towards increased global interdependence, even the Soviet Union is rethinking its traditional ways of doing business with the West. Mikhail Gorbachev is actively promoting joint ventures between Soviet enterprises and American companies, including Eli Lilly & Company, Cummins Engine, Occidental Petroleum Corporation, Combustion Engineering, Monsanto, Dresser Industries, Honeywell, Pepsico, and Philips. In conjunction with the Soviet Ministry of Oil Refining and Petrochemical Industry, Combustion Engineering has formed a joint venture, called Applied

Engineered Systems, to supply process-control technology for Soviet refineries. Pepsico will open two Pizza Huts in Moscow in 1988. Beginning January 1, 1988, 48,000 businesses in the Soviet Union were given financial independence and broad management autonomy. Gorbachev is rapidly moving the Soviet Union towards decentralizing business decision making and plans to reduce by 50 percent the employee staff of Gosplan, the central planning agency. He also intends to reduce the number of Moscow ministries from eighty to twenty. Gorbachev's overall policy to change the structure of business is called "glasnost" ("openness").

The Impact of Diverse Industrial Policies

Some domestic firms, such as Chrysler and Harley-Davidson, have been successful in persuading the United States government to aid them directly. When Honda, Kawasaki, Yamaha, and Suzuki shifted their focus from medium-sized motorcycles to large bikes, Harley-Davidson struggled to defend its domestic market. Nonetheless, Harley's market share dropped from 21 percent in 1979 to a meager 9 percent in 1983. After receiving help (in the form of restrictive tariffs) from the federal government, Harley's market share steadily climbed back to prior levels. By the time he gave a speech at a Harley plant in 1987, President Reagan could announce that the tariffs imposed to save the company were being lifted early, at Harley's request.

Perhaps the greatest threat to domestic firms engaged in international operations is the national and international debt situation. When countries become excessively leveraged, they frequently turn to slashing imports and boosting exports to generate trade surpluses capable of servicing their debt. Faced with these policies, domestic firms producing for export markets can often no longer import essential inputs. When a debtor country is successful in boosting its exports, domestic firms often encounter a protectionist backlash in foreign countries. According to the Small Business Administration, in 1987, the top five American industries with export potential were computers and peripherals hardware, telecommunications equipment and systems, computer software and services, medical instruments, equipment and supplies, and electronic parts.

Multinational business strategists can contribute to the solution of economic trade problems and improve their firms' competitive positions by maintaining and strengthening communication channels with domestic and foreign governments. Strategists are commonly on the front line of trade and financial crises around the world, so they often have direct knowledge of the gravity and interrelated nature of particular problems. Strategists should relay this knowledge and experience to national leaders. A steady stream of counsel and advice from international business strategists to policymakers and lawmakers can emphasize the deep interdependence that exists in the world economy, and the impossibility of global economic recovery when narrow, nationalist policies restrict trade and investment flows.

Strategists for multinational corporations must gain an understanding of foreign governments' industrial policies. Industrial policies differ from country to country as governments take different actions to develop their own economies. For example, cooperation between business and government in Japan is so good that some experts doubt whether a clear distinction exists there between government and business; some even use the term "Japan, Inc." when referring to the Japanese government and particularly the Ministry for International Trade and Industry (MITI). Industrial policies include providing government subsidies, promoting exports, restructuring industries, nationalizing businesses, imposing regulations, changing tax laws, instituting pollution standards, and establishing import quotas. The vicissitudes of foreign affairs make identifying and selecting from alternative strategies more challenging for MNCs than for their domestic counterparts.

> Strategic management has proven to be a valuable tool in the successful firm's repertoire. Firms traveling on the path of international business face more risks than their domestic counterparts, but also may reap greater rewards. Properly done, strategic management offers these firms a map to guide them on their journey through the perilous paths of international business.[22]

COMPARING BUSINESS AND MILITARY STRATEGY

A strong military heritage underlies the study of strategic management. In fact, the first strategic principles—including "objectives," "mission," "strengths," and "weaknesses"—may well have been formulated to address problems on the battlefield. In many respects business strategy is like military strategy, and military strategists have learned much over the centuries that can benefit business strategists today. Both business and military organizations try to use their own strengths to exploit competitors' weaknesses. If an organization's overall strategy is wrong (ineffective), then all the efficiency in the world may not be enough to allow success. Business or military success is generally not the happy result of accidental strategies. Rather, success is the product of continuous attention to changing internal and external conditions and the formulation and implementation of insightful adaptations to those conditions. The element of surprise provides great competitive advantages in both military and business strategy; information regarding opponents' or competitors' strategies and resources is also vitally important.

Of course, a fundamental difference between military and business strategy is that business strategy is formulated, implemented, and evaluated with an assumption of *competition,* whereas military strategy is based on an assumption of *conflict.* Nonetheless, military conflict and business competition are so similar that many techniques for formulating, implementing, and evaluating strategies apply equally to both. Business strategists have access to valuable insights that military thinkers have refined over time. For example, the Battle of Cannae (described in Exhibit 1–5) has come to symbolize the ultimate military planning and strategy and is considered by historians to be the best example of how superior strategy formulation and implementation can overcome an opponent's superiority in numbers and resources.

Both business and military organizations must adapt to change and constantly improve to be successful. Too often firms do not change their strategies when their environment and competitive conditions dictate the need to change. Gluck offers a classic military example of this:

> When Napoleon won it was because his opponents were committed to the strategy, tactics, and organization of earlier wars. When he lost—against Wellington, the Russians, and the Spaniards—it was because he, in turn, used tried-and-true strategies against enemies who thought afresh, who were developing the strategies not of the last war, but of the next.[23]

EXHIBIT 1–5 The Battle of Cannae

At dawn on the morning of August 2, 216 B.C., actions began in what was to become the Battle of Cannae, the most decisive battle in the history of warfare. Hannibal, who had led his Carthaginians across the Alps and into Italy in order to capture the land of his enemies, found his army of forty-two thousand opposed by a numerically superior force of seventy-two thousand fierce Roman warriors under Varro. Behind Hannibal's forces was the Aufidus River. He could neither escape nor avoid battle. Hannibal formulated an excellent strategy.

Hannibal divided his forces into an advanced weak center and strong flanks, both flanks resting on terrain features that would form a natural obstacle to the Roman advance. He deployed his cavalry on these flanks, the larger group to the left flank and a smaller group to the right. Varro, noting the disposition of Carthaginian infantry, immediately directed his forces to avoid the flanks and to crush the Carthaginian center by weight of numbers. Varro divided the Roman cavalry, sending approximately equal numbers to oppose the two Carthaginian cavalry units. This meant the Roman cavalry on the left was weaker than the Carthaginian cavalry opposing it. As Hannibal had planned, about sixty-five thousand Roman infantry were directed against the weaker Carthaginian center.

As the Roman mass rushed forward, the Carthaginian cavalry on the left attacked the smaller opposing Roman cavalry and destroyed it. Hannibal's cavalry then circled behind the Roman army to attack the other wing of Roman cavalry on the other Carthaginian flank. This other Roman cavalry force had been held in place by the smaller Carthaginian cavalry units. With superior numbers of Carthaginians attacking from two directions, the remaining Roman cavalry was defeated and put to flight.

Meanwhile, the main body of Roman infantry continued charging into the Carthaginian center. On orders from Hannibal, the center was slowly withdrawing, while the flanks held fast to their positions. The mass of Romans, ever increasing in density as Varro rushed more and more troops into what he perceived to be a disintegrating center, was drawn in between the two strong Carthaginian flanks.

Once the Roman army was completely encircled and without cavalry, Hannibal ordered his withdrawing center to attack. Simultaneously the strong Carthaginian infantry units on both flanks attacked. Packed so densely that they could not use their weapons effectively, and with their retreat cut off by Carthaginian cavalry at their backs, the Romans were slaughtered. More than sixty thousand Roman soldiers were killed in the Battle of Cannae. Hannibal demonstrated that a well-formulated and implemented strategy can enable an organization to overcome great odds.

Source: Adaptation from pp. 65–66 from *Encyclopedia of Military History*, Revised Edition by R. Ernest Dupuy and Trevor N. Dupuy. Copyright © 1970 by R. Ernest Dupuy and Data Memory Systems, Inc. Copyright 1977 by Data Memory Systems, Inc. Reprinted by permission of Harper & Row, Publishers, Inc. See also William Cohen, "War in the Marketplace," *Business Horizons* (March–April 1986): 10, 11.

CONCLUSION

All firms have a strategy, even if it is informal, unstructured, and sporadic. All organizations are heading somewhere, but unfortunately some organizations do not know where. The old saying "If you do not know where you are going, then any road will lead you there!" accents the need for organizations to use strategic-management concepts and techniques. The strategic-management process is becoming more and more widely used by small firms, large companies, nonprofit institutions, governmental organizations, and multinational conglomerates alike.

Organizations should take a proactive rather than a reactive approach to their environment, and should strive to influence, anticipate, and initiate rather than just respond to events. The strategic-management process embodies this approach to decision-making. It represents a logical, systematic, and objective approach for determining an enterprise's future direction. The stakes are generally too high for strategists to use intuition alone in choosing among alternative courses of action. Successful strategists take the time to think about their business, where they are with the business, and what they want to be as an organization, and then implement programs and policies to get from where they are to where they want to be in a reasonable period of time.

It is a known and accepted fact that people and organizations that plan ahead are much more likely to become what they want to become than those who do not plan at all. A "good" strategist plans and controls his plans, while a "bad" strategist never plans and then tries to control people! This textbook is devoted to providing you with the tools necessary to be a "good" strategist.

KEY TERMS AND CONCEPTS

Annual objectives
Business ethics
Corporate evolution
Economic nationalism
Environmental scanning
External audit
External opportunities
External threats
Forward integration
Horizontal diversification
Industrial policies
Internal audit
Internal strengths
Internal weaknesses
Intuition
Long-term objectives
Mission statement
Policies
Strategic management
Strategic-management process
Strategies
Strategists
Strategy evaluation
Strategy formulation
Strategy implementation

ISSUES FOR REVIEW AND DISCUSSION

1. Explain why business policy is often called a "capstone course."
2. Select one of the suggested readings at the end of this chapter. Go to your college library and find that article. Read the article and prepare a one-page written summary.
3. What aspect of strategy formulation do you think requires the most time? Why?
4. Why is strategy implementation often considered the most difficult stage in the strategic-management process?
5. How would strategy formulation differ for a small versus large organization? For a profit versus nonprofit organization?
6. Why is it so important to integrate intuition and analysis in strategic management?

7. Describe the importance of a formal mission statement.
8. Discuss relationships among objectives, strategies, and policies.
9. Why do you think some chief executive officers fail to use a strategic-management approach to decision making? Can you identify and describe a good alternative approach?
10. Discuss the importance of feedback in the strategic-management model.
11. How can strategists best assure that strategies formulated will be effectively implemented?
12. Give an example of a recent political development that changed the overall strategy of some organization.
13. Who are the major competitors of your college or university? What are their strengths and weaknesses? What are their strategies? How successful are these institutions compared to your college?
14. If you owned a small business, would you develop a code of business conduct? If yes, what variables would you include? If no, how would you assure that ethical business standards were being followed by your employees?
15. Would strategic-management concepts and techniques benefit foreign businesses as much as domestic firms? Justify your answer.
16. Compare business strategy and military strategy.

NOTES

1. Peter Drucker, *Management: Tasks, Responsibilities, and Practices* (New York: Harper & Row, 1974), 611.
2. Alfred Sloan, Jr., *Adventures of the White Collar Man* (New York: Doubleday, 1941), 104.
3. Quoted in Eugene Raudsepp, "Can You Trust Your Hunches?" *Management Review* (April 1960): 7.
4. Bruce Henderson, *Henderson on Corporate Strategy* (Boston: Abt Books, 1979), 6.
5. Michael Allen, "Strategic Management Hits Its Stride," *Planning Review* (September 1985): 6.
6. "Formal Integrated Long-Range Planning: Its Impact on Financial Risk Decisions," *Business Horizons* (March–April 1986): 80.
7. Robert H. Waterman, Jr., "How the Best Get Better," *Business Week* (14 September 1987): 99.
8. Rosemary Brady, "World Class," *Forbes* (18 June 1984): 133.
9. Saul Gellerman, "Why 'Good' Managers Make Bad Ethical Choices," *Harvard Business Review* (July–August 1986): 88.
10. Ibid., 88.
11. Drucker, *Management*, 462, 463.
12. John Pearce, II, and Fred David, "The Bottom Line on Corporate Mission Statements," *Academy of Management Executive* 1, no. 2 (May 1987): 109.
13. Ibid., 112.
14. Kraft, Inc., *Annual Report* (1986), 1.
15. Portland General Corporation, *Annual Report* (1986), 2, 3.
16. Weston Agor, "How Top Executives Use Their Intuition to Make Important Decisions," *Business Horizons* (January–February 1986): 6.
17. Some of these articles are: P. H. Thurston, "Should Smaller Companies Make Formal Plans?" *Harvard Business Review* (September–October 1983): 162–88; R. Robinson, J. Pearce, G. Vozikis, and T. Mescon, "The Relationship Between Stage of Development and Small Firm Planning and Performance," *Journal of Small Business Management* 22, no. 2 (April 1984): 45–52; L. Nagel, "Strategy Formulation for the Smaller Firm: A Practical Approach," *Long Range Planning* 14, no. 4 (August 1981): 115–120; P. G. Holland and W. Boulton, "Balancing the 'Family' and the 'Business' in Family Business," *Business Horizons*

(March–April 1984): 16–21; F. R. David, "Computer Assisted Strategic Planning for Small Businesses," *Journal of Systems Management* 36, no. 7 (July 1985): 24–33.

18. "How Academia Is Taking a Lesson from Business," *Business Week* (27 August 1984): 58.
19. Ravi Ramamurti, "Strategic Planning in Government—Dependent Businesses," *Long Range Planning* 19, no. 3 (June 1986): 68.
20. David Garfield, "The International Challenge to U.S. Business," *Journal of Business Strategy* 5, no. 4 (Spring 1985): 28, 29.
21. John Keane, "Focusing on the Corporate Future: Not a Trivial Pursuit," *Business Horizons* (January–February 1987): 31.
22. Ellen Fingerhut and Daryl Hatano, "Principles of Strategic Planning Applied to International Corporations," *Managerial Planning* (September–October 1983): 4–14. Also, Narendra Sethi, "Strategic Planning Systems for Multinational Companies," *Long Range Planning* 15, no. 3 (June 1982): 80–89.
23. Frederick Gluck, "Taking the Mystique out of Planning," *Across the Board* (July–August 1985): 59.

SUGGESTED READINGS

Agor, W. H. "How Top Executives Use Their Intuition to Make Important Decisions." *Business Horizons* (January–February 1986): 49–53.

Allen, M. G. "Strategic Management Hits Its Stride." *Planning Review* (September 1985): 6–9.

Bandrowski, J. F. "Orchestrating Planning Creativity." *Planning Review* (September 1985): 18–23.

Brache, A. "Taking the Strategic Planning Initiative." *Management Solutions* (June 1986): 36–42.

Cadbury, Sir Adrian. "Ethical Managers Make Their Own Rules." *Harvard Business Review* 65, no. 5 (September–October 1987): 69–73.

Carroll, A. B. "In Search of the Moral Manager." *Business Horizons* (March–April 1987): 7–15.

Cartwright, T. J. "The Lost Art of Planning." *Long Range Planning* 20, no. 2 (April 1987): 92–99.

Cohen, W. A. "War in the Marketplace." *Business Horizons* (March–April 1986): 10–20.

Diffenbach, J., and Higgins, R. B. "Strategic Credibility Can Make a Difference." *Business Horizons* (May–June 1987): 13–18.

Fannin, W. R., and Gilmore, C. B. "Developing a Strategy for International Business." *Long Range Planning* 19, no. 3 (1986): 81–85.

Gellerman, S. W. "Why 'Good' Managers Make Bad Ethical Choices." *Harvard Business Review* (July–August 1986): 85–90.

Gluck, F. W. "Taking the Mystique Out of Planning." *Across The Board* (August 1985): 56–61.

———. "A Fresh Look at Strategic Management." *Journal of Business Strategy* (Fall 1985): 4–19.

Godiwalla, Y. H. "Multinational Planning—Developing a Global Approach." *Long Range Planning* 19, no. 2 (April 1986): 110–116.

Hamermesh, R. G. "Making Planning Strategic." *Harvard Business Review* (July–August 1986): 115–120.

Hegarty W. H., and Hoffman, R. C. "Who Influences Strategic Decisions?" *Long Range Planning* 20, no. 2 (April 1987): 76–85.

Heskett, J. L. "Lessons in the Service Sector." *Harvard Business Review* (March–April 1987): 118–126.

Hornaday, R. W., and Wheatley, W. J. "Managerial Characteristics and the Financial Performance of Small Business." *Journal of Small Business Management* (April 1986): 1–7.

Hrebiniak, L. G., and Joyce, W. F. "The Strategic Importance of Managing Myopia." *Sloan Management Review* (Fall 1986): 5–14.

Ireland, R. D.; Hitt, M. A.; Bettis, R. A., and de Porras, D. A. "Strategy Formulation Processes: Differences in Perceptions of Strength and Weakness Indicators and Environmental Uncertainty by Managerial Level." *Strategic Management Review* 8, no. 5 (September–October 1987): 469–486.

Jauch, L. R., and Kraft, K. L. "Strategic Management of Uncertainty." *Academy of Management Review* 11, no. 4 (October 1986): 777–790.

Laczniak, G. R., and Naor, J. "Global Ethics: Wrestling with the Corporate Conscience." *Business* ly–September 1985): 3–10.

Litzinger, W. D., and Schaefer, T. E. "Business Ethics Bogeyman: The Perpetual Paradox." *Business Horizons* (March–April 1987): 16–21.

Loucks, V. R., Jr. "A CEO Looks at Ethics." *Business Horizons* (March–April 1987): 2–6.

McConkey, D. D. "Planning for Uncertainty." *Business Horizons* (January–February 1987): 40–45.

MacMillan, K. "Strategy: An Introduction." *Journal of General Management* 11, no. 3 (Spring 1986): 75–94.

Mason, J. "Developing Strategic Thinking." *Long Range Planning* 19, no. 3 (1986): 72–80.

Meredith, J. "The Strategic Advantages of New Manufacturing Technologies for Small Firms." *Strategic Management Journal* 8 (1987): 249–258.

Morris, Elinor. "Vision and Strategy: A Focus for the Future." *Journal of Business Strategy* 8, no. 2 (Fall 1987): 51–58.

Mushkat, M. "Improving the Prospects for Plan Acceptance in Public Organizations." *Long Range Planning* 20, no. 1 (February 1987): 52–66.

Noyes, T. E. "The Evolution of Strategic Planning at Signode." *Planning Review* (September 1985): 10–13.

Ohmae, K. "In Praise of Planning." *Planning Review* (September 1985): 4.

Payne, A. "New Trends in the Strategy Consulting Industry." *Journal of Business Strategy* (Summer 1986): 43–55.

Pearce, J. A. II; Freeman, E. B.; and Robinson, R. B., Jr. "The Tenuous Link between Formal Strategic Planning and Financial Performance." *The Academy of Management Review* 12, no. 4 (October 1987): 658–675.

Pearce, J. A. II; Robbins, D. K.; and Robinson, R. B., Jr. "The Impact of Grand Strategy and Planning Formality on Financial Performance." *Strategic Management Journal* 8 (1987): 125–134.

Peters, Thomas P. *Thriving on Chaos*. New York: Alfred A. Knopf, 1987.

Porter, M. E. "From Competitive Advantage to Corporate Strategy." *Harvard Business Review* (May–June 1987): 43–59.

Quinn, J. B., and Gagnon, C. E. "Will Services Follow Manufacturing into Decline?" *Harvard Business Review* (November–December 1986): 95–103.

Ramamurti, R. "Strategic Planning in Government-Dependent Businesses." *Long Range Planning* 19, no. 3 (June 1986): 62–71.

Ring, P. S., and Perry, J. L. "Strategic Management in Public and Private Organizations: Implications of Distinctive Contexts and Constraints." *Academy of Management Review* 10, no. 2 (1985): 276–286.

Rosenberg, L. J. and Schewe, C. D. "Strategic Planning: Fulfilling the Promise." *Business Horizons* (July–August 1985): 54–62.

Scholz, Christian. "Corporate Culture and Strategy—The Problem of Strategic Fit." *Long Range Planning* 20, no. 4 (1987): 78–87.

Schwaninger, M. "A Practical Approach to Strategy Development." *Long Range Planning* 20, no. 5 (October 1987): 74–85.

Slevin, Dennis, and Pinto, Jeff. "Balancing Strategy and Tactics in Project Implementation." *Strategic Management Review* 29, no. 1 (Fall 1987): 33–42.

Smith, Daniel C., and Prescott, J. "Demystifying Competitive Analysis." *Planning Review* 15, no. 5 (September–October 1987): 8–13.

TenDam, H. "Strategic Management in a Government Agency." *Long Range Planning* 19, no. 4 (August 1986): 78–86.

Waterman, Robert H., Jr. *The Renewal Factor: How the Best Get and Keep the Competitive Edge*. New York: Bantam, 1987.

THE COHESION CASE AND EXPERIENTIAL EXERCISES

Two special features of this text are introduced here: the Cohesion Case and Experiential Exercises. As strategic-management concepts and techniques are introduced in later chapters, they are applied to the Cohesion Case through Experiential Exercises, which are designed to give students a practical, working knowledge of strategic-management concepts and tools. Some additional Experiential Exercises do not relate specifically to the Cohesion Case.

Ponderosa, Inc. is an international operator and franchiser of steakhouses and Casa Lupita Mexican restaurants, and the updated Ponderosa case is an excellent Cohesion Case for several important reasons. First, Ponderosa is a multinational corporation, and so international issues can be considered. Second, Ponderosa is a multidivisional organization, thus allowing strategic-management concepts to be applied at the corporate, divisional, and functional levels. Third, Ponderosa is undergoing extensive strategic changes, having just been acquired by Asher Edelman, who took the company private at the beginning of 1988. Fourth, Ponderosa is a relatively small and simple organization with annual sales under $500 million. Finally, you probably are familiar with family steakhouses and maybe have eaten at a Ponderosa restaurant, so it will not take much time to "learn this business."

Part Six of this text provides some detailed information on "How to Prepare a Case Analysis" and "How to Give an Oral Presentation." After reading the text and applying concepts and tools to the Cohesion Case through Experiential Exercises, you should be well prepared to analyze business policy cases. The objectives of the case method are:

1. To give you experience applying strategic-management concepts and techniques to different organizations.
2. To give you experience applying and integrating the knowledge you have gained in prior courses and work experiences.
3. To give you decision-making experience in actual organizations.
4. To improve your understanding of relationships among the functional areas of business and the strategic-management process.
5. To improve your self confidence; since there is no one right answer to a case, you will gain experience justifying and defending your own ideas, analyses, and recommendations.
6. To improve your oral and written communication skills.
7. To sharpen your analytical and intuitive skills.

THE COHESION CASE

THE COHESION CASE

Ponderosa, Inc., 1988

FRED R. DAVID

For better or worse, the guard changed at Ponderosa on January 21, 1987, the day Asher B. Edelman completed a hostile takeover. Edelman paid about $235 million for Ponderosa, and Edelman's newly formed company, PON Acquisition Corporation, acquired 95 percent of Ponderosa's outstanding common stock. Edelman replaced Gerald Office as Chairman of the Board and Chief Executive Officer. Six members of Ponderosa's board of directors resigned and were replaced with Edelman's own directors. Other Ponderosa top managers were fired or resigned on that day, including Thomas Russo, executive vice president, Fred Gonzales, chief marketing officer, and Randy Lawson, chief financial officer. Time alone will tell whether January 21, 1987 was the darkest or the brightest day in Ponderosa's history. Turmoil or prosperity could be on the horizon for Ponderosa, whose headquarters are located at Dayton International Airport in Vandalia, Ohio (ZIP code 45377; Telephone 513–454–2400).

HISTORY

The first Ponderosa steakhouse opened in 1965 in Kokomo, Indiana. In 1969, at twenty-seven, Gerald Office became Chairman of the Board and President of Ponderosa. During the 1970s, Ponderosa's annual revenues increased every year to a high of $274 million in 1979 on net earnings of $13 million. Ponderosa's return on equity was 25.6 percent in 1979 and its debt/equity ratio was 1.46. The 1970s were a great decade for the company.

Ponderosa's fiscal year ends in the month of February. In fiscal 1980, Ponderosa created a wholly-owned subsidiary, ESI Meats, to operate a meat processing and freezer facility in Bristol, Indiana. The Bristol ESI plant is one of the largest freezer facilities under one roof in the world. In addition to supplying all company-owned and most franchised Ponderosa steakhouses with meat products, ESI distributes non-meat items such as french fries, seafood, desserts, and paper products.

Fiscal year 1981 was the first disappointing period of time for Ponderosa. Net income fell to $2.3 million from $13.1 million the year before. Return on stockholders' equity fell to 3.5 percent from 20.1 percent in 1980. Four of Ponderosa's top managers resigned or were fired in 1981. New strategies were put in place in hopes of restoring the company to prosperity.

Fiscal Year 1982

Ponderosa began concentric diversification in 1982 by acquiring Casa Lupita. Casa Lupita is a chain of Mexican dinner restaurants that serves a broad menu of Mexican and American foods and alcoholic beverages. Although Ponderosa does not have a single executive with experience in running Mexican restaurants, six Casa Lupita restaurants were opened in 1982. Mexican dinner chains enjoyed an average 15 percent to 20 percent annual growth in 1982.

Casa Lupita Mexican restaurants are designed to attract middle and upper income customers. They serve a variety of Mexican foods including chimichangas, enchiladas, burritos, tacos, and a wide variety of beef, seafood, and chicken specialties. Customers enjoy complete bar service with margaritas as the featured drink. The decor is classic Mexican and features stucco, Spanish colonial tiles, and live plants. Casa Lupita restaurants have a distinct physical separation between the bar and the dining areas.

Major competitors to Casa Lupita are El Pacho, El Chico, Monterey House, Taco Villa, Taco Plaza, Taco Bueno, Casa Olé, Ninfu's, and Chi Chi's. Tacos and tortillas are much less expensive than main courses of beef alone, so Mexican food profit margins are high during economic bad times. Casa Lupita meal tabs average almost double those of a Ponderosa steakhouse. Donald R. Jackson, Executive Vice President and chief financial officer, says, "Ten Casa Lupitas have the same impact on our bottom line as eighty Ponderosas." Several Casa Lupitas are located in converted Ponderosa steakhouses.

Also in 1982, Ponderosa began to expand internationally. The first international Ponderosa steakhouse restaurant was completed in Watford, England. Watford has a population of about eight hundred thousand and is twelve miles from London. Ponderosa's international market development strategy is targeted towards the United Kingdom, Australia, West Germany, Singapore, Malaysia, Indonesia, and Puerto Rico. Ponderosa's net income and return on stockholders' equity rebounded in fiscal 1982 to $8.3 million and 12.5 percent, respectively.

Fiscal Year 1983

Ponderosa's net income increased further in fiscal 1983 to $10.4 million on revenues of $385 million. The company began to emphasize expansion through licensee operations. In this year, Ponderosa opened ten new licensed steakhouses for a total of 235 licensed steakhouses in the United States and Canada; 447 company-owned steakhouses in the United States and one in England; and two company-owned and four licensed Casa Lupita restaurants in the United States. Ponderosa's 682 steakhouses are concentrated in the Northeast United States and Florida; only seventeen are located outside these areas.

During 1983, the company cut its debt/equity ratio nearly in half as it made improvements in cost effectiveness and operating efficiency. The company's marketing strategy was changed to emphasize heavy discounting and television advertising. A new advertising theme was adopted for fiscal 1984: "The Biggest Little Steakhouse in the U.S.A." Ponderosa began shifting its menu mix to higher priced offerings in 1983.

Fiscal Year 1984

A number of new programs were established in 1984. Ponderosa installed "The World's Biggest, Best Salad Buffet," a striking, thirty-foot long buffet of over fifty different items. Also introduced was "The World's Biggest, Best Breakfast Buffet." New marketing programs were instituted to reduce couponing and discounting. Total advertising expenditures in fiscal 1984 were approximately 4 percent of revenues, and much heavier emphasis was placed upon television media. Ponderosa's featured spokesman in its television ads was president Gerald Office. Newspaper advertisements that would focus on higher priced items were planned for fiscal 1985. Ponderosa constructed and opened three new Casa Lupita restaurants and purchased four previously licensed units in the Pacific Northwest. Also during fiscal 1984, Ponderosa began construction of a second restaurant in England and reached a territorial development agreement in the Far East for seven licensed units to be built in Singapore, Malaysia, and Indonesia over the next four years. The strategy of worldwide market development was selected because most restaurant companies operating overseas are of the fast food variety, not the family steakhouse type business.

During fiscal 1984, Ponderosa expanded its steakhouse menu to include a New York strip steak, a filet mignon, a porterhouse steak, chicken Italian, country fried steak, and a "Chicken Value Meal." Total revenues and net income increased to $429 million and $12.1 million, respectively. By the end of the year there were 436 company-owned Ponderosa steakhouses in the United States plus one in England, 221 licensed steakhouses in the United States and Canada, and nine company-owned Casa Lupita restaurants in the United States.

Fiscal Year 1985

During fiscal 1985, Ponderosa constructed eleven new Casa Lupita restaurants in New Jersey, Florida, Pennsylvania, Ohio, Michigan, and Illinois. Total revenues for fiscal

1985 increased to $513 million, but net income decreased to $8.4 million. Return on stockholders' equity for 1985 was 6 percent and the debt/equity ratio was 0.30.

Ponderosa designed and tested a steakhouse renovation program during fiscal 1985. This renovation included lighter color schemes, new smallwares, uniforms, more efficient layouts, and additional seating. The company also decentralized marketing decision-making to allow individual districts and restaurants to respond more quickly to local competitive pressure and customer preferences.

Some of Ponderosa's critics said the company should have been pursuing domestic market development rather than foreign market expansion, since there were still only two Ponderosa steakhouses in the southern United States (excluding Florida), no restaurants on the West Coast, only seven restaurants west of Texas, just one Ponderosa steakhouse in Texas, and no Ponderosa restaurants in California or the Carolinas. Critics asked, "Why is Ponderosa interested in putting restaurants in Malaysia, Singapore, and Indonesia instead of North Carolina, Louisiana, California, and other states with no Ponderosas?"

The Watford restaurant was enjoying exceptional success. Although its storefront location limited its seating capacity, customer counts were 50 percent larger than those recorded in the average American Ponderosa. A second Ponderosa steakhouse opened in Croydon (London) early in fiscal 1985. Ponderosa's long-term strategy in 1985 was to find joint venture partners who would develop the Ponderosa concept internationally. Ponderosa estimated that as many as one hundred of their steakhouses could operate successfully in Great Britain alone.

By the end of fiscal 1985, Ponderosa offered a breakfast buffet in over four hundred company-owned steakhouses and ninety licensed restaurants and produced over $60 million of new business. During the second quarter of fiscal 1985, prices for the all-you-can-eat breakfast buffet increased from $2.99 to $3.19 on weekdays and from $3.59 to $3.79 on weekends.

Fiscal Year 1986

In 1986 net income again declined by 55 percent to $3.7 million. Revenues in fiscal 1986 also decreased to $490 million. Earnings per share declined to $0.39 in 1986 compared to $0.92 in 1985, a 58 percent decline. These declines weakened Ponderosa. The company was further weakened in fiscal 1986 by having to defend itself from a hostile takeover by USA Cafes, the parent company of Bonanza steakhouses. The successful defense cost Ponderosa $2.6 million in investment banking and legal fees.

A number of new products were introduced in fiscal 1986, including the "No Stopping The Topping Sundae Bar" and a hot vegetable bar called the "Hot Spot." However, breakfast was removed from 260 company-owned steakhouses due to unsatisfactory profit levels. (One hundred seventy-eight company-owned and franchised steakhouses continued to serve breakfast.) Thirty new steakhouses were franchised during fiscal 1986 and thirty-five company-owned restaurants were sold to franchisees. Three new Casa Lupita restaurants were opened in fiscal 1986. The fourth Ponderosa in England opened in fiscal 1986. Franchised Steak & Salad Restaurants opened in Singapore, Taiwan, and the Republic of China.

During fiscal 1986, the corporate staff was cut to one-third of what it had been, with expected savings of $3.5 million a year starting in 1987. Plans for fiscal 1987 were to open sixty-seven new franchised steakhouses and two new Casa Lupita restaurants, to build twenty new company-owned steakhouse restaurants, to franchise eight new Steak & Salad Restaurants overseas, and to remodel seventy steakhouses. Ponderosa's long-term strategy was to have five hundred franchised steakhouses by fiscal 1991.

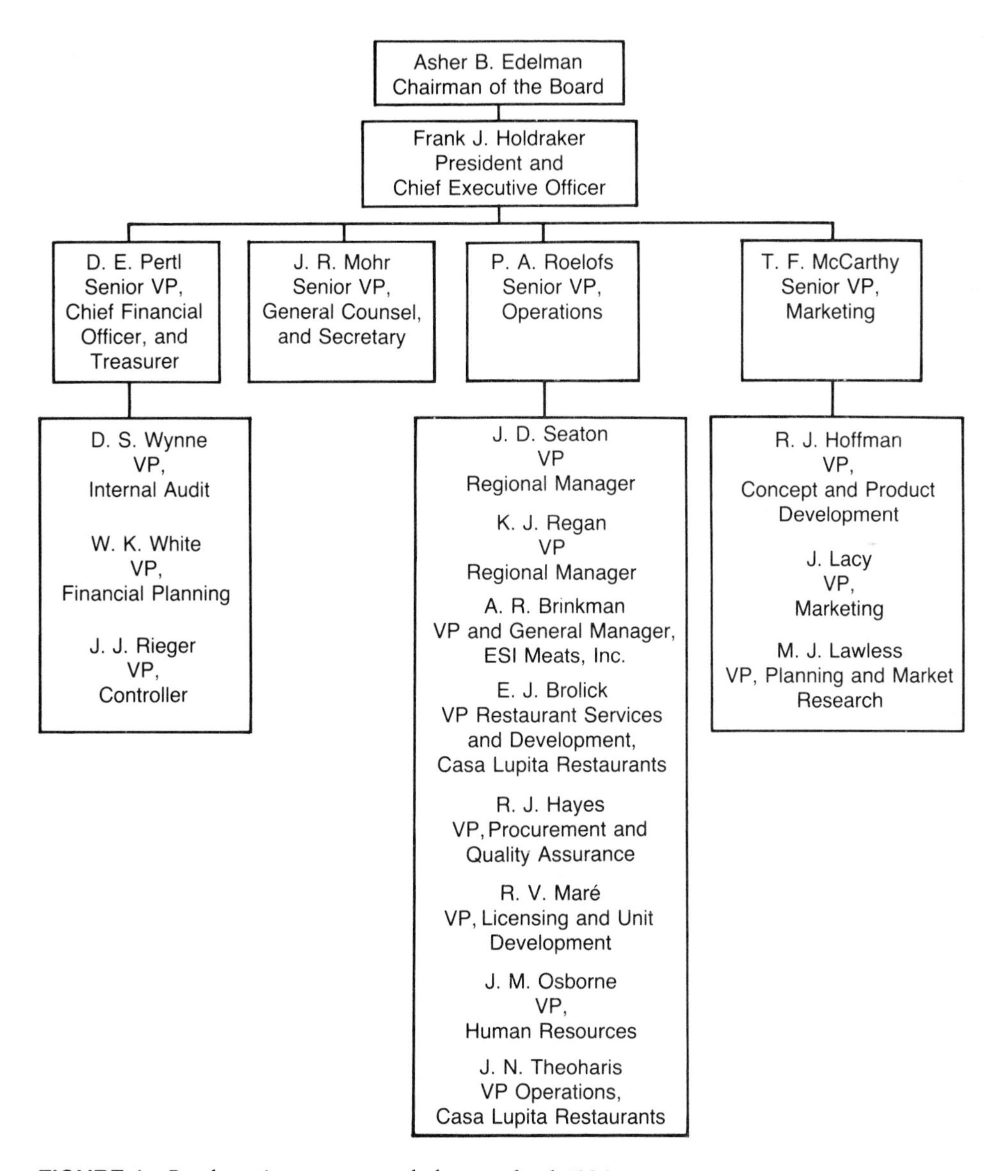

FIGURE 1 Ponderosa's organizational chart in fiscal 1986

Source: Based on information given in Ponderosa's 1987 *Annual Report,* p. 42.

EXHIBIT 1 Summary information regarding the purchase price of Ponderosa

(In thousands)		
Purchase Price		
The purchase price consists of the following:		
Cost to acquire 9,344,621 shares:		
Capital contribution (1,603,300 shares)	$ 38,617	
Acquired in tender offer (7,741,321 shares)	226,433	$265,050
Remaining common shares including redemption of outstanding options (519,810 shares)		15,100
Fees and expenses		9,597
Total Purchase Price		$289,747
Allocation of Purchase Price		
The allocation of the purchase price is as follows:		
Cash		$ 12,862
Accounts and notes receivable		4,589
Inventories		5,719
Assets held for sale		54,300
Property, plant, and equipment		188,371
Other assets		36,336
Accounts payable		(28,650)
Accrued expenses		(36,010)
Long-term obligations (including current portion)		(56,937)
Excess of cost over fair value of net assets acquired		109,167
Total Allocation of Purchase Price		$289,747

Source: Ponderosa's 1987 *Annual Report,* p. 31. Used with permission.

THE TAKEOVER YEAR

Then it happened. On December 2, 1986, PON Acquisition Corporation began an unsolicited tender offer to purchase all outstanding shares of common stock of Ponderosa. On January 21, 1987, PON Acquisition obtained 7.7 million shares of Ponderosa's common stock. In exchange, Ponderosa stockholders received $29.25 per share in cash, amounting to $15,100,000. These shares, together with the 1.6 million that PON already owned, constituted approximately 95 percent of the shares outstanding. On the same date, Gerald Office resigned under pressure as Chief Executive Officer and Chairman of the Board of Ponderosa. For fiscal year 1987, Mr. Office received a salary of $610,577, plus $6,378,133 pursuant to the "change of control" provisions, $1,731,358 for stock appreciation rights, and $48,619 of additional compensation. Due to a so-called golden parachute feature in his contract, he will receive from Ponderosa an annual salary of $500,000 through 1998.

Frank Holdraker (age 43) now serves as President and Chief Executive Officer of Ponderosa. David Pertl (age 35) is Vice President, Chief Financial Officer, and Treasurer. Asher Edelman (age 48) is Chairman of the Board of Directors. Current directors include Gerald Agranoff, Jamie Coulter, Frank Holdraker, Corey Horowitz and

EXHIBIT 2 Ponderosa's statement of consolidated income

(In thousands except per share data)	47 Weeks Ended January 21, 1987	Year Ended February 27, 1986	Year Ended February 28, 1985
Revenues			
Food sales	$461,363	$474,109	$499,411
Service fees and other income	18,915	16,195	13,891
Total Revenues	480,278	490,304	513,302
Cost and Expenses			
Cost of food sales	191,544	195,045	219,281
Restaurant operating expenses	233,382	255,457	247,532
Rent expense	16,952	19,094	18,089
General and administrative expenses	7,606	7,115	9,715
Interest expense	5,040	6,435	6,678
Takeover expenses	19,468	2,558	—
Total Cost and Expenses	473,992	485,704	501,295
Income Before Income Taxes	6,286	4,600	12,007
Income Taxes			
State, local and foreign	1,058	818	1,228
Federal			
Current	2,291	43	705
Deferred	844	(8)	1,670
Total Income Taxes	4,193	853	3,603
Net Income	$ 2,093	$ 3,747	$ 8,404
Net Income Per Share	$ 0.21	$ 0.39	$ 0.92
Average Shares Outstanding	9,752	9,680	9,161

Source: Ponderosa's 1987 *Annual Report*, p. 12. Used with permission.

Gerald Office. Office's resignation as a director of Ponderosa was effective on December 31, 1987.

Figure 1 illustrates Ponderosa's organization immediately following the takeover.

As a result of the acquisition, Ponderosa reported two financial statements in its 1987 *Annual Report;* one was for the forty-seven weeks ending January 21, 1987, and the other was for the five weeks ending February 26, 1987. For the forty-seven weeks ending January 21, Ponderosa's revenues declined further to $480 million and net income declined to $2.1 million from fiscal 1986. For the five weeks ending February 26, 1987, revenues were $54 million and net income was a negative $3.9 million.

Ponderosa's debt/equity ratio jumped from 0.45 on January 21, 1987 to 8.54 on February 26 due to takeover debts. Ponderosa incurred $19.5 million in debt due to the takeover including $8.682 million for severance payments to executive officers, $5.452 million for investment banking and legal fees, $5.108 million for payment of stock appreciation rights, and $226 thousand for other expenses. A summary of the Purchase Price and Allocation of Purchase Price is given in Exhibit 1.

EXHIBIT 3 Ponderosa's consolidated balance sheets

(In thousands) Assets	January 21, 1987	February 27, 1986
Current Assets		
Cash and short-term investments	$ 14,368	$ 11,804
Accounts and notes receivable	7,481	7,146
Recoverable federal income taxes	1,021	133
Inventories	20,463	16,804
Prepaid expenses	6,628	4,703
Total Current Assets	49,961	40,590
Property, Plant and Equipment		
Land and improvements	17,809	15,550
Buildings, leaseholds and improvements	155,847	146,395
Equipment	169,462	163,857
Construction in progress	15,786	2,248
Total Property, Plant and Equipment	358,904	328,050
Less accumulated depreciation and amortization	(144,188)	(135,225)
Net Property, Plant and Equipment	214,716	192,825
Other Assets	23,177	22,058
Total Assets	$287,854	$255,473

PONDEROSA'S INTERNAL OPERATIONS

Ponderosa obtained a $40 million revolving credit agreement among five banks during fiscal 1987; $20.5 million of that money was still available on February 26, 1987. However, Ponderosa is now in violation of certain loan covenants of this revolving credit agreement. Ponderosa's income statements for fiscal 1985, 1986, and 1987 are provided in Exhibit 2. The company's balance sheets for fiscal 1985, 1986, and 1987 are provided in Exhibit 3. Ponderosa's Statement of Changes in Consolidated Financial Position for fiscal 1985, 1986, and 1987 is given in Exhibit 4.

Edelman is changing Ponderosa's organizational culture. He has changed Ponderosa's logo or symbol from a globe to a pine tree, as illustrated in Figure 2. The green pine tree symbol appeared on the front cover of Ponderosa's 1987 *Annual Report* for

Liabilities and Stockholders' Equity	January 21, 1987	February 27, 1986
Current Liabilities		
Accounts payable	$ 29,256	$ 25,369
Accrued payroll and employee benefits	9,493	7,705
Accrued interest	675	590
Accrued insurance	4,245	3,271
Accrued expenses—Note J	16,840	8,634
Federal taxes payable	145	—
Current portion of long-term obligations—Note G	35,969	3,860
Total Current Liabilities	96,623	49,429
Notes Payable—Note G	5,698	22,917
Obligations under Capitalized Leases—Notes G and H	24,828	25,454
Deferred Federal Income Taxes	14,032	12,392
Stockholders' Equity—Notes K and L		
Preferred stock, no par value authorized 25,000,000 shares (none issued)	—	—
Common stock, par value $0.10 per share authorized 25,000,000 shares (issued 1987-10,444,147; 1986-10,403,211)	1,044	1,040
Additional paid-in capital	64,753	62,510
Retained earnings	85,959	87,313
Foreign currency translation	(623)	(688)
Less cost of shares in treasury (shares in 1987-644,711; 1986-707,711)	(4,460)	(4,894)
Total Stockholders' Equity	146,673	145,281
Total Liabilities and Stockholders' Equity	$287,854	$255,473

Source: Ponderosa's 1987 *Annual Report*, pp. 12, 14, 15. Used with permission.

the first time. Previous annual reports featured the globe symbol. Edelman explains the logo change in the company's 1987 *Annual Report* (from the inside front cover):

> The new Ponderosa logo reflects the contemporary needs of our customers. Customers identify the Company with the Ponderosa pine trees and the use of green, beige, and burgundy was found to have a wider appeal. The positive image conveyed by the new logo has resulted in the Company utilizing the new logo and its color scheme in the remodeling program, new signage, employee uniforms, and a variety of in-unit supplies. The continued and extensive usage of the logo is expected to reinforce positive recall of Ponderosa and the pleasant dining experience which it affords.

Ponderosa's advertising spending increased from $19.3 million in fiscal 1986 to $22.0 million in 1987. Fees received from franchises increased to $7.9 million in 1987 from $6.7 million in 1986 and $5.6 million in 1985.

EXHIBIT 4 Ponderosa's statement of changes in consolidated financial position

(In thousands)	47 Weeks Ended January 21, 1987	Year Ended February 27, 1986	Year Ended February 28, 1985
Cash Provided from Operations			
Net income	$ 2,093	$ 3,747	$ 8,404
Non-cash charges to net income			
Depreciation	21,433	22,920	21,015
Amortization	3,970	3,900	3,751
Deferred income taxes	1,640	782	1,857
Changes in working capital components			
Accounts and notes receivable	(335)	(1,032)	(876)
Federal income taxes	(888)	2,275	(745)
Inventories	(3,659)	271	(229)
Prepaid expenses	(1,925)	(757)	(847)
Accounts payable and accrued expenses	15,085	(1,633)	5,990
Cash Provided from Operations	37,414	30,473	38,320
Dividends paid or payable	(2,928)	(3,876)	(3,845)
Cash Provided Before Investing and Financing Activities	34,486	26,597	34,475
Investing Activities			
Additions to property, plant and equipment	(57,174)	(25,815)	(50,812)
Carrying value of property, plant and equipment disposals	13,850	2,245	3,197
Resources designated for construction and acquisitions	—	—	7,053
Other, net	(5,559)	(5,016)	(5,599)
Cash Used by Investing Activities	(48,883)	(28,586)	(46,161)
Financing Activities			
Proceeds from notes payable and capitalized lease obligations	22,171	21,146	2,719
Repayment of notes payable and capitalized lease obligations	(7,956)	(12,408)	(26,201)
Proceeds from stock issuance	—	—	30,023
ESOP and Retirement Savings Plan contributions and exercise of stock options	2,681	873	627
Foreign currency translation	65	295	(580)
Cash Provided from Financing Activities	16,961	9,906	6,588
Increase (Decrease) in Cash and Short-term Investments	2,564	7,917	(5,098)
Cash and Short-term Investments, Beginning-of-period	11,804	3,887	8,985
Cash and Short-term Investments, End-of-period	$14,368	$11,804	$ 3,887

Source: Ponderosa's 1987 *Annual Report*. Used with permission.

FIGURE 2 Ponderosa's logo before (left) and after (right) the Edelman takeover
Logos used with permission.

Ponderosa Steakhouse Division

As of April 1987, Ponderosa operated 407 steakhouses and franchised another 246 restaurants using the name "Ponderosa Steakhouse." The company had steakhouses in thirty-one states, the Virgin Islands, Puerto Rico, and Canada. Ponderosa also operates three restaurants and franchises five others under the name "Ponderosa Steak & Salad" in Singapore, England, the Republic of China, and Taiwan. In fiscal 1987, forty-nine new steakhouses were opened. Of these, forty-three were franchised and six were company-owned. Three steakhouses were franchised in international markets. Average customer counts per week in fiscal 1987 increased 14.4 percent from the previous fiscal year. (Approximately ninety million meals were served to Ponderosa customers during fiscal 1987.) Average weekly sales for lunch and dinner increased 17.6 percent from $16,784 in 1986 to $19,739 in 1987. Ponderosa attributes this growth to the following factors:

1. The remodeling of 117 steakhouses
2. The new marketing theme, "There's a Family Feeling at Ponderosa"
3. The dedication to quality, service, and cleanliness
4. Several new menu items, including seafood products and charbroiled chicken

Ponderosa maintains tight control over its licensed steakhouses by requiring licensee managers to complete the company's formal training program and to operate their restaurants like the company-operated steakhouses. However, license agreements do not require licensees to purchase any meat or supplies from ESI Meats nor do they require a set of regulated prices. Ponderosa retains the right to inspect franchise steak-

TABLE 1 Ponderosa's Steakhouse Division, 1984—1987

	1987	*1986*	*1985*	*1984*
Average weekly sales per restaurant	$20,406	$18,267	$19,376	$16,487
Average weekly customer count	4,302	4,003	4,284	3,999
Average check amount	$4.74	$4.56	$4.52	$4.12

houses and cancel licenses if company standards are not met. Table 1 presents statistics that describe Ponderosa's Steakhouse Division for fiscal years 1984 through 1987.

A Ponderosa steakhouse is generally staffed by fifty hourly employees and three managers. Each steakhouse has about 5,400 square feet with seating capacity for two hundred customers and parking available for one hundred automobiles. Ponderosa is remodeling the interior and exterior of its restaurants, including new signs, lighting, carpeting, furniture, and changes to the facade. In certain restaurants, windows are being added to create a more airy, open environment. As of February 1987, 117 steakhouses had been remodeled. The company plans to remodel seventy more in fiscal 1988. In addition, sixteen franchised restaurants have been remodeled and it is expected that twenty to twenty-five more will be remodeled by the end of 1988. Ponderosa encourages franchisees to remodel in accordance with approved plans by offering credit with a maximum of 10 percent of the remodeling costs.

Casa Lupita Restaurants

Casa Lupita restaurants offer a complete line of alcoholic and nonalcoholic beverages in a festive atmosphere featuring stucco, Spanish colonial tiles, and Mexican decor. Once recruited, Casa Lupita franchise licensees undergo a four-month training program that includes both classroom and hands-on experiences. Casa Lupita restaurants generally have one hundred hourly employees and five managers. The restaurants range in size from 5,000 to 11,400 square feet with seating for one hundred to 270 customers in the dining area and about seventy-five in the bar. Casa Lupita operates twenty-three restaurants and franchises three others in the United States. Casa Lupita's average sales per week increased to $36,718 in 1987, up 5.3 percent from the previous year. The average check per person was $9.92. Two new franchised Casa Lupita restaurants and two company-owned restaurants were opened in 1987. Food sales for company-owned Casa Lupitas in fiscal 1987, 1986 and 1985 were $39.3 million, $34.2 million, and $23.9 million, respectively.

Casa Lupita has restaurant franchise and exclusive area development agreements. The area development agreement calls for the franchisee to pay a startup fee of ten thousand dollars per restaurant. Casa Lupita's franchise requirements are generally the same as those for the Ponderosa Steakhouses. As of April 1987, the company had three area development agreements in which ten restaurants would be opened by 1992. Because of uncertainty surrounding the planned divestiture of Casa Lupita, Ponderosa has given indefinite extensions to the development schedules. Exhibit 5 sum-

EXHIBIT 5 The locations of Ponderosa steakhouses and Casa Lupita restaurants on April 30, 1987

	Steakhouses		Casa Lupitas		Total
	Company	Franchised	Company	Franchised	Restaurants
Arizona		2			2
California		2			2
Colorado		2			2
Connecticut	8	1			9
Delaware		1			1
Florida	28	19	6	2	55
Georgia	1	1			2
Illinois	44	7	1		52
Indiana	21	42			63
Iowa	4				4
Kansas	4				4
Kentucky	9	9			18
Massachusetts	6	3			9
Michigan	30	27	2		59
Minnesota	9	1			10
Missouri	19	3			22
New Hampshire		1			1
New Jersey	1	14	2		17
New York	51	11			62
North Carolina		1			1
North Dakota		2			2
Ohio	104	14	5		123
Oregon			1		1
Pennsylvania	27	34	1		63
Rhode Island	3	1	1		5
South Carolina		1			1
Utah		6			6
Vermont		2			2
Virginia		6			6
Washington		1	4		5
West Virginia	8	1			9
Wisconsin	30	4			34
United States	407	219	23	3	652
Puerto Rico		7			7
U. S. Virgin Islands		1			1
Canada		19			19
United Kingdom	3	1			4
Singapore		2			2
Taiwan, Republic of China		2			2
Total Restaurants	410	251	23	3	687

Source: Ponderosa's 1987 *Annual Report*, page 43. Used with permission.

marizes the location of all Ponderosa Steakhouse and Casa Lupita restaurants as of April 30, 1987.

ESI Meats, Inc.

ESI sales for 1985, 1986 and 1987 to company-owned restaurants were $76,960,000, $72,472,000, and $96,305,000, respectively. Sales to franchisees and others were $24,966,000, $27,391,000, and $45,218,000 during these years. The company is currently planning to divest of ESI, but if the divestiture occurs, ESI will still be required to supply Ponderosa and its franchisees. Ponderosa's cost of food sales as a percent of total food sales increased to 41.5 percent in fiscal 1987 from 41.1 percent in fiscal 1986, largely due to the increase in ESI sales. Food received from ESI has a higher percentage cost of sales.

Employee Benefits

There were approximately 24,300 Ponderosa employees as of April 30, 1987. About 70 percent of these employees were employed for thirty hours or less per week. Casa Lupita employed about 2,500 persons and ESI about 500. There is no union present at any Ponderosa facilities.

Ponderosa offers employees aged twenty-one and over who have completed one year of service a retirement savings plan. The plan allows employees to contribute up to 10 percent of their annual compensation before taxes and an additional 6 percent of their compensation after taxes to a variety of investment alternatives. Ponderosa matches 50 percent of each participant's allocation up to 2 percent of each participants' annual compensation. For fiscal 1987, 1986, and 1985, Ponderosa contributed $624,000, $733,000, and $618,000 respectively to the retirement savings plan.

Ponderosa also offers a company pension plan for employees aged twenty-one or over who have completed one year of service. Ponderosa contributed $270,000, $395,000, and $382,000 for 1987, 1986, and 1985, respectively, to the employee pension plan.

ENVIRONMENTAL FACTORS

The cost of beef significantly affects Ponderosa's cost of food. As the price of beef goes up, Ponderosa's costs increase. The nationwide trend or shift away from eating red meat to consuming poultry and fish represents a threat to Ponderosa. However, the American beef industry spent $44 million in 1987 to promote "The Lighter Side of Beef." A recent advertisement saying "Beef, Real Food For Real People" had Cybill Shepherd wondering whether she could trust someone who doesn't eat hamburgers. In another advertisement, James Garner offered his beef kabob recipe: just sirloin, no vegetables.

Public opinion polls clearly show a growing concern among the general public about residues from pesticides, herbicides, and other agricultural chemicals in restaurant foods. As a result, more and more patrons of national steakhouse chains, and other restaurants too, are eating out less, buying fresh food from supermarkets, or even growing their own gardens.

The Tax Reform Act of 1986 directly affects Ponderosa, too. Reduction in the corporate tax rate from 46 percent to 40 percent in 1987 and to 34 percent in 1988 represents an opportunity. However, the Tax Reform Act also provides retroactive elimination of the investment tax credit for property placed in service after December 31, 1985. This is a threat to Ponderosa because historically the investment tax credit was an important factor in reducing the Company's effective tax rate. Depreciation schedules have been extended from three years to five years on much equipment that Ponderosa uses, including automobiles and trucks. Other legislative threats facing the restaurant industry in general and Ponderosa require employers

- ☐ to pay Social Security taxes on all employees tips
- ☐ to pay minimum health care benefits to all employees
- ☐ to grant up to 18 weeks of unpaid parental leave every 2 years, and 26 weeks of unpaid disability a year
- ☐ to give advance notice of a mass layoff or business shutdown

Ponderosa's business is seasonal, and summer months normally generate higher average weekly sales than do the winter months. This is especially true in the Northeast and Midwest United States during harsh winters. In September, 1987, the United States Department of Commerce forecast that disposable personal income would increase 2 percent in 1988, compared to a 1.4 percent increase in 1987. The Commerce Department also forecast that employment rates will rise 1.6 percent in 1988 compared to 1.2 percent in 1987.

According to the 1987 *Gallup Annual Report on Eating Out,* 33 percent of all breakfast and dinner customers and 26 percent of all lunch customers are aged fifty or older. Older Americans still eat out less than younger adults, but the gap is narrowing. On a typical day, 36 percent of all adults eat out. Dining out increased by 6 percent between 1978 and 1986, but for the fifty and older group, it increased 21 percent. Where these people decide to eat is the important question for top managers of major restaurant chains such as Ponderosa. For example, older people are more than twice as likely to order seafood as individuals aged eighteen to forty-nine. However, older individuals are less than half as likely to purchase take-out food or want an extensive menu or wine list.

The United States Department of Commerce reported in June, 1987, that sales trends at the nation's restaurants slowed for the fourth consecutive month. Total revenues at restaurants and bars in the United States were $13.21 billion in June 1987. This was 5.3 percent higher than June 1986, but lower than the percentage increase in May. As interest rates rise and individuals have less disposable income, restaurants meals are one of the easiest places to cut household budgets.

Lobbying groups such as the National Restaurant Association and the Foodservice and Lodging Institute work hard in Washington, D.C., to head off legislation that could hurt restaurant business. Most of Ponderosa's employees are paid hourly rates as determined by federal and state minimum wage and tip credit laws. Consequently, pending legislation to boost the current minimum-wage rate by 40 percent (from

$3.35 an hour to $4.65 an hour by 1990) represents a threat to the restaurant industry. Other proposed legislation on tip-reporting and tax reform would limit deductions for business meals.

COMPETITION

Supermarkets are beginning to challenge restaurants by offering freshly prepared foods; delis and salad bars are becoming common in these nontraditional settings. For example, Food Emporium and Shopwell, both divisions of A & P Company, recently began offering a line of seven freshly prepared appetizers and salads and ten entrees daily. The supermarket challenge to restaurants is spreading rapidly from the New England states, Ponderosa's primary market area. Prepared ready- to-eat food sales are surging in supermarkets. Most customer surveys show that individuals perceive supermarket take-out food to be fresher, healthier, and of better quality than restaurant food. New hypermarkets, huge discount plus grocery shopping complexes, are offering one-stop shopping. Convenience stores are also challenging restaurants with take-out entrees. For example, 7–Eleven has eight thousand outlets and does more than $700 million in annual food-service sales.

The family steakhouse industry is intensely competitive. Quincy's, Bonanza, Sizzler, Western Sizzlin, Steak & Ale, Western Steer, Golden Corral, and Family Steakhouse compete directly with Ponderosa. For example, Golden Corral, based in Raleigh, N.C., has expanded to thirty-three states with 493 restaurants in 1987. Golden Corral's plan is to open eighty to one hundred new units annually through 1992. Restaurants such as Shoney's and Denny's are also considered competitors because Ponderosa offers chicken and seafood entrees. Here we examine Ponderosa's two major competitors further.

Sizzler Steakhouses

Sizzler Restaurants International, Inc. is a 62 percent-owned subsidiary of Collins Foods International, Inc. Collins Foods is one of the largest franchisees of Kentucky Fried Chicken (KFC) restaurants with 201 KFCs in the United States and 52 KFCs in Australia. Collins Foods also has 170 Naugles restaurants in the United States. Collins Foods' net income increased to $20.9 million in 1987 on revenues of $522 million, compared to a net income of $4.6 million in 1986 on revenues of $341.7 million. Company-owned Collins Foods' sales were up 15 percent to $169.5 million in 1986, compared to $146.8 million in 1985. Franchised Collins Foods' sales were up 13 percent to $335.5 million, compared to $296.5 million for the previous year. Collins Foods bought seventy-seven Rustler Steakhouses in 1985 and acquired the rights to twenty-four more in 1986. By June 1986, twenty Rustler Steakhouses had been converted to Sizzlers. Plans are to convert sixty more during fiscal 1987.

Los Angeles-based Sizzler had 331 franchised restaurants and 153 company-owned restaurants in 1986, up from 327 and 138, respectively, in 1985. Franchised Sizzler restaurants include locations in Alaska, Guam, Japan, Hawaii, Kuwait, and Saudi Arabia. There are three company-owned and one franchised Sizzler in Australia. Forty percent of all Sizzlers are in California. A total of forty-eight Sizzlers were remodeled in fiscal 1986. Sizzler's average customer count per restaurant increased 7.4 percent in 1986, and average monthly sales increased 11.6 percent per restaurant. Total sales for fiscal 1986 increased to $182 million from $159 million in 1985. Net income in 1986 was $11.7 million, up from $9.9 million in 1985. Most Sizzler restaurants have recently introduced an enhanced menu including fresh fish, a soup bar, fresh fruit, and an expanded salad bar. Sizzler is transforming its image as a budget steakhouse serving working-class customers to a casual dinner house catering to a more affluent clientele. Among all restaurant chains in the United States, Sizzler ranked eleventh in total television advertising expenditures for the first half of 1987. Sizzler spent $9.6 million, an increase of 32 percent over the company's 1986 first-half figures.

Bonanza Steakhouses

The Bonanza Restaurant Division is the dominant division of Dallas-based USA Cafes. As of September 1987, there were 588 Bonanza steakhouses operating under fifty-five area development agreements. Bonanza steakhouses are located throughout the United States (except in the Pacific Northwest), and in Canada, Puerto Rico, and Australia. Bonanza plans to open sixty-five restaurants in fiscal 1987. States with more than twenty-five Bonanza restaurants include Texas, Arkansas, Tennessee, Illinois, and Michigan. Plans are to begin expansion into the Far East soon.

Average annual sales per Bonanza restaurant were $840,000 in 1986, up from $776,000 in 1985, and $738,000 in 1984. Net income in fiscal 1986 exceeded 1985 by 35.4 percent. The average Bonanza restaurant had a 6 percent increase in total customers in 1986, while the average increase for the industry was only 1 percent. Chainwide sales for Bonanza in 1986 were $458 million compared to $420 million in 1985, a 9 percent increase, while the restaurant industry as a whole increased only 2 percent. Bonanza's average weekly sales per restaurant increased from $14,925 in 1985 to $16,155 in 1986. Bonanza served approximately ninety-four million people in 1986, compared to eighty-nine million in 1985. The average age of Bonanza's customers is thirty-two, down from thirty-nine a few years ago.

Bonanza is remodeling all of its restaurants to shed its traditional western image and to introduce a new, lighter, contemporary image. A sixty-item "Freshtastiks" food bar and new menu items that include broiled chicken and shrimp have been introduced. Bonanza restaurants are adding skylights over Freshtastiks food bars, replacing tile with carpet, using light-colored wood to replace dark interiors, and replacing wooden doors with glass doors. By the end of 1987, 73 percent of all its steakhouses were either recently remodeled or new. The Freshtastiks food bar continues to be a favorite, with 30 percent of Bonanza's customers ordering it as a meal in itself. Bonanza is also continuing to offer "regional menus." Bonanza serves Mexican food in the Southwest, broiled scallops in the Northeast, and catfish in the South. A total of 37 percent of Bonanza's sales come from steak; 20 percent comes from chicken and seafood entrees.

FUTURE OUTLOOK

Edelman plans to use franchising to expand Ponderosa's operations in new and existing markets. Ponderosa has both area development and individual agreements. Area development agreements give individuals the right to develop one or several steakhouses in a specific geographic area during a specific time period. Franchisees pay Ponderosa 4 percent of sales and must spend another 4 percent of gross sales on advertising, of which 0.5 percent is paid to Ponderosa for systemwide advertising. Ponderosa's franchising agreements require all building plans and sites for steakhouses be approved by Ponderosa. Franchised restaurants must offer approximately the same menu and operate in the same general manner as company-owned steakhouses. Initial franchise fees during fiscal 1988 increased to $25,000. On April 30, 1987, Ponderosa had sixteen area development agreements with sixteen different franchisees, who collectively plan to open 219 Ponderosa steakhouses over the next ten years, as follows: 1987 (23), 1988 (34), 1989 (40), 1990 (38), 1991 (31), 1992–1996 (53). There is no guarantee that these units will in fact be opened.

Asher Edelman took Ponderosa private on December 31, 1987. There will be no *Annual Report* or *Form 10K* for Ponderosa after that date. In addition to numerous hirings and firings, Edelman has made it clear that many other things will change at Ponderosa. He is seeking to dispose of the Casa Lupita chain of restaurants and ESI Meats. Rumors say Michael Grisanti, chairman and president of the National Restaurant Association, is interested in purchasing Casa Lupita. Edelman plans to consolidate office locations and administrative functions. He believes consolidation will save Ponderosa $7 million annually through improved efficiency.

Ponderosa currently owns three restaurants and franchises one in England. Taiwan, Singapore, and the Republic of China each have two Ponderosa Steak & Salad franchises. Edelman is trying to dispose of Ponderosa's company-owned steakhouses in England. He wants to develop in international markets only on a franchising basis. Food sales for Ponderosa's international division for fiscal 1987, 1986, and 1985 were $2.7 million, $2.4 million, and $1.7 million, respectively. Additional revenues from franchise fees for the same years were $147,000, $103,000, and $75,000 respectively.

Edelman is considering introducing a pasta bar and express buffet service at all Ponderosa restaurants. He plans to add an express salad line at lunch. In Ponderosa's 1987 *Annual Report,* Edelman summarizes his outlook for the company:

> We look forward to fiscal 1988 as we focus on steakhouse operations, continue the remodeling program, and put an increased emphasis on franchising. Our goal is to franchise an additional 55 steakhouses in fiscal 1988, with the long-term objective to be two-thirds franchised by fiscal 1991. About $20 million will be used for remodeling and maintenance of existing steakhouses. It is anticipated that capital expenditures will remain at reduced levels for the next several years. Ponderosa currently plans to remodel approximately 70 company-owned steakhouses in fiscal 1988, increasing the total number of remodeled steakhouses to about 190 by year-end. (P. 4)

Do you think Edelman's proposed strategies are right for Ponderosa? Was this takeover good or bad for Ponderosa's employees and customers? For Ponderosa's shareholders and creditors? What strategies would you recommend Ponderosa pursue now? How could the company best implement those strategies?

SUGGESTED READINGS

"Golden Corral—Rounding Up a Strong Team." *Restaurant Business* (20 July 1987): 86–94.

Romeo, Peter. "Grisanti's to Buy, Convert 19 Casa Lupitas." *Nation's Restaurant News* 21, no. 30 (20 July 1987): 2.

———. "Ponderosa Tries Pasta, Express Buffet Service." *Nation's Restaurant News* 21, no. 36 (31 August 1987): 3.

In addition to *Nation's Restaurant News* (a weekly newspaper of the food-service industry) and *Restaurant Business, Restaurants and Institutions* is a good publication for additional information about the restaurant industry.

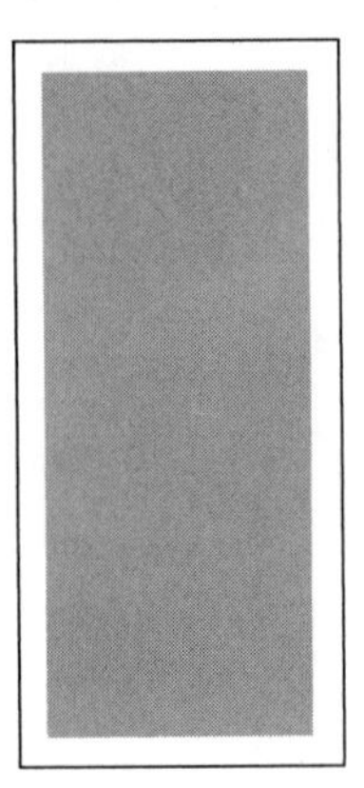

EXPERIENTIAL EXERCISES

EXPERIENTIAL EXERCISE 1A

Strategy Analysis for Ponderosa

PURPOSE

The purpose of this exercise is to give you experience identifying an organization's opportunities, threats, strengths, and weaknesses. This information is vital to generating and selecting among alternative strategies.

YOUR TASK

Step 1 At the top of a separate sheet of paper, write "Ponderosa's Opportunities." Halfway down this sheet, write "Ponderosa's Threats." At the top of another sheet of paper, write "Ponderosa's Strengths." Write "Ponderosa's Weaknesses" halfway down that sheet.

Step 2 From the Cohesion Case, identify what you consider to be Ponderosa's opportunities, threats, strengths, and weaknesses. List these key factors under the appropriate headings on the separate sheets of paper. Be sure to state each factor in specific terms.

Step 3 Compare your external and internal factors to factors developed by other students or the author. Keep this information for use in later exercises.

EXPERIENTIAL EXERCISE 1B

Examining Strategy Articles

PURPOSE

The purpose of this exercise is to familiarize you with strategy articles. Strategy articles can be found weekly in journals, magazines, and newspapers. By reading and studying strategy articles, you can gain a better understanding of the strategic-management process. Several of the best journals in which to find corporate-strategy articles are *Planning Review, Long Range Planning, Journal of Business Strategy,* and *Strategic Management Journal.* These journals are devoted to reporting the results of empirical research in strategic management. They apply strategic-management concepts to specific organizations and industries. They introduce new strategic-management techniques and provide short case studies on selected firms.

In addition to journals, many magazines regularly publish articles that focus on business strategies. Several of the best magazines to find applied strategy articles are *Dun's Business Month, Fortune, Forbes, Business Week, Inc. Magazine,* and *Industry Week.* A strategy article in one of these magazines generally introduces a particular organization's strategists, provides financial data on the company, identifies key competitors in the industry, and presents the firm's objectives and strategies.

Various newspapers, such as *USA Today, The Wall Street Journal, The New York Times,* and *Barrons,* consistently publish strategy stories. Articles published in newspapers are exceptionally timely. Newspapers cover strategy events when they occur, such as a joint venture being announced, a bankruptcy being declared, a new advertising campaign starting, a company being acquired, a division being divested, a chief executive officer being hired or fired, or a hostile takeover attempt.

In combination, journal, magazine, and newspaper articles can make the business policy course an exciting one. They allow current strategies of profit and nonprofit organizations to be identified and studied.

YOUR TASK

Step 1 Go to your college library and find a recent strategy article. Copy the article and bring it to class.

Step 2 Give a five-minute oral report summarizing the most important information in your article. Give your personal reaction to the article.

EXPERIENTIAL EXERCISE 1C

Developing a Code of Business Ethics

PURPOSE

This exercise can give you practice developing a code of business ethics. Research was recently conducted by the author to examine codes of business ethics from large manufacturing and service firms in the United States. The twenty-eight variables listed below were found to be included in a sample of more than eighty formal codes of business ethics. The variables are presented in order of how frequently they occurred. Thus, the first variable, "Conduct business in compliance with all laws," was the variable most often included in the sample documents; "Firearms at work are prohibited" was least often included.

1. Conduct business in compliance with all laws.
2. Payments for unlawful purposes are prohibited.
3. Avoid outside activities that impair duties.
4. Comply with all antitrust and trade regulations.
5. Comply with accounting rules and controls.
6. Bribes are prohibited.
7. Maintain confidentiality of records.
8. Participate in community and political activities.
9. Provide products and services of the highest quality.
10. Exhibit standards of personal integrity and conduct.
11. Do not propagate false or misleading information.
12. Perform assigned duties to the best of your ability.
13. Conserve resources and protect the environment.
14. Comply with safety, health, and security regulations.
15. Racial, ethnic, religious, and sexual harassment at work is prohibited.
16. Report unethical and illegal activities to your manager.
17. Convey true claims in product advertisements.
18. Make decisions without regard for personal gain.
19. Do not use company property for personal benefit.
20. Demonstrate courtesy, respect, honesty, and fairness.
21. Illegal drugs and alcohol at work are prohibited.
22. Manage personal finances well.
23. Employees are personally accountable for company funds.
24. Exhibit good attendance and punctuality.
25. Follow directives of supervisors.
26. Do not use abusive language.
27. Dress in businesslike attire.
28. Firearms at work are prohibited.

YOUR TASK

Step 1 Working alone for twenty minutes, write a code of business ethics for Ponderosa, Inc. Include as many variables listed above as you believe appropriate to Ponderosa's business. Limit your document to two hundred words or less.

Step 2 Join with three other students to form a team. Let everyone in your group read your code of business ethics, and read each of theirs in turn. As a group, select the best code of business ethics from the four being considered. This selection can be made by each person in the group rating each code on a 1 to 5 scale, where 5 = outstanding, 4 = excellent, 3 = good, 2 = fair, and 1 = weak. Add each person's ratings for each code to determine the best code; i.e., the highest score indicates the best code in the group.

Step 3 Submit the best code from your team to your professor for consideration as the "Best Code of Business Ethics in Class."

The Nature of Strategic Management

NOTABLE QUOTES

Strategic management is not a box of tricks or a bundle of techniques. It is analytical thinking and commitment of resources to action. But quantification alone is not planning. Some of the most important issues in strategic management cannot be quantified at all.

Peter Drucker

By taking over companies and breaking them up, corporate raiders thrive on failed corporate strategies. Fueled by junk bond financing and growing acceptability, raiders can expose any company to takeover, no matter how large or blue chip.

Michael Porter

Alice said, "Would you please tell me which way to go from here?" The cat said, "That depends on where you want to get to."

Lewis Carroll

Tomorrow always arrives. It is always different. And even the mightiest company is in trouble if it has not worked on the future. Being surprised by what happens is a risk that even the largest and richest company cannot afford, and even the smallest business need not run.

Peter Drucker

Planning. Doing things today to make us better tomorrow. Because the future belongs to those who make the hard decisions today.

Eaton Corporation

When organizations reach a fork in the road, forces are in motion that will, if not halted, drive a planning process towards the end-state of a self-perpetuating bureaucracy.

R.T. Lenz

Competing in the marketplace is like war. You have injuries and casualties, and the best strategy wins.

John Collins

2

OUTLINE

THE BENEFITS OF STRATEGIC MANAGEMENT

GUIDELINES FOR EFFECTIVE STRATEGIC MANAGEMENT

MERGERS, ACQUISITIONS, TAKEOVERS, AND LEVERAGED BUYOUTS

GENERIC TYPES OF STRATEGIES

GAINING COMPETITIVE ADVANTAGE

INTEGRATION STRATEGIES IN ACTION

INTENSIVE STRATEGIES IN ACTION

DIVERSIFICATION STRATEGIES IN ACTION

OTHER STRATEGIES IN ACTION

INTEGRATING STRATEGY AND CULTURE

Experiential Exercise 2A: Classifying Alternative Strategies for Ponderosa

Experiential Exercise 2B: Strategic Management at the Dynamic Computer Company

Experiential Exercise 2C: How Risky Are Various Alternative Strategies?

OBJECTIVES

After studying this chapter, you should be able to

- Describe the benefits of strategic management.
- Identify fourteen alternative types of generic business strategies.
- Identify and discuss numerous examples of organizations pursuing different types of strategies.
- Identify and discuss guidelines for pursuing various types of strategies.
- Discuss the importance of integrating strategic management and organizational culture.

This chapter describes the potential benefits of strategic management and the probable results of poorly conceived strategies. Generic types of strategies are defined and exemplified. Guidelines indicate when different types of strategies are most appropriate to pursue. Numerous examples of strategies in action are provided. Military and business strategies are compared and organizational culture issues are examined.

THE BENEFITS OF STRATEGIC MANAGEMENT

Many benefits can be derived from a strategic-management approach to decision making. First and perhaps foremost, strategic management allows an organization to initiate and influence (rather than just respond and react to) its environment and thus control its own destiny. Strategic-management concepts provide an objective basis for allocating resources and for reducing internal conflicts that can arise when subjectivity or intuition alone is the basis for major decisions. Strategic management allows an organization to take advantage of key environmental opportunities, to minimize the impact of external threats, to capitalize upon internal strengths, and to improve internal weaknesses. Strategic management allows organizations to anticipate and initiate change.

> In today's business environment, more than any preceding era, the only constant is change. Successful organizations effectively manage change, continuously adapting their bureaucracies, strategies, systems, products, and cultures to survive the shocks and prosper from the forces that decimate their competition.[1]

The strategic-management process, illustrated in Figure 2–1, can be an effective vehicle for generating synergy and esprit de corps among all managers and employees. William Dearden, chairman of Hershey Foods Corporation, attributes his company's success to strategic management. Hershey's sales and profits were up 12.2 percent and 11.6 percent, respectively, in 1987 over 1986. Dearden says:

> There is the strategic-management process. Planning for the long-term future has been entrenched as a way of life at Hershey, and we certainly plan to strengthen and rely on the process going forward.[2]

Financial Benefits

Many research studies have concluded that organizations using strategic-management concepts are more profitable and successful than those that do not. For example, Robinson's longitudinal study of 101 retail, service, and manufacturing firms over a three-year period concluded that businesses using strategic-management concepts showed significant improvement in sales, profitability, and productivity compared to firms without systematic planning activities; Buzzel and Heany's classic study reported that up to 80 percent of the improvement possible in a firm's profitability is achieved through changes in a company's strategic direction; Cook and Ferris report that the practices of high-performing firms reflect a more strategic orientation and a longer-term focus.[3] High-performing firms tend to do systematic planning to prepare for future fluctuations in their internal and external environments. Firms with planning systems more closely

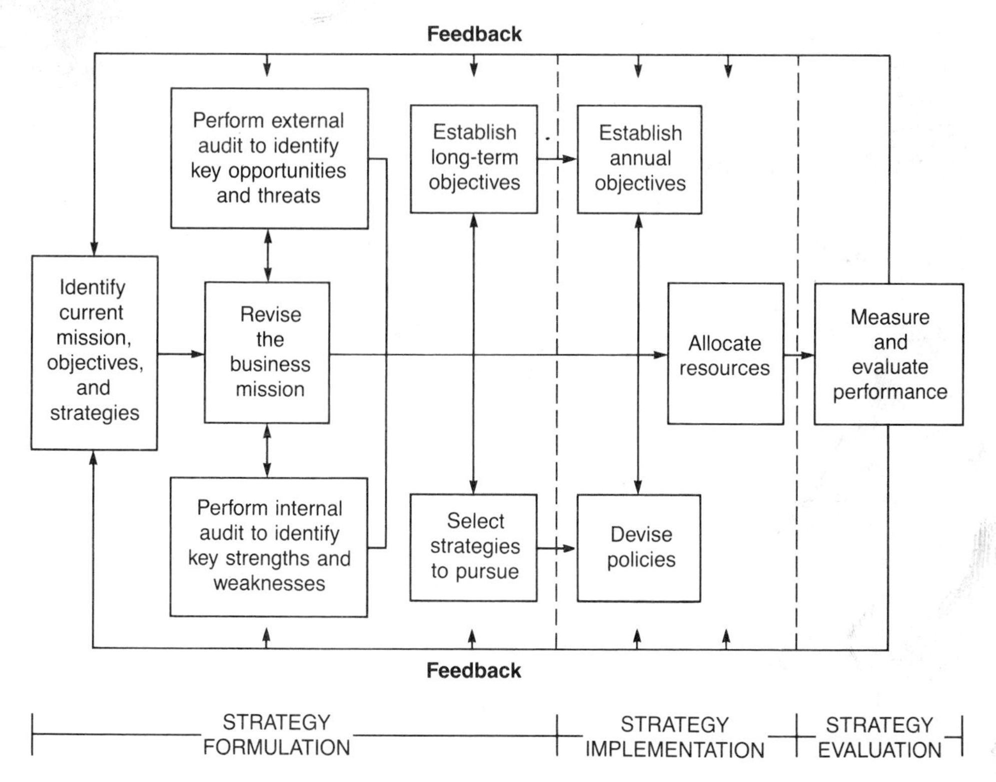

FIGURE 2–1 A comprehensive strategic-management model

resembling strategic-management theory generally exhibit superior long-term financial performance relative to their industry and also in absolute terms.

High-performing firms seem to make more informed decisions with good anticipation of both short- and long-term consequences. On the other hand, firms that perform poorly or not as well often engage in activities that are shortsighted and do not reflect good forecasting of future conditions. Michael Allen found that strategic management demonstrated impressive power by dramatically improving the performance of a number of major companies that had implemented it, including General Electric, American Express, Allied Corporation, Dun & Bradstreet, and Pitney Bowes.[4]

Strategists of low-performing organizations are often preoccupied with solving internal problems and meeting paperwork deadlines. They typically underestimate their competitors' strengths and overestimate their own firm's strengths. Strategists of low-performing organizations often attribute weak performance to uncontrollable factors such as a poor economy, technological change, or foreign competition. They often fail to appreciate or understand the need to devote sufficient time to formulating, implementing, and evaluating strategies that provide direction for the firm.

There has been almost a 70 percent turnover in the Fortune 500 list of companies from 1955 to 1988. Forty-one firms were dropped from the list in 1988 and replaced by others. Since 1980, approximately twenty thousand businesses annually have declared bankruptcy. Dun & Bradstreet Corporation reports that the number of business failures nationwide increases about 7 percent annually, while the number of business startups declines about 6 percent annually. Although many factors besides a lack of effective strategic management can lead to low performance, these statistics suggest that strategic-management concepts and techniques could be useful for many organizations.

Nonfinancial Benefits

Besides helping firms avoid financial demise, strategic management offers other benefits including an enhanced awareness of environmental threats, an improved understanding of competitors' strategies, increased employee productivity, reduced resistance to change, and a clearer understanding of performance-reward relationships. Strategic-management enhances the problem prevention capabilities of organizations, because it promotes interaction among managers at all levels. Strategic management often brings order and discipline to an enterprise. Yoo and Digman emphasize that strategic management is needed to cope with and manage uncertainty in decision making. They describe several benefits of strategic management:

1. It provides a way to anticipate future problems and opportunities.
2. It provides employees with clear objectives and directions for the future of the organization.
3. It results in more effective and better performance compared to non-strategic management organizations.
4. It increases employee satisfaction and motivation.
5. It provides timely information for decision makers.
6. It results in faster and better decision making and
7. It results in cost savings.[5]

A strategic-management approach to decision making is not a guarantee of success, but it can be the beginning of an efficient and effective managerial system. Strategic management may renew confidence in the current business strategy, or it may point to the need for corrective actions. The strategic-management process provides a basis for identifying and rationalizing the need for change to all managers and employees of a firm; it helps them see change as an opportunity rather than a threat. Greenley stresses that strategic management offers the following process and personnel benefits:

1. It allows for identification, prioritization, and exploitation of opportunities.
2. It provides an objective view of management problems.
3. It represents a framework for improved coordination and control of activities.
4. It minimizes the effects of adverse conditions and changes.
5. It allows major decisions to better support established objectives.
6. It allows more effective allocation of time and resources to identified opportunities.
7. It allows fewer resources and less time to be devoted to correcting erroneous or ad hoc decisions.
8. It creates a framework for internal communication among personnel.
9. It helps to integrate the behavior of individuals into a total effort.

10. It provides a basis for the clarification of individual responsibilities.
11. It gives encouragement to forward thinking.
12. It provides a cooperative, integrated, and enthusiastic approach to tackling problems and opportunities.
13. It encourages a favorable attitude towards change.
14. It gives a degree of discipline and formality to the management of a business.[6]

The Chrysler Corporation is a glowing example of an organization that has benefited immensely from strategic-management concepts. Lee Iacocca, chief executive officer at Chrysler, formulated and implemented a retrenchment strategy that turned the company around despite overwhelming internal weaknesses and external threats. Iacocca, a strong advocate of strategic management, says:

> When I came to Chrysler in 1979, the Michigan State fairgrounds were jammed with thousands of unsold, unwanted, rusting Chryslers, Dodges, and Plymouths. Foreign operations were leeching the lifeblood out of the company. And worst of all, cars were coming off the assembly line with loose doors, chipped paint, and crooked moldings.[7]

In 1980 Iacocca's annual salary was only $1.00. He says, "I didn't take $1 a year to be a martyr. I did it for good, cold, pragmatic reasons. I wanted our employees and our suppliers to be thinking: I can follow a guy who sets that kind of example."[8] Iacocca's strategic-management approach was instrumental in convincing the federal government to provide Chrysler with massive loan guarantees. His strategies paid off in Chrysler's successful comeback, and in 1986 he became the most highly paid corporate executive in America. His annual salary, plus bonus and stock options, was $20.5 million, which was $8 million higher than that of second-place Paul Fireman, chairman of Reebok International.

GUIDELINES FOR EFFECTIVE STRATEGIC MANAGEMENT

Although managers can expect numerous benefits to result from the strategic-management process, failing to follow certain guidelines can foster criticisms of the process and create problems for the organization. Strategic management must not become a self-perpetuating bureaucratic mechanism. Rather, it must be a self-reflective learning process that familiarizes managers in the organization with key strategic issues and feasible alternatives for resolving those issues. Strategic management must not become ritualistic, stilted, orchestrated, or too formal, predictable, and rigid. Words supported by numbers, rather than numbers supported by words, should represent the medium for explaining strategic issues and organizational responses. A key role of strategists is to facilitate continuous organizational learning and change. Robert Waterman emphasizes this, saying:

> Successful companies know how to keep things moving. If they share a habit pattern, it's the habit of habit breaking. Sometimes they seem to change for its own sake. IBM's chief executive, John Akers, says "IBM never reorganizes except for a good business reason, but if they haven't reorganized in a while, that's a good business reason." Successful companies are deliberate bureaucracy-busters. They delight in smashing pettifogging encumbrances that Harry Quadracci calls "playing office."[9]

R. T. Lenz offers some important guidelines for effective strategic management, as presented below:

> Keep the strategic-management process as simple and non-routine as possible. Eliminate jargon and arcane planning language. Remember, strategic management is a process for fostering learning and action, not merely a formal system for control.
>
> To avoid routinized behavior, vary assignments, team membership, meeting formats, and the planning calendar. The process should not be totally predictable, and settings must be changed to stimulate creativity.
>
> Emphasize word-oriented plans with numbers as back-up material. If managers cannot express their strategy in a paragraph or so, they either do not have one or do not understand it.
>
> Stimulate thinking and action that challenge the assumptions underlying current corporate strategy. Welcome bad news. If strategy is not working, managers desperately need to know it. Further, no pertinent information should be classified as inadmissible merely because it cannot be quantified.
>
> Build a corporate culture in which the role of strategic management and its essential purposes are understood. Do not permit "technicians" to co-opt the process. It is ultimately a process for learning and action. Speak of it in these terms. Attend to psychological, social, and political dimensions, as well as the information infrastructure and administrative procedures supporting it.[10]

An important guideline for effective strategic management is open-mindedness. A willingness and eagerness to consider new information, new viewpoints, new ideas, and new possibilities are essential. There must exist a spirit of inquiry and learning. Strategists such as chief executive officers, presidents, owners of small businesses, and heads of government agencies must commit themselves to listen to and understand managers' positions well enough to be able to restate those positions to the managers' satisfaction. In addition, managers throughout the firm should be able to describe the strategists' positions to the satisfaction of the strategists. This degree of discipline will promote understanding and learning.

No organization has unlimited resources. No firm can take on an unlimited amount of debt or issue an unlimited amount of stock to raise capital. Therefore, no organization can pursue all the strategies that potentially could benefit the firm. Strategic decisions always have to be made to eliminate some courses of action and to allocate organizational resources among others. Most organizations can afford to pursue only a few corporate-level strategies at any given time. It is a critical mistake for managers to pursue too many strategies at the same time, thereby spreading the firm's resources so thin that all strategies are jeopardized. Joseph Charyk, CEO of The Communication Satellite Corporation (COMSAT), says, "We have to face the cold fact that Comstat may not be able to do all it wants. By making hard choices on which ventures to keep and which to fold, we hope to boost our sales from $440 million in 1983 to $1 billion by 1989."[11]

Strategic decisions require tradeoffs such as long-range versus short-range considerations or maximizing profits versus increasing shareholders' wealth. These types of tradeoffs require subjective judgments and preferences. In many cases, a lack of objectivity in formulating strategy results in a loss of competitive posture and profitability.

Most organizations today recognize that strategic-management concepts and techniques can enhance the effectiveness of decisions. Subjective factors such as attitudes toward risk, concern for social responsibility, business ethics, and organizational culture will always affect strategy-formulation decisions, but organizations need to be as objective as possible in considering qualitative factors.

MERGERS, ACQUISITIONS, TAKEOVERS, AND LEVERAGED BUYOUTS

Acquisition and merger are two commonly used ways to pursue strategies. An *acquisition* occurs when a large organization purchases (acquires) a smaller firm, or vice versa. A *merger* occurs when two organizations of about equal size unite to form one enterprise. For example, Chrysler recently acquired American Motors Corporation (AMC), but Burroughs and Sperry merged to form Unisys. When an acquisition or merger is not desired by both parties, it can be called a *takeover* or *hostile takeover*.

Among mergers, acquisitions, and takeovers in recent years, same-industry combinations have predominated. For example, General Electric acquired RCA, Capital Cities acquired ABC, Greyhound acquired Trailways, Kraft acquired All American Gourmet, and Ramada acquired Rodeway Inns. In 1987 there were 3,701 mergers and acquisitions in the United States totaling $166 billion. Until recently, the idea of merger/acquisition was taboo in Japan, but now the Japanese are buying up large and small companies worldwide, especially in the United States. (Japanese acquisitions of companies abroad increased dramatically from 31 in 1985, to 78 in 1986 and over 100 in 1987.) Reasons for this activity include the strong yen, American protectionism, and a desire to diversify into new technologies. The Japanese "are over here in droves looking for things to buy," says an analyst for Donaldson Lufkin & Jenrette. "Many companies are looking around saying, 'If we are ever going to sell, now is the time.' Many more companies are putting themselves on the block."

Regarding "merger mania" restructuring in the United States, *Business Week* offers the following conclusion:

> It is clear now that restructurings are driven by a lot more than tax considerations, low stock prices, raiders' desire for a quick buck, and aggressive merger merchants on Wall Street. . . . Restructuring continues because U.S. industry needs it. Deregulation in industries from financial services to energy, from communications to transportation, has exposed managerial complacency and inefficient practices caused by years of shelter from market forces. . . . Plenty of companies have simply recognized that if they want to compete globally, they must slim down, toughen up, and focus on a narrower range of businesses.[12]

Some states are instituting laws to protect their businesses from takeover raiders. For example, in August 1987 Washington passed a law to protect Boeing, the state's largest employer, from a takeover attempt by Texas raider T. Boone Pickens. The law imposes a five year ban on the sale of assets to pay off debt in any company (with more than twenty thousand employees) that is taken over in a hostile raid. Although Boeing, with eighty-five thousand employees, is the only company in Washington fitting that description, the bill passed by huge margins in both houses.

In June, 1987, shares of Singer Company, a pure aerospace and defense contractor, began rising rapidly for no apparent reason. CEO Joseph Flavin became worried that a takeover attempt was being secretly arranged. Then, on August 7, 1987, T. Boone Pickens came forward and announced that his company, Mesa Limited Partnership, had acquired 4.4 percent of Singer stock and options to buy another 15 percent of the company. Singer's stock price increased to $53.25 a share, and the company's value rose to $1.1 billion (but still below analysts' estimates that the breakup value of Singer would be $70 per share). Financially troubled Singer's sales and profits declined 9.2 percent and 68.0 percent, respectively, in 1987 compared to 1986. For the other seventeen aerospace companies in the Fortune 500, sales and profits increased an average of five percent and four percent, respectively, in 1987.

Many companies buy back their own stock to avoid a takeover. For example, Golden Nugget, Inc., the Las Vegas casino operator, is buying back ten million shares of common stock outstanding. The buyback will thwart a possible takeover by New York real estate developer Donald Trump who owns 4.9 percent of Golden Nugget's stock. Even General Motors CEO Roger Smith is concerned about GM being the target of a corporate raider. Smith says, "You'd be crazy to assume you're immune." Smith has instituted a defensive strategy for GM to purchase 20 percent of its common stock between 1987 and 1990, roughly seventy million shares.

Mergers, acquisitions, and takeovers accounted for 498 corporate name changes in the first half of 1987. Divestitures accounted for another 152 name changes. An additional 150 corporate name changes were purely elective; for example, Primerica was American Can, Armtek was formerly Armstrong Tire, and Maxus Energy was Diamond Shamrock. A total of 919 American corporations changed their name in the first half of 1987, a 59 percent increase over 1986 figures.

Leveraged Buyouts

A *leveraged buyout* occurs when a company is taken private by a third party using borrowed funds, usually to avoid a hostile takeover. Borg-Warner, Owens-Illinois, and Jim Walter are examples of companies that obtained a leveraged buyout in 1987. Under this arrangement, the debt is paid back later through funds from operations and the sale of assets. Many banks, insurance companies, and other financial institutions are now getting into the buyout business, sometimes called "merchant banking." For example, in the leveraged buyout of Burlington Industries by Morgan Stanley, Morgan took 37 percent of Burlington's stock, Equitable Life Insurance took a 35 percent interest, and Bankers Trust took 28 percent of the stock in exchange for bank financing. The largest leveraged buyout during the fourth quarter of 1987 was the Thompson Company taking Southland Corporation private for $4 billion.

Merchant bankers usually sell companies acquired in leveraged buyouts in pieces and at high profits. In the most profitable leveraged buyout ever recorded, Kohlberg, Kravis Roberts (KKR) and Company acquired Beatrice in 1986 for $6.4 billion and then sold its divisions separately at huge premiums. Kohlberg divested 45 percent of its assets in from August 1986 to August 1987. Eight divisions sold separately for a total price of $4.07 billion: Playtex Bras/Girdles, Coca-Cola Bottler, Cold Storage, Bottled Water, Max Factor Cosmetics, and Dairy Products. Kohlberg is trying to sell the following additional divisions, separately or together, for an estimated total price of $6.0 billion: Tropicana Orange Juice, Hunt's Tomato Sauce, Orville Redenbacher Popcorn,

Wesson Oil, Stiffel Lamps, Samsonite Luggage, and Culligan Water Treatment. Nestlé, Unilever, and several foreign competitors are expected to bid to acquire Beatrice.

Merrill Lynch leads all American firms in leveraged buyouts. When Borg-Warner Corporation was about to be acquired in a hostile takeover by GAF Corporation in May, 1987, Merrill Lynch quickly took it private in a $4.78 billion leveraged buyout. Merrill Lynch did the same thing for Supermarkets General Corporation a month later for $2.07 billion when that company faced a hostile takeover by Dart Group Corporation.

GENERIC STRATEGIES

Generic strategies are applicable to all sizes and types of organizations. As defined and exemplified in Table 2–1, an enterprise can pursue at least fourteen *generic strategies:* forward integration, backward integration, horizontal integration, market penetration, market development, product development, concentric diversification, conglomerate diversification, horizontal diversification, joint venture, retrenchment, divestiture, liquidation, and a combination strategy. The term "generic" is used because strategy has countless variations. For example, market penetration can include adding salespersons, increasing advertising expenditures, couponing, and many other actions to increase market share in a given geographic area. Exhibit 2–1 reveals situations, conditions, and guidelines when the generic strategies are most appropriate to pursue.

GAINING COMPETITIVE ADVANTAGE

According to Michael Porter, generic strategies allow organizations to gain competitive advantage from three different bases: cost leadership, differentiation, and focus.[13] *Cost leadership* emphasizes producing standardized products at very low per-unit cost for many consumers who are price-sensitive. *Differentiation* refers to producing products and services considered unique industry-wide and directed at consumers who are relatively price-insensitive. *Focus* has to do with producing products and services that fulfill the needs of small groups of consumers. Porter explains that these bases for generic strategies imply different organizational arrangements, control procedures, and incentive systems. Larger firms with greater access to resources typically compete on a cost leadership and/or differentiation basis, whereas smaller firms generally compete on a focus basis. In an article refining Porter's work, Peter Wright emphasizes that midsize and large firms can effectively pursue focus-based strategies only in conjunction with differentiation- or cost leadership-based strategies.[14]

A number of cost elements affect the relative attractiveness of generic strategies, including economies or diseconomies of scale achieved, learning and experience curve effects, the percentage of capacity utilization achieved, and linkages with suppliers and distributors.[15] Other cost elements to consider in choosing among alternative strategies include the potential for sharing costs and knowledge within the organization, R and D costs associated with new product development or modification of existing products,

(*Text continues on p. 70.*)

TABLE 2–1 Alternative generic strategies defined and exemplified

Strategy	*Definition*	*Recent Example*
Forward Integration	Gaining ownership or increased control over distributors or retailers	Coca-Cola Company purchased its largest franchised bottler, JTL, for $1.4 billion.
Backward Integration	Seeking ownership or increased control of a firm's suppliers	Apple Computer Company created a new company-owned software subsidiary called Claris Corp.
Horizontal Integration	Seeking ownership or increased control over competitors	Delta bought Western Air Lines; Maytag bought Magic Chef.
Market Penetration	Seeking increased market share for present products or services in present markets through greater marketing efforts	Lance developed a salesforce of 2,300 persons in thirty-five states; Lance's strategy included no advertising expenditures.
Market Development	Introducing present products or services into new geographic areas	Kindercare plans to open one hundred new daycare units in 1988.
Product Development	Seeking increased sales by improving or modifying present products or services	Apollo Computer introduced a $57,900 high performance workstation for engineers.
Concentric Diversification	Adding new, but related, products or services	Union Pacific, a big Western railroad, bought Overnite Transportation, a big Eastern trucker.
Conglomerate Diversification	Adding new, unrelated products or services	Ford Motor Co. bought PMI Mortgage Insurance Co., the nation's fourth-largest mortgage insurance company.
Horizontal Diversification	Adding new, unrelated products or services for present customers	PepsiCo bought the Kentucky Fried Chicken Company.
Joint Venture	Two or more sponsoring firms forming a separate organization for cooperative purposes	DuPont and Xerox created a new company called DX Imaging to develop and manufacture copying equipment based on a new type of liquid toner technology.
Retrenchment	Regrouping through cost and asset reduction to reverse declining sales and profits	Firestone closed plants in Illinois, Oklahoma, and Iowa, due to shrinking demand for farm and off-highway tires.
Diversiture	Selling a division or part of an organization	BankAmerica sold the Charles Schwab division for $230 million.
Liquidation	Selling all of a company's assets, in parts, for their tangible worth	GenCorp liquidated the RKO General Broadcasting Group.
Combination	Pursuing two or more strategies simultaneously	Ralston Purina sold its Purina animal feed business to British Petroleum and at the same time bought Union Carbide's battery division.

EXHIBIT 2–1 Guidelines for situations when particular strategies are most effective

Forward Integration

- When an organization's present distributors are especially expensive, or unreliable, or incapable of meeting the firm's distribution needs
- When the availability of quality distributors is so limited as to offer a competitive advantage to those firms that integrate forward
- When an organization competes in an industry that is growing and is expected to continue to grow markedly; this is a factor because forward integration reduces an organization's ability to diversify if its basic industry falters.
- When an organization has both the capital and human resources needed to manage the new business of distributing its own products
- When the advantages of stable production are particularly high; this is a consideration because an organization can increase the predictability of the demand for its output through forward integration.
- When present distributors or retailers have high profit margins; this situation suggests that a company could profitably distribute its own products and price them more competitively by integrating forward.

Backward Integration

- When an organization's present suppliers are especially expensive, or unreliable, or incapable of meeting the firm's needs for parts, components, assemblies, or raw materials
- When the number of suppliers is few and the number of competitors is many
- When an organization competes in an industry that is growing rapidly; this is a factor because integrative-type strategies (forward, backward, and horizontal) reduce an organization's ability to diversify in a declining industry.
- When an organization has both the capital and human resources needed to manage the new business of supplying its own raw materials
- When the advantages of stable prices are particularly important; this is a factor because an organization can stabilize the cost of its raw materials and the associated price of its products through backward integration.
- When present suppliers have high profit margins, which suggests that the business of supplying products or services in the given industry is a worthwhile venture
- When an organization needs to acquire a needed resource quickly

Horizontal Integration

- When an organization can gain monopolistic characteristics in a particular area or region without being challenged by the federal government for "tending substantially" to reduce competition
- When an organization competes in a growing industry
- When increased economies of scale provide major competitive advantages
- When an organization has both the capital and human talent needed to successfully manage an expanded organization

- When competitors are faltering due to a lack of managerial expertise or a need for particular resources which your organization possesses; note that horizontal integration would not be appropriate if competitors are doing poorly because overall industry sales are declining.

Market Penetration

- When current markets are not saturated with your particular product or service
- When the usage rate of present customers could be significantly increased
- When the market shares of major competitors have been declining while total industry sales have been increasing
- When the correlation between dollar sales and dollar marketing expenditures has historically been high
- When increased economies of scale provide major competitive advantages

Market Development

- When new channels of distribution are available that are reliable, inexpensive, and of good quality
- When an organization is very successful at what it does
- When new untapped or unsaturated markets exist
- When an organization has the needed capital and human resources to manage expanded operations
- When an organization has excess production capacity
- When an organization's basic industry is rapidly becoming global in scope

Product Development

- When an organization has successful products that are in the maturity stage of the product life cycle; the idea here is to attract satisfied customers to try new (improved) products as a result of their positive experience with the organization's present products or services.
- When an organization competes in an industry that is characterized by rapid technological developments
- When major competitors offer better quality products at comparable prices
- When an organization competes in a high-growth industry
- When an organization has especially strong research and development capabilities

Concentric Diversification

- When an organization competes in a no-growth or a slow-growth industry
- When adding new, but related, products would significantly enhance the sales of current products
- When new, but related, products could be offered at highly competitive prices
- When new, but related, products have seasonal sales levels that counterbalance an organization's existing peaks and valleys
- When an organization's products are currently in the decline stage of the product life cycle
- When an organization has a strong management team

Conglomerate Diversification

- When an organization's basic industry is experiencing declining annual sales and profits
- When an organization has the capital and managerial talent needed to compete successfully in a new industry
- When the organization has the opportunity to purchase an unrelated business that is an attractive investment opportunity
- When there exists financial synergy between the acquired and acquiring firm; note that a key difference between concentric and conglomerate diversification is that the former should be based on some commonality in markets, products, or technology; whereas, the latter should be based more on profit considerations.
- When existing markets for an organization's present products are saturated
- When antitrust action could be charged against an organization that has historically concentrated on a single industry

Horizontal Diversification

- When revenues derived from an organization's current products or services would significantly increase by adding the new, unrelated products
- When an organization competes in a highly competitive and/or a no-growth industry, as indicated by low industry profit margins and returns
- When an organization's present channels of distribution can be used to market the new products to current customers
- When the new products have countercyclical sales patterns compared to an organization's present products

Joint Venture

- When a privately owned organization is forming a joint venture with a publicly owned organization; there are some advantages of being privately held, such as close ownership; there are some advantages of being publicly held, such as access to stock issuances as a source of capital. Sometimes, the unique advantages of being privately and publicly held can be synergistically combined in a joint venture.
- When a domestic organization is forming a joint venture with a foreign company; joint venture can provide a domestic company with the opportunity for obtaining local management in a foreign country, thereby reducing risks such as expropriation and harassment by host country officials.
- When the distinctive competencies of two or more firms complement each other especially well
- When some project is potentially very profitable, but requires overwhelming resources and risks; the Alaskan pipeline is an example.
- When two or more smaller firms have trouble competing with a large firm
- When there exists a need to introduce a new technology quickly

Retrenchment

- When an organization has a clearly distinctive competence, but has failed to meet its objectives and goals consistently over time

- When an organization is one of the weakest competitors in a given industry
- When an organization is plagued by inefficiency, low profitability, poor employee morale, and pressure from stockholders to improve performance
- When an organization has failed to capitalize on external opportunities, minimize external threats, take advantage of internal strengths, and overcome internal weaknesses over time; that is, when the organization's strategic managers have failed (and possibly been replaced by more competent individuals)
- When an organization has grown so large so quickly that major internal reorganization is needed

Divestiture

- When an organization has pursued a retrenchment strategy and it failed to accomplish needed improvements
- When a division needs more resources to be competitive than the company can provide
- When a division is responsible for an organization's overall poor performance
- When a division is a misfit with the rest of an organization; this can result from radically different markets, customers, managers, employees, values, or needs.
- When a large amount of cash is needed quickly and cannot be reasonably obtained from other sources
- When government antitrust action threatens an organization

Liquidation

- When an organization has pursued both a retrenchment strategy and a divestiture strategy, and neither has been successful
- When an organization's only alternative is bankruptcy; liquidation represents an orderly and planned means of obtaining the greatest possible cash for an organization's assets. A company can legally declare bankruptcy first and then liquidate various divisions to raise needed capital.
- When the stockholders of a firm can minimize their losses by selling the organization's assets

---

Source: Adapted from: F.R. David, "How Do We Choose Among Alternative Growth Strategies?" *Managerial Planning* 33, no. 4 (January–February 1985): 14–17, 22.

and labor costs, tax rates, energy costs, and shipping costs. A primary reason for pursuing forward, backward, and horizontal integration strategies is to gain cost leadership benefits.

Different generic strategies offer different degrees of differentiation. Differentiation does not guarantee competitive advantage, especially if standard products sufficiently meet customer needs or if rapid imitation by competitors is possible. Durable products protected by barriers to quick copying by competitors are most efficacious. Successful differentiation can mean greater product flexibility, greater compatibility, lower costs, improved service, less maintenance, greater convenience, or more features. Product development is an example of a generic strategy that offers the advantages of differentiation.

A successful focus strategy depends upon an industry segment that is of sufficient size, has good growth potential, and is not crucial to the success of other major competitors. Some generic strategies, such as market penetration and market development, offer substantial focusing advantages. Depending upon factors such as type of industry, size of firm, and nature of competition, various generic strategies could provide advantages in cost leadership, differentiation, and focus. Porter stresses the need during strategy-formulation activities to determine and weigh the ramifications that various alternative strategies have upon cost leadership, differentiation, and focus.

INTEGRATION STRATEGIES IN ACTION

Forward Integration

Forward integration involves gaining ownership or increased control over distributors or retailers. A company that is betting a large part of its future on forward integration is Melridge, Inc., the largest firm in the $7 billion American flower industry. Melridge is rapidly expanding its number and type of retail outlets. Supermarkets are Melridge's latest push. Americans spend only about $10 per person annually on flowers, compared to $20 per capita for Europeans. Only about 25 percent of all flowers purchased in the United States are for purposes other than "occasions" such as weddings and anniversaries. Melridge wants to increase this percentage, and its strategy is to use forward integration "to make buying flowers as American as eating hamburgers."

To help alleviate problems in obtaining retail shelf space in chains such as Computer Land Corporation and Businessland, Atari purchased Federated Group in 1987 for $67.3 million. Federated operates sixty-five consumer electronic stores in California, Texas, Arizona, and Kansas and will now become a major retail outlet for Atari products. Another company pursuing forward integration is Boeing, which loaned its major distributor, Allegis, $700 million in 1987, and received in return an order of eleven long-range 747–400s. Allegis, the parent company of United Airlines, was faced with a hostile takeover, so Boeing in effect "rescued" its major distributor. As part of this forward integration strategy, the $700 million in notes is convertible to 16 percent of Allegis's stock. Boeing's sales and profits declined 6 percent and 28 percent, respectively, in 1987 compared to 1986.

Another effective means of implementing forward integration is franchising. Approximately 1,900 companies in about fifty different industries in the United States used franchising in 1987 to distribute their product or service. Businesses can expand rapidly by franchising because costs and opportunities are spread among many individuals. In 1987, there were 342 American franchisors with outlets in foreign countries. The United States Department of Commerce expects an additional 192 American franchisors to operate in foreign markets by the end of 1988. The recreation, entertainment, and travel industries have the fastest annual growth in franchising; the number of franchises in these industries will grow by 24 percent annually through 1990. Construction and home services are the second fastest growing industries for franchising.

Backward Integration

Manufacturers and retailers purchase needed materials from suppliers. *Backward integration* is a strategy of seeking ownership or increased control of a firm's suppliers. Companies such as Apple, IBM, Unisys, Tandem, and Data General, for example, are allocating substantial resources to develop or acquire software businesses. The basic reason for backward integration strategies in the computer industry is that pretax margins on hardware have dropped from 40 percent in the early and mid-1980s to about 10 percent in the late 1980s. A sharp drop in hardware prices has occurred because many computers now look and function alike. In contrast, pretax margins on computer software products and services average about 25 percent. Kidder-Peabody estimates percentage revenues derived from software sales and services will exceed 45 percent by 1992. IBM recently formed a new internal division called Application Systems to develop software and expects it to boost IBM software revenues from 30 percent of total company revenues in 1987 to 50 percent in 1990. Apple has done the same thing with its new Claris subsidiary.

Many industries in the United States (such as the automotive and aluminum industries) are reducing their historical pursuit of backward integration. Instead of owning their own suppliers, more and more companies are using outside suppliers. Ford and Chrysler already buy over half of their components parts from outside suppliers such as TRW, Eaton, General Electric, Johnson Controls, and foreign suppliers. De-integration makes sense due to increased internationalization of industries. "Sources of supply have become global, but ownership is not," says Richard Cooper of Harvard. "Most countries won't permit the exploitation of their national patrimony." *Outsourcing,* whereby companies use outside suppliers, shop around, play one seller against another, and go with the best deal, is becoming more widely practiced. But backward integration is not a dead-end strategy. Sometimes it makes sense. Kathryn Rudie Harrigan of Columbia University Business School says: "Both forward and backward integration are a series of finetunings, of adjusting strategy to whatever makes sense at a particular point in time."

Horizontal Integration

Horizontal integration refers to the strategy of seeking ownership or increased control over a firm's competitors. One of the most significant trends in strategic management today is the increased use of horizontal integration as a growth strategy. Mergers, acquisitions, and takeovers among competitors allow for increased economies of scale and enhanced transfer of resources and competencies. Kenneth Davidson makes this observation about horizontal integration:

> The trend towards horizontal integration seems to reflect strategists' misgivings about their ability to operate many unrelated businesses. Mergers between direct competitors are more likely to create efficiencies than mergers between unrelated businesses, both because there is a greater potential for eliminating duplicate facilities and because the management of the acquiring firm is more likely to understand the business of the target.[16]

Horizontal integration is not a strategy without risk, as evidenced recently by Maxicare Health Plans. The nation's largest for-profit health maintenance organization

(HMO), Maxicare recently acquired a number of its competitors, including Health America and Healthcare USA. Maxicare's membership grew from 832,000 in June, 1986 to 2.3 million in July, 1987. But, during the same period, the horizontal integration strategy resulted in huge losses in net income and a stock price plunging from 28 to 11, despite a strong bull market. On sales of $1.8 billion in 1987, Maxicare incurred a loss in profits of negative $61 million.

Horizontal integration between large interstate banks is creating a new breed of institutions called "superregionals." First Fidelity Bancorp, the second largest bank holding company in New Jersey, recently merged with Fidelcor, a large Pennsylvania bank, to form the eighteenth largest bank holding company in the United States with $27 billion in assets. The nationwide trend in banking is for groups of banks in different geographic areas to combine until they control 75 percent or more of the assets in a region. Emergence of "superregionals" represents a major threat to large money-center banks such as Mellon and BankAmerica that continue to have problems with bad loans to third world countries.

Using horizontal integration, Computer Associates (CA) in mid-1987 surpassed Lotus Development and Microsoft as the largest computer software company in the world. CA did it by acquiring sixteen competitors in five years, including most recently Uccel for $800 million in stock. Chief executive officer Charles Wang of CA wants to see the firm's revenues divided evenly among systems utilities, personal computer software, and computer applications. In total, there were 305 horizontal integration mergers and acquisitions in the computer software industry in 1986, up 50 percent from 1985. This total was second only to similar mergers and acquisitions in the financial services industry.

In October, 1987, Tonka Corporation, the sixth-largest American toy company with 1986 sales of $293 million, acquired Kenner-Parker Toys (the fourth-largest American toy company with 1986 sales of $503 million) for $640 million. This horizontal integration deal made Tonka the third-largest American toy company behind Hasbro and Mattel, which had 1987 sales of $1.3 billion and $1.0 billion, respectively. Until the October buyout occurred, the third-largest toy company was Fisher-Price. Tonka has been hurt recently by not developing a new product to match the "Pound Puppies" that accounted for half of the company's 1986 sales or the "Go-Bots" that were so successful several years earlier.

INTENSIVE STRATEGIES IN ACTION

Market penetration, market development, and product development are sometimes referred to as "intensive strategies" because they require intensive efforts to improve a firm's competitive position with existing products.

Market Penetration

A *market penetration* strategy seeks to increase market share for present products or services in present markets through greater marketing efforts. This strategy is widely used as a lone strategy and in conjunction with other strategies. Market penetration includes increasing the number of salespersons, increasing advertising expenditures, offering extensive sales promotion items, or increasing publicity efforts. Wolverine Worldwide, the maker of Hush Puppies shoes, is an example of a firm that has chosen market penetration to reverse a loss ($13 million in 1986 on sales of $34 million). Wolverine has adopted a multimillion dollar advertising campaign featuring boxer Marvin Hagler, model Lauren Hutton, and former house speaker "Tip" O'Neill. The company is striving to change Hush Puppies' image from "fusty and old" to "young and lively."

Tandy Corporation, a computer firm that is pursuing market penetration extensively, has recently hired and trained 1,100 salespersons to sell their products outside the 385 Radio Shack Computer Centers and 6,498 ordinary Radio Shacks in the United States. The company plans to have 1,500 outside salespersons by 1988. Tandy's market share in personal computers was 16 percent in 1986, compared to 21 percent for IBM and 12 percent for Apple. To counter Tandy, IBM is using market penetration too, and added more than seven thousand salespersons for a total over 30,000 by the end of 1987, up from 23,000 at the end of 1986. In addition, IBM's sales force is being reorganized along industry lines, so that one group can develop expertise in aerospace companies, one in big banks, one in insurance companies, and so on. John Akers, IBM's CEO, is making videotape presentations to be used by managers and salespersons' worldwide. "I've chosen to use this as a rallying point," says Mr. Akers. The troops seem to be getting the message. "There's gonna be a lot of pressure this year," one IBM account executive was overheard saying. "Yeah," another responded. "It's war." IBM's sales and profits for 1987 increased 6 percent and 10 percent, respectively, compared to Tandy's sales and profits (10 percent and 34 percent).

Coca-Cola and Pepsi spend millions of dollars each year pursuing a market penetration strategy. Coke increased its advertising budget 15 percent in 1987 to $200 million. Coke presently has 39.9 percent of the market compared to Pepsi's 29.2 percent. Coke Classic is the number one soft drink in sales in the United States and Coke's Sprite has overtaken Pepsi's 7up. In the beer industry, Coors is the first beer company to use a market penetration strategy that directs some advertisements solely to women. Coors is spending more than $500,000 in 1987 for full-page beer ads in *Cosmopolitan, Glamour, People,* and *Women's Sports and Fitness* magazines. Women buy about 17 percent of the beer sold in the United States, accounting for $6.5 billion in sales. Coors expects industry's beer sales to women to exceed $9 billion by 1990, and its market penetration strategy is intended to increase the company's 8.5 percent market share.

Market Development

Market development involves introducing present products or services into new geographic areas. The climate for international market development has become more favorable recently. In many industries it is going to be hard to maintain a competitive edge by staying close to home. One firm that is staying at home to pursue market development in domestic markets is Food Lion. Based in Salisbury, N.C., Food Lion is one of the fastest growing and most profitable grocery chains in the United States. With 430 stores located exclusively in the Southeast, Food Lion's growth in stores averaged 29 percent a year between 1981 and 1988. While competitors are adding flower shops, takeout meals, and seafood counters to their stores, Food Lion's success is attributed to a no-frills, low price offering. Food Lion has been called the "Wal-Mart of the grocery industry." Food Lion's objective is to add 85 stores in 1987 and 105 more stores in 1988, with hopes of topping $5 billion in sales by 1990. Food Lion's sales increased 21 percent in 1987 to $2.9 billion.

Another company that is pursuing a market development strategy is Family Dollar Stores, but its sales and profit growth per store is decreasing dramatically. As a result, president and chief operating officer Lewis Levine resigned in 1987, as did Howard Levine, the company's senior vice president for merchandising. Virtually all Family Dollar's merchandise is priced below $18.00. Family Dollar currently has about 1,500 stores in thirty states; company sales declined in 1987 to $360 million from $488 million in 1986.

In 1987 several American banks began market development into Canada by purchasing securities firms. For example, First Chicago Corporation acquired a 30 percent stake in Toronto-based Wood Gundy Corporation. Also, Los Angeles-based Security Pacific Corporation acquired a 30 percent stake worth $75.8 million in Burns Fry, Ltd., one of Canada's largest securities firms. Security Pacific has previous experience with market development by acquiring securities firms in Asia and Europe; its revenues increased 13 percent in 1987 over 1986, but company profits declined 97 percent.

Product Development

Product development is a strategy that seeks increased sales by improving or modifying present products or services. Product development usually entails large research and development expenditures. Zenith is pursuing product development to stay alive in the color television industry; it has just developed a flat-tension television tube that produces ultrasharp color images with a perfectly flat face, eliminating glare and reflections. Zenith started manufacturing televisions with the new tube beginning in 1988, but Zenith computers began featuring the new tube in 1987. Analysts say, "Zenith will have the world on a string when people see the flat-mask technology in a television in 1988."

Ford Motor Company recently announced it will spend $900 million in 1988 and 1989 to develop a new line of auto and truck engines by retooling its tractor plant in Romeo, Michigan. Previously, Ford had planned to close the Romeo plant in 1988. Conversion and retooling of the plant will cost $500 million and worker training programs will cost another $400 million. The new line of engines will not come off assembly lines until the 1990s. Ford's 1987 sales and profits increased 14 and 41 percent, respectively, over 1986 figures.

Using a product development strategy, Jaguar PLC is one of Britain's best-known manufacturing comeback stories. The new Jaguar XJ6 Sedan went on sale in the United States in May, 1987 and listed for $40,500, while the more luxurious Vanden Plas model listed for $44,500. Jaguar's American car sales increased to twenty-five thousand in 1986, up from three thousand in 1980. Jaguar has also developed a competitive racing model to rebuild its image.

DIVERSIFICATION STRATEGIES IN ACTION

Concentric Diversification

Adding new, but related, products or services is widely called *concentric diversification.* Wal-Mart is using concentric diversification through the development of Hypermarket U.S.A. superstores that combine supermarket and general merchandise at discount prices under one roof covering over two hundred thousand square feet. Wal-Mart tested two of these stores in 1987 and plans to build numerous superstores in the 1990s. Superstores are already common in Europe. K-mart is also concentrically diversifying by building hypermarkets under a partnership arrangement with Bruno's, Inc. Bruno's is a 111-store supermarket chain headquartered in Birmingham, while K-mart is the world's second-largest retailer with more than 3,800 stores and 1987 sales of $25.8 billion. Hypermarkets will include restaurants, dry cleaners, financial services, and beauty salons.

Sears is another firm pursuing concentric diversification. Sears department stores are changing their looks to appear more like a grouping of specialty stores. Evidence of this strategy was Sears' recent acquisition of Eye Care Centers of America, a forty-one–store optical chain, for $52.4 million. Sears plans to internally develop other new departments, such as Trader Bay and Fieldmaster, through concentric diversification. Sears' sales in 1987 were $48.4 billion, up 9 percent from 1986.

Kindercare is also pursuing concentric diversification by acquiring financial services and insurance companies. The largest childcare company in the world, Kindercare presently has 1,200 centers in the United States and Canada. Kindercare has always provided insurance, finance, and real estate services to center operators, but acquiring businesses in these areas is considered by some analysts to be too risky. Kindercare recently bought American Savings and Loan Association in Florida for $138 million. Kindercare's revenues increased 55 percent in 1987 to $507 million, but profits declined 6 percent to $26.3 million.

Conglomerate Diversification

Adding new, unrelated products or services is called *conglomerate diversification.* Some firms pursue conglomerate diversification through acquisition based in part on an expectation of profits from breaking up the acquired firm and selling divisions to strategists with more experience in those businesses. Xerox, for example, is presently pursuing conglomerate diversification into financial services; it recently acquired Furman Selz Holding Corporation, a New York brokerage firm, for $110 million. With this acquisition, Xerox now derives about 27 percent of its $12.9 billion in annual revenues and 50 percent of profits from financial services such as insurance, leasing, mutual funds, and brokerage services.

A majority of companies that pursued conglomerate diversification in the 1970s and early 1980s are now deconglomerating. Richard West, dean of New York University's School of Business, says, "The stock market is rewarding deconglomerations, saying company assets are worth more separately than together. There is a kind of antisynergy, the whole being worth less than the parts." Conglomerate diversification, once a dominant strategy, is now on the retreat. Says Michael Porter of the Harvard Business School, "Management found they couldn't manage the beast." Hence, businesses are selling, or closing, less profitable divisions in order to focus on core businesses. Peters and Waterman's advice is to "stick to the knitting" and not to stray too far from the firm's basic areas of competence.

Horizontal Diversification

Adding new, unrelated products or services for present customers is called *horizontal diversification*. This strategy is not as risky as conglomerate diversification, because a firm should already be familiar with its present customers. For example, BellSouth Corporation (the telephone company) is diversifying into the education business by offering telecommunications and management training programs to its business customers. To implement this strategy, it has created a new division called BellSouth Educational Services, which has been accredited by the Southern Association of Colleges and Schools. It will mostly offer training to both current and new customers through courses that range from fiber optics design to performance evaluation. BellSouth's revenues and profits increased 7 percent and 5 percent, respectively, in 1987 compared to 1986.

Ford Motor Company is using horizontal diversification too, as evidenced by its recent entrance into the financial services business with the acquisition of PMI Mortgage Insurance Company, the nation's fourth-largest mortgage insurance company. Earlier, Ford had acquired First Nationwide Bank, the seventh-largest savings institution in the country. George Brown, Ford's vice president for strategic and diversification planning, says the number two automaker expects to use horizontal diversification to expand further its financial services operations. Ford's net profit increased a whopping 41 percent in 1987.to $4.6 billion.

OTHER STRATEGIES IN ACTION

Joint Venture

It is often advantageous for two or more companies to form a temporary partnership or consortium for the purpose of capitalizing on some opportunity. A *joint venture* occurs when two or more sponsoring firms form a separate organization for cooperative purposes; the sponsoring firms have shared equity ownership in the new entity. Besides joint ventures, other types of *cooperative arrangements* include research and development partnerships, cross-distribution agreements, cross-licensing agreements, cross-manufacturing agreements and joint-bidding consortia. Walt Disney Company and Metropolitan Life Insurance Company are pursuing a cooperative arrangement to develop the most costly exhibit yet at Epcot in Orlando. Costing $50 million and scheduled to open in October of 1989, the exhibit will include "Body Wars," a simulated ride through the human body, "Cranium Command," a theater featuring shows about the brain, and "Fitness Fairgrounds," featuring a "fun house of the five senses."

Some more successful recent joint ventures include Tri-Star Pictures (a Columbia Pictures, CBS, and Home Box Office venture), GEMCO (a venture between Merrill

Lynch and McGraw-Hill), PD Glycol (a venture between Dupont and PPG Industries), and Industrial Networking (a venture between General Electric and Ungermann-Bass). Joint ventures and cooperative arrangements are being used increasingly because they provide companies opportunities to improve telecommunications and networking, to acquire the larger capital required to develop new products and enter new markets, to globalize industries, and to take advantage of deregulation and rapid technological change. Joint ventures require strategists to overcome inhibitions about taking risks and sharing resources. A willingness to develop cooperative strategies can often enhance a firm's competitive position in a fashion that simply could not be done alone.

Kathryn Rudie Harrigan, professor of strategic management at Columbia, summarizes the trend towards increased joint venturing:

> In today's global business environment of scarce resources, rapid rates of technological change, and rising capital requirements, the important question is no longer, "Shall we form a joint venture?" Now the question is, "Which joint ventures and cooperative arrangements are most appropriate for our needs and expectations?" followed by, "How do we manage these ventures most effectively?"[17]

About twenty-seven large, technology-related joint ventures between American and Japanese companies were formed in 1986, including ones between Boeing and NEC, Vitelic and Tokyo Sanyo, LSI Logic and Toshiba, and Advanced Microsystems and Sony. In one such joint venture to boost its global market share of semiconductor chips up from 6 percent in 1987, Motorola formed a cooperative agreement with Toshiba to swap high technology and assistance in penetrating each other's geographic markets. Ralph Thompson, senior vice president of American Electronics Association, says, "Strategic partnerships are becoming an irrevocable piece of every company's strategy."

In 1986, transnational joint ventures and mergers within the twelve-nation European Economic Community (EEC) rose 18 percent. That trend is continuing as European companies recognize the need to achieve economies of scale to compete with larger American and Japanese firms. A new generation of managers in Europe is not constrained by national pride; they recognize the need to cooperate to compete in world markets. In 1987 there were three $2-billion-a-year joint ventures among European firms: ASEA (Sweden) and Brown Boveri (Switzerland), Philips (Netherlands) and GEC (Great Britain), and Thomson in France and Thorn EMI Ferguson (Great Britain).

Retrenchment

Retrenchment occurs when an organization regroups through cost and asset reduction to reverse declining sales and profits. Sometimes called a turnaround or reorganizational strategy, retrenchment is designed to fortify an organization's basic distinctive competence. During retrenchment, strategists work with limited resources and face pressure from shareholders, employees, and the media. Retrenchment can entail selling off land and buildings to raise needed cash, pruning product lines, closing marginal businesses, closing obsolete factories, automating processes, reducing the number of employees, and instituting expense control systems. Commodore has been pursuing a retrenchment strategy since the mid-1980s. Between 1985 and 1987, Commodore closed five plants and cut its payroll from 4,700 to 3,100. More than half of the employees at the company's West Chester, Pennsylvania, headquarters were fired. Commodore's strategy is to continue retrenchment, coupled with product development. The Amiga, a Commodore computer introduced in late 1987, is priced below $1,000 and represents a major hope for the firm in the future.

In some cases, *bankruptcy* can be an effective type of retrenchment strategy. Bankruptcy can allow a firm to avoid major debt obligations and to void union contracts. There are four major types of bankruptcy: Chapter 7, Chapter 11, Chapter 12, and Chapter 13.

Chapter 7 Bankruptcy is a liquidation procedure used only when a corporation sees no hope of being able to operate successfully or to obtain the necessary creditor agreement. All of the organization's assets are sold in parts for their tangible worth.

Chapter 11 Bankruptcy allows organizations to reorganize and "come back" after filing a petition for protection. Chapter 11 bankruptcy filings increased five-fold between 1980 and 1987. Three companies that operated under Chapter 11 bankruptcy during 1987 were among the best-performing stocks that year: A. H. Robins Co., a Richmond, Virginia-based health-care and consumer products company; Global Marine, a Houston-based offshore driller; and LTV Corp., a Dallas-based steelmaker. But some companies, such as Heck's and Endotronics, declare Chapter 11 bankruptcy and never recover. Heck's stock was the biggest loser of all New York Stock Exchange firms during the first quarter of 1987, and Endotronics stock fell from 35.5 in August 1986 to 1.0 in April 1987. Declaring Chapter 11 bankruptcy allowed the Manville Corporation and Continental Products to gain protection from liability suits filed over their manufacture of asbestos products. Million dollar judgments against Manville and Continental would have required company liquidation, so bankruptcy was a good decision for these two firms.

Chapter 12 Bankruptcy was created by the Family Farmer Bankruptcy Act of 1986. This law became effective in 1987 and provides special relief to family farmers with debt equal to or less than $1.5 million.

Chapter 13 Bankruptcy is a reorganization plan similar to Chapter 11 but available only to small businesses owned by individuals with unsecured debts of less than $100,000 and secured debts of less than $350,000. The Chapter 13 debtor is allowed to operate the business while a plan is being developed to provide for the successful operation of the business in the future.

Divestiture

Selling a division or part of an organization is called *divestiture*. Clarke and Gall emphasize that divestiture, a widely used strategy, may be necessary to balance a company's equity with its long-term risks or to balance short-term and long-term debt payments to optimize the cost of capital.[18] Divestiture is commonly used to generate funds for further strategic acquisitions or investments. For example, General Electric raised about $5 billion between 1982 and 1986 by divesting itself of 155 divisions and purchasing RCA with the proceeds. CBS recently divested itself of the company's magazine division (which had generated $14 million in profits in 1986 on sales of $407 million) for $650 million. The division included twenty-one popular magazines, such as *Woman's Day, Field & Stream,* and *Home Mechanix*. CBS strategists are now considering several options for investing their newly acquired cash, including buying more television stations, paying off the company's long-term debt, and buying back stock.

United Airlines' parent company, Allegis Corporation, based in Chicago, is trying to divest itself of all its nonairline assets. During the fourth quarter of 1987, Allegis Corporation sold Hertz Corporation for $1.3 billion and Hilton International Corporation for $1.1 billion. In 1988, Allegis plans to sell its Westin hotel chain for $1.8 billion, and its Covia air reservations unit for $500 million. Allegis's prior strategy of building a full-service travel empire failed.

Liquidation

Selling all of a company's assets, in parts, for their tangible worth is called *liquidation*. Liquidation is a recognition of defeat and consequently can be an emotionally difficult strategy. For example, container-shipping pioneer Malcolm P. McLean recently liquidated McLean Industries, the 115-year-old shipping company. Reorganization under Chapter 11 bankruptcy in 1987 failed. The company was 85 percent owned by Mr. McLean.

Another company that liquidated in 1987 was TransStar Airlines. TranStar sold its fifteen aircraft and all parts and equipment for $40 million to Continental Airlines. Liquidation is sometimes the best strategy to pursue for minimizing shareholders' losses. No organization can operate at a loss for too long a period of time.

Combination

Many, if not most, organizations pursue a *combination* of two or more strategies simultaneously, but a combination strategy can be exceptionally risky if carried too far. No organization can afford to pursue all the strategies that might benefit the firm. Organizations, like individuals, have limited resources. Both organizations and individuals must set priorities, choose among alternative strategies, and avoid excessive indebtedness. Organizations cannot do too many things well because resources and talents get spread thin and competitors gain advantage. In large diversified companies, a combination strategy is commonly employed when different divisions pursue different strategies. Organizations struggling to survive may employ a combination of several defensive strategies, such as divestiture, liquidation, and retrenchment simultaneously.

Digital Equipment is one firm that is successfully pursuing several strategies simultaneously, including product development and market penetration. For the fiscal year ending June 30, 1987, Digital's net income jumped 80 percent to $1.1 billion and its revenues increased 24 percent to $9.4 billion. Digital's product development strategy is evidenced by its introduction of a major new product every four weeks during 1986 and 1987. Digital's market penetration strategy consists of its hiring thousands of new salespersons. Digital had a total of 7,000 salespeople at the end of fiscal 1987, and was still hiring.

Waldenbooks, which has 1,100 book stores in shopping malls nationwide, is another company successfully pursuing a combination strategy. Through market development, Waldenbooks plans to open sixty to eighty new stores annually through 1991.

Using horizontal diversification, Waldenbooks is entering the computer software retailing business. It is also pursuing new product development by opening about forty new Waldenkids stores per year and is replacing the book sections at K-Mart stores with its own Reader's Market centers at the rate of about one hundred per year. For now, Waldenbooks' income statement and balance sheet look fine. However, competitors such as Barnes & Noble Bookstores, the nation's largest book retailer, watch as Waldenbooks' resources get spread across many strategies and areas.

INTEGRATING STRATEGY AND CULTURE

It is beneficial to view strategic management in relation to its cultural setting. Success is often determined by linkages between an organization's culture and strategies. The challenge of strategic management today is to bring about the changes in organizational culture and individual mind-sets necessary to support the formulation, implementation, and evaluation of strategies.

Organizational culture is a complex and paradoxical phenomenon that has no universal definition. It is difficult to pin down and remarkably resistant to change. Schein defines it as "a pattern of basic assumptions—invented, discovered, or developed by an organization as it learns to cope with its problem of external adaptation and internal integration—that has worked well enough to be considered valid and to be taught to new members as the correct way to perceive, think, and feel in reaction to those problems."[19] Organizational culture is a concept that captures the subtle, elusive, and largely unconscious forces that shape a workplace.

Cultural products, including values, beliefs, rites, rituals, ceremonies, myths, stories, legends, sagas, language, metaphors, symbols, heroes, and heroines, are exhibited as critical levers that strategists can use to influence and direct strategy formulation, implementation, and evaluation. Defined in Figure 2–2, cultural products should be considered more often in strategic-management practice and research. A conceptual model of the strategy-culture relationship is illustrated in Figure 2–3.

Organizational culture significantly affects strategic-management decisions. If strategies are legitimized by a firm's culture, then management can often implement changes swiftly and easily. However, if the firm's culture is not supportive, then strategic changes may be ineffective or even counterproductive. A firm's culture can become antagonistic to new strategies with the result being confusion and disorientation. Strategists should use the organization's culture to infuse individuals with enthusiasm for implementing strategies. Allarie and Firsirotu emphasize the need to link strategy and culture, contending that:

> Culture provides an explanation for the insuperable difficulties a firm encounters when it attempts to shift its strategic direction. Not only has the "right" culture become the essence and foundation of corporate excellence, it is also claimed that success or failure of reforms hinges on management's sagacity and ability to change the firm's driving culture in time and in tune with required changes in strategies.[20]

The potential value of organizational culture has not been fully realized in the study of strategic management. Ignoring the significance of strategy-culture linkages can

FIGURE 2–2 Cultural products and associated definitions

Rites	Relatively elaborate, dramatic, planned sets of activities that consolidate various forms of cultural expressions into one event, carried out through social interactions, usually for the benefit of an audience.
Ceremonial	A system of several rites connected with a single occasion or event.
Ritual	A standardized, detailed set of techniques and behaviors that manage anxieties, but seldom produce intended, technical consequences of practical importance.
Myth	A dramatic narrative of imagined events, usually used to explain origins or transformations of something. Also, an unquestioned belief about the practical benefits of certain techniques and behaviors that is not supported by facts.
Saga	An historical narrative describing the unique accomplishments of a group and its leaders, usually in heroic terms.
Legend	A handed-down narrative of some wonderful event that is based on history but has been embellished with fictional details.
Story	A narrative based on true events, sometimes a combination of truth and fiction.
Folktale	A completely fictional narrative.
Symbol	Any object, act, event, quality, or relation that serves as a vehicle for conveying meaning, usually by representing another thing.
Language	A particular form or manner in which members of a group use sounds and written signs to convey meanings to each other.
Metaphors	Short-hand words used to capture a vision or to reinforce old or new values.
Values	Life-directing attitudes that serve as behavioral guidelines.
Belief	An understanding of a particular phenomenon.
Heroes/ Heroines	Individuals whom the organization has legitimized to model behavior for others.

Source: Adapted from H. M. Trice and J. M. Beyer, "Studying Organizational Cultures Through Rites and Ceremonials," *Academy of Management Review* 9, no. 4 (October 1984): 655.

result in barriers to communication, lack of coordination, and an inability to adapt to changing conditions. It is important for strategists to understand their firm as a socio-cultural system. Failure to integrate a firm's culture with strategic-management activities can undermine organizational effectiveness.

CONCLUSION

The main appeal of any managerial approach is the expectation that it will enhance organizational performance. This is especially true of strategic management. Through involvement in strategic-management activities, managers and employees achieve a

FIGURE 2–3 A conceptualization of the relationship between strategic management and organizational culture

An Organization's Culture

Values and Beliefs	*Language and Metaphors*	*Rites, Rituals, and Ceremonies*	*Symbols*	*Heroes and Heroines*	*Myths, Stories, Legends, and Sagas*

Strategy Formulation	Strategy Implementation	Strategy Evaluation
Is our mission compatible with our culture? Do our external stakeholders understand our culture? Do our managers and employees understand our culture and our strategy? Do our strategies capitalize on our culture? Are our objectives reasonable considering our culture? Which heroes and heroines will actively support our strategies? culture?	Are our management policies and objectives consistent with our culture? Are our marketing and financial policies consistent with our culture? Is our organizational structure compatible with our culture? Is our resource allocation process consistent with our culture? What cultural products could be used to reinforce our new strategies?	Is our performance evaluation system consistent with our culture? Is the timing of our evaluation procedures consistent with our culture? Are our evaluative criteria consistent with our values and beliefs? Do we effectively monitor changes in our strategy and culture? Are proposed corrective actions appropriate considering our culture?

better understanding of an organization's priorities and operations. Strategic management allows organizations to be efficient, but more importantly, it allows them to be effective. Although strategic management does not guarantee organizational success, the process allows proactive rather than reactive decision making. Strategic management may represent a radical change in philosophy for some organizations, so strategists must be trained to anticipate and constructively respond to questions and issues as they arise.

KEY TERMS AND CONCEPTS

Acquisition
Backward integration
Bankruptcy
Combination strategy
Concentric diversification
Conglomerate diversification

Cooperative arrangements
Cost leadership
Cultural products
Differentiation
Diversification strategies
Divestiture
Focus
Forward integration
Franchising
Generic strategies
Horizontal diversification
Horizontal integration
Integrative strategies
Intensive strategies
Joint venture
Leveraged buyout
Liquidation
Market development
Market penetration
Merchant banking
Merger
Organizational culture
Outsourcing
Product development
Retrenchment
Takeover

ISSUES FOR REVIEW AND DISCUSSION

1. Identify guidelines that you think are most important for using strategic management effectively in organizations. Justify your answer.
2. What are some potential pitfalls or risks in using a strategic-management approach to decision making?
3. Give examples of market penetration, market development, and product development strategies pursued by organizations during the last six months.
4. Give examples of forward integration, backward integration, and horizontal integration strategies pursued by organizations during the last six months.
5. Give examples of concentric diversification, horizontal diversification, and conglomerate diversification strategies pursued by organizations during the last six months.
6. Give examples of joint venture, retrenchment, divestiture, liquidation, and combination strategies pursued by organizations during the last six months.
7. Select one of the current readings at the end of this chapter and find that article in your college library. Read the article and prepare a one-page summary.
8. Do you think hostile takeovers are unethical? Why or why not?
9. Explain why cultural products affect strategic-management activities so greatly.
10. Do you think cultural products affect strategy formulation, implementation, or evaluation the most? Why?
11. When a large bank acquires a small bank, to what extent should the small bank's culture be changed to fit the large bank's? How can this be done most effectively?
12. Do you think the President of the United States uses strategic management to make decisions? Why or why not? Could strategic management benefit his decision making? Why or why not?
13. What are the major advantages and disadvantages of diversification?
14. What are the major advantages and disadvantages of an integrative strategy?
15. In your opinion, what is the single major benefit of using a strategic-management approach to decision making? Justify your answer.
16. How would strategic management differ in profit and nonprofit organizations?
17. Why is it not advisable to pursue too many strategies at once?

NOTES

1. Robert Waterman, Jr., *The Renewal Factor: How the Best Get and Keep the Competitive Edge* (New York: Bantam, 1987). Also, see *Business Week* (14 September 1987): 100.
2. Hershey Foods Corporation, *Annual Report*, 1983: 3.
3. Richard Robinson, Jr., "The Importance of Outsiders in Small Firm Strategic Planning," *Academy of Management Journal* 25, no. 1 (March 1982): 80. Also, S. Schoeffler, Robert Buzzell, and Donald Heany, "Impact of Strategic Planning on Profit Performance," *Harvard Business Review* (March 1974): 137; Lawrence Rhyne, "The Relationship of Strategic Planning to Financial Performance," *Strategic Management Journal* 7 (1986): 432; and Deborah Cook and Gerald Ferris, "Strategic Human Resource Management and Firm Effectiveness in Industries Experiencing Decline," *Human Resource Management* 25, no. 3 (Fall 1986): 454.
4. Michael Allen, "Strategic Management Hits Its Stride," *Planning Review* 13, no. 5 (September–October 1985): 6.
5. Sanglin Yoo and Lester Digman, "Decision Support System: A New Tool for Strategic Management," *Long Range Planning* 20, no. 2 (April 1987): 117.
6. Gordon Greenley, "Does Strategic Planning Improve Company Performance?" *Long Range Planning* 19, no. 2 (April 1986): 106.
7. Lee Iacocca, "The Rescue and Resuscitation of Chrysler," *Journal of Business Strategy* 4, no. 1 (Summer 1983): 67.
8. "Executive Pay: Who Got What In 1986," *Business Week* (4 May 1987): 50.
9. Waterman, *Renewal Factor*, 112.
10. R. T. Lenz, "Managing the Evolution of the Strategic Planning Process," *Business Horizons* 30, no. 1 (January–February 1987): 39.
11. "COMSTAT: Caught in a Cash Crunch That May Ground Some Ventures," *Business Week* (21 May 1984): 86–87.
12. "Why Nothing Seems to Make a Dent in Dealmaking," *Business Week* (20 July 1987): 75.
13. Michael Porter, *Competitive Strategy: Techniques for Analyzing Industries and Companies* (New York: Free Press, 1980); also, Michael Porter, *Competitive Advantage: Creating and Sustaining Superior Performance* (New York: Free Press, 1985).
14. Peter Wright, "A Refinement of Porter's Strategies," *Strategic Management Journal* 8, no. 1 (January–February 1987): 94.
15. Porter, *Competitive Strategy*, 70–83.
16. Kenneth Davidson, "Do Megamergers Make Sense?" *Journal of Business Strategy* 7, no. 3 (Winter 1987): 45.
17. Kathryn Rudie Harrigan, "Joint Ventures: Linking for a Leap Forward," *Planning Review* 14, no. 4 (July–August 1986): 10.
18. Christopher Clarke and Francois Gall, "Planned Divestment—A Five-step Approach," *Long Range Planning* 20, no. 1 (February 1987): 17.
19. Edgar Schein, *Organizational Culture and Leadership* (San Francisco: Jossey-Bass, 1985), 9.
20. Y. Allarie and M. Firsirotu, "How to Implement Radical Strategies in Large Organizations," *Sloan Management Review* (Spring 1985): 19.

SUGGESTED READINGS

Aaker, D. A. "How to Select a Business Strategy." *California Management Review* 26, no. 3 (Spring 1984): 167–175.

Aggarwal, Raj. "The Strategic Challenge of the Evolving Global Economy." *Business Horizons* 30, no. 4 (July–August 1987): 38–44.

Batts, W. L. "Dart & Kraft From Merger to Strategic Management." *Planning Review* 30, no. 6 (November–December 1985): 12–17, 44.

Brache, A. "Taking the Strategic Planning Initiative." *Management Solutions* (June 1986): 36–42.

Clarke, C. J., and Gall, F. "Planned Divestment—A Five-step Approach." *Long Range Planning* 20, no. 1 (February 1987): 17–24.

David, F. R. "How Do We Choose Among Alternative Growth Strategies?" *Managerial Planning* 33, no. 4 (January–February 1985): 14–17, 22.

Davidson, K. M., "Do Megamergers Make Sense?" *Journal of Business Strategy* 7, no. 3 (Winter 1987): 49–59.

Deshpande, R., and Parasuraman, A. "Linking Corporate Culture to Strategic Planning." *Business Horizons* 29, no. 3 (May–June 1986): 28–37.

DeSouza, G. "The Best Strategies for Corporate Venturing." *Planning Review* 14, no. 2 (March–April 1986): 12–14.

Drucker, P. "Creating Strategies of Innovation." *Planning Review* 13, no. 6 (November–December 1985): 8–11.

Gardner, M. P. "Creating a Corporate Culture for the Eighties." *Business Horizons* 28, no. 1 (January–February 1985): 59–63.

Gilbert, X., and Strebel, P. "Strategies to Outpace the Competition." *Journal of Business Strategy* 8, no. 1 (Summer 1987): 28–35.

Goold, Michael, and Campbell, Andrew. "Many Best Ways to Make Strategy." *Harvard Business Review* 65, no. 6 (November–December 1987): 70–76.

Gray, D. H. "Uses and Misuses of Strategic Planning." *Harvard Business Review* 64, no. 1 (January–February 1986): 89–96.

Greenley, G. E. "Does Strategic Planning Improve Company Performance?" *Long Range Planning* 19, no. 2 (April 1986): 101–109.

Hardy, Cynthia. "Investing in Retrenchment: Avoiding the Hidden Costs." *California Management Review* 29, no. 4 (Summer 1987): 111–125.

Harrigan, K. R. "Matching Vertical Integration Strategies to Competitive Conditions." *Strategic Management Journal* 7, (1986): 535–555.

Harrigan, K. R. "Joint Ventures: Linking for a Leap Forward." *Planning Review* 14, no. 4 (July–August 1986): 10–14.

Harris, S., and Sutton, R. I. "Functions of Parting Ceremonies in Dying Organizations." *Academy of Management Journal* 29, no. 1 (March 1986): 5–30.

Hopkins, H. D. "Acquisition Strategy and the Market Position of Acquiring Firms." *Strategic Management Journal* 8, no. 6 (November–December 1987): 535–548.

James, B. G. "SMR Forum: Strategic Planning Under Fire." *Sloan Management Review* (Summer 1984): 57–61.

Jemison, D. B., and Sitkin, S. B. "Corporate Acquisitions: A Process Perspective." *The Academy of Management Review* 11, no. 1 (January 1986): 145–163.

Kelso, Louis, and Kelso, Patricia. "Leveraged Buyouts Good and Bad." *Management Review* (November 1987): 28–31.

Kilmann, R. H., Saxton, M. J., and Serpa, R. "Issues in Understanding and Changing Culture." *California Management Review* 28, no. 2 (Winter 1986): 87, 93–94.

Malik, Z. A., and Basu, S. "Formal Integrated Long-Range Planning: Its Impact on Financial Risk Decisions." *Business Horizons* 29, no. 2 (March–April 1986): 80–82.

Mason, J. "Developing Strategic Thinking." *Long Range Planning* 19, no. 3 (June 1986): 72–80.

Mayer, Robert. "Winning Strategies for Manufacturers in Mature Industries." *Journal of Business Strategy* 8, no. 2 (Fall 1987): 23–31.

Olson, J. E., and Cooper, T. A. "CEOs on Strategy: Two Companies, Two Strategies." *Journal of Business Strategy* 8, no. 4 (Summer 1987): 51–57.

Pascale, R. "The Paradox of Corporate Culture: Reconciling Ourselves to Socialization." *California Management Review* 28, no. 2 (Winter 1985): 26, 37–40.

Pearce, J. A., II, Freeman, E. B., and Robinson, R. B., Jr. "The Tenuous Link Between Formal Strategic Planning and Financial Performance." *Academy of Management Review* 12, no. 4 (October 1987): 658–675.

Pekar, P. "Joint Venture: A New Information System is Born." *Planning Review* 14, no. 4 (July–August 1986): 15–19.

Porter, M. E. "From Competitive Advantage to Corporate Strategy." *Harvard Business Review* 65, no. 3 (May–June 1987): 43–59.

Rafferty, J. "Exit Barriers and Strategic Position in Declining Markets." *Long Range Planning* 20, no. 2 (April 1987): 86–91.

Ramanujam, V., and Venkatraman, N. "Planning and Performance: A New Look at an Old Question." *Business Horizons* 30, no. 3 (May–June 1987): 19–25.

Ramanujam, V., Venkatraman N., and Camillus, J. C. "Multi-Objective Assessment of Effectiveness of Strategic Planning: A Discriminant Analysis Approach." *Academy of Management Journal* 29, no. 2 (June 1986): 347–372.

Rhyne, L. C. "The Relationship of Strategic Planning

to Financial Performance." *Strategic Management Journal* 7 (1986): 423–436.

Roberts, E. B., and Berry, C. A. "Entering New Businesses: Selecting Strategies for Success." *Sloan Management Review* (Spring 1985): 3–17.

Rosenberg, L. J., and Schewe, C. D. "Strategic Planning: Fulfilling the Promise." *Business Horizons* 28, no. 4 (July–August 1985): 54–62.

Schillaci, Carmela. "Designing Successful Joint Ventures." *Journal of Business Strategy* 8, no. 2 (Fall 1987): 59–63.

Schmidt, R. J. "Corporate Divestiture: Pruning for Higher Profits." *Business Horizons* 30, no. 3 (May–June 1987): 26–31.

Scholz, Christian. "Corporate Culture and Strategy—The Problem of Strategic Fit." *Long Range Planning* 20, no. 4 (August 1987): 78–87.

Schwaninger, M. "A Practical Approach to Strategy Development." *Long Range Planning* 20, no. 5 (October 1987): 74–85.

Shanklin, W. L. "Fortune 500 Dropouts." *Planning Review* 14, no. 3 (May–June 1986): 12–17.

Shrivastava, P. "Integrating Strategy Formulation with Organizational Culture." *Journal of Business Strategy* 5 (1985): 103–111.

Shrivastava, P. "Postmerger Integration." *The Journal of Business Strategy* 7, no. 1 (Summer 1986): 65–76.

Sutton, Robert I., and Callahan, Anita L. "The Stigma of Bankruptcy: Spoiled Organizational Image and Its Management." *Academy of Management Journal* 30, no. 3 (September 1987): 405–436.

Trice, H. M., and Beyer, J. M. "Studying Organizational Cultures Through Rites and Ceremonials." *Academy of Management Review* 9, no. 4 (October 1984): 653–669.

Varadarajan, P. R., and Ramanujam, V. "Diversification and Performance: A Reexamination Using a New Two-Dimensional Conceptualization of Diversity in Firms." *Academy of Management Journal* 30, no. 2 (June 1987): 380–393.

Venkatraman, N., and Ramanujam, V. "Measurement of Business Performance in Strategy Research: A Comparison of Approaches." *Academy of Management Review* 11, no. 4 (October 1986): 801–814.

Weidenbaum, Murray, and Vogt, Stephen. "Takeovers and Stockholders: Winners and Losers." *California Management Review* 29, no. 4 (Summer 1987): 157–168.

White, R. E. "Generic Business Strategies, Organizational Context and Performance: An Empirical Investigation." *Strategic Management Journal* 7 (1986): 217–231.

Wiener, D. P. "Deals of the Year." *Fortune* (2 February 1987): 68–74.

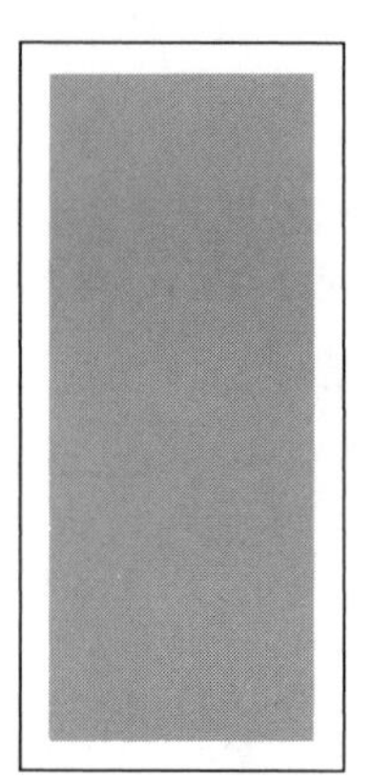

EXPERIENTIAL EXERCISES

EXPERIENTIAL EXERCISE 2A:

Classifying Alternative Strategies

PURPOSE

This exercise can improve your understanding of generic strategies by giving you experience classifying strategies. This skill will help you use the strategy-formulation tools presented later. The first five strategies are hypothetical and apply to Ponderosa. The last ten strategies are real and apply to different companies.

1. Ponderosa sells Casa Lupita.
2. Ponderosa builds two hundred new restaurants in Western Europe.
3. Ponderosa acquires the Bonanza Steakhouse chain.
4. Ponderosa begins building seafood restaurants nationwide. The restaurants are called "The Shrimper."
5. Ponderosa acquires the First Union National Bank, headquartered in Charlotte, North Carolina.
6. ITT Corporation, a large, diversified American firm and Generale d'Electricite, a French firm, recently created Alcatel, a telecommunications company. ITT has a 37 percent stake in Alcatel.
7. Coleco's new StarCom toys—male action figures that move via magnets and springs—are expected in 1987 to reverse the company's net loss of $112.2 million in 1986.

8. Wickes Companies just sold its British unit, Wickes PLC, to Cityquest PLC, a company formed by the unit's chairman, Henry Sweetbaum. Wickes PLC operates building supply and home improvement centers in the United Kingdom, Belgium, and the Netherlands.
9. Ford Motor Company is acquiring Aston Martin Lagonda Ltd., the British maker of ultraluxury cars. Aston Martin Lagonda produces about two hundred cars a year, with prices ranging from $145,000 to $170,000. The company has only four hundred employees.
10. Sears, Roebuck and Company announced in 1987 that it will close five of its twelve big, regional warehouses and eliminate thousands of jobs over the next several years.
11. Lomas and Nettleton Financial Corporation created a new subsidiary in 1987 called Lomas Capital Management Company to manage equity, fixed-income, and balanced funds, with an initial portfolio of $55 million. Entering the securities-management business is new for Lomas and Nettleton, the largest mortgage banking company in the United States.
12. Motel 6, an economy motel chain, recently acquired eleven properties, raising its inventory to 415 company-operated motels in forty states. Motel 6 is planning to expand along the Atlantic coast. Motel 6's 1986 occupancy levels were 66.7 percent, higher than industry average of 62.4 percent but below the company's 1985 average of 69.5 percent.
13. As the nation's largest air carrier, Texas Air recently acquired Eastern Airlines, People's Express, Frontier Airlines, Continental Airlines, and New York Air.
14. During 1987, General Motors Corporation shifted about 10 percent of its parts' production to outside suppliers.
15. Fairchild Industries is closing its Farmingdale, N. Y. aircraft plant and dismissing the plant's three thousand employees.

YOUR TASK

Step 1 Across the top of a separate sheet of paper, set up three columns with the following headings:

Type of Strategy	Attractiveness of Strategy ("High" or "Low")	Supporting Rationale

Step 2 Down the left side of your paper, number from 1 to 15. These numbers correspond to the strategies described above.

Step 3 For the strategies listed in the previous section, record under column one the type of strategy that best describes those actions. Under the second column record whether you think the strategy's attractiveness is "High" or "Low" for the organization. Record under column three a supporting rationale statement.

Step 4 Compare your answers to the author's answers, given by your professor.

EXPERIENTIAL EXERCISE 2B

Strategic Management at the Dynamic Computer Company

PURPOSE

This exercise can give you experience choosing among alternative growth strategies for a specific company. Remember that organizations cannot pursue all the strategies that potentially may benefit the firm. Difficult decisions have to be made to eliminate some options. Use the guidelines given in Exhibit 2–1 to complete this exercise.

THE STRATEGIC SITUATION

Dynamic Computer, Inc. (DCI) is a highly regarded personal computer manufacturer based in central California. DCI designs, develops, produces, markets, and services personal computer systems for individuals' needs in business, education, science, engineering, and the home. The company's main product is the Dynamic II personal computer system, complete with optional accessories and software. The company has recently announced a new system, the Dynamic III, that is aimed at large business firms. It is much more expensive than the Dynamic II.

Dynamic's computer systems are distributed in the United States and Canada by one thousand independent retail stores and internationally through twenty-one independent distributors that resell to 850 foreign retail outlets. Approximately seven hundred of the retail outlets in the United States and Canada are authorized service centers for Dynamic products, but none of the outlets sell Dynamic products exclusively. Many of these outlets are not marketing Dynamic's products effectively.

The American computer industry grew at an inflation-adjusted, compound annual rate of about 20 percent from 1958 through the late 1980s. In the 1990s, real annual growth in the computer industry is expected to average about 18 percent a year. The outlook for personal computers continues to be positive. However, this market is highly competitive and is characterized by rapid technological advances in both hardware and software. Margins on software are nearly double operating margins on hardware. New firms are entering the industry at an increasing rate and this has resulted in a decline in Dynamic's sales, earnings, and market share in recent years. Most computer companies expect software sales and services to represent 50 percent of their total revenues by 1990. Dynamic is concerned about its future direction and competitiveness. Selected financial information for Dynamic is given in Table 2B–1.

YOUR TASK

The owners of DCI have indicated a willingness to explore a number of alternative growth strategies for the future. They have hired you as a consultant to assist them in making strategic decisions regarding the future allocation of resources. The feeling is

TABLE 2B–1

	1987	*1988*	*1989*
Sales	$ 13,000,000	$ 12,000,000	$ 10,000,000
Net Income	3,000,000	1,000,000	500,000
Total Assets	180,000,000	200,000,000	250,000,000
Market Share	15%	12%	10%

that to sustain growth, the company must make some critical decisions. Dynamic is financially capable of investing in several projects. The owners wish to use their resources wisely to produce the highest possible return on investment in the future. They are considering the five alternative strategies:

1. Market penetration—establish a nationwide sales force to market Dynamic products to large firms that do not buy through independent retailers.
2. Product development—develop an "easier to use" computer for small business firms.
3. Forward integration—offer major new incentives to distributors who sell and service Dynamic products.
4. Backward integration—purchase a major outside supplier of software.
5. Conglomerate diversification—acquire Toys Unlimited, a large and successful toy manufacturer.

Based on the strategy guidelines given in Exhibit 2–1, your task is to offer specific recommendations to the strategists of DCI. Follow these steps:

Step 1 Across the top of a separate sheet of paper, set up five columns, with the following headings:

Individual Percentage Allocations	Group Percentage Allocations	Expert Percentage Allocations	The Absolute Difference Between Columns 1 and 3	The Absolute Difference Between Columns 2 and 4

Down the left side of your paper, number from 1 to 5. These numbers correspond to the five strategies listed above.

Step 2 Take ten minutes to determine how you would allocate DCI's resources among the five alternative strategies. Record your answers by placing individual percentage values for strategies 1 through 5 under column 1. Your only constraint is that the total resources allocated must equal 100%. Distribute resources in the manner you think will offer the greatest future return on investment and profitability.

Step 3 Join with two other students in class. Develop a set of group percentage allocations and record these values for strategies 1 through 5 under column 2. Do not change your individual percentage allocations once discussion begins in your group.

Step 4 As your professor reveals the author's percentage allocations and supporting rationale, record these values for strategies 1 through 5 under column 3.

Step 5 For each row, subtract column 3 values from column 1 values and record the absolute difference (ignore negatives) in column 4. Then, sum the column 4 values.

Step 6 For each row, subtract column 3 values from column 2 values and record the absolute difference (ignore negatives) in column 5. Then, sum the column 5 values.

Step 7 If the sum of column 4 values exceeds the sum of column 5 values, then your group allocation of DCI's resources was better than your individual allocation. However, if the sum of column 4 values is less than the sum of column 5 values, you were a better strategist than your group on this exercise. Strategic-management research indicates that group strategic decisions are almost always better than individual strategic decisions. Did you do better than your group? Why?

EXPERIENTIAL EXERCISE 2C

How Risky Are Various Alternative Strategies?

PURPOSE

This exercise focuses on how risky various alternative strategies are for organizations to pursue. Different degrees of risk are based largely on varying degrees of *externality*, that is, movement away from the present business into new markets, products, or totally different businesses.[1] In general, the greater the degree of externality, the greater the probability of loss resulting from unexpected events. High-risk strategies are generally less attractive than low-risk strategies.

YOUR TASK

Step 1 On a separate sheet of paper, number vertically from 1 to 10. Think of 1 as "least risky," 2 as "next least risky," and so forth to 10, "most risky."

Step 2 Write the following strategies beside the appropriate number to indicate how risky you believe the strategy is to pursue: horizontal integration, horizontal

1. James Belohlav and Karen Giddens-Emig, "Selecting a Master Strategy," *Journal of Business Strategy* 7, no. 3 (Winter 1987): 77.

diversification, liquidation, forward integration, backward integration, product development, market development, market penetration, joint venture, and conglomerate diversification.

Step 3 Grade your paper as your professor gives to you the author's answers and supporting rationale. Each correct answer is worth ten points. This exercise is based on a commonly accepted and published classification of strategies given in the footnote article.

PART TWO
STRATEGY FORMULATION

The Business Mission

NOTABLE QUOTES

A business is not defined by its name, statutes, or articles of incorporation. It is defined by the business mission. Only a clear definition of the mission and purpose of the organization makes possible clear and realistic business objectives.

Peter Drucker

A corporate vision can focus, direct, motivate, unify, and even excite a business into superior performance. The job of a strategist is to identify and project a clear vision.

John Keane

For strategists, there's a trade-off between the breadth and detail of information needed. It's a bit like an eagle hunting for a rabbit. The eagle has to be high enough to scan a wide area in order to enlarge his chances of seeing prey, but he has to be low enough to see the detail—the movement and features that will allow him to recognize his target. Continually making this trade-off is the job of a strategist—it simply can't be delegated.

Frederick Gluck

The best laid schemes of mice and men often go awry.

Robert Burns (paraphrased)

A strategist's job is to see the company not as it is . . . but as it can become.

John W. Teets
Chairman of Greyhound, Inc.

That business mission is so rarely given adequate thought is perhaps the most important single cause of business frustration.

Peter Drucker

Most of us fear change. Even when our minds say change is normal, our stomachs quiver at the prospect. But for strategists and managers today, there is no choice but to change.

Robert Waterman, Jr.

To be in hell is to drift, to be in heaven is to steer.

George Bernard Shaw

3

OUTLINE

OBJECTIVES

After studying this chapter, you should be able to

- Describe the nature and role of mission statements in strategic management.
- Identify the components of mission statement documents.
- Discuss the importance of mission statements in strategic management.
- Evaluate mission statements of different organizations.
- Write good mission statements.

This chapter focuses on the concepts and tools needed to evaluate and write business mission statements successfully. A practical framework for developing mission statements is provided. Actual mission statements from large and small organizations and profit and nonprofit enterprises are presented and critically examined.

WHAT IS OUR BUSINESS?

Current thought on mission statements is based largely on guidelines set forth in the mid-1970s by Peter Drucker, often called "the father of modern management" for his pioneering studies at General Motors Corporation and for his twenty-two books and hundreds of articles. *Harvard Business Review* calls Drucker, aged seventy-seven, "the preeminent management thinker of our time."

Drucker says asking the question, "What is our business?" is synonymous with asking the question, "What is our mission?" An enduring statement of purpose that distinguishes one organization from other similar enterprises, the *mission statement* is a declaration of an organization's "reason for being." It answers the pivotal question, "What is our business?" It is essential for effectively establishing objectives and formulating strategies. Sometimes called a *creed statement,* a statement of purpose, a statement of philosophy, a statement of beliefs, a statement of business principles, or a statement "defining our business," a mission statement reveals the long-term vision of an organization in terms of what it wants to be and whom it wants to serve. All organizations have a reason for being, even if strategists have not consciously transformed this into writing. As illustrated in Figure 3–1, a carefully prepared statement of mission is widely recognized by both practitioners and academicians as the first step in strategic management.

> A business mission is the foundation for priorities, strategies, plans, and work assignments. It is the starting point for the design of managerial jobs and, above all, for the design of managerial structures. Nothing may seem simpler or more obvious than to know what a company's business is. A steel mill makes steel, a railroad runs trains to carry freight and passengers, an insurance company underwrites fire risks, and a bank lends money. Actually, "What is our business?" is almost always a difficult question and the right answer is usually anything but obvious. The answer to this question is the first responsibility of strategists. Only strategists can make sure that this question receives the attention it deserves and that the answer makes sense and enables the business to plot its course and set its objectives.[1]

We can perhaps best understand a business mission by focusing on a business when it is first started. In the beginning, a new business is simply a collection of ideas. Starting a new business rests on a set of beliefs that the new organization can offer some product or service, to some customers, in some geographic area, using some type of technology, at a profitable price. A new business owner typically believes that the management philosophy of the new enterprise will result in a favorable public image and that this concept of the business can be communicated to and will be adopted by important constituencies. When the set of beliefs about a business at its inception are put into writing, the resulting document mirrors the same basic ideas that compose a

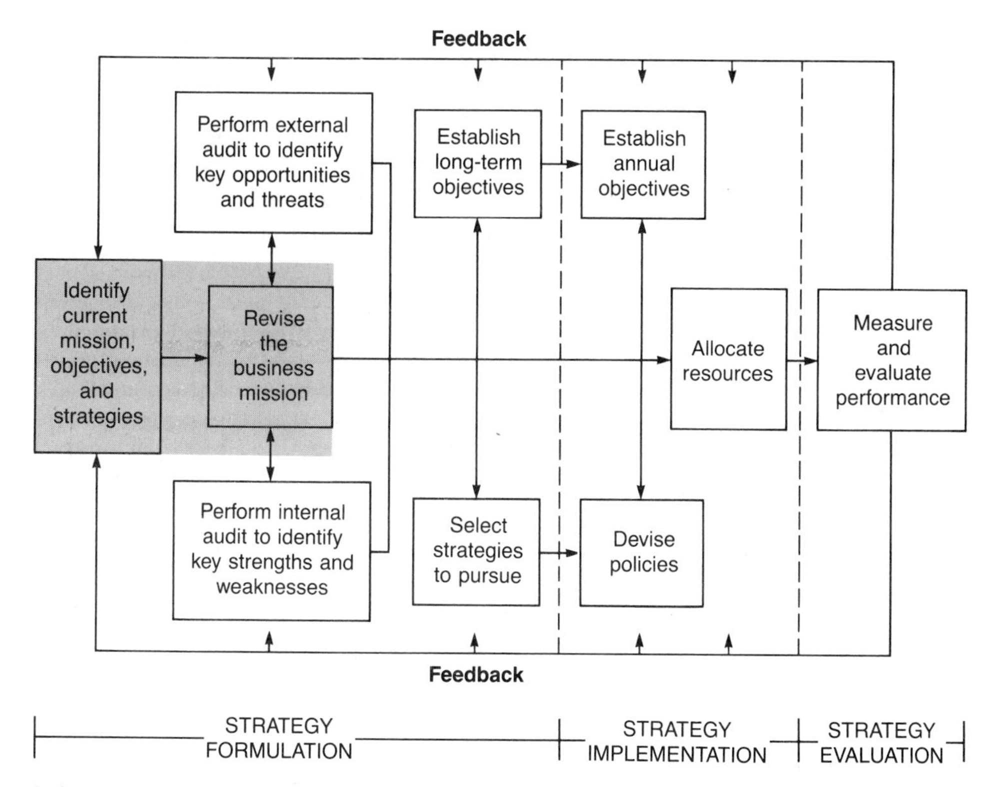

FIGURE 3–1 A comprehensive strategic-management model

mission statement. As a business grows, owners or managers find it necessary to revise the founding set of beliefs, but those original ideas usually are reflected in the revised statement of mission.

Business mission statements can often be found in the front of annual reports. The current mission statement of Eli Lilly and Company is one such example.

> Eli Lilly and Company is a research-based corporation that develops, manufactures, and markets human medicines, medical instrument systems, diagnostic products, agricultural products, and cosmetics. To guide its affairs, the company follows certain fundamental principles. These principles, which we believe are in the best long-term interests of all shareholders, are the following: The company is committed to the discovery and marketing of innovative products of the highest quality that offer benefits to customers in all of our markets. The company is dedicated to the highest levels of ethics, integrity, and excellence in research, manufacturing, marketing, and all other phases of its operations. The company recognizes a primary responsibility to its employees because of the key role employees play in the achievement of corporate goals. The company's objective is to attract and retain outstanding people at all levels and in all parts of the organization. We are committed to fair and equitable treatment of all employees and to policies and programs that offer the opportunity for employees to develop meaningful and rewarding careers. Eli Lilly feels an obligation to be a good corporate citizen wherever it operates.[2]

A good mission statement describes an organization's purpose, customers, products or services, markets, philosophy, and basic technology. According to Vern McGinnis, a mission statement should (1) define what the organization is and what the organization aspires to be, (2) be limited enough to exclude some ventures and broad enough to allow for creative growth, (3) distinguish a given organization from all others, (4) serve as a framework for evaluating both current and prospective activities, and (5) be stated in terms sufficiently clear to be widely understood throughout the organization.[3]

Some strategists spend almost every moment of every day on administrative and tactical concerns, and strategists who rush quickly to establish objectives and implement strategies often overlook developing a mission statement. This problem is widespread even among large organizations. Approximately 40 percent of large corporations in America have not yet developed a formal mission statement, but 60 percent do have a formal mission document.[4] An increasing number of organizations every day are developing formal mission statements.

THE IMPORTANCE OF A CLEAR MISSION

The importance of a mission statement to effective strategic management is well documented in the literature. A recent study comparing mission statements of Fortune 500 firms performing very well and firms performing less well concluded that high performers have more comprehensive mission statements than low performers.[5] King and Cleland recommend that organizations carefully develop a written mission statement for the following reasons:

1. To ensure unanimity of purpose within the organization.
2. To provide a basis, or standard, for allocating organizational resources.
3. To establish a general tone or organizational climate.
4. To serve as a focal point for individuals to identify with the organization's purpose and direction; and to deter those who cannot from participating further in the organization's activities.
5. To facilitate the translation of objectives into a work structure involving the assignment of tasks to responsible elements within the organization.
6. To specify organizational purposes and the translation of these purposes into objectives in such a way that cost, time, and performance parameters can be assessed and controlled.[6]

THE NATURE OF A BUSINESS MISSION

A Declaration of Attitude

A mission statement is a declaration of attitude and outlook more than a statement of specific details. It is usually broad in scope for at least two major reasons. First, a good mission statement allows for the generation and consideration of a range of feasible alternative objectives and strategies without unduly stifling management creativity. Excess specificity would limit the potential of creative growth for the organization. On the other hand an overly general statement that does not exclude any strategy alternatives could be dysfunctional. Apple Computer's mission statement, for example, should not open the possibility for diversification into pesticides, or Ford Motor Company's, into food processing.

Second, a mission statement needs to be broad to effectively reconcile differences among an organization's diverse *stakeholders,* the individuals and groups of persons who have a special stake or claim on the company. Stakeholders include employees, managers, stockholders, boards of directors, customers, suppliers, distributors, creditors, governments (local, state, federal, and foreign), unions, competitors, special interest groups, and the general public. Stakeholders affect and are affected by an organization's strategies, yet the claims and concerns of diverse constituencies vary and often conflict. For example, the general public is especially interested in social responsibility, whereas stockholders are more interested in profitability. Claims on any business may literally number in the thousands, and often include clean air, jobs, taxes, investment opportunities, career opportunities, equal employment opportunities, employee benefits, salaries, wages, clean water, and community services. All stakeholders' claims on an organization cannot be pursued with equal emphasis. A good mission statement indicates the relative attention that an organization will devote to meeting the claims of various stakeholders.

Reaching the fine balance between specificity and generality is difficult to achieve, but is well worth the effort. George Steiner offers the following insight on the need for a mission statement to be broad in scope:

> Most business statements of mission are expressed at high levels of abstraction. Vagueness nevertheless has its virtues. Mission statements are not designed to express concrete ends, but rather to provide motivation, general direction, an image, a tone, and a philosophy to guide the enterprise. An excess of detail could prove counterproductive since concrete specification could be the base for rallying opposition. Precision might stifle creativity in the formulation of an acceptable mission or purpose. Once an aim is cast in concrete it creates a rigidity in an organization and resists change. Vagueness leaves room for other managers to fill in the details, perhaps even to modify general patterns. Vagueness permits more flexibility in adapting to changing environments and internal operations. It facilitates flexibility in implementation.[7]

An effective mission statement arouses positive feelings and emotions about an organization. An effective mission statement is inspiring in the sense that it motivates readers to action. An effective mission statement generates the impression that a firm is successful, has direction, and is worthy of time, support, and investment. It reflects judgments about future growth directions and strategies based upon forward-looking external and internal analyses. A business mission should provide useful criteria for selecting among alternative strategies. A clear mission statement provides a basis for generating and screening strategic options. The statement of mission should be dynamic in orientation, allowing judgments about the most promising growth directions and those considered less promising.

A Resolution of Divergent Views

What are the reasons some strategists are reluctant to develop a statement of their business mission? First, the question "What is our business?" can create controversy. Raising the question often reveals differences among strategists in the organization. Individuals who have worked together for a long time and who think they know each other may suddenly realize that they are in fundamental disagreement:

> "What is our Mission?" is a genuine decision; and a genuine decision must be based on divergent views to have a chance to be a right and effective decision. Developing a business mission is always a choice between alternatives, each of which rests on different assumptions regarding the reality of the business and its environment. It is always a high-risk decision. A change in mission always leads to changes in objectives, strategies, organization, and behavior. The mission decision is far too important to be made by acclamation. Developing a business mission is a big step toward management effectiveness. Hidden or half-understood disagreements on the definition of a business mission underlie many of the personality problems, communication problems, and irritations that tend to divide a top-management group. Establishing a mission should never be made on plausibility alone, never should be made fast, and never should be made painlessly.[8]

Considerable disagreement among an organization's strategists over basic purpose and mission can cause trouble if not resolved. For example, unresolved disagreement over the business mission was one of the reasons for W. T. Grant's bankruptcy. As one executive reported:

> There was a lot of dissension within the company whether we should go the K-Mart route or go after the Montgomery Ward and J. C. Penney position. Ed Staley and Lou Lustenberger (two top executives) were at loggerheads over the issue, with the upshot being we took a position between the two and that consequently stood for nothing.[9]

Too often, strategists develop a statement of business mission only when their organization is in trouble. Of course, by then it is needed. Developing and communicating a clear mission during troubled times may indeed have spectacular results and may even reverse decline. However, to wait until an organization is in trouble to develop a mission statement is a gamble that characterizes irresponsible management. According to Drucker, the most important time to ask seriously "What is our business?" is when a company has been successful:

> Success always obsoletes the very behavior that achieved it, always creates new realities, and always creates new and different problems. Only the fairy story ends "They lived happily ever after." It is never popular to argue with success or to rock the boat. The ancient Greeks knew that the penalty of success can be severe. The management that does not ask "What is our mission?" when the company is successful is, in effect, smug, lazy, and arrogant. It will not be long before success will turn into failure. Sooner or later, even the most successful answer to the question "What is our business?" becomes obsolete.[10]

A Customer Orientation

A good mission statement effectively reflects the anticipations of customers. Rather than developing a product and then trying to find a market, the operating philosophy of organizations should be to identify customers' needs and then provide a product or service to fulfill those needs. Good mission statements identify the utility of a firm's products to its customers. This is why AT & T's mission statement focuses on communication rather than telephones, Exxon's mission statement focuses on energy rather than oil and gas, Union Pacific's mission statement focuses on transportation rather than railroads, and Universal Studios' mission statement focuses on entertainment instead of movies. An anonymous author offers a general admonition that is particularly relevant for a strategist attempting to develop a business mission statement:

> Do not offer me things.
> Do not offer me clothes. Offer me attractive looks.
> Do not offer me shoes. Offer me comfort for my feet and the pleasure of walking.
> Do not offer me a house. Offer me security, comfort, and a place that is clean and happy.
> Do not offer me books. Offer me hours of pleasure and the benefit of knowledge.
> Do not offer me records. Offer me leisure and the sound of music.
> Do not offer me tools. Offer me the benefit and the pleasure of making beautiful things.
> Do not offer me furniture. Offer me comfort and the quietness of a cozy place.
> Do not offer me things. Offer me ideas, emotions, ambience, feelings, and benefits.
> Please, do not offer me things.

A major reason for developing a business mission is to attract the customers who give meaning to an organization. A classic description of the purpose of a business reveals the relative importance of customers in a statement of mission:

> It is the customer who determines what a business is. It is the customer alone whose willingness to pay for a good or service converts economic resources into wealth and things into goods. What a business thinks it produces is not of first importance, especially not to the future of the business and to its success. What the customer thinks he/she is buying, what he/she considers value, is decisive—it determines what a business is, what it produces, and whether it will prosper. And what the customer buys and considers value is never a product. It is always utility, meaning what a product or service does for him. The customer is the foundation of a business and keeps it in existence.[11]

A Declaration of Social Policy

The words "*social policy*" embrace managerial philosophy and thinking at the highest levels of an organization. For this reason, social policy affects the development of a business mission statement. Social issues mandate that strategists consider not only what the organization owes its various stakeholders but also what responsibilities the firm has to consumers, environmentalists, minorities, communities, and other groups. After decades of debate on the topic of social responsibility, many firms still struggle to determine appropriate social policies.

The issue of social responsibility arises when a company establishes its business mission. The impact of society on business organizations is becoming more pronounced each year. Social policies directly affect a firm's customers, products and services, markets, technology, profitability, self-concept, and public image. An organization's social policy should be integrated into all strategic-management activities including the development of a mission statement. Carroll and Hoy assert that corporate social policy should be designed and articulated during strategy formulation, set and administered during strategy implementation, and reaffirmed or changed during strategy evaluation.[12] The emerging view of social responsibility holds that social issues should be attended to both directly and indirectly in determining strategies.

Firms should strive to engage in social activities that have economic benefits. For example, in 1987 Merck & Company developed the drug ivermectin for treating "river blindness," a disease caused by a fly-borne parasitic worm endemic in poor tropical areas of Africa, the Middle East, and Latin America. In an unprecedented gesture that reflected its corporate commitment to social responsibility, Merck then made ivermectin available at no cost to medical personnel throughout the world. Merck's action highlights the dilemma of "orphan drugs," which offer pharmaceutical companies no economic incentive for developing and distributing.

Despite differences in approaches, most American companies try to assure outsiders that they conduct business in a socially responsible way. The mission statement is an effective instrument for conveying this message. The Norton Company, for example, concludes its mission statement by saying:

> In order to fulfill this mission, Norton will continue to demonstrate a sense of responsibility to the public interest and to earn the respect and loyalty of its customers, employees, shareholders, and suppliers, and the communities in which it does business.[13]

COMPONENTS OF A MISSION STATEMENT

Mission statements can and do vary in length, content, format, and specificity. Most practitioners and academicians of strategic management consider an effective statement to exhibit nine characteristics or *mission statement components*. Since a mission statement is often the most visible and public part of the strategic-management process, it is important that it includes all of these essential components. Components and corresponding questions that a mission statement should answer are given here.

1. *Customers* Who are the enterprise's customers?
2. *Products or services* What are the firm's major products or services?
3. *Markets* Where does the firm compete?
4. *Technology* What is the firm's basic technology?
5. *Concern for survival, growth, and profitability* What is the firm's commitment towards economic objectives?
6. *Philosophy* What are the basic beliefs, values, aspirations, and philosophical priorities of the firm?
7. *Self-concept* What are the firm's major strengths and competitive advantages?
8. *Concern for public image* What is the firm's public image?
9. *Concern for employees* What is the firm's attitude towards employees?

Excerpts from the mission statements of different organizations are provided in Figure 3–2 to exemplify the nine essential components.

FIGURE 3–2 Examples of the nine essential components of a mission statement

1. *Customers*

   We believe our first responsibility is to the doctors, nurses, and patients, to mothers and all others who use our products and services. (Johnson & Johnson)

2. *Products or services*

   AMAX's principal products are molybdenum, coal, iron ore, copper, lead, zinc, petroleum and natural gas, potash, phosphates, nickel, tungsten, silver, gold, and magnesium. (AMAX)

   Standard Oil Company (Indiana) is in business to find and produce crude oil, natural gas, and natural gas liquids; to manufacture high quality products useful to society from these raw materials; and to distribute and market those products and to provide dependable related services to the consuming public at reasonable prices. (Standard Oil Company)

3. *Markets*

   We are dedicated to the total success of Corning Glass Works as a worldwide competitor. (Corning Glass Works)

   Our emphasis is on North American markets, although global opportunities will be explored. (Blockway)

4. *Technology*

   Control Data is in the business of applying micro-electronics and computer technology in two general areas: computer-related hardware; and computing-enhancing services, which include computation, information, education and finance. (Control Data)

   The common technology in these areas is discrete particle coatings. (Nashua)

5. *Concern for survival, growth, and profitability*

   In this respect, the company will conduct its operations prudently, and will provide the profits and growth which will assure Hoover's ultimate success. (Hoover Universal)

   To serve the worldwide need for knowledge at a fair profit by gathering, evaluating, producing and distributing valuable information in a way that benefits our customers, employees, authors, investors, and our society. (McGraw-Hill)

6. *Philosophy*

   We believe human development to be the worthiest of the goals of civilization and independence to be the superior condition for nurturing growth in the capabilities of people. (Sun Company)

   It's all part of the Mary Kay philosophy—a philosophy based on the golden rule. A spirit of sharing and caring where people give cheerfully of their time, knowledge, and experience. (Mary Kay Cosmetics)

7. *Self-concept*

   Crown Zellerbach is committed to leapfrogging competition within 1,000 days by unleashing the constructive and creative abilities and energies of each of its employees. (Crown Zellerbach)

8. *Concern for public image*

   To share the world's obligation for the protection of the environment. (Dow Chemical)

To contribute to the economic strength of society and function as a good corporate citizen on a local, state, and national basis in all countries in which we do business. (Pfizer)

9. *Concern for employees*

   To recruit, develop, motivate, reward, and retain personnel of exceptional ability, character and dedication by providing good working conditions, superior leadership, compensation on the basis of performance, an attractive benefit program, opportunity for growth and a high degree of employment security. (The Wachovia Corporation)

   To compensate its employees with remuneration and fringe benefits competitive with other employment opportunities in its geographical area and commensurate with their contributions toward efficient corporate operations. (Public Service Electric and Gas Company)

WRITING AND EVALUATING MISSION STATEMENTS

Perhaps the best way to develop a skill for writing and evaluating mission statements is to study actual company missions. Therefore, eight mission statements are presented in Exhibit 3–1. These statements are then evaluated in Table 3–1 based on the nine criteria presented in the previous section. Key parts of Mary Kay Cosmetics' mission statement are italicized for your convenience and study.

EXHIBIT 3–1 Mission statements of eight organizations

Avon Company
Avon's corporate mission is to expand aggressively our new, emerging businesses while continuing our historical growth as the world's leading beauty business. The Company's diverse operations enhance our access to profitable, consistent growth. Our strong financial position will enable us to fund most growth opportunities through internal sources. (Avon Company, *Annual Report, 1982,* p. 1.)

Penn State University
Penn State's fundamental responsibility is to provide programs of instruction, research, and public service, and thus act as an instrument of self-renewal and development for the Commonwealth. As Pennsylvania's land-grant university, Penn State must preserve and enhance its distinctive qualities.

While the modern university maintains links to the past and serves to maintain cultural values, its most extensive task at present is to help people to understand the great changes taking place in our society. People must have the skills and the learning habits that will make it possible for them to educate themselves over a lifetime. The rapid rate of change in contemporary society dictates that the University's programs adjust without undue delay to meet the needs of students and society.

University programs of research and other creative and scholarly activities are essential if the University is to contribute to the solution of the social, scientific, and technical problems of society, and discharge effectively its upper-division and graduate teaching responsibilities. The University must also serve the Commonwealth directly through its programs of extension, continuing education, and other public service programs designed to meet the needs of citizens throughout the state.

By encouraging the enrollment of students from all segments of society and from other states and nations, the University provides the intellectual arena in which the search for rational solutions to societal problems can be nurtured, and in which teaching and learning can be the pivotal function. In performing this function, it is essential that the University foster independent thought and open discussion of alternatives. (Pennsylvania State University, *Baccalaureate Catalog, 1982–1983*)

University of Idaho

In the widest sense, the mission of the University of Idaho, a publicly supported, land-grant institution, is to serve the people of the state and nation as a major center of learning for the advancement, preservation, dissemination, and use of knowledge. Deriving from this multifaceted mission are the functions to be performed and the objectives to be achieved through the interaction of the various components and publics of the university. (University of Idaho, *Bulletin and General Catalog, 1983/1985,* p. 9.)

Nashua Corporation

Nashua Corporation provides products and services in four business segments: office systems and supplies, coated papers and tapes, computer products, and photo products. Most of the product lines in these four areas relate to discrete particle technology. This technology addresses a broad range of market applications in which various substrates are coated with particles that can be activated by light, heat, magnetism, pressure, electrical current and other stimuli. Nashua products are sold internationally by wholly owned foreign subsidiaries and more than 90 distributors. Foreign sales and export sales from the United States totaled $317.7 million and represented 53 percent of the company's total sales in fiscal 1982. (Nashua Corporation, *Annual Report, 1982,* p. 2.)

The General Tire & Rubber Company

Broadly diversified, The General Tire & Rubber Company occupies major business positions in basic, high technology, and service industries, supplying a wide range of products and services to industrial, consumer, and governmental markets. An historic innovator in the rubber industry, the Company is a large domestic tire manufacturer and maintains a full line of passenger and truck tires for the original-equipment and replacement markets. The Company's Chemicals/Plastics/Industrial Products Group furnishes an extensive variety of products to the automotive, construction, appliance, and other industries and is a leader in the production of wallcoverings and athletic products. Aerojet General, through advanced technology, research, and manufacture, is a vital component of the nation's aerospace and defense capability. RKO General, a pioneer in radio and television broadcasting, also has important interests in soft drink bottling, hotel development and management, theatrical productions for pay television and movie production, audio tape and floppy disk reproduction, and airline transportation. Far more than its name implies, General Tire has achieved strength through diversity. (The General Tire & Rubber Company, *Annual Report, 1983,* p. 1.)

Harsco Corporation

The mission of Harsco Corporation is to be a leading international manufacturer, marketer, and distributor of diverse goods and services, principally for industrial, commercial, construction, and defense applications. The Corporation is committed to providing innovative engineering solutions to specialized problems where technology and close attention to customer service can differentiate it from commodity production or job-shop operations. (Harsco Corporation, *Annual Report, 1982,* p. 1.)

Economics Laboratory

Our mission is to establish Economics Laboratory as a leading developer and marketer of chemical specialty products and systems. This mission is dedicated to providing superior products and services, supported by unique technology or marketing, which satisfy the needs of our customers to improve their results and productivity, conserve resources, and preserve the quality of the environment. (Economics Laboratory, *Annual Report, 1982,* p. 1.)

Mary Kay Cosmetics

Choices. A woman's life is filled with them. Her busy world demands choices about how she uses her time, juggles her commitments and reaches her goals. But whatever her lifestyle, Mary Kay is right for the times.

Because we understand a woman's needs and care about meeting them. We do more than just sell a woman cosmetics. We teach a personalized skin-care regimen, help her discover her own glamour look, and provide continuing service to assure that her skin care and beauty programs stay consistent with her changing *needs.*

Our corporate goal for the 1980s is to be the finest teaching-oriented skin-care organization in the world. We're doing that by teaching women about their skin and how to care for it. Our program is based on a personal relationship with an individual Beauty Consultant, who guides, instructs, and counsels each of her clients.

Women appreciate the service and knowledge they get from their Mary Kay Beauty Consultant. Our careful quality assurance and research means we're so confident about our products that we offer a 100-percent satisfaction guarantee.

We can do this because Mary Kay understands the way women want to look and live, offering products and services to meet their needs in the '80s. Equally important, we care about our customers—and make sure they know it. Because customers don't care how much we know until they know how much we care.

It's all part of the Mary Kay philosophy—a philosophy based on the golden rule. A spirit of sharing and caring where people give cheerfully of their time, knowledge, and experience.

Our management believes strongly in human resources. Excellent compensation, recognition, opportunity for growth, and pride motivate our employees, as well as 196,755 independent Beauty Consultants. A key element in the Mary Kay success equation is the Company's organizational structure which stimulates individual and group creativity, communication, and performance. This results in a high level of personal satisfaction, which in turn is reflected in high productivity.

This success-oriented attitude leads everyone to new heights and greater achievements. Achievements which are based on discipline and determination, and mean growth for each individual as well as the Company. (Mary Kay Cosmetics, *Annual Report, 1982,* p. 5.)

Table 3–1 An evaluation matrix of mission statements quoted in Exhibit 3–1

	EVALUATIVE CRITERIA				
Organizations	*Customers*	*Products/ Services*	*Markets*	*Technology*	*Concern for Survival*
Avon Company	no	yes	yes	no	yes
Penn State Univ.	yes	yes	yes	yes	no
Univ. of Idaho	yes	yes	yes	no	no
Nashua Corporation	no	yes	yes	yes	no
Economics Lab	yes	yes	no	yes	yes
Harsco Corporation	yes	yes	yes	yes	no
General Tire & Rubber	yes	yes	yes	yes	no
Mary Kay Cosmetics	yes	yes	yes	yes	yes

There is no one best mission statement for a particular organization, so good judgment is required in evaluating mission statements. In Table 3–1, a "yes" indicates that the given mission statement answers *satisfactorily* the question posed in Exhibit 3–1 for the respective evaluative criteria. For example, the "yes" under "customers" for the Penn State University mission statement means this statement answers "Who are Penn State's customers?" Notice that "people of the Commonwealth" are Penn State's customers. A "no" would mean a particular mission statement does not answer or answers *unsatisfactorily* the key question associated with one of the ten evaluative criteria. For example, note that the Avon mission statement does not identify the company's customers. Table 3–1 indicates that the Penn State University and Mary Kay Cosmetics mission statements are the "best" and the Nashua mission statement is the "worst" of the examples. As exemplified by the Economics Laboratory statement, mission statements do not have to be lengthy to be effective. The mission statements in the examples are weakest in the area of "philosophy"; they are strongest in the areas of "products or services" and "self-concept."

Why specifically does the Mary Kay Cosmetics mission statement receive a "yes" on all nine criteria? The Mary Kay mission statement reveals the firm's *customers* to be women. The company's *product* is a "personalized skin care regimen." Mary Kay's *market* or geographic area is the world. Mary Kay's *technology* is based on "quality assurance and research." The company's *concern for survival* is evident since the statement describes the desire for "high productivity" and "growth of the company." The company's *philosophy* is "based on the golden rule." Mary Kay's *self-concept* is "to be the finest teaching-oriented skin care organization in the world." The Mary Kay mission statement expands upon this self-concept to reflect a *concern for public image*. The *concern for employees* component is indicated by the sentence "Excellent compensation, recognition, opportunity for growth, and pride motivate our employees."

> Market research at Mary Kay indicates that the woman of the '90s demands things that work, buys brand names she knows, and wants value and quality. She prefers competent, personal service and convenient, enjoyable shopping. She is looking for financial security,

	EVALUATIVE CRITERIA			
	Philosophy	*Self-Concept*	*Concern for Public Image*	*Concern for Employees*
Avon Company	no	no	no	no
Penn State Univ.	yes	yes	yes	no
Univ. of Idaho	no	no	no	no
Nashua Corporation	no	yes	no	no
Economics Lab	yes	yes	yes	no
Harasco Corporation	no	yes	no	no
General Tire & Rubber	no	yes	no	no
Mary Kay Cosmetics	yes	yes	yes	yes

increased time with her family, and feelings of "group membership" that help her gain a sense of identity. She wants to make her own choices. In light of this market research, Mary Kay Cosmetics today has a new, shorter mission statement as follows:

> To achieve preeminence in the manufacturing and marketing of personal care products by providing personalized service, value and convenience to Mary Kay customers through our independent sales force.[14]

In multidivisional organizations, strategists should ensure that divisional units perform strategic-management tasks, including the development of a statement of mission. Each division should use strategic-management concepts and techniques to develop its own mission statement, consistent with and supportive of the corporate mission. Divisional mission statements are important for motivating middle- and lower-level managers and employees.

An effective mission statement addresses strategic concerns at the corporate, divisional, and functional levels of an organization. Anchor Hocking is an example of a multinational organization that has developed an overall corporate mission statement and a statement for each of its eight divisions. (See Exhibit 3.2.)

EXHIBIT 3–2 Anchor Hocking Corporation strategic plan: mission statements

The Anchor Hocking Corporation
The mission of Anchor Hocking Corporation's management is to profitably provide goods and services to customers in such a way as to enhance shareholder/owner values, as exhibited by the dividends paid and the increase in market valuation of the corporation's stock.

Consumer and Industrial Division
C. & I. Division is committed to becoming a competitive, technically efficient market-focused organization, characterized by distinctive, quality products, either manufactured or acquired, innovativeness, and achievement of financial goals.

Household Products Group
We meet selected consumer, industrial, and foodservice market needs throughout the United States and targeted foreign countries by developing, manufacturing, acquiring, and marketing a focused line of products and services which maximize the group's current and future resources and optimize real growth and profit opportunities.

Plastics, Inc. Division
As the major plastics arm of the Household Products Group of Anchor Hocking Corporation, to be an innovative manufacturer and supplier of high-quality plastics products to the transportation, foodservice, premium, food processor, and consumer markets.

Utilizing broad-based plastics technology and a variety of processes and materials, to supply both customized and standard products to meet the ongoing and developing needs of these domestic and international markets, through its own sales force and distribution and/or those of the parent corporation.

Administrative Services Division
To provide with maximum efficiency, the services required by the operating units of the Company in the areas of
—information systems
—human resources
—facilities management

Foodservice & Trading Company
To provide supplies and services throughout the world for the preparation, storing, and serving of food—away from home. Products provided include glassware, china and ceramicware, metal holloware, plasticware, and related table-top supplies; product sourcing is both self-manufactured and secured from domestic and foreign manufacturers.

Carr-Lowrey Division
The Carr-Lowrey Division's management mission is to promote growth and profitability in markets now being served (toiletries and cosmetics, 75-to-90 percent; other—pharmaceutical, floral, food, lighting, and specialty glassware, 10-to-25 percent) while diversifying into other markets.

All products are designed, engineered, and manufactured in the Baltimore plant and marketed by our own sales forces in Baltimore, New York, Chicago, Los Angeles, and Raleigh, North Carolina.

Our primary tasks are to improve sales growth and profitability through promotion of our manufacturing, technical, and marketing strengths, and quality products that are competitively aggressive.

International Division
Our mission is to build a growing, profitable export business by selling products of Anchor Hocking and related products in world markets, and to license patents, know-how, and technical assistance both from and to Anchor Hocking with industrial organizations throughout the world, excluding the U.S.A. We also investigate possibilities for investing, on a minority basis only, in non-North American manufacturing facilities.

The Closure Group
The mission for the Closure Group is to build a growing, profitable business by designing, producing, and marketing plastic, metal, and combination metal/plastic closures, specialty plastic packages, plastic molds, packaging machinery, and services to meet the known needs of food, toiletries, cosmetics, and household-product packagers. The Closure Group produces products in its own facilities and markets its products through its own organizations in the United States and Canada. Brokers and independent agents are used to sell these products in other countries through our International Division.

Source: Anchor Hocking Corporation, internal reports, 1985.

An organization that fails to develop a comprehensive and inspiring mission statement loses the opportunity to present itself favorably to existing and, perhaps more importantly, to potential stakeholders. Unquestionably, all organizations need customers, employees, and supporters. The business mission statement is an effective vehicle for communicating with important internal and external constituencies. The principal value of a mission statement as a tool of strategic management is derived from its specification of the ultimate aims of a firm:

> It provides managers with a unity of direction that transcends individual, parochial, and transitory needs. It promotes a sense of shared expectations among all levels and generations of employees. It consolidates values over time and across individuals and interest groups. It projects a sense of worth and intent that can be identified and assimilated by company outsiders. Finally, it affirms the company's commitment to responsible action, which is symbiotic with its needs to preserve and protect the essential claims of insiders for sustained survival, growth, and profitability of the firm.[15]

CONCLUSION

Every organization has a unique purpose and reason for being. This uniqueness should be reflected in a statement of mission. The nature of a business mission can represent either a competitive advantage or disadvantage for the firm. An organization achieves a heightened sense of purpose when its strategists develop and communicate a clear business mission. Drucker says developing a clear business mission is the "first responsibility of strategists." A good mission statement reveals an organization's customers, products or services, markets, technology, concern for survival, philosophy, self-concept, concern for public image, and concern for employees. These nine basic components serve as a practical framework for evaluating and writing mission statements.

A well designed mission statement is essential for formulating, implementing, and evaluating strategy. Developing and communicating a clear business mission is one of the most commonly overlooked tasks in strategic management. Without a clear statement of mission, a firm's short-term actions can be counterproductive to long-term interests. A mission statement should always be subject to revision, but it will require changes only infrequently if carefully prepared.

Effective mission statements stand the test of time. A mission statement is an essential tool for strategists, a fact illustrated in a short story told by Porsche CEO Peter Schultz: "Three people were at work on a construction site. All were doing the same job, but when each was asked what his job was, the answers varied. 'Breaking rocks,' the first replied. 'Earning a living,' responded the second. 'Helping to build a cathedral,' said the third."

> Few of us can build cathedrals. But to the extent we can see the cathedral in whatever cause we are following, the job seems more worthwhile. Good strategists and a clear mission help us find those cathedrals in what otherwise could be dismal issues and empty causes.[16]

KEY TERMS AND CONCEPTS

Concern for employees
Concern for public image
Concern for survival, growth, and profitability
Creed statement
Customers
Markets
Mission statement
Mission statement components
Philosophy
Products or services
Self-concept
Social policy
Stakeholders
Technology

ISSUES FOR REVIEW AND DISCUSSION

1. Do local service stations need to have a written mission statement? Why or why not?
2. Why do you think organizations that have a comprehensive mission tend to be high performers? Does having a comprehensive mission cause high performance?
3. Explain why a mission statement should not include strategies and objectives.
4. What is your college or university's "self concept?" How would you state that in a mission statement?
5. Explain the principal value of a mission statement.
6. Why is it important for a mission statement to be conciliatory?
7. In your opinion, what are the three most important components to include in writing a mission statement? Why?
8. How would the mission statements of a profit and a nonprofit organization differ?
9. Write a business mission statement for an organization of your choice.
10. Go to your nearest library and look in the annual reports of corporations. Find a mission statement, make a photocopy of the document, bring the copy to class, and evaluate the document.
11. Who are the major stakeholders of the bank that you do business with locally? What are the major claims of those stakeholders?
12. Select one of the suggested readings at the end of this chapter. Look that article up in your college library and give a five-minute oral report to the class summarizing the article.

NOTES

1. Peter Drucker, *Management: Tasks, Responsibilities, and Practices* (New York: Harper & Row, 1974), 61.
2. Eli Lilly and Company, *Annual Report* (1986).
3. Vern McGinnis, "The Mission Statement: A Key Step in Strategic Planning," *Business* 31, no. 6 (November–December 1981): 41.
4. John Pearce, II, and Fred David, "Corporate Mission Statements: The Bottom Line," *Academy of Management Executives* 1, no. 2 (May 1987): 110.
5. Ibid., 110.
6. W. R. King and D. I. Cleland, *Strategic Planning and Policy* (New York: Van Nostrand Reinhold, 1979), 124.
7. George Steiner, *Strategic Planning: What Every Manager Must Know* (New York: The Free Press, 1979): 160.
8. Drucker, *Management,* 78, 79
9. "How W. T. Grant Lost $175 Million Last Year," *Business Week* (25 February 1975): 75.
10. Drucker, *Management,* 88.
11. Drucker, *Management,* 61.
12. Archie Carroll and Frank Hoy, "Integrating Corporate Social Policy into Strategic Management," *Journal of Business Strategy* 4, no. 3 (Winter 1984): 57.
13. The Norton Company, *Annual Report* (1981).
14. Mary Kay Cosmetics, Internal Report. Used with permission.
15. John Pearce, II, "The Company Mission as a Strategic Tool," *Sloan Management Review* 23, no. 3 (Spring 1982): 74.
16. Robert Waterman, Jr., *The Renewal Factor: How the Best Get and Keep the Competitive Edge* (New York: Bantam, 1987). Also, *Business Week* (14 September 1987): 120.

SUGGESTED READINGS

Ackoff, Russel. "Mission Statements." *Planning Review* 15, no. 4 (July–August 1987): 30–32.

Aggarwal, Raj. "The Strategic Challenge of the Evolving Global Economy." *Business Horizons* 30, no. 4 (July–August 1987): 38–44.

Bettinger, C. "Behind the Mission statement." *ABA Banking Journal* 127, no. 10 (October 1985): 154–160.

Byars, Lloyd. "Organizational Philosophy and Mission Statements." *Planning Review* 15, no. 4 (July–August 1987): 32–36.

Cochran, D., and David, F. R. "The Communication Effectiveness of Organizational Mission Statements." *Journal of Applied Communication Research* 14, no. 2 (Fall 1986): 108–118.

Cochran D.; David, F. R.; and Gibson, K. "A Framework for Developing an Effective Mission Statement." *Journal of Business Strategies* 2, no. 2 (Fall 1985): 4.

David, F. R. "The Company Mission: Its Nature and Purpose." *Long Range Planning* (1988): in press.

Hunter, J. C. "Managers Must Know the Mission: 'If It Ain't Broke Don't Fix It.' " *Managerial Planning* 33, no. 4 (January–February 1985): 18–22.

McGinnis, V. J. "The Mission Statement: A Key Step in Strategic Planning." *Business* 31, no. 6 (November–December 1981): 39–43.

Pearce, J. A., II. "The Company Mission as a Strategic Tool." *Sloan Management Review* 23, no. 3 (Spring 1982): 15–24.

Pearce, J. A., II, and David, F. R. "Corporate Mission Statements: The Bottom Line." *Academy of Management Executive* 1, no. 2 (May 1987): 109–116.

Peters, Thomas P. *Thriving on Chaos* (New York: Knopf, 1987).

Staples, W. A., and Black, K. U. "Defining Your Business Mission: A Strategic Perspective." *Journal of Business Strategies* 1, no. 1 (Spring 1984): 33–39.

Want, J. H. "Corporate Mission." *Management Review* 75, no. 8 (August 1986): 46–50.

Waterman, Robert H., Jr., *The Renewal Factor: How the Best Get and Keep the Competitive Edge*. (New York: Bantam, 1987).

EXPERIENTIAL EXERCISES

EXPERIENTIAL EXERCISE 3A

Writing a Mission Statement for Ponderosa

PURPOSE

There is no one best mission statement for a given organization. To write a mission statement that includes desired components and at the same time is inspiring and reconciliatory requires careful thought. Mission statements should not be too lengthy; statements under two hundred words are desirable.

YOUR TASK

Step 1 Take twenty minutes to write a mission statement for Ponderosa that does not exceed two hundred words. Scan the case for needed details as you prepare your mission statement.

Step 2 Join with three other classmates. Read each other's mission statements silently. As a group, select the best of your team's mission statements.

Step 3 Read that best mission statement to the class.

EXPERIENTIAL EXERCISE 3B

Evaluating Mission Statements

PURPOSE

A business's mission statement is an integral part of strategic management. It provides direction for formulating, implementing, and evaluating strategic activities. This exercise will give you practice evaluating mission statements, a skill that is prerequisite to writing an effective mission statement.

YOUR TASK

Step 1 On a separate sheet of paper, construct an evaluation matrix like the one presented in Table 3–1. Evaluate the mission statements presented in this exercise on the basis of the nine criteria.

Step 2 Record a "yes" in all cells of the evaluation matrix where the respective mission statement satisfactorily meets the desired criteria. Record a "no" in all cells where the respective mission statement does not meet the stated criteria.

The mission of F. W. Woolworth Co. is to provide value to consumers in North America, Germany, and Australia through distinctly individual but complementary retailing businesses. These businesses are being managed, on a decentralized basis, to generate levels of profit that reward investors, sustain long-term growth, provide competitive rewards for employees, and benefit the communities in which they live and work. (*F. W. Woolworth Company*)

The purpose of Sunwest Bank is to provide financial and related services in a manner that: Maintains a level of earnings to support our growth and expansion, and sustains the confidence of those that invest in us. Anticipates and fulfills our customers' needs at a high level of product quality and staff performance. Provides a rewarding and challenging environment for our employees. Responds and contributes to the social and economic well-being of the community and markets we serve. (*Sunwest Bank*)

The leader in diverse markets, we are developing new technologies and applying them to products and systems in our four principal businesses—Aerospace, Electronics, Automotive and General Industries. Our 103,000 employees, more than 17,000 of them engineers and scientists, are dedicated to excellence in everything they do, from implementing new technologies, to managing complex systems, to making products of the highest quality. This effort is serving the needs and meeting the challenges of today's society. It also has given Rockwell International a momentum for continued outstanding financial performance. (*Rockwell International*)

Public Service Electric and Gas Company is an investor-owned, business-managed public utility, franchised by the State of New Jersey. Its primary purpose is to provide safe, reliable, and economical electric and gas service to its customers at just and reasonable rates.

In furtherance thereof, it is the aim of the corporation to afford its stockholders a return on their investment equivalent to that of other investments of similar risks, and to compensate its employees with remuneration and fringe benefits competitive with other employment opportunities in its geographical area and commensurate with their contributions toward efficient corporate operations. (*Public Service Electric and Gas Company*)

To serve in a fair, balanced and exemplary manner the interests of shareholders, customers, employees and the public through adherence to high standards of financial soundness, customer service, employee professionalism, business ethics, corporate citizenship, and profitability.

To protect the shareholder investment and customer deposits entrusted in the organization by maintaining sound assets, reliable funds sources, adequate reserves, a strong capital position and other characteristics necessary to an overall financial condition which inspires confidence and provides stability.

To earn profits sufficient to afford shareholders an attractive appreciation of their investment, to provide meritorious employee compensation, to give quality customer service, to meet public responsibilities, to maintain a strong equity base, to finance future growth and to assure the organization's continued vitality.

To recruit, develop, motivate, reward, and retain personnel of exceptional ability, character, and dedication by providing good working conditions, superior leadership, compensation on the basis of performance, an attractive benefit program, opportunity for growth, and a high degree of employment security.

To provide for customers and market segments, Wachovia is privileged to serve the fullest practical range of basic, progressive, competitive and quality deposit, loan, operational investment and other permissible financial services, consistent with the organization's mission, objectives, strategy and capacity.

To meet responsibilities to communities, states and the nation by performing and behaving in a manner which contributes to economic and social progress, by giving to worthy charitable causes, by participating in public interest activities, and by complying with applicable laws and regulations. (*Wachovia Corporation*)

The External Assessment

NOTABLE QUOTES

Positive trends in the environment breed complacency. That underscores a basic point: In change there is both opportunity and challenge.

Clifton Garvin

The opportunities and threats existing in any situation always exceed the resources needed to exploit the opportunities or avoid the threats. Thus, strategy is essentially a problem of allocating resources. If strategy is to be successful, it must allocate superior resources against a decisive opportunity.

William Cohen

Organizations pursue strategies that will disrupt the normal course of industry events and forge new industry conditions to the disadvantage of competitors.

Ian C. MacMillan

The idea is to concentrate our strength against our competitor's relative weakness.

Bruce Henderson

There was a time in America when business was easier. We set the pace for the rest of the world. We were immune to serious foreign competition. Many of us were regulated, therefore protected. No longer. Today's leaders must recreate themselves and their ways of doing business in order to stay on top or stay competitive.

Robert H. Waterman, Jr.

Competitive strategy must grow out of a sophisticated understanding of the rules of competition that determine an industry's attractiveness.

Michael Porter

The majority of our strategic successes were ideas that we borrowed from the marketplace, usually from a small regional or local competitor. In each case, what we did was spot a promising new idea, improve on it, and then out-execute our competitor.

Andy Pearson

4

OUTLINE

OBJECTIVES

After studying this chapter, you should be able to:

- Describe how to conduct an external strategic-management audit.
- Explain Michael Porter's model for competitive analysis.
- Identify key sources of environmental information.
- Discuss important forecasting tools used in strategic management.
- Discuss the importance of monitoring environmental trends and events.
- Explain how to develop a Competitive Profile Matrix and an EFE Matrix.

This chapter examines the tools and concepts needed to conduct an external strategic-management audit (sometimes called environmental scanning, environmental audit, or industry analysis). An *external audit* focuses on identifying and evaluating trends and events beyond the control of a single firm, for example, increased foreign competition, population shifts to the Sunbelt, a maturing society, information technology, and the computer revolution. An external audit reveals key opportunities and threats confronting an organization, so that managers can formulate strategies to take advantage of the opportunities and avoid or reduce the impact of threats. This chapter presents a practical framework for gathering, assimilating, and analyzing environmental information.

PERFORMING AN EXTERNAL AUDIT

The existence and magnitude of economic, social, cultural, demographic, geographic, political, governmental, legal, technological, and competitive changes underlie the need for an effective external audit. Increasing levels of environmental uncertainty are having a major impact upon all products, services, markets, and organizations in the United States. By identifying and evaluating when, where, how, and why relevant trends and events will affect them, organizations can use the external audit to formulate and implement strategies more successfully. Figure 4–1 illustrates how the external audit fits into the strategic-management model.

An external audit results in a finite list of the opportunities that could benefit a business most and the threats that should be avoided. As the term "finite" suggests, the external audit is not aimed at developing an exhaustive list of every possible factor that could influence a business. Rather, it is aimed at identifying key variables that offer actionable responses. The firm should be able to respond either offensively or defensively to the identified factors by formulating strategies that take advantage of external opportunities or that minimize the impact of potential threats. Some organizations survive solely because they recognize and take advantage of environmental opportunities. For example, the proliferation of personal computers during the early 1980s was an external opportunity that Dennis Hayes exploited as chief executive officer of Hayes Microcomputer Products (HMP). HMP is a small, private company near Atlanta that has gained 70 percent of the retail market for modems.

The increasing complexity of today's business environment is evidenced by more countries' developing the capacity and the will to compete aggressively in world markets. Foreign businesses and countries are eager to improve their economic conditions and are willing to learn, adapt, innovate, and invent to compete successfully in the marketplace. (For example, there are more competitive new technologies in Europe and the Far East today than ever before.) American businesses can no longer beat foreign competitors with ease.

Most organizations practice some form of environmental analysis as part of their planning process. Nearly 75 percent of chief executive officers of the Fortune 500 companies report that their firms perform environmental analysis and achieve numerous benefits from doing so.[1] Another 16 percent report that they do not have organized

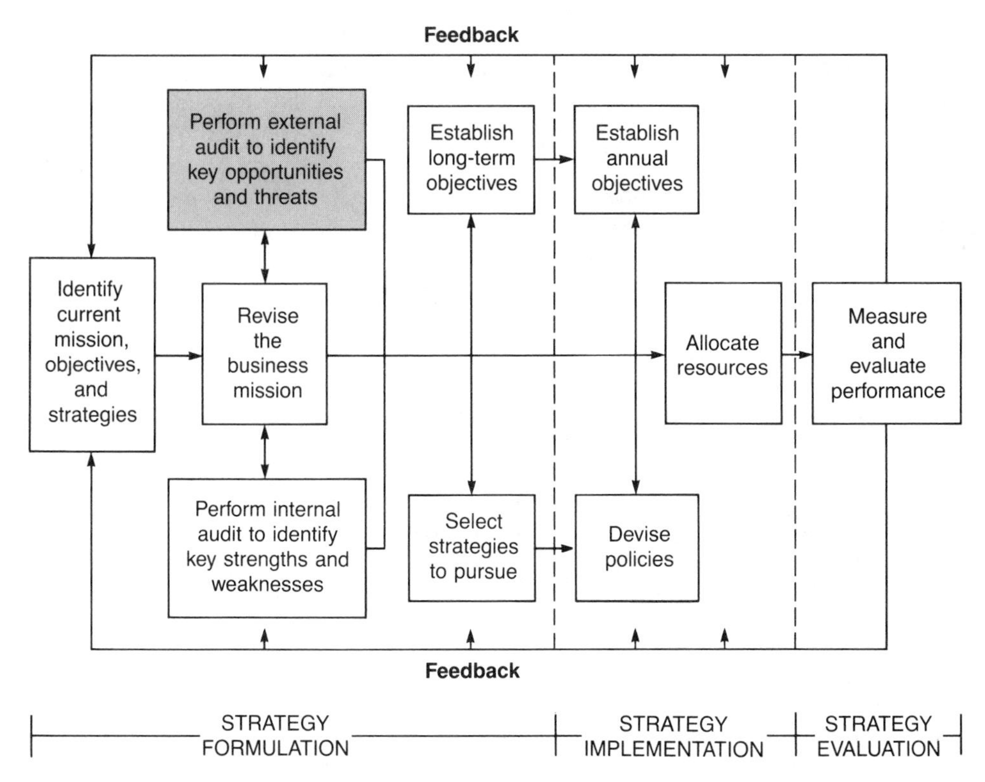

FIGURE 4–1 A comprehensive strategic-management model

environmental analysis but probably should. Only 11 percent report that their firms do not conduct external audits and have no plans to begin.

One successful approach to performing an external audit is to assign various sources of information to particular individuals and then require them to submit periodic scanning reports. In addition to providing timely strategic information, this approach provides the derived benefit of involving many employees and managers in the strategy-formulation process, which greatly enhances strategy-implementation efforts. On-line data bases provide an alternative resource for gathering strategic information. Strategists should decide what approach is most appropriate for their organization.

Information Technology

Information has always been a key business asset, but only recently has information become recognized as a powerful tool for conducting an external audit. The quantity and quality of environmental and competitive information available to organizations have increased dramatically in recent years. Advances in computer technology, telecommunications, data access and storage devices, on-line data bases, graphics equipment, and software have created a wide spectrum of new opportunities and threats for organizations. *Information technology (IT)* is changing the very nature of opportunities and threats facing many industries by altering the life cycles of products, increasing the speed of distribution, creating new products and services, erasing limitations of traditional geographic markets, and changing the historical tradeoff between production standardization and flexibility. IT is altering economies of scale, changing entry barriers, and changing the relationship between industries and various suppliers, creditors, customers, and competitors. As an example, consider the airline industry's business travel market:

> Given the current rate of development in telecommunications and office technology, video conferences may become a major substitute for some business air travel soon. This would significantly affect the airline industry's business travel market. Strategists today must address a crucial question: What impact will IT have on our industry over the next five to ten years in terms of products and services, markets, and production economies?[2]

Information technologies such as *electronic data interchange* (EDI) are rapidly changing the way America does business. EDI allows companies to lower inventory levels, improve customer service, and reduce payroll expenses by sending specially formatted documents such as invoices and purchase orders from one company's computer to another's. EDI is enabling organizations to perform external audits more effectively and to gain competitive advantages in world markets. *Business Week* gives the following example of EDI in use:

> In businesses such as the $55 billion textile industry, which has suffered as retailers doubled their purchases of cheap Asian apparel over the past five years, adopting EDI has become a way to get an edge over foreign rivals. Led by textile magnate Roger Milliken, 220 top retail and clothing executives convened earlier this year [1987] to back industry-standard formats for purchase orders, shipping documents, and other forms. Their purpose is to beat Asian rivals by making it easier for retailers to deal with U.S. suppliers. "This is the beginning of a revolution in our industry," says Milliken.[3]

The era of the mainframe computer is giving way to a proliferation of affordable microcomputers that are almost as powerful. This trend is creating a new basis for competition in virtually all industries and has generated new buyers, new suppliers, new products, and new services. The microcomputer revolution represents a great opportunity for innovative young companies. Entrenched industrial leaders face more competition than ever before from small firms using advanced microcomputer technology.

KEY EXTERNAL FORCES

Environmental forces can be divided into five major categories: (1) economic forces, (2) social, cultural, demographic, and geographic forces, (3) political, legal, and governmental forces, (4) technological forces, and (5) competitive forces. Relationships between key environmental forces and an organization are depicted in Figure 4–2.

Changes in environmental forces translate into changes in consumer demand for both industrial and consumer products and services. Environmental forces affect the types of products developed, the nature of positioning and market segmentation strategies, the types of services offered, and the choice of businesses to acquire or sell.

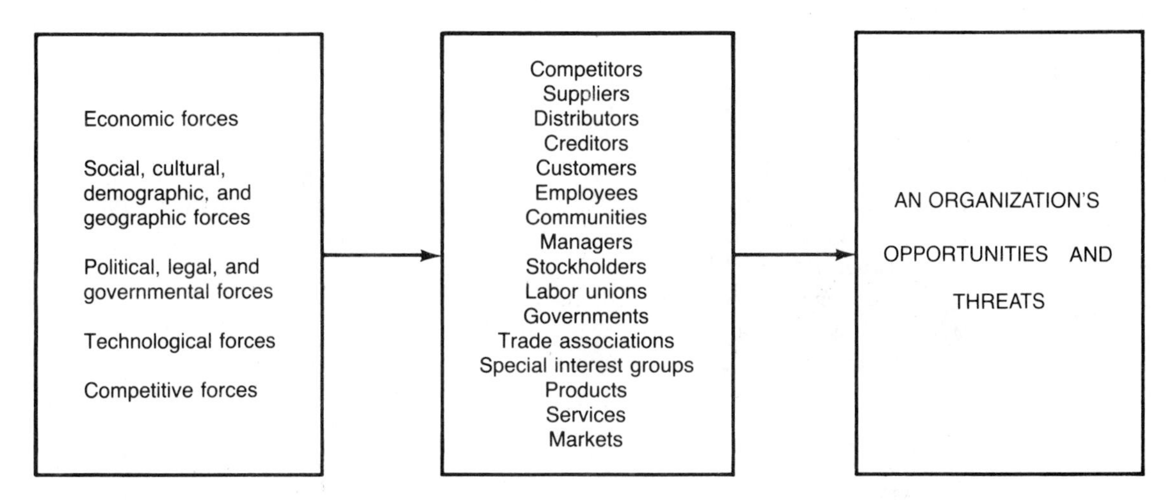

FIGURE 4–2 Relationships between key environmental forces and an organization

Environmental forces also directly affect supply, or input, dimensions of an organization. For instance, a petroleum company may do environmental analysis to assess relative levels of oil available in the world; a securities firm may monitor printing of foreign currency to identify opportunities or threats associated with exchange rates in various markets. Identifying and evaluating environmental opportunities and threats enables organizations to develop a clear mission, to design strategies to achieve long-term objectives, and to develop policies to achieve annual objectives.

Economic Forces

On October 19, 1987, now known as Black Monday, the New York Stock Exchange dropped 508.32 points. What happened that day emphasizes the turbulent economic environment that faces strategists today. Inflation and economic flux have caused sweeping changes in the buying patterns of consumers during the 1980s. As consumers perceive that more money is buying them less, many have adopted the much publicized "buy now, save later" motto. Both consumer debt and governmental debt levels have soared in the 1980s at the expense of future security. As a percent of disposable income, consumer savings fell to only 3.2 percent in 1987, the lowest rate ever recorded. Numerous states are increasing taxes to reduce debt. Some states, such as Florida, are now taxing services such as legal services and haircuts.

The steady growth in per capita real income and the rapid increase in the number of two-income households is an economic trend in America. As affluence increases, individuals place a premium on time. Improved customer service, immediate availability and trouble-free operation of products, and dependable maintenance and repair services are becoming more important. Americans today are more willing than ever to pay the price for good service if it limits inconvenience.

Economic factors have a direct impact on the potential attractiveness of various strategies. For example, if money is tight, then funds needed for diversification may be too costly or unavailable. As interest rates rise, discretionary income declines and the demand for discretionary goods falls. As stock prices increase, the desirability of equity as a source of capital for market development increases. As the stock market rises, consumer and business wealth expands. Between August 1982 and August 1987 the stock market's rise from below 1,000 to over 2,700 expanded net wealth in the United States by almost $1.9 trillion. Then on Black Monday, the New York Stock Exchange plunged 22.6 percent. A summary of economic variables that often represent opportunities and threats for organizations is provided in Exhibit 4–1.

Between 1985 and 1988, the American dollar declined 45 percent against the yen, the Swiss franc, and the German mark; however, during that same period, it held steady against the Canadian dollar and the Korean won and rose 370 percent against the Mexican peso, 300 percent against the Brazilian cruzeiro, 100 percent against the Venezuelan bolivar, and 15 percent against the Australian dollar. The pharmaceutical, tourism, entertainment, motor vehicles, aerospace, and forest products industries benefited greatly from the dollar's fall against the yen, franc, and mark, but agricultural and petroleum industries were hurt by the dollar's rise against the currencies of Mexico, Brazil, Venezuela, and Australia. Because American companies face competition from different foreign countries, trends in the dollar's value have significant and unequal effects on companies in different industries and operating in different areas.

Social, Cultural, Demographic, and Geographic Forces

Social, cultural, demographic, and geographic changes have a major impact upon virtually all products, services, markets, and customers. Small and large and profit and nonprofit organizations in all industries are both staggered and challenged by the opportunities and threats arising from changes in social, cultural, demographic, and geographic variables. In every way, the United States is much different in the 1980s than it was in the 1970s, and the 1990s promise even greater changes.

Social, cultural, demographic, and geographic variables are shaping the way Americans live, work, produce, and consume. Recent changes in the structure of the family are indisputable. There were 2.4 million marriages in the United States during 1987, up one percent from the 1986 total. But the number of divorces in the United States declined one percent in 1987, to 1.1 million. Consumers are becoming more educated, the population is aging, narcissism is replacing the Protestant work ethic, minorities are becoming more influential, people are looking for local rather than federal solutions to problems, the fixation on youth is diminishing, and more women are entering the work force. The United States Census Bureau projects that Hispanics will rise from 7 percent of the population in 1987 to 14 percent by 2010, when they will become a larger minority than Blacks in America. A steady decline in the view of work as an expression of identity is evidenced in America and many foreign countries. There appears to be a weaker commitment to the work environment and ethic, more questioning of corporate values and procedures, more job turnover and absenteeism, and more demand for businesses to assume social functions such as childcare and retirement counseling for employees. New trends are creating a different type of consumer and consequently a need for different products, different services, and different strategies. For example, by 1991, one hundred thousand people in the United States will be suffering from AIDS, and nearly ten million Americans will carry the AIDS virus but show no

EXHIBIT 4–1 Key economic variables to be monitored

Shift to a service economy in the U.S.
Availability of credit
Level of disposable income
Propensity of people to spend
Interest rates
Inflation rates
Economies of scale
Money market rates
Federal government budget deficits
Gross national product trend
Consumption patterns
Unemployment trends
Worker productivity levels
Value of the dollar in world markets
Stock market trends
Foreign countries' economic conditions
Import/export factors
Demand shifts for different categories of goods and services
Income differences by region and consumer groups
Price fluctuations
Exportation of labor and capital from the U.S
Monetary policies
Fiscal policies
Tax rates
European Economic Community (EEC) policies
Organization of Petroleum Exporting Countries (OPEC) policies
Coalitions of Lesser Developed Countries (LDC) policies

symptoms; these developments represent an opportunity for pharmaceutical companies to develop and market a cure for AIDS.

The number of births is increasing in the United States. An estimated 3.8 million babies were born in the United States during 1987, up 3 percent from 1986. The 1987 total is the largest number of births reported since 1964. However, the world's population is still increasing—by 150 persons every minute. It passed the five billion mark in July 1987 and is expected to hit six billion in 1999.

Individuals aged eighty-five and over are increasing in percentage of the population faster than any other age group in America and throughout the world. The trend toward an older America is good news for firms such as home builders, furniture producers, computer manufacturers, travel services, pharmaceutical firms, and auto makers, but it could be bad news for distributors of clothing for children and adolescents, child-care facilities, toy manufacturers, and beer producers. The aging American society is demanding in new products, services, markets, and personnel policies as well as a new look at advertising, a decreased emphasis on schools, an increased emphasis on health care, a growing market for luxury items, and a drop in crime rates. The aging American population affects the strategic orientation of nearly all organizations. For example, apartment complexes for the elderly, with one meal a day, transportation, and utilities included in the rent, increased to 180,000 units nationwide in 1987. Called lifecare facilities, the complexes are expected to increase in number to 815,000 by 1995. Some well-known companies building these facilities include Avon, Marriott, and Hyatt. By the year 2005, individuals aged 65 and older in the United States will rise to 13 percent of the total population; Japan's elderly population ratio will rise to 17 percent, and West Germany's, to 19 percent.

Americans are also on the move in a population shift to the South and West (Sunbelt) and away from the Northeast and Midwest (Frostbelt). The Internal Revenue Service is now providing the Census Bureau with massive computer files of demographic data. By comparing individual address changes from year to year, the Census Bureau now publishes extensive information about population shifts from state to state. For example, Colorado loses residents heavily to California and Arizona, but gains residents from Illinois, Iowa, Nebraska, and Wyoming. The movement of families from cities to suburbs is almost as dramatic as shifts from state to state and region to region in the country. Early in 1987, the Corporation for Enterprise Development (CED) determined the most attractive and least attractive areas for economic development in the United States. All states were rated on four broad indexes: economic performance, business vitality, resources and capacity, and government policy. The CED concluded that the six leading states in America for business and economic development are Arizona, California, Connecticut, Massachusetts, Minnesota, and Colorado. Northeastern states are best overall; Alabama and Tennessee ranked lowest of all fifty states. This type of information is helpful and in many cases essential for successful strategy formulation and strategy implementation. Population trends and business development research have many strategy implications including where to locate new plants and distribution centers and where to focus marketing efforts.

Many organizations are altering their basic strategies as a result of population changes. Among metropolitan areas with more than one million residents, the cities that had the greatest population growth between 1980 and 1986 were Phoenix (+26%), Dallas-Fort Worth (+25%), Atlanta (+20%), San Antonio (+19%), Tampa-St. Petersburg (+19%), San Diego (+18%), Sacramento (+17%), and Houston (+17%). According to *Inc. Magazine,* the following twenty metropolitan areas are the nation's fastest-growing on the basis of job generation, new business start-ups, and percentage of thriving young companies:[4]

1. Austin, Texas
2. Orlando, Florida
3. Phoenix, Arizona
4. Dallas-Ft. Worth, Texas
5. Tucson, Arizona

6. San Antonio, Texas
7. Raleigh-Durham, North Carolina
8. Manchester-Nashua, New Hampshire
9. Atlanta, Georgia
10. Huntsville, Alabama
11. Washington, D.C.- Maryland and Virginia
12. Albuquerque, New Mexico
13. San Diego, California
14. Charleston, South Carolina
15. Nashville, Tennessee
16. Jacksonville, Florida
17. Melbourne-Titusville, Florida
18. Tallahassee, Florida
19. El Paso, Texas
20. Portsmouth-Dover, New Hampshire

A summary of important social, cultural, demographic, and geographic variables that represent opportunities or threats for virtually all organizations is given in Exhibit 4–2.

EXHIBIT 4–2 Key social, cultural, demographic, and geographic variables

Childbearing rates
Number of special interest groups
Number of marriages
Number of divorces
Number of births
Number of deaths
Immigration and emigration rates
Social security programs
Life expectancy rates
Per capita income
Location of retailing, manufacturing, and service businesses
Attitudes toward business
Life-styles
Traffic congestion
Inner city environments
Average disposable income
Value placed on leisure time
Trust in government
Attitudes toward government
Attitudes toward work
Buying habits

EXHIBIT 4–2 Continued

Ethical concerns
Attitudes toward saving
Sex roles
Attitudes toward investing
Racial equality
Use of birth control
Average level of education
Government regulation
Attitudes toward retirement
Attitudes toward leisure time
Attitudes toward product quality
Attitudes toward customer service
Pollution control
Attitudes toward foreign peoples
Energy conservation
Social programs
Number of churches
Number of church members
Social responsibility
Attitudes toward authority
Attitudes toward careers
Population changes by race, age, sex, and level of affluence
Population changes by city, county, state, region, and country
Regional changes in tastes and preferences
Number of women and minority workers
Number of high school and college graduates by geographic area

Political, Governmental, and Legal Forces

Federal, state, local, and foreign governments are major regulators, deregulators, subsidizers, employers, and customers of organizations in the United States. Political, governmental, and legal factors can therefore represent key opportunities or threats for both small and large organizations. For industries and firms that depend heavily on government contracts or subsidies, political forecasts can be the most important part of an external audit. Changes in patent laws, antitrust legislation, and lobbying activities can affect firms significantly. The increasing global interdependence among economies, markets, governments, and organizations makes it imperative that firms consider the possible impact of political variables on the formulation and implementation of competitive strategies. For example, scores of American companies are abandoning operations in South Africa due to that country's apartheid policies. By May 1987 only ten

TABLE 4–1 Risk forecast for 85 countries for 1988–1992

Country	*Regime*	*Inflation*	*Turmoil*	*Transfer*	*Investment*	*Export*	*Growth*
China	Reformers	10.0%	Moderate	B+	B−	C+	5.0%
Libya	Qaddafi	8.0%	High	C+	C+	C+	1.0%
France	Mitterrand	3.8%	Moderate	B+	B+	B+	2.5%
Sudan	Mahdi	30.0%	Very High	D−	C	D−	−3.0%
USSR	Gorbachev	2.2%	Low	A−	B	B+	4.5%
Israel	Nat. Unity	12.0%	Moderate	B−	A−	B	3.5%
Brazil	Sarney	150%	Moderate	C	C+	C−	4.0%

Source: William Coplin and Michael O'Leary, "World Political/Business Risk Analysis for 1988," *Planning Review* (September–October 1988): 34–39. (Note: Only seven of eighty-five countries are included here.)

American companies had more than one thousand employees in South Africa, including Mobil (3,013 employees), RJR Nabisco, Goodyear Tire & Rubber, USG Corporation, Caltex Petroleum, Johnson & Johnson, Emhart Corporation, United Technologies, American Brands, and Joy Manufacturing.

A number of nationally known firms forecast political, governmental, and legal variables, including Frost & Sullivan, Probe International, and Arthur D. Little (ADL). ADL forecasts the political environment in foreign countries by examining five criteria: (1) social development, (2) technological advancement, (3) abundance of natural resources, (4) level of domestic tranquility, and (5) type of political system. ADL has found that political unrest follows whenever a country's development in any one of these areas gets too far ahead of the other. Ford, Dupont, Singer, and PepsiCo are among the many companies that use forecasts developed by outside firms to identify key political and governmental opportunities and threats.

Political forecasting can be especially critical and complex for multinational firms that depend on foreign countries for natural resources, facilities, or lands, distribution of products, special assistance, or customers. *Planning Review* annually publishes an extensive political risk forecast for eighty-five countries worldwide; an excerpt from the 1988 political forecast is given in Table 4–1.

Increasing global competition toward the year 2000 accents the need for accurate political, governmental, and legal forecasts. Many companies will have to become familiar with the capital markets of Europe and Asia and with trading currency futures. East Asian countries have already become world leaders in labor-intensive industries. Frederick Gluck, director of McKinsey & Company, concludes that a world market is emerging from what previously was a multitude of distinct national markets and that the climate for international business in the late 1980s and 1990s is becoming much more favorable than in recent years due to changes in the oil, currency, and labor markets. Mass communication and high technology are creating similar patterns of consumption in diverse cultures worldwide. This means that many companies may find it difficult to survive by relying solely on domestic markets.

> It is no exaggeration that in an industry that is, or is rapidly becoming, global, the riskiest possible posture is to remain a domestic competitor. The domestic competitor will watch as

> more aggressive companies use this growth to capture economies of scale and learning. The domestic competitor will then be faced with an attack on domestic markets using different (and possibly superior) technology, product design, manufacturing, marketing approaches, and economies of scale. A few examples suggest how extensive the phenomenon of world markets has already become. Hewlett-Packard's manufacturing chain reaches halfway around the globe, from well-paid, skilled engineers in California to low-wage assembly workers in Malaysia. General Electric has survived as a manufacturer of inexpensive audio products by centralizing its world production in Singapore.[5]

Local, state, and federal laws, regulatory agencies, and special interest groups can have a major impact on the strategies of small, large, profit, and nonprofit organizations. Many companies have abandoned plans or strategies in the past because of political or governmental actions. For example, many nuclear power projects have been halted and many steel plants shut down because of pressure from the Environmental Protection Agency (EPA). Other federal regulatory agencies include the Food and Drug Administration (FDA), the National Highway Traffic and Safety Administration (NHTSA), the Occupational Safety and Health Administration (OSHA), the Consumer Product Safety Commission (CPSC), the Federal Trade Commission (FTC), the Securities and Exchange Commission (SEC), the Equal Employment Opportunity Commission (EEOC), the Federal Communications Commission (FCC), the Federal Maritime Commission (FMC), the Interstate Commerce Commission (ICC), the Federal Energy Regulatory Commission (FERC), the National Labor Relations Board (NLRB), and the Civil Aeronautics Board (CAB). Local, state, and federal laws, regulations, and political pressures represent significant opportunities and threats for many organizations. For example, in 1987 OSHA imposed a record $2.6 million penalty against the Occidental Petroleum Corporation. OSHA accused the company of underreporting 1,038 job-related injuries and illnesses. The largest fine previously imposed by OSHA was levied in 1987 against Chrysler Corporation, which paid $1.6 million for exposing workers to lead and arsenic. Chrysler did not contest the fine. A summary of political, governmental and legal variables that can represent key opportunities or threats to organizations is provided in Exhibit 4–3.

Technological Forces

Revolutionary technological changes and discoveries such as superconductivity, computer engineering, "thinking" computers, robotics, unmanned factories, miracle drugs, space communications, space manufacturing, lasers, cloning, satellite networks, fiber optics, biometrics, and electronic funds transfer are having a dramatic impact on organizations. New microprocessor-based equipment and process technologies such as computer-aided design and manufacturing (CAD/CAM), direct numerical control (DNC), computer-centralized numerical control (CNC), flexible production centers (FPC), equipment and process technology (EPT), and computer-integrated manufacturing (CIM) are burgeoning. Superconductivity advancements alone, which increase the power of electrical products by lowering resistance to current, are expected to revolutionize business operations in the 1990s, especially in the transportation, utility, healthcare, electrical, and computers industries.

EXHIBIT 4–3 Important political, governmental, and legal variables

Government regulations or deregulations
Changes in tax laws
Special tariffs
Political action committees
Voter participation rates
Number, severity, and location of government protests
Number of patents
Changes in patent laws
Environmental protection laws
Level of defense expenditures
Legislation on equal employment
Level of government subsidies
Antitrust legislation
Sino-American relationships
Soviet-American relationships
European-American relationships
African-American relationships
Import-export regulations
Government fiscal and monetary policy changes
Political conditions in foreign countries
Special local, state, and federal laws
Lobbying activities
Size of government budgets
World oil, currency, and labor markets
Location and severity of terrorist activities
Local, state, and national elections

Technological forces such as these represent major opportunities and threats that must be considered in formulating strategies since they can dramatically affect an organization's products, services, markets, suppliers, distributors, competitors, customers, manufacturing processes, marketing practices, and competitive position. Technological advancements can create new markets, result in a proliferation of new and improved products, change the relative competitive cost positions in an industry, and render existing products and services obsolete. Technological changes can reduce or eliminate cost barriers between businesses, create shorter production runs, create shortages in technical skills, and result in changing values and expectations of employees, managers, and customers. Technological advancements can create new competitive advantages that are more powerful than existing advantages. No company or industry today is insulated against emerging technological developments. In high-tech industries, identification and evaluation of key technological opportunities and threats can be the most important part of the external strategic-management audit.

Organizations that have traditionally limited efforts to improve technologies to what they can fund after they meet marketing and financial requirements urgently need a reversal in thinking. The pace of technological change is increasing and the changes are coming from different directions, such as from "unrelated" industries, universities, and foreign competitors. An emerging consensus holds that technology management is one of the key responsibilities of strategists. Firms should pursue strategies that take advantage of technological opportunities to achieve sustainable, competitive advantages in the marketplace. The key lies in formulating the right technology strategy and, ultimately, integrating it into the strategic-management process:

> In the business environment of the 1990s, we believe that technology-based issues will underlie nearly every important decision that strategists make. Crucial to those decisions will be the ability to approach technology planning analytically and strategically. We also believe that technology can be planned and managed using formal techniques similar to those used in business and capital investment planning. An effective technology strategy is built on a penetrating analysis of technology opportunities and threats, and an assessment of the relative importance of these factors to overall corporate strategy.[6]

In practice, critical decisions about technology are too often delegated to lower organizational levels or are made without an understanding of their strategic implications. Many strategists spend countless hours determining market share, positioning products in terms of features and price, forecasting sales and market size, and monitoring distributors; yet too often technology does not receive the same respect:

> The impact of this oversight is devastating. Firms not managing technology to ensure their futures may eventually find their futures managed by technology. Technology's impact reaches far beyond the "high-tech" companies. Although some industries may appear to be relatively technology-insensitive in terms of products and market requirements, they are not immune from the impact of technology; companies in smokestack as well as service industries must carefully monitor emerging technological opportunities and threats.[7]

Not all sectors of the economy are equally affected by technological developments. For example, the communications, electronics, aeronautics, and pharmaceutical industries are much more volatile than the textile, forestry, and metals industries. Strategists in industries affected by rapid technological change must especially identify and evaluate technological opportunities and threats. Some key questions about technology that should be asked during the external audit are presented in Exhibit 4–4.

EXHIBIT 4–4 Key questions to ask in assessing the technological environment

- What are the technologies within the corporation?
- Which technologies are utilized in the firm's business? products? components and parts?
- How critical is each technology to each of these products and businesses?
- Which of these technologies are shared among different products and businesses?
- Which technologies are contained in purchased parts and material?
- Which of these external technologies might become critical and why? Will they remain available outside the firm?
- What was the evolution of these technologies over time? In which companies were these technological changes initiated?
- What is the likely evolution of these technologies in the future?
- What have been the firm's investments in critical technologies over time?

- What were the investments and investment patterns of its leading technological competitors? Historical? Planned?
- What has been the investment in the product and in the process side of these technologies? For the firm and for its competitors? Design? Production? Implementation and service?
- What is the subjective ranking of different firms in each of these technologies?
- What are the firm's businesses and products?
- What are the parts and components of these products?
- What is the cost and value-added structure of these parts, components, products, and businesses?
- What has been the historical financial and strategic performance of the business, and what are the implications of these trends? In terms of cash generation and earnings characteristics? Investment requirements? Growth? Market position and market share?
- What are the applications of the firm's technologies?
- In which does the firm currently participate and why? In which does the firm not participate and why?
- How attractive is each of these applications as an investment opportunity in terms of its market growth, its potential for profit improvement, and/or its potential for increasing technological leadership?

  —Underlying growth characteristics?

  —Evolution of customer needs and requirements?

  —Current and emerging market segments; segment growth rates?

  —Competitive positioning and likely strategies of key competitors?
- How critical are the firm's technologies to each of these applications?
- What other technologies are critical to the external applications?
- How do the technologies differ in each of these applications?
- What are the competing technologies in each application? What are the determinants of substitution dynamics?
- What is and will be the degree of technological change in each of these technologies?
- What are the applications that the firm should consider entering?
- What should be the priorities of technological resource investment?
- What technological resources are required for the firm to achieve its current business objectives?
- What should be the level and rate of corporate technology investments?
- Which technological investments should be curtailed or eliminated?
- What additional technologies will be required in order to achieve the current corporate business objectives?
- What are the implications of the technology and business portfolios for corporate strategy?

Source: Boris Petrov, "The Advent of the Technology Portfolio." Reprinted by permission from the *Journal of Business Strategy*, Fall 1982. Published by Warren, Gorham & Lamont, Inc. Boston, Mass.

One organization making significant changes in strategy due to technological advancements is Deere & Company, which has recently invested millions in new equipment and process technology. But Deere is making massive technology investments for reasons other than to save on manufacturing costs. Rather, it is striving to improve quality, reliability, customer service and response, while reducing inventories and lead times. Deere's revenues increased 17.6 percent in 1987 over 1986.

Competitive Forces

Analyzing competitors means identifying and evaluating rival firms' strengths, weaknesses, capabilities, opportunities, threats, objectives, and strategies. Collecting and evaluating information concerning competitors is essential to performing an external audit effectively. Identifying major competitors is not always easy because many firms have multiple divisions that compete in different industries. Most multidivisional firms do not provide sales and profit information on a divisional basis for competitive reasons. Furthermore, many firms are privately held and do not publish any financial or marketing information. Despite these problems, financial information on the leading competitors in particular industries can be found in a number of publications. For example, the top competitors in five different industries are identified in Table 4–2.

Questions such as those presented in Figure 4–3 are important to answer in performing an external audit. The more information and knowledge a firm can obtain on its major competitors, the more likely it can formulate and implement effective strategies. Major competitors' weaknesses can represent external opportunities; major competitors' strengths may represent key threats. The increasing emphasis on competitive analysis in the United States is evidenced by some corporations putting this function on their organizational charts and appointing a "Director of Competitive Analysis." Computer-based filing systems can assimilate newspaper clippings, annual reports, and similar information about competitors. It is important to study an organization's competitors carefully when preparing a business policy case analysis.

GAINING COMPETITIVE ADVANTAGE

Probably the two most widely read books on competitive analysis in this decade are Michael Porter's *Competitive Strategy* (Free Press, 1980) and *Competitive Advantage* (Free Press, 1985). Exhibit 4–5 summarizes Porter's ideas. According to Porter, five competitive forces create vital opportunities and threats to organizations: (1) new entrants, (2) substitute products or services, (3) bargaining power of suppliers, (4) bargaining power of buyers, and (5) rivalry among existing firms.

In a recent article, Porter stresses the need for strategists to perform cost-benefit analyses to evaluate "sharing opportunities" among a firm's existing and potential business units.[8] Sharing activities and resources enhances competitive advantage by lowering costs or raising differentiation. In addition to sharing, Porter stresses the need for firms to "transfer" skills and expertise among autonomous business units effectively in order to gain competitive advantage.

TABLE 4–2 The five top competitors in five different industries in 1987

Company	*1987 Sales in $ Millions*	*Percent Change from 1986*	*1987 Profits in $ Millions*	*Percent Change from 1986*
		Aerospace		
United Technologies	17,170	10	591.7	1130
Boeing	15,355	−6	480.0	−28
McDonnell Douglas	13,146	4	313.0	13
Lockheed	11,321	11	436.0	6
General Dynamics	9,344	5	437.3	NM
		Banking		
Citicorp	27,988	19	−1,138.0	NM
Chase Manhattan	10,745	14	−894.8	NM
BankAmerica	10,193	−19	−955.0	NM
Manufacturers Hanover	7,757	−3	−1,140.3	NM
Security Pacific	7,618	13	15.7	−97
		Computers and peripherals		
IBM	54,217	6	5,258.0	10
Digital Equipment	10,391	24	1,284.3	49
Xerox	10,320	10	578.0	18
Unisys	9,713	31	578.0	NM
Hewlett-Packard	8,542	18	707.0	35
		Publishing		
Time	4,190	11	250.0	−34
Dun & Bradstreet	3,359	8	393.0	16
Times Mirror	3,155	7	266.5	−35
Gannett	3,079	10	319.4	16
Tribune	2,160	6	141.5	−52
		Telephone Companies		
American Tel. & Tel.	51,209	−5	2,044.0	551
GTE	15,421	2	1,118.8	−6
BellSouth	12,269	7	1,664.8	5
NYNEX	12,084	7	1,276.5	5
Bell Atlantic	10,298	4	1,240.4	6

In contrast to Porter's competitive approach for gaining advantages, strategies that stress cooperation among firms are being used more and more. Grossack and Heenan assert that this notion is not easily accepted by many Americans, weaned on the ideology of the traditional competitive model of the firm; they often wrongly view cooperation with skepticism and suspicion.[9] And indeed joint ventures and cooperative arrangements among competitors demand a certain amount of trust to combat paranoia

FIGURE 4–3 Key questions about competitors

1. What are the major competitors' strengths?
2. What are the major competitors' weaknesses?
3. What are the major competitors' objectives and strategies?
4. How will the major competitors most likely respond to current economic, social, cultural, demographic, geographic, political, governmental, technological, and competitive trends affecting our industry?
5. How vulnerable are the major competitors to our alternative company strategies?
6. How vulnerable are the alternative strategies to successful counterattack by our major competitors?
7. How are the products or services positioned relative to our major competitors?
8. To what extent are new firms entering and old firms leaving this industry?
9. What key factors have resulted in the present competitive position in this industry?
10. How have the sales and profit rankings of major competitors in the industry changed over recent years? Why have these rankings changed that way?
11. What is the nature of supplier and distributor relationship in this industry?
12. To what extent could substitute products or services be a threat to competitors in this industry?

EXHIBIT 4–5 Michael Porter on competitive analysis

The intensity of competition in an industry is neither a matter of coincidence nor bad luck. Rather, competition is rooted in the underlying economic structure of an industry and this goes well beyond the behavior of current competitors. The state of competition in an industry depends on five basic competitive forces: (1) the threat of new entrants, (2) the threat of substitute products or services, (3) the bargaining power of suppliers, (4) the bargaining power of buyers, and (5) the rivalry among existing firms. The collective strength of these forces determines the ultimate profit potential in the industry. Not all industries have the same potential. They differ fundamentally in their ultimate profit potential as the collective strength of the forces differs; the forces range from intense in industries like tires, paper, and steel—where no firm earns spectacular returns—to relatively mild in industries like oil-field equipment and services, cosmetics, and toiletries—where high returns are quite common.

The goal of competitive analysis in an organization or a business unit is to find a position in the industry where the company can best defend itself against these competitive forces or can influence them in its favor. Since the collective strength of the forces may well be painfully apparent to all competitors, the key for developing strategy is to delve below the surface and analyze the sources of each. Knowledge of these underlying sources of competitive pressure highlights the critical strengths and weaknesses of the company, animates its positioning in the industry, clarifies the areas where strategic changes may yield the greatest payoff, and highlights the areas where industry trends promise to hold the greatest significance as either opportunities or threats.

In coping with the five competitive forces, there are three potentially successful generic strategic approaches to outperforming other firms in an industry: (1) overall cost leadership, (2) differentiation, and (3) focus. Sometimes a firm can successfully pursue more than one approach as its primary target, though this is rarely possible. The first strategy, overall cost leadership, requires aggressive construction of efficient-scale facilities, vigorous pursuit of cost reductions from experience, tight cost and overhead control, avoidance of marginal customer accounts, and cost minimization in areas like R&D, service, sales force, advertising, and so on. For example, Briggs and Stratton's success in small horsepower gasoline engines is attributable to an overall cost leadership approach. The second strategy, differentiation, requires creating something unique with the firm's product or service, such as superior customer service, superior technology, or a superior dealer network. For example, Caterpillar is known for dealer network and excellent spare parts availability. The final generic strategy is focusing on a particular buyer group, segment of the product line, or geographic market. The entire focus strategy is built around serving a particular target very well, and each functional policy is developed with this in mind. For example, Fort Howard Paper focuses on a narrow range of industrial-grade papers, avoiding consumer products vulnerable to advertising battles and rapid introductions of new products.

---

about whether one firm will injure the other. However, multinational firms are becoming more globally cooperative, and increasing numbers of domestic firms are joining forces with competing foreign firms to reap mutual benefits. Nielson identifies four types of cooperative mutual gain strategies.[10]

1. Trading Different and Complementary Resources—An example is the manufacturing/advertising agreement between Lotus and IBM.
2. Pooling Similar Resources and Risks—An example is the Microelectronics and Computer Technology Corporation based in Austin, Texas. This a pooled R & D effort.
3. Expanding Total Demand—An example is industry-level advertising. Instead of advertising just your own brand, you advertise for the whole category.
4. Expanding Number of Players—Joint venture arrangements involving more than two firms are an example.

In 1987 Intel and Texas Instruments recently agreed to a cooperative mutual gain strategy whereby the two firms will swap semiconductor designs and manufacturing technologies for developing computer chips and act as alternate suppliers for each other. This technology exchange will allow both companies to gain market share in the burgeoning market for application-specific integrated circuits (ASICs), the fastest growing segment of the semiconductor industry with projected world sales reaching $5 billion by 1990. For both companies, sales and profits increased dramatically in 1987.

According to *Fortune,* many organizations now spy on competitors, using means that include:

1. buying competitors' garbage
2. buying competitors' products and dissecting them
3. taking plant tours anonymously
4. counting tractor-trailer trucks leaving competitors' loading bays
5. studying aerial photographs
6. analyzing labor contracts
7. analyzing help-wanted ads

8. quizzing customers and buyers about the sales of competitors' products
9. infiltrating customers' and competitors' business operations
10. questioning suppliers to find out how much competitors are manufacturing
11. using customers to put out phony bid requests
12. encouraging key customers to reveal competitive information
13. questioning competitors' former employees
14. interviewing consultants who may have worked with competitors directly or indirectly
15. hiring key managers away from competitors
16. conducting phony job interviews to get competitors' employees to reveal information
17. sending engineers to trade meetings to question competitors' technical employees, and
18. questioning potential employees who may have in the past worked with competitors.[11]

Some of these activities are illegal and/or unethical, but determining which is often a matter of opinion or a jury.

SOURCES OF INFORMATION.

A wealth of strategic information is available to organizations from both published and unpublished sources. Environmental information can be obtained through unpublished sources such as customer surveys, market research, speeches at professional meetings, conversations with stakeholders, interviews, and aerial photographs. Published sources of strategic information include periodicals, journals, reports, government documents, abstracts, books, directories, and manuals.

Indexes

A number of excellent indexes reveal the location of strategic information by subject, topic, source, author, company, and industry. Indexes can save managers considerable time and effort by identifying and evaluating environmental opportunities and threats. A description of major indexes available for locating environmental information is provided in Table 4–3.

On-line Data bases

In addition to indexes, *on-line data bases* are being used increasingly to locate strategic information. On-line data bases allow individuals who have no computer programming skills at all to search hundreds of publications efficiently for information by subject, industry, name of organization, Standard Industrial Classification (SIC) code, type of product, geographic area, type of publication, and so forth. The *Directory of Online Databases* gives a description of nearly all available data base services. An excellent on-line data base for accessing economic information is *Economics Abstracts Interna-*

TABLE 4–3 Major indexes that reference economic, social, political, technological, and competitive information

Name of Index	*Type of Information*	*Description*
Applied Science & Technology Index	Technological	A subject index that covers over 200 selected journals in the fields of aeronautics and space science, automation, chemistry, construction, earth sciences, electricity and electronics, engineering, industrial and mechanical arts, materials, mathematics, metallurgy, physics, telecommunication, transportation, and related subjects. *ASTI* is published monthly.
Business Periodicals Index	Economic Social Political Technological Competitive	This is probably the best known index for its overall subject coverage of selected periodicals in the following fields of business: accounting, advertising and public relations, automation, banking, communications, economics, finance and investments, insurance, labor, management, marketing, taxation, and also specific businesses, industries and trades. This index also includes a review of books appearing in the journals it indexes, listed together under the heading "Book Reviews." *BPI* is published monthly.
Funk & Scott Index of Corporations & Industries	Competitive	This is the best index for current information on companies and industries. It covers a wide selection of business, industrial and financial periodicals and also a few brokerage house reports. The yellow pages in the weeklies and the green pages in cumulated issues list articles (or data in articles) on all SIC (Standard Industrial Classification) industries; the white pages list articles on companies. Since many of the entries refer to very brief citations, it is important to note that major articles are designated by a black dot, which precedes the abbreviated title of the journal. *F & S* is published weekly.
F & S Index International	Competitive Political	A companion of the index above, covering articles on foreign companies and industries that have appeared in some 1,000 foreign and domestic periodicals and other documents. It is arranged in three parts: (1) by SIC number or product; (2) by region and country; (3) by company, *F & SI* is published monthly.
Public Affairs Information Service Bulletin	Social[a] Political	This is a selective subject listing in the areas of economic and social conditions, public administration, and international relations, published in English throughout the world. The important differences in this index are: (1) it only selectively indexes journals, to cover those articles pertinent to its subject coverage; (2) it covers not only periodical articles but also selected books, pamphlets, government publications, and reports of public and private agencies. There is a companion index called *Public Affairs*

TABLE 4–3 Continued

		Information Service: Foreign Language Index. The *PAIS* is published weekly.
Readers' Guide to Periodical Literature	Economic Social Political Technological Competitive	A very popular author and subject index to periodicals published in the United States. The *RGPL* is published bimonthly.
Social Sciences Index	Social Economic Political	A subject and author index to articles in over 260 journals that cover the fields of anthropology, area studies, economics, environmental science, geography, law and criminology, medical sciences, political science, psychology, public administration, sociology, and related subjects. At the back of each issue is an author listing of book reviews that appear in the indexed journals. The *SSI* is published quarterly.
New York Times Index	Economic Social Political Technological Competitive	This is an excellent and very detailed index of articles published in the *New York Times* newspaper. The index is arranged alphabetically and includes many helpful cross-references. The *NYTI* is published bimonthly.
Wall Street Journal/ Barron's Index	Economic Social Political Technological Competitive	A valuable index of *Wall Street Journal* and *Barron's* articles. Each issue is in two parts, corporate news and general news. The index includes a list of book reviews. The *WSJI* is published monthly.

Source: Adapted from Lorna M. Daniells, *Business Information Sources* (Los Angeles: University of California Press, 1976) 14–17.

[a]"Social" includes cultural, demographic, and geographic information; "Political" includes governmental and legal information.

tional. For social, cultural, demographic, and geographic information, *Sociological Abstracts* is a good on-line data base. Another widely used data base for political, governmental and legal information is the *Public Affairs Information Service (PAIS) International.* The *National Technical Information Service (NTIS)* is an excellent on-line data base for technology-related information. One of the best for locating information on competitors is *PIS Indexes,* which incorporates the *F & S Index of Corporations & Industries.*

Several other data bases are widely used, including *ABI/Inform,* the largest reference business data base providing information for strategists. This data base has 650 business and management publications on-line and makes information from many areas, including finance, economics, manufacturing, technology, human resources, and data processing, accessible. Most of the data accessible by *ABI/Inform* is updated weekly. *Disclosure II* is another on-line data base that includes financial and statistical information on about 8,500 publicly owned companies and is updated weekly. *PTS U. S. Time Series* and *PTS International Time Series* are data bases that monitor over 150,000 time series. Time series measure variables such as productivity rates, consumption patterns, prices, foreign trade, population statistics, income levels, and agricultural factors over a period of time. The *PTS U. S. Time Series* is updated three times a year and the *PTS International Time Series* is updated monthly; graphic displays of information from these sources are available. Another commonly used data base is the *Harvard Business Review/Online,* often called the *HBR/Online.* It covers a wide range of subjects that include accounting, organizational behavior, marketing, industry analysis, international trade, business ethics, computers, time management, and strategic management. The subscriber can print a full text of every article, citation, or abstract published in the *Harvard Business Review* from 1976 to the present.

Three other excellent data bases tailored specifically for home users are *Compuserve, The Source,* and Dow Jones *On Line.* All three of these services have grown over 100 percent annually since 1980. The *Directory of Online Databases* is an excellent reference book on data bases, which is published twice a year and describes about 1,800 on-line data bases offered by nine hundred organizations. It can be ordered from Caudra Associates, Inc. for $75 per year (2001 Wilshire Blvd., Suite 305, Santa Monica, California, 90403).

Library Publications

Important published sources of environmental information are provided in Exhibits 4–6 through 4–10. Some of the most widely used sources are described in Table 4–4.

EXHIBIT 4–6 Sources of social, cultural, demographic, and geographic information

American Statistics Index
Demographic Yearbook
Social Indicators and Social Reporting
Brookings Institution Report
Ford Foundation Report
World Bank Atlas
Annals of the American Academy of Political and Social Sciences
Conference Board, *Business Outlook*
Yearbook of International Organizations
County Business Patterns

Great Britain Central Statistical Office, *Social Trends*
Public opinion polls
Census of Population
Census of Housing
Census of Agriculture
Census of Manufactures
Guide to Consumer Markets
County and City Data Book
United Nations Educational, Scientific, and Cultural Organization, *Statistical Yearbook*
Dun & Bradstreet, *Principal International Businesses*
Chamber of Commerce publications
City directories
Telephone directories

EXHIBIT 4–7 Sources of political and governmental information

Monthly *Catalog of United States Government Publications*
Federal Register
Directory of American Firms Operating In Foreign Countries
Code of Federal Regulations
Congressional Information Service publications
Bureau of National Affairs publications
Chamber of Commerce publications
Kiplinger Washington Letter
Lobbyists
U.S. Congress, *Official Congressional Directory*
Census of Governments
American Statistics Index
Congressional Information Service Annual

EXHIBIT 4–8 Sources of technological information

Scientific and Technical Information Source
Trade journals and industrial reports
Annual Report of the National Science Foundation
Research and Development Directory
Patent records
World Guide to Trade Associations
University reports
Congressional reports
Department of Defense Annual Reports
Proceedings to professional meetings

EXHIBIT 4–9 Sources of economic information

Economic Outlook
American Register of Exporters and Importers
Worldcasts
Federal Reserve Bank of St. Louis, *Rates of Change in Economic Data for Ten Industrial Countries.*
Handbook of Basic Economic Statistics
National Bureau of Economic Research publications
Marketing Economic Guide
U.S. Council of Economic Advisors, *Economic Indicators*
Chase Econometric Associates' publications
U.S. Bureau of Labor Statistics, *Monthly Labor Review*
U.S. Bureau of Labor Statistics, *Handbook of Labor Statistics*
U.S. Bureau of the Census, *Statistical Abstract of the U.S.*
Survey of Business
Business Conditions Digest
Survey of Manufactures

U.S. Department of Commerce, *Survey of Current Business*
U.S. Department of Commerce, *Business Statistics*
U.S. Department of Commerce, *Long-Term Economic Growth*
U.S. Department of Commerce, *Foreign Economic Trends and Their Implications for the United States*
U.S. Industrial Outlook
Securities and Exchange Commission *Survey of Buying Power*
United Nations, *Yearbook of International Trade Statistics*
U.S. Board of Governors of the Federal Reserve System, *Federal Reserve Bulletin*
Kiplinger Washington Letter
Guide to Foreign Trade Statistics
Census of Retail Trade
Census of Wholesale Trade
Index of Economic Articles

EXHIBIT 4–10 Sources of information on competitors

Annual reports of companies
Directory of Corporate Affiliations
Securities and Exchange Commission, *10K Reports*
U.S. Industrial Outlook
Value Line Investment Survey
Moody's Industrial Manual
Moody's Investors Service
Moody's Handbook of Common Stocks
Moody's Bank and Finance Manual
Moody's Municipal & Government Manual
Moody's Public Utilities Manual
Moody's Transportation Manual
Dun & Bradstreet, *Million Dollar Directory*
Dun & Bradstreet, *Reference Book*
Dun & Bradstreet, *Key Business Ratios*
Standard and Poor's Corp., *Industry Surveys*
Standard and Poor's Corp., *Standard Corporation Records*
Standard and Poor's Corp., *Analyst's Handbook*
Standard and Poor's Corp., *Earnings Forecaster*
Standard and Poor's Corp., *Bond Guide*
Standard and Poor's Corp., *Security Owners Stock Guide*
Standard and Poor's Corp., *The Outlook*
Standard and Poor's *Register of Corporations, Directors, and Executives*
Starch Marketing
U.S. Industrial Directory
U.S. Internal Revenue Service, *Statistics of Income: Corporation Income Tax Returns*
Robert Morris Associates, *Annual Statement Studies*
Troy, Leo, *Almanac of Business and Industrial Financial Ratios*
Fortune 500 Directory
Trade association publications
County Business Patterns

EXHIBIT 4–10 Continued

County and City Data Book
Fortune
Dun's Business Month
Industry Week, "Trends and Forecasts"
Industry Week, "Financial Analysis of Industry"
Business Week, "Survey of Capital Requirements of Nonfinancial Corporations"
Business Week, "Annual Survey of International Corporate Performance"
Business Week, "Survey of Corporate Performance"
Business Week, "Investment Outlook"
Business Week, "Annual Survey of Bank Performance"
Barron's
Forbes, "Annual Report on American Industry"
Nation's Business, "Lesson of Leadership"
Census of Manufactures
Encyclopedia of Associations
Facts on File
U.S. Department of Commerce, *Overseas Business Reports*
U.S. Department of Commerce, *International Economic Indicators and Competitive Trends*
Barometer of Small Business
Dow Jones & Co., *Dow Jones Investor's Handbook*
Wall Street Transcript
F & S Index of Corporate Change
Investment Dealers' Digest
Conference Board Record
Conference Board, *Business Outlook*
Local newspapers

TABLE 4–4 Key sources of external information

Source	*Brief Description*
Statistical Abstract of the U.S. (published annually)	Provides social, demographic, geographic, political, and economic information about the United States.
United States Industrial Outlook (published annually)	Provides industry forecasts, profiles, data, trends, and projections. Industries are classified by type of business and by SIC Code.
Survey of Business (published quarterly)	Provides information concerning the economic outlook of specific industries. Many graphs are given.
Business Conditions Digest (published monthly)	Provides charts and graphs of past, present, and forecasted unemployment rates, productivity and income data, consumption patterns, and prices of products and services.
Survey of Manufacturers (published annually)	Provides manufacturing data for many industries, including the value of inventories, plant and equipment expenditures, book values of assets, rental payments, etc.

Predicasts (published quarterly)	A guide to corporate organization developments, including liquidations, name changes, new companies, joint ventures, bankruptcies, and divestitures
Survey of Buying Power (published annually)	Provides information on households, population shifts, disposable income, and retail sales by geographic area.
Federal Reserve Bulletin (published monthly)	Includes congressional reports, staff studies, announcements, legal developments in the monetary and banking systems.
Forbes (published weekly)	A magazine that focuses on current business issues and topics
Business Week (published weekly)	A magazine that contains current business news, including corporate strategy articles
Fortune (published biweekly)	A popular magazine that reports news and events in the business world
Federal Register (published daily)	Gives all public regulations and legal notices issued by federal agencies.
Trade journals	Provide news, forecasts, changes, and developments in particular industries. Examples are *Hardware Ace* and *The Underwriter.*
Securities and Exchange Commission's *10K Reports* (published annually)	Gives detailed descriptive and financial information on a specific company.
Annual reports (published annually)	Published by corporations for shareholders and interested parties. Reveal company plans, organization, and financial condition.
Moody's Industrial Manual (published annually)	Provides information on firms' capital structure, history, financial condition, and bond ratings.
The Dun & Bradstreet Corporation, Three Century Drive Parsippany, New Jersey 07054	Publishes many reference indexes, including *Market Profile Analysis, Dun's Business Rankings, The Billion Dollar Directory, Who Owns Whom,* and *Principal International Businesses.*
United States Census of Manufactures (published annually)	Presents manufacturing data by state and area within states. Includes data on employment, payroll, number of workers, hours, wages, capital expenditures, and the like.
Value Line (published weekly)	Provides investment information on companies and industries. Evaluates companies and industries on financial criteria.
Guide to Consumer Markets (published annually)	Provides detailed consumer information on the distribution and prices of goods and services, labor force changes, and other key areas.
Chambers of commerce	Provide valuable local business information such as traffic patterns, location of particular businesses, household income levels, etc.
Facts on File (published weekly)	Weekly summaries of world business news are provided.

FORECASTING TOOLS AND TECHNIQUES

Forecasts are educated assumptions about future trends and events. Forecasting is a complex activity due to numerous relationships among factors such as technological innovation, cultural changes, new products, improved services, stronger competitors, shifts in government priorities, changing social values, unstable economic conditions, and unforeseen events. Many strategists rely upon published environmental forecasts to identify key environmental opportunities and threats effectively.

Many of the publications cited in Exhibit 4–6 through Exhibit 4–10 forecast environmental variables. Several examples include *Industry Week*'s "Trends and Forecasts," *Business Week*'s "Investment Outlook," Standard & Poor's *Earnings Forecaster,* and the *U. S. Industrial Outlook.* The reputation and continued success of these publications depend to some extent upon accurate forecasts, so published sources of information can offer the best projections available for some variables.

When published forecasts of key internal or external variables are not available, then organizations must develop their own projections. Most organizations forecast (project) their own revenues and profits annually. Organizations sometimes forecast market share or customer loyalty information in local areas. Since forecasting is so important in strategic management and since the ability to forecast (in contrast to the ability to *use* a forecast) is so important, selected tools are examined further here.

Forecasting tools can be broadly categorized into two groups: quantitative techniques and qualitative techniques. Quantitative forecasts are most appropriate when historical data is available and when the relationships among key variables are expected to remain the same in the future. The three basic types of quantitative forecasting techniques are econometric models, regression, and *trend extrapolation. Econometric models* are based on simultaneous systems of regression equations that forecast variables such as interest rates and money supply. With the advent of sophisticated computers, econometric models have become the most widely used approach for forecasting economic variables.

All quantitative forecasts, regardless of statistical sophistication and complexity, are based on historical relationships among key variables. *Linear regression,* for example, is based on the assumption that the future will be just like the past—which, of course, it never is. As historical relationships become less stable, quantitative forecasts become less accurate.

The six basic qualitative approaches to forecasting future environmental conditions are: (1) sales-force estimate, (2) juries of executive opinion, (3) anticipatory surveys or market research, (4) scenario forecasts, (5) delphi forecasts, and (6) brainstorming. Qualitative or judgmental forecasts are particularly useful when historical data is not available or when constituent variables are expected to change significantly in the future.

Due to advancements in computer technology, quantitative forecasting techniques are usually cheaper and faster than qualitative methods. Some quantitative techniques, such as multiple and linear regression, can generate "measures of error" that allow a manager to estimate the degree of confidence associated with a given forecast. Forecasting tools must be used carefully, or the results can be more misleading than helpful, but qualitative techniques require more intuitive judgment than do quantitative ones,

TABLE 4–5 The costs, popularity, and complexity of quantitative versus qualitative forecasting techniques

Quantitative Techniques	*Cost*	*Popularity*	*Complexity*
Econometric Models	High	High	High
Regression	High	High	Medium
Trend Extrapolation	Medium	High	Medium
Qualitative Techniques	*Cost*	*Popularity*	*Complexity*
Sales-force Estimate	Low	High	Low
Juries of Executive Opinion	Low	High	Low
Anticipatory Surveys and Market Research	Medium	Medium	Medium
Scenario	Low	Medium	Low
Delphi	Low	Medium	Medium
Brainstorming	Low	Medium	Medium

Source: Adapted in part from J.A. Pearce II and R.B. Robinson, Jr., "Environmental Forecasting: Key to Strategic Management," *Business* (July–September 1983): 6.

and managers may end up "forecasting" what they would like to occur. The cost, popularity, and complexity of different forecasting techniques are compared in Table 4–5.

No forecast is perfect and some forecasts are even wildly inaccurate. This fact accents the need for strategists to devote sufficient time and effort to study the underlying bases for published forecasts and to develop internal forecasts of their own. Key external opportunities and threats can be effectively identified only through good forecasts. Accurate forecasts can provide major competitive advantages for organizations. Forecasts are vital to the strategic-management process and to the success of organizations.

INDUSTRY ANALYSIS: THE COMPETITIVE PROFILE MATRIX

Of all the environmental trends and events that can affect a firm's strategic position, competitive forces are often considered to have the greatest impact. The *Competitive Profile Matrix* identifies a firm's major competitors and their particular strengths and weaknesses.

There are five steps required to develop a Competitive Profile Matrix. First, strategists need to identify key success factors in the industry by studying the particular industry and, through negotiation, reaching a consensus on the factors most critical to success. These key factors can vary over time and by industry. According to Porter's framework for competitive analysis (as described in Exhibit 4–5), relationships with suppliers or distributors are often a key success factor. Other variables commonly used include market share, breadth of product line, economies of scale, foreign affiliates, proprietary and key account advantages, price competitiveness, the effectiveness of advertising and promotion, the location and newness of facilities, capacity and productivity, place on the experience curve, financial position, product quality, R & D advantages/position, caliber of personnel, and general image. The Competitive Profile Matrix should comprise five to fifteen of the key success factors.

The second step is to assign a weight to each key success factor to indicate its relative importance to success in the industry. Appropriate weights can be determined by comparing successful competitors with unsuccessful competitors. The weight assigned to each factor must range from 0.0 (not important) to 1.0 (very important). The assigned weights are applicable to all competitors; the weight column sums to 1.0. Third, strategists should assign a rating to each competitor to indicate that firm's strength or weakness on each key success factor (1 = major weakness, 2 = minor weakness, 3 = minor strength, and 4 = major strength). To the extent possible, the ratings for each competitor should be based on objective information. Fourth, the weight assigned to each key success factor must be multiplied by the corresponding rating for each competitor to determine a weighted score for each firm. The weighted score indicates the relative strength or weakness of each competitor on each key success factor. The final step in developing a Competitive Profile Matrix is to sum the weighted score column for each competitor. This results in a *total weighted score* for each firm, which reveals the relative overall strength of the sample firm compared to each major competitor. The highest total weighted score indicates the strongest competitor while the lowest total weighted score reveals perhaps the weakest firm. The total weighted score ranges from 1.0 (lowest) to 4.0 (highest).

A sample Competitive Profile Matrix is provided in Table 4–6. In this example, financial position is the most important key success factor, as indicated by a weight of 0.40. The sample company is strongest in product quality as evidenced by a rating of 4; competitor 1 is strongest on price competitiveness with a rating of 4; and competitor

TABLE 4–6 A Competitive Profile Matrix

		Sample Company		*Competitor 1*		*Competitor 2*	
Key Success Factors	*Weight*	*Rating*	*Weighted Score*	*Rating*	*Weighted Score*	*Rating*	*Weighted Score*
Market Share	0.20	3	0.6	2	0.4	2	0.4
Price Competitiveness	0.20	1	0.2	4	0.8	1	0.2
Financial Position	0.40	2	0.8	1	0.4	4	1.6
Product Quality	0.10	4	0.4	3	0.3	3	0.3
Customer Loyalty	0.10	3	0.3	3	0.3	3	0.3
Total Weighted Score			2.3		2.2		2.8

Note: Since a weighted score of 2.5 is average, the sample company and competitor 1 are below average. Competitor 2 is above average.

TABLE 4–7 A Competitive Profile Matrix for Holiday Inn Corporation

		Holiday		*Hilton*		*Marriott*	
Key Success Factors	*Weight*	*Rating*	*Wt. Score*	*Rating*	*Wt. Score*	*Rating*	*Wt. Score*
Brand Recognition	0.05	4	0.20	4	0.20	3	0.15
Service	0.15	4	0.60	4	0.60	3	0.45
Occupancy Rate	0.15	3	0.45	3	0.45	3	0.45
Market Segmentation	0.08	4	0.32	2	0.16	3	0.24
Market Share	0.15	4	0.60	3	0.45	2	0.30
Gaming Properties	0.10	4	0.40	4	0.40	1	0.10
Financial Strength	0.18	1	0.18	4	0.72	3	0.54
Location of Properties	0.10	4	0.40	3	0.30	3	0.30
Contemporary Facilities	0.04	4	0.16	3	0.12	3	0.12
Total Weighted Score	1.00		3.31		3.40		2.65

Note: Holiday is stronger than Marriott but weaker than Hilton as indicated by its total weighted score of 3.31.

2 has the best financial position and is the strongest firm overall as indicated by a rating of 4 and a total weighted score of 2.80 respectively. Competitor 1 is the weakest firm as evidenced by a total weighted score of 2.2. Competitors' strengths and weaknesses often represent major opportunities and threats for organizations.

An example Competitive Profile Matrix for Holiday Inn is given in Table 4–7. Note that compared to Hilton, Ramada, and Marriott, Holiday Inn has the highest market share but is weakest on financial strength. Among the competitors, Hilton has the highest total weighted score, 3.40.

However, just because one firm receives a 3.2 rating and another receives a 2.8 rating in a Competitive Profile Matrix, it does not follow that the first firm is 20 percent better than the second. Numbers reveal the relative favorableness or competitiveness of firms, but their apparent precision is only an illusion. Numbers are not magic. Consequently, in developing strategy-formulation analytical matrices such as the Competitive Profile Matrix, alter the ratings and weights to consider various scenarios. The aim is not to arrive at a "single magic number," but rather to assimilate and evaluate information in a meaningful way that aids in decision making. The Competitive Profile Matrix also provides the strategist with necessary input for developing an External Factor Evaluation Matrix.

INDUSTRY ANALYSIS: THE EXTERNAL FACTOR EVALUATION (EFE) MATRIX

An External Factor Evaluation (EFE) Matrix allows strategists to summarize and evaluate environmental information. There are five steps in developing an EFE Matrix:

1. List the firm's key opportunities and threats.
2. Assign a weight that ranges from 0.0 (not important) to 1.0 (very important)

to each factor. The weight assigned to a given factor indicates the relative importance of that factor to success in a given industry. The summation of all weights assigned to the factors must total 1.0.

3. Assign a one-to-four rating to each factor to indicate whether that variable represents a major threat (rating = 1), a minor threat (rating = 2), a minor opportunity (rating = 3), or a major opportunity (rating = 4) to the organization.
4. Multiply each factor's weight by its rating to determine a weighted score for each variable.
5. Sum the weighted scores for each variable to determine the total weighted score for an organization.

Regardless of the number of key opportunities and threats included in an EFE Matrix, the highest possible total weighted score for an organization is 4.0 and the lowest possible total weighted score is 1.0. The average total weighted score is therefore 2.5. A total weighted score of 4.0 indicates that an organization competes in an attractive industry and has abundant external opportunities, while a total score of 1.0 would characterize an organization that competes in an unattractive industry and faces severe external threats.

The recommended number of key opportunities and threats to include in the EFE Matrix is from ten to fifteen (an example is provided in Table 4–8). Note that government deregulation is the most important environmental factor affecting this industry. The firm in the example has two major opportunities: the population shift to the American West and computerized information systems. Its one major threat is rising interest rates. The total weighted score of 2.7 indicates that it is just above average in its efforts to capitalize on environmental opportunities and avoid threats.

Table 4–9 shows an EFE Matrix developed for Winn-Dixie Stores. Increasing competition is the major environmental threat facing Winn-Dixie. The company's total weighted score is 2.71.

TABLE 4–8 An example of an External Factor Evaluation Matrix

Key External Factor	*Weight*	*Rating*	*Weighted Score*
Rising interest rates	0.20	1	0.20
Population shift to the American West	0.10	4	0.40
Government deregulation	0.30	3	0.90
A major competitor's expansion strategy	0.20	2	0.40
Computerized information system	0.20	4	0.80
Total	1.00		2.70

Note: (1) For simplicity, this sample EFE Matrix has only five key factors. At least ten factors should be included in an EFE Matrix.
(2) The total weighted score of 2.70 is above the average of 2.50.

TABLE 4–9 An EFE Matrix for Winn-Dixie Stores, Inc.

Key External Factor	*Weight*	*Rating*	*Weighted Score*
Tax Reform	0.10	3	0.30
Rising Insurance Costs	0.09	2	0.18
Technological Changes	0.04	2	0.08
Rising Interest Rates	0.10	2	0.20
Population Shift to the South	0.14	4	0.56
Demographic Lifestyle Changes:			
Working Women	0.09	3	0.27
Male Shoppers	0.07	3	0.21
Demographic Composition Changes:			
Aging Market	0.10	4	0.40
Ethnic Groups	0.12	3	0.36
Increasing Competition	0.15	1	0.15
	1.00		2.71

Note: The total weighted score of 2.71 indicates that Winn-Dixie is above average in its competitive position to capitalize on opportunities and avoid threats in its industry.

STRATEGIC CONCERNS OF MULTINATIONAL FIRMS

An increasing number of organizations are exploring business opportunities in world markets. David Shanks, manager of the Strategic Management Unit of Arthur D. Little, suggests three major factors driving many domestic firms into international operations: (1) the maturing economies of industrialized nations, (2) the emergence of new geographic markets and business arenas, and (3) the globalization of financial systems.[12] The typical evolution of a domestic firm into a *multinational corporation* (MNC) is illustrated in Figure 4–4.

Special concerns and problems confront a firm involved in international operations. Multinational corporations face unique and diverse environmental risks such as expropriation of assets, currency losses through exchange rate fluctuations and revaluations, unfavorable foreign court interpretations of contracts and agreements, social-political disturbances, import-export restrictions, tariffs, and trade barriers. Strategists in MNCs are often confronted with the need to be globally competitive and nationally responsive at the same time. With the rise in world commerce, government and regulatory bodies are more closely monitoring foreign business practices. The United States Foreign Corrupt Practices Act, for example, defines "corrupt practices" in many areas of business. A sensitive issue is that some MNCs violate legal and ethical standards of the home, but not the host, country.

A complicating factor for many international firms is the historical propensity of some MNCs to interfere in the internal affairs of *less developed countries (LDCs)*. International Telephone and Telegraph (ITT), for example, was implicated in mastermind-

FIGURE 4–4 The typical evolution of a MNC

---------->	-------->	--------->	--------->	----------->	-------->	
Begin Export Operations	*Conduct Licensing Activities*	*Add Foreign Sales Represen-tatives*	*Build Foreign Manufac-turing Facilities*	*Establish a Foreign Division of the Firm*	*Establish Several Foreign Business Units*	A MNC

Adapted from: C. A. Bartlett, "How Multinational Organizations Evolve," *Journal of Business Strategy* (Summer 1982): 20–32. Also, D. Shanks, "Strategic Planning for Global Competiton," *Journal of Business Strategy* (Winter 1985): 83.

ing the overthrow of Allende's socialist government in Chile in 1973. In the past, foreign corporations have removed certain key decisions from host governments, forced a floating of the exchange rate by buying foreign exchange, exploited natural resources, and shaped the socioeconomic structures of host countries in ways that enhanced their own prospects for further growth. Some critics say American oil companies, with their major interests, were largely responsible for American involvement in the Vietnam War. It is important that MNC strategists today be more sensitive to the socioeconomic developmental aspirations of host countries to avoid unilateral breaches of contracts by LDCs.

Before entering international markets, firms should scan relevant journals and patent reports, seek the advice of academic and research organizations, participate in international trade fairs, and conduct extensive research to broaden their contacts and diminish the risk of doing business in the new markets. Firms could also reduce the risks of doing business internationally by obtaining insurance from the United States government's Overseas Private Investment Corporation (OPIC).

Globalization of Industries

Despite the historical social costs of hosting a foreign business, more and more countries around the world are welcoming foreign investment and capital. As a result, labor markets have steadily become more international. East Asian countries have become market leaders in labor-intensive industries. Brazil offers abundant natural resources and rapidly developing markets. Germany offers skilled labor and technology. The drive to improve the efficiency of global business operations is leading to greater functional specialization by locations and countries. This is not limited to a search for the familiar low cost labor in Latin America or Asia. Other considerations include the cost of energy, availability of resources, inflation rates, existing tax rates, and the nature of trade regulations.

MNCs are increasingly having to monitor different countries' relative strengths and withdraw from areas of relative disadvantage. The People's Republic of China for example announced early in 1985 that "Marx's principles are irrelevant to much of what is going on in China today." China is encouraging direct Western investment more and more. Since 1985, several dozen American corporations have started business operations in China, including thirteen major oil companies, R. J. Reynolds, Gillette, McDonnell Douglas, 3M, and American Motors. However, foreign investment in China has been on the decline since the end of 1985. Foreign investment in China fell 12 percent in 1987 to $20 billion. Analysts say China has not done enough to alter a perception among foreigners that many problems still exist there for doing business, such as demands from corrupt and greedy officials, difficulties in getting foreign exchanges, and problems with raw material suppliers.

It is clear that different industries become global for different reasons. Convergence of income levels and standardization is what made designer clothing a universal product. The need to amortize massive R & D investments over many markets is a major reason why the aircraft industry became global. Knowing when and if one's industry will globalize is an invaluable piece of business intelligence. Knowing how to use that intelligence for one's competitive advantage is even more important. For example, when MNCs choose a technology, they look around the world for the best technology and select one that has the most promise for the largest number of markets. When MNCs design a product, they design it to be marketable in as many countries as possible. When MNCs manufacture a product, they select the lowest cost source, which may be Japan for semiconductors, Sri Lanka for textiles, Malaysia for simple electronics, and Europe for precision machinery. MNCs design manufacturing systems to accommodate world markets. These are all reasons why one of the riskiest strategies for a domestic firm is to remain solely a domestic firm if the industry is rapidly becoming global.

The ability to identify and evaluate strategic opportunities and threats in an international environment is rapidly becoming a prerequisite competency for strategists. The number and sometimes subtle nuances of competing in international markets are seemingly infinite; language, culture, politics, attitudes, and economies are several variables that differ significantly across countries. MNCs face complex political, economic, legal, social, and cultural environments. Communications within a MNC can be exceedingly difficult due to time, distance, and cultural barriers between home and host countries. The availability, depth, and reliability of economic and marketing information vary extensively across countries, as does industrial structures, business practices, and the number and nature of regional organizations. Differences between domestic and multinational operations that affect strategic management are summarized in Table 4–10.

TABLE 4–10 Differences between U.S. and multinational operations that affect strategic management

Factor	*U.S. Operations*	*International Operations*
Language	English used almost universally	Local language must be used in many situations
Culture	Relatively homogeneous	Quite diverse, both between countries and within a country
Politics	Stable and relatively unimportant	Often volatile and of decisive importance

TABLE 4–10 Continued

Economy	Relatively uniform	Wide variations among countries and between regions within countries
Government interference	Minimal and reasonably predictable	Extensive and subject to rapid change
Labor	Skilled labor available	Skilled labor often scarce, requiring training or redesign of production methods
Financing	Well-developed financial markets	Poorly developed financial markets. Capital flows subject to government control
Market research	Data easy to collect	Data difficult and expensive to collect
Advertising	Many media available; few restrictions	Media limited; many restrictions; low literacy rates rule out print media in some countries
Money	U.S. dollar used universally	Must change from one currency to another; changing exchange rates and government restrictions are problems
Transportation/communication	Among the best in the world	Often inadequate
Control	Always a problem. Centralized control will work	A worse problem. Centralized control won't work. Must walk a tightrope between overcentralizing and losing control through too much decentralizing
Contracts	Once signed, are binding on both parties, even if one party makes a bad deal	Can be voided and renegotiated if one party becomes dissatisfied
Labor relations	Collective bargaining; can lay off workers easily	Often cannot lay off workers; may have mandatory worker participation in management; workers may seek change through political process rather than collective bargaining
Trade barriers	Nonexistent	Extensive and very important

Source: R. G. Murdick, R. C. Moor, R. H. Eckhouse, and T. W. Zimmerer, *Business Policy: A Framework for Analysis*, 4th ed. (Columbus, Ohio: Grid Publishing Company, 1984), p. 275.

JAPAN: ITS CULTURE AND BUSINESS ENVIRONMENT

Japan is changing rapidly. Masakagu Yamazaki uses the term "*flexible individualism*" to summarize the changes occurring in Japanese society and business. A comparison of educational levels of Japanese and American young people appears in Exhibit 4–11. Young Japanese call their parents "fossils" or "tombstones." Workaholic attitudes in

EXHIBIT 4–11 The educational levels of young Japanese and young Americans compared

	Americans	*Japanese*
Literacy Rate	80.0%	99.0%
High school completion rate	72.7%	90.0%
Length of School Year	180 days	240 days
High school seniors spending less than five hours per week on homework	76.0%	35.0%
Financing of Education:		
National	6.2%	47.3%
State	49.0%	28.1%
Local	44.8%	24.6%
Teacher Salaries	Determined locally	By national law, teachers are paid 10% more than the top civil servant.

Sources: U.S. Department of Education, Japanese Ministry of Education.

Japan are being replaced by greater emphasis on leisure activities and consumption of leisure products and services. The value of the yen doubled between 1985 and 1987 and resulted in the Japanese buying foreign products, services, and assets in large quantities. "Made outside Japan" no longer means "shoddy" to the Japanese. For example, Shuwa Corporation, a large real estate company in Tokyo, is just one of many Japanese firms now buying large assets worldwide. Shuwa recently bought the Washington D.C. headquarters building of *U. S. News and World Report* for about $80 million. Shuwa also bought The Arco Plaza in Los Angeles and the ABC building in New York.

Technology and research and development have become a basic mission of the Japanese government and nearly all Japanese firms. It is a mission of the whole country. Rising incomes, an aging population, and more women in the work force are increasing the demand for services in all sectors of the Japanese economy. Japan estimates that its trade deficit with the United States will decline to about $20 billion in 1990, from $59 billion in 1986, due to diversified exports, expanded imports, and the strong yen.

There are a number of American success stories in Japan. For example, Eastman Kodak has 20 percent of the Japanese market for film, Procter & Gamble has 50 percent of the market for disposable diapers, Warner-Lambert has 70 percent of the market for razors, Coca-Cola has 60 percent of the market for soft drinks, IBM has 40 percent of the market for computers, and Caterpillar has 43 percent of the market for bulldozers. However, many American firms have been unsuccessful in entering Japanese markets. Why? Business analysts nearly always cite reasons that are beyond the control of a single firm, such as trade barriers, the strong position of the yen, Japan's complex distribution system, nationalistic buying habits, and different business practices. Nonetheless, foreign firms do control many factors that affect doing business in Japan.

The Japanese economy no longer depends on exports for growth. Exports declined almost 16 percent in 1986. In contrast, imports from Europe surged 57 percent, and from the United States, 13 percent. Auto imports increased 97 percent in 1986 and consumer electronics imports increased 39 percent. Japan is clearing barriers that once discouraged firms from distributing or manufacturing products and services in Japan. This trend presents great opportunities for many domestic firms. Some of Japan's major objectives for the next five years are:

1. To deregulate the economy.
2. To institute aggressive policies to improve residential housing.
3. To increase imports of manufactured goods.
4. To raise agricultural productivity.
5. To reduce the average number of working hours per individual per year to 1,800 (compared to 1,924 in the United States and 1,659 hours in West Germany).
6. To institute a five-day work week for all government offices and financial institutions.
7. To give more foreign aid to underdeveloped countries.[13]

The Japanese government plans to invest $40 billion or more from 1986 to 2000 to develop a futuristic space shuttle, a colony of space platforms, and an orbiting factory for manufacturing "Made in Space" products. Many aerospace companies in the United States and worldwide consider the Japanese market to be a great opportunity and are developing strategies to capitalize on Japan's commitment to commercialize space.

CONCLUSION

Due to increasing turbulence in business environments around the world, the external audit has become an explicit and vital part of the strategic-management process. This chapter provided a framework for collecting and evaluating economic, social, cultural, demographic, geographic, political, governmental, legal, technological, and competitive information. Firms that do not identify, monitor, forecast, and evaluate key environmental forces may fail to anticipate emerging opportunities and threats and, consequently, pursue ineffective strategies, miss opportunities, and invite organizational demise.

A major responsibility of strategists is to develop an effective external-audit system. The external-audit approach described in this chapter can be effectively used by any size or type of organization. Typically the external audit is more informal in small firms, but the need to understand environmental trends and events is no less important for these firms. The Competitive Profile Matrix and EFE Matrix can help the strategist assess the environment but they must be accompanied by good intuitive judgment. Multinational firms especially need a systematic and effective external audit system because environmental forces and cultures vary greatly among foreign countries.

KEY TERMS AND CONCEPTS

Business Periodicals Index
Competitive advantage
Competitive analysis
Competitive Profile Matrix
Computer-aided design and manufacturing (CAD/CAM)
Cooperative mutual gain strategies
Director of competitive analysis
Directory of Online Databases
Econometric models
Electronic data interchange (EDI)
Environmental analysis
Environmental forces
Environmental scanning
External audit
External Factor Evaluation (EFE) Matrix
Flexible individualism
F&S Index of Corporations & Industries
Information technology (IT)
Linear regression
Multinational corporations (MNCs)
On-line data bases
Spying on competitors
Standard and Poor's Corporation *Industry Surveys*
Statistical Abstract of the United States
Total weighted score
Trend extrapolation
U.S. Industrial Outlook
Value Line Investment Survey
Wall Street Journal/Barron's Index

ISSUES FOR REVIEW AND DISCUSSION

1. Explain how to conduct an external strategic-management audit.
2. Identify a recent economic, social, political, or technological trend that significantly affects financial institutions.
3. Discuss the following statement: Major opportunities and threats usually result from an interaction among key environmental trends rather than from a single external event or factor.
4. Identify two industries experiencing rapid technological change and three industries that are experiencing little technological change. How does the need for technological forecasting differ in these industries? Why?
5. The three most prominent beverage companies in America are Coca-Cola, Anheuser-Busch, and PepsiCo. Imagine that you are a strategist for PepsiCo. Construct a Competitive Profile Matrix that includes these competitors using information available in your college library and your own judgment.
6. What major forecasting techniques would you use to identify (1) economic opportunities and threats and (2) demographic opportunities and threats? Why are these techniques most appropriate?
7. How does the external audit affect other components of the strategic-management process?
8. As owner of a small business, explain how you would organize a strategic information scanning system. How would you organize such a system in a large organization?
9. Construct an EFE Matrix for your university. What key success factors did you include? How did your weights, ratings, weighted scores, and total weighted score compare to another student's EFE Matrix?
10. Make an appointment with a librarian at your university to learn how to use on-line data bases. Report your findings in class.
11. Give some advantages and disadvantages of cooperative versus competitive strategies.

12. As a local bank strategist, explain when you would use qualitative versus quantitative forecasts.
13. What is your forecast for interest rates and the stock market in the next several months? As the stock market moves up, do interest rates always move down? Why? What are the strategic implications of these trends?
14. Explain how information technology affects strategies of the organization where you most recently worked.
15. Let's say your boss develops an EFE Matrix that includes sixty-two factors. How would you suggest that she reduce the number of factors to twenty?
16. Select one of the suggested readings at the end of this chapter. Prepare a one page written summary that includes your personal opinion of the article.

NOTES

1. John Diffenbach, "Corporate Environmental Analysis in Large U.S. Corporations," *Long Range Planning* 16, no. 3 (June 1983): 109.
2. Gregory Parsons, "Information Technology: A New Competitive Weapon," *Sloan Management Review* 25, no. 1 (Fall 1983): 5.
3. Susan Gelford, "An Electronic Pipeline That's Changing the Way America Does Business," *Business Week* 3, no. 4 (3 August 1987): 80.
4. "Hot Spots," *Inc. Magazine* 10, no. 3 (March 1988): 75.
5. Frederick Gluck, "Global Competition in the 1990s," *Journal of Business Strategy* (Spring 1983): 22, 24.
6. John Harris, Robert Shaw, Jr., and William Sommers, "The Strategic Management of Technology," *Planning Review* 11, no. 1 (January–February 1983): 28, 35.
7. Susan Levine and Michael Yalowitz, "Managing Technology: The Key to Successful Business Growth," *Management Review* 72, no. 9 (September 1983): 44.
8. Michael Porter, "From Competitive Advantage to Corporate Strategy," *Harvard Business Review* 65, no. 3 (May–June 1987): 43.
9. Irvin Grossack and David Heenan, "Cooperation, Competition, and Antitrust: Two Views," *Business Horizons* 29, no. 5 (September–October 1986): 27.
10. Richard Nielson, "Cooperative Strategies," *Planning Review* 14, no. 2 (March–April 1986): 16.
11. Steven Flax, "How to Snoop on Your Competitors," *Fortune* (14 May 1984): 29–33.
12. David Shanks, "Strategic Planning for Global Competition," *Journal of Business Strategy* 5, no. 3 (Winter 1985): 80.
13. "Japan Goes International," *Business Week* (13 July 1987): 47.

SUGGESTED READINGS

Aggarwal, Raj. "The Strategic Challenge of the Evolving Global Economy." *Business Horizons* 30, no. 4 (July–August 1987): 38–44.

Ansoff, H. I. "Strategic Management of Technology." *Journal of Business Strategy* 7, no. 3 (Winter 1987): 40–48.

Ball, R. "Assessing Your Competitor's People and Organization." *Long Range Planning* 20, no. 2 (April 1987): 32–41.

Barrett, F. D. "Strategies for the Use of Artificial and Human Intelligence." *Business Quarterly* 51, no. 2 (Summer 1986): 18–27.

Briggs, W. "Software Tools for Planning: DSS and AI/Expert Systems." *Planning Review* 13, no. 5 (September–October 1985): 36–45.

Chakravarthy, B. S., and Perlmutter, H. V. "Strategic Planning for a Global Business." *Columbia Journal of World Business* 10, no. 2 (Summer 1985): 3–10.

Coplin, W. D., and O'Leary, M. K. "World Political/ Business Risk Analysis for 1987." *Planning Review* 15, no. 1 (January–February 1987): 34–40.

Drucker, P. F. "Keeping U.S. Companies Productive." *Journal of Business Strategy* 7, no. 3 (Winter 1987): 12–15.

Filho, P. V. "Environmental Analysis for Strategic Planning." *Managerial Planning* 33, no. 4 (January–February 1985): 23–30.

Ghoshal, S., and Kim, S. K. "Building Effective Intelligence Systems for Competitive Advantage." *Sloan Management Review* 28, no. 1 (Fall 1986): 49–58.

Gilbert, X., and Strebel, P. "Strategies to Outpace the Competition." *Journal of Business Strategy* 8, no. 1 (Summer 1987): 28–35.

Goold, Michael, and Campbell, Andrew. "Many Best Ways to Make Strategy." *Harvard Business Review* 65, no. 6 (November–December 1987).

Grossack, I., and Heenan, D. A. "Cooperation, Competition and Antitrust: Two Views." *Business Horizons* 29, no. 5 (September–October 1986): 24–28.

Hayward, R. G. "Developing an Information Systems Strategy." *Long Range Planning* 20, no. 2 (April 1987): 100–113.

Henderson, J. C.; Rockart, J. F.; and Sifonis, J. G. "Integrating Management Support Systems into Strategic Information Systems Planning." *Journal of Management Information Systems* 4, no. 1 (Summer 1987): 5–24.

Hitt, M. A., and Ireland, R. D. "Building Competitive Strength in International Markets." *Long Range Planning* 20, no. 1 (February 1987): 115–122.

Keiser, B. "Practical Competitor Intelligence." *Planning Review* 15, no. 5 (September–October 1987): 14–19.

Kogut, B. "Designing Global Strategies: Profiting From Operational Flexibility." *Sloan Management Review* 27, no. 1 (Fall 1985): 27–38.

Lauglaug, A. S. "A Framework for the Strategic Management of Future Type Technology." *Long Range Planning* 20, no. 5 (October 1987): 21–41.

Nielson, R. P. "Cooperative Strategies." *Planning Review* 14, no. 2 (March–April 1986): 16–20.

Porter, M. E. *Competitive Advantage: Creating and Sustaining Superior Performance*. New York: Free Press, 1985.

———. *Competitive Strategy: Techniques for Analyzing Industries and Companies*, New York: Free Press, 1980.

———. "From Competitive Advantage to Corporate Strategy." *Harvard Business Review* 65, no. 3 (May–June 1987): 43–59.

Prescott, J. E., and Smith, D. C. "A Project-based Approach to Competitive Analysis." *Strategic Management Journal* 8, no. 5 (September–October 1987): 411–424.

Reimann, B. C. "Personal Computers Empower Strategic Management." *Planning Review* 14, no. 6 (November–December 1986): 28–34.

Schnaars, S. P. "How to Develop and Use Scenarios." *Long Range Planning* 20, no. 1 (February 1987): 105–114.

Shanks, D. "Strategic Planning for Global Competition." *Journal of Business Strategy* 5, no. 3 (Winter 1985): 80–89.

Smith, Daniel C., and Prescott, J. E. "Demystifying Competitive Analysis." *Planning Review* 15, no. 5 (September–October 1987): 8–13.

Sommers, W. P.; Nemec, J.; and Harris, J. M. "Repositioning With Technology: Making it Work." *Journal of Business Strategy* 7, no. 3 (Winter 1987): 16–27.

Willis, R. "What's Happening to America's Middle Managers?" *Management Review* 76, no. 1 (January 1987): 24–33.

Wright, P. "Strategic Management Within a World Parameter." *Managerial Planning* 33, no. 10 (January–February 1985): 33–36.

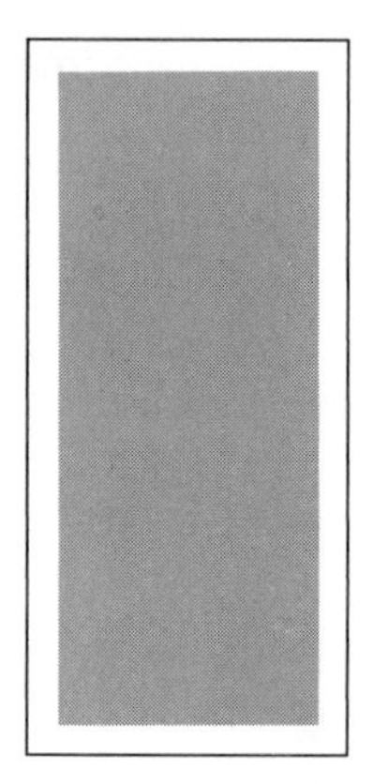

EXPERIENTIAL EXERCISES

EXPERIENTIAL EXERCISE 4A

Developing a Competitive Profile Matrix for Ponderosa

PURPOSE

Monitoring competitors' performance and strategies is a key aspect of an external audit. This exercise is designed to give you practice evaluating the relative strengths and weaknesses of organizations in a given industry, and assimilating that information in the form of a Competitive Profile Matrix.

YOUR TASK

Step 1 Turn back to the Cohesion Case and review the section on competitors.

Step 2 Take out a separate sheet of paper and prepare a Competitive Profile Matrix that includes Ponderosa, Sizzler, and Bonanza.

Step 3 Compare your matrix to the author's. Discuss any major differences.

EXPERIENTIAL EXERCISE 4B

Developing an EFE Matrix for Ponderosa

PURPOSE

This exercise will give you practice developing an EFE Matrix. An EFE Matrix summarizes the results of an external audit. It is an important tool widely used by organizations and by students in preparing business policy case analyses.

YOUR TASK

Step 1 Join two other individuals in class and, together, prepare an EFE Matrix for Ponderosa.

Step 2 Go to the board and record your total weighted score in a column that includes the total weighted scores recorded by the other teams. Put your initials after your score to identify it as your team's.

Step 3 Compare your total weighted score to the total weighted score given in the author's analysis.

Step 4 Examine differences between your EFE Matrix and the author's EFE Matrix. Discuss any major differences.

EXPERIENTIAL EXERCISE 4C

The Library Search

PURPOSE

This exercise will help you become familiar with important sources of environmental information available in your college library. A key part of preparing an external audit is to examine published sources of information for relevant economic, social, cultural, demographic, geographic, political, governmental, technological, and competitive trends and events. Environmental opportunities and threats must be identified and evaluated before strategies can be formulated effectively.

Twenty commonly used sources of information are listed here. Ten of the twenty sources are briefly described in the following section.

1. *Wall Street Journal*
2. *Census of Retail Trade*
3. *Rand McNally Atlas & Marketing Guide*
4. *Value Line*
5. *Business Periodicals Index*
6. *Survey of Buying Power*
7. Standard & Poor's Publications
8. Robert Morris Associates, *Annual Statement Studies*
9. Annual Reports of specific companies
10. *Standard Industrial Classification Manual*
11. Moody's Publications
12. *Dun & Bradstreet Million Dollar Directory Series*
13. *Survey of Business*
14. *Statistical Abstract of the United States*
15. *Census of Manufactures*
16. *Predicast's F & S Index*
17. *The Wall Street Transcript*
18. *The U. S. Industrial Outlook*
19. *Industry Week*
20. *Barron's*

SHORT DESCRIPTIONS OF TEN INFORMATION SOURCES

1. This source contains financial information divided by industry into six manuals published annually with weekly updates: *Bank and Finance Manual, International Manual, OTC Industrial Manual, Industrial Manual, Public Utility Manual,* and *The Transportation Manual.* Information is provided on a specific company's history, subsidiaries, product or service, major plants and properties, financial ratios, bond ratings, and stock ratings. A monthly *Bond Record* and *Bond Survey* are also published. Bonds are rated on a scale from AAA (best) to C (worst) and stock is rated from aaa (best) to c (worst).

2. This source publishes three quarterly reports, the *OTC, ASE,* and *NYSE,* as well as a monthly *Bond Guide* and *Stock Guide.* The quarterly reports include information on each company about (1) earnings and dividend forecasts, (2) a near-term and long-term outlook statement, (3) company stock prices, (4) price-earnings ratios, (5) dividends, (6) bond yields, and (7) stock ratings. In addition, comparative financial information is provided by industry. Stocks are rated A+ (best) to C (worst). The *Bond Guide* lists new offerings, rating changes, and current bond ratings from AAA (best) to D (worst). *Corporation Records* contains company information and *Industry Surveys* contains financial comparisons and projections.

3. This source is published yearly by all publicly held corporations. It includes a summary of the company's past performance and future plans. It usually includes a discussion of the company's mission, purpose, policies, goals, objectives, strategies, and culture.

4. This source contains financial data on manufacturing, wholesaling, retailing, service, and contracting businesses. Key industry average financial ratios are given by Standard Industrial Classification (SIC) Code for the four most recent years.

5. This source provides detailed statistics on social, political, and economic trends in the United States. For example,

Women-owned firms—number and receipts by industry

Industry	*All Firms*	*Number Women-Owned*	*% of All Firms*
All	9833	702	7.1
Building	1107	21	1.9
Manufacturing	287	19	6.6

6. This is a monthly index of articles published in magazines. The articles are indexed by subject, which includes industries, corporations, and individuals.

7. This publication contains detailed information, in five volumes, on 450 manufacturing industries in every state, including for each: number of establishments, value of shipments, cost of materials, capital expenditures, assets, rents, inventories, employment, and payrolls.

8. This source is published in three volumes that include all companies with a net worth over $500,000. Companies are listed alphabetically by business name. Volume I includes businesses with net worth over $1,670,000; Volume II includes businesses with net worth from $847,000 to $1,670,000; and Volume III covers businesses with $500,000 to $847,000 net worth. Each entry gives a specific company's name, address, type of business, top executives' names and titles, annual sales, number of employees, principal bank, and SIC code. Listings are cross-referenced geographically, alphabetically, and by industry.

9. This source is published five days a week and is devoted to businessmen and businesswomen. Regular features include: "What's New," "Special Reports," "The Outlook," and detailed results of the previous day's NYSE, ASE, and commodities markets. An index for the articles appearing in this publication is available. The front section of the index list articles on companies and the back section lists articles by industry or subject.

10. This publication provides statistics by state, Standard Metropolitan Statistical Areas (SMSAs), and areas outside SMSAs for about one hundred different kinds of retail enterprises. The data includes number of establishments, sales, payroll, and employment. This publication is updated and reprinted every five years.

YOUR TASK

Step 1 On a separate sheet of paper, number from 1 to 20. These numbers correspond to the publications listed.

Step 2 Go to your college library and determine which ten publications from the list of twenty are described in the preceding section. Write the name of the publication beside the appropriate number on your paper if it is described.

Step 3 For the ten publications not described below, write a short description.

This exercise was edited by Kelly Janousek, Social Sciences Librarian at Mississippi State University.

The Internal Assessment

NOTABLE QUOTES

Like a product or service, the planning process itself must be managed and shaped, if it is to serve executives as a vehicle for strategic decision-making.

Robert Lenz

Strategic management does not lessen the importance of managerial ability, courage, experience, intuition, or even hunch—just as scientific biology and systematic medicine have not lessened the importance of these qualities in physicians.

Peter Drucker

Efficient operations aren't enough to gain competitive advantage. Organizations must be effective.

Elizabeth Haas

A pertinent question for fire-fighting type managers to ask themselves is: How many of today's problems are yesterday's opportunities gone unaddressed or underaddressed?

John Keane

Weak leadership can wreck the soundest strategy.

Sun Zi

A firm that continues to employ a previously successful strategy eventually and inevitably falls victim to a competitor.

William Cohen

It is the ability of an organization to move information and ideas from the bottom to the top and back again in continuous dialogue that the Japanese value above all things. As this dialogue is pursued, strategy evolves.

Rosenberg and Schewe

An organization should approach all tasks with the idea that they can be accomplished in a superior fashion.

Thomas Watson, Jr.

5

OUTLINE

THE INTERNAL AUDIT

RELATIONSHIPS AMONG THE FUNCTIONAL AREAS OF BUSINESS

MANAGEMENT

MARKETING

FINANCE/ACCOUNTING

PRODUCTION/OPERATIONS

RESEARCH AND DEVELOPMENT

INTERNAL-AUDIT CHECKLISTS

DIMENSIONS OF ORGANIZATIONAL CULTURE

THE INTERNAL FACTOR EVALUATION (IFE) MATRIX

Experiential Exercise 5A: Performing a Financial Ratio Analysis for Ponderosa

Experiential Exercise 5B: Constructing an IFE Matrix for Ponderosa

OBJECTIVES

After studying this chapter, you should be able to

- Describe how to perform an internal strategic-management audit.
- Discuss key interrelationships among the functional areas of business.
- Identify the basic functions or activities of management, marketing, finance/accounting, production/operations, and research and development.
- Explain the importance of financial ratio analysis.
- Develop an Internal Factor Evaluation (IFE) Matrix.

This chapter provides a framework for conducting an *internal strategic-management audit,* which is a means of identifying and evaluating organizational strengths and weaknesses in the functional areas of business, including management, marketing, finance/accounting, production/operations, and research and development. Relationships among these areas of business are examined. Strategic implications of important functional area concepts are examined.

THE INTERNAL AUDIT

The internal audit part of the strategic-management process is highlighted in Figure 5–1. Internal strengths and weaknesses, coupled with external opportunities and threats and a clear statement of mission, provide the basis for establishing objectives and strategies.

Organizations that use strategic management ideas chart their future with the intention of capitalizing upon internal strengths and overcoming weaknesses. According to William King, a task force of managers from different units of the organization, supported by staff, should be charged with determining the ten to fifteen most important strengths and weaknesses that should influence the future of the organization:

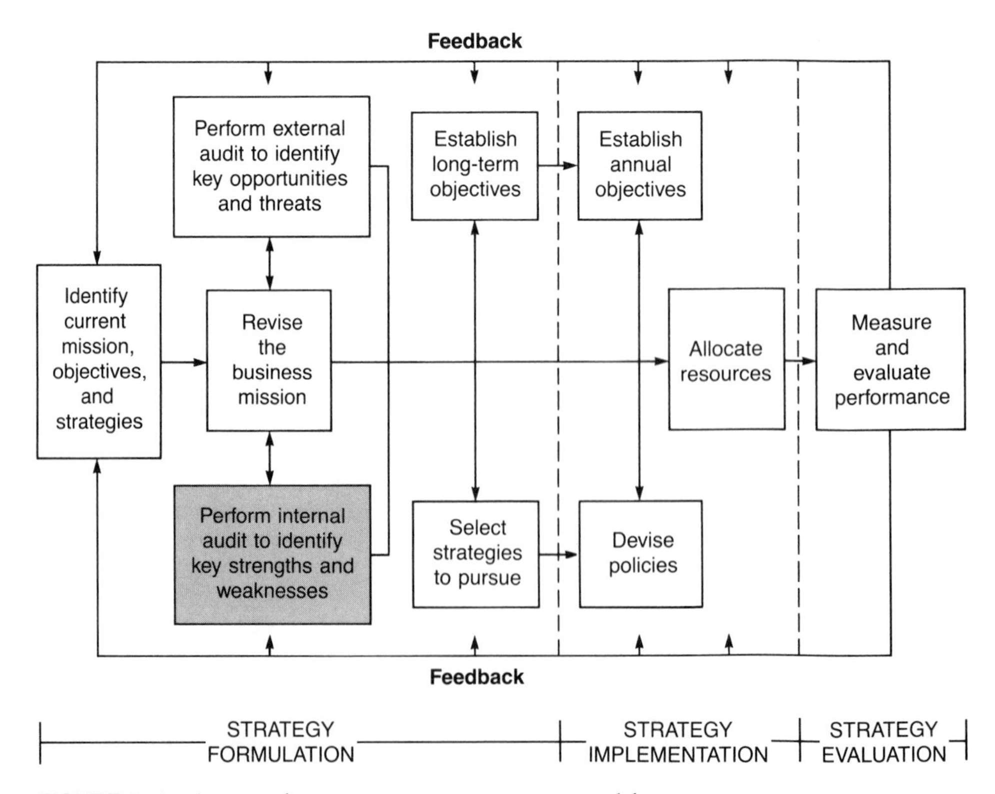

FIGURE 5–1 A comprehensive strategic-management model

The development of conclusions on the ten to fifteen most important organizational strengths and weaknesses can be, as any experienced manager knows, a difficult task, when it involves managers representing various organizational interests and points of view. Developing a twenty page list of strengths and weaknesses could be accomplished relatively easily, but a list of the ten to fifteen most important ones involves significant analysis and negotiation. This is true because of the judgments that are required and the impact which such a list will inevitably have as it is used in the formulation, implementation, and evaluation of strategies.[1]

RELATIONSHIPS AMONG THE FUNCTIONAL AREAS OF BUSINESS

Strategic management is sometimes misperceived as a unidirectional flow of strategies, objectives, policies, and decisions from corporate to divisional to functional level managers. Actually, however, it is a highly interactive process and requires effective coordination of all the functional areas of a business. There are an infinite number of relationships among management, marketing, finance/accounting, production/operations, and R&D activities. For example, financial problems could restrict the number of feasible options available to operations managers, or R & D managers could develop such successful products that marketing managers would need to set higher objectives. Although the strategic-management process is overseen by strategists, success requires that managers from all functional areas work together to provide ideas and information. Ansoff recently summarized this need as follows:

> During the first fifty years, successful firms focused their energies on optimizing the performance of one of the principal functions: production/operations, R & D, or marketing. Today, due to the growing complexity and dynamism of the environment, success increasingly depends on a judicious combination of several functional influences. This transition from a single-function focus to a multifunction focus is essential for successful strategic management.[2]

A failure to recognize and understand relationships among the functional areas of business can be detrimental to the strategic-management process, and the number of those relationships that must be managed increases dramatically with a firm's size, diversity, geographic dispersion, and the number of products or services offered. Governmental and nonprofit enterprises have traditionally not placed sufficient emphasis on relationships among the business functions. For example, some state governments, utilities, universities, and hospitals have only recently begun to establish marketing objectives and policies that are consistent with their financial capabilities and limitations.

Evaluating financial ratios also exemplifies the complexity of relationships among the functional areas of business. A declining return on investment or profit margin ratio could be the result of ineffective marketing, poor management policies, research and development errors, or other factors. The effectiveness of strategy formulation, implementation, and evaluation activities hinges upon a clear understanding of how major business functions affect one another, and effective strategies achieve a coordinated effort among all the functional areas of business. For example, in the case of planning, George says:

> We may, of course, conceptually separate planning for the purpose of theoretical discussion and analysis, but in practice, neither is it a distinct entity nor is it capable of being separated. The planning function is mixed with all other business functions and, like ink once mixed with water, it cannot be set apart. It is spread throughout and is a part of the whole of managing an organization.[3]

MANAGEMENT

The *functions of management* consist of five basic activities: planning, organizing, motivating, staffing, and controlling (see Table 5–1).

Planning

The only thing certain about the future of any organization is change, and *planning* is the essential bridge between the present and the future that increases the likelihood of achieving desired results. Planning is the cornerstone of effective strategy formulation.

TABLE 5–1 The basic functions of management

Function	*Description*	*Most Important at What Stage of the Strategic Management Process?*
Planning	Planning consists of all those managerial activities related to preparing for the future. Specific tasks include forecasting, establishing objectives, devising strategies, developing policies, and setting goals.	Strategy Formulation
Organizing	Organizing includes all those managerial activities that result in a structure of task and authority relationships. Specific areas include organizational design, job specialization, job descriptions, job specifications, span of the control, unity of command, coordination, job design, and job analysis.	Strategy Implementation
Motivating	Motivating involves efforts directed towards shaping human behavior. Specific topics include leadership, communication, work groups, behavior modification, delegation of authority, job enrichment, job satisfaction, needs fulfillment, organizational change, employee morale, and managers' morale.	Strategy Implementation
Staffing	Staffing activities are centered on personnel or human resource management. Included are wage and salary administration, employee benefits, interviewing, hiring, firing, training, management development, employee safety, affirmative action, equal employment opportunity, union relations, career development, personnel research, discipline policies, grievance procedures, and public relations.	Strategy Implementation
Controlling	Controlling refers to all those managerial activities directed towards assuring that actual results are consistent with planned results. Key areas of concern include quality control, financial control, sales control, inventory control, expense control, analysis of variances, rewards, and sanctions.	Strategy Evaluation

But though it is considered the foundation of management, it is commonly the task managers neglect most. Planning is also essential for successful strategy implementation and strategy evaluation, because organizing, motivating, staffing, and controlling activities are dependent upon good planning.

To be effective, planning must begin at the top of an organization and filter down. The major reason for beginning at the corporate level is that top management must establish a firm's mission, strategies, and long-term objectives before divisional and functional managers can effectively set annual objectives and institute policies. The three levels of planning, shown in Figure 5–2, are analogous to the three levels of strategic management: corporate, divisional, and functional.

There are some important reasons why planning has a positive impact on organizational and individual performance. First, planning allows an organization to identify and take advantage of environmental opportunities and minimize the impact of environmental threats. Planning is more than extrapolating from the past and present into the future. It includes forecasting the likelihood that future events and trends could be harmful or beneficial to an enterprise. An organization can develop synergy through planning. *Synergy* exists when everyone pulls together as a team that knows what it wants to achieve; synergy is the 2 + 2 = 5 effect. By establishing and communicating clear objectives, employees and managers can work together towards desired results. Synergy can result in powerful competitive advantages. Planning also allows a firm to

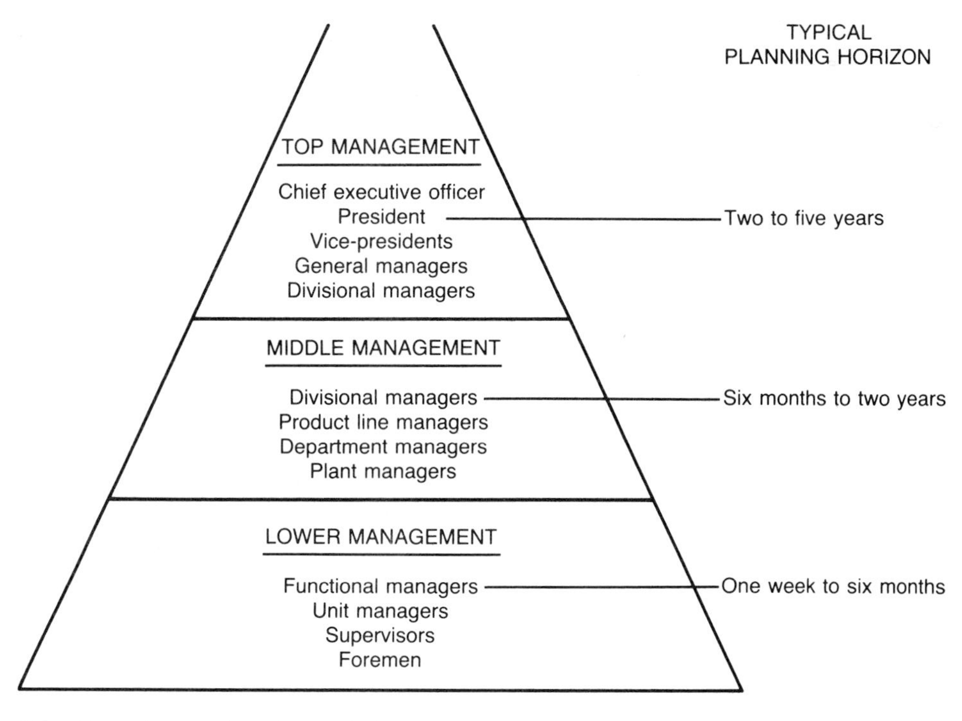

FIGURE 5–2 The three levels of planning

adapt to changing environments and thus shape its own destiny. The strategic-management process can be viewed as a formal planning process that allows an organization to pursue proactive rather than reactive strategies. Successful organizations strive to control their own future rather than merely to react to external forces and events as they occur. Historically, organisms and organizations that have not adapted to changing environments have become extinct. Swift adaptation is needed today more than ever before because changes in business environments worldwide are accelerating.

Organizing

The purpose of *organizing* is to achieve coordinated effort by defining tasks and determining authority relationships. Organizing means determining who does what and who reports to whom. A well organized firm can formulate, implement, and evaluate strategies much more effectively than a disorganized firm. The organizing function of management can be viewed as consisting of three sequential activities: breaking tasks down into jobs (work specialization), combining jobs to form departments (departmentalization), and delegating authority.

Breaking tasks down into jobs requires development of job descriptions and job specifications. These tools enable managers to match people to jobs effectively. They also clarify for both employee and supervisor what a given job entails and are essential components in the performance evaluation process. Combining jobs to form departments results in an organizational structure. Changes in strategy often require changes in structure because structure dictates how resources are allocated.

Delegating authority is an important organizing activity, as evidenced in the old saying that "you can tell how good a manager is by observing how his department functions when he isn't there." Employees today are more educated and more capable of participating in organizational decision making than ever before. In most cases, they expect to be delegated authority and responsibility. Delegation of authority is embedded in the strategic-management process at Johnson & Johnson, a firm described as a prime example of good organizing and delegating:

> The people running Johnson & Johnson's divisions enjoy autonomy unheard of in most corporations. Most divisions have their own boards. J & J's corporate headquarters staff is a scant 750 people. And only one management layer separates division presidents from the 14-member executive committee to whom they report. J & J's earnings growth in the last 10 years has averaged 13% annually.[4]

Johnson & Johnson's net profit for 1987 increased 152 percent over 1986, to $833 million, while company sales increased fourteen percent to $8.012 billion.

Motivating

Motivating can be defined as the process of influencing people to act. Motivation explains why some people work hard and others do not. Objectives, strategies, and policies have little chance of succeeding if employees and managers are not motivated to implement strategies once they are formulated. The motivating function of management includes at least four major components: leadership, group dynamics, communication flows, and organizational change.

To motivate an organization's human resources, strategists must be willing to negotiate, must have a heightened sense of corporate social responsibility, must be willing to give up some authority, and must take responsibility for the career development of managers. Good strategists motivate managers and employees to achieve high levels of productivity. They are good leaders.

> Leadership is not a magnetic personality. That can just as well be demagoguery. It is not "making friends and influencing people." That is flattery. Leadership is the lifting of a person's vision to higher sights, the raising of a person's performance to a higher standard, the building of a person's personality beyond its normal limitations.[5]

Group dynamics play a major role in employee morale and satisfaction. Informal groups or coalitions form in every organization. The norms of coalitions can range from being very positive to very negative toward management. It is important therefore that strategists try to identify the composition and nature of informal groups in an organization to facilitate strategy formulation, implementation, and evaluation.

Communication is a third major component in motivation. Poor communications can derail the strategic-management process. An organization's system of communication greatly affects whether strategies can be implemented successfully. Good two-way communication is vital for gaining employees' support for departmental objectives and policies. Top-down communication encourages bottom-up communication. The strategic-management process becomes a whole lot easier when subordinates are encouraged to discuss their concerns, reveal their problems, provide recommendations, and give suggestions.

> Communication always makes demands. It demands that the recipient become somebody, do something, believe something. It appeals to motivation. If communication fits in with the aspirations, the values, the purposes of the recipient, it is powerful. If it goes against a person's aspirations, values, and motivation, it is likely not to be received at all or, at best, to be resisted. By and large, therefore, there is no communication unless the message can key into the recipient's own values, at least to some degree.[6]

The Dana Corporation exemplifies an excellent communication system (see Exhibit 5–1). Dana's net profits increased sixty-four percent in 1987 to $141 million, while company sales increased twelve percent to over $4 billion. Citicorp is another organization that has an excellent communication system; an important element of its strategic-management philosophy is that good two-way communication offers major competitive advantages:

> Citi is an open society that encourages people to speak their minds, in sharp contrast to such banks as Chase and First Chicago where strategists have installed electronic voting machines so managers can voice their opinions anonymously. Moreover, at Citi, the belief is sacred that anyone with a good idea should have the chance to try it out. The philosophy at Citi is to "let a thousand flowers bloom." This may explain why Citi, whose electronic network connects with 6,500 corporate offices around the world, is far ahead of competitors.[7]

EXHIBIT 5–1 Listen, Listen, Listen

Listening, really listening, is tough and grinding work, often humbling, sometimes distasteful. It's a fairly sure bet that you won't like that lion's share of what you hear. Little wonder that many senior executives avoid doing it.

But Dana Corporation isn't among them. Walk into a factory of the $3.7 billion auto parts manufacturer, and you notice big blue posters all over the place. The caption of the poster says: "Write a letter to your chairman." On the bottom left-hand corner of the poster is a thick pad of tear sheets, already stamped and addressed to Chairman Mitchell at Dana headquarters in Toledo. Across the top of the card is printed: "A letter to the chairman," and below that the words "Dear Gerry."

Mitchell gets 3,000 of these letters every year. He reads them all and with staff help replies to every one. It's one of the ways he stays in touch with 36,000 employees worldwide. He figures about 60% of the letters are routine gripes and bitches; the rest contain information about important people, products, and processes. Each year he makes 50 scheduled and 100 unscheduled visits to plants.

Listening is central to success (renewal), but, as Mitchell demonstrates, it is not a passive activity. You don't just wait for information to come to you. And you can't expect a small circle of peers to provide you with a current or complete account of what's happening. Instead you should listen around the hierarchy, and you need to do it yourself.

Source: Robert Waterman, Jr., "The Renewal Factor," *Business Week* (14 September 1987): 108. Reprinted from September 14, 1987 issue of *Business Week* by special permission, copyright © 1987 by McGraw Hill, Inc.

Staffing

The management function of *staffing* is also called *personnel management* or *human resource management.* Human resource managers assist line managers in performing staffing activities such as recruiting, interviewing, testing, selecting, orienting, training, developing, caring for, evaluating, rewarding, disciplining, promoting, transferring, demoting, and dismissing employees. Staffing activities play a major role in strategy-implementation efforts, and for this reason human resource managers are becoming more actively involved in the strategic-management process.

The complexity and importance of human resource activities have increased to such a degree that all but the smallest organizations often need a full-time human resource manager. Numerous court cases that directly affect staffing activities are decided each day. Organizations and individuals can be penalized severely for not following federal, state, and local laws and guidelines related to staffing. Line managers simply cannot stay abreast of all the legal developments and requirements regarding staffing. The human resources department is meant to effectively coordinate line managers' actions in the staffing area so that an organization as a whole meets legal requirements; it also provides needed consistency in administering company rules, wages, practices, and policies. Strategists are becoming increasingly aware of how important human resources are to effective strategic management. In the future, the human resource or staffing function of management is expected to become even more proactive, anticipating and initiating rather than merely responding. Waterman describes staffing activities among successful companies:

> Successful (renewing) companies are busy taking out layers of management, cutting staff, and pushing decisions down. Nucor Corporation runs a successful, near billion-dollar steel enterprise from a headquarters office and complement of seven people in a Charlotte, N.C., shopping mall. At Dana Corporation, President Woody Morcott and others take extraordinary pride in the fact that today there are only five layers between the chief executive's office and the person on the factory floor. In the mid-1970s there were 14. . . .Leaner organizations set the stage for success (renewal). They make each one of us more important. They empower the individual.[8]

Controlling

The *controlling* function of management includes all those activities undertaken to assure that actual operations conform to planned operations. All managers in an organization have controlling responsibilities, such as conducting performance evaluations and taking necessary actions to minimize inefficiencies. The controlling function of management is particularly important for effective strategy evaluation. Controlling consists of four basic steps:

1. Establishing performance standards
2. Measuring individual and organizational performance
3. Comparing actual performance to planned performance standards
4. Taking corrective actions

Measuring individual performance is often conducted ineffectively or not at all in organizations. Some reasons for this shortcoming are that the evaluation process can create confrontations that most managers prefer to avoid, can take more time than most managers are willing to give, and can require skills that most managers lack. No single approach to measuring individual performance is without limitations. Therefore, an organization should examine various methods such as the graphic rating scale, the behaviorally anchored rating scale, or the critical incident method, and then develop or select a performance appraisal instrument that best suits the firm's needs.

MARKETING

Marketing can be described as the process of defining, anticipating, creating, and fulfilling customers' needs and wants for products and services. Joel Evans and Barry Berman suggest nine basic *functions of marketing*: (1) customer analysis, (2) buying, (3) selling, (4) product and service planning, (5) pricing, (6) distribution, (7) marketing research, (8) opportunity analysis, and (9) social responsibility.[9] Understanding these functions helps the strategist identify and evaluate marketing strengths and weaknesses.

Customer Analysis

Customer analysis, the examination and evaluation of consumer needs, desires, and wants, involves administering customer surveys, analyzing consumer information, evaluating market positioning strategies, developing customer profiles, and determining optimal market segmentation strategies. The information generated by customer analysis can be essential in developing an effective mission statement. Customer profiles can reveal the demographic characteristics of an organization's customers. Buyers, sellers, distributors, salesmen, managers, wholesalers, retailers, suppliers, and creditors can all participate in gathering information to identify customers' needs and wants successfully. Successful organizations continually monitor present and potential customers' buying patterns.

IBM declared 1987 to be the "Year of the Customer" and initiated the theme by inviting two hundred of its largest corporate customers to Orlando, Florida for a free vacation. It used the vacation as an opportunity to discuss products and company strategies, and customers had unusual access to IBM's top managers. "I've never seen anything like it," said William Trischler, director of the corporate data center at Westinghouse Electric Corporation.[10] With a stock-market value of over $68 billion on March 18, 1988, IBM ranked number one among the *Business Week* 1,000 United States companies.

Buying

The second function of marketing is buying. *Buying* means obtaining the goods and services needed to produce and sell a product or service. Buying consists of evaluating alternative suppliers, selecting the best suppliers, arranging acceptable terms with suppliers, and procurement. The buying process can be complicated by such factors as price controls, recession, foreign trade restrictions, strikes, walkouts, and machine breakdowns. Even the weather can significantly disrupt the procurement of needed supplies. Quite often, the question arises whether to "make or buy" needed supplies and services. (Recall that backward integration, gaining control over suppliers, is a particularly attractive strategy when suppliers are unreliable, costly, or incapable of meeting company needs.)

Selling

Successful strategy implementation generally rests upon the ability of an organization to sell some product or service. *Selling* includes many marketing activities such as advertising, sales promotion, publicity, personal selling, sales force management, customer relations, and dealer relations. These activities are especially critical when a firm pursues a market penetration strategy. The effectiveness of various selling tools for consumer and industrial products varies. Personal selling is most important for industrial-goods companies, and advertising is most important for consumer-goods companies. In the case of cigarettes, for example, companies like Philip Morris and R. J. Reynolds are having to use elaborate sales techniques that include massive discounting and couponing. Many organizations use magazines for the bulk of their advertising. The top five magazines based on total adult readership in 1987 were *TV Guide* (43.2 million), *Reader's Digest* (37.5 million), *People* (24.6 million), *National Geographic* (23.6 million), and *Time* (23.2 million). For the world's second largest toy company, Mattel, Inc., advertising and promotion expenditures declined from 19 percent of sales in 1986, to 18 percent in 1987, to 16 percent in 1988.

Product and Service Planning

Product and service planning includes activities such as test marketing; product and brand positioning; devising warranties; packaging; determining product options, product features, product style, and product quality; deleting old products; and providing for customer service. Product and service planning is particularly important when a company is pursuing product development or diversification. One of the most effective product and service planning techniques is *test marketing*. Test markets allow an organization to pretest alternative marketing plans and to forecast the future sales of a new product. In conducting a test market, an organization must decide how many test cities to include, which cities to include, how long to run the test, what information to collect during the test, and what action to take after the test has been completed. Test marketing is more frequently used by consumer-goods companies than by industrial-goods companies. Test marketing can allow an organization to avoid great losses by revealing weak products and ineffective marketing approaches before large-scale production begins.

Pricing

Four major stakeholders affect *pricing* decisions: consumers, governments, channel members (distributors), and competitors. Sometimes an organization will pursue a forward integration strategy primarily to gain better control over prices charged to consumers. Governments can impose various limitations such as price fixing, price discrimination, minimum prices, unit pricing, price advertising, and price controls. For example, the Robinson-Patman Act prohibits manufacturers and wholesalers from discriminating in price among channel-member purchasers if competition is injured. Competing organizations must be careful not to coordinate discounts, credit terms, or condition of sale; not to discuss prices, markups, and costs at trade association meetings; and not to arrange to issue new price lists on the same date, to rotate low bids on contracts, or to uniformly restrict production to maintain high prices. Strategists should view price from both a short-run and long-run perspective, because competitors can copy price changes with relative ease. Often a dominant firm will aggressively match all price cuts by competitors.

Distribution

Distribution includes warehousing, physical distribution channels, distribution coverage, retail site locations, sales territories, inventory levels and location, transportation carriers, wholesaling, and retailing. Most producers today do not sell their goods directly to consumers. Many marketing entities act as intermediaries between producers and consumers and provide a variety of functions. They bear a variety of names such as wholesalers, retailers, brokers, facilitators, agents, middlemen, vendors, or simply distributors. Distribution becomes especially important when a firm is striving to implement a market development or forward integration strategy. Some of the most complex and challenging decisions facing a firm concern product distribution. Intermediaries flourish in our economy because many producers lack the financial resources and expertise to carry out direct marketing. Manufacturers who could afford to sell directly to the public often can gain greater returns by expanding and improving their current operations with such intermediaries. Even General Motors would find it very difficult to buy out its more than 18,000 independent dealers.

Successful organizations identify and evaluate alternative ways to reach their ultimate market. Possible approaches vary from direct selling, to using just one wholesaler and retailer, to using many levels and numbers of intermediaries. Each channel alternative should be evaluated according to economic, control, and adaptive criteria. That is, organizations should consider the costs and benefits of various wholesaling and retailing options. They must consider the need to motivate and control channel members and the need to adapt to environmental changes in the future. Once a marketing channel is chosen, an organization usually must adhere to it for an extended period.

Marketing Research

Marketing research is the systematic gathering, recording, and analyzing of data about problems relating to the marketing of goods and services. Marketing research can uncover critical strengths and weaknesses, and marketing researchers employ numerous scales, instruments, procedures, concepts, and techniques to gather information. Marketing research activities support all of the major business functions of an organization. Organizations that possess excellent marketing research skills have a definite strength in pursuing generic strategies.

> The President of PepsiCo says, "Looking at the competition is the company's best form of market research. The majority of our strategic successes are ideas that we borrow from the marketplace, usually from a small regional or local competitor. In each case, we spot a promising new idea, improve on it, and then out-execute our competitor."[11]

Reebok is a company that attributes much of its success to extensive market research. "I think people who want to put Reebok into a boom—bust sort of theory don't really know that Reebok is closely tied to its customers," says Christine King, an analyst at Kidder, Peabody & Co. "Reebok, unlike a lot of firms in the industry, does market research. Reebok sits down and talks to people who buy their shoes." Reebok has a 43 percent share of the American market for tennis shoes, ahead of rivals Nike and Adidas.

Opportunity Analysis

The eighth function of marketing, *opportunity analysis,* is an appraisal of the costs, benefits, and risks associated with marketing-related decisions. Three steps are required to perform a *cost/benefit analysis*: (1) compute the total costs associated with a decision, (2) estimate the total benefits from the decision, and (3) compare the total costs with the total benefits. As expected benefits exceed total costs, an opportunity becomes more attractive. Sometimes the variables included in a cost/benefit analysis cannot be quantified or even measured, but usually reasonable estimates can be made to allow the analysis to be performed. One key factor to be considered is risk. Cost/benefit analyses should also be performed when a company is weighing social responsibilities.

Social Responsibility

The final function of marketing is to determine *social responsibility*. Social responsibility includes a company's obligation to offer products and services that are safe, ethical, and reasonably priced. Demands by special interest groups on business organizations have greatly increased in the 1980s. Arguments still rage today though about how socially responsible firms should be. A clear social policy can represent a major strength for organizations, whereas a poor social policy can be a weakness. One problem with the contemporary view of social responsibility many firms hold is that it is based on a mistaken notion:

> What is especially unfortunate is how many strategists have misinterpreted or misunderstood the concept of social responsibility. Many of them have viewed social responsibility as a focus which detracts from or is counter to their profit minded pursuits. Although there may be some clearly distinct economic versus social concerns, there is a rather broad area in which economic and social concerns are consistent with one another. It is corporate activities which fall into this area that provide the more realistic view of social responsibility, that is, activities that are profitable but at the same time are socially responsible. When a firm engages in social activities, it must do so in a way that receives economic advantages. The net effect is that the firm simultaneously achieves social and economic objectives. This concept also recognizes that social activity can lead to economic rewards and that businesses should attempt to create such a favorable situation.[12]

Problems concerning social responsibility can arise from unexpected sources. For example, General Motors was recently sued by the southern Ohio town of Norwood for $318.3 million over "breach of contract." A town of 26,000 residents, Norwood claimed that GM must pay "alimony" for closing a local assembly plant that employed 4,200 workers and paid 40 percent of the town's taxes. GM had previously promised to expand, and as a result Norwood had built schools and added municipal services. General Motors' revenues for 1987 declined 1 percent from 1986 to $10.2 billion.

FINANCE/ACCOUNTING

Financial condition is often considered the single best measure of a firm's competitive position and overall attractiveness to investors. Determining an organization's financial strengths and weaknesses is essential to formulating strategies effectively. A firm's liquidity, leverage, working capital, profitability, asset utilization, cash flow, and equity can eliminate some strategies as being feasible alternatives. Financial factors often alter existing strategies and change implementation plans.

Finance/Accounting Functions

According to James Van Horne, the *functions of finance/accounting* comprise three decisions: the investment decision, the financing decision, and the dividend decision.[13] *Financial ratio analysis* is the most widely used method for determining an organization's strengths and weaknesses in the investment, financing, and dividend areas. Since the functional areas of business are so closely related, financial ratios can signal strengths or weaknesses in management, marketing, production, and research and development activities.

The *investment decision,* sometimes called *capital budgeting,* is the allocation and reallocation of capital and resources to projects, products, assets, and divisions of an organization. Once strategies are formulated, capital budgeting decisions are required to implement those strategies successfully. The *financing decision* concerns determining the best financing mix or capital structure for the firm and includes examining various methods by which the firm can raise capital (for example, by issuing stock, increasing debt, selling assets, or using a combination of these approaches). The financing decision must consider both short-term and long-term needs for financing and working capital. Two key financial ratios that indicate whether a firm's financing decisions have been effective are the debt-to-equity ratio and the debt-to-total-assets ratio.

Dividend decisions concern issues such as the percentage of earnings paid to stockholders, the stability of dividends paid over time, and the repurchase or issuance of stock. Dividend decisions determine the amount of funds that are retained in a firm compared to the amount paid out to stockholders. Three financial ratios that are helpful in evaluating a firm's dividend decisions are the earnings-per-share ratio, the dividends-per-share ratio, and the price-earnings ratio. The benefits of paying dividends to investors must be balanced against the benefits of retaining funds internally, and there is no set formula on how to balance this tradeoff. For the reasons listed here, dividends are sometimes paid out even when funds could be better reinvested in the business or when the firm has to obtain outside sources of capital:

1. Paying cash dividends is customary. Failure to do so could be thought of as a stigma. A dividend change is considered a signal about the future.
2. Dividends represent a sales point for investment bankers. Some institutional investors can buy only dividend-paying stocks.
3. Shareholders often demand dividends, even in companies with great opportunities for reinvesting all available funds.
4. There exists a myth that paying dividends will result in a higher stock price.

Basic Types of Financial Ratios

Financial ratios are computed from an organization's income statement and balance sheet. Computing financial ratios is like taking a picture, because both results reflect a situation at just one point in time. Comparing ratios over time and to industry averages is more likely to result in meaningful statistics that can be used to identify and evaluate strengths and weaknesses. Trend analysis, illustrated in Figure 5–3, is a useful technique that incorporates both the time and industry average dimensions of financial ratios. Four major sources of industry-average financial ratios are:

1. Dun & Bradstreet's *Industry Norms and Key Business Ratios*—Fourteen different ratios are calculated in an industry-average format for eight hundred different types of businesses. The ratios are presented by Standard Industrial Classification (SIC) number and are grouped by annual sales into three size categories.
2. Robert Morris Associates, *Annual Statement Studies*—Sixteen different ratios are calculated in an industry-average format. Industries are referenced by SIC num-

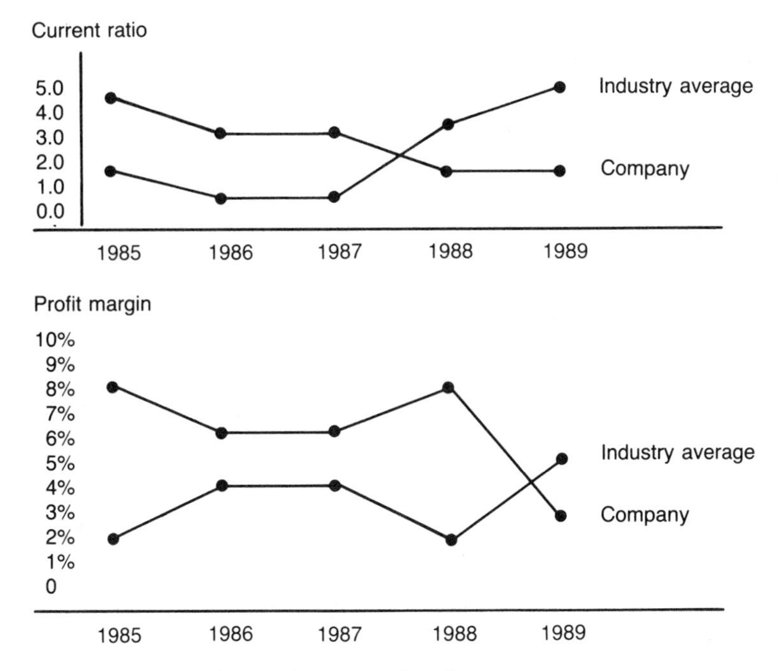

FIGURE 5–3 A financial ratio trend analysis

bers published by the Bureau of the Census. The ratios are presented in four size categories by annual sales and "for all firms" in the industry.

3. Troy *Leo's Almanac of Business & Industrial Financial Ratios*—Twenty-two financial ratios and percentages are provided in an industry-average format for all major industries. The ratios and percentages are given for twelve different company-size categories and for all firms in a given industry.
4. Federal Trade Commission Reports—The FTC publishes quarterly financial data including ratios on manufacturing companies. FTC reports include analyses by industry group and asset size.

Table 5–2 provides a summary of key financial ratios showing how each ratio is calculated and what each ratio measures, but it is not cast in stone. All of the ratios are not significant for all industries and companies. (For example, Ponderosa has no inventory of finished goods. Accounts receivable turnover and average collection period are not very meaningful to a company that does primarily a cash receipts business.) These key financial ratios can be classified into five types:

1. *Liquidity ratios* measure a firm's ability to meet maturing short-term obligations.
   - ☐ Current ratio
   - ☐ Quick or acid-test ratio
2. *Leverage ratios* measure the extent to which a firm has been financed by debt.
   - ☐ Debt-to-total-assets ratio
   - ☐ Debt-to-equity ratio

TABLE 5–2 A summary of key financial ratios

Ratio	*How Calculated*	*What It Measures*
Liquidity Ratios		
Current ratio	$\frac{\text{Current assets}}{\text{Current liabilities}}$	The extent to which a firm can meet its short-term obligations
Quick ratio	$\frac{\text{Current assets—inventory}}{\text{Current liabilities}}$	The extent to which a firm can meet its short-term obligations without relying upon the sale of its inventories
Leverage Ratios		
Debt-to-total-assets ratio	$\frac{\text{Total debt}}{\text{Total assets}}$	The percentage of total funds that are provided by creditors
Debt-to-equity ratio	$\frac{\text{Total debt}}{\text{Total stockholders' equity}}$	The percentage of total funds provided by creditors versus by owners
Long-term-debt-to-equity ratio	$\frac{\text{Long-term debt}}{\text{Total stockholders' equity}}$	The balance between debt and equity in a firm's long-term capital structure
Times-interest-earned ratio	$\frac{\text{Profits before interest and taxes}}{\text{Total interest charges}}$	The extent to which earnings can decline without the firm becoming unable to meet its annual interest costs.
Activity Ratios		
Inventory turnover	$\frac{\text{Sales}}{\text{Inventory of finished goods}}$	Whether a firm holds excessive stocks of inventories and whether a firm is selling its inventories slowly compared to the industry average
Fixed-assets turnover	$\frac{\text{Sales}}{\text{Fixed assets}}$	Sales productivity and plant and equipment utilization
Total-assets turnover	$\frac{\text{Sales}}{\text{Total assets}}$	Whether a firm is generating a sufficient volume of business for the size of its assest investment
Accounts-receivable turnover	$\frac{\text{Annual credit sales}}{\text{Accounts receivable}}$	(In percentage terms) the average length of time it takes a firm to collect credit sales
Average collection period	$\frac{\text{Accounts receivable}}{\text{Total sales/365 days}}$	(In days) the average length of time it takes a firm to collect on credit sales
Profitability Ratios		
Gross profit margin	$\frac{\text{Sales minus cost of goods sold}}{\text{Sales}}$	The total margin available to cover operating expenses and yield a profit
Operating profit margin	$\frac{\text{Earnings before interest and taxes (EBIT)}}{\text{Sales}}$	Profitability without concern for taxes and interest
Net profit margin	$\frac{\text{Net income}}{\text{Sales}}$	After-tax profits per dollar of sales
Return on total assets (ROA)	$\frac{\text{Net income}}{\text{Total assets}}$	After-tax profits per dollar of assets; this ratio is also called return on investment (ROI).
Return on stockholders' equity (ROE)	$\frac{\text{Net income}}{\text{Total stockholders' equity}}$	After-tax profits per dollar of stockholders' investment in the firm
Earnings per share (EPS)	$\frac{\text{Net income}}{\text{Number of shares of common stock outstanding}}$	Earnings available to the owners of common stock
Growth Ratios		
Sales	Annual percentage growth in total sales	Firm's growth rate in sales
Income	Annual percentage growth in profits	Firm's growth rate in profits
Earnings per share	Annual percentage growth in EPS	Firm's growth rate in EPS
Dividends per share	Annual percentage growth in dividends per share	Firm's growth rate in dividends per share
Price-earning ratio	$\frac{\text{Market price per share}}{\text{Earnings per share}}$	Faster-growing and less risky firms tend to have higher price-earnings ratios

- ☐ Long-term debt-to-equity ratio
- ☐ Times-interest-earned (or coverage) ratio

3. *Activity ratios* measure how effectively a firm is using its resources.
   - ☐ Inventory-turnover ratio
   - ☐ Total-assets turnover
   - ☐ Fixed-assets turnover
   - ☐ Average collection period
4. *Profitability ratios* measure management's overall effectiveness as shown by the returns generated on sales and investment.
   - ☐ Gross profit margin
   - ☐ Operating profit margin
   - ☐ Net profit margin
   - ☐ Return on total assets (ROA)
   - ☐ Return on stockholders' equity (ROE)
   - ☐ Earnings per share
5. *Growth ratios* measure the firm's ability to maintain its economic position in the growth of the economy and industry.
   - ☐ Sales
   - ☐ Net income
   - ☐ Earnings per share
   - ☐ Dividends per share
   - ☐ Price-earnings ratio

Financial ratios analysis is not without some limitations. First of all, financial ratios are based on accounting data, and firms differ in their treatment of such items as depreciation, inventory valuation, research and development expenditures, pension plan costs, mergers, and taxes. Also, seasonal factors can influence comparative ratios. Therefore, conformity to industry composite ratios does not establish with certainty that a firm is performing normally or that it is well managed. Likewise, departures from industry averages do not always indicate that a firm is doing especially well or badly. For example, a high inventory-turnover ratio could indicate efficient inventory management and a strong working capital position, but it could also indicate a serious inventory shortage and a weak working capital position.

It is important to recognize that a firm's financial condition depends not only on the functions of finance, but also on many other factors that include (1) management, marketing, production/operations, and research and development decisions, (2) actions by competitors, suppliers, distributors, creditors, customers, shareholders, and (3) economic, social, demographic, political, governmental, and technological trends. So, financial ratio analysis, like all other analytical tools, should be used wisely.

PRODUCTION/OPERATIONS

The *production/operations function* of a business consists of all those activities that transform inputs into goods and services. Production/operations management deals with inputs, transformations, and outputs that vary across industries and environments. A

EXHIBIT 5–2 The basic functions of production management

Function	Description
1. Process	Process decisions concern the design of the physical production system. Specific decisions include choice of technology, facility layout, process flow analysis, facility location, line balancing, process control, and transportation analysis.
2. Capacity	Capacity decisions concern determination of optimal output levels for the organization—not too much and not too little. Specific decisions include forecasting, facilities planning, aggregate planning, scheduling, capacity planning, and queuing analysis.
3. Inventory	Inventory decisions involve managing the level of raw materials, work in process, and finished goods. Specific decisions include what to order, when to order, how much to order, and materials handling.
4. Work Force	Work force decisions are concerned with managing the skilled, unskilled, clerical, and managerial employees. Specific decisions include job design, work measurement, job enrichment, work standards, and motivation techniques.
5. Quality	Quality decisions are aimed at assuring that high-quality goods and services are produced. Specific decisions include quality control, sampling, testing, quality assurance, and cost control.

Source: R. Schroeder, *Operations Management* (New York: McGraw-Hill Book Co., 1981): 12.

manufacturing operation transforms or converts inputs such as raw materials, labor, capital, machines, and facilities into finished goods. Service operations transform inputs into needed services. Roger Schroeder suggests that production/operations management comprises five functions or decision areas: process, capacity, inventory, work force, and quality (see Exhibit 5–2).

Production/operations activities often represent the largest part of an organization's human and capital assets. In most industries, the major costs of producing a product or service are incurred within operations, so production/operations can have great value as a competitive weapon in a company's overall strategy. Strengths and weaknesses in the five functions of production can mean the success or failure of an enterprise. For example, Goodyear's outstanding production facilities and procedures have resulted in its having a secure grip on one-third of the American tire business and nearly one-fifth of the world market.

There is much reason for concern that many organizations have not taken sufficient account of the capabilities and limitations of the production/operations function in formulating strategies. Scholars contend that this neglect has had unfavorable consequences on corporate performance in America. In Table 5–3, James Dilworth outlines several types of strategic decisions that a company might make and considers production/operations implications of those decisions. Production capabilities and policies can also greatly affect strategies:

> Given today's decision-making environment with shortages, inflation, technological booms, and government intervention, a company's production/operations capabilities and policies

TABLE 5–3 Impact of strategy elements on production management

Possible Elements of Strategy	*Concomitant Conditions That May Affect the Operations Function and Advantages and Disadvantages*
1. Compete as low-cost provider of goods or services	Discourages competition. Broadens market. Requires longer production runs and fewer product changes. Requires special-purpose equipment and facilities.
2. Compete as high-quality provider	Often possible to obtain more profit per unit, and perhaps more total profit from a smaller volume of sales. Requires more quality-assurance effort and higher operating cost. Requires more precise equipment, which is more expensive. Requires highly skilled workers, necessitating higher wages and greater training efforts.
3. Stress customer service	Requires broader development of service people and service parts and equipment. Requires rapid response to customer needs or changes in customer tastes, rapid and accurate information system, careful coordination. Requires a higher inventory investment.
4. Provide rapid and frequent introduction of new products	Requires versatile equipment and people. Has higher research and development costs. Has high retraining costs and high tooling and changeover in manufacturing. Provides lower volumes for each product and fewer opportunities for improvements due to the learning curve.
5. Strive for absolute growth	Requires accepting some projects or products with lower marginal value, which reduces ROI. Diverts talents to areas of weakness instead of concentrating on strengths.
6. Seek vertical integration	Enables company to control more of the process. May not have economies of scale at some stages of process. May require high capital investment as well as technology and skills beyond those currently available within the organization.
7. Maintain reserve capacity for flexibility	Provides ability to meet peak demands and quickly implement some contingency plans if forecasts are too low. Requires capital investment in idle capacity. Provides capability to grow during the lead time normally required for expansion.
8. Consolidate processing (Centralize)	Can result in economies of scale. Can locate near one major customer or supplier. Vulnerability: one strike, fire, or flood can halt the entire operation.
9. Disperse processing of service (Decentralize)	Can be near several market territories. Requires more complex coordination network: perhaps expensive data transmission and duplication of some personnel and equipment at each location. If each location produces one product in the line, then other products still must be transported to be available at all locations. If each location specializes in a type of component for all products, the company is vulnerable to strike, fire, flood, etc. If each location provides total product line, then economies of scale may not be realized.
10. Stress the use of mechanization, automation, robots	Requires high capital investment. Reduces flexibility. May affect labor relations. Makes maintenance more crucial.
11. Stress stability of employment	Serves the security needs of employees and may develop employee loyalty. Helps to attract and retain highly skilled employees. May require revisions of make-or-buy decisions, use of idle time, inventory, and subcontractors as demand fluctuates.

may not be able to fulfill the demands dictated by strategies. In fact, they may dictate corporate strategies. It is hard to imagine that an organization can formulate strategies today without first considering the constraints and limitations imposed by its existing production/operations structure.[14]

RESEARCH AND DEVELOPMENT

The fifth major area of internal operations that should be examined for specific strengths and weaknesses is research and development (R & D). Many firms today conduct no R & D, and yet many other companies depend on successful R & D activities for survival. Firms pursuing a product development strategy especially need to have a strong R & D orientation. Total R & D expenditures by American companies increased 7 percent in 1987 over 1986 (compared to a 8.1 percent increase in 1986). American companies spent an average of 3.4 percent of sales on R & D in 1987. Organizations invest in R&D because they believe that such investment will lead to superior product or services and give them competitive advantages. Research and development expenditures are directed at developing new products before competitors do, improving product quality, or improving manufacturing processes to reduce costs.[15]

When companies are acquired, R & D departments are often pared down or eliminated due to "redundancy." For example, when General Electric acquired RCA in June of 1986, it sold RCA's research laboratories to SRI International. The proliferation of mergers, acquisitions, and takeovers in the United States is one reason for forecasters' fears that total R & D spending in the United States is poised for a downturn. Other worrisome trends are burgeoning trade deficits, waning competitiveness, and the rapidly rising cost of R & D. Declines in R & D would hurt virtually all the generic types of strategies described in Chapter 2, especially product development.

The federal government is encouraging cooperative agreements between academic and industrial researchers. The National Science Foundation (NSF) recently established thirty-nine collaborative industry-university centers and thirteen Engineering Research Centers. By 1989, NSF plans to add twelve more Engineering Research Centers and ten Basic Science and Technology Centers at major universities.

Internal and External R & D

Cost distributions among R & D activities vary by company and industry, but total R & D costs generally do not exceed manufacturing and marketing start-up costs. Four approaches to determining R & D budget allocations are commonly used: (1) financing as many project proposals as possible, (2) using a percentage-of-sales method, (3) budgeting about the same amount that competitors spend for R & D, or (4) deciding how many successful new products are needed and working backwards to estimate the required R & D investment.

R & D in organizations can take two basic forms: (1) internal R & D where an organization operates its own R & D department, and/or (2) contract R & D where a firm hires independent researchers or independent agencies to develop specific products.

Many companies use both approaches to develop new products. For example, Grumman Corporation spent $167 million on R & D in 1986: $88 million externally and $79 million internally. A widely used approach for obtaining outside R & D assistance is to pursue a joint-venture with another firm. R & D strengths (capabilities) and weaknesses (limitations) play a major role in strategy formulation and strategy implementation.

Most firms have no choice but to continually develop new and improved products because of changing consumer needs and tastes, new technologies, shortened product life cycles, and increased domestic and foreign competition. A shortage of ideas for new products, increased global competition, increased market segmentation, strong special-interest groups, and increased government regulation are several factors making the successful development of new products more and more difficult, costly, and risky. In the pharmaceutical industry, for example, only one out of every ten thousand drugs created in the laboratory ends up on pharmacists' shelves. Campbell Soup Company received an award in 1988 for introducing 354 new products (more than any other company had introduced) during the preceding three years. Scarpello, Boulton, and Hofer emphasize that different generic strategies require different R & D capabilities:

> The focus of R & D efforts can vary greatly depending on a firm's competitive strategy. Some corporations attempt to be market leaders and innovators of new products, while others are satisfied to be market followers and developers of currently available products. The basic skills required to support these strategies will vary, depending on whether R & D becomes the driving force behind competitive strategy. In cases where new product introduction is the driving force for strategy, R & D activities must be extensive. The R & D unit must then be able to advance scientific and technological knowledge, exploit that knowledge, and manage the risks associated with ideas, products, services, and production requirements.[16]

INTERNAL-AUDIT CHECKLISTS

The checklists of questions provided in this section can be helpful in determining specific strengths and weaknesses in the functional areas of business. An answer of "no" to any one question could indicate a potential weakness although the strategic significance and implications of negative answers will of course vary by organization, industry, and severity of the weakness. Positive or "yes" answers to the checklist questions suggest potential areas of strength. The checklists provided in Exhibits 5–3 through 5–7 are not all inclusive, but they can facilitate internal-audit efforts.

EXHIBIT 5–3 A management audit checklist

Planning

1. Does the organization have clearly stated goals and objectives?
2. Does the organization have an overall strategy for competing in its basic industry?
3. Does the organization monitor and forecast relevant trends in the economic, political, social, and technological environments?

EXHIBIT 5–3 Continued

4. Does the organization monitor and anticipate competitors' actions and reactions in the marketplace?
5. Does the organization monitor and anticipate the needs of key customers, suppliers, distributors, creditors, shareholders, and employees?
6. Does the organization have an effective budgeting process?
7. Does the organization use a strategic-management approach to corporate decision making?
8. Does the organization have a written mission statement?
9. Does the organization have contingency plans?
10. Does the organization have synergy?
11. Does the organization allocate resources based on stated goals?
12. Does the organization have objectives, strategies, goals, and policies that are mutually consistent, supportive, and clearly communicated?

Organizing

1. Does the enterprise have a clear organizational structure as evidenced by a formal organizational chart?
2. Does the organizational chart reflect the most desirable structure for the firm?
3. Does the organizational chart exhibit acceptable spans of control?
4. Are similar activities appropriately grouped together in the organizational chart?
5. Are staff functions, such as personnel, shown appropriately in the organizational chart?
6. Is the unity of command principle adhered to in the organizational chart?
7. Do the organization's managers delegate authority well?
8. Does the organization have and use written job descriptions?
9. Does the organization have and use written job specifications?
10. Are the organization's jobs meaningful, rewarding, and challenging?

Motivating

1. Is employee morale high?
2. Is managerial morale high?
3. Is job satisfaction high?
4. Is a participative management style used?
5. Is creativity encouraged?
6. Are absenteeism rates in the organization low?
7. Are turnover rates in the organization low?
8. Have managers identified the number and composition of informal groups in the organization?
9. Are the norms of informal groups in the organization favorable to management?
10. Does a good system for two-way communication exist in the organization?
11. Are managers in the organization good leaders?
12. Does the organization have a good system of rewards and sanctions?

13. Does the organization and its employees adapt well to changes?
14. Are employees able to satisfy individual needs through the organization?
15. Are department policies reasonable and supportive of stated goals?

Staffing

1. Does the organization have a personnel manager or human resource department?
2. Does the organization hire employees only after careful recruiting, interviewing, testing, and selecting?
3. Does the organization provide employee training and management-development programs?
4. Does the organization provide reasonable employee benefits?
5. Does the organization have an effective performance evaluation system?
6. Does the organization have a good wage and salary administration system?
7. Does the organization have stated grievance procedures?
8. Does the organization have stated disciplinary policies?
9. Does the organization have a career planning system for its employees?
10. Does mutual trust and respect exist between line managers and personnel managers in the organization?
11. Are working conditions in the organization clean and safe?
12. Does the organization have equal employment opportunities?
13. Does the organization have an affirmative action program?
14. Does the organization promote employees from within?
15. Does the organization provide employee counseling?
16. Are union-management relations good in the organization?
17. Does the organization have a code of ethics?

Controlling

1. Does the organization have an effective financial control system?
2. Does it have an effective sales control system?
3. Does it have an effective inventory control system?
4. Does it have an effective expense control system?
5. Does it have an effective production control system?
6. Does it have an effective management control system?
7. Does it have an effective quality control system?
8. Does it have computer-assisted control systems?
9. Have productivity standards been established in all departments of the organization?
10. Does the organization regularly monitor favorable and unfavorable variances in the control process?
11. Are corrective actions taken promptly to improve unfavorable variances?
12. Are rewards and sanctions in the organization supportive of established control systems?
13. Is unethical behavior effectively controlled in the organization?
14. Are the organization's control systems prompt, accurate, and thorough?

EXHIBIT 5–4 A marketing audit checklist

A Marketing Systems Audit

1. Is the marketing intelligence system producing accurate, sufficient, and timely information about marketplace developments with respect to customers, prospects, distributors and dealers, competitors, suppliers, and various publics?
2. Are company decision makers asking for enough marketing research, and are they using the results?
3. Is the company employing the best methods for market and sales forecasting?
4. Is the marketing planning system well conceived and effective?
5. Is sales forecasting and market potential measurement soundly carried out?
6. Are sales quotas set on a proper basis?
7. Are the control procedures adequate to ensure that the annual goals are being achieved?
8. Does management periodically analyze the profitability of products, markets, territories, and channels of distribution?
9. Are marketing costs periodically examined?
10. Is the company well organized to gather, generate, and screen new-product ideas?
11. Does the company do adequate concept research and business analysis before investing in new ideas?
12. Does the company carry out adequate product and market testing before launching new products?

A Marketing Productivity Audit

1. What is the profitability of the company's different products, markets, territories, and channels of distribution?
2. Should the company enter, expand, contract, or withdraw from any business segments and what would be the short- and long-run profit consequences?
3. Do any marketing activities seem to have excessive costs? Can cost-reducing steps be taken?

A Marketing Function Audit

1. What are the product-line objectives? Are these objectives sound? Is the current product line meeting the objectives?
2. Should the product line be stretched or contracted upward, downward, or both ways?
3. Which products should be phased out? Which products should be added?
4. What is the buyers' knowledge and attitudes toward the company's and competitors' product quality, features, styling, brand names, etc.? What areas of product strategy need improvement?
5. What are the pricing objectives, policies, strategies, and procedures? To what extent are prices set on cost, demand, and competitive criteria?
6. Do the customers see the company's prices as being in line with the value of its offer?
7. What does management know about the price elasticity of demand, experience curve effects, and competitors' prices and pricing policies?

8. To what extent are price policies compatible with the needs of distributors and dealers, suppliers, and government regulation?
9. What are the distribution objectives and strategies?
10. Is there adequate market coverage and service?
11. How effective are the following channel members: distributors, dealers, manufacturers' representatives, brokers, agents, etc.?
12. Should the company consider changing its distribution channels?
13. What are the organization's advertising objectives? Are they sound?
14. Is the right amount being spent on advertising? How is the budget determined?
15. Are the ad themes and copy effective? What do customers and the public think about the advertising?
16. Are the advertising media well chosen?
17. Is the internal advertising staff adequate?
18. Is the sales promotion budget adequate? Is there effective and sufficient use of sales promotion tools such as samples, coupons, displays, sales contests?
19. Is the publicity budget adequate? Is the public relations staff competent and creative?
20. What are the organization's sales-force objectives?
21. Is the sales force large enough to accomplish the company's objectives?
22. Is the sales force organized along the proper principles of specialization (territory, market, product)? Are there enough (or too many) sales managers to guide the field sales representatives?
23. Does the sales-compensation level and structure provide adequate incentive and reward?
24. Does the sales force show high morale, ability, and effort?
25. Are the procedures adequate for setting quotas and evaluating performances?
26. How does the company's sales force compare to competitors' sales forces?

Source: Philip Kotler, *Marketing Management: Analysis, Planning and Control,* © 1984, pp. 767–70. Adapted by permission of Prentice-Hall, Inc., Englewood Cliffs, New Jersey.

EXHIBIT 5–5 A financial audit checklist

Liquidity

1. Have the firm's liquidity ratios been increasing over time?
2. Are the firm's liquidity ratios above industry averages?

Leverage

1. Have the firm's leverage ratios been increasing over time?
2. Are the firm's leverage ratios below industry averages?

Activity

1. Have the firm's activity ratios been moving favorably over time?
2. Do the firm's activity ratios compare favorably with industry averages?

EXHIBIT 5–5 Continued

Profitability

1. Have the firm's profitability ratios been increasing over time?
2. Are the firm's profitability ratios above industry averages?

Growth

1. Have the firm's growth ratios been increasing over time?
2. Are the firm's growth ratios above industry averages?

EXHIBIT 5–6 A production audit checklist

Process

1. Are facilities located effectively?
2. Are facilities designed effectively?
3. Should the organization be integrated backward or forward to a greater extent?
4. Are transportation costs for receiving and shipping excessive?
5. Is the process technology that is being used appropriate?
6. Is an effective and efficient flow or sequence of operations being used to convert inputs into outputs?
   - Line flow—characterized by a linear sequence of operations used to make the product or service; extremely efficient but also extremely inflexible. Examples are cafeterias and automobile assembly lines.
   - Intermittent flow—characterized by production in batches at intermittent intervals; equipment and labor are organized into work centers by similar types of skill or equipment. Examples are the flow operations used by fast-food restaurants and hospitals.
   - Project flow—characterized by a sequence of operations used to produce a unique product; no real product flow; used when there is a great need for creativity and uniqueness. Examples are developing a new product or building a ship.
7. Is the product or service being made to order, made to stock, or both? Is this activity most effective and efficient?
   - Made to order—processing activities are keyed to individual customer orders; process consists of customer placing an order, firm responding with a price and delivery date, and customer accepting or rejecting the offer. Delivery time and control of order flow are critical. Examples are a restaurant operation and painting a portrait.
   - Made to stock—process consists of producing a standardized product line; inventories are maintained to meet, say, a 95 percent service level of orders. Forecasting, inventory management, and capacity planning are critical. Examples are a furniture plant and oil refinery.

Capacity

1. Is overall demand for the product or service regularly and effectively forecasted?
2. Are appropriate economies of scale achieved?
3. Are factories, warehouses, and stores located effectively?

4. Are there an appropriate number of factories, warehouses, and stores?
5. Are factories, warehouses, and stores of an appropriate size?
6. Have aggregate planning costs been determined and minimized?
   - Hiring and firing costs
   - Overtime and undertime costs
   - Inventory-carrying costs
   - Subcontracting costs
   - Part-time labor costs
   - Cost of stockout or back order
7. Are loading, scheduling, and dispatching activities performed effectively?
8. Have strategies been developed for dealing with nonuniform demand?
9. Does the firm have an effective and efficient production control system?

Inventory

1. Have the costs of producing or buying needed inventories been examined?
2. Have inventory carrying costs been determined?
3. Have inventory ordering costs been determined?
4. Have purchasing, receiving, and shipping costs been determined?
5. Have stockout costs been determined?
6. Have service level versus inventory level considerations been examined?
7. Have appropriate production lot sizes been determined?
8. Does the firm have an effective inventory control system?
   - Single-bin system
   - Two-bin system
   - Card-file system
   - Computerized system
   - Economic Order Quantity (EOQ) system
   - Materials Requirements Planning (MRP) system
   - Order-point systems

Work Force

1. Have time and motion studies been completed on all operations-related jobs?
2. Have production jobs been designed effectively and efficiently?
3. Are production management employees competent, efficient, and motivated?
4. Are production standards clear, reasonable, and effective?
5. Have productivity rewards and sanctions been established?
6. Have reasonable and effective operations policies been established?
7. Are absenteeism and turnover rates low among production employees?
8. Is employee morale high among production employees?
9. Are the firm's operations managers effective leaders?

EXHIBIT 5–6 Continued

Quality

1. Does the organization have an effective and efficient quality control system?
2. Have the following quality control costs been determined and evaluated?
   - Prevention costs, such as the cost of training and development programs, and marketing studies to determine customers' quality needs and desires?
   - Appraisal costs, such as the cost of determining the quality of incoming raw materials, sampling procedures, finished goods inspections and tests, and operating laboratories?
   - Internal failure costs, such as the cost of scrap material, downtime, retesting, and inspections?
   - External failure costs, such as the cost of refunds, repairing products, replacing products, and settling customer complaints?

Source: R. Schroeder, *Operations Management* (New York: McGraw-Hill, 1981), 528

EXHIBIT 5–7 A research and development audit checklist

1. Has the organization examined the research and development practices in its basic industry?
2. Does the organization have the personnel needed to conduct successful research and development?
3. Does the organization have the facilities and equipment needed to conduct successful research and development?
4. Does the organization have the information flows and resources needed to conduct successful research and development?
5. Has the organization investigated the relative benefits of focusing R&D efforts on existing versus new products?
6. Has the organization examined the tradeoffs between developing new and improved products on the one hand, and developing new and improved production processes on the other?
7. Has the organization established a research and development department?
8. Does the organization allocate sufficient human and capital resources to conduct successful research and development?
9. Does the organization capitalize on available sources of new product ideas?
10. Is the organization prepared to take the risk of instituting long periods of research without discovering ideas that have commercial value?
11. Is the organization prepared to take the risk of financing long periods of product development and testing without eventual successful marketing of the product?
12. Does the organization have, or can it obtain, needed capital to exploit discoveries if and when they are made?
13. Has the organization examined the potential benefits of using outside agencies or individuals to conduct basic and applied research for the firm?
14. Has the organization established clear research and development goals and policies?

15. Does the organization understand the research and development strategies of its major competitors?
16. Has the organization considered joint ventures in research and development?
17. Is the organization knowledgeable about domestic and foreign licenses, royalty fees, patents, trademarks, and other regulatory concerns applicable to research and development activities in its basic industry?
18. Does the organization have an overall research and development strategy?

DIMENSIONS OF ORGANIZATIONAL CULTURE

Dimensions of organizational culture permeate all the functional areas of business. It is something of an art to uncover the basic values and beliefs that are buried deeply in an organization's rich collection of stories, language, heroes, and rituals, but cultural products can represent important strengths and weaknesses. Culture is an aspect of organizations that can no longer be taken for granted in performing an internal strategic-management audit, because culture and strategy must work together.

The strategic-management process takes place largely within a particular organization's culture. Lorsch found that executives in successful companies are emotionally committed to the firm's culture, but he concluded that culture can inhibit strategic management in two basic ways.[17] First, managers frequently miss the significance of changing external conditions because they are blinded by strongly held beliefs. Second, when a particular culture has been effective in the past, the natural response is to stick with it in the future, even during times of major strategic change. An organizations's culture must support the collective commitment of its people to a common purpose. It must foster competence and enthusiasm among managers and employees.

Successful strategic management requires a well coordinated sequence of actions, which aim, in a conscious way, to reorient and restructure an organization's culture. For this reason, a clear understanding of supportive and nonsupportive dimensions of an organization's culture is important internal information for strategists. Some tension between culture and a firm's strategy is inevitable, but the tension should be monitored so that it does not reach a point where relationships are severed and the culture becomes antagonistic. The resulting disarray among members of the organization would disrupt strategy formulation, implementation, and evaluation.

THE INTERNAL FACTOR EVALUATION (IFE) MATRIX

The final step in conducting an internal strategic-management audit is to construct an *IFE Matrix*. This strategy-formulation tool summarizes and evaluates the major strengths and weaknesses in the functional areas of a business, and it also provides a basis for identifying and evaluating relationships among those areas. Intuitive judgments are required in developing an IFE Matrix, so the appearance of a scientific approach should not be interpreted to mean this is an all-powerful technique. Analogous to the EFE Matrix described in Chapter Four, an IFE Matrix can be developed in five steps:

1. Identify the organization's key strengths and weaknesses.
2. Assign a weight that ranges from 0.0 (not important) to 1.0 (all-important) to

each factor. The weight indicates the relative importance of each factor to being successful in a given industry. Regardless of whether a key factor is an internal strength or weakness, factors considered to have the greatest impact on performance should be assigned highest weights. The summation of all weights assigned to the factors must total 1.0.

3. Assign a 1 to 4 rating to each factor to indicate whether that variable represents a major weakness (rating = 1), a minor weakness (rating = 2), a minor strength (rating = 3), or a major strength (rating = 4).
4. Multiply each factor's weight by its rating to determine a weighted score for each variable.
5. Sum the weighted scores for each variable to determine the total weighted score for the organization.

Regardless of how many factors are included in an IFE Matrix, the total weighted score can range from a low of 1.0 to a high of 4.0, with the average score being 2.5. Total weighted scores well below 2.5 characterize organizations that are weak internally, whereas scores significantly above 2.5 indicate a strong internal position. Like the EFE Matrix, an IFE Matrix should include from ten to fifteen key factors. The number of factors has no effect upon the range of total weighted scores because the weights always sum to 1.0.

An example of an IFE Matrix is provided in Table 5–4. Note that the firm's major weakness is the absence of an organizational structure, as indicated by a rating of 1, whereas the firm's major strength is product quality, which received a rating of 4. Organizational structure and employee morale have the greatest impact on organizational performance as indicated by assigned weights of .30 and .22 respectively. The total weighted score of 2.31 indicates that the firm is just below average in its overall internal strategic position. Table 5–5 shows an IFE Matrix for Chrysler. Chrysler's revenues increased 16 percent in 1987, but net profits declined 8 percent. Chrysler's chief

TABLE 5–4 A sample Internal Factor Evaluation Matrix

Key Internal Factor	*Weight*	*Rating*	*Weighted Score*
Employee morale is low.	0.22	2	0.44
Product quality is excellent.	0.18	4	0.72
Profit margins exceed industry average.	0.10	3	0.30
Excess working capital is available.	0.15	3	0.45
No organizational structure exists.	0.30	1	0.30
No research and development staff is employed.	0.05	2	0.10
Total	1.00		2.31

Note: 1) For simplicity, this sample IFE Matrix has only six key factors. At least ten factors should be included in an IFE matrix.

2) The total weighted score of 2.31 is below the average of 2.50.

TABLE 5–5 An IFE Matrix for Chrysler

Key Internal Factor	*Weight*	*Rating*	*Weighted Score*
1. Chrysler's breakeven point has been reduced from 2.4 million to 1.5 million vehicles.	.15	3	0.45
2. Chrysler's vehicle quality has increased 35 percent.	.10	3	0.30
3. Chrysler's productivity has increased from 10 to 20 vehicles annually per employee.	.10	3	0.30
4. Chrysler's management has undergone a massive reorganization.	.15	3	0.45
5. Chrysler's 7/70,000 warranty is the best in the industry.	.10	4	0.40
6. Chrysler has increased its R & D expenditures to $7.5 billion.	.15	3	0.45
7. The AMC acquisition has increased Chrysler's debt/equity ratio to 60 percent.	.10	1	0.10
8. The AMC acquisition has expanded Chrysler's product line.	.05	3	0.15
9. Chrysler has cut its white-collar workers from 40,000 to 20,000.	.05	3	0.15
10. Chrysler's costs have been cut by $1200 per vehicle.	.05	3	0.15
Total	1.00		2.90

Note: The total weighted score of 2.90 indicates that Chrysler is above average in its internal position.

executive officer, Lee Iacocca, was the second highest paid business executive in 1987. His 1987 compensation was $17.9 million. Note that Chrysler has a total weighted score of 2.90.

In multidivisional firms, each autonomous division or strategic business unit should construct an IFE Matrix. Divisional matrices can then be integrated to develop an overall corporate IFE Matrix. The IFE Matrix, Competitive Profile Matrix, EFE Matrix, and a clear statement of mission provide the basic information needed to formulate competitive strategies successfully.

CONCLUSION

The notion that periodic audits of a firm's internal operations are vital to organizational health continues to be discussed in boardrooms across America. Many companies still prefer to be judged solely on their bottom-line performance. However, an ever-increasing number of successful organizations are using the internal audit to gain competitive advantages over rival firms. Systematic methodologies for performing strength-weakness assessments are not well developed in the strategic-management literature, but it is clear that managers must identify and evaluate important internal factors to formulate and choose among alternative strategies effectively.

KEY TERMS AND CONCEPTS

Buying
Capital budgeting
Controlling
Cost/benefit analysis
Customer analysis
Distribution
Dividend decision
Financial ratio analysis
Financing decision
Functions of finance/accounting
Functions of management
Functions of marketing
Functions of production/operations
Human resource management
Internal audit
Internal Factor Evaluation (IFE) Matrix
Investment decision
Marketing research
Motivating
Opportunity analysis
Organizing
Personnel Management
Planning
Pricing
Social responsibility
Staffing
Synergy
Test marketing

ISSUES FOR REVIEW AND DISCUSSION

1. Explain why determining the relative importance of strengths and weaknesses to include in an IFE Matrix can require substantial negotiation among managers.
2. How can delegation of authority contribute to effective strategic management?
3. Diagram a formal organizational chart that reflects the following positions: a president, two executive officers, four middle managers and eighteen lower-level managers. Now, diagram three overlapping and hypothetical informal group structures. How can this in-

formation be helpful to a strategist in formulating and implementing strategy?

4. How could a strategist's attitude towards social responsibility affect a firm's strategy? What is your attitude towards social responsibility? Plot your attitude on a scale of one to ten, with one indicating a position like Ralph Nader's and ten indicating a position like John Galbraith's.
5. Which of the three basic functions of finance/accounting do you feel is most important in a small electronics manufacturing concern? Justify your position.
6. Do you think aggregate R & D expenditures for American firms will increase or decrease next year? Why?
7. Explain how you would motivate managers to implement a major new strategy.
8. Why do you think production/operations managers are often not directly involved in strategy-formulation activities? Why can this be a major organizational weakness?
9. Give two examples of staffing strengths and two examples of staffing weaknesses of an organization with which you are familiar.
10. Would you ever pay out dividends when your firm's annual net profit is negative? Why? What effect could this have on a firm's strategies?
11. If a firm has zero debt in its capital structure, is that always an organizational strength? Why or why not?
12. Describe the production/operations system in a police department.
13. After conducting an internal audit, a firm discovers a total of one hundred strengths and one hundred weaknesses. What procedures could then be used to determine the most important of these? Why is it important to reduce the total number of key factors?
14. Select one of the suggested readings at the end of this chapter. Look that article up in your college library. Give a five minute oral report to the class summarizing the article and your views on the topic.

NOTES

1. William King, "Integrating Strength-Weakness Analysis into Strategic Planning," *Journal of Business Research* 11, no. 4 (1983): 481. Copyright 1983 by Elsevier Science Publishing Co., Inc. Reprinted by permission.
2. Igor Ansoff, "Strategic Management of Technology," *Journal of Business Strategy* 7, no. 3 (Winter 1987): 38.
3. Claude George, Jr., *The History of Management Thought,* 2nd ed. (Englewood Cliffs, N. J.: Prentice-Hall, 1972), 174.
4. "Changing a Corporate Culture," *Business Week* (14 May 1984): 130, 131.
5. Peter Drucker, *Management Tasks, Responsibilities, and Practice* (New York: Harper & Row, 1973), 463.
6. Ibid., 487.
7. "The New Shape of Banking," *Business Week* (18 June 1984): 108.
8. Robert Waterman, Jr. "The Renewal Factor," *Business Week* (14 September 1987): 104.
9. J. Evans and B. Berman, *Marketing* (New York: Macmillan, 1982), 17.
10. "The Business Week Top 1000," *Business Week* (15 April 1988): 174.
11. Quoted in Robert Waterman, Jr., "The Renewal Factor," *Business Week* (14 September 1987): 108.
12. James Chrisman and Archie Carroll, "Corporate Responsibility—Reconciling Economic and Social Goals," *Sloan Management Review* 25, no. 2 (Winter 1984): 61. Also, P. Arlow and M. Gannon, "Social Responsiveness, Corporate Structure, and Economic Performance," *Academy of Management Review* 7, no. 2 (April 1982): 239.
13. J. V. Horne, *Financial Management and Policy* (Englewood Cliffs, N. J.: Prentice-Hall, 1974), 10.

14. W. Boulton and B. Saladin, "Let's Make Production-Operations Management Top Priority for Strategic Planning in the 1980s," *Managerial Planning* 32, no. 1 (July–August 1983): 19.

15. Vida Scarpello, William Boulton, and Charles Hofer, "Reintegrating R & D into Business Strategy," *Journal of Business Strategy* 6, no. 4 (Spring 1986): 50.

16. Ibid., 50, 51.

17. John Lorsch, "Managing Culture: The Invisible Barrier to Strategic Change," *California Management Review* 28, 2 (1986): 95–109.

SUGGESTED READINGS

Burack, E. H. "Linking Corporate Business and Human Resource Planning: Strategic Issues and Concerns." *Human Resource Planning* 8, no. 3 (1985): 133–145.

Collier, D. W. "How Management Should Use R & D to Set New Directions." *Journal of Business Strategy* 7, no. 2 (Fall 1986): 75–78.

Cook, D. S., and Ferris, G. R. "Strategic Human Resource Management and Firm Effectiveness in Industries Experiencing Decline." *Human Resource Management* 25, no. 3 (Fall 1986): 441–457.

Cravens, D. W. "Strategic Forces Affecting Marketing Strategy." *Business Horizons* 29, no. 5 (September–October 1986): 77–86.

Drucker, P. F. "Keeping U.S. Companies Productive." *Journal of Business Strategy* 7, no. 3 (Winter 1987): 12–15.

Fox, H. W. "Financial ABCs of Test-Marketing." *Business Horizons* 29, no. 5 (September–October 1986): 63–70.

Gordon, I. "Exit Marketing Concept—Enter Competitive Concept." *Business Quarterly* 51, no. 2 (Summer 1986): 28–32.

Ireland, R. D.; Hitt, M. A.; Bettis, R. A.; and de Porras, D. A. "Strategy Formulation Processes: Differences in Perceptions of Strength and Weaknesses Indicators and Environmental Uncertainty by Managerial Level." *Strategic Management Journal* 8, no. 5 (September–October 1987): 469–486.

Johnson, A. "MRP? MRPH? OPT? CIM? FMS? JIT? Is Any System Letter-Perfect?" *Management Review* 75 (September 1986): 22–27.

Kaplan, R. S. "Yesterday's Accounting Undermines Production." *Harvard Business Review* 62, no. 4 (July–August 1984): 95–101.

Kogut, B. "Designing Global Strategies: Profiting From Operational Flexibility." *Sloan Management Review* 27, no. 1 (Fall 1985): 27–38.

Lenz, R. T., and Lyles, M. A. "Managing Human Problems in Strategic Planning Systems," *Journal of Business Strategy* 60, no. 4 (Spring 1986): 57–66.

Meredith, J. R. "The Strategic Advantages of the Factory of the Future." *California Management Review* 29, no. 3 (Spring 1987): 27–41.

Miller, D. "Configuration of Strategy and Structure: Towards a Synthesis." *Strategic Management Journal* 7, no. 3 (1986): 233–249.

"Understanding the R & D Culture." *Management Review* 75 (December 1986): 34–39.

Miller, E. L.; Beechler, S.; Bhatt, B.; and Nath, R. "The Relationship Between the Global Strategic Planning Process and the Human Resource Management Function." *Human Resource Planning* 9, no. 1 (May–June 1986): 9–23.

Nielsen, Richard P. "Cooperative Strategy in Marketing." *Business Horizons* 30, no. 4 (July–August 1987): 61–68.

Peters, Thomas P. *Thriving on Chaos*. New York: Knopf, 1987.

Power, D. "Linking R & D to Corporate Strategy." *Management Review* 75 (December 1986): 28–33.

Ramanujam, V., and Venkatraman, N. "Planning System Characteristics and Planning Effectiveness." *Strategic Management Journal* 8, no. 5 (September–October 1987): 453–468.

Sandberg, C. M.; Lewellen, W. G.; and Stanley, K. L. "Financial Strategy: Planning and Managing the Corporate Leverage Position." *Strategic Management Journal* 8, no.1 (January–February 1987): 15–24.

Scarpello, V.; Boulton, W. R.; and Hofer, C. W. "Reintegrating R & D into Business Strategy." *Journal of Business Strategy* 7, no. 4 (Winter 1987): 49–56.

Scholz, Christian. "Corporate Culture and Strategy—The Problem of Strategic Fit." *Long Range Planning* 20, no. 4 (August 1987): 78–87.

Waterman, Robert, Jr. "The Renewal Factor." *Business Week* (14 September 1987): 98–120.

Weidenbaum, M. L. "Learning to Compete." *Business Horizons* 29, no. 5 (September–October 1986): 2–12.

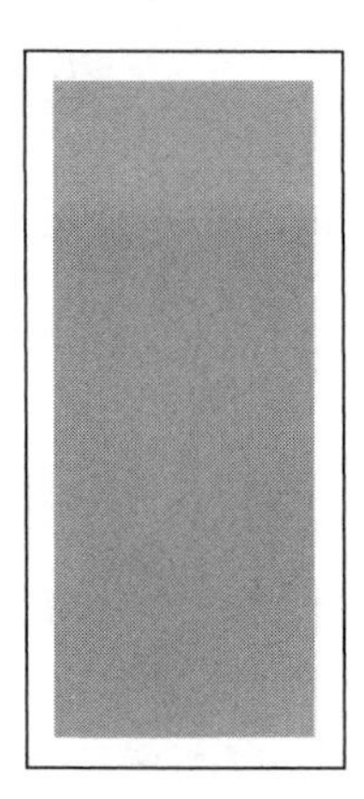

EXPERIENTIAL EXERCISES

EXPERIENTIAL EXERCISE 5A

Performing a Financial Ratio Analysis for Ponderosa

PURPOSE

Financial ratio analysis is one of the best techniques for identifying and evaluating internal strengths and weaknesses. Stock brokerage firms and potential investors look closely at firms' financial ratios, making detailed comparisons to industry averages and to previous periods of time. Financial ratio analyses represent vital input information for developing an IFE Matrix.

YOUR TASK

Step 1 On a separate sheet of paper, number from 1 to 20. Referring to Ponderosa's Income Statement and Balance Sheet (pp. 33–51), calculate twenty 1985, 1986, and 1987 financial ratios for the company. Use Table 5–2 as a reference. Record your values in three columns, 1985, 1986, and 1987.

Step 2 Go to your college library and find industry average financial ratios for the restaurant industry. Record the industry average values in a fourth column on your paper.

Step 3 In a fifth column, indicate whether you consider each ratio to be a strength, a weakness, or a neutral factor for Ponderosa.

EXPERIENTIAL EXERCISE 5B

Constructing an IFE Matrix for Ponderosa

PURPOSE

This exercise will give you experience developing an IFE Matrix. This strategic-management tool is designed to be completed with several other students in class because strategy formulation is a group-oriented process in organizations. Identifying and prioritizing factors to include in an IFE Matrix creates good discussion among functional and divisional managers.

YOUR TASK

Step 1 Working alone, develop an IFE Matrix for Ponderosa.

Step 2 Join with two other individuals to form a three-person team. Examine each other's IFE Matrices for Ponderosa.

Step 3 Develop a team IFE Matrix for Ponderosa.

Step 4 Compare your individual IFE Matrix and your team's IFE Matrix to the author's IFE Matrix presented by your professor. Was your total weighted score closer to the author's score, or was your team's total weighted score closest? Discuss any major differences.

Step 5 What strategies do you think would allow Ponderosa to capitalize on its major strengths? What strategies would allow Ponderosa to improve upon its major weaknesses?

Strategy Analysis and Choice

NOTABLE QUOTES

Objectives are not commands; they are commitments. They do not determine the future; they are the means to mobilize resources and energies of an organization for the making of the future.

Peter Drucker

Life is full of lousy options.

General P. X. Kelley

When a crisis forces choosing among alternatives, most people will choose the worst possible one.

Rudin's Law

Strategy isn't something you can nail together in slap-dash fashion by sitting around a conference table.

Terry Haller

A firm that continues to employ a previously successful strategy eventually and inevitably falls victim to a competitor.

William Cohen

Planning is often doomed before it ever starts, either because too much is expected of it or because not enough is put into it.

T. J. Cartwright

To acquire or not to acquire, that is the question.

Robert J. Terry

There are few things that distinguish competent from incompetent strategists as sharply as performance in balancing objectives. There is no formula for doing the job. Each business requires its own balance—and it may require a different balance at different times.

Peter Drucker

6

OUTLINE

OBJECTIVES

After studying this chapter, you should be able to:

- Describe a practical three-stage framework for generating and choosing among alternative strategies.
- Explain how to develop a TOWS Matrix, a SPACE Matrix, a BCG Matrix, an IE Matrix, and a QSPM.
- Identify important behavioral, cultural, political, ethical, and social responsibility considerations in strategy analysis and choice.
- Discuss the role of intuition in strategic analysis and choice.
- Discuss the appropriate role of a board of directors in choosing among alternative strategies.

Strategic analysis and choice largely involves making subjective decisions based on objective information. This chapter introduces important concepts that can help strategists generate feasible alternatives, evaluating those alternatives, and choose a specific course of action. Behavioral aspects of strategy formulation are described, including politics, culture, ethics, and social responsibility considerations. Modern tools for formulating strategies are described and the appropriate role of a board of directors is discussed.

LONG-TERM OBJECTIVES

As indicated by the shaded portion of Figure 6–1, this chapter focuses on establishing long-term objectives, generating alternative strategies, and selecting strategies to pursue. Long-term objectives represent the results expected from pursuing certain strategies. Strategies represent the actions to be taken to accomplish these long-term objectives. The time frame for objectives and strategies should be consistent, usually from two to five years.

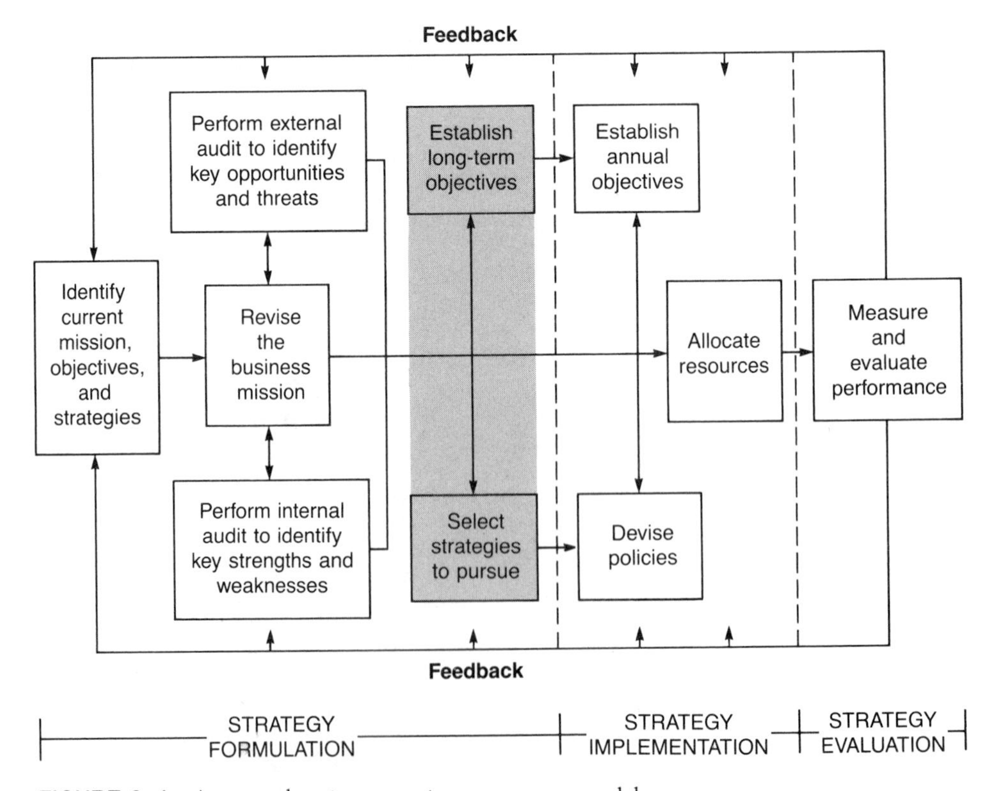

FIGURE 6–1 A comprehensive strategic-management model

An increasing number of successful strategists recognize that establishing long-term objectives and strategies must be a give and take process. In practice, organizations generally establish objectives and strategies concurrently. Therefore, the strategic-management model reveals with multidirectional arrows a symbiotic relationship between establishing objectives and establishing strategies. Objectives become crystallized as feasible strategies are formulated and selected.

The Nature of Long-term Objectives

Objectives should be quantitative, measurable, realistic, understandable, challenging, hierarchical, obtainable, and congruent among organizational units. Each objective should also be associated with a timeline. Objectives are commonly stated in terms such as growth in assets, growth in sales, profitability, market share, degree and nature of diversification, degree and nature of vertical integration, earnings per share, and social responsibility. Clearly established objectives offer many benefits. They provide direction, allow synergy, aid in evaluation, establish priorities, reduce uncertainty, minimize conflicts, stimulate exertion, and aid in both the allocation of resources and the design of jobs.

Long-term objectives are needed at the corporate, divisional, and functional levels in an organization. They are an important measure of managerial performance. Many practitioners and academicians attribute a significant part of American industry's competitive decline to the short-term, rather than long-term, strategy orientation of American managers. Arthur D. Little argues that bonuses or merit pay for managers today must be based to a greater extent on long-term objectives and strategies. A general framework for relating objectives to performance evaluation is provided in Table 6–1; a particular organization could tailor these guidelines to meet its own needs. In any case, incentives should be attached to both long-term and annual objectives.

Clearly stated and communicated objectives are vital to success for many reasons. First, objectives help stakeholders understand their role in an organization's future. Objectives also provide a basis for consistent decision making by managers whose values and attitudes differ; by reaching a consensus on objectives during strategy-formulation activities, an organization can minimize potential conflicts later during implementation.

TABLE 6–1 Varying performance measures by organizational level

Organization Level	*Basis for Annual Bonus or Merit Pay*
Corporate	75% based on long-term objectives 25% based on annual objectives
Divisional	50% based on objectives 50% based on goals
Functional	25% based on objectives 75% based on goals

Objectives set forth organizational priorities and stimulate exertion and accomplishment. They serve as standards by which individuals, groups, departments, divisions, and entire organizations can be evaluated. Objectives provide the basis for designing jobs and organizing activities to be performed in an organization. Objectives provide direction and allow for organizational synergy. Without long-term objectives, an organization would drift aimlessly towards some unknown end!

Apple Computer's long-term objective for the Macintosh computer is to achieve 18 percent of the business market by 1990 and to obtain overall company revenues of more than $5 billion by the mid-1990s. "We want to be the third center of gravity in computers, along with IBM and DEC," says Apple's chairman John Sculley. Macintosh's market share of the business market was 7 percent in 1986 and 9 percent in 1987. Apple Computer's revenues increased 50 percent in 1987 to $3.0 billion, while company profits increased 80 percent to $280 million.

Managing by Objectives

Wal-Mart is one firm that has clearly established long-term objectives. Sam Walton, CEO of Wal-Mart (and possibly the richest person in America), expects his firm's revenues to increase from $15.9 billion in 1987 to $33 billion in 1990. His long-term objective is to double the number of Wal-Mart Stores by 1992, from 1,023 in 1987 to 2,046. Wal-Mart's revenues increased 34 percent in 1987, and profits increased 39 percent.

An unknown educator once said, "If you think education is expensive, try ignorance." The idea behind this saying also applies to establishing objectives. Strategists should avoid these alternatives to managing by objectives:

- ☐ Managing by Extrapolation—adheres to the principle "If it ain't broke, don't fix it." The idea is to keep on doing about the same things in the same ways, because things are going well.
- ☐ Managing by Crisis—based on the belief that the true measure of a really good strategist is her ability to solve problems. Since there are plenty of crises and problems to go around for every person and every organization, strategists ought to bring their time and creative energy to bear on solving the most pressing problems of the day. Managing by crisis is actually a form of reacting rather than acting and of letting events dictate the whats and whens of management decisions.
- ☐ Managing by Subjectives—built on the idea that there is no general plan for which way to go and what to do, just do the best you can to accomplish what you think should be done. In short, "do your own thing, the best way you know how," (sometimes referred to as "the mystery approach to decision making" because subordinates are left to figure out what is happening and why).
- ☐ Managing by Hope—based on the fact that the future is laden with great uncertainty and that if we try and do not succeed, then we hope our second (or third) attempt will succeed. Decisions are predicated on the hope that they will work and that good times are just around the corner, especially if luck and good fortune are on our side.[1]

A COMPREHENSIVE STRATEGY-FORMULATION FRAMEWORK

Important strategy-formulation techniques can be integrated into a three-stage decision-making framework, as shown in Figure 6–2. The tools presented in the framework are applicable to all sizes and types of organizations and can help strategists identify, evaluate, and select strategies.

Stage 1 of the formulation framework consists of the Competitive Profile Matrix, EFE Matrix, and the IFE Matrix. Stage 1 is called the *Input Stage* because the three tools summarize the basic input information needed for Stage 2 analyses. Stage 2, the *Matching Stage,* focuses upon generating feasible alternative strategies by aligning key external and internal factors. Stage 2 techniques include the Threats-Opportunities-Weaknesses-Strengths (TOWS) Matrix, the Strategic Position and Action Evaluation (SPACE) Matrix, the Boston Consulting Group (BCG) Matrix, the Internal-External (IE) Matrix, and the Grand Strategy Matrix. Stage 3, the *Decision Stage,* involves a single technique, the Quantitative Strategic Planning Matrix (QSPM). QSPM uses input information derived from Stage 1 to objectively evaluate feasible alternative strategies identified in Stage 2; it reveals the relative attractiveness of alternative strategies and thus provides an objective basis for selecting specific strategies. All nine techniques included in the strategy-formulation framework require integration of intuition and analysis. Autonomous divisions in an organization commonly use strategy-formulation techniques to develop strategies and objectives. Divisional analyses provide a basis for identifying, evaluating, and selecting among alternative corporate-level strategies.

Modern strategy-formulation tools presented in this chapter can be invaluable in helping strategists assimilate and evaluate information, but strategists themselves, not analytical tools, are always responsible and accountable for strategic decisions. In a recent article, Lenz emphasizes that the shift from a words-oriented to a numbers-oriented planning process can give rise to a false sense of certainty; it can reduce dialogue, discussion, and argument as a means to explore understandings, test assumptions, and foster organizational learning.[2] Strategists must be conscious of this possibility and use analytical tools to facilitate (rather than diminish) communication. Without objective information, biases, politics, and *halo error* (the tendency to put too much weight on a single factor) tend to play a dominant role in the strategy-formulation process.

THE INPUT STAGE

Procedures for developing an IFE Matrix, a Competitive Profile Matrix, and a EFE Matrix were presented in the previous two chapters. These tools require strategists to quantify subjectivity during early stages of the strategy-formulation process. Making "small" decisions in the input matrices regarding the relative importance of internal and external factors allow strategists to make final strategy decisions more effectively. Good intuitive judgment is always needed in determining appropriate weights and ratings.

Sometimes a key internal factor can be both a strength and a weakness; a key external factor can be both an opportunity and a threat. When this is so, the factor should be included twice in the appropriate matrix and a weight and rating should be

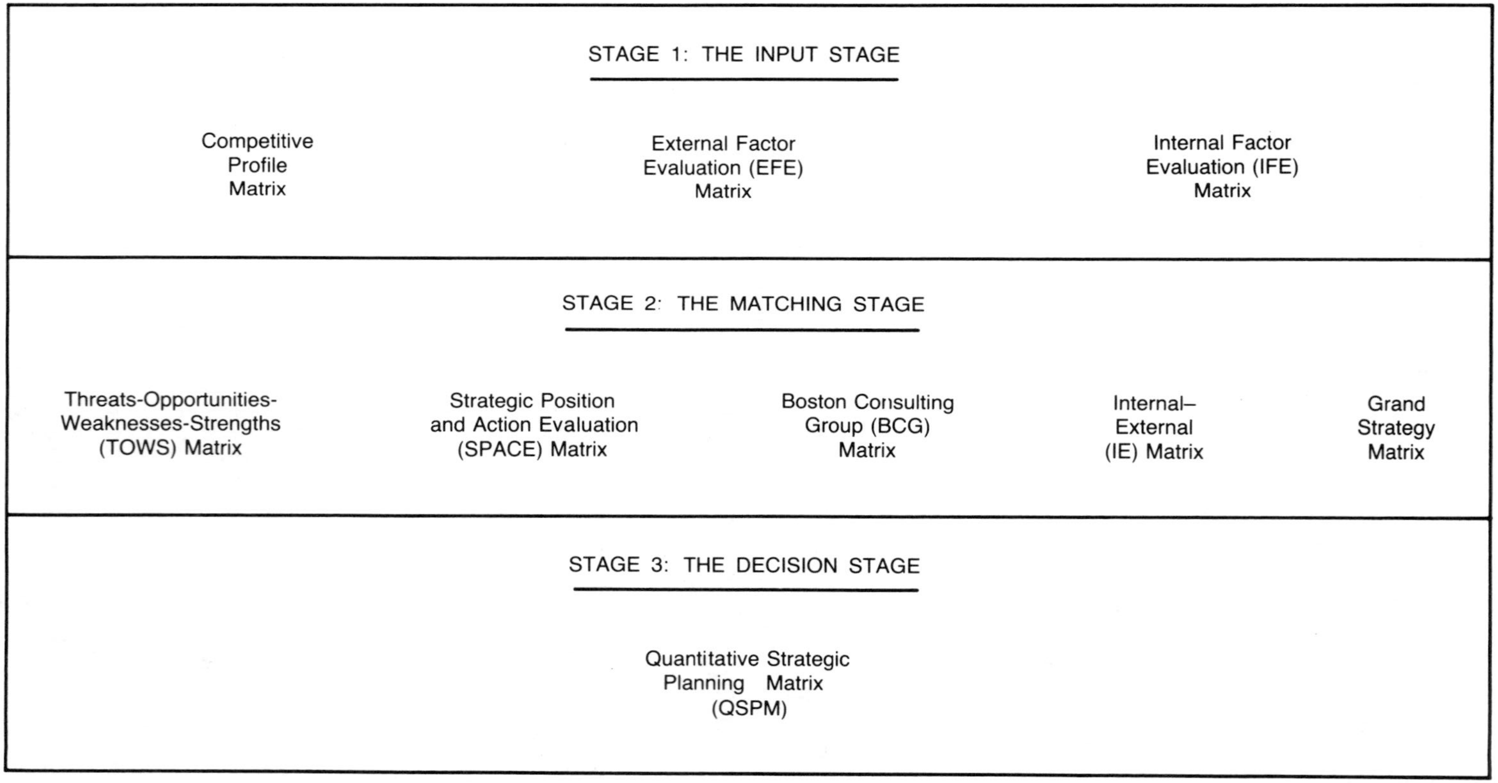

STAGE 1: THE INPUT STAGE

Competitive Profile Matrix

External Factor Evaluation (EFE) Matrix

Internal Factor Evaluation (IFE) Matrix

STAGE 2: THE MATCHING STAGE

Threats-Opportunities-Weaknesses-Strengths (TOWS) Matrix

Strategic Position and Action Evaluation (SPACE) Matrix

Boston Consulting Group (BCG) Matrix

Internal–External (IE) Matrix

Grand Strategy Matrix

STAGE 3: THE DECISION STAGE

Quantitative Strategic Planning Matrix (QSPM)

FIGURE 6–2 The strategy-formulation analytical framework

assigned to each statement. For example, the Playboy logo both helps and hurts Playboy Enterprises: the logo attracts customers to Playboy casinos, clubs, and the magazine, but it also keeps the Playboy cable channel out of many markets.

THE MATCHING STAGE

The matching stage of the strategy-formulation framework consists of five techniques that can be used in any sequence: the TOWS Matrix, the SPACE Matrix, the BCG Matrix, the IE Matrix, and the Grand Strategy Matrix. These tools rely upon input information derived from Stage 1 (the Competitive Profile Matrix, EFE Matrix, and IFE Matrix) to match internal strengths or weaknesses with external opportunities or threats. Matching internal and external factors is the key to effectively generating feasible alternative strategies! For example, a firm with excess working capital (an internal strength) could take advantage of the aerospace industry growing 40 percent annually (an external opportunity) by acquiring a firm in the aerospace industry. This example portrays simple one-to-one matching. In most situations, internal and external relationships are more complex and the matching process requires multiple alignments for each strategy generated. The basic concept of matching is exemplified in Table 6–2.

Any organization, whether military, product-oriented, service-oriented, governmental, or even athletic, must develop and execute good strategies to win. A good offense without a good defense, or vice versa, usually leads to defeat. Every organization has some internal strengths and weaknesses and external opportunities and threats that can be aligned to formulate feasible alternative strategies.

The Threats-Opportunities-Weaknesses-Strengths (TOWS) Matrix

The Threats-Opportunities-Weaknesses-Strengths *(TOWS) Matrix* is an important matching tool that helps managers develop four types of strategies: SO Strategies, WO Strategies, ST Strategies, and WT Strategies.[3] Matching key external and internal fac-

TABLE 6–2 Matching key internal and external factors to formulate alternative strategies

Key Internal Factor		*Key External Factor*		*Resultant Strategy*
Excess working capital (an internal strength)	+	40% annual growth of the aerospace industry (an external opportunity)	=	Acquire Aerospace, Inc.
Insufficient capacity (an internal weakness)	+	Exit of two major foreign competitors from the industry (an external opportunity)	=	Pursue horizontal integration by buying competitors' facilities
Strong R&D expertise (an internal strength)	+	Decreasing numbers of young adults (an external threat)	=	Develop new products for older adults
Poor employee morale (an internal weakness)	+	Strong union activity (an external threat)	=	Develop a new employee-benefits package

tors is the most difficult part of developing a TOWS Matrix and requires good judgment; and there is no one best set of matches. Note in Table 6–2 that the first, second, third, and fourth strategies are SO, WO, ST, and WT strategies respectively.

SO Strategies use a firm's internal strengths to take advantage of external opportunities. All managers would like their organizations to be in a position where internal strengths can be used to take advantage of trends and events in the environment. For example, Mercedes Benz, with its technical know-how and reputation for quality (internal strengths), could take advantage of the increasing demand for luxury cars (external opportunity) by building a new manufacturing plant (SO Strategy). Organizations generally will pursue WO, ST, or WT Strategies in order to get into a situation where they can apply SO Strategies. When a firm has major weaknesses, it will strive to overcome them, making them strengths. When an organization faces major threats, it will seek to avoid them in order to concentrate on opportunities.

WO Strategies aim at improving internal weaknesses by taking advantage of external opportunities. Sometimes key external opportunities exist, but a firm has internal weaknesses that prevent it from exploiting those opportunities. For example, there may be a high demand for electronic devices to control the amount and timing of fuel injection in automobile engines (opportunity), but a certain auto parts manufacturer may lack the technology required for producing these devices (weakness). One possible WO Strategy would be to acquire this technology by forming a joint venture with a firm having competency in this area. An alternative WO Strategy would be to hire and train people with the required technical capabilities.

ST Strategies use a firm's strengths to avoid or reduce the impact of external threats. This does not mean that a strong organization should always meet threats in the external environment head-on. General Motors found this out in the 1960s when Ralph Nader (an external threat) exposed safety hazards of the Corvair automobile. GM used its strength (size and influence) to ridicule Nader and the direct confrontation caused more problems than expected. In retrospect, this ST Strategy was probably inappropriate for GM at the time.

WT Strategies are defensive tactics directed at reducing internal weaknesses and avoiding environmental threats. An organization faced with numerous external threats and internal weaknesses may indeed be in a precarious position. In fact, such a firm may have to fight for its survival, merge, retrench, declare bankruptcy, or choose liquidation.

A schematic representation of the TOWS Matrix is provided in Figure 6–3. Note that a TOWS Matrix is composed of nine cells. As shown, there are four key factor cells, four strategy cells, and one cell that is always left blank (the upper left cell). The four strategy cells, labeled SO, WO, ST, and WT, are developed after completing the four key factor cells, labeled S, W, O, and T. There are eight steps involved in constructing a TOWS Matrix:

1. List the firm's key external opportunities.
2. List the firm's key external threats.
3. List the firm's key internal strengths.
4. List the firm's key internal weaknesses.

Always leave blank	**STRENGTHS—S** 1. 2. 3. 4. 5. 6. List 7. strengths 8. 9. 10.	**WEAKNESSES—W** 1. 2. 3. 4. 5. 6. List 7. weaknesses 8. 9. 10.
OPPORTUNITIES—O 1. 2. 3. 4. List 5. opportunities 6. 7. 8. 9. 10.	**SO STRATEGIES** 1. 2. 3. 4. Use strengths 5. to take 6. advantage of 7. opportunities 8. 9. 10.	**WO STRATEGIES** 1. 2. 3. 4. Overcome 5. weaknesses 6. by taking 7. advantage of 8. opportunities 9. 10.
THREATS—T 1. 2. List 3. threats 4. 5. 6. 7. 8. 9. 10.	**ST STRATEGIES** 1. 2. Use 3. strengths 4. to avoid 5. threats 6. 7. 8. 9. 10.	**WT STRATEGIES** 1. 2. Minimize 3. weaknesses 4. and 5. avoid 6. threats 7. 8. 9. 10.

FIGURE 6–3 The TOWS Matrix

5. Match internal strengths with external opportunities and record the resultant SO Strategies in the appropriate cell.
6. Match internal weaknesses with external opportunities and record the resultant WO strategies.
7. Match internal strengths with external threats and record the resultant ST strategies.
8. Match internal weaknesses with external threats and record the resultant WT strategies.

Some other example SO, WO, ST, and WT strategies are given as follows:

1. A strong financial position (internal strength) coupled with unsaturated foreign markets (external opportunity) could suggest market development to be an appropriate SO Strategy.

2. A lack of technical expertise (internal weakness) coupled with a strong demand for computer services (external opportunity) could suggest the WO Strategy of acquiring a high-tech computer company.
3. A strong distribution system (internal strength) coupled with intense government deregulation (external threat) could suggest concentric diversification to be a desirable ST Strategy.
4. Poor product quality (internal weakness) coupled with unreliable suppliers (external threat) could suggest backward integration to be a feasible WT Strategy.

The purpose of each Stage 2 matching tool is to generate feasible alternative strategies, not to select or determine which strategies are best! Not all of the strategies developed in the TOWS Matrix and the other Stage 2 matching tools will be selected for implementation. Figure 6–4 is a TOWS Matrix for the Chrysler Corporation. Chrysler is the third largest automaker in the United States; the company controls 15 percent of the domestic market for automobiles and 20 percent of the market for trucks. It recently purchased American Motors Corporation for $1.6 billion and Lamborghini for $ 4.5 million. Chrysler's revenues increased 16 percent in 1987 to $26.3 billion, but profits declined 8 percent to $1.3 billion.

The strategy-formulation guidelines provided in Chapter 2 can enhance the process of matching key internal and external factors. For example, when an organization has both the capital and human resources needed to distribute its own products (internal strength) and distributors are unreliable, costly, or incapable of meeting the firm's needs (external threat), then forward integration can be an attractive ST Strategy. When a firm has excess production capacity (internal weakness) and its basic industry is experiencing declining annual sales and profits (external threat), then concentric diversification can be an effective WT Strategy. It is important to use specific, rather than generic, strategy terms when developing a TOWS Matrix.

The Strategic Position and Action Evaluation (SPACE) Matrix

The Strategic Position and Action Evaluation *(SPACE) Matrix,* another important Stage 2 "matching" tool, is illustrated in Figure 6–5. Its four-quadrant framework indicates whether aggressive, conservative, defensive, or competitive strategies are most appropriate for a given organization. The axes of the SPACE Matrix represent two internal dimensions (*financial strength* [FS] and *competitive advantage* [CA]) and two external dimensions (*environmental stability* [ES] and *industry strength* [IS]). These four factors are the most important determinants of an organization's overall strategic position.[4]

Depending upon the type of organization, numerous variables could comprise each of the dimensions represented on the axes of the SPACE Matrix. Some variables commonly included are given in Exhibit 6–1. For example, return on investment, leverage, liquidity, working capital, and cash flow are commonly considered determining factors of an organization's financial strength. Like the TOWS Matrix, the SPACE Matrix should be tailored for a particular organization being studied and based on factual information to the extent possible.

	STRENGTHS—**S**	WEAKNESSES—**W**
	1. Product quality improved 35% from 1985 to 1987 2. Chrysler's labor costs are lower than Ford or GM's 3. Chrysler's Gulfstream Aerospace jets lead industry 4. Chrysler's breakeven point has decreased from 2.4 to 1.5 million vehicles 5. Chrysler has 50% of mini-van market	1. AMC acquisition raises debt/equity ratio to 60% 2. Fixed assets are 42% of total assets (4 times industry average) 3. Chrysler has fewer joint ventures than Ford or GM 4. Chrysler's operations are confined to Canada, Mexico, and the United States
OPPORTUNITIES—**O** 1. Low value of the dollar 2. Aerospace and defense industries are growing 20% per year 3. Consumers' disposable income is increasing 5% per year 4. Interest rates are declining 5. GM's new Saturn project is having problems	**SO** STRATEGIES 1. Acquire an aerospace company (S3, O2) 2. Export 50% more mini-vans (S1, S5, O1)	**WO** STRATEGIES 1. Form an aerospace joint venture company (W3, O2) 2. Build a manufacturing plant in Europe (W4, O4)
THREATS—**T** 1. Foreign imports are gaining market share 2. Unrest in the Middle East could increase gas prices 3. Ford has an excellent new line of cars	**ST** STRATEGIES 1. Boost advertising expenditures 50% (S1, S5, T1, T3)	**WT** STRATEGIES

FIGURE 6–4 A TOWS Matrix for the Chrysler Corporation

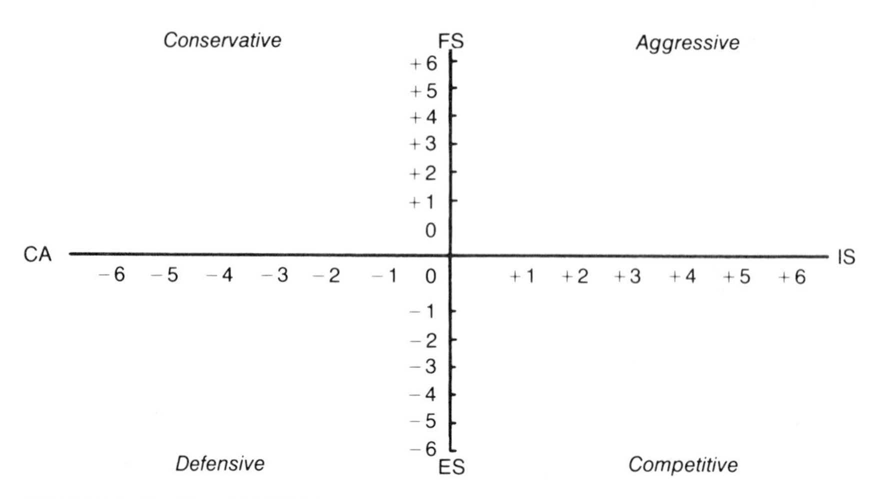

FIGURE 6–5 The SPACE Matrix

Source: H. Rowe, R. Mason, and K. Dickel, *Strategic Management and Business Policy: A Methodological Approach* (Reading, Massachusetts: Addison-Wesley Publishing Co., © 1982): 155. Reprinted with permission.

EXHIBIT 6–1 Examples of factors that comprise the SPACE Matrix axes

INTERNAL STRATEGIC POSITION	EXTERNAL STRATEGIC POSITION
Financial Strength (FS)	**Environmental Stability (ES)***
Return on investment	Technological changes
Leverage	Rate of inflation
Liquidity	Demand variability
Working capital	Price range of competing products
Cash flow	Barriers to entry into market
Ease of exit from market	Competitive pressure
Risk involved in business	Price elasticity of demand
Competitive Advantage (CA)	**Industry Strength (IS)**
Market share	Growth potential
Product quality	Profit potential
Product life cycle	Financial stability
Customer loyalty	Technological know-how
Competition's capacity utilization	Resource utilization
Technological know-how	Capital intensity
Control over suppliers and distributors	Ease of entry into market
	Productivity, capacity utilization

Source: H. Rowe, R. Mason, and K. Dickel, *Strategic Management & Business Policy: A Methodological Approach* (Reading, Mass.: Addison-Wesley Publishing Company, Inc., © 1982), 155–156. Reprinted with permission.

*A stable environment represents a better strategic position than an unstable environment.

The steps required in developing a SPACE Matrix are as follows:

1. Select a set of variables to comprise financial strength (FS), competitive advantage (CA), environmental stability (ES), and industry strength (IS).
2. Assign a numerical value ranging from +1 (worst) to +6 (best) to each of the variables that comprise the FS and IS dimensions. Assign a numerical value ranging from −1 (best) to −6 (worst) to each of the variables that comprise the ES and CA dimensions.
3. Compute an average score for FS, CA, IS, and ES by summing the values given to the variables of each dimension and dividing by the number of variables included in the respective dimension.
4. Plot the average scores for FS, IS, ES, and CA on the appropriate axis in the SPACE Matrix.
5. Add the two scores on the *x*-axis and plot the resultant point on X. Add the two scores on the *y*-axis and plot the resultant point on Y. Plot the intersection of the new *xy* point.
6. Draw a *directional vector* from the origin of the SPACE Matrix through the new intersection point. This vector reveals the type of strategies recommended for the organization: aggressive, competitive, defensive, or conservative.

Some examples of strategy profiles that can emerge from a SPACE analysis are shown in Figure 6–6. The directional vector associated with each profile suggests the type of strategies to pursue: aggressive, conservative, defensive, or competitive. When a firm's directional vector is located in the *aggressive quadrant* of the SPACE Matrix, an organization is in an excellent position to use its internal strengths to (1) take advantage of external opportunities, (2) overcome internal weaknesses, and (3) avoid external threats. Therefore, market penetration, market development, product development, backward integration, forward integration, horizontal integration, conglomerate diversification, concentric diversification, horizontal diversification, or a combination strategy can all be feasible, depending on the specific circumstances that face the firm.

The directional vector may appear in the *conservative quadrant* (upper left quadrant) of the SPACE Matrix, which implies staying close to the firm's basic competencies and not taking excessive risks. Conservative strategies most often include market penetration, market development, product development, and concentric diversification. The directional vector may also be located in the lower left or *defensive quadrant* of the SPACE Matrix, which suggests that the firm should focus on improving internal weaknesses and avoiding external threats. Defensive strategies include retrenchment, divestiture, liquidation, and concentric diversification. Finally, the directional vector may be located in the lower right or *competitive quadrant* of the SPACE Matrix indicating competitive strategies. Competitive strategies include backward, forward, and horizontal integration, market penetration, market development, product development, and joint venture.

SPACE Matrix analysis for Mellon Bank is provided in Exhibit 6–2. Mellon is the thirteenth largest bank in the United States and the largest bank in Pennsylvania. Bad loans to third world countries, coupled with increased competition in the banking industry, have resulted in Mellon's experiencing a net profit loss of $844 million in 1987.

Aggressive Profiles

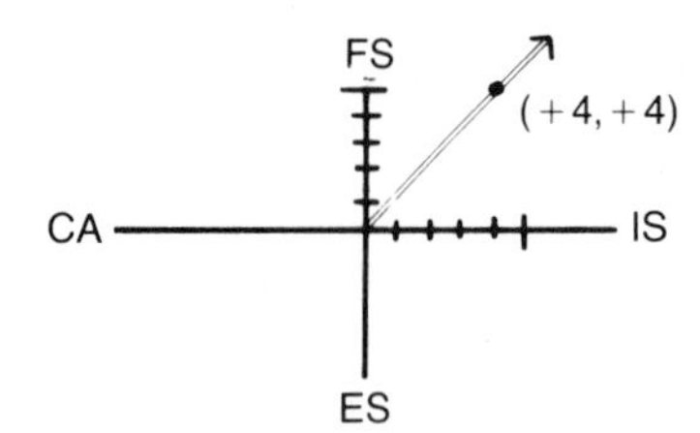

A financially strong firm that has achieved major competitive advantages in a growing and stable industry

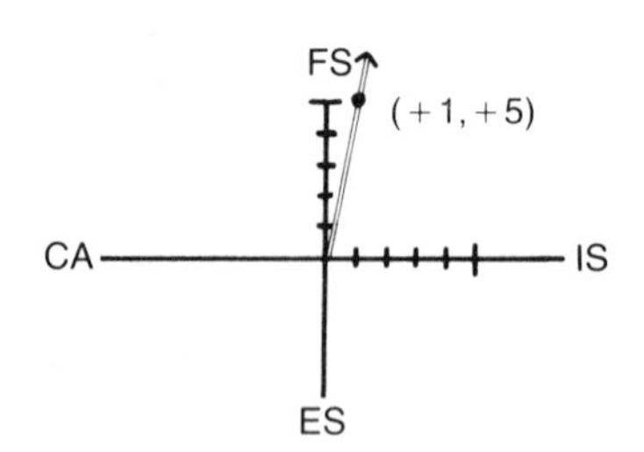

A firm whose financial strength is a dominating factor in the industry

Conservative Profiles

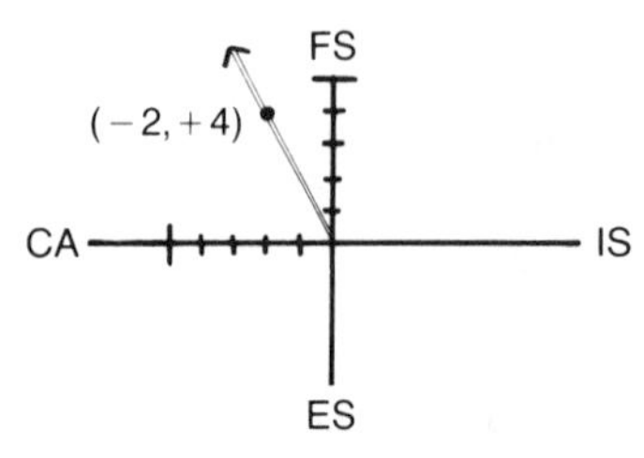

A firm that has achieved financial strength in a stable industry that is not growing; the firm has no major competitive advantages.

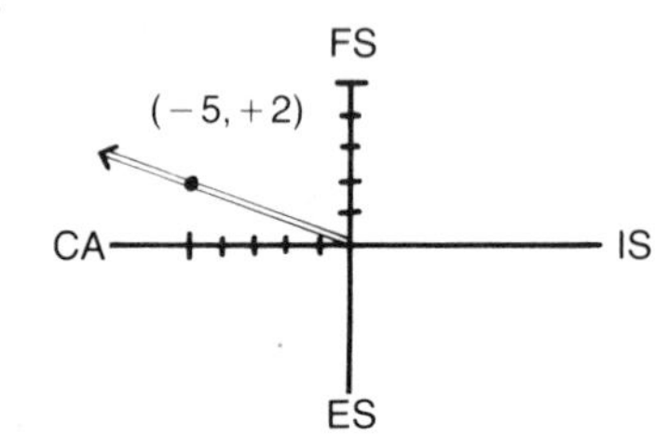

A firm that suffers from major competitive disadvantages in an industry that is technologically stable but declining in sales

Competitive Profiles

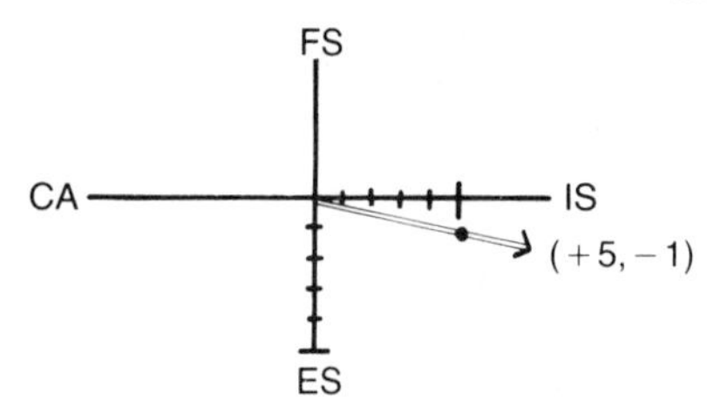

A firm with major competitive advantages in a high-growth industry

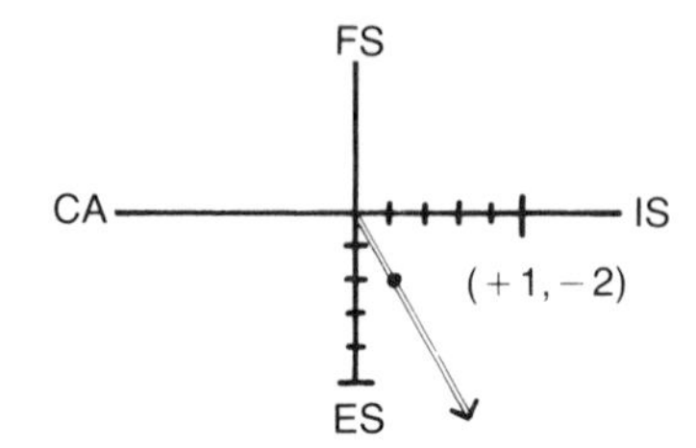

An organization that is competing fairly well in an unstable industry

Defensive Profiles

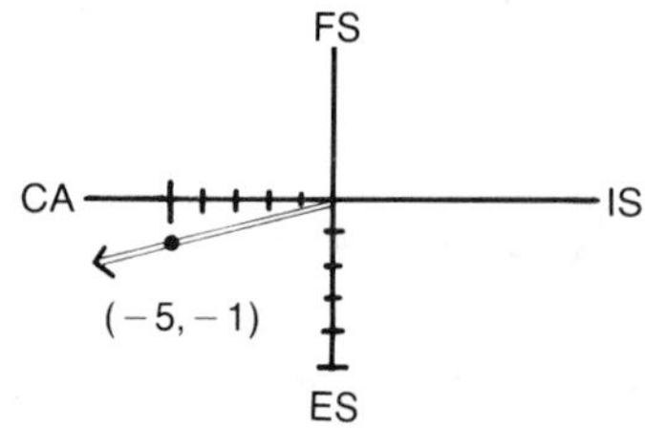

A firm that has a very weak competitive position in a negative growth, stable industry

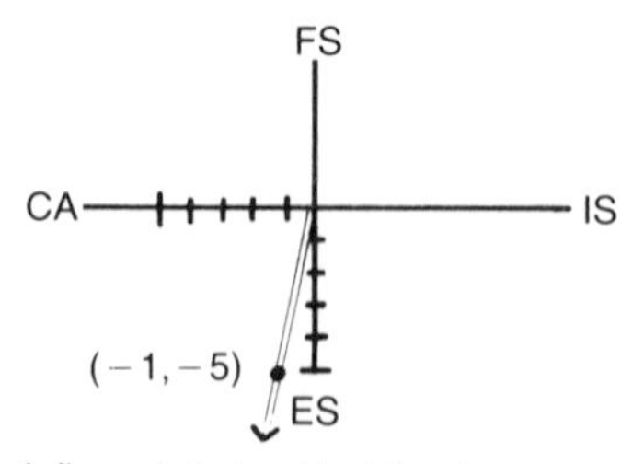

A financially troubled firm in a very unstable industry

FIGURE 6–6 Examples of strategy profiles. (Source: H. Rowe, R. Mason, and K. Dickel, *Strategic Management and Business Policy: A Methodological Approach* (Reading Massachusetts: Addison-Wesley Publishing Co., © 1982): 155. Reprinted with permission.)

EXHIBIT 6–2 A SPACE Matrix for Mellon Bank

	Ratings
Financial Strength	
Mellon's primary capital ratio is 7.23 percent, which is 1.23 percent over the generally required ratio of 6 percent.	1.0
Mellon's return on assets is negative 0.77, compared to a bank industry average ratio of positive 0.70.	1.0
Mellon's 1986 net income was $183 million, down 9 percent from 1985.	3.0
Mellon's 1986 revenues increased 7 percent from 1985 to $3.46 billion.	4.0
	9.0
Industry Strength	
Deregulation provides geographic and product freedom.	4.0
Deregulation increases competition in the banking industry.	2.0
Pennsylvania's interstate banking law allows Mellon to acquire banks in New Jersey, Ohio, Kentucky, The District of Columbia, and West Virginia.	4.0
	10.0
Environmental Stability	
Lesser developed countries are experiencing high inflation and political instability.	−4.0
Headquartered in Pittsburgh, Mellon has historically been heavily dependent on the steel, oil, and gas industries. These industries are depressed.	−5.0
Banking deregulation has created instability throughout the industry.	−4.0
	−13.0
Competitive Advantage	
Mellon provides data processing services for more than 450 institutions in 38 states.	−2.0
Superregional banks, international banks, and non-banks are becoming increasingly competitive.	−5.0
Mellon has a large customer base.	−2.0
	−9.0

Conclusion

ES Average is −13.0/3 = −4.33 IS Average is +10.0/3 = 3.33
CA Average is −9.0/3 = −3.00 FS Average is +9.0/4 = 2.25

Directional Vector Coordinates: x axis: −3.00 + (+3.33) = +0.33
y axis: −4.33 + (+2.25) = −2.08

** Mellon should pursue Competitive Type Strategies

The Boston Consulting Group (BCG) Matrix

Autonomous divisions (or profit centers) of an organization make up what is called a "*business portfolio.*" When a firm's divisions compete in different industries, a separate strategy often must be developed for each business. The Boston Consulting Group *(BCG) Matrix,* and Internal-External (IE) Matrix are designed specifically to enhance a multidivisional firm's efforts to formulate strategies.

The BCG Matrix graphically portrays differences among divisions in terms of relative market share position and industry growth rate.[5] The BCG Matrix allows a multidivisional organization to manage its "portfolio of businesses" by examining the relative market share position and the industry growth rate of each division relative to all other divisions in the organization. *Relative market share position* is defined as the ratio of a division's own market share in a particular industry to the market share held by the largest rival firm in that industry. Relative market share position is given on the *x*-axis of the BCG Matrix. The midpoint on the *x*-axis is usually set at .50 corresponding to a division that has half the market share of the leading firm in the industry. The *y*-axis represents the industry growth rate in sales, measured in percentage terms. The growth rate percentages on the *y*-axis could range from −20 to +20 percent, with 0.0 being the midpoint. These numerical ranges on the *x* and *y* axes are often used, but other numerical values could be established as deemed appropriate for particular organizations.

An example of a BCG Matrix appears in Figure 6–7. Each circle represents a separate division. The size of the circle corresponds to the proportion of corporate revenue generated by that business unit, and the pie slice indicates the proportion of corporate profits generated by that division. Divisions located in Quadrant I of the BCG Matrix are called Question Marks, those located in Quadrant II are called Stars, those located in Quadrant III are called Cash Cows, and finally those divisions located in Quadrant IV are called Dogs.

- ☐ *Question Marks*—Divisions in Quadrant I have a low relative market share position, yet compete in a high-growth industry. Generally, these firms' cash needs are high and their cash generation is low. These businesses are called Question Marks because the organization must decide whether to strengthen them by pursuing an intensive strategy (market penetration, market development, or product development) or to sell them.
- ☐ *Stars*—Quadrant II businesses (often called Stars) represent the organization's best long-run opportunities for growth and profitability. Divisions with a high

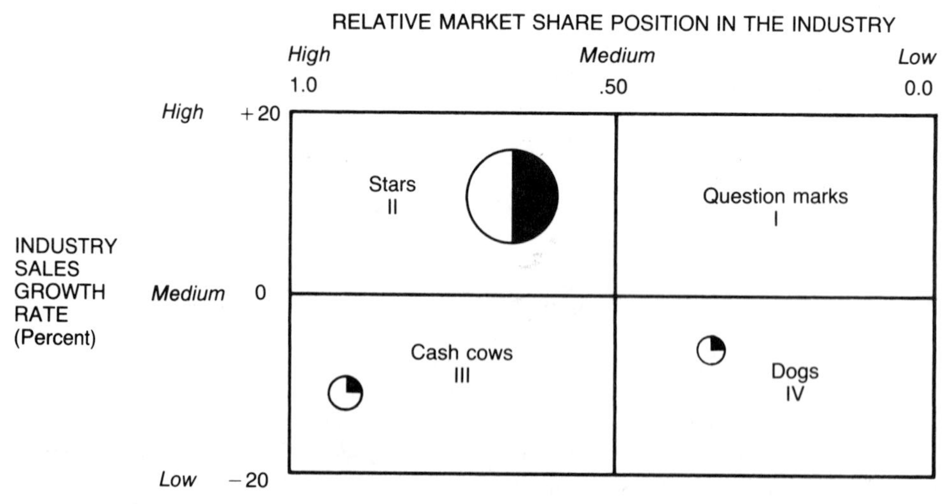

FIGURE 6–7 The BCG Matrix

relative market share and a high industry growth rate should receive substantial investment to maintain or strengthen their dominant positions. Forward, backward, and horizontal integration; market penetration; market development; product development; and joint ventures are all appropriate strategies for these divisions to consider.

- *Cash Cows*—Divisions positioned in Quadrant III have a high relative market share position but compete in a low-growth industry. Called Cash Cows because they generate cash in excess of their needs, they are often "milked." Many of today's Cash Cows were yesterday's Stars. Cash Cow divisions should be managed to maintain their strong position for as long as possible. Product development or concentric diversification may be attractive strategies for strong Cash Cows. However, as a Cash Cow division becomes weak, retrenchment or divestiture can become more appropriate.
- *Dogs*—Quadrant IV divisions of the organization have a low relative market share position and compete in a slow-or-no-market-growth industry; they are Dogs in the firm's portfolio. Because of their weak internal and external position, these businesses often are liquidated, divested, or trimmed down through retrenchment. When a division first becomes a Dog, retrenchment can be the best strategy to pursue, because many Dogs have bounced back, after strenuous asset and cost reduction, to become viable, profitable divisions.

The major benefit of the BCG Matrix is that it draws attention to the cash flow, investment characteristics, and needs of an organization's various divisions. The divisions of many firms evolve over time: Dogs become Question Marks, Question Marks become Stars, Stars become Cash Cows, and Cash Cows become Dogs, in an ongoing counterclockwise motion. Less frequently, Stars become Question Marks, Question Marks become Dogs, Dogs become Cash Cows, and Cash Cows become Stars (in a clockwise motion). In some organizations no cyclical motion is apparent. Over time, organizations should strive to achieve a portfolio of divisions that are Stars.

One example of a BCG Matrix is provided in Figure 6–8, which illustrates an organization composed of five divisions with annual sales ranging from $5,000 to $60,000. Division 1 has the greatest sales volume, so the circle representing that division is the largest one in the Matrix. The circle corresponding to Division 5 is the smallest since its sales volume ($5,000) is least among all the divisions. The pie slices within the circles reveal the percent of corporate profits contributed by each division. As shown, Division 1 contributes the highest profit percentage, 39 percent. Notice in the diagram that Division 1 is considered a Star, Division 2 is a Question Mark, Division 3 is also a Question Mark, Division 4 is a Cash Cow, and Division 5 is a Dog.

The BCG Matrix, like all analytical techniques, has some limitations. For example, viewing all businesses as either a Star, Cash Cow, Dog, or Question Mark is an oversimplification; many businesses fall right in the middle of the BCG Matrix and are thus not easily classified. Then too, the BCG Matrix does not reflect whether or not various divisions or their industries are growing over time; that is, the matrix has no temporal qualities, but rather is a snapshot of an organization at a given point in time. Finally, other variables besides relative market share position and industry growth rate

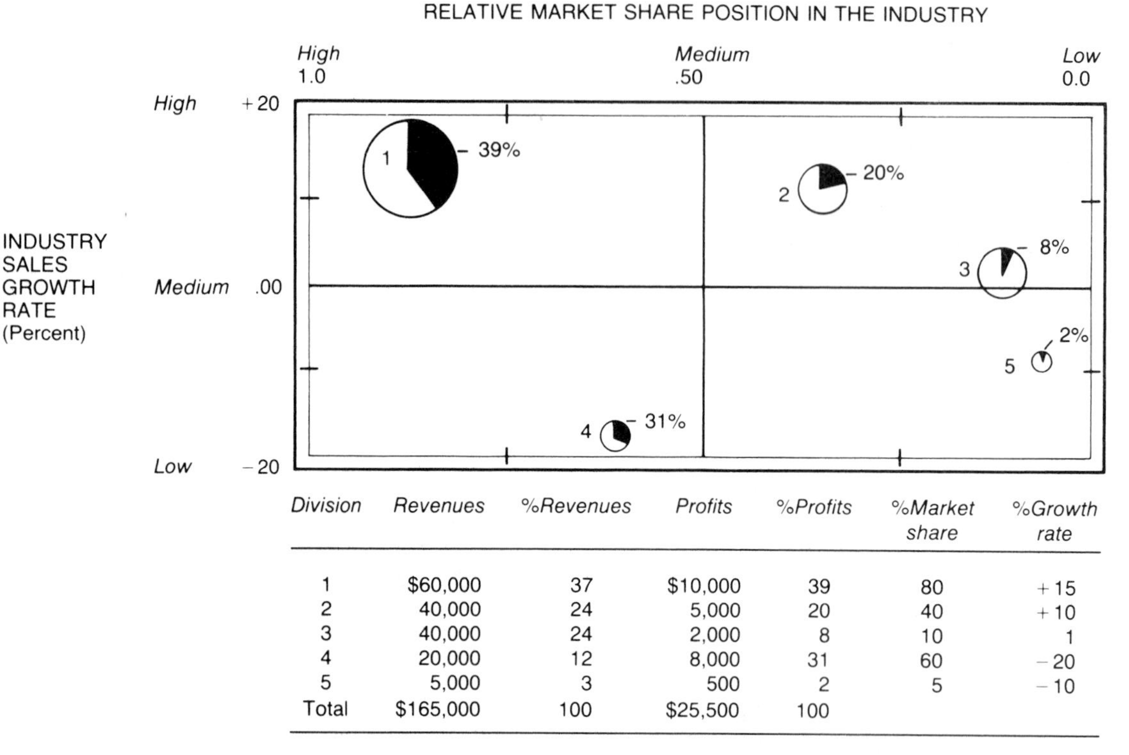

Division	Revenues	%Revenues	Profits	%Profits	%Market share	%Growth rate
1	$60,000	37	$10,000	39	80	+15
2	40,000	24	5,000	20	40	+10
3	40,000	24	2,000	8	10	1
4	20,000	12	8,000	31	60	−20
5	5,000	3	500	2	5	−10
Total	$165,000	100	$25,500	100		

FIGURE 6–8 An example of a BCG Matrix

Note: The IE was developed from the General Electric (GE) Business Screen Matrix. For a description of the GE Matrix, see: Michael Allen, "Diagramming GE's Planning for What's WATT," in *Corporate Planning: Techniques and Applications*, ed. R. Allio and M. Pennington (New York: AMACOM, 1979).

in sales, such as size of the market and competitive advantages, are important in making strategic decisions about various divisions.

Lockheed Corporation recently identified its Seattle shipyard as a Dog and announced that it hoped to divest itself of that division. The shipyard lost $3.5 million in 1986 on sales of $112 million. Lockheed also intends to sell two Question Mark divisions, the Cal Comp computer graphics subsidiary and its information processing unit. With the proceeds from these sales, Lockheed strategists are considering a major stock buyback to defend the organization against a possible takeover. For the year 1987, Lockheed's sales and profits increased 11 percent and 6 percent respectively over 1986.

The Internal-External (IE) Matrix

The *Internal-External (IE) Matrix* positions an organization's various divisions in a nine-cell display (see Figure 6–9).[6] The IE Matrix is similar to the BCG Matrix in that both tools involve plotting organizational divisions in a schematic diagram; this is why they are both called portfolio matrices. Also, the size of each circle represents the percentage sales contribution of each division and pie slices reveal the percentage profit contribution of each division in both the BCG and IE Matrix.

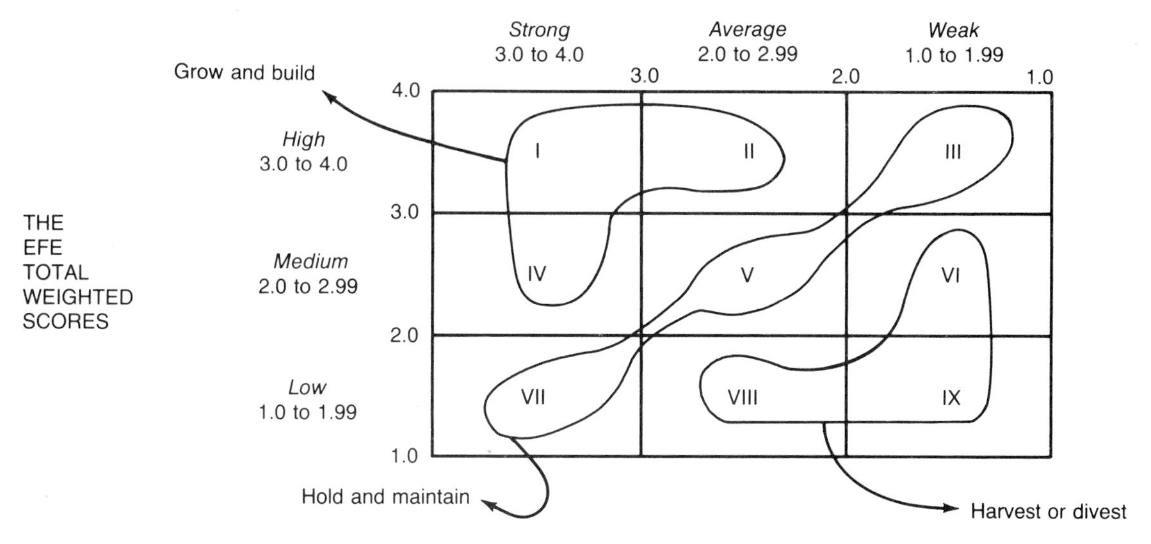

FIGURE 6–9 The Internal-External (IE) Matrix

But there are some important differences between the BCG Matrix and IE Matrix. The axes are different. Also, the IE Matrix requires more information about the divisions than the BCG Matrix. Further, the strategic implications of each matrix are different. For these reasons, strategists in multidivisional firms often develop both the BCG and the IE Matrix in formulating alternative strategies. A common practice is to develop a BCG matrix and an IE Matrix for the present, and then develop projected matrices to reflect the future. This practice forecasts the expected effect of current strategic decisions on an organization's portfolio of divisions.

The IE Matrix is based on two key dimensions: the IFE total weighted scores on the *x*-axis and the EFE total weighted scores on the *y*-axis. Recall that each division of an organization should construct an IFE Matrix and an EFE Matrix for its part of the organization. The total weighted scores derived from the divisions allow construction of the corporate level IE Matrix. On the *x*-axis of the IE Matrix, an IFE total weighted score of 1.0 to 1.99 represents a weak internal position, a score of 2.0 to 2.99 is considered average, and a score of 3.0 to 4.0 is strong. Similarly, on the *y*-axis, an EFE total weighted score of 1.0 to 1.99 is considered low, a score of 2.0 to 2.99 is medium, and a score of 3.0 to 4.00 high. A schematic diagram of the IE Matrix is provided in Figure 6–9.

The IE Matrix can be divided into three major regions that have different strategy implications. First, the prescription for divisions that fall into cells I, II, or IV can be described as "Grow and Build." Intensive (market penetration, market development, and product development) or integrative (backward integration, forward integration, and horizontal integration) strategies can be most appropriate for these divisions. Second, divisions that fall into cells III, V, or VII can best be managed with "Hold and Maintain" strategies; market penetration and product development are two commonly employed strategies for these types of divisions. Third, a common prescription for divisions that fall into cells VI, VIII, or IX is "Harvest or Divest." Successful organizations are able to achieve a portfolio of businesses positioned in or around cell I in the IE Matrix.

An example of a completed IE Matrix is given in Figure 6–10, which depicts an organization composed of four divisions. As indicated by the positioning of the circles, "Grow and Build" strategies are appropriate for Division 1, Division 2, and Division 3. Division 4 is a candidate for "Harvest or Divest." Division 2 contributes the greatest percentage of company sales and thus is represented by the largest circle. Division 1 contributes the greatest proportion of total profits, since it has the largest percentage pie slice.

The Grand Strategy Matrix

In addition to the TOWS Matrix, SPACE Matrix, BCG Matrix, and IE Matrix, the *Grand Strategy Matrix* has become a popular tool for formulating alternative strategies. All organizations can be positioned in one of the Grand Strategy Matrix's four strategy quadrants. A firm's divisions could likewise be positioned. As illustrated in Figure 6–11, the Grand Strategy Matrix is based on two evaluative dimensions: competitive

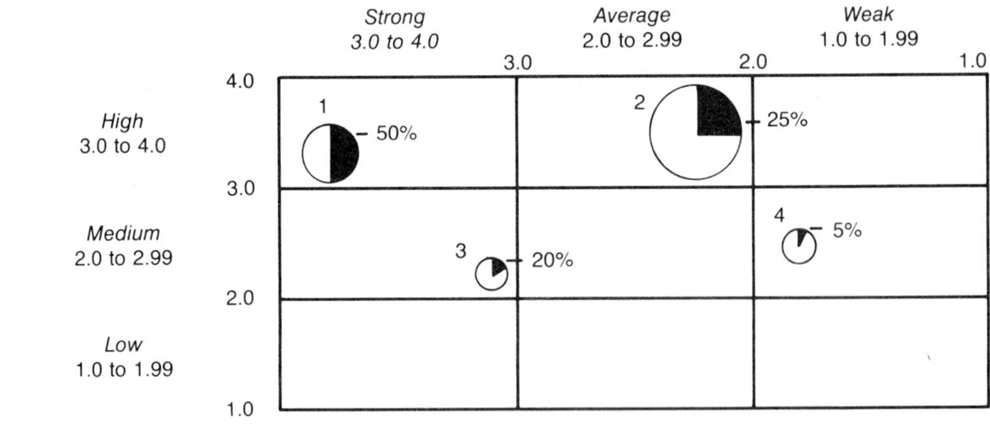

Division	Sales	Percent sales	Profits	Percent profits	IFE scores	EFE scores
1	$100	25	10	50	3.6	3.2
2	200	50	5	25	2.1	3.5
3	50	12.5	4	20	3.1	2.1
4	50	12.5	1	5	1.8	2.5
Total	400	100	20	100		

FIGURE 6–10 An example IE Matrix

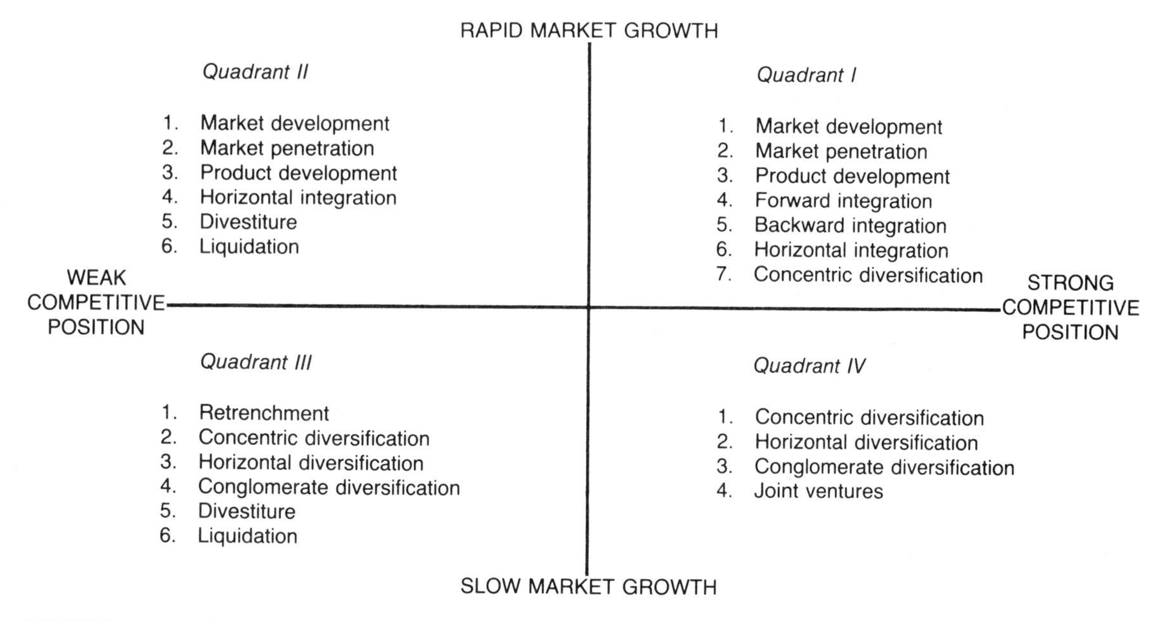

FIGURE 6–11 The Grand Strategy Matrix

Source: Adapted from Roland Christensen, Norman Berg, and Malcolm Sulter, *Policy Formulation and Administration* (Homewood, Ill.: Richard D. Irwin, 1976), 16–18.

position and market growth. Appropriate strategies for an organization to consider are listed in sequential order of attractiveness in each quadrant of the matrix.

Firms located in Quadrant I of the Grand Strategy Matrix are in an excellent strategic position. For these firms, continued concentration on current markets (market penetration and market development) and products (product development) are appropriate strategies. It is unwise for a Quadrant I firm to shift notably from its established competitive advantages. When a Quadrant I organization has excessive resources, then backward, forward, or horizontal integration may be effective strategies. When a Quadrant I firm is too heavily committed to a single product, then concentric diversification may reduce the risks associated with a narrow product line. Quadrant I firms can afford to take advantage of external opportunities in many areas; they can aggressively take risks when necessary.

Firms positioned in Quadrant II need to evaluate their present approach to the marketplace seriously. Although their industry is growing, they are unable to compete effectively, and they need to determine why the firm's current approach is ineffectual and how the company can best change to improve its competitiveness. Since Quadrant II firms are in a rapid-market-growth industry, an intensive strategy (as opposed to integrative or diversification) is usually the first option that should be considered. However, if the firm is lacking a distinctive competence or competitive advantage, then horizontal integration is often a desirable alternative. As a last result, divestiture or liquidation should be considered. Divestiture can provide funds needed to acquire other businesses or buy back shares of stock.

Quadrant III organizations compete in slow-growth industries and have weak competitive positions. These firms must make some drastic changes quickly to avoid further demise and possible liquidation. Extensive cost and asset reduction (retrenchment) should be pursued first. An alternative strategy is to shift resources away from the current business into different areas. If all else fails, the final options for Quadrant III businesses are divestiture or liquidation.

Finally, Quadrant IV businesses have a strong competitive position but are in a slow-growth industry. These firms have the strength to launch diversified programs into more promising growth areas. Quadrant IV firms have characteristically high cash flow levels and limited internal growth needs and can often pursue concentric, horizontal, or conglomerate diversification successfully. Quadrant IV firms may also pursue joint ventures.

THE DECISION STAGE

The Quantitative Strategic Planning Matrix (QSPM)

The *Quantitative Strategic Planning Matrix (QSPM)* is used at Stage 3 of the strategy-formulation analytical framework.[7] This technique objectively suggests which alternative strategies are best. The QSPM uses input from Stage 1 analyses and matching results from Stage 2 analyses to "decide" objectively among alternative strategies. That is, the Competitive Profile Matrix, EFE Matrix, and IFE Matrix that comprise Stage 1, coupled with the TOWS Matrix, SPACE Analysis, BCG Matrix, IE Matrix, and Grand Strategy Matrix that make up Stage 2 provide the needed information for setting up the QSPM (Stage 3). QSPM is a tool that allows strategists to evaluate alternative strategies objectively, based on internal strengths and weaknesses and environmental opportunities and threats. Like other strategy-formulation analytical tools, QSPM requires intuitive decisions in assigning weights and ratings. It should be used carefully.

The basic format of the QSPM is illustrated in Table 6–3. Note that the left column of QSPM consists of key internal and external factors (from Stage 1), and the top row consists of feasible alternative strategies (from Stage 2). Specifically, the left column of a QSPM consists of information obtained directly from the EFE Matrix and IFE Matrix. In a column adjacent to these key factors, the respective ratings received by each factor in the EFE Matrix and IFE Matrix are recorded. The top row of a QSPM consists of alternative strategies derived from the TOWS Matrix, SPACE Matrix, BCG Matrix, IE Matrix, and Grand Strategy Matrix. These matching tools usually generate similar feasible alternatives. However, not every strategy suggested by the matching techniques has to be evaluated in a QSPM. Strategists should use good intuitive judgment in selecting strategies to include in a QSPM.

Conceptually, the QSPM determines the relative attractiveness of various strategies based on the extent that key internal and external factors are capitalized upon or improved. The relative attractiveness of each strategy within a set of alternatives is computed by determining the cumulative impact of each key internal and external factor. Any number of sets of alternative strategies can be included in the QSPM, and any number of strategies can comprise a given set. But only strategies within a given set are evaluated relative to each other. For example, one set of strategies may include con-

TABLE 6–3 The Quantitative Strategic Planning Matrix—QSPM

Key Factors	*Ratings*	*Strategy 1*	*STRATEGIC ALTERNATIVES* *Strategy 2*	*Strategy 3*
Internal Factors				
Management				
Marketing				
Finance/Accounting				
Production/Operations				
Research and Development				
External Factors				
Economy				
Political/Legal/Governmental				
Social/Cultural/Demographic				
Technological				
Competitive				

Internal Factors: 1 = major weakness; 2 = minor weakness; 3 = minor strength; 4 = major strength
External Factors: 1 = major threat; 2 = minor threat; 3 = minor opportunity; 4 = major opportunity

centric, horizontal, and conglomerate diversification, whereas another set may include issuing stock and selling a division to raise needed capital. These two sets of strategies are totally different, and the QSPM evaluates strategies only within sets. Note in Table 6–3 that three strategies are included and they comprise just one set. A more detailed example of the QSPM is provided in Table 6–4.

This example illustrates all of the components of the QSPM: Key Factors, Strategic Alternatives, Ratings, Attractiveness Scores, Total Attractiveness Scores, and Sum Total Attractiveness Score. The three new terms just introduced, (1) Attractiveness Scores, (2) Total Attractiveness Scores, and (3) Sum Total Attractiveness Score, are defined and explained as the six steps required to develop a QSPM are discussed.

Step 1 **List the firm's key internal strengths/weaknesses and external opportunities/threats in the left column of the QSPM.** This information should be taken directly from the IFE Matrix and the EFE Matrix. A minimum of five key internal factors and five key external factors should be included in the QSPM. Remember that each factor should be stated in specific terms.

Step 2 **Assign Ratings to each key internal and external factor.** These Ratings are identical to those in the IFE Matrix and the EFE Matrix. The Ratings are presented in a straight column just to the right of the key internal and external factor statements, as shown in Table 6–4.

Step 3 **Examine the Stage 2 (matching) matrices and identify alternative strategies that the organization should consider implementing.** Record these strategies in the top row of the QSPM. Group the strategies into sets if appropriate.

Step 4 **Determine the Attractiveness Scores.** They are defined as numerical values that indicate the relative attractiveness of each strategy in a given set of

TABLE 6–4 A sample Quantitative Strategic Planning Matrix

Key Factors	Rating	*Strategic Alternatives* Acquire Financial Services, Inc. AS*	TAS*	Acquire Food Services, Inc. AS*	TAS*	Rationale for Attractiveness Score
Internal Factors						
Top management team has fifteen years' experience.	3	4	12	2	6	Fifteen years' experience is in financial services
We have excess working capital of $2 million.	4	2	8	3	12	Food Services is valued at $2 million.
All of our twenty plants are located in the Northeast United States.	1	2	2	4	4	Food Services is located in the Sunbelt.
Our R&D department is outstanding.	3	—	—	—	—	This item does not affect the strategy choice.
Our Return on Investment (ROI) ratio of .12 is lowest in the industry.	1	2	2	3	3	ROI at Food Services is higher than at Financial Services.
External Factors						
Interest rates are expected to rise to 15 percent in 1987.	2	3	6	4	8	Rising rates will hurt the financial services business.
Population of the South is expected to grow by 15.3 million between 1980 and 2000.	3	4	12	2	6	Many new houses and apartments will be built and financed.
The financial services industry is expected to grow by 40 percent in 1986.	4	4	16	2	8	This 40 percent growth is in financial services.
Two major foreign competitors are entering the industry.	1	1	1	3	3	Food Services, Inc. is not affected by this entry.
President Reagan is expected to deregulate the industry.	2	—	—	—	—	This item does not affect the strategy choice.
SUM TOTAL ATTRACTIVENESS SCORE			59		50	

*AS = Attractiveness Score; TAS = Total Attractiveness Score

Attractiveness Score: 1 = not acceptable; 2 = possibly acceptable; 3 = probably acceptable; 4 = most acceptable

Internal Ratings: 1 = major weakness; 2 = minor weakness; 3 = minor strength; 4 = major strength

External Ratings: 1 = major threat; 2 = minor threat; 3 = minor opportunity; 4 = major opportunity

Note: Multiplying the rating times the attractiveness score is based upon the premise that to capitalize on strengths and take advantage of opportunities is more important for firms than improving weaknesses and avoiding threats. Some strategists do not agree with this premise and therefore do not compute the total attractiveness scores. They simply sum the attractiveness scores to determine the relative attractiveness of strategies using the QSPM.

alternatives. Attractiveness Scores are determined by examining each internal or external factor, one at a time, and asking the question "Does this key factor have an effect on the choice of the strategies being evaluated?" If the answer to this question is YES, then the strategy should be evaluated relative to that key factor. Specifically, Attractiveness Scores should be assigned to each strategy in a given set of alternatives, where 1 = the strategy is not acceptable, 2 = the strategy is possibly acceptable, 3 = the strategy is probably acceptable, and 4 = the strategy is most acceptable. However, if the answer to the above question is NO, indicating that the respective key factor has no effect upon the specific choice being made, then do not assign Attractiveness Scores to the strategies in that set. Note in Table 6–4 that the "outstanding R&D Department" (an internal strength) has no significant effect upon the choice being made between acquiring the finance service versus the food company, so "blank" lines are placed in that row of the QSPM. "Two major foreign competitors are entering the industry" is a major external threat that results in an Attractiveness Score of "1" for "Acquire Financial Services," compared to an Attractiveness Score of "3" for the "Acquire Food Services" strategy. These scores indicate that acquiring Financial Services, Inc. is "not an acceptable strategy" whereas acquiring Food Services, Inc. is "probably an acceptable strategy," considering this single external threat.

Step 5 **Compute the Total Attractiveness Scores**. Total Attractiveness Scores are defined as the product of multiplying the Ratings (Step Two) by the Attractiveness Scores (Step Four) in each row. The Total Attractiveness Scores indicate the relative attractiveness of each alternative strategy, considering only the impact of the adjacent internal or external factor. Total Attractiveness Scores for each alternative are provided in Table 6–4. The higher the Total Attractiveness Score, the more attractive the strategic alternative (considering only the respective internal or external factor).

Step 6 **Compute the Sum Total Attractiveness Score**. It is the summation of the Total Attractiveness Scores in a strategy column of the QSPM. Sum Total Attractiveness Scores reveal which strategy is most attractive in each set of alternatives. Higher scores indicate more attractive strategies, considering all the relevant internal and external factors that could impact the strategic decisions. The magnitude of the difference between the Sum Total Attractiveness Scores in a given set of strategic alternatives indicates the relative desirability of one strategy over another. (In the example, the Sum Total Attractiveness Score of 59, compared to 50, indicates that Financial Services, Inc. should be acquired.)

Positive Features and Limitations of the QSPM

A positive feature of the QSPM is that sets of strategies can be examined sequentially or simultaneously. For example, corporate-level strategies could be evaluated first, followed by divisional-level strategies, and then functional-level strategies. There is no limit to the number of strategies that can be evaluated or the number of sets of strategies that can be examined at once using the QSPM.

Another positive feature of the QSPM is that it requires strategists to integrate pertinent internal and external factors into the decision process. Developing a QSPM makes it less likely that key factors will be overlooked or weighted inappropriately. A QSPM draws attention to important relationships that affect strategy decisions. Although developing a QSPM requires a number of subjective decisions, making small decisions along the way enhances the probability that the final strategic decisions will be best for the organization. A QSPM can be adapted for use by small and large, profit and nonprofit organizations and can be applied to virtually any type of organization. A QSPM can especially enhance strategic choice in multinational firms because many key factors and strategies can be considered at once. It also has been applied successfully by a number of small businesses.[8]

The QSPM is not without some limitations. First, it always requires subjective judgments and educated guesses. The ratings and attractiveness scores are judgmental decisions even though they should be based on objective information. Negotiation among strategists throughout the strategy-formulation process, including development of a QSPM, is constructive and enhances the strategic decisions. Constructive discussion among strategists may arise because of genuine differences of interpretation of information and varying opinions of what is really the appropriate strategy. Another limitation of the QSPM is that it can be only as good as the prerequisite information and matching analyses upon which it is based.

CULTURAL ASPECTS OF STRATEGY CHOICE

All organizations have a culture. Culture includes the set of shared values, beliefs, attitudes, customs, norms, personalities, and heroes that describe a firm. Culture is the unique way an organization does business. Culture is the human dimension that creates solidarity and meaning, and inspires commitment and productivity. Culture can actively and forcefully begin to work against an organization when strategy changes are made. All human beings have a basic need to make sense of their world, to feel in control, and to make meaning. When events threaten meaning, individuals react defensively. Managers and employees may even sabotage new strategies in an effort to recapture the status quo.

It is beneficial to view strategic management from a cultural perspective because success often rests upon the degree of support that strategies receive from a firm's culture. If a firm's strategies are supported by cultural products such as values, beliefs, rites, rituals, ceremonies, stories, symbols, language, and heroes, then managers can often implement changes swiftly and easily. However, if a supportive culture does not exist and is not cultivated, then strategy changes may be ineffective or even counterproductive. A firm's culture can become antagonistic to new strategies and the result of that antagonism may be confusion and disarray.

Strategies that require fewer cultural changes may be more attractive because extensive changes can take considerable time and effort. Whenever two firms merge, culture-strategy linkages become especially important to evaluate and consider. For example, Michael Blumenthal, chairman of the board and chief executive officer of Unisys Corporation (the company formed by the merger of Sperry and Burroughs), describes the culture of Unisys as a conscious distillation of the best customs, mores, symbols, and principles from Sperry and Burroughs; Unisys is not merely a balanced mix of Sperry and Burroughs. Unisys' revenues increased 3 percent in 1987 to $9.7 billion.

When two or three companies from different countries form a joint venture, such as the recent venture among Honeywell, NEC Corporation of Japan, and Compagnie des Machines Bull of France, merging corporate cultures can be a major problem. Jerome Meyer, a Honeywell executive, is president and CEO of the new organization, the first multinational computer company. "We've not had an alliance of these dimensions before, with its geographic diversity and cultural conflict," said Michael Geran, an analyst with E. F. Hutton, Inc. "The skill to run it will be a tremendous challenge." He predicted that Mr. Meyer would become primarily "a referee." Honeywell's sales declined 5.7 percent in 1987 to $6.68 billion.

Culture provides an explanation for the difficulties a firm encounters when it attempts to shift its strategic direction, as described below:

> Not only has the 'right' corporate culture become the essence and foundation of corporate excellence, but success or failure of needed corporate reforms hinges on management's sagacity and ability to change the firm's driving culture in time and in tune with required changes in strategies.[9]

THE POLITICS OF STRATEGY CHOICE

All organizations are political. Unless managed, political maneuvering consumes valuable time, subverts organizational objectives, diverts human energy, and results in the loss of some valuable employees.[10] Sometimes political biases and personal preferences get unduly embedded in strategy choice decisions. Internal politics affect the choice of strategies in all organizations. The hierarchy of command in an organization, combined with the career aspirations of different people and the need to allocate scarce resources, guarantees the formation of coalitions of individuals who strive to take care of themselves first and the organization second, third, or fourth. Coalitions of individuals often form around key strategy issues that face an enterprise. A major responsibility of strategists is to guide the development of coalitions, to nurture an overall team concept, and to gain the support of key individuals and groups of individuals.

In the absence of objective analyses, strategy decisions are too often based on the politics of the moment. With development of improved strategy-formulation tools, political factors become less important in making strategic decisions. In the absence of objectivity, political factors sometimes dictate strategies, and this is unfortunate. Managing political relationships is an integral part of building enthusiasm and esprit de corps in an organization. Don Beeman and Tom Sharkey offer the following guidelines for minimizing the negative aspects of organizational politics:

1. Make clear the bases and processes for performance evaluation.
2. Differentiate rewards among high and low performers.
3. Make sure rewards are as immediately and directly related to performance as possible.

4. Minimize resource competition among managers.
5. Replace resource competition with externally oriented objectives.
6. Where highly cohesive political empires exist, break them apart by removing or splitting the most dysfunctional subgroups.
7. Be keenly sensitive to managers whose mode of operation is personalization of political patronage. Approach these persons with a directive to "stop political maneuvering." If it continues, remove them from the position and preferably the company.[11]

In a classic study of strategic management in nine large corporations, the political tactics of successful and unsuccessful strategists were examined.[12] Successful strategists were found to let weakly supported ideas and proposals die through inaction and to establish additional hurdles or tests for strongly supported ideas considered unacceptable but not openly opposed. Successful strategists kept a low political profile on unacceptable proposals and strived to let most negative decisions come from subordinates or a group consensus, thereby reserving their own personal vetoes for big issues and crucial moments. Successful strategists did a lot of chatting and informal questioning to stay abreast of how things are progressing and to know when to step in to intervene. They led strategy but did not dictate it. They gave few orders, announced few decisions, depended heavily on informal questioning, and sought to probe and clarify until a consensus emerged.

Successful strategists generously and visibly rewarded key thrusts that succeed. They assigned responsibility for major new thrusts to "champions," the individuals most strongly identified with the idea or product and whose future is linked to its success. They stayed alert to the symbolic impact of their own actions and statements, so as not to send a false signal that could stimulate movements in unwanted directions.

Successful strategists ensured that all major power bases within an organization were represented in or had access to top management. They interjected new faces and new views into considerations of major changes. (This is important because new employees and managers generally have more enthusiasm and drive than employees who have been with the firm a long time. New employees do not "see the world the same old way" and act as screens against changes.) Successful strategists minimized their own political exposure on highly controversial issues and in circumstances where major opposition from key power centers was likely. In combination, these findings provide a basis for managing political relationships in an organization.

Since strategies must be effective in the marketplace and capable of gaining internal commitment, the following tactics used by politicians for centuries can aid strategists:

- ☐ *Equifinality:* It is often possible to achieve similar results using different means or paths. Strategists should recognize that achieving a successful outcome is more important than imposing the method of achieving it. It may be possible to generate new alternatives that give equal results but with far greater potential for gaining commitment.
- ☐ *Satisficing:* Achieving satisfactory results with an acceptable strategy is far better than failing to achieve 'optimal' results with an unpopular strategy.

- *Generalization:* Shifting focus from specific issues to more general ones may increase strategists' options for gaining organizational commitment.
- *Focus on Higher-order Issues:* By raising an issue to a higher level, many short-term interests can be postponed in favor of long-term interests. For instance, by focusing on issues of survival, the auto and steel industries were able to persuade unions to make concessions on wage increases.
- *Provide Political Access on Important Issues:* Strategy and policy decisions with significant negative consequences for middle managers will motivate intervention behavior from them. If middle managers do not have an opportunity to take a position on such decisions in appropriate political forums, they are capable of successfully resisting the decisions after they are made. Providing such political access provides strategists with information that might otherwise not be available and that could be useful in managing intervention behavior.[13]

THE ROLE OF A BOARD OF DIRECTORS

The widespread lack of involvement by boards of directors in the strategic-management process is slowly changing in America. Historically, boards of directors have mostly been "insiders" who would not second-guess top executives on strategic issues. It has generally been understood that strategists are responsible and accountable for implementing strategy, so they should formulate strategy, not board members. Consequently, chief executive officers usually avoided discussions of overall strategy with directors because the results of those discussions often restricted their freedom of action. The judgments of board members were seldom used on acquisitions, divestitures, large capital investments, and other strategic matters. Often the board would meet only annually to fulfill its minimum legal requirements; in many organizations boards served merely a traditional legitimizing role.

Today, boards of directors are composed mostly of "outsiders" who are becoming more involved in an organization's strategic management. In a recent study of 1,300 large corporations in the United States, nearly 40 percent of the boards of directors reported that they were actively involved in their firms' strategic-management process.[14] The major reason for the expanded role of boards of directors is that stockholders, government agencies, and customers are filing legal suits against directors for fraud, omissions, inaccurate disclosures, lack of due diligence, and culpable ignorance about a firm's operations with increasing frequency. *Business Week* recently concluded that board members face a one in five chance of being sued. Liability insurance for directors has become exceptionally expensive and has caused numerous directors to resign.

Two recent rulings have particularly affected the role of a board of directors in the strategy-formulation process. First, the Supreme Court of Delaware ruled that the directors of the Trans Union Corporation violated the interests of shareholders when they hastily accepted a takeover bid from the Marmon Group; that ruling erodes the so-called business judgment rule, which protects directors from liability as long as their decisions represent a good-faith effort to serve the best interests of the corporation. One clear signal from the Trans Union case is that haste can be costly for board members.

In another landmark ruling that illustrates how boards of directors are increasingly being held responsible for the overall performance of organizations, the Federal Deposit Insurance Corporation forced Continental Illinois to accept the resignations of ten of the troubled bank's outside directors. The impact of increasing legal pressures on board members is that directors are demanding greater and more regular access to financial performance information.

And just as directors are beginning to place more emphasis on staying informed about the organization's health and operations, they are also taking a more active role in assuring that publicly issued documents are accurate representations of the firm's status. It is becoming widely recognized that a board of directors has legal responsibilities to stockholders and society for all company activities, for corporate performance, and for assuring that a firm has an effective strategy. Failure to accept responsibility for auditing or evaluating a firm's strategy is considered a serious breach of a director's duties.

A direct response of increased pressures on directors to stay informed and execute their responsibilities is that audit committees are becoming commonplace. Milton Lauenstein proposes that a board of directors should conduct an annual strategy audit in much the same fashion as it reviews the annual financial audit.[15] In performing such an audit, a board could work jointly with operating management and/or seek outside counsel. The questions provided in Exhibit 6–3 illustrate the areas that a strategy audit might encompass, but, of course, not all of these questions apply to every situation and organization.

EXHIBIT 6–3 A board of directors strategy audit framework

- Is the company adequately informed about its markets? What further information would be worth the cost of getting? How should it be obtained?
- How well informed is the company about its competitors? How well is it able to forecast what competitors will do under various circumstances? Is there a sound basis for such competitive appraisals? Is the company underestimating or overestimating its competitors?
- Has management adequately explored various ways of segmenting its market? To what extent is it addressing market segments in which the company's strengths provide meaningful advantages?
- Are the products and services the company proposes to sell ones that it can provide more effectively than competitors? What is the basis for such a belief?
- Do the various activities proposed in the strategy provide synergistic advantages? Are they compatible?
- Does the proposed strategy adequately address questions of corporate objectives, financial policy, scope of operations, organization, and integration?
- What specific resources (personnel, skills, information, facilities, technology, finances, relationships) will be needed to execute the strategy? Does the company already possess these resources? Has management established programs for building these resources and overall competence which will provide telling competitive advantages over the long run?

- To what extent does the strategy define a unique and appropriate economic role for the company? How different is it from the competitors' strategy?
- Has the issue of growth rate been raised? Are there good reasons to believe that investment in growth will pay off? Does the company's track record support such a conclusion?
- Does the proposed dividend policy reflect the company's growth policy, based on a demonstrated ability or inability to reinvest cash flow advantageously? Or is it just a "safe" compromise, conforming to what others usually do?
- Is management capable of implementing the strategy effectively? What leads to this conclusion?
- How and to what extent is the strategy to be communicated to the organization? Is it to be distributed in written form? If competitors are aware of the company's strategy, will that help or hurt?
- What provision is to be made for employing the strategy as a guide to operating decisions? To what extent is it to be used by the board? How?
- How is it to be kept up-to-date? Are there to be regular reviews? How often and by whom?
- Has a set of long-range projections of operations following the strategy been prepared? Have the possible results of following alternative strategies been prepared?
- Does the strategy focus on the few really important key issues? Is it too detailed? Does it address genuine business questions (as opposed to "motherhood" statements)?
- In its strategic thinking, has management avoided the lure of simplistic approaches such as:

  Growth for growth's sake?

  Diversification for diversification's sake?

  Aping the industry leader?

  Broadening the scope in order to secure "incremental" earnings?

  Assuming it can execute better than competitors without objective evidence that such is the case?
- Are there other issues, trends, or potential events that should have been taken into account?

Source: Milton Lauenstein, "Boards of Directors: The Strategy Audit," *Journal of Business Strategy* 4, no. 3 (Winter 1984): 90, 91. Reprinted with permission.

The trend among corporations toward decreased diversification, increased takeover activity, increased legal pressures, multidivisional structures, and multinational operations augments the problem of keeping directors informed. Boards should play a role beyond that of performing a strategic audit. They should provide greater input and advice in the strategy-formulation process to assure that strategists are providing for the long-term needs of the firm. This is being done through the formation of three other types of board committees: nominating committees to propose candidates for the board and senior officers of the firm; compensation committees to evaluate the performance of top executives and determine the terms and conditions of their employment; and public policy committees to give board-level attention to company policies and performance on subjects of concern such as business ethics, consumer affairs, and political activities.[16] Two example individuals who serve on ten corporate boards of directors and who receive an annual compensation of more than $100,000 for board services are former President Gerald Ford and former Commerce Secretary Juanita Kreps.

CONCLUSION

The essence of strategy formulation is an assessment of whether an organization is doing the right things and how it can be more effective in what it does. Every organization should be wary of becoming a prisoner of its own strategy, because even the best strategies become obsolete sooner or later. Strategies should never be cast in stone. Regular reappraisal of strategy helps management avoid complacency. Objectives and strategies should be consciously developed and coordinated and should not merely evolve out of day-to-day operating decisions. An organization with no sense of direction and no coherent strategy precipitates its own demise. When an organization does not know where it wants to go, it usually ends up some place it does not want to be! Every organization needs to consciously establish and communicate clear objectives and strategies.

Modern strategy-formulation tools and concepts are described in this chapter and integrated into a practical three-stage framework. Tools such as the TOWS Matrix, SPACE Matrix, BCG Matrix, IE Matrix, and QSPM can significantly enhance the quality of strategic decisions, but they should never be used to dictate the choice of strategies. Behavioral, cultural, and political aspects of strategy generation and selection are always important to consider and manage. Due to increased legal pressure from outside groups, boards of directors are assuming a more active role in strategy analysis and choice. This is a positive trend for organizations.

KEY TERMS AND CONCEPTS

Aggressive quadrant
Attractiveness Scores (AS)
Board of directors
Business portfolio
Boston Consulting Group (BCG) Matrix
Cash Cows
Competitive Advantage (CA)
Competitive quadrant
Conservative quadrant
Decision stage
Defensive quadrant
Directional vector
Dogs
Environmental Stability (ES)
Financial Strength (FS)
Grand Strategy Matrix
Halo error
Industry Strength (IS)
Input stage
Internal-External (IE) Matrix
Matching
Matching stage
Quantitative Strategic Planning Matrix (QSPM)
Question Marks
Relative market share position
SO Strategies
ST Strategies
Stars
Strategic Position and Action Evaluation (SPACE) Matrix

Strategy-formulation framework
Sum Total Attractiveness Scores
Threats-Opportunities-Weaknesses-Strengths (TOWS) Matrix
Total Attractiveness Scores (TAS)
WO Strategies
WT Strategies

ISSUES FOR REVIEW AND DISCUSSION

1. How would application of the strategy-formulation framework differ from a small to a large organization?
2. What types of strategies would you recommend for an organization that achieves total weighted scores of 3.6 on the IFE and 1.2 on the EFE?
3. Given the following information, develop a SPACE Matrix for the XYZ Corporation.
   FS = +2 ES = −6 CA = −2
   IS = +4
4. Given the information in the table below, develop a BCG Matrix and an IE Matrix.
5. Explain the steps involved in applying QSPM.
6. How would you develop a set of objectives for your school of business?
7. What do you think is the appropriate role of a board of directors in strategic management? Why?
8. Discuss the limitations of various strategy-formulation analytical techniques.
9. Explain why cultural factors should be an important consideration in analyzing and choosing among alternative strategies.
10. How are the TOWS Matrix, SPACE Analysis, BCG Matrix, IE Matrix, and Grand Strategy Matrix similar? How are they different?
11. How would profit and nonprofit organizations differ in their application of the strategy-formulation framework?
12. Select an article given from the suggested readings for this chapter and prepare a report on that article for your class.

Divisions	*Profits*	*Sales*	*Relative Market Share*	*Industry Growth Rate*	*IFE Total Weighted Scores*	*EFE Total Weighted Scores*
1	10	100	0.2	+.20	1.6	2.5
2	15	50	0.5	+.10	3.1	1.8
3	25	100	0.8	−.10	2.2	3.3

NOTES

1. These four alternatives were first presented in Steven C. Brandt, *Strategic Planning in Emerging Companies* (Reading, Massachusetts: Addison-Wesley, 1981).
2. R. T. Lenz, "Managing the Evolution of the Strategic Planning Process," *Business Horizons* 30, no. 1 (January–February 1987): 37.
3. Heinz Weihrich, "The TOWS Matrix: A Tool for Situational Analysis," *Long Range Planning* 15, no. 2 (April 1982): 61.
4. A. Rowe, R. Mason, and K. Dickel, *Strategic Management and Business Policy: A Methodological Approach* (Reading, Massachusetts: Addison-Wesley, 1982), 155.
5. Boston Consulting Group, *Perspectives on Experience* (Boston: The Boston Consulting Group,

1974). Also, Barry Hedley, "Strategy and the Business Portfolio," *Long Range Planning* 10, no. 1 (February 1977): 9.

6. This technique is similar to the General Electric Business Screen, but the axes are labeled more clearly and the scoring procedure is improved in this text.
7. Fred David, "The Strategic Planning Matrix—A Quantitative Approach," *Long Range Planning* 19, no. 5 (October 1986): 102.
8. Fred David, "Computer-Assisted Strategic Planning in Small Businesses," *Journal of Systems Management* 36, no. 7 (July 1985): 24–34.
9. Y. Allarie, and M. Firsirotu, "How to Implement Radical Strategies in Large Organizations," *Sloan Management Review* 26, no. 3 (Spring 1985): 19. Another excellent article is P. Shrivastava, "Integrating Strategy Formulation with Organizational Culture," *Journal of Business Strategy* 5, no. 3 (Winter 1985): 103–111.
10. Don Beeman, and Thomas Sharkey, "The Use and Abuse of Corporate Politics," *Business Horizons* 30, no. 2 (March–April 1987): 30.
11. Ibid.
12. James Brian Quinn, *Strategies for Change: Logical Incrementalism* (Homewood, Illinois: Richard D. Irwin, 1980), 128–145. These political tactics are listed in A. Thompson and A. Strickland, *Strategic Management: Concepts and Cases* (Plano, Texas: Business Publications, 1984), 261.
13. William Guth, and Ian MacMillan, "Strategy Implementation Versus Middle Management Self-Interest," Strategic Management Journal 7, no. 4 (July–August 1986): 321.
14. John Henke, Jr., "Involving the Board of Directors in Strategic Planning, *Journal of Business Strategy* 7, no. 2 (Fall 1986): 89.
15. Milton Lauenstein, "Boards of Directors: The Strategic Audit," *Journal of Business Strategy* (Winter 1984): 87–91.
16. Murray Weidenbaum, "Updating the Corporate Board," *Journal of Business Strategy* 7, no. 1 (Summer 1986): 80.

SUGGESTED READINGS

Aaker, D. A. "How to Select a Business Strategy." *California Management Review* 26, no. 3 (Spring 1984): 167–175.

Aggarwal, Raj. "The Strategic Challenge of the Evolving Global Economy." *Business Horizons* 30, no. 4 (July–August 1987): 38–44.

Aram, J. D., and Cowen, S. S. "The Directors' Role in Planning: What Information Do They Need?" *Long Range Planning* 19, no. 2 (April 1986): 117–124.

Baum, L., and Byrne, J. A. "The Job Nobody Wants." *Business Week* (8 September 1986): 56–61.

Beeman, D. R., and Sharkey, T. W. "The Use and Abuse of Corporate Politics." *Business Horizons* 30, no. 2 (March–April 1987): 26–30.

Bhide, A. "Hustle as Strategy." *Harvard Business Review* 64, no. 5 (September–October 1986): 59–65.

Clarke, C. J., and Gall, F. "Planned Divestment—A Five-step Approach." *Long Range Planning* 20, no. 1 (February 1987): 17–24.

Davidson, William H. "Creating and Managing Joint Ventures in China." *California Management Review* 29, no. 4 (Summer 1987): 77–94.

Denison, D. R. "Bringing Corporate Culture to the Bottom Line." *Organizational Dynamics* (Fall 1984): 5–14.

Ghoshal, S. "Global Strategy: An Organizing Framework." *Strategic Management Journal* 8, no. 5 (September–October 1987): 425–440.

Goold, Michael, and Campbell, Andrew. "Many Best Ways to Make Strategy." *Harvard Business Review* 65, no. 6 (November–December 1987).

Hardy, Cynthia. "Investing in Retrenchment: Avoiding the Hidden Costs." *California Management Review* 29, no. 4 (Summer 1987): 111–125.

Henke, J. W. "Involving the Board of Directors in Strategic Planning." *The Journal of Business Strategy* 7, no. 2 (Fall 1986): 87–95.

Hopkins, H. D. "Acquisition Strategy and the Market

Position of Acquiring Firms." *Strategic Management Journal* 8, no. 6 (November–December 1987): 535–548.

Jemison, D. B., and Sitkin, S. B. "Corporate Acquisitions: A Process Perspective." *Academy of Management Review* 11, no. 1 (January 1986): 145–163.

Kesner, I. F., and Dalton, D. R. "Boards of Directors and the Checks and Balances of Corporate Governance." *Business Horizons* (September–October 1986): 17–23.

Kesner, I. F.; Victor, B.; and Lamont, B. T. "Board Composition and the Commission of Illegal Acts: An Investigation of Fortune 500 Companies." *Academy of Management Journal* 29, no. 4 (December 1986): 789–799.

Kim, W. C., and Mauborgne, R. A. "Cross-Cultural Strategies." *Journal of Business Strategy* 7, no. 4(Spring 1987): 28–35.

Lenz, R. T., and Lyles, M. A. "Managing Human Problems in Strategic Planning Systems." *The Journal of Business Strategy* 60, no. 4 (Spring 1986): 57–66.

MacMillan, K. "Strategy: Portfolio Analysis." *Journal of General Management* 11, no. 4 (Summer 1986): 94–112.

Mayer, Robert. "Winning Strategies for Manufacturers in Mature Industries." *Journal of Business Strategy* 8, no. 2 (Fall 1987): 23–31.

Miesing, P. "Limitations of Matrix Models as a Strategic Planning Tool." *Managerial Planning* 31, no. 6 (May–June 1983): 42–45.

Morris, Elinor. "Vision and Strategy: A Focus for the Future." *Journal of Business Strategy* 8, no. 2 (Fall 1987): 51–58.

Pawling, J. D. "The Crisis of Corporate Boards: Accountability vs. Misplaced Loyalty." *Business Quarterly* 51, no. 2 (Summer 1986): 71–73.

Perkins, R. B. "Avoiding Director Liability." *Harvard Business Review* 64, no. 3 (May–June 1986): 8–14.

Porter, M. E. "From Competitive Advantage to Corporate Strategy." *Harvard Business Review* 65, no. 3 (May–June 1987): 43–59.

Roberts, E. B., and Berry, C. A. "Entering New Businesses: Selecting Strategies for Success." *Sloan Management Review* 26, no. 3 (Spring 1985): 3–17.

Schillaci, Carmela. "Designing Successful Joint Ventures." *Journal of Business Strategy* 8, no. 2 (Fall 1987): 59–63.

Schmidt, R. J. "Corporate Divestiture: Pruning for Higher Profits." *Business Horizons* 30, no. 3 (May–June 1987): 26–31.

Scholz, Christian. "Corporate Culture and Strategy—The Problem of Strategic Fit." *Long Range Planning* 20, no. 4 (August 1987): 78–87.

Schwaninger, M. "A Practical Approach to Strategy Development." *Long Range Planning* 20, no. 5 (October 1987): 74–85.

Weidenbaum, M. L. "Updating the Corporate Board." *Journal of Business Strategy* 7, no. 1 (Summer 1986): 77–83.

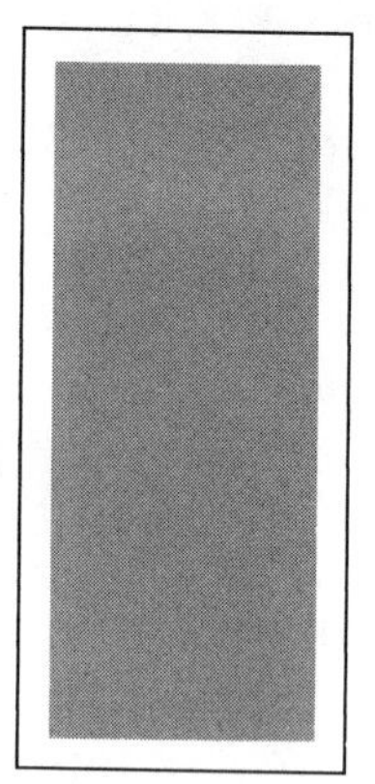

EXPERIENTIAL EXERCISES

EXPERIENTIAL EXERCISE 6A

Developing a TOWS Matrix for Ponderosa

PURPOSE

The most widely used strategy-formulation technique among American firms is the TOWS Matrix. This exercise requires development of a TOWS Matrix for Ponderosa. Matching key internal and external factors in a TOWS Matrix requires good intuitive and conceptual skills. You will improve with practice in developing a TOWS Matrix.

YOUR TASK

Recall from earlier experiential exercises that you have already determined Ponderosa's external opportunities/threats and internal strengths/weaknesses. This information could be used in completing this exercise. Follow the steps outlined below:

Step 1 On a separate sheet of paper, construct a large nine-cell diagram that will represent your TOWS Matrix. Label the cells appropriately.

Step 2 Record Ponderosa's opportunities/threats and strengths/weaknesses appropriately in your diagram.

Step 3 Match external and internal factors to generate feasible alternative strategies for Ponderosa. Record SO, WO, ST, and WT Strategies in appropriate cells of the TOWS Matrix. Use the proper notation to indicate the rationale for the strategies. You do not necessarily have to have strategies in all four strategy cells.

Step 4: Compare your TOWS Matrix to other students' TOWS Matrix. Discuss any major differences.

EXPERIENTIAL EXERCISE 6B

Developing a SPACE Matrix for Ponderosa

PURPOSE

Should Ponderosa pursue aggressive, conservative, competitive, or defensive strategies? Develop a SPACE Matrix for Ponderosa to answer this question.

YOUR TASK

Step 1 Join with one other person in class and develop a joint SPACE Matrix for Ponderosa.

Step 2 Compare your SPACE Matrix to the author's SPACE Matrix. Discuss any major differences.

EXPERIENTIAL EXERCISE 6C

Developing a BCG Matrix for Ponderosa

PURPOSE

Portfolio matrices are widely used by multidivisional organizations to help identify and select strategies to pursue. A BCG analysis could identify particular divisions to receive fewer resources and others to receive more resources. It may identify some divisions to be divested and others to be acquired. This exercise can give you practice developing a BCG Matrix.

YOUR TASK

Step 1 Place the following five column headings at the top of a separate sheet of paper: Divisions, Revenues, Profits, Relative Market Share Position, Industry Growth Rate.

Step 2 Complete a BCG Matrix for Ponderosa.

Step 3 Compare your BCG Matrix to another student's matrix. Discuss any major differences.

EXPERIENTIAL EXERCISE 6D

Developing a QSPM for Ponderosa

PURPOSE

This exercise can give you practice developing a Quantitative Strategic Planning Matrix to determine the relative attractiveness of various strategic alternatives.

YOUR TASK

Step 1 Join two other students in class to develop a joint QSPM for Ponderosa.

Step 2 Go to the blackboard and record your strategies and their Sum Total Attractiveness Scores. Compare your team's strategies and total attractiveness scores to other teams.

Step 3 Compare your QSPM to the author's QSPM. Discuss any major differences.

EXPERIENTIAL EXERCISE 6E

Formulating Individual Strategies

PURPOSE

Individuals and organizations are alike in many ways. Each has competitors and each should plan for the future. Every individual and organization has some internal strengths and weaknesses and faces some external opportunities and threats. Both individuals and organizations establish objectives and allocate resources. These and other similarities make it possible for individuals to use many strategic-management concepts and tools. This exercise is designed to demonstrate how the TOWS Matrix can be used by an individual to plan his or her own future. As one nears completion of a college degree and begins interviewing for jobs, planning can be particularly important.

YOUR TASK

On a separate sheet of paper, construct a TOWS Matrix. Develop the TOWS matrix by including what you consider to be your major external opportunities, your major external threats, your major strengths, and your major weaknesses. An external opportunity, for example, may be that your university offers a graduate program that interests you; an internal weakness may be a low grade point average. Match key external and internal factors by recording in the appropriate cell of the matrix alternative strategies or actions that would allow you to capitalize upon your strengths, overcome your weaknesses, take advantage of your external opportunities, and minimize the impact of external threats. Be sure to use the appropriate matching notation in the strategy cells of the matrix. Since every individual (and organization) is unique, there is no one right answer to this exercise.

EXPERIENTIAL EXERCISE 6F

The Mach Test

PURPOSE

The purpose of this exercise is to enhance your understanding and awareness of the impact that behavioral and political factors can have on strategy analysis and choice.

YOUR TASK

Step 1 On a separate sheet of paper, number from 1 to 10. For each of the ten statements given below, record a 1, 2, 3, 4, or 5 to indicate your attitude, where:

1 = I disagree a lot
2 = I disagree a little
3 = My attitude is neutral
4 = I agree a little
5 = I agree a lot

1. The best way to handle people is to tell them what they want to hear.
2. When you ask someone to do something for you, it is best to give the real reason for wanting it, rather than giving a reason than might carry more weight.
3. Anyone who completely trusts anyone else is asking for trouble.
4. It is hard to get ahead without cutting corners here and there.
5. It is safest to assume that all people have a vicious streak, and it will come out when they are given a chance.
6. One should take action only when it is morally right.
7. Most people are basically good and kind.
8. There is no excuse for lying to someone else.
9. Most people forget more easily the death of their father than the loss of their property.
10. Generally speaking, people won't work hard unless they're forced to do so.

Step 2 Add the number you recorded beside statements 1, 3, 4, 5, 9, and 10. This sum is Subtotal One. For the other four statements, reverse the numbers you recorded, so a 5 becomes a 1, 4 becomes 2, 2 becomes 4, 1 becomes 5, and 3 remains a 3. Then add those four numbers to get Subtotal Two. Finally, add Subtotal One and Subtotal Two to get your Final Score.

YOUR FINAL SCORE

Your Final Score is your Machiavellian Score. Machiavellian principles are defined in a dictionary as "manipulative, dishonest, deceiving, and favoring political expediency over morality." These tactics are not desirable, are not ethical, and are not recommended in the strategic-management process! You may however encounter some highly Machiavellian individuals in your career, so beware.

It is important for strategists not to manipulate others in the pursuit of organizational objectives. Individuals today recognize and resent manipulative tactics more than ever before. J. R. Ewing (on *Dallas*) is a good example of someone who is a high Mach (score over 30).

The National Opinion Research Center used this short form in a random sample of American adults and found the national average Final Score to be 25.[1] The higher your score, the more Machiavellian (manipulative) you tend to be. The following scale is descriptive of individual scores on this test:

below 16:	Never uses manipulation as a tool.
16 to 20:	Rarely uses manipulation as a tool.
21 to 25:	Sometimes uses manipulation as a tool.
26 to 30:	Often uses manipulation as a tool.
Over 30:	Always uses manipulation as a tool.

TEST DEVELOPMENT

The Mach (Machiavellian) test was developed by Dr. Richard Christie, whose research suggests the following tendencies:

1. Men are generally more Machiavellian than women.
2. There is no significant difference between high Machs and low Machs on measures of intelligence or ability.
3. Although high Machs are detached from others, they are not detached in a pathological sense.
4. Machiavellian scores are not statistically related to authoritarian scores.
5. High Machs tend to be in professions that emphasize the control and manipulation of individuals; for example, lawyers, psychiatrists, and behavioral scientists.
6. Machiavellianism is not significantly related to major demographic characteristics, such as educational level or marital status.
7. High Machs tend to come from a city or have urban backgrounds.
8. Older adults tend to have lower Mach scores than younger adults.[2]

A classic book on power relationships, *The Prince,* was written by Niccolo Machiavelli. Several excerpts from *The Prince* are given below:

> Men must either be cajoled or crushed, for they will revenge themselves for slight wrongs, while for grave ones they cannot. The injury therefore that you do to a man should be such that you need not fear his revenge.
>
> We must bear in mind. . .that there is nothing more difficult and dangerous, or more doubtful of success, than an attempt to introduce a new order of things in any state. The innovator has for enemies all those who derived advantages from the old order of things, while those who expect to be benefited by the new institution will be but lukewarm defenders.
>
> A wise prince, therefore, will steadily pursue such a course that the citizens of his state will always and under all circumstances feel the need for his authority, and will therefore always prove faithful to him.
>
> A prince should seem to be merciful, faithful, humane, religious, and upright, and should even be so in reality; but he should have his mind so trained that, when occasion requires it, he may know how to change to the opposite.[3]

1. Richard Christie and Florence Geis, *Studies in Machiavellianism* (Academic Press, 1970). Material in this exercise adapted with permission of the authors and the Academic Press.
2. Christie and Geis: 82–83.
3. Machiavelli, *The Prince* (New York: The Washington Press, 1963).

PART THREE STRATEGY IMPLEMENTATION

Implementing Strategies: Management Issues

NOTABLE QUOTES

The ideal organizational structure is a place where ideas filter up as well as down, where the merit of ideas carries more weight than their source, and where participation and shared objectives are valued more than executive orders.

Edson Spencer

"Poor Ike; when he was a general, he gave an order and it was carried out. Now, he's going to sit in that office and give an order and not a damn thing is going to happen."

Harry Truman

Management, in the last analysis, means the substitution of thought for brawn and muscle, of knowledge for folkways and superstition, and of cooperation for force. It means the substitution of responsibility for obedience to rank, and of authority of performance for authority of power.

Peter Drucker

Organizations are creatures of habit just like people. They are cultures, heavily influenced by the past.

Robert H. Waterman, Jr.

Of course objectives are not a railroad timetable. They can be compared to a compass bearing by which a ship navigates. A compass bearing is firm, but in actual navigation, a ship may veer off its course for many miles. Without a compass bearing, a ship would neither find its port nor be able to estimate the time required to get there.

Peter Drucker

The opportunities and threats existing in any situation always exceed the resources needed to exploit the opportunities or avoid the threats. Thus, strategy is essentially a problem of allocating resources. If a strategy is to be successful, it must allocate superior resources against a decisive opportunity.

William Cohen

The best game plan in the world never blocked or tackled anybody.

Vince Lombardi

7

OUTLINE

OBJECTIVES

After studying this chapter, you should be able to:

- Explain why strategy implementation is more difficult than strategy formulation.
- Discuss the importance of annual objectives and policies in achieving organizational commitment for strategies to be implemented.
- Explain why organizational structure is so important to strategy implementation.
- Describe important relationships between production/operations variables and strategy implementation.

The strategic-management process does not end when strategists decide what strategy or strategies to pursue. There must be a translation of strategic thought into strategic action. Implementing strategy affects an organization from top to bottom; it impacts all the functional areas of a business. It is beyond the purpose and scope of this text to examine all of the functional business concepts and tools important in the strategy-implementation process. Only issues central to strategy implementation are examined. This chapter focuses on management issues most important to strategy implementation, while Chapter 8 focuses on marketing, finance/accounting, and R & D issues.

MANAGEMENT PERSPECTIVES ON STRATEGY IMPLEMENTATION

The strategy-implementation stage of strategic management is represented by the shaded portion of Figure 7–1. Successful strategy formulation does not guarantee successful strategy implementation. It is always more difficult to do something (strategy implementation) than to say you are going to do it (strategy formulation)! Although inextricably linked, strategy implementation is fundamentally different from strategy formulation. Strategy formulation and implementation can be contrasted in the following ways:

- ☐ Strategy formulation is the positioning of forces before the action.
- ☐ Strategy implementation is the managing of forces during the action.
- ☐ Strategy formulation focuses on effectiveness.
- ☐ Strategy implementation focuses on efficiency.
- ☐ Strategy formulation is primarily an intellectual process.
- ☐ Strategy implementation is primarily an operational process.
- ☐ Strategy formulation requires good intuitive and analytical skills.
- ☐ Strategy implementation requires special motivation and leadership skills.
- ☐ Strategy formulation requires coordination among a few individuals.
- ☐ Strategy implementation requires coordination among many persons.

Strategy-formulation concepts and tools do not differ greatly for small, large, profit, or nonprofit organizations. However, strategy implementation varies considerably among different types and sizes of organizations. Implementing strategy includes such actions as altering sales territories, adding new departments, closing facilities, hiring new employees, changing an organization's pricing strategy, developing financial budgets, developing new employee benefits, establishing cost control procedures, changing advertising strategies, building new facilities, training new employees, and transferring managers among divisions. These types of activities obviously differ greatly between manufacturing, service, and governmental organizations.

In all but the smallest organizations, the transition from strategy formulation to strategy implementation requires a shift in responsibility from strategists to divisional and functional managers. Implementation problems can arise because of this shift in

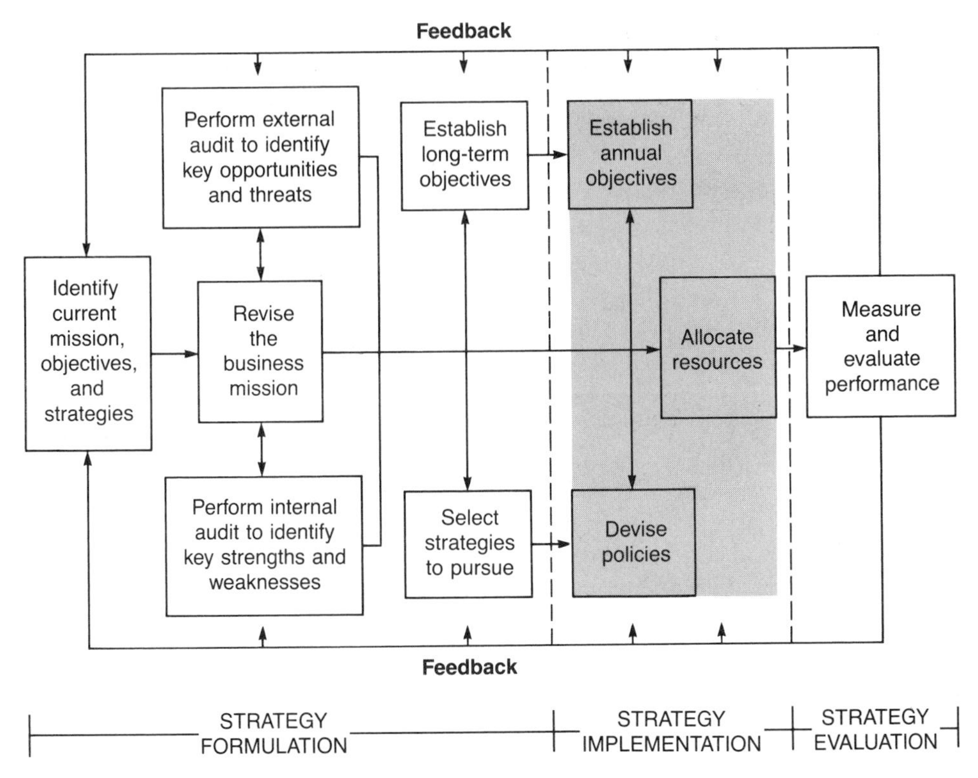

FIGURE 7–1 A comprehensive strategic-management model

responsibility, especially when strategy-formulation decisions come as a surprise to middle- and lower-level managers. Managers and employees are motivated more by perceived self-interests than by organizational interests, unless the two coincide. Therefore, it is essential that divisional and functional managers be involved as much as possible in strategy-formulation activities. Of equal importance, strategists should be involved as much as possible in strategy-implementation activities.

Management issues central to strategy implementation include establishing annual objectives, devising policies, allocating resources, altering an existing organizational structure, revising reward and incentive plans, minimizing resistance to change, matching managers with strategy, developing a strategy-supportive culture, adapting production/operations processes, and developing an effective human resource function. Management changes are necessarily more extensive when strategies to be implemented move a firm in a major new direction.

Managers throughout an organization should participate early and directly in strategy-implementation decisions. Their role in strategy implementation should build upon prior involvement in strategy-formulation activities. Top management's expressed personal commitment to strategy implementation is a necessary and powerful motivational force for middle- and lower-level managers. Too often, top managers and strategists are "too busy" to actively support strategy-implementation efforts, and their lack of interest can be detrimental to organizational success. The rationale for objectives and strategies should be clearly communicated throughout an organization. Major competitors' accomplishments, products, plans, actions, and performance should be presented. Major external opportunities and threats should be communicated, and managers' and employees' questions should be answered. Top-down flow of communication is essential for developing bottom-up support.

ANNUAL OBJECTIVES

Establishing *annual objectives* is a decentralized activity that directly involves all managers in an organization. Active participation in establishing annual objectives can lead to acceptance and commitment. Annual objectives are essential for strategy implementation because they (1) represent the basis for allocating resources, (2) are a primary mechanism for evaluating managers, (3) are the major instrument for monitoring progress towards achieving long-term objectives, and (4) establish organizational, divisional, and departmental priorities. For all of these, and other, reasons, considerable time and effort should be devoted to ensuring that annual objectives are well conceived, consistent with long-term objectives, and supportive of strategies to be implemented. Approving, revising, or rejecting annual objectives is much more than a rubber stamp activity. Two well-known writers once described the purpose of annual objectives as follows:

> Annual objectives serve as guidelines for action, directing and channeling efforts and activities of organization members. They provide a source of legitimacy in an enterprise by justifying activities to stakeholders. They serve as standards of performance. They serve as an important source of employee motivation and identification. They give incentives for employees to perform. They provide a basis for organizational design.[1]

Clearly stated and communicated objectives are critical to success in all types and sizes of firms. Annual objectives, stated in terms of profitability, growth, and market share by business segment, geographic area, customer groups, and product, are common in organizations. Figure 7–2 illustrates how the Stamus Company could establish annual objectives based on long-term objectives. Table 7–1 reveals associated revenue figures that correspond to the objectives outlined in Figure 7–2. Note that, according to plan, the Stamus Company will slightly exceed its long-term objective of doubling company revenues in two years.

Figure 7–2 also reflects how a hierarchy of annual objectives can be established based on an organization's structure. Objectives should be consistent across hierarchical levels and form a network of supportive aims. *Horizontal consistency of objectives* is as important as *vertical consistency*. For instance, it would not be effective for manufacturing to achieve more than its annual objective of units produced if marketing could not sell the additional units.

Annual objectives should be measurable, consistent, reasonable, challenging, clear, communicated throughout the organization, characterized by an appropriate time dimension, and accompanied by commensurate rewards and sanctions. Too often, objectives are stated in generalities, with little operational usefulness. Annual objectives such as "to improve communication" or "to improve performance" are not clear, spe-

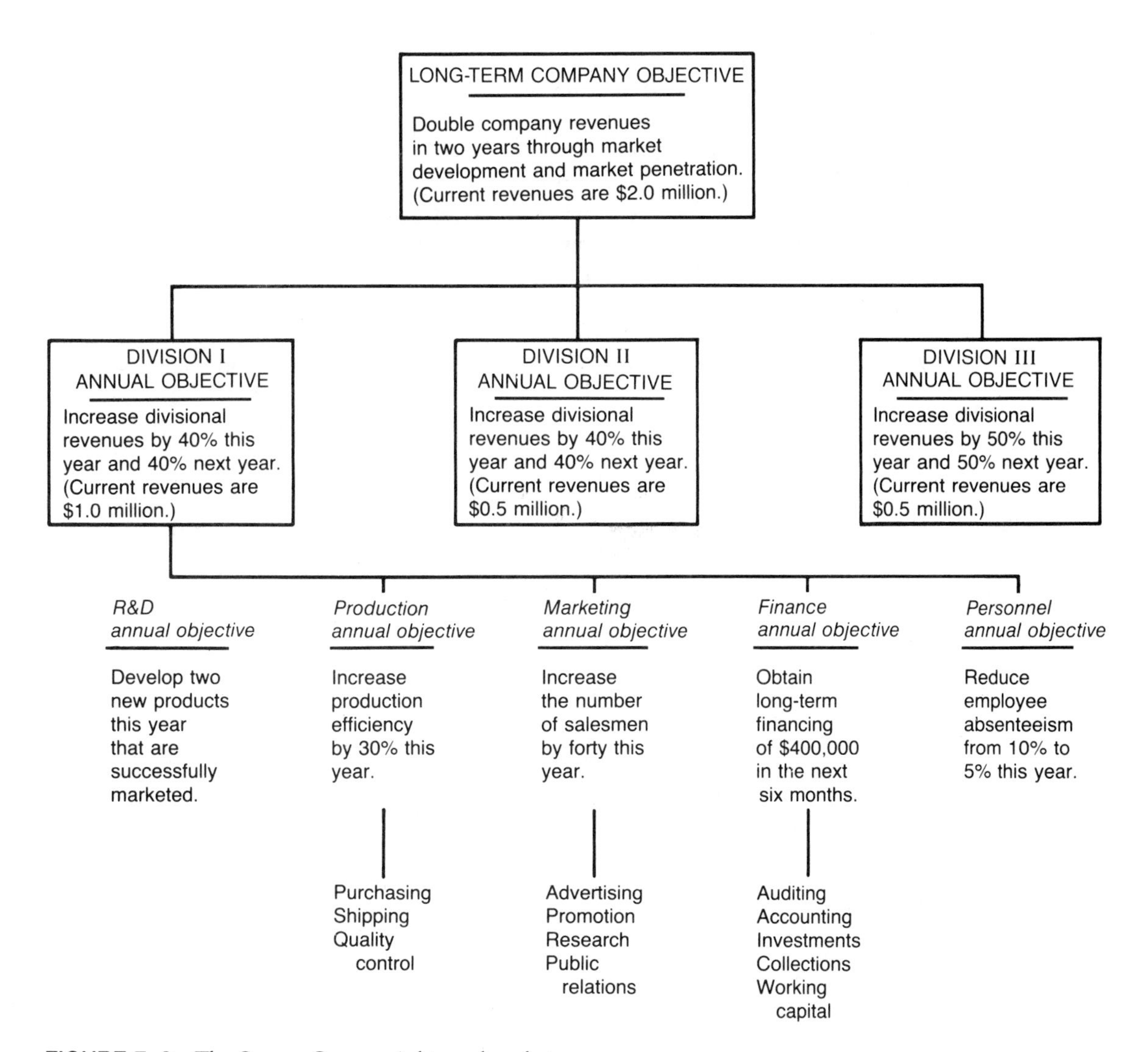

FIGURE 7–2 The Stamus Company's hierarchy of aims

TABLE 7–1 The Stamus Company's revenue expectations (in millions of dollars)

	1988	*1989*	*1990*
Division I Revenues	1.0	1.400	1.960
Division II Revenues	0.5	0.700	.980
Division III Revenues	0.5	0.750	1.125
Total Company Revenues	2.0	2.950	4.065

cific, or measurable. Objectives should state quantity, quality, cost, and time and also be verifiable. Terms such as "maximize," "minimize," "as soon as possible," and "adequate" should be avoided.

Annual objectives should be compatible with employees' and managers' values and should be supported by clearly stated policies. More of something is not always better! Improved quality or reduced cost may, for example, be more important than quantity. It is important to tie rewards and sanctions to annual objectives, so that employees and managers understand that achieving objectives is critical to successful strategy implementation. Clear annual objectives do not guarantee successful strategy implementation, but they do increase the likelihood that personal and organizational aims can be accomplished. Overemphasis on achieving objectives can result in undesirable conduct, such as faking the numbers, distorting the records, and letting objectives become ends in themselves. Managers must be alert to these potential problems.

POLICIES

Changes in a firm's strategic direction do not occur automatically. On a day-to-day basis, policies are needed to make a strategy work. Policies facilitate solving repetitive or recurring problems and guide the implementation of strategy. Broadly defined, *policy* refers to specific guidelines, methods, procedures, rules, forms, and administrative practices established to support and encourage work towards stated goals.[2] Policies are instruments for strategy implementation. Policies set boundaries, constraints, and limits on the kinds of administrative actions that can be taken to reward and sanction behavior; they clarify what can and cannot be done in pursuit of an organization's objectives.

Policies let both employees and managers know what is expected of them, thereby increasing the likelihood that strategies will be implemented successfully. They provide a basis for management control, allow coordination across organizational units, and reduce the amount of time managers spend making decisions. Policies also clarify what work is to be done by whom. They promote delegation of decision making to appropriate managerial levels where various problems usually arise. Many organizations have a policy manual that serves to guide and direct behavior. A 1987 study by *Business Week* found that 30 percent of all corporations in the United States have instituted "No Smoking" policies. This number is expected to increase to 80 percent by 1990.[3]

Policies can apply to all divisions and departments (for example, "We are an equal opportunity employer"). Some policies apply to a single department ("Employees in this department must take at least one training and development course each year"). Whatever their scope and form, policies serve as a mechanism for implementing strategies and obtaining objectives. Policies should be stated in writing whenever possible. They represent the means for carrying out strategic decisions. Examples of policies that support a company strategy, a divisional objective, and a departmental objective are given in Exhibit 7–1.

Here are some other questions or behaviors that may require answers in the form of management policies:

☐ To offer extensive or limited management-development workshops and seminars?
☐ To centralize or decentralize employee-training activities?
☐ To recruit through employment agencies, college campuses, and/or newspapers?
☐ To promote from within or hire from the outside?
☐ To promote on the basis of merit or on the basis of seniority?
☐ To tie executive compensation to long-term and/or annual objectives?
☐ To offer numerous or few employee benefits?
☐ To negotiate directly or indirectly with labor unions?
☐ To delegate authority for large expenditures or to retain this authority centrally?
☐ To allow much, some, or no overtime work?
☐ To establish a high- or low-safety stock of inventory?
☐ To use one or more suppliers?
☐ To buy, lease, or rent new production equipment?
☐ To stress quality control greatly or not?
☐ To establish many or only a few production standards?
☐ To operate one, two, or three shifts?
☐ To discourage using insider information for personal gain
☐ To discourage sexual harassment
☐ To discourage smoking at work
☐ To discourage insider trading
☐ To discourage moonlighting

EXHIBIT 7–1 A hierarchy of policies

Company Strategy: Acquire a chain of retail stores to meet our sales growth and profitability objectives.

Supporting policies:

1. "All stores will be open from 8:00 AM to 8:00 PM Monday through Saturday." (This policy could increase retail sales if stores currently are open only forty hours a week.)
2. "All stores must submit a Monthly Control Data Report." (This policy could reduce expense-to-sales ratios.)
3. "All stores must support company advertising by contributing 5 percent of their total monthly revenues for this purpose." (This policy could allow the company to establish a national reputation.)
4. "All stores must adhere to the uniform pricing guidelines set forth in the Company Handbook." (This policy could help assure customers that the company offers a consistent product in terms of price and quality in all its stores.)

Divisional Objective: Increase the division's revenues from $10 million in 1988 to $15 million in 1989.

Supporting policies:

1. "Beginning in January 1989, this division's salespersons must file a weekly activity report that includes the number of calls made, the number of miles traveled, the number of units sold, the dollar volume sold, and the number of new accounts opened." (This policy could assure that salespersons do not place too great an emphasis in certain areas.)
2. "Beginning in January 1989, this division will return to its employees 5 percent of its gross revenues in the form of a Christmas bonus." (This policy could increase employee productivity.)
3. "Beginning in January 1989, inventory levels carried in warehouses will be decreased by 30 percent in accordance with a Just-In-Time manufacturing approach." (This policy could reduce production expenses and thus free funds for increased marketing efforts.)

Production Department Objective: Increase production from 20,000 units in 1988 to 30,000 units in 1989.

Supporting policies:

1. "Beginning in January 1989, employees will have the option of working up to twenty hours of overtime per week." (This policy could minimize the need to hire additional employees.)
2. "Beginning in January 1989, perfect attendance awards in the amount of $100 will be given to all employees who do not miss a workday in a given year." (This policy could decrease absenteeism and increase productivity.)
3. "Beginning in January 1989, new equipment must be leased rather than purchased." (This policy could reduce tax liabilities and thus allow more funds to be invested in modernizing production processes.)

RESOURCE ALLOCATION

Resource allocation is a central management activity that allows for strategy execution. In organizations that do not use a strategic-management approach to decision making, resource allocation is often a politicized activity. Strategic management enables resources to be allocated according to priorities established by annual objectives. Nothing could be more detrimental to strategic management and to organizational success than for resources to be allocated in ways not consistent with priorities indicated by approved annual objectives.

All organizations have at least four types of resources that can be used to achieve desired objectives: financial resources, physical resources, human resources, and technological resources. Strategies are not implemented merely by allocating resources appropriately. Allocating resources to particular divisions and departments does not mean that strategies will be successfully implemented. A number of factors commonly prohibit effective resource allocation, including an over-protection of resources, too great an emphasis on short-run financial criteria, organizational politics, vague strategy targets, a reluctance to take risks, and a lack of sufficient knowledge.[4]

Below the corporate level, there often exists an absence of systematic thinking about resources allocated and strategies of the firm. Yavitz and Newman explain why:

> Managers normally have many more tasks than they can do. Managers must allocate time and resources among these tasks. Pressure builds up. Expenses are too high. The CEO wants a good financial report for the third quarter. Strategy formulation and implementation activities often get deferred. Today's problems soak up available energies and resources. Scrambled accounts and budgets fail to reveal the shift in allocation away from strategic needs to currently squeaking wheels.[5]

The real value of any resource-allocation program lies in the resulting accomplishment of an organization's objectives. Effective resource allocation does not guarantee successful strategy implementation because programs, personnel, controls, and commitment must breathe life into the resources provided. Strategic management itself is sometimes referred to as a "resource-allocation process."

MANAGING CONFLICT

Interdependency of objectives and competition for limited resources often leads to conflict. *Conflict* can be defined as a disagreement between two or more parties on one or more issues. Establishing annual objectives can lead to conflict because different individuals have different expectations and different perceptions, schedules create pressure, personalities are incompatible, and misunderstandings between line and staff occur. For example, a collection manager's objective of reducing bad debts by 50 percent in a given year may conflict with a divisional objective to increase sales by 20 percent.

Establishing objectives can lead to conflict because managers and strategists must make tradeoffs, such as whether to emphasize short-term profits or long-term growth, profit margin or market share, market penetration or market development, growth or stability, high risk or low risk, and social responsiveness or profit maximization. Conflict is unavoidable in organizations, so it is important that conflict be managed and resolved before dysfunctional consequences affect organizational performance. Conflict is not always bad. An absence of conflict sometimes signals indifference and apathy. Conflict can serve to "energize" opposing groups into action and may help managers identify problems.

Various approaches for managing and resolving conflict can be classified into three categories: avoidance, defusion, and confrontation. *Avoidance* includes such actions as ignoring the problem in hopes that the conflict will resolve itself or physically separating the conflicting individuals (or groups). *Defusion* can include playing down differences between conflicting parties while accentuating similarities and common interests, compromising so that there is neither a clear winner nor loser, resorting to majority rule, appealing to a higher authority, or redesigning present positions. *Confrontation* is exemplified by exchanging members of conflicting parties so that each can gain an appreciation of the other's point of view, focusing on superordinate goals such as company survival, or holding a meeting whereby conflicting parties present their views and work through their differences.

MATCHING STRUCTURE WITH STRATEGY

Changes in strategy often require changes in the way an organization is structured for two major reasons. First, structure largely dictates how objectives and policies will be established. For example, the format for objectives and policies established under a geographic organizational structure is couched in geographic terms. Objectives and policies are stated largely in terms of products in an organization whose structure is based on product groups. The structural format for developing objectives and policies can significantly impact all other strategy-implementation activities. Second, structure dictates how resources will be allocated. If an organization is structured based on customer groups, then resources will be allocated in that manner. Similarly, if an organization's structure is set up along functional business lines, then resources are allocated by functional areas. Unless new or revised strategies place emphasis in the same areas as old strategies, structural reorientation commonly becomes a part of strategy-implementation.

In a classic study of seventy large American corporations, Alfred Chandler concluded that changes in strategy lead to changes in organizational structure.[6] Structure, he says, should be designed to facilitate the strategic pursuit of a firm, and therefore, structure follows strategy. Chandler found a particular sequence to be often repeated as organizations grow and change strategy over time; this sequence is depicted in Figure 7–3.

There is no one optimal organizational design or structure for a given strategy or type of organization. What is appropriate for one organization may not be appropriate for a similar firm, although successful firms in a given industry do tend to organize themselves in a similar way. For example, consumer-goods companies tend to emulate the divisional structure-by-product form of organization. Small firms tend to be functionally structured (centralized). Medium size firms tend to be divisionally structured (decentralized). Large firms tend to use an SBU (strategic business unit) or matrix structure. As organizations grow, their structures generally change from simple to complex as a result of concatenation, or the linking together of several basic strategies.[7] In 1988 General Foods Corporation, a division of Philip Morris, reorganized into three separate operating companies—General Foods USA, General Foods Coffee & Interna-

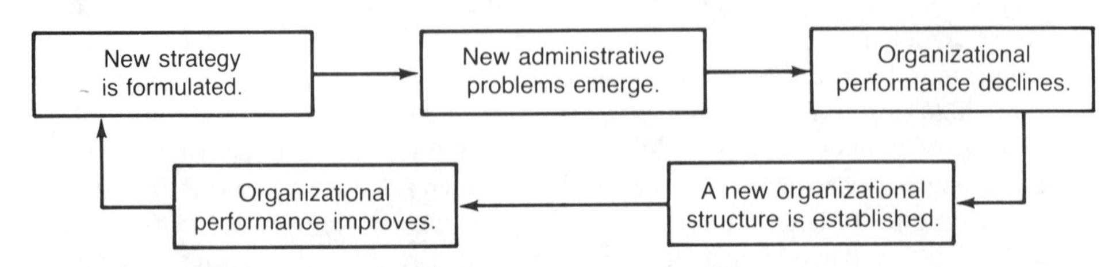

FIGURE 7–3 Chandler's strategy–structure relationship

tional, and Oscar Mayer Foods (to market meat products)—to cut costs and eliminate two thousand staff jobs.

Numerous internal and external forces affect an organization; no firm could change its structure in response to every one of these forces, because to do so would lead to chaos. However, when a firm changes its strategy in response to one or more of these forces, the existing organizational structure may become ineffective. Symptoms of an ineffective organizational structure include too many levels of management, too many meetings attended by too many people, too much attention being directed towards solving interdepartmental conflicts, too large a span of control, and too many unachieved objectives. Changes in structure can facilitate strategy-implementation efforts, but changes in structure should not be expected to make a bad strategy good, or to make bad managers good, or to make bad products sell.

It is undeniable that structure can and does influence strategy.[8] Strategies formulated must be workable, so if a certain new strategy requires massive structural changes, that fact would make the strategy less attractive. In this way, structure can shape the choice of strategies. But a more important concern is determining what types of structural changes are needed to implement new strategies and how these changes can best be accomplished. We can examine this issue by focusing on seven basic types of organizational structure: functional, divisional by geographic area, divisional by product, divisional by customer, divisional by process, strategic business unit (SBU), and matrix.

The Functional Structure

The most widely used structure is the functional or centralized type, because this structure is the simplest and least expensive of the seven alternatives. A *functional structure* groups tasks and activities by business function such as production/operations, marketing, finance/accounting, research and development, and personnel. A university may structure its activities by major functions that include academic affairs, student services, alumni relations, athletics, maintenance, and accounting. Besides being simple and inexpensive, a functional structure also promotes specialization of labor, encourages efficiency, minimizes the need for an elaborate control system, and allows rapid decision making. Some disadvantages of a functional structure are that it forces accountability to the top, minimizes career-development opportunities, and is sometimes characterized by low employee morale, line-staff conflicts, poor delegation of authority, and inadequate planning for products and markets.

The Divisional Structure

The *divisional* or *decentralized structure* is the second most common type used by American businesses. As a small organization grows, it becomes increasingly difficult to manage different products and services in different markets. Some form of divisional structure generally becomes necessary to motivate employees, control operations, and compete successfully in diverse locations. The divisional structure can be organized in one of four basic ways: by geographic area, by product or service, by customer, or by process. Within a divisional structure, functional activities are performed centrally and in each separate division.

A divisional structure has some clear advantages. First and perhaps foremost, accountability is clear. That is, divisional managers can be held responsible for sales and profit levels. Since a divisional structure is based on extensive delegation of authority, managers and employees can easily see the results of their good or bad performance. As a result, employee morale is generally higher in a divisional structure than it is in a centralized structure. Other advantages of the divisional design are that it creates career development opportunities for managers, allows local control of local situations, leads to a competitive climate within an organization, and allows new businesses and products to be added easily.

The divisional design is not without some limitations, however. Perhaps the most important limitation is that a divisional structure is costly, for a number of reasons. First, each division requires functional specialists who must be paid. Second, there exists some duplication of staff services, facilities, and personnel; for instance, functional specialists are also needed centrally (at headquarters) to coordinate divisional activities. Third, managers must be well qualified since the divisional design forces delegation of authority; better qualified individuals require higher salaries. A divisional structure can also be costly because it requires an elaborate, headquarters-driven control system. Finally, certain regions, products, or customers may sometimes receive special treatment, and it may be difficult to maintain consistent, company-wide practices. Nonetheless, for most large organizations and many small firms, the advantages of a divisional structure more than offset the potential limitations.

A *divisional structure by geographic area* is appropriate for organizations where strategies need to be tailored to fit the particular needs and characteristics of customers in different geographic areas. This type of structure can be most appropriate for organizations that have similar branch facilities located in widely dispersed areas. A divisional structure by geographic area allows local participation in decision making and improved coordination within a region. The Internal Revenue Service, the American Red Cross, the Small Business Administration, A & P, and Sears, Roebuck are examples of organizations that use the geographic type of divisional structure.

The divisional structure by product is most effective for implementing strategies when specific products or services need special emphasis. Also this type of structure is widely used when an organization offers only a few products or services, or when an organization's products or services differ substantially. The divisional structure allows strict control and attention to product lines, but it may also require a more skilled management force and reduced top-management control. General Motors, Dupont, and Proctor & Gamble use divisional structure by product to implement strategies.

When a few major customers are of paramount importance and many different services are provided to these customers, then a *divisional structure by customer* can be the most effective way to implement strategies. This structure allows an organization to cater effectively to the requirements of clearly defined customer groups. For example, book publishing companies often organize their activities around customer groups such as colleges, secondary schools, and private commercial schools. Some airline companies have two major customer divisions: passengers and freight or cargo services. Merrill Lynch is organized into separate divisions that cater to different groups of customers, including wealthy individuals, institutional investors, and small corporations. Merrill

Lynch's revenues increased 13 percent in 1987 to 10.9 billion, but company profits fell 17 percent to $391 million.

A *divisional structure by process* is similar to a functional structure, since activities are organized according to the way work is actually performed. However, a key difference between these two designs is that functional departments are not accountable for profits or revenues, whereas divisional process departments are evaluated on these criteria. An example of a divisional structure by process is a manufacturing business organized into six divisions: electrical work, glass cutting, welding, grinding, painting, and foundry work. In this case, all operations related to these specific processes would be grouped under the separate divisions. Each process (division) would be responsible for generating revenues and profits. The divisional structure by process can be particularly effective in achieving objectives when distinct production processes represent the thrust of competitiveness in an industry.

The Strategic Business Unit (SBU) Structure

As the number, size, and diversity of divisions in an organization increase, it becomes increasingly difficult for strategists to control and evaluate divisional operations. Increases in sales often are not accompanied by similar increases in profitability. The span of control becomes too large at top levels of the firm. For example, in a large conglomerate organization composed of ninety divisions, the chief executive officer could have difficulty even remembering the first names of divisional presidents. In multidivisional organizations, an SBU structure can greatly facilitate strategy-implementation efforts.

The *SBU structure* groups similar divisions into strategic business units and delegates authority and responsibility for each unit to a senior executive who reports directly to the chief executive officer. This change in structure can facilitate strategy implementation by improving coordination between similar divisions and channeling accountability to distinct business units. In the ninety-division conglomerate just mentioned, the ninety divisions could perhaps be regrouped into ten SBUs according to certain common characteristics, such as competing in the same industry, being located in the same area, or having the same customers. Two disadvantages of an SBU structure are that it requires an additional layer of management, which increases salary expenses, and the role of the group vice-president is often ambiguous. However, these limitations often do not outweigh the advantages of improved coordination and accountability. Atlantic Richfield is an example of a firm that successfully uses an SBU type structure. Atlantic Richfield's 1987 revenues and net profits increased 12 percent and 99 percent respectively over 1986.

The Matrix Structure

A *matrix structure* is the most complex of all designs. The complexity of the matrix structure stems from its dependence upon both vertical and horizontal flows of authority and communication (hence the term "matrix"). In contrast, functional and divisional structures depend primarily on vertical flows of authority and communication. Other characteristics of a matrix structure that contribute to overall complexity include dual lines of budget authority (a violation of the unity-of-command principle), dual sources of reward and punishment, shared authority, dual reporting channels, and a need for an extensive and effective communication system. Despite its complexity, the matrix structure is widely used in many industries, including construction, health care, research, and defense.

In order for a matrix structure to be effective, great attention should be paid to such things as thorough participative planning, training, clear mutual understanding of roles and responsibilities, excellent internal communication, and mutual trust and confidence. The matrix structure is being used more frequently by American businesses because firms are pursuing strategies that add new products, customer groups, and technology to their range of activities. Out of these changes are coming product managers, functional managers, and geographic-area managers, all of whom have important strategic responsibilities. When several variables such as product, customer, technology, geography, functional area, and line of business have roughly equal strategic priorities, a matrix organization can be an effective structural form.

LINKING PERFORMANCE AND PAY TO STRATEGIES

American businesses need to align strategy, performance, and pay more closely. Compensation programs in many American corporations have rewarded executives handsomely for poor performance.[9] This low correlation between corporate performance and executive's pay characterizes American businesses for a number of reasons. First, an "increased pay for increased size" phenomenon exists. Second, too much emphasis is placed on short-term performance. Staff control of pay systems, a related problem, often prevents line managers from using financial compensation as a strategic tool. Flexibility regarding managerial and employee compensation is needed to allow short-term shifts in compensation that can stimulate efforts to achieve long-term objectives.

How can an organization's reward system be more closely linked to strategic performance? How can decisions on salary increases, promotions, merit pay, and bonuses be more closely aligned to support the long-term strategic objectives of the organization? There are no widely accepted answers to these questions, but a dual bonus system based on both annual objectives and long-term objectives is becoming common. The percentage of a managers' annual bonus attributable to short-term versus long-term results should vary by hierarchical level in the organization. A chief executive officer's annual bonus could for example be determined on a 75 percent short-term and 25 percent long-term basis. It is important that bonuses not be based solely on short-term results, because such a system ignores long-term company strategies and objectives.

The most important and commonly used long-term performance criterion is earnings per share (EPS). Bristol-Myers, General Electric, and Honeywell all use EPS as the gauge in determining bonuses. At Honeywell, for example, fifty-one senior executives covered by the plan receive long-term performance awards only if earnings per share grow at least 9 percent annually over four years as calculated by the company's own formula. If earnings per share grow by 17 percent or more, executives receive maximum awards. Honeywell's earnings per share increased in 1987 to 5.75 from 0.28 in 1986.

Criteria such as sales, profit, production efficiency, quality, and safety could also serve as bases for an effective bonus system. If an organization meets certain understood, agreed-upon profit objectives, every member of the enterprise should share in the harvest. A bonus system can be an effective tool for motivating individuals to support strategy-implementation efforts. According to the Hay Compensation Report in 1987, average bonuses as a percentage of annual salary increased from 35 percent to 48 percent between 1983 to 1987 for top executives; this ratio increased from 26 percent to 35 percent for senior managers and from 18 percent to 22 percent for middle managers during the same time period.

In addition to a dual bonus system, a combination of reward-strategy incentives including salary raises, stock options, fringe benefits, promotions, praise, recognition, criticism, fear, increased job autonomy, awards, and profit sharing can be utilized to encourage managers and employees to push hard for successful strategy implementation. The range of options for getting people, departments, and divisions to actively support strategy-implementation activities in a particular organization is almost limitless. Motivational incentives can be positive, negative, intrinsic, or extrinsic. In the final analysis, a successful reward-performance system allows for blended fulfillment of both short-term and long-term organizational and personal objectives.

MANAGING RESISTANCE TO CHANGE

No organization or individual can escape change. But the thought of change raises anxieties because people fear economic loss, inconvenience, uncertainty, and a break in normal social patterns. Almost any change in structure, technology, persons, or strategies has the potential to disrupt comfortable interaction patterns. For this reason, people resist change. The strategic-management process itself can impose major changes on individuals and processes. Reorienting an organization to get people to think and act strategically is not an easy task.

> The level of familiarity with strategic thinking in the U.S. is high, but acceptance is low. U.S. management has to undergo a cultural change, and it's difficult to force people to change their thinking; it's like ordering them to use personal computers. One obstacle is that top executives are often too busy fighting fires to devote time to developing managers who can think strategically. Yet, the best-run companies recognize the need to develop managers who can fashion and implement strategy.[10]

Resistance to change can be considered the single greatest threat to successful strategy implementation. Resistance in the form of sabotaging production machines, absenteeism, filing unfounded grievances, and an unwillingness to cooperate regularly occurs in organizations. People often resist strategy implementation because they do not understand what is happening or why changes are taking place. In that case, employees may simply need accurate information. Successful strategy implementation hinges upon managers' ability to develop an organizational climate conducive to change. Change must be viewed as an opportunity rather than as a threat by managers and employees.

Resistance to change can emerge at any stage or level of the strategy-implementation process. Although there are various approaches for implementing changes, three commonly used strategies are: a force change strategy, an educative change strategy, and a rational or self-interest change strategy. A *force change strategy* involves giving orders and enforcing those orders; this strategy has the advantage of being fast, but it is plagued by low commitment and high resistance. The *educative change strategy* is one which presents information to convince people of the need for change; the disadvantage of an educative change strategy is that implementation becomes slow and difficult. However, this type of strategy evokes greater commitment and less resistance than does the force strategy. Finally, a *rational* or *self-interest change strategy* is one that attempts to convince individuals that the change is to their personal advantage. When this appeal is successful, strategy implementation can be relatively easy. However, implementation changes are seldom to everyone's advantage.

The rational change strategy is the most desirable, so this approach is examined a bit further. Managers can improve the likelihood of successfully implementing change by carefully designing change efforts. Jack Duncan describes a rational or self-interest change strategy as consisting of four steps. First, employees are invited to participate in the process of change and the details of transition; participation allows everyone to give opinions, to feel a part of the change process, and to identify their own self-interests regarding the recommended change. Second, some motivation or incentive to change is required; self-interest can be the most important motivator. Third, communication is needed so that people can understand the purpose for the changes. Giving and receiving feedback is the fourth step; everyone enjoys knowing how things are going and how much progress is being made.[11]

Igor Ansoff summarizes the need for strategists to manage resistance to change as follows:

> Observation of the historical transitions from one orientation to another shows that, if left unmanaged, the process becomes conflict-laden, prolonged, and costly in both human and financial terms. Management of resistance involves anticipating the focus of resistance and its intensity. Second, it involves eliminating unnecessary resistance caused by misperceptions and insecurities. Third, it involves mustering the power base necessary to assure support for the change. Fourth, it involves planning the process of change. Finally, it involves monitoring and controlling resistance during the process of change.[12]

Due to diverse internal and external forces, change is a fact of life in organizations. The rate, speed, magnitude, and direction of changes vary over time by industry and organization. Strategists should strive to create a work environment where change is recognized as necessary and beneficial, so that individuals can adapt to change more easily. Adopting a strategic-management approach to decision-making can itself require major changes in the philosophy and operations of a firm.

Strategists can take a number of positive actions to minimize managers' and employees' resistance to change. For example, individuals who will be affected by a change should be involved in the decision to make the change and in decisions about how to implement change. Strategists should anticipate changes and develop and offer training and development workshops so managers and employees can adapt to those changes. They also need to communicate the need for changes effectively. The strategic-management process can be described as a process of managing change. Here Robert Waterman describes how successful (renewal) organizations involve individuals to facilitate change:

Implementation starts with, not after, the decision. When Ford Motor Company embarked on the program to build the highly successful Taurus, management gave up the usual, sequential design process. Instead they showed the tentative design to the work force and asked their help in devising a car that would be easy to build. Team Taurus came up with no less than 1,401 items suggested by Ford employees. What a contrast from the secrecy that characterized the industry before! When people are treated as the main engine rather than interchangeable parts, motivation, creativity, quality, and commitment to implementation go up.[13]

CREATING A STRATEGY-SUPPORTIVE CULTURE

Strategists should strive to preserve, emphasize, and build upon aspects of an existing *culture* that support proposed new strategies. Aspects of an existing culture that are antagonistic to a proposed strategy should be identified and changed when implementing new strategies. Substantial research indicates that new strategies are often market driven and dictated by competitive forces. For this reason, changing a firm's culture to fit a new strategy is usually more effective than changing a strategy to fit an existing culture. Numerous techniques are available to alter an organization's culture, including recruitment, training, transfer, promotion, restructuring an organization's design, role modeling, and positive reinforcement.

Schwartz and Davis suggest four guidelines for changing an existing culture to effectively match a new strategy:

1. Identify the relevant culture and subcultures in the organization through individual and small-group meetings. Develop a list of simply stated beliefs about "the way it is" in the organization and of current imperatives for how to behave. Review these until there is a consensus about the central norms in the culture.
2. Organize these statements about the firm's culture in terms of manager's tasks and key relationships.
3. Assess the risk that the organization's culture presents to the realization of the planned strategic effort. This is done by first determining the importance of the culture products and then determining their compatibility with the intended strategy.
4. Identify and focus on those specific aspects of the organization's culture that are highly important to successful strategy formulation, implementation, and evaluation. It may then be possible to develop alternative organizational approaches that better fit the existing culture, as well as to design planned programs to change those aspects of culture that are the source of the problem.[14]

Schein indicates that the following elements are most useful in linking culture to strategy:

1. Formal statements of organizational philosophy, charters, creeds, materials used for recruitment and selection, and socialization.
2. Designing of physical spaces, facades, buildings.
3. Deliberate role modeling, teaching, and coaching by leaders.
4. Explicit reward and status system, promotion criteria.
5. Stories, legends, myths, and parables about key people and events.
6. What leaders pay attention to, measure, and control.

7. Leader reactions to critical incidents and organizational crises.
8. How the organization is designed and structured.
9. Organizational systems and procedures.
10. Criteria used for recruitment, selection, promotion, leveling off, retirement, and "excommunication" of people.[15]

Deal and Kennedy emphasize that making strategic changes in an organization always threatens a culture:

> . . . people form strong attachments to heroes, legends, the rituals of daily life, the hoopla of extravaganza and ceremonies, and all the symbols of the workplace. Change strips relationships and leaves employees confused, insecure, and often angry. Unless something can be done to provide support for transitions from old to new, the force of a culture can neutralize and emasculate strategy changes."[16]

In the personal and religious side of life, the impact of loss and change is easy to see.[17] Memories of loss and change often haunt individuals and organizations for years. Ibsen says, "Rob the average man of his life illusion and you rob him of his happiness at the same stroke."[18] When attachments to a culture are severed in an organization's attempt to change direction, employees and managers often experience deep feelings of grief. This phenomena commonly occurs when environmental conditions dictate the need for a new strategy. Managers and employees often struggle to find meaning in a situation that changed many years past. Some people find comfort in memories; others find solace in the present. Weak linkages between strategic management and organizational culture can jeopardize performance and success.

AT & T divested itself of the local operations of its twenty-two wholly owned local telephone companies in 1984. The "old" corporate culture at AT & T could be described as consisting of lifetime careers, intense loyalty to the company, up-from-the-ranks management succession, dedication to the service ethos, and management by consensus. As AT & T moved from a regulated monopoly to a highly competitive environment in the 1980s, the company made numerous changes to create a culture that supported the new strategy; it redesigned its organizational structure, articulated its value system explicitly, provided management training to modify behavior in support of new values, revised recruiting aims and practices, and modified old symbols. AT & T abandoned its familiar logo, a bell with a circle, and adopted a new logo, a globe circled by electronic communications, that symbolizes its new strategies to compete with U.S. Sprint and MCI. AT & T's new culture contributed to a 551 percent increase in the company's net profits in 1987 compared to 1986.

PRODUCTION/OPERATIONS CONCERNS WHEN IMPLEMENTING STRATEGIES

Production/operations capabilities, limitations, and policies can significantly enhance or inhibit attainment of objectives. Production processes typically constitute more than 70 percent of a firm's total assets. A major part of the strategy-implementation process takes place at the production site. Production-related decisions such as plant size, plant location, product design, choice of equipment, kind of tooling, size of inventory, inventory control, quality control, cost control, use of standards, job specialization, employee training, equipment and resource utilization, shipping and packaging, and technological innovation can have a dramatic impact on the success or failure of strategy-implementation efforts.

> There was a time when people were 'factors of production,' managed little differently from machines or capital. No more. The best people will not tolerate it. And if that way of managing ever generated productivity, it has the reverse effect today. While capital and machines either are or can be managed toward sameness, people are individuals. They must be managed that way. When companies encourage individual expression, it is difficult for them not be successful (renew). The only true source of success in a company is the individual.[19]

Examples of adjustments in production systems that could be required to implement various strategies are provided in Table 7–2 for both profit and nonprofit organizations. For instance, note that when a bank formulates and selects a strategy to add ten new branches, a production-related implementation concern is site location.

Just in Time (JIT) production approaches can significantly reduce the costs of implementing strategies. With JIT, parts and materials are delivered to a production site just as they are needed, rather than being stockpiled as a hedge against late deliveries. Harley-Davidson reports that at one plant alone, JIT freed $22 million previously tied up in inventory and greatly reduced reorder lead time. *Industry Week* gives the following observation about JIT:

> Most of the nation's 1000 largest industrial companies are experimenting with, or preparing to implement, "Just in Time" manufacturing schemes. Suppliers who can't, or won't, play by the new rules are finding themselves on the sidelines. "Just in Case" just isn't good enough any more.[20]

Failure to match production/operations policies with strategy can have disastrous results. For example, Babcock and Wilcox (B & W) not long ago located a manufacturing facility for nuclear pressure containers in a cornfield in southwestern Indiana.

TABLE 7–2 Production management and strategy implementation

Type of Organization	*Strategy Being Implemented*	*Production System Adjustments*
Hospital	Adding a cancer center (Product Development)	Purchase specialized equipment and add specialized people.
Bank	Adding ten new branches (Market Development)	Perform site location analysis.
Beer brewery	Purchasing a barley farm operation (Backward Integration)	Revise the inventory control system.
Steel manufacturer	Acquiring a fast-food chain (Conglomerate Diversification)	Improve the quality control system.
Computer company	Purchase a retail distribution chain (Forward Integration)	Alter the shipping, packaging, and transportation systems.

The reason was to tap an unspoiled labor market. In spite of a massive training program to turn farmers into technicians, poor quality, slow delivery, and discipline problems plagued this B & W facility from its inception. Factors that should be studied before locating production facilities include the availability of major resources, the prevailing wage rates in the area, transportation costs related to shipping and receiving, the location of major markets, political risks in the area or country, and the availability of trainable employees.

For high-technology companies, production costs may not be as important as production flexibility, because major product changes can be needed often. Industries such as biogenetics and plastics rely on production systems that must be flexible enough to allow frequent changes and rapid introduction of new products into the market. On the other hand, for consumer goods, production costs are often more important than production flexibility. Production resources carefully and purposefully deployed to support strategy-implementation activities can effectively serve as a fulcrum for competitive leverage.

Organizations that fail to match manufacturing policies and product strategy effectively get into trouble. For example, Warwick Electronics at one time was the only supplier of color televisions to Sears, Roebuck and Company. Warwick depended on Sears for almost 75 percent of its sales. As technology changed and price competition increased, Warwick failed to adjust production operations appropriately. Warwick was soon forced to sell its television business to Sanyo. An article in *Harvard Business Review* explains why organizations like Warwick get into trouble:

> They too slowly realize that a change in product strategy alters the tasks of a production system. These tasks, which can be stated in terms of requirements for cost, product flexibility, volume flexibility, product performance, and product consistency, determine which manufacturing policies are appropriate. As strategies shift over time, so must production policies covering the location and scale of manufacturing facilities, the choice of manufacturing process, the degree of vertical integration of each manufacturing facility, the use of R & D units, the control of the production system, and the licensing of technology.[21]

HUMAN RESOURCE CONCERNS WHEN IMPLEMENTING STRATEGIES

Strategists are typically more comfortable and confident with strategic-management techniques and procedures than with human resource problems that arise during strategy implementation. A well-designed strategic-management system can fail if insufficient attention is given to the human resource dimension. Human resource concerns when implementing strategies can usually be traced to one of three basic causes: (1) disruption of social and political structures, (2) failure to match individuals' aptitudes with implementation tasks, and (3) inadequate support from strategists for implementation activities.[22]

Strategy implementation poses a threat to many managers and employees in an organization. New power and status relationships are anticipated and realized. New formal and informal groups are formed whose values, beliefs, and priorities may be largely unknown. Managers and employees may become engaged in resistance behavior as their roles, prerogatives, and power in the firm change. Disruption of social and political structures that accompany strategy execution must be anticipated and considered during strategy formulation and managed during strategy implementation.

A concern in matching managers with strategy is that jobs have specific and relatively static responsibilities, while people are dynamic in their personal development. Commonly used methods to match managers with strategies to be implemented include transferring managers, developing leadership workshops, offering career development activities, promotions, job enlargement, and job enrichment.

A number of other guidelines can help ensure that human relationships facilitate rather than disrupt strategy-implementation efforts. Specifically, managers should do a lot of chatting and informal questioning to stay abreast of how things are progressing and to know when to intervene. Managers can build support for strategy-implementation efforts by giving few orders, announcing few decisions, depending heavily on informal questioning, and seeking to probe and clarify until a consensus emerges. Key thrusts that succeed should be rewarded generously and visibly. A sense of humor is important, too; according to Adia Personnel Services, 72 percent of personnel executives nationwide say that humor is appropriate in discussions with colleagues; 63 percent say humor is appropriate in job interviews; 58 percent say humor is appropriate in performance reviews; and 53 percent say humor is appropriate in tense meetings.

It is surprising that so often during strategy formulation, individual aptitudes, values, skills, and abilities needed for successful strategy implementation are not considered. It is rare that a firm selecting new strategies or significantly altering existing strategies possesses the right line and staff personnel in the right positions for successful strategy implementation. The need to match individual aptitudes with strategy-implementation tasks should be considered in strategy choice.

Inadequate support from strategists for implementation activities too often undermines strategy-formulation. Chief executive officers, small business owners, government agency heads, and other strategists must be personally committed to strategy implementation and express this commitment in highly visible actions. Strategists' formal statements about the importance of strategic management must be consistent with actual support and rewards given for activities completed and objectives reached. Otherwise, stress created by inconsistency can cause uncertainty among managers and employees at every level.

Perhaps the best method for preventing and overcoming human resource problems in strategic management is to actively involve as many managers as possible in the process. Although time consuming, this approach builds understanding, trust, commitment, and ownership and reduces resentment and hostility. The true potential of strategy formulation and implementation resides more in people than analytical techniques.

CONCLUSION

Successful strategy formulation does not at all guarantee successful strategy implementation. Although inextricably interdependent, strategy formulation and strategy implementation are characteristically different. In a single word, strategy implementation means "change." It is widely agreed that "the real work begins after strategies are formulated." Successful strategy implementation requires support, discipline, motivation, and hard work from all managers and employees. It is sometimes frightening to think that a single individual can sabotage strategy-implementation efforts irreparably.

It is not enough to formulate the right strategies, because managers and employees must be motivated to implement those strategies. Management issues considered central to strategy implementation include matching organizational structure with strategy, linking performance and pay to strategies, creating an organizational climate conducive to change, managing political relationships, creating a strategy-supportive culture, adapting production/operations processes, and managing human resources. Establishing annual objectives, devising policies, and allocating resources are central strategy-implementation activities common to all organizations. Depending on the size and type of organization, other management issues could be equally important to successful strategy implementation.

KEY TERMS AND CONCEPTS

Annual objectives
Avoidance
Conflict
Confrontation
Culture
Defusion
Devise policies
Divisional structure by geographic area, product, customer, or process
Educative change strategy
Establish annual objectives
Force change strategy
Functional structure
Horizontal consistency of objectives
"Just in Time"
Matrix structure
Policies
Rational change strategy
Resistance to change
Resource allocation
Strategic business unit (SBU) structure
Vertical consistency of objectives

ISSUES FOR REVIEW AND DISCUSSION

1. Allocating resources can be a political and ad hoc activity in firms that do not use strategic management. Why is this true? Does adopting strategic management assure easy resource allocation? Why?
2. Compare strategy formulation with strategy implementation in terms of each being an "art" or a "science."
3. Describe the relationship between annual objectives and policies.
4. Identify a long-term objective and two supporting annual objectives for a familiar organization.
5. Identify and discuss three policies that apply to your present business policy class.
6. Explain the following statement: Horizontal consistency of goals is as important as vertical consistency.
7. Describe several reasons why conflict may occur during objective-setting activities.
8. In your opinion, what approach to conflict resolution would be best for resolving a dis-

agreement between a personnel manager and a sales manager over the firing of a particular salesman? Why?

9. Describe the organizational culture of your college or university.
10. Explain why organizational structure is so important in strategy-implementation.
11. In your opinion, how many separate divisions could an organization reasonably have without using an SBU type organizational structure? Why?
12. Would you recommend a divisional structure by geographic area, product, customer, or process for a medium-sized bank in your local area? Why?
13. What are the advantages and disadvantages of decentralizing the wage and salary function of an organization? How could this be accomplished?
14. Consider a college organization that you are familiar with. How did management issues affect strategy implementation in that organization?
15. As production manager of a local newspaper, what problems would you anticipate in implementing a strategy to increase the average number of pages in the paper by 40 percent?
16. Select an article from the suggested readings at the end of this chapter. Read the article and give a summary report to the class revealing your thoughts on the topic.

NOTES

1. A. G. Bedeian and W. F. Glueck, *Management,* 3rd ed. (Chicago: The Dryden Press, 1983), 212.
2. Most authors consider procedures and rules to be policies. Procedures can be defined as chronological steps that must be followed to complete a particular action, such as completing an application form. Rules can be defined as actions that can or cannot be taken, such as "No Smoking." Neither a procedure nor a rule provides much latitude in decision making, so some writers do not consider either to be a policy.
3. "No Smoking Sweeps America," *Business Week* (27 July 1987): 40.
4. Boris Yavitz and William Newman, *Strategy in Action: The Execution, Politics, and Payoff of Business Planning* (New York: The Free Press, 1982), 195.
5. Yavitz and Newman, *Strategy in Action,* 200.
6. Alfred Chandler, *Strategy and Structure* (Cambridge, Massachusetts: MIT Press, 1962).
7. Ibid., 14.
8. A. Hax and N. Majluf, "Organization Design: A Case Study on Matching Strategy and Structure," *Journal of Business Strategy* 4, no. 2 (Fall 1983): 72–86.
9. Alfred Rappaport, "How To Design Value-Contributing Executive Incentives," *Journal of Business Strategy* 4, no. 2 (Fall 1983): 49. For a criticism of executive compensation programs, see L. Brindisi, Jr., "Why Executive Compensation Programs Go Wrong," *Wall Street Journal.* Also, see H. Platt and D. McCarthy, "Executive Compensation: Performance and Patience," *Business Horizons* 28, no. 1 (January–February, 1985): 48–53.
10. Perry Pascarella, "The Toughest Turnaround of All," *Industry Week* (2 April 1984): 33. Reprinted with permission from Industry Week, April 2, 1984. Copyright Renton Publishing Inc., Cleveland, Ohio.
11. Jack Duncan, *Management* (New York: Random House, 1983): 381–90.
12. H. Igor Ansoff, "Strategic Management of Technology," *Journal of Business Strategy* 7, no. 3 (Winter 1987): 38.
13. Robert Waterman, Jr., "How the Best Get Better," *Business Week,* (14 September 1987): 104.
14. H. Schwartz and S. M. Davis, "Matching Corporate Culture and Business Strategy," *Organizational Dynamics* (Summer 1981): 30–48.
15. E. H. Schein, "The Role of the Founder in Creating Organizational Culture," *Organizational Dynamics* (Summer 1983): 13–28.
16. T. Deal and A. Kennedy, *Corporate Cultures: The*

Rites and Rituals of Corporate Life (Reading, Massachusetts: Addison-Wesley, 1982).

17. T. Deal and A. Kennedy, "Culture: A New Look Through Old Lenses," *The Journal of Applied Behavioral Science* 19, no. 4 (1983): 498–504.
18. H. Ibsen, "The Wild Duck," in O. G. Brochett and L. Brochett (Eds.), *Plays for the Theater* (New York: Holt, Rinehart & Winston, 1967). Also, R. Pascale, "The Paradox of 'Corporate Culture': Reconciling Ourselves to Socialization," *California Management Review* 28, 2 (1985): 26, 37–40.
19. Robert Waterman, Jr., "The Renewal Factor," *Business Week* (14 September 1987): 100.
20. "Just in Time: Putting the Squeeze on Suppliers," *Industry Week* (9 July 1984): 59.
21. Robert Stobaugh and Piero Telesio, "Match Manufacturing Policies and Product Strategy," *Harvard Business Review* 61, no. 2 (March–April 1983): 113.
22. R. T. Lenz and Marjorie Lyles, "Managing Human Resource Problems in Strategy Planning Systems, *Journal of Business Strategy* 60, no. 4 (Spring 1986): 58.

SUGGESTED READINGS

Barney, J. B. "Organizational Culture: Can It Be a Source of Sustained Competitive Advantage?" *The Academy of Management Review* 11, no. 3 (July 1986): 656–665.

Beeman, D. R. and Sharkey, T. W. "The Use and Abuse of Corporate Politics." *Business Horizons* 30, no. 2 (March–April 1987): 26–30.

Brossy, Roger and Shaw, Douglas. "Using Pay to Implement Strategy." *Management Review* 77 (September 1987): 44–48.

Burack, E. H. "Linking Corporate Business and Human Resource Planning: Strategic Issues and Concerns." *Human Resource Planning* 8, no. 3 (September 1985): 133–145. Also, Frederickson, J. W. "The Strategic Decision Process and Organizational Structure." *Academy of Management Review* 11, no. 2 (April 1986): 280–297.

Cook, D. S. and Ferris, G. R. "Strategic Human Resource Management and Firm Effectiveness in Industries Experiencing Declining." *Human Resource Management* 25, no. 3 (Fall 1986): 441–457.

Denison, D. R. "Bringing Corporate Culture to the Bottom Line." *Organizational Dynamics* (Fall 1984): 5–14.

Deshpande, R. and Parasuraman, A. "Linking Corporate Culture to Strategic Planning." *Business Horizons* 29, no. 3 (May–June 1986): 28–34.

Drucker, P. F. "Keeping U.S. Companies Productive." *Journal of Business Strategy* 7, no. 3 (Winter 1987): 12–15

Dyer, W. G. and Dyer, W. G., Jr. "Organization Development: System Change or Culture Change?" *Personnel* 63, no. 2 (February 1986): 14–22.

Gardner, M. P. "Creating a Corporate Culture for the Eighties." *Business Horizons* 28, no. 1 (January–February 1985): 59–63.

Ghoshal, S. "Global Strategy: An Organizing Framework." *Strategic Management Journal* 8, no. 5 (September–October 1987): 425–440.

Giasi, R. W. "Finding Suitable Objectives." *Managerial Planning* 32, no. 3 (November–December 1983): 43–45.

Goold, M. and Campbell, A. "Many Best Ways to Make Strategy." *Harvard Business Review* 65, no. 6 (November–December 1987): 70–76.

Gray, D. H. "Uses and Misuses of Strategic Planning." *Harvard Business Review* 64, no. 1 (January–February 1986): 89–96.

Gupta, A. K. "SBU Strategies, Corporate-SBU Relations, and SBU Effectiveness in Strategy Implementation." *The Academy of Management Journal* 30, no. 4 (September 1987): 477–500.

Guth, W. D. and MacMillan, I. C. "Strategy Implementation Versus Middle Management Self-Interest." *Strategic Management Journal* 7, no. 4 (1986): 313–327.

Harris, S. and Sutton, R. I. "Functions of Parting Ceremonies in Dying Organizations." *Academy of Management Journal* 29, no. 1 (March 1986): 5–30.

Hergert, M. "Strategic Resource Allocation Using Divisional Hurdle Rates." *Planning Review* 15, no. 1 (January–February 1987): 28–32.

Isenberg, D. J. "The Tactics of Strategic Opportunism." *Harvard Business Review* 65, no. 2 (March–April 1987): 92–97.

Johnson, A. "MRP? MRPH? OPT? CIM? FMS? JIT?

Is Any System Letter-Perfect?" *Management Review* 75 (September 1986): 22–27.

Kanter, R. M.; Summers, D. V.; and Stein, B. A. "The Future of Work." *Management Review* 75 (July 1986): 30–33.

Kilmann, R. H.; Saxton, M. J.; and Serpa, R. "Issues in Understanding and Changing Culture." *California Management Review* 28, no. 2 (Winter 1986): 87, 93–94.

Kogut, B. "Designing Global Strategies: Profiting From Operational Flexibility." *Sloan Management Review* 27, no. 1 (Fall 1985): 27–38.

Lee, S. M. and Shim, J. P. "Zero Base Budgeting—Dealing with Conflicting Objectives." *Long Range Planning* 17, no. 5 (October 1984): 103–110.

Lenz, R. T. and Lyles, M. A. "Managing Human Problems in Strategic Planning Systems." *Journal of Business Strategy* 60, no. 4 (Spring 1986): 57–66.

Lieberman, M. B. "The Learning Curve, Diffusion, and Competitive Strategy." *Strategic Management Journal* 8, no. 5 (September–October 1987): 441–452.

Meredith, J. R. "The Strategic Advantages of New Manufacturing Technologies for Small Firms." *Strategic Management Journal* 8, no. 3 (May–June 1987): 249–258.

Meredith J. R. "The Strategic Advantages of the Factory of the Future." *California Management Review* 29, no. 3 (Spring 1987): 27–41.

Miller, D. "Configuration of Strategy and Structure: Towards a Synthesis." *Strategic Management Journal* 7, no. 3 (May–June 1986): 233–249.

Miller, D. "Strategy Making and Structure: Analysis and Implications for Performance." *Academy of Management Journal* 30, no. 1 (March 1987): 7–32.

Miller, E. L.; Beechler, S.; Bhatt, B.; and Nath, R. "The Relationship Between the Global Strategic Planning Process and the Human Resource Management Function." *Human Resource Planning* 9, no. 1 (March 1986): 9–23.

Mullen, T. P. and Stumpf, S. A. "The Effect of Management Styles on Strategic Planning." *The Journal of Business Strategy* 7, no. 3 (Winter 1987): 60–86.

Nutt, P. C. "Identifying and Appraising How Managers Install Strategy." *Strategic Management Journal* 8, no. 1(1987): 1–14.

Nutt, P. C. "Tactics of Implementation." *Academy of Management Journal* 29, no. 2 (June 1986): 230–261.

Pascale, R. "The Paradox of 'Corporate Culture': Reconciling Ourselves to Socialization." *California Management Review* 28, no. 2 (1985): 26, 37–40.

Peters, Thomas P. *Thriving on Chaos* (New York: Alfred A. Knopf, 1987).

Ramanujam, V. and Venkatraman, N. "Planning System Characteristics and Planning Effectiveness." *Strategic Management Journal* 8, no. 5 (September–October 1987): 453–468.

Rosenberg, L. J. and Schewe, C. D. "Strategic Planning: Fulfilling the Promise." *Business Horizons* 28, no. 4 (July–August 1985): 54–62.

Scholz, Christian. "Corporate Culture and Strategy—The Problem of Strategic Fit." *Long Range Planning* 20, no. 4 (August 1987): 78–87.

Sethi, S. P. and Namiki, N. "Top Management Compensation and Performance." *Journal of Business Strategy* 7, no. 4 (Spring 1987): 37–43.

Shrivastava, P. "Integrating Strategy Formulation with Organizational Culture." *Journal of Business Strategy* 5, no. 3 (Winter 1985): 103–111.

Slevin, Dennis and Pinto, Jeff. "Balancing Strategy and Tactics in Project Implementation." *Strategic Management Journal* 29, no. 1 (Fall 1987): 33–42.

Trice, H. M. and Beyer, J. M. "Studying Organizational Cultures Through Rites and Ceremonials." *Academy of Management Review* 9, no. 4 (October 1984): 653–669.

Usry, M. F. "Organizing Capital Expenditure Resource Allocation and Control Systems." *Managerial Planning* 31, no. 6 (May–June 1983): 18–21, 10.

Walton, R. E. "People Policies for the New Machines." *Harvard Business Review* 65, no. 2 (March–April 1987): 98–106.

Waterman, Robert H., Jr. *The Renewal Factor: How the Best Get and Keep the Competitive Edge.* (New York: Bantam Books, 1987).

Weidenbaum, M. L. "Learning to Compete." *Business Horizons* 29, no. 5 (September–October 1986): 2–12

Weihrich, H. "How To Set Goals That Work for Your Company—And Improve the Bottom Line!" *Management Review* 17 (February 1982): 60–65.

Weihrich, H. "A Hierarchy and Network of Aims." *Management Review* (January 1982): 47–54.

Winer, L. "How to Add Goal-Directed Creativity to Planning." *Managerial Planning* 32, no. 3 (November–December 1983): 30–37.

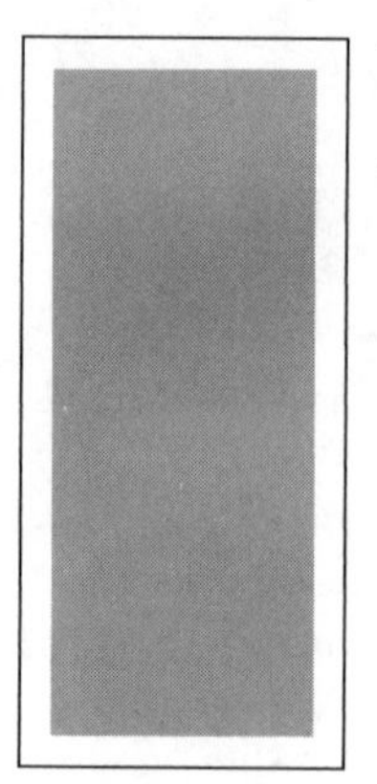

EXPERIENTIAL EXERCISES

EXPERIENTIAL EXERCISE 7A

Establishing Policies at Ponderosa

PURPOSE

This exercise can give you experience establishing policies to support Ponderosa's annual objectives.

YOUR TASK

Think of yourself as the manager of a Ponderosa steakhouse. You have just read Ponderosa's *Statement of Organization Philosophy*. One section in this document (provided in Exhibit 1) is entitled "Recognizing Individual Qualities." Now develop some policies that you feel would be supportive of that philosophy.

EXHIBIT 1 Ponderosa's philosophy on recognizing individual qualities

We value individuality. We will not try to make everyone fit into the same mold. By allowing people to be themselves, we expect to bring fresh ideas and increased productivity to our business. We will maintain a working environment, both physical and mental, that supports a high level of employee performance and energy.

In this environment, there will still be the basic requirements of discipline and policy adherence in order to maintain consistency and order. Beyond these basic elements, we expect to create an environment that fosters development of the following human qualities:

- ☐ Pride, one of the essential forces that moves us.
- ☐ Self-reliance and the ability to handle delegated authority independently.
- ☐ Courage to be open with one another and to change our minds as we receive new facts and new insights from each other.
- ☐ Self-determination. With the knowledge that people grow at different rates and have varying needs, we will create an attitude of trying to bring out the best in people, giving them the opportunity to shape their own lives and careers.

Source: Ponderosa, Inc., *Statement of Organization Philosophy*, 1983, p. 11.

EXPERIENTIAL EXERCISE 7B

Revising Ponderosa's Organizational Chart

PURPOSE

Developing and altering organizational charts is an important skill for strategists to possess. This exercise can improve your skill in altering an organization's hierarchical structure.

YOUR TASK

On a separate sheet of paper, diagram an organizational chart that you believe would best suit Ponderosa's needs. Provide as much detail in your chart as possible, including the names of individuals and the titles of positions. Use Ponderosa's present organizational chart, given in the Cohesion case (p. 33), as a diagram to start with.

EXPERIENTIAL EXERCISE 7C

Matching Managers with Strategy

PURPOSE

For many years, strategists believed that good managers could adapt to handle any situation. Consequently, strategists rarely replaced or transferred managers as the need arose to implement new strategies. Today, this situation is changing. Research supports the notion that certain management characteristics are needed for certain strategic situations.[1] Chase Manhattan Bank, Heublien, Texas Instruments, Corning Glass, and General Electric are examples of companies that match managers to strategic requirements.

This exercise can improve your awareness and understanding of particular managerial characteristics that have been found to be most desirable for implementing certain types of strategies. Having the right managers in the right jobs can determine the success or failure of strategy-implementation efforts. This exercise is based on a recently published framework that has proved to be useful in "matching managers to strategy."[2]

YOUR TASK

Your task is to match specific managerial characteristics with particular generic strategies. Four broad types of strategies are examined:

1. Retrenchment/Turnaround
2. Intensive (market penetration, market development, and product development)
3. Liquidation/Divestiture
4. Integration (backward, forward, and horizontal)

Five managerial characteristics have been found to be associated with each of these strategies. On a separate sheet of paper, write down the four types of strategy. Beside each strategy, record the appropriate letter of the five managerial characteristics that you believe are most needed to successfully implement those strategies. Each of the managerial characteristics in the following list should be used only once in completing this exercise.

a. Is technically knowledgeable—"knows the business"
b. Is "callous"—tough-minded, determined, willing to be the bad guy
c. Is "Take Charge"-oriented—strong leader
d. Is a good negotiator
e. Wants to be respected, not necessarily liked
f. Has good analytical ability
g. Is low glory-seeking—willing to do dirty jobs; does not want glamour

h. Has excellent staffing skills
i. Handles pressure well
j. Is a risk taker
k. Has good relationship-building skills
l. Is oriented to getting out the most efficiency, not growth
m. Anticipates problems—"Problem Finder"
n. Has strong analytical and diagnostic skills, especially financial
o. Is an excellent business strategist
p. Has good communication skills
q. Has personal magnetism
r. Is highly analytical—focuses on costs/benefits; does not easily accept current ways of doing things
s. Has good interpersonal influence

1. Marc Gerstein and Heather Reisman, "Strategic Selection: Matching Executives to Business Conditions," *Sloan Management Review* 24, no. 2(Winter 1983): 33–47.
2. "Strategic Selection," 37.

Implementing Strategy: Marketing, Finance/Accounting, and Research and Development Issues

NOTABLE QUOTES

Effective organizational responses are retarded not so much by failing to recognize what needs to be done, as by not doing what ought to be done.

John Keane

Most of the time, strategists should not be formulating strategy at all; they should be getting on with implementing strategies they already have.

Henry Mintzberg

The best plan is only a plan, that is, good intentions. Unless commitment is made, there are only promises and hopes, but no plan.

Peter Drucker

Organizations should approach all tasks with the idea that they can be accomplished in a superior fashion.

Thomas Watson, Jr.

My job is to make sure the company has a strategy and that everybody follows it.

Kenneth Olsen

Just being able to conceive bold new strategies is not enough. A strategist must also be able to translate his or her strategic vision into concrete steps that "get things done."

Richard G. Hamermesh

There is no "perfect" strategic decision. One always has to pay a price. One always has to balance conflicting objectives, conflicting opinions, and conflicting priorities. The best strategic decision is only an approximation—and a risk.

Peter Drucker

The real question isn't how well you're doing today against your own history, but how you're doing against your competitors.

Donald L. Kress

8

OUTLINE

OBJECTIVES

After studying this chapter, you should be able to:

- Explain market segmentation and product positioning as strategy-implementation tools.
- Discuss procedures for determining the worth of a business.
- Explain why pro forma financial analysis is a central strategy-implementation tool.
- Explain how to evaluate the attractiveness of debt versus stock as a source of capital to implement strategies.
- Discuss the nature and role of research and development in strategy implementation.

Strategies have no chance of being implemented successfully in organizations that do not market goods and services well, or in firms that cannot raise needed working capital, or in firms that produce technologically inferior products. This chapter examines marketing, finance/accounting, and research and development issues that are central to effective strategy implementation. Special topics include market segmentation, market positioning, evaluating the worth of a business, determining to what extent debt and/or stock should be used as a source of capital, developing pro forma financial statements, and contracting research and development outside the firm. As described in the last chapter, good leadership and good management are essential for success in marketing, finance/accounting, and research and development.

IMPLEMENTING STRATEGIES SUCCESSFULLY

The quarterback can call the best play possible in the huddle, but that does not mean the play will go for a touchdown. The team may even lose yardage, unless the play is executed (implemented) well. Less than 10 percent of strategies formulated are successfully implemented. There are many reasons for this low success rate, including failure to segment markets appropriately, paying too much for a new acquisition, and falling behind competitors in research and development.

Strategy implementation directly affects the lives of plant managers, division managers, department managers, sales managers, product managers, project managers, personnel managers, staff managers, supervisors, and all employees. Many of these individuals may have not participated in the strategy-formulation process at all and may not appreciate, understand, or even accept the work and thought that went into strategy formulation. There may even be foot-dragging or resistance on their part. In some cases, managers and employees may attempt to sabotage strategy-implementation efforts in hopes that the organization will return to its old ways. The strategy-implementation stage of the strategic-management process is shaded in Figure 8–1.

MARKETING ISSUES IN STRATEGY IMPLEMENTATION

Countless marketing variables affect the success or failure of strategy implementation, and the scope of this text does not allow addressing all those issues. However, two variables are of central importance to strategy implementation: market segmentation and product positioning. Ralph Biggadike asserts that market segmentation and product positioning must rank as marketing's most important contributions to strategic management.[1] Some examples of marketing decisions that may require policies are:

1. To use exclusive dealerships or multiple channels of distribution.
2. To use heavy, light, or no TV advertising.
3. To limit (or not) the share of business done with a single customer.
4. To be a price leader or a price follower.
5. To offer a complete or limited warranty.
6. To reward salespeople based on a straight commission or a combination salary/commission.

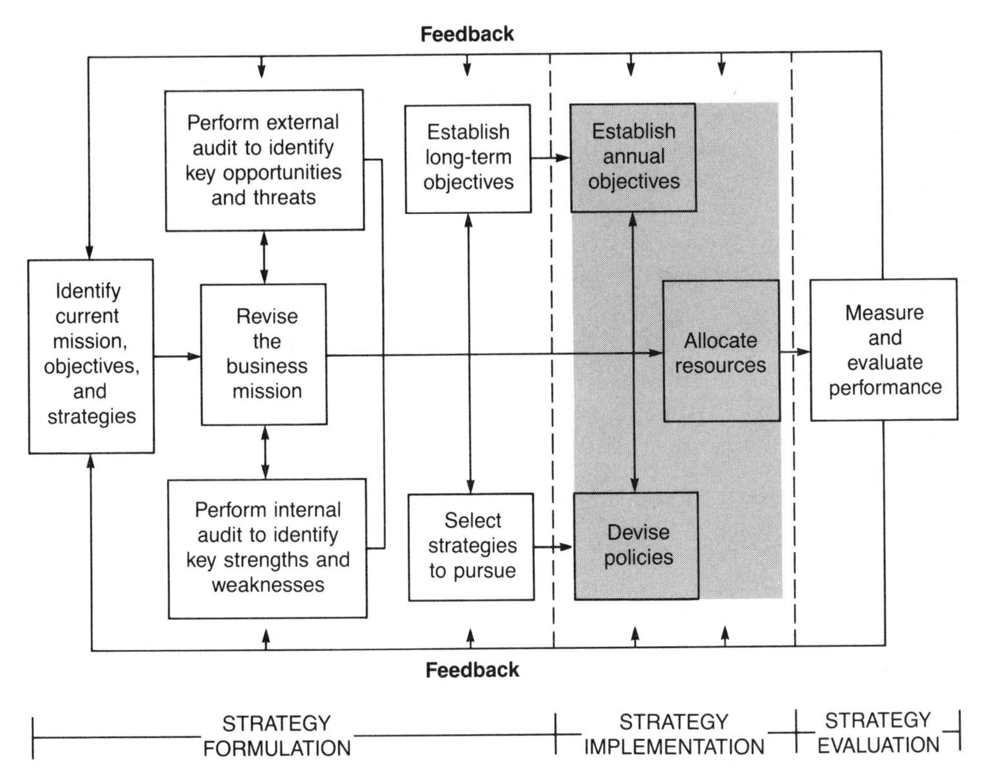

FIGURE 8–1 A comprehensive strategic-management model

Market Segmentation

Market segmentation is widely used in implementing strategies, especially for small and specialized firms. *Market segmentation* can be defined as "the subdividing of a market into distinct subsets of customers according to needs and buying habits."[2] Market segmentation is an important variable in strategy implementation for at least three major reasons. First, strategies such as market development, product development, market penetration, and diversification require increased sales through new markets and products. To implement these strategies successfully, new or improved market-segmentation approaches are required. Second, market segmentation allows a firm to operate with limited resources since mass production, mass distribution, and mass advertising are not required. Market segmentation can enable a small firm to compete successfully with a large firm by maximizing per-unit profits and per-segment sales. Finally, market segmentation decisions directly affect *marketing-mix variables:* product, place, promotion, and price, as indicated in Table 8–1.

Geographic and demographic bases for segmenting markets are the most commonly employed (Table 8–2). Beer producers, for example, have generally divided the light beer market into three segments:

> The light beer market can be meaningfully separated into three motivation segments: those who are calorie-conscious, those who prefer less alcohol, and those who prefer a lighter

TABLE 8–1 The marketing mix component factors

Product	*Place*	*Promotion*	*Price*
Quality	Distribution channels	Advertising	Level
Features and options	Distribution coverage	Personal selling	Discounts and allowances
Style	Outlet locations	Sales promotion	Payment terms
Brand name	Sales territories	Publicity	
Packaging	Inventory levels and locations		
Product line	Transportation carriers		
Warranty			
Service level			
Other services			

Source: E. Jerome McCarthy, *Basic Marketing: A Managerial Approach*, 9th ed. (Homewood, Ill.: Richard D. Irwin, Inc., 1987) p. 37–44 (1st ed., 1960).

taste. In fact, it is possible for one person to consume light beer on three separate occasions for three different reasons. The situation may therefore dictate the segment the consumer falls into.[3]

Evaluating potential market segments requires strategists to determine the characteristics and needs of consumers, analyze consumer similarities and differences, and develop consumer group profiles. Segmenting consumer markets is generally much simpler and easier than segmenting industrial markets, because industrial products, such as electronic circuits, have multiple applications and appeal to diverse customer groups. Market-segmentation matrices and decision trees can facilitate implementing strategies effectively. An example of a matrix for segmenting the lawn fertilizer market is provided in Figure 8–2. Similar matrices could be developed for almost any market, product, or service. Market segmentation strategies in the men's fragrance business are described as follows:

> The men's fragrance business breaks into four segments based on price. At the bottom are Mennen's Skin Bracer, Brut 33, and Aqua Velva that are sold mainly in food and drug stores and are priced below $4 for a 3 ounce bottle. The next tier, at about $4 to $5 for 4 ounces, is Old Spice and English Leather. Next, are the mass prestige brands, with twice the amount of scent as after-shaves, led by Chaps and Stetson at $10 and up. Above that are expensive department store brands, such as Obsession for Men, Aramis, Polo, Georgio, and beyond. Old Spice is the best selling men's fragrance in the world, with sales above $180 million annually.[4]

One of the most rapidly growing market segments in the publishing industry is magazines for college students. Some of the leading magazines targeted directly for college students are *Newsweek on Campus, Dorm, College Woman, College Musician, Panache, Business Week Careers,* and *Texas College Student.* David Hadlock, a professor of publication design at California State University, Long Beach, says, "These magazines talk about things that marketing people have determined are college students' interests."

TABLE 8–2 Alternative bases for market segmentation

Variable	*Typical Breakdowns*
Geographic	
Region	Pacific, Mountain, West North Central, West South Central, East North Central, East South Central, South Atlantic, Middle Atlantic, New England
County Size	A, B, C, D
City or SMSA size	Under 5,000; 5,000–20,000; 20,000–50,000; 50,000–100,000; 100,000–250,000; 250,000–500,000; 500,000–1,000,000; 1,000,000–4,000,000; 4,000,000 or over
Density	Urban, suburban, rural
Climate	Northern, southern
Demographic	
Age	Under 6, 6–11, 12–19, 20–34, 35–49, 50–64, 65+
Sex	Male, female
Family size	1–2, 3–4, 5+
Family life cycle	Young, single; young, married, no children; young, married, youngest child under 6; young, married, youngest child 6 or over; older, married, with children; older, married, no children under 18; older, single; other
Income	Under $2,500; $2,500–$5,000; $5,000–$7,500; $7,500–$10,000; $10,000–$15,000; $15,000–$20,000; $20,000–$30,000; $30,000–$50,000; $50,000 and over
Occupation	Professional and technical; managers, officials, and proprietors; clerical, sales; craftsmen, foremen; operatives; farmers; retired; students; housewives; unemployed
Education	Grade school or less; some high school; high school graduate; some college; college graduate
Religion	Catholic, Protestant, Jewish, other
Race	White, black, Oriental
Nationality	American, British, French, German, Scandinavian, Italian, Latin American, Middle Eastern, Japanese
Psychographic	
Social class	Lower lowers, upper lowers, lower middles, upper middles, lower uppers, upper uppers
Lifestyle	Straights, swingers, longhairs
Personality	Compulsive, gregarious, authoritarian, ambitious
Behavioral	
Use occasion	Regular occasion, special occasion
Benefits sought	Quality, service, economy
User status	Nonuser, ex-user, potential user, first-time user, regular user
Usage rate	Light user, medium user, heavy user
Loyalty status	None, medium, strong, absolute
Readiness stage	Unaware, aware, informed, interested, desirous, intending to buy
Attitude toward product	Enthusiastic, positive, indifferent, negative, hostile

Source: Philip Kotler, *Marketing Management: Analysis, Planning and Control,* © 1984, p. 256. Reprinted by permission of Prentice-Hall, Inc., Englewood Cliffs, New Jersey.

Heavy users	High income	Central city
		Suburban
		Rural
	Low income	Central city
		Suburban
		Rural
Light users	High income	Central city
		Suburban
		Rural
	Low income	Central city
		Suburban
		Rural
Nonusers	High income	Central city
		Suburban
		Rural
	Low income	Central city
		Suburban
		Rural

FIGURE 8–2 Tools for segmenting the lawn fertilizer market

Source: Fred Winter, "Market Segmentation: A Tactical Approach," *Business Horizons* (January–February 1984): 60, 61.

Product Positioning

Deciding what target customers to focus marketing efforts upon sets the stage for deciding how to meet the needs and wants of particular consumer groups. *Product positioning,* widely used for this purpose, entails developing schematic representations that reflect how your products or services compare to competitors' on dimensions most important to success in the industry. The following steps are required in product positioning:

1. Select key criteria that effectively differentiate products or services in the industry.
2. Diagram a two-dimensional product positioning map with specified criteria on each axis.
3. Plot major competitors' products or services in the resultant four quadrant matrix.
4. Identify areas in the positioning map where the company's products or services could be most competitive in the given target market. Look for vacant areas (niches).
5. Develop a marketing plan to position the company's products or services appropriately.

Since just two criteria can be examined on a single product positioning map, multiple maps are often developed to assess various approaches to strategy implementation. *Multidimensional scaling* could be used to examine three or more criteria simultaneously, but this technique requires computer assistance and is beyond the scope of this text. Some examples of product positioning maps are illustrated in Figure 8–3.

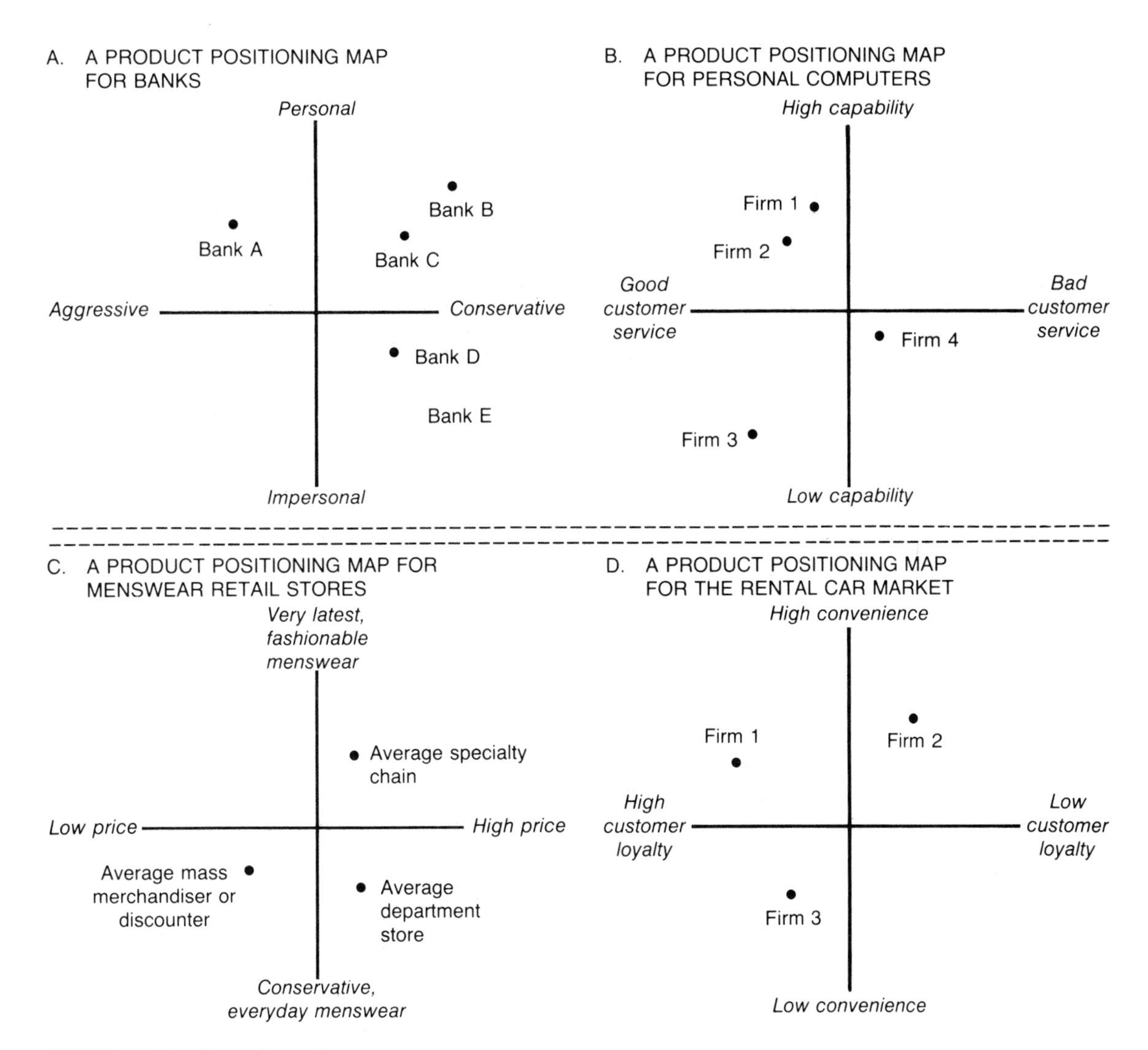

FIGURE 8–3 Example product positioning maps

Some rules of thumb for using product positioning as a strategy-implementation tool are:

1. Look for the hole or *vacant niche*. The best strategic opportunity might be an unserved segment.
2. Don't squat between segments. Any advantage from squatting (such as a larger target market) is offset by a failure to satisfy one segment. In decision-theory terms, the intent here is to avoid suboptimization by trying to serve more than one objective function.
3. Don't serve two segments with the same strategy. Usually, a successful strategy with one segment cannot be directly transferred to another segment.

4. Don't position yourself in the middle of the map. The middle usually means a strategy that is not clearly perceived to have any distinguishing characteristics. This rule can vary with the number of competitors. For example, when there are only two competitors, as in U.S. presidential elections, the middle becomes the preferred strategic position.[5]

FINANCE/ACCOUNTING ISSUES IN STRATEGY IMPLEMENTATION

In this section, we examine several finance/accounting concepts considered to be central to strategy implementation: acquiring needed capital, developing pro forma financial statements, preparing financial budgets, and evaluating the worth of a business. Some examples of decisions that may require finance/accounting policies are:

1. To raise capital with short-term debt, long-term debt, preferred stock, or common stock
2. To lease or buy fixed assets
3. To determine an appropriate dividend payout ratio
4. To use LIFO, FIFO, or a market-value accounting approach
5. To extend the time of accounts receivable
6. To establish a certain percentage discount on accounts paid within a specified period of time
7. To determine the amount of cash that should be kept on hand

Acquiring Capital to Implement Strategies

Successful strategy implementation often requires additional capital. Besides net profit from operations, two basic sources of capital for an organization are debt and equity. Determining an appropriate mix of debt and equity in a firm's capital structure can be vital to successful strategy implementation. An *Earnings Per Share/Earnings Before Interest and Taxes (EPS/EBIT) analysis* is the most widely used technique for determining whether debt, stock, or a combination of debt and stock, is the best alternative for raising capital to implement strategies. This technique involves an examination of the impact that debt versus stock financing has on earnings per share, under various assumptions as to EBIT.

Theoretically, an enterprise should have enough debt in its capital structure to boost its return on investment by applying debt to products and projects earning more than the cost of the debt. In low earnings periods, too much debt in the capital structure of an organization can endanger stockholders' return and jeopardize company survival. Fixed debt obligations generally must be met, regardless of circumstances. This does not mean that stock issuances are always better than debt for raising capital. Some special concerns with stock issuances are dilution of ownership, effect on stock price, and the need to share future earnings with all new shareholders.

Without going into detail on other institutional and legal issues related to the debt versus stock decision, EPS/EBIT may be best explained by working through an example. Let's say the Brown Company needs to raise $1 million to finance implementation of a

TABLE 8–3 EPS/EBIT analysis for The Brown Company (in millions)

	Common Stock Financing			*Debt Financing*			*Combination Financing*		
	Recession	*Normal*	*Boom*	*Recession*	*Normal*	*Boom*	*Recession*	*Normal*	*Boom*
EBIT	$2.0	$ 4.0	$ 8.0	$2.0	$ 4.0	$ 8.0	$2.0	$ 4.0	$ 8.0
Interest[a]	0.0	0.0	0.0	.10	.10	.10	.05	.05	.05
EBT	2.0	4.0	8.0	1.9	3.9	7.9	1.95	3.95	7.95
Taxes	1.0	2.0	4.0	.95	1.95	3.95	.975	1.975	3.975
EAT	1.0	2.0	4.0	.95	1.95	3.95	.975	1.975	3.975
# Shares[b]	.12	.12	.12	.10	.10	.10	.11	.11	.11
EPS[c]	8.33	16.66	33.33	9.5	19.50	39.50	8.86	17.95	36.14

Notes:
[a]The annual interest charge on $1 million at 10% is $100,000 and on $0.5 million is $50,000.
[b]To raise all of the needed $1 million with stock, 20,000 new shares must be issued, raising the total to 120,000 shares outstanding. To raise one half of the needed $1 million with stock, 10,000 new shares must be issued, raising the total to 110,000 shares outstanding.
[c]EPS = Earnings After Taxes (EAT) divided by (Number of shares outstanding)

market-development strategy. The company's common stock currently sells for $50 per share, and 100,000 shares are outstanding. The prime interest rate is 10 percent and the company's tax rate is 50 percent. The company's earnings before interest and taxes (EBIT) next year are expected to be $2 million, if a recession occurs, $4 million if the economy stays as is, and $8 million if the economy significantly improves. EPS/EBIT analysis can be used to determine if all stock, all debt, or some combination of stock and debt is the best capital financing alternative. The EPS/EBIT analysis for this example is provided in Table 8–3.

As indicated by the EPS values of 9.5, 19.50, and 39.50 in Table 8–3, debt is the best financing alternative for the Brown Company if a recession, boom, or normal year is expected. An EPS/EBIT chart can be constructed to determine the break-even point where one financing alternative becomes more attractive than another. Figure 8–4 indicates that issuing common stock is the least attractive financing alternative for the Brown Company.

EPS/EBIT analysis is a valuable tool for making capital financing decisions needed to implement strategies, but several considerations should be made whenever using this technique. First, profit levels may be higher for stock or debt alternatives when EPS levels are lower. For example, looking only at the earnings after taxes (EAT) values in Table 8–3, the common stock option is the best alternative regardless of economic conditions. If the Brown Company's mission includes strict profit maximization, as opposed to the maximization of stockholders' wealth or some other criterion, then stock rather than debt is the best choice of financing.

Another consideration when using EPS/EBIT analysis is flexibility. As an organization's capital structure changes, so does its flexibility for considering future capital needs. Using all debt or all stock to raise capital in the present may impose fixed

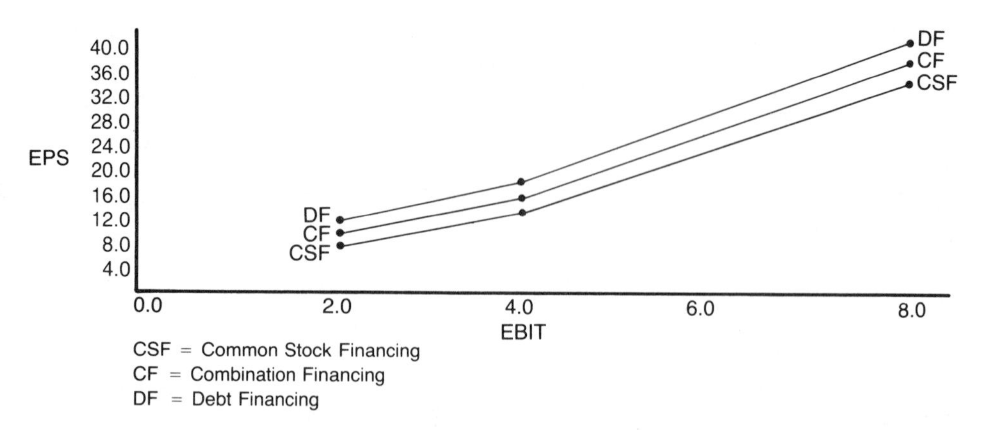

FIGURE 8–4 An EPS/EBIT chart for the Brown Company

obligations, restrictive covenants, or other constraints that could severely reduce a firm's ability to raise additional capital in the future. Control is also a concern. When additional stock is issued to finance strategy implementation, ownership and control of the enterprise are diluted. This can be a serious concern in today's business environment of hostile takeovers, mergers, and acquisitions. Also, dilution of ownership can be an overriding concern in closely held corporations, where stock issuances affect the decision-making power of majority stockholders. For example, the Smucker family owns 30 percent of the stock in Smucker's, a well-known jam and jelly company. When Smucker's acquired Dickson Family, Inc., the company used mostly debt rather than stock in order not to dilute the family's ownership.

When using EPS/EBIT analysis, timing in relation to movements of stock prices, interest rates, and bond prices becomes important. In times of depressed stock prices, debt may prove to be the most suitable alternative from both a cost and a demand standpoint. However, when the cost of capital (interest rates) is high, stock issuances become more attractive. Interest rates remained below 10 percent in 1985–1987 and many organizations (and individuals) became highly leveraged. A recent Federal Reserve Board study warns that "many firms now are highly leveraged and would be too vulnerable to adverse economic or financial developments." During the 1985–1987 period, corporations raised $483.4 billion through debt, but equity financing fell to $226.1 billion. Between January 1984 and October 1987, the bull stock market steadily reduced the ratio of debt to the market value of equity from over 83 percent to a fifteen-year low of 61 percent. But, uncertainty surrounding the October 1987 stock market crash drove the ratio of debt to the market value of equity back over 80 percent by the beginning of 1988.

Pro Forma Financial Statements

Pro Forma (projected) financial statement analysis is a central strategy-implementation technique because it allows an organization to examine the expected results of various actions and approaches. This type of analysis can be used to forecast the impact of various implementation decisions (for example, to increase promotion expenditures by 50 percent to support a market-development strategy, to increase salaries by 25 percent to support a market penetration strategy, to increase research and development expenditures by 70 percent to support product development, or to sell $1 million of common stock to raise capital for diversification). Nearly all financial institutions require at least three years of projected financial statements whenever a business seeks capital. A pro forma income statement and balance sheet allows an organization to compute projected financial ratios under various strategy-implementation scenarios. When compared to prior years and to industry averages, financial ratios provide valuable insights into the feasibility of various strategy-implementation approaches.

A pro forma income statement and balance sheet for the Litten Company is provided in Exhibit 8–1. The pro forma statements for Litten are based on five assumptions: (1) the company needs to raise $45 million to finance expansion into foreign markets, (2) $30 million of this total will be raised through increased debt and $15 million through common stock, (3) sales are expected to increase 50 percent, (4) three new facilities, costing a total of $30 million, will be constructed in foreign markets, and (5) land for the new facilities is already owned by the company. Note in Exhibit 8–1 that Litten's strategies and their implementation are expected to result in a sales increase from $100 million to $150 million in the forecasted year and a net increase in income (from $6 million to $9.75 million).

There are six steps in performing pro forma financial analysis:

1. Prepare the pro forma income statement before the balance sheet. Start by forecasting sales as accurately as possible.
2. Use the percentage-of-sales method to project cost-of-goods-sold (CGS) and the expense items in the income statement. For example, if CGS is 70 percent of sales in the prior year (as it is in Exhibit 8–1), then use that same percentage to calculate CGS in the future year—unless there is reason to use a different percentage. Items such as "interest," "dividends," and "taxes" must be treated independently and cannot be forecasted using the percentage-of-sales method.
3. Calculate the projected net income.
4. Subtract from the net income any dividends to be paid and add the remaining net income to "retained earnings." Reflect the "retained earnings" total on both the income statement and balance sheet, because this item is the key link between the two projected statements.
5. Project the balance sheet items, beginning with retained earnings and then forecasting stockholders' equity, long-term liabilities, current liabilities, total liabilities, total assets, fixed assets, and current assets (in that order). Use the "cash" account as the plug figure; that is, use the cash account to make the assets total the liabilities. Then, make appropriate adjustments. For example, if the "cash" needed to balance the statements is too small (or too large), make appropriate changes to borrow more (or less) money than planned.
6. List comments (remarks) on the projected statements. Anytime a significant change is made in an item from a prior year to the projected year, an explanation (remark) should be provided. Remarks are essential because otherwise pro formas are meaningless.

EXHIBIT 8–1 A pro forma income statement and balance sheet for the Litten Company (in millions)

Pro Forma Income Statement	Prior Year 1988	Projected Year 1989	Remarks
Sales	100	150.00	50% increase
Cost of goods sold	70	105.00	70% of sales
Gross margin	30	45.00	
Selling expense	10	15.00	10% of sales
Administrative expense	5	7.50	5% of sales
Earnings before interest and taxes	15	22.50	
Interest	3	3.00	
Earnings before taxes	12	19.50	
Taxes	6	9.75	50% rate
Net income	6	9.75	
Dividends	2	5.00	
Retained earnings	4	4.75	

Pro Forma Balance Sheet			
Assets			
Cash	5	7.75	Plug figure
Accounts receivable	2	4.00	Incr. 100%
Inventory	20	45.00	
Total current assets	27	56.75	
Land	15	15.00	
Plant and equipment	50	80.00	Add 3 new @ $10 million each
Less: depreciation	10	20.00	
Net plant and equipment	40	60.00	
Total fixed assets	55	75.00	
Total assets	82	131.75	
Liabilities			
Accounts payable	10	10.00	
Notes payable	10	10.00	
Total current liabilities	20	20.00	
Long-term debt	40	70.00	Borrowed $30 million
Common stock	20	35.00	Issued 100000 shares @ $150 each
Retained earnings	2	6.75	2 + 4.75
Total liabilities and new worth	82	131.75	

Financial Budgets

A *financial budget* is a document that details how funds will be obtained and spent for a specified period of time. Annual budgets are most common, although the period of time for a budget can range from daily to over ten years. Fundamentally, financial budgeting is a method for specifying what must be done to complete strategy implementation successfully. Financial budgeting should not be thought of as a tool for limiting expenditures but rather as a method for obtaining the most productive and profitable use of an organization's resources. Financial budgets can be viewed as the planned allocation of a firm's resources, based on forecasts of the future.

There are almost as many different types of financial budgets as there are types of organizations. Some common types of budgets include cash budgets, operating budgets, sales budgets, profit budgets, factory budgets, capital budgets, expense budgets, divisional budgets, variable budgets, flexible budgets, and fixed budgets. When an organization is experiencing financial difficulties, budgets are especially important in guiding strategy implementation. Perhaps the most common type of financial budget is the *cash budget*. The Financial Accounting Standards Board mandated in November 1987 that every publicly held company in the United States must issue an annual cash-flow statement in addition to the usual financial reports. Effective July 15, 1988, the new statement must include all receipts and disbursements of cash in operations, investments, and financing. It will supplement the "statement on changes in financial position" currently included in the annual reports of all publicly held companies.

An example of a cash budget for the Toddler Toy Company is provided in Table 8–4. Note that Toddler is not expecting to have surplus cash until November of 1989.

Financial budgets have some limitations. First, budgetary programs can become so detailed that they are cumbersome and overly expensive. Overbudgeting or underbudgeting can cause problems. Second, financial budgets can become a substitute for objectives. A budget is a tool and not an end in itself. Third, budgets can hide inefficiencies if based solely on precedent rather than periodic evaluation of circumstances and standards. Finally, budgets are sometimes used as instruments of tyranny that result in frustration, resentment, absenteeism, and high turnover. To minimize the effect of this last concern, managers should increase the participation of subordinates in preparing budgets.

Evaluating the Worth of a Business

Evaluating the worth of a business is central to strategy implementation because integrative, intensive, and diversifying strategies are often implemented by acquiring other firms. Other strategies, such as retrenchment and divestiture, may result in a division of an organization, or the firm itself, being sold. Approximately twelve thousand transactions occur each year in which businesses are bought or sold in the United States. In all these cases it is necessary to establish the financial worth or cash value of a business to successfully implement strategies.

All the various methods for determining a business's worth can be grouped into three main approaches: what a firm owns, what a firm earns, or what a firm will bring in the market. But it is important to realize that valuation is not an exact science. The

TABLE 8–4 A six-month cash budget for the Toddler Toy Company in 1989

Cash Budget (in thousands)	*July*	*Aug.*	*Sept.*	*Oct.*	*Nov.*	*Dec.*	*Jan.*
Receipts:							
Collections	$12,000	$21,000	$31,000	$35,000	$22,000	$18,000	$11,000
Payments:							
Purchases	$14,000	$21,000	$28,000	$14,000	$14,000	$ 7,000	
Wages and salaries	1,500	2,000	2,500	1,500	1,500	1,000	
Rent	500	500	500	500	500	500	
Other expenses	200	300	400	200	200	100	
Taxes	—	8,000	—	—	—	—	
Payment on machine	—	—	10,000	—	—	—	
Total payments	$16,200	$31,800	$41,400	$16,200	$16,200	$ 8,600	
Net cash gain (loss) during month	−$4,200	−$10,800	−$10,400	$18,800	$ 5,800	$ 9,400	
Cash at start of month if no borrowing is done	6,000	1,800	−9,000	−19,400	−600	5,200	
Cumulative cash (cash at start plus gains or minus losses)	$ 1,800	−$ 9,000	−$19,400	−$ 600	$ 5,200	$14,600	
Less: Desired level of cash	−5,000	−5,000	−5,000	−5,000	−5,000	−5,000	
Total loans outstanding to maintain $5,000 cash balance	$ 3,200	$14,000	$24,400	$ 5,600	—	—	
Surplus cash	—	—	—	—	$ 200	$ 9,600	

valuation of a firm's worth is based on financial facts, but common sense and intuitive judgment must enter into the process. It is difficult to assign a monetary value to such factors as a loyal customer base, a history of growth, legal suits pending, dedicated employees, a favorable lease, a bad credit rating, or good patents, which may not be reflected in a firm's financial statements. Also, different valuation methods will yield different totals for a firm's worth, and no prescribed approach is best for a certain situation. Evaluating the worth of a business truly requires both qualitative and quantitative skills.

The first approach in evaluating the worth of a business is determining its net worth or stockholders' equity. Net worth represents the sum of common stock, additional paid-in capital, and retained earnings. After calculating net worth, add or subtract an appropriate amount for goodwill (such as high customer loyalty) and overvalued or undervalued assets. This total provides a reasonable estimate of a firm's monetary value.

The second approach to measuring the value of a firm grows out of the belief that the worth of any business should be based largely on the future benefits its owners may derive through net profits. A conservative rule of thumb is to establish a business's worth as five times the firm's current annual profit. A five year average profit level could also be used. When using this approach, remember that firms normally suppress earnings in their financial statements to minimize taxes.

The third approach, letting the market determine a business's worth, involves two methods. First, base your firm's worth on the selling price of a similar company. However, a problem is that sometimes comparable figures are not easy to locate even though substantial information is available in major libraries on firms that buy or sell to other firms. An alternative approach is called the *price-earnings ratio method.* To use this method, divide the market price of the firm's common stock by the annual earnings per share and multiply this number by the firm's average net income for the past five years.

Business evaluations are becoming routine in many situations. In addition to buying or selling a business, there are other strategy-implementation reasons why a firm should determine its business worth. Employee plans, taxes, retirement, mergers, acquisitions, expansion plans, banking relationships, death of a principal, divorce, partnership agreements, and IRS audits are other reasons for a periodic valuation. It is just good business to have a reasonable understanding of what your firm is worth. This knowledge protects the interests of all parties involved.

During 1987, Georgia-Pacific bought U.S. Plywood for $215 million, Kraft bought Quaker Oats for $235 million, Primerica bought Smith Barney for $750 million, and British Petroleum bought Standard Oil (Ohio) for $7.56 billion. Although the total number of acquisitions and buyouts dropped 13 percent in 1987 compared to 1986, the number of foreign companies buying American firms increased 50 percent.

RESEARCH AND DEVELOPMENT ISSUES IN STRATEGY IMPLEMENTATION

Research and development personnel can play an integral part in strategy implementation. These individuals are generally charged with developing new products and improving old products in a way that will allow effective strategy implementation.

R & D employees and managers perform tasks such as the transfer of complex technology, adjustment of processes to local raw materials, adaptation of processes to local markets, and alteration of products to particular tastes and specifications. Strategies such as product development, market penetration, and concentric diversification require that new products be successfully developed and that old products be significantly improved. But the level of management support for R & D is often constrained by resource availability:

> If U.S. business is to maintain its position in the global business competition, then R & D support will have to become a major U.S. commitment. U.S. managers cannot continue to ignore it or take funds away from it for short-term profits and still have long-term strategic options. If one runs away from more aggressive product and process strategies, one should not be surprised by the fact that competitive advantages are lost to foreign competitors.[6]

Technological improvements that affect consumer and industrial products and services shorten product life cycles. Companies in virtually every industry are relying more and more upon the development of new products and services to fuel profitability and growth. Exhibit 8–2 provides a breakdown of R & D expenditures in 1987 for the ten American companies that spent the most on R & D. American companies in 1987 increased their R & D expenditures 7 percent and this represented a record 3.4 percent average of all sales dollars being devoted to R & D.[7] Many firms in 1987 increased R & D expenditures substantially over 1986, including Genentech by 110 percent, Compaq Computer by 77 percent, and Harley-Davidson by 223 percent. Increasing R & D expenditures reflects a realization among American strategists that foreign competitors are becoming more technologically advanced.

Surveys suggest that "the most successful organizations use a R & D strategy that ties internal strengths to external opportunities and is linked with objectives."[8] Well-formulated R & D policies effectively match market opportunities with internal capabilities and provide an initial screen to all ideas generated. R & D policies can enhance strategy-implementation efforts to:

EXHIBIT 8–2 Ranking the top ten American companies in R & D spending in 1987

In Total Dollars (Millions)		*In Percent of Sales*	
1. General Motors	$4,361	1. Centocar	53.7
2. IBM	3,998	2. Alza	36.9
3. Ford Motor	2,514	3. Continuum	31.0
4. AT & T	2,453	4. Genentech	30.9
5. Du Pont	1,223	5. Cullinet Software	28.5
6. General Electric	1,194	6. Standard Microsystems	26.2
7. Digital Equipment	1,010	7. Advanced Micro Devices	24.9
8. Eastman Kodak	992	8. Cypress Semiconductor	24.4
9. Hewlett-Packard	901	9. Daisy Systems	23.8
10. United Technologies	879	10. Evans & Southerland	22.8

Source: Adapted from *Business Week.* (20 June 1988): 140.

TABLE 8–5 Research and development involvement in selected strategy-implementation situations

Type of Organization	*Strategy Being Implemented*	*R & D Activity*
Pharmaceutical company	Product development	Develop a procedure for testing the effects of a new drug on different subgroups.
Boat manufacturer	Concentric diversification	Develop a procedure to test the performance of various keel designs under various conditions.
Plastic container manufacturer	Market penetration	Develop a more durable container.
Electronics company	Market development	Develop a telecommunications system.

1. Emphasize product or process improvements.
2. Stress basic or applied research.
3. Be leaders or followers in R & D.
4. Develop robotics or manual-type processes.
5. Spend a high, average, or low amount of money on R & D.
6. Perform R & D within the firm or to contract R & D to outside firms.
7. Use university researchers or private-sector researchers.

A recent study by Ruekert and Walker stresses the need for effective interactions between R & D departments and other functional departments in implementing different types of generic business strategies.[9] Conflict between marketing, finance/accounting, and R & D departments commonly arises and can be minimized with clear policies and objectives. Table 8–5 gives some examples of R & D activities that could be required for successful implementation of various strategies.

SmithKline Beckman Corporation is one company that is counting heavily on R & D to implement a product development strategy. SmithKline's R & D spending increased from 8 percent of sales in 1982 to 10 percent in 1987. The company recently built a new $200 million research facility. SmithKline has high hopes for fenoldopam, a heart drug, leukotrienes, an asthma drug, and carvedilol, a hypertension drug. For 1987, SmithKline's revenues increased 16 percent to $4.3 billion, and profits increased 9 percent over 1986 to $570 million.

CONCLUSION

Successful strategy implementation depends upon cooperation among all functional and divisional managers in an organization. Marketing departments are commonly charged with implementing strategies that require significant increases in sales revenues in new areas and with new or improved products. Finance and accounting managers must devise effective strategy-implementation approaches at low cost and minimum risk to the firm. R & D managers have to transfer complex technologies or develop new technologies to successfully implement strategies. The nature and role of marketing, finance/accounting, and R & D activities coupled with management activities described in Chapter 7, largely determine organizational success.

KEY TERMS AND CONCEPTS

Cash budget
EPS/EBIT analysis
Financial budgets
Marketing-mix variables
Market segmentation
Price-earnings ratio method
Product positioning
Pro forma financial statement analysis
Multidimensional scaling
Research and development
Retained earnings
Vacant niche

ISSUES FOR REVIEW AND DISCUSSION

1. Suppose your company has just acquired a firm that produces battery-operated lawn mowers, and strategists want to implement a market-penetration strategy. How would you segment the market for this product? Justify your answer.
2. Explain how you would estimate the total worth of a business.
3. Diagram and label clearly a product positioning map that includes four colleges and universities in your state.
4. Explain why EPS/EBIT analysis is a central strategy-implementation technique.
5. How would the R & D role in strategy implementation differ in small versus large organizations?
6. Discuss the limitations of EPS/EBIT analysis.
7. Explain how marketing, finance/accounting, and R & D managers' involvement in strategy formulation can enhance strategy implementation.
8. Is the following statement true or false? "Retained earnings on the balance sheet are not monies available to finance strategy implementation." Explain.
9. Explain why pro forma financial statement analysis is considered to be both a strategy-formulation and a strategy-implementation tool.
10. Describe some marketing, finance/accounting, and R & D activities that a small restaurant chain might undertake to expand into a neighboring state.
11. Select one of the suggested readings at the end of this chapter, find that article in your college library, and prepare a five minute oral report for the class to summarize it.

NOTES

1. Ralph Biggadike, "The Contributions of Marketing to Strategic Management," *Academy of Management Review* 6, no. 4 (October 1981): 624.
2. Philip Kotler, *Marketing Management* (Englewood Cliffs, N.J.: Prentice-Hall, 1976), 144.
3. Fred Winter, "Market Segmentation: A Tactical Approach," *Business Horizons* 27, no. 1 (January–February 1984): 59.
4. Jeff Trachtenberg, "The Sweet Smell of Success," *Forbes* (10 August 1987): 92.

5. Biggadike, "Contributions," 627.
6. Vida Scarpello, William Boulton, and Charles Hofer, "Reintegrating R & D into Business Strategy," *Journal of Business Strategy* 6, no. 4 (Spring 1986): 55.
7. "A Perilous Cutback in Research Spending," *Business Week* (20 June 1988): 139.
8. T. Kuczmarski and S. Silver, "Strategy: The Key to Successful New Product Development," *Management Review* 71, no. 7 (July 1982): 27.
9. R. Ruekert and O. Walker, "Interactions Between Marketing and R & D Departments in Implementing Different Business Strategies," *Strategic Management Journal* 8, no. 3 (1987): 233–248.

SUGGESTED READINGS

Brossy, Roger and Shaw, Douglas. "Using Pay to Implement Strategy." *Management Review* 76, no. 9 (September 1987): 44–48.

Collier, D. W. "How Management Should Use R & D to Set New Directions." *The Journal of Business Strategy* 7, no. 2 (Fall 1986): 75–78.

Cravens, D. W. "Strategic Forces Affecting Marketing Strategy." *Business Horizons* 29, no. 5 (September–October 1986): 77–86.

Daltas, A. and McDonald, P. "Barricades to Strategic Marketing Thinking." *Planning Review* 15, no. 1 (January–February 1987): 8–15.

———. "Corning Converts to Strategic Marketing." *Planning Review* 15, no. 2 (March–April 1987): 38–39.

Fox, H. W. "Financial ABC's of Test-Marketing." *Business Horizons* 29, no. 5 (September–October 1986): 63–70.

Gordon, I. "Exit Marketing Concept—Enter Competitive Concept." *Business Quarterly* 51, no. 2 (Summer 1986): 28–32.

Hopkins, H. D. "Acquisition Strategy and the Market Position of Acquiring Firms." *Strategic Management Journal* 8, no. 6 (November–December 1987): 535–548.

Isenberg, D. J. "The Tactics of Strategic Opportunism." *Harvard Business Review* 65, no. 2 (March–April 1987): 92–97.

Johnson, A. "How To Measure Your Company's Value." *Nation's Business* 71, no. 4 (April 1983): 68, 70.

Kanter, R. M.; Summers, D. V.; and Stein, B. A. "The Future of Work." *Management Review* 75, no. 7 (July 1986): 30–33.

Kaplan, R. S. "Yesterday's Accounting Undermines Production." *Harvard Business Review* 62, no. 4 (July–August 1984): 95–101.

Miller, D. B. "Understanding the R & D Culture." *Management Review* 75, no. 12 (December 1986): 34–39.

Murray, K. B. and Montanari, J. R. "Strategic Management of the Socially Responsible Firm: Integrating Management and Marketing Theory." *Academy of Management Review* 11, no. 4 (October 1986): 815–827.

Nielsen, Richard P. "Cooperative Strategy in Marketing." *Business Horizons* 30, no. 4 (July–August 1987): 61–68.

Nutt, P. C. "Identifying and Appraising How Managers Install Strategy." *Strategic Management Journal* 8, no. 1 (1987): 1–14.

———. "Tactics of Implementation." *Academy of Management Journal* 29, no. 2 (June 1986): 230–261.

Power, D. "Linking R & D to Corporate Strategy." *Management Review* 75, no. 12 (December 1986): 28–33

Rodnick, R. "Getting the Right Price for Your Firm." *Nation's Business* 72, no. 3 (March 1984): 70, 71.

Ruekert, R. W. and Walker, O. C. "Interactions Between Marketing and R & D Departments in Implementing Different Business Strategies." *Strategic Management Journal* 8, no. 3 (May–June 1987): 233–248.

Sandberg, C. M.; Lewellen, W. G.; and Stanley, K. L. "Financial Strategy: Planning and Managing the Corporate Leverage Position." *Strategic Management Journal* 8, no. 1 (January–February 1987): 15–24.

Scarpello, V.; Boulton, W. R.; and Hofer, C. W. "Reintegrating R & D into Business Strategy." *The Journal of Business Strategy* 6, no. 4 (Spring 1986): 45–55.

Shapiro, B. and Thomas, B. "How to Segment Industrial Markets." *Harvard Business Review* 62, no. 3 (May–June 1984): 104–110.

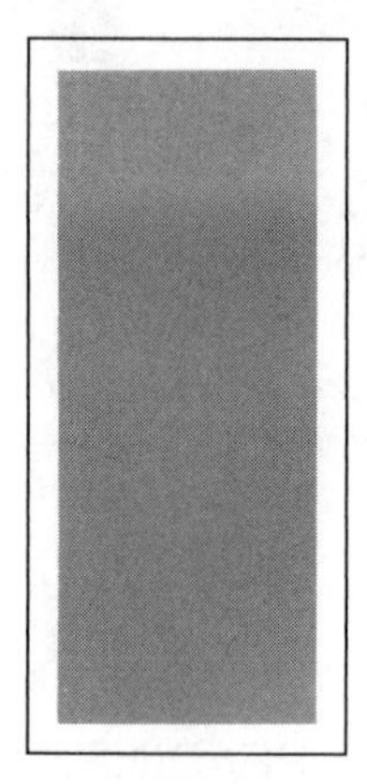

EXPERIENTIAL EXERCISES

EXPERIENTIAL EXERCISE 8A

Developing Product Positioning Maps for Ponderosa

PURPOSE

Organizations continually monitor how their products and services are positioned relative to competitors. This information is especially useful for marketing managers, but is also used by other managers and strategists.

YOUR TASK

Step 1 Work with one other student in class.

Step 2 On a separate sheet of paper, develop four product positioning maps for Ponderosa. Include Bonanza and Sizzler in your map, along with Ponderosa.

Step 3 Go to the blackboard and diagram one of your product positioning maps.

Step 4 Compare your product positioning maps to other students'. Discuss any major differences.

EXPERIENTIAL EXERCISE 8B

Performing an EPS-EBIT Analysis for Ponderosa

PURPOSE

An EPS-EBIT analysis is one of the most widely used techniques for determining the extent that debt and/or stock should be used to finance strategies to be implemented. This exercise can give you practice performing EPS-EBIT analysis.

YOUR TASK

Let's say Ponderosa needs to raise $100 million to build seventy-five new Ponderosa steakhouses in 1988. Determine whether Ponderosa should use all debt, all stock, or a 50/50 combination of debt and stock to finance this market development strategy. Assume a 40 percent tax rate and a 10 percent interest rate. Develop an EPS-EBIT chart to reflect your analysis. Compare your analysis and chart to the author's analysis. What are the major differences? What questions do you have regarding the differences?

EXPERIENTIAL EXERCISE 8C

Preparing Pro Forma Statements for Ponderosa

PURPOSE

This exercise is designed to give you experience preparing pro forma financial statements. Pro forma analysis is a central strategy-implementation technique because it allows managers to anticipate and evaluate the results of various strategy-implementation approaches.

YOUR TASK

Step 1 Work with a classmate. Develop a 1988 pro forma income statement and balance sheet for Ponderosa. Assume that Ponderosa plans to build 75 new steakhouses in 1988 and plans to obtain 50 percent financing from a bank and 50 percent financing from a stock issuance. Make other assumptions as needed and state them clearly in written form on your analysis.

Step 2 Compute Ponderosa's current ratio, debt to equity ratio, and return on investment ratio for 1986, 1987, and 1988. How do your 1988 projected ratios compare to the 1986 and 1987 ratios? Why is it important to make this comparison?

Step 3 Compare your pro forma statements to other students' and to the author's pro forma analysis. What major differences exist between your analysis and the others?

EXPERIENTIAL EXERCISE 8D

Determining the Cash Value of Ponderosa

PURPOSE

It is simply good business practice to periodically determine the financial worth or cash value of your company. This exercise gives you practice in this activity using several methods.

YOUR TASK

Step 1 Calculate the financial worth of Ponderosa based on the net worth or stockholders' equity, the future value of Ponderosa's earnings, and price-earnings ratio.

Step 2 In a single dollar amount, how much is Ponderosa worth?

Step 3 Compare your analyses and conclusions to the author's.

PART FOUR
STRATEGY EVALUATION

Strategy Review, Evaluation, and Control

NOTABLE QUOTES

Complicated controls do not work. They confuse. They misdirect attention from what is to be controlled to the mechanics and methodology of the control.

Seymour Tilles

Organizations are most vulnerable when they are at the peak of their success.

R. T. Lenz

While strategy is a word that is usually associated with the future, its link to the past is no less central. Life is lived forward but understood backward. Managers may live strategy in the future, but they understand it through the past.

Henry Mintzberg

Unless strategy evaluation is performed seriously and systematically, and unless strategists are willing to act on the results, energy will be used up defending yesterday. No one will have the time, resources, or will to work on exploiting today, let alone to work on making tomorrow.

Peter Drucker

There is no guarantee we will be successful. But we will not fail through indecision or inaction. If we err, and we will from time to time, it will not be because we failed to take action.

James E. Olsen

I have a duty to the soldiers, their parents, and the country, to remove immediately any commander who does not satisfy the highest performance demands. It is a mistake to put a person in a command that is not the right command. It is therefore my job to think through where that person belongs.

George C. Marshall

We all tend to see our institutions as permanent and lasting forever. Indeed, a view of the world from inside an institution is fatally flawed by confidence in the institution's unvulnerability.

Edith Weiner

9

OUTLINE

THE NATURE OF STRATEGY EVALUATION
A STRATEGY-EVALUATION FRAMEWORK
PUBLISHED SOURCES OF STRATEGY-EVALUATION INFORMATION
CHARACTERISTICS OF AN EFFECTIVE EVALUATION SYSTEM
CONTINGENCY PLANNING
AUDITING
USING COMPUTERS TO EVALUATE STRATEGIES

Experiential Exercise 9A: Preparing a Strategy-Evaluation Report
Experiential Exercise 9B: Analyzing Ponderosa's Strategy-Evaluation Model

OBJECTIVES

After studying this chapter, you should be able to:

- Describe a practical framework for evaluating strategies.
- Explain why strategy evaluation is complex, sensitive, and yet essential to organizational success.
- Discuss the importance of contingency planning in strategy evaluation.
- Discuss the role of auditing in strategy evaluation.

The best formulated and implemented strategies become obsolete as a firm's internal and external environments change. It is essential, therefore, that strategists systematically review, evaluate, and control the execution of strategies. This chapter presents a framework that can guide managers' efforts to evaluate strategic-management activities, to make sure they are working, and to make timely changes.

THE NATURE OF STRATEGY EVALUATION

The strategic-management process results in decisions that can have significant, long-lasting consequences. Erroneous strategic decisions can inflict severe penalties and can be exceedingly difficult, if not impossible, to reverse. Most strategists agree, therefore, that strategy evaluation is vital to an organization's well-being; timely evaluations can alert management to problems or potential problems before a situation becomes critical. Strategy evaluation includes examining the underlying bases of a firm's strategy, comparing expected results with actual results, and taking corrective actions to ensure that performance conforms to plans. The strategy-evaluation stage of the strategic-management process is illustrated in Figure 9–1.

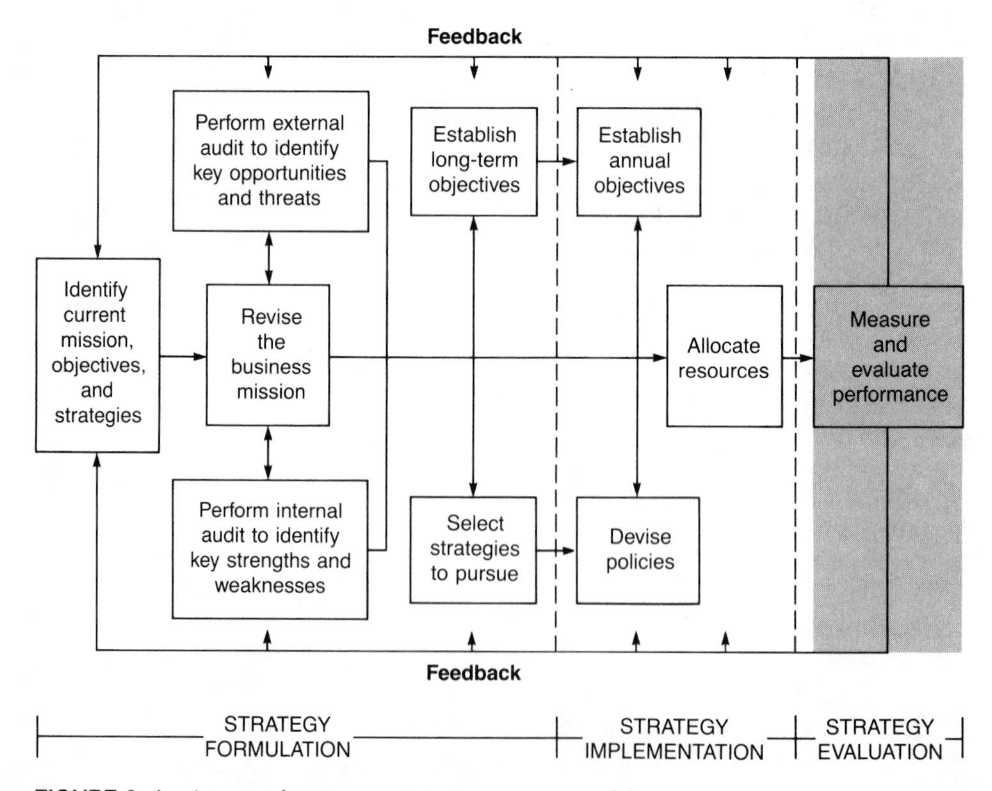

FIGURE 9–1 A comprehensive strategic-management model

Adequate and timely feedback is the cornerstone of effective strategy evaluation. Strategy evaluation can be no better than the information on which it operates. Too much pressure from top managers may result in lower managers contriving numbers they think will be satisfactory. Strategists for Boy Scouts of America recently determined that membership figures coming in from the field had been falsified. The drive to increase membership had motivated people to increase the number of new members reported, but had not motivated them to increase the number of Boy Scouts actually enrolled.[1]

Strategy evaluation can be a complex and sensitive undertaking. Too much emphasis on evaluating strategies may be expensive and counterproductive. No one likes to be evaluated too closely! Dalton and Lawrence emphasize that the more managers attempt to evaluate the behavior of others, the less control they have. Yet, too little or no evaluation can create even worse problems.[2] Strategy evaluation is essential to ensure that stated objectives are being achieved.

In many organizations strategy evaluation is simply an appraisal of how well an organization has performed. Have the firm's assets increased? Has there been an increase in profitability? Have sales increased? Have productivity levels increased? Have profit margin, return on investment, and earnings per share ratios increased? Some firms argue that their strategy must have been correct if the answers to these types of questions are affirmative. Well, the strategy or strategies may have been correct, but this type of reasoning can be misleading, because strategy evaluation must have both a long-run and short-run focus. Strategies often do not affect short-term operating results until it is too late to make needed changes. Braniff Airlines, for example, did not know that their worldwide market development would result in bankruptcy until hundreds of new planes had been purchased and extensive resources committed.

It is impossible to demonstrate conclusively that a particular strategy is optimal or even to guarantee that it will work. One can, however, evaluate it for critical flaws. Richard Rumelt offers four criteria that could be used to evaluate a strategy: *consistency, consonance, advantage,* and *feasibility*. Described in Exhibit 9–1, consonance and advantage are mostly based on a firm's external assessment, whereas consistency and feasibility are largely based on an internal assessment.

EXHIBIT 9–1 Rumelt's criteria for evaluating strategies

Consistency

A strategy should not present inconsistent goals and policies. Organizational conflict and interdepartmental bickering are often symptoms of a managerial disorder, but these problems may also be a sign of "strategic inconsistency." Rumelt offers three guidelines to help determine if organizational problems are due to inconsistencies in strategy.

- If managerial problems continue despite changes in personnel, and if they tend to be issue-based rather than people-based, then strategies may be inconsistent.
- If success for one organizational department means, or is interpreted to mean, failure for another department, then strategies may be inconsistent.
- If policy problems and issues continue to be brought to the top for resolution, then strategies may be inconsistent.

Consonance
Consonance refers to the need for strategists to examine *sets of trends* as well as individual trends in evaluating strategies. A strategy must represent an adaptive response to the external environment and to the critical changes occurring within it. One difficulty in matching a firm's key internal and external factors in the formulation of strategy is that most trends are the result of interactions among other trends. For example, the daycare explosion came about as a combined result of many trends that included a rise in the average level of education, increased inflation, and an increase in women in the work force. Thus, while single economic or demographic trends might appear steady for many years, there are waves of change going on at the interaction level.

Feasibility
A strategy must neither overtax available resources nor create unsolvable subproblems. The final broad test of strategy is its feasibility; that is, can the strategy be attempted within the physical, human, and financial resources of the enterprise? The financial resources of a business are the easiest to quantify and are normally the first limitation against which strategy is evaluated. It is sometimes forgotten, however, that innovative approaches to financing are often possible. Devices such as captive finance subsidiaries, sale-leaseback arrangements, and tying plant mortgages to long-term contracts have all been used effectively to help win key positions in suddenly expanding industries. A less quantifiable, but actually more rigid limitation on strategic choice is that imposed by individual and organizational capabilities. In evaluating a strategy it is important to examine whether an organization has demonstrated in the past that it possesses the abilities, competencies, skills, and talents needed to carry out a given strategy.

Advantage
A strategy must provide for the creation and/or maintenance of a competitive advantage in a selected area of activity. Competitive advantages normally are the result of superiority in one of three areas: 1) resources, 2) skills, or 3) position. The idea that the positioning of one's resources can enhance their combined effectiveness is familiar to military theorists, chess players, and diplomats. Position can also play a crucial role in an organization's strategy. Once gained, a good position is defensible—meaning so costly to capture that rivals are deterred from full-scale attacks. Positional advantage tends to be self-sustaining, as long as the key internal and environmental factors that underlie it remain stable. This is why entrenched firms can be almost impossible to unseat, even if their raw skill levels are only average. Although not all positional advantages are associated with size, it is true that larger organizations tend to operate in markets and use procedures that turn their size into advantage, while smaller firms seek product/market positions that exploit other types of advantage. The principal characteristic of good position is that it permits the firm to obtain advantage from policies that would not similarly benefit rivals without the same position. Therefore, in evaluating strategy, organizations should examine the nature of positional advantages associated with a given strategy.

Source: Adapted from Richard Rumelt, "The Evaluation of Business Strategy," in W. F. Glueck, ed., *Business Policy and Strategic Management* (New York: McGraw-Hill, 1980), 359–67.

Strategy evaluation is necessary for all sizes and kinds of organizations. According to Dale Zand, strategy evaluation should initiate managerial questioning of expectations and assumptions, should trigger a review of objectives and values, and should stimulate creativity in generating alternatives and formulating criteria of evaluation.[3] Regardless of the size of the organization, a certain amount of "management by wandering around" at all levels is essential to effective strategy evaluation. Strategy-evaluation activities should be performed on a continuing basis, rather than at the end of specified periods of time or just after problems occur. Waiting until the end of the year, for example, could result in a firm "closing the barn door after the horses have already escaped."

Evaluating strategies on a continuous rather than a periodic basis allows benchmarks of progress to be established and more effectively monitored. Some strategies take years to implement and, consequently, associated results may not become apparent for years. Successful strategists combine patience with a willingness to take corrective actions promptly when necessary. There always comes a time when corrective actions are needed in an organization! Centuries ago, a writer, perhaps Solomon, made these observations about change:

There is a time for everything,
a time to be born and a time to die,
a time to plant and a time to uproot,
a time to kill and a time to heal,
a time to tear down and a time to build,
a time to weep and a time to laugh,
a time to mourn and a time to dance,
a time to scatter stones and a time to gather them,
a time to embrace and a time to refrain,
a time to search and a time to give up,
a time to keep and a time to throw away,
a time to tear and a time to mend,
a time to be silent and a time to speak,
a time to love and a time to hate,
a time for war and a time for peace.[4]

In a recent study that examined the timing of strategy evaluation in many organizations, Lindsay and Rue hypothesized that strategy-evaluation activities would be conducted more frequently as environmental complexity and instability increased.[5] However, the researchers found a surprising inverse relationship between "planning review frequency" and organizational environment. Top managers in dynamic environments performed strategy-evaluation activities less frequently than those in stable environments. Lindsay and Rue concluded that forecasting is more difficult under complex and unstable environmental conditions, so strategists may see less need for frequent evaluation of their long-range plans. Evidence for this conclusion was stronger for large firms than for small ones.

Strategy evaluation is important because organizations face dynamic environments in which key internal and external factors often change quickly and dramatically. Success today is no guarantee for success tomorrow! An organization should never be lulled into complacency with success! Countless firms have thrived one year only to struggle for survival the following year. Organizational demise can come swiftly, as evidenced by the examples described in Exhibit 9–2.

A STRATEGY-EVALUATION FRAMEWORK

Numerous internal and external problems commonly prohibit firms from achieving long-term objectives and annual objectives. Internally, ineffective strategies may have been chosen, or good strategies may have been chosen, but implementation activities

EXHIBIT 9–2 Two examples of organizational demise

Coleco Industries, Inc.

Coleco enjoyed great success in 1985 with products like Cabbage Patch Kids. The company had 1985 earnings of $82.9 million and sales of $776 million. But, at the end of 1986, Coleco's net worth or stockholders' equity (assets minus liabilities) was negative $7.7 million. The company's 1986 earnings were negative $112.2 and sales declined 35 percent from 1985 to $501 million. Sales of Cabbage Patch Kids alone declined 62 percent in 1986 to $230 million from $600 million in 1985. Coleco went from boom to bust in just one year. For the year 1987, Coleco's earnings were negative $105.4 million on sales of $504 million.

LTV Corporation

LTV Corporation thought it had a bad year in 1985, incurring a loss of $723.9 million on sales of $8.2 billion. But, at the end of 1986, LTV incurred the largest annual loss ever recorded by a corporation, negative $3.25 billion on sales of $7.27 billion. At the end of 1986, LTV's new worth was negative $2.56 billion. These losses were incurred despite a major six month strike at LTV's major competitor, USX, the nation's largest steelmaker. LTV is the nation's second largest steelmaker, but the company also has extensive aerospace and energy assets. LTV is currently operating under Chapter 11 of the federal Bankruptcy Code. For 1987, LTV's revenues increased 4 percent to $7.58 billion, while profits were $502.6 million.

were poor, or stated objectives may be too optimistic. Externally, actions by competitors, changes in demand, changes in technology, economic changes, demographic shifts, and governmental actions may prohibit objectives from being accomplished. So, strategy evaluation must focus on potential internal and external problems. Internal strengths or weaknesses and external opportunities or threats that represent the bases of current strategies must continually be monitored for change. It is not a question of whether these factors will change, but rather, when they will change and in what ways. Here are some initial questions to address in evaluating strategies:

1. Are our internal strengths still strengths?
2. Have we added other internal strengths? If so, what are they?
3. Are our internal weaknesses still weaknesses?
4. Do we now have other internal weaknesses? If so, what are they?
5. Are our external opportunities still opportunities?
6. Are there now other external opportunities? If so, what are they?
7. Are our external threats still threats?
8. Are there now other external threats? If so, what are they?
9. Are we vulnerable to a hostile takeover?

Another important strategy-evaluation activity is to measure organizational performance. This activity includes comparing expected results to actual results, investigating deviations from plans, evaluating individual performance, and examining progress being made towards meeting stated objectives. Both long-term and annual objectives are commonly used in this process. Criteria for evaluating strategies should be measurable and easily verifiable. Criteria that predict results may be more important than those that reveal what already has happened. For example, strategists do not want to find out that sales last quarter were 20 percent under what were expected. More importantly, they need to know that sales next quarter may be 20 percent below standard unless some action is taken to counter the trend. Really effective control requires accurate forecasting.[6]

The final strategy-evaluation activity, taking corrective actions, requires making changes to reposition a firm competitively for the future. Some examples of changes that may be needed are altering an organization's structure, replacing one or more key individuals, selling a division, or revising a business mission. Other changes could include establishing or revising objectives, devising new policies, issuing stock to raise capital, adding additional salespersons, allocating resources differently, or developing new performance incentives. Taking corrective actions does not necessarily mean that existing strategies will be abandoned or even that new strategies must be formulated.

> The probabilities and possibilities for incorrect or inappropriate action increase geometrically with an arithmetic increase in personnel. Any person directing an overall undertaking must check on the actions of the participants as well as the results that they have achieved. If either the actions or results do not comply with preconceived or planned achievements, then corrective actions are needed.[7]

Table 9–1 summarizes strategy-evaluation activities in terms of key questions that should be addressed, alternative answers to those questions, and appropriate actions for an organization to take. Notice that corrective actions are almost always needed, except when (1) internal and external factors have not significantly changed, *and* (2) a firm is progressing satisfactorily towards achieving stated objectives. Relationships among strategy-evaluation activities are illustrated in Figure 9–2.

TABLE 9–1 A strategy-evaluation assessment matrix

Have Major Changes Occurred in the Firm's Internal Strategic Position?	*Have Major Changes Occurred in the Firm's External Strategic Position?*	*Has the Firm Progressed Satisfactorily Toward Achieving Its Stated Objectives?*	*Result*
no	no	no	Take corrective actions
yes	yes	yes	Take corrective actions
yes	yes	no	Take corrective actions
yes	no	yes	Take corrective actions
yes	no	no	Take corrective actions
no	yes	yes	Take corrective actions
no	yes	no	Take corrective actions
no	no	yes	Continue present strategic course

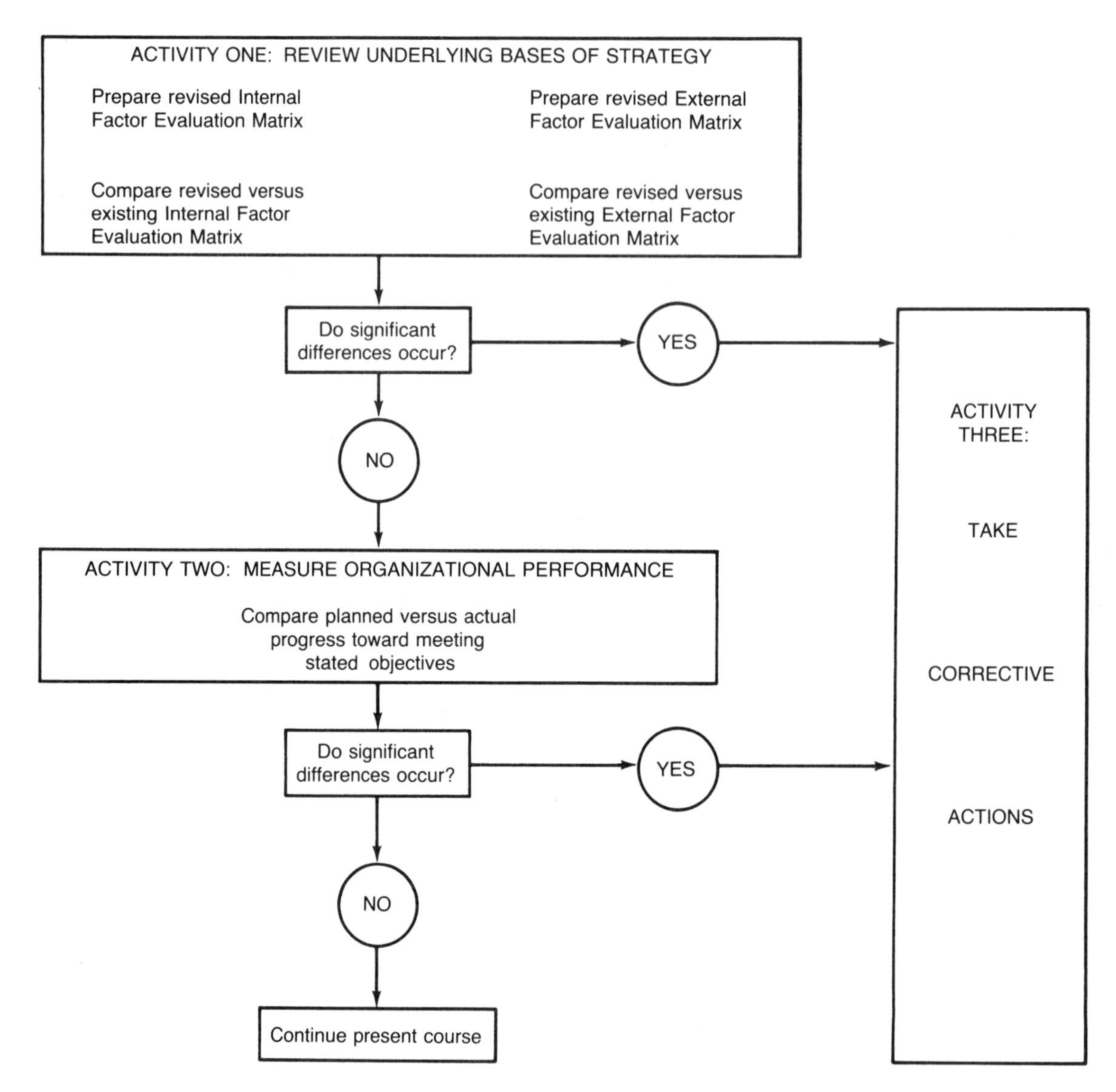

FIGURE 9–2 A strategy-evaluation framework

Reviewing Bases of Strategy

As illustrated in Figure 9–2, *reviewing the underlying bases of an organization's strategy* could be approached by developing a revised EFE Matrix and IFE Matrix. A revised IFE Matrix should focus on changes in the organization's management, marketing, finance/accounting, production/operations and R & D strengths and weaknesses. A revised EFE Matrix would show how a firm's position has changed relative to major competitors. This analysis could address such questions as:

1. How have competitors reacted to our strategies?
2. How have competitors' strategies changed?
3. Have major competitors' strengths and weaknesses changed?
4. Why are competitors making certain strategic changes?
5. Why are some competitors' strategies more successful than others?
6. How satisfied are our competitors with their present market position and profitability?
7. How far can our major competitors be pushed before retaliating?
8. How could we more effectively cooperate with our competitors?

Measuring Organizational Performance

Failure to make satisfactory progress towards accomplishing long-term or annual objectives signals a need for corrective actions. Myriad factors—such as unreasonable policies, unexpected turns in the economy, unreliable suppliers or distributors, or ineffective strategies—can result in unsatisfactory progress towards meeting objectives. Problems can result from ineffectiveness (not doing the right things) or inefficiency (doing the right things poorly).

Determining which objectives are most important in the evaluation of strategies can be difficult. Strategy evaluation is based on both quantitative and qualitative criteria. Selecting the exact set of criteria for evaluating strategies depends on a particular organization's size, industry, strategies, and management philosophy. An organization pursuing a retrenchment strategy, for example, could have an entirely different set of evaluative criteria from an organization pursuing a market-development strategy. Perhaps the most commonly used quantitative criteria to evaluate strategies are financial ratios, which strategists use to make three critical comparisons: (1) compare the firm's performance over different time periods, (2) compare the firm's performance to competitors', and (3) compare the firm's performance to industry averages. Some key financial ratios that are particularly useful as criteria for strategy evaluation include:

1. Return on investment
2. Return on equity
3. Profit margin
4. Market share
5. Debt to equity
6. Earnings per share
7. Sales growth
8. Asset growth

But there are some potential problems associated with using quantitative criteria for evaluating strategies. First, most quantitative criteria are geared to annual objectives rather than long-term objectives. Also, different accounting methods can provide different results on many quantitative criteria. Third, intuitive judgments are almost always involved in deriving quantitative criteria. For these and other reasons, qualitative criteria are also important in evaluating strategies. Human factors such as high absenteeism and turnover rates, poor production quality and quantity rates, or low employee satisfaction can be underlying causes of declining performance. Marketing, finance/

accounting, or R & D factors can also cause financial problems. Seymour Tilles identifies six qualitative questions that are useful in evaluating strategies:

1. Is the strategy internally consistent?
2. Is the strategy consistent with the environment?
3. Is the strategy appropriate in view of available resources?
4. Does the strategy involve an acceptable degree of risk?
5. Does the strategy have an appropriate time framework?
6. Is the strategy workable?[8]

Some additional key questions that reveal the need for qualitative or intuitive judgments in strategy evaluation are:

1. How good is the firm's balance of investments between high risk and low risk projects?
2. How good is the firm's balance of investments between long-term and short-term projects?
3. How good is the firm's balance of investment between slow-growing markets and fast-growing markets?
4. How good is the firm's balance of investments among different divisions?
5. To what extent are the firm's alternative strategies socially responsible?
6. What are the relationships among the firm's key internal and external strategic factors?
7. How are major competitors likely to respond to particular strategies?

Taking Corrective Actions

No organization can survive as an island; no organization can escape change! Taking corrective actions is necessary to keep an organization on track toward achieving stated objectives. In his thought-provoking books, *Future Shock* and *The Third Wave,* Alvin Toffler argues that business environments are becoming so dynamic and complex that they threaten people and organizations with *future shock,* which occurs when the nature, types, and speed of changes overpower an individual or organization's ability and capacity to adapt. Strategy evaluation enhances an organization's ability to adapt successfully to changing circumstances. Brown and Agnew refer to this notion as "corporate agility."[9]

Taking corrective actions raises employees' and managers' anxieties. Research suggests that participation in strategy-evaluation activities is one of the best ways to overcome individuals' resistance to change. According to Erez and Kanfer, individuals accept change best when they have a cognitive understanding of the changes, a sense of control over the situation, and an awareness that necessary actions are going to be taken to implement the changes.[10]

Strategy evaluation can lead to strategy-formulation changes, strategy-implementation changes, both formulation and implementation changes, or no changes at all. Strategists cannot escape having to revise strategies and implementation approaches sooner or later. Hussey and Langham offer the following insight on taking corrective actions:

> Resistance to change is often emotionally based and not easily overcome by rational argument. Resistance may be based on such feelings as loss of status, implied criticism of present competence, fear of failure in the new situation, annoyance at not being consulted, lack of understanding of the need for the change, or insecurity in changing from well-known and fixed methods. It is necessary, therefore, to overcome such resistance by creating situations of participation and full explanation when changes are envisaged.[11]

Corrective actions should place an organization in a better position to capitalize upon internal strengths, to take advantage of key external opportunities, to avoid, reduce or mitigate external threats, and to improve internal weaknesses. Corrective actions should have a proper time horizon and an appropriate amount of risk. They should be internally consistent and socially responsible. Perhaps most importantly, corrective actions strengthen an organization's competitive position in its basic industry. Continuous strategy evaluation keeps strategists close to the pulse of an organization and provides information needed for an effective strategic-management system. Carter Bayles describes the benefits of strategy evaluation as follows:

> Evaluation activities may renew confidence in the current business strategy or point to the need for actions to correct some weaknesses, such as erosion of product superiority or technological edge. In many cases, the benefits of strategy evaluation are much more far-reaching, for the outcome of the process may be a fundamentally new strategy that will lead, even in a business that is already turning a respectable profit, to substantially increased earnings. It is this possibility that justifies strategy evaluation, for the payoff can be very large. [12]

PUBLISHED SOURCES OF STRATEGY-EVALUATION INFORMATION

A number of publications are helpful in evaluating a firm's strategies. For example, in its May and June issues each year, *Fortune* identifies and evaluates the Fortune 1,000 (the largest manufacturers) and the Fortune 50, (the largest retailers, transportation companies, utilities, banks, insurance companies, and diversified financial corporations in the United States). In these issues, *Fortune* also ranks the best and worst performers on various factors such as return on investment, sales volume, and profitability. In its January issue each year, *Fortune* evaluates organizations in twenty-five industries. Eight key attributes serve as evaluative criteria: quality of management; innovativeness; quality of products or services; long-term investment value; financial soundness; community and environmental responsibility; ability to attract, develop, and keep talented people; and use of corporate assets. *Fortune's* 1988 evaluation of firms in four industries are revealed in Exhibit 9–3.

Another excellent evaluation of corporations in America, "The Annual Report on American Industry," is published annually in the January issue of *Forbes*. It provides a detailed and comprehensive evaluation of hundreds of American companies in many different industries. *Business Week, Industry Week,* and *Dun's Business Month* also periodically publish detailed evaluations of American businesses and industries. Although published sources of strategy-evaluation information focus primarily on large, publicly held businesses, the comparative ratios and related information are widely used to evaluate small businesses and privately owned firms as well.

EXHIBIT 9–3 *Fortune's* 1988 ranking of companies in four industries

Life insurance

Northwestern Mutual leads in management and financial strength, but Prudential gets the palm for innovation.

Rank	Last Year	Company	Score
1	1	Northwestern Mutual Life	7.03
2	2	Prudential	6.61
3	4	Aetna Life	6.44
4	6	Metropolitan Life	6.36
5	7	Connecticut General Life	6.15
6	5	Travelers	6.12
7	9	John Hancock Mutual	5.97
8	10	Equitable Life Assurance	5.89
9	3	Teachers Insurance & Annuity	5.85
10	8	New York Life	5.83

Aerospace

Boeing, still first in its industry, fell out of the top ten this year, scores of all the aerospace companies sank.

Rank	Last Year	Company	Score
1	1	Boeing	7.70
2	2	Martin Marietta	6.99
3	3	Rockwell International	6.76
4	4	Lockheed	6.61
5	6	McDonnell Douglas	6.54
6	7	Travelers	6.27
7	8	General Dynamics	6.25
8	5	Northrop	6.19
9	9	Textron	5.77
10	10	Allied-Signal	5.71

Commercial banking

J. P. Morgan rules the roost in this industry at a time when most banks are socking away reserves against bad LDC loans.

Rank	Last Year	Company	Score
1	1	J. P. Morgan	8.03
2	3	Bankers Trust New York	7.08
3	2	Citicorp	7.06
4	—	Wells Fargo & Co.	6.92
5	4	Security Pacific	6.76
6	5	First Interstate Bancorp	5.91
7	7	Chase Manhattan	5.48
8	6	Chemical New York	5.41
9	8	Manufacturers Hanover	4.68
10	10	BankAmerica	3.21

Food

Sara Lee remains the best managed food company.

Rank	Last Year	Company	Score
1	1	Sara Lee	7.50
2	3	General Mills	7.30
3	2	Pillsbury	6.82
4	6	ConAgra	6.82
5	5	Kraft[3,4]	6.81
6	4	Ralston Purina	6.81
7	7	Borden	6.59
8	8	Archer Daniels Midland	6.19
9	9	CPC International	6.06
10	—	Occidental Petroleum	5.30

Source: Ellen Schultz, "America's Most Admired Corporations," *Fortune* (18 January 1988): 42–45.

CHARACTERISTICS OF AN EFFECTIVE EVALUATION SYSTEM

Strategy evaluation must meet several basic requirements to be effective. First, strategy-evaluation activities must be economical; too much information can be just as bad as too little information, and too many controls can do more harm than good. Strategy-evaluation activities should be meaningful; they should specifically relate to a firm's objectives. They should provide managers with useful information about tasks over which they have control and influence. Strategy-evaluation activities should provide timely information; on occasion and in some areas, managers may need information daily. For example, when a firm has diversified by acquiring another firm, evaluative information may be needed frequently. However, in an R & D department, daily or even weekly evaluative information could be dysfunctional. Approximate information that is timely is generally more desirable as a basis for strategy evaluation than accurate information that does not depict the present. Frequent measurement and rapid reporting may frustrate control rather than give better control. The time dimension of control must coincide with the time span of the event being measured.

Strategy evaluation should be designed to provide a true picture of what is happening. For example, in a severe economic downturn, productivity and profitability ratios may drop alarmingly, while employees and managers are actually working harder. Strategy evaluations should portray this type of situation fairly. Information derived from the strategy-evaluation process should facilitate action and should be directed to those individuals in the organization who need to take action based on it. Managers commonly ignore evaluative reports that are provided for informational purposes only; all managers do not need to receive all reports. Controls need to be action-oriented rather than information-oriented.

The strategy evaluation should not dominate decisions; it *should* foster mutual understanding, trust, and common sense. No department should fail to cooperate with another in evaluating strategies. Strategy evaluations should be simple, not too cumbersome, and not too restrictive. Complex strategy-evaluation systems often confuse people and accomplish little. The test of an effective evaluation system is its usefulness, not its complexity.

Large organizations require a more elaborate and detailed strategy-evaluation system because it is more difficult to coordinate efforts among different divisions and functional areas. Managers in small companies often communicate with each other and their employees daily and do not need extensive evaluative reporting systems. Familiarity with local environments usually makes gathering and evaluating information much easier for small organizations than for large businesses.[13] But the key to an effective strategy-evaluation system may be the ability to convince participants that failure to accomplish certain objectives within a prescribed time is not necessarily a reflection of their performance.[14] There is no one ideal strategy-evaluation system. The unique characteristics of an organization, including its size, management style, purpose, problems, and strengths, can determine a strategy evaluation and control system's final design. Robert Waterman offers the following observation about successful organizations' strategy evaluation and control systems:

> Successful companies treat facts as friends and controls as liberating. Morgan Guaranty and Wells Fargo not only survive but thrive in the troubled waters of bank deregulation, because

their strategy evaluation and control systems are sound, their risk is contained, and they know themselves and the competitive situation so well. Successful companies have a voracious hunger for facts. They see information where others see only data. They love comparisons, rankings, anything that removes decision-making from the realm of mere opinion. Successful companies maintain tight, accurate financial controls. Their people don't regard controls as an imposition of autocracy, but as the benign checks and balances that allow them to be creative and free.[15]

CONTINGENCY PLANNING

Regardless of how carefully strategies are formulated, implemented, and evaluated, unforeseen events such as strikes, boycotts, natural disasters, foreign competitors, and government actions can make a strategy obsolete. To minimize the impact of potential threats, organizations should develop contingency plans as part of the strategy-evaluation process. *Contingency plans* can be defined as alternative plans that can be put into effect if certain key events do not occur as expected. Only high-priority areas require the insurance of contingency plans. Strategists cannot and should not try to cover all bases by planning for all possible contingencies. But in any case, contingency plans should be as simple as possible.

When strategy-evaluation activities reveal the need for a major change quickly, an appropriate contingency plan can be executed in a timely way. Contingency plans can promote a strategist's ability to respond quickly to key changes in the internal and external bases of an organization's current strategy. For example, if underlying assumptions about the economy turn out to be wrong and contingency plans are ready, then managers can make appropriate changes promptly.

In some cases, internal or external conditions present unexpected opportunities. When such opportunities do occur, contingency plans allow an organization to capitalize on them quickly. Linneman and Chandran have found in their research that contingency planning gives users such as DuPont, Dow Chemical, Consolidated Foods, and Emerson Electric three major benefits: it permits quick response to change, it prevents panic in crisis situations, and it makes managers more adaptable by encouraging them to appreciate just how variable the future can be; they suggest that effective contingency planning involves a seven-step process as follows:

1. Identify both beneficial and unfavorable events that could possibly derail the strategy or strategies.
2. Specify trigger points. Calculate about when contingent events are likely to occur.
3. Assess the impact of each contingent event. Estimate the potential benefit or harm of each contingent event.
4. Develop contingency plans. Be sure that contingency plans are compatible with current strategy and are economically feasible.
5. Assess the counterimpact of each contingency plan. That is, estimate how much each contingency plan will capitalize on or cancel out its associated contingent event. Doing this will quantify the potential value of each contingency plan.

6. Determine early warning signals for key contingent events. Monitor the early warning signals.
7. For contingent events with reliable early warning signals, develop advance action plans to take advantage of the available lead time.[16]

AUDITING

A frequently used tool in strategy evaluation is the audit. *Auditing* is defined by the American Accounting Association (AAA) as "a systematic process of objectively obtaining and evaluating evidence regarding assertions about economic actions and events to ascertain the degree of correspondence between those assertions and established criteria, and communicating the results to interested users."[17] People who perform audits can be divided into three groups: independent auditors, government auditors, and internal auditors. Independent auditors basically are certified public accountants (CPAs) who provide their services to organizations for a fee; they examine the financial statements of an organization to determine whether they have been prepared according to generally accepted accounting principles (GAAP) and whether they fairly represent the activities of the firm. Independent auditors use a set of standards called generally accepted auditing standards (GAAS). Public accounting firms often have a consulting arm that provides strategy-evaluation services. Two government agencies, the General Accounting Office (GAO) and the Internal Revenue Service (IRS), employ government auditors responsible for making sure that organizations comply with federal laws, statutes, and policies. GAO and IRS auditors can audit any public or private organization. The third group of auditors are those employees within an organization who are responsible for safeguarding company assets, for assessing the efficiency of company operations, and for ensuring that generally accepted business procedures are practiced. To evaluate the effectiveness of an organization's strategic-management system, internal auditors often seek answers to the questions posed in Exhibit 9–4. Aaron Kelly developed the Planning Process Audit (PPA) presented in Exhibit 9–5.

USING COMPUTERS TO EVALUATE STRATEGIES

The usefulness of computers in facilitating strategy evaluation should not be overlooked. When properly designed, installed, and operated, a computer network can efficiently acquire information promptly and accurately. Computers can allow diverse strategy-evaluation reports to be generated for different levels and types of managers. For example, strategists will want reports concerned with whether the mission, objectives, and strategies of the enterprise are being achieved. Middle managers could require strategy-implementation information such as whether construction of a new facility is on schedule or a product's development is proceeding as expected. Lower-level managers could need evaluation reports that focus on operational concerns such as absenteeism and turnover rates, productivity rates, and the number and nature of grievances. Computers are being used more and more to integrate reports and enhance strategy evaluation at all levels in organizations.

EXHIBIT 9–4 Key strategy-evaluation questions

1. Do you feel that the strategic-management system exists to provide service to you in your day-to-day work? How has it helped you in this respect?
2. Has the strategic-management system provided the service that you feel was promised at the start of its design and implementation? In which areas has it failed and excelled, in your opinion?
3. Do you consider that the strategic-management system has been implemented with due regard to costs and benefits? Are there any areas in which you consider the costs to be excessive?
4. Do you feel comfortable using the system? Could more attention have been paid to matching the output of the system to your needs and if so, in what areas?
5. Is the system flexible enough in your opinion? If not, where should changes be made?
6. Do you still keep a personal store of information in a notebook or elsewhere? If so, will you share that information with the system? Do you see any benefits in so doing?
7. Do you think that the strategic-management system is still evolving? Can you influence this evolution and, if not, why not?
8. Does the system provide you with timely, relevant, and accurate information? Are there any areas of deficiency in this respect?
9. Do you think that the strategic-management system makes too much use of complex procedures and models? Can you suggest areas in which less complicated techniques might be used to advantage?
10. Do you consider that there has been sufficient attention paid to the confidentiality and security of the information in the system? Can you suggest areas for improvement of these aspects of its operation?

Source: K.J. Radford, *Information Systems for Strategic Decisions*, © 1978, pp. 220–21. Reprinted by permission of Prentice-Hall, Inc., Englewood Cliffs, N.J. Also, Lloyd Byars, *Strategic Management* (New York: Harper & Row, 1984), 237.

EXHIBIT 9–5 The Planning Process Audit

1. To what extent do you feel top management has been committed to the pursuit of stated corporate strategy?
2. To what extent do you feel committed to the pursuit of stated corporate strategy?
3. Has top management's decision making been consistent with stated corporate strategy?
4. Has decision making been more or less centralized than anticipated?
5. Do you feel you have received sufficient resource support (financial and human) to pursue your stated plans?
6. Do everyday, operational plans seem to support the overall corporate strategy?
7. How would you rate the extent and quality of the coordination of plans among functional areas/departments/divisions?
8. How would you rate the extent and quality of the communication of plans to lower organizational levels?

9. Does the reward system (pay, promotions, etc.) seem to be tied to your planning efforts?
10. Do the written plans seem to adequately represent the actual goals toward which managers seem to be working?
11. How complex is the present planning process?
12. How formal is the present planning process?
13. Do you feel you have the right types and amounts of external information to fulfill your planning responsibilities?
14. Do you feel you have the right types and amounts of internal information to fulfill your planning responsibilities? If not, what other internal information do you feel you need?
15. Would any other training help you do a better job of planning? If Yes, what other specific training would help?
16. What are the major problems of the current planning systems?
17. How might the planning process be improved upon?

Source: C. Aaron Kelly, "Auditing the Planning Process," *Managerial Planning* 32, no. 4 (January–February 1984): 13. Used with permission.

For over a decade, we have been reading about the senior executive "war room" and what more recently has been termed "the office of the future," a room containing a number of computer terminals with graphic displays. There the chief executive officer of an organization spends most of the day monitoring the firm's internal and external environment and formulating, implementing, and evaluating strategies. The corporate war room may never become a reality, but computers are becoming an integral part of strategic-management systems. Computers now offer strategists integration, uniformity, analysis, and economy in evaluating strategic-management activities.

Today's business environment has become so competitive that strategists are being forced to extend planning horizons and to make decisions under greater and greater degrees of uncertainty. As a result, more information has to be obtained and assimilated to formulate, implement, and evaluate strategic decisions. In any competitive situation, the side with the best intelligence (information) usually wins; computers enable managers to evaluate vast amounts of information quickly and accurately.

A limitation of computer-based systems to evaluate and monitor strategy execution is that personal values, attitudes, morals, preferences, politics, personalities, and emotions are not programmable. This limitation accents the need to view computers as a tool, rather than as actual decision-making devices. Computers can significantly enhance the process of effectively integrating intuition and analysis in strategy-evaluation. The General Accounting Office of the United States Government offers the following conclusions regarding the appropriate role of computers in strategy evaluation:

> The aim is to enhance and extend judgment. Computers should be looked upon not as a provider of solutions, but rather as a framework which permits science and judgment to be brought together and made explicit. It is the explicitness of this structure, the decision-maker's ability to probe, modify, and examine "What if?" alternatives, that is of value in extending judgment.[18]

CONCLUSION

This chapter presents a strategy-evaluation framework that can facilitate accomplishment of annual and long-term objectives. Effective strategy evaluation allows an organization to capitalize on internal strengths as they develop, to exploit external opportunities as they emerge, to recognize and defend against environmental threats, and to improve internal weaknesses before they become detrimental.

Strategists in successful organizations take the time to formulate, implement, and then evaluate strategies deliberately and systematically. Good strategists move their organization forward with purpose and direction, continually evaluating and improving the firm's internal and external strategic position. Strategy evaluation allows an organization to shape its own future rather than constantly being shaped by remote forces that have little or no vested interest in the well being of the enterprise. Computers are being used more and more to facilitate this process. A key to effective strategy evaluation and to successful strategic management is an integration of intuition and analysis.

> A potentially fatal problem is the tendency for analytical and intuitive issues to polarize. This polarization leads to strategy evaluation that is dominated by either analysis or intuition, or to strategy evaluation that is discontinuous, with a lack of coordination among analytical and intuitive issues.[19]

KEY TERMS AND CONCEPTS

Advantage
Auditing
Consistency
Consonance
Contingency planning
Feasibility
Future shock
Management by wandering around
Measuring organizational performance
Planning process audit (PPA)
Reviewing the underlying bases of an organization's strategy
Revised IFE Matrix
Revised EFE Matrix
Taking corrective actions

ISSUES FOR REVIEW AND DISCUSSION

1. Why has strategy evaluation become so important in today's business environment?
2. BellSouth Services is considering putting divisional EFE and IFE matrices online for continual updating. How would this affect strategy evaluation?
3. What types of quantitative and qualitative criteria do you think Sam Walton, CEO of Wal-Mart, uses to evaluate the company's strategy?
4. As owner of a local, independent supermarket, explain how you would evaluate the firm's strategy.
5. Under what conditions are corrective actions not required in the strategy-evaluation process?

6. Identify types of organizations that may need to evaluate strategy more frequently than others. Justify your choices.
7. As executive director of the state forestry commission, in what way and how frequently would you evaluate the organization's strategies?
8. Identify some key financial ratios that would be important in evaluating a bank's strategy.
9. As owner of a chain of hardware stores, describe how you would approach contingency planning.
10. Strategy evaluation allows an organization to take a proactive stance towards shaping its own future. Discuss the meaning of this statement.
11. Select an article listed in the suggested readings for this chapter. Give a five-minute oral report to the class summarizing the article and your thoughts on the particular topic.

NOTES

1. Cortlandt Camman and David Nadler, "Fit Control Systems to Your Managerial Style," *Harvard Business Review* 54, no.1 (January–February 1976): 65.
2. Gene Dalton and Paul Lawrence, *Motivation and Control in Organizations* (Homewood, Illinois: Richard D. Irwin, 1971), 5.
3. Dale Zand, "Reviewing the Policy Process," *California Management Review* 21, no.1 (Fall 1978): 37.
4. Eccles. 3: 1–8.
5. W. Lindsay and L. Rue, "Impact of the Organization Environment on the Long-Range Planning Process: A Contingency View," *Academy of Management Journal* 23, no. 3 (September 1980): 402.
6. George Steiner, *Strategic Planning: What Every Manager Must Know* (New York: The Free Press, 1979), 269.
7. Claude George, Jr., *The History of Management Thought* (Englewood Cliffs, N.J.: Prentice-Hall, 1968), 165–166.
8. John Brown and Neil Agnew, "Corporate Agility," *Business Horizons* 25, no.2 (March–April 1982): 29.
9. M. Erez and F. Kanfer, "The Role of Goal Acceptance in Goal Setting and Task Performance," *Academy of Management Review* 8, no. 3 (July 1983): 457.
10. D. Hussey and M. Langham, *Corporate Planning: The Human Factor* (Oxford, England: Pergamon Press, 1979), 138.
11. Carter Bayles, "Strategic Control: The President's Paradox," *Business Horizons* 20, no.4 (August 1977): 18.
12. Peter Drucker, *Management Tasks, Responsibilities and Practice* (New York: Harper & Row, 1973), 503.
13. George Rice, Jr., "Strategic Decision Making in Small Business," *Journal of General Management* 9, no. 1 (Autumn 1983): 64.
14. Timothy Brady, "Six Step Method to Long Range Planning for Non-profit Organizations," *Managerial Planning* 32, no. 4 (January–February 1984): 49.
15. Robert Waterman, Jr., "How the Best Get Better," *Business Week* (14 September 1987): 105.
16. Robert Linneman and Rajan Chandran, "Contingency Planning: A Key to Swift Managerial Action in the Uncertain Tomorrow," *Managerial Planning* 29, no.4 (January–February 1981): 23–27.
17. American Accounting Association, *Report of Committee on Basic Auditing Concepts* (1971), 15–74.
18. GAO Report PAD–80–21, 17.
19. Michael McGinnis, "The Key to Strategic Planning: Integrating Analysis and Intuition," *Sloan Management Review* 26, no.1 (Fall 1984): 49.

SUGGESTED READINGS

Dyment, J. J. "Strategies and Management Controls for Global Corporations." *Journal of Business Strategy* 7, no.4 (Spring 1987): 20–26.

Kelley, C. A. "Auditing the Planning Process." *Managerial Planning* 32, no. 4 (January–February 1984): 12–14.

King, William. "Evaluating the Effectiveness of Your Planning." *Managerial Planning* 33, no. 2 (September–October 1984): 4–8, 26.

Lauglaug, A. S. "A Framework for the Strategic Management of Future Type Technology." *Long Range Planning* 20, no. 5 (October 1987): 21–41.

Mayer, Robert. "Winning Strategies for Manufacturers in Mature Industries." *Journal of Business Strategy* 8, no. 2 (Fall 1987): 23–31.

McGinnis, M. A. "The Key to Strategic Planning: Integrating Analysis and Intuition." *Sloan Management Review* 26, no.1 (Fall 1984): 45–52.

Pearce, J. A., II; Freeman, E. B.; and Robinson, R. B., Jr. "The Tenuous Link Between Formal Strategic Planning and Financial Performance." *The Academy of Management Review* 12, no. 4 (October 1987): 658–675.

Ramanujam, V. and Venkatraman, N. "Planning System Characteristics and Planning Effectiveness." *Strategic Management Journal* 8, no. 5 (September–October 1987): 453–468.

Schreyogg, G. and Steinmann, H. "Strategic Control: A New Perspective." *Academy of Management Review* 12, no. 1 (January 1987): 91–103.

Siegel, J. G. and Rubin, M. S. "Corporate Planning and Control Through Variance Analysis." *Managerial Planning* 33, no. 2 (September–October 1984): 35–39, 49.

EXPERIENTIAL EXERCISES

EXPERIENTIAL EXERCISE 9A

Preparing a Strategy-Evaluation Report

PURPOSE

This exercise can give you experience locating strategy-evaluation information in your college library. Published sources of information can significantly enhance the strategy-evaluation process.

YOUR TASK

Step 1 Use *F & S Index of Corporations and Industries*, and *Business Periodicals Index* in your college library to locate strategy-evaluation information on Ponderosa. List five to ten articles written in the last six months that relate to Ponderosa or the restaurant industry.

Step 2 Summarize your research findings by preparing a strategy-evaluation report for your professor. Include in your report a summary of Ponderosa's strategies in fiscal 1988 (or 1989), a summary of Ponderosa's performance in fiscal 1988 (or 1989), and a summary of your conclusions regarding the effectiveness of Ponderosa's strategies.

EXPERIENTIAL EXERCISE 9B

Analyzing Ponderosa's Strategy-Evaluation Model

PURPOSE

This exercise asks you to evaluate Ponderosa's strategy-evaluation procedures as described in an article published in *Planning Review*. Mark Lawless, vice president and director of corporate planning at Ponderosa, wrote the article in 1984 to describe Ponderosa's strategy-evaluation system. The article, entitled "Investment and Strategy Evaluation: A Personal Computer Model," is presented in Exhibit 9B.

YOUR TASK

Read Mr. Lawless's strategy-evaluation article. In a one-page paper, give your assessment of the strategy-evaluation procedures described in the article. Ponderosa's strategies have changed significantly since 1984, so include your thoughts about how the model may have contributed positively or negatively to Ponderosa's strategic changes.

EXHIBIT 9B Investment and strategy evaluation: a personal computer model

A standard chore for most planning departments in strategically managed companies is evaluating capital spending strategies and alternatives. To make these evaluations, planners need to consider both financial and nonfinancial criteria since there are minimum financial requirements that have to be met before a potential investment can be taken seriously. No matter how attractive an opportunity may seem, it will fall by the wayside unless specific financial conditions—such as investment hurdle rates—can be satisfied.

The investment hurdle rate is simply the minimum acceptable return on investment—based on the degree of risk, expected inflation, and the return on riskless investments (such as Treasury Bills). Return on investment (ROI) usually sets the basic criteria for evaluating an investment, and the most widely accepted measure of ROI is now the internal rate of return.

In order to make the best possible evaluation of an investment opportunity, management usually requests a variety of detailed scenarios. But putting these scenarios together can be a lengthy business. Even worse, the exercise can muddle the investment criteria and dull the judgment of the analysts.

This article offers an analysis tool that quickly screens the investment performance and permits an objective view of the requirements. The technique is based on my investment analysis model for investment and strategy screening, with a case study of its application for Ponderosa, Inc. The model can be used by any business and is quite easy to alter to fit particular business considerations, although it's not essential to do this to benefit from the model's simulation capabilities in "generic form."

Strategy Analysis

Ponderosa, Inc. is a major diversified company in the food service industry. Its dominant business is a chain of family steakhouses concentrated in the heartland area of the United States. The company owns a meat-processing plant that sells most of its products to the Ponderosa Steakhouses, and it recently acquired and is expanding a Mexican specialty restaurant business. This portfolio of businesses was designed to provide the basic synergies essential to developing restaurant chains, to balancing market opportunities and risks, and to providing a level of vertical integration that would strengthen the businesses' cost-value equation. Given this portfolio, a major strategic issue is how to grow the business through unit addition.

Ponderosa has been considering several expansion alternatives: first of all, building and operating the units, its primary vehicle for growth up to now; second, licensing the concept on a market or individual unit basis, Ponderosa's secondary source of previous expansion. A third, and extremely interesting option would be a joint venture with some other investor.

The present case concerns the feasibility of Ponderosa's expanding in United Kingdom markets. One U.K. company-owned-and-operated steakhouse has provided a good learning base. The specific requirements of a joint-venture arrangement were considered to determine what variable cost and profit structures were required, considering the operating characteristics of the steakhouse and the potential for change.

Information obtained from several different banking institutions indicated that Ponderosa would need a 15–20 percent return over a five-year time horizon. The specific evaluations were:

Investment:	$1.1 million with $.5 million residual value at the end of five years
Fixed Cost:	$180 thousand plus $20 thousand per year
Customer Traffic:	305 thousand per year (5,865 per week)
Average Check:	$4.75 plus $.25 annually
Cash Flow Pattern:	.1 .2 .3 .2 .2
Variable Costs (% of sales):	
Food:	43–47%
Labor:	17–19%
Advertising:	3–4%
Licensing Fee:	4%
Other Variables:	5–7%
Total Variable Cost:	72–81%
Variable Profit:	19–28%

Although the 19–28 percent range for variable profit was considered achievable, these are relatively thin margins, considering:

- The five-year time horizon for return.
- The investment requirement.
- The fixed cost structure.
- The uniqueness of the asset as reflected in the relatively low residual value at the end of the period.

The residual value estimate was very conservative, taking into account only the worth of the furniture and equipment in a sale of the assets, not the sale of the restaurant or the goodwill value of its name. A long hard look at these factors cast considerable doubt on the unit's ability to achieve the necessary return on investment.

Another concern was the estimated volume of customer traffic and the average expenditure per customer. The average check is essentially determined by the market positioning of the concept, the target customer, prevailing economic conditions, and the product mix. The level of customer traffic is affected by the same factors—the average check, alternatives facing the consumer, and the capacity limits of the restaurant. Average check and customer traffic tend to vary inversely with one another, so the most desirable combinations of check size and volume were a significant consideration. Using all available economic and demographic data, as well as site and size considerations, we estimated customer volumes between 286,000 and 315,000 per year. These volumes were consistent with an average check of $4.75 in the initial year, sustainable with check increases of 5 percent annually (that is, averaging between $4.75 and $5.75 over the five-year period).

We studied a series of simulations to determine the requisite operating features, given the business parameters we'd outlined. These simulations (Table 1) used a model adapted to the food service industry from a generic model.

TABLE 1*

1. Desired ROI:	15%	18%	20%
2. Required Variable Profit ($000)	635	705	753
Expected Level	368	368	368
3. Required Sales Level ($000)	2760	3062	3274
Expected Level	1600	1600	1600
4. Required Variable Profit % of Sales	39%	44%	47%
Expected Level	19–28% (23%)	19–28% (23%)	19–28% (23%)

*Values shown are average annual values (specific values vary by year).

Table 1 shows that the expected business performance fell short of what we needed to satisfy the requirements for a successful joint venture. Nevertheless, this option still had several clear advantages that made it a desirable long-term strategy. It permitted risk sharing, a more timely expansion of the business into new markets, and the integration of domestic and U.K. businesses.

We then set out to find alternatives that could eventually make the joint venture a viable approach. We determined that we needed to:

- Reduce investor requirements for return and timing.
- Reduce initial investment through unit design changes.
- Modify menu and service systems to increase operating margins.
- Institute additional cost controls to improve efficiency.
- Develop marketing programs to increase the level of achievable sales.
- Various combinations of the above.

Management chose the last alternative since it was the approach most likely to produce favorable conditions for a joint venture, and Ponderosa's International Development subsidiary is currently acting on this program.

How sensitive are the results to the areas of potential action? Using the 15 percent ROI level scenario, the following changes were evaluated. A $200,000 reduction in the initial investment reduces the required variable profit by $86,000 and 5 percentage points. A $30,000 reduction in annual fixed costs reduces the required variable profit by an additional $30,000 and 2 percentage points. These two actions alone could lower the required variable profit from 39 percent of sales to 32 percent of sales. An increase of 1 percentage point in advertising expenditures, leading to a 10 percent increase in the average check, would give an additional 3-percentage-point reduction in the required variable profit percentage (although it wouldn't reduce the required dollar amount of variable profit). This would reduce the percentage of required variable profit to 29 percent.

As you can see, relatively small changes in some of the business parameters result in significant changes in what is needed to produce the desired ROI.

Source: Mark Lawless, "Investment and Strategy Evaluation: A Personal Computer Model," *Planning Review* (May 1984): 24–27. Used with permission.

PART FIVE
CASE ANALYSIS

Appendix: How to Analyze a Business Policy Case

NOTABLE QUOTES

The essential fact that makes the case method an educational experience of the greatest power is that it makes the student an active rather than a passive participant.

Wallace B. Donham

The great aim of education is not knowledge, but action.

Herbert Spencer

Two heads are better than one.

Unknown Author

Good writers do not turn in their first draft. Ask someone else to read your written case analysis, and read it out loud to yourself. That way, you can find rough areas to clean up.

Lawrence Jauch

One reaction frequently heard is, "I don't have enough information." In reality, strategists never have enough information, because some information is not available and some is too costly.

William Glueck

I keep six honest serving men. They taught me all I know. Their names are What, Why, When, How, Where, and Who.

Rudyard Kipling

Don't recommend anything you would not be prepared to do yourself it you were in the decision maker's shoes.

A. J. Strickland, III

A picture is worth a thousand words.

Unknown Author

OUTLINE

WHAT IS A BUSINESS POLICY CASE?

GUIDELINES FOR PREPARING CASE ANALYSES

PREPARING A CASE FOR CLASS DISCUSSION

PREPARING A WRITTEN CASE ANALYSIS

MAKING AN ORAL PRESENTATION

50 TIPS FOR SUCCESS IN CASE ANALYSIS

OBJECTIVES

After studying this appendix, you should be able to:

- Describe the case method for learning strategic-management concepts.
- Identify the steps in preparing a comprehensive written case analysis.
- Describe how to give an effective oral case analysis presentation.

The purpose of this appendix is to help you analyze business policy cases successfully. Guidelines for preparing written and oral case analyses are given, and suggestions for preparing cases for class discussion are presented. Steps to follow in preparing case analyses are provided. Guidelines for making an oral presentation are described.

WHAT IS A BUSINESS POLICY CASE?

A *business policy case* describes an organization's internal and external environment and raises issues concerning the firm's mission, strategies, objectives, and policies. Most of the information in a business policy case is established fact, but some information may be opinions, judgments, and beliefs. Business policy cases are more comprehensive than those you may have studied in other courses. They generally include a description of related management, marketing, finance/accounting, production/operations, R & D, and environmental issues. (Ponderosa is an example business policy case.) A business policy case puts the reader on the scene of the action by describing a firm's situation at some point in time. Business policy cases are written to give you practice applying strategic-management concepts. The case method for studying strategic management is often called *learning by doing*.

GUIDELINES FOR PREPARING CASE ANALYSES

The Need for Practicality

There is no such thing as a complete case, and no case ever gives you all the information you need to conduct analyses and make recommendations. Likewise, in the business world, strategists never have all of the information they need to make decisions: information may be unavailable, too costly to obtain, or may take too much time to obtain. So, in preparing business policy cases, do what strategists do every day; make reasonable assumptions about unknowns, state assumptions clearly, perform appropriate analyses, and make decisions. *Be practical.* For example, in performing pro forma financial analysis, make reasonable assumptions, state them appropriately, and proceed to show what impact your recommendations are expected to have on the organization's financial position. Avoid saying, "I don't have enough information." You can always supplement the information provided in a case with research in your college library. Library research is encouraged in case analyses.

The Need for Justification

The most important part of analyzing cases is not what strategies you recommend, but rather, how you support your decisions and how you propose that they be implemented. There is no single best solution or one right answer to a case, so *give ample justification* for your recommendations. This is important. In the business world, strategists usually do not know if their decisions are "right" until resources have been allocated and consumed. Then it is too late to reverse the decisions. This cold fact accents the need for careful integration of intuition and analysis in preparing business policy case analyses.

The Need for Realism

Avoid recommending a course of action beyond an organization's means. *Be realistic.* No organization can possibly pursue all the strategies that could potentially benefit the firm. Estimate how much capital will be required to implement what you recommend. Determine whether debt, stock, or a combination of debt and stock could be used to obtain the capital. Make sure your recommendations are feasible. Do not prepare a case analysis that omits all arguments and information not supportive of your recommendations. Rather, present the major advantages and disadvantages of several feasible alternatives. Try not to exaggerate, stereotype, prejudge, or overdramatize. Strive to demonstrate that your interpretation of the evidence is reasonable and objective.

The Need for Specificity

Do not make broad generalizations such as "the company should pursue a market penetration strategy." *Be specific* by telling what, why, when, how, where, and who! Failure to use specifics is the single major shortcoming of most oral and written case analyses! For example, in an internal audit, say, "the firm's current ratio fell from 2.2 in 1987 to 1.3 in 1988 and this is considered to be a major weakness" instead of "the firm's financial condition is bad." Rather than concluding from a SPACE Matrix that a firm should be defensive, be more specific, saying "the firm should close three plants, lay off 280 employees, and divest of its chemical division, for a net savings of $20.2 million in 1988." Use ratios, percentages, numbers, and dollar estimates. Businessmen and businesswomen dislike generalities and vagueness.

The Need for Originality

Do not necessarily recommend the course of action that the firm actually undertook, even if those actions resulted in improved revenues and earnings. The aim of case analysis is for you to consider all the facts and information relevant to the organization at the time, generate feasible alternative strategies, choose among those alternatives, and defend your recommendations. Put yourself back in time to the point when strategic decisions were being made by the firm's strategists. Based on information available then, what would you have done? Support your position with charts, graphs, ratios, analyses, and the like—not a revelation from the library. You can become a good strategist by thinking through situations, making management assessments, and proposing plans yourself. *Be original.*

The Need to Contribute

Strategy formulation, implementation, and evaluation decisions are commonly made by a group of individuals rather than by a single person. Therefore, your professor may divide the class into three- or four-person teams to prepare written or oral case analyses. Members of a strategic-management team, in class or in the business world, differ on their aversion to risk, their concern for the short-run versus long-run, their attitudes towards social responsibility, and on other key factors. There are no perfect people, so there are no perfect strategists. Be open-minded to others' views. *Be a good listener and a good contributor.*

PREPARING A CASE FOR CLASS DISCUSSION

Your professor may ask you to prepare a case for class discussion. Preparing a case for class discussion means that you need to read the case before class, make notes regarding the organization's internal strengths and weaknesses and external opportunities and threats, perform appropriate analyses, and come to class prepared to offer and defend some specific recommendations.

The Case Method versus Lecture Approach

The case method of teaching is radically different from the traditional lecture approach where little or no preparation is needed by students before class. The *case method* involves a classroom situation where students do most of the talking: your professor facilitates discussion by asking questions and encouraging student interaction regarding ideas, analyses, and recommendations. Be prepared for a discussion along the lines of "what would you do, why would you do it, when would you do it, and how would you do it?" Prepare answers to the following types of questions:

1. What are the organization's major strengths and weaknesses?
2. How would you describe the organization's financial condition?
3. What are the firm's most important external opportunities and threats?
4. What are the firm's existing strategies and objectives?
5. Who are the firm's competitors and what are their strategies?
6. What objectives and strategies do you recommend for this organization? Explain your reasoning.
7. How could the organization best implement what you recommend? What implementation problems do you envision? How could the firm avoid or solve those problems?

The Cross-Examination

Do not hesitate to take a stand on the issues and to support your position with objective analyses and outside research. Strive to apply strategic-management concepts and tools in preparing your case for class discussion. Seek defensible arguments and positions. Support opinions and judgments with facts, reasons, and evidence. Crunch the numbers before class! Be willing to describe your recommendations to the class without fear of disapproval. Respect the ideas of others, but be willing to "go against the grain" of majority opinion when you can justify a "better" position.

Business policy case analysis gives you the opportunity to learn more about yourself, your colleagues, strategic management, and the decision-making process in organizations. The rewards of this experience will depend upon the effort you put forth, so do a good job. Discussing business policy cases in class is exciting and challenging. Expect views counter to those you present. Different students will place emphasis on different aspects of an organization's situation and submit different recommendations for scrutiny and rebuttal. *Cross-examination* discussions commonly arise, just as they occur in a real business organization. Avoid being a "silent observer."

PREPARING A WRITTEN CASE ANALYSIS

In addition to asking you to prepare a case for class discussion, your professor may ask you to prepare a written case analysis. Preparing a written case analysis is similar to preparing a case for class discussion, except written reports are generally more structured and more detailed. There is no ironclad procedure for preparing a written case analysis because cases differ in focus and the type, size, and complexity of the organizations being analyzed vary as well.

When writing a strategic-management report or case analysis, avoid jargon, vogue words, redundant words, acronyms, abbreviations, sexist language, or ethnic or racial slurs; watch your spelling! Use short sentences and paragraphs and simple words and phrases. Arrange issues and ideas from the most important to the least important. Arrange recommendations from the least controversial to the most controversial. Use the active voice rather than the passive voice for all verbs; for example, say, "Our team recommends the company diversify" rather than "It is recommended by our team to diversify." Use many examples to add specificity and clarity. Tables, figures, pie charts, bar charts, time lines, and other kinds of exhibits help communicate important points and ideas. Sometimes, a picture *is* worth a thousand words.

The Executive Summary

Your professor may ask you to focus your written case analysis on a particular aspect of the strategic-management process, such as "to identify and evaluate the organization's existing mission, objectives, and strategies," or "to propose and defend specific recommendations for the company," or "to develop an industry analysis by describing the competitors, products, selling techniques, and market conditions in a given industry." These types of written reports are sometimes called *executive summaries*. An executive summary usually ranges from three to five pages of text in length, plus exhibits.

Steps in Preparing a Comprehensive Written Analysis

In preparing a comprehensive written analysis, you could follow the steps outlined here, which follow the stages in the strategic management process and the chapters in this text.

Step 1 Identify the firm's existing mission, objectives, and strategies.

Step 2 Develop a mission statement for the organization.

Step 3 Identify the organization's external opportunities and threats.

Step 4 Construct a Competitive Profile Matrix.

Step 5 Construct an EFE Matrix.

Step 6 Identify the organization's internal strengths and weaknesses.

Step 7 Construct an IFE Matrix.

Step 8 Prepare a TOWS Matrix, SPACE Matrix, BCG Matrix, IE Matrix, Grand Strategy Matrix, and QSPM as appropriate. Give advantages and disadvantages of alternative strategies.

Step 9 Recommend specific long-term objectives and strategies. Show how much your recommendations will cost.

Step 10 Specify how your recommendations can be implemented and what results you expect. Prepare forecasted ratios and pro forma financial statements. Present a timetable or agenda for action.

Step 11 Recommend specific annual objectives and policies.

Step 12 Recommend procedures for strategy review and evaluation.

MAKING AN ORAL PRESENTATION

Sometimes your professor will ask you to prepare a business policy case analysis, individually or as a group, and present your analysis to the class. Oral presentations are usually graded on two parts: content and delivery. *Content* refers to the quality, quantity, correctness, and appropriateness of analyses presented, including such dimensions as logical flow through the presentation, coverage of major issues, use of specifics, avoidance of generalities, prevalence of mistakes, and feasibility of recommendations. *Delivery* includes such dimensions as audience attentiveness, clarity of visual aids, appropriate dress, persuasiveness of arguments, tone of voice, eye contact, and posture. Great ideas are of no value unless others can be convinced of their merit through clear communication. The guidelines presented here can help you make an effective formal oral presentation.

Organizing the Presentation

Begin your presentation by introducing yourself and giving a clear outline of topics to be covered. If a team is presenting, specify the sequence of speakers and the areas each person will address. At the beginning of an oral presentation, try to capture your audience's interest and attention. You could do this by displaying some products made by the company, or telling an interesting short story about the company, or sharing an experience that you had related to the company, its products, or services. A light or humorous introduction can be effective.

Be sure the setting of your presentation is well organized, with chairs, flip charts, a transparency projector, and whatever else you plan to use. Arrive at least fifteen minutes early to the classroom to organize the setting and be sure your materials are ready to go. Make sure everyone can see your visual aids well.

Controlling Your Voice

An effective rate of speaking ranges from a hundred to 125 words per minute. Practice your presentation out loud to determine if you are going too fast. Individuals commonly speak too fast when nervous. Breathe deeply before and during the presentation to help yourself slow down. Have a cup of water available; pausing to take a drink will wet your throat, give you time to collect your thoughts, control your nervousness, slow you down, and signal to the audience a change in topic.

Avoid a monotone by placing emphasis on different words or sentences. Speak loud and clear, but don't shout. Silence can be used effectively to break a monotone voice. Stop at the end of each sentence, rather than running sentences together with "and" or "uh."

Managing Body Language

Be sure not to fold your arms, or lean on the podium, or put your hands in your pocket, or put your hands behind you. Keep a straight posture with one foot slightly in front of the other. Do not turn your back to the audience, which is not only rude but also your voice would not project well. Avoid using too many hand gestures. On occasion, leave the podium or table and walk towards your audience, but do not walk around too much. Never block the audience's view of your visual aids.

Maintain good eye contact throughout the presentation. This is the best way to persuade your audience. There is nothing more reassuring to a speaker than to see members of the audience nod agreement or smile. Try to look everyone in the eye at least once during your presentation, but focus more on individuals who look interested than on persons who seem bored. Use humor and smiles as appropriate throughout your presentation to stay in touch with your audience. A presentation should not be dull!

Speaking from Notes

Be sure not to "read" to your audience, because that puts people to sleep. Perhaps worse than "reading" is "memorizing." Do not try to memorize anything. Rather, practice using notes unobtrusively. Make sure your notes are written clearly, so you will not flounder trying to read your own writing. Include only main ideas on your note cards. Keep note cards on a podium or table if possible, so that you won't drop them or get them out of order; walking with note cards tends to be distracting.

Constructing Visual Aids

Make sure your visual aids are clearly legible to individuals in the back of the room. Use color to highlight special items. Avoid putting complete sentences on visual aids.

Rather, use short phrases and then elaborate on the issues as you make your presentation. Generally there should be no more than four to six lines of text on each visual aid. Use clear headings and subheadings. Be careful about spelling and grammar; use a consistent style of lettering. Use masking tape or an easel for posters: do not hold posters in your hand. Transparencies and handouts are excellent aids; however, be careful not to use too many handouts or your audience may look at them instead of you during the presentation.

Answering Questions

It is best to field questions at the end of your presentation, rather than during the presentation itself. Encourage questions and take your time to respond to each one. Answering questions can be persuasive because it involves you with the audience. If a team is giving the presentation, the audience should direct questions to a specific person. During the question and answer period, be polite, confident, and courteous. Avoid verbose responses. Do not get defensive with your answers, even if a hostile or confrontational question is asked. Staying calm during potentially disruptive situations such as a cross examination reflects self confidence, maturity, and poise. Stand up throughout the question-answer period.

FIFTY TIPS FOR SUCCESS IN CASE ANALYSIS

1. View your case analysis and presentation as a product that must have some competitive factor to differentiate it favorably from the case analyses of other students.
2. Prepare your case analysis far enough in advance of the due date to allow time for reflection and practice. Do not procrastinate.
3. Develop a mindset of "why," continually questioning assumptions and assertions (your own as well as others').
4. The best ideas are lost if not communicated to the reader, so as ideas develop, think of their most appropriate presentation.
5. Maintain a positive attitude about the class, working with problems rather than against them.
6. Keep in tune with your professor and understand his or her values and expectations.
7. Since business policy is a capstone course, seek the help of professors in other specialty areas as needed.
8. Other students will have strengths in functional areas that will complement your weaknesses, so develop a cooperative spirit that moderates competitiveness in group work.
9. Read your case frequently as work progresses so you don't overlook details.
10. When preparing a case analysis as a group, divide into separate teams to work on the external analysis and internal analysis. Each team should write its section as if it were to go into the paper; then give each group member a copy.
11. At the end of each group session, assign each member of the group a task to be completed for the next meeting.

12. Have a good sense of humor.
13. Capitalize on the strengths of each member of the group; volunteer your services in your areas of strength.
14. Set goals for yourself and your team; budget your time to attain them.
15. Become friends with the library.
16. Foster attitudes that encourage group participation and interaction. Do not be too hasty to judge group members.
17. Be creative and innovative throughout the case analysis process.
18. Be prepared to work. There will be times when you will have to do more than your "share." Accept it, and do what you have to do to move the team forward.
19. Think of your case analysis as if it were really happening; do not reduce case analysis to a mechanical process.
20. To uncover flaws in your analysis and to prepare the group for questions during an oral presentation, assign one person in the group to actively play the "devil's advocate."
21. Do not schedule excessively long group meetings; two-hour sessions are about right.
22. A goal of case analysis is to improve your ability to think clearly in ambiguous and confusing situations; do not get frustrated that there is no "single best answer."
23. Push your ideas hard enough to get them listened to, but then let up; listen to others and try to follow their lines of thinking; follow the flow of group discussion, recognizing when you need to get back on track; do not repeat yourself or others unless clarity or progress demands repetition.
24. Do not confuse symptoms with causes; do not develop conclusions and solutions prematurely; recognize that information may be misleading, conflicting, or wrong.
25. Work hard to develop the ability to formulate reasonable, consistent, and creative plans; put yourself in the strategist's position.
26. Develop confidence in using quantitative tools for analysis; they are not inherently difficult; it is just practice and familiarity you need.
27. Develop a case-writing style that is direct, assertive, and convincing; be concise, precise, fluent, and correct.
28. Have fun when at all possible. It is frustrating at times, but enjoy it while you can; it may be several years before you are playing CEO again.
29. Acquire a professional typist and proofreader. Do not perform either task alone.
30. Strive for excellence in writing and technical preparation of your case. Prepare nice charts, tables, diagrams, and graphs. Use color and unique pictures. No messy exhibits!
31. In group cases, do not allow personality differences to interfere. When they occur, they must be understood for what they are and put aside.
32. Do not forget that the objective is to learn; explore areas with which you are not familiar.
33. Pay attention to detail.

34. Think through alternative implications fully and realistically. The consequences of decisions are not always apparent. They often affect many different aspects of a firm's operations.
35. Get things written down (drafts) as soon as possible.
36. Read everything that other group members write, and comment on them in writing. This allows group input into all aspects of case preparation.
37. Provide answers to such fundamental questions as what, when, where, why, and how.
38. Adaptation and flexibility are keys to success; be creative and innovative.
39. Do not merely recite ratios or present figures. Rather, develop ideas and conclusions concerning the possible trends. Show the importance of these figures to the corporation.
40. Support reasoning and judgment with factual data whenever possible.
41. Neatness is a real plus; your case analysis should look professional.
42. Your analysis should be as detailed and specific as possible.
43. A picture speaks a thousand words, and a creative picture gets you an "A" in many classes.
44. Let someone else read and critique your paper several days before you turn it in.
45. Emphasize the "Strategy Selection" and "Strategy Implementation" sections. A common mistake is to spend too much time on the external or internal analysis parts of your paper. Always remember that the "meat" of the paper or presentation is the strategy selection and implementation sections.
46. Make special efforts to get to know your group members. This leads to more openness in the group and allows for more interchange of ideas. Put in the time and effort necessary to develop these relationships.
47. Be constructively critical of your group members' work. Do not dominate group discussions. Be a good listener and contributor.
48. Learn from past mistakes and deficiencies. Improve upon weak aspects of other case presentations.
49. Learn from the positive approaches and accomplishments of other classmates.
50. Be considerate, dependable, reliable, and trustworthy.

SUGGESTED READINGS

Holcombe, M., and Stein, J. *Presentations for Decision Makers*. Belmont, California: Lifetime Learning Publications, 1983.

———. "*Writing for Decision Makers*. Belmont, CA: Lifetime Learning Publications, 1981.

Jeffries, J., and Bates, J. *The Executive's Guide to Meetings, Conferences, and Audiovisual Presentations*. New York: McGraw-Hill, 1983.

Shurter, R., Williamson, J. P., and Broehl, W. *Business Research and Report Writing*. New York: McGraw-Hill, 1965.

Strunk, W., and White, E. B. *The Elements of Style*. New York: Macmillan, 1978.

Zall, P., and Franc, L. *Practical Writing in Business and Industry*. North Scituate, Massachusetts: Duxbury Press, 1978.

PART SIX
CASES

CASES

Lomas & Nettleton Financial Corporation—1988

FRED DAVID
Auburn University

Lomas & Nettleton is a diversified financial institution that does business in mortgage banking, retail banking, commercial leasing, short-term lending, life insurance, and real estate development. Lomas & Nettleton is greatly affected by movements in interest rates and the stock market. On October 19, 1987, known as Black Monday, the New York Stock Exchange fell a composite 508 points, the worst single-day drop in history. Jess Hay, Lomas & Nettleton's chief executive officer, is concerned that this crash may signal the beginning of a recession or depression, which may reduce individuals' disposable income to the purchase of insurance, homes, and real estate.

Headquartered in Dallas, Texas, Lomas & Nettleton's net income declined from $54.5 million in 1986 to $45.5 million in 1987, down 17 percent. Earnings per share declined from $2.19 to $1.49. Lomas & Nettleton now faces a hostile takeover attempt and some major strategic decisions. Fiscal 1988 promises to be a pivotal year for the company.

HISTORY

John Lomas founded Lomas & Nettleton in 1894 in New Haven, Connecticut. In 1963, Lomas & Nettleton was acquired by Wallace Investments, Inc. The company changed its name in 1965 to the Lomas & Nettleton Financial Corporation. As indicated in Exhibit 1, Lomas & Nettleton acquired the servicing portfolio of T. J. Bettes in 1968, making it the nation's largest mortgage banking company. Lomas & Nettleton has acquired a number of mortgage companies since 1968, including United Mortgage in 1970, Northwest Mortgage in 1971, Great Lakes Mortgage in 1979, Advance Mortgage Corporation in 1983, and Jefferson National Life Insurance Company in 1985.

In 1986, Lomas & Nettleton began to experience increased economic pressures, high delinquency rates on mortgages, increased foreclosures, and greater losses on liquidations. Hurt by these trends, Lomas & Nettleton began diversifying to lessen the severity of cyclical declines in the housing industry. The following three companies were acquired in fiscal 1987 as part of a corporate concentric diversification strategy:

1. Union Life Insurance Company in December 1986 for $52.5 million. This expands Lomas & Nettleton's operations into the insurance industry.

EXHIBIT 1 A chronological history of Lomas & Nettleton Financial Corporation

1894	L & N was founded in New Haven, Connecticut.
1963	Wallace Investments, Inc. purchased L & N.
1965	Wallace Investments, Inc. changed its name to the L & N Financial Corp.
1968	L & N acquired the servicing portfolio of T. J. Bettes Co.
1969	L & N Mortgage Investors, a real estate investment trust, was formed.
1970	L & N acquired United Mortgage Servicing Corp. in Virginia, providing a base of operations in the Southeast.
1971	L & N acquired the Northwest Mortgage, Inc. in the state of Washington, providing a base of operations in the Northwest.
1972	L & N acquired the Kardon Investment Co. in Pennsylvania, providing a base of operations in the Northeast.
1979	L & N acquired the portfolio of National Homes Acceptance Corp. in Indiana and the Great Lakes Mortgage Corp. of Chicago. These acquisitions established L & N as the first truly national mortgage banking operation.
1981	L & N formed L & N Housing Corp., a real estate investment trust located in Maryland.
1982	L & N purchased Vista Mortgage Realty, Inc. and formed a joint venture with Oppenheimer & Co. to own and operate Advance Mortgage Corp.
1983	L & N formed the L and N Securities Corp. to provide relocation financial services and act as a broker-dealer.
1984	Employee Participation Idea Councils were implemented at L & N.
1985	L & N acquired Jefferson National Life Insurance Company.
1987	L & N acquired Union Life Insurance Company, MNet Corporation, and Ellco.

Source: New Employee Orientation Program, Dallas, Texas; Lomas and Nettleton Financial Group, 1982.

2. MNet Corporation in December 1986 for $293.7 million. This enables Lomas & Nettleton to enter retail banking.
3. Equitable Life Leasing Corporation in June 1987 for $253.4 million in stock and $9.9 million in cash and notes. "Ellco" is involved in leasing advanced technology equipment.

A chronological list of major events in Lomas & Nettleton's history is provided in Exhibit 1.

LOMAS & NETTLETON DIVISIONS

Mortgage Banking

Mortgage banking involves originating real estate loans and marketing them to institutional lenders. This activity forms the core of Lomas & Nettleton's operations. Lomas & Nettleton is the largest mortgage servicer for the Federal National Mortgage Association (FNMA) and currently is the largest issuer of securities backed by the guarantee of the Government National Mortgage Association. Lomas & Nettleton obtains applications for mortgage loans principally through established contacts with real estate developers, brokers, and builders. Through its mortgage banking division, Lomas & Nettleton provides long-term financing for home buyers and developers of commercial projects such as apartment complexes, office buildings, shopping centers, and industrial facilities. The major revenue sources for Lomas & Nettleton's mortgage banking division are loan administration, loan interest, and marketing gains, as indicated in Exhibit 2.

Loan administration involves collecting and sending principal and interest installments to investors, maintaining escrow accounts for taxes and insurance, assessing the quality of hazard insurance, managing bad loans, aiding in foreclosure cases, and informing customers about the physical condition of properties. Mortgage loans are currently serviced under arrangements with 962 investors, including savings and loans, banks, pension funds, FNMA, and insurance companies. The mortgage banking divi-

EXHIBIT 2 Sources of revenue (by percent)

	Fiscal		
	1987	*1986*	*1985*
Loan administration	47	52	59
Loan interest	26	30	27
Marketing gains	22	13	8
Other	5	5	6
	100	100	100

sion of Lomas & Nettleton provides data processing services to other financial institutions and also provides certain administrative and advisory services to issuers of mortgage revenue bonds.

Mortgage banking continues to be the major profit center for Lomas & Nettleton, but the percent of corporate revenues contributed by this division declined from 60.6 percent in 1986 to 47.6 percent in 1987. Given the company's diversification strategy, this percentage is expected to decline further to 25.1 in 1988. Lomas & Nettleton's mortgage banking portfolio in 1987 consisted of 653,152 loans, valued at approximately $21.5 billion, as shown in Exhibit 3. These loans are secured by properties in 50 states and the District of Columbia, as shown in Exhibit 4. Lomas & Nettleton's three largest regions in terms of mortgage loans and principle amounts are the Southeast, Central, and Midwest United States. The company's largest concentration of activities is in Texas, California, Illinois, Florida, Arizona, Pennsylvania, Virginia, Colorado, Utah, and Minnesota.

Retail Banking

Lomas & Nettleton entered the retail banking business in December 1986 with the acquisition of MNet Corporation. MNet provides administrative and financial services to individual as well as commercial customers. The largest bank credit card program in the United States is operated by MNet, serving approximately 700 banks. MNet has several subsidiary companies, including MBank USA. MNet's assets are predominantly credit card receivables. MNet offers such products as bonds, options, stocks, insurance, and financial management services.

Commercial Leasing

Lomas & Nettleton entered commercial leasing in June 1987 with the acquisition of Equitable Life Leasing Corporation (Ellco). Ellco specializes in buying and leasing ad-

EXHIBIT 3 Lomas & Nettleton's mortgage banking portfolio

Portfolio balance at beginning of the year		$21,299,782
Additions and reductions during the year		
Servicing retained on mortgage production		
Single-family	$3,428,797	
Commercial and multi-family	296,189	
	3,724,986	
Servicing acquired by purchase	2,779,213	
Total additions		6,504,199
		27,803,981
Amortization, satisfactions and sales		(6,300,699)
Portfolio balance at June 30, 1987		$21,503,282

Source: From Lomas & Nettleton's 1987 *Annual Report*. Used with permission.

EXHIBIT 4 Properties secured by Lomas & Nettleton's loans

	Number of Loans	Principal Amount (000)
State		
Alabama	9,822	$ 210,326
Alaska	1,678	171,048
Arizona	29,395	889,015
Arkansas	3,979	167,040
California	97,085	3,192,547
Colorado	17,757	796,527
Connecticut	5,810	292,858
Delaware	2,714	70,595
District of Columbia	1,127	38,501
Florida	36,586	1,040,807
Georgia	18,191	451,552
Hawaii	959	68,048
Idaho	9,518	304,793
Illinois	37,117	1,277,757
Indiana	19,715	441,813
Iowa	7,549	213,149
Kansas	4,071	122,798
Kentucky	3,537	46,467
Louisiana	11,888	332,187
Maine	818	31,268
Maryland	11,950	464,359
Massachusetts	1,416	78,577
Michigan	24,129	389,191
Minnesota	21,292	885,456
Mississippi	3,985	86,937
Missouri	5,544	120,611
Montana	4,814	188,382
Nebraska	2,273	110,799
Nevada	3,344	143,971
New Hampshire	145	5,032
New Jersey	6,302	361,145
New Mexico	6,598	192,561
New York	357	54,877
North Carolina	9,542	293,971
North Dakota	804	47,343
Ohio	25,466	412,197
Oklahoma	11,416	239,058
Oregon	5,142	220,593
Pennsylvania	31,179	720,999
Rhode Island	210	4,255
South Carolina	6,493	163,370
South Dakota	699	22,019
Tennessee	13,773	334,345
Texas	69,560	3,129,377
Utah	18,371	747,625
Vermont	434	19,048
Virginia	23,239	935,958
Washington	17,001	625,712
West Virginia	505	17,327
Wisconsin	5,983	255,139
Wyoming	1,870	73,952
	653,152	$21,503,282
Type of property		
Single-family	651,123	$19,926,579
Multi-family and commercial	2,029	1,576,703
	653,152	$21,503,282
Type of loan		
FHA	318,587	$ 7,704,332
VA	234,565	6,630,037
Conventional	100,000	7,168,913
	653,152	$21,503,282

Source: From Lomas & Nettleton's 1987 *Annual Report*. Used with permission.

vanced technology equipment, such as computers and office automation equipment. After credit of the customer has been approved, Ellco enters into an agreement with the lessee, purchases the equipment from a vendor, and delivers the equipment to the lessee. The lessee is responsible for insuring and maintaining the equipment. The lease usually calls for monthly payments of a fixed amount. The leased equipment is recorded at cost on the balance sheet of Ellco and is depreciated over the time of the lease. Lomas & Nettleton projects that commercial leasing will contribute the largest percent to total revenue in 1988 with 27.8 percent, just exceeding mortgage banking's contribution.

Life Insurance

Lomas & Nettleton has two life insurance subsidiaries, Mayflower National Life Insurance Company and Lomas Financial Security Insurance Company. These institutions provide credit life, mortgage redemption, accident and health insurance, and life insurance. All of Lomas & Nettleton's current life insurance operations have been transferred to Jefferson National Life (JNL) Insurance Company. Lomas & Nettleton's life insurance operations offer a variety of services, including mortgage redemption, credit life, accident and health insurance, term, and universal life insurance.

Lomas & Nettleton's life insurance revenues for fiscal 1987 were approximately $1.4 billion, compared to $498 million in fiscal 1986. Operations in this division are located in 42 states and the District of Columbia. Lomas & Nettleton employs approximately 2,700 agents in their life insurance operations and insures about 500,000 individuals. Life insurance coverage in force for fiscal 1987 was approximately $11.6 billion, up from $6.4 billion in 1986.

Short-Term Lending

Lomas & Nettleton's short term lending in real estate consists of providing first mortgage construction, development, and acquisition loans. First mortgage construction loans provide financing for the sites and construction of residential as well as commercial properties. These loans typically do not exceed five years. Lomas & Nettleton originates short-term construction loans through Lomas & Nettleton Mortgage Investors, Lomas & Nettleton Housing Corporation, and Lomas & Nettleton Management & Company. Short-term loans are provided to home builders and to commercial developers. Special projects often financed include the acquisition of land, the development of streets, the installation of sewer systems, and the construction of residential and commercial housing.

Real Estate Development

Lomas & Nettleton has invested heavily in new, multi-family rental projects in major metropolitan areas. These projects are owned jointly with real estate developers. Lomas & Nettleton's investment philosophy has been to focus almost exclusively on new projects. To minimize construction risks, Lomas & Nettleton issues a commitment to the developer for the lesser of a predetermined amount or his cost in the project. The developer then obtains construction financing from another financial source that underwrites timely completion of the project within a stated budget. Only after satisfactory completion of the project in accordance with approved plans and specifications does Lomas & Nettleton fund the investment.

This division of Lomas & Nettleton acquires land in major development areas, contracts to have the utilities, drainage, sewers, and streets installed, and then sells the developed land. Major markets for this division are California, Florida, and Texas. As of fiscal 1987, assets in this division were approximately $416 million, representing approximately 7.5 percent of the company's total assets. This division contributed approximately $6.1 million to the company's net income in 1987, as compared to $7.9 million in 1986.

INTERNAL OPERATIONS

Offices and Subsidiaries

Lomas & Nettleton's corporate offices are located in Dallas, Texas. Divisional offices of Lomas & Nettleton and their respective locations are

Division	*Location*
Mortgage Banking	Dallas, Texas
Short-term Lending	Dallas, Texas
Real Estate Development	Dallas, Texas
Life Insurance	Indianapolis, Indiana
Commercial Leasing	San Diego, California
Retail Banking	Wilmington, Delaware

Lomas & Nettleton has over 160 offices located in 41 states. The company services loans in all fifty states and the District of Columbia. Lomas & Nettleton has more offices in the individual states of California, Florida, Texas, Virginia, and Pennsylvania than any other state. They have no offices in New York, New Jersey, Delaware, New Hampshire, Maine, Rhode Island, and Hawaii. The company has no offices in foreign countries.

Financial Information

Revenues for 1987 were $632.4 million compared to $393 million in 1986. Net income for fiscal 1987 was $45.4 million, down from $54.5 million in 1986, a 17 percent decline. This decline in net income was due to a $25 million increase in reserves for possible losses. Dividends per share were up 28 percent in fiscal 1987, from $.93 per share in 1986. A breakdown of the company's sales revenues, percent of total revenues, operating profits, and identifiable assets by operating division for 1985, 1986, and 1987 is shown in Exhibit 5. Lomas & Nettleton's income statements and balance sheets for these fiscal years are given in Exhibit 6 and Exhibit 7, respectively. Lomas & Nettleton's statement of consolidated cash flows is given in Exhibit 8.

EXHIBIT 5 Lomas & Nettleton's sales revenues, percent of total revenues, operating profits, and identifiable assets by operating division

Division	Revenues 1985	1986	1987	1988 (projected)
Mortgage banking	$194.0	$238.3	$300.7	$ 308.0
Commercial leasing	—	—	—	342.0
Retail banking	—	—	87.1	227.0
Life insurance	19.0	69.4	145.4	231.0
Short-term lending	48.4	63.3	72.1	94.0
Real estate development	24.4	22.3	27.1	28.0
	$285.8	$393.3	$632.4	$1,230.0

Division	Percentages of Aggregate Revenues 1985	1986	1987	1988 (projected)
Mortgage banking	67.9	60.6	47.6	25.1
Commercial leasing	—	—	—	27.8
Retail banking	—	—	13.8	18.4
Life insurance	6.7	17.7	23.0	18.8
Short-term lending	16.9	16.1	11.4	7.6
Real estate development	8.5	5.6	4.2	2.3
	100.0	100.0	100.0	100.0

	Gross Income Total (000)	%	Direct Expense (000)	Net Total (000)	%
Mortgage banking	$300,742	47.6	$272,175	$28,567	38.8
Short-term lending	72,017	11.4	48,959	23,058	31.3
Life insurance	145,386	23.0	134,438	10,948	14.8
Retail banking	87,101	13.8	82,050	5,051	6.9
Real estate development	27,110	4.2	21,028	6,082	8.2
	$632,356	100.0	$558,650	73,706	100.0
Deduct unallocated expenses					
General and administrative				(13,332)	
Taxes				(14,926)	
Net income				$45,448	

Activity	Assets Employed at June 30, 1987 Amount (000)	% of Total
Mortgage banking	$1,184,335	21.3
Commercial leasing	1,240,706	22.3
Retail banking	1,306,341	23.5
Life insurance	622,522	11.2
Short-term lending	759,514	13.6
Real estate development	416,422	7.5
Unallocated	35,052	.6
	$5,564,892	100.0

Source: From Lomas & Nettleton's 1987 *Annual Report*, p. 31. Used with permission.

Organization

The Chairman and Chief Executive Officer of Lomas & Nettleton Financial Corporation is Jess Hay. Lomas & Nettleton has a fourteen member Board of Directors. As illustrated by the organizational chart in Exhibit 9, Ted Enloe is President of Lomas & Nettleton, and Albert N. Rohnstedt is vice chairman. Assisting Ted Enloe are the executive vice presidents David Kelly, Jr. in charge of Control and John F. Sexton in charge of finance.

THE ENVIRONMENT

Loan Growth

Consumer loan growth slowed dramatically in 1986 to 6.5 percent, from 15 percent in 1985. Many consumers reached their debt limits in 1986, as indicated by installment debt as a percent of disposable income reaching 19.9 percent, an all-time high. Most consumers can now increase their rate of borrowing only at the rate of growth of income.

Commercial and industrial loan growth declined substantially in 1986 to 3.8 percent from 5.5 percent in 1985. Capital spending declined in 1986, and many corporations flocked to the bond markets to lock in lower interest rates on long-term debt, in preference to short-term bank debt. Large corporate customers, more and more, are

EXHIBIT 6 Statement of consolidated income of Lomas & Nettleton Financial Corporation and subsidiaries (*in thousands, except per share amounts*)

	1987	1986	1985
REVENUES			
Interest	$194,384	$118,472	$ 85,955
Mortgage servicing	110,012	94,770	89,924
Insurance premiums	106,122	46,948	19,038
Gain on sales	92,053	51,753	39,492
Commissions and fees	79,266	49,060	41,006
Investment	45,410	23,964	4,607
Other	5,109	8,315	5,733
	632,356	393,282	285,755
EXPENSES			
Interest	162,084	101,743	70,197
Personnel	139,941	106,072	89,550
Insurance benefits	94,442	38,855	5,937
General and administrative	67,342	41,087	40,150
Depreciation and amortization	63,638	31,742	24,829
Provision for losses	45,885	7,365	4,459
	573,332	326,864	235,122
Income before federal income tax	59,024	66,418	50,633
Federal income tax	13,576	11,955	9,113
Net income	$ 45,448	$ 54,463	$ 41,520
Net income per share:			
Primary	$1.49	$2.19	$1.87
Fully diluted	$1.45	$1.83	$1.61
Average number of shares:			
Primary	30,529	24,801	22,170
Fully diluted	44,463	37,432	30,050
Cash dividends paid per share	$1.19	$ .93	$ .77

Source: From Lomas & Nettleton's 1987 *Annual Report*, p. 31. Used with permission.

sidestepping financial institutions and going directly to capital markets themselves. On the other hand, small businesses are turning more and more to banks for capital.

Real estate loan growth was strong in both 1985 (11.6 percent) and 1986 (10.3 percent). However, most of this growth was in residential mortgages. In contrast, construction lending slowed to about 1 percent in 1987, reflecting the overbuilt condition of many metropolitan markets and tax reform's negative effects.

Tax Reform

The 1986 Tax Reform Act requires that banks pay taxes on reserves for loan losses and no longer deduct 80 percent of the borrowing costs on tax exempt bonds. Depreciation schedules are extended under the new tax legislation, thus making multifamily housing less attractive as investments. The 20 percent alternative minimum tax provision of the new tax law will also significantly hurt financial institutions. These aspects of the new tax law will negatively affect Lomas & Nettleton's business, while a de-

EXHIBIT 7 Consolidated balance sheet of Lomas & Nettleton Financial Corporation and subsidiaries (*in thousands*)

	1987	1986
ASSETS		
Cash and cash equivalents	$ 208,676	$ 13,290
First mortgage loans held for sale	551,398	699,755
Receivables	1,791,913	709,792
Investments	2,006,391	583,114
Foreclosed real estate	50,588	24,131
	3,848,892	1,317,037
Less allowance for losses	(68,474)	(4,466)
	3,780,418	1,312,571
Fixed assets — net	156,566	125,910
Prepaid expenses and other assets	131,656	84,406
Purchased future income	534,272	190,486
Goodwill	201,906	29,279
	$5,564,892	$2,455,697
Escrow, agency and fiduciary funds (segregated in separate bank accounts and excluded from corporate assets and liabilities) — see contra	$ 515,812	$ 563,141

crease in the overall corporate tax rate could benefit Lomas & Nettleton. The net effect of the new tax law is for the federal government to obtain $10 billion in extra taxes from financial services firms between 1987 and 1992.

Bank Deregulation

Up until 1985, the banking industry was predominantly regulated by two acts, the McFadden Act of 1927 and the Glass Steagall Act of 1933. The McFadden Act was intended to reduce excessive competition by prohibiting banks from having branches across state lines. This act allowed banks to have virtually exclusive rights within their respective territories. The Glass Steagall Act prohibited banks from involvement in investment banking. These acts restricted banks as to markets they could serve and products they could offer.

In 1985, the Supreme Court basically overturned the McFadden Act. This decision gave states the right to determine the destiny of their banks. A result of this has

EXHIBIT 7 continued

	1987	1986
LIABILITIES AND STOCKHOLDERS' EQUITY		
Notes payable	$2,437,634	$ 949,550
Accounts payable	218,915	88,865
Life insurance reserves	402,831	246,064
Deferred federal income tax	46,384	41,983
Term notes payable	1,320,092	371,044
Convertible subordinated debentures	436,026	422,311
Redeemable preferred stock	35,000	—
Stockholders' Equity:		
Convertible preferred stock	254,166	—
Common stock — 37,085 and 34,027 shares issued, respectively	74,170	45,369
Other paid-in capital	256,041	177,255
Retained earnings	129,918	142,564
Unrealized gain (loss) on marketable equity securities	(3,604)	197
Less common stock held in treasury at cost — 5,587 and 5,082 shares, respectively	(42,681)	(29,505)
	668,010	335,880
	$5,564,892	$2,455,697
Liability for escrow, agency and fiduciary funds — see contra	$ 515,812	$ 563,141

Source: From Lomas & Nettleton's 1987 *Annual Report*, pp. 32–33. Used with permission.

been the creation of superregional banking giants that are dominating the industry. Some example superregional banks are Banc One in Ohio, Bank of New England in Massachusetts, First Union in North Carolina, NBD in Michigan, Norwest in Minnesota, PNC Financial in Pennsylvania, Security Pacific in California, SunTrust in Georgia, First Interstate in California, and Sovran Financial in Virginia. There is a trend toward nationwide banking resulting from less restrictive state laws on the location of bank branches. The distinction between different types of financial institutions is becoming blurred.

The Rate-lock Crisis

In April of 1987, interest rates unexpectedly increased 2 percent. This increase caused Lomas & Nettleton and other lenders to be unable to profitably close outstanding loans, resulting in a "rate-lock crisis." A rate-lock occurs when a mortgage banker and

EXHIBIT 8 Statement of consolidated cash flows of Lomas & Nettleton Financial Corporation and subsidiaries (*in thousands*)

	1987	1986	1985
Net cash flow from operating activities:			
Net income	$ 45,448	$ 54,463	$ 41,520
Noncash charges deducted in determining net income:			
Depreciation and amortization	63,638	31,742	24,829
Provision for losses	45,885	7,365	4,459
Accretion of interest to principal of debt	13,831	7,438	—
Deferred federal income tax	4,401	13,889	13,141
Income before noncash charges	173,203	114,897	83,949
Net change in sundry receivables, payables and other assets	(42,618)	(79,910)	(23,713)
Gain from investing activities	(101,815)	(60,400)	(43,940)
Net cash flow from (used by) operating activities	28,770	(25,413)	16,296
Cash flows from lending and investing activities:			
Origination of first mortgage loans	(3,428,797)	(2,389,010)	(1,164,482)
Sales of first mortgage loans	3,581,236	2,093,537	1,110,248
Advances on mortgage notes receivable	(466,868)	(419,258)	(250,370)
Collections on mortgage notes receivable	291,676	157,627	139,953
Net increase in credit card receivables	(195,658)	—	—
Purchases of investments	(1,793,745)	(309,590)	(142,776)
Sales of investments	1,613,601	273,058	153,384
Additions to foreclosed properties	(40,991)	(35,955)	(15,167)
Sales of foreclosed property	27,698	25,217	8,947
Net additions to fixed assets	(37,292)	(36,418)	(30,611)
Purchases of future income rights	(116,695)	(46,110)	(62,919)
Sales of mortgage servicing	69,148	16,782	4,243
Cash paid for acquisitions, net of cash acquired	(125,423)	(86,574)	—
Net cash used by lending and investing activities	(622,110)	(756,694)	(249,550)
Cash flows from financing activities:			
Net proceeds from note payable borrowings	641,949	371,776	115,733
Proceeds from term note borrowings	262,388	157,487	51,613
Repayment of term notes	(68,922)	(34,434)	(10,156)
Issuance of debentures	—	315,750	100,000
Retirement of debentures	—	(1,550)	(12,662)
Issuance of common stock	1,874	1,914	790
Purchase of treasury stock	(13,176)	(189)	(19)
Dividends paid	(35,387)	(22,219)	(16,946)
Net cash provided by financing activities	788,726	788,535	228,353
Net increase (decrease) in cash	$ 195,386	$ 6,428	$ (4,901)
Schedule of noncash investing and financing activities:			
Acquisition of companies:			
Net assets acquired other than debt assumed	$(2,127,273)	$ (86,408)	$ —
Less: Debt assumed	1,482,773	—	—
Redeemable preferred stock assumed	35,000	—	—
Term notes issued	118,944	—	—
Preferred stock issued	292,866	—	—
Common stock issued	44,190	—	—
Cash paid to acquire companies	$ (153,500)	$ (86,408)	$ —

Source: From Lomas & Nettleton's 1987 *Annual Report*, p. 35. Used with permission.

EXHIBIT 9 Lomas & Nettleton's organizational chart in 1987

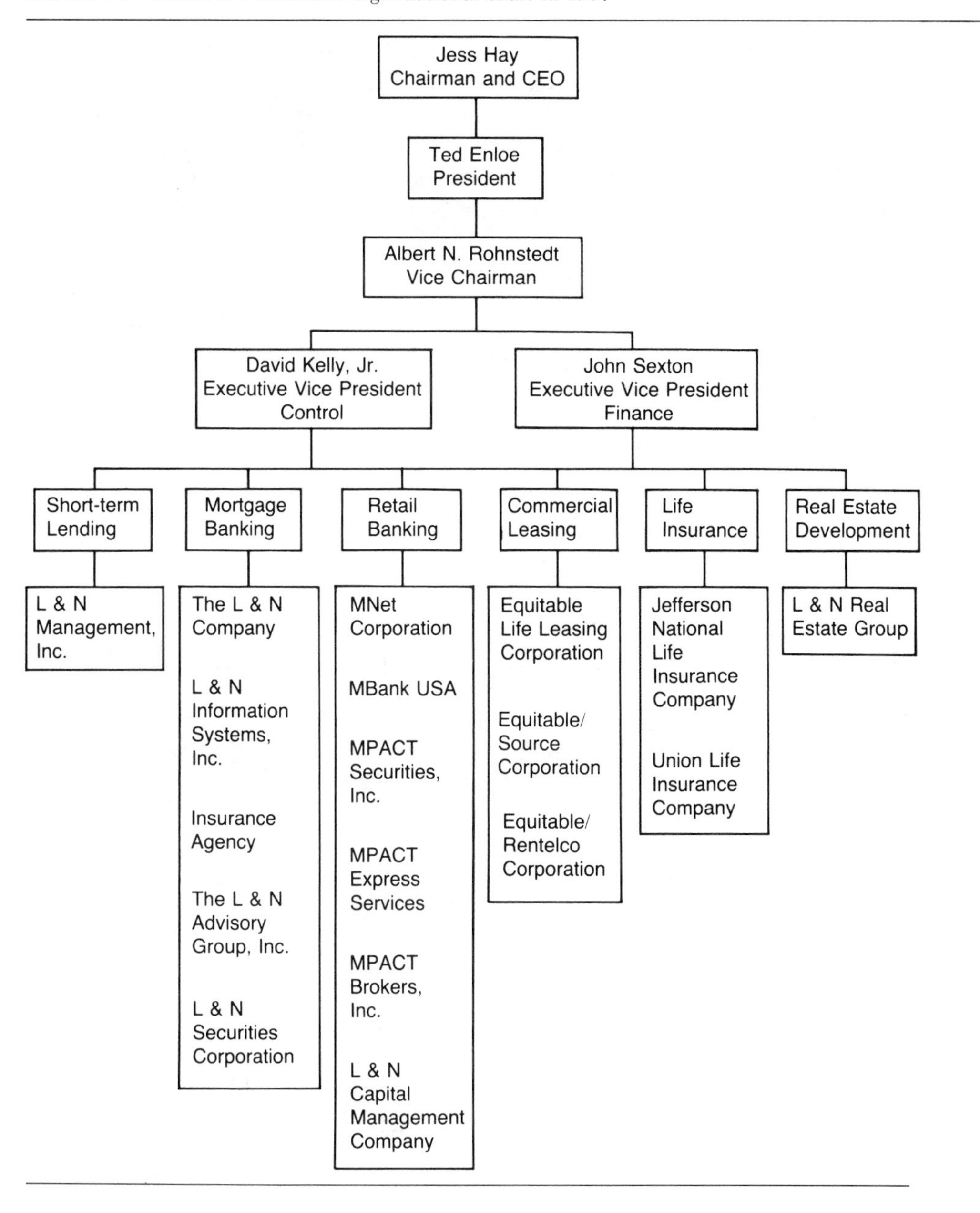

customer enter into an agreement stating the interest rate. This takes place before actual closing of the loan. When interest rates increase quickly, mortgage bankers cannot profitably close loans. Lomas & Nettleton's business is negatively affected by quickly increasing interest rates. Analysts report that 200 mortgage lenders went out of business as a result of the April 1987 interest rate increase.

Because of the lock-in crisis, consumer complaints concerning mortgages have increased, resulting in legislators and regulatory agencies becoming involved. New laws are being passed to more closely regulate mortgage banks, thus protecting customers. For example, mortgage bankers now have to make additional disclosures to their customers. Some states require the loan processing time and procedure to be explained in detail and put in writing for the borrower. Also, if a loan is not processed in a specified length of time, the deposit must be returned to the customer. The Federal Government is considering a number of procedures to regulate lock-ins, such as prohibiting lenders from locking in a rate for a specified length of time, requiring that agreements be delivered within three days, and requiring lenders to honor agreements. Mortgage bankers can expect future investigations, additional legislation, and more paperwork.

Black Monday

The stock market crash in October 1987 created widespread conservative thinking on the part of builders and real estate developers. Consumers are now more cautious in making large purchases for homes or equipment. Many individuals and businesses lost substantial capital, as stocks plunged unexpectedly. The crash contributed to overall credit quality declining in 1987 for the fourth consecutive year. Credit quality problems nationwide have been concentrated mostly in industries such as shipping, agriculture, and real estate, but now are becoming common in many industries.

COMPETITION

Industry Consolidation

Due to the deregulation of financial services, Lomas & Nettleton competes with retail banks, mortgage banking companies, insurance companies, and brokerage firms. Increased competition is making the mortgage banking business more complex and risky. Consolidations are running rampant. Some analysts suggest that the 12,000 plus financial institutions in the United States will shrink to 150 by the year 2000. Increased size offers greater access to capital markets. Smaller institutions often cannot afford the heavy capital investment needed to keep up with technological changes. Corporations more and more are limiting the number of financial institutions with whom they maintain relationships, thus opting for large institutions with sufficient lending limits and a full range of services.

Diversified financial firms such as American Express, Transamerica, and Merrill Lynch are now offering insurance, travel, financing, and deposit-taking functions under one umbrella. Even nonfinancial firms such as Sears, American Can, General Motors, and Ford are accumulating huge financial empires by acquiring savings & loans, mortgage bankers, consumer finance companies, retail-oriented brokerage houses, and insurance companies. Financial information on Lomas & Nettleton's major competitors in the financial services industry is given in Exhibit 10.

Norwest Corporation

Lomas & Nettleton has historically considered its major competitor to be Norwest Corporation. Norwest has 283 banking offices in the United States, 574 financial offices, 44 mortgage offices, and 83 leasing, insurance, and venture capital offices.

EXHIBIT 10 The performance of L & N's major competitors in 1986 and 1987

	Sales ($ millions)		*Profits ($ millions)*		*Return on Equity (percent)*	
Company	*1986*	*1987*	*1986*	*1987*	*1986*	*1987*
Banks						
Citicorp	23,496	27,988	1,058.0	−1138.0	12.8	−17.0
Chase Manhattan	9,460	10,745	585.4	−894.8	12.3	−29.3
Manufacturers Hanover	7,965	7,757	410.7	−1140.3	11.7	−57.7
J. P. Morgan	6,672	6,834	872.5	83.3	17.6	1.5
First Interstate Bancorp	5,290	5,080	337.9	−556.2	12.2	−27.9
First Union	2,537	2,626	278.7	283.1	17.4	15.9
Suntrust	2,463	2,561	245.1	282.8	16.3	16.9
Norwest	2,420	2,298	121.7	−29.8	9.5	−4.0
Banc One	1,415	1,960	164.7	208.9	16.6	14.4
Non-Banks						
Aetna Life & Casualty	20,483	22,114	714.3	867.4	12.5	14.0
American Express	14,652	17,768	1,110.2	533.0	20.3	12.2
Merrill Lynch	9,606	10,868	469.2	390.6	17.4	12.2
Salomon	6,789	6,003	516.0	142.0	15.4	4.5
American General	6,160	7,158	538.0	555.0	12.1	12.1
Transamerica	6,080	7,174	224.4	354.3	9.4	14.1
Lincoln National	5,999	6,960	214.0	236.1	10.2	10.8
First Boston	1,309	1,322	180.6	108.9	20.0	10.3
Morgan Stanley Group	2,463	3,148	201.3	230.9	27.5	23.2
PaineWebber Group	2,412	2,437	75.0	74.6	12.2	10.0

Adapted from *Business Week*, April 17, 1987: 115, 134, 135, and 136; and April 15, 1988: 234, 236.

Headquartered in Minneapolis, Minneosta, Norwest's net income increased more than 13 percent in 1986 to $121.7 million. Earnings per share were $3.64 for the year, an increase of 13.8 percent over 1985. With an average 8.2 percent primary capital ratio, Norwest ranks near the top of the 30 largest bank holding companies in the United States. Norwest's non-performing assets decreased to $419 million at the end of 1986, down from a peak of $603 million in 1985. Actual net credit losses for the year were $201.6 million, compared with a credit loss provision of $247.8 million. When completed in 1988, the 57-story Norwest Center in downtown Minneapolis will serve as the home base for 1,500 Twin Cities employees.

FUTURE OUTLOOK

Some analysts say the United States has become overbanked, with too many institutions duplicating services to consumers and too many loan officers calling on the same companies. This has contributed to bloated overhead expenses in the whole industry. If this assessment is correct, do you think Lomas & Nettleton should acquire other financial institutions to gain economies of scale and reap the benefits of increased size? What type of firms should Lomas & Nettleton seek, i.e., mortgage banking, commercial leasing, retail banking, life insurance, or real estate? Alternatively, should present divisions or subsidiaries of Lomas & Nettleton be divested? This issue looms heavily on the mind of Jess Hay.

There are other important strategic decisions that face Jess Hay in 1988. For example, since the stock market crash, numerous stock brokerage companies have offered themselves for sale or declared bankruptcy. Some analysts emphasize this as an opportunity for Lomas & Nettleton. Should Lomas & Nettleton enter the stock brokerage or securities business by acquiring a company such as PaineWebber? Would acquiring PaineWebber reduce the possibility of Lomas & Nettleton, itself, facing a hostile takeover attempt? What is your specific recommendation to Mr. Hay?

Lomas & Nettleton's major competitor, Norwest, is expanding rapidly in international markets. Should Lomas & Nettleton expand into Canada, Europe, or Japan by opening offices in these geographic areas? Lloyd Johnson, chief executive officer of Norwest, gives the following information in Norwest's 1986 Annual Report:

> International products and services continue to be an important part of the services we offer our customers. While our foreign loan commitments have declined, use of fee-based international products and services has markedly increased. Regional customers continue to rely on Norwest as a source of international expertise (p. 4).

Jess Hay recognizes that Lomas & Nettleton cannot pursue every strategy that could possibly benefit the company. Strategists such as Mr. Hay must make important decisions to eliminate some strategic options and allocate resources to others. Strategy implementation concerns dictate the need to manage change effectively. How could Lomas & Nettleton best implement the specific strategies that you recommend to Mr. Hay? Would additional financing be needed, and if so, how much and of what type? Should Lomas & Nettleton's organizational chart be altered to implement your recommended strategies?

PaineWebber—1987

ELLEN H. SIDES
Auburn University

What does world-famous tennis champion Jimmy Conners have in common with an individual investor? They both might say, "Thank you, PaineWebber." Advertising has been an important key to PaineWebber's strategy. "Thank You, PaineWebber," has become one of the nation's most widely recognized advertising slogans. Research studies show that PaineWebber holds a leading position in consumer awareness, although advertising expenditures are among the lowest of all investment firms. The link with Connors gave PaineWebber an image of a highly competitive firm with the ability for making clients "winners." The ad won PaineWebber a coveted Gold Lion Award at the 1984 Cannes Film Festival. PaineWebber recently signed legendary golf pro Arnold Palmer to a similar advertising contract.

PaineWebber sponsors major sports events such as the PaineWebber Classic Professional Tennis Tournament in Sanigal Harbour, Florida, and the PaineWebber World Seniors Invitational Pro Golf Event in Charlotte, North Carolina. These events have helped PaineWebber retain a strong market position. New York-based PaineWebber is the fourteenth largest diversified financial company in the United States. PaineWebber continues to invest heavily in the securities brokerage business to strengthen the firm's overall competitive position. However, some observers say PaineWebber must successfully broaden its presence into other markets, such as insurance, commercial banking, and investment banking. Deregulation of the banking industry is a threat to PaineWebber as large U.S. and world banks enter the securities brokerage business.

HISTORY

In 1879, Charles Cabot Jackson and Laurence Curtis opened a financial services office on Congress Street in Boston, Massachusetts. A year later, William Paine and Wallace Webber opened a competing office on Congress Street. Paine, Webber, Jackson & Curtis was formed in 1942 with the merger of PaineWebber and Co. and Jackson and Curtis. The new firm boasted 23 branch offices. Paine, Webber, Jackson & Curtis became a full service financial firm with the acquisition of F. S. Smithers & Co. and Mitchum, Jones & Templeton, Inc.

PaineWebber Incorporated was established in 1974 as the holding company for Paine, Webber, Jackson & Curtis. To further expand its products and services, PaineWebber has acquired a number of financial companies since 1974, including Mitchell Hutchins, Blyth Eastman Dillon, Rotan Mosle Financial Corporation, First Mid America, and Rouse Real Estate Finance. A historical profile of PaineWebber is provided in Exhibit 1.

EXHIBIT 1 A history of PaineWebber Group, Incorporated

1879	Charles Cabot Jackson and Laurence Curtis opened an office on Congress Street in Boston, Massachusetts.
1880	William A. Paine and Wallace C. Webber opened their office up the street.
1899	PaineWebber and Co. opened its first branch office in Houghton, Michigan.
1942	PaineWebber and Co. merged with Jackson and Curtis to become Paine, Webber, Jackson & Curtis. The firm now boasted twenty-three branch offices.
1963	Paine, Webber, Jackson & Curtis moved their headquarters from Boston to New York.
1967	Paine, Webber, Jackson & Curtis made its first acquisition, Barrett, Fitch, North and Co., of Kansas City.
1970	Paine, Webber, Jackson & Curtis incorporated and acquired the principal offices of Abbott, Proctor & Paine.
1972	Paine, Webber, Jackson & Curtis, Inc. went public through the acquisition of Abacus Fund, Inc., a listed, closed-end investment company.
1973	Paine, Webber, Jackson & Curtis, Inc. became a full service financial firm with the acquisitions of F. S. Smithers & Co. and Mitchum, Jones & Templeton, Inc. The former enhanced their capability in the fixed income area, while the latter strengthened their position on the West Coast. The firm also opened offices in London and Tokyo.
1974	PaineWebber, Inc. was established as the holding company for Paine, Webber, Jackson & Curtis, Inc. The firm further strengthened its retail capabilities with the acquisition of DuPont Walston, Inc.
1977	PaineWebber acquired Mitchell Hutchins, Inc., one of America's leading equity research firms.
1979	PaineWebber merged with Blyth Eastman Dillon, adding seventy more branch offices and giving them their first investment banking subsidiary.
1983	PaineWebber gained direct access to two of the nation's growth areas by acquiring two regional securities firms: Rotan Mosle Financial Corp., strong in the Southwest, and First Mid America, headquartered in Lincoln, Nebraska.
1984	The firm brought its subsidiaries under the PaineWebber name and created a new management structure. PaineWebber acquired Rouse Real Estate Finance, one of the nation's twenty largest non-bank owned mortgage companies.
1985	PaineWebber moved its world headquarters to the "PaineWebber Building," bringing the firm's major decision makers under one roof.
1986	PaineWebber moved selective administrative functions to the new Administrative and Data Centers in Lincoln Harbor, New Jersey.

Source: "The Investor's Guide to PaineWebber." (New York, New York: PaineWebber Group Inc., 1986).

INTERNAL OPERATIONS

PaineWebber Group is a holding company that, together with its operating subsidiaries, forms one of the largest investment service firms in the world. To keep pace with changing market conditions and the increasingly varied needs of clients,

PaineWebber offers a full range of products and services to an expanding base of individual, institutional, corporate, and governmental clients. The company provides investment services through its broker-dealer subsidiary, PaineWebber Incorporated (PWI). PWI's primary services are aligned into two operating groups: Consumer Markets and Capital Markets.

Consumer Markets

The Consumer markets group consists of a domestic branch office system and a consumer products area. PWI provides investment services to individual and institutional clients, including the purchase and sale, as principal and agent, of securities, option contracts, commodity and financial futures contracts, tax-advantaged investments, selected insurance products, and money market, commodity, bond, and mutual funds.

In August 1986, PaineWebber instituted a branch group reorganization for the Consumer Markets group, combining the Eastern and Western branch groups into one unit with one director. In addition, the 12 divisions formerly in those two groups were realigned to form eight units. Separate subsidiaries in the Consumer Market group conduct specialized investment services. For example, Mitchell Hutchins Asset Management, Inc. provides investment, advisory, and portfolio management services to institutions, individuals, and mutual and money market funds. PaineWebber Properties, Inc. designs products to meet capital needs of real estate firms. Rotan Mosle Financial Corporation is one of the leading securities firms in the southwestern United States.

Particular product emphasis in the Consumer Products group has been given to proprietary products that place assets under PaineWebber's direction, such as mutual funds, RMAs (Resource Management Accounts), and IRA's. In 1986, PaineWebber introduced Olympus, a domestic growth fund, and two highly successful tax-exempt funds. The PaineWebber Master Series, a new family of mutual funds, was introduced in 1986 and complements the firm's Family of Funds (introduced in 1984).

PaineWebber continues to be an industry leader with unit trusts, groupings of tax-free bonds. A unique new product, the Pathfinders Unit Trust, offers common stocks selected for above average growth, combined with zero-coupon bonds to hedge market risk. The new Personal Security Loan Account (PSLA), enabling clients to borrow funds for personal needs against their accounts at very competitive rates, continued to grow and be profitable. PSLA accumulated more than $144 million in loans outstanding during 1986. PaineWebber strives to create, package, and sell products that meet the needs of their clients.

Capital Markets

The Capital Markets group consists of PWI's investment banking activities, institutional fixed income, and equity sales and trading. Through this group, PWI provides financial advice to, and raises capital for, a broad range of clients, including corporations, major institutions, and public agencies. PWI manages public offerings, provides advice in connection with mergers and acquisitions, privately places securities directly with institutional investors, and effects venture capital placements.

PWI also has separate subsidiaries for conducting more specialized aspects of the Capital Markets group's investment services. Mortgage Investment Banking Incorporated is active in both publicly and privately placed real estate financing transactions, including the establishment of real estate investment trusts and the issuance of collateralized mortgage obligations. PaineWebber Real Estate Securities, Inc. is one of the industry's largest dealers in securities guaranteed by various agencies of the U.S. Government, including Government Mortgage Association and Federal Home Loan Mortgage Corporation.

As one of the nation's largest non-bank owned mortgage companies, PaineWebber Mortgage Finance, Inc. provides PWI with a complete range of real estate skills and products to participate fully in the field of real estate finance. Through its offices in Maryland, Virginia, and the District of Columbia, this subsidiary originates residential and commercial mortgage loans that it sells to investors while retaining the rights to service the loans thereafter. Also, it purchases servicing rights to loans originated by others. In fiscal 1985, this subsidiary ranked sixth in underwritings and continues to be a key mortgage banking force in the Baltimore and Washington markets. A new commercial loan office was opened in Kansas City, Kansas, in 1986 with plans to open additional branches in both the Northeast and Southeast.

With increased foreign demand for financial services, PaineWebber has placed a greater emphasis on its PaineWebber International subsidiary. This subsidiary provides investment services for institutional and retail brokerage activities, Eurobond sales and trading, as well as investment banking for clients outside the United States. The ten office locations of this subsidiary are: New York, London, Geneva, Zurich, Paris, San Juan, Athens, Hong Kong, Tokyo, and Miami. The Miami office opened in 1986 to serve clients in South America.

OFFICES AND SUBSIDIARIES

PaineWebber headquarters, located in the new PaineWebber building in mid-town Manhattan, has brought together, for the first time, all the major operating subsidiaries of the company. The organization's principal line of business is providing investment products and services to its customers worldwide. Although the Consumer Markets and Capital Markets groups of PaineWebber Incorporated are the principal providers of these services, other significant subsidiaries of PaineWebber and their respective locations are

Subsidiary	*Location*
PaineWebber Incorporated	New York, New York
PaineWebber Properties Incorporated	New York, New York
PaineWebber Incorporated of Puerto Rico	Puerto Rico
Rotan Mosle Financial Corporation	Houston, Texas
Rotan Mosle, Inc.	Houston, Texas
PaineWebber Capital, Incorporated	New York, New York
PaineWebber Real Estate Securities Inc.	Columbia, Maryland
PaineWebber International Banking Corp.	New York, New York

Mitchell Hutchins Asset Management, Inc.	New York, New York
PaineWebber Mortgage Finance Holding Co.	New York, New York
PaineWebber Mortgage Finance, Inc.	Columbia, Maryland

PaineWebber's branch office system includes 292 offices located in 47 states, the District of Columbia, and British Columbia. This number changes yearly with the opening of new offices, acquisition of offices from other firms, and the relocation or closing of existing PaineWebber offices. PaineWebber's strength lies in the northeastern states, Florida, and California. Regional offices and their locations are as follows:

Regional Office	*Location*
New England	Boston, Massachusetts
Eastern	New York, New York
Mid-Atlantic	Columbus, Ohio
Central	Chicago, Illinois
Northwestern	San Francisco, California
Southwestern	Los Angeles, California
Southern	Palm Beach, Florida
Southeastern	Washington, D.C.

ORGANIZATION

Donald B. Marron is the chairman, president, and chief executive officer for PaineWebber Group Incorporated. PaineWebber has a ten member Board of Directors. Marron is also the chairman and chief executive officer of the principal subsidiary, PaineWebber Incorporated. Assisting Marron is the President of the Consumer Markets group, Donald Nickelson, and Frank Marsell, advisory director of PaineWebber Capital Markets. Three divisions of PaineWebber Incorporated—Administration/Operations/Systems, Research, and Finance—provide overlapping services for the entire organization. Exhibit 2 illustrates the organizational structure of PaineWebber.

Financial Information

PaineWebber Group Incorporated is a diversified financial company with a broad range of revenue-producing services. A breakdown of the company's revenues and expenses for 1982 through 1986 are shown in Exhibit 3. PaineWebber's income statements and balance sheets for recent years are given in Exhibit 4 and Exhibit 5. Exhibit 6 gives PaineWebber's Statement of Consolidated Changes in Financial Position for 1983 through 1986.

COMPETITION

PaineWebber competes directly with numerous other brokers, dealers, investment banking firms, investment advisors, commercial banks, and insurance companies. PaineWebber principally serves the brokerage securities industry, where the firm is

EXHIBIT 2 Organizational chart for PaineWebber Group, Inc.**

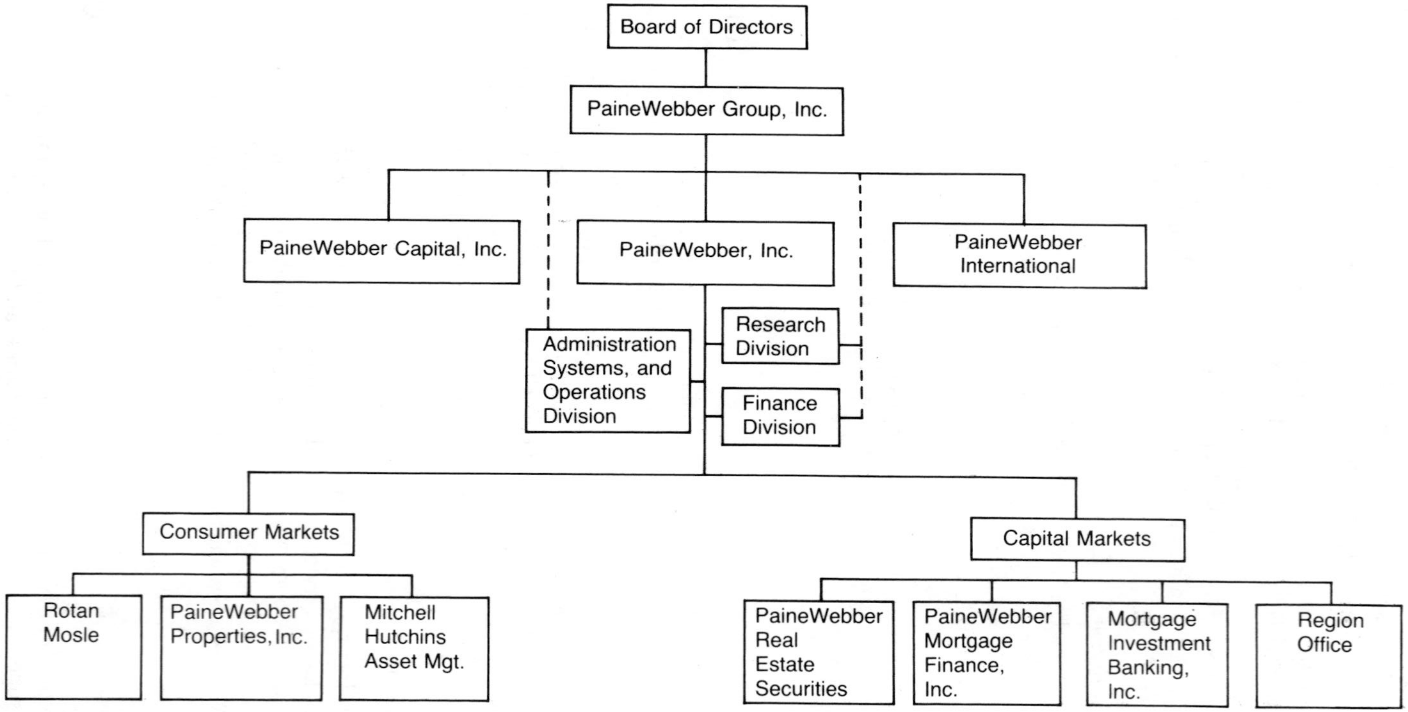

Board of Directors

PaineWebber Group, Inc.

PaineWebber Capital, Inc.

PaineWebber, Inc.

PaineWebber International

Administration Systems, and Operations Division

Research Division

Finance Division

Consumer Markets

Rotan Mosle

PaineWebber Properties, Inc.

Mitchell Hutchins Asset Mgt.

Capital Markets

PaineWebber Real Estate Securities

PaineWebber Mortgage Finance, Inc.

Mortgage Investment Banking, Inc.

Region Office

**Based on information from the 1986 *Annual Report (Form 10–K)*, PaineWebber, Group, Inc.

EXHIBIT 3 PaineWebber's five-year financial summary (*dollars in thousands except per share amounts*)

	1986		1985		1984		1983		1982	
	Amount	%	Amount	%	Amount	%	Amount	%	Amount	%
Revenues										
Commissions										
Listed securities	$ 344,832	14.5	$ 256,579	13.6	$ 241,935	15.6	$ 322,312	20.9	$ 204,747	17.2
Mutual funds	190,583	8.0	98,238	5.2	44,552	2.9	35,115	2.3	5,972	.5
Options	66,445	2.8	48,918	2.6	49,392	3.2	56,362	3.7	42,408	3.6
Tax-advantaged investments	48,326	2.0	39,761	2.1	45,550	2.9	49,794	3.2	30,581	2.6
Commodities	46,870	2.0	44,385	2.4	39,806	2.5	39,399	2.6	27,934	2.3
Over-the-counter securities	42,313	1.8	28,849	1.5	28,183	1.8	45,373	2.9	18,690	1.5
Insurance	22,590	0.9	20,296	1.1	11,880	.8	10,369	.7	12,196	1.0
	761,959	32.0	537,026	28.5	461,298	29.7	558,724	36.3	342,528	28.7
Interest										
Resale agreements	394,978	16.6	370,136	19.6	323,827	20.9	187,241	12.2	225,945	19.0
Securities inventory	186,573	7.8	185,092	9.8	113,751	7.3	100,562	6.5	67,999	5.7
Client margin accounts	135,818	5.7	123,723	6.6	151,326	9.7	105,286	6.8	139,445	11.7
Other	82,496	3.4	82,155	4.4	42,389	2.7	28,520	1.9	24,440	2.0
	799,865	33.5	761,106	40.4	631,293	40.6	421,609	27.4	457,829	38.4
Principal transactions										
Corporate securities	270,576	11.4	173,056	9.2	98,424	6.3	123,040	8.0	65,013	5.4
United States government and agency obligations	71,906	3.0	52,244	2.8	75,949	4.9	89,466	5.8	53,198	4.5
Municipal obligations	57,564	2.4	46,465	2.4	42,059	2.7	66,149	4.3	55,765	4.7
	400,046	16.8	271,765	14.4	216,432	13.9	278,655	18.1	173,976	14.6
Investment banking										
Selling concessions and underwriting fees:										
Corporate obligations	92,316	3.8	56,938	3.0	53,699	3.5	69,829	4.5	31,645	2.7
Municipal obligations	47,015	2.0	36,587	1.9	30,677	2.0	77,306	5.0	74,603	6.3
Underwriting management fees:										
Corporate obligations	19,846	.8	13,776	.7	12,667	.8	18,364	1.2	9,945	.8
Municipal obligations	23,267	1.0	17,750	.9	9,135	.6	17,378	1.1	8,746	.7
Private placement and other fees	112,228	4.7	84,198	4.6	61,555	4.0	55,345	3.6	52,350	4.4
	294,672	12.3	209,249	11.1	167,733	10.9	238,222	15.4	177,289	14.9
Other	128,178	5.4	105,930	5.6	76,650	4.9	43,526	2.8	40,677	3.4
Total revenues	$2,384,720	100.0	$1,885,076	100.0	$1,553,406	100.0	$1,540,736	100.0	$1,192,299	100.0

EXHIBIT 3 continued

	1986		1985		1984		1983		1982	
	Amount	%	Amount	%	Amount	%	Amount	%	Amount	%
Expenses										
Employee compensation and related expenses	$ 995,002	41.7	$ 736,354	39.0	$ 621,901	40.0	$707,292	45.9	$486,271	40.8
Interest	719,813	30.2	691,833	36.7	564,750	36.4	330,595	21.4	363,010	30.4
Communications	97,506	4.1	86,474	4.6	86,881	5.6	79,764	5.2	75,142	6.3
Office and equipment rental	87,468	3.7	76,313	4.0	63,936	4.1	61,995	4.0	54,000	4.5
Business development	84,051	3.5	71,490	3.8	65,786	4.2	56,232	3.6	47,662	4.0
Brokerage, clearing and exchange fees	48,578	2.0	40,782	2.2	33,712	2.2	38,562	2.5	25,727	2.2
Other expenses	207,374	8.7	125,763	6.7	107,043	6.9	89,694	5.9	72,203	6.1
Total expenses	2,239,792	93.9	1,829,009	97.0	1,544,009	99.4	1,364,134	88.5	1,124,015	94.3
Earnings before taxes on income	144,928	6.1	56,067	3.0	9,397	.6	176,602	11.5	68,284	5.7
Provision (benefit) for taxes on income	73,329	3.1	22,243	1.2	(3,622)	(.2)	86,000	5.6	32,345	2.7
Net earnings	$ 71,599	3.0	$ 33,824	1.8	$ 13,019	.8	$ 90,602	5.9	$ 35,939	3.0
Earnings per share and dividends										
Earnings per common and common equivalent share:										
Primary	$2.51		$1.36		$.61		$4.42		$1.89	
Fully diluted	2.46		1.36		.61		4.32		1.89	
Weighted average common and common equivalent shares:										
Primary	25,483,000		20,935,000		20,123,000		20,520,000		19,180,000	
Fully diluted	26,965,000		20,935,000		20,123,000		21,292,000		19,180,000	
Dividends declared per share:										
Common stock	$.49		$.48		$.48		$.42		$.29	
Preferred stock:										
$2.25 Convertible Exchangeable	2.25		1.48							
Series B					7.50		7.50		7.50	
Series C									7.50	
Series D					4.50		9.00		9.00	

Source: *Form 10–K,* PaineWebber Group, Inc., 1986. Used with permission.

EXHIBIT 4 PaineWebber's consolidated statements of earnings (*in thousands of dollars except per share amounts*)

	1986	1985	1984
Revenues			
Commissions	$ 761,959	$ 537,026	$ 461,298
Interest	799,865	761,106	631,293
Principal transactions	400,046	271,765	216,432
Investment banking	294,672	209,249	167,733
Other	128,178	105,930	76,650
	2,384,720	1,885,076	1,553,406
Expenses			
Employee compensation and related expenses	995,002	736,354	621,901
Interest	719,813	691,833	564,750
Communications	97,506	86,474	86,881
Office and equipment rental	87,468	76,313	63,936
Business development	84,051	71,490	65,786
Brokerage, clearing and exchange fees	48,578	40,782	33,712
Other	207,374	125,763	107,043
	2,239,792	1,829,009	1,544,009
Earnings before taxes on income	144,928	56,067	9,397
Provision (benefit) for taxes on income	73,329	22,243	(3,622)
Net earnings	$ 71,599	$ 33,824	$ 13,019
Earnings applicable to common and common equivalent shares (primary)	$ 63,838	$ 28,391	$ 12,346
Earnings per common and common equivalent share			
Primary	$2.51	$1.36	$.61
Fully diluted	2.46	1.36	.61

Source: *Form 10–K,* PaineWebber Group, Inc., 1986. Used with permission.

considered to be one of the best in that field. Competitive pressures from discount brokerage firms and commercial banks, increased investor sophistication, an increase in the variety of investment products, and numerous mergers and acquisitions have resulted in a few well capitalized national firms. Although E. F. Hutton and Merrill Lynch are the industry leaders, other large competitors are Salomon, Bear Stearns, Morgan Stanley Group, and First Boston. These companies have hefty capital to back up risky trades and underwritings. Exhibit 7 shows PaineWebber's 1986 standing in sales, profits, assets, and earnings per share as compared to the top nonbank financial companies in the United States.

PaineWebber's biggest challenge comes in the field of investment banking. Industry salwarts such as Morgan Stanley, Shearson Lehman Brothers, Drexel Burnham Lambert, and Bear Stearns are among the leading competitors in this field. In addi-

EXHIBIT 5 PaineWebber's consolidated balance sheets (*in thousands of dollars except share and per share amounts*)

	1986	1985
Assets		
Cash, including interest bearing deposits	$ 119,159	$ 116,688
Cash and securities (securities at market value of $25,977 in 1986; $21,685 in 1985) on deposit in compliance with Federal and other regulations	124,786	77,565
Receivable from brokers and dealers	1,315,589	1,642,580
Receivable from clients	2,258,433	1,983,493
Securities inventory, at market value:		
United States government and agency obligations	760,564	1,278,612
State and municipal obligations	378,882	380,261
Commercial paper and other short-term debt	743,134	984,846
Corporate debt securities	283,518	497,499
Corporate equity securities	723,564	597,106
Securities purchased under resale agreements, at resale prices	6,667,119	4,632,937
First mortgage notes held for resale	232,650	83,635
Assets of special purpose subsidiaries	496,130	816,252
Office equipment and leasehold improvements, net	122,783	103,986
Dividends and interest receivable	100,376	115,183
Other assets	399,063	278,152
	$14,725,750	$13,588,795

tion, Merrill Lynch, Goldman Sacks, First Boston, and Salomon have substantial market share.

Due to the increasing popularity of discount brokers PaineWebber has been forced to begin trade discounting, which involves reducing commission rates paid by the consumer. Discounting on trades has become more frequent since 1975 when negotiable commissions were instituted. The popularity of discount brokers has been a major factor in giving investors discount opportunities with full-service firms such as

EXHIBIT 5 continued

	1986	1985
Liabilities and Stockholders' Equity		
Bank loans	$ 1,719,355	$ 2,058,776
Payable to brokers and dealers	1,211,713	1,103,637
Payable to clients (including free credit balances of $301,560 in 1986; $317,100 in 1985)	964,472	842,194
Dividends and interest payable	144,556	117,136
Securities sold but not yet purchased, at market value:		
United States government and agency obligations	1,297,632	1,363,313
State and municipal obligations	11,534	44,953
Corporate debt securities	70,200	108,182
Corporate equity securities	346,133	459,699
Securities sold under repurchase agreements, at repurchase prices	6,753,049	5,382,438
Liabilities of special purpose subsidiaries	488,719	801,719
Accrued taxes on income	81,885	78,585
Accrued compensation and related expenses	262,176	174,768
Other accrued liabilities and accounts payable	333,681	323,629
Dividends payable to stockholders	3,468	2,491
	13,688,573	12,861,520
Term debt	403,812	295,865
	14,092,385	13,157,385
Stockholders' equity:		
$2.25 Convertible Exchangeable Preferred Stock, $25 stated value, shares issued and outstanding: 1986 — 3,449,000; 1985 — 3,449,600	83,517	83,533
Common stock, $1 par value, 100,000,000 shares authorized; shares issued and outstanding: 1986 — 26,687,759; 1985 — 20,764,916	26,688	20,765
Additional paid-in capital	289,097	131,554
Retained earnings	252,612	200,957
	651,914	436,809
Unamortized cost of restricted stock awards	(18,549)	(3,342)
Common stock held in treasury, at cost: 87,500 shares in 1985	—	(2,057)
	633,365	431,410
	$14,725,750	$13,588,795

Source: *Form 10–K,* PaineWebber Group, Inc., 1986. Used with permission.

PaineWebber. Exhibit 8 illustrates broker commissions as a percentage of overall trade value for Merrill Lynch, Shearson Lehman, Prudential-Bache, Kidder Peabody, and PaineWebber.

The American economy is becoming more and more service oriented. Changes in the tax laws, low interest and money market rates, and instability in the stock market are factors affecting this trend. The development of new services presents a constant challenge to PaineWebber and its competitors.

EXHIBIT 6 PaineWebber's consolidated statements of changes in stockholders' equity (*in thousands of dollars except per share amounts*)

	$2.25 Convertible Exchangeable Preferred Stock	Common Stock	Additional Paid-in Capital	Retained Earnings	Unamortized Cost of Restricted Stock Awards	Treasury Stock	Total
Balance at September 30, 1983	$ —	$19,573	$110,793	$179,331	$ —	$ —	$309,697
Common stock issued in exchange for 9% Series D Convertible Preferred Stock	—	746	10,454	—	—	—	11,200
Exercise of stock options and awards of restricted stock, net	—	179	4,138	—	(3,518)	—	799
Net earnings	—	—	—	13,019	—	—	13,019
Dividends:							
Common stock, $.48 per share	—	—	—	(9,514)	—	—	(9,514)
Preferred stock	—	—	—	(639)	—	—	(639)
Accretion of redeemable preferred stock	—	—	—	(34)	—	—	(34)
Balance at September 30, 1984	—	20,498	125,385	182,163	(3,518)	—	324,528
Issuance of $2.25 Convertible Exchangeable Preferred Stock	83,543	—	—	—	—	—	83,543
Exercise of stock options and awards of restricted stock, net	—	267	5,561	—	176	—	6,004
Purchases of treasury stock	—	—	—	—	—	(2,057)	(2,057)
Redemption of redeemable preferred stock	—	—	598	—	—	—	598
Conversion of preferred stock	(10)	—	10	—	—	—	—
Net earnings	—	—	—	33,824	—	—	33,824
Dividends:							
Common stock, $.48 per share	—	—	—	(9,920)	—	—	(9,920)
Preferred stock	—	—	—	(5,110)	—	—	(5,110)
Balance at September 30, 1985	83,533	20,765	131,554	200,957	(3,342)	(2,057)	431,410
Common stock issued in public offering, net	—	4,954	133,201	—	—	—	138,155
Purchases of treasury stock	—	—	—	—	—	(2,307)	(2,307)
Common stock issued in connection with options, restricted stock awards and other employee benefit plans, net	—	969	24,326	—	(15,207)	4,364	14,452
Conversion of preferred stock	(16)	—	16	—	—	—	—
Net earnings	—	—	—	71,599	—	—	71,599
Dividends:							
Common stock, $.49 per share	—	—	—	(12,183)	—	—	(12,183)
Preferred stock	—	—	—	(7,761)	—	—	(7,761)
Balance at September 30, 1986	$83,517	$26,688	$289,097	$252,612	$(18,549)	$ —	$633,365

Source: *Form 10–K*, PaineWebber Group, Inc., 1986. Used with permission.

EXHIBIT 7 The leading brokerage firms in the United States in 1986

Company	*Sales ($ millions)*	*Profits ($ millions)*	*Assets ($ millions)*	*Earnings (per share)*
Salomon	6789	516.0	78164	3.45
Merrill Lynch	9606	469.2	53013	4.44
Bear Stearns	2349	223.8	51914	2.06
Morgan Stanley Group	2463	201.3	29190	8.42
First Boston	3258	180.6	48618	5.14
E. F. Hutton	2760	−106.4	23572	2.90
PaineWebber Group	2412	75.0	15717	2.51

Source: *Form 10–K,* PaineWebber Group Inc., 1986.

Consumer attitudes toward saving have been changing in recent years. As an increasing number of consumers adopt a motto of "buy now save later," companies like PaineWebber have been forced to develop products that will attract the consumer to save. Saving for the future implies investing in a product that will earn a high return.

More and more companies are beginning to offer many of the services provided by companies like PaineWebber. Commercial banks, savings and loan associations, and insurance companies have all expanded their traditional service lines to include financial security plans such as IRA's, mutual funds, and various other investment op-

EXHIBIT 8 Scheduled broker commission rates as a percentage of the overall trade value

Number of Shares	*Merrill Lynch*	*Shearson Lehman*	*Prudential-Bache*	*Kidder Peabody*	*Paine-Webber*
		Share Price: $5			
25	25.0	10.0	28.0	7.6	17.0
100	10.0	7.0	7.9	7.1	7.2
1000	3.8	4.0	4.1	3.5	4.0
		Share Price: $10			
25	10.0	7.0	7.9	3.9	7.2
100	3.6	2.9	3.2	3.2	3.0
1000	1.8	2.1	2.1	1.9	2.0
		Share Price: $70			
25	3.6	3.0	3.3	2.6	3.1
100	1.4	1.4	1.6	1.5	1.5
1000	1.0	1.0	1.1	1.0	1.1

Source: "Talking Price: Full-Service Brokers Often Offer Discounts on Trades," *Wall Street Journal* (16 July, 1987), 31. Reprinted by permission of the *Wall Street Journal,*

portunities. To counter this competition, financial service firms are diversifying and expanding their services. The industry continues to increase in complexity as these organizations find it difficult to specialize in one or two services.

OUTLOOK FOR 1987

According to Mr. Marron, plans for 1987 include increasing merchant banking activities where company capital is invested in transactions such as mergers and leveraged buyouts. Mr. Marron believes tax reform legislation in 1986 will have a favorable impact on the company's after-tax earnings, since the needs of investors will change, creating a need for new products, services, and advice. PaineWebber needs to develop new products and services to accommodate the changing needs of investors. What specific recommendations would you offer Mr. Marron?

PaineWebber has been plagued recently by an outbreak of lawsuits. Earnings per share in fiscal 1986 were reduced by $0.60 when the firm had to add $31 million to its litigation reserve as a result of a judgment rendered in a commodities trading case. Further, three PaineWebber executives were indicted in March and April 1987 on money-laundering charges. The defendants allegedly helped wealthy clients hide cash from the Internal Revenue Service. PaineWebber suspended the three officials and has given the U.S. Attorney's Office full cooperation during the investigation. No charges were filed against the company itself. In addition, five former top brokers filed a 1986 lawsuit against PaineWebber for fraud in hiring. The five ex-brokers claim they were hired to draw their large client bases and then were fired by PaineWebber. Executive titles and six-figure bonuses were allegedly given to the plaintiffs to lure them away from employment with major competitors. These activities indicate a need for PaineWebber to develop and communicate a clear code of business ethics.

Donald Marron is concerned about PaineWebber's future. Should PaineWebber allocate millions of dollars to become a powerhouse investment banker? Should PaineWebber expand its line of insurance products? Should PaineWebber attempt to takeover a major bank such as Citicorp or Bank of Boston? What effect would such a takeover have on PaineWebber's operations and financial condition? Should PaineWebber intensify foreign operations by opening offices in major European cities? Would such a strategy give PaineWebber the lead in the international markets? Should PaineWebber increase acquisitions in presently weak regions such as the Southeast, Midwest and West?

If interest rates and inflation continue to rise, what effect will this have on the investment industry? How should PaineWebber's strategy change in the event of a major fall in the stock market or a recession?

SUGGESTED READINGS

"International Investment Strategy." *Wall Street Transcript.* 24 March, 1986, 81, 300.

"PaineWebber Ex-Top Broker Is Indicted." *Wall Street Journal.* 13 March, 1987.

"PaineWebber Says Per-Share Profit is Flat, Net Jumps." *Wall Street Journal.* 26 January, 1987, 13.

"PaineWebber Sees Sharp Jump in Net for December 31 Period." *Wall Street Journal.* 21 January, 1986, 17.

"PaineWebber Sued By Five Ex-Brokers for Deceit in Hiring." *Wall Street Journal*. 31 March, 1987, 16.

"Service 500." *Fortune*. 9 June, 1986, 27.

"The Forbes 500 Annual Directory." *Forbes*. 27 April, 1987, 199–231.

"Two Suspended PaineWebber Officials Indicated on Money Laundering Charges." *Wall Street Journal*. 3 April, 1987, 4.

"Why PaineWebber is on a Hiring Binge." *Fortune*. 30 September, 1985, 105.

BankAmerica Corporation—1987

MILES Y. BASSIL
Auburn University
PATRICIA HOBAUGH BASSIL
Auburn University
FRED DAVID
Auburn University

In February 1987, Tom Clausen, chairman and chief executive officer of BankAmerica, was meeting with his top managers to evaluate the impact of Brazil's decision. Brazil had just announced its suspension of interest and principal repayments to its creditors. The government and corporations of Brazil owed BankAmerica $2.74 billion or 2.6 percent of the bank's assets.

"We can't afford to take a $2.7 billion loss on just one customer," said Frank Newman, vice chairman and chief financial officer.[1] "Our capital ratio would fall below the Federal Reserve's requirements, and we might have a run on the bank when customers hear of the loss," he explained.

Glenhall Taylor, vice chairman—credit policy, favored waiting for a while before making any major decisions about the Brazilian debt crisis. "You know, we've got a major problem," he told his colleagues. "Last year, we lost about $1 billion on our domestic portfolio, alone, and things have not changed much since then."

"That's why we are here gentlemen," said Clausen. "As you know, we have to evaluate the ramifications of Brazil's decision on the survival of our corporation. The Brazilian problem is only a small portion of our troubled loan portfolio. We also have to consider the strengths and weaknesses of our other assets before we decide what to do," he explained.

HISTORY

BankAmerica, once the largest bank holding corporation in the world, had its beginning as a small Italian bank in San Francisco, California. Started in 1904 to serve the Italian community of North Beach, the Bank of Italy grew to become the third largest bank in the United States by 1927. Its founder, A. P. Giannini, believed in the branch banking system and opened 276 branches in over 200 localities in California by 1927.

In 1930, the Bank of Italy was renamed Bank of America. By 1953, the Bank of America had expanded to 538 branches in 317 California towns and nine branches overseas. Bank of America became a subsidiary of the BankAmerica Corporation in April of 1969, six months after the holding company was formed.

In 1974, BankAmerica acquired GAC Finance (renamed FinanceAmerica Corporation). Two subsidiaries, BankAmerica Mortgage Company and BankAmerica International Realty Corporation, merged in 1977. In 1978, BankAmerica expanded international operations by forming a subsidiary called BankAmerica Overseas Finance Corporation. BankAmerica diversified into brokerage services in 1983 by acquiring Charles Schwab & Company. In the same year, BankAmerica moved one step closer to interstate banking by acquiring the Seafirst Corporation that wholly owned the Seattle First National Bank in Washington. The Hertz Corporation and BankAmerica entered into a joint venture in 1985 that was named the BankAmerica Acceptance Corporation. In this venture, BankAmerica provides financing services for the sale of Hertz cars in California.

Turmoil in 1986

Following a huge loss of $640 million in the second quarter of 1986, BankAmerica found itself in a weak position. Rumors began to circulate in California that the bank would collapse. BankAmerica's stock price continued to decline on the New York Stock Exchange. There was increased pressure on President and CEO Samuel Armacost to take action or resign. BankAmerica's problems originated in the 1970s when bankers believed that governments don't default on loans, only individuals and businesses do. Armacost was faced with the consequences of his predecessor's short-sighted strategies.

During the summer of 1986, BankAmerica publicly denied rumors of impending failure. Customer anxiety was appeased, but management prepared for possible takeover attempts. Armacost realized that BankAmerica held several subsidiaries and divisions that were not essential to its core business. He knew that the value of those subsidiaries taken as parts could be worth more than the entire corporation as a whole. Thus, during 1986, BankAmerica's strategies were to suspend dividend payments on common stock, to sell BankAmerica Acceptance to General Electric, and to sell its Los Angeles headquarters building.

A Takeover Attempt

In October 1986, First Interstate Bancorp announced a hostile takeover attempt of BankAmerica for $2.78 billion ($18/share). BankAmerica's Board of Directors then asked for and received Mr. Armacost's resignation. Tom Clausen was named Chairman and CEO. Clausen's immediate job was to decide whether to accept or reject the takeover offer. First Interstate soon sweetened its bid to $3.39 billion (slightly less than $22/share), but Clausen and the Board of Directors refused the offer. Rather, they continued divesting assets, including Charles Schwab for $230 million and Banca d'America e d'Italia for $603 million. This latter company was BankAmerica's subsidiary in Italy. Divestiture of these two highly profitable divisions was a major factor in the withdrawal of the hostile takeover attempt in February 1987.

Clausen continued Armacost's strategy of shedding assets to buoy the corporation's capital ratio. By the end of 1986, BankAmerica had 1,119 branches, 19 representative offices, and 278 affiliate offices in over 53 countries. BankAmerica's two major subsidiaries, Bank of America and Seafirst Corporation, had 1,053 domestic branches, 66 foreign branches, and 17 international representative offices in 1986. By year-end 1986, BankAmerica employed 73,465 individuals.

Early in 1987, Mr. Clausen reorganized BankAmerica and brought in new top management. He sold the Consumer Trust Services division, a unit of BankAmerica Trust, to Wells Fargo in California. Other recent developments are listed in Exhibit 1.

EXHIBIT 1 Recent developments at BankAmerica

Date	*Event*
1985	Sold San Francisco world headquarters properties.
	Sold a large Japanese property resulting in a $58 million pretax gain.
	Sold 20.6% stake in Corner Banca, Switzerland.
	Sold 50% stake in Banco Internacionale, Brazil.
	Sold FinanceAmerica to Chrysler Financial.
1986	
Jan	Suspended dividend payment on common stock.
Mar	Sold Los Angeles headquarters properties.
Sep	Went to the media to deny rumors of its collapse.
Oct	Sold BankAmerica Trust Company of New York's securities clearing and custody operations to Security Pacific, NY.
Oct	Sold BankAmerica Acceptance (Auto leasing venture with Hertz Corp.) to GE Credit.
Oct	Hostile takeover attempt by First Interstate Bancorp for $2.78 billion ($18/share).
Oct	Resignation of Samuel H. Armacost (President & CEO) and return of former president A. W. Clausen as Chairman and CEO.
Oct	Takeover bid sweetened to $3.39 billion ($21.75/share).
Nov	Rejected takeover bid.
Dec	Sold Banca d'America e d'Italia to Deutsche Bank.
1987	
Jan	Sold 43% majority stake in Charles Schwab & Co. brokerage services to its founder Charles Schwab.
Feb	Sold BankAmerica Finance (Mortgage subsidiary in the UK) to Bank of Ireland, UK.
Feb	Withdrawal of takeover bid by First Interstate.
Feb	Brazil announced its suspension of interest and principal repayments.
Mar	Sold Bankhaus Centrale Credit and B of A Card Services division in W. Germany to Banco Santander, W. Germany.
Mar	Sold the Consumer Trust Services Division (a unit of BankAmerica Trust) to Wells Fargo, California.

INTERNAL STRUCTURE

BankAmerica is principally a bank holding corporation with the majority of its operations in California. Its largest two holdings are Bank of America and Seafirst Corporation. (Note that BankAmerica is the holding company, and Bank of America is the commercial bank). Bank of America manages its various operations through three major profit centers or strategic business units: the Retail Bank, the World Banking Division, and BankAmerica Systems Engineering. The Seattle First National Bank is the sole division of Seafirst Corporation. An organizational chart for BankAmerica is provided in Exhibit 2.

EXHIBIT 2 Organizational structure of BankAmerica

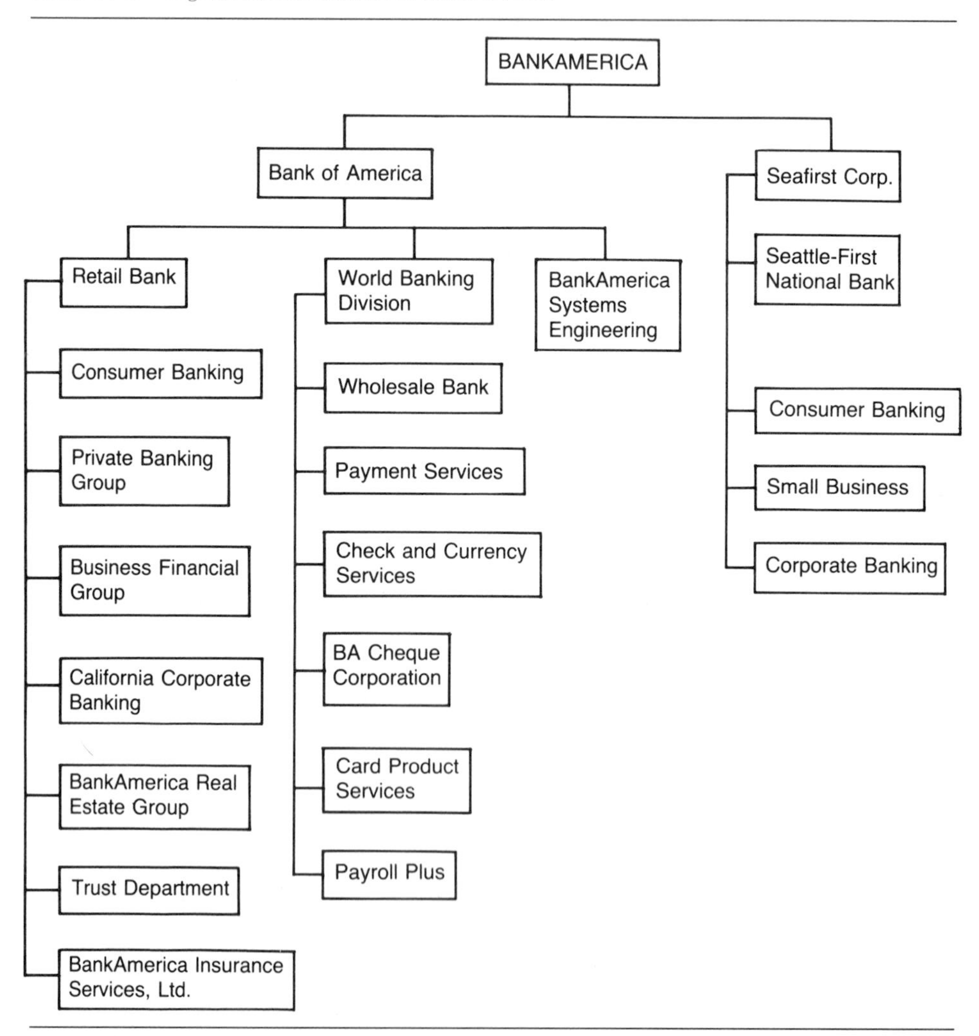

Source: Based on information provided in the 1986 *Annual Report*, pp. 6–15.

THE RETAIL BANK

The Retail Bank, a division of Bank of America, focuses on the needs of small businesses and individuals. In 1986, the Retail Bank was restructured to reduce costs and improve customer service. It served clients through more than 1,100 offices that included 895 branches and 156 convenience banking locations. Specialized banking offices included 30 home loan centers and 12 real estate loan centers in California, as well as 30 private banking offices worldwide. The Retail Bank's base of customers accounts for about one of every four households in California.

In January 1986, legal restrictions on interest-bearing accounts were dismantled in California. In response, the Retail Bank introduced Investors Checking Plus, a personal checking account that pays a variable rate of interest based on the account's balance and the prevailing interest rate. The Retail Bank's network of VERSATELLER automated teller machines (ATMs) became the largest full-service system in California. In addition, VERSATELLER cards could be used to pay for purchases at more than 1,800 California retail outlets in point-of-sale networks. The bank also offers credit card services through its World Banking Division).

As part of a cost cutting program that began in 1985, 40 branches were consolidated, eliminating several staff positions. Service was enhanced by the expansion of specialized service units to give customers easier access to bank products and information. The centralization process continued in 1986, with 3,500 staff level positions being eliminated from the Retail Bank. This was possible by moving many processing operations from branches into regional centers, thus utilizing economies of scale and automation. As a result, non-essential support operations were eliminated, and California regional administrative offices were reduced from seven to four.

Other Retail Bank Divisions

The Bank of America Private Banking Group offers an array of banking, investment, and asset management services designed to meet the needs of very wealthy customers. Eighteen facilities are located nationwide, but only three are outside California. Preferred Banking was introduced in 1986 in 125 offices to provide personalized services to affluent customers.

The Business Financial Group is committed to serving and expanding its base of 370,000 small business customers ranging from start-up enterprises to companies with gross sales of $10 million. Credit authority is localized, so customers receive attention from officers with primary knowledge of the customer's needs. California Corporate Banking, another Retail Bank division, deals with medium-sized companies that have sales from $10 million to $500 million. In California, Bank of America holds a 40 percent market share of this segment.

BankAmerica Real Estate Group was reorganized in 1984 and originated about $2 billion in residential mortgage loans in 1986, up from $950 million in 1985. To take advantage of the Tax Reform Act of 1986, CustomLine Equity, a new home equity line of credit, was offered for California residents. The Retail Bank's Trust Department manages pension plans and individual retirement accounts. In addition, an Insurance Division offers customers highly specialized insurance products. In 1985, the

Insurance Division became a broker to Lloyds of London and opened BankAmerica Insurance Services Ltd. in London and BankAmerica Insurance Brokers, Inc. in New York. Charles Schwab & Co. was a division of the Retail Bank before its divestiture in January 1987.

THE WORLD BANKING DIVISION

The World Banking Division was reorganized in 1986 to include (1) the Wholesale Bank and (2) Payment Services. This profit center provides banking operations to major corporations, governments, and financial institutions. Many customers use BankAmerica's facilities in multiple locations and require integrated lending, investment banking, and corporate payment services. BankAmerica Capital Markets Group has become a key player in the profit center's strategy. According to Euromoney Capital Markets Guide, the group ranked first in 1985 as lead arranger for committed Euronote facilities worldwide. Bank of America ranked as the number two underwriter of municipal notes for the United States in 1986.

The Wholesale Bank

The Wholesale Bank is segmented geographically into four divisions: North America; Asia; Europe, Middle East, and Africa; and Latin America/Caribbean. As part of its reorganization plan, the centralization of international administration in San Francisco eliminated an entire layer of management and resulted in a reduction of about 2,200 positions in the World Banking Division. Global network operations continued to be expanded by International Banking Systems (IBS), an integrated global data base of information that supports transaction processing as well as marketing and management information. IBS is expected to facilitate a wide range of financial services and products to meet the changing needs of institutional network clients. In 1986, IBS was expanded from Europe to include Hong Kong, Puerto Rico, and Panama. Additional locations throughout North America and Asia are targets for IBS expansion in 1987.

Payment Services

Payment Services, also known as Corporate Payments Division, provides check and currency processing, credit cards, information access, cash management, payroll services, and electronic point-of-sale support activities. The sales force of Payment Services coordinates activities with the Retail Bank and the Wholesale Bank to enhance communication and distribution efforts.

Other World Banking Divisions

Check and Currency Services provides depository and distribution services for the bank and for high volume and middle market customers. Through two major processing centers in San Francisco and Los Angeles, and about 30 centers throughout California, 10 million items (mostly checks) are processed each day. In addition, Check and Currency Services receives and supplies more than $3 billion in cash each month.

BA Cheque Corporation, a World Bank division that sells travelers cheques, expanded its global network of refund locations. By adding Visa and MasterCard to its proprietary BankAmerica travelers cheques, the bank increased its market share of the travelers cheque market to 15 percent.

Card Products and Services provides payments and credit card services to more than 77,000 merchants nationwide and six million credit card accounts. This division also provides debit card payments to merchants and financial institutions. Debit cards allow the user to withdraw funds directly from his/her checking account. The user does not borrow money with a debit card, instead he/she merely uses the debit card as a "plastic" check.

The computerized payroll system, Payroll Plus, has been expanded to the national marketplace. In 1986, Payroll Plus was selected to provide weekly electronic payroll deposit services to 90,000 employees of McDonnell Douglas, the aerospace company. In addition, Payroll Plus is one of eight systems that provide General Motors' monthly payments electronically to about 20,000 suppliers.

In addition to interest revenues, the World Banking Division generates fee-based revenues. These revenue sources are designed to reduce the bank's dependence on traditional credit products that are highly sensitive to economic cycles domestically and abroad. Moreover, the fee-based services in the banking industry are highly competitive. BankAmerica maintains a good profit margin in this sector due to its reliance on advanced technology and economies of scale.

BANKAMERICA SYSTEMS ENGINEERING

BankAmerica Systems Engineering (BASE) manages the bank's data processing centers in San Francisco, Los Angeles, Concord (California), New York, Hong Kong, and Croydon (United Kingdom). It is also responsible for managing, developing, and applying technology. BASE is currently working on 20 major technological projects to meet present and future corporate requirements. The projects are expected to improve service quality and speed, to help the corporation control and reduce the costs of worldwide banking, and to increase internal productivity. BASE is implementing the Global Data Network to provide high quality voice and data telecommunications throughout Bank America's California and international networks. This network is designed to support the International Banking System and to improve the performance of VERSATEL by reducing telecommunication expenses. BASE is also working on a Customer Information File Network that will provide complete information on customer accounts with Bank of America, thus improving customer service and enhancing the bank's ability to market additional products and services.

THE SEAFIRST CORPORATION

Seafirst Corporation reinforces BankAmerica's position as a primary financial institution in the Pacific Northwest. As parent of Seattle First National Bank in Washington, Seafirst serves an estimated 800,000 customers through 158 branches. In 1986, Seafirst reorganized its branch banking system to improve customer service. The reorganization resulted in reducing layers of management and centralizing non-customer related activities such as credit administration and other support functions. Currently, Seafirst holds the largest market share of all banks in Washington, 45 percent of the consumer segment, 28 percent of the small business market, and 58 percent of the corporate banking market.

BANKAMERICA'S FINANCIAL CONDITION

A consolidated balance sheet and income statement are provided for 1985–1986 in Exhibits 3 and 4, respectively. In 1980, BankAmerica reported record earnings of $643 million or $4.39 per share. In 1984, the company reported its most recent net profit, $346 million. During 1985 and 1986, the company lost $337 million and a record $518 million, respectively. Total assets peaked in 1982, slightly exceeding $122.4 billion. In 1986, total assets declined to $104.2 billion, a 12.1 percent decline from the previous year.

Domestic net interest revenue decreased by 5 percent in 1986 to $3.2 billion and accounted for about 80 percent of total net interest revenue. The decline was a result of an increase in nonaccrual loans by $810 million, as illustrated in Exhibit 5. Restructured loans and loans past due 90 days or more decreased in 1986 by $202 million and $158 million, respectively. The increase in nonaccrual loans was the principal reason for the decline in BankAmerica's net interest margin to 3.79 percent, as indicated in Exhibit 6. Another contributing factor to the decline in net interest revenue for 1986 was the increased costs (interest paid) on Eurodollar time deposits, which constitute a primary source of overseas funds. However, the weak dollar in 1986 partially offset the effects of higher Eurodollar costs. As a result, foreign net interest revenue fell to $639 million in 1986.

Exhibit 7 shows that noninterest revenue increased 10 percent in 1986 to $2.35 billion. This revenue source is broken into three categories: fees and commissions, trading revenue and gain on sale of assets. Fees and Commissions revenue increased by 11 percent to $1,411 million. Trading revenue increased by 43.6 percent to $530 million, and net gain on sale of assets was $411 million. Brokerage commissions will decline drastically in 1987 due to the recent sale of the Charles Schwab & Co. discount brokerage unit. Trading revenues are highly volatile as shown in Exhibit 7. Finally, the net gain on sale of assets includes pretax gains of $286 million from the sale of Banca d'America e d'Italia, $77 million from the sale of the Los Angeles headquarters properties, and $58 million from the sale of a Japanese property.

As part of its reorganization efforts, BankAmerica's management has placed special emphasis on controlling the growth of noninterest expenses. Noninterest expenses grew to $4.49 billion—up 12 percent from the previous year as shown in Exhibit 8. Personnel cutbacks were equivalent to the reduction of 9,600 full-time staff members during 1986. Excluding the effects of sales of subsidiaries, staff levels declined 6,600 in 1986. The new management team expects to make further staff reductions to achieve high employment efficiencies. Despite staff reductions, personnel expenses increased 6 percent in 1986 due to increased severance costs of $66 million and a decrease in the dollar's value against foreign currencies. Advertising expenses rose 14

EXHIBIT 3 Consolidated balance sheet of BankAmerica Corporation

(dollar amounts in millions)	December 31, 1986	1985
Assets		
Interest-earning deposits	**$ 3,917**	$ 7,937
Investment securities (market value: **1986–$5,595**; 1985–$5,858)	**5,702**	5,948
Trading account assets	**3,203**	3,148
Federal funds sold and securities purchased under resale agreements	**3,496**	1,751
Loans (net of unearned income)	**73,955**	84,326
Less: Allowance for possible credit losses	**2,172**	1,584
Net loans	**71,783**	82,742
Cash and noninterest-earning deposits	**9,116**	7,637
Premises and equipment	**1,892**	1,950
Customers' liability for acceptances	**1,985**	3,791
Accrued interest receivable	**744**	1,214
Other real estate owned	**476**	470
Other assets	**1,875**	1,953
Total Assets	**$104,189**	$118,541
Liabilities and Stockholders' Equity		
Domestic deposits:		
Interest-bearing	**$ 43,851**	$ 47,693
Noninterest-bearing	**18,336**	16,586
Foreign deposits:		
Interest-bearing	**18,722**	28,480
Noninterest-bearing	**1,296**	1,452
Total deposits	**82,205**	94,211
Federal funds purchased and securities sold under repurchase agreements	**3,031**	2,810
Commercial paper	**182**	839
Other short-term borrowings	**4,215**	3,135
Liability on acceptances	**1,985**	3,791
Accrued interest payable	**547**	858
Other payables and accrued liabilities	**3,377**	2,963
Intermediate-term debt	**2,606**	3,333
Long-term debt	**862**	856
Subordinated capital notes	**1,141**	1,198
Total liabilities	**100,151**	113,994
Commitments and contingencies		
Stockholders' Equity		
Preferred stock	**709**	709
Common stock, par value $1.5625 (authorized: 200,000,000 shares; issued: **1986–155,566,222 shares**; 1985-153,990,425 shares)	**243**	241
Additional paid-in capital—special preferred	**—**	8
Additional paid-in capital—common	**965**	945
Retained earnings	**2,225**	2,802
Cumulative translation adjustments	**(90)**	(145)
Common stock in treasury, at cost (**1986–622,668 shares**; 1985–575,168 shares)	**(14)**	(13)
Total stockholders' equity	**4,038**	4,547
Total Liabilities and Stockholders' Equity	**$104,189**	$118,541

Source: BankAmerica *Annual Report,* 1986, p. 42. Used with permission.

EXHIBIT 4 Consolidated statement of operations for BankAmerica Corporation

(dollar amounts in millions, except per share data)	1986	1985	1984
Interest on loans	**$ 7,982**	$ 9,342	$10,022
Loan fees	**508**	456	431
Interest and dividends on investment securities:			
Taxable interest	**419**	451	531
Nontaxable interest	**37**	51	63
Dividends	**6**	7	8
Interest on trading account assets	**241**	195	131
Interest on deposits	**626**	854	1,090
Interest on federal funds sold and securities purchased under resale agreements	**195**	217	307
Net leasing revenue	**117**	162	212
Total interest revenue	**10,131**	11,735	12,795
Interest on deposit liabilities	**5,375**	6,591	7,809
Interest on other short-term borrowings	**430**	535	698
Interest on intermediate-term debt	**367**	387	255
Interest on long-term debt	**83**	82	80
Interest on subordinated capital notes	**83**	98	33
Total interest expense	**6,338**	7,693	8,875
Net interest revenue	**3,793**	4,042	3,920
Provision for credit losses	**2,004**	2,180	861
Net interest revenue after provision for credit losses	**1,789**	1,862	3,059
Trading account profit and commissions	**67**	36	51
Investment securities profit	**79**	30	11
Foreign exchange trading profit	**141**	170	117
Deposit account service charges	**332**	304	274
Merchant fees on credit cards	**195**	167	162
Brokerage commissions	**214**	133	91
Other fees and commissions	**670**	663	648
Net gain on sales of assets	**411**	509	65
Other revenue	**243**	133	184
Total noninterest revenue	**2,352**	2,145	1,603
Personnel	**2,341**	2,210	2,156
Net occupancy—premises	**513**	462	441
Equipment—rentals, depreciation, and maintenance	**385**	388	342
Nonrecurring loss from escrow and trust operations	**—**	—	95
Other expense	**1,252**	1,374	1,174
Total noninterest expense	**4,491**	4,434	4,208
Income (loss) before income taxes	**(350)**	(427)	454
Provision for (benefit from) income taxes	**168**	(90)	108
Net Income (Loss)	**$ (518)**	$ (337)	$ 346
Net income (loss) applicable to common stock	**$ (577)**	$ (407)	$ 267
Average number of common shares outstanding (amounts in thousands)	**154,277**	152,300	150,668
Earnings (loss) per common share	**$ (3.74)**	$ (2.68)	$ 1.77
Dividends declared per common share	**—**	1.16	1.52

Source: BankAmerica *Annual Report,* 1986, p. 41. Used with permission.

EXHIBIT 5 BankAmerica's nonaccrual loans, restructured loans, and loans past due 90 days or more

(dollar amounts in millions)[a]	1986	1985	1984
Nonaccrual			
Domestic:			
Real estate	**$1,298**	$ 620	$ 419
Consumer installment	**29**	6	4
Commercial, industrial, and financial institutions	**1,033**	831	790
Agricultural	**205**	228	213
Lease financing	**63**	56	58
	2,628	1,741	1,484
Foreign:			
Governments and official institutions	**430**	344	561
Banks and other financial institutions	**108**	114	96
Commercial and industrial	**754**	935	1,119
Other loans	**47**	23	29
	1,339	1,416	1,805
	$3,967	$3,157	$3,289
Restructured			
Domestic:			
Real estate	**$ 31**	$ 139	$ 137
Commercial, industrial, and financial institutions	**5**	99	45
Agricultural	**1**	9	8
Lease financing	**7**	—	2
	44	247	192
Foreign:			
Commercial and industrial	**18**	19	26
Other loans	**2**	—	—
	20	19	26
	$ 64	$ 266	$ 218
Past Due 90 Days or More			
Domestic:			
Real estate	**$ 97**	$ 219	$ 374
Consumer installment	**70**	91	68
Commercial, industrial, and financial institutions	**65**	63	172
Agricultural	**3**	17	20
Lease financing	**7**	16	23
	242	406	657
Foreign:			
Governments and official institutions	**—**	—	4
Banks and other financial institutions	**—**	—	21
Commercial and industrial	**39**	37	58
Other loans	**4**	—	1
	43	37	84
	$ 285	$ 443	$ 741

[a]Certain amounts in prior periods have been reclassified to conform to the current presentation.

Source: BankAmerica *Annual Report,* 1986, p. 32. Used with permission.

EXHIBIT 6 BankAmerica's net interest revenue, average earning assets, and the net interest margin

(dollar amounts in millions)	1986	1985	1984
Net interest revenue:[a]			
Domestic	**$ 3,211**	$ 3,380	$ 3,301
Foreign	**639**	739	743
	$ 3,850	$ 4,119	$ 4,044
Average earning assets:			
Domestic	**$ 65,311**	$ 67,525	$ 65,560
Foreign	**36,236**	36,884	38,396
	$101,547	$104,409	$103,956
Net interest margin:[ab]			
Domestic	**4.92%**	5.00%	5.04%
Foreign	**1.76**	2.00	1.93
Corporate	**3.79**	3.94	3.89

[a]Taxable-equivalent.
[b]Ratio of net interest revenue (taxable-equivalent) to average earning assets.

Source: BankAmerica *Annual Report,* 1986, p. 21. Used with permission.

EXHIBIT 7 BankAmerica's noninterest revenue (in millions of dollars)

	Year Ended December 31,		
	1986	*1985*	*1984*
Fees and Commissions			
Deposit account service charges	332	304	274
Merchant fees on credit cards	195	167	162
Brokerage commissions	214	133	91
Other fees and commissions	670	663	648
Subtotal	**1,411**	**1,267**	**1,175**
Trading Revenue			
Trading account profit and commissions	67	36	51
Investment securities profit	79	30	11
Foreign exchange trading profit	141	170	117
Net gain on sales of loans	71	13	1
Other	172	120	183
Subtotal	**530**	**369**	**363**
Net gain excluding sale of assets	1,941	1,636	1,538
Net gain on sale of assets[a]	411	509	65
Total Noninterest Revenue	**2,352**	**2,145**	**1,603**

Note: [a] Assets sold include premises, equipment and operations

Source: Adapted from BankAmerica 1986 *Annual Report.*

EXHIBIT 8 BankAmerica's noninterest expenses

(dollar amounts in millions)	1986	1985	1984	Change 1986 over 1985	Change 1985 over 1984
Personnel	**$2,341**	$2,210	$2,156	6 %	3 %
Net occupancy—premises	**513**	462	441	11	5
Equipment—rentals, depreciation, and maintenance	**385**	388	342	(1)	13
Communications	**244**	239	231	2	3
Costs and writedowns associated with other real estate owned	**102**	135	39	(24)	246
Professional services	**106**	118	101	(10)	17
Stationery and supplies	**85**	95	94	(11)	1
Advertising	**79**	69	74	14	(7)
Travel	**60**	67	71	(10)	(6)
Nonrecurring loss from trust and escrow operations	**—**	—	95	—	(100)
Other	**576**	651	564	(12)	15
	$4,491	$4,434	$4,208	1	5

Source: BankAmerica *Annual Report,* 1986. Used with permission.

percent in 1986, reflecting the company philosophy to strengthen its position in the western U.S. market.

PORTFOLIO ANALYSIS

Loan Portfolio and Net Credit Losses

BankAmerica's loan portfolio is well diversified in both the domestic and foreign markets, as indicated in Exhibit 9. Real estate, consumer installment, agricultural, financial institution, and lease financing loan categories are mostly domestic and highly concentrated on the West Coast. The commercial and industrial loan category includes loans made through the Business Financial Group and California Corporate Banking division to multinational corporations and domestic government bodies. Foreign loans are spread among industrialized and developing nations as illustrated in Exhibit 10. The Brazilian, Mexican, and Venezuelan governments owed BankAmerica $1.96 billion, $1.415 billion, and $794 million, respectively, in 1986. These three governments' debts constituted 4 percent of BankAmerica's total assets. In addition, Brazil, Mexico, and Venezuela owed a total of $6.5 billion or 6.2 percent of the Bank's assets.

BankAmerica's ratio of net credit losses to average loan outstandings was 1.75 percent in 1986, down from 1.91 percent in 1985, but up from 1.1 percent in 1984, as shown in Exhibit 11. Industry analysts believed the banking industry as a whole, and BankAmerica in particular, should have recognized more losses in previous years

EXHIBIT 9 BankAmerica's loan outstandings

(dollar amounts in millions)	1986	1985	1984	1983	1982
Domestic loans:					
Real estate	**$17,847**	$19,887	$19,882	$19,368	$18,067
Consumer installment	**12,570**	14,375	13,348	11,648	9,499
Commercial and industrial	**18,258**	20,616	20,813	18,450	15,874
Agricultural	**1,175**	1,610	1,966	2,136	1,828
Financial institutions	**2,209**	1,580	1,532	1,066	1,257
Lease financing	**1,002**	1,501	1,868	2,015	1,925
Foreign loans	**20,894**	24,757	25,637	27,674	28,177
	$73,955	$84,326	$85,046	$82,357	$76,627

Source: BankAmerica *Annual Report*, 1986, p. 30. Used with permission.

EXHIBIT 10 BankAmerica's cross-border outstandings exceeding 1% of total assets

(dollar amounts in millions)[abcd]	December 31,	Governments and Official Institutions	Banks and Other Financial Institutions	Commercial and Industrial	Total Cross-Border Outstandings	Cross-Border Outstandings as a Percentage of Total Assets
Japan	**1986**	**$ —**	**$1,421**	**$1,947**	**$3,368**	**3.2%**
	1985	—	1,706	1,812	3,518	3.0
	1984	—	1,837	2,001	3,838	3.3
Brazil	**1986**	**1,963**	**591**	**187**	**2,741**	**2.6**
	1985	1,869	732	198	2,799	2.4
	1984	2,054	455	212	2,721	2.3
Mexico	**1986**	**1,415**	**340**	**745**	**2,500**	**2.4**
	1985	1,423	366	794	2,583	2.2
	1984	1,419	357	913	2,689	2.3
United Kingdom	**1986**	**206**	**414**	**1,352**	**1,972**	**1.9**
	1985	401	487	787	1,675	1.4
	1984	373	779	2,188	3,340	2.8
Venezuela	**1986**	**794**	**221**	**245**	**1,260**	**1.2**
	1985	734	343	373	1,450	1.2
	1984	991	108	409	1,508	1.3
Canada	**1986**	**29**	**172**	**588**	**789**	**0.8**
	1985	10	576	778	1,364	1.2
	1984	46	1,075	640	1,761	1.5
South Korea	**1986**	**161**	**219**	**307**	**687**	**0.7**
	1985	383	408	502	1,293	1.1
	1984	517	121	454	1,092	0.9
France	**1986**	**18**	**217**	**378**	**613**	**0.6**
	1985	93	741	189	1,023	0.9
	1984	163	1,077	333	1,573	1.3

[a]Cross-border outstandings reported in prior periods have been restated for Japan, Mexico, United Kingdom, Canada, South Korea, and France.
[b]Cross-border outstandings include the following assets, primarily in U.S. dollars, with borrowers or customers in a foreign country: loans, accrued interest, acceptances, interest-earning deposits with other banks, other interest-earning investments, and other monetary assets. Material local currency outstandings which are neither hedged nor funded by local currency borrowings are included in cross-border outstandings. Guarantees of outstandings of borrowers of other countries are considered outstandings of the guarantor. Loans made to, or deposits placed with, a branch of a foreign bank located outside the foreign bank's home country are considered loans to, or deposits with, the country in which the foreign bank is headquartered. Outstandings of a country do not include amounts of principal or interest which are supported by written, legally enforceable guarantees by guarantors from other countries or the amount of outstandings to the extent they are secured by tangible, liquid collateral held and realizable by BankAmerica outside the country.
[c]At December 31, 1986, commitments in excess of 10% of cross-border outstandings were as follows: $2,558 million for United Kingdom, $1,129 million for France, $824 million for Canada, $540 million for Japan, $464 million for Mexico, and $388 million for South Korea.
[d]No country, with the exception of Brazil, Mexico, and Venezuela, which are discussed separately, had nonaccrual, restructured, or past due 90 days or more loans in excess of 10% of cross-border outstandings at December 31, 1986.

Source: BankAmerica *Annual Report*, 1986, p. 29. Used with permission.

due to the deteriorating economic condition of several domestic industries and national economies abroad. As consumer indebtedness and individual bankruptcies continued to increase in the 1980s, consumer losses in 1986 rose to $279 million. This figure includes net credit card losses of $166 million and dealer auto financing losses of $56 million.

EXHIBIT 11 BankAmerica's net credit losses

(dollar amounts in millions)	1986 Net Credit Losses	1986 Percent of Loan Outstandings[a]	1985 Net Credit Losses	1985 Percent of Loan Outstandings[a]	1984 Net Credit Losses	1984 Percent of Loan Outstandings[a]
Domestic loans:						
Real estate	**$ 244**	**1.26%**	$ 173	0.86%	$ 39	0.20%
Consumer installment	**279**	**1.99**	238	1.68	128	1.05
Commercial and industrial	**345**	**2.05**	279	1.54	330	1.88
Agricultural	**72**	**5.50**	152	8.70	78	3.77
Financial institutions	**6**	**0.31**	2	0.14	1	0.13
Lease financing	**14**	**1.10**	43	2.75	29	1.53
Foreign loans	**459**	**1.85**	712	2.84	302	1.13
	$1,419	**1.75**	$1,599	1.91	$907	1.10

Source: BankAmerica *Annual Report*, 1986, p. 36. Used with permission.

Nonperforming Loans

Nonperforming loans include loans placed on a nonaccrual basis, restructured loans, and loans past due 90 days or more. BankAmerica experienced an increase in its nonperforming loans from 4.58 percent of loan outstandings at the end of 1985 to 5.84 percent in 1986. Several analysts criticized the bank's management for not recognizing the majority of these loans as a credit loss for 1986. During the year, the corporation received interest payments of $160 million on nonaccrual loans. These payments were not included in interest revenue. Instead, they were used to reduce the principal balance of loans outstanding as required by Generally Accepted Accounting Principles (GAAP). Interest owed on nonaccrual loans is counted as principal reducing income only when cash payments are received.

Allowance For Possible Credit Losses

The $2.17 billion allowance for possible credit losses was allocated to different segments as shown in Exhibit 12. The largest losses of $752 million and $452 million were allocated to foreign loans and to the commercial and industrial segment, respectively. However, the agricultural segment received the largest relative allocation (11.99 percent) of loan outstandings in that segment. The level and allocation of each allowance reflect management's best judgment of the risks associated with the loan outstandings. The foreign segment allowance does not include any provisions for Brazil's recent announcement to suspend interest payments on its debt.

Capital Ratio Requirements

The Federal Depository Insurance Corporation (FDIC) requires that all member banks maintain a primary capital ratio of at least 5.5 percent. The primary capital ratio is defined as the ratio of primary capital over total assets including the allowance for possible credit losses (*i.e.*, total assets + allowance). Primary capital is defined as stockholders' equity plus allowance for possible credit losses, minority interest in the equity of consolidated subsidiaries, and subordinated capital notes. Total capital ratio is the ratio of primary capital plus qualifying intermediate and long-term debt over total assets plus allowance for possible credit losses.

EXHIBIT 12 BankAmerica's allowance for possible credit losses

	1986		1985		1984	
(dollar amounts in millions)	Allowance[a]	Percent of Loan Outstandings	Allowance[a]	Percent of Loan Outstandings	Allowance[a]	Percent of Loan Outstandings
Domestic loans:						
Real estate	**$ 393**	**2.20%**	$ 117	0.59%	$ 69	0.35%
Consumer installment	**258**	**2.06**	226	1.57	91	0.68
Commercial and industrial	**452**	**2.47**	300	1.45	198	0.95
Agricultural	**141**	**11.99**	107	6.65	30	1.53
Financial institutions	**32**	**1.45**	12	0.75	3	0.20
Lease financing	**8**	**0.84**	14	0.92	16	0.87
Foreign loans	**752**	**3.60**	744	3.01	225	0.88
	2,036	**2.75**	1,520	1.81	632	0.74
Unallocated	**136**	**—**	64	—	371	—
	$2,172	**2.94**	$1,584	1.88	$1,003	1.18

[a]The allowance for possible credit losses is allocated by applying loss factors to the related loan outstandings and from estimates of probable future losses.

Source: BankAmerica *Annual Report,* 1986, p. 33. Used with permission.

The Federal Reserve Board considers banks with total capital ratios of less than 6.0 percent to be undercapitalized. Institutions with total capital ratios above 6.0 percent, but below 7.0 percent, are in a minimally acceptable capitalization region. Total capitalization ratios above 7.0 percent are presumed adequate.

During 1984 and 1985, BankAmerica's total capital ratio was 6.61 percent and 6.88 percent, respectively, as shown in Exhibit 13. In 1986, shareholders' equity decreased by $504 million to $4.04 billion. By increasing its allowance for possible

EXHIBIT 13 BankAmerica's primary and total capital

(dollar amounts in millions)	1986	1985	1984
Capital Components			
Stockholders' equity	**$4,038**	$4,547	$5,119
Subordinated capital notes	**1,141**	1,198	799
Minority interest	**10**	8	9
Allowance for possible credit losses	**2,172**	1,584	1,003
Primary capital	**7,361**	7,337	6,930
Secondary capital—qualifying debt	**1,245**	931	914
Total Capital	**$8,606**	$8,268	$7,844
Capital Ratios			
Primary capital[a]	**6.92%**	6.11%	5.84%
Total capital[b]	**8.09**	6.88	6.61

[a]Primary capital ratio = (stockholders' equity plus the allowance for possible credit losses, minority interest in equity of consolidated subsidiaries, and subordinated capital notes) divided by (total assets plus the allowance for possible credit losses).
[b]Total capital ratio = (primary capital plus certain qualifying intermediate- and

Source: BankAmerica's *Annual Report,* 1986, p. 27. Used with permission.

credit losses and selling several portions of its asset base, BankAmerica was able to increase its total capital ratio of 8.09 percent. However, if the corporation continues to post record losses, its total capital ratio is likely to drop below the regulatory requirement. To build the corporation's capital resources, Clausen and his management team plan to sell other non-core assets and to issue debt and equity securities as needed.

INDUSTRY AND ENVIRONMENT

In the last several years, many U.S. banks have experienced an increase in the number of failed commercial loans associated with the agriculture, energy, and construction industries. An abundant supply of farm products has led to lower prices, lower earnings, and a reduction in agricultural land values. In many cases, the value of the collateral land is much less than the original loans. This also holds true for the energy sector. Lower oil prices and declining earnings have reduced land values in the same manner as in agriculture. Overbuilding in the construction industry has produced empty office and residential buildings with no revenues.

Consumer debt reached an all-time high in 1986, resulting in record personal bankruptcies. Bank failures in 1985 and 1986 registered record highs of 120 and 138, respectively. Another form of consumer debt that came to haunt many banks in the mid-1980s was the credit card. Increased competition for this lucrative market resulted in the issuance of many new credit cards. Unfortunately, numerous consumers taking advantage of new cards were not credit worthy, resulting in large losses for banks.

The domestic debt crisis is just one of many external threats facing U.S. banks. Loans made to Third World countries in the early 1980s resulted in significant debt amounts being rescheduled for payment and suspension of interest payment. Latin America has been an area of major concern. Brazil, Mexico, and Venezuela have all suffered from inflation, while simultaneously undergoing a recession. Current economic conditions in these countries have made repayment of these loans next to impossible. Even with highly creative debt restructuring agreements, many banks are realizing that they will never receive full value on their loans.

Brazil reached an agreement with its foreign lenders in September 1986 on restructuring its debt. Under the restructuring plan, cross-border debts that matured in 1985 were to be repaid over a seven-year period. Cruzado equivalents of the restructured debts were deposited in the Central Bank of Brazil. However, the cruzado's value continued to decline against the dollar, and the Brazilian economy did not grow as expected. As a result, on February 20, 1987, the Brazilian government advised the international lending institutions that all interest payments due to them would be held at the Central Bank of Brazil instead of being transferred to the financial institutions.

Mexico and Venezuela are facing problems similar to Brazil's. Both countries rely heavily on income generated from oil exports. Oil prices have declined from a record high of $35/barrel in 1983 to a record low of $9.50/barrel in December 1986. In light of continuing uncertainties regarding world petroleum markets, Mexico and Venezuela are also considering suspending their interest payments and restructuring their foreign debts.

To add insult to injury, many banks' large corporate customers are turning elsewhere for short-term borrowing. Lower interest rates on commercial paper have become more advantageous to the industrial borrower. In an attempt to counter the commercial paper market, banks are forced to cut loan rates. Reducing interest rates, however, results in losses on these loans after selling costs are subtracted. These losses are being incurred in the hopes that the industrial borrower will also use other financial services provided by the bank and therefore bring the bank a profit from fee-based revenues.

Deregulation

When the Supreme Court upheld the regional interstate banking pacts in June 1985, it paved the way for a multitude of interstate bank mergers. As a result, banks have the means to cross state lines to acquire business. Although many states will only reciprocate with other states in their region, a number of states have a "trigger" clause written into their interstate banking agreements. This "trigger" permits national banks from outside the state's region to enter the state after a particular date, in most cases sometime around 1990. A total of 27 states have regional banking laws, including California, Oregon, Michigan, the Carolinas, and Florida. Fifteen states do not allow any form of interstate banking, including mostly Rocky Mountain states, plus Vermont, Massachusetts, and Delaware. Eight states allow national interstate banking, including Texas, Arizona, Washington, New York, West Virginia, Maine, Kentucky, and Connecticut. Several large banks anxiously await the day when they can enter new territories.

Deregulation of the banking industry has allowed commercial banks to compete with other types of financial institutions in respect to the interest paid on deposit accounts. Before the Deregulation Act of 1980, commercial banks could not offer more than 5¼ percent interest on deposit accounts. These commercial banks experienced large withdrawals as deposits were placed elsewhere in accounts paying a much higher return. The Deregulation Act not only allowed for the gradual elimination of the interest rate ceiling, but also permitted interest bearing checking accounts. Since banking institutions were forced to increase their interest payments to customers, they had to turn to other revenue sources to maintain profitability. To compensate, service charges and loan initiation fees increased substantially. During 1985, banks derived, on the average, 27.2 percent of their income from fee-based revenues, 18.2 percent from income on investments, and 54.5 percent from income on loans.

As interest rates and fees rise, banks continually look for ways to reduce costs. The increased use of electronic funds transfer (EFT) between banks allows funds to be transferred almost instantaneously. The amount of paperwork and processing time is reduced considerably, resulting in higher profit margins to the bank. The use of automated teller machines (ATM's) by customers is convenient to the bank as well as the client. The customer obtains 24-hour banking privileges while the bank reduces its transaction processing expenses. The use of electronic communication has yet to reach its fullest potential in the banking industry. Banks are turning more to telecommunications for the latest financial information on multinational corporate accounts, fund transfers, ATM transactions, and point-of-sale transaction processing. These services combined provide for decreased costs with increased speed and accuracy.

BANKAMERICA'S COMPETITION

Competition from American Banks

BankAmerica's two largest rivals are New York-based Citicorp and Chase Manhattan. In California, BankAmerica's largest competitor is First Interstate Bancorp. BankAmerica's capital ratios are compared to Citicorp's and Chase's in Exhibit 14. BankAmerica's total capital ratio is lowest among the three national banks. Similarly, BankAmerica's net interest margin is lowest when compared to Citicorp, Chase, and First Interstate, as shown in Exhibit 15. BankAmerica's loan loss ratio to average loan outstandings is the highest of all four banks, as indicated in Exhibit 16.

EXHIBIT 14 Comparison of BankAmerica's capital ratios with its major competitors

	Primary		*Total*	
	1986	*1985*	*1986*	*1985*
Citicorp	6.80%	6.20%	10.90%	9.10%
Chase	6.95%	6.87%	9.27%	9.23%
BankAmerica	6.92%	6.11%	8.09%	6.88%

EXHIBIT 15 Net interest margin on average earning assets of major competitors

	1986	*1985*
Citicorp	3.95%	3.98%
Chase	4.25%	4.03%
First Interstate	5.32%	5.43%
BankAmerica	3.79%	3.94%

EXHIBIT 16 Loan losses as a percentage of average loans outstanding

	1986	*1985*
Citicorp	1.16%	0.91%
Chase	0.76%	0.52%
First Interstate	1.21%	1.01%
BankAmerica	1.75%	1.91%

Citicorp, guided by its chairman John Reed, is the largest bank in the United States, with assets over $196 billion. Reed's goal is to build an even stronger company for the future. One growth area Citicorp is focusing upon is retail banking. Citicorp has subsidiaries or affiliates in 40 states, thus giving it a broad base for consumer contact. Citicorp has acquired banks in Arizona, a state that allows nationwide banking. It has also acquired several failing thrifts in California, Florida, and Nevada at bargain prices.

While Citicorp has a considerable amount of loans outstanding to Third World countries, it has been steadily increasing its loan loss reserves in 1985 and 1986 in anticipation of problems with their repayment. As a result of Brazil's announcement, Citicorp is likely to make a $3 billion provision to its loan loss reserves that would result in a second quarter 1986 loss of more than $2.5 billion.

Chase Manhattan Bank became the second largest U.S. bank in March 1987. Like Citicorp, Chase Manhattan increased its consumer banking interests by purchasing banks in Arizona. It added further to its interstate base by acquiring collapsing institutions in Maryland and Ohio. As the second largest lender to Latin American countries after Citicorp, Chase has also increased its provision for losses on these loans.

On the western front, BankAmerica faces a great deal of competition in the California market. Besides BankAmerica, Californians can choose from Security Pacific, Wells Fargo, and First Interstate Bancorp. First Interstate is of the most concern to BankAmerica, even though it is a much smaller bank. When First Interstate attempted a takeover of BankAmerica in late 1986, BankAmerica successfully resisted. For now, First Interstate will watch and wait. Such a takeover would give First Interstate a firm hold on the California market and would make it the second largest bank in the country. A strong base in California would help to support First Interstate's growing operations in 17 other states.

Competition from Foreign Banks

A more recent form of competition for the commercial bank is the advent of foreign banks operating in the United States. With the increasing number of imports to the United States, many countries found it to their advantage to establish banks in this country. With the International Banking Act (IBA) of 1978, foreign banks were finally required to meet some of the restrictions already imposed upon domestic banks. Not only must foreign banks follow the reserve requirement stipulated by the Federal Reserve, but they are also required to select a "home" state for their primary banking business. The "home" state rule was intended to restrict the interstate banking privileges that foreign banks previously had. The IBA, however, does not give U.S. banks equal footing with foreign banks. Due to a grandfather clause, foreign banks already providing non-banking services such as security activities were allowed to continue these services. Foreign banks were also given the right to change their home state one time, thus gaining an avenue for continued interstate expansion.

By the end of 1985, there were over 600 foreign bank offices in the United States with over $440 billion in assets. Over half of these offices were located in New York and most of the remaining ones in California, Florida, and Illinois. These locations were not selected by chance but were carefully chosen to compete in lucrative markets that are traditionally served by large American banks.

Competition from Nonbanks

Commercial banks not only face competition from other banks, but they also encounter competition from other types of financial institutions. Historically, commercial banks have been inclined to ignore the consumer market and focus energies on commercial endeavors. Filling the gap in consumer services are thrifts, nonbank companies, and nonbank banks.

Thrifts consist of savings and loans, mutual savings banks and credit unions, all originated with the consumer's interest in mind. Traditionally, they met the consumer's need for borrowing that the large commercial banks were unwilling to satisfy. When thrifts started to offer money market accounts in the 1970s, they began to attract patrons of commercial banks. Commercial banks were unable to compete on this frontier until the Deregulation Act of 1980 was approved.

The Bank Holding Company Act of 1956 and its amendment of 1970 state that:

> A bank is any institution which 1) accepts deposits that the depositor has a legal right to withdraw on demand, *and* 2) engages in the business of making commercial loans.[2]

This definition is important to nonbank companies. Since these businesses do not fit the definition of a bank, they are not subject to the rules and regulations imposed on banks. For example, nonbanks are not required to keep a specified amount of deposits on reserve with the Federal Reserve, therefore enabling them to invest money in a more profitable manner. The greatest advantage for a nonbank is its ability to conduct business across state lines. Until recently, interstate banking could not be conducted by commercial banks, but nonbanks have been free to conduct interstate transactions at will. Nonbank companies such as American Express, Merrill Lynch, and Sears have taken advantage of this loophole.

Since nonbank companies are exempt from banking regulations, they are able to offer services to their clients that the commercial bank cannot. Insurance, real estate, and security brokerage services are just some of the offerings that can be made by a nonbank company. Many nonbank companies enter the financial services business with a pre-established customer base to draw from. Sears and Merrill Lynch, for example, both have huge databases and thousands of customers. Since these customers already have a working relationship with the company, added financial services can provide the customer with one-stop service.

A "nonbank bank" is a commercial bank that has abandoned operations in either demand deposits or commercial loans. Since it does not fit the definition of a bank, a nonbank bank does not fall under regulations concerning nonbanking services or interstate banking. Several bank holding companies have gone this route to bypass interstate banking regulations.

FUTURE OUTLOOK

The year 1986 has been a period of retrenchment, regrouping, takeover attempts, and change. BankAmerica's determination to return to profitability is hindered by continuous credit quality problems. Mr. Clausen has to decide whether to take a large loss on Brazil's debt or to restructure the loans. Making an additional $1 billion allowance for credit losses during 1987 would likely result in BankAmerica reporting a $1.4 billion loss for the year. This would further weaken the bank's capital ratio and depress the stock price. Further issuance of stock may then be very difficult. Would you restructure BankAmerica's foreign loans or take the loss now?

Mr. Clausen could continue to sell assets, but he may soon rid the corporation of its most profitable divisions. Some analysts suggest that BankAmerica should sell Seafirst Corporation for as much as $600 million. This sale could result in a $200 million pre-tax profit for the corporation. However, BankAmerica's long-term strategy of being a leading financial institution in the western United States would be compromised. Would you recommend selling Seafirst at this point in time?

What additional steps should BankAmerica take to improve its total capital ratio, while simultaneously improving profitability? Should BankAmerica issue stock and debt to increase the total capital? Should BankAmerica acquire another bank to expand operations? How could BankAmerica take advantage of BASE's technological knowledge by introducing new fee-based services? Mr. Clausen must address these and other strategic issues in the days ahead. What specific recommendations would you offer to Mr. Clausen?

ENDNOTES

1. The quotes in the first section of this case signify possible conversations rather than actual statements.
2. Compton, Eric. *The New World of Commercial Banking* (Lexington, Mass.: Lexington Books, 1987), p. 293–94.

Hanson–1987

RICHARD REED
Washington State University

> "It is our true policy to steer clear of permanent alliance with any portion of the foreign world." [George Washington (1732–1799), Farewell Address, September 17, 1796]

Against a background of more and more acquisitions in the United States by foreign firms, this case study concentrates on one specific takeover situation and the company that instigated the action. Through the last months of 1985 and into 1986, the U.S. company, SCM (previously Smith Corona Marchant) fielded a white knight, Merrill Lynch, in response to an aggressive takeover attempt made by the U.K. company, Hanson Trust. In its white knight role of protector against the hostile Hanson bid, Merrill Lynch proposed an agreed-upon counter-bid. Part of SCM's defensive strategy was to lock-up the most profitable parts of the corporation, for immediate purchase by Merrill Lynch, in the event that the counter-bid failed. A long and bitter battle for control of SCM's stock was finally settled when U.S. courts ruled the lock-up was illegal. If SCM's tactic had been successful, Hanson Trust would have been left with an expensive and pointless portfolio addition that would have marred its outstanding domestic and foreign acquisition record.

FOREIGN ACQUISITIONS (1980–86)

Direct foreign investment in the United States is increasing.[1] British investment is up from $14.1 billion in 1980 to $51.4 billion in 1986. During those same years, Dutch investment has increased from $19.1 billion to $42.9 billion, and Japanese investment has risen from $4.7 billion to $23.4 billion. The story is the same for Canadian, West German, and Swiss foreign investment. These investments are aimed mainly at industry and real estate. Sir James Goldsmith (British), now notorious in the United States for his attempted control of Goodyear, bought Crown-Zellerbach for its huge forest holdings in Oregon and Washington State. Unilever (Dutch) has bought Chesebrough-Ponds, British Petroleum now has Sohio, Bridgestone (Japanese) acquired Firestone, Hoechst (West German) took over Celanese, Heileman Brewing agreed to be bought out by the (Australian) Bond Corporation, and, amid the continuing list, Hanson Trust acquired SCM.

Numerous factors combine to make the United States attractive to foreign investors. There are the obvious things like political stability and size of market, but these have existed for some time and do not explain the surge of foreign takeovers. More recent events have brought about the dramatic increase. First, and most apparent, is the devalued U.S. dollar. While its reduced value curbs imports and boosts exports, the reverse side of the coin is that American domestic assets suddenly appear to be low-priced in terms of the Japanese yen, the British pound, the French franc, the German mark, and others. Real estate is considered a bargain, and, despite the existence of a bull market between 1982 and 1987, company stocks remain a good buy. Second, and equally apparent, is the continuing trend toward the internationalization of business. Through their hugely successful export activities, Pacific rim countries have accrued earnings and become more familiar with American culture and business practices. Consequently, they are now able to acquire and operate U.S. companies with relative equanimity.

A third factor which indirectly fueled foreign investment in the United States was the slowing of Western economies in the early 1980s. The increased propensity for European companies to acquire U.S. firms resulted from the shake-out effects the recession had in more marginal economies. Many European companies were forced to adopt imaginative strategies, such as stock buy-backs. Others rationalized and cut away unproductive fat and then aggressively pursued longer-term gains through acquisition. Only the better-managed and more cost-effective companies survived. These lean and aggressive survivors now observe U.S. companies that would "benefit" from their hard learned management skills. The American companies being targeted for acquisition typically have some potential for increased profitability. They have never had the pressing economic need to fully develop the skills necessary for strict control of costs and releasing synergies. The companies have not had the need, or have not been prepared to look beyond their traditional domestic boundaries for new opportunities and growth.

BACKGROUND AND HISTORY OF HANSON TRUST

Hanson Trust plc[2] is a company that knew the secret of efficient operation coupled with growth by takeover long before the last recession forced other British companies into using the same strategy. By making judicious acquisitions, strictly controlling its subsidiaries' capital expenditures, and keeping efficiency high, Hanson Trust has come a long way since its humble beginnings a little over twenty years ago.

In 1964, the Wiles Group Ltd. was a relatively small British company. It was based in Yorkshire, in the north of England, and operated in the agricultural services field. That year saw two key events occur that would initiate the transformation of the company into the Hanson Trust of today. First, the Wiles Group became a quoted company on the London Stock Exchange, thus providing facilities for increasing its capital base. Second, it acquired Oswald Tillotson Ltd., another relatively small British company engaged in commercial vehicle distribution. James Hanson (now Lord Hanson), who was a director of the acquired company, became chairman of the Wiles Group in the following year, 1965.

Under Lord Hanson's direction, the Wiles Group embarked upon a series of acquisitions that were also concentric diversifications. In 1967, a construction equipment and distribution company was purchased for 0.7 million pounds (nearly $1.7 million). Table 1 provides exchange rates between the U.K. pound and the U.S. dollar. An agricultural sack rental company was purchased for just over 3 million pounds in mid-1968 and, at the end of that year, a brick manufacturer was acquired for nearly 5 million pounds. In 1969, the company's name was changed to Hanson Trust, Ltd., and further acquisitions followed in construction equipment distribution, brick manufacturing, and engineering. Hanson Trust's obvious strategy of acquiring companies in low-technology but stable industries was now well established. The company was associated with an equally obvious rationalization program that produced improved levels of profit from the acquired assets. Between 1964 and 1973, before-tax profit climbed from 0.14 million pounds to 8.2 million pounds, a fifty-eightfold increase in ten years.

In 1973, Gordon White (now Sir Gordon White KBE) was dispatched from London with the aim of establishing Hanson Trust in the United States. The company entered the United States with an initial equity investment of only $3,000.[3] Sir Gordon's first major acquisition was Seacoast Products, a producer of animal feedstuffs and edible oil. The acquisition was achieved through a leveraged buy-out with assets of the target company being used as collateral against loans. Originally called J. Howard Smith, Seacoast was purchased on a deferred basis for $32 million. From the very first year, Seacoast produced a cash flow which helped facilitate other acquisitions. A textile company, Indian Head (now Carisbrook Industries), was acquired in 1975 and was followed by Hygrade Foods in 1976. Interstate United (food services), Templon (textiles), and McDonough (building materials) were acquired over the period 1977–81. In total, Hanson Trust spent over $0.3 billion in acquisitions in the first eight years of its U.S. operation.

From this (small) beginning, the company has balanced its U.S.-U.K. portfolio to the extent that by 1986, sales topped $6 billion, of which the U.S. operations provided 45 percent. U.S. profits accounted for 51 percent of the total. Hanson Trust has become one of the largest British investors in the United States and, in the process, has earned Sir Gordon White the reputation of being a top corporate raider[4].

TABLE 1 Currency exchange rates (1967–86) for U. S. dollars and U. K. pounds

Year	*One U. S. Dollar in U. K. Pounds*	*One U. K. Pound in U. S. Dollars*
1967	0.4155	2.4067
1968	0.4194	2.3843
1969	0.4166	2.4004
1970	0.4174	2.3959
1971	0.4091	2.4442
1972	0.3999	2.5008
1973	0.4080	2.4510
1974	0.4273	2.3403
1975	0.4501	2.2216
1976	0.5541	1.8048
1977	0.5731	1.7449
1978	0.5212	1.9184
1979	0.4712	2.1224
1980	0.4300	2.3258
1981	0.4940	2.0243
1982	0.5721	1.7480
1983	0.6597	1.5159
1984	0.7482	1.3366
1985	0.7707	1.2974
1986	0.6776	1.4758

Source: *Statistics Abstract for the United States.*

Structurally, Hanson Trust reflects the geographic split in its operations. Lord Hanson is overall company chairman and chairman of the British operations. American operations, Hanson Industries, Inc., has Sir Gordon White as chairman. While responsibilities for the control of operational activities remain clearly separate, decisions on acquisitions remain less clear.

For more than twenty years, Hanson Trust has maintained a growth rate and growth in earnings that have made it one of the top performing British companies of today and have elevated Hanson Industries into the top twenty percent of the *Fortune* 500. The company's ten-year record for 1977–86 is shown in Table 2. Between 1977 and 1986, sales increased ninefold and were matched by earnings per share, which increased more than 890 percent. The phenomenal growth record that has been achieved and maintained is in large part due to the continued policy of acquisition. This strategy has led to both conglomeration and diversification. Because the diversifications have moved beyond being related, to become unrelated in nature, a smoothing effect on earnings has been realized. Also, by operating simultaneously in the

TABLE 2 Hanson Trust review (1977–86)

U. K. Pounds (million)	*1986*	*1985*	*1984*	*1983*	*1982*	*1981*	*1980*	*1979*	*1978*	*1977*
Income										
Sales	4312	2674	2382	1484	1148	856	684	658	605	477
Profit (before tax)	469	264	169	91	60	50	39	31	26	24
Earnings per share[a]	14.3	10.6	7.6	4.7	3.7	3.3	2.5	2.0	1.7	1.6
Assets Less Liabilities										
Tangible assets	1074	603	685	289	211	129	92	91	70	57
Investments	40	187	17	11	4	4	6	7	1	1
Current assets	5551	2062	1443	962	547	458	216	210	161	135
Current liabilities	2486	907	754	565	323	196	142	150	102	67
Financed by										
Share capital	814	500	164	106	55	27	27	27	17	17
Reserves	774	625	247	323	134	138	94	80	58	50
Long-term debt	1972	640	797	186	188	191	42	40	42	41
Liability provisions	619	180	183	82	62	39	9	11	13	18
Total	**4179**	**1945**	**1391**	**697**	**439**	**395**	**172**	**158**	**130**	**126**
Assets per share[a]	**54**	**52**	**31**	**33**	**19**	**16**	**12**	**11**	**9**	**8**

Note: [a] In pence (one hundred pence = one U. K. pound), fully diluted.
Source: Hanson Trust Annual Report and Accounts, 1986.

United Kingdom and the United States, the potency of the diversification has been increased further. While the 1985 financial results were not as outstanding as earlier years (see Tables 2 and 3), the currency exchange rate worked in Hanson Trust's favor when U.S. earnings were translated into U.K. pounds. In 1986, Hanson Trust saw a return to the previous (real) levels of growth.

PRODUCT MARKETS AND ORGANIZATION

In 1984, Hanson Trust described itself as "an industrial management company".[5] This statement reflects the company's policy of maintaining a discrete distance from the operational activities of its subsidiaries. Less obviously, the statement also reflects the company's policy of avoiding research-and-development-intensive industries.

The essence of the company's philosophy is to provide "essential goods and services to proven markets, with definable future prospects."[6] Hanson Industries (U.S.) is controlled by a chief operating officer (COO), D. H. Clarke, and operates in the low technology industries of food products, food services, building products, furniture and furnishings, yarns and fabrics, consumer products (Endicott Johnson footwear)

TABLE 3 Hanson Trust income statement and balance sheet (1985–86) years ending September 30 (U. K. Pounds in millions)

	1986	*1985*
Income Statement		
Sales	4312.0	2674.0
Cost of goods sold[a]	3889.0	2387.0
Operating Profit	**423.0**	**287.0**
Other income	296.0	99.0
Interest expense	250.0	122.0
Income before Tax	**469.0**	**264.0**
Provisions for tax	104.0	60.0
Net Income	**365.0**	**204.0**
Balance Statement		
Assets		
Cash	1623.0	1131.0
Marketable securities	123.0	45.0
Receivables	754.0	297.0
Inventories	913.0	452.0
Other current assets	2138.0	137.0
Total Current Assets	**5551.0**	**2062.0**
Property and equipment[b]	1074.0	603.0
Advances to subsidiaries	40.0	187.0
Total Assets	**6665.0**	**2852.0**
Liabilities		
Notes payable	1187.0	433.0
Accounts payable	379.0	188.0
Accrued expenses	839.0	245.0
Other current liabilities	81.0	41.0
Total Current Liabilities	**2486.0**	**907.0**
Deferred charges	95.0	52.0
Long-term debt	1972.0	640.0
Other long-term liabilities	524.0	128.0
Total Liabilities	**5077.0**	**1727.0**
Net common stock[c]	814.0	500.0
Capital surplus	244.0	358.0
Retained earnings	517.0	254.0
Other	13.0	13.0
Shareholders' Equity	**1588.0**	**1125.0**
Total Liabilities and Net Worth	**6665.0**	**2852.0**

Notes: [a] Includes administration expense
[b] Net of depreciation
[c] Issued as 25 pence common stock (100 pence = one U. K. Pound
Source: Compact Disclosure, 1987.

and housewares, engineering, and lighting. The U.K. activities are controlled by A.G.L. Alexander (COO) and remain in equally basic and low technology industries: retailing, battery manufacture, yarns and threads, engineering, and building products. Following the acquisition of London Brick for 245 million pounds in 1984, and the subsequent forming of the Hanson Brick Company through the amalgamation of London Brick and its existing subsidiary, Butterley Building Materials, the company has become the largest brick manufacturer in the world.[7] Table 4 gives a breakdown of activities by operating divisions for both the United States and the United Kingdom. Divisions on both sides of the Atlantic include consumer goods, building products, industrial products, and food.

Each COO heads up a small team that exerts financial control over the subsidiary companies. This control includes developing the budgets, targets and plans necessary for translating strategy into action. Stock options are used to encourage managers to think as shareholders, and thus improve profitability and return on capital. Additionally, the decentralized system of control puts each manager in the position of being firmly responsible for, and in charge of, daily operations without interference from the corporate level. This "hands off" approach to operations also extends to other aspects of the acquired company's organization and culture. However, the minimal interference approach excludes all capital expenditures which do require a corporate blessing before they can be undertaken. Hanson Trust recently employed consultants to devise an incentive plan for corporate executives who bear the major responsibility for the company's continued growth.

HANSON'S TAKEOVER STRATEGY

In the early days, the company's acquisitions had the potential to generate profit without the need for substantial reinvestment. Takeovers were usually arranged for family tax reasons, or to ensure profitability or even survival. Where possible, original managements were kept intact after acquisition, but with Hanson Trust's increasing size, there has been a subtle but distinct change in Hanson Trust's policy for acquisition and post-acquisition control. Targets now include firms with untapped earnings potential, and tactics for takeover have become more aggressive as takeover target size has increased. Even though, where possible, managements are retained, profitability is instilled into the culture through managerial performance and appraisal criteria.

Today, the stated objectives of Hanson Trust are "to increase earnings per share and dividends annually . . ."[8]. The strategy for achieving these objectives is to locate the target, make the acquisition—often for cash—streamline its operations, and then let it run as a profit center by its own means but with an expectation of internal growth. A good example of this strategy in action is one of Hanson Trust's larger and more recent acquisitions; Berec plc (formerly Ever Ready).[9] After the takeover in 1981, Berec's name was changed to the British Ever Ready Company to reflect both its original name and the product for which the company was famous: batteries. In a very short time, Hanson turned Berec around from a position of declining profitability to one of strength through the simple expedient of improving efficiencies and divesting non-profitable activities. Corporate staff and research activities were reduced to

TABLE 4 Hanson Trust Divisional activities (1985–86)

	1986		*1985*	
	Sales	*Profit*	*Sales*	*Profit*
United States (In U.S. $ million[a])				
Consumer Products	761	60	615	45
Carisbrook's—specialty textile machinery, yarns, soft furnishings, apparel				
Blue Mountain Industries—twines, recreational products				
Crawford's—soft furnishings				
Franklyn—yarns				
Templon—yarns				
Native Textiles—knit lace and tricot fabrics				
Endicott Johnson—footwear				
Georgia Book—footwear				
Teters—artificial flowers				
Building Products	608	78	546	69
USI Lighting (Columbia Lighting, Keystone Lighting, Prescolite)—lighting fixtures and controls				
MW Manufacturers—windows, doors				
Brown Mouldings—wood moldings				
Superlite Builder Supply—concrete and masonry products				
Duke City Lumber—lumber				
Ames—tools				
Industrial[b]	917	150	325	43
A & S Building Systems—pre-engineered buildings				
Leon Plastics—parts for autos, cabinets, computers				
Axelson—office furniture				
Huron—custom machining, fabrication				
Office Group America—office furniture				
Allied Paper—office supplies, business forms				
Food	487	20	253	7
Durkee Industrial Foods—oils, frozen bakery products confectionery coatings				
Hygrade—hotdogs, hams, chicken products				
Ground Round—restaurants				
	2773	**308**	**1739**	**164**

continued

TABLE 4 continued

	1986		1985	
	Sales	*Profit*	*Sales*	*Profit*
United Kingdom				
Consumer Products[c]	2319	135	835	86
British Ever Ready—batteries				
Allders—department stores, duty free shops				
Building Products	344	89	323	82
Hanson Brick (London Brick, Butterly Bricks)—fletton and non-fletton bricks				
Crabtree Electrical—electrical products				
Industrial	323	39	316	37
Lindustries (Delanair, Smith Meters, Barbour Campbell)—auto heaters and air-conditioners, meters, yarns, threads				
Robert Morton—brewing equipment				
SLD—pumps, conveyor equipment				
St. Albans Rubber—wet suit sheeting				
Dufaylite—fire proofing				
Food[c]	437	33	—	—
Ross (Ross Young's, Ross Foods, Young's Seafoods)—frozen foods, frozen meals				
HP Foods—sauces, soups				
Lea & Perrins—sauces				
Marfleet—canned foods, healthfoods				
	3423	296	1474	205
	6196	604	3213	369
Businesses owned in 1985 and sold in 1986		—	630	35
Other income less central expense		—	—	(40)
		667	3843	364

Notes: [a] All information restated at 1.437 dollars to the pound

[b] Includes some income from SCM for 1986

[c] Includes some income from Imperial for 1986

Source: *Hanson Trust Annual Report,* 1984.

manageable proportions, and direction was refocussed on the core activity of dry cell batteries. This slumbering company was returned to being an efficient battery producer; in contrast to the 1981 pre-acquisition profits of 10 million pounds on sales of 241 million, the company produced 1985 profits of 31 million pounds on sales of 128 million. British Ever Ready still produces 70 percent of the zinc batteries sold in Britain. Its products are also sold in substantial numbers in third world countries.

Selling off non-profitable or marginal assets (activities) from its new acquisitions has been used to great effect by Hanson Trust. About half of the 95 million pounds spent on the acquisition of Berec was recovered from the sale of assets to Duracell and others. In 1981, when McDonough was bought for $180 million, some $50 million was recouped from the sale of its cement manufacturing activities. While these assets accounted for almost 28 percent of the total cost, they were responsible for only one tenth of the companies profits. In addition to releasing $50 million for further Hanson Trust acquisitions, McDonough's return on investment was instantly improved by 25 percent.

Central staffing at Hanson Trust is very small. Major responsibilities include financial control of the conglomerate and a constant search for attractive takeover candidates. Hanson Trust's affinity for leanness at the top has become a major factor in its impressive stretch of profitability.

SCM

SCM was a large industrial company that in 1985 attained just over $2 billion in sales with a net income of about $42 million, as indicated in Table 5. Activities and products included the production of chemicals, Glidden Paints, Smith Corona typewriters, Allied Paper, and Durkee Foods. The chemicals division which, among other things, produces pigments, led SCM with 1985 sales over $538 million and an operating income of nearly $74 million, as seen in Table 6. Coatings and resins operations were second with sales and operating profits of $687 million and $50 million, respectively. While paper products and foods turned in profits of only $23 million each on sales of $361 million and $422 million, they performed better than the typewriter division, which had losses of $47 million on $176 million sales.

Paul H. Elicker, chairman and chief executive officer, was in the midst of rationalizing and restructuring the company when Hanson Trust started its bid for takeover. Chairman Elicker's plan included the infusion of $365 million to improve technology in the chemical and coatings divisions. In 1985, a new adhesives plant was added, a new coatings plant was completed at Huron, Ohio, and work had started on the doubling in size of a coatings plant at Carrollton, Texas.

SCM had recently sold its popular Proctor-Silex division and acquired additional titanium oxide operations from Laporte Industries. Titanium oxide is used in the manufacture of paints, plastic packaging, vinyl siding, vinyl pipes, and numerous rubber products. Technology was upgraded in pigment plants at Ashtabula, Ohio, and Stallingborough in England. This, along with the appointment of D. George Harris, president of the chemicals division since 1981, emphasized chemicals as the new core of SCM's business.

TABLE 5 SCM income statement and balance sheet (1984–85) (years ending June 30, dollars in millions)

	1985	*1984*
Income Statement		
Sales	2175.4	1963.3
Cost of goods sold[a]	2084.0	1873.7
Operating Profit	**91.4**	**89.6**
Other income	2.5	4.5
Interest expense	39.8	29.2
Income before Tax	**54.1**	**64.9**
Provisions for tax	12.3	23.1
Net Income	**41.8**	**41.8**
Balance Sheet		
Assets		
Cash	15.5	10.6
Marketable securities	34.6	40.5
Receivables	339.4	313.2
Inventories	375.0	382.7
Other current assets	22.6	23.6
Total Current Assets	**787.1**	**770.6**
Property and equipment[b]	560.6	562.8
Deposits and other assets	42.8	29.0
Total Assets	**1390.5**	**1362.3**
Liabilities		
Notes payable	82.3	45.2
Accounts payable	130.1	127.0
Accrued expenses	138.9	159.9
Other current liabilities	23.0	22.0
Total current liabilities	**374.3**	**354.1**
Deferred charges	68.9	69.0
Long-term debt	335.7	260.4
Other long-term liabilities	21.7	22.8
Total liabilities	**800.6**	**706.3**
Net common stock[b]	52.2	59.5
Capital surplus	141.9	197.9
Retained earnings	403.9	406.6
Other	(8.1)	(8.0)
Shareholders' equity[c]	**589.9**	**656.0**
Total liabilities and net worth	**1390.5**	**1362.3**

Notes: [a] Includes administration expense.
[b] Net of depreciation.
[c] At June 30, 1985, major reported holdings were, Citibank, 9.6 per cent; Hanson Trust plc, 27.6 per cent; Hanson Holdings Netherlands BV, 19.8 per cent; Halcyon, 7.9 per cent; HSCM Industries, 5.6 per cent.

Source: Compact Disclosure, 1987.

TABLE 6 SCM divisional results (1982–85)[a] (in millions of dollars)

	1985	*1984*	*1983*	*1982*
Chemicals				
Net sales	538.9	360.7	250.6	248.6
Operating income	73.7	36.9	15.1	22.4
Return on sales (%)	13.7	10.2	6.0	9.0
Depreciation	N/A	15.0	16.8	10.7
Capital expenditure	N/A	49.7	9.6	29.8
Total Assets	**N/A**	**316.9**	**266.6**	**272.7**
Coatings and Resins				
Net sales	687.3	654.6	575.8	552.0
Operating income	49.9	51.4	36.7	32.2
Return on sales (%)	7.3	7.8	6.4	5.8
Depreciation	N/A	8.6	9.3	7.6
Capital expenditure	N/A	16.1	9.8	16.9
Total Assets	**N/A**	**348.9**	**330.0**	**311.2**
Paper Products				
Net sales	361.7	351.7	315.9	327.8
Operating income	23.1	21.0	15.3	33.3
Return on sales (%)	6.4	6.0	4.9	10.2
Depreciation	N/A	10.1	9.8	8.7
Capital expenditures	N/A	10.9	12.4	14.3
Total Assets	**N/A**	**167.5**	**155.1**	**146.7**
Foods				
Net sales	422.1	393.3	354.8	389.9
Operating income	23.0	17.2	28.6	18.2
Return on sales (%)	5.4	4.4	8.1	4.7
Depreciation	N/A	4.7	3.8	3.9
Capital expenditures	N/A	10.0	9.8	6.0
Total Assets	**N/A**	**160.3**	**145.9**	**148.1**
Typewriters				
Net sales	176.3	198.5	164.3	177.4
Operating loss	47.4	15.9	11.6	23.8
Return on sales (%)	—	—	—	—
Depreciation	N/A	6.6	6.2	6.6
Capital expenditures	N/A	6.8	6.4	7.5
Total Assets	**N/A**	**149.1**	**148.6**	**148.6**

Note: [a] Excludes income (expenditure) and profit (loss) from other unspecified sources.
Source: SCM *Annual Report*, 1985.

As part of the restructuring plan, SCM had recently bought the Baltimore Spice Company in an effort to reduce its food division's reliance upon edible oils. The company also started up a confectionery coating plant in Illinois. In 1985, Smith Corona was being restructured to concentrate on electric and electronic typewriters, as manual machines were being de-emphasized. Employment in the typewriter division was reduced by more than 2,000 people, and the asset base was in the process of being reduced from a high of $149 million to less than $100 million.

In actual (unadjusted) terms, SCM's revenues generally increased during the ten years, 1975–84 (see Table 7). In real (adjusted for inflation) terms, revenues declined. From the figures for 1982 and 1983, sales showed a slight dip, and gross profit followed that trend. However, the profit dip was disproportionately large. Over this period, sales fell some 6 percent from $1.76 billion in 1981 to $1.66 billion in 1983; gross income fell 48 percent from $73 million to $38 million. Net income fell 43 percent from $56.5 million to $24.5 million. The dip in earnings corresponds with Elicker's efforts at retrenchment and restructuring, which were aimed at turning SCM around from the worrying (adjusted) trend. Results for 1984 and 1985 show that the strategy was starting to have effect. Arguably, Paul Elicker's selected strategies were

TABLE 7 SCM review (1976–85) (in millions of dollars)

	1985	*1984*	*1983*	*1982*	*1981*	*1980*	*1979*	*1978*	*1977*	*1976*
Income										
Sales	2175	1963	1663	1703	1761	1745	1628	1406	1289	1244
Profit—before tax	54	65	38	35	73	83	79	47	69	56
Earnings per share[a]	N/A	4.05	2.45	2.88	5.44	5.17	4.59	3.75	3.70	3.04
Assets										
Tangible assets	561	563	406	436	404	350	327	305	279	251
Working capital	413	417	430	351	361	369	362	279	285	288
Total Assets	1391	1362	1113	1124	1078	1009	980	845	768	740
Financed by										
Shareholders equity	N/A	530	506	499	489	455	414	372	344	314
Long-term debt	336	260	277	240	238	229	245	190	201	210
Book value per share[a]	N/A	54.3	52.7	52.7	51.7	47.5	43.4	40.4	37.4	34.2
Other Data										
Number of employees[b]	N/A	20.9	24.5	25.5	27.6	27.4	28.6	27.4	25.5	27.1
U. S. index of inflation[c]	340	343	351	356	371	405	459	510	550	586

Notes: [a] In dollars, fully diluted

[b] In thousands

[c] Purchasing power of the dollar, in producer prices; 1967 = 1000

Source: SCM *Annual Report and Accounts*, 1984; Compact Disclosure, 1987; and, *Statistical Abstract of the United States*.

well conceived and appropriate for a multi-product company suffering from stagnation and decline. However, it can also be argued that the strategies were implemented too late to save the company from being a suitable target for Hanson Trust.

Hanson Trust has become a free-world expert at transforming mature and marginally profitable firms into cash generators, and SCM's chemicals operations constituted a substantial cash generator that would fit well in Hanson's cash-cow portfolio. Additionally, the incumbent management at SCM had displayed their ability to concentrate on profitability improvement, thus compounding the company's attractiveness by offering a fit with Hanson's preference for retaining existing management.

THE BATTLE FOR SCM

On August 22, 1985, Hanson Trust announced a $755 million tender offer for any or all shares of SCM. Although the offer was made at the $60 per share level for the 12 million plus shares that were outstanding, trading was halted on the first day at $58 and was not reopened. Analysts predicted a $3 to $4 billion sales potential for SCM in the coming years and valued the opening offer as too low.[10]

Two days later, the SCM board unanimously agreed to ask shareholders to reject the $60 per share offer. It was stated that the takeover offer came as a surprise to Chairman Elicker who made the not unexpected comment, "We feel the shareholder has been served well by this management and can continue to be served well. . . .".[11] Trading was resumed, and the company's shares closed at $64.125 amid expectations of an increased offer. At this stage, there were no public considerations of defense strategies using tactics like leveraged buy-outs, but it was suggested by SCM's managers that a better offer may be forthcoming for its shareholders.[12]

Hanson Trust's cash offer could have been covered by its very substantial cash reserves, but, instead, Hanson Trust chose debt as a means of financing the purchase. Favorable borrowing rates in the United States made the obtaining of loans an attractive proposition. In this way, the company remained flexible enough to consider other takeovers.

During the first frantic days of the aggressive takeover challenge, Merrill Lynch was called in to act as SCM's financial advisor. It was also rumored that Merrill Lynch may become a possible partner in a leveraged buy-out. On August 25, SCM announced that "golden parachutes" had been previously voted into effect. These golden parachutes would richly compensate any existing SCM executive who left the company at any date up to two years after an outside party had acquired 20 percent or more of the company's stock. This defensive tactic has been used successfully in the past by other companies to discourage attempted acquisitions.

In the three days that had elapsed since Hanson Trust announced its $755 million bid, SCM had responded vigorously and clearly signalled its intent to fight the takeover attempt. The stage had been set for a corporate battle. On the New York Stock Exchange, SCM shares closed at $67.875 amid speculation of competing bids from other interested firms.

On August 29, SCM and its financial consultant Merrill Lynch announced plans to initiate a $70 per share ($868 million) leveraged buy-out of SCM. SCM had been negotiating with the bankers Kolberg Kravis and Merrill Lynch. A retort to the rumored leveraged buy-out was forthcoming from Hanson Trust, and on September 4, they raised their offer to $72 per share. Experts did not expect the bidding to go much higher and conceded that SCM had achieved its goal of increasing the common stock price.[13]

It took one week for SCM's white knight, Merrill Lynch, to consider a response to the increased offer made by Hanson Trust, but, on September 11, Merrill Lynch came forward with a $74 per share, two-thirds leveraged buy-out offer. SCM's management instantly accepted. Normally, it might be expected that this would have signalled the end of the contest, but Hanson Trust's actions made it abundantly clear that the battle was not over. In a matter of hours, they retracted their $72 bid and acquired approximately 25 percent of SCM's common stock from large institutional investors for the price of $73.50. This move entailed wide ranging legal implications.

SCM charged that in purchasing the stock on the market, Hanson Trust took part in an illegal tender offer, thus violating federal law. A temporary restraining order was won against Hanson Trust prohibiting any further purchases of SCM shares and, as security, the 3.1 million shares that had been acquired were held in escrow. Hanson Trust denied that it had taken this action to acquire one third of SCM's common stock in order to block the two thirds leveraged buy-out planned by Merrill Lynch.[14] It was disclosed that the leveraged buy-out planned by SCM and Merrill Lynch was, in fact, a "poison pill" and contained a "crown jewel lock up" option. Upon the accumulation of one-third of SCM shares by a hostile suitor, certain divisions of SCM would immediately be sold to Merrill Lynch at a substantial discount. Since these divisions constituted the most valuable operations of SCM, the action would make SCM virtually worthless to Hanson Trust as a subsidiary.

On October 2, 1985, the U.S. Federal District Court ruled in favor of Hanson Trust in its September 11 buy-up of SCM stock. Interpreting the Williams Act, which regulates takeovers, judges ruled that the purchases were legal because they were made from a few sophisticated investors and arbitragers, not the general market.[15] Since they were sophisticated investors, it had to be assumed that they were aware of the implications of their actions and had not been duped by Hanson.

The next day, upon news of the ruling, Merrill Lynch began to prepare to exercise the SCM lock-up option, but, before any action could be taken, it had to be ascertained whether Hanson Trust had actually acquired one-third of SCM's stock. This new legal controversy centered around the level of diluted or undiluted SCM stock holdings. Hanson Trust filed a suit claiming that SCM and Merrill Lynch unlawfully conspired to obtain and exercise the previously described lock-up option. One source close to the British conglomerate commented upon the filing, "the gloves are off".[16] In other words, the legal action was taken as a sign that Hanson Trust intended to fight to the bitter end for SCM.

On October 9, Hanson Trust made yet another new offer for SCM stock. The price now stood at $75. The bid was made in response to Merrill Lynch's move to exercise the $74 lock-up option after the courts ruled that Hanson Trust did hold one-third of SCM's common stock. Two days later on October 11, in the face of the latest Hanson Trust bid, SCM offered $74 per share for two thirds of its outstanding stock. At this time, some 85 percent of SCM's common stock was outstanding. The move was interpreted as one that was designed to assure SCM shareholders that they would receive at least $74 dollars per share in the event that the lock-up option was exercised.[17] On the stock exchange, trading closed at $72.50, with Wall Street expecting one of the suitors to prevail. Major stockholders such as PaineWebber, who held about 5 percent of SCM's stock, felt that the $75 per share cash offer was better than the Merrill Lynch bid. William Kaye, head of PaineWebber's takeover trading section commented, "I can't understand why we, as shareholders, aren't being allowed to choose what is obviously a better offer."[18] Not only was the Hanson Trust bid more generous in terms of the amount being offered, but it could also be considered superior in content. Hanson Trust was offering $75 cash for any or all of the stock. SCM was offering $74 made up of $10 cash and $64 in preferred stock for two thirds of common stock, while Merrill Lynch's offer, for any or all stock, was comprised of $59.20 cash and $14.80 worth of "junk bonds".

THE COURTS' RULINGS

Two court rulings with far reaching implications were handed down in the Hanson Trust-SCM battle. Both involved tactics used to foil takeovers, and they will influence future attempts at acquisition and defense. The first court ruling favored Hanson Trust in its September 11 stock buy up. When Merrill Lynch increased its bid for SCM shares to $74, Hanson Trust immediately bought a large number of SCM shares on the open market. SCM claimed that this action constituted an illegal tender offer and brought suit. The Williams Act, which regulates takeovers, was interpreted to say that the action was legal because the purchase of the shares was from "sophisticated investors," not the general market. The opinion stated in the case was that the Williams Act was in use to protect investors without full information. The parties from which Hanson Trust purchased the shares were ruled to be sophisticated and therefore in full knowledge. Substantial discussion has been generated as to how investors may be identified as being sophisticated. This decision may influence other acquisitive conglomerates to take similar action in the face of stern takeover defenses. Many stock purchase scenarios might be engineered by takeover specialists and sophisticated investors to utilize the benefits of this opinion. Initially, it was felt most white knights would, from here on, require the presence of lock-up options in order to secure their positions in the event of a move such as that made by Hanson Trust.

The second decision handed down in the Hanson Trust-SCM battle provided a major signal regarding the use of lock-up options. In December 1985, the New York Federal District Court originally ruled that the Merrill Lynch-SCM lock-up option was valid. However, upon appeal in January 1986, that ruling was overturned. In essence, the opinion of the court was that SCM and Merrill Lynch illegally conspired to obtain and exercise the crown jewel lock-up option. The use of this tactic was therefore ruled illegal. As a result of Merrill Lynch's $74 offer, Hanson made a $75 per share offer pending a court decision in their favor. Once the ruling to disallow lock-up options was handed down, the door opened for SCM shareholders to tender their shares to Hanson Trust.

The opinion on lock-up options is expected to have some long-range effects on current takeover strategies. First of all, as would be expected, the use of lock-up options will fall substantially as a result of their minimized defensive power. Ripple effects will be seen in the decreased use of white knights. Along with the ruling on stock purchase from sophisticated investors, this decision limits the security a white knight can attain in a hostile situation. A white knight may now have stock bought out from under its leveraged buy-out offer (given certain circumstances) as well as lose the security given to it in constructing a lock-up. Although the actual impact of these judgments remain to be seen, their effects are sure to be substantial.

THE FINAL DAYS

On January 8, 1986, a Federal District Appeals Court ruled in favor of Hanson Trust concerning the use of the Merrill Lynch-SCM lock-up option. SCM's request for further appeal was denied since no offer larger than Hanson's $75 per share was made. The $930 million (cash) takeover was completed by Friday, January 10, when SCM shareholders met the tender offer deadline.

Managements of both companies, acquirer and acquired, arranged for the takeover to be orderly and for SCM to be admitted as a subsidiary of Hanson Industries, Inc., the American half of Hanson Trust. The agreement formally ended one of 1985's most bitter takeover battles. Paul Elicker, SCM's chairman, and D. George Harris, president of the chemicals division, were retained in their existing positions, and they pledged their efforts to the Hanson Trust shareholders.

. . . AND AFTER

In November 1986, ten months after the acquisition, Hanson recouped over three-fourths of the $930 million paid for SCM. Glidden Paints was sold to Imperial Chemical Industries plc[19] for $580 million, and Durkee Foods was sold to Reckitt and Colman plc[20] for $140 million. This left Hanson Industries with the highly profitable chemicals division of SCM and the restructured typewriter division which, by the end of 1986, had been returned to profitability.

In 1987, Sir Gordon White closed a deal to acquire Kaiser Cement for $200 million. He also announced a $1.8 billion deal to acquire Kidde, a manufacturer of various items that include Farberware kitchen utensils, fire extinguishers, office supplies, leather seating, Rexair home cleaners, Jacuzzi Whirlpool Baths, and, among other things, Progress Lighting fixtures. Sales in 1986 for Kidde were $2.4 billion, and operating profits amounted to nearly $160 million. This move doubles Hanson Industries' employment roster to about 70,000 people.

As 1987 heads rapidly towards 1988, the questions must be asked: Where does Hanson Trust go from here? Can it sustain its growth? And, will its "hands off" approach to structural and organizational culture issues continue to be successful with future acquisitions. There is no evidence to suggest that the company intends to change its strategy. In fact, the opposite is the more likely scenario. *Fortune* reports that Hanson Trust's "war-chest" currently stands at $6 billion, second only to Ford's at $9 billion, and that Sir Gordon White is now searching for an acquisition large enough to double Hanson Trust's revenues.[21]

A second rhetorical question concerns whether the onslaught of foreign acquisitions will continue. Part of the answer is apparent in the recent trend for some U.S. companies to get "leaner and meaner."[22] Smaller, efficient, and vibrant companies like Apple, Cray Research, and Marion Laboratories lead the way and epitomize "lean and mean" in the select group of firms that are competitive high-performers. Some of the larger, more established companies like Dow Chemical, Ford, and Westinghouse Electric also fall into this category. But, paradoxically, while U.S. output per hour worked has increased more than 6 percent since 1980, the international competitiveness of U.S. companies (measured in terms of worldwide market share) has declined by the same amount. Whether the re-awakening philosophies of dynamism, efficiency and innovation in business will reach the majority of American companies and stem the tide of foreign takeovers remains to be seen.

Perhaps the final word should go to Sir Gordon White. The following is taken from an article in *Time* in which Sir Gordon was interviewed:

> . . . . .new managers like Sir Gordon White are giving their American troops a pep talk. Says he: "In the U.S., you haven't got the drive to export. It's often very difficult to convince managers in companies we've bought that they should flog [sell] their products in Britain. They say 'Why go to all of that trouble when I can sell in the U.S.?' "
>
> White would be only too happy to discover more American corporations that need to be taken over and set straight. . . . . . With all those tempting treasure chests of undervalued wealth in view, it is small wonder that Sir Gordon and his many foreign imitators still want to buy, buy, buy.[23]

ENDNOTES

1. For more discussion on direct foreign investment in the United States, see *Time,* 14 September, 1987, 52–62.
2. plc = public limited company.
3. Due to currency exchange regulations, $3000 was the maximum sum that could be transferred from the United Kingdom for foreign investment. This rule no longer applies.
4. *Fortune,* September 28, 1987, carries an article on the top twelve corporate raiders in which Sir Gordon White, along with Sir James Goldsmith and Carl Icahn, receives the highest (most aggressive) rating on a "shark fin" rating scale of one fin to four fins.
5. Hanson Trust *Annual Report* and Accounts, 1984.
6. Hoare Gosset Limited (Analysts), October 1986.
7. Hanson Trust *Annual Report* and Accounts, 1984.
8. Hanson Trust *Annual Report* and Accounts, 1986.
9. Not related to Ever Ready batteries, United States of America.
10. *New York Times,* 22 August, 1985.
11. *Wall Street Journal,* 26 August, 1985.
12. Ibid, 23 August, 1985.
13. Ibid, 4 September, 1985.
14. Ibid, 3 September, 1985.
15. Ibid, 2 October, 1985.
16. Ibid, 10 October 1985.
17. Ibid, 11 October 1985.
18. Ibid, 18 October 1985.
19. Imperial Chemical Industries (ICI) is a $15+ billion company with about 350 subsidiaries, worldwide. ICI produces general, specialty, agricultural and petrochemicals, plus pharmaceuticals, fibers, explosives, fertilizers, colors, and paints.

20. Recritt and Colman (R&C), a British foods, toiletries and household products company, firmly established itself in U.S. and European markets in early 1985 with the purchase of Airwick for 500 million Swiss francs ($215 million) from Ciba Geigy. The purchase of Durkee Foods is simply an extension of R&C's push for internationalization.

21. *Fortune,* 28 September, 1987, 54.

22. *Business Week,* 5 October 1987, 78–88.

23. *Time,* 14 September, 1984, 62.

The Limited, Inc.—1987

JILL AUSTIN
Middle Tennessee State University
FRED DAVID
Auburn University

"My vision of the business is always to have a large one. When I had two stores, ten stores seemed like a lot. I like to believe that trees can grow to the sky. None have yet, but that doesn't mean it's impossible." Leslie Wexner, chairman of The Limited, seems almost mystic about the continuing growth of his Limited stores. In the last five years, The Limited, Inc. has more than tripled in size to almost 2,700 stores. Net sales increased 32 percent in 1986 to $3.1 billion, and net income rose 57 percent to $227.8 million.

Leslie Wexner's merchandising strategy has made The Limited successful. Instead of offering a wide variety of types of clothing, the stores offer a limited assortment of women's "sportswear" in large quantities and a variety of colors. In 1982 the company acquired Lane Bryant (the largest retailer of women's special size clothing), Roaman's (a women's special size clothing store and catalog), and Victoria's Secret (a lingerie store). Pic-A-Dilly stores were purchased in 1984, and Lerner Stores and Henri Bendel were acquired in 1985. The Limited, Inc., headquartered in Columbus, Ohio, has grown to become the largest women's apparel specialty store and mail order retailer in the United States. The company's strategy formulation and implementation efforts are led by Leslie Wexner, a bachelor who maintains residences in four U.S. cities. Owning 30 percent of The Limited's stock, Wexner's personal fortune of about $2.7 billion makes him one of America's dozen richest people.

HISTORY

In 1963, Leslie Wexner borrowed $10,000 from an aunt and a bank to open The Limited's first store. During its first year in operation, this store achieved sales of $157,000. Wexner believed that providing quality fashionable sportswear at medium prices would lead to success, so he opened other Limited stores. By the late 1970s, The Limited began a twofold strategy of market development and product development. As shown in Exhibit 1, new stores were opened and acquired to appeal to women of different ages, different sizes, and different budget limits.

The Carter Hawley Hale Takeover Attempt

Probably the greatest disappointment to Leslie Wexner in the 23-year history of The Limited is the failed takeover attempt of Carter Hawley Hale Stores, Inc. On April 4, 1984, Leslie Wexner submitted an offer to buy Carter Hawley Hale for $1.1 billion. The offer was to purchase 20,300,000 shares of Carter Hawley Hale stock at $30 per share. At the time of the offer, Carter Hawley Hale consisted of 124 department

EXHIBIT 1 The Limited's acquisitions 1980–1986

	Date Started	*Date Acquired*	*Number of Stores Fiscal Year Ending* 1982	1983	1984	1985	1986
Retail Divisions							
Limited	1963		489	521	562	597	652
Limited Express	1980		30	70	133	218	286
Lane Bryant		1982	222	245	322	401	579
Victoria's Secret		1982	6	16	46	93	167
Sizes Unlimited (consolidated with Pic-A-Dilly)		1982	78	85	349	293	247
Roamans (Merged into Sizes Unlimited)		1982					
Pic-A-Dilly (Merged into Sizes Unlimited)		1984					
Lerner		1985				750	750
Henri Bendel		1985				1	1
Totals			**825**	**937**	**1,412**	**2,353**	**2,682**
Mail Order Divisions							
Brylane		1982					
Lane Bryant							
Roaman's							
Lerner Woman							
Sue Brett							
Lerner Sport							
Tall Collection							
Victoria's Secret		1982					
Limited	1987						

EXHIBIT 2 Financial information for Carter Hawley Hale (in millions of dollars per share amounts)

	1983	*1984*	*1985*	*1986*
Gross revenue	3632.7	3724.3	3977.9	4089.9
Net income	56.6	27.1	50.6	66.7
Long-term debt	521.5	548.7	697.6	707.5
Net worth	783.5	648.1	659.4	624.2
Earnings per share	1.61	—	1.05	1.81

stores, 117 specialty stores, and 841 bookstores. As of January 1987, Carter Hawley Hale operated 115 department stores and 185 specialty stores. Some of the store names associated with Carter Hawley Hale include: Broadway, Thalhimer Brothers, Neiman-Marcus, Bergdorf Goodman, and Contempo Casuals. Selected financial data for Carter Hawley Hale is shown in Exhibit 2.

The Limited started accumulating Carter Hawley Hale stock before the takeover attempt and owned about 700,000 shares at the time of its offer. The Limited had plans to borrow $609 million to finance the buy-out. Carter Hawley Hale filed suit in federal court to stop The Limited's takeover attempt, claiming that The Limited failed to disclose information about potential antitrust problems. General Cinema Corporation, a large theater and soft-drink company, attempted to stop The Limited's takeover by acquiring $300 million of Carter Hawley Hale preferred stock. The stock, convertible to common stock in one year, allowed General Cinema to obtain substantial voting rights in Carter Hawley Hale. In addition, Carter Hawley Hale began buying some of its own stock to counteract The Limited's takeover plans. During six trading days, Carter Hawley Hale acquired 17.9 million of its own shares at an average price of $26.

The Securities and Exchange Commission ruled that the Carter Hawley Hale purchase of its own stock was a "tender offer" of its own and should have been registered with the SEC. The SEC filed a suit in federal court to force Carter Hawley Hale to distribute enough shares to stockholders to bring the total number of shares outstanding to the level before the company began purchasing its own stock. These legal developments stalled Wexner's takeover attempt. All litigation in connection with The Limited's offer to purchase shares of Carter Hawley Hale stock was dismissed by the parties, but Leslie Wexner is still waiting and even now would like to take over Carter Hawley Hale.

The Year 1986

The year 1986 was a good one for The Limited. Sales increased to $3.1 billion, and income increased to $227.8 million. Four new support divisions were created: Limited Store Planning, Limited Real Estate, Limited Distribution Services, and Limited Credit Services. Four hundred thirty-one new stores were opened during the year.

Ground was broken for a $70 million addition to the Columbus Distribution Complex (already the largest of its kind in the world). Long-term debt was decreased from $390 million to about $70 million. Plans are underway to combine several Limited stores into a "one-stop department store" type environment, and a new location was selected on Madison Avenue in New York for the Henri Bendel store.

CURRENT BUSINESS STRUCTURE (1987)

The Limited, Inc. is presently organized into 13 major operating divisions that include seven different store types, one mail order division, and five support operations. All stores are wholly company owned and managed. The thirteen divisions are described briefly here:

1. *Limited Stores*—This is the flagship division of the organization. Originally, merchandise in these stores was targeted at women between the ages of 16 and 25. Limited Stores have now shifted their orientation to women in the 25 to 44 age group. These stores focus on the sale of medium-priced fashion clothing consisting of skirts, blouses, sweaters, pants, coats, suits, dresses, and accessories. The fastest growing brands in America are sold here. Outback Red, Moods by Krizia, Venezia, and Forenza are private label brands made especially for The Limited through Mast Industries. Most of the 652 Limited stores are located in regional shopping centers or malls across the United States.
2. *Limited Express*—Wexner began to experiment with the Limited Express concept as an expansion possibility. Limited Express is a "Neon-lit high tech" store that sells a unique assortment of popular-priced sportswear. These fashions are the latest in American and international styles. Limited Express stores are designed to appeal to women between the ages of 15 and 25. The 286 Limited Express stores in operation are located mostly in shopping malls. An average Limited Express store has 2,600 square feet, compared to the typical Limited store which averages 4,000 square feet.
3. *Lerner*—The Lerner stores sell clothing of current styles at budget prices. The Limited purchased the 800-store Lerner chain in 1985 for $297 million. The average size of these stores is 6,400 square feet. Presently, there are 750 Lerner stores in operation in malls and shopping centers across the United States.
4. *Victoria's Secret*—These stores specialize in the sale of European and American designer lingerie. The store sells high quality lingerie with prices ranging from $5 to $2,000. This division focuses on women aged 25 to 45, but gifts purchased by men account for a significant portion of the total sales. The stores are decorated as Victorian parlors. There are 167 Victoria's Secret stores, most of which are located in southern California. On the average, these stores contain 1,700 square feet. Victoria's Secret also publishes a mail order catalog four times per year.
5. *Lane Bryant*—Lane Bryant had been in operation for 80 years and was actually larger than The Limited at the time of purchase. Lane Bryant's market is primarily women between 30 and 50 years of age. The store specializes in

the sale of medium-priced clothing for the "special-sized woman" (sizes 14 and up). The merchandise assortment includes blouses, sweaters, skirts, pants, coats, suits, dresses, intimate apparel, and accessories. Nearly all Lane Bryant stores were originally located in regional shopping centers, but Wexner has targeted almost 500 shopping malls that presently have Limited Stores to be future bases for Lane Bryant outlets. Since about 40 percent of American women are size 14 or larger, Wexner plans to open 200 new Lane Bryant stores in 1987. That means the company will be hiring two regional managers, 32 district managers, 200 store managers, 400 lower-level supervisors, and thousands of sales clerks. Presently, there are 579 Lane Bryant stores, each containing about 4,000 square feet of merchandising space.

6. *Sizes Unlimited*—These stores sell bargain-priced, first-quality sportswear, dresses, and accessories beginning at size 14. The 240-store Pic-A-Dilly chain (purchased in 1985) and Roaman's (purchased in 1982) were merged into "Sizes Unlimited". There are presently 247 Sizes Unlimited stores in major U.S. markets. A typical Sizes Unlimited store contains 3,500 square feet of selling space and is located in a "smaller" shopping center.
7. *Brylane*—This division is the nation's largest catalog retailer. Brylane catalogs sell women's "special-sized" apparel and shoes. Catalogs include: Lane Bryant, Lerner Sport, Lerner Woman, Roaman's, and Tall Collection. This division of the Limited maintains a distribution center in Indianapolis, Indiana, where all mail orders are shipped and received.
8. *Henri Bendel*—In 1985, The Limited purchased this upscale, fashion store. The store offers the best in clothing and accessories from international designers. Prices are designed for the "fashion conscious," not the "budget conscious" shopper. The Henri Bendel store is located in New York City. Plans are underway to open stores in the top 40 markets in the United States. This is the only "high priced" store owned by The Limited.
9. *Mast Industries*—The business of this division is to arrange for the manufacture and import of women's clothing from around the world, and to wholesale this merchandise to The Limited's stores and other companies. Mast specializes in high quality products that are produced at low costs. Much of the merchandise imported by Mast is marked with one of The Limited's own labels: Forenza, Outback Red, Moods by Krizia, Venezia, or Hunter's Run. Leslie Wexner believes that having their own brands allows The Limited to keep merchandise inventory current and unique. In 1986, Mast purchased inventory from about 6,000 suppliers and factories around the world. Presently, the company is trying to locate more domestic suppliers and would like to pursue more joint manufacturing ventures. Mast has a joint venture agreement with Daewoo, a South Korean company, to open a wool sweater factory in Costa Rica.
10. *Distribution Services*—The Limited's distribution center is in Columbus, Ohio. The Center is now 1.5 million square feet and has a capacity to handle 5,000 retail stores. More than 60 percent of the U.S. population is located within a 500-mile radius of Columbus, so Wexner feels this is an ideal location for a distribution center. Another advantage of the Columbus location is

its nearness to New York City, the port where incoming merchandise produced in foreign countries is received by Mast Industries. All merchandise arriving in New York is shipped directly to the distribution center for allocation among The Limited's stores. A computerized distribution system aids distributors in their selections for each store's inventory. This system allows The Limited to monitor inventory levels, the merchandise mix, and the sales patterns at each store so that appropriate adjustments can be made as needed.

11. *Limited Store Planning*—This division designs store layout and develops merchandising techniques for all of The Limited's retail divisions.
12. *Limited Real Estate*—This Limited division handles store leases for the seven store divisions.
13. *Limited Credit Services*—The credit division handles consumer credit for both the retail and mail order divisions.

COMPETITION

The retail sale of women's clothing is a very competitive business. Competitors of The Limited include nationally, regionally, and locally owned department stores, specialty stores, and mail order catalog businesses. Some of The Limited's major competitors are: Casual Corner, Petrie Stores, Marshall Fields, Carsons Pirie Scott, May Department Stores, Boston Stores, Gimbels, Dayton Hudson Stores, Carter Hawley Hale Stores, Brooks Fashion Stores, Peck and Peck, The Body Shop, Talbots, Lots to Love, Castner Knott, McRae's, Red Rooster, Sears, and J.C. Penney. A discussion of two of The Limited's major competitors follows.

Casual Corner (U.S. Shoe)

In 1987, U.S. Shoe Corporation operated approximately 600 Casual Corner Stores. Casual Corner attempts to appeal to fashion-conscious working women as do The Limited Stores. Casual Corner stores are usually located in major shopping centers and malls. U.S. Shoe operates other clothing specialty stores that compete with subsidiaries of The Limited. For example, Ups'n Downs is designed for the 14- to 21-year-old woman, much like The Limited Express. U.S. Shoe also sells intimate apparel through mail order in their "Intimique" catalog. Exhibit 3 gives financial information for the 1,367-store chain (including Casual Corner, Ups'n Downs, J. Riggins, Lens Crafters, and shoe brands such as Pappagallo, Red Cross, and Joyce). Specialty retailing accounts for approximately 55 percent of sales for U.S. Shoe.

Petrie Stores Corporation

Petrie Stores sells women's clothing for teens, juniors, young misses, and "special sized" women. Some of the store names for the 1,350 Petrie store chain include: Petrie's, Marianne, Stuarts, David's, Hartfields, Three Sisters, and Plus. This corporation also owns approximately 25 percent of Toys "R" Us, Inc. More than 90 percent of the

EXHIBIT 3 Financial information for U. S. Shoe Corporation (in millions of dollars except per share amount)

	1983	*1984*	*1985*	*1986*
Gross revenue	1507.8	1717.4	1920.2	2003.3
Net income	75.2	53.4	71.8	25.5
Long-term debt	49.6	45.6	92.2	143.5
Net worth	390.2	427.8	477.3	488.8
Earnings per share	1.71	1.21	1.62	.57

company stores are located in shopping centers and malls. Selected financial information for Petrie Stores is shown in Exhibit 4.

Department Stores

Competition from department stores is increasing. J.C. Penney's now sells designer brands. Sears also is becoming more competitive, especially with the Cheryl Tiegs Collection. Both of these stores operate major mail order businesses. Competition for The Limited, Inc. is practically every department store that sells women's fashions in the United States, and especially those stores located in shopping malls.

FINANCIAL CONDITION

The Limited's income statements and balance sheets for four years ending January 1987 are provided in Exhibit 5 and Exhibit 6, respectively. These statements reveal increasing levels for sales, income, assets, and shareholders' equity. A consolidated statement of The Limited's shareholders' equity is given in Exhibit 7. The Limited's rapid growth in number of stores during the last five years is evidenced in Exhibit 8.

EXHIBIT 4 Financial information for Petrie Stores Incorporated (in millions of dollars except per share amount)

	1983	*1984*	*1985*	*1986*
Gross revenue	625.6	951.1	1160.8	1198.4
Net income	47.6	54.6	77.9	73.7
Long-term debt	55.1	317.3	475.8	475.6
Net worth	297.6	322.7	476.7	517.8
Earnings per share	1.15	1.30	1.76	1.50

EXHIBIT 5 Income statements for The Limited, Inc. (in millions of dollars except per share amounts)

	1983	*1984*	*1985*	*1986*
Net sales	1085.9	1343.1	2387.1	3142.7
Cost of goods, sold, occupancy and buying costs	758.3	938.8	1668.3	2180.9
Gross income	327.6	404.3	718.8	961.8
General, administrative, and store operating expenses	192.2	231.2	442.6	523.6
Operating income	135.4	173.1	276.2	438.2
Interest expense	(10.2)	(16.7)	(41.2)	(45.9)
Other income, net	9.8	1.1	4.3	2.5
Income before income taxes	134.9	157.5	239.3	394.8
Provision for income taxes	64.0	65.0	94.0	167.0
Net Income	**70.9**	**92.5**	**145.3**	**227.8**
Net Income Per Share	**.59**	**.51**	**.80**	**1.21**

Source: The Limited, Inc. 1986 and 1985 *Annual Reports*.

FUTURE OUTLOOK

According to Leslie Wexner, the main desire of The Limited, Inc. is to satisfy customer needs. He feels that company operations must be changed as customer needs change. Wexner believes that The Limited should pursue several strategies:

1. A new concept in Limited stores is being tested. The Limited, Limited Express, and Victoria's Secret have been combined into one store that will allow one-stop "department store-like" shopping.
2. Wexner is interested in department store sales. He believes most department stores are "dinosaurs," but since they sell about 40 percent of women's clothing, he would like to determine how to make the concept successful for The Limited.
3. Wexner plans to find more domestic suppliers for the apparel sold by The Limited, mainly because of foreign trade legislation.
4. The company plans to begin selling menswear. About 15 mens' stores will be opened in 1987 in the company's Limited Express division. These men's stores will sell sportswear, including slacks, shirts, and sweaters. Mr. Wexner says men want the same European style and quality in clothes that The Limited offers for women. He expects menswear to one day comprise 30 percent to 40 percent of sales at the Limited Express division.

EXHIBIT 6 Balance sheet for The Limited, Inc. (in thousands of dollars)

	Feb. 1984	*Feb. 1985*	*Feb. 1986*	*Feb. 1987*
Assets				
Current assets				
Cash and equivalents	1,282	7,494	12,948	3,256
Accounts receivable	44,201	45,912	62,077	72,878
Inventories	115,608	190,014	320,305	361,489
Prepayments and other	8,339	13,056	20,994	31,608
Total Current Assets	**169,430**	**256,476**	**416,324**	**469,231**
Property and equipment	261,815	267,528	648,314	734,727
Investment in and advances to finance subsidiaries	13,730	23,672	74,795	105,503
Other assets	13,894	19,476	72,077	67,628
Total Assets	**377,396**	**567,152**	**1,211,510**	**1,377,089**
Liabilities and Shareholders' Equity				
Current liabilities				
Accounts payable	65,134	103,010	184,368	169,112
Accrued expenses	42,224	47,719	103,381	131,829
Income taxes payable	7,801	9,378	9,253	33,963
Deferred income taxes	14,140	29,109	56,416	—
Total Current Liabilities	**129,299**	**189,216**	**353,418**	**334,904**
Senior long-term debt	21,763	60,139	213,744	70,420
Subordinated convertible debt	—	—	175,000	—
Deferred income taxes	33,758	42,394	44,506	169,414
Other long-term liabilities	—	—	20,767	20,809
Shareholder's equity				
Common stock	29,590	29,807	59,917	94,398
Paid-in capital	18,088	22,466	24,695	199,424
Retained earnings	144,898	223,130	319,463	487,720
Total Shareholders' Equity	**192,576**	**275,403**	**404,075**	**781,542**
Total Liabilities and Shareholders' Equity	**377,396**	**567,152**	**1,211,510**	**1,377,089**

Source: The Limited, Inc. 1983–1986 *Annual Reports.*

5. Plans are being made to quadruple the size of some Limited stores. The company expects to open 10 "supersized" stores (15,000 to 20,000 square feet) in 1987.

Other future strategies are being considered such as expanding catalog sales, entering foreign markets, expanding the number of domestic stores, and acquiring other companies such as Carter Hawley Hale. Perhaps a market penetration strategy of extensive advertising is needed. Currently The Limited does no advertising, relying instead on walk-in traffic in malls. The Limited does not have unlimited resources, of

EXHIBIT 7 Consolidated statement of shareholders' equity (in thousands of dollars)

	Common Stock			
Balance	*Number of Shares Outstanding*	*Par Value*	*Paid-in Capital*	*Retained Earnings*
Jan. 28, 1984	59,180	$24,590	$ 18,088	$144,898
Feb. 2, 1985	59,614	29,807	22,466	233,130
Feb. 1, 1986	119,834	59,917	24,695	319,463
Jan. 31, 1987	188,796	94,398	199,424	487,720

Source: The Limited, Inc., 1986 *Annual Report.*

EXHIBIT 8 Growth in stores for The Limited, Inc.

Fiscal Year	*Stores at Beginning of Year*	*Stores Acquired During Year*	*Stores Opened During Year*	*Stores Closed During Year*	*Stores at End of Year*
1982	430	343	52	—	825
1983	825	—	116	4	937
1984	937	240	240	5	1,412
1985	1,412	799	267	125	2,353
1986	2,353	—	431	102	2,682

Source: The Limited, Inc., Form 10–K, January 31, 1987, p. 2.

course. The company cannot pursue all of the strategic alternatives that could benefit the firm, so major strategic decisions must be made.

If Wexner can develop a plan to continue improving The Limited's position in the women's specialty clothing industry, perhaps he is correct in saying that "trees really do grow to the sky." However, critics warn that The Limited will soon face several serious problems that include: (1) investor disenchantment because of Wexner's risk-taking attitude, (2) difficulty finding reliable foreign suppliers, (3) manufacturing import problems caused by protectionist trade laws, (4) difficulty finding qualified managers for new positions, (5) a saturation of Limited stores in U.S. malls, and (6) financial instability. A recent article in *Forbes* is concluded as follows:

> Leslie Wexner is a promotional and merchandising genius. He has found that women will rush to buy clothes bearing a phony Italian or psuedo-Australian label—even though the designs are knockoffs and the articles made in Taiwan or Hong Kong—and that the secret to fashion merchandising is speed of delivery. These are smart insights, but they are neither profound nor capable of endless application. Leslie Wexner—and investors—ought to recall the story of Galileo, who went blind because he stared too long at the stars.[1]

Leslie Wexner currently ponders some other issues of concern:

1. What are the advantages and disadvantages of The Limited, Inc. acquiring Carter Hawley Hale? Is the $1.1 billion offered in 1984 still reasonable?
2. Is The Limited, Inc. expanding too rapidly? Is the company becoming too diversified?
3. How could The Limited, Inc. compete more effectively with other women's retail clothing stores?
4. How could The Limited improve its market positioning and market segmentation strategies? Are they effective?
5. What impact would The Limited's strategic alternatives have on the company's financial statements for 1987? How much would each alternative cost, and could The Limited raise that amount of capital?
6. When a firm is taken over by another, yet top management of the acquired firm does not support the takeover, what strategy implementation problems could this cause for the acquiring firm?
7. How serious are the problems that critics say will face The Limited in the future?

REFERENCES

Hymowitz, Carol. "Limited Inc's. Apparel Won't Be Limited to Women Anymore; Menswear Planned." *Wall Street Journal.* 19 May, 1987.

O'Reilly, Brian. "Leslie Wexner Knows What Women Want." *Fortune.* 19 August, 1985, 154–60.

Solomon, Jolie. "Limited's Sales, Earnings Rose in its First Period." *Wall Street Journal.* 13 May, 1987.

Solomon, Jolie. "Limited Inc., Citing U.S. Trade Policy, to Boost Domestic Sources for Apparel." *Wall Street Journal.* April 1987.

The Limited Becomes People Mover. *Chain Store Age Executive.* February 1986, 54–55.

Weiner, Steven. "The Unlimited?" *Forbes.* 6 April, 1987, 76–80.

ENDNOTE

[1]Weiner, Steven. "The Unlimited?" *Forbes.* 6 April, 1987, 76–80.

Federated Department Stores, Inc.—1987

CHARLOTTE D. SUTTON
Auburn University

When you think of department stores, you likely think first of Sears, J.C. Penney, or Montgomery Ward. On a more regional level you might think of Dillard's, Nordstrom, or Macy's. One is not likely to think, however, of Federated Department Stores—despite the fact that Federated is the nation's largest multi-division department store operator with sales of more than $10.5 billion. Its lack of name recognition is a result of operating its stores under a host of names, including Rich's, Bloomingdale's, Burdines, Bullock's, Abraham & Straus, Filene's, Foley's, and I. Magnin, each a leader in its own geographical area.

COMPANY HISTORY

Federated Department Stores was founded in 1851 when Simon Lazarus, an emigre from Germany, opened a one-room men's clothing store in Columbus, Ohio. The store would eventually become the anchor of the Federated chain, but it was not until 1929 when Fred Lazarus, Jr. was cruising on a yacht with three friends that the Federated Department Store chain was actually born. On the yacht with Lazarus was S.F. Rothschild, president of Abraham & Straus in Brooklyn; Louis Kirstein, who ran Filene's of Boston; and Samuel Bloomingdale. The four formed an alliance, and the retail chain was launched. In 1945, the team bought Foley's, the largest department store in Houston. They also acquired the Boston Store (1948), Burdines and Goldsmith's (1957), Rike's (1959), Bullock's (1964), and Rich's, the largest department store in Atlanta (1976). Most of Federated's acquisitions were respected stores with rich heritages dating back before 1910.

Today, Federated has more than 620 stores, and its merchandise could more than fill twenty-two Empire State Buildings. In addition to 225 department stores, Federated operates almost one hundred discount stores (which Federated calls mass merchandising stores), 127 supermarkets, and 203 other stores, primarily specialty stores.

In all, Federated has fifteen operating divisions, including 10 department store chains which remain the core of Federated's operations. Federated considers three of its department store chains (Bullock's, I. Magnin, and Bloomingdale's) to be "up-scale," catering to a more elite customer. Federated offers catalog sales through the three "up-scale" divisions. Catalog sales increased 11 percent during 1986 to a combined total of $75 million

Federated's other divisions include The Children's Place, which has 163 children's apparel and three women's accessories stores; MainStreet, a new division of moderately priced department stores; Filene's Basement, a division of mass merchandising stores; Gold Circle/Richway, another mass merchandising division; and Ralphs supermarkets.

Exhibit 1 shows Federated's 1986 performance by division. Exhibit 2 reveals the sales and operating profits of Federated's business segment.

EXHIBIT 1 Federated's 1986 performance by division

Division	*Number of Stores*	*Sales (million)*	*Operating area*
Abraham & Straus	15	$ 778.6	New York, Pennsylvania, New Jersey
Bloomingdale's	16	1050.0	Throughout United States
Bullock's	22	751.8	California, Nevada, Arizona
Burdines	29	809.7	Florida
The Children's Place	166	161.8	Throughout United States
Filene's	16	390.8	Throughout Northeast
Filene's Basement	22	252.1	Pennsylvania, Massachusetts, New York
Foley's	37	1107.0	Throughout Southwest
Gold Circle	76	969.2	North and Southeast
Goldsmith's	6	174.0	Tennessee
Lazarus	32	904.7	Ohio, Indiana, Kentucky, West Virginia
I. Magnin	26	317.1	Primarily Western United States
MainStreet	15	109.3	Illinois, Michigan
Ralphs	127	2045.7	Primarily California
Rich's	20	690.6	Throughout Southeast

Source: Federated Department Stores, Inc., 1986 *Annual Report,* 16–20.

Federated considers itself a decentralized organization. Recognizing that each region of the country has a different market, Federated has encouraged its various divisions to develop their own personalities, style and merchandise, depending upon the target market.

FEDERATED'S STRATEGY FOR THE 1980S

During the early 1980s, Federated put great emphasis on expansion and remodeling existing stores. Much of Federated's remodeling and expansion efforts have been concentrated on the company's department store divisions. From 1984 to 1986, the organization began forty major remodeling and expansion projects involving 22 percent of Federated's department store selling space at a cost of $300 million. Exhibit 3 reveals the capital expenditures made.

During 1986 alone, Federated opened fifty new stores, with capital expenditures of more than $500 million, a 41 percent increase over 1985. Although Federated plans to spend $2 billion between 1986–1990 on capital projects, Federated management reports that it is now "prudently" developing new stores to fill needs in existing markets and "to broaden the company's influence." Among its capital expenditure

EXHIBIT 2 Federated's business segments

Operating Profit by Business Segment[1]

(millions) Fiscal Year	Department Stores Amount	% of Sales	Mass Merchandising Amount	% of Sales	Supermarkets Amount	% of Sales	Other Amount	% of Sales
1986	$628.7	9.0%	$31.8	3.3%	$59.2	2.9%	$(6.9)	(1.3)%
1985	621.9	9.3	39.0	3.7	58.7	3.2	(9.5)	(2.3)
1984	619.7	9.4	31.8	3.0	43.9	2.6	(2.7)	(.8)
1983	637.5	10.7	39.1	3.9	49.2	3.3	5.3	2.1
1982	494.0	9.1	23.4	2.8	37.0	2.9	10.0	5.3

Sales by Business Segment

(millions) Fiscal Year	Department Stores Amount	% of Total	Mass Merchandising Amount	% of Total	Supermarkets Amount	% of Total	Other Amount	% of Total
1986	$6,974.3	66.3%	$ 969.2	9.2%	$2,045.7	19.5%	$523.2	5.0%
1985	6,684.7	67.0	1,057.9	10.6	1,813.6	18.2	421.8	4.2
1984	6,566.6	67.9	1,059.9	11.0	1,711.3	17.7	334.5	3.4
1983	5,970.3	68.7	991.1	11.4	1,473.7	17.0	254.5	2.9
1982	5,412.2	70.3	822.9	10.7	1,275.7	16.6	188.1	2.4

Note: [1]Operating profit represents the pre-tax profit from operations of the divisions.

Source: Federated Department Stores, Inc. 1986 *Annual Report*, p. 32.

projects, Federated plans to remodel all seventy-six of its Gold Circle stores. Federated will also be replacing many of its older, smaller Ralphs supermarket locations with larger operations.

Federated is particularly optimistic about the potential of three divisions that the company considers "growth vehicles." Company officials believe MainStreet, Filene's Basement, and The Children's Place have the potential to broaden the company's total market penetration while expanding geographic diversity. Federated's hopes may be well founded. In the past five years, sales within the three divisions have grown almost three-fold, reaching more than $523 million in 1986. During 1986, Federated opened twenty-two new locations within those divisions in twelve new markets.

EXHIBIT 3 Federated's capital expenditures by store type 1984–1986 (millions of dollars)

	1984	*1985*	*1986*
Department stores	$207.6	$243.4	$266.3
All other stores	73.9	107.5	237.5

Source: Federated Department Stores, Inc. 1986 *Annual Report*, p. 7.

Federated is also optimistic about a series of stores spun off of Federated's ever-popular Bloomingdale's. The boutique-style shops, known as Bloomie's Express, are to be located in airports and eventually shopping centers and hotels. Two Bloomie's Express stores were opened in 1986 on a pilot basis in Kennedy International Airport in New York to take advantage of international travelers wanting to carry something home with Bloomingdale's name on it.

While Federated has continued to expand its operations, it has also closed stores that did not meet performance standards, including the entire Gold Triangle home furnishings discount chain. In its efforts to upgrade its Ralphs stores, the company also closed eighteen of its smaller Ralphs locations. In addition, Federated closed its Abraham & Straus stores in the Philadelphia market, choosing instead to concentrate the division's efforts on the New York/New Jersey area.

Federated's most recent strategy to reduce costs has included a reorganization of both its corporate offices and divisions, resulting in a consolidation of duplicated corporate functions as well as mergers of some of its divisions. In 1986, Federated completed the merger of its two up-scale discount divisions, Gold Circle and Richway, into a single, $1.1 billion, 76-store operation. During 1986, Federated also merged its Ohio-based Lazarus and Shillito Rikes department store divisions into a single, 32-store division operating under the Lazarus name. In January 1987, Federated completed the merger of its two Texas department store divisions (Sanger Harris and Foley's) under the Foley's banner.

Federated's renewed interest in expansion and marketing is reflected in the 1987 appointment of Norman S. Matthews as president and chief operating officer. With a background in advertising, marketing and discount operations, Matthews joined Federated less than ten years ago. He is expected to draw heavily on his marketing background and has already noted the need for the store divisions to have "lots of marketing focus" to keep up in today's rapidly changing and competitive retail market.[1]

FINANCIAL STRUCTURE

In fiscal 1986, Federated had sales totaling more than $10.5 billion, an increase of 5.4 percent. However, net income was up only 0.3 percent to $287.6 million. Federated management attributed the relatively poor showing in its earnings to several unusual expenses, some of which were the result of repositioning strategies designed to improve the company's financial position beginning in 1987. The following are highlights of actions affecting Federated's financial structure during 1986:

1. The repurchase and retirement of 4.4 million shares of Federated outstanding common stock resulted in an after-tax expense of $14.3 million. Federated also repurchased $297 million of its outstanding long-term Sinking Fund Debentures and Euronotes with coupon rates above 10 percent. The repurchase resulted in a $14.3 million after-tax expense, but helped to lower interest expenses from $86.4 million in 1985 to $79.8 million in 1986.
2. The merger of the Sanger Harris and Foley's divisions resulted in an after-tax expense of $15.7 million. The merger, instigated to promote long-term operating efficiencies, was expected to have a modest positive impact on earnings in 1987 and more significant positive effects beginning in fiscal 1988.

3. The Tax Reform Act of 1986 repealed the investment tax credit for property placed in service after 1985. The act reduced the company's tax credit from $16.4 million in fiscal 1985 to $4.9 million in 1986. The act also institutes changes in tax accounting for inventories and taxation on income from credit sales and bad debts. Those changes will result in an initial reduction in company tax benefits, but the tax reform will reduce Federated's federal tax rate from 46 percent to 34 percent in 1988.
4. The acquisition and opening of fourteen Ralphs Giant stores and four superstores required capital expenditures of more than $158 million. Federated management sees Ralphs supermarkets as a major growth opportunity for the company.
5. A $4.4 million after-tax increase in expenses for department store remodeling, expansion and openings was incurred in 1986.
6. An aggressive expansion program of Filene's Basement, MainStreet, and The Children's Place, costing $3.1 million, exceeded 1985's expenditures in that area by 36.7 percent. The program resulted in the opening of 22 stores.
7. The sale of ownership interests in two major shopping centers in Texas and Tennessee resulted in a sizable taxable income. The after-tax gain on the sale was $18.6 million. The sale represented the completion of the strategic disposition of all wholly owned shopping centers as well as all other major interests in shopping center developments. The transactions were timed to take advantage of capital gains tax provisions repealed by the incoming tax reform act.

Historically, Federated has followed a conservative fiscal policy. However, it has the financial clout resulting from an approximate $500 million cash flow annually. Even in poor years, when earnings may decline, the overall cash flow tends to be high. (See Exhibits 4–6.)

FEDERATED'S COMPETITION

Federated's competition takes two forms. First, the company competes on a national scale with other diversified retailing firms. Federated holds first place in that competition, followed closely by May Department Store Co. and more distantly by Dayton Hudson. Federated also competes on a more limited basis with individual department store chains, typically referred to as divisions. Although Federated's top ranked division (Foley's) achieved only seventh place in 1986, Federated placed seven of its ten department store divisions in the top twenty. Exhibit 7 discusses Federated's top diversified competition, May Department Store Co. Exhibit 8 provides information on Federated's top-ranked divisional competitor, Dillard Department Store.

May Department Store Co.

In 1986, May acquired New York-based Associated Dry Goods Corporation for approximately $2.7 billion worth of stock. The merger created a $10 billion company, and May became the second largest multi-division department store operator in the country—second in size only to Federated. Following the acquisition, May divested the Joseph Horne department store and Sycamore Store specialty chain that came

EXHIBIT 4 Balance sheet for Federated Department Stores, Inc.

(in thousands)	*January 31, 1987*	*February 1, 1986*
Assets		
Current Assets:		
Cash	$ 101,097	$ 54,270
Accounts receivable	1,554,402	1,607,012
Merchandise inventories	1,405,992	1,320,097
Supplies and prepaid expenses	42,508	43,448
Total Current Assets	3,103,999	3,024,827
Property and Equipment — net	2,451,629	2,249,624
Other Assets	132,110	79,192
Total Assets	$5,687,738	$5,353,643
Liabilities and Shareholders' Equity		
Current Liabilities:		
Notes payable and long-term debt due within one year	$ 240,053	$ 42,749
Accounts payable and accrued liabilities	1,249,149	1,125,626
Income taxes	119,149	320,748
Total Current Liabilities	1,608,351	1,489,123
Deferred Income Taxes	420,042	186,091
Deferred Compensation and Supplementary Retirement	204,890	189,648
Long-Term Debt	791,901	781,513
Shareholders' Equity:		
Preferred stock	—	—
Common stock	118,876	62,196
Capital in excess of par value of common stock	25,597	98,506
Retained earnings	2,538,612	2,569,404
Less treasury stock at cost	20,531	22,838
Total Shareholders' Equity	2,662,554	2,707,268
Total Liabilities and Shareholders' Equity	$5,687,738	$5,353,643

Source: Federated Department Stores, Inc. 1986 *Annual Report,* p. 23.

with the package. May now has seventeen department store divisions, including the prestigious Lord & Taylor department stores; Caldor and Venture discount stores; Loehmann's off-price women's apparel chain; and Volume Shoe Corporation, which operates Payless ShoeSource.

Stuart Robbins, a retail analyst with Donaldson, Lufkin & Jenrette feels the Associated Dry Goods acquisition was a good move for May. "The combination will be a powerhouse in the general merchandising field. It will be just about as big as Federated and will grow twice as fast," he said. He projected that May will see a 15 percent annual earnings growth during the next five years.[2]

May Department Store Co. has a total of 2,793 stores. During 1986, May had sales of $10.3 billion, an increase of 8.7 percent over the previous year. May is beginning an aggressive capital spending program, with plans to lay out $3 billion between 1986 and 1990. The capital expenditure program is the largest in the company's his-

EXHIBIT 5 Statement of income for Federated Department Stores, Inc.

(in thousands, except per share data)	*52 Weeks Ended January 31, 1987*	*52 Weeks Ended February 1, 1986*	*53 Weeks Ended February 2, 1985*
Net Sales, including leased department sales of $324,200, $294,300 and $264,000	$10,512,425	$9,978,027	$9,672,336
Cost of sales, including occupancy and buying costs	7,698,628	7,314,725	7,097,683
Selling, publicity, delivery and administrative expenses	2,103,315	1,962,537	1,893,649
Provision for doubtful accounts	50,558	45,599	33,924
Interest expense — net	79,801	86,386	116,259
Unusual items — net	13,082	35,054	(42,609)
Total costs and expenses	9,945,384	9,444,301	9,098,906
Income Before Income Taxes and Extraordinary Item	567,041	533,726	573,430
Federal, state and local income taxes	265,100	247,100	244,100
Income Before Extraordinary Item	301,941	286,626	329,330
Extraordinary item — loss on early extinguishment of debt, net of tax effect of $14,527	(14,341)	—	—
Net Income	$ 287,600	$ 286,626	$ 329,330
Earnings Per Share of Common Stock:			
Income before extraordinary item	$3.12	$2.94	$3.38
Extraordinary item	(.15)	—	—
Net income	$2.97	$2.94	$3.38
Fully Diluted Earnings Per Share:			
Income before extraordinary item	$3.05	$2.87	$3.30
Extraordinary item	(.14)	—	—
Net income	$2.91	$2.87	$3.30

Source: Federated Department Stores, Inc. 1986 *Annual Report,* p. 22.

tory. It calls for fifty-nine new department stores, fifty-two discount stores, and more than 1,300 specialty stores, the largest number of new units during any five-year period in the company's history.

UPHEAVAL IN THE RETAIL INDUSTRY

In the past few years, the retailing industry has experienced dramatic change. As David Schulz wrote, "The tremors that had been shaking up retailing in recent years burst into a full-fledged earthquake in 1986, causing much upheaval, as entire companies were swallowed and shock waves reverberated throughout the industry. In no year in recent memory has the overall profile of multi-division retailing companies changed so dramatically."[3]

EXHIBIT 6 Ratio analysis for Federated Department Stores, Inc.

Fiscal Year Ending	*2/1/86*	*2/2/85*	*1/28/84*
Quick ratio	1.12	0.97	0.89
Current ratio	2.03	1.77	1.58
Sales/cash	183.86	91.99	134.71
Selling, General, and Administrative sales	0.20	0.20	0.20
Receivables turnover	6.21	6.26	6.09
Receivables days sales	57.98	57.53	59.13
Inventories turnover	7.32	7.36	7.70
Inventories days sales	49.20	48.92	46.75
Net sales/working capital	6.50	7.40	8.87
Net sales/plant & equipment	4.44	4.44	4.05
Net sales/current assets	3.30	3.21	3.27
Net sales/total assets	1.86	1.83	1.77
Net sales/employees	75306	N/A	70247
Total liabilities/total assets	0.49	0.52	0.52
Total liabilities/invested capital	0.76	0.84	0.87
Total liabilities/common equity	0.98	1.07	1.10
Times interest earned	7.18	5.93	6.99
Long term debt/equity	0.29	0.28	0.27
Total debt/equity	0.29	0.28	0.27
Total assets/equity	1.98	2.07	2.10
Pretax income/net sales	0.05	0.06	0.07
Pretax income/total assets	0.10	0.11	0.12
Pretax income/invested capital	0.15	0.18	0.20
Pretax income/common equity	0.20	0.23	0.26
Net income/net sales	0.03	0.03	0.04
Net income/total assets	0.05	0.06	0.07
Net income/invested capital	0.08	0.10	0.11
Net income/common equity	0.11	0.13	0.15

Source: Company Records and Compact Disclosure, 1987.

The upheaval is due, in large part, to the slowing of shopping center construction. Although many companies are continuing to open new stores, available prime shopping space is diminishing. Thus many companies are eyeing competitors as possible takeover targets, and the result is the massive restructuring of the retail industry. In 1986, eight companies constituted the Standard and Poor's department store index. During that year alone, three were acquired or taken private, and a fourth is likely to

EXHIBIT 7 Retail corporate results for fiscal 1986

Company (Total Sq. Ft.)	*Store Total by Type (Fiscal year change)*	*Sales (Millions)*	*% Gain or Decline*	*Earnings (Millions) Net Actual*	*% Gain or Decline*
Federated	631 Total (+17)	$10,512 Total	5.4%	$287,600	0.3%
61,600,000	225 Dept (+8)	6,974 Dept	4.3		
	203 Other (+19)	523 Other	23.9		
	76 Mass (−)	969 Mass	−8.4		
	127 Super (−)	2,048 Super	12.8		
May Department Store Co.	2,793 Total (+371)	$10,376 Total[a]	8.7	$381,000	9.8
76,013,000	286 Dept (−15)	6,503 Dept	6.1		
	115 Caldor (+6)	1,411 Caldor	5.4		
	65 Venture (+3)	1,129 Venture	12.5		
	90 Loehmann (+9)	351 Loehmann	9.0		
	2,210 Shoe (+343)	934 Shoe	34.0		
Dayton Hudson	475 Total (−731)[b]	$ 9,259 Total	12.2	$310,000	9.3
47,672,000	37 Dept. (−)	1,566 Dept	8.1		
	246 Target (+20)	4,355 Target	10.8		
	175 Merv (+27)	2,862 Merv	13.3		
	17 Spec (+7)	476 Spec	36.4		

[a]Adjusted to show acquisition of Associated Dry Goods in October 1986
[b]Includes divestiture of B. Dalton Bookseller, Dec. 27, 1986
Source: David P. Schulz, "Stores' Annual Ranking," *Stores* (July 1987): 18.

be split into two separate, publicly traded companies. Even Federated has been the subject of takeover talks. Late in 1986, Dart Group Corporation, with almost $500 million in cash, was rumored to be interested in Federated. Dart has previously (and unsuccessfully) chased such retailers as Safeway, Revco, and Jack Eckerd. Both Revco and Jack Eckerd took themselves private to avoid being taken over by Dart.

Analysts predict that changes in the retailing industry will continue through 1987. The new tax law may discourage some retail investment, but stimulate takeover attempts of established stores. Since the new law makes depreciation schedules longer, developers will be attracted to properties that can produce income quickly. Established stores in existing shopping centers may provide that quick return.

While a great deal of trading has taken place, most of the real estate will continue to be run as retail operations. The result will likely intensify the already competitive conditions as marginally productive space is acquired by more efficient operators.

Some experts now feel the retail industry is "overstored," which bodes ill for all but the strongest of competitors. The retailers' rule of thumb is that the store with the highest sales in any given market is very profitable. The store with the second highest sales is profitable. The Number 3 store is only marginal, while the store with the fourth highest sales is losing money.

EXHIBIT 8 Top twenty department store divisions

Rank	*Company/division (headquarters)*	*Affil.*	*Units*	*Sq. Ft. (000)*	*Volume (000,000)*
1.	Dillard's (Little Rock)	(Ind)	115	15,588	$1,851.4
2.	Nordstrom (Seattle)	(Ind)	53	5,098	1,629.9
3.	Macy's (New York)	(RHM)	22	7,710	1,575.0
4.	Dayton Hudson (Minneapolis)	(DH)	37	7,791	1,566.3
5.	Macy's (New Jersey)	(RHM)	24	6,550	1,440.0
6.	Macy's (California)	(RHM)	25	5,682	1,335.0
7.	Foley's (Houston)	(Fed)	37	8,003	1,107.0
8.	Bloomingdale's (New York)	(Fed)	16	4,269	1,050.0
9.	The Broadway (Southern California)	(CHH)	43	7,459	1,045
10.	Saks Fifth Avenue (New York)	(Bat)	44	N/A	1,005
11.	Marshall Field (Chicago)	(Bat)	25	6,825	925
12.	Lazarus (Cincinnati)	(Fed)	32	7,385	904.7
13.	Lord & Taylor (New York)	(May)	45	5,954	865
14.	Neiman-Marcus (Dallas)	(CHH)	22	3,230	850
15.	May Co. (California)	(May)	34	6,411	814
16.	Burdines (Miami)	(Fed)	29	5,069	809.7
17.	Abraham & Straus (Brooklyn)	(Fed)	15	5,578	778.6
18.	Bullock's (California)	(Fed)	28	4,805	751.8
19.	Emporium-Capwell (San Francisco)	(CHH)	22	5,268	710
20.	Rich's (Atlanta)	(Fed)	20	4,878	690.6

Key:

Bat—Batus Retail Group

CHH—Carter Hawley Hale

DH—Dayton Hudson Corp.

Fed—Federated Department Stores

Ind—Independent

May—May Department Stores

RHM—R. H. Macy & Co. Inc.

Source: David P. Schulz, "Stores' Annual Ranking," *Stores* (July 1987): 14.

EXHIBIT 9 Three-year comparison of Federated, May, and Dillard's department stores

	Sales (millions)			*Net Income (thousands)*			*EPS*		
	1986	*1985*	*1984*	*1986*	*1985*	*1984*	*1986*	*1985*	*1984*
Federated	10,512.4	9,978.0	9,672.3	255.6	286.6	329.3	3.12	2.94	3.38
May	10,376.0	9,542.0	8,835.0	381.0	347.0	327.0	2.44	2.20	2.10
Dillard's	1,851.4	1,601.3	1,277.3	74.5	66.9	49.5	2.35	2.29	1.82

Source: Company Records.

Not only are retailers having to deal with excessive competition, but they are also facing a slower growth in demand for general merchandise, especially apparel. Sales per square foot, a frequently used measure of productivity for department stores, are lower than they were a decade ago, considering inflation. The Marketing Science Institute predicts that spending on apparel will rise only 0.8 percent through 1990, compared to a 2.4 percent increase in sales of overall general merchandise. The relatively poor outlook for apparel sales is attributed to a declining teenage population that fueled earlier retail sales and an increasing population of older Americans, who have less need for clothing than do younger, working Americans.

Retail sales are also expected to be affected by an uncertain stock market. The Oct. 19, 1987, crash, in which the stock market lost 508 points, reduced the potential buying power of stockholders by $850 billion—the equivalent of six years of savings. The crash couldn't have come at a worse time for the retail industry: 19 percent of total retail sales occur during November and December. Even with a stabilizing of the stock market, consumer anxiety is expected to affect retail sales for some time to come. In fact, two out of three Americans polled three weeks following Black Monday said they expected an economic downturn during the following year.

Facing the problem of an increasingly competitive and slow-growing market, most retailers are looking for ways to lower their costs by consolidating regional department

EXHIBIT 10 Two-year comparison of Federated, May, and Dillard's department stores

	Profit Ratio		*Debt/Equity Ratio*		*Current Ratio*	
	1986	*1985*	*1986*	*1985*	*1986*	*1985*
Federated	2.7	2.9	.30	.29	1.93	2.03
May	3.7	4.6	.48	.41	2.20	2.06
Dillard's	4.0	4.2	.34	.15	2.20	1.56

Source: Company Records.

store divisions. Consolidations provide the benefits of economies of scale in purchasing, advertising, and administration. Companies are also looking for ways to reduce distribution costs using technological advances such as computer-assisted bar code scanning, on-line receiving, and merchandise tracking. Through such measures, companies are able to reduce inventory costs, speed up merchandise turnover, and move merchandise into stores more quickly.

Department stores have found themselves caught between off-price chains, which offer much of the same designer-brand merchandise at discount prices, and specialty stores, which offer customers more personal service. In trying to find the right balance between customer service and competitive prices, more and more stores are placing a renewed emphasis on customer service and a decreasing emphasis on product promotions.

Retail companies such as Nordstrom's have switched to all-commissioned sales forces to try to stimulate attention to customers. Nordstrom's sales clerks also keep records of customers' dress sizes and fashion preferences. In some Nordstrom stores, music from grand pianos entertains shoppers of the store's most elegant dresses. The strategy appears to be working. Nordstrom's sales per square foot were $322 in 1986, up from $243 in 1983, a 33 percent increase. That figure compares to sales of $138 and $118 per square foot for Foley's, Federated's top-ranked division, and Dillard's, respectively.

In an effort to attract customers, particularly career women with limited shopping time, some stores have also begun offering "personal shoppers," in-store dry cleaning, and tailoring services. Although such services often mean an increase in prices, many department stores now believe that a significant number of customers are willing to pay for more personal attention.

The changing demographic characteristics of the American shopper are also forcing a change in many department stores. With the decline of the middle class and the increasing size of the upper and lower classes, some market analysts predict a decline in the middle-income department store. These analysts suggest that stores such as Zayre, Wal-Mart, and Mervyn's will meet the needs of lower- and middle-income Americans shopping for discounted prices while department stores reposition themselves to meet the needs of households with annual incomes of more than $50,000. Such households currently control approximately a third of all personal income, and may control as much as half of all personal income by the year 2000. The decreasing number of middle-income families suggests that the most successful retailers may well have to abandon strategies focusing on that segment of the market.[4]

FUTURE OUTLOOK

Federated is among those companies adopting repositioning strategies to try to attract higher-income customers. Federated is expanding its moderate and better merchandise lines as well as continuing to develop its private label. Federated also plans to continue to focus energies and resources on its Ralphs, MainStreet, and Filene's Basement divisions, believing those divisions are positioned to offer significant growth and earnings in the years to come.

Financially, Federated management is expecting 1987 to be "a good to very good year," according to Donald J. Stone, vice chairman of Federated Department Stores. While Federated suffered a decline in earnings in 1984 and 1985, earnings picked up in 1986, despite the depressed conditions in the Southwest where the company had two major divisions (Foley's and Sanger Harris). He predicts 1987 sales will be even better. Still, the economy is confusing even the experts. Stone reports, "We can't get our economist to make a firm projection for more than three months at a time. But as far as we can tell, the economy appears to be shaping up a little better in 1987 than in 1986." Stone believes the conflicting economic currents and competitive retailing environment will lead all retailers to work hard to keep or increase their shares of the market.[5]

Like most retailers, Federated is examining other strategies that would help it retain its top position in retail sales. While Federated has already consolidated several of its divisions, further consolidation is a possibility. Such consolidations offer increased economies of scale and efficiencies. Possible mergers might include Federated's two mass merchandising divisions, Filene's Basement and Gold Circle/Richway. Federated might also consider mergering some of its smaller divisions, such as Goldsmith's, with other divisions operating within the same region.

Another possibility which would increase economies of scale is a move from a decentralized structure to a more centralized organizational design. If buying and advertising decisions for all the divisions were made at headquarters, the company would be able to better take advantage of economies of scale.

Federated must also consider the nation's changing demographics. With the declining size of the middle class, Federated must consider how to best adapt. If it is attempting to appeal to higher-income customers, how might it best attract them? If customer service is the answer, what services should the company offer?

Given the changing demographics, should the company continue to expand its mass merchandising divisions—moving beyond its current locations in the eastern sections of the United States, perhaps even into Europe? Or, considering the ever-increasing number of discount stores, should Federated withdraw from discount operations altogether?

Finally, but perhaps most importantly, Federated must consider the upheaval in the retail industry in which acquisitions are continually changing the complexion of the industry. Federated must first determine the best strategy to prevent an unwanted takeover such as that considered by the Dart Group Corporation. Rumors suggest that R.H. Macy and Campeau Corporation are preparing bids to acquire Federated. Although Federated has already repurchased 4.4 million shares of outstanding stock, the company may want to repurchase even more stock to assure the continuation of its current leadership.

Federated may want to consider some acquisitions of its own. A company such as Nordstrom's could move Federated into markets in which it may now have difficulty obtaining prime locations. Federated may even want to consider diversifying out of retail into other areas which may be promising industries for the future.

ENDNOTES

1. Solomon, Jolie. "Federated Stores Taps Matthews to Post of President and Chief Operating Officer." *The Wall Street Journal.* 6 March, 1987, 36.
2. "ADG Acquisition Turns May into Super Power." *Chain Store Age Executive.* September 1986, 145–46.
3. Schulz, David P. "Upheaval for Multi-Divisionals." *Stores.* July 1987, 17.
4. "Retailing Basic Analysis: The Velocity of Assets." *Standard & Poor's Industry Surveys.* 22 January, 1987, 79–86.
5. Barmash, Isadore. "A Bit Better Than This Year." *Stores.* December 1986, 5–8.

Sears, Roebuck, & Company—1987

KEITH ROBBINS
George Mason University

Conspicuously headquartered in the tallest building in the world, Sears, Roebuck, and Company is the world's largest retailer of general merchandise. (See Exhibit 1 for information on the Sears tower.) Revenues for the year ended December 31, 1986 exceeded $44 billion; as shown in Exhibit 2, this ranked sixth among U.S. industrial firms trailing only corporate giants GM, Exxon, Ford, IBM, and Mobil. Sears has evolved into a multibusiness enterprise—a far cry from the mail order firm which Richard Sears established in Minneapolis in 1886. Today, Sears is comprised of three primary business divisions: retail merchandising, insurance, and financial services.

It is Chairman Edward Brennan's vision that Sears' customer of the future will not only buy his work shirts and sabre saws at Sears, but will also finance and insure his home through Sears, entrust his savings to Sears, write his checks on a Sears ac-

EXHIBIT 1 The Sears Tower

In 1969 Sears announced plans to build a national headquarters in downtown Chicago. Designed to handle projected growth through the year 2000, the 110-story structure contains 4.5 million gross square feet of space, making it the largest private office building in the world.

Additional statistics:

- ☐ At 1,454 feet above ground, it is the world's tallest building.
- ☐ Construction began in 1970 and was completed in 1974.
- ☐ Materials included: 76,000 tons of steel, 2 million cubic feet of concrete, 16,000 bronze-tinted windows, 1,500 miles of electrical wiring and 80 miles of elevator cable.
- ☐ Has the most complete fire safety system ever designed for a high rise building including 40,000 sprinkler heads.
- ☐ Total population of the Tower is about 12,000.

Source: *Sears Yesterday and Today,* 1986, p. 20.

EXHIBIT 2 The *Business Week* 1986 top 10 in sales

	Billions of Dollars	*% Change from 1985*
1. General Motors	$102.8	7%
2. Exxon	71.6	−19
3. Ford	62.7	19
4. IBM	51.3	2
5. Mobil	44.9	−20
6. Sears Roebuck	44.3	9
7. General Electric	35.2	24
8. AT & T	34.1	−1
9. Texaco	32.6	−31
10. DuPont	27.1	−8

Source: *Business Week,* 17 April 1987, p. 32.

count, open an IRA, buy stocks, bonds, and mutual funds through Sears, and procure auto, health, and life insurance, all through Sears.

HISTORY

Exhibit 3 presents a chronological listing of highlights from Sears' first 100 years. Many of the vents represent the responsiveness of Sears to major demographic and sociological trends which swept the United States during a century of unprecedented change.

A former railway worker, Richard Sears began the R. W. Sears Watch Company in Minneapolis in 1886. He had grown up in a small rural community where the only merchandise outlet was the general store. These general stores were typified by stockouts and high markups. Sears envisioned an alternative to the general store: by operating a mail order business out of a large warehouse, he could eliminate the costly middleman by mailing goods directly to the customer, and he could purchase in quantities sufficiently large to warrant discounts from many manufacturers.

He realized the savings in shipping costs that would be afforded by a more centralized location, particularly one with access to railway routes serving the major U.S. cities. Chicago was the logical choice, and the operation was relocated there in 1893. Shortly thereafter, Mr. Sears hired a young watchmaker named Alvah Roebuck, and the firm became Sears, Roebuck, and Company. The key success factor for the young entrepreneurs was that they could provide customers a wide range of goods at substantial savings over the traditional general store due to volume buying and shipment of goods via railways and later through rural free delivery and parcel post.

By 1895, Sears was producing a 532-page catalog and had realized an annual sales volume of more than $750 thousand. In 1901, the company went public with its first-

EXHIBIT 3 A chronology of the evolution of Sears, Roebuck and Company

1886	Richard Sears starts selling watches to supplement his income as station agent at North Redwood, Minnesota.
1887	Sears settles in the company's first Chicago location and hires a watchmaker named Alvah C. Roebuck.
1888	Date of the earliest catalog featuring only watches and jewelry.
1893	Corporate name of firm becomes Sears, Roebuck and Co.
1896	First large general catalog.
1906	First catalog merchandise distribution center opens in Chicago.
1911	Sears establishes testing laboratory.
1916	Savings and Profit Sharing Fund of Sears employees is established.
1924	General Robert E. Wood—the man responsible for Sears' entry into retail—joins the company.
1925	First Sears retail store opens in catalog center on Chicago's west side.
1931	Allstate insurance company established.
1945	Sears' sales exceed $1 billion.
1952	Simpson-Sears, Ltd., established.
1973	Sears moves its national headquarters to the Sears Tower.
1980	CEO Edward Telling reorganizes Sears. Seraco group formed by uniting several financial services already owned by Sears, the largest of these, Homart Development Company, focuses on the development of commercial real estate and has become the nation's third largest developer of shopping centers. At this point Sears is a semi-holding company consisting of Merchandising, Allstate, and Seraco.
1981	Acquired Dean Witter Reynolds, the fifth largest securities brokerage, and Coldwell Banker, nation's largest real estate broker.
1982	Began World Trade operations. Reorganized from three business groups (Merchandising, Allstate, and Seraco) into five (Merchandising, Allstate, Dean Witter, Coldwell Banker, and Sears World Trade).
1983	Opened 33 financial centers in Sears stores, where shoppers can purchase securities, insurance policies, and real estate brokerage services. Began Merchandising Head Edward Brennan's 5–year plan highlighted by "Stores of the Future"; elegantly and tastefully decorated outlets offering more name brand merchandise. Introduced new slogan: "There's more for your life at Sears."
1985	Introduced Discover credit card to be honored by 25,000 retail outlets.
1986	Sears celebrates 100 years of business. Edward Telling resigns as Chairman and CEO and is replaced by Edward Brennan. Sears World Trade, which has been suffering seriously declining performance, merges with the Merchandise Group.
1987	Sears announces its plan to open specialty stores, which in many cases will compete directly with existing stores.

ever offering of common and preferred stock (it has remained a publicly held firm thereafter). The company soon outgrew its original five-story building, and in 1906, a 40-acre, $5 million facility was built on the west side of Chicago. Simultaneously, Sears opened its second distribution center in Dallas.

Sears' history of success has been largely due to its remaining abreast of the needs of a dramatically shifting consumer population. By 1925, industrialization had led to a significant migration of individuals into the cities and away from rural agricultural areas. Sears could no longer sustain its ambitious growth objectives by relying solely on rural catalog customers. General Robert E. Wood, a Sears vice president (later to become president and chairman), campaigned vigorously to open retail stores. Chain stores were becoming ever more prominent across the country and were cutting into Sears' mail-order business. In 1914, there were about 24,000 chain stores; by 1929, there were 150,000. Wood argued that unless Sears opened retail centers to serve the urban population, the company would end up serving only a small portion of the total buying public.

Wood thus opened Sears' first retail store in Chicago adjacent to its existing mail order facility; it was an instant success. The retail operation expanded to 128 stores in 1928, to 324 stores in 1929, and to 400 stores in 1933. It was calculated that during one 12-month period during the late 1920s, Sears averaged a new store opening every other day.

The automobile, by this time, was beginning to radically alter American life styles; Gen. Wood again correctly predicted that it would soon become a standard and highly valued investment for their typical customer. Recognizing the opportunity, Sears began to offer low-cost auto insurance to its customers through the mail. This new business was organized in 1931 and named the Allstate Insurance Company after a popular line of Sears tires. In 1933, Sears began offering over-the-counter insurance sales in its stores.

A critical point in the evolution of Sears into the corporate giant of today occurred subsequent to the conclusion of World War II. Many retailers of the time, including its fiercest rival, Montgomery Ward, predicted a crushing recession after the war and decided to halt any plans for expansion. Sears planners disagreed and launched a rapid expansion into the suburbs. Where did America wind up shopping? As a result of these bold initiatives, customers today shop at 854 conveniently located Sears retail stores in shopping malls and suburban areas in the United States.

THE BUSINESSES OF SEARS, ROEBUCK AND COMPANY

Exhibit 4 presents a profile of the four major business groups of Sears. While there have been many changes in retailing over the years, there were no major changes in the composition of Sears, Roebuck and Company until 1981. Then, Sears acquired the nation's largest real estate broker, Coldwell Banker and Company. That same year, the company also acquired the nation's fifth-largest brokerage house, Dean Witter Reynolds Organization, Inc.

In 1982, Sears formed Sears World Trade Incorporated, a general trading company designed to import and export trade items as well as engage in other trade support services. In 1983, Sears World Trade, Inc. extended its service into the agricultural business world by offering its services to many agrarian underdeveloped nations. The primary purpose of the World Trade subsidiary was to offer management, technological, and financial services to U.S. and foreign firms that are expanding into overseas markets.

EXHIBIT 4 The businesses of Sears, Roebuck and Company—1987

MERCHANDISING **(61% of revenues)**

- ☐ established 1886.
- ☐ distributes goods and services in United States.
- ☐ provides credit services to consumers.
- ☐ conducts retail merchandising services in Central and South America, Canada, and Puerto Rico.
- ☐ has four U.S. regions, 854 retail stores.
- ☐ has 2,778 sales offices.
- ☐ operates in forty-three Mexican retail stores.

ALLSTATE **(29% of revenues)**

- ☐ established 1931.
- ☐ second largest property and liability insurer in United States.
- ☐ provides insurance and financial services.
- ☐ serves fifty states, Washington, D.C., Virgin Islands, and Canada.
- ☐ has sales facilities in Sears retail outlets.
- ☐ has large independent agent force.

DEAN WITTER **(8% of revenues)**

- ☐ acquired 1981.
- ☐ consists of Dean Witter Reynolds Organization, Inc. and Sears Savings Bank.
- ☐ offers a full range of investments and services including stocks, bonds, and options traded on all major securities exchanges as well as over-the-counter market.
- ☐ headquartered in New York, offers these investment-related services in the financial service centers of many Sears retail stores.

COLDWELL BANKER **(2% of revenues)**

- ☐ acquired 1981.
- ☐ consists of Coldwell Banker, the country's largest full-service real estate company, and Homart Development Co., one of the industry leaders in commercial property development.
- ☐ invests in, develops, operates, manages, and acts as a broker in real estate and provides various related real estate services, primarily in the United States.
- ☐ residential division helps people buy and sell homes, and handles mortgage financing, title insurance, general insurance, appraisals, escrow, and relocation services.
- ☐ Homart, founded in 1959, develops regional shopping malls.
- ☐ headquartered in Los Angeles.

In 1983, Sears opened the Financial Network Centers, a test company in many major U.S. markets. These centers, located in Sears retail stores, offer customers many financial services, including mortgage and property-casualty insurance. Nearly two dozen task forces, comprised of individuals from the ranks of Sears' new and old businesses, began exploring possible strategies in areas ranging from mortgage banking to telecommunications. The purpose of these task forces was to explore possibilities for attracting Sears' 40 million customer base to its financial services. The strategies developed within these task forces began hitting the marketplace in mid-1983:

> Dean Witter recently began rolling out an array of new offerings—including tax-exempt unit trusts and a line of credit that allows homeowners to borrow against their home equity—that are aimed squarely at Sears' middle-America stronghold. Through vertical integration—which Sears will achieve, for example, with its mortgage-backed securities by originating, insuring, and packaging the loans, then selling them through Dean Witter to investors—the retailer hopes to attain cost savings that will allow it to score with more competitive pricing. Add to that Sears' massive distribution network of 831 retail stores, 2,388 catalog outlets, 1,950 stand-alone Allstate Insurance sales offices, 355 Dean Witter offices, 87 Allstate Savings & Loan Assn. branches in California, and several hundred real estate locations. Sears is "in a unique position . . . to be complete masters of our destiny." (*Business Week.* 13 June, 1983, p. 116)

In the fall of 1985, Sears unveiled its Discover credit card. The card was touted as the first "true financial services card." In addition to charging purchases at restaurants and retailers, Discover users open savings accounts and get cash from automatic teller machines nationwide. Sears hired 600 salespeople to persuade retail and service establishments to accept Discover before the national launch. (*Fortune.* 27 May, 1985.)

Competitors in the credit card business estimate that it will cost Sears at least $30 million to establish the card. Sears does, however, have an advantage: it already has the names, addresses, and credit histories of some 60 million Americans who have a Sears store credit card, 28 million of whom use it actively. Most of the 28 million already carry Visas and/or MasterCards, but Sears is offering incentives to use Discover instead. Consumers who sign up for Discover within the first two years get the card free. By comparison, banks typically charge between $12 to $25 annually for Visa and MasterCard, and American Express charges $45 annually for its standard green card. Additionally, Sears offers rebates of up to 1 percent on a customer's annual credit balance. (*Fortune.* 14 October, 1985.)

The legacy of Edward Telling is comprised of bold moves undertaken to transform Sears into the "great American corporation:"

> The merchandising and insurance businesses were already securely in place, and good beginnings had been made toward building financial and real estate services through the operations of Allstate Insurance and the Holmart Development Corporation, the wholly owned subsidiary which had been created in the 1950s to handle shopping center projects in which Sears was interested. Apparently it was Telling's original intention to build his "great American corporation" from these existing Sears components. Then, in 1981, the opportunity arose to greatly accelerate the process by means of two strategic acquisitions: Dean Witter Reynolds, a leading full-line investment house, and Coldwell Banker, the nation's largest real estate firm—two moves which came almost simultaneously and shook the finance and real estate communities to their foundations.
>
> There are those on Wall Street who look askance at Sears' new policy, just as a half century before the financial gurus of their grandfather's generation scoffed at General Wood's audacious entry into retailing . . . It is too early to pass judgement on the new Sears strategy. On the surface it looks good. But it will take time to prove, and meanwhile it carries a very high level of risk . . . The course ahead is rough and filled with dangers, both seen and unseen. Yet, as General Wood often said, "If your strategy is right, you can make a lot of mistakes learning how to make it work." (*Worthy.* 1984, pp. 264–67)

In January of 1986, Sears' 100th birthday, Edward Brennan succeeded Edward Telling as president and chief executive officer of Sears. Like Telling, Brennan was a merchandising man who got his start at Sears selling ties, underwear, and pajamas in the men's furnishings department. He ascended to the position of president of the merchandising group in 1980. Michael Bozic was named to replace Brennan as CEO of the Merchandise group. Heading the other business groups of Sears were Donald Craib—Allstate, Arthur Hill—Coldwell Banker, and Robert Gardiner—Dean Witter. Late in 1986, Sears World Trade, Inc., which had been plagued by several years of poor performance (losses of $10.5, $24.8, and $12.1 million in 1985, 1984, and 1983, respectively), was merged into the Merchandise Group.

SEARS TODAY

Organization

Sears, Roebuck and Company is a diversified general merchandise, insurance, real estate, financial services and world trading company. As depicted in the organization chart of Exhibit 5, the family of companies that comprise Sears today are: Sears Merchandise Group, Allstate Insurance Group, Coldwell Banker Real Estate Group, and Dean Witter Financial Services Group. Sears, Roebuck and Company, therefore, is a holding company comprised of four major businesses; each is set up as an autonomous group headed by its own chairman and chief executive officer, who is responsible for running the business. The four group chairmen report to the corporate chairman of Sears, Roebuck and Company, as do corporate officers, who assist the chairman in setting goals, monitoring performance, coordinating functions, and reporting results.

Sears' Corporate Vision

Sears' corporate philosophy, displayed in Exhibit 6, has always stressed responsiveness to customer needs. The philosophy focuses on four fundamental factors that management contends are essential to future success: Sears must be aggressive, responsive, innovative, and consistent.

The Discover Card was certainly an aggressive effort, the first major bank credit card to be introduced in twenty years. The Merchandise Group best exemplifies Sears' efforts to be responsive to customer preferences. During 1986, Sears developed localized merchandising programs for small and mid-sized stores and continued to implement its national remodeling program to improve retail store performance. To be innovative, Sears has offered novel services previously unavailable on a national scale. For example, Coldwell Banker and Dean Witter have joined forces to offer homebuyers one-stop access to competitive home mortgages and related financial services. An example is the annuity products developed by Allstate and distributed through Dean Witter. Sears recognizes that these success factors must be pursued in a fashion which is consistent with the principles on which Sears was established initially: taking care of the customer is the cardinal rule of success.

EXHIBIT 5 Organization chart—Sears, Roebuck and Company, 1987.

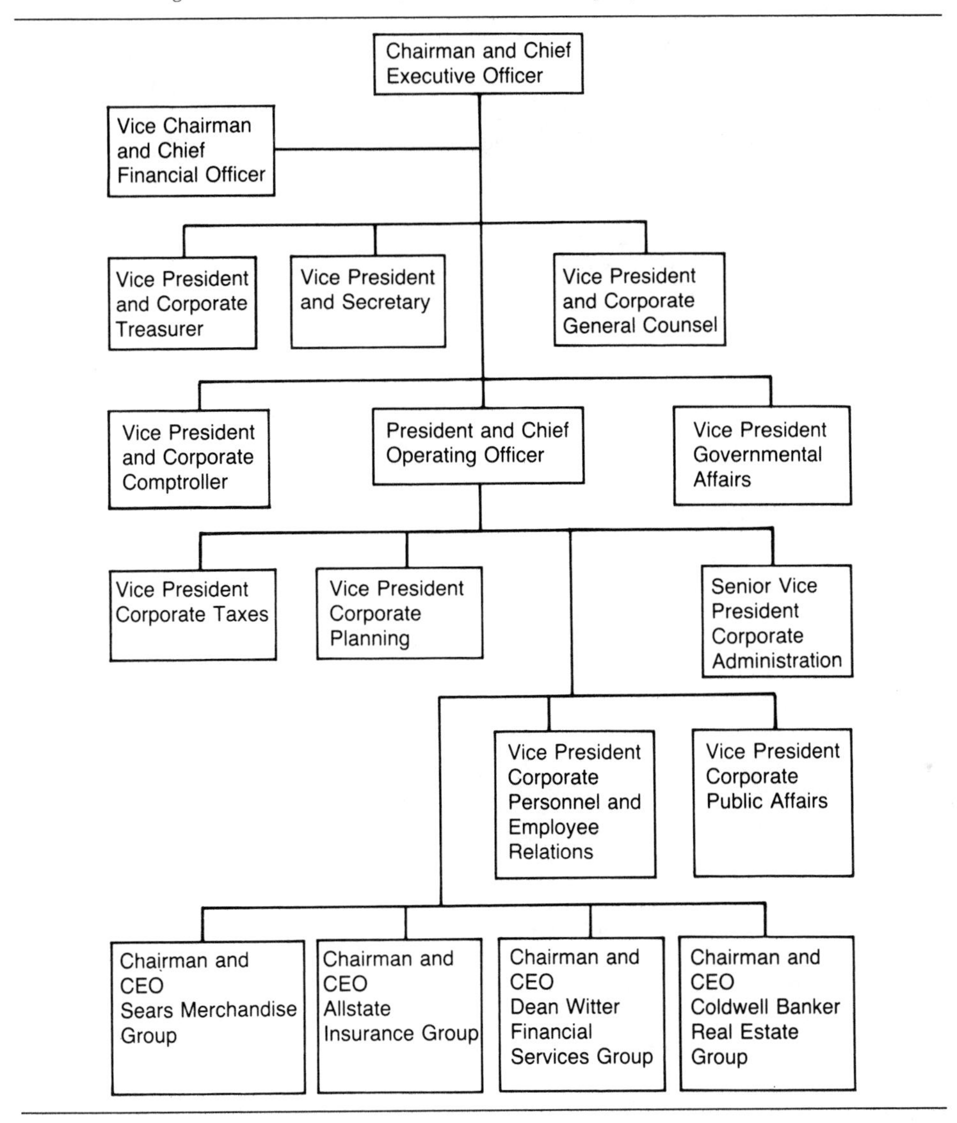

SEARS' PRIMARY COMPETITION IN NONFOOD RETAILING

The primary competitors in nonfood retailing are listed in Exhibit 7 along with their respective sales, market value, and net income. Sears is the market share leader. Sears competes most directly with other general retailers; the most significant of these are Wal-Mart, J. C. Penney, and Kmart.

EXHIBIT 6 Sears' Corporate Philosophy

Sears, Roebuck, and Co., a family of diversified businesses, is the leader in providing and distributing quality products and services to consumers. We will engage in those commercial opportunities that leverage the distinctive capabilities of our existing businesses.

We are committed to our most valued asset, our reputation for integrity.

We dedicate ourselves to the principle that serving the customer is of prime importance.

We strive to provide our shareholders with a foundation for consistent and profitable investment growth. Our attractiveness to investors will be enhanced by the additional value created through our family of companies' coordinated activities.

We will manage ourselves as strong, decentralized business groups reporting to the Chairman of the Board. In their commitment to further objectives consistent with approved plans and the overall direction of the corporation, our groups will be supported by an efficiently structured corporate organization.

We will be a low cost provider, managing with efficiencies of scale, building upon a foundation of competitive cost advantages, and maximizing the productivity of resources which contribute directly to serving our customers.

We will allocate resources among our enterprises based upon an evaluation of their long-term relative profitability and the financial goals established by the corporation. We will maintain an overall capital structure which is stable, cost efficient, and which provides an appropriate balance between financial leverage and business risk.

We will develop and distribute proprietary products and services when our reputation and skills add value and provide the opportunity to achieve greater profitability.

Our commitment to strategic planning is integral to managing our businesses and thinking long term.

We will be a leader in developing innovative applications of proven technology.

We will provide all employees—regardless of their sex, race, age, religion, disability, or ethnic background—with an environment in which to maximize their potential and their contribution to our success, and we will see to it that they share in that success in meaningful ways.

We will faithfully fulfill our social and citizenship responsibilities.

We will communicate with customers, employees, shareholders, governments and the general public with the company's traditional devotion to integrity in order to enhance our reputation, advance company goals, and clarify company policy and activities.

Source: Sears, Roebuck and Co., 1986 *Annual Report*, p. 6.

Wal-Mart

Wal-Mart operates 980 discount stores primarily in small town settings in twenty-two states. Wal-Mart stores represent the major shopping outlets in rural areas. They carry a wide assortment of merchandise for one-stop shopping convenience. Wal-Mart also owns forty-six Sam's Wholesale Club units, a members only outlet featuring lower prices on selected merchandise in a warehouse setting. Launched in 1983, the "wholesale clubs" are no-frills stores twice the size of Wal-Marts and located in large metropolitan areas. Sam's Wholesale Clubs sell mostly name-brand, high-turnover items on a phenominally low mark-up of 7 percent, as opposed to the typical retail

EXHIBIT 7 The *Business Week* top 10 nonfood retailers—1986

	Market Value			Sales		Profits	
	Top 1000 Rank	*$ Millions*	*Percent Change from 1985*	*$ Millions*	*Percent Change from 1985*	*$ Millions*	*Percent Change from 1985*
Industry Composite	*7*	*127046*	*32*	*194725*	*14*	*6193.4*	*16*
1. Sears, Roebuck	14	19608	9	44281	9	1351.3	4
2. Wal-Mart Stores	19	16436	49	11909	41	450.1	37
3. Limited	48	9039	80	3143	32	227.8	57
4. K-Mart	57	8188	46	23812	8	570.0	21
5. J. C. Penney	68	7471	46	14740	7	530.0	34
6. May Dept. Stores	72	7377	124	10328	9	381.0	10
7. Toys 'R' Us	116	5081	43	2445	24	152.2	27
8. Federated	131	4612	20	10512	5	301.9	5
9. Dayton Hudson	132	4585	−9	9259	12	255.0	−10
10. Melville	146	3959	17	5262	10	238.3	8

Source: *Business Week,* 17 April, 1987, p. 146.

mark-up of 50 percent. Memberships to the clubs are sold on a yearly basis to businesses; whereas, individuals are assessed a 5 percent surcharge on purchases.

Wal-Mart's sales increased by $2 billion in fiscal 1987. According to Donald F. Spindel, a stock analyst with A. G. Edwards & Sons Inc. in St. Louis, Wal-Mart does well in discount retailing for a number of reasons. Most important, he believes, is its policy of bottom-to-top and top-to-bottom communication which permits a great sales idea at one location to be immediately implemented at more than 950 others. Furthermore, according to Spindel, "Wal-Mart dares to dare. They really promote change. Anytime you promote change, there are going to be instances where you try something and it doesn't work . . . so you abandon it." He quickly adds that abandoned approaches have been rare at Wal-Mart: "If they do anything wrong, I have a hard time seeing it." (*Business Week Careers,* February/March 1987)

Sales for the three fiscal years ended January 31, 1987, and the respective total and comparable store increases (actual increases due to improvements in operations of existing stores) over the three-year period are shown in Table 1.

Wal-Mart is the mass retailing success story of the 1980s. Since 1972, it has grown rapidly from twenty-eight stores and $45 million in sales. It has been referred to as the classic niche chain in retailing. It puts "too many" stores in any one portion of its midwestern and southwestern turf in order to discourage its larger competitors (primarily Sears and Kmart) from entry. (Peters and Waterman, 1982)

TABLE 1

Fiscal Year	*Sales (millions)*	*Total Increases*	*Comparable Store Increases*
1987	$11,909	41%	13%
1986	8,451	32	9
1985	6,400	37	15

J. C. Penney

J.C. Penney is one of the largest retailers of family apparel, home furnishings, and leisure lines operating nearly 2,000 stores in fifty states, Puerto Rico, and Belgium. Approximately one fourth of its stores are what J. C. Penney refers to as metropolitan market stores. These stores are located primarily in premier regional shopping centers in the suburbs, while the traditional soft line stores are in older generation shopping centers and business districts serving the more densely populated mature suburbs and urban sectors of these markets. J. C. Penney also operates 359 Thrift and Treasury Drug Centers throughout the United States.

J.C. Penney is the fourth-largest retailer in the United States. It has recently been emphasizing designer apparel in an effort to appeal to the tastes of an increasingly affluent and image-conscious consumer. It has discontinued its automotive service centers in keeping with its increasing emphasis on soft goods. Accordingly, J.C. Penney no longer offers major appliances, paint, hardware, and lawn and garden supplies.

After several years of declining profits, 1986 figures indicate that J.C. Penney's repositioning strategy may be beginning to pay off. (See Table 2.)

For J.C. Penney, 1986 was a year of record earnings and sales. The company's income before an extraordinary charge rose to $530 million, 33.5 percent above the $397 million earned in 1985. Gross margin increased during 1986 due to lower mark-

TABLE 2 Financial highlights

	1986	*1985*	*1984*
Sales (millions)	$14740	13747	13451
Sales of JCP stores and catalog	13390	12634	12372
Percent increases	6.0	2.1	12.1
Retail income (millions)	497	386	407
Percent increase (decrease)	28.8	(5.1)	(7.7)
Percent of sales	3.4	2.8	3.0
Net income (millions)	478	397	435
Net income per share	7.06	5.31	5.81
Dividends per share	2.48	2.36	2.36
Capital expenditures (millions)	350	426	505

downs and well-controlled inventories. During 1986, J.C. Penney opened a total of forty-one stores and closed 120 stores. In addition, thirty-seven free-standing catalog sales centers were added as well as 146 independent catalog sales merchants.

For 1987, the company plans to open sixteen department stores in regional shopping centers and thirty geographic stores in smaller markets as well as thirty drug stores and thirty-five free-standing catalog sales centers. Finally, in the summer of 1987, J.C. Penney will launch the first consumer-controlled, cable-television-delivered home shopping and information service, called "Telaction," that will enable consumers, at their convenience, to buy or browse for merchandise and services offered by some of the America's and Europe's leading companies.

Kmart

Kmart Corporation is the nation's largest chain of discount stores operating more than 2,100 stores in every state except Alaska and Hawaii. The company's first store was opened in 1962, and since then, Kmart has had a profound effect on general merchandise retailing. Kmart was the first to introduce the discount department store on a national scale. Recently, the company has been concentrating on improving profit margins across its retail units. In addition to its Kmart department stores, the company also operates Walden book stores, Pay Less drugstores, and Builders Square hardware. In 1986, Kmart opened 195 new specialty stores, increasing total square feet of selling area to over 16 million, in its attempt to position each company for profitable future growth.

Kmart Corporation achieved record sales and profits in 1986, as evidenced by the five year summary shown in Table 3.

Kmart's plan for the coming years is to steadily improve overall market share while substantially improving the rate of profitability for each dollar of sales that is generated. The most obvious component of this strategy is the conversion of many former Kmarts, typically those which exhibited marginal performance, into specialty stores. For instance, during 1986 eight of the fourteen domestic Kmarts closed were converted to specialty retail locations: six locations to Builders Square stores, and two locations to Pay Less Wonder World stores.

Finally, Kmart is engaged in a massive recapitalization program. During 1986, 207 Kmart stores were completely refurbished. The refurbishments centered around an im-

TABLE 3

	Five Year Summary		
Year	*Sales (000s)*	*Net Income*	*EPS*
1986	23,812,000	570,000	2.84
1985	22,035,000	472,000	2.42
1984	20,762,000	503,000	2.58
1983	18,380,000	491,000	2.53
1982	16,611,000	255,000	1.34

proved merchandise mix emphasizing apparel and new fixturing and floor plans, which created a more pleasant and convenient shopping atmosphere. In addition, Kmart's investment in a $50 million satellite network serves the communication needs of domestic Kmart stores, and its rapid installation of point-of-sale systems not only speeds customer service but also rapidly assesses customer buying trends and enables Kmart to alter inventory accordingly.

INDUSTRY OUTLOOK

According to Harold Greene of *Standard & Poor*

> . . . the retail trade industry should show steady progress over the remainder of the year (1987) and continue through 1988 . . . General merchandise sales will advance at an annual rate of 5–6% in both years, but a number of leading retailers should do better. The overstored and intensely competitive market will continue to put pressure on earnings, but this will be offset by lower income tax rates and benefits derived from cost-cutting programs such as divisional consolidations, distribution efficiencies, overhead expense reductions, and expanding applications of electronic technologies. The combination of lower taxes, cost reductions, and more balanced inventories should allow earnings gains to exceed sales gains. This was generally the pattern for the first quarter of 1987 and it should prevail for the full year. (Greene, p. R61)

A majority of the dominant general merchandise retailers showed strong earnings gains in the first quarter of 1987. These gains resulted from a combination of factors: strong Easter sales, lower federal tax rates, the success of cost-containment measures, and a mild rate of inflation. It is expected that full-year earnings for general merchandise retailers should be fairly good.

There is a notion among analysts that America has become overstored—that there is an oversaturation of retailing alternatives throughout most of the nation. Therefore, retailing giants can no longer expect to grow simply by opening new stores in untapped areas. This notion has triggered a major restructuring of the retailing industry. Increasingly, retailers are beginning to focus their efforts more narrowly on the promising niches within the market.

One such niche is specialty retailing, where the store emphasizes a vast selection of closely related product lines.

> Specialty stores have numerous advantages. Site selection is facilitated by the marketing studies that mall developers conduct. The cost of opening a store is relatively low which minimizes the investment risk and permits a short payback period. Proprietary credit cards are not generally offered, which limits working capital needs primarily to inventory. Cash flow generation is strong. Reflecting small store size and efficient space utilization, they generate higher sales per square foot vis-a-vis department stores. *Stores Magazine* reported that specialty stores generated sales of $178 per square foot in 1985, 18% greater than $151 for department stores. Advertising costs as a percentage of sales are lower for specialty stores: they depend on both regular mall traffic and traffic spurts resulting from anchor store sales promotions, which receive heavy advertising support. The narrow merchandise lines of specialty stores lend themselves to more effective buying and more efficient use of electronic systems for inventory control and management information sys-

> tems. Because the cost of opening a store is comparatively low, it is also easier for specialty chains to achieve geographic diversification, which lessens their risk in the event of regional economic downturns. Since most stores are small and general purpose facilities, they can be recycled without much difficulty if unsatisfactory performance warrants closing. This reduces the likelihood of being encumbered by unexpired lease obligations. (Greene, p. R62)

Specialty stores do have some disadvantages. Due to the relatively low entry barriers, overstoring is a frequent problem. Another problem is that specialty stores have in the past focused on a narrow line of merchandise which turned out to be a fad and therefore had a very short product life cycle, such as the numerous citizen's band radio outlets which emerged in the mid-1970s.

There are many examples of major retailers which have entered the specialty retailing market, such as Kmart in hardware, J.C. Penney in drugstores, Montgomery Ward in appliance stores, and Woolworth in shoes. They have adopted an "if you can't beat 'em, join 'em" philosophy. (*Standard & Poor's Industry Surveys.* 22 January, 1987, p. R82)

Merchandising's Decade of Strategic Change

Sears' retailing division experienced sagging performance during the early 1970s. Consequently, for the first time in its history Sears began to alter its merchandising strategies. First, it upgraded its products in an attempt to attract customers who had previously frequented department stores. Sensing little improvement in performance, the firm reversed itself by slashing prices in an effort to attract customers who typically shopped at the discount chains. According to a *Forbes* analysis of 1980

> Sears, Roebuck and Company had never really recovered from a series of merchandising missteps of the early 1970s when, in 1980, the $30 billion giant reported a $7 million retailing loss in the first quarter. It had lost much of its market to Kmart and others, and retailing was falling far behind Sears' highly profitable insurance operation, Allstate. (*Forbes.* 21 July, 1980)

Sears' retailing woes were the subject of national attention:

> The Sears, Roebuck and Company of the late '70s was in danger of dying. The glory years of the USA's largest retailer had faded. Sears men watched in horror as the stock fell from $62 a share in 1972 to $14.50 in 1980. Sales dropped to all-time lows. Observers likened Sears to a great ship "dead in the water, helpless and adrift . . ." (*USA Today.* 14 October, 1987, p. 14)

At this time, Edward Brennan was appointed chief executive officer of the retailing division formed during the conversion to a holding company structure. Through a massive retrenchment effort (cost savings of $125 million by consolidating nine headquarter operations into five and voluntary retirement of more than 1,400 middle and senior level managers), merchandising experienced its first successive years of increased earnings during the decade. Even so, Brennan was deeply concerned; he recognized major trends among consumers that were inconsistent with Sears' age-old strategy of "one stop shopping".

> . . . a consulting firm specializing in the retail industry, notes that a generation ago Sears, Penney, and Ward dominated the middle-American market. Now he says the discounters are doing twice the sales volume of the three combined. 'The mass merchants' formula for presenting a store with a full assortment of goods is really obsolete . . . It just won't work for growth.'
>
> Even Sears seems to be questioning the all-things-for-all-people way of retailing. For the past few years it has been examining every one of the 800 product lines that it sells in catalogues as well as in stores. Where it is already a market leader—in so called hard goods like radial tires, lawn tractors, car batteries, washers and dryers—Sears says it will work on new products, presentations, and advertising to maintain dominance. The company also aims to strengthen its soft goods lines, especially apparel and home furnishings, where Sears is not a major player but sees opportunities to increase market share. Products that don't sell well and won't increase Sears' market penetration are to be eliminated. (*Fortune*. 4 April, 1983, p. 134)

In 1983, Sears opened its first store of the future. This new store makes everything visually more appealing. By the end of the year, Sears had twelve stores of the future where the key concept was a remerchandising of nearly 730 product lines into a shopping environment that was as attractive and inviting as it was logical and disciplined. Modeled on the store within a store concept, popularized by Bloomingdale's and Macy's, the new Sears contain areas for selling telephones, insurance, stocks, and real estate, as well as clothing, appliances, hardware, and automotive supplies—all in an effort to efficiently remain the country's most comprehensive retailer. (*Fortune*. 4 April, 1983)

Sears' store of the future was just one component of a five-year, $1.7 billion remodeling program for its merchandise group. Due to a shortage of what it considered to be desirable new shopping mall locations, Sears pursued increased per-unit revenues by refurbishing stores and shifting to strongly focused departments such as electronics, housewares, and automotive (*Business Week*. 21 November, 1983). Initially, the results were promising; 1984 was a good year. However, as shown in Exhibit 8, Sears' retail sales have grown just 2.2 percent since 1984 while industrywide revenues have increased at twice that rate. Net income over the same period dropped 18.7 percent, to $736 million.

Many of the problems relate to inefficiencies at Sears (selling and administrative costs account for 29 percent of sales, compared with 24 percent at Kmart and 18 percent at Wal-Mart), but analysts point to vacillating pricing strategies and ineffectual marketing as more fundamental problems. Sears has thus far been largely unsuccessful in its attempts to become an established name in high fashion despite its signature Cheryl Tiegs and Stefanie Powers apparel lines. (*Business Week* 6 July 1987). This was painfully accentuated when *The Wall Street Journal* characterized Sears' long-term apparel retailing prospects as grim. (*Wall Street Journal*. 18 November 1986).

Sears and Specialty Retailing

As Sears continues its efforts to revitalize its merchandising division, one of the critical issues it must resolve is whether to enter specialty retailing. If it chooses to do so, then the obvious issues become how, in what areas, and on how large a scale. All of this

EXHIBIT 8 Sears' financial data

millions

Revenues	**1986**	1985	1984	1983	1982
Sears Merchandise Group					
Merchandising	**$22,092**	$21,549	$21,671	$20,439	$18,779
Credit	**2,068**	2,098	1,894	1,404	1,158
International	**2,914**	2,905	2,943	3,246	730
Sears Merchandise Group total	**27,074**	26,552	26,508	25,089	20,667
Allstate Insurance Group					
Property-liability insurance	**9,698**	8,244	7,551	7,004	6,487
Life-health insurance	**2,884**	2,089	1,404	1,079	930
Non-insurance	**56**	46	34	41	42
Allstate Insurance Group total	**12,638**	10,379	8,989	8,124	7,459
Dean Witter Financial Services Group					
Securities-related	**2,563**	2,031	1,845	1,544	1,110
Consumer banking	**852**	826	651	564	487
Dean Witter Financial Services Group total	**3,415**	2,857	2,496	2,108	1,597
Coldwell Banker Real Estate Group	**1,152**	949	826	704	470
Corporate and Other	**489**	424	359	196	120
Inter-group transactions	**(487)**	(446)	(350)	(338)	(293)
Total	**$44,281**	$40,715	$38,828	$35,883	$30,020
Income before income taxes, equity in net income of unconsolidated companies and minority interest					
Sears Merchandise Group					
Merchandising	**$ 885**	$ 738	$1,196	$1,182	$ 826
Credit	**502**	582	483	285	35
International	**98**	94	16	(27)	(46)
Sears Merchandise Group total	**1,485**	1,414	1,695	1,440	815
Allstate Insurance Group					
Property-liability insurance	**441**	261	363	373	310
Life-health insurance	**177**	164	124	96	88
Non-insurance	**3**	(1)	1	6	5
Allstate Insurance Group total	**621**	424	488	475	403
Dean Witter Financial Services Group					
Securities-related	**154**	(3)	(94)	138	72
Consumer banking	**(212)**	21	24	52	(17)
Dean Witter Financial Services Group total	**(58)**	18	(70)	190	55
Coldwell Banker Real Estate Group	**151**	130	121	76	72
Corporate and Other	**(374)**	(332)	(332)	(289)	(263)
Total	**$1,825**	$1,654	$1,902	$1,892	$1,082
Net income	**1986**	1985	1984	1983	1982
Sears Merchandise Group					
Merchandising	**$ 458**	$ 447	$ 656	$ 654	$ 456
Credit	**253**	294	243	144	18
International	**25**	25	6	(17)	(42)
Sears Merchandise Group total	**736**	766	905	781	432
Allstate Insurance Group					
Property-liability insurance	**631**	490	505	469	399
Life-health insurance	**117**	114	155	83	74
Non-insurance	**2**	1	1	3	2
Allstate Insurance Group total	**750**	605	661	555	475

continued

EXHIBIT 8 continued

millions

Net income	**1986**	1985	1984	1983	1982
Dean Witter Financial Services Group					
Securities-related	**80**	—	(45)	69	36
Consumer banking	**(117)**	13	12	31	(9)
Dean Witter Financial Services Group total	**(37)**	13	(33)	100	27
Coldwell Banker Real Estate Group	**94**	86	76	48	52
Corporate and Other	**(192)**	(167)	(154)	(142)	(125)
Total	**$1,351**	$1,303	$1,455	$1,342	$ 861

millions

	1986	1985
Assets		
Investments		
Bonds and redeemable preferred stocks, at amortized cost (market $12,257.4 and $9,571.6)	**$11,377.0**	$ 9,619.5
Mortgage loans	**7,031.4**	6,417.8
Common and preferred stocks, at market (cost $1,954.4 and $1,632.2)	**2,458.0**	2,095.5
Real estate	**1,692.5**	1,394.8
Total investments	**22,558.9**	19,527.6
Receivables		
Retail customers	**12,408.4**	12,260.1
Brokerage clients	**3,275.6**	3,260.0
Insurance premium installments	**1,301.1**	1,096.9
Discover Card	**1,271.9**	20.4
Finance installment notes	**870.5**	738.9
Other	**1,913.9**	1,286.5
Total receivables	**21,041.4**	18,662.8
Securities purchased under agreements to resell	**5,228.7**	10,655.3
Property and equipment, net	**4,593.0**	4,541.3
Merchandise inventories	**4,013.0**	4,115.2
Cash and invested cash (note 5)	**2,984.4**	2,357.2
Trading account securities, at market value	**2,565.0**	3,764.4
Other assets	**3,010.2**	2,793.1
Total assets	**65,994.6**	66,416.9
Liabilities		
Long-term debt (note 6)	**10,066.7**	9,906.6
Insurance reserves	**9,952.1**	8,053.6
Deposits and advances	**6,623.2**	5,278.8
Accounts payable and other liabilities	**5,925.4**	5,576.2
Securities sold under agreements to repurchase	**5,887.9**	12,022.9
Unearned revenues	**4,412.9**	3,560.3
Short-term borrowings (note 5)	**4,306.0**	3,996.0
Payable to brokerage clients	**2,845.3**	2,633.5
Deferred income taxes (note 4)	**2,451.3**	2,341.6
Securities sold but not yet purchased, at market value	**477.2**	1,253.8
Total liabilities	**52,948.0**	54,623.3

continued

EXHIBIT 8 continued

millions	1986	1985
Commitments and contingent liabilities (notes 3, 7, 8, 9)		
Shareholders' equity (note 9)		
Preferred shares ($1 par value, 2.5 shares outstanding)	**250.0**	250.0
Common shares ($.75 par value, 376.6 and 364.1 shares outstanding)	**286.1**	277.4
Capital in excess of par value	**1,982.6**	1,489.7
Retained income	**10,367.6**	9,681.4
Treasury stock (at cost)	**(89.0)**	(106.2)
Unrealized net capital gains on marketable equity securities	**364.1**	336.1
Cumulative translation adjustments	**(114.8)**	(134.8)
Total shareholders' equity	**$13,046.6**	$11,793.6

must be assessed under the knowledge that if it does enter specialty retailing, then it will be subjecting itself to the possibility of competing subsidiaries: general merchandising with specialty merchandising. Specialty retailing runs against the very foundation of Sears—the synergies of multiple businesses under the same roof. Yet, Sears cannot escape the reality that specialty retailers such as Toys R Us, Circuit City, the Foot Locker, and True Value have eroded its once strong image in toys, consumer electronics, shoes, and hardware/tools, respectively. These are the critical strategic issues facing the merchandising group at Sears.

REFERENCES

"A Big Remodeling Job at Sears." *Business Week.* 21 November, 1983, 54.

"The Business Week Top 1000: America's Most Valuable Companies." *Business Week.* (Special Issue, 17 April, 1987, 31–36.

"Can Sears Get Sexier But Keep the Common Touch?" *Business Week.* 6 July, 1987, 93–94.

"A Fuller Deck." *Fortune.* 27 May, 1985, 9–10.

Greene, Harold. "Retailing Current Analysis." *Standard & Poor's Industry Surveys.* 30 July, 1987: section 2, R61–R64.

J. C. Penney Inc., 1986 *Annual Report.*

K Mart Corporation, 1986 *Annual Report.*

Morrison, Anne. "Sears' Overdue Retailing Revival." *Fortune.* 4 April, 1983, 133–37.

Moss, Phil. "What It's Like to Work for Wal-Mart." *Business Week Careers.* February/March 1987, 24–26.

Peters, T. J., and Waterman, R. H. Jr. *In Search of Excellence.* (Harper & Row: New York, 1982).

"Saga of How Sears Survived the '70s." *USA Today.* 14 October, 1987, 14.

Sears, Roebuck and Company, 1986 *Annual Report.*

"Sears Yesterday and Today." Sears, Roebuck, and Company: 1986.

Simpson, Janice. "Business Schools—and Students—Want to Talk Only About Success." *Wall Street Journal.* 15 December, 1986, 31–32.

"Synergy Begins to Work for Sears' Financial Supermarket." *Business Week.* 13 June, 1983, 116–117.

Wal-Mart Stores Inc., 1986 *Annual Report.*

Williams, Monci. "Sears Roebuck's Struggling Financial Empire." *Fortune.* 14 October, 1985, 40–44.

Worthy, James C. *Shaping an American Institution* (University of Illinois Press: Chicago, 1984).

Bevell's True Value Hardware, Inc.—1987

FREDERICK C. HAAS
Virginia Commonwealth University

During the peak pre-Christmas sales period of 1986, Bevell's True Value Hardware faced its biggest challenge in recent years. Ames Discount Department Store, one unit of a 306-store regional chain, opened near Blackstone, Virginia. The grand opening was advertised heavily. This store competed directly with Bevell's in two major product lines: housewares and toys. Throughout October and early November, Robert Daniels, Bevell's president, witnessed a drop in sales in these product categories. Bevell's personnel were keenly aware that the competitive picture had changed because of the Ames store.

BEVELL'S INTERNAL OPERATIONS

Product Lines Sales

Bevell's Hardware is a franchise of Cotter & Company that sells True Value Products. Each of Cotter's approximately 8,000 True Value franchise holders owns ten shares of Cotter stock worth $100 per share. Cotter offers legal advice, store layout planning, market surveys, store performance evaluations, uniforms (for lease or purchase), insurance, trucks (for lease only), and cars and equipment to each of its True Value stores. Cotter negotiates the sale of True Value franchises for any individual who requests the service. Daniels uses some of these services. is satisfied with them, and feels the fees are justifiable. He is in the process of having Cotter provide an improved layout for Bevell's housewares display area.

Bevell's Hardware carries several thousand individual items grouped in nine categories. These categories, along with 1986 percent contributions to total sales, are as follows:

1. Hardware	15–20%
2. Housewares	3–7% (seasonal)
3. Paint	3–4%
4. Plumbing Supplies	9%
5. Electrical Supplies	10%
6. Tools	5–7%
7. Lawn and Garden	10–14% (seasonal)
8. Sporting Goods/Toys	0–2% (seasonal)
9. Building Supplies	35–50% (anything *not* in the main showroom)

FIGURE 1 Organization chart for Bevell's True Value Hardware, Inc., January 1987

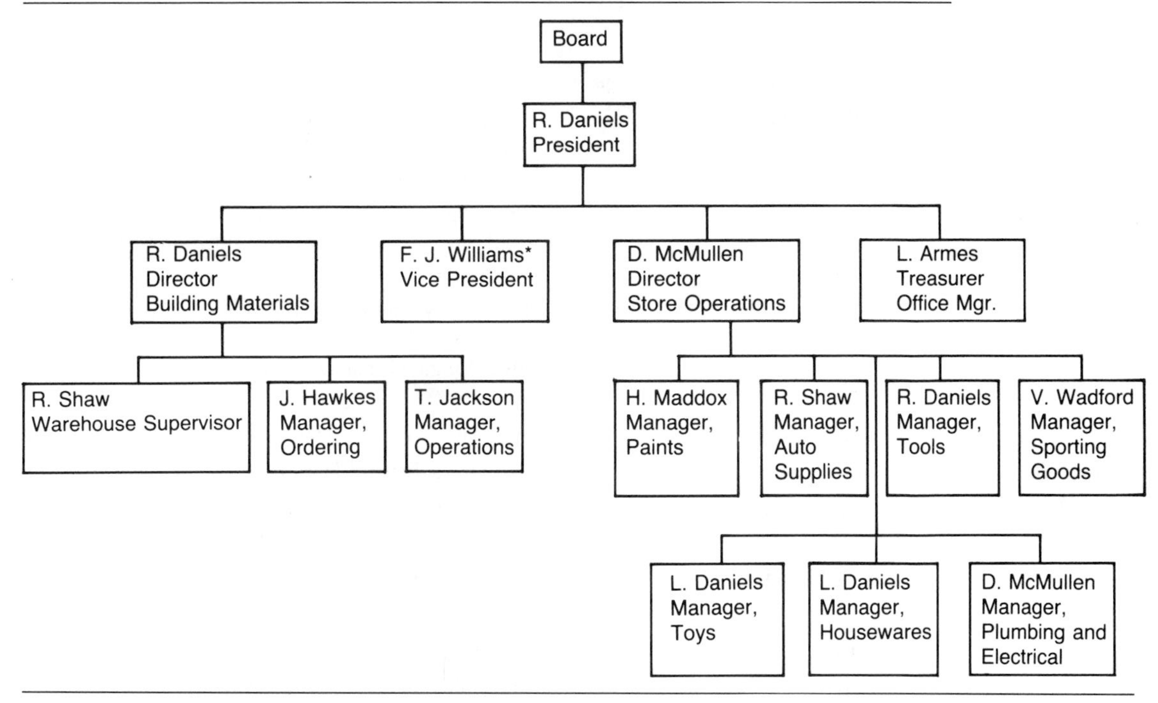

*Major stockholder involved in planning but not in operations

Organization and Personnel

The organizational structure of Bevell's Hardware has evolved and expanded as a result of growth characterized by increasing sales, expanded product lines and enlarged facilities. A representation of that organizational structure is shown in Figure 1.

Employee turnover is very low, and there is a waiting list of applicants who would like to work at Bevell's Hardware. The average employee has several years experience selling the varied product lines at Bevell's Hardware or similar stores. Regular customers know Bevell's employees on a first-name basis. A brief experience profile of the full-time employees is provided in Figure 2. Bevell's pay scale and employee benefits are competitive with those of other employers in the community. There is no union at the store and little union representation in the locality. Both store and warehouse employees show a strong career-oriented attitude concerning their employment.

Advertising and Selling

Bevell's advertising expenditures average 1.5 percent of sales. In late 1986, advertising expenditures were increased to 2 percent of sales because of increased competition from the recently opened local unit of Ames. There is a significant seasonal fluctuation. During the most recent two-year period, about 20 percent of advertising expen-

FIGURE 2 Employee experience profiles

Full-Time Employees

Name	Age	Profile
Robert Daniels	47	President and operations manager of Bevell's for nine years. Prior experience in fast foods management.
Laura Armes	33	fifteen years experience at Bevell's Hardware; oversees customer billing and other financial details.
Lynn Daniels	42	Thoroughly familiar with Bevell's Hardware (president's wife); develops media advertising and manages housewares and toys.
Eleanor Hudson	50	five years at Bevell's Hardware.
Thomas Jackson	33	six years at Bevell's Hardware.
Herbert Maddox	31	eleven years at Bevell's Hardware.
Dewey McMullen	53	twelve years experience hardware; eight years at Bevell's Hardware.
Mary Ellen Prue	32	two years at Bevell's Hardware.
Richard Shaw	40	five years at Bevell's Hardware.
Mary Slaw	57	thirty plus years experience in other hardware stores; two years at Bevell's Hardware.
Vicki Wadford	33	Experience at Ace Hardware prior to two and a half years at Bevell's Hardware.
Barbara Wampler	47	seven years at Bevell's Hardware; works in billing and customer accounts.
Lorena Watts	55	two years at Bevell's Hardware.
Regular Part-Time Employees (three days per week)		
Bess Alder	68	eighteen years at Bevell's Hardware.
Paul Black	62	twenty-three years at Bevell's Hardware.
James Hawkes	67	thirty-three years at Bevell's Hardware.
Jerry Stroup	55	six years at Bevell's Hardware.

ditures have gone to mass mailings, 52 percent to radio and TV spot advertising, 20 percent to newspaper advertising, and 8 percent to miscellaneous advertising, such as promotional contests. Daniels believes that spot advertising on radio and TV has the best results, but he has made no formal attempt to verify this belief. Advertising is concentrated primarily on the Blackstone area, where more than 50 percent of the store's repeat customers reside. Some advertising is directed to the residents of Nottoway County, where Blackstone is located.

Mass mailing typically had been a multi-page publication that Cotter & Company produces and sends to 13,000 Bevell's customers. These circulars are mailed four times a year with seasonal emphasis: spring (gardening), summer (paints and home care), fall, and Christmas issues. Newspaper ads are placed in *The Courier-Record,* Blackstone's newspaper. They feature one or several inventory items at a time. A heavy seasonal emphasis is placed on spot radio ads that usually feature one high ticket item during the period of heaviest demand, such as a riding lawn mower or a Christmas gift item. To counter the Ames store's heavy advertising, more frequent three- and four-column-inch specials were being used during the fourth quarter of 1986.

The showroom area of the Bevell's store and some areas in the warehouses are designed for customer self-service. Small items are stocked on shelves, in bins, or on racks, as appropriate, at selected point in the store and warehouse. Customers who are familiar with these locations and know what they want to purchase can serve themselves. Payment is made by cash, check, or credit card. Recording cash registers provide a record of type of sales by inventory category (hardware, paint, or building supplies, for example) on a paper tape printout. These registers are not linked to a computer and do not serve any function in inventory control or replenishment. Customers can charge purchases, and billing is monthly.

Customers needing assistance can be served by any of the salespeople. However, if there is a special need, the salesperson responsible for that area is consulted. Bulky or heavy items, such as power tools and lumber, are loaded at the warehouse onto a Bevell's delivery truck or the customer's vehicle.

Store and Warehouse Facilities

Bevell's Hardware occupies three buildings and has outside yard storage for materials that can be exposed to the weather. A layout of the buildings is provided in Figure 3.

The Bevell's store is a one story, cement block building of 11,700 square feet and opening on two streets. The store is the major sales area. It houses office and employee facilities plus some storage of small, fast-selling items. During April 1986, the concrete block store front (facing the parking lot) was improved aesthetically with a covering of exterior siding boards and a roof that tied two building segments together. Sidewalk, curb, and gutters were installed by Bevell's Hardware along this face of the building. Blackstone resurfaced the street running between the parking lot and the store.

Bevell's attached warehouse building is a steel trussed, framed and sheathed, concrete-floored building having 7,000 square feet with a 25-foot ceiling. Its floor is designed for heavy vehicles, and the space is used for storage and display of bulky building materials. There is also an unattached warehouse, which is an old wooden building having 12,000 square feet on the main level, plus a 3,000 square-foot balcony, a 4,000 square-foot cellar, and several shed roofs attached to its exterior walls. This space is used for storage and display of bulky building materials.

Finally, an outside yard storage area of 20,000 square feet is used to store building materials not subject to weather damage. This area will be fenced as soon as a draining problem is resolved.

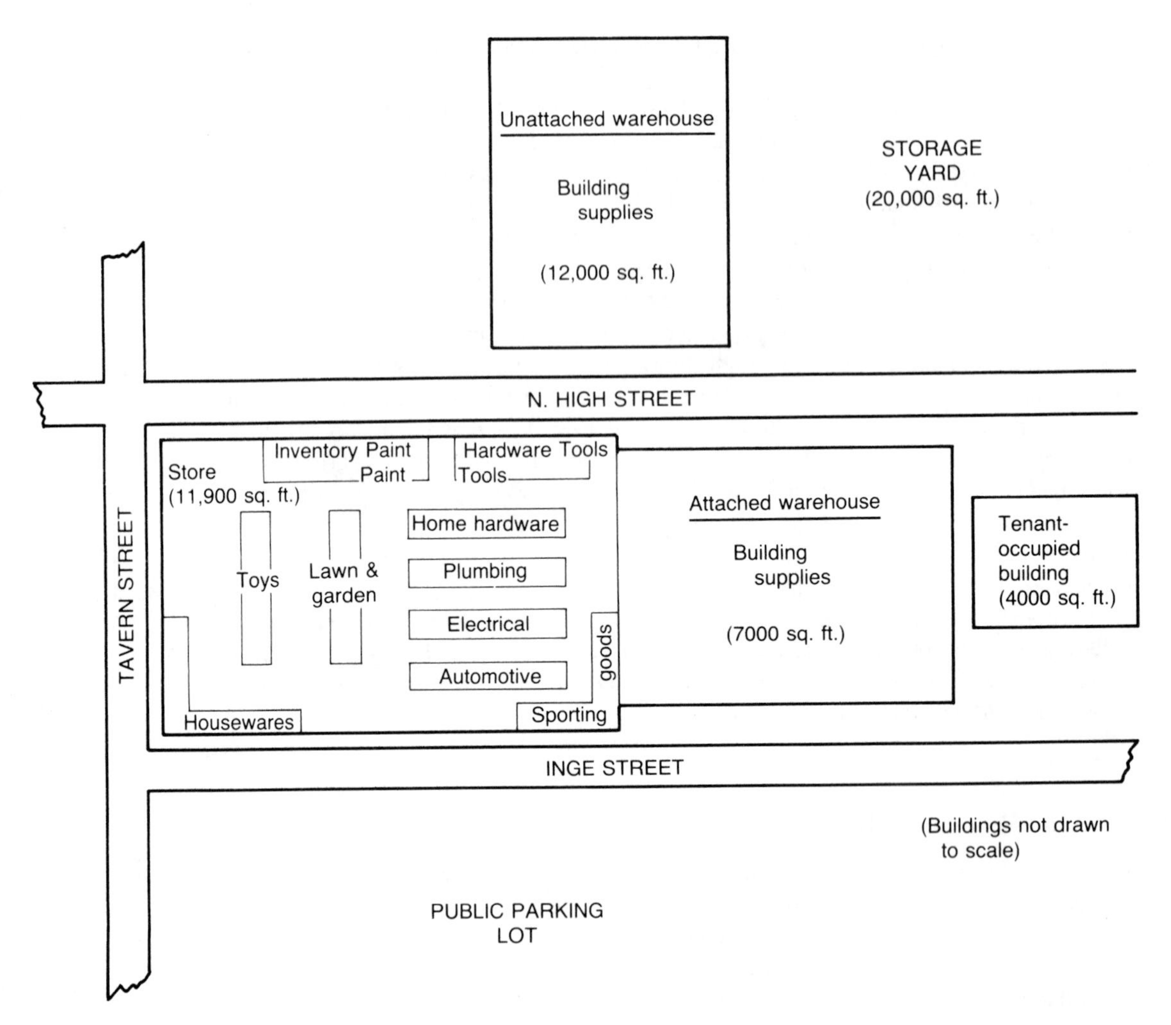

FIGURE 3 Layout of Bevell's buildings

Financial Details

Bevell's Hardware purchases accounting services from a certified public accountant in Blackstone. During fiscal 1983, a computer terminal was provided in the store. A four-digit identification number was assigned to all charge customers when the accounting function was computerized. This number serves several purposes for Bevell's office staff, who use it when compiling charges for billing and crediting account payments. Grouping customers for various purposes can be done using this control number. Bevell's payroll was computerized in the fourth quarter of 1986.

Bevell's historical financial data are given on the balance sheet in Figure 4 and the income statement in Figure 5. An important financial rearrangement was made during fiscal year 1983 when Bevell's purchased the buildings and furnishings it had

FIGURE 4 Bevell's True Value Hardware, Inc., balance sheet

	1986	*1985*	*1984*	*1983*	*1982*
Assets					
Current Assets					
Cash in bank/on hand	$ 169,935	$126,836	$104,152	$ 91,879	$ 92,389
Accounts receivable	235,030	247,204	203,285	175,156	190,427
Notes and loans receivable	13,864	3,950	3,950	4,152	4,324
Inventory	238,829	235,657	251,249	249,909	202,030
Prepaid expenses	0	735	3,652	5,738	1,376
Estimated corporates taxes	0	0	7,044	0	0
Investments	17,137	11,338	4,612	0	0
Total Current Assets	**$ 674,795**	**$625,720**	**$577,944**	**$526,834**	**$490,546**
Long-term					
Land	35,334	39,875	39,875	39,875	8,573
Buildings, equipment and vehicles (net)	187,398	179,449	190,556	72,913	36,968
Other assets	157,911	148,402	143,738	169,220	2,011
Total Assets	**$1,055,438**	**$993,446**	**$952,113**	**$808,842**	**$538,098**
Liabilities and Equity					
Current Liabilities					
Accounts payable	187,425	197,947	166,890	141,407	107,858
Notes and loans payable	138,131	152,174	203,916	109,567	138,812
Accrued expenses	0	0	33,354	0	1,321
Taxes due	10,258	14,443	8,317	50,339	46,288
Mortgage payments due	5,605	0	0	5,476	0
Total Current Liabilities	**$ 341,419**	**$364,564**	**$412,477**	**$306,789**	**$294,279**
Long-Term Debt					
Mortgage notes and other notes payable	200,383	205,988	215,730	269,524	100,000
Deferred income tax	7,828	9,404	3,914	0	0
Total Long-Term Debt	**208,211**	**215,392**	**219,644**	**0**	**0**
Total Liabilities	**$ 549,630**	**$579,956**	**$632,122**	**$576,213**	**$394,279**
Stockholders equity					
Cap. stock	1,000	1,000	1,000	1,000	1,000
Add't. paid in capital	2,350	2,350	2,350	0	0
Retained earnings	502,458	410,139	316,641	231,629	142,819
Total Equity	$505,808	$413,489	$319,991	$232,629	$143,819
Total Liabilities and Equity	**$1,055,438**	**$993,446**	**$952,113**	**$808,842**	**$538,098**

Note: Buildings and equipment which the business had been leasing were purchased during the 1983 fiscal year. Bevell's fiscal year is May 1 to April 30.

been leasing. As a part of the purchase program, $82,500 was borrowed for renovation of existing facilities and construction of a new warehouse to replace an existing, obsolete one. The purchase was financed by $275,000 in industrial development bonds issued by the Industrial Development Authority of the Town of Blackstone and purchased by a Blackstone bank. This purchase gave Bevell's Hardware a fixed monthly

FIGURE 5 Bevell's True Value Hardware, Inc. income statement

	1986	1985	1984	1983	1982
Sales (Net)	**$2,071,243**	**$1,667,070**	**$1,571,876**	**$1,435,549**	**$1,390,573**
Cost of goods sold					
Beginning inventory	235,654	251,245	237,071	202,030	212,712
Purchases	1,600,300	1,263,485	1,190,556	1,059,551	1,025,494
Freight and related expenses	34,423	26,333	32,528	34,144	19,497
Ending inventory	[238,829]	[235,654]	[251,246]	[249,909]	[202,030]
Total Cgs.	**1,631,548**	**1,305,409**	**1,208,909**	**1,045,816**	**1,055,673**
Gross Profit	**$ 439,695**	**$ 361,661**	**$ 362,967**	**$ 389,733**	**$ 334,900**
Deduct Operating Exp.					
Warehouse and store	42,911	34,633	34,887	43,900	78,636
Selling, General and administrative Expenses	283,116	208,025	228,925	227,416	240,258
Total Operating Expenses	**$ 326,027**	**$ 242,658**	**$ 263,812**	**$ 271,316**	**$ 318,894**
Profit (loss) from OPNS	113,668	119,003	99,155	118,417	16,006
Other income	74,686	72,332	69,107	58,474	61,892
Total Income	**$ 188,354**	**$ 191,335**	**$ 168,262**	**$ 176,891**	**$ 77,898**
Other expense	36,528	39,212	32,822	24,328	10,000
Income (before tax)	151,826	152,123	135,440	152,563	67,898
Federal and state income tax	59,507	58,625	50,428	63,753	18,370
Net income (loss)	**$ 92,319**	**$ 93,498**	**$ 85,012**	**$ 88,810**	**$ 49,528**
Ret. earn. begin.	**$ 410,139**	**$ 316,641**	**$ 231,629**	**$ 142,819**	**$ 93,291**
Ret. earn. ending	**$ 502,458**	**$ 410,139**	**$ 316,641**	**$ 231,629**	**$ 142,819**
Earnings Per Share	**$923**	**$935**	**$850**	**$888**	**$495**

Note: Building and equipment which the business had been leasing were purchased during the 1983 fiscal year. Bevell's Fiscal year is May 1 to April 30.

bond payment of $2,386.51 (instead of monthly lease payments totalling $1,916.67 plus 3 percent of gross sales over $1 million). A substantial decrease in monthly cash outflow resulted.

BEVELL'S EXTERNAL ENVIRONMENT

Market Area Served

Blackstone is located in Nottoway County, Virginia. The 1980 Census indicated a town population of 3,624 people, 30.4 percent white females, 26.9 percent white males, 24.0 percent black females, and 18.7 percent black males. Over 84 percent of the town residents are native Virginians, with 39 percent being high school graduates and 12.6 percent having completed four or more years of college study. The median family income in Blackstone in 1986 was $20,744, while the Nottoway County per

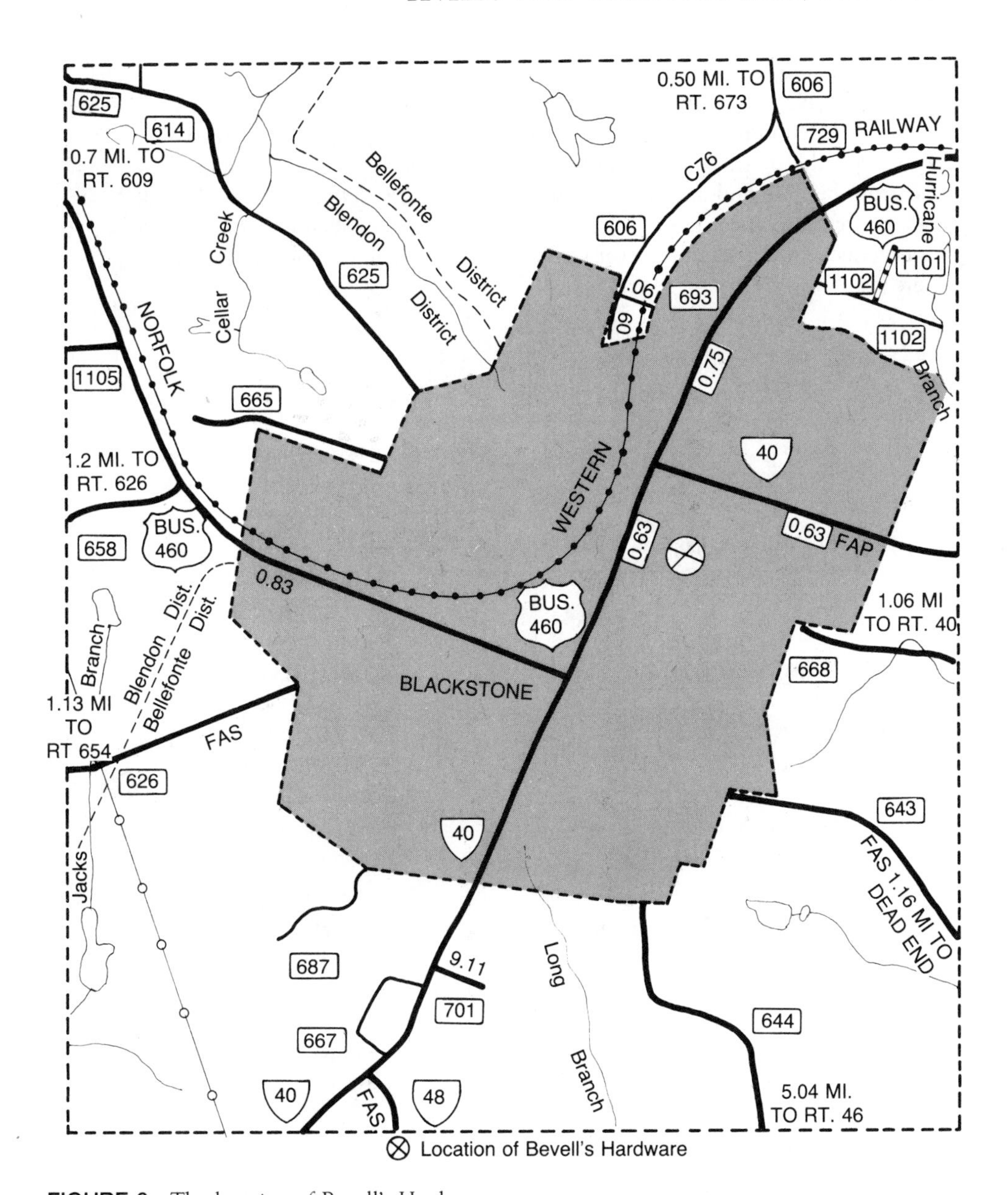

FIGURE 6 The location of Bevell's Hardware

Source: Commonwealth of Virginia, General Highway Map, Nottoway County

capita income was $9,954. A map of Blackstone showing Bevell's location is given in Figure 6.

Competing Stores

The newly opened Ames store will provide heavy competition in housewares and toys. Another wide line supplier, Kenbridge Mfg. and Supply Company, has an Ace Hardware franchise that carries all of Bevell's product categories in greater or lesser variety. Kenbridge is located 11 miles southwest of Blackstone. Daniels believes Bevell's Hardware and Kenbridge Supply compete in the territory lying between them. He believes, however, that both Bevell's and Kenbridge have great difficulty in shipping past one another because building supplies often require costly delivery by large flat bed trucks. Compared to competitors, Bevell's Hardware offers a central location, a wide variety of products, and generally lower prices. The major competitors are described in Figure 7.

FIGURE 7 Competitive businesses

Business	*Competing Lines*
Ames	Toys and housewares
Blackstone Emporium	Floor Coverings
Blackstone Fuel and Supply Co.	Hand tools Paints and sundries Lawn and garden
Dollar General Variety Store	Electrical supplies Paint and sundries Sporting goods Housewares
Eppes Supply	Primarily automotive supplies
Freeman Auto Parts	Hand tools Automotive supplies
Janet's Nook	Arts and crafts supplies
Pennington Aluminum Products	Building siding materials Doors and windows
Planters Southern States	All of Bevell's categories except building supplies
Sears Catalog Stores	All of Bevell's categories except building supplies
Sheffield furniture	Floor coverings
Sheffield TV and Appliance	TVs and appliances
Super Dollar Variety Stores	Housewares Hardware Electrical supplies Paint and sundries Toys
United Motor Parts	Hand tools Automotive supplies
Western Auto	All of Bevell's categories except building supplies

Factors Affecting Customer Income

News of industry openings and closings in the area commanded top billing in *Courier-Record* columns during 1986, Virginia Apparel should be in operation soon. A new $8 million North American Reiss plant in the town's industrial park is expected to employ 200 workers. Plans are progressing for construction of a 30,000 square-foot plant for Eastern Wood Fibers Corporation that will employ twenty-five workers.

Ames Department Store in the Blackstone Shopping Center provides about forty jobs with seasonal highs of double that number. Three more stores are now under construction in the shopping center. A new shopping center with a Food Lion supermarket and several other stores has been announced for Route 40 South. Land has been rezoned for an apartment project, a car dealership, a motel and several other businesses on Route 606, the town's link to the U.S. 460 bypass. Blackstone's other large employers, Velvet Textile, Taylor-Ramsey Furniture, Blackstone Kilns, Southeastern Lumber, and Nottoway Lumber, are all in full production.

Cotter & Company—Bevell's Parent

Daniel A. Cotter, president and chief executive officer, assumed active direction of Cotter & Company on January 1, 1983. His father, John M. Cotter, chartered the company in January 1948 and managed its growth for 35 years. The company is a manufacturer and wholesaler of hardware and housewares. It is wholly owned by the retail outlets it serves. These outlets, including Bevell's Hardware, consist of more than 8,000 True Value stores throughout the United States. Also, there are approximately 840 combination True Value Hardware and V&S Variety Stores and 920 V&S Variety Stores. Revenues increased from $1.459 billion in 1983 to $1.734 billion in 1986. Daniel A. Cotter took command of a vertically integrated, well established organization that he described as a "very tight ship."

The Cotter Company is a member-owned wholesaler of hardware, variety, and related products, including sporting goods. It is the largest wholesaler of hardware and related items in the United States. The company also manufactures paint, lawn, and garden products (including snow throwers) and hardware-related products. For reporting purposes, the company operates in a single industry as a member-owned wholesaler cooperative.

Membership in the company entitles Bevell's and the other members to use certain company trademarks and trade names, which Cotter promotes and advertises throughout the country. These include the federally registered collective membership trademarks indicating membership in "True Value Hardware Stores" and "V&S Variety Stores" collective groups sponsored by the company.

Cotter serves its members by purchasing products in quantity lots and selling them to members in smaller lots, thus passing along any savings to members in the form of lower prices and/or patronage dividends. Conventions and meetings are held for members in order to keep them better informed about industry trends and new merchandise availability.

Cotter also provides each of its members with an illustrated catalog showing the products available to the member stores. Sales to members are divided into three categories, as follows: (1) warehouse shipment sales (approximately 46 percent of total sales); (2) direct/drop shipment sales (approximately 41 percent of total sales); and (3) relay sales (approximately 13 percent of total sales). Warehouse shipment sales are sales of products purchased, warehoused, and resold by the company upon order from the members. Direct shipments sales are sales of products purchased by the company but delivered directly to the members. A relay sale is the sale of a product purchased by the company in response to the request of several members for it. The product is not normally held in inventory and is not suitable for direct shipment.

Cotter employs approximately 3,700 persons on a full-time basis. Due to the widespread geographical distribution of Cotter's operations, employee relations are governed by the practices prevailing in the particular area where the facility is located and are generally dealt with locally. Approximately 65 percent of the company's hourly wage employees are covered by collective bargaining agreements that are usually effective for periods of three years. In general, the company considers its relationship with its employees to be good.

PAST AND PRESENT OPERATING STRATEGIES

When asked to explain the steady and rapid sales growth of Bevell's Hardware during his years as president, Daniels cited several factors that have promoted profitable sales.

- ☐ Sufficient and correct inventory that is reviewed and upgraded continually.
- ☐ Purchase of inventory at the lowest cost.
- ☐ Freedom given to the department managers to experiment with inventories and sales techniques.
- ☐ Emphasis on tie-in sales.
- ☐ Emphasis on seasons, including preplanned inventory buildup, in-store promotions used in advertising, and direct selling.

Under Daniels' direction, Bevell's Hardware has been carrying an inventory averaging 15–16 percent of sales. He believes that some items, such as power tools and gasoline-powered gardening tools, have to be displayed and demonstrated to be sold effectively. He feels also that many hardware and building supply items sales are lost if customers have to wait for delivery, because resulting construction delays are costly to contractors.

Purchases come from three sources. First, Bevell's Hardware can buy directly from any manufacturer whenever the purchase is sufficient to obtain a suitable price and terms. Second, the company can buy through True Value Relays, which provides a computer-based method for placing mixed item, various quantity orders. These mixed orders are offered by the Cotter True Value organization to member stores on a continuing basis. Third, Bevell's may buy from the Cotter True Value warehouse stock. Relay purchase is the least costly source, while purchase from the True Value warehouse is the most costly. Daniels' target is to average one third of inventory purchases from each of these sources.

Tie-in sales are emphasized at Bevell's Hardware, especially in building materials. For example, the sale of wall paneling usually results in the purchase of nails, glue, moldings, and tools to aid with the installation. Drop ceiling panels and insulation put on sale also create tie-in sales, as do the sale of numerous other items. Another sales strategy is to expand the inventory of seasonal items as the selling period approaches and to advertise heavily. A picture of Bevell's Hardware is given in Figure 8.

Looking Toward the Future

For the next several years, Daniels plans to continue improving his present location rather than branching out to other sites, even though he is aware of the limited growth potential in the town and county. Daniels believes the time and resources needed to locate and purchase another business and integrate it into Bevell's Hardware, or to establish another branch site, can be better spent developing the present location.

At the present location, Daniels expects to expand existing lines as sales projections indicate the need. He plans to improve the store layout and customer service wherever possible. New lines will be added and perhaps some lines will be discontinued or deemphasized. He notes that wood stove sales have virtually disappeared. He thinks he can expand Bevell's share of the market in several selected building supply, hardware, and housewares lines. He notes that Kenbridge Construction is putting heavy emphasis on contracting and has recently undertaken several large construction projects. This move is taking some emphasis away from the Ace Hardware operation. Therefore, Bevell's may be able to attract some new customers as a result.

The most recent and serious challenge, however, is the Ames Discount Department Store. Although Ames overlaps with only two of Bevell's merchandise categories, housewares and toys, Daniels is planning a vigorous weekly campaign to promote five to ten leading products in various departments through radio spots and newspaper classified ads. Long-term, Daniels hopes that Bevell's Hardware can increase sales and continue to operate profitably.

FIGURE 8 A photo of Bevell's Hardware

Dick's Place—1987

FREDERICK C. HAAS
Virginia Commonwealth University

The door to Bill Paulette's office swung open, and his business partner, Bob Borum, entered and sat down. "Morning Bob," said Bill, without looking up from the report he was reading. "How's it going at our Richmond store?"

"We are still having problems with some car owners who buy their Armstrong and Michelin tires from the buyers clubs. As you know, Bill, some of these clubs sell tires to their members and charge extra for mounting and balancing. Others do not mount or balance the tires they sell. Their customers go to full service tire dealers, including us, with tires we did not sell. The customers sometimes get angry when we charge them for mounting and balancing," explained Bob.

"Well, we certainly can't do it free," Bill agreed. "It's bad enough the way these buyers clubs are taking away our sales without our being expected to provide services that they don't. That's how some clubs underprice us. All their customers get is the tire, which they take from the store to their cars or trucks themselves. As you well know, there frequently is little advice on what tires to buy, no one to explain fully the features of the different tires and no mounting or balancing. On the other hand, we include all this in our price."

"Sure, we realize all that," Bob griped, "but many of these customers don't, and that's a real problem for all of the people in my shop. Bill, I've been thinking that we should make a clear statement in our newspaper advertising that our prices do include mounting and balancing. Then, customers can make a more accurate assessment of how much they actually are saving by buying at the discounters who charge extra for these services."

Bill Paulette agreed immediately. "Great idea, Bob. Before you leave here, let's set up an ad with that statement in it. I've been thinking of doing more advertising. We should tell the potential recap customers about our new computer-controlled recapping machine. We have it running now; would you like to see it?"

Bob nodded his head, "Sure would, Bill. One hundred twenty-five thousand dollars for one machine really impresses me. We once could build a retail outlet like Blackstone for that kind of money." The two men got up and left the office, heading for the recapping plant in another part of the Amelia building. The Labor Day, 1987, advertisement for Dick's Place is given in Figure 1.

THE COMPANY

Named for its founder, Richard A. Johns, Jr., who established the business in 1941, Dick's Place is now managed by William Paulette, co-owner (with Robert Borum) and president. The company is organized as a closely held corporation that sells new and

FIGURE 1 1987 Labor Day advertisement for Dick's Place

recapped truck and passenger car tires. The Dick's Place organization chart is shown in Figure 2.

Dick's Place has three facilities located in different market areas: Amelia, Blackstone, and Richmond. A commercial sales representative, working out of the Richmond location, calls on truck fleet owners in the greater Richmond area and surrounding counties selling new truck tires and recapping service. All recapping is done at the Amelia location. A brief historical profile of Dick's Place follows:

1941 Founded by R. A. Johns, Jr., with $360 total capital as a wayside service station on a secondary road in Amelia County, Virginia.
1943 Became a truck stop on Route 360, an east-west arterial highway crossing Virginia.
1951 Moved to Amelia and occupied a rented building.
1955 Relocated to a new building built for tire sales and tire recapping.
1965 The building was completely destroyed by a fire set by Halloween fireworks, but some of the stock and recapping equipment was saved. The business was moved to its present location.

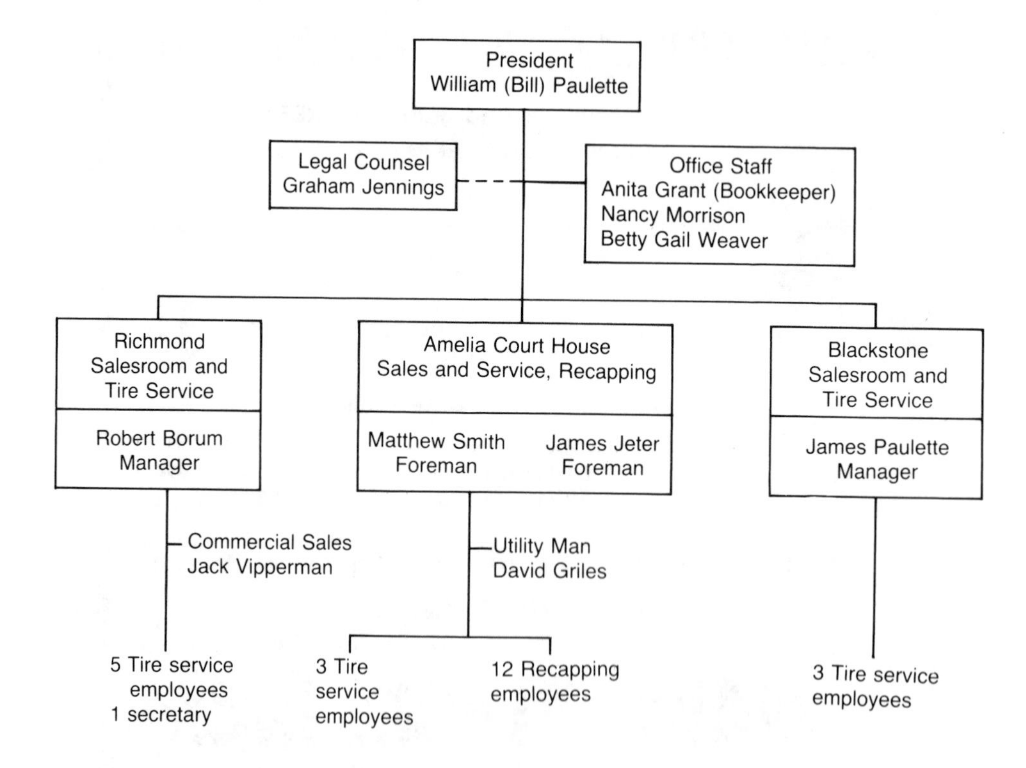

FIGURE 2 Dick's Place organization chart

1972 Richmond facility established in a rented building.
1980 Blackstone facility established in a new building (leaseback arrangement).
1984 Richmond facility established in a new building (leaseback arrangement).

Gross sales of $2.85 million for 1986 were about $50,000 less than for 1985, and net income decreased about $13,000. This was the first decrease over a previous year since 1983. Besides the new kind of competition being seen at the Richmond location, both Amelia and Blackstone sales had been adversely affected by reduced incomes for customers, primarily logging contractors and farm equipment operators.

Positive Factors of the Business

A large pool of satisfied, repeat customers had been established by giving good service and competitively priced products. Another strength of Dick's Place are the employees who provide total customer satisfaction. There is very low turnover. Employees see Dick's Place as providing career employment. Managers and employees of the three facilities are highly motivated.

Dick's Place serves both rural and urban markets in a number of Virginia counties and cities. Although the three facilities service different markets, they are close enough to each other to permit a cross-flow of products and services as needed to provide efficient customer sales and service.

Among its three locations, Dick's Place has five road service trucks that are dispatched to customers having a tire failure on the road. Three of these trucks are located at the Richmond facility, one is at Amelia, and one is located in Blackstone. Purchasing is done at the Amelia headquarters for all Dick's Place locations, and two affiliated tire sales companies, Denton's Tire Service (Farmville) and Perdue Tire Company (Hopewell). Billing is centralized in Amelia.

Problems of the Business

Neither tires nor tire rubber scrap is welcome in the typical county landfill because they do not deteriorate. Dick's Place pays a fee for each tire and each load of rubber scrap taken to the landfills. Alternate disposal for tires is sought and sometimes found when someone wishes to fill a ditch or ravine, or can use the discarded tires for some other purpose. Disposal of scrap rubber particles has recently been arranged. They are being burned by a high temperature incinerator that supplies steam for an Amelia business.

The proliferation of buyers cooperatives is a growing threat facing Dick's Place. Company-owned and affiliated retail outlets of major tire manufacturers also represent stiff competition for Dick's Place. Product supply, accounting, financial advice and support, training, legal support, and other services are provided to these dealers by the tire manufacturers. The independent dealer must obtain these services by purchase or contract in the competitive market.

Decreased demand occurred in 1985 for truck tires used by logging workers who could not compete with the prices of Canadian lumber. Farm tire usage also declined in 1985 due to the generally depressed farm economy. Bill Paulette estimated that the Amelia sales totals were off $100,000, and the Blackstone sales totals were off $75,000 because of these two reasons. However, the excise tax placed on the Canadian lumber imported into the United States caused some resumption of lumbering in Amelia County in 1986.

Disposal of unusable tire bodies and scrap rubber generated by the recapping process creates both a problem (since rubber is not welcomed on the county landfills) and an expense for handling and hauling. Limited capacity and inefficient movement of tires at the Amelia facility are another problem. For example, recapped tires not belonging to a particular customer are inventoried on an upper floor. Multi-level product movement is more difficult and time-consuming and, consequently, more costly than one-level movement. Management has felt that the investment either to upgrade (if it is possible) or replace this building could not be made in the near future.

BUSINESS AREAS

Retail Sales, Truck and Passenger Car Tires

The sales mix on a dollar basis has averaged as follows:

- ☐ Truck Tire Sales — 50 percent
- ☐ Passenger Car Tire Sales — 15 percent
- ☐ Truck Tire Recapping — 20 percent
- ☐ Passenger Car Tire Recapping — 15 percent

The sales mix shifts in reaction to economic factors. Elements that increase consumer disposable income tend to cause an increase in new passenger car tires; whereas, decreases tend to favor sales of recaps. Truck tire sales and recapping services sales react to the volume of freight traffic, which is also influenced by economic factors. A highway hauler truck typically has eighteen wheels and carries one or two spare tires. A common-size tire for these trucks [11R 22.5] lists for approximately $280, and there was a federal excise tax of $29.75 in 1986. To equip such a truck with a full set of new tires requires an investment of about $6,000. Recapping this size tire by the hot capping process costs an average of $64. There is no tax on recapping. These cost factors virtually assure that truck tires with sound, undamaged cord bodies and sidewalls will be recapped as many times as possible. A radial cord truck tire is expected to run about 100,000 miles on the original tread and an equal amount of road miles on each of two recaps for a 300,000 mile service life.

At all its locations, Dick's Place sells and mounts new tires of several brands in a wide range of sizes. Warranty work and any other tire performance adjustments are provided also. All of these locations have a full range of vehicle lifting equipment. Each location also has pneumatic and electrical tools for mounting and demounting wheels on cars, and tires on the wheel rims. But Dick's place does not do automobile repairs, tune-ups, alignment, or brake work. Providing these services has been considered but never undertaken.

Recapping Process and Recap Sales

Customers desiring recapping services may obtain them at any of the locations by either leaving their tires for recapping or swapping them for inventoried tires already recapped. A customer having his or her tires recapped obtains a warranty only on the recapping since Dick's Place cannot guarantee the tire body. A customer purchasing a recapped tire from inventory obtains a warranty on the tire body because it has been examined for damage *and* the recapping.

Tires from all locations that appear suitable for recapping are sent to the Amelia location, recapped by either the hot or cold process, and returned to the location from which they were sent. The hot recapping process includes these steps:

1. Inspection of the tire on a specially designed tool that exposes the tire's interior while the operator looks for broken cords or other damage. Tires found unsuitable for recapping are discarded at this point.
2. Buffing of the tire surface so the new rubber cap can be applied cleanly and smoothly. Each tire is given a number at this point.
3. Inspection of the buffed tire for hidden damage.
4. Inflation and capping of the tire on a machine that applies a coating of heated rubber as directed by a computer program that controls the tread size and thickness being applied.
5. Curing of the tire in a heated mold while the tire is inflated to high pressure. At this point, the tread design is impressed by the mold.
6. Clean up of the tire, which requires the removal of small rubber spikes, mould marks, and other blemishes. A visual inspection of the tire.
7. Inventory or return to customer of completed recapped tire. There are some by-products of the recapping process that create a disposal problem. One of these is a large quantity of discarded used tire bodies unsuitable for recapping. Another by-product is several tons per month of rubber scrap—small particles buffed off the tires during the recapping process.

The Cold Cap Process

The cold capping process costs about $10 to $15 more than hot capping for the various truck tire sizes, but it produces a harder, better wearing tread.

For cold capping, steps 1, 2, and 3 for casing inspection and preparation are performed in the same way as for hot capping, then:

4. A layer of very sticky rubber is applied to the surface of the casing where the new tread will be applied.
5. A precut-to-width rubber strip that has the tread design already in it is then cut to length and wrapped around the casing on top of the sticky surface.
6. The tire casing is then put into a smooth sided mold, inflated to 250 pounds by means of a tube, and subjected to a ton of pressure to make the cold rubber cap seat firmly and evenly.
7. Clean up and inspection.
8. Inventory or return to customer of completed recapped tire.

Bill led Bob Borum into the recapping plant when in full operation. They went directly to the new machine, being careful not to interfere with any of the workers. "Watch the hot cap process Bob," suggested Bill, "he has just mounted a 10:00R20 truck tire casing on the spindle and is checking the chart for the required settings." They watched the machine operator key the settings into the machine by pushing a series of buttons on the control panel. Then he pulled the strip of 1½ inch wide heated rubber compound and pressed it against the tire. He pushed the start button, and the tire began to rotate. An even strip of rubber was then placed on the tire casing, overlapping continuously as it was moved across the tread area.

"Well, Bill," Bob remarked, "you and I have seen this many times. As a matter of fact, we've both done it. Why does this recapper cost so much money? We could have done a lot of other things for that much investment." "Sure we could have, Bob," Bill responded quickly, "But this machine lays ten pounds of rubber a minute versus six for the older one we've been using. It also is much more accurate. That light shining across the edge of the rubber strip coming out of the machine keeps it in perfect alignment. The slightest deviation is instantly picked up by the electric eye that immediately makes an adjustment. On the older machine, the rubber strip ran in groves. It could deviate considerably before the operator recognized the problem and manually made a correction. In addition, the older machine's settings were made by a feeler touching raised points on a hard plastic pattern. As it got worn, the settings shifted. This one is entirely electronic so no wear occurs. This new recapper will give us the best recaps available with the present technology."

LOCATION AND FACILITIES LAYOUT

Dick's Place is headquartered in Amelia. This facility houses the administrative offices from which Bill Paulette directs the operation of the business. Purchasing, billing (averaging a volume of about 1,000 bills per month), and administrative and clerical functions are centralized here. The recapping factory here also services all the locations by receiving tires and shipping recapped tires to them daily. The factory also has a tire sales room as well as mounting and service bays capable of handling either cars or trucks. Dick's Place owns this building. This location contributed 38 percent of sales in 1986.

The newest facility, in Richmond, Virginia, was first occupied in January 1984. It is a few miles west of the city limits in Chesterfield County and about 40 miles east of the Amelia headquarters. This location contributed 42 percent of fiscal year 1986 sales. It is located on Route 360, a major highway leading to and through the city. Robert Borum, the manager there, is also a co-owner (with Bill Paulette) and secretary-treasurer of Dick's Place. While depending primarily upon Amelia for his supply of tires and recapping services, he has considerable autonomy in buying locally when necessary, selling tires, servicing customers, and maintaining the facilities. These facilities include a sales area with customer waiting area, a large tire storage area with $100,000 to $150,000 in tire inventory, and a four-bay service area capable of handling both cars and trucks. There is room for two more service bays.

The Blackstone facility in Nottoway County, Virginia, was built in 1980. It is managed by James Paulette, the president's brother. This location contributed 20 percent of fiscal year 1986 sales. While not as large as either the Amelia or the Richmond facility, it offers the same products and services. It has a sales room with customer waiting facilities and a combined storage and service area that has two bays capable of handling cars and trucks. Blackstone depends on Amelia for its new and recapped tires. James Paulette exercises the same degree of autonomy as does the Richmond manager. Photos of all Dick's Place facilities are provided in Figure 3.

Both the Richmond and the Blackstone facilities were built under the direction of and are owned by the Paulette-Borum Investment Company, formed for that purpose. They are leased to Dick's Place, long-term. The Investment Company also owns various other investment properties. Among them are two church buildings, a seven-unit trailer park, a laundromat, a furniture store, a mechanic's shop, and a house. All these properties are located in or near Amelia.

MARKETS SERVED

Dick's Place is represented in the Richmond Yellow Pages by a two-line listing. There are more than eighty listings for new-tire dealers, and thirty more for tire recappers. Advertising is placed in the Richmond newspapers daily and the Amelia and Blackstone weekly newspapers on a regular basis.

From its Amelia and Blackstone locations, Dick's Place services a number of rural counties in an area known as the Piedmont region. Within a 50-mile radius of one or the other of these locations are residents of Amelia, Brunswick, Charlotte, Cumberland, Lunenburg, Nottoway, and Prince Edward counties as well as parts of others. This area had a 1980 combined population of 87,430 with a 1990 projection of 91,700, a 4.88 percent increase.

From these locations to some extent, but primarily from the Richmond unit, Dick's Place serves the Richmond Standard Metropolitan Statistical Area (SMSA) having a 1980 population of 630,015 with a 1990 projection of 720,300, a 15.6 percent projected increase. Customers residing in a number of other Coastal Plains Region counties not included in the Richmond SMSA—such as Hanover, Goochland, and Powhatan Counties—also are within easy driving range of these Dick's Place locations. These three counties had a combined 1980 population of 75,221 and were forecasted to have 93,900 residents in 1990, a 24.8 percent increase.

Population projection for the three current Dick's Place units by five-year intervals are shown in Figure 4. Dick's Place executives believe they are experiencing a more rapid population growth in Richmond and Amelia than these projections anticipated. The Blackstone area has not experienced a rapid growth. There is a general belief among local business owners that the 1980 census projections were overly pessimistic.

PRESIDENT'S PLANS FOR THE FUTURE

In 1986, the Richmond store's sales of $1,199,520 were $114,000 higher than Amelia, where sales totaled $1,085,280. The Blackstone store sold $571,235 in new and recapped tires. Dick's Place balance sheets and income statements are provided in Fig-

FIGURE 3 The Richmond (top), Amelia (center), and Blackstone (bottom) locations of Dick's Place

FIGURE 4 Population projections for locations in which Dick's Place has sales facilities

County	*Base Year 1980*	*1985*	*1990*	*1995*	*2000*
Amelia	8,405	8,700	9,200	9,500	9,900
Nottoway	14,666	14,600	15,000	15,100	15,300
Richmond SMSA[1]	630,015	679,157	728,399	769,500	810,700
Totals	**653,086**	**702,457**	**752,500**	**794,100**	**835,900**
10 year cumulative growth			15.2%		11.08%
20 year cumulative growth					27.99%

Notes: [1]Richmond Standard Metropolitan Statistical Area includes the City of Richmond and Henrico County and Chesterfield County where Dick's Place facility is located.

ures 5 and 6, respectively. This is the first time Richmond has outsold the Amelia location. If the present sales growth continues, the Richmond facility probably will have to be expanded to handle the increasing customer traffic.

Long-term, company executives see the need to rework or replace the Amelia facility. While the location is believed suitable, they are not optimistic concerning the possibility of modernizing the old building, or relocating to another building in the area. However, the tire recapping machinery and the tire mounting and balancing equipment has been maintained and replaced, as needed. This practice has kept these functions efficient despite inadequacies of the building. Acquiring other branch locations is possible, but not probable.

Another possibility is having more affiliated outlets. A Farmville location, called Denton's Tire Service, had been a part of Dick's Place until 1982, but it is now a well-established tire sales and service outlet. Denton's does not do a sufficient volume of business to buy factory-direct. Dick's Place purchases for and supplies Denton's Tire, charging a percentage mark-up over wholesale on new tires. Dick's Place also provides Denton's with recapped tires. In 1983, the Perdue Tire Company in Hopewell was established with capital borrowed from Dick's Place. This capital has been repaid. Perdue is on the same new tire and recapped tire supply basis as Denton's Tire.

Adding services such as tune-ups, automobile repairs, alignments, and brake repairs at all three present locations is not currently being considered.

FIGURE 5 Dick's Place, balance sheet (all figures in dollars)

	1986	*1985*	*1984*	*1983*	*1982*
Assets					
Current Assets					
Cash	177,094	194,215	247,369	231,373	108,962
Accounts receivable—Trade	405,367	415,617	375,550	389,495	352,925
Inventory (LC or M)	348,258	286,024	247,288	244,475	238,572
Prepaid taxes	6,435	0	35,176	0	21,403
Total Current Assets	**937,154**	**895,856**	**905,383**	**865,343**	**721,862**
Property Plant and Equipment					
Land	135,798	135,798	116,143	70,000	70,000
Building	362,329	362,329	303,563	48,505	48,505
Equipment and furniture	343,846	327,415	300,699	274,550	251,152
Vehicles	87,478	86,378	75,533	66,621	50,087
Leasehold improvement	18,241	18,241	18,241	18,242	18,242
	947,692	930,161	814,179	477,918	437,986
Loss: Accumulated depreciation and amortization	498,679	415,768	337,236	267,952	229,895
Net Property, Plant and Equipment	**449,013**	**514,393**	**476,943**	**209,966**	**208,091**
Other Assets					
Employee savings account	0	0	0	0	10,675
Loans receivable—employees	8,195	12,245	10,347	12,639	16,840
Loans and notes receivable—other	22,600	31,428	40,009	35,126	32,645
Total Other Assets	**30,795**	**43,673**	**50,356**	**47,765**	**60,160**
Total Assets	**1,416,962**	**1,453,922**	**1,432,682**	**1,123,074**	**990,113**
Liabilities					
Current Liabilities					
Accounts payable—trade	305,129	404,245	449,458	337,639	348,263
Notes payable—bank	100,000	0	0	0	0
Current portion of long-term liabilities	52,691	47,799	51,899	43,250	38,923
Accrued salaries and wages	9,166	33,250	49,450	97,602	27,419
Employee savings plan	0	0	0	0	5,456
Payroll taxes accrued and withheld	1,765	2,156	1,875	989	1,199
Sales and excise taxes payable	8,968	7,492	5,947	6,637	7,372
Income taxes payable	0	13,944	0	37,644	0
Total Current Liabilities	**477,719**	**508,886**	**558,629**	**523,761**	**428,632**
Long-term Liabilities					
Notes payable—R. A. Johns, Jr.	390,438	427,253	461,274	199,706	220,261
Notes payable—bank	46,875	58,287	17,878	38,990	57,358
Notes payable—stockholders	0	0	0	3,259	15,259
	437,313	485,540	479,152	241,955	292,878
Less: Current portion (above)	52,691	47,786	51,899	43,250	38,923
Long-term Liabilities	**384,622**	**437,754**	**427,253**	**198,705**	**253,955**
Total Liabilities	**862,341**	**946,640**	**985,882**	**722,466**	**682,587**
Stockholders' Equity					
Common stock outstanding	7,500	7,500	7,500	7,500	7,500
Additional paid in capital	67,500	67,500	67,500	67,500	67,500
Retained earnings	511,376	464,038	403,556	357,364	264,282
	586,376	539,038	478,556	432,364	339,282
Less: Treasury stock (at cost)	31,755	31,756	31,756	31,756	31,756
Total Stockholders' Equity	**554,621**	**507,282**	**446,800**	**400,608**	**307,526**
Total Liabilities and Stockholders' Equity	**1,416,962**	**1,453,922**	**1,432,682**	**1,123,074**	**990,113**

FIGURE 6 Dick's Place, income statements (all figures in dollars)

	1986	1985	1984	1983	1982
Sales	**2,856,035**	**2,913,283**	**2,738,048**	**2,575,354**	**2,669,256**
Cost of goods sold	1,914,208	1,926,799	1,840,523	1,691,031	1,862,688
Gross Profit	941,827	986,484	897,525	884,323	806,568
Operating Expenses					
Salaries and wages	500,040	511,923	499,588	517,185	465,192
Advertising, entertainment, and promotion	22,054	23,689	17,608	12,431	7,991
Bad debts	21,698	25,329	9,218	(5,072)	34,727
Bank discounts	748	1,225	1,601	1,793	1,587
Collection fees	2,599	1,882	1,021	1,308	629
Depreciation and amortization	82,911	93,970	74,522	48,281	41,517
Donations	4,940	13,040	7,752	5,982	2,000
Dues and subscriptions	1,831	1,869	1,041	837	908
Employee savings plan	0	0	0	6,155	6,535
Employee group insurance	22,738	14,048	10,203	7,585	6,330
Insurance	40,690	37,807	22,894	20,302	30,435
Legal accounting	4,465	1,792	4,370	2,600	4,265
Office supplies and postage	9,328	8,849	9,262	6,512	9,093
Rent	64,180	65,930	64,019	43,063	44,609
Taxes and licenses	49,075	45,067	50,237	38,229	39,120
Telephone	11,232	12,530	9,785	8,796	9,227
Uniform service	256	504	2,336	4,129	3,876
Utilities	40,075	39,877	44,822	41,034	46,098
Vehicle expenses	28,605	31,275	30,550	17,659	32,244
Total Operating Expenses	**907,465**	**930,606**	**860,829**	**778,809**	**776,384**
Income from Operations	**34,362**	**55,878**	**36,696**	**105,514**	**30,184**
Other Income					
Bad debt recovery	16,067	10,751	0	0	0
Gain on sales of property and equipment	0	4,468	2,716	1,175	8,994
Interest and discounts	33,214	32,087	34,625	36,975	2,882
Rent	28,201	23,350	15,345	14,079	5,400
Total Other Income	**77,482**	**70,656**	**52,687**	**52,229**	**17,276**
Total Income	**111,844**	**126,534**	**89,383**	**157,743**	**47,460**
Other Expense					
Repair and utilities rental property	4,449	1,210	0	0	0
Interest	45,648	43,813	36,107	22,415	28,484
Total other expense	50,097	45,023	36,107	22,415	28,494
Income Before Taxes	**61,747**	**81,511**	**53,276**	**135,328**	**18,976**
Provisions for Income Taxes	14,408	21,027	7,084	42,247	2,489
Net Income	47,339	60,484	46,192	93,081	16,487

Woodland Video—1987

RICHARD J. WARD
Bowling Green State University

It had all the appearances of being "one of those days." The weather was typical for a midwestern mid-January—snowy, windy, and very, very cold. I wasn't at work an hour, when my wife called to report our second appliance failure of the year (1987 was shaping up to be a banner year for my appliance repair person). I had just finished meeting with a student who thought that the grade on his paper was far too harsh. Since I thought I had been far too generous, our exchange of views on the subject had been intense. Next, I answered my telephone, I woefully found myself talking to Jim Mason.

Mason, a colleague from our College of Music, had a justly earned reputation for being the "kiss of death" for the new businesses he was forever starting. To date, Jim had started at least 10 different ventures that I knew about, and only his second, a musical instrument store, had been successful. Jim had sold the music store to get funding for his third effort, and he promptly lost it all in the only pizza outlet in our community to ever fail.

Thinking it over, Jim had concluded that lack of adequate capital was the primary cause of his downfall. Starting with his fourth business venture, he sought out "silent partners" among his colleagues, citing his one success and the "can't miss" nature of his new idea as investment justifications. We quickly learned to avoid Jim whenever the word was out that he was looking for a new partner. Unfortunately for me, the latest rumors suggested that Mason was looking again!

For lack of a better response, I put on a cheerful front. "Good morning, Professor Mason. What can I do for you?" In my mind, I added, "said the fly to the spider!"

Jim's phone style was to get right to the point. "I've heard that your students have studied the videocassette industry," he said. "Not exactly," I explained. "You see, I split my class up into teams, and I let each team pick an industry to analyze. One team chose to analyze the videocassette rental industry. They did a good job of it, but, as I recall, they didn't deal with the production and distribution of blank videocassettes."

"Perfect!" Jim exclaimed. "I beg your pardon," I responded in confusion. "Did they write a report, and do you have a copy of it?" he asked, ignoring my confusion. "Yes, and yes," I responded, "but I don't understand . . ."

"I need a copy of that report," Jim said, cutting me off. "I'm thinking of opening a videocassette rental store, and it will be a great help. Can I stop over at your place tonight to pick it up? While I'm at it, I can get your reactions to—what did my banker call it—oh, yeah, my business plan, since you teach business courses. Of course, assuming you don't mind . . .," he finished lamely.

"Well . . ." I hesitated, trying to think of some reason why I wouldn't be able to see him. "Great!" he said, taking advantage of the pause. "I'll be over about 7 P.M. Don't forget to get a copy of that report."

I hung up the phone with a sigh. It seemed that I was going to be invited to join one of Mason's business schemes. I started rehearsing alternative ways of saying that all my funds were tied up for the foreseeable future, but they all sounded lame.

I decided that my best bet was to find a flaw in his plan to open a video store. Towards that end, I found the report he had mentioned and refreshed my memory about its contents. The student team had briefly summarized the videocassette recorder industry and then discussed the videocassette rental industry in detail.

THE VIDEOCASSETTE RECORDER INDUSTRY

The industry that produces and markets prerecorded videocassettes prefers to label itself as the video software industry, perhaps in homage to its "hardware cousin," the videocassette recorder industry. The video software industry is a classic example of derived demand, as basic demand for the industry's product depends almost exclusively upon demand for the videocassette recorder, or VCR. Although some individuals will rent a VCR to view videocassettes, the number of videocassettes that can be sold or rented is essentially determined by "VCR penetration," the proportion of "TV households" (households owning one or more TV sets) that also own a VCR.

The first "home-use" VCR was offered for sale in 1975, and cumulative VCR sales totalled 250,000 units by 1979. At that time, the most practical use for a VCR was "time-shifting," the recording of a TV program at its scheduled broadcast time in order to watch it at a more convenient time. Motion picture producers saw the VCR's potential for their industry, but they elected to wait for better VCR penetration before entering this new market. As a result, the early video software wholesalers and retailers had very little product to offer their new customers. In a 1979 *Time* survey of its VCR-owning readers, only half of the VCR owners purchased prerecorded programming, and half of that was X-rated. The majority of these prerecorded programs were purchased through the mail.[1]

In early 1981, when cumulative VCR purchases totaled approximately 1 million units, several motion picture studios formed subsidiaries to market videocassette versions of their products. As these firms started to produce video software for sale and rental, the VCR started to become a more desirable product in the minds of many potential owners. At about the same time, VCR manufacturers started to move from skim pricing to penetration pricing, hoping to achieve better profits at the higher volumes resulting from lower price levels.

The strategy worked better than anyone expected. In 1982, 2 million VCRs were sold, and in 1983, that number doubled. Sales levels almost doubled again in 1984, reaching 7.5 million units. In 1985, VCR sales reached a rate of 1 million units a month, and that rate has continued throughout 1986.

However, every sale of a new VCR does not constitute a new VCR household. Some original VCR owners are discovering that their worn-out VCR is more expensive to repair than replace. Other new VCRs are purchased as upgrades for less-sophisticated original equipment, and some households are taking advantage of lower prices to purchase a second VCR for the second TV. Taking such purchases into consideration, one study estimates that there are approximately 31 million VCR households as of September 1986, representing a 35.7 percent VCR penetration of TV households.[2] Some industry observers predict growth of about 5 million VCR households over the next year.

To sum up the growth of the VCR industry, there has been a classic pattern of development in the decade or so that the industry has been in existence. After a period of slow initial growth, the VCR industry enjoyed a period of explosive expansion. As the industry approaches maturity, forecasts suggest a slower rate of growth over the next four to five years. The typical projection sees VCR penetration doubling by the early 1990s, but warns of the consequences to any firm that plans on continuing growth if the VCR industry fails to maintain its present sales rate of 1 million units per month.

THE VIDEO SOFTWARE INDUSTRY

The video software industry has its own names for its manufacturing, wholesaling, and retailing functions. Firms that record videocassettes are called studios, and distributors perform the industry's wholesale function. Video software dealers are the retail outlets that rent or sell prerecorded videocassettes to the end-use consumer. As more than 90 percent of all prerecorded videocassettes contain motion pictures, the merchandising of motion picture videocassettes will be the focal point in the following discussion of the video software industry.

Studios

Many videocassette studios are fully owned subsidiaries of major motion picture producer organizations. These producers sell the right to record and market motion pictures to their videocassette studios in the same way they sell print distribution rights to theater distribution organizations. Most subsidiary studios are free to deal with motion picture producers other than their parent organizations.

The copying process used by a videocassette studio is highly automated. Some studios use a master tape player and a large number of "slave" tape recorders. These units copy tapes at "real-time," with a two-hour tape taking two full hours to copy. Other studios use a new high-speed tape copying system. Such systems can make copies in 100 to 150 times the speed of "real-time," reproducing a two-hour program in 1½ to 2 minutes. With either system, blank tape is copied in large reels, cut to cassette size, and wound onto empty cassette shells. Improvements in videotape recording technology and a downward trend in the price of tape and cassette shells has pushed the variable cost of a motion picture videocassette down to approximately $5 per unit.

Primary promotion of a motion picture videocassette occurs when the film is advertised before and during theatrical release. In addition, word of mouth reaction to the motion picture plays a powerful role in its success as a videocassette. The videocassette version of the motion picture receives relatively little additional promotion. There might be a four-color, full-page ad in magazines aimed at VCR owners. In addition, the video software dealer usually is provided with point-of-purchase material at little or no cost, and co-op advertising support on a refund basis.

Studios price their videocassettes in terms of a suggested retail price to the end-use purchaser, less appropriate markups. Distributors are charged 64 percent of retail price and are expected to charge 80 percent of the retail price to video software dealers. This pricing structure allows both the wholesaler and the retailer a 25 percent markup. Of course, quantity and payment discounts alter the actual price paid by both wholesalers and retailers.

If the retail price is high—currently $39.95 or more—it is known in the trade as a "rental" price. A "rental-priced" videocassette is expected to be sold to only a few end-users due to the high price of the cassette. The only significant purchasers will be a fixed number of video software dealers, who will use a few cassette copies to generate rental revenue. Since the video software dealer pays the same price for the cassette whether it is to be sold or rented, a high price is the studio's way of obtaining what it believes to be a proper share of the dealer's rental revenue.

The highest rental price—currently $79.95—is reserved for the "A" title, a successful motion picture that has recently finished theatrical service. The $69.95 rental price is used for titles that weren't quite so successful (or are a little older). The lower rental prices—$39.95 to $59.95—are assigned to "catalog" titles, which are priced according to their original popularity.

At the other end of the pricing spectrum is the "sell-through" price, set low by the studios in hopes of encouraging end-user purchases. Some "A" titles (such as *Raiders of The Lost Ark* and *Indiana Jones and The Temple of Doom*) may be offered on videocassette at an original sell-through price of $29.95. However, sell-through pricing most often is presented as a price reduction with a "limited time offer" format. A studio might offer twenty titles with common sell-through prices (from $19.95 to 29.95) as a Christmas promotion.

Studios prefer that their videocassettes be sold rather than rented to end-use consumers. About 150,000 copies of a successful motion picture videocassette can be sold to video software dealers at rental prices.[3] If the cassette could be marketed successfully at sell-through prices, the potential market should be a large fraction of the nation's 31 million VCR households.

If sell-through pricing carries the potential for higher revenue, it also carries a much higher risk. A motion picture videocassette is an impulse purchase. Thus, a large inventory of a sell-through cassette must be developed to minimize stockout potential. Should production exceed demand, there is only minimal salvage value for the excess, as each cassette must be erased and delabeled before it can be put to other uses (assuming that the tape was already cut to a standard length). To compound the problem, sales volume (as opposed to hypothetical market potential) is very difficult to predict for a motion picture videocassette offered at an original sell-through price. Of course, a price increase from sell-through to rental levels is not possible, as rental outlets will have purchased all their needs at sell-through prices.

Due to the risk involved, studios are reluctant to rely upon sell-through pricing. Rental pricing, on the other hand, is a relatively low-risk decision. With even mediocre theatrical success, a new rental-priced videocassette should generate predictable sales to video software dealers and known revenues to the studio. If a title is released at rental prices, the studio could always change to sell-through pricing after "skimming" the rental market.

Thus, rental pricing has been the far safer merchandising route for the studios. Indeed, this conservative approach has been highly profitable. For example, in 1982, CBS/Fox Home Video was started with $142 million of owners' equity. In 1983, CBS/Fox earned net profits of $22.7 million on revenues of $141.6 million, and in 1984 it earned net profits of $51 million on revenues of $215.6 million. By the end of 1984, CBS/Fox had paid out $60 million in cumulative dividends to its parent corporations.[4]

However, as studios improve their skill at predicting sales levels for motion picture videocassettes offered at sell-through pricing, and as increasing VCR penetration enhances sell-through market potential, a growing proportion of "A" title releases at sell-through prices seems likely. In fact, some observers suggest that motion picture producers and their videocassette studios will use theatrical release of future films as a method to promote and insure successful videocassette sales.

In the more immediate future, however, motion picture producers are said to be contemplating significant increases in the $5 million or so that is the current "asking price" for cassette rights to a major motion picture. If such an increase occurs, a logical consequence would be a corresponding increase (of $10 or so) in the rental price charged by the studios.

Distributors

The wholesaling segment of the video software industry is growing at a significantly faster pace than the industry as a whole. As an illustration, one trade publication listed a total of twenty-nine multi-branch and thirty-seven single-branch distributors in February 1986. In October, the same listing showed that three single-branch distributors had ceased operations and two distributors had closed one of their multiple-branch outlets. However, nine distributors had added a new branch to their operations, and sixteen new distributors had entered the video software market. In eight months, the total number of distributor outlets had grown approximately 15 percent from a base of 138 outlets.

This growth has a number of causes. Existing distributors have been routinely adding branch outlets to obtain significant quantity discounts and to spread administrative costs over higher sales levels. Record, audio tape, and book wholesalers have sought synergistic effects by expansion into videocassette distribution. Some video software dealers have found increased efficiency through backward integration into wholesaling.

However, the primary consequence of this "excess" growth has been a great deal of competitive pressure being placed on distributors. Because VCR growth gives studios no motive to lessen price control, distributors cannot rely on price to offset increased competition. Instead, they must remain price competitive, charging what become standard prices for videocassette stock. Likewise, dealers are offered standard quantity discounts (such as a 5 percent discount on this month's orders when last month's orders totaled at least $1,000), and standard cash payment discounts (2 percent 10/net 30).

The only effective competitive tool available to distributors is service, backed by an extensive stock of titles. Thus, distributors are constantly reminding present and new dealers (primarily through trade journal advertising) that faster, more helpful responses cannot be obtained from any other distributor. Dealers who dial toll-free numbers are greeted by computer-supported sales personnel who will verify that requested stock is on-hand and guarantee that it will be shipped within 24 hours.

The typical distributor shares the studios' desire for more purchases by end-use consumers, as the resulting increase in volume would put few strains on the distributor's administrative overhead. However, limited margins prohibit the distributor from absorbing the risk of overestimating demand for sell-through titles. As long as studios refuse to take back excess stock, distributors will also refuse to honor "stock adjustment" requests from dealers. Most dealers, in turn, will refuse to take all the risk of stocking titles for sale.

Most distributors are treating the excess supply of wholesalers as a temporary phenomenon which will evaporate as VCR penetration continues. Until that time, the goal of most distributors is to "ride out" what they perceive as a minor shakeout in their segment of the video software industry.

Video Software Dealers

Current industry estimates place the total number of video software dealer outlets at 20,000 nationwide, in addition to the estimated 15,000 other retail stores that also rent or sell videocassettes. Depending on the source cited, between 2,000 and 4,000 of these 20,000 dealer outlets belong to one of several video store franchise systems. Another 5,000 dealer stores belong to independent chains, defined as collections of two or more outlets under common ownership. Most of the remaining outlets are so-called "mom-and-pop" stores, single-store dealerships typically managed by the owner.

Several video software store archetypes can be seen among those 20,000 outlets. Video "superstores" occupy one end of the size spectrum. Virtually every motion picture ever recorded on videocassette is included in their inventory, which often exceeds 10,000 cassettes. These stores generate annual rental revenue of $250,000 or more and supplement that revenue with sales of cassettes, VCRs, and related supplies. Superstores usually are found in large metropolitan communities, as they require a large customer base for profitable operation. Their typical competitive edge is the ability to expertly satisfy all of their customers' video needs at reasonable prices.

"Neighborhood" video stores can be found in the middle of the size continuum. These stores typically stock 2,000 to 3,000 cassettes and generate annual rental revenues in the range of $100,000 to $150,000. Found in smaller communities and in the neighborhood centers of larger communities, these stores rely on convenience and service to satisfy a limited customer base. In addition to cassette rental, neighborhood stores also rent video equipment. If they sell prerecorded videocassettes, it will be to customer order rather than from inventory. These stores most likely require customers to purchase video club memberships, although this practice is disappearing under competitive pressure.

The smallest video rental outlets typically offer videocassettes as a sideline to their normal business. These "convenience" outlets include grocery stores, convenience stores, drug stores, and even an occasional car wash. These stores stock only the most popular titles in an inventory of approximately 200 cassettes. The stores rely on customers who are drawn by the primary product mix to rent cassettes on an impulse basis. While some convenience outlets might stock blank cassettes as part of their normal product mix, their video business is limited to cassette rental. In many cases, these outlets share rental revenue with a videocassette rack jobber.

The basic nature of the videocassette rental "product" creates some unique problems for the video software dealer. Although the normal rental videocassette has a physical life of about three years, its usefulness to video software dealers is far more limited. To their continuing frustration, dealers find they have virtually no control over the useful life of their rental cassettes.

Once a motion picture producer believes no more significant revenue can be obtained from theatrical distribution of a film, that film will be released for videocassette distribution. For most "A" titles, the cassette release date occurs approximately six to seven months after initial theatrical release. This is the starting date for the videocassette's useful life. The ending date is determined by the motion picture producer's decision to release the film to pay TV. This decision, which normally occurs six to seven months after cassette release, is based on the conclusion that videocassette sales have peaked.

The videocassette's useful life will end before the actual pay TV release date because pay TV tends to promote its latest acquisitions a month or two before they are actually shown. Furthermore, initial enthusiasm for a given videocassette will wear off as customers start to pay more attention to the next new cassette releases. Thus, most motion picture videocassettes will have a shelf life of six to seven months, and a primary revenue-generating life of two to three months.

The short revenue-generating life of a videocassette gives video software dealers cash flow headaches. Dealers must pay cash "up front" for the videocassette that will generate revenue in small quantities over a two- to three-month period. Long before that revenue period is completed, new cassettes will become available to the dealer (at a rate of about 400 films per year). Failure to acquire these new cassettes at the earliest possible date simply means the new cassettes will have a shorter revenue-generating life when they are acquired, as some customers will have rented competitors' promptly acquired copies of the cassette.

Industry studies and dealer experiences have shown that the video software customer has virtually no loyalty to the dealer. Renting a videocassette is an impulse decision, and the customer wants convenience in carrying out that decision. Convenience translates into an outlet that is easy to reach, a selection process that is easy to implement, and a rental transaction that is quick. Above all, the customer wants the desired videocassette to be readily available. If the desired cassette cannot be found, the customer will seek the cassette at a nearby competitive outlet unless sales personnel persuade the customer to consider an alternative title. As long as the dealer's prices are generally competitive, specific rental price does not seem to be an important issue to the customer.

Stocking more copies of popular titles would seem to be a logical method of retaining customers. Unfortunately, dealers can easily overstock titles, with a disastrous impact on cash flow and profits. As a simplified example, assume that a dealer has a total of 300 customers who wish to see a given new title. Also assume that each copy of that title costs the dealer $60 (near the normal dealer purchase price for an "A" title), and that rental revenue per copy is $2 per day.

If only one copy of the title is purchased and rented out, the dealer could make a "profit" (revenue minus investment only; overhead not considered) of $540 if the 300th customer were willing to wait about ten months to see the cassette. If ten copies are purchased, the dealer will "break even" (total revenue = total investment) if the 300th customer is willing to wait only thirty days to see the cassette. If the dealer purchases 20 copies, the 300th customer only needs to wait fifteen days to see the cassette, but the dealer will incur a "loss" totaling half the investment made in the cassette copies.

The basic problem is that revenue generated does not change as the number of cassettes (and the total amount invested) increases. For this reason, dealers tend to stock relatively few copies of even popular cassettes. As illogical as it might otherwise sound, dealers are willing to risk customer movement to other dealers in order to protect their own profits.

In this example, the dealer would probably stock five copies, make the 300th customer wait sixty days, and hope to make a "profit" of $300. The dealer will "break even" on the investment in five copies if no more than 150 of the 300 customers turn to competitors. If all competitors behave with similar logic, then some customers will have to wait up to sixty days to see the cassette.

Understandably, customer dissatisfaction with such long waits has opened market niches for a variety of direct and indirect competitors to the video software dealer. Cable TV owners are experimenting with pay-per-view systems, which give cable customers access to three or four first-run motion pictures per month, well in advance of cassette and normal pay TV release. Some video franchise owners are experimenting with pay-per-rental systems, in which dealers, in return for low purchase prices ($6 per cassette) and advance release (about sixty days before normal cassette release), share rental revenues with suppliers on a 50/50 basis. A number of diverse locations such as apartment buildings, malls, and health clubs are experimenting with credit-card-driven, cassette-rental vending machines. Last but certainly not least, a number of customers continue to experiment with casual or intentional piracy, the illegal copying of videocassettes.

However, increasing direct competition is causing the greatest damage to the video software dealer. Early profits, growing demand, and ease of entry have caused the retail level of the video software industry to grow faster than market demand, and retailers are now experiencing a serious shakeout. As John Power, executive director of the American Video Association explains, "The movie rental business is a neighborhood business. The product is exactly the same from store to store, and the number of stores that can be opened in a given geographic area is about to reach its maximum in many parts of the country."[5]

Industry statistics back up Mr. Power's concerns. According to one study, the most successful video stores processed an average of 4,593 cassette rentals in November 1983. At an average price of $4.70 per rental, these stores generated a monthly gross rental revenue of $21,568. Two years later, these stores had improved their average monthly revenue to $22,646, a 5 percent increase. However, this revenue was achieved by renting an average of 8,235 cassettes (an increase of 79 percent) at an average price of $2.75 (a decrease of 71 percent).[6] The direct cause of the declining price has been increased competition, and it has forced the most successful stores to work significantly harder to essentially maintain the same revenue.

For stores that do not have a sufficient competitive edge, reduced revenue occurs whether the owner works harder or not. Research on the gross annual revenue of large samples of video stores reports a continuing decline from the peak year of 1983. In that year, gross median annual revenue of the sample was $250,000. That statistic dropped to $190,000 in 1984 and $160,000 in 1985. The forecast is for a further drop in 1986.[7]

Two examples reinforce the point. In early 1984, one dealer opened a store in Grand Junction, Colorado, a community of 80,000. Initial revenues topped $1,500 per week, even though the town already supported sixteen other videocassette outlets. By early 1985, however, there were sixty outlets, and rental prices had dropped from $3 a day to as low as 69 cents per day. The dealer suffered a 50 percent drop in revenue and closed the store in May 1985.[8]

Another, less drastic example concerns a dealer who opened the first video rental outlet in a Philadelphia suburb in 1982. By 1986, five other stores were in operation within three miles of this outlet, and the dealer's sales had dropped from a peak of $150,000 in 1984 to $100,000 in 1986. Although the store has been "on the market" for some time, no buyers have been found; the owner is now considering closing the store.[9]

Video software dealers who are surviving the shakeout rely on one or more competitive edges to differentiate themselves from competitors. One such edge is a superior breadth of selection. Another is a highly motivated work force that suggests alternate films when a desired cassette is unavailable and that inquires about a customer's willingness to purchase a cassette upon its rental return. A third edge is a high-traffic location, readily available to customers on some other errand who get struck by the rental impulse. Finally, the large size that comes from past success, chain operation, or franchise affiliation translates into purchasing and promotion efficiency.

THE LOCAL MARKET

Bowling Green is a county seat located along Interstate 75, approximately 20 miles south of Toledo, Ohio. Home of Bowling Green State University, the community also functions as a supply center for area farms. In addition, Bowling Green serves as a "bedroom community" for individuals employed in the Toledo area. The 1980 census puts the population of Bowling Green at about 25,000, in addition to the 16,000 students who attend the University.

Bowling Green supports one daily newspaper, an FM radio station, and a combined AM/FM station. In addition, the university provides a student-run newspaper, student-run AM and FM radio stations, and a PBS-affiliated TV station. A cable TV company offers thirty area and satellite-transmitted channels and four premium channels: The Disney Channel, HBO, The Movie Channel, and PASS, a regional sports channel. Area residents also have access to five Toledo TV stations (three network affiliates, an independent, and a PBS affiliate), a Toledo-based daily/Sunday newspaper, and a number of AM and FM radio stations serving the Toledo area.

Bowling Green is bisected by two major streets, running north/south and east/west, which divide the town into four distinctive quadrants. The northeast quadrant contains the university's 1,200-acre campus and older homes that now are used primarily for off-campus student housing. The southeast quadrant, which contains most of the community's apartments, also is dedicated to off-campus student housing. The southwest quadrant includes the most expensive homes to be found in Bowling Green, and the northwest quadrant includes the newest suburban development projects. The two western quadrants are predominately zoned for single-family dwellings, and homes in these areas are prized for their distance from the university.

The two major streets define the community's retail business centers. "Downtown" occurs at the intersection of these two streets, and it contains the traditional retail outlets found in most midwestern communities. The Bowling Green Downtown Business Association is concerned about maintaining the viability of this shopping district. One of its major projects was a clean-up, paint-up, fix-up program for the downtown area. Recently, the group persuaded Bowling Green's city council to construct a major parking lot within one block of the downtown center.

Bowling Green's eastern retail center is located at the community's main exit from Interstate 75 and includes a number of outlets designed to serve the traveler. The eastern retail center also includes the community's first shopping mall. This L-shaped mall contains one large unit and several smaller units connected by an outdoor walkway. For a number of reasons, the mall has fallen on "hard times" and now contains unrelated businesses attracted more by low rental rates than by any ability of the mall to generate customer traffic.

Zoning prohibits retail development at Bowling Green's western boundary and encourages new housing development in that area. The community's western expansion has supported growth in the two retail centers located at the northern and southern boundaries of Bowling Green. Each of these retail centers contains at least one major grocery store and at least one major mass merchandising outlet. Both centers contain a number of smaller outlets designed to draw on the traffic generated by the major stores. The southern center has more outlets at present, but the "balance of power" is expected to tip toward the northern center when a new, 57-store, enclosed shopping mall is completed there in May 1987.

Competition

Presently, videocassettes can be rented at nine locations in Bowling Green. Of those nine, the outlet with the largest selection is the Video Spectrum, which boasts of more than 5,000 VHS cassettes in inventory. Located at the southern edge of the downtown retail center, the Video Spectrum was Bowling Green's first video rental outlet. Furthermore, it is the community's only video specialty store, dealing exclusively in videocassettes and related merchandise.

Recent growth in competition has forced the Video Spectrum to permit a waiver of its $15.00 lifetime "membership fee" as a prerequisite for cassette rental. The firm's basic rental price is $1.95 for the first night; members are charged an additional $1.00 for each consecutive night after the first. VCRs are available for rent at $4.95 per night. A variety of conditional "special" rental prices are offered to members.

The Video Spectrum appears to put most of its extensive promotion budget into print, placing weekly display ads in both the community and the campus newspapers.

These ads, located near TV listings whenever possible, point out new titles in stock and stress the breadth of selection. Coupons are offered in quarterly direct mail packets, and reminder ads are placed in a variety of local media. For example, a Video Spectrum ad can be seen on the cable TV channel used to publish program listings.

Bowling Green's second-largest video rental outlet is Barney's Video, which contains an estimated 1,500 VHS and Beta cassettes. Although operated as a separate video specialty store, Barney's Video is physically connected to Barney's Convenience Mart, which features self-service gasoline pumps as well as customary convenience store stock. The combined facility is located in the middle of Bowling Green's northern retail center.

Barney's Video offers an optional $10.00 annual membership, and the store provides members with a variety of conditional "special" rental prices. These special prices are featured in Barney's weekly newspaper display ads, which also stress new cassettes in stock. The basic rental charge is $1.99 per night; Barney's encourages fast cassette turnaround by not offering a discount for extended rental periods. VCRs are available for rent at $5.99 per night.

The Video Connection, Bowling Green's third-largest video rental outlet, also is associated with a convenience store. The Video Connection's 1,000 VHS cassettes occupy about 25 percent of the Dairy Mart's floor space. A member of a regional convenience store chain, the Dairy Mart is located about five blocks east of the downtown retail center and about two blocks from the western edge of Bowling Green State University. The Video Connection is the nearest video cassette outlet for the 9,000 students who live in university dormitories.

Video Connection customers may purchase a $25.00 lifetime membership, a $10.00 annual membership, or rent cassettes without any membership. Members qualify for a variety of conditional price "specials" and receive a specified number of "free" cassette rentals. The basic rental price is $1.99 for the first night, $1.50 more for the second night, an additional $1.00 for the third night. VCRs are available at $6.99 per night. Promotion, aimed at members only, is limited to a direct mail newsletter featuring new cassette arrivals and discount coupons.

All three major grocery stores in Bowling Green have entered the video cassette rental business, although with varying degrees of enthusiasm. Kroger, located in the northern retail center, stocks about 500 VHS cassettes and charges $1.99 for the first night. Food Town stocks about 100 VHS titles in its northern retail center store (also at $1.99 for the first night) and does not stock cassettes at all in its southern retail center store. Churchill's, a smaller regional chain, stocks about 1,000 VHS cassettes in its southern retail center store and charges $1.89 for the first night. All three stores charge $1.00 for each additional night the cassette is rented.

These three grocery stores offer "free" membership as a means of obtaining the customer's name and address. Correspondingly, no price "specials" are available to customers. None of these stores promotes its videocassettes, relying instead on normal customer traffic to generate cassette rentals. VCRs are available at Churchill's for $4.95 per night and at Kroger's for $5.95 per night; Food Town does not stock VCRs.

Phillips TV, an appliance store located in the northern retail center, became Bowling Green's second cassette rental outlet as a logical outgrowth of its TV and VCR sales. Customers may purchase a $15 lifetime membership, a $10 annual membership, or rent cassettes without any membership. Members qualify for competitive rental rates on Phillips' approximately 500 VHS and Beta cassettes. However, the non-member rate is $3.00 for a one-night rental, $4.15 for a two-night rental, and $5.00 for a three-night rental. VCRs can be rented at $4.99 per night. While cassette rental opportunities might be mentioned in newspaper display ads featuring appliances, Phillips TV normally does not promote its videocassettes.

An unusual competitor is the Wood County Public Library, located in the downtown retail center. The library stocks approximately 100 VHS and Beta titles, about half of which are obtained from a rotating inventory shared by a regional library consortium. To check out a cassette for three nights, patrons are charged a fee of $1, which is applied to purchasing new titles. The library does not rent VCRs and does not promote its cassette stock.

Bowling Green's newest videocassette competitor is Lawson's, a convenience store located in the southern retail center. Its 150 VHS titles are presented in a display case that occupies about 5 percent of the store's floor space. The display case includes a TV/VCR combination that continually runs previews of available cassettes. Beyond this point-of-purchase effort, no cassette rental promotion seems likely.

Lawson's offers a "free" membership (as a means of recording customer names and addresses) and presently is giving one free rental for every new membership. As an introductory measure, Lawsons is pricing its cassettes at 99 cents per night. In the long run, prices are expected to climb to $1.95 per night. VCRs can be rented at $4.95 per night; the price is not expected to change.

Lawson's experience with videocassette rental is being watched carefully by the Sterling Dairy Store, another convenience store located near the university. The store manager has been informally polling customers concerning their tastes and preferences in videocassette rentals and has hinted that 100 or so titles might be stocked in the near future.

In addition, "teaser" ads in both the local and campus newspapers suggest that another video rental outlet will open in the near future. These ads suggest the outlet will compete on the basis of low prices, extensive selection, and convenience. Not only will the outlet be located closer to campus than any other cassette rental store, but it also will offer such service features as "drive-up" windows for returning rented cassettes.

JIM'S BUSINESS PLAN

Evening arrived, and so did Jim. He was brimming with excitement as he explained his plans for Woodland Video, the name he planned to give to his newest business venture. "The key to this operation," Jim said, "is the Woodland Mall. You see, every other video outlet in Bowling Green has some way to draw customers into the store. For the Video Spectrum, it's the large inventory. For the convenience and grocery stores, it's their main merchandise lines. I won't have any other products to offer, and I simply can't afford to match the inventory of the Video Spectrum. I can succeed only if I find a location that brings a large number of potential customers past my door. The Woodland Mall will give me those potential customers!"

The mall that Jim mentioned—The Woodland Mall—does not yet exist. It is under construction at the northern end of Bowling Green's northern retail center and is scheduled to open this May. It had been bitterly opposed by members of the downtown retail center, who believe it will significantly, perhaps fatally, damage sales in the downtown area. The mall will have 200,000 total square feet, and it will be "anchored" at one end by a 35,000-square-foot J. C. Penney store and at the other end by a 40,000-square-foot Elder-Beerman outlet.[10] There will be a five-screen cinema and a food service area with a cluster of six independent specialty food outlets. Fifty other retail outlets are planned, and space is available for six kiosks along the center of the enclosed walkway. At the last count, twenty outlets (including the two anchor stores, the cinema, and one food outlet) had signed mall leases.

"I'm going to rent the kiosk closest to the Penney's store," Jim continued. "It will cover 12 feet by 14 feet, which is just right for my needs! It will cost me $15,000 per year or 6 percent of gross revenue, whichever is greater, and I will have to sign a 10 year lease. There also will be a maintenance assessment of $1,200 per year. My guess is that utilities will run $100 per month, and my basic phone bill should be about $35 a month.

"I'll even be required to build my own kiosk!" Jim said. My contractor thinks he can construct it for about $5,000. There will be floor-to-counter display shelves for empty videocassette boxes on the two longer sides and one of the shorter sides of the kiosk. The remaining side, facing the Penney's store, will be my customer service area. All four sides will have a two-foot-wide counter, and four corner posts will hold up a ceiling and overhead fluorescent signs that say 'Woodland Video.' Inside the kiosk, the back of the display shelves will hold the videocassettes.

"It's going to cost me $6,000 to buy a computer, complete with video store software, Jim added. "But it will be worth it to have a system that tracks performance of each cassette, keeps detailed records on each customer, automatically prices and prints a customized receipt for each transaction, manages a reservation system, and keeps track of cash flow and a thousand other details necessary to run a video store. The computer will even hook up to a cash register drawer, so I won't have to buy a separate cash register. Except for a keyboard and monitor on the customer service counter, the whole system will sit on a shelf under that counter.

"I'm going to spend another $3,000 to buy a laser printer and desktop publishing software," Jim said. "I plan to use the store's quiet times to prepare a top-notch, biweekly newsletter, which will be mailed to all of my customers. Besides highlighting new cassette arrivals, providing independent film reviews, and suggesting how to care for video equipment, the newsletter will include coupons for such specials as 'two-for-one' rentals. As long as I pay an annual bulk mailing fee of $100 and keep each newsletter under four ounces, the postage charge will be only 12.5 cents per newsletter. Of course, my computer will keep the customer mailing list up to date and print the mailing labels.

"Any questions?" Jim asked as he paused to catch his breath. "Only one at this point," I responded. "Exactly what will you be renting?"

"I guess I forgot to mention that," replied Jim with an embarassed laugh. "I'm going to stock only the 'hottest' videocassettes. I'm going to have an inventory of 200 titles, with two copies of the 100 'best sellers' and one copy of 100 other 'hot' titles, for a total of 300 cassettes. Each month, I'll sell the slowest moving 10 percent of my inventory to a used tape dealer, for about $20 per cassette. I'll replace those cassettes with new titles, using the same ratio of two 'best seller' copies to one copy of other films. This way, I'll maintain a constant inventory and won't outgrow my store. I'll always have the titles with the greatest demand in stock. My whole inventory should turn over within a year!

"I'm going to charge $1.50 per night for each cassette, which will make me the lowest price outlet in Bowling Green," added Jim. "However, that'll be a flat rate. With the lowest price in town, I won't give discounts for multiple-night rentals. I will have a mandatory membership policy, but it will only cost the customer $5.00 per year. That will offset my low rental price, and it won't be so high that it turns potential customers away. For that fee, the customer will get a bar code membership card, so I can quickly complete each rental transaction. Furthermore, each Woodland Video member will be sent my biweekly newsletter, something no Bowling Green competitor now offers.

"My plan is to work the 'impulse angle'" Jim said. "A potential customer walks by my kiosk, sees an available 'hot' title, notices how little it costs, and decides to rent it now. Even if the customer is not yet a member, I don't think $5 will stand in the way of renting a desired and available cassette. Thanks to my computer, the customer gets the cassette, a customized receipt, and departs within 20 seconds. Stopping back the next day is no problem. Since the customer will be in the mall anyway, she can shop for something else she needs. My cassette will be back in stock, ready for the next customer."

Jim sipped his coffee, which was growing cold. While I warmed it up, I inserted another question into our conversation. "Besides your newsletter, do you plan to do any other promotion, or will you rely on your 'impulse angle'?"

"Glad you asked," Jim responded. "The 'impulse angle' will only work once the customer is in the mall, and it won't work at all if the customer has already rented the cassette from a competitor. I've got to advertise so that potential customers start to think of me as a good way of obtaining cassettes. I plan to match Barney's and Video Spectrum, my major competitors. They insert weekly ads in both the *Sentinal-Tribune* and the *BG News,* so I will do the same. A weekly 12-column-inch ad in the *Sentinal-Tribune* will cost me $55, and a weekly 18-column-inch ad in the *BG News* will cost $80.

"Let's see," mused Jim, "what have I missed? Oh yes, my store will be open the same hours as the mall: 10 to 9 daily and 12 to 5 on Sundays. The store will be staffed by college students as part-time employees; I'll pay them $3.50 per hour.

"So," said Jim, looking eager for a positive response, "what do you think?"

"It sounds interesting," I waffled, looking for some way to postpone making a judgement. A mental light bulb clicked on. I decided that I might as well get the issue out into the open. "We missed something, something really important," I said. "How are you going to finance this deal? You had said something about a banker . . .?"

"Yes," Jim replied. "Frankly, that's why I came over to talk to you." I mentally cringed, anticipating the 'touch' I felt sure was coming. But Jim surprised me. "I have an appointment with my banker tomorrow morning. I have developed a pro forma

EXHIBIT 1 Woodland Video, Pro forma income statement, fiscal year ending May 14, 1988

Revenue		
Video tape rental	($1.50 × 360 days × 150 tapes[1])	$81,000
Club memberships	($5.00 × 520 members[2])	2,600
Sale of used tapes	($20.00 × 30 tapes/month × 12)	7,200
Total Revenue		**$90,800[3]**
Expenses		
Tape purchases[4]	($64.00 × 30 tapes/month × 12)	$23,040
Kiosk amortization	($5,000/10 years)	500
Equipment depreciation	($9,000/5 years)	1,800
Computer supplies	(paper, printer toner, etc.)	1,200
Other supplies	(membership cards, etc.)	600
Rent	(per lease)	15,000
Maintenance fee	(per lease)	1,200
Utilities	($100 × 12 months)	1,200
Phone	($50 × 12 months)	600
Bulk mailing fee	(per post office)	100
Newsletter postage	($.125 × 520 members × 26)	1,690
Newspaper advertising	($135 × 52 weeks)	7,020
Other promotion	(coupon revenue losses, etc.)	5,000
Wages	($3.50 × 106 hours/week[5] × 52)	19,292
Social Security taxes	($19,292 × 7.15%)	1,380
Interest expense	($33,000 × 10.5%)	3,465
Total expenses		**$83,087**
Net Income Before Taxes		**$7,713**

Notes: [1] These estimates assume that each of Woodland Video's 300 tapes is rented every other day.

[2] 54,000 tape rentals per year (see note 1) divided by 104 rentals per member per year.

[3] Sales tax is not included in these estimates, either as revenue or expense.

[4] This figure more accurately should be described as 100% depreciation (less salvage value, which these estimates treat as revenue) of all tapes that are sold as used. However, unless a tape price increase occurs, an amount equal to 100% depreciation must be paid for each replacement tape.

[5] One employee will be on hand during all 71 hours that the store is open each week. A second employee will be working during the peak 35 hours of the store's weekly operation.

income statement and balance sheet (see Exhibits 1 and 2). I can only put up $10,000 for this business; it's all I can beg, borrow, or steal. The bank will have to put up the rest, and the banker hasn't been too enthusiastic. He said he wanted to see some details before making a commitment. So I am using you as a 'dry run' for tomorrow's presentation. How do you think my banker will react to my plans? Will

EXHIBIT 2 Woodland Video, Pro forma balance sheet, May 15, 1987 (opening day)

Assets	
Cash (approximate cash outflow for 1 month)	$ 6,100
Inventory ($64.00/tape × 300 tapes)	19,200
Kiosk (carried as a leasehold improvement)	5,000
Equipment (computer, printer, and software)	9,000
Prepaid rent (1 month deposit; 1 month advance rent)	2,500
Prepaid maintenance	1,200
Total Assets	**$43,000**
Liabilities	
Long Term Debt (5 years; 10.5% APR; monthly payments)	$33,000
Owners' Equity	
Capital	$10,000
Total Liabilities and Owners' Equity	**$43,000**

he be impressed? Should I change anything? What do you think?" Jim sat on the edge of his chair, waiting for my response.

ENDNOTES

1. *Video Store.* November 1986, 19.
2. *Video Store.* November 1986, 38.
3. *Billboard.* 17 May, 1986, 50.
4. *Video.* June 1986, 174.
5. *Video Store.* February 1986, 8.
6. *Video Store.* February 1986, 32.
7. *Video Store.* October 1986, 30.
8. *Business Week.* 2 September, 1985, 34.
9. *Wall Street Journal.* 14 July, 1986, 21 (Eastern Edition).
10. Elder-Beerman is a department store based in Dayton, Ohio, with 26 units in Ohio and Indiana.

Winn-Dixie—1987

SHARON WOOD
Auburn University
FRED DAVID
Auburn University

Years ago, putting dinner on the table meant a full afternoon of shopping for mom. The milk and eggs arrived every morning via the milkman, but the rest of the meal required a number of shopping stops. Meat came from the local butcher who carved beef and pork to your request and passed on a few cooking tips or recipes with every order. Next stop was the vegetable stand, where locally grown fruit and vegetables were the fare. The aroma from the bakery was tantalizing; from this stop came breads and maybe something sweet for dessert. Canned goods, cleaning products, crackers, noodles, frozen foods, and a variety of other items came from the corner grocery store. Finally, mom picked up grandma's prescription at the drug store and flowers for the dining room table at the florist.

Times sure have changed! In the 1980s, the era of "one-stop shopping" has become a reality in the food industry. The 100,000-square-foot Real Superstore Supermarket in Lafayette, Louisiana, houses thirty aisles of groceries, clothing, hardware, a private post office, a branch bank, a jewelry store, and an on-site dental clinic. The 212,000-square-foot Fred Meyer Supermarket in Beaverton, Oregon, sells everything from home computers to fifty-two varieties of mustard. To remain competitive, supermarket chains such as Winn-Dixie have had to rethink their corporate strategies.

HISTORY

Winn-Dixie's beginning can be traced to Burley, Idaho, in the early 1900s. William Davis, owner and operator of Burley's general store stocked a wide variety of "groceries," called "dry goods" then. Like most general store owners of that time, Davis ran his business on a charge and deliver basis. In 1914, another merchant opened a shop in Burley, and Davis found himself in competition. The other merchant operated on a "cash and carry" basis. The cash and carry concept was so well received in Burley that soon Davis was forced to liquidate.

Davis and his family moved to Lemon City, a small suburb of Miami, Florida, and purchased a grocery store in 1925 with $10,000 borrowed capital. Rockmoor Grocery, as it was called, was a family affair. Mrs. Davis kept the books and paid the bills; their four sons contributed in various ways to help make the store a success. By 1934, the Davis family was operating thirty-four stores in southern Florida. These stores were called "Table Supply Stores." At this point, Rockmoor Grocery had grown into quite a large operation.

Mr. Davis died in 1934, leaving the management of Rockmoor to his four sons. Dano Davis became president, James Davis, treasurer, and Austin Davis and Tine Davis, vice presidents. The Davis brothers in 1939 purchased seventy-eight Winn & Lovett Grocery Company stores located in Florida and Georgia. Headquarters for their company was established in Jacksonville, Florida, and the firm assumed the Winn & Lovett name.

Following World War II, Winn and Lovett acquired Margaret Ann Stores in Florida, King Stores in Georgia, Wylie Stores in Alabama, Eden and Ballentine Stores in South Carolina, Penney Stores in Mississippi, and Steiden Stores in Kentucky. The firm changed its name to Winn-Dixie Stores in 1955 when it merged with Dixie Home Stores in North and South Carolina.

Winn-Dixie acquired Ketner and Milner Stores in the Carolinas and Hill Stores in Louisiana and Alabama. Expansion continued in 1967 to include eleven stores in Nassau and Freeport in the Bahama Islands. Recent acquisitions include Foodway and Buddies retail stores and facilities in the Southwest, as well as the retail assets of Kimbell, Inc.

Winn-Dixie's phenomenal growth has transformed a family-owned grocery business into the thirteenth largest retailing company in the world. As of June 25, 1986, Winn-Dixie had 1,262 supermarkets in operation with 123 of these stores measuring more than 35,600 square feet each.

INTERNAL OPERATIONS

All Winn-Dixie stores are located in the southern United States, with the majority in the Southeast. Winn-Dixie currently operates facilities in Florida, Georgia, North Carolina, South Carolina, Alabama, Mississippi, Louisiana, Kentucky, Tennessee, Indiana, Virginia, Texas, and Oklahoma. More than one-third of all Winn-Dixie's 1,262 stores are located in Florida, where the company competes directly with Publix, a 300-store chain. Exhibits 1 and 2 give the location of Winn-Dixie's stores, distribution centers, and manufacturing and processing plants.

Winn-Dixie Hope Lodge

Winn-Dixie demonstrated interaction with the community and response to social needs by opening the Winn-Dixie Hope Lodge in 1986. The Lodge is a "home away from home" for cancer patients receiving treatment at Shands Hospital. Winn-Dixie made a million dollar pledge toward building the facility, with matching grants from their Florida and south Georgia associates and the Winn-Dixie Foundation. The facility is run by the American Cancer Association.

Employees

Winn-Dixie employs more than 76,000 workers whom they refer to as "associates." Long-term employee loyalty is seen throughout Winn-Dixie's corporate staff. Of sixteen regional vice presidents at Winn-Dixie, all but two have been with the company for twenty-five years or more. Of the company's seventeen corporate officers, eleven fall into the 25-year-and-over category. Four vice presidents have been with Winn-Dixie for more than forty years. Though this seems amazing for our mobile society, it is not unusual for the grocery industry, which still supports the idea of working your

EXHIBIT 1 Winn-Dixie store locations, 1987

States	*Number of Stores*
Alabama	100
Georgia	123
Florida	447
Kentucky	56
Indiana	4
Louisiana	91
Mississippi	22
North Carolina	156
Oklahoma	6
South Carolina	93
Tennessee	37
Texas	83
Virginia	44
	1,262

Source: Winn-Dixie's 1986 *Annual Report,* 20.

way from the bottom up. Winn-Dixie utilizes a Strategic Business Unit (SBU) form of organizational structure, as illustrated in Exhibit 3.

Finance

Winn-Dixie's balance sheets for 1985 and 1986 and income statements for 1984, 1985 and 1986 are provided in Exhibits 4 and 5, respectively. Winn-Dixie's 1986 current ratio of 1.66 exceeded the industry average of 1.3. Winn-Dixie's inventories, determined by the LIFO method, constitute 40.44 percent of total assets, higher than the industry average of 34.7 percent.

Revenues for 1986 equaled $8.2 billion, the fifty-second straight year of increasing sales. This figure represents an increase of 5.8 percent over revenues earned in 1985 and compares favorably to an industry average increase of 5.5 percent. Winn-Dixie's gross profit margin of 21 percent has been maintained since 1977, but it is below the industry average of 23.9 percent. Net income for fiscal 1986 amounted to $116 million, an increase of $8.5 million or 7.87 percent over 1985 earnings.

Analysts believe that Winn-Dixie's ambitious capital expansion program has temporarily reduced the firm's earnings. However, the store expansion program should prove worthwhile in coming years. Winn-Dixie already believes this expansion program is profitable, as evidenced by their increase in earnings per share: $2.84 in 1986, up from $2.64 in 1985, a 7.58 percent change. Winn-Dixie reported a 17 percent return on equity (ROE) for fiscal year 1986 and 1985. Winn-Dixie's goal of earning a record $9 billion in sales for fiscal 1987 looks as if it may be attained.

EXHIBIT 2 Winn-Dixie—Locations and facilities

Alabama	
Montgomery	Distribution Center Plant: milk bottling; bread, bread products, and sweet goods; pizza
Florida	
Jacksonville	Two Distribution Centers Plants: bread and bread products; detergents; paper bags, coffee, tea and spices
Madison	Plant; meat processing
Miami	Distribution Center Plants: bread and bread products; milk bottling
Orlando	Distribution Center Plants: jams, jellies, mayonnaise, salad dressing, peanut butter and condiments; canned and bottled carbonated beverages
Bartow	Plant: egg processing
Plant City	Plant: ice cream and milk bottling
Pompano	Distribution Center
Sarasota	Distribution Center
Tampa	Distribution Center
Georgia	
Atlanta	Distribution Center Plant: canned and bottled carbonated beverages
Gainesville	Plant: oleomargarine; natural cheese cutting and wrapping; processed cheese and pimento cheese
Valdosta	Plant: crackers and cookies
Kentucky	
Louisville	Distribution Center
Louisiana	
New Orleans	Distribution Center Plant: milk bottling
North Carolina	
Charlotte	Distribution Center
Raleigh	Distribution Center
High Point	Plant: milk bottling and cultured products
South Carolina	
Greenville	Distribution Center Plants: bread and bread products; milk bottling and ice cream
Texas	
Fort Worth	Distribution Center Plants: canned and bottled carbonated beverages; milk bottling; corrugated boxes and bags

Source: Winn-Dixie's 1986 *Form 10–K*, p. 2.

EXHIBIT 3 Winn-Dixie's organizational chart in 1986.

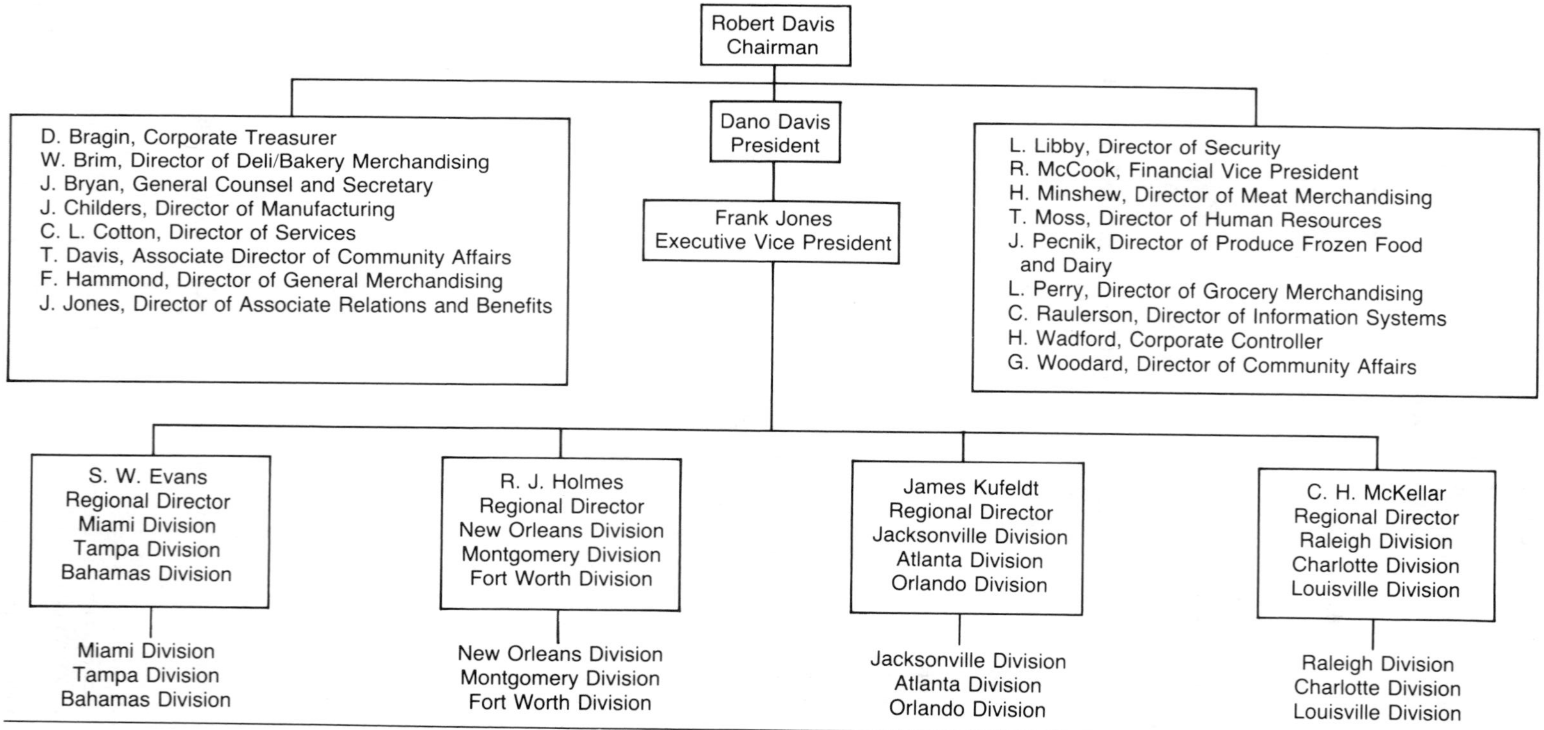

Robert Davis
Chairman

D. Bragin, Corporate Treasurer
W. Brim, Director of Deli/Bakery Merchandising
J. Bryan, General Counsel and Secretary
J. Childers, Director of Manufacturing
C. L. Cotton, Director of Services
T. Davis, Associate Director of Community Affairs
F. Hammond, Director of General Merchandising
J. Jones, Director of Associate Relations and Benefits

Dano Davis
President

Frank Jones
Executive Vice President

L. Libby, Director of Security
R. McCook, Financial Vice President
H. Minshew, Director of Meat Merchandising
T. Moss, Director of Human Resources
J. Pecnik, Director of Produce Frozen Food and Dairy
L. Perry, Director of Grocery Merchandising
C. Raulerson, Director of Information Systems
H. Wadford, Corporate Controller
G. Woodard, Director of Community Affairs

S. W. Evans
Regional Director
Miami Division
Tampa Division
Bahamas Division

Miami Division
Tampa Division
Bahamas Division

R. J. Holmes
Regional Director
New Orleans Division
Montgomery Division
Fort Worth Division

New Orleans Division
Montgomery Division
Fort Worth Division

James Kufeldt
Regional Director
Jacksonville Division
Atlanta Division
Orlando Division

Jacksonville Division
Atlanta Division
Orlando Division

C. H. McKellar
Regional Director
Raleigh Division
Charlotte Division
Louisville Division

Raleigh Division
Charlotte Division
Louisville Division

Source: Inferred from Winn-Dixie's 1986 *Annual Report*, p. 20.

EXHIBIT 4 Winn-Dixie's consolidated balance sheets—June 25, 1986, and June 26, 1985.

June 25, 1986 and June 26, 1985

Assets	**1986**	1985
	Amounts in thousands	
Current assets:		
Cash and marketable securities	**$ 180,556**	117,322
Receivables, less allowance for doubtful items of $532,000 ($492,000 in 1985)	**73,715**	57,404
Merchandise inventories at lower of cost or market less LIFO reserve of $151,512,000 ($145,301,000 in 1985)	**548,060**	503,953
Prepaid expenses	**27,359**	26,089
Total current assets	**829,690**	704,768
Investments and other assets:		
Investment in tax benefit leases	**2,129**	4,488
Investments in and advances to foreign subsidiary not consolidated	**1,409**	1,274
Other assets	**22,653**	15,515
Total investments and other assets	**26,191**	21,277
Prepaid income taxes	**16,079**	4,031
Net property, plant and equipment	**483,394**	,508,662
	$1,355,354	1,238,738

Liabilities and Shareholders' Equity	**1986**	1985
Current liabilities:		
Accounts payable	**$ 293,888**	279,017
Accrued wages and salaries	**57,518**	56,553
Accrued expenses	**121,307**	94,977
Current obligations under capital leases	**2,644**	2,973
Income taxes	**24,167**	20,755
Total current liabilities	**499,524**	454,275
Long-term liabilities:		
Obligations under capital leases	**74,102**	69,672
Other long-term debt	**24,950**	25,290
Total long-term liabilities	**99,052**	94,962
Reserve for insurance claims and self-insurance	**52,220**	42,724
Shareholders' equity:		
Common stock of $1 par value. Authorized 50,000,000 shares; issued 42,298,577 shares (45,798,577 shares in 1985)	**42,299**	45,799
Retained earnings	**675,827**	688,962
	718,126	734,761
Less cost of common stock held for associates' stock purchase plan and other corporate purposes, 987,651 shares (4,872,111 shares in 1985)	**13,568**	87,984
Total shareholders' equity	**704,558**	646,777
Commitments and contingent liabilities (Note 8)		
	$1,355,354	1,238,738

EXHIBIT 5 Winn-Dixie's consolidated statements of earnings—years ended June 25, 1986, June 26, 1985, and June 27, 1984.

Years Ended June 25, 1986, June 26, 1985 and June 27, 1984	1986	1985	1984
	Amounts in thousands except per share data		
Net sales	$8,225,244	7,774,480	7,302,369
Cost of sales, including warehousing and delivery expenses	6,371,124	6,061,220	5,708,341
Gross profit on sales	1,854,120	1,713,260	1,594,028
Other operating expenses:			
Operating and administrative	1,632,935	1,511,778	1,383,223
Taxes other than income taxes	98,388	92,696	85,374
Total other operating expenses	1,731,323	1,604,474	1,468,597
Operating income	122,797	108,786	125,431
Cash discounts and other income, net	82,927	74,854	80,546
	205,724	183,640	205,977
Interest:			
Interest on long-term liabilities	10,486	9,709	10,371
Other interest	2,860	1,336	103
Total interest	13,346	11,045	10,474
Earnings before income taxes	192,378	172,595	195,503
Income taxes	75,987	64,700	79,587
Net earnings	$ 116,391	107,895	115,916
Earnings per share	$ 2.84	2.64	2.83

Marketing

Traditionally for Winn-Dixie and the supermarket industry, marketing has meant putting weekly ads in the local newspaper. Changes occurring in the marketplace over the last decade, however, have forced the industry to reassess their marketing strategies. Winn-Dixie's "The Beef People" theme has been deemphasized in recent times. Price-oriented messages are becoming a more frequent theme for Winn-Dixie's advertising. In addition, Winn-Dixie focuses more on the nutrition craze, moving away from "meat and potatoes" advertising toward "light" products, and stressing the need for exercising. One television advertisement depicts a woman doing aerobics who claims, "I'm going to do it. I'm gonna lose 10 pounds. So I'm starting at Winn-Dixie. From now on, I'm going for low fat, low sugar, and low prices." Winn-Dixie ads are still marked with the familiar motto: "Winn-Dixie, America's Supermarket." They have added a new singing theme: "Winn-Dixie's changing right with you."

Although newspaper advertising and television are the most popular media forms used by Winn-Dixie, direct mail, radio advertising, and outdoor advertising are also used. Winn-Dixie spends about one percent of sales on advertising. This figure is about average for the industry. Winn-Dixie now offers new store formats and sizes, expanded product lines and departments, and new advertising strategies. "Large and upscale" accurately describe Winn-Dixie's new Marketplace stores. Fifteen Marketplace stores have been opened by Winn-Dixie in the past few years. Marketplace stores average more than 45,900 square feet, exceeding the national average of 43,830 square feet. Classified as "superstores" by the grocery industry, these stores include a larger number of products and departments than traditional supermarkets. Winn-Dixie's superstores project a "one-stop shopping" image. Winn-Dixie is locating these stores in traditional southern towns and fast-paced metropolitan areas.

In 1985, Winn-Dixie entered the warehouse store market with the opening of its first Table Supply Store. These "no frills" stores provide service departments, such as fresh seafood and produce. They range in size from 45,000 to 73,000 square feet. Five Table Supply stores were opened in 1986: one in Orlando, Florida, and four in south Florida. Another Table Supply store is scheduled to open in Macon, Georgia, in 1987. The marketing theme behind Table Supply is low prices. To attract price-conscious shoppers, Winn-Dixie advertises prices at Table Supply to be the "absolutely positively" lowest food prices in the area.

In addition to building new stores, Winn-Dixie has remodeled and enlarged a number of their older stores. In 1986, Winn-Dixie closed eighty-eight low-performing stores. The closed stores averaged 20,400 square feet. Winn-Dixie is adding a number of new departments and services to their stores, including in-store pharmacies, (fourteen were added to stores in 1986), gourmet cheese departments, and upscale bath shops. Regional product lines are also being added to attract different ethnic or geographic groups. Shoppers find enchiladas and tortillas in Texas stores, exotic spices and shellfish in Louisiana stores, and southern-fried catfish in southern Georgia stores. Another departure from Winn-Dixie's traditional store format is seen in the decor. New stores are airy, spacious, and modern with skylighting and spotlighting.

COMPETITORS

For supermarkets, competition comes in many forms. Fast food chains such as McDonalds and Wendy's are more aggressively competing for individuals' food dollar by accepting credit cards, offering home delivery, emphasizing low calorie food, and being more personable. Convenience stores like 7-Eleven, White Hen Pantry, and Circle K are expanding their product lines to become more like supermarkets. Convenience store sales increased 5.8 percent in 1986; whereas, supermarket sales rose 4.6 percent.

Winn-Dixie's primary competition comes from the more than 30,000 supermarkets operated in the United States, 17,000 of which are chain operations. Winn-Dixie's major competitors by region are listed in Exhibit 6. Winn-Dixie is especially concerned with supermarkets that operate in the Southeast, including Kroger, Publix, and Cub Foods. Kroger and Minneapolis-based Cub Foods are now vying for revenues in "hot-spot regions" such as Atlanta, Birmingham, and Houston. These companies are not building traditional supermarkets, but rather have superstores and warehouse stores that are upscale, modern, and full-service. Kroger has captured the largest market share in Atlanta. Publix has increased their marketing efforts in Florida. Other major chains such as Albertsons, Tom Thumb, Food Lion, and Big Star are major competitors in Texas and the Carolinas. Additional competition includes non-chain and small chain supermarket operators located throughout the United States. There are also the smaller "Mom and Pop" stores and "non-food" stores such as K-Mart, Revco, and Texaco that sell assorted food products. Common supermarket store formats are defined in Exhibit 7.

EXHIBIT 6 Supermarket store formats, defined, and 1986 market share

Conventional supermarkets—Under 30,000 total square feet	53.9%
Superstores—Over 30,000 total square feet, expanded food and nonfood selection	26.2%
Combination stores—Over 30,000 total square feet and at least 25 percent of area in general merchandise	4.5%
Limited assortment stores—Carries less than 1,000 items and offers few if any perishables with a "no frills" shopping environment	0.2%
Warehouse stores—Over 30,000 square feet; emphasizes lower prices at the expense of customer service	13.0%
Superwarehouse—Over 100,000 total square feet; emphasizes lower prices at the expense of customer service	1.1%
Hypermarket—Over 100,000 total square feet, expanded food and nonfood selection	1.1%

Source: Adapted from *The Food Marketing Industry Speaks 1986* (The Food Marketing Institute) and *Progressive Grocer,* April 1987.

Kroger

Kroger, the second-largest supermarket chain in the United States, is a strong competitor in many of Winn-Dixie's markets. Kroger has 27 percent of the market in Atlanta, compared to 19 percent for Food Giant (Cub Foods), 15 percent for Winn-Dixie, and 11 percent for the Atlantic & Pacific Tea Company (A&P). Kroger's ability to lead the Atlanta market is attributed to increased advertising expenditures and a greater emphasis on general merchandise, "one-stop shopping," and low prices. Kroger has broadened its product line, built superstores and combination stores, and experimented with a number of different store themes. Twenty Kroger stores now contain full-service bank branches. Kroger opened its first liquor store in 1984.

EXHIBIT 7 Per capita disposable income information

Years	*In 1986 Dollars*	*Percent of Total Disposable Income Spent on Food*
1980	8,421	12.1
1981	9,243	11.8
1982	9,724	11.6
1983	10,340	11.2
1984	11,265	10.8
1985	11,817	10.9
1986	12,312	10.0

Source: The Food Marketing Institute, *The Food Marketing Industry Speaks 1985,* p. 5.

Kroger is not without problems, however. In 1985, Kroger closed 100 unprofitable stores and reduced its staff by 25 percent. Kroger put its weak drugstore chain up for sale. Although these moves earned Kroger the title of *Forbes* most improved food distributor in 1986, Kroger's woes are not yet over. The U.S. Department of Labor's May 1987 *Monthly Labor Review* reported that Kroger is still trying to pare down its costs. Workers in Virginia, Tennessee, and Ohio all received pay cuts in lieu of closing stores. Kroger said the wage cuts were necessary to compete with discount and non-union stores.

Publix

Publix is Winn-Dixie's major competitor in Florida. Founded in 1930, Publix is the largest full-service supermarket chain in the South. Headquartered in Lakeland, Florida, Publix employs more than 40,000 people and has annual sales of about $3.5 billion. At the end of 1986, Publix was operating 321 supermarkets in Florida, after opening thirty-four new stores in 1986. Publix plans to continue expansion by adding new stores, remodeling existing stores, and opening new distribution centers. Like many other firms in the industry, Publix is taking advantage of the "one-stop shopping" craze by building new stores that include pharmacy departments, automatic teller machines, and related amenities. Publix officials feel the population growth in the state of Florida will contribute to a bright future for their company.

Cub Foods

Many of Atlanta's changes in the supermarket industry last year were sparked by the opening of the first Cub Foods store. *Supermarket News* said that Atlanta may very well remember 1986 as the "Year of the Cub." Cub Foods, owned by Super Valu Stores of Minnesota, opened its first store in Atlanta in 1985 in an agreement with Food Giant. It was a 75,000-square-foot superwarehouse store. Within months of Cub Foods' entrance into the Atlanta market, Grand Union, A & P, and Winn-Dixie all introduced new, upscale, full-service store formats. Although the first Cub Foods store "created a stir" among competitors, its sales were below forecasted expectations due to poor store location and union difficulties. Super Valu has announced plans to build more Cub Food stores in the South.

ENVIRONMENTAL ISSUES

Demographic trends that affect Winn-Dixie's strategies include more small families, more two-income families, more disposable income, an increasing number of men shopping for themselves or their families, and an increasing number of working women having to better manage their shopping schedules. Immigration for the United States is increasing, and supermarkets now recognize ethnic groups as distinct market segments. Different "ethnic" tastes have brought about many regionally unique product lines and marketing campaigns. On the East Coast, Italian cuisine is most popular; Mexican cuisine is most popular in the Midwest and Rocky Mountain states;

Chinese cuisine is most popular in the northern United States, from Michigan to California.

A recent study of 2,000 men and women aged 18 to 65 from all fifty states revealed the following findings, which affect the supermarket industry:

1. Almost half of all nonworking women shop for food twice a week or more; men shop once a week or less; most working women shop once a week.
2. Fridays and Saturdays are still the top food-shopping days, but Sunday is gaining in popularity.
3. Women aged 18 to 34 say they are cooking more now. The reverse is true of women aged 50 to 65. Far more women than men like to cook.
4. About 63 percent of women and 56 percent of men say they are eating more healthfully now than they did two years ago.
5. As for ethnic foods, Italian and Chinese are the most popular, but Cajun foods are gaining rapidly.[1]

Insurance Costs

Seventy-five percent of all supermarket chain executives say that insurance costs are a major problem, according to *Progressive Grocer's 1986 Annual Report.* More than 86 percent of all chain store owners report increases in their insurance in 1986. Some owners claim that in 1986 their rates doubled or tripled, or even worse, they were unable to attain insurance at any cost. Tort reform has been a key issue in many state legislative sessions. Under civil law, a tort is a wrong inflicted by one person against another. The goal of tort reform is to limit the dollar amounts awarded in liability cases. This in turn, limitation, would allow insurance companies to offer policies at lower rates. Only five states have passed significant tort reform bills as of October 1986: Connecticut, Colorado, Michigan, New Hampshire, and Washington.

Technology

Scanning, customer-scanning, automatic teller machines, profit-tracking software, scanning software, computer coupon dispensaries, and computerized store directories are just a few of the technological innovations in the food industry. The objective of these innovations include higher operating efficiency, more information, more accurate information, improved inventory control, and improved services for customers.

The use of scanning is the most widespread innovation in the industry. The advantages of using scanners include quicker service for customers, more accurate accounting, and a better understanding of consumer demand. Deterrents to using these systems range from high initial costs to increased customer complaints concerning the lack of a sales price on the actual goods. Various software companies now sell helpful packages that can be used in conjunction with scanning equipment. Winn-Dixie has found the benefits of scanning to outweigh the costs. The company has installed scanning equipment in 80 to 90 percent of its stores. Winn-Dixie is experimenting with the use of computerized inventory controls, efficient storage and stocking systems, and other methods to improve the customer's "shopping flow."

Economic Influences

Low inflation, low interest rates, and small increases in the consumer price index have allowed retail sales to show increases from 7 to 14 percent annually since 1980. Economists are predicting, however, that inflation will begin to rise in the next few years and the economic climate of the early 1980s will stabilize or decline in the later part of the decade. Increases in the inflation rate can be damaging to Winn-Dixie's bottom line.

Winn-Dixie is already responding to a decline in the percentage of disposable income spent on food. Although per capita disposable income has increased annually, the percentage of the total spent on food has decreased, as seen in Exhibit 8. Winn-Dixie's response to this trend has been to add a number of non-food services to its stores, such as pharmacies, greeting cards, floral shops, and cosmetics.

Tax reform has had a positive effect on the retail food industry. Winn-Dixie claims that high tax rates of the past have been a financial burden for the company. The tax reform bill will reduce Winn-Dixie's corporate tax ceiling from 45 percent to 34 percent. Winn-Dixie expects its customers to enjoy a reduction in personal taxes, increasing their disposable income. Depreciation schedules have been shortened, and this factor could slow the building of supermarkets.

Carryout Foods

According to *Restaurants USA*, the number of consumers ordering takeout dinners doubled from 1982 to 1985. The National Restaurant Association adds that in a study of 1,000 consumers, 56 percent bought takeout food more than twice a week. The Food Marketing Institute reports that less than 10 percent of all carryout food is purchased from the supermarket. A breakdown of where takeout food is purchased is given in Exhibit 9. This trend is being fueled by the increase in working women. Some supermarket chains are already taking advantage of this marketing niche. First

EXHIBIT 8 Where do households purchase takeout foods?

Sources	*Percent of Households*
Fast food store	43
Restaurant carryout	38
Supermarket carryout	10
Some other place	2
None/not applicable	4
It varies	1
Not sure	3

Source: The Food Marketing Institute, *Trends 1987—Consumer Attitudes and the Supermarket*, p. 37.

EXHIBIT 9 Winn-Dixie's major competitors by region, 1987

State	*Competitor(s)*
Florida	Publix
Georgia	Kroger, Cub Foods, Piggly Wiggly, A&P
Carolinas	Food Lion, Kroger, Big Star
Texas	Kroger, Tom Thumb, Skaggs/Alphabeta, Albertsons

National Supermarket Stores offer complete dinners in microwavable dishes. Kroger in Atlanta has a a 64-foot Sushi bar where you can purchase eight pieces of Sushi for $4.99. Kings Supermarket in New Jersey offers items such as rosemary roasted potatoes, tortellini pesto, and honey glazed roast duck. *Advertising Age* predicts the supermarket carryout trend will gain momentum in the future.

The Aging Market

America's elderly are the healthiest, wealthiest, and longest-lived generation of people in history. Since a high percentage of Winn-Dixie stores are located in Florida, a known retirement area, the elderly market is substantial and important. Supermarkets more and more are offering products especially for older citizens and are advertising in a way that is not degrading.

The Hispanic Shopper

In Winn-Dixie's market, Hispanics represent a majority of the population in cities such as Miami, San Antonio, and El Paso. Hispanics are growing in numbers in many other areas. Some retailers, including Winn-Dixie, have begun to market to this group, as well as to other ethnic groups such as Asians and Latin Americans. According to an article in *American Demographic's* May 1987 issue, Hispanic shoppers use coupons more often and spend 15 to 20 percent more of their disposable income on groceries than the average American. Supermarkets are targeting marketing campaigns toward ethnic groups by offering ethnic food products and by employing people with foreign language skills.

FUTURE OUTLOOK

Slow and conservative change has been the mainstay of Winn-Dixie's strategies for many of its sixty-two years of existence. This element is seen in the "beef people" slogan that Winn-Dixie continues to use and in the management staff members who still earn promotions by moving up through the ranks. Although these traditions have worked well in the past, the late 1980s have brought in new ideas of what grocery stores are and how they should be operated. Winn-Dixie's greatest challenge of the future may be identifying ways to differentiate itself from competitors who are looking for ways to lure Winn-Dixie's customers into their stores. Product and/or store differentiation may be the key to gaining larger market share. Winn-Dixie has only recently started to reposition itself from an industry follower to an industry leader. Its reactive stance may not have been a hindrance in the past, but changes in the supermarket industry necessitate more proactive strategies in the future. The number and type of stores that Winn-Dixie builds and the particular products and services offered will be critical to success.

Various strategies that Winn-Dixie could consider in the future include staying open twenty-four hours a day, seven days a week; offering self-service food checkout lines; presenting videos in meat and produce departments to show how to cook; and placing digital displays on shelves so customers can push a button to get a price. *Progressive Grocer* reports that 55 percent of all supermarkets now offer camera film processing service, 45 percent use scanning, and 44 percent have hot take-out food. Winn-Dixie could offer these services in more of its stores. James Wood, chairman of New Jersey-based A&P, the nation's oldest and fourth-largest grocery-store chain, says, "We have upgraded food selling in America to a level that's higher than anywhere else in the world."

Winn-Dixie's plans for 1987 include opening nearly 100 stores that average about 40,000 square feet each, enlarging or remodeling about fifty stores, and closing about seventy-five stores that average 20,000 square feet each. Are these planned openings, remodelings, and closings financially feasible? Should Winn-Dixie locate new stores in states such as Indiana and Oklahoma where the company has only four and six stores, respectively? Should it expand into states with no Winn-Dixie stores, such as Arkansas, Maryland, and New York? What combination or mix of supermarkets, Marketplaces, and Table Supply warehouse stores should Winn-Dixie strive to achieve in the future? Winn-Dixie opened fourteen pharmacies in its stores in fiscal 1986; should this trend be continued? What specific strategies would you recommend to Dano Davis and Robert Davis, Winn-Dixie's president and chairman, respectively? How could your recommended strategies best be implemented?

SUGGESTED READINGS

"Do Real Men Shop?" *American Demographics.* March 1987, 13.

Food Marketing Institute. *Trends.* 1987, 35.

Food Marketing Institute. *Food Marketing Industry Speaks 1986.* 1986, 103–105.

Frenner, Denise. "From Piano to Sushi Bars, Grocers Jazz Up Service." *Advertising Age.* 4 May, 1987, S–1, S–2.

Kotkin, Joel. "Selling to the New America." *Inc.* July 1987, 44–51.

"Most Improved." *Forbes.* 12 January, 1987, 131.

"New Cubs, Kiogers Sparkling Innovation in Atlanta." *Supermarket News.* 21 April, 1986, 4A.

Progressive Grocer: 54th Annual Report of the Grocery Industry. April 1987, 7, 13, 14, 17.

Shaw, Russell. "Winn-Dixie Adds New Ideas to Old Traditions." *Advertising Age.* 28 April, 1986, S–16, S–20.

"Taking to Take-Out." *American Demographics.* March 1987, 13–14.

"The Top 1000 U.S. Companies Ranked by Industry." *Business Week.* 17 April, 1987, 146.

U.S. Department of Labor. "Kroger Workers Forego Bonus Plan to Save Jobs." *Monthly Labor Review.* March 1987, 42–43.

Valentino, Cynthia. "In a Fragmented Market, Grocers Cover the Niches." *Advertising Age.* 4 May, 1987, S–8–S–15.

Winn-Dixie Stores, Inc. *Form 10–K/Annual Report* for the Fiscal Year Ended June 25, 1986.

Wolfe, David B. "The Ageless Market." *American Demographics.* July 1987, 27–29, 55, 56.

ENDNOTES

1. Clements, Mark. *Parade Magazine.* 25 October, 1987, 8–12.

The Kroger Company—1987

KEITH ROBBINS AND SHAKER ZAHRA
George Mason University

The Kroger Company celebrated its 100th anniversary in 1983. Over the past century, Kroger has become one of the most successful and innovative companies in its industry. Yet, the birthday celebrations were overshadowed by gloomy forecasts for the company's future. The industry was expected to become more competitive while experiencing a meager growth rate. These forecasts brought Kroger's management little comfort; the company was competing on many fronts. The competitors included supermarket chains, independent grocers, drug stores, fast-food chains, and convenience stores. Industry profit margins were declining, and price competition was intensifying.

Kroger's response was to initiate an aggressive restructuring program during 1984. The purpose was to achieve a successful company turnaround, to redefine the business concept and sharpen Kroger's competitive position. The essential elements of the program were set forth in Kroger's turnaround strategy. This strategy revolved around a thorough examination of Kroger's business mix, disposal of unprofitable segments and units, lowering of operating costs via employee layoffs, and redeployment of corporate assets to better utilize them in growth markets. The dilemma for Kroger was how to implement the turnaround strategy without detriment to its image as the most productive company in its industry. The 1984–1987 period was a most challenging transitional point in Kroger's life, and it did not proceed peacefully.

HISTORY

A chronology of the highlights from Kroger's past are presented in Exhibit 1. Barney H. Kroger founded The Kroger Company as the Great Western Tea Company in 1883 in Cincinnati, Ohio. Kroger firmly believed that quality products were essential to cultivating customer loyalty. He repeatedly sampled the products to ensure high quality.

EXHIBIT 1 The Kroger timeline

1883	The first store opens at 66 East Pearl Street in Cincinnati.
1884	Barney Kroger buys out partner and opens a second store. Kroger is one of the first grocery stores to advertise regularly in newspaper.
1901	Kroger is first grocery company to operate its own bakeries.
1902	With forty stores and $1.75 million in annual sales, the Kroger Grocery & Baking Company is incorporated.
1908	Kroger's growing chain numbers 136 stores in Cincinnati, Dayton, Columbus, and northern Kentucky.
1912	In its first long-distance expansion, Kroger opens twenty-five stores in St. Louis, Missouri.
1928	B. H. Kroger sells his company stock and retires from active management.
1935	Fifty Kroger stores take on the new "supermarket" style.
1938	B. H. Kroger dies at age 78.
1946	Kroger Grocery & Baking Company officially becomes The Kroger Co.
1952	Kroger sales top $1 billion.
1955	Kroger joins six other firms to found the Top Value Stamp Co.
1961	The first SupeRx Drug Store opens in Millford, Ohio.
1962	Kroger achieves its first $2 billion sales year.
1968	In just five years Kroger's sales mushroom another $1 billion and go beyond $3 billion.
1972	Kroger's first superstore opens in Barberton, Ohio.
1975	Kroger sales exceed $5 billion.
1978	Lyle Everingham is named Kroger's president and chief executive officer.
1979	Kroger becomes the nation's second largest food retailing company.
1980	Company sales top $10 billion.
1981	Kroger merges with Dillion Companies, Inc. and begins new era as coast-to-coast operator of food, drug, and convenience stores, and the manufacturer of more than 4,000 food and nonfood products.

Source: *The Kroger Story: A Century of Innovation.*

Mr. Kroger was a disciple of word-of-mouth advertising: that the best endorsement is a satisfied customer. He attracted new customers from referrals and kept them by providing quality products. Kroger always maintained the idea that customers were important and key to his business. A considerable number of his regular customers were farmers and lower-income families.

Although word-of-mouth was the primary promotional vehicle, Kroger also utilized the media. Kroger used full-page ads in local newspapers as early as the 1890s—a practice unheard of at the time. Additionally, Kroger revolutionized the idea of bulk purchasing. Scale economies in purchasing allowed him to advertise lower prices.

Kroger began to expand through Cincinnati. His stores had been family managed, but as the chain expanded, Kroger was forced to hire managers outside of the family. He was fortunate in that most of the managers were hard working and conscientious. However, when managers failed to perform satisfactorily, Kroger was not hesitant to terminate their employment.

As the company grew, Kroger continued to personally supervise all store operations to ensure the quality that bred customer loyalty. Kroger devoted much of his energies to cost control. He was the industry leader in pursuing cost reductions due to process innovations. In order to gain greater control over product cost and quality, Kroger vertically integrated into manufacturing staple items.

The Great Western Tea Company continued to expand. The stores used wagon routes to deliver groceries. Kroger supplemented direct sales with mail-order operations. The mail-order operation was particularly lucrative in rural Pennsylvania and West Virginia. Popular mail-order items included coffee, tea, pepper, dried peas, and spices.

In 1902, The Great Western Tea Company was incorporated as The Kroger Grocery and Baking Company. At this time Kroger began to pursue expansion outside of Cincinnati. Kroger's first target for expansion was Hamilton, Ohio. Subsequently, Kroger moved into Dayton and Columbus, Ohio.

Kroger's disposition to innovate and take risks became more evident. For example, Kroger was the first grocer to establish bakeries within the stores. The idea proved to be very profitable. Kroger also took another bold step and opened a meat market/butcher shop in selected stores.

Kroger successfully integrated horizontally and vertically. Both the introduction of the bakery and meat center were major innovations and achievements. Kroger acquired facilities that would complement his stores; he bought trucks and established delivery services. Kroger also developed and managed warehouses and distribution centers to reduce operational costs, control quality, and meet changing customer preferences. These efforts were major factors in Kroger's early success.

Kroger's first national expansion was signaled by the purchase of a chain of stores in St. Louis in 1912. As highway and railroad conditions improved, Kroger was able to expand to other cities, including Detroit, Indianapolis, Springfield, and Toledo.

Kroger was a major contributor to the fund raising campaign supporting World War I during 1917. Thereafter, the company continued to expand in areas adjacent to Cincinnati. The strategy was to acquire financially distressed grocery chains. This strategy fueled the rapid expansion experienced by Kroger during the 1920s. Kroger's centralized management structure was considered essential in turning around the purchased grocers.

In 1928, Mr. Kroger sold all of his stock in the company but continued his association with the company by serving on the board of directors. During the great depression, he repurchased many shares of company stock to demonstrate his confidence in Kroger's long-term viability. Finally, in 1931 after the confidence in the firm was no longer an issue, Kroger resigned from the board of directors, severing his official ties with the company.

Barney Kroger died in 1938, leaving The Kroger Company as a legacy to his managerial skills. His influence pervades the company to this day.

Kroger in the 1980s

Today, Kroger's top-management team adheres to the same principles instituted by Barney Kroger decades ago. Over the years, Kroger acquired businesses and stores through both horizontal and vertical integration. During that time, the company has grown to be a leader in its industry. An important transition for the company was its emphasis on cultivating the supermarket chain concept during the 1930s and 1940s. This goal was accomplished through a series of carefully chosen acquisitions that facilitated Kroger's entry into Georgia and Texas. Thus, Kroger's acquisitions were carefully selected according to their regional strengths.

COMPANY STRATEGIES

Company Mission

Kroger's current mission statement is presented in Exhibit 2. Once a grocery and bakery-oriented operation, Kroger has evolved into a company composed of four strategic business units: food, convenience, drug stores, and food manufacturing. The entrepreneurial spirit pioneered by its founder still guides Kroger's management today. The overall corporate goal is "to become the very best food and drug retailing company" (*Annual Report,* 1985, 2).

To achieve this ambitious goal, the firm stresses a strategy that centers on the idea of flexible responsiveness. Flexible responsiveness entails the following: 1) understanding the changing nature of the competitive environment, 2) redefining the product mix and, if necessary, the business portfolio to meet customer needs, and 3) being selective in corporate activities to ensure that high quality is maintained in the chosen lines of business.

EXHIBIT 2 The Kroger Mission Statement

Our principal objective is to be a performance-proven leader in the distribution and merchandising of food, and related products and services to the consumer.

We will serve customers, primarily through retail stores in the United States, and whenever doing so will provide a value to them and a profit opportunity for the company.

We will invest in manufacturing and distribution facilities whenever this course will improve our profit potential and increase the value received by customers of company-owned or affiliated retail outlets.

We will satisfy the needs of consumers as well as, or better than, the best of our competitors, and in so doing, we will grow as a company and meet the expectations of our employees and shareowners.

We will encourage our employees to be active and responsible citizens in the communities in which we operate, and we will allocate resources for activities which enhance the quality of life for our customers, employees and the general public.

Kroger's strategy of flexible responsiveness had significant implications for the company's business portfolio, internal organization, corporate social involvement, and ultimately, financial performance. In the following sections, each of these four areas will be examined to better understand how the top-management team articulated the company's business concept and philosophy over the years.

Flexible Responsiveness

Joe Pichler, president of Kroger, summarized his views of what customers expect from the company: "They're looking for convenience, price, variety, service, ... and they want it all" (1986 *Annual Report*, p. 5). Guided by this belief, the strategy of flexible responsiveness stresses careful selection of location, convenience, added utility through swift customer service, large selection of items, and differentiation.

Regarding location, Kroger estimates that each new store costs about $5 to $6 million. As a result, sophisticated analytical models are utilized to determine the potential profitability of a proposed store, and the proper mix of merchandise to be offered in a given location.

Kroger's top-management team is well aware of the trend toward "one-stop shopping" that has transformed the industry in recent years. In response to this trend, combination stores (that is, drug and food stores) were emphasized. These stores have a wide assortment of items ranging from pharmacies and video rental areas to pizza shops, salad bars, and home floral delivery departments. The new stores emphasize prepared meals, seafoods, and many other items. At Kroger, convenience implies variety.

Differentiation is an important dimension of Kroger's strategy. This factor is best reflected in store formats which vary by locale. Examples include the City Market on a Navaho Indian reservation in New Mexico, the Welcome super warehouse in Greenville, South Carolina, and the Turkey Hill Minit Market in south central Pennsylvania.

This search for uniqueness in a highly competitive market has been accompanied by increased attention to controlling costs. This focus was perceived to be a top corporate priority because grocery store profits averaged about one percent of sales. To achieve the goal of reducing costs, several steps were undertaken. Integration efforts continued by moving into wholesaling through increasing the company's warehousing facilities. However, in some markets, the firm did the opposite by contracting with outside wholesalers to provide store needs. This arrangement was particularly evident in Texas and Florida. Kroger also entered into a joint-venture arrangement in Michigan to experiment with the idea of entering grocery wholesaling more aggressively.

Kroger's retrenchment included the closing of 100 unprofitable stores during 1986. Staff reductions were attained primarily through a generous early retirement program. The rationale was to replace higher salaried senior personnel with fewer, lower-salaried new employees. The reductions in employees were most pronounced in the data processing and accounting departments. Kroger was attempting to streamline its staff personnel.

In summary, Kroger's flexible responsiveness was comprised of five interrelated concepts: 1) consumer-driven marketing, 2) contemporary facilities and ideas, 3) disciplined asset review, 4) rigorous cost control, and 5) increased shareholder's value.

BUSINESS SEGMENTS

In 1984, Kroger had four business groups: food stores, convenience stores, drug stores, and food manufacturing. During the period 1984–1987, Kroger pursued a massive reorientation of each of the business segments.

Food Stores

According to *Forbes* (11 January, 1988), over 90 percent of Kroger's sales and profits came from its supermarkets. Kroger Food Stores comprise the second-largest supermarket chain in the country. Indeed, despite rising emphasis on food manufacturing, the food stores remain the most important segment of the company by far. The supermarket industry also remains the most fiercely competitive business in which the company competes.

The late 1970s witnessed double-digit inflation and a severe general economic recession. Many grocers responded to the shocks by reducing prices to stimulate sales volume. As a result, price wars became widespread among retailers throughout the country. These price wars, coupled with miscalculations on the part of management, had a particularly adverse affect on Kroger; operating costs were eating into profit margins even as Kroger was reducing prices to remain competitive with other grocers.

Kroger was quick to reduce prices to forestall or prohibit entry into its lucrative markets. One of Kroger's most successful markets had been the Indianapolis area in which it operated thirty-four stores. Rumor had it that another chain, SuperValue Stores, was about to enter this market. In order to prevent entry, Kroger reduced its prices significantly prompting one SuperValue executive to remark that "the prices they (Kroger) used ... were significantly below what we would have come in with."

In fact, Kroger's pricing strategy, commonly referred to as zone pricing, led to widespread accusations of predatory pricing among the competition. Zone pricing was ostensibly intended to permit flexibility in meeting local competitive challenges. In practice, it gave zone managers the ability to lower their prices to the point where existing competition was reduced and the threat of entry by new companies was minimized.

In another price-related case, Kroger refused to go along with the evolving industry trend to double or triple the value of manufacturers' coupons. These coupons were intended to encourage purchase of national brands. Kroger's management thought that by not redeeming these coupons, consumers' defection from its brands to national brands could be thwarted. Later, management changed its position due to the strong trend of increasing consumer preference for national brands.

Perhaps one of the worst strategic miscalculations committed by Kroger management related to the acquisition of Dillon in 1983. An important consideration behind the $608 million acquisition was access to new markets. Dillon operated 219 supermarkets and 350 convenience stores, mainly in Arizona, California, Colorado, and Kansas (*Wall Street Journal,* 26 January, 1983). Dillon was expected to complement Kroger's existing stores, which were located primarily in the Midwest.

The deal went sour when, according to the *Wall Street Journal,* "Dillon was already locked into long-term supply agreements, and Kroger underestimated the difficulty of renegotiating them" (31 May, 1984, p.1).

The difficulties faced by the Food Stores Group over the past decade were not unique to Kroger. Slower economic and population growth, a major recession, shifting customer attitudes, and intensified competition were causes of industrywide distress. However, some industry observers contended that Kroger was particularly vulnerable due to its entrepreneurial philosophy. Despite abundant warnings, Kroger's management continued its practices as the "nation's most innovative grocer." Experimentation continued in efforts to determine optimal product mix, to introduce new items, and to broaden the company's geographic scope. The problem, according to many industry observers, was not the innovative thrust of Kroger's strategy, per se. The problem was the breadth of the efforts. To many, these activities lacked a clear focus.

How did Kroger respond to its increasingly unfavorable environment? It instituted a six-step strategy: 1) it placed a greater emphasis on merchandising activities, 2) it stepped up its promotional activities, 3) it intensified its customer/market research activities, 4) it selectively increased the number of stores, 5) it introduced new services into its supermarkets, and 6) it increased its international operations.

The company placed a greater emphasis on merchandising activities, primarily to lower costs and respond more expediently to changing customer expectations. Merchandising, food manufacturing, and retailing were interrelated at Kroger to a greater degree than within any other supermarket chain.

Promotional activities were increased with a renewed commitment to advertising and in-store promotion. As a result, several "special event sales" were staged using a wide range of promotional media including print and electronic advertising, and store displays. One such "special event" was Kroger's involvement in a program aimed at weight loss using the Rotation Diet. This brought the company a great deal of visibility and increased sales in participating stores. In fact, Kroger's experience with the Rotation Diet became a model for other supermarket stores to follow.

Kroger intensified its customer research efforts. These activities have been linked to merchandising to ensure timely response to customer needs. Individual stores were encouraged and expected to become thoroughly familiar with their customers.

The number of stores within the Supermarket Group has been increased via new store development, store remodeling, and selective acquisitions. Interestingly, the growth in the number of new stores has been limited, but store space has been expanded by nearly 85 percent.

Expansion was achieved through new store development or remodeling, and acquisition as in the case of the Dillon's chain. To help finance this expansion, poorly performing stores were closed. In 1982, the year preceding the Dillon acquisition, 178 stores were closed. Another 128 were closed in 1984, sixty-three in 1985, and 100 in 1986. Proceeds from these closings were deployed to increase corporate expansion in the Sunbelt and Southwest. This expansion focus was evidenced by the fact that two-thirds of the new stores built by Kroger in 1983 were in one of these regions. These changes reflected management perception of shifting population demographics. Most of the store closings occurred in the Midwest.

New services were offered in Kroger's supermarkets. Recognizing the popularity of "one-stop shopping," Kroger increased its in-store financial centers, which are run by Capital Venture Corporation. Today, some Kroger stores in Ohio, Texas, Georgia, and North Carolina contain the financial centers. These centers sell insurance, money market and mutual funds, and individual retirement accounts.

Kroger also responded to the fast-food establishments with its Greenhouse restaurants. Resembling greenhouses, these in-store restaurants primarily offered fast-food and ethnic specialties as part of a limited menu.

Finally, the company attempted to increase its international presence. For example, Kroger marketed its store-branded merchandise through a large Japanese supermarket chain. The brands were included as the "American Section" of the Japanese stores.

Food Manufacturing Group

The purpose of the Food Manufacturing Group is to supply "private label food products for the company's retail stores, as well as outside customers" (*Annual Report,* 1985, p.12). Interestingly, Kroger consolidates the sales and earnings of the Manufacturing Group with those of the food stores. In 1987, Kroger had 41 food manufacturing and processing facilities.

The Food Manufacturing Group has received increased attention recently. One reason is management's recognition that this group complements Kroger's main business line, the Supermarket Group. A second reason is that manufacturing allows the firm to quickly respond to changing customer preferences by producing customized alternatives frequently not immediately available from other manufacturers.

In 1984, Kroger enacted a new strategy for the Food Manufacturing Group. This strategy has four main themes. The first is to make this division more market-driven. In operational terms, this meant that the group was expected to produce privately labelled products that appealed to Kroger's shoppers and competed with national brands. The second theme was increased attention by the group to developing a solid external customer base of independent and smaller regional grocers. The group was also interested in procuring more government contracts.

Consistent with the strategy of the Food Stores Group, the third theme for the Manufacturing Group focused on effective asset management to control costs and improve productivity. The fourth dimension of the Food Manufacturing Group's strategy was especially exciting. The group has entered into a joint venture with Corning Glass Works to utilize biotechnology to produce commercial food products from dairy products. In 1985, Eastman Kodak Company became a partner in this joint venture, which was renamed Nutrisearch International Corporation.

The Convenience Store Group

Like other supermarket chains, in recent years Kroger has placed a great deal of emphasis on its Convenience Store Group. In fact, the number of stores grew at a significantly higher rate than the food store segment: from 352 in 1983 to 735 in 1986.

These stores were designed to meet the growing trend toward convenience. As a result, stores were stocked with items generally consumed within 24 hours of purchase. Some of the recent convenience stores were designed to include seating for onsite consumption of microwave snacks.

Drug Store Group

In 1960, Kroger acquired a small but growing chain of drug stores. The chain was established by James P. Herring in 1954 and had seven stores in New Jersey and New York. Kroger's decision to buy this chain was due to the company's belief that many customers would enjoy the convenience of side-by-side food and drug stores.

Mr. Herring was asked by Kroger's management to build a national chain of drug stores. Kroger called its drug stores SupeRx, and the first of these was built next door to a Kroger Food Store in Milford, Ohio. Within two years, Herring had built sixty-six stores. Expansion over the next decade continued at an average rate of forty new stores per year. By 1983, there were 575 SupeRx drug stores in twenty states.

In the early 1980s, Kroger decided to reorganize SupeRx operations to make them more efficient and to improve the image of the chain. Subsequently, SupeRx began to emphasize convenience, which became its strategic focus. SupeRx was made more convenient through the addition of a wide range of impulse items to complement its wide range of non-traditional services. Thus, SupeRx became much more than a drug store. A typical store contained an optical shop, a photo shop, soft drinks, and picnic supplies, in addition to the pharmacy. By 1985, many Kroger Food Stores included a SupeRx Drug Store under the same roof. The purpose was to achieve economies in company operations and to better seize opportunities that were created in response to the market's demand for convenience.

To further its growth into the health care market, Kroger acquired Hook's Drug Stores in May 1985. Hook's had a long record of success in pharmaceutical retailing in Indiana, Ohio, Kentucky, Illinois, and Michigan. Hook's also included nineteen convalescent aid centers.

Hook's Chairman J. Douglas Reeves was appointed to the position of executive vice president of SupeRx in 1986. Kroger's plans for SupeRx included expanding the company's nursing home business and pursuing special arrangements with suppliers in order to truly become a discount drug retailer. Kroger also implemented an ambitious program to upgrade SupeRx's facilities concurrent to the redefinition of marketing strategy. As a result, Kroger added ten convalescent homes and forty-one new SupeRx drug stores, as well as renovated forty-two existing facilities for 1986. Kroger also planned to install computer pharmacies in all stores by the end of 1986. These computer pharmacies would process data on customer preferences, monitor inventories to facilitate reordering, and in general enhance the level of customized service.

These plans never came to fruition. Despite the improved performance of the Drug Store Group in 1985, its contribution to company revenues was a modest 6 percent. In July 1986, in a radical reversal of its plans, Kroger announced its intentions to sell some SupeRx units. Among the options announced by Kroger was the formation of a private company to buy most of the SupeRx chain as a spinoff to shareholders or the outright sale of SupeRx. On December 22, 1983, Rite Aid Corporation announced that it had reached a definitive agreement to acquire 115 of Kroger's SupeRx drug stores. The 1986 *Annual Report* disclosed that the company was concluding the sale of its drug stores through a series of private transactions. In 1987, Kroger actually divested its free-standing drug stores. Kroger planned to use the proceeds from the divestment to reduce its long-term debt and to repurchase outstanding shares of company stock.

INTERNAL ORGANIZATION

Redefinition of the business concept was paralleled by a strong emphasis on decentralization of operations. The purpose was twofold: to expedite implementation of the flexible responsiveness strategy, and to enhance employee participation in decision making. As Walter Dryden, senior vice president, stated: "Much of what is driving Kroger today is a vigorous push for more widespread and shared decision making; that is, decisions which are made closest to the customer. It is expected that broadened responsibility will create a variety of marketplace responses more in tune with today's fast-changing retail environment" (Kroger, 1986 *Annual Report,* p. 11). Thus, Kroger's earlier emphasis on uniformity of policy and procedures has been replaced by a carefully planned program of participation.

How does Kroger implement its decentralization strategy? Kathy Miller, manager of human resources, believes it begins with the recruiting process. Increasingly, Kroger is looking for people with leadership skills and the ability to make changes: people who are able to motivate others and are willing to take risks.

To further instill a sense of participation, Kroger implemented an employee stock option. By the end of 1986, more than 96,000 Kroger employees were also shareholders, the result of a payroll deduction program and other incentives offered by the company.

These steps were considered necessary to increase employee satisfaction and performance. Indirectly, the steps described above were a response to the company's growing recognition of the difficulty of undertaking a major strategic transition with a unionized workforce. On many occasions, Kroger's initiatives to reduce cost through labor savings led to employee strikes. Union-management relations deteriorated to the point that Kroger threatened to shut down its stores if wage concessions were not accepted.

Participative management and quality of working life helped employees deal with another aggressive workforce reduction program initiated by management. Early retirement, voluntary terminations, and layoffs were implemented across all levels of the organization.

The central figure behind these sweeping changes in Kroger's strategy was Chairman and Chief Executive Officer Lyle Everingham. Everingham has been associated with Kroger for more than 40 years, having first joined Kroger as a store clerk in 1946. He was a major figure in the revamping of the Food Store Group's merchandising strategy during the 1970s.

Industry publications depicted a power struggle within Kroger between Everingham and his would-be successor, William Kagler. President and Chief Operating Officer Kagler was apparently in favor of a more gradual strategic transformation. The two disagreed on many of the steps taken to actualize Kroger's strategy, resulting in Kagler's resignation from the company in 1986. Many industry analysts contended that the real reason for Kagler's resignation was Everingham's belief that Kagler was actively attempting to supplant him as CEO. Joseph Pichler was promoted to the position vacated by Kagler.

In 1987, many of the strategies implemented by Kroger were showing initial evidence of success. "The company's restructuring, in which approximately 12 percent of our asset base was disposed of or sold, has had several beneficial effects. The disposal of 100 unprofitable supermarkets stemmed a cash flow drain and freed management to direct attention toward profitable activities. The sales of SupeRx drug stores and Hook Drug, Inc., generated proceeds which have been used to reduce debt and to increase shareholder value through stock buybacks. Expenses were reduced through early retirement programs and administrative consolidations. And perhaps most important, our primary mission—the profitable operation of convenience-oriented retail stores—stands today in sharp focus" (Kroger 1986 *Annual Report,* p.2).

Kroger has rededicated itself to the basic principles which guided Barney Kroger during the inception of the company: quality, value, service, and inventiveness in all facets of company operation. The changes in the store mix are presented in Exhibit 3.

PRIMARY COMPETITORS

Exhibit 4 contains a list of the primary competitors in food retailing ranked according to size. Asset and profit data are also included in the listing. Three competitors are described in more detail below to provide a sense of the state of competition within the industry. Safeway and A&P were chosen because in the past they have competed most closely with Kroger on a national basis. Southland was chosen because it represents a new challenge to the industry in general and illustrates the demand for convenience from the American consumer.

Safeway

Safeway is the largest retail grocery chain in the world. At fiscal year-end 1986, the company operated 1,909 domestic stores: 1,681 stores were in twenty-one of the twenty-four states west of the Mississippi River, and 228 stores were located in the Mid-Atlantic region. The company operated 244 stores in Canada.

Safeway offers the usual assortment of products: meats, dairy items, canned goods, and beverages. Safeway also includes floral departments, liquor and gourmet shops,

EXHIBIT 3 Kroger's store mix: 1981–1986

Year	*Food*	*Drug*	*Convenience*
1981[1]	1285	493	—
1982[1]	1199	563	—
1983[1]	1428	606	352
1984	1318	618[2]	443
1985	1367[2]	872	643
1986	1298	—	735

Notes: [1] Data were collected from the *Wall Street Journal,* May 31, 1984; other figures were compiled from Kroger's 1985 and 1986 Annual Reports.

[2] Forty-four stores previously classified as drug stores were included with food stores.

EXHIBIT 4 Competitor financial data (in millions of dollars)

Company	*1984*	*1985*	*1986*
Revenues			
A & P	5222	5878	6615
Safeway	19642	19651	—
Southland	7998	8578	8578
Operating Income			
A & P	88	87	119
Safeway	423	428	—
Southland	172	282	245
General and Administrative Expenses			
A & P	1092	1267	1452
Safeway	4214	4351	—
Southland	1487	1630	1748
Net Income			
A & P	48	216	88
Safeway	185	231	—
Southland	160	213	200

delicatessens, and appliance sections in many of its stores. Safeway also owns the Food Barn chain (wholesale food) and the Liquor Barn chain (wholesale liquor).

According to Moody's Industrial Manual, Safeway "operates extensive distribution, manufacturing, and processing facilities. A complex of 26 distribution warehousing centers, 14 freestanding warehouses and a fleet of approximately 1,700 tractor-trailer combinations plus 2,200 additional trailers and other vehicles, all of which are generally serviced and maintained at the Co.'s facilities, are used to supply supermarkets. [Safeway] . . . operates 86 milk manufacturing and processing facilities, including 19 fluid milk plants, 18 bakeries, 13 ice cream plants, 5 soft drink bottling plants, 5 meat processing plants, 5 egg candling plants, 3 fruit and vegetable processing plants, 4 cheese plants, 2 jam and jelly plants, 2 household cleaning products plants and 10 other manufacturing and processing plants as of Jan. 3, 1987." (*Moody's Industrial Manual,* 1987, p. 6134)

During 1986, Safeway became a privately held corporation as a result of a leveraged buyout by the investment firm of Kohlberg Kravis Roberts & Company. Since then, the company has continued to place a strong emphasis on the one-stop-shopping concept; multiple goods and services are provided within "megastores." These megastores feature approximately 28,000 different items at deep discount prices (*Grocer's Spotlight,* December 1985, p. 51).

Safeway has pharmacies in 410 of its stores. In-store banks offer Safeway customers the convenience of transacting financial business while doing their grocery shopping.

Southland

The Southland Corporation is the country's largest operator and franchisor of convenience stores. The convenience stores primarily operated under the name 7-Eleven. At the end of 1986, Southland included 7,672 7-Eleven convenience stores in the United States and Canada, 465 Chief Auto Parts stores, five distribution centers, six food processing centers, 346 High Dairy stores, 163 Quik Mart and Super-7 outlets, and 50 percent equity interest in Citgo Petroleum Corporation. Southland also manufactures and distributes specialty chemicals, ice, and safes. The company is divided into two business segments: convenience retailing and food processing.

The 7-Eleven outlets sell convenience, which management defines as, "giving customers what they want, when they want it, and where they want it." Consequently, over 80 percent of 7-Eleven stores are open twenty-four hours, offering merchandise ranging from rental televisions to floor polishing machines to prepared foods.

Over the past few years, Southland has continued its domination of the convenience store industry by offering new products and services to its customers. By 1982, 7-Eleven had become the largest gasoline retailer in the United States, offering gasoline at 44 percent of all locations. In 1986, the company sold 2.05 billion gallons of gasoline at retail.

Two other noteworthy 7-Eleven innovations were the introduction of automatic teller machines (ATM's) and fast food to its convenience stores. By the end of 1986, ATM's were installed in 1,500 stores. The company's fast-food capabilities were greatly enhanced during 1986. There are in-store delicatessans at more than 3,600 locations, and freshly prepared hot dogs and nachos are sold at 6,500 locations. Southland most recently has entered into joint ventures with Hardee's and Church's Fried Chicken in order to offer branded fast food at many outlets.

Southland has been expanding rapidly into the suburbs. These neighborhood locations are easily accessible for quick in and out shopping. The 7-Eleven convenience store emphasizes personal, courteous service and clean, modern stores. The principal customer groups include early and late shoppers, weekend and holiday shoppers and customers who may need only a few items at any one time and desire rapid service. (*Moody's Industrial Manual,* 1987)

A&P

The Great Atlantic and Pacific Tea Company (A&P) was founded in 1869 and for the next century was the undisputed king of the supermarket chains. In 1973, Safeway surpassed A&P in revenues, marking the beginning of a severe financial downturn for the company. Today, A&P is once again a financially stable company thanks to the leadership of Chief Executive Officer James Wood, who accomplished one of the most dramatic turnarounds in the history of corporate America.

Today, A&P is the fourth-largest grocery store chain in America. A&P operates 1,045 stores in the eastern, southern, and midwestern portions of the United States and in Canada. A&P's stores are of two basic types: traditional supermarkets and superstores (supermarket-drug combination stores). The company has 849 retail stores in the United States that are operated under the names Super Fresh, Kohl's, Pantry Pride, and Family Mart in addition to the long-standing A&P. Family Marts are A&P's superstores, and are located exclusively in the Southeast.

All A&P stores carry groceries, meats, produce, and other items commonly sold in the retail food business. Most stores offer fresh fish and contain a bakery and cheese department. A&P stores carry both national brands and private-label merchandise as well as certain generic (nonbranded) products. The private-label and generic products are typically lower in price than the comparable national brand. What distinguishes the superstores is that they offer prescription and over-the-counter drug services and a larger selection of both food and nonfood merchandise.

As A&P began to regain its stability in the mid-1980s, the company pursued growth through a series of acquisitions. Two of the acquisitions were the Kohl and Pantry Pride chains in Wisconsin and Virginia, respectively. In 1985, A&P implemented a $345-million modernization plan for its existing stores. The stores are being remodeled with an emphasis on special departments such as delis, bakeries, gourmet meats, and seafood. Also, in 1985, A&P embarked on an ambitious plan that called for initiating construction of, on average, one new store per week through 1988. The plan calls for a total of 106 new stores: half Future Stores and half Sav-a-Centers.

INDUSTRY TRENDS

Last year, Americans spent $166 billion in supermarkets. According to James Wood, CEO of A&P, "We have upgraded food-selling in America to a level that's higher than anywhere else in the world" (*Parade Magazine,* 25 October 1987, 4). A 1987 survey conducted by the Food Marketing Institute found that the three most important factors cited by shoppers in their selection of a supermarket were quality fruit and vegetables, wide selection, and quality meats. The study found that saving time was considered to be a major factor by 80 percent of consumers. It is not surprising then that the two dominant trends among supermarkets are one-stop shopping and upscale specialty shops.

According to industry analyst Michael VerMuelen, "Round-the-clock hours, an increased emphasis on prepared foods, and chains dedicated to specific segments—whether it's harried one-stop shoppers or spend thrift yuppies in search of the latest, most expensive cheese—all reflect a new industrywide commitment to providing better customer service" (*Parade,* 25 October, 1987, 5).

There have been major shifts in supermarket consumer behavior over the past two decades. Red meat sales have declined by about a third, whereas, fresh fish and poultry sales have increased dramatically. According to Don Byerly, owner of a trend-setting chain of upscale, ultra-service supermarkets in the Minneapolis area, "in the future, we'll be designing smaller meat departments, bigger delis, bigger restaurants, bigger bakeries. From our point of view, the future is in prepared foods, lighter fare and healthier foods too" (*Parade,* 25 October, 1987, 5).

The two recent stars among the general merchandise categories are photo needs and blank videotapes. The stagnant categories have been automotive, light bulbs, and soft goods. While general merchandise has been losing space in many stores, it is important to note that these categories are generally more profitable than traditional supermarket categories.

As Lyle Everingham notes, the most significant trend affecting the grocery industry is the demand for convenience. "The big change is the phenomenon of the working mother and of two-income family units, for whom time is at an extreme premium. In addition, the growth in the number of elderly people and the rise of more single-person households have made one-stop shopping more important because of its convenience" (Kroger *Annual Report,* 1986). Consequently, Kroger has been, for several years, one of the most aggressive promoters of the superstore concept.

INDUSTRY OUTLOOK

Food price disinflation and stiffening competition within the industry have contributed to an increasingly hostile operating environment for the supermarket industry. There have been a series of acquisitions and mergers which have reduced the number of competitors and generally enhanced the strength of the established firms.

Standard & Poor's offers the following appraisal of overall industry prospects: "... we view the earnings prospects for food retailers in the year ahead as reasonably good. The more astute operators have enhanced their ability to strike the right balance between aggressive pricing on recession-resistant merchandise and opportunistic marketing of a broadening array of specialty foods and non-food items formerly the province of other retail trade classes. By persevering on the cost-control front, while harnessing their traffic-generating ability to more profitable product categories and appropriating incremental business from non-food retailers, the industry should be able to sustain its improved profitability. Technology-driven advances in food distribution and more sophisticated processing of market information and profit analysis also should facilitate these more aggressive marketing strategies" (Standard & Poor's *Industry Surveys,* 22 January, 1987, 95).

Most analysts are predicting moderate but steady expansion in the overall economy for 1987. Standard & Poor's forecasts the real GNP growth rate to be 2.7 percent for 1987. Food prices are projected to increase at an annual rate of approximately 3 percent. In combination, these factors will tend to suppress price levels for staple items. The firms that will experience greater profitability, therefore, are the ones that have been remodeled to include a greater proportion of higher-margin perimeter departments such as bakeries and delis.

Progressive Grocer reported that supermarket sales rose 5.24 percent during 1986, reflecting a meager 1.7 percent increase in the price of food-at-home. This increase is well below the 3.6 percent gain in overall inflation as measured by the consumer price index.

The supermarket industry has reached a state of maturation for two primary reasons: slow population growth and overstoring as a result of low interest loans to finance construction. Studies by the Marketing Research Institute suggest a decline in

EXHIBIT 5 Kroger's consolidated balance sheet (in thousands of dollars).

	January 3, 1987	December 28, 1985
ASSETS		
Current assets		
Cash and temporary cash investments	$ 212,156	$ 105,510
Receivables	264,853	215,414
Inventories:		
FIFO cost	1,435,269	1,696,590
Less LIFO reserve	(238,031)	(223,834)
	1,197,238	1,472,756
Property held for sale	100,891	88,022
Deferred income taxes	27,209	
Prepaid and other current assets	148,384	119,431
Total current assets	1,950,731	2,001,133
Notes receivable	35,878	34,218
Property, plant and equipment		
Land	176,846	147,343
Buildings and land improvements	453,800	461,894
Equipment	1,731,578	1,685,093
Leaseholds and leasehold improvements	480,629	485,389
Leased property under capital leases	260,337	269,430
	3,103,190	3,049,149
Allowance for depreciation and amortization	(1,134,718)	(1,112,228)
Property, plant and equipment, net	1,968,472	1,936,921
Investments and other assets	121,366	205,535
Total Assets	$4,076,447	$4,177,807
LIABILITIES		
Current liabilities		
Current portion of long-term debt	$ 117,215	$ 35,730
Current portion of obligations under capital leases	5,825	5,920
Notes payable	10,341	122,170
Accounts payable	912,371	986,729
Other current liabilities	537,196	487,788
Accrued income taxes	114,297	89,124
Accrual for special charge	75,763	
Total current liabilities	1,773,008	1,727,461
Long-term debt	561,258	710,890
Obligations under capital leases	196,981	214,586
Deferred income taxes	292,176	314,390
Other long-term liabilities	98,253	21,810
Total Liabilities	2,921,676	2,989,137

continued

EXHIBIT 5 continued

	January 3, 1987	December 28, 1985
SHAREOWNERS' EQUITY		
Preferred capital stock, cumulative, voting, par $100		
Issued: 1986 - 1,250,000 Auction Preferred shares, Series A and B		
1985 - None	**125,000**	
Common capital stock, par $1, at stated value		
Issued: 1986 - 97,814,920 shares		
1985 - 97,045,616 shares	**409,953**	396,387
Accumulated earnings	**938,752**	980,003
Common stock in treasury, at cost		
1986 - 13,750,999 shares		
1985 - 9,679,944 shares	**(318,934)**	(187,720)
Total Shareowners' Equity	**1,154,771**	1,188,670
Total Liabilities and Shareowners' Equity	**$4,076,447**	$4,177,807

per capita spending on food-at-home for the balance of the decade. This decline is due to the rapid growth in the elderly and infant population segments. These two groups traditionally consume less food. Exacerbating the situation will be the continued increase in the number of working women and male shoppers who are more disposed to dining outside the home.

Slow sales growth is a particularly serious problem for supermarkets due to their inherently high overhead and low profit margins. Industry net margins typically average a mere 1.0 percent of revenues.

FINANCIAL PERFORMANCE

Kroger's current balance sheet and income statements are displayed in Exhibits 5 and 6, respectively. The corporate retrenchment program continues to show strong signs of success. The company has reduced its asset base by 12 percent and has completed its sale of SupeRx and Hook Drugs. The proceeds continue to be used to finance remodeling of traditional stores and to reduce long-term obligations.

The fourth quarter of 1986 was a time of exceptionally solid performance. Revenues for the year totaled $17.1 billion, representing a 7 percent increase over 1985. Pre-tax earnings from continuing operations of $279.6 million were slightly ahead of 1985 pre-tax earnings of $277.0 million. Net income was slightly lower in 1986 due to special one-time charges for restructuring and the creation of a charitable foundation. In summary, all facets of Kroger including supermarkets, convenience stores, and manufacturing saw increased operating earnings during 1986.

A general summary of Kroger's financial performance for the years 1977–1986 is presented in Exhibit 7. The early 1980s witnessed a significant drop in Kroger's net

EXHIBIT 6 Kroger's consolidated statement of earnings and accumulated earnings for years ended January 3, 1987, December 28, 1985 and December 29, 1984 (in thousands, except per share amounts) (1985 and 1984 restated for discontinued operations).

	1986 (53 Weeks)	1985 (52 Weeks)	1984 (52 Weeks)
Sales, Continuing Operations	**$17,122,518**	$15,966,620	$15,063,414
Costs and expenses			
Merchandise costs, including warehousing and transportation	**13,170,911**	12,282,282	11,575,943
Operating, general and administrative	**3,163,718**	2,926,489	2,797,674
Rent	**226,070**	202,121	195,774
Depreciation and amortization	**211,159**	194,715	181,996
Dividend and interest income	**(12,744)**	(17,830)	(23,171)
Interest expense	**103,765**	101,862	95,618
Special charge	**164,025**		
Total	**17,026,904**	15,689,639	14,823,834
Earnings from continuing operations before taxes based on income	**95,614**	276,981	239,580
Taxes based on income	**39,846**	117,418	96,382
Earnings from continuing operations	**55,768**	159,563	143,198
Results of discontinued operations	**(4,275)**	21,187	13,435
Net Earnings	**$ 51,493**	$ 180,750	$ 156,633
Accumulated Earnings			
Beginning of year	**$ 980,003**	$ 887,606	$ 820,944
Net earnings	**51,493**	180,750	156,633
Cash dividends on common stock	**(89,428)**	(88,353)	(89,971)
Cash dividends on preferred stock	**(3,316)**		
End of year	**$ 938,752**	$ 980,003	$ 887,606
Earnings Per Common Share			
From continuing operations	**$ .60**	$1.81	$1.59
From discontinued operations	**(.05)**	.24	.15
Net earnings	**$ .55**	$2.05	$1.74
Cash Dividends Per Common Share	**$1.025**	$1.00	$1.00
Average Common Shares Outstanding	**86,871**	88,347	89,866

EXHIBIT 7 Kroger's ten-year summary (amounts prior to 1986 restated for discontinued operations).

	1986(b)	1985	1984
OPERATIONS (In thousands of dollars, except per common share amounts)			
Sales, continuing operations	**$17,122,518**	15,966,620	15,063,414
Earnings from continuing operations before taxes based on income	**$ 95,614**	276,981	239,580
Taxes based on income	**$ 39,846**	117,418	96,382
Earnings from continuing operations	**$ 55,768**	159,563	143,198
Per common share(a)			
Earnings from continuing operations	**$ .60**	1.81	1.59
Dividends on common stock	**$ 1.025**	1.00	1.00
BALANCE SHEET STATISTICS (In thousands of dollars, except per common share amounts)			
Inventories	**$ 1,197,238**	1,472,756	1,245,985
Working capital	**$ 177,723**	273,672	276,522
Property, plant and equipment, net	**$ 1,968,472**	1,936,921	1,846,436
Total assets	**$ 4,076,447**	4,177,807	3,687,326
Long-term debt	**$ 561,258**	710,890	577,842
Obligations under capital leases	**$ 196,981**	214,586	200,815
Shareowners' equity	**$ 1,154,771**	1,188,670	1,148,776
Per common share(a)	**$ 12.25**	13.61	12.74
OTHER STATISTICS (In thousands of dollars, except stock prices)			
Cash provided from operations	**$ 441,446**	392,305	380,743
Capital expenditures	**$ 474,627**	362,436	310,029
Rent	**$ 226,070**	202,121	195,774
Interest expense	**$ 103,765**	101,862	95,618
Common stock price range (a)	**$ 21⅜-35**	19-25	14⅝-19¾
RETAIL FACILITIES (Areas in thousands of square feet)			
Stores — end of year			
Food stores	**1,298**	1,367	1,318
Convenience stores	**735**	643	443
Total square feet — end of year			
Food stores	**45,054**	45,751	43,939
Convenience stores	**1,786**	1,527	1,057

(a) In 1986, the Company declared a two-for-one stock split. All share and per share amounts have been restated to reflect this split.
(b) 1980 and 1986 were fifty-three week years.
(c) In 1979, the Company changed from the First-In, First-Out (FIFO) method of valuing certain of its inventories to the Last-In, First-Out (LIFO) method.

profit margin, sales per share, and cash flow per share. It does appear that strategic moves by Kroger resulted in improved performance since 1984.

How has Kroger fared relative to its competitors? *Forbes* "40th Annual Report on American Industry" includes the grocery industry (see Exhibit 8). Kroger's performance over the past five years is close to the industry median level for most measures.

EXHIBIT 7 continued

1983	1982	1981	1980(b)	1979(c)	1978	1977
14,446,823	14,045,270	13,275,039	11,981,245	10,370,722	8,953,032	7,597,646
185,679	276,356	274,654	206,658	180,394	187,489	142,060
72,002	95,109	102,916	78,796	71,997	82,719	63,002
113,677	181,247	171,738	127,862	108,397	104,770	79,058
1.24	1.91	1.87	1.45	1.23	1.20	.91
.955	.88	.785	.70	.63	.445	.38
1,151,131	1,108,786	951,773	900,095	896,147	796,183	703,358
339,701	368,266	405,065	246,011	271,211	320,461	311,844
1,769,339	1,610,693	1,339,626	1,138,287	962,018	814,377	728,186
3,529,813	3,319,699	2,964,017	2,483,504	2,232,134	2,023,767	1,843,236
665,386	604,007	477,501	311,036	269,026	239,172	247,060
212,406	194,195	187,516	173,268	169,561	165,856	153,958
1,072,852	1,086,345	1,000,049	835,066	762,194	692,894	611,169
11.99	11.65	10.67	9.42	8.63	7.91	7.06
365,139	299,232	423,566	362,986	174,008	217,170	176,947
368,895	464,380	324,280	298,766	242,324	168,543	127,944
187,134	169,712	144,262	129,994	110,966	96,203	82,555
89,110	69,815	55,358	44,044	36,408	35,879	36,912
16⅞-21½	11¾-23⅝	9⅝-14	7-11⅞	8¾-13½	6⅜-9¼	5⅞-7¼
1,428	1,418	1,475	1,459	1,438	1,406	1,384
352	352	349	333	326	290	189
46,077	44,088	43,615	40,846	38,341	36,113	33,729
809	807	800	732	718	638	400

Note, however, that the rate of revenue increase has slowed over the past 12 months. Earnings per share, on the other hand, were significantly higher over the past year.

Kroger professes confidence in its future. Despite its unsteady recent past, Kroger believes that its restructuring program, though expensive, has given it a competitive advantage: additional flexibility in merchandising and distribution. Kroger believes it will outdistance its competition due to its enhanced ability to rapidly respond to changing customer tastes.

EXHIBIT 8 Comparative financial performance: Kroger compared to industry

Financial Measure	*Kroger*	*Industry Median**
Return on Equity (5 yr avg)	12.8%	19.3%
Return on Equity (1986)	14.9	14.9
Sales Growth (5 yr avg)	9.7	9.0
Sales Growth (1986)	3.7	5.6
EPS (5 yr avg)	−18.9	12.6
EPS (1986)	81.1	15.4

Note: * The group consists of the following companies: American Stores, Lucky Stores, Albertson's, Winn-Dixie, Stop & Shop, Kroger, and A & P.

Source: 40th Annual Report on American Industry, *Forbes* (January 11, 1988): 131.

SUPER 8 MOTELS—1987

DR. E. J. GAINOK
Northern State College
(Aberdeen, South Dakota)

Super 8 Motels, Inc. is a fast-growing chain of economy lodging motels located in forty-one states and two Canadian provinces. Super 8 Motels ranks third nationally in the economy lodging field, with 25,655 rooms in 404 motels as of January 1, 1987. Key officers of the corporation are Dennis Brown, co-founder and chairman of the board; Ronald J. Rivett, co-founder and vice-chairman; Dennis Bale, vice-chairman and chief executive officer; and Loren D. Steele, president. These four individuals are members of the board of directors and principal stockholders of the privately held corporation. Super 8 is headquartered in Aberdeen, South Dakota.

Super 8 Motels likes to think of its operation in terms of "Yesterday, Today, and Tomorrow." This "where have we been, where are we now, and where are we going" attitude is often found in fast-growing organizations. Since Super 8 is a relatively new organization, entrepreneurial spirit continues to be a driving force.

YESTERDAY

In 1972, attorney Dennis A. Brown and businessman Ronald J. Rivett formed a partnership to bring economy lodging to South Dakota. After two years of planning, the first Super 8 Motel opened in Aberdeen in September, 1974. It provided travelers comfortable sleeping accommodations for $8.88. It had no conference rooms, no

swimming pool, no restaurant, and only a functional lobby. This first Super 8 Motel was built near the local Holiday Inn to attract overflow and cost-conscious travelers. In the mid-70s, bargain hunting and cost consciousness prevailed among both business and recreational travelers. (Super 8's 1986 lodging room price was $28.00 for a single room.)

Economy lodging, as we know it today, dates back to 1962. Prior to that year, "Mom and Pop" motels provided economy lodging with a variety of operations. The lodging industry is currently segmented into economy, mid-range, and luxury motels. The first economy motel chian was Motel 6, which originated in California. Mid-range motels such as Holiday and Ramada comprise the largest segment of the lodging industry. But, they do not provide elaborate facilities, as do the Hyatt, Marriott and Hilton luxury motels.

The number of economy motel rooms increased from 15,000 to 326,000 during the period 1968–1986. At this time, economy rooms represented about 13 percent of all available lodging, and this share continues to increase annually. The basic concept of budget motels is often expanded to include lounges, restaurants, meeting rooms, pools, saunas, and game rooms. However, the general public continues to perceive the budget motel as consisting of guest rooms only. Suppliers of this type of lodging provide comfortable accommodations at a price well below (20–40 percent of) full-service lodging.

TODAY

Currently, there are fifteen major economy motel chains operating in the $36-billion United States lodging industry. The typical Super 8 is a "luxury economy motel" with between 21 and 165 guest rooms. As indicated in Exhibit 1, there were 323 Super 8 Motels at the end of 1985; 404 by January 1987, and another 100 properties scheduled for completion during 1987. Super 8 lays claim to being one of the fastest-growing economy motel chains in the country.

EXHIBIT 1 Growth of Super 8 Motels

Year	*New Motels*	*Total Motels*	*Income (in dollars)*[1]
1974	1	1	
1975	3	4	
1976	9	13	33,000.00
1977	20	33	83,000.00
1978	24	57	267,000.00
1979	14	71	447,000.00
1980	17	88	743,000.00
1981	22	110	1,081,000.00
1982	29	139	1,560,000.00
1983	48	187	2,220,000.00
1984	62	249	3,280,000.00
1985	74	323[2]	4,030,000.00
1986	81	404[2]	4,836,000.00
1987	100	502	15,000,000.00
1988–1990[3]	248	750	$25,000,000.00

Notes: [1] Four percent of gross room rent
[2] Franchise terminations subtracted
[3] Estimated

Super 8 is organized to operate its own units as well as assist owners in building and operating franchised motels. More than 90 percent of all Super 8 Motels are owned by individual franchisees. The location of the chain's motels are given in Exhibit 2. To purchase a franchise for a typical sixty-unit motel, an investor needs $100,000; $20,000 for the cost of the franchise and $80,000 for the initial payment for real estate, construction, and motel furnishing. The chain charges its franchisees 4 percent royalty and 2 percent advertising fees, based on gross room revenue.

Super 8 attributes its rapid growth to several factors, including product, support services, motel developers, and locations. The management has adapted its concept of economy lodging to particular markets. For example, the architectural differences required in South Florida and South Dakota were noted, and buildings (product) were then designed to meet the needs and aesthetics of the local area while incorporating the standard ingredients in the Super 8 formula. Each room must meet the minimum size, have carpeting, tub/shower combinations, free color TV, direct dial telephones, and approved furnishings. Super 8 provides support services that include a nationwide Superline toll-free reservation system, marketing services, management training, a V.I.P. Club for guests, graphic arts support, and quality review through quarterly inspection of each motel.

Super 8 Motels are developed primarily by existing franchisees. Management likes to think that this reflects well on services provided by the franchisor. When consider-

EXHIBIT 2 The locations of Super 8 Motels (January 1, 1987)

Alabama	4	Nebraska	22
Alaska	4	Nevada	4
Arizona	12	New Hampshire	1
Arkansas	12	New Jersey	4
California	29	New Mexico	13
Colorado	24	New York	19
Connecticut	6	North Carolina	6
Delaware	1	North Dakota	14
Florida	6	Ohio	11
Georgia	12	Oklahoma	4
Idaho	8	Oregon	3
Illinois	24	Pennsylvania	17
Indiana	15	South Carolina	5
Iowa	24	South Dakota	27
Kansas	15	Tennessee	2
Kentucky	14	Texas	11
Louisiana	3	Utah	6
Maine	1	Vermont	2
Maryland	8	Virginia	21
Massachusetts	4	Washington	11
Michigan	7	West Virginia	4
Minnesota	32	Wisconsin	25
Missouri	22	Wyoming	16
Montana	22		

Note: As of January 1, 1987, 404 properties were open. Of the 557 properties listed in this exhibit, 155 were due to open after January 1, 1987. Super 8 Motels or motels under development at this time. Motels in all 50 states is a 1987 goal.

ing locations, Super 8 Motels has a product for virtually any community. Motels currently range in size from 21 to 165 guest rooms, with the average being 63 rooms. This flexibility enables investors with limited funding to become motel owners.

Since Super 8 Motels directs most of its marketing effort toward the frequent traveler, it attempts to assure that there will be no surprises. It has developed a guest profile and identified opportunities that alert management to new wants and needs of guests. The goal is to assume the customer receives what he or she expects—accommodations similar to those provided at the last Super 8 Motel where he or she was a guest. *Consumer Report* and the *1987 Consumer Guide Issue,* recognized Super 8 Motels as one of the top three economy chains in quality of service and guest satisfaction.

To coordinate activities more effectively, Super 8 Motels recently constructed national headquarters buildings in Aberdeen, which are staffed to develop new properties, to support independent franchise groups, and to help individual developers. As shown in Figure 1, the Super 8 Corporation is organized functionally into four support

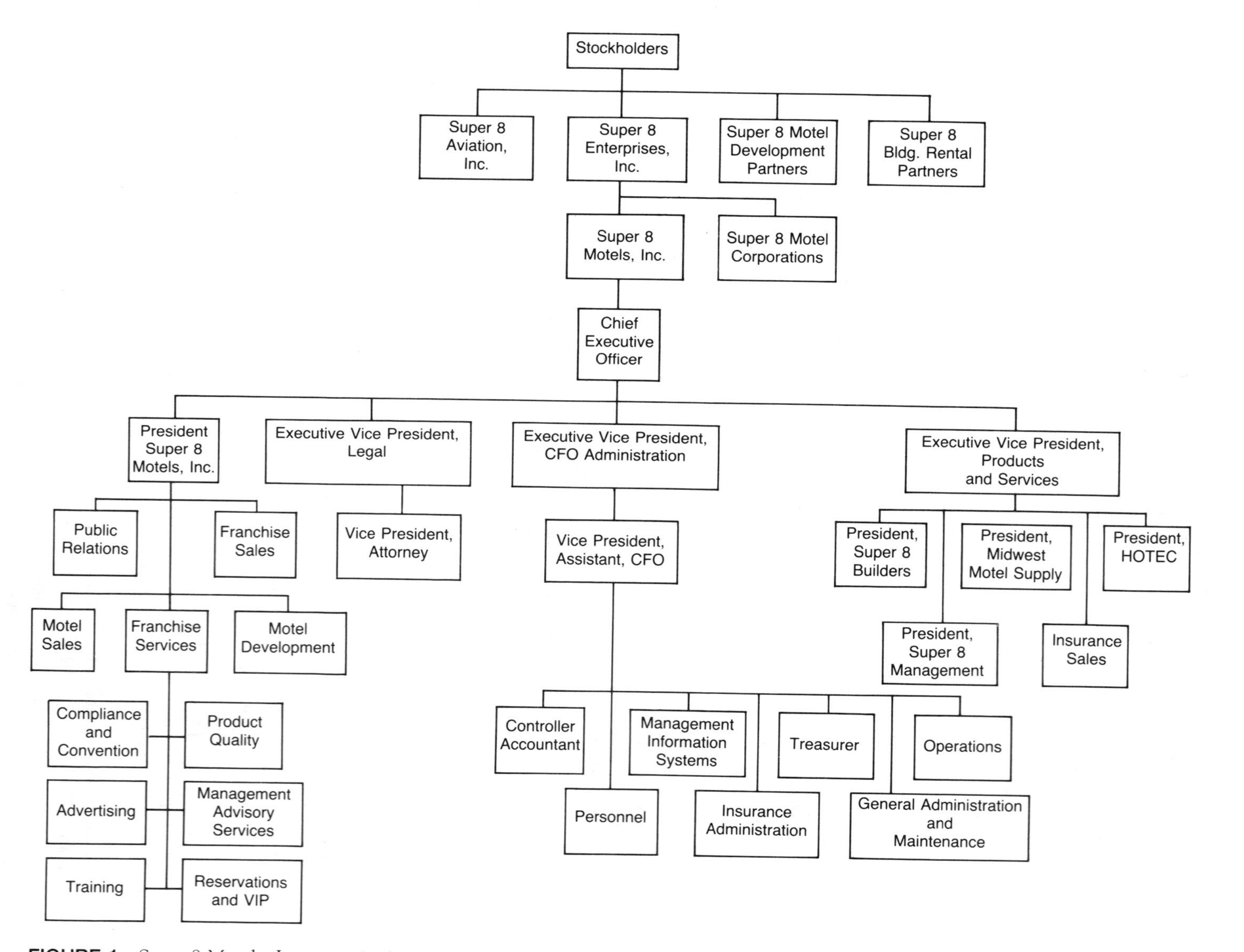

FIGURE 1 Super 8 Motels, Inc. organization.

Source: Super 8 Motels internal documents.

groups: Super 8 Builders, Incorporated, which builds properties; Hospitality Technology Incorporated, which markets telephones and satellite equipment to other busnesses as well as Super 8 Motels; Midwest Motel Supply, which provides furniture, equipment, carpeting, and all types of supplies to Super 8 Motels; Super 8 Management Incorporated, which provides management services to fifty-seven Super 8 Motels, including company-owned units located in Aberdeen; and insurance services. The headquarters facility also houses the legal and administrative offices and the computerized reservation system.

Aberdeen is a city of approximately 28,500 people serving northeast South Dakota's agricultural area in the north plains. Although the city is served by a commuter airline, with transportation to Minneapolis, Fargo, and Denver, this service does not meet Super 8's needs. Therefore, the Super 8 Motels chain recently expanded its aviation department to include three full-time pilots and three aircraft, one of which is a nine-passenger jet. Early in 1985, Super 8 Motels purchased a small aviation company and now provides charter service to the public.

FINANCIAL CONDITION

Super 8 Motels' consolidated balance sheets for 1984, 1985, and 1986 are provided in Exhibit 3. Exhibit 4 gives consolidated statements of income for these years. An affiliate company, Super 8 Builders, constructed thirty-eight motels (2,300 rooms), for a gross in excess of $37 million in 1986. Midwest Motel Supply had revenues of more than $11 million for 1986, and Super 8 Management Incorporated, expanded its operations to fifty-seven properties currently open and forty-three in the development stages. Hospitality Technology Incorporated (Hotech), which markets telephones and satellite equipment, expanded its revenues to $1.7 million, and total gross revenues for Super 8 were over $57 million in 1986.

TOMORROW

There is no doubt that Super 8 Motels' growth has been good. Since January 1986, one new Super 8 Motel has been opened every ninety-seven hours, and projections are for 100 new motels to open in 1987. Sustaining or increasing this level of operation is a monumental management task in terms of planning, organizing, staffing, motivating, and controlling. Management must coordinate activities involving three separate and distinct types of motel operations: (1) franchisees with only one small property, (2) franchisees with two or more properties, or authority over a state or region, and (3) corporation-owned properties. Maintaining control as the organization grows is a primary concern of Super 8's management.

The corporate plans are designed to make Super 8 the first national budget chain in all fifty states, with 500 motels by the end of 1987. Super 8 plans to open new motels primarily in small and medium-sized communities, as well as some in metropolitan areas.

EXHIBIT 3 Super 8, Inc., and subsidiaries: Consolidated balance sheet (summarized)

	1986	*1985*	*1984*
Assets			
Current assets	$12,732,740	$ 7,524,296	$ 5,047,742
Investments	74,103	107,112	145,512
Property and equipment	34,798,189	27,900,695	15,807,604
Notes receivable	2,707,136	2,005,509	1,410,883
Cost in excess of purchased subsidiaries	1,274,416	1,333,480	1,392,544
Other assets	3,739,904	2,092,994	528,496
Total Assets	**$55,326,488**	**$40,964,086**	**$24,332,781**
Liabilities and Equity			
Current liabilities	$10,012,411	$ 8,895,474	$ 4,060,983
Long-term debt	39,893,867	27,210,067	16,273,238
Deposits	334,773	168,037	85,000
Deferred taxes	627,859	296,700	220,700
Equity*			
Preferred stock	2,497,249	2,497,249	2,497,249
Common stock	1,000	1,000	1,000
Excess over par	25,108	25,108	25,108
Retained earnings	1,934,221	1,870,451	1,169,503
Total Liabilities	**$ 4,457,578**	**$ 4,393,808**	**$ 3,692,860**
	$55,326,488	**$40,964,086**	**$24,332,781**

Note: *Preferred stock—5,000,000 authorized; 2,497,249 issued and outstanding
Common stock—100,000,000 authorized; 100,000 issued and outstanding; $.01 par value

COMPETITION

Motel 6, founded in 1963, was the first economy chain. In 1963, a room at a Motel 6 cost just $6 a night. The room had a shower stall but no bath tub or TV. By 1987, more than 60 economy lodging chains were operating, with more than 2,400 properties and 250,000 rooms nationwide plus numerous non-chain operations.

Super 8 Motels, Inc., has plans to improve its market share in a competitive market. With Marriott, Holiday Inn, and others bringing competition to economy lodging, Super 8 has to pay closer attention to marketing a useful product. In 1986, standard hotel occupancy rates rose by 4.4 percent, and budget motels increased by 0.2 percent.

Marriott has begun a Courtyard Franchise System and has signed contracts for more than 125 hotels, whose rates range from $40 to $60 per night. Howard Johnson's is introducing Park Square Inns with rates of $45 to $60. Carlson Properties,

EXHIBIT 4 Super 8 Motels, Inc., and subsidiaries: Statements of income (year ending December 31)

	1986	*1985*	*1984*
Revenues			
Franchise fees			
Initial	$ 1,365,000	$ 1,227,500	$ 1,191,000
Recurring	5,591,015	4,178,959	2,979,617
Construction	27,191,302	13,650,119	8,438,835
Lodging	10,868,086	6,974,929	5,148,476
Furnishings and supplies	9,466,515	6,438,729	4,856,465
Telephone equipment	1,389,509	1,002,381	725,956
Accounting fees	464,630	313,444	133,177
Rental income	143,573	164,740	146,790
Management fees	380,336	326,964	169,123
Other income	925,403	759,971	445,344
	$57,785,369	**$35,037,736**	**$24,234,783**
Costs and Expenses			
Administrative and general	$ 8,190,636	$ 5,620,108	$ 4,067,375
Construction	24,606,367	12,815,153	8,109,244
Motel operations	6,243,970	3,795,527	2,635,576
Furnishings and supplies	8,731,672	6,084,501	4,644,820
Telephone equipment	982,966	744,926	625,038
Interest	4,305,385	2,843,045	1,984,933
Depreciation	2,647,417	1,647,509	1,149,235
Amortization	280,894	109,019	71,674
Terminated offering costs	521,710		
Net Loss Sale of Motels	763,585		
	$57,274,602	**$33,659,788**	**$23,287,895**
Income before income taxes and extraordinary item	**$ 510,667**	**$ 1,377,948**	**$ 946,888**
Income Taxes			
Current	$ 447,000	$ 243,000	$ 40,400
Deferred		234,000	313,600
Provision in lieu of taxes			84,500
	$ 447,000	**477,000**	**438,500**
Income before extraordinary item	**63,667**	**$ 900,948**	**$ 508,388**
Extraordinary Item			
Tax benefit from utilization of loss carryforward			$ 84,500
Net income	**$ 63,667**	**$ 900,948**	**$592,888**

which owns and operates the Radisson Hotels, plans to open a Country Inn chain, with eighty-five motel rooms on four to five acres, with a $35.00 room rate. Holiday Inn is introducing Park Inns to compete in the economy motel industry.

With recent changes in federal tax laws developers, lenders, and investors are beginning to look at the lodging industry in a different manner. They are looking for results in operations rather than long-term real estate, capital gains, and even tax shelters. Additionally, Days Inns, Motel 6, Econo Lodge and the other top fifty motels are continuing to add rooms ranging in rates from $16.95 to $65.00. The industry is alive and thriving.

To remain competitive, Super 8 is doing more than adding rooms. The chain ended 1986 by increasing the occupancy rate from 65 to 66 percent through mid-March, and in 1987, the chain showed a 2½ percent increase over 1986 in overall occupancy. The corporation plans to refrain from tying up funds in real estate for future development on a long-term basis, and the corporation will build motels only to be sold to franchisees or the public. This is related to possible future action of taking the corporation public rather than being privately held. The corporation will also accept quality motel conversions in markets where new construction is not feasible. Super 8 anticipates conversions would add 10–15 percent to the growth rate.

Super 8 assisted its franchisees in making its product more appealing by conducting 1,358 motel inspections in 1986; 80 percent of the motels were rated excellent or good. Super 8 trained 104 persons at corporate headquarters and performed fifty-one training visits on site. It received more than 87,000 survey responses from Super 8 guests, with 93 percent indicating they would make repeat visits.

The economy lodging segment is currently segmented into three tiers: upper, middle, and lower. The upper tier offers rooms at 20–25 percent less than the market-area average rate. Example chains are Dillon Inns, Drury Inns, Hampton Inns, La Quinta Motor Inns, Lexington Hotel Suites, Signature Inns, Skylight Inns, and Texas Inns. These motels will offer amenities above and beyond sleeping accommodations. Generally, they have pools, saunas, and restaurants; most are company owned.

The middle tier offers rooms at 20–40 percent less than the market-area average rate. Examples are Red Roof Inns, Exel Inns, Super 8 Motels, Budgetel Inns, Comfort Inns, Econo Lodges, Knight's Inns, and Shoney's Inns. These motels have only a minimum of amenities. They are usually located near restaurants.

The lower tier offers rooms at 50 percent below the market average. Motel 6 is the dominant chain in the lower tier. Motel 6 offers nationwide, year-round rates at all locations. These motels are designed primarily for the budget-conscious traveler. Clean, no-frills lodging at a reasonable price is what is offered.

The top ten economy lodging chains in the United States are described in Exhibit 5.

ISSUES, CONCERNS, AND STRATEGIES

As Super 8 Motels enter the 1987–1990 era, a number of issues and concerns face the corporation's top management. It is important that Super 8 have a clear understanding of its internal strengths and weaknesses as well as external opportunities and threats to

EXHIBIT 5 The top ten economy lodging chains in the United States in 1986 (by number of guest rooms)

Chain Name	*Ownership Structure*	*Number of Inns*	*Number of Rooms*	*Geographic Concentration*
Days Inn	Co-owned/ franchised	318	49,500	Eastern and Western United States
Motel 6	Co-owned	401	45,000	Throughout United States
Econo Lodges	Franchised	354	27,900	Throughout United States
La Quinta Motor Inns	Co-owned/ franchised	192	25,100	Throughout United States
Super 8 Motels	Co-owned/ franchised	390	24,795	Throughout United States/Canada
Comfort Inns	Co-owned/ franchised	231	18,200	Throughout United States/Canada
Red Roof Inns	Co-owned	146	15,900	Eastern United States
Hospitality International	Franchised	186	15,800	Eastern United States
Knights Inn	Co-owned	76	8,300	Eastern United States
Hampton Inns	Co-owned/ franchised	67	8,200	Throughout United States

effectively establish strategies, objectives, and policies for the future. Some of the most important issues and concerns facing Super 8 are as follows:

1. Should Super 8 utilize equity financing, liability financing, or a combination of both to continue expansion? Can and should Super 8 continue to add a new motel every 97 hours?
2. How many motels should the corporation own? What would be the best mix of corporate-owned and franchised units? Is Super 8's policy to have 10 percent of the motels company-owned a good one? How should Super 8 assist franchisees in financing? Using various scenarios, what are the profit contributions of franchise versus company-owned units?
3. What kind of organizational structure is needed to deal with Super 8's dispersed motels and the mix of corporate managers and franchisees? As the organization continues to grow, would a divisional structure by geographic area be more effective than the functional structure now being used? How would you redesign Super 8's structure to be more effective?
4. How can Super 8 maintain quality lodging at economy rates? Travelers staying at one Super 8 Motel expect the same accommodations at the next Super

8 Motel. How can Super 8 best minimize franchisees' "milking" their business without realistic reinvestment, maintenance, and refurbishing?

5. What are Super 8's long-range objectives? Will economy motel competition grow, remain stable, or decline? Will luxury and mid-range priced motel chains see profitability in economy lodging and attempt to move into this competitive arena? In 1986, average occupancy for budget motels increased by .2 percent.
6. Is Super 8's $20,000 initial franchise fee reasonable? What about the 4 percent royalty and 2 percent advertising fees?
7. Super 8 Motels are normally located at sites near other motels and restaurants. Is this preferable to building restaurants at existing Super 8 Motels? Are choice sites at high prices worth the investment?
8. Should Super 8 Motels offer swimming pools, saunas, or other amenities found in mid-range and luxury motels/hotels? What incentives could Super 8 offer for repeat business? Could the firm do these things and continue rapid market development?
9. How important are controls for Super 8, Inc? What form should controls take in terms of inspections, reports, audits, and accounting procedures?
10. Should Super 8's headquarters be relocated elsewhere besides Aberdeen, South Dakota? If so, where? Aberdeen presents travel complications, although these problems have been somewhat minimized due to the acquisition of three aircraft with assigned pilots.
11. Who are Super 8's key competitors, and what are their strategies? How is Super 8 positioned in the economy lodging industry, in terms of price, location, convenience, service, and accommodations?

HOLIDAY CORPORATION—1987

PHILIPPE LINDSAY AND FRED DAVID
Auburn University

In November 1986, the management of Holiday Corporation announced a $65 per share dividend. Considering that the stock was trading at $72 per share, this caught the public totally by surprise. The move increased Holiday's debt to $2.5 billion. Holiday remains in a tenuous position until the debt can be reduced, but the recapitalization plan was successful in warding off a hostile takeover attempt. The recapitalization plan provides for top management to receive stock that increases their holdings from 1.5 percent to more than 10 percent. The plan limits voting rights to individuals who own more than 10 percent of outstanding stock. While the plan leaves Holiday with an admitted negative net worth of $1 billion, Holiday officials argue that this number is just an accounting figure. They say it does not represent the true value of Holiday's assets that currently have an estimated value of about $3.5 billion.

HISTORY

In 1951, Kemmons Wilson, a Memphis businessman, returned from a family vacation to Washington, D.C. He had noticed a lack of quality, inexpensive, air-conditioned hotels on his trip and realized that such a hotel would have great potential. He began plans for the first Holiday Inn to be built in Memphis. It would have 120 air-conditioned rooms, a swimming pool, a restaurant, phones in every room, free ice, and free parking. The inn was finished in 1952, and during the next year and a half, three more inns were built in the Memphis area. The phenomenal success of these properties led Wilson to develop the idea of a national chain, and he began looking for additional investors to provide the necessary support for such an undertaking.

Wallace Johnson, a Tennessee developer and homes builder, formed a partnership with Wilson in 1954. Known as Holiday Inns of America, Inc., the partnership experienced slow but profitable growth. It became apparent that in order to achieve the kind of growth envisioned by Wilson, it would be necessary to sell stock. The first public offering of 120,000 shares sold at $9.75 per share. The dramatic growth that followed led Holiday to vertically diversify into other industries. In 1957, Inn Keepers Supply Company was formed to supply Holiday and other firms with items such as restaurant equipment and motel supplies. A year later, Holiday Press was formed for the purpose of printing menus, stationery, place mats, advertising flyers, and the *Holiday Inn Passport Directory.*

In 1963, Holiday signed an advertising agreement with Gulf Oil to allow traveling motorists to charge Holiday Inn services on Gulf charge cards. For the first time, it was now possible to travel anywhere in the United States and be able to purchase food, lodging, and automotive services on a single credit card. Other portions of the agreement included building Gulf stations next door to Holiday Inns wherever possible, including a large amount of Gulf advertising in Holiday Inn advertisements, and vice versa.

Continued growth and expansion led Holiday to institute its HOLIDEX computerized reservation system, the most revolutionary concept the industry had ever seen. By the late-1960s, Holiday Inn expansion efforts were so prolific that, on average, a new inn opened every three days. This rapid growth continued until the Arab Oil Embargo of 1974. As domestic travel declined due to gasoline shortages, occupancy rates plummeted, and profits fell 64 percent during fiscal 1974. During this time, a competitor, Days Inn of America, was founded by offering nice rooms for $8 a night and a guaranteed full tank of gas for customers. The growth of other budget chains in the mid-1970s led Holiday to reassess its corporate strategy.

In September 1978, Holiday announced a joint venture with L & M Walter Corporation to build two casinos, valued at $75 million and $175 million, in Atlantic City, New Jersey. A second acquisition was completed in August 1979 with the announcement of the purchase of a 40 percent interest in Riverboat Casinos of Las Vegas for $17 million. Holiday continued its ambitious expansion program and in 1979 acquired a family restaurant chain, Perkins Cake & Steak, Inc. Holiday was also beginning to realize enormous profits from its casinos. In 1980, Holiday absorbed Harrah's of Reno as an operating subsidiary serving the gaming market.

In the early 1980s, Holiday developed two innovative new products, Embassy Suites and the Hampton Inns. Embassy Suites was an all-suite product aimed at the luxury market and targeted to business and leisure customers, while the Hampton Inn was a limited-service hotel chain aimed at the budget-minded traveler. A recent review of these two segments shows that Embassy Suites is the leader in its segment and Hampton Inn is in sixth place (in number of rooms) in a crowded segment with more than fifty entrants.

In 1985, Holiday acquired a 50 percent interest in Residence Inns. This product, aimed at the extended-stay segment, is the market leader, and it boasts an average stay of more than twelve days per guest. Due partially to Holiday's success and insiders owning only 15 percent of the company, Holiday became a potential takeover candidate in 1986. Donald Trump and other persons were mentioned as unfriendly suitors who sought control of Holiday. Holiday opposed any takeover attempts and initiated the $2.1 billion recapitalization plan in November 1986. The plan was approved by shareholders in February 1987 and was labeled "suicidal" by some analysts. In order to pay huge interest charges on the long-term debt created by the recapitalization plan, Holiday has begun an aggressive campaign to sell hotels and enter into long-term management agreements for these properties. While the divestiture/sales efforts will undoubtedly result in lower revenues in the future, Holiday believes that these revenue losses can be offset by more effective managerial procedures. Only time will tell, but Holiday has temporarily silenced industry critics and continues to be a viable and financially sound corporation in spite of its unfavorable debt position.

INTERNATIONAL MARKETS

The foreign market is becoming more important for Holiday as the domestic market becomes saturated and companies look abroad for new investment opportunities. Exhibit 1 provides a listing of Holiday's locations and holdings worldwide.

The worldwide lodging industry can be broken into five regions: Africa and the Middle East; Asia/Australia; Europe; Latin/South America; and North America. Exhibit 2 gives a summary of vital characteristics of these regions. A major customer base in these markets is Americans traveling abroad. When the value of the dollar is high, American tourists travel to foreign countries much more than when the value of the dollar is low. Exhibit 3 gives a percentage breakdown by region of American travelers to foreign lands.

Africa/The Middle East

Recent trends in the African and Middle Eastern lodging industry have generally been unfavorable. Figures for 1986 indicate that total revenue was down 6.0 percent on a per-room basis, and the rate of return was down 2.4 percent. In addition, the average daily room rate declined to $54.24, compared to $60.50 a year earlier. Income before taxes was also down 6.4 percent from the previous year. All of these declines can be primarily attributed to poor economies and politically unstable conditions in the southern Africa region.

EXHIBIT 1 Holiday Inn worldwide locations (as of December 1, 1987)

Region		*Number of Locations*
I. Africa/The Middle East		41
Africa	31	
Middle East	10	
II. Asia/Australia		33
Asia	31	
Australia	2	
III. Europe		58
IV. Latin/South America		18
Mexico	14	
South America	4	
V. North America		1420
United States	1364[1]	
Canada	47	
Carribbean	9	

Top Ten Countries of the World (Number of Holiday Inn Locations)

1. United States	1364	6. Mexico	14
2. Canada	47	7. France	10
3. South Africa	22	8. Japan	8
4. West Germany	19	9. China	7
5. England	14	10. Malaysia	6

Region	*United States Locations*[2]	*Number of Locations*
1. Southeast	(Fla., Ga., Tenn., La., Ky., Ala., Miss.)	361
2. Midwest	(Ohio, Mich., Ill., Ind., Mo., Minn., Wis., Iowa)	290
3. Middle Atlantic	(Va., S.C., D.C., Md., Del.)	203
4. Southwest	(Tex., Okla., Ariz., Ark., N.Mex.)	175
5. Northeast	(N.Y., N.J., Mass., Pa., W.Va., Conn., Maine, R.I., Vt., N.H.)	160
6. West	(Calif., Wash., Nev., Oreg.)	95
7. North Central	(Colo., Kans., Wyo., Nebr., Utah, S.Dak., N.Dak., Idaho, Mont.)	77
8. Pacific	(Hawaii, Alaska)	3
Total		**1364**

Top Ten States (by number of Holiday Inn Locations)

1. Florida	141	6. North Carolina	61
2. Texas	114	7. Georgia	55
3. California	75	8. Illinois	53
4. Ohio	66	9. Virginia	53
5. New York	62	10. Tennessee	48

[1] Total is lower than 1986 figures due to divestiture of several properties

[2] In order of most locations to least locations per region

EXHIBIT 2 International Market Data (in percentages)

	International Composite	*Africa/ Middle East*	*Asia/ Australia*	*Europe*	*Latin America*	*North America*			
						Total	*Canada*	*U.S.*	*Carribean*
Source of Business									
Domestic	50.2	24.4	49.2	42.1	58.2	76.9	79.7	89.8	15.4
Foreign	49.8	75.6	50.8	57.9	41.8	23.1	22.3	10.2	84.6
Percent of repeat business	40.0	36.9	38.2	34.9	46.3	45.2	52.4	43.9	25.7
Percent of advance reservations	82.7	69.8	87.4	90.7	79.1	75.3		71.7	
Composition of Market									
Government officials	7.1	9.2	5.7	3.4	4.8	8.7	10.2	0.4	2.9
Businesspersons	38.3	39.9	38.5	39.4	48.5	34.9	27.7	44.7	13.3
Tourist/tour groups	34.4	29.7	43.5	36.0	29.0	31.0	33.0	24.1	77.2
Conventions	10.5	5.2	5.7	12.1	6.2	16.0	18.0	15.8	2.9
Other	9.7	16.8	6.6	9.1	7.4	9.4	11.1	8.1	3.7

Source: Adapted from 1986 *Worldwide Hotel Industry*, Horwath & Horwath, 29, 60.

EXHIBIT 3 American guests as a percent of occupancy in hotels by region

	U.S.	*Canada*	*Total*
Africa/Middle East	10.5	1.5	12.0
Asia/Australia	14.1	3.1	17.2
North America	54.9	29.4	84.3
Europe	21.2	2.3	23.5
Latin America	24.9	6.2	31.1

Source: Adapted from 1986 *Worldwide Hotel Industry*, Horwath & Horwath, 61.

Asia/Australia

Conditions in the Asian and Australian markets are only slightly better than the African and Middle Eastern markets. Recent figures indicate that total revenue was down 8.9 percent, and the rate of return ws down 2.1 percent (on a per-room basis) from a year earlier. The average daily room rate was down $6.59—to $43.19—from a year earlier. Income before taxes was 31.8 percent lower than a year earlier.

Much of this decline can be attributed to currency fluctuations that have had an unfavorable impact on the lodging industry. Tourists remain the largest market segment, followed closely by business travelers. Almost 90 percent of all rooms are booked on an advance basis.

Europe

The European market made substantial progress according to 1986 figures. Total revenues were up 20.1 percent, and income before taxes rose 8.7 percent on a per-room basis from the previous year. Room occupancy rates were also up 0.8 percent from a year earlier, but the region had the lowest percentage of repeat business of any region. Businessmen make up the largest European segment, followed closely by tourists.

Latin/South America

This region covers Mexico, Central America, and South America. Occupancy rates were up 9.5 percent in 1986 to 67.9 percent, while the average daily rate per room rose slightly to $46.34. Total revenue nearly doubled, while income before taxes stood at $2,143 on a per-room basis. Latin America and the Caribbean have been favorably affected by Pan American Airlines' divestiture of the Asian/Pacific corridor and increased focus upon the Latin American region. In addition, American, Eastern, and Delta Airlines have also expanded flights to these areas.

North America

The North American market consists of three segments: Canada, the United States, and the Caribbean. As a whole, the region's performance mirrored typical trends in other regions. Total revenues were down 12.5 percent, while the rate of return was down 1.6 percent on a per-room basis. The average daily rate per room fell to $50.85 from $56.88 a year earlier. This decline can be attributed largely to declining rates in the United States, which are due to the emergence of the economy market segment. The average daily rate increased in both Canada and the Caribbean. Income before taxes was 44.1 percent higher on a per-room basis.

The performance of the U.S. lodging industry in 1986 was much higher than originally anticipated. The national occupancy rate was 64.7 percent, a rebound from a five-year downward trend. Several factors contributed to this rebound, including a sharp 21.9 percent drop in gasoline prices that boosted domestic travel. Also in 1986, terrorist activities in Europe and the nuclear accident in the Soviet Union resulted in a decrease in American tourists abroad. Worried vacationers booked domestic rather than foreign vacations. In the United States, total revenues were up 4.8 percent in 1986, led by 8.1 percent and 7.5 percent increases in the Northeast and West, respectively.

U.S. hotel room inventory increased 6 percent in 1985 and another 7 percent in 1986. What started out as "unique" products, such as all-suite and economy facilities, have now developed into significant industry segments. The distinction between these markets becomes more clouded each day. Many analysts believe that developers and national chains have overvalued segmentation in the market and that consumers are becoming confused with the overwhelming number of products available.

ECONOMIC FACTORS

Changes in federal and state tax laws have caused a significant decline in all non-residential construction, including hotels. This decline could lead to a long-run improvement in hotels' performance, preventing further overbuilding, and focusing more attention on the feasibility of a hotel before it is built. New tax laws also make hotels less attractive to investors due to tougher syndication rules, longer depreciation schedules, and higher minimum tax rates.

Another tax implication that will have a negative impact upon the hotel/lodging industry is the planned reduction of business entertainment deductions to 80 percent. This reduction will undoubtedly cause a decrease in the number of business guests nationwide. Also, travel for business education is no longer deductible, contributing to a further reduction in business traffic.

There are a number of economic factors that could have a positive impact upon the U.S. lodging industry. For example, gasoline prices are expected to remain at relatively low levels, stimulating domestic travel. An increase in foreign tourism is expected as a result of the dollar's decline. Tourism markets, such as New York, Las Vegas, Hawaii, and California, will benefit the most from these developments.

THE COMPETITION

Major chains account for more than 60 percent of all hotel rooms in the United States. A listing of the top ten hotel chains in the United States is given in Exhibit 4. Holiday's major competitors include Best Western International, Hilton Inns, Sher-

EXHIBIT 4 Top American lodging chains (as of September 1986), ranked by number of rooms

Chain	*Number of Rooms*	*Number of Properties*
1. Holiday Inns	266,927	1,486
2. Best Western International	164,761	1,833
3. Hilton Hotels	100,061	285
4. Sheraton	99,347	412
5. Ramada Inns	85,373	526
6. Marriott Hotels	65,914	145
7. Quality Inns	59,283	484
8. Howard Johnson's	55,788	464
9. Days Inn	48,053	297
10. Motel 6	45,157	405

aton Inns, Ramada Inns, Quality International, The Marriott Corporation, Days Inn of America, and Howard Johnson. A segmented listing of major competitors is given in Exhibit 5.

Best Western International

Best Western is headquartered in Phoenix, Arizona, and is currently the second-largest hotel chain in the world. The chain is made up of independently owned and operated hotels throughout the world. Presently, there are 1,826 Best Western hotels in the United States (165,807 rooms). Best Western has properties in both the mid-price and luxury markets, with restaurants, swimming pools, and recreation areas. Preferred locations for Best Western are key urban and commercial areas, such as downtown or at the airport. Best Western is well established throughout the United States and is concentrating expansion efforts in the northeastern United States.

Hilton Inns

Hilton Hotels is headquartered in Beverly Hills, California, and has two chains: Hilton Inns and Cresthil by Hilton. In September 1987, Hilton had 270 U.S. properties and more than 96,000 rooms. All of these rooms represented Hilton Inns, because Cresthil by Hilton's first property does not open until late 1987. Cresthil is a low-rise hotel aimed at the budget-minded traveler. Hilton Inns presently serve the upper mid-priced market with full service hotels of at least 100 rooms, a restaurant, several meeting rooms, and a swimming pool. The average size is 275 rooms; the average occupancy rate is 62 percent. Hilton is currently targeting the Northeast and South as regions for aggressive expansion activity.

EXHIBIT 5 U.S. lodging information

	As of September 1987		*Additions Planned through 1988*	
	Properties	*Rooms*	*Properties*	*Rooms*
Best Western	1,826	165,807	180	16,380
Days Inns	536	78,372	264	34,628
Hilton Corporation				
Hilton Inns	222	55,190	15	3,000
Cresthil by Hilton	0	0	8	1,248
Holiday Corporation				
Embassy Suites Hotels	75	18,085	89	21,860
Hampton Inn Hotels	150	18,000	20	24,000
Holiday Inn Hotels	1,263	226,599	34	6,139
H. I. Crowne Plaza Hotels	5	1,759	1	238
Howard Johnson's	384	46,376	48	7,100
Quality International				
Comfort Inns	309	27,400	120	11,000
Quality Inns	474	57,000	71	9,000
Clarion Hotels	34	10,300	26	7,700
Comfort Suites	5	800	20	2,800
Quality Suites	4	700	31	5,100
Clarion Suites	0	0	10	2,000
Ramada Corporate				
Ramada Inns	487	78,698	60	10,000
Rodeway Inns	160	18,000	61	7,930
Sheraton Inns	333	72,443	0	0

Hilton operates two casino hotels in Las Vegas—the Flamingo Hilton and the Las Vegas Hilton. The casino division accounted for 33 percent of Hilton's sales and 52 percent of profits in 1985. Both casinos are averaging above 85 percent occupancy and are Las Vegas' two largest hotels. In 1986, Hilton's revenue was up $33.4 million to $680.7 million, but profits fell $2.4 million to $97.8 million. Hilton's financial situation remains strong with record earnings of $4.85 and $5.70 per share expected in 1987 and 1988, respectively. The international sector is expected to provide a growth opportunity for Hilton's properties overseas, such as the Gold Coast Conrad casino-hotel in Australia. Hilton may not use its trademark abroad because it is currently owned by Allegis, the parent of United Airlines.

Marriott Corporation

Marriott is a diversified company that owns hotels, catering kitchens, franchised restaurants, and other food contract businesses. It currently operates the Marriott Hotels, Courtyard by Marriott, and Residence Inns. Marriott is developing several other lodging products such as Fairfield Inns, a low-priced budget chain. Marriott owns and operates Bob's Big Boy, Roy Rogers and Howard Johnson's Restaurants.

Despite saturated market conditions, Marriott has aggressively expanded its room base in recent years. Marriott has leveraged itself by developing properties, selling them to investors, and obtaining long-term management contracts on the properties. Net income was $191.7 million in 1986, up $24.3 million from 1985, and revenues were $5.3 billion, up over $1 billion from the previous year.

Ramada Inns

As of January 1987, Ramada had 569 properties containing 96,500 rooms. These properties were distributed over mid-priced Ramada Inns, budget-priced Rodeway Inns, and Ramada's luxury product—Ramada Renaissance. Ramada owns Tropicana Casinos, which has locations in Atlantic City and Las Vegas. Renovations and expansion activities are underway at both properties. Ramada reported revenues of $687 million and $583.2 million in 1986 and 1985, respectively, with profits of $10.3 and $13.8 million over the same periods.

Quality International

Quality Inns International is headquartered in Silver Springs, Maryland. It currently has three segments: Comfort Inns/Suites, aimed at the economy/limited-service market; Quality Inn/Suites, a mid-priced chain aimed at the general public; and Clarion Inns/Suites, a luxury chain aimed at business and upper-end customers. There is currently no particular region that Quality is targeting, but it does have aggressive expansion plans for each of the three chains. Quality International is developing a fourth chain called McSleep Inns. While McDonald's has filed suit claiming that the use of "Mc" is part of their trademark, McSleep Inns are based on a principle similar to that of their fast-food counterparts. The McSleep Inn concept is quite simple: provide upscale furnishings in a down-sized guestroom that developers can build for about $3,000 a room and charge $25 per night. The concept could have universal appeal and establish some benchmark for consistent quality.

FINANCE

Holiday Inn Hotel Group is the world's largest hotel chain with 1,633 hotels and 316,164 rooms in more than fifty-one countries. Holiday Inn pioneered innovations such as free parking, color televisions, swimming pools, in-room movies, and the HOLIDEX computerized reservation system. Holiday currently has more than 250,000 employees. Holiday's income statement and balance sheets are provided in Exhibit 6 and Exhibit 7, respectively.

EXHIBIT 6 Statements of income, Holiday Corporation and consolidated subsidiaries.

(In thousands, except per share amounts)	January 2, 1987	January 3, 1986	December 28, 1984
			Fiscal Year Ended
Revenues			
Hotel	$ 952,007	$1,049,652	$1,003,730
Gaming	689,989	664,328	644,098
Other	5,792	90,492	111,990
	$1,647,788	$1,804,472	$1,759,818
Operating income			
Hotel			
Operations	$ 140,982	$ 194,267	$ 169,480
Property transactions	67,333	82,073	26,093
Gaming			
Operations	112,925	119,915	123,298
Property transactions	4,784	192	1,144
Other			
Operations	(6,959)	3,409	12,721
Property transactions	23,552	4,205	3,790
	342,617	404,061	336,526
Corporate expense	(40,579)	(30,420)	(20,195)
Interest, net of interest capitalized	(135,741)	(148,192)	(86,550)
Recapitalization expenses	(12,900)	-	-
Other income (expense), net	3,224	(1,186)	-
Income before income taxes and extraordinary item	156,621	224,263	229,781
Provision for income taxes	(53,251)	(82,978)	(98,806)
Income before extraordinary item	103,370	141,285	130,975
Extraordinary gain on termination of pension plan, net of income taxes of $8,462	-	8,738	-
Net income	$ 103,370	$ 150,023	$ 130,975
Income per common and common equivalent share			
Income before extraordinary item	$ 4.15	$ 5.06	$ 3.59
Extraordinary item	-	.32	-
Net income	$ 4.15	$ 5.38	$ 3.59
Average common and common equivalent shares outstanding	24,893	27,900	36,487

In 1986, Holiday opened 171 new hotels. Revenues were $1.65 billion, down 8.7 percent from 1985. This decrease was primarily due to Holiday selling properties, such as the Residence Inn hotel chain and assets. Holiday's 1986 earnings per share and net income declined to $4.15 and $103.4 million from $5.38 and $150 million in 1985, respectively. Continued declines like these could make it difficult for the com-

EXHIBIT 7 Balance sheets, Holiday Corporation and consolidated subsidiaries.

(In thousands, except share amounts)	January 2, 1987	January 3, 1986
Assets		
Current assets		
Cash	$ 59,822	$ 51,199
Temporary cash investments, at cost which approximates market	14,355	21,188
Receivables, including notes receivable of $16,076 and $16,968, less allowance for doubtful accounts of $24,416 and $22,302	180,102	173,285
Supplies, at lower of average cost or market	33,869	40,100
Deferred income tax benefits	6,597	-
Prepayments	12,246	11,743
Other current assets	19,742	21,139
Total current assets	326,733	318,654
Investments in nonconsolidated affiliates, at equity	111,739	185,519
Notes receivable due after one year, net of deferred gain of $44,000 and $40,758, and other investments	123,764	123,473
Property and equipment, at cost		
Land, buildings, improvements and equipment	2,029,978	2,124,442
Accumulated depreciation and amortization	(483,069)	(448,706)
	1,546,909	1,675,736
Excess of cost over net assets of businesses acquired, amortized evenly over 40 years	63,886	65,733
Deferred charges and other assets	105,158	78,455
	$2,278,189	$2,447,570
Liabilities and Stockholders' Equity		
Current liabilities		
Accounts payable	$ 117,037	$ 109,336
Long-term debt due within one year	169,879	166,609
Accrued expenses	190,151	199,515
Total current liabilities	477,067	475,460
Long-term debt	992,538	1,087,762
Deferred credits and other long-term liabilities	48,662	85,239
Deferred income taxes	121,189	136,624
Commitments and contingencies-See pages 45, 47, and 48		
Stockholders' equity		
Capital stock		
Preferred stock, $100.00 par value, authorized-150,000 shares, none issued	-	-
Special stock, authorized-5,000,000 shares		
Series A-$1.125 par value, redeemable at $105.00, convertible into 1.5 shares of common stock, outstanding-170,171 and 331,235 shares (excluding 98,072 shares held in treasury)	191	373
Series B-$1.125 par value, none issued	-	-
Common stock, $1.50 par value		
Authorized-120,000,000 shares, outstanding-23,592,569 and 25,191,781 shares (excluding 17,246,828 and 15,399,219 shares held in treasury)	35,389	37,788
Capital surplus	205,717	212,510
Retained earnings	404,655	423,012
Cumulative foreign currency translation adjustments	(63)	(2,239)
Restricted stock	(7,156)	(8,959)
Total stockholders' equity	638,733	662,485
	$2,278,189	$2,447,570

pany to fulfill the *Holiday Hospitality Promise,* which states: "Customers must be satisfied with every aspect of their stay, or the price of the portion they were displeased with will be refunded."

HOLIDAY'S INTERNATIONAL OPERATIONS

Holiday wants to double its international presence by 1995. In 1987, Holiday plans to add 4,400 rooms (17 hotels). More than twenty-seven international properties are currently planned or under construction. If considered separately, Holiday's international group would be the eighth largest hotel chain in the world, recently surpassing the 50,000 room mark. By the end of 1987, Holiday's International group will have 220 hotels in fifty-four countries. This group has undergone major development pushes in both the Asia/Pacific region and the Europe/Africa/Middle East region. By 1995, Holiday hopes to have fifty-five hotels in the Asia/Pacific region, up from twenty-eight today, and 192 in the Europe/Africa/Middle East region, more than double its current presence.

Europe/Africa

Holiday's primary overseas focus is on the European region. Although the population of Western Europe is roughly the same as the U.S. population, Holiday has only sixty-five hotels in this region, compared with more than 1,400 in the United States. Holiday's recent expansion effort includes opening five Holiday Inn Crowne Plazas in Hamburg, Munich, Amsterdam, Manchester (England), and Lisbon (Portugal).

In early 1987, Holiday Inn Hotel Group announced plans to introduce a chain of limited-service hotels in international markets, starting in Western Europe. Holiday projects 130 such properties by 1996; each will have sixty to 150 rooms, a small restaurant/lounge, and fewer frills than the typical Holiday Inn. Projected daily rates would be $47, and Holiday is targeting the commercial business traveler in suburban areas and smaller European cities.

Holiday currently has hotels in Malta, Morocco, and other regions of Africa, but its holdings are limited in this region. Current plans do not include any significant expansion efforts due to the political instability of this region.

Asia/Pacific

Holiday's presence in the Asia/Pacific region is somewhat limited. It currently has seven properties in China, six in Malaysia, two in Australia, and one in India. A Holiday Hotel opened in Phucket, Thailand, in early 1987. Four additional hotels are either under construction or planned in China. China represents an untapped resource for the international lodging industry, and Holiday has become the early leader in efforts to open this market.

HOLIDAY'S DOMESTIC OPERATIONS

The hospitality leader in the United States, Holiday Inn Hotels is the core business of a continually expanding portfolio that includes Embassy Suites, an all-suite hotel brand, Hampton Inn, a limited-service economy brand, and Holiday Inn Crowne Plaza, a luxury brand found in major metropolitan areas. Until recently, Holiday owned a 50 percent interest in Residence Inn, an extended-stay hotel product. Due to economic pressures created by Holiday's November 1986 recapitalization, Holiday sold this segment, but plans to develop a similar line in the future. Holiday's hotel/casino brand, Harrah's, was acquired in 1980 and remains the gaming industry's acknowledged leader. Together, these brands comprised more than 1,900 hotels throughout the United States. During 1987, Holiday will reach a milestone of having 2,000 hotels open. In 1986, Holiday opened, on average, more than three hotels per week.

Holiday Inn Hotels

Studies show that 96 percent of all U.S. travelers have stayed at a Holiday Inn. Estimated revenues from this segment totaled $4.6 billion in 1986, up from $4.5 billion in 1985. The division has a 39 percent share of the mid-priced market. Recent developments in this segment have resulted in more than 300 hotels being eliminated from the Holiday Inn hotel system during the past five years. Obsolete hotels have been replaced by newer and larger facilities. The average age of a Holiday Inn hotel room (including renovations) is now less than five years.

As of December 1987, this division consisted of 1,580 Holiday Inn hotels, including nineteen Holiday Inn Crowne Plazas. These hotels are located in fifty-one countries, but almost all are located in the United States. Exhibit 8 shows a breakdown of licensed versus company-owned facilities for Holiday Inns and other brands. Occupancy rates have dropped steadily, averaging 71 percent, 67.8 percent, and 65.2 percent in 1984, 1985, and 1986, respectively. Average room rates have risen from $50.84 in 1984 to $57.03 in 1986.

Hampton Inn Hotels

Hampton Inns serve the business and leisure traveler desiring quality accommodations at economy prices. The typical price range is between $30 and $40 per night. The Hampton Inn Hotel Division added sixty-eight new hotels in 1986 to finish the year with 106 hotels. Revenues from Hampton totaled 59.4 million in 1986, compared to $10.5 million in 1985. This growth record makes Hampton Inn one of the fastest-growing hotel chains in the world. Exhibit 9 gives a top ten listing of the fastest-growing economy/limited-service chains and shows that Hampton Inn placed fifth with 5,500 rooms to be added, representing 6.5 percent of the total additional rooms to be added to this segment during 1987. The average occupancy and daily revenue per occupied room in 1986 are 69.1 percent and $34.26, respectively, up from 57.2 percent and $32.67 in 1985.

EXHIBIT 8 Holiday Corporation's licensed and company-owned facilities, compared

	Licensed		*Company Owned*			
Fiscal Year	*Number of Hotels*	*Number of Rooms*	*Number of Hotels*	*Number of Rooms*	*Occupancy Rate*	*Average Daily Revenue Per Room*
Holiday Inn Hotels						
1986	1,442	262,485	126	31,784	65.2%	$57.03
1985	1,484	263,405	133	32,657	67.7	54.14
1984	1,485	259,462	170	41,325	71.0	50.89
Hampton Inn Hotels						
1986	95	12,024	11	1,370	69.1	34.26
1985	30	3,736	8	963	57.2	32.67
1984	1	123	2	229	—	30.59
Embassy Suites						
1986	38	8,987	9	2,032	71.5	72.69
1985	28	6,098	13	2,935	66.8	69.73
1984	12	2,366	9	1,908	76.3	66.97

Source: Adapted from Holiday Corporation 1986 *Annual Report*, p. 35.

Embassy Suites

Embassy Suites, Holiday's luxury all-suite product, is the industry leader in this segment with a 52 percent market share. Embassy is targeted at the upscale business traveler who desires more space and amenities than found in the traditional hotel. Embassy Suites were recognized in a major independent consumer survey as the best hotel in the mid- or upper-price category. Embassy Suites had seventy-three properties in twenty-two states, with seventeen hotels under construction at the end of 1986. Embassy's revenues for 1986 totaled $257.8 million, up from $153.5 million in 1985. As of January 1987, Embassy Suites Hotels had fifteen properties under management contract and had interests in joint ventures for an eleven additional hotels. Occupancy rates for 1984, 1985, and 1986 were 76.3, 66.8, and 71.5 percent, respectively. Average daily rates increased from $66.97 in 1984 to $72.69 in 1986.

GAMING INTERESTS

Among the leaders in the hotel-casino industry, Holiday accounts for nearly 10 percent of total gaming revenues nationwide. Holiday is the only company that has properties in all four major gaming markets in the United States, including: Harrah's Reno (Nevada), Harrah's Lake Tahoe (Nevada), The Holiday Inn Casino in Las Vegas, and Harrah's Marina in Atlantic City. These properties all have loyal customer bases. The

EXHIBIT 9 Fastest growing limited service/economy chains (based on number of rooms expected to open in 1987)

Chain	*Number of Rooms to be Added in 1987*	*Percent of Total, Industry Segments Additional Rooms*
1. Days Inn	11,500	13.6
2. Comfort Inns	8,700	10.3
3. Rodeway Inns	7,500	8.9
4. Super 8 Motels	7,000	8.3
5. Hampton Inn Hotels	5,500	6.5
6. Knights Inn	4,900	5.8
7. Econo Lodges	4,300	5.1
8. Travel Lodge	4,300	5.1
9. National 9 Motels	4,200	5.0
10. Motel 6	3,700	4.4

Source: Laventhol & Horwath Survey.

Lake Tahoe facility has won Mobil's five-star award and the American Automobile Associations (AAA) five-diamond award for ten consecutive years.

Holiday's strategy of focusing on the middle-to upper-income customers provides the best opportunity to maximize gaming revenues and profits. All of Holiday's gaming facilities have been extremely successful at retaining high occupancy rates for their casinos. These rates have averaged between 85 and 90 percent over the past four years.

Two transactions have recently taken place in the gaming segment of the Holiday Corporation. On May 16, 1986, Holiday sold its 50 percent interest in the Trump Casino Hotel for $76 million. On December 31, 1986, the company purchased Barney's Club, a small casino in Lake Tahoe. Barney's has subsequently been remodeled and reopened in mid-1987. In 1986, Harrah's opened 244 new suites at Harrah's Marina hotel/casino in Atlantic City. As a result of this expansion, revenues increased 12.0 percent from 1985 levels and added to Harrah's market share. Gaming income is expected to grow 5 percent annually over the next five years.

RECENT STRATEGIES

Sale of Residence Inns

In June 1987, Holiday announced plans to sell its 50 percent interest in Residence Inns to the Residence Inn Company. Following this development, Marriott purchased the Residence Inns Company in August 1987. Holiday's actions have been criticized by industry officials, since Residence Inns is a highly successful chain of ninety properties, has a 91 percent share of its markets, and is expected to have more than 300 properties by 1990. Holiday's management acknowledges the success of Residence Inns and is expected to develop a similar line of hotels to target this segment. To justify the sale, Holiday officials point to the recapitalization plan and to the very good offer that it received from the Residence Inns Company.

Holiday's Build-to-Sell Strategy

Holiday has a build-to-sell strategy whereby the company builds properties, finds a buyer, and obtains a long-term management contract on the property. Holiday recently exercised this strategy by selling eighteen Hampton Inns to the Fox Corporation while retaining long-term managerial rights on these properties. This strategy allows for rapid growth by providing funds to invest in additional hotel development. The build-to-sell strategy was formulated with the hopes of: 1) increasing leverage; 2) reducing capital intensity; 3) unlocking appreciation through the sale of real estate assets; and 4) distributing asset sales proceeds to shareholders. Since this strategy was implemented, Holiday has sold all or part of 86 hotels, generating $760.3 million in after-tax proceeds. The company used these funds to repurchase 12 million shares of stock in 1985 and 1986. In addition, by retaining managerial control, Holiday receives a continuing income stream from these properties. The act of producing revenues from a decreased asset base increases Holiday's returns and reduces ongoing capital requirements associated with ownership.

Domestic Developments

Although the Holiday Inn Hotel Group continues to expand at the rate of one new property every five days, this figure is somewhat misleading. Over the last five years, Holiday has dropped more than 300 properties. The company explains that these properties have ceased to be competitive or failed to meet the high standards of Holiday. Other companies, such as Days Inns, have aggressively targeted Holiday and attempted to lure Holiday's franchises into their camps. Days Inns has printed a series of advertisements directly criticizing Holiday's recapitalization plan and questioning Holiday's ability to adequately support franchises in the future. Industry analysts also question Holiday's ability to support franchisees in the future and are worried about the effects of this recapitalization.

Streamlining Operations

Holiday has recently announced the combination of Holiday Inns, Hampton Inns, and Embassy Suites into a single operating unit. This act will enable these divisions to share finance, accounting, human resources, and legal functions. Each division will continue to operate individual marketing, planning, and franchising activities.

THE FUTURE

Holiday Corporation's top management currently faces many strategic decisions that will determine whether the company's future will be gloomy or rosy. A pressing decision in particular is how best to reduce Holiday's massive debt obligation of $2.5 billion. Also, should Holiday continue as planned to add sixty-five more properties in Western Europe by 1996 and to add four more properties in China before 1990? Should Holiday continue adding about 150 new hotels annually in the United States? In what geographic areas of the United States and world would you recommend adding new Holidays? Should Holiday add to its current 106 Hampton Inns and thirty-nine Embassy Suites? How could Holiday more effectively streamline its organizational structure? Should Holiday acquire (or divest) additional casinos? Financially, are Holiday's strategies feasible and practical, or are they suicidal as some critics say? What specific recommendations would you offer to Holiday's top management?

Atlantic Southeast Airlines, Inc.—1987

BLANE BRIAN MOONEY
Auburn University

Have you ever ridden on an Embraer Brasilia? Chances are, you have if you've ever used Atlantic Southeast Airlines (ASA) for travel. This 30-seat airplane is one of the company's latest additions to a growing fleet of modern, state-of-the-art aircraft. ASA is the nation's fourth-largest regional air carrier, providing high frequency airline service between Hartsfield Atlanta International Airport (ATL) and twenty-seven other airports in the Southeast. The rapidly growing company also provides service between the Dallas/Fort Worth International Airport (DFW) and six other airports in the Southwest. ASA's flights are utilized primarily by business and military passengers to make connections with flights operated by Delta Air Lines, Inc. (Delta) and various other carriers at Atlanta and Dallas.

ASA was founded in 1979 by George F. Pickett, Jr., Robert L. Priddy, and John W. Beiser, all of whom resigned from merger-bound Southern Airways in January of the same year. On July 21, 1982, the company had an initial public offering of its common stock at $6.50 per share. The company has been able to maximize the use of its aircraft by operating with a hub-and-spoke system where all flights originate or terminate at a central location. This concept has resulted in one of the lowest per-seat-mile operating costs in the industry. ASA's breakeven load factor of 34.6 percent may well be the lowest of any airline in the United States.

As shown in Exhibit 1, ASA's "revenue passengers carried" has grown from less than 200 thousand in 1982 to well over 1 million in 1986. Operating revenues have increased by an equally impressive 600 percent. ASA's operating margin at year-end 1986 was 20.1 percent, one of the highest of any commercial airline in the country.

EXHIBIT 1 ASA's growth table (figures in thousands)

	1982	*1983*	*1984*	*1985*	*1986*
Operating revenues	13,182	23,785	43,762	75,318	92,295
Income from operations	2,898	3,299	10,739	15,218	18,523
Stockholders' equity	7,181	12,908	18,214	28,536	77,071
Revenue passengers carried	198	358	614	982	1,156

Additionally, ASA's net margin of 11.4 percent was after a 42.5 percent effective tax rate.

ASA's extraordinary success can be seen by evaluating the performance of its common stock. Due to stock splits and price increases, an initial investment of $650.00 for 100 shares of stock in 1982 would have grown to $6,100.00 when the stock reached its highest level ($15.25) in 1986.[1] This remarkable increase represents an 838 percent return on investment in less than four years.

At year-end 1986, ASA's financial position was the strongest in its history. Stockholder's equity exceeded $77 million, and working capital was at an all time high of almost $50 million. ASA's growth and cash infusion was so great during early 1986 that on July 15, the company incorporated ASA Investments, Inc. as a wholly owned subsidiary whose sole purpose is to invest cash assets of the company not currently needed for business operations. As of December 31, 1986, the company had transferred $36 million to the newly formed organization.

Although ASA begins 1987 cash rich, it faces numerous threats in its external environment. A hostile takeover attempt could be imminent. Consolidation in the airline industry is giving ASA's competitors greater and greater economies of scale. This could price ASA out of the market. Republic Express recently forced ASA out of the Memphis, Tennessee, market. American Eagle is trying to do the same thing to ASA at the Dallas/Fort Worth airport. These kinds of trends have ASA worried. ASA's top management realizes that success today is no guarantee at all for success tomorrow.

THE EMERGENCE OF ASA

In October 1978, the Airline Deregulation Act was enacted by Congress. This legislation led to the birth of ASA. The three founders of the company were all working for Southern Airways, which was about to become a part of Republic Airlines in an impending merger. They saw deregulation as a golden opportunity to enter the local service airline industry.

As Southern was absorbed by Republic, many south-central U.S. communities would be left with drastically reduced service as local routes were abandoned in favor of jet service to larger, more profitable markets. The three young executives knew the time was right to launch a commuter airline to fill this void in service created by the major carriers. In January 1979, they resigned from Southern and began forming their airline.

Led by Pickett, who later became president and chief executive officer, the three drew heavily on the marketing experience and contacts they had obtained while working for Southern. They were able to accurately predict several markets that were destined for reductions in service by the major carriers. Under the Deregulation Act, some communities were guaranteed air service by the Essential Airline Service clause which prevented the last carrier in a given city from abandoning that route unless a replacement carrier was found. ASA was able to take advantage of the major carriers' strong desires to abandon these unprofitable routes. Using smaller turbo-prop aircraft, the founders were confident they could turn those abandoned routes into profitable ones by implementing the hub-and-spoke concept, using Atlanta, Georgia, as the central hub for all flights.

ASA's Rapid Expansion

ASA began operations in June 1979 with one de Havilland Twin Otter doing five round trips a day over an 82-mile route between Atlanta and Columbus, Georgia. By the end of that year, ASA had carried 12,174 passengers. During 1980, four Embraer Bandeirantes were acquired, and service was expanded. By 1982, ASA had entered into interline agreements with Eastern, Piedmont, USAir and Delta Air Lines. Between 1979 and 1982, ASA's success and growth was limited only by its relatively limited access to capital. New markets were opened in each of these years, and record profits were being recorded just as often.

To obtain needed capital for expansion, ASA issued an initial public offering of 800,000 common shares of stock at $6.50 each. This capital infusion set the stage for continued growth and rapid expansion. In April 1983, ASA acquired Coastal Air, Limited, a regional air carrier doing business as Southeastern Airlines, serving nine markets in the Southeast. This acquisition also added six badly needed aircraft to ASA's system. Subsequent to this acquisition, four unprofitable markets were eliminated from the route system.

The Delta Connection

Perhaps the most significant event in ASA's history occurred in May 1984, when the company became a member of the "Delta Connection" program. This program has benefitted ASA by incorporating it into Delta's strong marketing program. Under this program, ASA's flights are listed using Delta's two-letter C.R.S. (Computer Reservations System) code in reservations terminals worldwide and in the Official Airline Guide. The "DL" designation gives ASA flights the same priority listing as Delta's and has resulted in much higher bookings. ASA passengers also receive the advantage of through-fares, credit in Delta's Frequent Flyer program, and the benefit of special promotions offered by Delta.

The Delta Connection program was designed to maximize the complimentary equipment and service of each company in order to increase the number of passengers carried by each carrier. ASA's operations and philosophy are geared toward providing service to short-haul regional markets with an efficient fleet of turbo-prop aircraft. Delta's system compliments ASA's by extending the service area throughout the United States and the world with jet aircraft that are more suited to larger markets and long-haul routes.

A necessary component of the Delta Connection program is the coordination of flight schedules between the two carriers. ASA's flights in Atlanta and Dallas/Fort Worth are designed to minimize connecting times between the company's flights and those of Delta's. In 1986, more than 80 percent of ASA's passengers connected to or from a Delta flight, attesting to the success of the program.

Stock Splits

The Delta Connection program has been so successful that ASA's stock prices began to climb at a rate never before seen by the company. In November 1984, ASA's board of directors declared a three-for-two stock split. Again, the price climbed higher. Two additional splits were authorized within the next twelve months: a two-for-one split in April 1985, and a four-for-three split in August of the same year. Throughout 1986, ASA's stock price has fluctuated from a low of $9.62 to a high of $15.25. Exhibit 2 shows the company's quarterly financial data, including the stock prices for 1985 and 1986.

ASA's Second Hub

ASA's decided to expand into the Memphis market as a second hub in late 1984; it proved to be a poor decision. This expansion was at the request of Delta Airlines, which had made an equally poor decision to expand its operations at Memphis in an attempt to obtain a larger share of the market. Delta and ASA were not able to successfully compete with the more dominant carrier, Republic, and its commuter partner, Republic Express. Republic's market share at Memphis was an overwhelming 85 percent.

Fortunately for ASA, the whole Memphis operation never amounted to more than 10.8 percent of its available seat miles. Average load factors from the Memphis-based operations were much lower than ASA's 43 percent system average. Delta was equally unhappy with its Memphis operations. Republic's announcement and subsequent merger with Northwest Airlines further strengthened the carrier's presence in Memphis and put additional pressure on Delta and ASA. After ASA entered the Memphis market, Republic expanded its operations threefold. Delta did not follow through with earlier plans to expand and, in fact, announced reductions in the number of flights offered. Delta and ASA essentially admitted defeat and began to search elsewhere for expansion opportunities.

The DFW Expansion

In mid-1986, ASA announced plans to establish a new hub at the Dallas/Fort Worth International Airport as requested by Delta Airlines. Operations were scheduled to begin on December 15, 1986, with a nominal five-city route structure. ASA was not

EXHIBIT 2 ASA's quarterly financial data

	First	Second	Third	Fourth	Year
1986					
Operating revenues	$21,082,000	$23,719,000	$24,499,000	$22,994,000	$92,295,000
Operating income	2,969,000	5,158,000	5,322,000	5,074,000	18,523,000
Net income	1,562,000	2,796,000	3,159,000	3,019,000	10,536,000
Net income per share	.15	.25	.24	.23	.87
Average weighted shares outstanding	10,662,000	11,015,000	13,334,000	13,339,000	12,098,000
Stock Price Data					
High	14.38	15.25	11.75	11.62	15.25
Low	10.75	11.25	9.62	10.25	9.62
1985					
Operating revenues	$14,598,000	$21,029,000	$21,283,000	$18,408,000	$75,318,000
Operating income	2,772,000	6,326,000	4,926,000	1,194,000	15,218,000
Net income	1,923,000	4,119,000	2,978,000	1,305,000	10,325,000
Net income per share	.18	.39	.28	.12	.97
Average weighted shares outstanding	10,660,000	10,660,000	10,660,000	10,660,000	10,660,000
Stock price data					
High	8.53	13.31	16.50	13.38	16.50
Low	3.70	7.50	9.75	8.75	3.70

Source: ASA *Annual Report,* 1986.

Delta's first choice. Delta had first approached Comair Inc., a Delta Connection partner based in Cincinnati, Ohio, about the possibility of replacing Rio Airways, the Delta Connection partner at DFW at that time. Rio had been hurt by intense competition and the relatively low yields characteristic of that market. In addition, Comair's research revealed that traffic potential could not offset those low yields and refused to sink its resources into the Dallas market.

ASA, on the other hand, felt that by shifting resources from Memphis to Dallas, Delta would be in a better position to increase its market share. ASA was also eager to abandon the no-win situation in Memphis. Most industry analysts argued, however, that more effective competition would not bring fares up, and only better yields could make DFW a money-making market. Many saw this move by ASA as a repeat of the Memphis mistake.

Before deciding to reallocate its Memphis resources to the DFW hub, ASA had considered purchasing Rio Airways. After researching the smaller carrier's financial records, maintenance system, and overall company operations, ASA decided against the acquisition.[2] A key factor in this decision was costs it would simply cost too much to integrate Rio's aircraft maintenance operations into ASA's (the two carriers used different types of maintenance systems). These costs essentially eliminated the financial incentives of acquiring the airline.

Delta's Investment in ASA

In addition to wanting the carrier in DFW, Delta also wanted to solidify its relationship with ASA. The failure of Rio as a Delta Connection partner and the loss of Ransome Airlines, a connection partner in the Northeast which sold out to another major carrier, led to a major decision by Delta. In May 1986, Delta and ASA jointly announced that each company's board of directors had approved a purchase by Delta of approximately 20 percent of the voting securities of ASA. This purchase involved 2,665,000 newly issued shares of ASA's common stock at a price of $14.25 per share, for a total consideration to ASA of almost $30 million. This proposal was carried out in June 1986.

This stock purchase by Delta, coupled with the stock owned by employees, directors, and their families, accounts for more than 40 percent of ASA's common stock. Due to this near-majority ownership, a hostile takeover would be extremely difficult, if not impossible.

ASA's Route System

ASA's route system currently includes service between Atlanta and twenty-seven other cities in Georgia, Florida, Alabama, South Carolina, North Carolina, Mississippi, Tennessee, Virginia, and West Virginia. Also included is service between Dallas and five other cities in Texas and Arkansas. Exhibits 3 and 4 reveal ASA's current route map and route system data for all markets served on December 31, 1986.

ASA's Flight Equipment

ASA's operating fleet consists of thirty-eight turbo-prop airplanes. Exhibit 5 shows relevant data concerning the numbers of each type of aircraft and ownership information.

Over short-haul routes, ASA's turbo-prop aircraft are more fuel efficient and can be operated more economically than jet aircraft, which are operated by most major air carriers. Due to their operating economy, ASA's aircraft can be operated profitably over short-haul routes with lower passenger load factors than larger jet aircraft. These elements and the relatively small size of the company's aircraft make it feasible for ASA to provide high-frequency service in markets with relatively low volumes of passenger traffic.

In September 1986, ASA signed the largest aircraft purchasing agreement in the history of the regional airline industry. The $109 million contract with Embraer calls for the delivery of 22 Brasilia airplanes at the rate of one per month beginning in March 1987. ASA also obtained the rights from Air Midwest to purchase six more Brasilias at a cost of $31 million.

ASA became the first U.S. airline to take delivery of the new-technology Embraer Brasilias in 1986. The 30 passenger turbo-prop aircraft has been warmly received by its passengers. With a true air speed of 285 knots and a cruising altitude between 21,000 and 25,000 feet, the Brasilia has allowed ASA to expand its market radius from 250 statute miles to 350 statute miles.

EXHIBIT 3 ASA's route map.

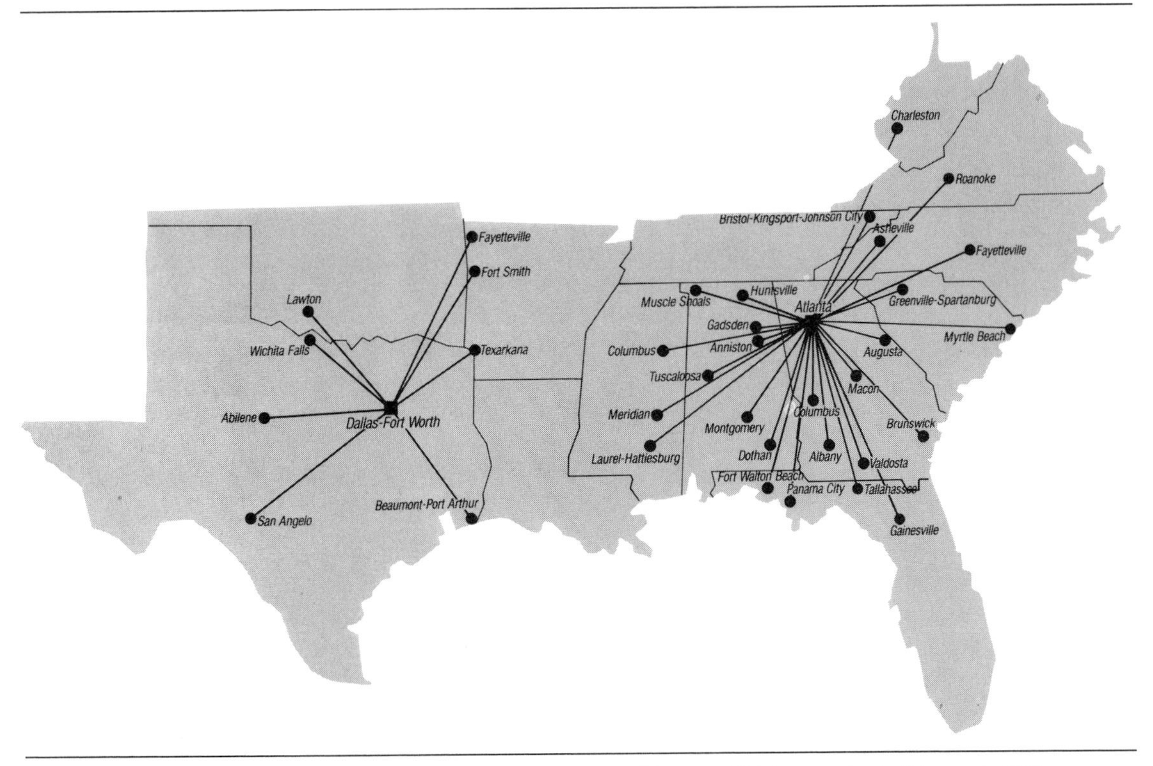

Note: Service to San Angelo, Texas, Beaumont/Port Arthur, Texas, and Lawton, Oklahoma to begin February 1, 1987.
Source: ASA *Annual Report,* 1986

Pilot training for the new Brasilias is done at night at the overnight stations. Embraer is currently building a flight simulator for the aircraft that should be available in the summer of 1987. Flight training for any new aircraft is very expensive. The necessary ground training and flight time can last as long as four weeks.

Each of ASA's aircraft is routed through Macon, Georgia, for periodic maintenance and checks. While the company has developed a sizeable line maintenance system in Atlanta, the more extensive maintenance is performed at its massive facility in Macon. Performing this maintenance at night allows the company to maximize aircraft usage during normal flight hours.

As shown in Exhibit 5, ASA's current fleet includes 22 leased aircraft. The minimum future lease payments have decreased from $21,784,275 in 1985 to $15,536,622 in 1986. Note also that many of these leases expire in 1987.

Marketing

ASA markets its passenger, air freight, and small package services primarily through direct sales activities and advertising programs. The direct sales activities focus on

EXHIBIT 4 ASA's route system

Atlanta, Georgia			
Airport Served	*Air Mileage from Atlanta Airport*	*Date Service Commenced*	*Flights Operated per Week*
Albany, Ga.	146	8/1/82	88
Anniston, Ala.	82	2/15/81	62
Asheville, N.C.	164	8/1/82	66
Augusta, Ga.	143	4/24/83	44
Brunswick, Ga.	238	6/1/81	50
Charleston, W.V.	363	2/1/86	40
Columbus, Ga.	83	6/27/79	80
Dothan, Ala.	171	10/31/82	88
Fayetteville, N.C.	330	11/1/85	66
Fort Walton Beach, Fla.	250	11/15/82	82
Gadsden, Ala.	98	7/15/81	25
Gainesville, Fla.	300	10/1/85	66
Golden Triangle, Miss.	241	12/15/84	62
Greenville/Spartanburg, S.C.	154	4/25/82	68
Huntsville, Ala.	151	6/15/84	122
Laurel/Hattiesburg, Miss.	308	12/15/84	26
Macon, Ga.	79	3/20/80	124
Meridian, Miss.	267	11/1/84	38
Montgomery, Ala.	147	6/1/82	54
Muscle Shoals, Ala.	198	10/1/82	52
Myrtle Beach, S.C.	323	9/1/86	40
Panama City, Fla.	247	3/1/84	79
Roanoke, Va.	357	12/15/85	40
Tallahassee, Fla.	223	12/15/85	70
Tri-Cities, Tenn.	227	10/31/82	66
Tuscaloosa, Ala.	186	11/15/82	52
Valdosta, Ga.	208	9/9/81	80

Dallas/Fort Worth, Texas			
Airport Served	*Air Mileage from DFW Airport*	*Date Service Commenced*	*Flights Operated per Week*
Abilene, Tex.	163	12/15/86	106
Fayetteville, Ark.	268	12/15/86	50
Fort Smith, Ark.	225	12/15/86	50
Texarkana, Ark.	176	12/15/86	66
Wichita Falls, Tex.	115	12/15/86	92

Note: Regular service is provided on all routes every weekday, with reduced service on weekends.

EXHIBIT 5 ASA's flight equipment

Type of Aircraft	*Owned*	*Leased*	*Expiration Dates*
Embraer Brasilia (30-passenger)	9	0	Not applicable
deHavilland Dash 7 (48-passenger)	1	4	Two in 1987; one in 1991; one in 1994.
Embraer Bandeirante (15-, 17-, or 19-passenger)	6	10	All ten in 1987
Shorts SD360 (35-passenger)*	0	8	Five in 1994; three in 1995.

Note: *ASA has the option to terminate seven of the Shorts SD360 leases each year, and the remaining one lease in 1988.

such high-volume sources of business as travel agencies and military ticket outlets. Special incentives for travel agents, such as free passes and familiarization trips, are used to encourage booking on ASA and Delta. These passes are generally on a space-available basis and constitute a negligible cost for the airline.

ASA also uses billboards, direct mail, newspapers, radio, and selected magazines and trade publications to promote its service. Cooperative advertising with Delta is used extensively to promote both ASA and Delta flight segments. Point-of-purchase displays are occasionally used to advertise specific flights and/or discount fares. ASA's affiliation with Delta, as a Delta Connection partner, also has a significant impact on operations and is sometimes referred to as a "marketing" agreement.

Exhibit 10 shows that ASA spent $7,992,857 on reservations, sales, and advertising in 1986. This amount is up from $6,276,490 in 1985. It is important to note that these figures include travel agency commissions as well as advertising expenditures. Specific figures on the percentage of tickets sold through travel agencies are not made available to the public. Generally speaking, a travel agency receives ten percent of the face amount of a given ticket in commission, which is paid by the airline and costs the consumer nothing.

Personnel

As of December 31, 1986, ASA had approximately 1,050 employees, of which 430 were ground service personnel, 425 were flight personnel, 130 were maintenance personnel, and the remainder were management and clerical employees. There is no union affiliation, and current relations with employees are good.

As is true with most commuter airlines, the employees of ASA tend to be much younger than those of the major carriers. Most beginning station agents have little or no previous training or experience in the travel industry. The approximate starting salary for a full-time agent is $11,700. This figure progresses to a maximum of almost $17,000 after four years of service. Overtime varies from station to station, depending on flight frequency and passenger loads.

Because ASA's reservations are handled by Delta agents, the station agent is generally the first ASA employee to come in contact with the customer. ASA and Delta have recognized this factor for some time and have provided joint training for most agents. This training currently concentrates on the technical aspects of the job, such as computer reservation systems, passenger bookings, and other ground service procedures. Little emphasis is placed on customer service. The task of emphasizing customer service and satisfaction is left to the station managers. This procedure creates some problems in many stations where the manager already words a 50- or 60-hour week. Usually, little time is available for on-the-job training. Pickett has always been quick to attribute ASA's success to the dedication of its employees.

Exhibit 6 shows ASA's organizational structure and lists the principal officers of the company. As the company grows, ASA does not hesitate to add additional personnel at the executive level. Most senior-level officers are former Southern employ-

EXHIBIT 6 ASA's organizational chart and key personnel.

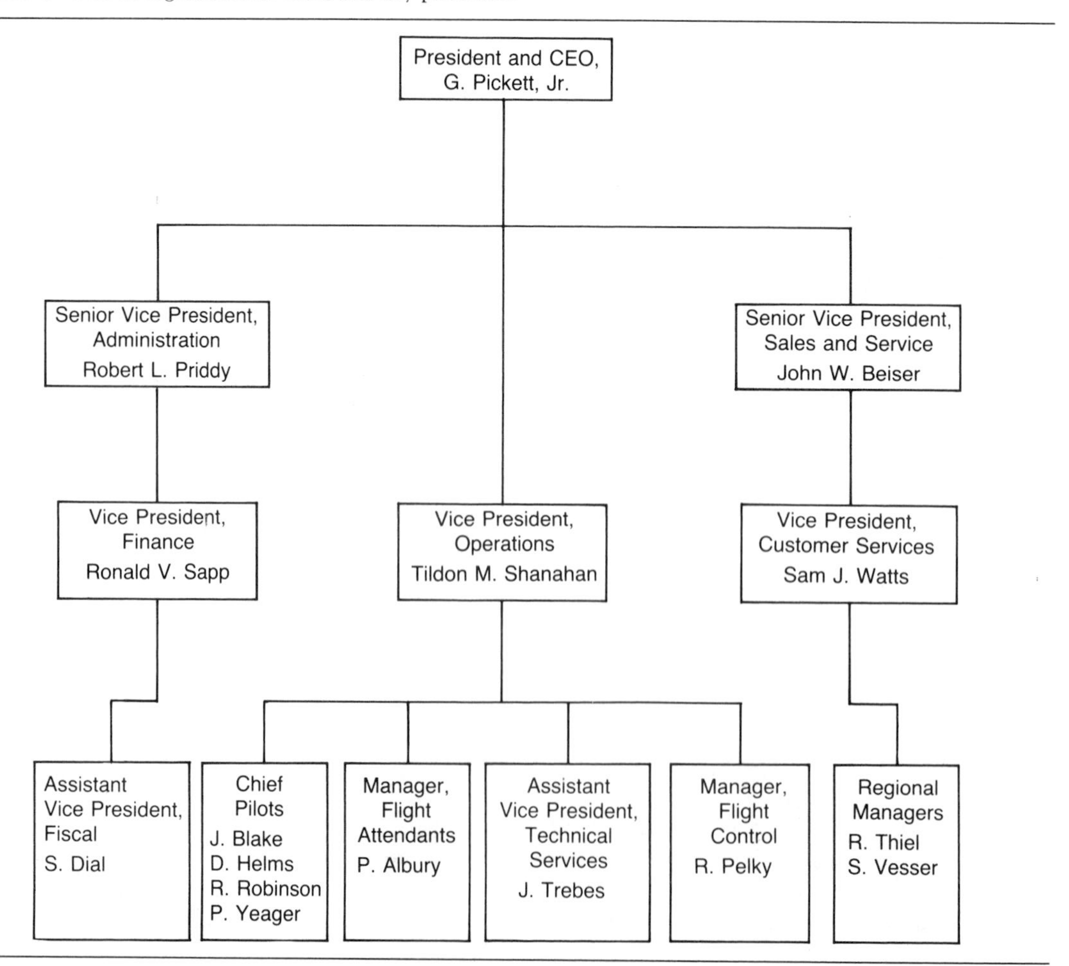

ees who have been acquainted with ASA's founders for many years. Both the regional manager and station manager positions are filled from within the company. This procedure often creates problems because the employees are young and have little or no supervisory experience. ASA occasionally provides assistance for these new managers by temporarily assigning an experienced manager at the station until the new manager is able to assume operations.

COMPETITION

ASA competes primarily with other air carriers and with ground transportation, such as automobiles, trains, and buses. Many of ASA's flight segments are less than 150 miles. These routes are especially susceptible to ground transportation competition. Due to the high frequency and low capacity offered by ASA in most routes, its services are utilized primarily by business and military travelers. The ability of ASA to compete with other carriers and ground transportation depends upon the public's acceptability of ASA's aircraft and ASA's provision of convenient, frequent, and reliable service to its markets at reasonable rates. With respect to other carriers, ASA's primary competition comes from Eastern Metro Express in Atlanta and American Eagle in Dallas. Both of these carriers are wholly owned subsidiaries of a large company, Metro Airlines, Inc. A third commuter operating from the DFW hub is Metro Express II, which does business as an American Eagle carrier similar to Metro Airlines, Inc. Metro Express II is owned by the President and Chairman of the Board for Metro Airlines, Inc., Edmond A. Henderson.

American Eagle

In 1984, Metro Airlines became an American Eagle carrier feeding American Air Lines in the same way that ASA feeds Delta. American has a firm 60 percent market share at DFW. Metro is solidly entrenched as the dominant commuter at DFW primarily due to American's overwhelming market share. Exhibit 7 shows the Metro route map for its DFW operations.

Competition at the DFW hub may prove to be just as fierce for ASA as that in Memphis. Whereas Republic Airlines had an 85 percent market share compared to Delta's 15 percent in Memphis, American has a 60 percent share compared to Delta's 22 percent at DFW. The comparison is not quite as bad, but far from favorable. Delta does have plans to embark on a massive expansion program with hopes of nearly equaling the service provided by American. However, remember that Delta had similar plans for its Memphis hub.

It has become apparent in the airline industry that the market share of the major carrier dictates the relative market share for its commuter partners. Unless Delta can cut into American's 60 percent share, it is not likely that ASA will break Metro's firm hold on the regional market. ASA and Delta will, however, almost certainly obtain some of the remaining 18 percent market share that is currently held in small parts by several other carriers.

Only time will tell if the DFW expansion will prove as frivolous as the earlier-abandoned Memphis operation. Although ASA and Delta officials flatly deny it, there

EXHIBIT 7 American Eagle (Metro) route map.

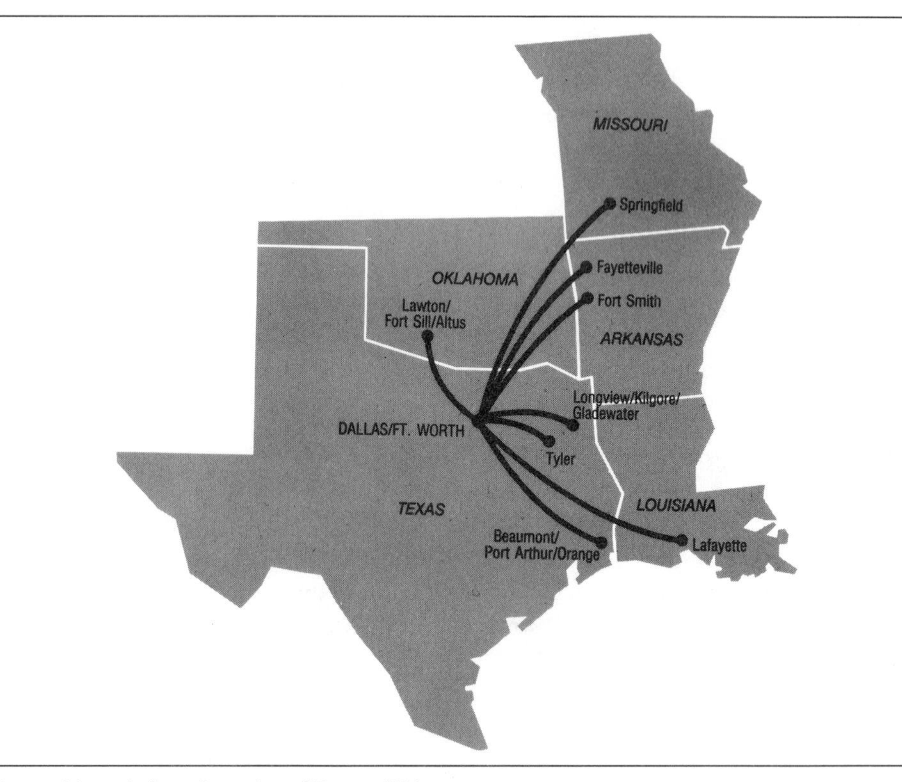

Source: Metro Airlines, Inc., *Annual Report,* 1986.

is a rumor in the airline industry that Delta has guaranteed ASA against initial losses for its new operations.

Eastern Metro Express

ASA competes with Eastern Metro Express between Atlanta and the following cities: Albany, Augusta, Columbus, and Macon, Georgia; Asheville, North Carolina; Dothan, Huntsville, and Montgomery, Alabama; Fort Walton Beach and Panama City, Florida; Myrtle Beach, South Carolina; and Tri-Cities, Tennessee. Exhibit 8 shows these and other cities served by Eastern Metro Express.

ASA is headquartered in Atlanta, as is Delta Air Lines, the dominant carrier in that market. Delta's position should adequately protect ASA's market share in the Southeast. Delta has the lowest consumer complaint record among all major carriers.

Operating as American Eagle and Eastern Metro Express, Metro's average system load factor was 54.6 percent in 1986. While the figure is considerably better than ASA's 43 percent average, Metro's breakeven load factor of 53 percent is almost 20 percent higher than ASA's breakeven point of 34.6 percent. Exhibit 9 shows Metro's

EXHIBIT 8 Eastern Metro Express route map.

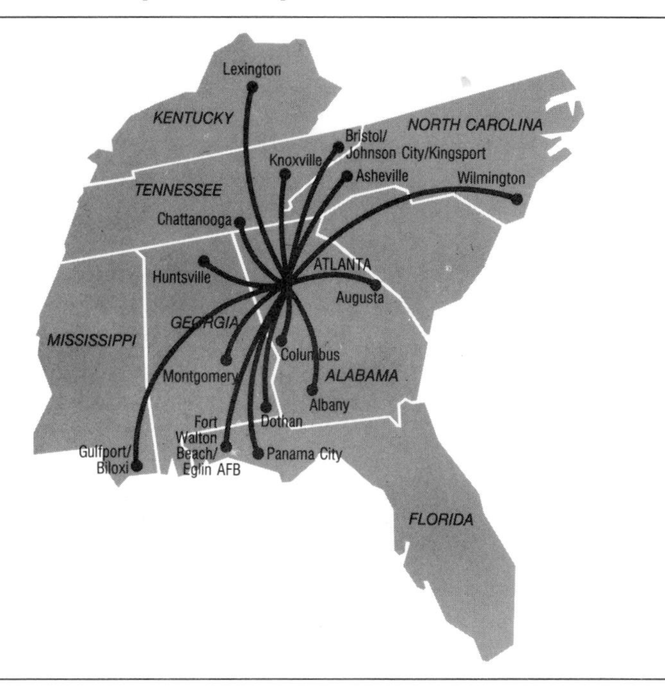

Source: Metro Airlines, Inc., *Annual Report,* 1986.

consolidated statements of income. Exhibits 10–13 give additional financial information for ASA.

AIRLINE DEREGULATION

The Airline Deregulation Act of 1978 has driven airline ticket prices down considerably. After falling an average of 6 percent in 1986, ticket prices may go even lower in 1987. Price wars and "Maxsaver" fare promotions have been good for the consumer but disastrous for many carriers. Braniff Airlines has yet to recover from its troubles. Even the largest carrier, United Air Lines, has had to impose cost restrictions and layoffs to remain competitive. Airlines were allowed to abandon unprofitable routes after the act was passed. The void created by the major carriers' withdrawals from these routes became ASA's niche in the market. Many communities aren't happy with the smaller aircraft, but most welcome the increased frequency in flights.

One negative consequence of deregulation has been the reduction in the quality of service provided to passengers. Airline customers are doing a record amount of complaining. Flight delays are the expected, rather than the exception, and many carriers actually lock their passengers on board an aircraft when they know that a delay is to occur. This procedure is practiced to prevent the passengers from changing to other carriers. Bumped baggage is probably the chief complaint concerning com-

EXHIBIT 9 Metro's consolidated statements of income.

	Year Ended April 30,		
	1986	1985	1984
Operating revenues:			
Passenger	**$74,332**	$54,049	$33,401
Cargo, mail and other	**1,119**	1,037	926
Federal compensation payments	**—**	571	1,013
Aircraft lease revenue	**328**	1,195	1,392
	75,779	56,852	36,732
Operating expenses:			
Flight operations	**16,278**	11,284	8,367
Fuel	**11,268**	8,400	6,120
Maintenance	**15,991**	12,034	10,056
Passenger service	**18,311**	11,171	5,557
Promotion and sales	**611**	882	776
General and administrative	**5,445**	2,987	2,284
Depreciation and amortization	**4,371**	3,021	2,693
	72,275	49,779	35,853
Operating income	**3,504**	7,073	879
Other income (expense):			
Interest expense, net	**(1,315)**	(1,198)	(1,389)
Gain on sale of assets, net	**1,735**	7	128
	420	(1,191)	(1,261)
Income (loss) before provision for (benefit of) income taxes	**3,924**	5,882	(382)
Provision for (benefit of) income taxes	**(599)**	1,667	(388)
Net income	**$ 4,523**	$ 4,215	$ 6
Weighted average number of shares outstanding	**3,783**	3,556	3,546
Earnings per common share	**$ 1.20**	$ 1.19	$ .00

Source: Metro Airlines, Inc., *Annual Report*, 1986.

muter airlines. This "bumping" occurs when a given flight is booked to capacity and little weight allowance is available for luggage. For example, ASA's 35-passenger Shorts SD360 can only carry fifty-five pieces of luggage. This 55-piece limit can only be carried under ideal weather conditions and on short flights. The irony is that each passenger is "allowed" to check two pieces of luggage. Essentially, the airlines are betting that not everyone will check the maximum allowance. They are right some of the time but wrong just as often!

Hardly a day goes by that we don't hear about airline safety violations, passenger dissatisfaction, and near collisions caused by the shortage of air traffic control personnel. Flight restrictions are almost certain to be imposed at the nation's busiest airports. It can be assumed that the commuter airlines, with their high frequency and low capacity mode of operations, will feel the crux of these restrictions.

Deregulation has made competition so tough that many airlines are simply forced from the industry. Instead of breaking up the monopolies that many carriers enjoyed prior to deregulation, the situation has somewhat worsened. The top five airlines now control a staggering 85 percent of the airline passenger traffic in the United States. Fortunately for ASA, Delta is one of these five.

EXHIBIT 10 ASA's consolidated statements of income.

	Years Ended December 31		
	1986	1985	1984
Operating revenues:			
Passenger	**$88,591,485**	$72,981,539	$41,817,054
Other	**3,703,531**	2,336,528	1,944,946
	92,295,016	75,318,067	43,762,000
Operating expenses:			
Flying operations	**30,019,850**	28,328,686	15,171,195
Maintenance	**12,513,143**	9,132,157	4,157,505
Aircraft and traffic servicing	**12,664,674**	9,427,549	4,586,867
Reservations, sales and advertising	**7,992,857**	6,276,490	3,886,537
General and administrative	**5,473,764**	4,341,512	3,225,692
Depreciation and amortization	**4,934,889**	2,451,015	1,822,523
Miscellaneous and transport related	**173,210**	142,537	173,068
	73,772,387	60,099,946	33,023,387
Income from operations	**18,522,629**	15,218,121	10,738,613
Nonoperating (income) expenses:			
Interest:			
Income	**(2,073,282)**	(938,090)	(541,167)
Expense	**2,561,269**	1,093,361	1,125,933
Other, net	**(301,617)**	(31,983)	(127,957)
	186,370	123,288	456,809
Income before income taxes	**18,336,259**	15,094,833	10,281,804
Income taxes—Note E:			
Current	**2,110,000**	1,461,000	2,430,000
Deferred	**5,690,000**	3,309,000	2,551,000
	7,800,000	4,770,000	4,981,000
NET INCOME	**$10,536,259**	$10,324,833	$ 5,300,804
Net income per share	**$ .87**	$ .97	$ .50
Weighted average number of shares outstanding—Note G	**12,098,239**	10,659,801	10,656,750

Source: ASA's *Annual Report*, 1986.

Many industry analysts do not believe that the "shake-down" is over yet. Mergers, acquisitions, and bankruptcies will continue to plague the industry. Other analysts believe that profitability will continue as fare wars abate, yields firm, and the consolidation trend continues.

Consumer rights advocates are becoming more vocal about the poor service and declining safety in the airline industry. There are even some calls for reregulation by Congress and various other parties. A group of senators recently warned that if the

EXHIBIT 11 Five-year selected financial and operating data.

FINANCIAL DATA	**1986**	1985	1984	1983	1982
Operating revenues	**$92,295,000**	$75,318,000	$43,762,000	$23,785,000	$13,182,000
Income from operations	**18,523,000**	15,218,000	10,739,000	3,299,000	2,898,000
Income before taxes	**18,336,000**	15,095,000	10,282,000	2,178,000	1,582,000
Net income	**10,536,000**	10,325,000	5,301,000	1,803,000	1,482,000
Net income per share	**.87**	.97	.50	.17	.20
Average weighted shares	**12,098,000**	10,660,000	10,657,000	10,320,000	7,533,000
Stockholders' equity	**77,071,000**	28,536,000	18,214,000	12,908,000	7,181,000
Stockholders' equity per share	**5.78**	2.68	1.71	1.25	.95
Property and equipment (net)	**74,860,000**	47,027,000	15,383,000	14,703,000	14,417,000
Long-term debt (net)	**40,032,000**	28,490,000	7,340,000	8,795,000	10,703,000
Total assets	**143,704,000**	77,666,000	37,993,000	27,621,000	25,410,000
OPERATING DATA					
Revenue passengers carried	**1,156,000**	982,000	614,000	358,000	198,000
Available seat miles (000)	**514,000**	402,000	210,000	141,000	68,000
Revenue passenger miles (000)	**222,000**	170,000	98,000	53,000	25,000
Passenger load factor	**43.2%**	42.4%	46.7%	37.9%	37.6%
Break-even load factor	**34.6%**	33.9%	35.7%	34.4%	33.1%
Average passenger trip length (miles)	**192**	174	160	148	128
Flights per week (end of period)	**2,084**	1,801	1,426	870	564

Source: ASA's *Annual Report,* 1986.

federal aviation officials do not order the airlines to at least publish information on flight delays, cancellations, and lost luggage, Congress will!

ASA's FUTURE

There are many threats facing ASA in the near future. The airline's rapid growth and tremendous success has not come without growing pains. One problem area that occurs every year is what to do about salary increases. ASA's workers have received a pay raise slightly higher than the rate of inflation each year since the company's inception. But with the inflation rate currently at relatively low levels and agent salaries approaching $20,000, this practice may need to be altered. Employees aren't satisfied with a 3 or 4 percent raise when the company is making a substantial profit. For many

EXHIBIT 12 ASA's balance sheets.

	December 31	
ASSETS	**1986**	1985
CURRENT ASSETS		
Cash and cash equivalents	**$ 53,356,875**	$13,787,673
Accounts receivable—shareholder	**4,994,513**	-0-
—other	**3,431,722**	8,478,845
Refundable income taxes	**237,930**	1,563,000
Expendable parts	**1,711,077**	1,030,538
Other current assets	**803,055**	899,310
Total current assets	**64,535,172**	25,759,366
PROPERTY AND EQUIPMENT—Note B		
Flight equipment	**81,356,946**	51,604,339
Other property and equipment	**3,564,125**	2,961,457
Advance payments on property and equipment	**3,535,670**	565,604
	88,456,741	55,131,400
Less accumulated depreciation and amortization	**(13,596,657)**	(8,104,137)
	74,860,084	47,027,263
OTHER ASSETS		
Excess of cost over fair value of tangible assets acquired	**3,811,237**	3,916,374
Other assets	**497,117**	963,393
	4,308,354	4,879,767
	$143,703,610	$77,666,396
LIABILITIES AND SHAREHOLDERS' EQUITY		
CURRENT LIABILITIES		
Current portion of long-term debt	**$ 5,074,780**	$ 4,009,648
Accounts payable—shareholder	**389,780**	-0-
—other	**5,487,018**	5,146,328
Air traffic liability	**248,105**	2,795,971
Accrued payroll and related expenses	**1,616,386**	1,112,060
Other accrued expenses	**1,532,232**	1,035,503
Income taxes payable	**254,282**	232,256
Total current liabilities	**14,602,583**	14,331,766
LONG-TERM DEBT—Note B	**40,031,848**	28,489,898
DEFERRED INCOME TAXES—Note E	**11,998,600**	6,308,600
SHAREHOLDERS' EQUITY—Notes B, G, and H		
Common Stock, $.10 par value; authorized 20,000,000 shares; issued and outstanding shares 1986—13,338,813; 1985—10,660,313	**1,333,882**	1,066,032
Capital in excess of par	**45,242,614**	7,512,276
Retained earnings	**30,494,083**	19,957,824
	77,070,579	28,536,132
COMMITMENTS—Notes B, C and F		
	$143,703,610	$77,666,396

Source: ASA's *Annual Report*, 1986.

EXHIBIT 13 ASA's consolidated statements of changes in financial position.

	Years Ended December 31		
	1986	1985	1984
SOURCE OF FUNDS			
Net income	**$10,536,259**	$10,324,833	$ 5,300,804
Add (subtract) items not affecting working capital:			
Depreciation and amortization	**4,934,889**	2,451,015	1,822,523
Increase in allowance for maintenance	**1,536,684**	1,396,771	158,397
Deferred income taxes	**5,690,000**	3,309,000	2,551,000
Other	**(264,647)**	130	(116,532)
Total from operations	**22,433,185**	17,481,749	9,716,192
Proceeds from sale of property and equipment	**5,617,700**	17,707	492,218
Increase in long-term debt	**22,413,145**	25,159,055	-0-
Decrease in other assets	**365,254**	2,209	-0-
Decrease in advance payments on equipment purchases	**5,439,425**	5,577,496	-0-
Issuance of common stock	**37,998,188**	1,137	6,500
	$94,266,897	$48,239,353	$10,214,910
APPLICATION OF FUNDS			
Purchase of property and equipment	**$36,481,222**	$35,148,406	$ 2,460,017
Increase in advance payments on equipment purchases	**8,409,491**	5,744,205	379,053
Increase in other assets	**-0-**	-0-	171,075
Payments and current maturities on long-term debt	**10,871,195**	4,009,648	1,454,774
Redemption of fractional shares	**-0-**	4,317	375
Increase in excess of cost over fair value of tangible assets acquired	**-0-**	-0-	160,931
Increase in working capital	**38,504,989**	3,332,777	5,588,685
	$94,266,897	$48,239,353	$10,214,910
SUMMARY OF NET CHANGES IN WORKING CAPITAL			
Increase (decrease) in current assets:			
Cash and cash equivalents	**$39,569,202**	$ 2,812,997	$ 6,475,893
Accounts receivable	**(52,610)**	3,127,304	2,530,692
Refundable income taxes	**(1,325,070)**	1,563,000	-0-
Expendable parts	**680,539**	474,544	84,615
Other current assets	**(96,255)**	308,757	405,999
	38,775,806	8,286,602	9,497,199
Increase (decrease) in current liabilities:			
Current portion of long-term debt	**1,065,132**	2,554,873	(1,101,746)
Accounts payable	**730,470**	2,410,719	1,670,385
Air traffic liability	**(2,547,866)**	1,340,162	653,715
Accrued payroll and related expenses	**504,326**	189,104	315,199
Other accrued expenses	**496,729**	636,010	(19,212)
Income taxes payable	**22,026**	(2,177,043)	2,390,173
	270,817	4,953,825	3,908,514
INCREASE (DECREASE) IN WORKING CAPITAL	**$38,504,989**	$ 3,332,777	$ 5,588,685

Source: ASA's *Annual Report,* 1986.

carriers, high labor rates, coupled with low yields, causes severe financial distress. These conditions could be especially important in the event of an economic downturn. Salary reductions are difficult to administer without alienating the work force.

Another key concern for ASA is, where will the carrier be if the industry is, in fact, reregulated? ASA, like most commuter airlines, is notorious for delayed baggage, crew delays, and the overbooking of flights. What impact would these shortcomings have on the carrier in a regulated environment?

With ASA catering to the business and military traveler, what affect will the rapidly developing telecommunications industry have on its services. Video conferences and information transfer systems may well become substitutes for some business air travel in the next five years. Should ASA diversify outside the airline industry, or should it go after the vacation traveler? More disposable income may mean increased air travel by America's vacationers.

A final item is worth consideration. What would happen to ASA should Delta decide to discontinue the Delta Connection program and terminate all ties with the carrier? As mentioned earlier, Delta has fewer customer complaints than any major airline. If legislation is passed requiring airlines to publish information about flight delays, lost luggage, and cancellations, ASA's disclosures will almost certainly have a negative impact on Delta's excellent reputation. What can ASA do to prepare for the possibility of independent status?

ENDNOTES

1. ASA's stock is traded on the National Market System under the NASDAQ symbol ASAI.
2. Through later agreements, Braniff began to feed the struggling Rio at DFW, and Trans Star, a Houston-based carrier, began to provide joint fares at Austin, Texas.

Con-Way Central Express—1987

ROBERT CROWNER
Eastern Michigan University

Jerry Detter was finishing the last session of the "New Employee Orientation Seminar" at the Sheraton in Ann Arbor. He was standing in front of a banner with "TEAM" on it. The word was done in the Con-Way Central Express (CCX) colors of orange and brown. Jerry was likening CCX to bailing twine. "Each strand in bailing twine," he said, "is very weak, but when you twist all of the strands together, you have a twine that is very strong and not easily broken." The acronym "TEAM", Jerry added, stands for Together Each Accomplishes Much. "TEAM sums up my belief as to why, by any measure, CCX has been so successful since its inception in 1983," said Jerry.

In 1986, CCX, a subsidiary of Consolidated Freightways, Inc., provided short-haul overnight freight service to points in the Midwest, including the states of Michigan, Illinois, Indiana, Iowa, Kentucky, Ohio, Pennsylvania, Minnesota, and Wisconsin. Its headquarters were located in a 7600-square-foot office on the south side of Ann Arbor, Michigan, in a commercial/light industry park. The company was founded on June 20, 1983, in a farm house nicknamed "Tara", which looked like it had barely survived the Civil War. CCX, which began operations in 1983 with seventy-two employees and eleven terminals, had 1500 employees at thirty-eight locations in 1986—just three and a half years later. During this same period, revenues increased over twenty-five times, which is even more amazing given the trucking industry shakeout that was causing many firms to go bankrupt.

THE PARENT COMPANY

Consolidated Freightways, Inc. (CFI), the parent company of CCX, is a large worldwide freight handler with five principal business lines: long-haul trucking; regional trucking, where CCX is one of three subsidiaries; air freight; international ocean container service; and specialized truckload and forwarding service. Its balance sheet for 1984 through 1986 are shown in Exhibit 1, and its income statements for 1983 through 1986 are shown in Exhibit 2.

CFI pioneered many innovations in the transportation industry. Today, many of them—such as the use of double trailers—are standard in the less-than-truckload (LTL) transportation business. The latest innovation was the establishment in 1983 of the Con-Way regional freight companies, Con-Way Eastern Express (CEX), Con-Way Western Express (CWX), and CCX. The opportunity to begin the regional businesses was ripe due to the deregulation of the trucking industry, which began with the passage of the Motor Carrier Act of 1980. Con-Way Eastern Express was begun by purchasing an existing carrier, while CCX and Con-Way Western Express were formed as new companies. By the end of 1986, CFI had invested $50 million in CCX and in turn had a subsidiary that was growing very rapidly and returning excellent profits. In September 1986, *Forbes* estimated that the three regional companies of CFI would generate $15 million in profits on sales of $150 million for 1986.

Consolidated Freightways Motor Freight (CFMF), the long-haul division of CFI, accounted for revenues of about $1.5 billion in 1986. CFMF has terminals and operates in many of the same cities as the regional subsidiaries; however, it sells to different markets since the average length of its haul is 1000 miles. Thus, CFMF does not directly compete with the regional units.

INTRAPRENEURING

To say that Jerry Detter, the president of CCX, has charisma seems trite. For when one sees him in action, he epitomizes the idea. Most employees agree he was—and continues to be—the driving force that created and sustains CCX. Jerry was 38 years old when CFI asked him to start CCX. He figured he was "young enough to start over" if the project failed, but he was confident it would succeed.

Jerry joined CFI as a terminal dock worker immediately after graduating in the bottom third of his high school class. He said he was only reading at the fifth grade level at the time and realized quickly he needed to improve himself. By the time he was 23, he was a terminal manager, and by age 28, he managed the largest terminal in the United States. It had 1200 employees, which he was able to reduce to 900 five years later. He had been with CFI for eighteen years and was a division manager responsible for twenty-three terminals at the time he was selected to start CCX.

Originally, CFI proposed to buy a company rather than start a new regional carrier from scratch. The accountants said it would cost $11 million to turn the proposed acquisition around, but Jerry thought it would take four times as much. Jerry convinced CFI to start a new company, and the proposed acquisition went out of business within ninety days, affirming his judgment. The original concepts for the company were simple and remain so today. Overnight delivery service was to be provided at least 95 percent of the time at a competitive cost using union-free labor. The company would provide superior efficiency and flexibility and would stress teamwork and profit sharing. Jerry likened CCX to a speedboat, which can make quick turns and adjust rapidly to the marketplace and competitors. Although the management concepts and style at CCX are atypical of the industry, they are unique at CFI.

At a two-and-a-half-day employee orientation seminar in February 1987, a number of comments were made by the employees regarding the company and Jerry's leadership. Some of those comments follow:

> It's great to talk to the president personally and think he really cares about your ideas.
>
> I like the honesty of this company.
>
> The company takes care of its equipment and provides good equipment.
>
> The company pays above-average wages, with profit sharing.
>
> CCX is intense, but I like it.
>
> There is real teamwork here. Everyone tries to help. The spirit and profit sharing are great.

Ninety-five percent of the drivers are former union members. Jerry encourages this because those drivers have something to compare CCX to and are appreciative of the different climate. The employees, in turn, appreciate the union-free environment.

THE TRUCKING INDUSTRY

The U.S. trucking industry can be segmented in several different ways. First, one can classify the for-hire carrier versus the private carrier. For-hire carriers are considered part of the trucking industry, while private carriers are not since they are solely owned by individual companies and only transport that company's freight. Private carriers typically are not subject to the same detailed regulations as for-hire carriers. By 1980, private carriers probably numbered 100,000.

For-hire carriers can, in turn, be divided into intracity truckers and over-the-road truckers. Expenditures for local cartage in 1986 still represented 40 percent of all ex-

EXHIBIT 1 Consolidated Freightways, Inc. and Subsidiaries: Balance sheet (in thousands of dollars)

	1984	*1985*	*1986*
Current Assets			
Cash	34,185	31,176	41,372
Marketable securities	107,409	77,599	94,041
Net accounts receivable	198,640	226,484	249,522
Notes receivable	11,511	13,556	24,891
Operating supplies	23,897	22,470	27,485
Prepaid expenses	37,476	46,567	48,066
Prepaid income taxes	14,478	7,845	14,057
Total Current Assets	**427,596**	**425,697**	**499,434**
Other Assets			
Marketable securities for investment	120,300	123,056	151,685
Notes receivable due through 1990	10,149	9,525	7,053
Operating rights and goodwill, net	19,689	18,915	20,447
Investment in tax benefit leases	8,042	7,460	5,999
Investment in CF Financial Services		4,986	5,267
Deferred Charges and Other Assets	9,159	6,275	12,463
Total Other Assets	**167,339**	**170,217**	**202,914**
Property, Plant and Equipment			
Land	48,660	54,235	63,818
Buildings and improvements	204,918	234,694	249,577
Motor carrier equipment	446,492	515,945	574,153
Other equipment and leasehold improvements	106,699	118,889	129,335
Total	806,769	923,763	1,016,883
Less accumulated depreciation	(341,130)	(386,104)	(443,791)
Total Net Property	**465,639**	**537,659**	**573,092**
Total Assets	**1,060,574**	**1,133,573**	**1,275,440**

EXHIBIT 1 continued

	1984	*1985*	*1986*
Current Liabilities			
Accounts payable and accrued liabilities	229,926	226,574	290,810
Federal and other income taxes	5,800	584	
Accrued claims cost	38,823	35,983	47,049
Current maturities of long-term debt	19,347	9,971	6,688
Total Current Liabilities	**293,896**	**273,112**	**344,547**
Long-Term Debt	62,645	62,539	58,700
Deferred Items	151,197	194,128	207,145
Total liabilities	**507,738**	**529,779**	**610,392**
Shareholders' Equity			
Common stock, $.625 par value	17,579	17,647	26,570
Capital in excess of par value	61,863	63,622	57,758
Cumulative translation adjustment	(5,839)	(8,176)	(7,120)
Retained earnings	520,183	571,926	630,228
Less treasury stock	(40,950)	(41,225)	(42,388)
Total Shareholders' Equity	**552,836**	**603,794**	**665,048**
Total Liabilities and Shareholders' Equity	**1,060,574**	**1,133,573**	**1,275,440**

EXHIBIT 2 Consolidated Freightways, Inc. and Subsidiaries: Income statement (in thousands of dollars)

	1983	*1984*	*1985*	*1986*
Revenues				
Surface transportation	1,173,866	1,480,156	1,616,567	1,843,177
Air freight	181,229	224,753	265,575	281,290
Total	**1,355,095**	**1,704,909**	**1,882,142**	**2,124,467**
Costs and Expenses				
Surface transportation				
Operating expenses	864,599	1,121,968	1,215,678	1,353,368
Selling and administrative expenses	159,512	192,076	213,519	262,648
Depreciation	58,934	65,420	79,096	86,875
Total	**1,083,045**	**1,379,464**	**1,508,293**	**1,702,891**
Air freight				
Operating expenses	137,235	168,361	214,589	238,781
Selling and administrative expenses	33,077	35,889	43,423	43,825
Depreciation	2,243	2,993	3,602	3,925
Total	**172,555**	**207,243**	**261,614**	**286,531**
Operating Income				
Surface transportation	90,821	100,692	108,274	140,286
Air freight	8,674	17,510	3,961	(5,241)
Total	**99,495**	**118,202**	**112,235**	**135,045**
Other Income				
Investment income	23,618	20,991	22,446	16,203
Interest expense	(9,893)	(7,379)	(6,159)	(7,298)
Miscellaneous, net	(162)	(3,079)	(1,103)	3,440
Total	**13,563**	**10,533**	**15,184**	**12,345**
Income Before Taxes	**113,058**	**128,735**	**127,419**	**147,390**
Income Taxes	**47,594**	**54,270**	**48,128**	**58,281**
Net Income	**65,464**	**74,465**	**79,291**	**89,109**
Net Income per Share	**$1.62**	**$1.88**	**$2.06**	**$2.31**

penditures on motor freight service. Intrastate cartage represented 60 percent of the tonnage carried. Intracity carriers are subject to state regulation.

Over-the-road carriers are subject to federal regulation and intermodal competition. Regulated carriers can, in turn, be divided into common carriers, who provide service to the general public, and contract carriers, who do not haul for the general public but provide specialized service to individual shippers. There were an estimated 193,000 self-employed truckers (contract carriers) in 1980. There were three classes of regulated carriers in 1980 based upon the annual amount of revenue they handled:

- ☐ Class I—In excess of $3,000,000
- ☐ Class II—Between $500,000 and $3,000,000
- ☐ Class III—Less than $500,000

The common carriers can be regular route carriers or irregular route carriers. Regular route carriers of general freight operate through terminals where LTL cargoes are received, sorted, and consolidated into truckload lots for subsequent movement to other terminals where the same process is reversed. Such terminals also serve as points for switching cargoes between carriers. Thus, regular route carriers are in the distribution business, and the terminal network required to perform this service requires a much larger capital investment than is necessary for contract carriers. In addition, their terminal operations make them more labor intensive and, therefore, more costly and dependent upon good terminal management.

The trucking industry from 1978 through 1984 was relatively stable in regard to ton-miles carried and employment, as shown in Table 1.

Regulation of the trucking industry was established by the Motor Carrier Act of 1935 during the Great Depression in order to overcome destructive competition, chaotic price structures, and market forces which were thought to be unreliable for producing satisfactory results. It was a movement away from the free market toward socialism. The lack of stability in the industry was thought to be due to the ease of entry with little capital required, owners being free to send their trucks anywhere they wished, and each operator being able to set his own rates.

The Act provided for the Interstate Commerce Commission to control entry into the interstate market, define and limit operations within the market, and control the rates charged. The control of entry was accomplished by requiring a "certificate of public convenience and necessity" for any carrier who sought new or extended routes. This certificate required a hearing in which existing competitors in the market could contest the need for the new carrier. As might be expected, the majority of the operating rights by the mid-1970s were obtained under the grandfather clause of the Act. The protective nature of regulatory policy reduced the risk which would have been encountered in a competitive industry and provided a good opportunity to grow with the general economy.

TABLE 1 Intercity ton-miles (billions)

Year	*Number*	*Percent of U.S. Total*	*Employment (000's)*
1978	599	24.3	1212
1979	608	23.6	1249
1980	555	22.3	1189
1981	527	21.7	1168
1982	520	23.1	1128
1983	548	23.7	1133
1984	602	23.6	1212

Source: Transportation Policy Associates, *Transportation in America: Regualtion of the Trucking Industry.*

The control of operations was provided by requiring the Commission to specify the nature and extent of authorized service that individual carriers could offer. As a result of this power, a congressional study in 1945 showed that 62 percent of intercity certificates had been limited to special commodities and only 32 percent of intercity carriers had general commodity authority which was subject to numerous exceptions. Furthermore, more than one-third of the intercity carriers were limited in obtaining income-generating backhauls, and one-tenth were prohibited from taking return loads for compensation. Route restrictions forced carriers to travel unnecessary distances, often partially or totally empty. Of regular route carriers, only 30 percent had full authority to serve all intermediate points on their routes, and 10 percent had no such authority.[1]

In order to facilitate the massive job of controlling rates in the interstate trucking industry, the Commission encouraged regulated carriers to use rate bureaus to jointly make rates. By 1980, ten major general freight rate bureaus were operating in different parts of the country. From their beginning, these rate bureaus clearly used price fixing, which was illegal under U.S. antitrust laws. This dilemma was "resolved" by the Reed-Bullwinkle Act of 1948, which theoretically preserved the right to make individual rates. The Act required the proposing carrier to show that the proposed rate was just, reasonable, and compensatory. However, the delays and litigation caused by this requirement effectively precluded individual rate making.

Deregulation of the Trucking Industry

Deregulation of the trucking industry began in 1977 with some administrative changes and culminated in the Motor Carrier Act of 1980. This Act altered all of the three factors involved in regulation: entry policy, operating authority, and rate making. Ease of entry was facilitated in two ways: the burden of proof of public convenience and necessity was eased, and the basis for protest by existing carriers was constrained. These changes caused the number of applications for operating authority to grow from 12,700 in 1979 to 22,735 in 1980 and to more than 29,000 in the twelve months following passage of the Act. Grants of authority to new entrants grew from 690 in 1979 to 1,423 in 1980 and to 2,452 in the following twelve months. Two years after the passage of the Act, applications were averaging about 1,100 per month, 43,000 new certificates had been issued, and about 8,000 new carriers had been granted operating authority.[2]

Rate making was altered by the Act to permit carriers to take independent rate actions without the potential procedural obstacles previously mounted by the rate bureaus. These obstacles included the power to delay filing of the proposal and the right to notify other members of the proposed rate change prior to action being taken.

Deregulation served to weaken the elaborate set of barriers to competition among existing carriers. It also produced another incentive which enhanced competition: added capacity. The operating restrictions previously in place had tied up capacity through inefficiencies. Elimination of the restrictions freed up this capacity for productive use.

Although the rate bureaus continue to operate, a shakeout occurred in the trucking industry in the three years following the passage of the Act. This shakeout was caused by the economic climate as well as the increased competition made possible by the Act. Rate reductions became more common, and carriers had stronger incentives to control costs, including wages negotiated with the Teamsters Union. Management could no longer afford to minimize confrontation with the Teamsters.

The trend toward non-union carriers which had begun to develop prior to the 1980 Act was accentuated after the passage of the Act. In 1983, non-union employees constituted 44 percent of the drivers and helpers, 42 percent of the vehicle maintenance personnel, and 69 percent of the cargo handlers. In 1983, Class I non-union carriers were able to generate 2.5 times as much revenue per dollar of compensation as the unionized carriers. Table 2 summarizes the costs and revenue relationships:

The LTL motor freight industry has higher rates than the truckload segment because it is a distribution network and as such is more labor intensive. Rate increases over time have brought LTL rates to the point where they reflect the full cost of handling such freight. The competitive advantage has gone to those firms with the lowest labor-productivity costs. Many anticipate a further shakeout of the weak firms in the industry, which will make those least able to control and reduce their labor costs the first to go.

The economic benefits from deregulation exceed the original government estimates by a factor of 10, ranging from $56 to $90 billion annually. Not only have transportation costs themselves been reduced but also, more importantly, much of the increased efficiency is due to better management of inventory and delivery systems. In effect "just-in-time" inventory concepts were facilitated. Exhibit 3 shows the components of 1986 U.S. logistics cost.

The performance of transportation services must be consistent and dependable if investments in inventory are to be controlled. Prior to deregulation, producers and distributors either built excessive inventory or operated their own trucks in order to overcome the poor service provided by many carriers. The competition fostered by deregulation has forced better service.

TABLE 2 Average annual pay and productivity per employee for Class I carriers, 1983

	Union	*Lightly Unionized*	*Non-union*	*Union / Non-union*
Wages	$27,293	$21,734	$18,630	1.46
Benefits	4,096	1,365	897	4.57
Compensation	31,389	23,099	19,527	1.61
Revenues	52,555	57,219	81,097	.65
Ratio of Revenue to Compensation	1.67	2.48	4.15	.40

Source: ICC databank of trucking industry statistics.

EXHIBIT 3 Components of 1986 U.S. logistics cost

Distribution Service	*Cost (in billions of dollars)*
Inventory Carrying/Holding	
Carrying	98
Warehousing	
Public	6
Private	50
Total	**56**
Total Carrying/Holding	**154**
Transportation	
Motor carriers	
Public carriers	54
Private and shipper affiliated carriers	75
Local freight carriers	76
Total Motor Carriers	**205**
Railroads	29
Water carriers	18
Oil pipelines	9
Air carriers	6
Forwarders, brokers and agents (net)	1
Total Nonmotor Carriers	**63**
Shipper-related services	3
Total Transportation	**271**
Distribution administration	18
Total	**443**

Source: Robert V. Delaney, "The Disunited States: A Country In Search of an Efficient Transportation Policy," *CATO Policy Analysis,* No. 84 (March 10, 1987): 3.

MARKETING

The marketing activities of CCX are managed by Bryan Millican. He graduated from the University of Waterloo in Canada with a bachelor's degree in mathematics and computer science and later received his master's degree in business administration from the University of Western Ontario. He began working in the trucking industry in Canada when he was 16 and has had extensive experience in data processing and marketing. He accepted the job at CCX after talking to Jerry Detter without even knowing his salary because he liked the opportunity and the fact that CCX was open for new thoughts. He normally spends 50 percent of his 60-hour week on the road seeing how customers perceive the marketing programs and how employees use the programs. Due to his background in computers, Bryan personally wrote many of the programs that are used locally by CCX.

CCX uses a three-phase marketing strategy. The first phase is to get market awareness as a regional carrier. CCX began with terminals in the eleven major cities in the central states region. Jerry Detter wanted to get the "biggest bang for the buck." Next, more key cities were added, followed by secondary cities, and finally the network was spread out to encompass the entire area.

One of the key factors CCX stresses is time on-time service. It aims to deliver 96 percent of the freight the next day; CCX was operating at 97 percent in late 1986. Regional trucking is much more sensitive to time than national trucking. Coverage between major freight centers within the region is also emphasized, along with financial stability or staying power. Exhibit 4 shows how terminals were added from 1983 through 1986 to carry out these policies.

The second phase of CCX's marketing strategy is the penetration of the market area. CCX is at this point now; it is in the top twenty-five in the country in terms of tonnage handled. The company is now proceeding into the third phase, which is domination of the Midwest market, with premier service and coverage.

CCX began with 700 points of service, is now at 6,500 points, and is looking forward to an expansion of fifteen more terminals to include 10,000 points of service in 1987. CCX's present market share is more than 10 percent, and Bryan Millican's goal is to have 20 percent of the market by June 1988. Jerry Detter sees a 45 percent growth in revenue in 1987—which would put CCX among the top twenty in the country—and a 25 percent share of the market by 1990. All of this growth is to be accomplished with a tight administrative and selling expense budget, which was 5.5 percent of revenues in 1986.

The selling strategy for CCX, as developed by Bryan, consists of these elements:

Try us; test our product.

Identify time-sensitive customers.

Make it easy for customers to deal with us—keep it simple.

Strive for error-free shipping.

Pricing

The industry has been reluctant to raise prices in the recent years after deregulation due to the severe competition and shakeout that it has experienced. Many freight companies have gone bankrupt as a result of these factors. CCX tries to differentiate itself from competition by the quality of its service, meaning consistent, realistic, next-day delivery with practically error-free shipping.

The trucking industry, as noted previously, has traditionally used rate bureaus for its rate base system (which is not related to mileage the freight travels). Most trucking firms still use this system even after deregulation, which allowed other systems to be used. The rate base system can result in different freight costs between the same terminals, depending upon which direction the freight is traveling. The freight class sys-

EXHIBIT 4 CCX terminal locations in the year added

	1983	*1984*	*1985*	*1986*
Michigan				
Detroit	X			
Grand Rapids	X			
Battle Creek		X		
Pontiac			X	
Holland				X
Flint				X
Jackson				X
Ohio				
Toledo	X			
Cleveland	X			
Columbus	X			
Cincinnati	X			
Dayton			X	
Akron			X	
Findlay				X
Pennsylvania				
Pittsburgh	X			
Sharon/Newcastle			X	
Erie			X	
Indiana				
Indianapolis	X			
South Bend		X		
Fort Wayne		X		
Kokomo			X	
Evansville			X	

tem, when used to extend freight costs as used by most firms, is not based on logic. For example, the freight class 200 is not double the 100 class but exceeds two times the 100 class.

CCX has a different pricing system. By staying out of the rate bureaus and not being part of a cartel, CCX is perceived as having lower prices. Actually, some of CCX's rates are higher and some are lower than those of the competition. The CCX system is based on a ZIP code model and is totally driven by mileage. An individual printout is given to each customer, so there is no need for elaborate, difficult-to-use tariff guides. Savings to CCX from this simplified system are estimated to be $150,000

EXHIBIT 4 continued

	1983	*1984*	*1985*	*1986*
Illinois				
Chicago	X			
Palatine		X		
Aurora			X	
Des Plaines				X
Bloomington				X
Danville				X
Wisconsin				
Milwaukee	X			
Janesville		X		
Green Bay			X	
Fond Du Lac				X
Minnesota				
Minneapolis	X			
Iowa				
Quad Cities	X			
Kentucky				
Louisville			X	
Lexington				X
Missouri				
St. Louis				X

to $400,000 annually since no highly paid rate clerk technicians are required. Furthermore, the customers appreciate the simplicity.

There are nineteen classes of freight, as defined by the National Motor Freight Classification (NMFC) system, in CCX's pricing system. Class 100 is established as the base level of rates. Classes are based on elements such as the freight's density, weight, stowability, susceptibility to damage, and valuation. For instance, rough steel plate is Class 50, and light bulbs are Class 200. In the CCX system, once the class number is established, it is easy to calculate that class's rate by using a multiplier to the Class 100 base rate. There is a minimum charge of $38 for less than 250 pounds.

All of the 100,000 shipments per month are rated by the computer. The only input needed is the originating point based on the three digit ZIP code, destination ZIP code, weight, and class of the freight. The average revenue per 100 pounds of freight handled by CCX is $6.50.

Jerry Detter believes, "there is no bad freight, just bad rates." The typical customer is not very analytical and judges the price based on the discount level given. On balance, CCX's rates are about 5 percent above the rate bureaus since a better product is provided, but a discount is offered on each shipment since the customer expects it. CCX rarely loses a customer entirely.

The decision maker for the customer is typically the shipping and receiving manager or the warehouse manager. CCX has sought small-to medium-sized shippers and has stayed away from the big companies, although larger accounts are being emphasized now. Big companies are moving toward using one carrier, and part of CFI's strategy is to be able to service this kind of account anywhere. The average CCX customer uses the company three times per week, with two shipments each time at a charge of $2,500 per month.

Terry Hartley is the pricing manager. He is responsible for coordinating bids, negotiations with customers, and regulatory compliance. He supervises two employees who work on auditing rates. The pricing manager makes 80 percent of the pricing adjustments, but Jerry Detter OK's all adjustments. Of the requests for adjustments submitted, 20 percent are rejected outright. Ninety-two percent of the business is sold at the base price.

Sales

The drivers at CCX are called driver salesmen, and they actually do sell. In fact, 20 percent of the business is maintained by them, and they distribute 30 percent of CCX's promotional literature. In the company seminars, a list of "Things CCX Driver Salesmen Must Do To Increase CCX Revenues" is discussed with the new driver salesmen. The list includes the following twelve items:

Always be courteous.

Always treat the customer with professional respect—if ever in doubt, contact your terminal manager. Never argue.

Ask for business at every opportunity.

Stress CCX service excellence on every call (comments regarding service on inbound bills, testimonials, promotional materials, and CCX's on-time percentage).

Create awareness of CCX services that a customer has never used (new terminals, additional points, inbound traffic, protective service).

Get multiple bills per stop.

Hand out CCX promotional literature, and get it up on the walls (stickers, dispatch cards, route maps, etc.).

36 percent discount on every shipment—make sure every customer knows that.

Make customers aware of the many features and benefits of CCX:

Itemize best service in the central states

A CFI Company

Very low claims ratio

Professional, experienced people

Easy to use

Simple (and very competitive) pricing program

Union free company

Coverage of thousands of points on a direct basis daily

Hats and other promotional materials—use them to increase your business (scratch pads, dispatch cards with Cox telephone number, stickers, hats).

The 30-second sales call . . .

Leads to your Account Managers (via your T.I.P. program).

Bryan Millican believes the CCX driver salesmen know more about their company than most managers in other companies. CCX believes its sales training is the best in the trucking industry.

Exhibit 5 shows the organization chart for CCX. As the chart indicates, all line responsibility flows through the terminal managers in the operations area. Bryan Millican does have a dotted line relationship to the field account managers and does make calls on customers with them. There are one to five of these account managers assigned to each terminal for a total of seventy-seven, and they make nine to ten calls per day. Generally, each account manager has about 200 accounts and calls on the large ones twice a month and the medium-size ones once a month. Each manager has a revenue quota which increases monthly. The revenue quota for each terminal is set by a committee that includes Jerry Detter, Bryan Millican, Dick Palazzo, the vice president of operations, and Kevin Schick, the controller.

Telemarketing is another important aspect of CCX's sales strategy. Pat Jannausch is manager of the Account Management Center (AMC). She has a reputation for being particularly good at training, which undoubtedly results from her teacher experience prior to joining CCX. She has twenty-one people working in the Center who account for 12 percent of the sales. Each person makes thirty-five to forty telephone sales calls per day, which averages out to one call per customer every six weeks. The Center handles 11,000 of the company's 32,000 accounts. The center's accounts tend to be small. However, once an account is obtained by the Center, it stays a Center account regardless of how big it becomes. The Center's calls cost about $6.50 each, and the Center makes about 250,000 direct mailings annually. Potential customers are obtained by referring to the Harris Directory and Dun & Bradstreet's Directory, by talking to recipients of freight from CCX, by getting referrals from driver salesmen, and by canvassing shippers of specific commodities such as electronics firms that may be involved in "just-in-time" inventory systems. There is a four week training program for AMC account managers. An income statement with full absorption of overhead is generated for the Center.

EXHIBIT 5 Con-Way Central Express organization chart

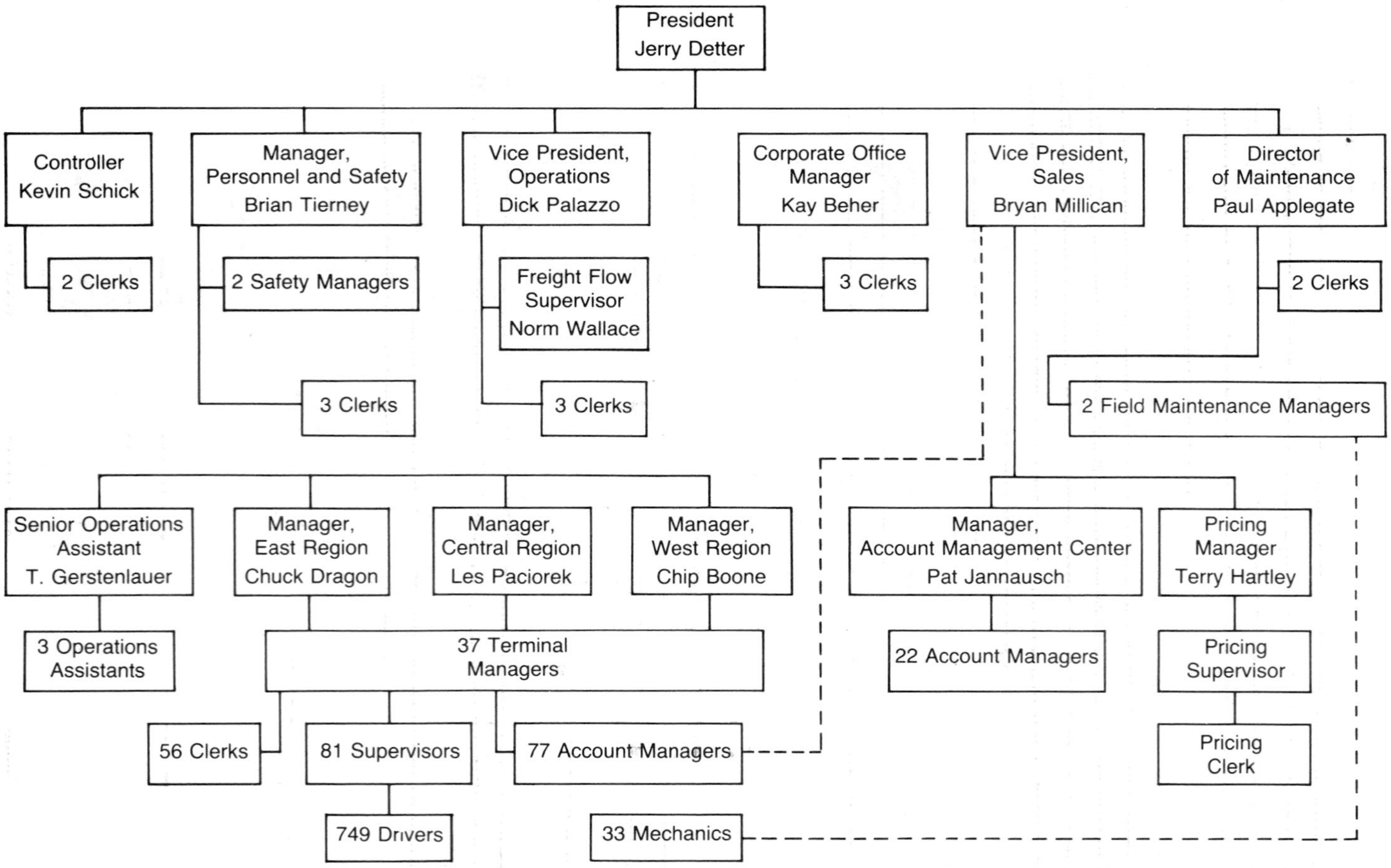

Promotion

Most of the advertising for CCX is done by the parent company, CFI, in the form of image advertising in trade magazines and general business magazines such as *Forbes* and *Fortune*. Due to the high cost of advertising and the regional nature of CCX's operations, little advertising is done. For instance, a single-page color ad run three times per year costs $20,000. Very little advertising is done by CCX in the Yellow Pages and the various industrial guides. Most of CCX's expenditures are for promotional items—literature, printed brochures and pamphlets, and some specialty items.

Bryan personally does all of the advertising layout work for the promotional literature used locally by CCX. Local typesetting services are used, but the actual printing of the pieces is done by CFI in its central printing shop. Printed material costs about $200,000 per year. Total marketing expense for CCX, which initially ran 20 percent of revenue, now runs about 5 percent and is expected to drop further.

As is probably true in any industry, there are ethical issues that arise in the trucking industry. Some carriers use entertainment in lieu of price competition. Others give gifts. As a policy, CCX gives any discount earned to the company paying the shipping bill. Gifts are not given beyond the normal promotional material (such as CCX hats, model trucks, and pens). Entertainment is less than 1 percent of marketing expense.

Competition

The central states region, in which CCX operates, is the most competitive area of the United States. The revenue from the region exceeds $1 billion, and it is estimated by CCX that there are more than 4,000 carriers operating in the market. Table 3 summarizes CCX's estimate of the revenue handled by its top thirty-five competitors in the central states region.

Not all of these carriers are profitable. CCX estimates that the operating ratio for these thirty-five carriers varies from 84 percent at best to 126 percent at worst. Given these estimates, it is not difficult to see why bankruptcies have been common and are continuing.

According to Jerry Detter, the strongest but not the largest competitor is TNT Holland. TNT Holland was formerly known as Holland Motor Express before being

TABLE 3 Central states revenues

	Central States Revenue	*Percent of Revenue*
Top 10 carriers	$ 621,000	57.6%
11–20	286,000	26.5
21–25	98,000	9.1
26–35	73,000	6.8
Total	**$1,078,000**	**100.0%**

acquired by TNT Pilot Freight Carriers, a subsidiary of Thomas Nationwide Transportation of Australia, in 1985. Holland had $128,680,000 in revenue in 1986, having doubled in size in the last eight years. It has thirty terminals in Illinois, Indiana, Kentucky, Michigan, Missouri, Ohio, Tennessee, Iowa, and Wisconsin and serves 2,854 points. CCX serves 76 percent more points with 23 percent more terminals and provides service to Pennsylvania and Minnesota as well but does not cover Tennessee. Holland currently is discounting its prices.

ANR Freight System, formerly ATL (Associated Truck Lines), operates in all states that CCX does plus some other ones outside the central states region. ANR has a large network of terminals and agency stations (eighty-one in CCX's market area) and serves more than 8,000 points. ANR's revenue for 1986 was $175 million, which was down 5 percent for the same period in 1985. Its on-time service level was recently reported to be 80 percent, with a goal of 85 percent. ANR is estimated to have 12 to 14 percent of the central states market.

OPERATIONS

Dick Palazzo, vice president of operations, is 47-years-old and has had 24 years experience with CFMF, starting as a clerk and finishing as a division manager prior to joining CCX. Dick was with Jerry Detter from the beginning. He serves as the sounding board for everyone. Dick studied Industrial Management for the equivalent of two to three years at the University of Akron from 1959 through 1966. He typically works sixty to seventy hours a week, spending about 50 percent of his time in the field.

Terminals and Freight Assembly Centers

CCX's operational area is divided into three regions: Eastern, Central , and Western, with a regional manager in charge of each region. CCX began operations without regional managers but added two in 1985 when the number of terminals increased to twenty-seven. Again, a regional manager was added in 1986 when the number of terminals was increased to thirty-seven.

Under these three regions are thirty-seven terminals, which are supervised by a terminal manager aided in three instances by an assistant terminal manager. The terminals have a total of 1,410 truck doors, which handled about 625,000 tons of freight in 1986. The 749 driver salesmen are supervised directly by eighty-one supervisors. The terminal managers also have direct responsibility for seventy-seven account managers and fifty-nine clerks. The typical terminal manager spends about 10 percent of his time selling with account managers or personally. CCX would like to see 30–40 percent of the time spent on selling.

Each of the five normal work days, the driver salesmen pick up and deliver freight between the hours of 8 A.M. and 4 P.M. over routes determined by the mix of customers that day. Weekends are not normally worked since freight picked up on Friday will be available for delivery on Monday morning in the normal course of events. At 8 P.M., the line haul drivers drive a tractor and two 28-foot trailers either to a

Freight Assembly Center or to a meet and turn point about equidistant between two terminals where the trailers are exchanged and driven back to the original terminal.

In conjunction with seven of the terminals, there are Freight Assembly Centers located at Aurora, Illinois; Indianapolis, South Bend, and Fort Wayne, Indiana; and Toledo, Columbus, and Cleveland, Ohio. Exhibit 6 shows a map of the CCX system indicating terminals, freight assembly centers, and meet-and-turn points. Every night between 11 P.M. and 3 A.M., freight is brought into these Centers from the various terminals, unloaded, sorted, and reloaded onto another trailer that is going to the final destination of the freight. Upon arriving at the Center and after checking in, drivers, who are paid by the mile on a line haul, begin working on an hourly basis until they resume driving back to their original terminal. The loading is done on a progressive basis rather than by staging the material by delivery sequence on the dock prior to loading. The driver salesman making deliveries to customers the next day determines the final delivery sequence.

EXHIBIT 6 Con-Way Central Express System map

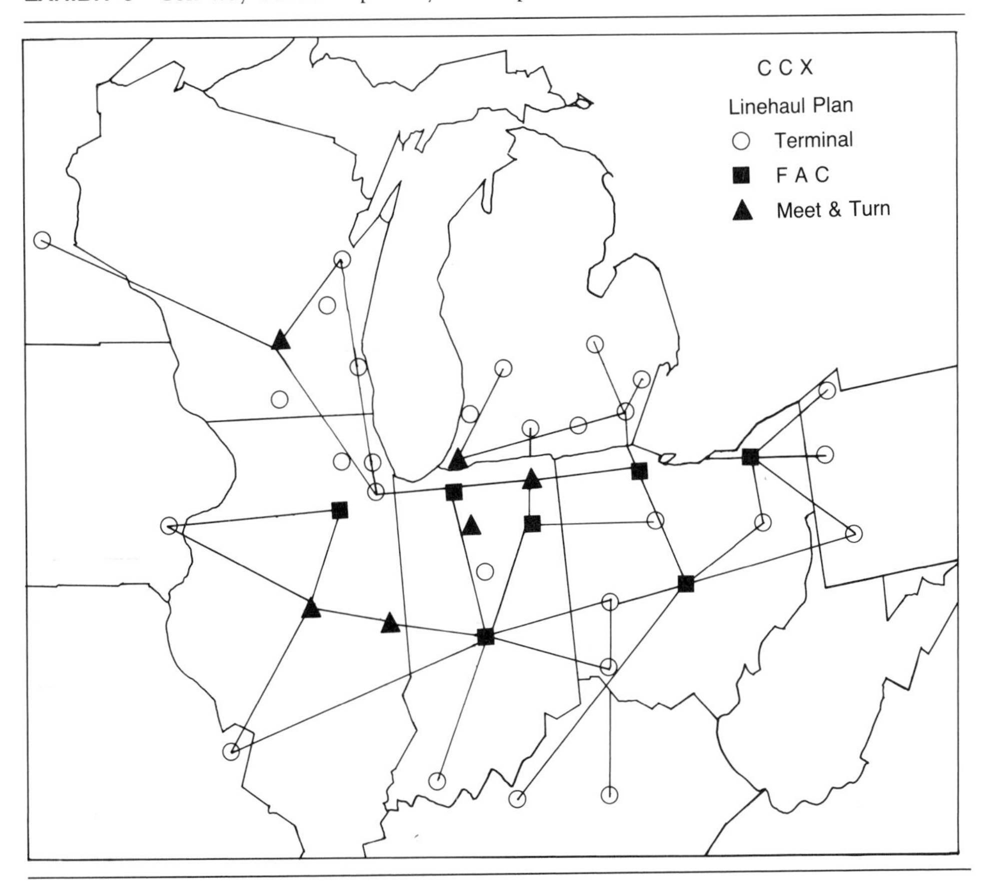

The control of line haul activities is the responsibility of Norm Wallace, the freight flow supervisor. He has three employees working for him at the central office in Ann Arbor. With the aid of the computer, they develop the line haul report, which is used to control truck operations transferring freight overnight. They balance pounds and linear feet of space—regardless of how high the freight is stacked—on each trailer in and out of each terminal by each "lane," which is the path between the terminals and/or centers. In case of an imbalance in one direction, an empty trailer will be sent along or carried back as circumstances may require. One of the key reports used in controlling shipments is the loading manifest shown in Exhibit 7. In 1987, line haul costs were 20.6 percent of revenues, and terminal costs were 54.5 percent of revenues.

Operations Control

Operations are controlled by a number of reports. The production report, known as the "244," is submitted daily and weekly (see Exhibit 8) by each terminal and is done by hand by the terminal manager or his assistant manager. This report goes to the regional managers, Dick Palazzo, and CFI's Portland, Oregon, computer center. The two operations assistants supervised by Tom Gerstenlauer, senior operations assistant, check the calculations, highlight substandard items, and send a rebuttal back to the regional managers about errors and problems. This activity shows the reports are actively being used. A monthly "244" report is submitted by each terminal manager within three days from the end of the month along with a trial income and expense statement. By the 13th to 15th of the month, a computer recap of the 244 is received by Dick Palazzo and, in turn, is transmitted to the terminals with comments.

Dick daily monitors the morning report, which includes revenue, wages, labor/wages, percent overtime, equipment out of service, number of shipments that did not move, any shipments not billed, and any bills that were brought back because they were not delivered. He also monitors the empty miles report, which shows the empty trailers and the lanes in which they occurred. The actual payroll figures are checked against the various reports, and the service factor is checked on a weekly basis in light of the on-time statistics. Annually, Dick sets revenue, productivity, labor, and claims goals for all terminals.

Another element of Dick Palazzo's job is handling new terminal expansion. The regional managers do a lot of the leg work, but Dick personally makes the final decisions and arranges for leases or purchases. A terminal is usually 50-feet wide and is leased by the door. The cost of leasing is about $150 per month per door. The cost of building a terminal is $18,000 per door. Originally, all terminals were leased, but now nine are owned through CFI.

The operations assistants conduct audits at each terminal with a goal of two per terminal per year. The audits cover all aspects of operations and operating statistics. The audits are written by hand in the field and are later typed with references to the master manual. The operations assistants also conduct seminars for clerical and supervisory personnel on a semi-annual or quarterly basis on such topics as handling hazardous materials, outbound loading, and handling OS&D (over, short, and damaged) freight. Another assistant is to be added in 1987.

EXHIBIT 7 Con-Way Central Express loading manifest

04145-QO (10/86)

LOADING MANIFEST

TRAILER NUMBER	MID	LOADING LOC. SIC	RESP RDC	TRAILER NUMBER	DEST SIC
	TCON			–	

DESTINATION	DATE	TOTAL WEIGHT	% CUBE	BILLS	TIME/DATE CLOSED	LOAD RELEASE NUMBER
		/	/			841501

ORIGIN	SWEPT	NAILS PULLED	HOLES REPAIRED	WHEELS CHOCKED

SPECIAL INSTRUCTIONS/REMARKS (38 CHARACTER LIMIT)

WEIGHT CARRIED FORWARD	CUBE	BILLS

LINE NO.	PIECES	WEIGHT	ID	H/M	PRO NUMBER	LINE NO.	PIECES	WEIGHT	ID	H/M	PRO NUMBER
1						23					
2						24					
3						25					
4						26					
5						27					
6						28					
7						29					
8						30					
9						31					
10						32					
11						33					
12						34					
13						35					
14						36					
15						37					
16						38					
17						39					
18						40					
19						41					
20						42					
21						43					
22						44					
SUB TOTAL ▶						SUB TOTAL ▶					

LOADING DIAGRAM (IDENTIFY MARKS)

TOP VIEW — NOSE / REAR — SIDE

SIDE VIEW — NOSE / REAR — BOTTOM

MARKS

1. C/ ______ D/ ______
2. C/ ______ D/ ______

TOTAL ▶		CUBE	BILLS

SEAL NUMBER	CHANGED SEAL NUMBER

HEATER: ☐ YES ☐ NO — UNIT NO.

PLACARDS: ☐ YES ☐ NO — TYPE

AUTHORITY:

DO NOT LOAD CLASS A OR B POISONS IN A TRAILER CONTAINING MATERIAL THAT IS MARKED AS OR KNOWN TO BE FOODSTUFF, FEED OR ANY OTHER EDIBLE MATERIAL INTENDED FOR CONSUMPTION BY HUMANS OR ANIMALS.

SPECIAL INSTRUCTIONS (TYPES OF HAZARDOUS MATERIAL) INFORMATION USEFUL TO UNLOADER CONCERNING LOAD, ETC.

EXHIBIT 8 Con-Way Central Express weekly production report

WEEKLY TERMINAL PRODUCTION and COST REPORT

04244-20 (3/83)

HAND WRITTEN PREFERABLE (LEGIBLE)

Terminal Cleveland OH. Code XCL Week Ending 5-16-87

FREIGHT HANDLING	LABOR				TONNAGE IN CWT UNITS				PERFORMANCE			
	A	B	C	D	E	F	G	H	I	J	K	L
FUNCTION	Std. Hrs.	Hrs. Worked	Prem. Hrs.	P/R Cost	Inbound CWT	Outbound CWT	Reship CWT	Total CWT	Std. Lbs./M.H.	Lbs/M.H.	Cost/CWT	$ Variance
1. Direct P&D 266	128	141	12 (24)	1904	3617	4720	XXXX	8337	6500	5913	.23	(310)
2. Cross Dock 379	541	582	16 (31)	6895	14878	14956	4229	34063	6300	5853	.20	(657)
3. City Liner P&D 262	933	1062	50 (98)	13955	14878	14956	XXXX	29843	3200	2810	.47	(2246)
4. Direct Peddle	XXXX	XXXX	XXXX	XXXX			XXXX		XXXX	XXXX	XXXX	XXXX
5. LTL Peddle 239							XXXX					
6. Frt. Not Handled	XXXX	XXXX	XXXX	XXXX			XXXX		XXXX	XXXX	XXXX	XXXX
7. Vol. Tsfr (Over 10M)	XXXX								XXXX			XXXX
8. Weekly Total	1602	1985	78 (153)	22754	18495	19676	4229	42400	XXXX	XXXX	.54	XXXX
9. LTL	XXXX	XXXX	XXXX	XXXX			XXXX		XXXX	XXXX	XXXX	XXXX

% OF CITY LINER AND PEDDLE CWT TO LTL CWT ______ % OF I/B AND O/B CROSS DOCK CWT TO LTL CWT ______ % DIRECT TONNAGE ______

OTHER TERMINAL ACTIVITIES	LABOR			HOOKS	PERFORMANCE		
	B	C	D	H	I	J	K
FUNCTION	Hrs. Worked	Prem. Hrs.	P/R Cost	Total Hooks	Std. Hks./Hrs.	Hooks/Hrs	Cost/Hooks
10. Hostling - Term Yard 382	15	-	177	98		6.5	1.81
11. Hostling - Pig/Pike 236							
12. Dispatch – L/H 212			XXXX				
13. Dispatch – P&D 226							
14. Term. & Bldg. Repairs 392							
15. Other Term. Labor *							
16. Weekly Total	15	-	177				

M — CITY LINER P&D STOPS: 2565 (2.13 · sph)

V. LOAD FACTOR		
No. of Trailers	Trailer Type	Avg. Load
	SEMI'S	
237	DUBS	11421

22. Explanation and Comments

2706674

(* *Hours entered on line 15 must be explained in this section.*)

OFFICE FUNCTION (Std. Bills/M.H.)	LABOR			PERFORMANCE	
	B	C	D	J	K
	Hrs. Worked	Prem. Hrs.	P/R Cost	Bill/M.H.	Cost/Bills
17. Billing 321 322	50	4 (4)	443	35	.26
18. Cashiering & Other 325 361 359 363	170	10 (16)	1476	XXXX	XXXX
19. Sub Total	220	14 (24)	1919	15	.57
20. Sales Clerical – Terminal 422				XXXX	XXXX
21. Weekly Total	220	14 (24)	1919	XXXX	XXXX

NUMBER OF BILLS

- E Inbound Bills 1600
- F Outbound Bills 1736
- G Billed for Other Term. 0
- Total Outbound Bills 1736
- H Total In & Out Bills 3336
- U Reship Bills 404

MARKETING REVENUE	E Total I/B Rev.	F Total O/B Rev.	Total I/O
Wkly.Ttl.Rev.	131936	130592	262528
Wkly.Qual.Rev.	129390	130592	XXXX
Qual. Rev. Quota	126206	124529	XXXX
Qual. % Quota	102.5	104.9	XXXX
Ttl. Rev. Cwt	7.13	6.64	XXXX
Ttl. Rev. Pr. Yr.	104982	106904	211886

RECEIVED
CON-WAY CENTRAL EXPRESS
MAY 19 1987
BY ______ YCO

% OVERTIME HOURS TO HOURS WORKED			
FUNCTION	HRS. WORKED	O.T. HOURS	%
Frt. Handling	1785	153	8.6
Oth. Term. Act.	15	-	0
Office	220	24	10.9

PAYROLL TO REVENUE SUMMARY		CURRENT WEEK	WEEK OF PRIOR YR.
N	Mean Revenue	128715	105562
P	Total Terminal Payroll	24850	19850
R	% P/R to Mean Revenue	19.3	18.8
	Std. % P/R to Rev.	20.0	-

Litho in U.S.A.

Claims control is another function of the Operations Department. In 1985, there were 3,580 claims for loss or damage paid for a total of $506,827. The ratio of paid claims to shipments was 1/164. The projected claims and payments for 1986 were expected to be 5,350 and $905,000, respectively. In light of the rapid increase in CCX's business, this projection if attained would actually amount to only 1 claim per 177 shipments.

EQUIPMENT AND MAINTENANCE

CCX's investment in equipment has grown substantially since 1983, as Table 4 verifies.

Each tractor costs about $40,000, and each trailer costs about $12,000. A tractor lasts about 750,000 miles or five years and requires a new engine at 400,000 miles. A dolly carries the front part of the double trailer much like the tractor does the lead trailer. A hostler is a small tractor-type vehicle that is used to move trailers around a Freight Assembly Center instead of using a road tractor.

At the end of 1986, CCX had ten service shops employing thirty-three mechanics to service the fleet of vehicles listed previously. Paul Applegate, director of maintenance, manages the maintenance activities through two field maintenance managers who do extensive traveling. Maintenance expenditures are distributed as follows: tractors: 56.1 percent, trailers: 33.3 percent, washing: 7.3 percent, and fork lifts: 3.3 percent.

Three system-wide maintenance meetings are held each year at different shops. A preventative maintenance program is carried out. Maintenance expenditures over $500 must be approved by Paul Applegate. Warranty claims are controlled and administered through a warranty clerk. Tractors are in use about 20 hours per day, except when they are in the shop for major maintenance.

PERSONNEL & SAFETY

Brian Tierney is the manager of personnel and safety. He is 33-years-old and has a degree in political science from Loyola University in New Orleans. He began working for CFI after graduation at the York, Pennsylvania, consolidation center, where he

TABLE 4 CCX's investment in equipment

	1983	*1986*
Tractors	43	621
Trailers	127	1524
Dollies	40	410
Fork lifts	11	113
Hostlers	0	10

Source: CCX internal documents.

participated in a training program that lasted for 45 weeks. After the program, he spent nine months as office manager in Philadelphia and four years in Portland, Oregon, as a member of the internal audit staff. He first met Jerry Detter in October 1977. Jerry had kept in touch and finally had asked Brian to join CCX. Initially, Brian did preliminary interviewing for terminal personnel recruited from blind ads and recommendations from CFI. Brian described the organization on June 20 when the first freight was hauled as a, "25-year-old trucking company with one day of experience."

One of Brian's key responsibilities is maintaining the personnel policy manual. One copy of the manual is kept in each terminal where employees can read it. When changes are made to the manual, all copies are returned to Ann Arbor and are updated simultaneously. These measures are taken to insure accuracy and to prevent the manual from falling into unfriendly hands such as the Teamsters. CCX retains the services of an Atlanta law firm that specializes in giving advice to non-union companies.

About 70 percent of Brian's time is spent on "crisis management," including such things as terminations and major accidents. The balance of his time is spent on planning things such as training sessions and the driver championship contest.

Safety is very important to CCX, considering that 50 million miles are driven each year. The Department of Transportation as well as state agencies have jurisdiction over trucking companies and do perform random inspections. Weekly comparisons are made by CCX regarding preventable accidents. Safety achievement awards are given yearly. The low accident frequency for 1986 is quite impressive: one per 750,000 road miles, one per 4,200 city driving hours, and one industrial injury per 8,300 hours worked. The safety program is carried out by two managers reporting to Brian Tierney.

CCX has a mandatory drug testing program. Each employee is tested once a year and is given thirty days notice of the test. Less than 3 percent of new employees and less than 1 percent of present employees test positive. Rehabilitation is stressed for those who are using drugs, and an unpaid leave is given to undergo rehabilitation.

About 80 percent of the work force for CCX is regular employees. The balance of the work force is supplemental employees. Since the trucking business is seasonal, with July and late December being the slowest periods, most companies lay off employees during these slow times. CCX does not lay off regular employees but rather discontinues supplemental employees. Supplemental employees usually move into regular employee status after six to nine months since CCX is expanding rapidly. This period gives CCX a good opportunity to evaluate each employee, and it gives the supplemental employee time to evaluate CCX as a permanent employer.

The pay levels are evaluated each June, and changes are made as indicated by competitive factors. Supplemental workers make $10.30 per hour. The hourly pay schedule for regular employees is shown in Table 5.

Overtime is not paid for line haul driving since the driver is paid by the mile. Overtime is paid for work in excess of 8 hours per day and 40 hours per week for local operations employees even though government regulations do not require it. Employee benefits include comprehensive health insurance covering major medical, dental, vision, and hospitalization; group life insurance; pension plan; tuition refund plan; stock

TABLE 5 Hourly pay schedule

	Drivers	*Mechanics*
Initial rate	$10.80	$12.40
After 6 Months	13.50*	
After 12 Months	11.70	
After 24 Months	12.40	
After 36 Months	13.50	

*A $.50 premium is paid to lead men.
Source: CCX internal documents.

purchase plan; a vacation plan of two weeks per year rising to three weeks at eight years and four weeks at fifteen years; nine paid holidays; sick leave; funeral leave; and jury duty leave. Uniforms for all employees are provided by CCX, which is also a valuable marketing tool since this practice is not common in the industry. Probably the most important benefit from the employee's standpoint is the Incentive Compensation Plan. Under this plan, CCX paid bonuses of $700,000 in 1984, $2,000,000 in 1985 and $3,200,000 in 1986, with individual employees receiving the maximum or close to the maximum provided for their wage level.

Supplemental employees are screened for drugs, their driver records are checked, a road test is given, and three interviews are held before they are hired. Each new employee is given one week's training working with four drivers and a supervisor. Upon attaining regular status, employees attend an orientation seminar for three days. It is conducted by Jerry Detter and his executive group and is designed to familiarize employees with personnel policies and procedures and company benefits and to establish an effective avenue for communications.

Regular employees are reviewed for job performance at 30-, 60-, 90-, and 180-day intervals, and yearly thereafter. The seven categories which are evaluated are job knowledge, work execution, job relationships, meeting job demands, dependability, job conduct, and safety. The evaluations are held privately on a face-to-face basis by the immediate supervisor.

CCX believes one of the key differences between itself and others in the industry is its emphasis on communication with its employees at all levels. CCX has an Employee Involvement Committee made up of Dick Palazzo, Paul Applegate, Brian Tierney, and three drivers from each region. This committee meets four times per year to discuss any subject of interest. CCX has an annual meeting for all sales and management personnel; about 200 attend, to review the year's performance. Regional meetings are held four times each year. They include a reception and dinner on Saturday night and a Sunday breakfast followed by a four-hour meeting for all regular employees of the region. About every six weeks, a Saturday morning breakfast followed by a two-hour discussion is held for the employees of each terminal. Attendance at these latter meetings is voluntary, but usually about 80 percent of the employees attend.

All of these meetings are designed to maintain the open communications needed in a union-free environment. In addition, Jerry Detter has a uniform, and he works on a dock or truck about every eight weeks to maintain first-hand contact with the work force.

FINANCE

Kevin Schick is the controller for CCX. He is 35-years-old and has a degree in accounting and finance from Marquette University and an MBA with a major in accounting from Northwestern University. Before joining CCX in April 1983, he had worked in various accounting positions for Motorola, Evans Products' transportation division (Monon Trailer), and MDSI in Ann Arbor.

Since the accounting activities for CCX are handled by CFI in Portland on their main frame computer, Kevin serves as a major liaison between CCX and Portland. He has a small staff of two clerks; one does accounts payable, and the other does capital expenditure appropriations and analysis work. Both work on spreadsheets using a PC computer. They help free Kevin's time for longer-term planning. Kevin does a one-year detailed financial plan plus four additional years of a strategic plan showing projected revenues, costs, capital expenditures, and net working capital. The input for this plan comes from regional and terminal managers, with Jerry Detter and his executive staff setting basic parameters such as tonnage and competitors' reactions. Kevin then puts in the detail assumptions working with Jerry, and to some extent with Dick Palazzo, on a one-to-one basis. The plans have worked out well: about 80 percent to 90 percent of the costs can be nailed down easily. Kevin reviews the final strategic plan with Jerry before submitting it to CFI.

Kevin says he has an entrepreneurial taste and fulfills the role of a "corporate wet blanket," which is the role often taken by the financial executive. He submits a weekly forecast compiled from various internal reports to the Portland computer center, which in turn submits it to CFI's home office in Palo Alto. Kevin also submits a "week that was" management report to Palo Alto which is really an exception report. Each month, after the books are closed, he prepares a monthly analysis for Jerry's signature to be sent to Palo Alto. Kevin also does a quarterly forecast on a rolling four quarter basis.

Kevin prepares the narrative for the capital expenditure report. One of CCX's advantages has been its easy access to capital through CFI. Both the payback method using two to three years and the net present value method using 15 percent are utilized in evaluating capital expenditures. CCX remitted 5.1 percent of its revenues to CFI in 1986 to cover the "interest on funds used." Kevin sees some tightening of capital availability from CFI occurring because other entities of CFI are requiring capital also. After all, CCX has become quite well established and must compete with other divisions.

When commenting on Jerry's leadership, Kevin says Jerry is the "spiritual leader of the drivers who can crawl inside the driver's mind." He believes Jerry's biggest value to CCX is his operational mind which can visualize the future. Kevin anticipates the shakeout in the trucking industry will continue for another three or four years. The service factor will be of prime importance to the customer.

THE FUTURE

When thinking about the future, Jerry Detter is just as enthusiastic as he is in describing the path of CCX thus far. Plans are under way to lease a new building being constructed near the present home office. Phase one will include 14,000 square feet, with phase two expanding to 20,000 square feet over a one-and-a-half year period. The new facility will include a training center for seventy-two people and a cafeteria and kitchen. CCX is paying the local Sheraton hotel so much for the frequent training sessions that a center for CCX can be justified. Thus far more than 1,300 employees have been trained. Proposed capital expenditure needs for 1987 are $20 million. Jerry is looking for a 25 percent market share of the Midwest trucking market within a few years. After that goal is reached? Well, Jerry Detter is never short of ideas!

ENDNOTES

1. Charles R. Perry, *Deregulation and the Decline of the Unionized Trucking Industry* (Philadelphia: Industrial Research Unit, The Wharton School, University of Pennsylvania, 1986), p. 27.

2. Ibid, p. 76.

THE AUDUBON ZOO—1987

CLAIRE J. ANDERSON
Loyola University
CAROLINE FISHER
Loyola University

The Audubon Zoo was the focus of national concern in the early 1970s. Well-documented stories told of animals kept in conditions described as an "animal ghetto",[1] "the New Orleans antiquarium," and even "an animal concentration camp."[2] In 1971, the Bureau of Governmental Research recommended a $5.6 million zoo improvement plan to the Audubon Park Commission and the City Council of New Orleans. The local *Times Picayune* commented on the new Zoo: "It's not going to be quite like the 'Planet of the Apes' situation in which the apes caged and studied human beings but something along those broad general lines".[3] The new Zoo confined

The authors wish to acknowledge the contributions of graduate students Martha McGraw Hamilton and Devvie Longo who aided in the research and who contributed many helpful suggestions in the development of the case. This case was designed for classroom discussion only. It was not meant to depict effective or ineffective handling of administrative situations.

people to bridges and walkways while the animals roamed amidst grass, shrubs, trees, pools, and fake rocks. The gracefully curving pathways, generously lined with luxuriant plantings, gave the visitor a sense of being alone in a wilderness, although crowds of visitors might be only a few yards away.

THE DECISION

The Aubudon Park Commission launched a $5.6 million development program, based on the Bureau of Governmental Research plan for the Zoo, in March 1972. A bond issue and a property tax dedicated to the Zoo were put before the voters, with renovations to begin the day following passage. The New Orleans City Planning Commission finally approved the master plan for the Aubudon Park Zoo in September 1973. But the institution of the master plan was far from smooth.

The Zoo Question Goes Public

A revenue-generating proposal was put to the voters by Mayor Moon Landrieu on Nov. 7, 1972. When it passed by an overwhelming majority, serious discussions began about what should be done. Over two dozen special interests were ultimately involved in choosing whether to renovate/expand the existing facilities or move to another site. Expansion became a major community controversy. Some residents opposed the zoo expansion, fearing "loss of green space" would affect the secluded character of the neighborhood. Others opposed the loss of what they saw as an attractive and educational facility.

Most of the opposition came from the Zoo's affluent neighbors. Zoo Director John Moore ascribed the criticism to "a select few people who have the money and power to make a lot of noise." He went on to say "[T]he real basis behind the problem is that the neighbors who live around the edge of the park have a selfish concern because they want the park as their private backyard."[4] Legal battles over the expansion plans continued until early 1976. At that time, the 4th Circuit Court of Appeals ruled that the expansion was legal.[5] An out-of-court agreement with the Zoo's neighbors (The Upper Audubon Association) followed shortly.

Physical Facilities

The expansion of the Audubon Park Zoo took it from 14 to 58 acres. The Zoo was laid out in geographic sections: the Asian Domain, World of Primates, World's Grasslands, Savannah, North American Prairie, South American Pampas, and Louisiana Swamp, according to the Zoo Master Plan developed by the Bureau of Governmental Research. Additional exhibits included the Wisner Discovery Zoo, Sea Lion Exhibit, and Flight Cage. See Exhibit 1 for a map of the new Zoo.

EXHIBIT 1 A map of the Audubon Park Zoo

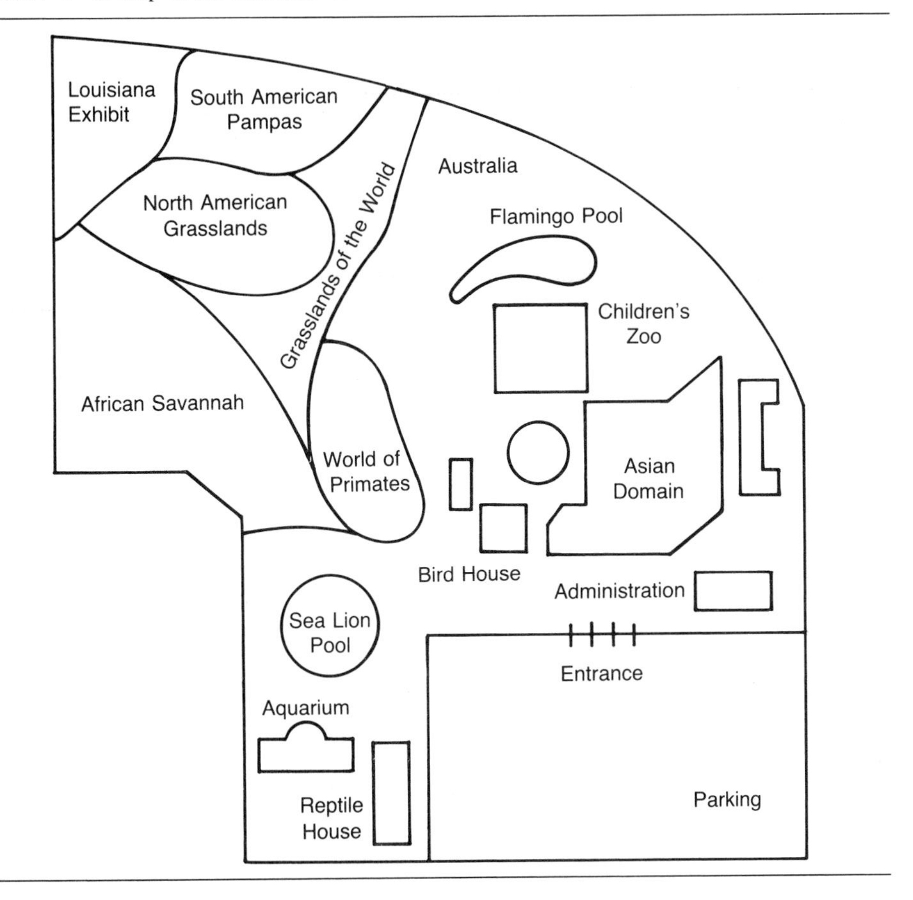

PURPOSE OF THE ZOO

The main outward purpose of the Audubon Park Zoo was entertainment. Many of the promotional efforts of the Zoo were aimed at creating an image of the Zoo as an entertaining place to go. Obviously, such a campaign was necessary to attract visitors to the Zoo. Behind the scenes, the Zoo also preserved and bred many animal species, conducted research, and educated the public.

NEW DIRECTIONS

One of the first significant changes made was the institution of an admission charge in 1972. Admission to the Zoo had been free to anyone prior to the adoption of the renovation plan. Ostensibly, the initial purpose behind instituting the admission

EXHIBIT 2 Number of admissions and admission charges

Year	Number of Paid Admissions	Number of Member Admissions	Admission Charges	
			Adult	Child
1972	163,000		$0.75	$0.25
1973	310,000			
1974	345,000			
1975	324,000			
1976	381,000			
1977	502,000			
1978	456,000		1.00	0.50
1979	561,000		1.50	0.75
1980	707,000		2.00	1.00
1981	741,000		2.50	1.25
1982	740,339	78,950	3.00	1.50
1983	835,044	118,665	3.50	1.75
1984	813,025	128,538	4.00	2.00
1985	854,996	144,060	4.50	2.00
1986	915,492	187,119	5.00	2.50
1987	439,264*	93,327*		

*Through the end of the second quarter
Source: The Audubon Zoo.

charge was to prevent vandalism,[6] but the need for additional income was also apparent. Despite the institution of and increases in admission charges, admissions numbers increased dramatically (see Exhibit 2).

OPERATIONS

Friends of the Zoo

The Friends of the Zoo was formed in 1974 and incorporated in 1975 with 400 original members. The stated purpose of the Friends was to increase support and awareness of the Audubon Park Zoo. Initially, the Friends of the Zoo tried to increase interest and commitment to the Zoo, but the group's activities increased dramatically over the following years to where it was involved in funding, operating, and governing the Zoo.

The Friends of the Zoo had a 24-member governing board. Yearly elections were held for six members of the Board who served four-year terms. The Board oversaw the policies of the Zoo and set guidelines for memberships, concessions, fund raising, and marketing. Actual policy-making and operations were controlled by the Audubon

Park Commission, however, which set policies such as Zoo hours and admission prices.

Through its volunteer programs, the Friends of the Zoo staffed many of the Zoo's programs. Volunteer members of the Friends of the Zoo served as "edZOOcators," education volunteers who were specially trained to conduct interpretive education programs, and "Zoo Area Patrollers," who provided general information about a geographic area of the Zoo and helped with crowd control. Other volunteers assisted in the Commissary, Animal Health Care Center, and Wild Bird Rehabilitation Center or helped with membership, public relations, graphics, clerical work, research, or horticulture.

Fund Raising

The Audubon Park Zoo and the Friends of the Zoo raised funds through five major types of activities: Friends of the Zoo membership, concessions, Adopt An Animal, Zoo-To-Do, and capital fund drives. Zoo managers from around the country came to the Audubon Park Zoo for tips on fund raising.

Membership

Membership in the Friends of the Zoo was open to anyone. The membership fees increased over the years, as summarized in Exhibit 3. Yet, the number of members increased steadily, from the original 400 members in 1974 to 33,000 members in 1987. Membership allowed free entry to the Audubon Park Zoo and many other zoos around the United States. Participation in Zoobilation (evenings at the Zoo for annual members only) and the involvement in the many volunteer programs described earlier were other benefits of membership.

EXHIBIT 3 Membership fees and membership

Year	*Family Membership Fees*	*Individual Membership Fees*	*Number of Memberships*
1979	$20	$10	1,000
1980	20	10	7,000
1981	20	10	11,000
1982	25	15	18,000
1983	30	15	22,000
1984	35	20	26,000
1985	40	20	30,000
1986	45	25	32,000
1987	45	25	33,000

Source: The Audubon Zoo.

Increasing membership required a special approach to marketing the Zoo. Chip Weigand, director of marketing for the Zoo, stated

> . . . [I]n marketing memberships we try to encourage repeat visitations, the feeling that one can visit as often as one wants, the idea that the Zoo changes from visit to visit and that there are good reasons to make one large payment or donation for a membership card, rather than paying for each visit. . . [T]he overwhelming factor is a good zoo that people want to visit often, so that a membership makes good economical sense.

In 1985, the Zoo announced a new membership designed for businesses, the Audubon Zoo Curator Club, with four categories of membership: Bronze, $ 250; Silver, $ 500; Gold, $ 1000; and Platinum, $ 2500 and more.

Concessions

The Friends of the Zoo took over the Audubon Park Zoo concessions for refreshments and gifts in 1976, through a public bidding process. The concessions were run by volunteer members of the Friends of the Zoo, and all profits went directly to the Zoo. Prior to 1976, concession rentals brought in $15,000 in a good year. Profits from operation of the concessions by the Friends of the Zoo brought in $400,000 a year by 1980, and the concessions were budgeted to bring in more than $900,000 in profits for 1987.

Adopt An Animal

Zoo Parents paid a fee to "adopt" an animal; the fee varied with the animal chosen. Zoo Parents' names were listed on a large sign inside the Zoo. They also had their own celebration, Zoo Parents Day, held at the Zoo yearly.

Zoo-To-Do

Zoo-To-Do was a black-tie fund raiser held annually with live music, food and drink, and original, high-class souvenirs such as posters or ceramic necklaces. Admission tickets, limited to 3,000 annually, were priced starting at $100 per person. A raffle was conducted in conjunction with the Zoo-To-Do, with raffle items varying from an opportunity to be Zoo Curator for the day to the use of a Mercedes Benz for a year. Despite the rather stiff price, the Zoo-To-Do was a popular sellout every year. Local restaurants and other businesses donated most of the necessary supplies, decreasing the cost of the affair. In 1985, the Zoo-To-Do raised almost $500,000 in one night, more money than any other non-medical fund raiser in the country.[7]

Advertising

The Audubon Zoo launched impressive marketing campaigns in the 1980s. The Zoo received ADDY awards from the New Orleans Advertising Club year after year.[8] In 1986, the film "Urban Eden," produced by Alford Advertising and Buckholtz Productions Inc. in New Orleans, finished first among forty entries in the "documentary films, public relations" category of the 8th Annual Houston International Film Festival. The first place Gold Award recognized the film for vividly portraying the Audubon Zoo as a conservation, rather than a confining, environment.

During the same year, local television affiliates of ABC, CBS, and NBC produced independent TV spots using the theme "One of the World's Greatest Zoos Is in Your

Own Back Yard . . . Audubon Zoo!" Along with some innovative views of the Audubon Zoo being in someone's backyard," local news anchor personalities enjoyed "monkeying around" with the animals, and the Zoo enjoyed some welcome free exposure.[9]

In 1986 and 1987, the advertising budgets were a little more than $150,000, the total public relations budgets were more than $300,000, and the total marketing budgets were more than $1 million each year, including salaries. The marketing budgets included development or fund raising and membership as well as public relations and advertising. Percentage breakdowns of the public relations budget for 1987 can be found in Exhibit 4.

The American Association of Zoological Parks and Aquariums reported that most zoos find the majority of their visitors live within a single population center in close proximity to the park.[10] Thus, in order to sustain attendance over the years, zoos must attract the same visitors repeatedly. A large number of the Zoo's promotional programs and special events were aimed at achieving that goal.

Progress was slow among non-natives. For example, Simon Schuster, a reputed publishing firm, in its 218-page 1983–84 *Guide to New Orleans,* managed only a three-

EXHIBIT 4 Public relations and media budgets (by percentage of total expenditures)

Category	*1986*	*1987*
Salaries and overtime		24.3
Education, travel and subscriptions		1.1
Printing and duplicating		2.4
Professional services		1.5
Tourist brochures for hotel rooms		3.6
Special events		24.1
News releases		0.4
Entertainment		0.7
Photography		0.9
Miscellaneous supplies		0.6
Advertising		40.3
Media Budgets		
TV and radio	28.0	46.3
Special promotion contingency	32.3	13.2
Tourist publications	10.5	9.2
Streetcar and bus	6.9	7.3
Magazines	4.2	5.0
Newspaper		1.1
Production	18.1	17.8

Source: The Audubon Zoo.

word allusion to a "very nice zoo." A 1984 study found that only 36 percent of the visitors were tourists, and even this number was probably influenced to some extent by an overflow from the World's Fair.

Promotional Programs

The Audubon Park Zoo and the Friends of the Zoo conducted a multitude of very successful promotional programs. The effect was to have continual parties and celebrations going on, attracting a variety of people to the Zoo (and raising additional revenue). Exhibit 5 lists the major annual promotional programs conducted by the Zoo.

In addition to these annual promotions, the Zoo scheduled concerts of well-known musicians, such as Irma Thomas, Pete Fountain, The Monkeys, and Manhattan Transfer, and other special events throughout the year. As a result, a variety of events occurred each month.

EXHIBIT 5 Audubon Park Zoo promotional programs

Title (Activity)	*Month(s)*
Photography Contest	January
Fit for Life (Aerobics)	March
Zoo-To-Do for Kids	April
Easter Family Days	April
Zoo-To-Do	May
Musical Zoo Revue (Symphony Concert)	May
Summer Concert Series	April to August
Breakfast with the Beasts	June
Ice Cream Sunday	June
Zoobilation (Members Party)	June
Play-Doh Invitational (Architects compete with Play-Doh designs)	June
Teddy Bear Affair (Teddy Bear Contests)	August
Press Party	September
Symphony Run	September
Louisiana Swamp Festival	October
Halloween	October
Beast Ballet (Ballet Performance)	November
Annual Essay Contest	November
Holiday Celebration	December
Annual Members' Christmas Sale	December

Source: The Audubon Zoo.

Many educational activities were conducted all year long. These included (1) a Junior Zoo Keeper program for seventh and eighth graders, (2) a Student-Intern program for high school and college students, and (3) a ZOOmobile, which took live animals to such locations as special education classes, hospitals, and old age homes.

Admission Policy

The Audubon Park Commission recommended the institution of an admission charge. Arguments against such a charge generally held that it results in an overall decline in attendance and a reduction of non-gate revenues. Proponents held that gate charges control vandalism, produce greater revenues, and result in increased public awareness and appreciation of the facility. In the early 1970s, no major international zoo failed to charge admission, and 73 percent of the 125 United States zoos charged admission.

The commission argued there is no such thing as a free zoo; someone must pay. If the Zoo is tax supported, then locals carry a disproportionate share of the cost. At the time, neighboring Jefferson Parish was growing by leaps and bounds and surely would bring a large, non-paying constituency to the new Zoo. Further, as most zoos are tourist attractions, the commission felt tourists should pay since they contribute little to the local tax revenues.

The average yearly attendance for a zoo may be estimated using projected population figures multiplied by a "visitor generating factor." The average visitor generating factor of 14 zoos similar in size and climate to the Audubon Zoo was 1.34, with a rather wide range from a low of .58 in the cities of Phoenix and Miami to a high of 2.80 in Jackson, Mississippi.

Attracting More Tourists and Other Visitors

A riverboat ride on the romantic paddle-wheeled *Cotton Blossom* took visitors from downtown to the Zoo. Originally, the trip began at a dock in the French Quarter, but the departure point was later moved to a dock immediately adjacent to New Orleans' newest attraction, the Riverwalk, a Rouse development, on the site of the 1984 Louisiana World Exposition. Not only was the riverboat ride great fun, but it also lured tourists and conventioneers from the downtown attractions of the French Quarter and the new Riverwalk to the Zoo, some six miles upstream. A further allure of the riverboat ride was a return trip to downtown on the New Orleans Streetcar, one of the few remaining trolley cars in the United States. The Zoo Cruise not only drew more visitors, but it also generated additional revenue—through landing fees paid by the New Orleans Steamboat company—and kept traffic out of uptown New Orleans.[11]

FINANCIAL STATUS

The Zoo's ability to generate operating funds has been ascribed to the dedication of the Friends of the Zoo, continued increases in attendance, and creative special events and programs. A history of adequate operating funds allowed the Zoo to guarantee

EXHIBIT 6 Operating budget

Year	*Operating Budget*	*Gov't. Support*	*Self-Generated*
1978	$1,700,000	$700,000	$1,000,000
1980	2,800,000	840,000	1,960,000
1986	4,469,000	460,000	4,009,000

Source: The Audubon Zoo.

capital donors that their gifts would be used to build and maintain top-notch exhibits. See Exhibit 6 for sources of operating budgets over the years. The 1986 combined balance sheet and statement of revenue and expense for the Park Commission are in Exhibits 7 and 8.

Capital Fund Drives

The Audubon Zoo Development Fund was established in 1973. Corporate/Industrial support of the Zoo has been very strong—many corporations have underwritten construction of Zoo displays and facilities. A partial list of major corporate sponsors is in Exhibit 9. A sponsorship was considered to be for the life of the exhibit. The development department operated on a 12 percent overhead rate, which meant 88 cents of every dollar raised went toward the projects. By 1987, the Master Plan for development had been 75 percent completed. The fund raising goal for 1987 was $1,600,000.

MANAGEMENT

The Zoo Director

Ron Forman, Audubon Zoo director, was called a "zoomaster extraordinaire" and was described by the press as a "cross between Doctor Doolittle and the Wizard of Oz," as a "practical visionary" and as "serious, but with a sense of humor."[12] A native New Orleanian, Mr. Forman quit an MBA program to join the city government as an administrative assistant and found himself doing a business analysis project on the Audubon Park. Once the city was committed to a new Zoo, Forman was placed on board as an assistant to the Zoo director, John Moore. In early 1977, Moore gave up the battle between the "animal people" and the "people-people,"[13] and Forman took over as Park and Zoo director.

Forman was said to bring an MBA-meets-menagerie style to the Zoo, which was responsible for transforming the zoo from a public burden into an almost completely self-sustaining operation. The result not only benefited the citizens of the city, but also added a major tourist attraction to the economically troubled city of the 1980s.

EXHIBIT 7 Audubon Park Commission combined balance sheet (December 31, 1986)

	Operating Fund	*Enterprise Fund*	*Designated Funds*	*Total*
Assets				
Current Assets				
Cash				
Noninterest-bearing	$ 12,108	$ 0	$ 131,411	$ 143,519
Interest-bearing	306,483	0	0	306,483
Time certificates of deposit	301,493	0	107,402	408,895
Investments	100	0	0	100
Accounts receivable:				
Friends of the Zoo, Inc.	321,774	0	1,177	322,951
Other	13,240	7,842	75,698	96,780
Due from Operating Fund	0	309,208	320,463	629,671
Due from Enterprise Fund	0	0	300,000	300,000
Due from other designated funds	0	0	66,690	66,690
Prepaid expenses	166,862	3,371	0	170,233
Total Current Assets	**1,122,060**	**320,421**	**1,002,841**	**2,445,322**
Fixed Assets				
Equipment	0	159,455	0	159,455
Less accumulated depreciation	0	75,764	0	75,764
Total Fixed Assets	**0**	**83,691**	**0**	**83,691**
Total Assets	**$1,122,060**	**$404,112**	**$1,002,841**	**$2,529,013**
Liabilities				
Cash overdraft	$ 39,700	$ 0	$ 0	$ 39,700
Accounts payable:				
City of New Orleans	267,185	0	0	267,185
Friends of the Zoo, Inc.	0	72,658	0	72,658
Other	68,805	7,099	0	75,904
Payroll taxes payable	14,337	0	0	14,337
Accrued salaries	7,973	1,579	0	9,552
Due to Operating Fund	0	0	46,899	46,899
Due to Enterprise Fund	309,208	0	0	309,208
Due to designated funds	273,564	300,000	0	573,564
Due to other designated funds	0	0	66,690	66,690
Total Liabilities	**980,772**	**381,336**	**113,589**	**1,475,697**
Fund Equities				
Fund balances	141,288	0	889,252	1,030,540
Retained earnings	0	22,776	0	22,776
Total Fund Equities	**141,288**	**22,776**	**889,252**	**1,053,316**
Total Liabilities and Fund Equities	**$1,122,060**	**$404,112**	**$1,002,841**	**$2,529,013**

EXHIBIT 8 Audubon Park Commission statement of revenue, expenditures and changes in operating fund balance—Actual and budgeted (Year ended December 31, 1986)

	Annual Budget	*Actual*	*Percent of Budget*
Revenue			
Intergovernmental			
City of New Orleans	$ 600,000	$ 450,000	75.0%
State of Louisiana	25,000	10,913	43.7
Other governmental	25,000	0	0.0
Total Intergovernmental	**650,000**	**460,913**	**70.9**
Charges for Services			
Animal rides	115,000	127,671	111.0
Binocular receipts	4,000	2,604	65.1
Education programs	10,000	930	9.3
Events	10,000	4,701	47.0
Food and drink	458,000	569,259	124.3
Gift Shops	140,000	136,369	97.4
Mombasa Railroad	40,000	40,030	100.1
Race fees	30,000	30,844	102.8
Swimming pool	17,000	15,992	94.1
Tennis	0	10,167	0.0
Train	10,000	0	0.0
Travel program	14,000	5,508	39.3
Zoo admissions	2,420,000	2,718,254	112.3
Total Charges for Services	**3,268,000**	**3,662,329**	**112.1**
Interest Income	**10,000**	**34,867**	**348.7**
Miscellaneous			
Animal sales	10,000	38,446	384.5
Aquarium campaign	0	124	0.0
Friends of the Zoo	525,000	640,869	122.1
Miscellaneous	12,000	8,569	71.4
Riverboat	35,000	36,278	103.7
Stables	8,400	7,887	93.9
Total Miscellaneous	**590,400**	**732,173**	**124.0**
Total Revenue	**4,518,400**	**4,890,282**	**108.2%**

EXHIBIT 8 continued

Expenditures	*Annual Budget*	*Actual*	*Percent of Budget*
Personal Services			
Life insurance	$ 2,000	$ 23,106	1,155.3
Medical insurance	100,000	103,321	103.3
Pension	150,000	160,543	107.0
Payroll taxes	198,000	155,961	78.8
Salaries—Regular	1,883,652	1,959,205	104.0
Salaries—Overtime	59,570	61,937	104.0
Terminal leave	10,000	1,169	11.7
Uniform allowance	19,900	17,287	86.9
Workmen's compensation	50,000	38,779	77.6
Total Personal Services	**2,473,122**	**2,521,308**	**101.9**
Contractual Services			
Advertising	131,200	111,863	85.3
Aquarium	90,000	248,082	275.6
Building repairs	5,400	18,790	348.0
Communications	100	166	166.0
Convention and travel	29,950	32,445	108.3
Delivery and parking	10,850	12,639	116.5
Dues and subscriptions	7,910	7,636	96.5
Duplicating services	14,500	5,021	34.6
Entertainment	5,800	12,350	212.9
Equipment rental	22,750	12,215	53.7
Insurance	260,000	254,079	97.7
Laboratory services	8,100	9,762	120.5
License fees	550	1,108	201.5
Minor repairs	10,300	12,265	119.1
News releases	6,000	1,551	25.9
Penguins	0	10,957	0.0
Personal contracts	46,200	0	0.0
Postage and freight	40,350	33,322	82.6
Printing	18,700	9,207	49.2
Professional services	342,890	362,050	105.6
Swimming pool	48,000	42,835	89.2
Telephone	40,000	50,634	126.6
Utilities	40,000	41,902	104.8
Vehicle repairs	10,000	12,307	123.1
Waste removal	18,800	18,011	95.8
Total Contractual Services	**1,208,350**	**1,321,197**	**109.3**

EXHIBIT 8 continued

Expenditures	*Annual Budget*	*Actual*	*Percent of Budget*
Supplies and Materials			
Amphitheater	$ 3,400	$ 2,264	66.6
Art and essay	900	518	57.6
Artifacts	1,000	0	0.0
Building supplies	57,750	63,151	109.4
Display supplies	32,100	17,172	53.5
Educational supplies	10,050	49,626	493.8
Electrical supplies	10,300	25,283	245.5
Events	50,200	45,989	91.6
Feed and forage	187,780	172,398	91.8
Fuel	38,000	23,874	62.8
Graphics supplies	4,500	8,152	181.2
Hand tools	4,000	3,120	78.0
Horticultural supplies	20,000	17,788	88.9
Hospital and laboratory supplies	15,300	13,711	89.6
Janitorial and cleaning	51,500	50,018	97.1
Junior keeper	500	817	163.4
Medical supplies	1,750	1,300	74.3
Minor equipment	28,950	30,384	105.0
Motor vehicle supplies	30,000	10,285	34.3
Office supplies	34,150	29,768	87.2
Photographic supplies	5,150	6,138	119.2
Plants, shrubs, and trees	18,300	16,574	90.6
Police supplies	1,500	3,128	208.5
Public information	0	638	0.0
Read the Zoo	7,000	7,675	109.6
Safari carts	3,000	1,136	37.9
Special education	10,000	12,731	127.3
Teacher inservice	6,000	2,562	42.7
Uniforms	5,060	4,329	85.6
Zoomobile	3,000	1,138	37.9
Total Supplies and Materials	**641,140**	**621,667**	**97.0**

EXHIBIT 8 continued

Expenditures	*Annual Budget*	*Actual*	*Percent of Budget*
Equipment			
Animals	$ 22,400	$ 14,359	64.1
Automotive	40,000	56,722	141.8
Communications	1,150	847	73.7
Construction projects	50,000	32,418	64.8
Educational and recreational	0	96	0.0
General plant	7,000	5,621	80.3
Hospital and medical	4,200	2,947	70.2
Office furniture and equipment	8,500	35,897	422.3
Total Equipment	**133,250**	**148,907**	**111.8**
Other Expenditures			
Claims	12,000	10,385	86.5
Miscellaneous	1,000	19,461	1,946.1
Total Other Expenditures	**13,000**	**29,846**	**229.6**
Total Expenditures	**4,468,862**	**4,642,925**	**103.9**
Excess of Revenue over Expenditures	**49,538**	**247,357**	**499.3**
Other Financing Uses			
Operating transfers out	49,538	150,000	302.8
Excess of Revenue and Other Financing Sources over Expenditures and Other Uses	$ 0	**97,357**	
Operating Fund Balance at Beginning of Year		**43,931**	
Operating Fund Balance at End of Year		**$ 141,288**	

Staffing

The Zoo used two classes of employees: civil service, through the Audubon Park Commission, and non-civil service. The civil service employees included the curators and zoo keepers. They fell under the jurisdiction of the city civil service system. Employees who worked in such areas as public relations, advertising, concessions, and fund raising were hired through the Friends of the Zoo and were not part of the civil service system. See Exhibit 10 for further data on staffing patterns.

EXHIBIT 9 Major corporate sponsors

Amoco Corporation
American Express
J. Aron and Company
Breaux Mart
Chevron USA, Inc.
Conoco, Inc.
Consolidated Natural Gas Corporation
D. H. Holmes, Ltd.
Dr. G. H. Tichenor Antiseptic Company
Exxon Corporation
First National Bank of Commerce
Freeport-McMoran, Inc.
Frischhertz Electric Company
Goudchaux/Maison Blanche
Hibernia National Bank
Kentwood Spring Water
Louisiana Coca-Cola Bottling Company, Ltd.
Louisiana Land and Exploration Company
McDonald's Operations of New Orleans
William B. Reily and Company
Texaco USA
Trammell Crow Company
Wendy's of New Orleans
Whitney National Bank
Frank B. Williams and Company

Source: The Audubon Zoo.

THE ZOO IN THE LATE 80s

A visitor to the new Audubon Zoo could quickly see why New Orleanians were so proud of their Zoo. In a city that has a reputation as one of the dirtiest in the nation, the Zoo was virtually spotless. The Zoo's cleanliness was a result of adequate staffing and the clear pride of both those who worked at and those who visited the zoo. One of the first points made by volunteers guiding school groups was that anyone seeing a piece of trash on the ground must pick it up.[14] A 1986 city poll showed that 93 percent of the citizens surveyed gave the Zoo a high approval rating—an extremely high rating for any public facility.

Kudos came from groups outside the local area as well. Delegates from the American Association of Zoological Parks and Aquariums ranked the Audubon Zoo as one

EXHIBIT 10 Employee Structure

Year	*Number of Paid Employees*	*Number of Volunteers*
1972	36	
1973	49	
1974	69	
1975	90	
1976	143	
1977	193	
1978	184	
1979	189	
1980	198	
1981	245	
1982	305	
1983	302	56
1984	419	120
1985	454	126
1986	426	250
1987	358*	287*

*Through the end of the second quarter
Source: The Audubon Zoo.

of the three top zoos of its size in America. In 1982, the American Association of Nurserymen gave the Zoo a Special Judges Award for its use of plant materials. In 1985, the Audubon Park Zoo received the Phoenix Award from the Society of American Travel Writers for its achievements in conservation, preservation, and beautification.

By 1987, the Zoo was virtually self-sufficient. The small amount of money received from government grants amounted to less than 10 percent of the budget. The Master Plan for the development of the Zoo was 75 percent complete, and the reptile exhibit was scheduled for completion in the fall. The organization had expanded with a full complement of professionals and managers. (See Exhibit 11 for the organizational structure of the Zoo.)

While the Zoo made great progress in 15 years, all was not quiet on the political front. In a court battle, the city won over the state on the issue of who wielded ultimate authority over Audubon Park and Zoo. Indeed, the Zoo benefited from three friendly mayors in a row, starting with Moon Landrieu, who championed the new Zoo, to Ernest "Dutch" Morial, to the 1987 mayor, Sidney Barthelemy, who threw his support to both the Zoo and a proposed aquarium, championed by Ron Forman.

EXHIBIT 11 Organizational structure of the Audubon Park Zoo

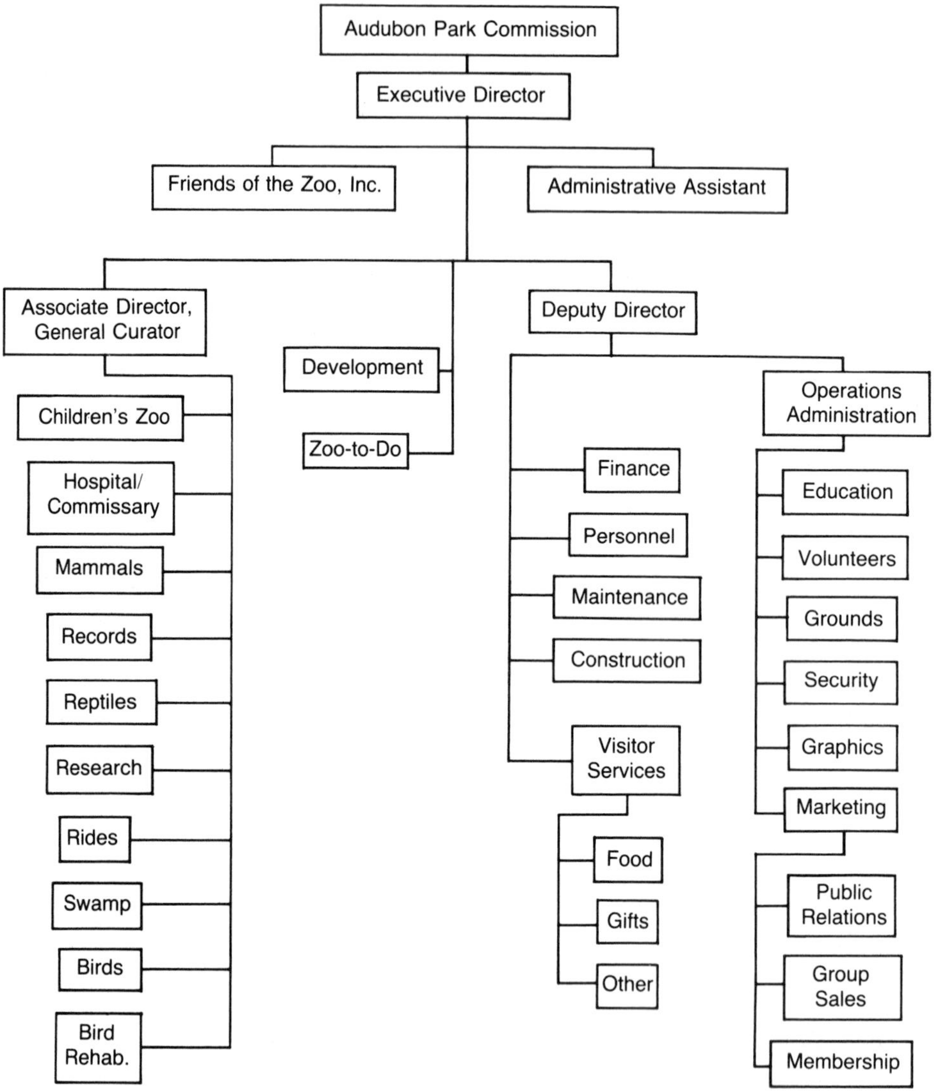

- Audubon Park Commission
  - Executive Director
    - Friends of the Zoo, Inc.
    - Administrative Assistant
    - Associate Director, General Curator
      - Children's Zoo
      - Hospital/ Commissary
      - Mammals
      - Records
      - Reptiles
      - Research
      - Rides
      - Swamp
      - Birds
      - Bird Rehab.
    - Development
    - Zoo-to-Do
    - Deputy Director
      - Finance
      - Personnel
      - Maintenance
      - Construction
      - Visitor Services
        - Food
        - Gifts
        - Other
      - Operations Administration
        - Education
        - Volunteers
        - Grounds
        - Security
        - Graphics
        - Marketing
          - Public Relations
          - Group Sales
          - Membership

THE FUTURE

New Directions for the Zoo

Zoo Director, Ron Forman, demonstrated that zoos have almost unlimited potential. A 1980 *New Orleans* magazine article cited some of Forman's ideas, ranging from a safari train to a breeding center for rare animals. The latter has an added attraction as a potential money-maker, since an Asiatic lion cub, for example, sells for around $10,000. This wealth of ideas was important because expanded facilities and programs are required to maintain attendance at any public attraction. The most ambitious of Forman's ideas was for an aquarium and riverfront park to be located at the foot of Canal Street.

Although the Zoo enjoyed political support in 1987, New Orleans was suffering from a high unemployment rate and a generally depressed economy resulting from the depression in the oil industry. Some economists were predicting the beginning of a gradual turnaround in 1988, but any significant improvement in the economy was forecasted to be years away. In addition, the Zoo operated in a city where many attractions competed for the leisure dollar of citizens and visitors. The Audubon Zoological Garden had to vie with the French Quarter, Dixieland jazz, the Superdome, and even the greatest of all attractions in the city—Mardi Gras.

The New Orleans Aquarium

In 1986, Forman and a group of supporters proposed the development of an aquarium and riverfront park to the New Orleans City Council. In November 1986, the electorate voted to fund an aquarium and a riverfront park by a 70 percent margin—one of the largest margins the city has ever given to any tax proposal. Forman[15] hailed this response as a vote of confidence from the citizens as well as a mandate to build a world-class aquarium that would produce new jobs, stimulate the local economy, and create an educational resource for the children of the city.

Even after the approval of the bond proposal by the voters, the New Orleans City Council had many decisions to make. Up for grabs was the management structure of the aquarium. Should it be placed within the same organization as the Audubon Zoo or under a separate structure? Where should the aquarium be located, and how large should it be?

A feasibility study prepared by Harrison Price Company[16] projected a probable 863,000 visitors by the year 1990, with 75 percent of the visitors coming from outside the metropolitan area. The location of the new aquarium was to be adjacent to the Riverwalk, providing a logical pedestrian link for visitors between New Orleans' major attractions, the Riverwalk and the Jax Brewery (a shopping center in the French Quarter).

The aquarium would face major confrontations from several interest groups: riverfront developers, the Vieux Carre Commission (preservationists of the Old French Quarter), the Dock Board (responsible for riverfront property usage), the National Park Service, and businesses from downtown and other parts of the city. Several of these groups argued that the proposed site was not safe from river accidents. One counter-plan was for the aquarium to be located on the west bank of the Mississippi River. The west bank, while a part of metropolitan New Orleans, was accessible from downtown only by two major bridges and ferry boats. The east bank of the city contained the major tourist and visitor attractions: the French Quarter, Convention Center, Lakefront (Lake Pontchartrain) restaurants and lake facilities, the historic Garden District, and major shopping areas. A different downtown site was pushed by an opposing political group.

Meanwhile, the Audubon Zoo had its own future to plan. The new physical facilities and professional care paid off handsomely in increased attendance and new animal births. But the Zoo could not expand as its existing location due to lack of land within the city. Forman and the Zoo staff considered several alternatives. One was incorporating the new aquarium. Another was little "neighborhood" zoos to be located all over the city. A third was a separate breeding area to be located outside the city boundaries where land was available. With the Zoo running smoothly, the staff seemed to need new challenges to tackle, and the Zoo needed new facilities or programs to continue increasing attendance. Exhibits 12, 13, and 14 provide additional information for developing strategies for the Audubon Zoo.

EXHIBIT 12 Chronology of events for the new zoo

1972	The Aubudon Zoological Society asked the Aubudon Park Commission to institute an admission charge "in an amount sufficient to reduce the possibility of vandalism but not so great as to inhibit visits by family groups and less affluent members of the community" (*Times Picayune*, 29 April, 1972).
1973	The City Planning Commission approved a master plan for the Aubudon Park Zoo calling for $3.4 million for upgrading—later phases will call for an additional $2.1 million—to be completed by 1978.
1974	Friends of the Zoo formed with 400 members to increase support and awareness of the Zoo.
1975	Phase I renovations began— $25 million public and private funds—14 acres to be expanded to 58 acres.
1977	John Moore went to Albuquerque; Ron Forman took over as Park and Zoo director.
1978	Phase II began.
1980	Phase III began.
1980	First full-time education staff went on duty at the Zoo.
1980	Last animal removed from antiquated cage—a turning point in Zoo history.
1981	Contract signed allowing New Orleans Steamboat Company to bring passengers from downtown to the Park.
1981	Delegates from the American Association of Zoological Parks and Aquariums ranked the Aubudon Zoo as one of the top three zoos in America of its size.
1981	Zoo accredited.
1982	The Aubudon Park Commission reorganized under Act 352, which required the Commission to contract with a nonprofit organization for the daily management of the Park.

EXHIBIT 13 Respondent characteristics of zoo visitors according to visitation frequency (in percentages)

Respondent Characteristic	Number of Zoo Visits Over Past Two Years: Four or More	Two or Three	One or None	Never Visited Zoo
Age				
Under 27	26	35	31	9
27 to 35	55	27	15	3
36 to 45	48	32	11	9
46 to 55	18	20	37	25
Over 55	27	29	30	14
Marital Status				
Married	41	28	20	11
Not Married	30	34	24	13
Children at Home				
Yes	46	30	15	9
No	34	28	27	12
Interest in visiting the Orleans aquarium				
Very interested, with emphasis	47	26	18	9
Very interested, without emphasis	45	24	23	12
Somewhat	28	37	14	11
Not too interested	19	32	27	22
Vote intention on aquarium				
For, with emphasis	46	33	16	5
For, without emphasis	39	31	16	14
Against or don't know	11	40	32	17
Member of FOTZ				
Yes	67	24	5	4
No, but heard of it	35	30	24	12
No, and never heard of it	25	28	35	13
Interest in joining FOTZ (nonmembers only)				
Very interested/somewhat	50	28	14	8
Not interested/don't know	33	29	26	12

EXHIBIT 14 Relative importance of seven reasons for respondent's not visiting the zoo more often (in percents)

Reason (Close Ended)	*Very Important with Emphasis*	*Very Important without Emphasis*	*Somewhat Important*	*Unimportant*
The distance of the zoo from where you live	7	11	21	60
The cost of a visit to the zoo	4	8	22	66
Lack of interest in zoo animals	2	12	18	67
The parking problem on weekends	7	11	19	62
Boredom with repeatedly seeing the same exhibits	5	18	28	49
The excessive heat during the summer months	25	23	22	30
Activity just not considered	8	19	26	48

END NOTES

1. *Times Picayune.* 30 March, 1975.
2. *Times Picayune.* 20 January, 1976.
3. Millie Ball. "The New Zoo of '82." *Dixie Magazine, Sunday Times Picayune.* 24 June, 1979.
4. *Times Picayune.* 30 March, 1975.
5. *Times Picayune.* 20 January, 1976.
6. *Times Picayune.* 29 April, 1972.
7. *Jefferson Business.* August 1985.
8. Ibid.
9. *Advertising Age.* 17 March, 1986.
10. Karen Sausmann, ed. *Zoological Park and Aquarium Fundamentals.* (Wheeling, W. Va: American Association of Zoological Parks and Aquariums, 1982): 111.
11. *Times Picayune.* 30 November, 1981.
12. Steve Brooks. "Don't Say 'No Can Do' to Audubon Zoo Chief." *Jefferson Business.* 5 May, 1986.
13. Ross Yuchey. "No Longer is Heard a Discouraging Word at the Audubon Zoo." *New Orleans.* August 1980, 53.
14. Yuchey, p. 49.
15. *At the Zoo.* Winter 1987.
16. Feasibility Analysis and Conceptual Planning for a Major Aquarium Attraction, prepared for the City of New Orleans, March 1985.

REFERENCES

Beaulieu, Lovell. "It's All Happening at the Zoo." *The Times Picayune.* 28 January, 1978.

Ball, Millie. "The New Zoo of '82." *Dixie Magazine, Sunday Times Picayune.* 25 June, 1979.

Brooks, Steve. "Don't Say 'No Can Do' to Audubon Zoo Chief." *Jefferson Business.* 5 May, 1986.

Bureau of Governmental Research, City of New Orleans. *Audubon Park Zoo Study, Part I, Zoo Improvement Plan,'' August 1971* (New Orleans: Bureau of Governmental Research).

Bureau of Governmental Research, City of New Orleans. *Aubudon Park Zoo Study, Part II, An Operational*

Analysis. August 1971 (New Orleans: Bureau of Governmental Research).

Donovan, S. "The Audubon Zoo: A Dream Come True." *New Orleans.* May 1986, 52–66.

Feasibility Analysis and Conceptual Planning for a Major Aquarium Attraction, prepared for the City of New Orleans. March 1985.

Forman, R., J. Logsdon, and J. Wilds. *Audubon Park: An Urban Eden.* (New Orleans: The Friends of the Zoo, 1985).

Poole, Susan. *Frommer's 1983–84 Guide to New Orleans.* (New York: Simon & Schuster, 1983).

Sausmann, K., ed. *Zoological Park and Aquarium Fundamentals,* (Wheeling, W. Va.: American Association of Zoological Parks and Aquariums, 1982).

Yuchey, R. "No Longer is Heard a Discouraging Word at the Audubon Zoo." *New Orleans.* August 1980, 49–60.

Zuckerman, S., ed. *Great Zoos of the World.* (Colorado: Westview Press, 1980).

The Classic Car Club of America—1987

MATTHEW C. SONFIELD
Hofstra University

THE 'COLLECTOR CAR' HOBBY

The "collector car" hobby in the United States is a broad and wide-reaching activity involving a large number of Americans. Basically, a "collector car" is any automobile owned for purposes other than normal transportation. The most widely read collector car magazine, *Hemmings Motor News,* had a circulation of more than 250,000 in January 1987, and its circulation had been steadily growing for many years. Thus, a figure of 300,000–400,000 would probably be a conservative estimate of the number of Americans engaged in this hobby.

"Collector car" is a loose term, covering vehicles from turn-of-the-century "horseless carriages" to currently built but limited-production cars, such as Italian super sportscars and American convertibles. Naturally, owners of collector cars enjoy the company of other persons with similar interests; thus, a wide variety of car clubs exist to suit almost any particular segment of this vast hobby market. The largest of these clubs, the Antique Automobile Club of America, caters to owners of virtually all cars 25 years old or older, and has a membership of more than 50,000.

HISTORY AND BACKGROUND

The Classic Car Club of America, Inc. (CCCA) was formed in 1952 by a small group of enthusiasts interested in the luxury cars of the late 1920s and 1930s. Certain high-priced, high-quality, and limited-production cars were designated as "Classic Cars," and the period of 1925–1942 was chosen as the "Classic Era." It was felt that cars built prior to 1925 had not yet reached technical maturity, and that after World War II, the quality of most so-called luxury cars had succumbed to the economic pressures of mass production.

Over the years, the list of CCCA-recognized Classics was modified and expanded, and the time period was extended to 1948 to include certain pre-World-War-II models that continued in production for a few years after the war. While all cars included on the list were of considerably higher price and quality than the mass-production cars of this era, there was also a wide variance in original price and quality of these recognized Classics. For example, in 1930 a new Ford Model A *(not a Classic)* cost about $450. Two of the many CCCA-recognized Classics of that year are the Auburn Eight, which was priced as low as $1195, and the Duesenberg Model J, which sold in the $12,000–$14,000 range. The Auburn, although a car of middle price and quality, is considered a Classic because its styling was exceptional at the time. In comparison, the Duesenberg was the highest priced and most exotic American car of the era; it carried custom-built bodies and was bought by an exclusive clientele of movie stars, playboys, and other super-rich personalities. Most Classics fell somewhere between these two extremes, with original prices in the $2000–$5000 range. Table 1 lists those cars recognized as Classics by the CCCA in 1987.

CCCA ACTIVITIES AND ORGANIZATION

When the CCCA's 1986 fiscal year ended on October 31, 1986, the club had 4,869 members as indicated by the following:

Active (regular membership—1987 dues $30/yr)	3885
Associate (for spouses, no publications—$5/yr)	773
Life (one-time charge of $420, after 10 years)	160
Life associate (spouse of life member—$42)	45
Honorary (famous car designers, etc.)	6
	4869

CCCA members receive a variety of benefits from their membership. A magazine, *The Classic Car,* is published four times a year. High in quality, it features full-color photos of Classics on the front and back covers, and it contains 48 pages of articles and black-and-white photos of Classics and CCCA activities. A CCCA *Bulletin* is also published eight times per year; it contains club and hobby news, technical columns, and members' and commercial ads for Classic Cars, parts, and related items. A further publication is the club's *Handbook and Directory,* published annually. It contains information such as the CCCA by-laws and judging rules, as well as a listing of current members and the Classic Cars they own.

The CCCA also sponsors three types of national events each year. The Annual Meeting in January includes business meetings and a car judging meet; it is held in a different U.S. location each year. In July, a series of "Grand Classic" judging meets are held simultaneously in a number of locations around the country. In 1986, 369 Classics were judged or exhibited at six different Grand Classics from coast to coast.

TABLE 1 CCCA recognized classic cars

A.C.	Farman*	N.A.G.*
Adler*	Fiat*	Nash*
Alfa Romeo	FN*	Packard*
Alvis*	Franklin*	Peerless*
Amilcar*	Frazer-Nash*	Peugot*
Armstrong-Siddeley*	Hispano-Suiza*	Pierce-Arrow
Aston Martin*	Horch	Railton*
Auburn*	Hotchkiss*	Raymond Mays*
Austro-Daimler	Hudson*	Renault*
Ballot*	Humber*	Reo*
Bentley	Invicta	Revere
Benz*	Isotta-Fraschini	Riley*
Blackhawk	Itala	Roamer*
B.M.W.*	Jaguar*	Rochet Schneider*
Brewster*	Jensen*	Rohr*
Brough Superior*	Jordan*	Rolls-Royce
Bucciali*	Julian*	Ruxton
Bugatti	Kissell*	Squire
Buick*	Lagonda*	S.S. and S.S. Jaguar*
Cadillac*	Lanchester*	Stearns-Knight
Chenard-Walcker*	Lancia*	Stevens-Duryea
Chrysler*	La Salle*	Steyr*
Cord	Lincoln*	Studebaker*
Cunningham	Lincoln Continental	Stutz
Dagmar*	Locomobile*	Sunbeam*
Daimler*	Marmon*	Talbot*
Darracq*	Maserati*	Talbot-Lago*
Delage*	Maybach	Tatra*
Delahaye*	McFarlan	Triumph*
Delaunay Belleville*	Mercedes	Vauxhall*
Doble	Mercedes-Benz*	Voisin
Dorris	Mercer	Wills Ste. claire
Duesenberg	M.G.*	Willys-Knight*
du Pont	Minerva*	
Excelsior*		

*Indicates that only certain models of this make are considered Classic; other 1925–1948 custom-bodied cars not listed may be approved as classic upon individual application.

At CCCA judging meets, cars are rated by a point system which takes into account the authenticity of restoration and the general condition of the car, both cosmetically and mechanically.

Each summer, the club sponsors one or more "Classic CARavans" in various parts of the United States and Canada. The CARavan is a tour in which more than 100 Classics join together in a week-long planned itinerary.

The CCCA also has technical advisors available to assist members, and it makes available for sale to members certain club-related products, such as hats and ties with a Classic Car design.

The club is managed by a 15-person Board of Directors, with the usual officers such as president, vice presidents, treasurer, and secretary. All board members are club member volunteers (from all over the United States) who have shown a willingness and ability to help run the CCCA, and who have been elected by the total membership to 3-year terms of office. The board members are not reimbursed for their expenses, which include attending monthly board meetings, most of which are held at headquarters offices rented in Des Plaines, Illinois. The only paid employees of the club are a part-time secretary and the publications editor. An organization chart of the CCCA is shown in Exhibit 1.

In addition to belonging to the National CCCA, the majority of members also pay dues and belong to a local CCCA Region. In 1987, there were twenty-five regions throughout the United States. (See Exhibit 2.) Each region sponsors a variety of local activities for members and their Classics as well as publishes its own magazine or newsletter. Many of the regions also derive revenues from the sale of Classic Car replacement parts or service items, offered to all members of the national club.

CURRENT PROBLEMS FACING THE CCCA

While the officers and directors of the CCCA believe the club is strong, both financially and in its value to its members, a variety of concerns about the future exist.

Of primary concern is the effect of inflation upon the club's ability to maintain its current level of service and benefits to the membership. In particular, the cost of publications, and headquarters office administration and rent have risen considerably in recent years. The board of directors has responded by watching costs carefully and raising annual dues several times (from $10 in the 1960s to the current $30). However, it recognizes that certain cost increases are unavoidable and that raising dues too high will result in a loss of members. (Financial statements are provided in Table 2.)

One way to overcome this problem is to increase the number of members, thus creating greater revenues for the club. The directors know that many Classic owners do not belong to the CCCA. While CCCA members owned about 7,000 Classics in 1987, no one really knows how many Classics and owners are not in the club. Club efforts in recent years to increase membership have been targeted at these Classic-owning non-member individuals. Letters have been sent to past members who failed to renew their CCCA membership (about 5 percent–10 percent each year). In addition, region officers have contacted local non-CCCA members known to own Clas-

EXHIBIT 1 Classic Car Club of America—organization chart

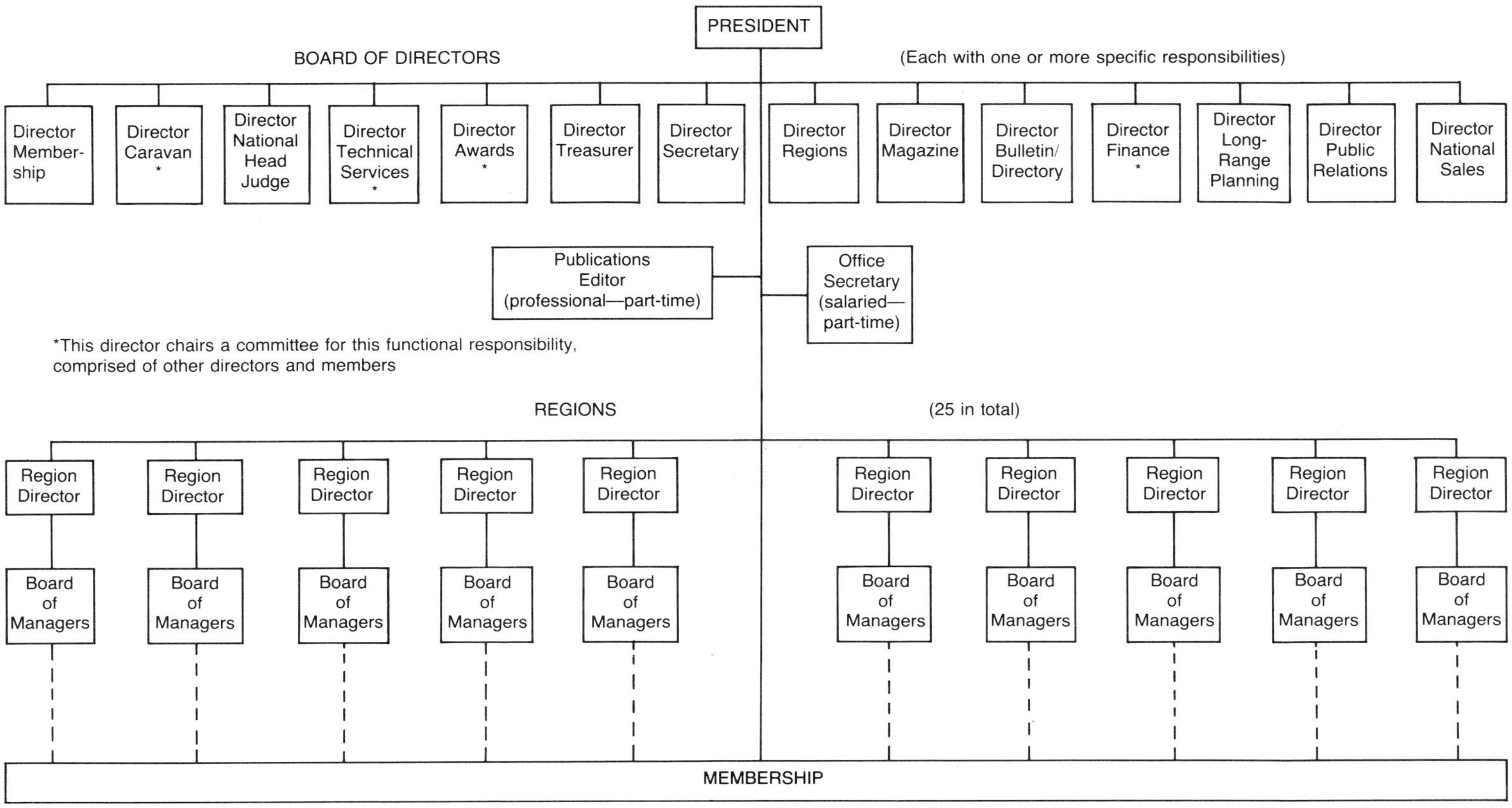

PRESIDENT

BOARD OF DIRECTORS

(Each with one or more specific responsibilities)

Director Member-ship
Director Caravan *
Director National Head Judge
Director Technical Services *
Director Awards *
Director Treasurer
Director Secretary
Director Regions
Director Magazine
Director Bulletin/ Directory
Director Finance *
Director Long-Range Planning
Director Public Relations
Director National Sales

Publications Editor (professional—part-time)

Office Secretary (salaried—part-time)

*This director chairs a committee for this functional responsibility, comprised of other directors and members

REGIONS

(25 in total)

Region Director — Board of Managers (×10)

MEMBERSHIP

EXHIBIT 2 Map showing boundaries of regions of Classic Car Club of America

sics. Finally, a few articles about CCCA activities as well as paid CCCA membership advertisements have been placed in various old car hobby magazines.

Furthermore, while many CCCA members do not own Classics, the majority do, because much of the pleasure of belonging to the club derives from participating in the various activities with a Classic Car. Thus, while Classic enthusiasts who do not own a Classic might also be an appropriate target for CCCA new membership efforts, the primary focus has been on persons currently owning a Classic.

The club's membership recruitment efforts have been only moderately successful. While new members have offset the annual 5 to 10 percent attrition rate, total membership has only risen about 2 percent per year in recent years, and most of the increase has been in Associate Memberships (spouses of existing members).

Yet, unless the listing of recognized Classics is expanded, the number of Classics in existence is fixed, and with it, by-and-large, is the number of Classic owners. Opinions vary within the CCCA with regard to expanding the current listing of Classics. While there is some debate over adding further makes and models within the current 1925–1948 year limits, the main controversy concerns whether or not to add cars built after 1948.

A minority of members favor this post-1948 expansion and make several arguments. They say that some high-quality cars were built after 1948, and these cars should also be considered "Classic." Furthermore, they argue that the club currently is not attracting young members (only 20 percent of CCCA members are under age 45) because younger people are less able to afford the cost of a Classic and are unable to "identify" as easily with a 1925–1948 car as they can with a car of the 1950s or 1960s. While prices of Classics vary greatly, depending upon the make of car, its condition, and type of body, all prices rose significantly in the 1970s and 1980s. Also, many current CCCA members own Classics due to nostalgia for the cars of their youth.

On the other hand, most members of the board of directors, along with a clear majority of the membership, argue against expansion of the list of Classics past 1948. The primary argument is that a Classic Car is more than just a high quality luxury car. Rather, it is the product of a "Classic Era," when the truly wealthy lived a separate life style from the rest of the population, and when an elite group of auto makers and custom body craftsmen were willing and able to produce cars to meet this upper-class life style. By the end of World War II, it is argued, social upheavals ended this life style, and economic pressures closed down the custom body builders and most of the independent luxury car makers, with the remaining luxury cars generally becoming simply bigger, heavier, and better-appointed versions of other cars made by multi-line manufacturers. Thus, expanding beyond 1948 would alter the basic focus and "philosophy" of the club.

Furthermore, it is argued, while a few truly special car models were made after 1948, the quantities produced were small, and the addition of these cars to the list would bring in few new members to the CCCA.

Beyond the board's concerns about the future financial strength of the club, there is a concern about the use of members' Classics and the nature of CCCA activities. As previously mentioned, the value of Classics has risen significantly over the years. In 1952, when the club was founded, most people viewed Classics as simply "old

TABLE 2 CCCA financial statements (cash flow basis)

	Fiscal Year					
	1986	*1985*	*1984*	*1983*	*1982*	*1981*
Receipts						
Active dues (dues received for current fiscal year)	$ 58,926	$ 78,663	$ 39,999	$ 47,950	$ 43,900	$ 41,199
Prepaid active dues (dues received for next fiscal year)	61,560	55,079	17,350	54,975	47,370	33,440
Associate dues	2,061	3,279	931	972	978	801
Prepaid associate dues	2,165	1,851	685	1,227	762	648
Life membership	1,799	840	2,975	7,310	5,375	6,775
Publications	2,987	2,661	3,665	3,429	3,472	4,202
Bulletin advertising	8,618	3,318	4,992	3,662	3,396	1,459
Magazine advertising	3,329	750	1,900	3,567	1,658	2,752
Awards (member registration fees for meets, etc.)	5,234	5,779	5,439	5,240	5,091	5,230
CARavan (current fiscal year)	4,760	47,678	2,400	5,300	5,646	5,900
CARavan (prepaid for next fiscal year)	7,400	4,241	23,041	6,360	1,500	1,550
National sales items (badges, jewelry, ties, etc.)	5,002	5,136	6,155	5,235	4,045	609
Interest earned	5,466	2,588	11,772	10,416	8,750	9,957
Regional insurance (reimbursement from regions)	2,280	1,845	1,780	1,110	1,550	1,300
Miscellaneous and foreign exchange	931	9,725	3,071	877	13,884	322
Total Receipts	**$172,518**	**$223,433**	**$126,155**	**$157,630**	**$147,377**	**$116,144**
Assets						
Bank balance	$ 36,605	18,466	11,296	5,356	1,891	5,485
Investments (at cost: money market funds, C.D.s, etc.)	71,148	59,885	27,296	96,966	89,397	85,636
(includes life membership fund)	(42,962)	(37,325)	(36,845)	(37,245)	(29,800)	(24,225)

TABLE 2 continued

	Fiscal Year					
	1986	*1985*	*1984*	*1983*	*1982*	*1981*
Liabilities: None						
Disbursements						
Bulletin	$ 22,651	$ 19,538	$ 20,734	$ 16,828	$ 19,165	$ 13,739
Magazine	44,697	47,972	45,788	46,598	52,624	33,756
Directory	11,647	1,784	11,739	16,181	9,277	9,237
Awards (judging, meetings, trophies, etc.)	3,386	4,038	20,378	8,888	9,648	10,025
General administration	12,658	11,801	14,664	8,786	7,573	10,843
Office (salaries, rent, etc.)	29,431	27,750	27,326	28,573	21,824	16,934
CARavan	6,323	46,924	29,777	5,069	5,564	4,252
National sales items	2,204	2,623	2,784	1,710	4,123	126
Membership (recruitment)	4,872	7,246	2,950	5,670	3,401	1,619
Regional insurance	2,250	2,800	1,924	1,600	1,177	1,279
Regional relations	0	27	302	454	462	431
Computer services	8,137	9,339	4,493	3,678	3,611	8,011
Miscellaneous and Foreign Exchange	861	456	426	2,562	8,762	1,142
Taxes	470	1,377	6,599	0	0	0
Total Disbursements	**$149,587**	**183,675**	**189,884**	**146,597**	**147,211**	**111,394**
Excess Receipts over Disbursements	**$ 22,931**	**39,758**	**(63,729)**	**11,033**	**166**	**4,750**

cars," and these cars could generally be bought for a few hundred to a few thousand dollars. Today, Classics are viewed as a major investment item, and professional dealers and auctions are a significant factor in the marketplace. While some less-exotic and unrestored Classic models can be found for under \$10,000, most sell for \$10,000–\$75,000, and the most desirable Classics (such as convertible models with custom bodies, and cars with 12- and 16-cylinder engines) can sell for \$100,000 and more. (A very small number of *super*-desirable Classics have recently sold in the \$500,000–\$1,000,000 range, and an "*ultimate*-desirable" 1931 Bugatti Royale sold in 1986 for more than \$8 million!) Furthermore, judging meets have become very serious events, with high scores adding significantly to a Classic's sales value. Thus, many highly desirable and/or top-scoring Classics are now hardly driven at all and are trailered to and from judging meets. While most Classic owners still enjoy driving their cars, the club's emphasis may be moving from driving to judging, and this possible shift upsets many CCCA members.

Still another concern of some members involves possible future gasoline shortages in the United States. If such a shortage again arose, how would the public view Classic Cars and the old car hobby in general? Would the ownership and driving of cars for non-transportation purposes be considered unpatriotic or anti-social?

Membership Survey

In response to these various concerns, the CCCA board established a Long Range Planning Committee to study issues about the future of the club and to make recommendations to the board. In late 1983, a membership questionnaire was developed and sent to all members along with their 1984 membership renewal material. The response rate was excellent—about 75 percent of the club's members returned a completed questionnaire with their 1984 dues. Exhibit 3 presents this questionnaire and a tabulation of quantifiable responses.

It is more difficult to summarize the responses to the open-ended questions. While no one sentiment represented a majority or even a large minority of the membership, some themes were frequently repeated:

- ☐ A concern about trailered cars and professionally restored cars competing with other Classics in judging.
- ☐ Too much emphasis in the CCCA on judging, and not enough emphasis on driving—a focus on cosmetics rather than mechanics.
- ☐ To attract younger members, the club must expand the listing of Classics beyond 1948.
- ☐ "The ________ (which I happen to own) should be recognized as a Classic. It is as fine a car as the ________, which is recognized by the CCCA as a Classic."
- ☐ The CCCA should not dilute the meaning of "Classic." Hold fast to the 1925–1948 limits.

EXHIBIT 3 1983 membership questionnaire

Please help your National Board of Directors guide the CCCA in the path that you desire by completing this questionnaire and returning it with your membership renewal.

1. I have been a member of the CCCA

☐ less than 2 years	☐ 2–5 years	☐ 5–10 years	☐ more than 10 years
11%	20%	18%	51%

2. I live in the ______________region (or state if there is no region)

3. My age is

☐ under 25	☐ 25–34	☐ 35–44	☐ 45–54	☐ 55–64	☐ 65 and over
1%	3%	17%	30%	28%	22%

4. I am a member of a CCCA Region ☐ yes 69% ☐ no 31%

   If not, why not? ______________

5. I have attended

   64% ☐ One or more Grand Classics
   19% ☐ One or more National CCCA CARavans
   24% ☐ One or more Annual Meetings
   52% ☐ One or more Regional Events

6. I belong to ______ (how many) other car clubs.

0	1	2	3	4	5	6	7	8	9	10&+
9%	19%	23%	17%	12%	7%	5%	2%	2%	1%	3%

   I am more active in some of these clubs than I am in the CCCA. ☐ yes 44% ☐ no 56%

   If "yes," why? ______________

7. Compared to other car clubs, the CCCA is

☐ the best	☐ better than most	☐ average	☐ poor
31%	47%	21%	1%

8. Compared to other car clubs, the value I receive for my CCCA dues is

☐ the best	☐ better than most	☐ average	☐ poor
27%	40%	31%	3%

9. Overall, I rate "*THE CLASSIC CAR*" magazine

☐ excellent	☐ good	☐ fair	☐ poor
74%	24%	1%	0%

10. Overall, I rate the "*CCCA BULLETIN*"

☐ excellent	☐ good	☐ fair	☐ poor
35%	51%	13%	1%

EXHIBIT 3 continued

11. In "*THE CLASSIC CAR,*" the types of articles I enjoy most are:
Rate each: 3 = enjoy a great amount 2 = enjoy a fair amount 1 = enjoy a little 0 = do not enjoy

2.3 Grand Classic articles
1.5 Annual Meeting articles
2.1 CARavan articles
2.7 Stories and photos of members' cars
2.8 Historic articles on classic cars or coachbuilders
2.4 Technical articles
2.5 Restoration articles
2.4 Articles on car collections or car museums
2.4 Articles on classic car designers
2.7 Car photos from the Classic Era
2.3 Reprints from classic era publications
1.5 Book reviews
1.6 Articles on regional events
1.3 Articles on non-CCCA car events
1.7 Classic car humor
1.8 Letters to the editor
____ Other: ____________

12. I would prefer
28% ☐ to continue to have the *HANDBOOK-DIRECTORY* published every year
72% ☐ to have it published every other year if a significant savings to the club would result

13. Currently the club's By-Laws require that 7 candidates run each year for election to 5 open National Board positions. While this gives the membership a choice in their voting, it also means that the two least-known candidates generally lose and will not seek election to the Board again.
I think it is important to continue the system of 7 candidates for 5 positions. ☐ yes 64% ☐ no 36%

14. With regard to the CCCA's listing of recognized Classic Cars,
69% ☐ I basically think the current listing is good
28% ☐ I think the listing should be expanded
3% ☐ I think the listing should be reduced
Comments: ____________

15. With regard to the CCCA 100-point judging system,
86% ☐ I basically think the current system is good
14% ☐ I think the system could be improved
If so, how: ____________

16. Overall, I would rate the Grand Classics as

☐ excellent 50%   ☐ good 30%   ☐ fair 2%   ☐ poor 1%   ☐ don't know 17%

17. Overall, I would rate the Annual Meetings as

☐ excellent 15%   ☐ good 22%   ☐ fair 5%   ☐ poor 0%   ☐ don't know 59%

18. Overall, I would rate the CARavans as

☐ excellent 28%   ☐ good 16%   ☐ fair 2%   ☐ poor 0%   ☐ don't know 54%

19. I think the CCCA should have additional National Judging Meets.   ☐ yes 23%   ☐ no 77%

If "yes," what type? ______

20. I think the CCCA could be improved by:

______

Other comments: ______

Thank you for your assistance.

FUTURE DIRECTION OF THE CCCA

In 1987, the CCCA Board of Directors was studying these issues. The board members knew that they could not ignore the problem of rising costs, and that the response must go beyond raising dues. While the survey clarified some of the membership opinions, the board did not view this survey as a ballot, with the board obligated to follow the majority preference in every question area.

As they met for their monthly Board of Directors meeting, the fifteen officers and directors of the CCCA asked themselves the following questions:

1. How do we deal with rising costs to the club?
2. What should be our policy with regard to future dues increases?
3. Should we consider the reduction of CCCA services to our membership in the future?
4. Is expansion of the listing of recognized Classic Cars desirable?
5. What are the alternative ways to increase membership in the club?
6. How can younger people be attracted to the CCCA?
7. Are there other sources of revenue for the club?
8. Were important questions not included in the 1983 membership survey that should be included in a future survey?
9. Are there other long-range issues or concerns that the club has not yet addressed?

Walt Disney—1987

HORACE HOLMES
Mississippi State University
REATHER HOLMES
Mississippi State University

A new movie out there is fast becoming one of the season's biggest hits. It features comedy star Bette Midler as a sometime porno actress, whose language would make a New York City cab driver blanch. Active movie goers might know that *Outrageous Fortune* also stars Shelley Long and was released by Touchstone Pictures. But few would know that Touchstone is a unit of Walt Disney Company. That's right, Walt Disney, as in Bambi and Thumper. The fantasy factory that gave America squeak-clean dreams filled with cuddly creatures is now bringing you R-rated movies. Walt would be appalled. Or maybe not. "Walt would love what's going on with his company," says Roy E. Disney, vice-chairman of the board and nephew of the founder. "We've become an idea company again."

It was not long ago that Disney seemed to have run out of ideas. In the two decades following Walt's death in 1966, the company stagnated. A revolution in the way Hollywood makes and sells movies had passed Disney by, leaving Mickey looking a little shopworn. The movie studio seemed unable to do anything but turn out costly bombs, and Disney, once a staple of the small screen, had disappeared from TV. That disappearance left the company dangerously dependent on its theme parks. The Walt Disney Company, formerly Walt Disney Productions, is a diversified international enterprise engaged in family entertainment and community development. Disney has operations in four business segments: Theme Parks and Resorts (formerly Entertainment and Recreation), Filmed Entertainment, Community Development, and Consumer Products. Disney employs approximately 32,000 people.

THEME PARKS AND RESORTS

The Walt Disney World Complex

The Walt Disney World Complex, located near Orlando, Florida, includes the Magic Kingdom and Epcot Center theme parks, hotels, villas, a shopping village, conference center, campgrounds, golf courses, and other recreational facilities. Disney receives royalties on revenues generated by the Tokyo Disneyland theme park near Tokyo, Japan, which is owned and operated by a Japanese corporation. While the Disneyland Park and the Walt Disney World Complex are operated on a year-round basis, historically the greater part of their business is in the spring and summer seasons, with other peak periods during Christmas, Easter, and on holidays.

On December 18, 1985, Disney announced that it had signed a letter of intent with governmental authorities in France to develop Euro Disneyland on a site approximately 20 miles east of Paris, France. Plans for the project include a Magic Kingdom, similar to Disneyland, the Walt Disney World Magic Kingdom in the United States, and Tokyo Disneyland in Japan, as well as a resort, residential, and commercial complex. Disney is continuing to negotiate a definitive agreement with French authorities. If an agreement is successfully concluded, it is expected that the first elements of the project, including the Magic Kingdom, will begin operations in five to six years. Disney plans to seek qualified investors in The French company that will be formed to own the Euro Disneyland project. Disney will also be an equity investor. It is contemplated that Disney will be entitled to receive royalties and management fees for its role as operator of the project under contracts to be concluded with the French company.

Construction is under way on the Disney-MGM Studio Tour, a third, separately gated complex at the Walt Disney World Complex. This facility will offer entertainment experiences and function as a working film studio. Production capabilities will complement Disney's Burbank studio operations. MGM is not a partner in the Studio Tour attractions, but Disney has licensed rights to the MGM Entertainment Co. name and portions of MGM's film library. In addition, Disney would use logos, film excerpts, and other memorabilia as part of a ride-through tour.

The Magic Kingdom consists of six principal areas designated as Main Street, Liberty Square, Frontierland, Tomorrowland, Fantasyland, and Adventureland. Each of these areas feature theme rides and attractions, restaurants, refreshment stands, and souvenir shops. A number of Magic Kingdom attractions are sponsored by corporate participants.

Epcot is an acronym for Experimental Prototype Community of Tomorrow. Epcot Center consists of two major theme areas: Future World and World Showcase. Future World dramatizes certain historical developments and addresses the challenges facing the world today. World Showcase presents a community of nations, focusing on the culture, traditions, and accomplishments of people around the world. It includes as a central showplace, the American Adventure pavilion, that highlights the history of the American people. Other nations represented are Canada, Mexico, Japan, China, France, the United Kingdom, Italy, Germany, Morocco, and Norway (scheduled to open in 1988).

A number of the attractions at Epcot Center are also sponsored by corporate participants, including General Motors (World of Motion), Exxon (Universe of Energy), Kraft (The Land), AT&T (Spaceship Earth), American Express and Coca-Cola (the American Adventure), General Electric (Horizons), Kodak (Journey into Imagination), Sperry (Epcot Computer Central in CommuniCore), and United Technologies (The Living Seas). Epcot Center is linked to the Magic Kingdom by monorail.

Disney owns and operates three resort hotels at the Walt Disney World Complex that have a present capacity of approximately 2,200 rooms, as well as the Fort Wilderness camping and recreational area that has a present capacity of approximately 1,200 sites. The 1986 average occupancy rates for the three resort hotels and Fort Wilderness were 92 percent and 85 percent, respectively.

Disney has also developed approximately 1,200 acres known as the Walt Disney World Village, including 585 villas, a unique shopping facility, a complete clubhouse facility, and a conference center. The Walt Disney World Conference Center consists of rooms and banquet facilities. Occupancy rates for all villas averaged 81 percent for 1986.

The occupancy rates for Disney's resort hotels, Fort Wilderness, and villas have not varied substantially over the past five years. However, Disney is continuing to expand hotel room and villa capacity. Disney has commenced construction on the 900-room Grand Floridian Beach Resort Hotel, located near the Magic Kingdom and scheduled to open in spring 1988. In 1988, a new nighttime entertainment complex, *Pleasure Island,* will open at the Walt Disney World Village. The 6-acre complex will contain theme parks, nightclubs, merchandise locations, specialty restaurants, and food outlets. At the Walt Disney World Village Hotel Plaza, seven major hotels are situated on property leased from Disney. These hotels have approximately 3,500 guest rooms.

Recreational activities include golfing (three championship golf courses), tennis, sailing, water skiing, swimming, horseback riding, and other leisure-time activities. Many of the recreational activities are centered around the beaches of Bay Lake, a natural lake located wholly within the Complex. There is a lagoon-style expansion of Bay Lake located between the Magic Kingdom and the resort hotels.

Disneyland Park California

Disney owns 320 acres and has under long-term lease an additional 24 acres of land in Anaheim, California. Disneyland Park consists of seven principal areas: Fantasyland, Adventureland, Frontierland, Tomorrowland, New Orleans Square, Main Street, and

Bear Country. Each of these areas features theme rides and attractions, restaurants, refreshment stands, and souvenir shops. Disney periodically revitalizes the shows and presentations and adds new attractions to maintain the continuing appeal of Disneyland Park and to increase in-park capacity. Disney markets these new attractions as well as the entire Disneyland Park through national and local advertising and promotional activities. In June 1986, Disneyland hosted the "Great American Race," an annual transcontinental antique car rally that began at the park and concluded in New York during the Statue of Liberty centennial celebration. Also in June, Disneyland opened Big Thunder Ranch, a re-creation of an 1800s horse ranch, featuring a petting barnyard with farm animals, pastures with grazing horses, a ranch house, and demonstrations of horseshoeing, harness-making, and wool spinning. Big Thunder Barbecue Restaurant, featuring chicken and ribs, is set to open in April 1987. New attractions in 1986 included a 3-D film, *Captain Eo,* featuring Michael Jackson and presented in the Kodak 3-D theater in Tomorrowland. *Star Tours,* a new attraction co-produced with George Lucas, opened in January 1987. This was the first attraction to introduce computer-programmed flight simulator technology to theme park guests.

Disneyland Park Tokyo

Tokyo Disneyland, owned and operated by the Oriental Land Company, Ltd., has been firmly established as a leading international theme park. Tokyo Disneyland opened in 1983 and lured more than 10 million visitors its first year—almost outdrawing the Anaheim original. The biggest single day was December 31, 1986, when 130,000 Japanese braved near-freezing temperatures for an all-night bash, complete with countdown, fireworks, and Minnie Mouse in a kimono.

Further enriching its vitality and appeal during 1986 was the opening of the "Cinderella Castle Mystery Tour" and other new attractions. In 1987, the Tokyo park should attract 11 million guests who will spend more than $500 million. By design, the atmosphere is all-American. In the late 1970s, the park's planners agonized over whether to add Japanese touches. They finally decided to make it look and feel like an experience in the States, says Toshio Kagami, managing director of the Oriental Land Company. Now they consider the all-American atmosphere to be the biggest factor in the park's success.

Two additional attractions opened at Toyko Disneyland in 1986. Alice's Tea Party began spinning guests in giant teacups around its teapot centerpiece in March. In July, the park introduced "American Journeys in Circle-Vision 360," with nine encircling screens enabling guests to experience the sensation of actually "being there." The 3-D spectacular, *Captain Eo,* is scheduled to open in Tomorrowland in 1987. Under construction for opening in 1987 is Big Thunder Mountain Railroad. The park is similar in size and concept to Disneyland Park and is located approximately 6 miles from downtown Tokyo.

Disneyland France

Euro Disneyland, scheduled to open by early 1991, will occupy about 1,000 acres and is expected to attract 10 million visitors in its first year. Under a preliminary agreement, the site will be developed by an as-yet-unformed French company in which

Disney will have a minority stake. Disney will manage the park and receive royalties on ticket sales and concessions.

Announcement of the deal came after nearly a year of intense competition between France and Spain. In the spirit of Scrooge McDuck, Disney had sought generous incentives from the two governments, and Spain, at least, was willing to comply, offering sweeteners estimated at more than $250 million. In the end, however, Disney opted for Paris, with its big permanent population, central location, and year-round stream of visitors. The French did not disclose what subsidies, if any, they offered, but they did agree to extend the suburban Paris commuter line to the new park, thus linking it directly by rail to the rest of Europe.

Euro Disneyland will earn most of its profits from satellite developments around the park. A 15-year master plan calls for up to 5,000 hotel rooms, along with shopping centers, office buildings, campgrounds, and other facilities. The amenities would cost an estimated $1.2 billion, about as much as the park itself, and would create some 10,000 jobs.

FILMED ENTERTAINMENT

Disney produces and acquires live-action motion pictures and produces animated motion pictures for distribution to the theatrical, television, and home video markets. Disney also produces original television shows for the networks and first-run syndication markets. Disney distributes its films through its own distribution and marketing companies in the United States and through foreign subsidiaries. Disney provides programming for and operates The Disney Channel, a pay television programming service.

Theatrical Films

Walt Disney Pictures, a wholly owned subsidiary, produces live-action and animated motion pictures under the Walt Disney Pictures label, and live-action motion pictures under the Touchstone Pictures label. Films produced and released under the name of Walt Disney Pictures are designed to appeal to family audiences that have traditionally supported Disney's product. Films produced and released under the Touchstone Pictures label are designed to appeal more to the teenage and adult segments of the public, thereby broadening the scope of Disney's product. Disney announced that by 1988, production levels are targeted to increase to approximately fifteen films each year. This level is comparable with other major motion picture companies.

Network Television

In 1985, Walt Disney re-entered the television market after an absence of two years with a prime-time situation comedy series, "The Golden Girls," distributed by Touchstone Television, and two animated cartoon series for Saturday morning, "The Adventures of the Gummi Bears" on NBC and "The Wuzzles" on CBS, distributed by Walt Disney Television. Disney operates in the television market under the Touchstone and Walt Disney labels, which are delineated in a similar manner as the two motion picture production labels.

Television Syndication

In 1985, Walt Disney formed a new subsidiary, Buena Vista Television, Inc., to license theatrical and television films to the domestic television syndication market. Previously, only "The Mickey Mouse Club" had been released to the television syndication market. Disney Magic-I and Wonderful World of Disney, major packages of Disney feature films and television programming, respectively, were licensed for broadcasting in the fall of 1986 and continuing over several years. The feature film package includes twenty-one motion pictures and four made-for-television movies. The television program package includes 178 hours of animated, live-action, adventure, and true-life films.

Home Video and Pay Television

Disney distributes selected Walt Disney Pictures and Touchstone Pictures products into the domestic and foreign home video markets. Approximately 325 titles, including 150 feature films and ninety cartoons and animated featurettes are now available to the home entertainment market with additional programming scheduled. For the 1987 Christmas season, Disney released in the domestic home video market its animated classic *Sleeping Beauty.*

In 1985 and 1986, Disney made available a number of feature films to the pay television services, as well as to its wholly owned subsidiary, The Disney Channel. In April 1986, Disney negotiated an agreement with Showtime/The Movie Channel to exclusively distribute Touchstone Pictures and selected Walt Disney Pictures films over the next five years, commencing with *Down and Out in Beverly Hills.*

The Disney Channel

The Disney Channel is the Company's nationwide pay television service that provides twenty-four hours of family entertainment daily. Approximately 20 percent of The Disney Channel is original programming. The new shows developed solely for original use by The Disney Channel include dramatic, adventure, comedy, and educational series, as well as documentaries and first-run television movies. In addition, entertainment specials include shows originating from both the Walt Disney World Complex and the Disneyland Park. The balance of the programming consists of products acquired from third parties (almost 50 percent), and products from the Walt Disney Theatrical Film and Television Programming Library.

COMMUNITY DEVELOPMENT

Disney develops, primarily in Florida, comprehensively planned resort and primary-home communities. Disney also develops commercial and industrial properties within or near many of its planned communities and provides general real estate brokerage, financing, and resort and property management services. These activities are conducted through Disney's subsidiary, Arvida Disney Corporation.

Arvida's development approach is to enhance the value of its real estate by applying to it successive phases of the community development process. Land is analyzed with respect to the market, absorption rate, and development costs, issues and potentials. Based on this analysis, Arvida proceeds to take the necessary steps for regulatory approvals. Arvida may then commence development of the infrastructure (such as road and water management systems) and subsequently may develop the architectural design, itself. All portions of the property can be sold at any stage of this process based on market conditions, development costs, and other factors.

Arvida attempts to have available residential units that appeal to a wide range of buyers, from those purchasing homes for the first time to high-income buyers seeking second homes in a resort area. Communities planned by Arvida usually include various amenities such as lakes and open space, clubhouses, golf courses, tennis courts, and swimming pools. Communities may have a diversity of housing products, ranging from single-family homes to mid-rise condominiums. Some developments may consist of a single product, such as high-rise condominiums.

Arvida is involved in the construction of neighborhood shopping centers, office buildings, and other commercial and industrial properties in or near its communities. In developing the infrastructure of its communities and building its own housing products, Arvida usually functions as a general contractor with its supervisory employees coordinating and monitoring all work on the project. Arvida from time to time also hires firms for general contracting. In 1985, Arvida introduced its largest residential, commercial, and industrial development project, the 10,000-acre Weston community located west of Fort Lauderdale, Florida.

CONSUMER PRODUCTS

Disney licenses the name Walt Disney, its characters, its literary properties, and its songs and music to various manufacturers, retailers, printers, and publishers. It also produces audio products primarily for the children's market and produces film, audio, and computer software products for the educational market. Disney licenses and distributes these products throughout the world. Foreign operations include ten subsidiaries and eighteen marketing offices throughout the world; these operations account for about 45 percent of the total revenues for Consumer Products.

Merchandising and Publication Licensing

Merchandise categories that have been licensed include apparel, toys, gifts, housewares, stationery, and domestic items such as sheets and towels. Publication categories that have been licensed include continuity-series books, book sets, art and picture books, comic books, weekly and monthly magazines (in foreign countries), and newspaper comic strips. The Walt Disney name and characters have been used in major promotions involving soft drinks, photographic products, and fast-food restaurants, among others.

Record and Music Publishing

The Records and Music Publishing Division produces, manufactures, and distributes records, audio cassettes and compact discs under the Disneyland and Buena Vista labels. The division also publishes music through two companies, Walt Disney Music and Wonderland Music, whose purpose is to exploit the song copyrights created for Disney's records, films, and television programs, to develop new songs, and to develop print music.

Revenues are generated through domestic retail sales, direct marketing, and international licensing. Domestic retail sales are the largest source of revenues and represent about 10 million records, audio cassettes, and related materials sold annually. Direct marketing is a growing means of distribution for the division, with about 100 million offers made to consumers annually through catalogs, coupon packages, and television.

International licensing consists of more than thirty licensees outside the United States who produce and distribute Disney-based products in about sixty countries and eighteen languages. Disney released its first domestic compact disc in October 1986 with *Fantasia* and plans to release additional titles on compact disc in 1987.

Educational Media

The Educational Media Division produces and distributes audio-visual materials to the educational market. These materials include 16 millimeter films, videocassettes, filmstrips, computer software, read-alongs, posters, and other teaching aids. The division currently has about 300 titles in its library and produces or acquires about twenty new titles in film and video format and ten to fifteen new filmstrip sets each year. Program content ranges from general guidance topics to specific academic subjects, such as reading or spelling, and is based on both Disney and non-Disney material. Sales are made to schools through a regional sales force and through direct mail. The division also runs the Epcot Teacher's Center at Epcot Center in the Walt Disney World Complex. It provides learning materials and exhibits based on Epcot's various science themes of energy, communications, transportation, and land use.

EXTERNAL FACTORS

Fears of foreign travel and the falling value of the dollar are hurting tourism industry abroad, but cheaper gasoline prices and a string of movie hits are pulling Americans out of their homes and into theaters, hotels, and casinos. Americans gave the leisure and recreation industry some of the best overall profits ever in 1986. Average earnings per share for the leisure and recreation industry were up 7.7 percent in 1986, compared with only 2.8 percent for all of U.S. industry. Revenues climbed 10.4 percent, more than double the all-industry median. Those trends are expected to continue into 1987 as well.

During 1986, Paramount's new head, Frank Mancuso, produced one hit after another, including *Top Gun* and *Crocodile Dundee,* thus regaining the top spot for Paramount as Hollywood's biggest box office success and doubling its market share to 20 percent. Disney, too, hit big, tripling its box office share to 10 percent.

"The most important thing we've done with this company is to stay away from emotional investments in overpriced media assets," says Michael Eisner, chairman of The Walt Disney Company. During 1986, that strategy paid off handsomely enough to make his company the most improved of any in the industry for the year. Instead of chasing after high-priced TV stations or movie theaters, Eisner raised $500 million in two limited partnerships for films and invested in areas of proven Disney expertise, such as feature films, TV syndication, pay cable, videocassettes, and toy licensing—all areas in which success brings healthy cash flow rewards.

COMPETITION

Disney's theme parks and resorts compete with all other forms of entertainment and recreational activities. Various factors influencing industry profitability are not directly controllable, such as economic conditions, amount of available leisure time, oil prices, and weather patterns. The company believes its theme parks and resorts benefit substantially from Disney's reputation in the entertainment industry for excellent quality and from the synergism with activities in other business segments of Disney.

The most serious challenge to Disney comes from Harcourt Brace Jovanovich (HBJ), a publisher and theme park operator with 1986 revenues of $1.3 billion. HBJ, which moved it corporate headquarters to Orlando from New York in 1984, already owns four amusement areas in and around Orlando: Sea World, home of Shamu the killer whale; Cypress Gardens, regarded by many as the premier tourist attraction in central Florida; Places of Learning, which boasts, among other things, the nation's largest children's bookstore; and Boardwalk and Baseball, a newly opened complex of ball fields and shops whose main attraction, starting next year, will be the Kansas City Royals during spring training.

With revenues derived from about 21 million tourists per year, the Orlando business community is rooting for HBJ to make a fight of it with Disney World. Says one businessman who is currently negotiating with HBJ: "It's clear that Disney is trying to soak up every available entertainment dollar at a location very far removed from Orlando."

HBJ has acquired the old Circus World amusement park (once owned by Mattel), converting it into the Boardwalk and Baseball complex at a cost of $22 million. HBJ is giving volume discounts, selling three-day combined tickets, so that tourists can visit all of the company's Orlando sights at a lower cost than a single-day trip to any single attraction. That marketing shift helped the parks gain 17 percent in income in 1986 over 1985.

Orlando supports HBJ for a major reason: HBJ's location is closer to downtown and the Orange County convention center. That location keeps tourist dollars closer to home and helps change the demographic mix. "From not being on anyone's list," says Abraham Pizam, director of the Dick Pope Sr. Institute for Tourism Studies at the University of Central Florida, "Orlando is now number 8 in convention traffic, and growing rapidly, for the next three years."

The convention business is helping to shift traffic away from Disney World. Although Disney reported 23.9 million attendees at its two U.S. theme parks in 1986, that number is inflated by a three-day unlimited admission pass. Pizam estimates that as many as half of the 21 million tourists who come to Orlando each year never set foot inside the Magic Kingdom. Such figures have drawn newcomers into the fray. MCA, the owner of Universal Studios in Hollywood, plans to open an entertainment complex and movie studio about 10 miles south of HBJ's Sea World in early 1989. The complex is in an embryonic stage, and, like Disney World and Sea World, it is also along Interstate 4. Although the Florida Division of Tourism forecasted a steady 5 percent annual growth in Orlando tourism three years ago, growth in the past two years has been running at better than 15 percent. For the first quarter of 1987, tourism is up even higher, close to 17 percent.

Also, the rise of an adult entertainment market in Orlando is being boosted by major convention business. The Church Street Station complex derives a huge and profitable business not only from tourism, but also from the 25,000 sailors at the Naval Training Center just outside of town. Orlando Entertains, owned by British entrepreneur Robert Earl, is making a run at the market with three dinner theaters, all opened since 1983. Each has a different theme, running the gamut from King Henry's Feast to Ft. Liberty, a Wild West show in Kissimmee.

Disney's filmed entertainment businesses—theatrical films, television programming products, syndication, pay television, home video markets, and The Disney Channel's pay programming service—compete with all forms of entertainment. The major competitors in this market are Paramount Pictures, MCA, Warner, Orion, and MGM. The Company also competes to obtain creative talents, story properties, and market share, which are essential to the success of Disney's filmed entertainment businesses.

A number of companies produce and/or distribute theatrical and television films, exploit products in the home video market, and provide pay television programming service. Disney produces and distributes films designed for family audiences and believes it is a significant source of such films. The animated feature-length films of Disney have been preeminent and, with respect to these films, Disney has experienced relatively little competition. Disney's competitive position in the live-action theatrical film and television programming markets may be affected by the quality of and public response to such films produced and distributed by it as well as by the quality and number of competing films offered to theaters, television networks, cable television operators, and consumers at large.

Disney competes in its character merchandising and other licensing activities with other licensors of characters, brand and celebrity names, entertainment, and other licensable properties. The chief competitors in this market are Marvel, Sesame Street, and Hanna Barbara. Disney competes with several other companies in the record and music publishing business.

FUTURE ISSUES AND CONCERNS

Disney plans to sell the Arvida Disney Corporation real estate unit to JMB Realty trust for about $400 million in cash and notes. Disney bought Arvida in 1984 for about $200 million in stock. Disney also plans to raise an additional $1.2 billion by selling it's four-year-old Epcot Center in Orlando to a master limited partnership.

Some of that money is planned for continuing development of Disney's still-vast Florida holdings, including several new hotels and a $300 million combined movie studio and tour attraction. Roughly $150 million is planned for purchase of a 17 percent stake in the new European Disneyland. But the rest, Disney officials say privately, is earmarked for at least one major entertainment investment by 1990.

Disney has been frustrated with its acquisitions and plans to play the now-familiar Hollywood game of vertical integration by buying distribution outlets for the products of its studios. A staff of six strategic planners has spent a year studying a list of targets. So far, though, other players have kept the prizes from Disney's grasp. The Company studied the 360-screen Mann Theater chain, bought by Gulf & Western in October for $220 million. It eyed the independent New York TV station WOR-TV, which MCA agreed to buy for $387 million in 1986.

Disney critics argue that Eisner and Wells have worked no fancier magic than to raise prices at Disney's theme parks. Admission prices had failed to keep pace with inflation, and the new management hiked them by 45 percent over two years. There are critics of Disney's big push into TV and movies. Two of Disney's four prime-time TV shows have been received poorly—"The Ellen Burstyn Show," that ABC has cancelled, and "Sidekicks," one of the lowest-rated shows of the year. Another recent feature film from Disney, *The Color of Money,* has performed well below expectations.

The company is pushing into TV syndication. Almost overnight it has grabbed a large chunk of the market for syndicated programs, an area where other studios have been cleaning up for years. Disney is also vigorously expanding its foreign presence. Videocassette sales are soaring in Britain, Spain, and Israel. Mickey and Donald are now prime-time stars on Chinese TV, Tokyo Disneyland is booming, and by 1992, millions of Europeans will probably be visiting a new French Disneyland.

The U.S. theme parks are growing, too. Besides the studio and tour at the Walt Disney World complex in Orlando, work will soon begin on Typhoon Lagoon, a 50-acre park with water slides and wave machines. Disney also plans to build as many as four new hotels in Orlando. The company is planning a new park in southern California and considering several sites for its first regional entertainment center, which will combine restaurants, night spots, and shopping malls.

The search for new assets is another part of Eisner's strategy to reduce the company's heavy reliance on theme parks and hotels. Those operations contributed $403.7 million in operating income last year, about 70 percent of the company's total. In 1974, theme parks and hotels contributed less than 40 percent of operating income.

When Eisner arrived at Disney, movies and TV accounted for only about 13 percent of company profits. Disney officials would like to triple that proportion. Eisner has set an ambitious goal of releasing fifteen to eighteen films a year, up from ten in 1986. A dozen will be pictures with adult themes, released under the Touchstone label. The rest will be either new children's movies or reissues of such classics as *Snow White and the Seven Dwarfs.* "The theme parks may be the heart of this company," Eisner says, "but the movie business is its soul."

In 1987, the studio is likely to release fifteen films, the highest total in its history. The goal is to get as many movies as possible into the long entertainment pipeline, collecting not only box office receipts but also added revenues from home video sales and contracts with pay and broadcast TV. The strategy is already paying off.

Touchstone's *Ruthless People* and *Down and Out in Beverly Hills* were among the top ten box office hits of 1986. *Down and Out* followed up with record video rentals of more than $10 million. In addition, Disney signed a five-year, $200 million deal giving Showtime/The Movie Channel Inc. cable rights to as many as fifty Touchstone films. Mining extra revenue from hit singles is nothing new in Hollywood. But while other studios spend an average of nearly $16 million per movie, Disney spends about $11 million. "Our movie philosophy is to go for singles and doubles when we make our films," says Eisner. "If you go for the home run all the time, you strike out a lot."

To keep costs down, the Disney studio signs such stars as Midler, Newman, and Richard Dreyfuss to long-term commitments to direct and produce their own films. The studio entices virtually all of its stars to take reduced salaries in return for a percentage of box office receipts and other sales. Disney executives "know what they want and how to get it," says Midler, who has signed to do three more films for Disney. "Right now they want to make comedies, and they are making the best in town."

Moviemaking is a risky business, of course. A series of punishments at the box office could stunt Disney's comeback. And even though the studios are revving up, much of the payoff is years away. But it wasn't long ago that critics were saying Disney was too cautious, paying its way by selling off the family heirlooms. Not so today. For now, and with luck for well into the future, the wearer of the Magic Kingdom's crown can enjoy a prosperous reign.

Disney's Consumer Products Division plans to open its second The Disney Store in 1987 at San Francisco's Pier 39 tourist attraction. Disney opened its first test outlet in March in the Glendale Galleria, a regional shopping mall outside Los Angeles. "Disney's strategy is to test two different markets—the regional mall and a festival atmosphere with high tourist foot traffic—to see where the product is more acceptable." Disney plans to open six more stores, bringing its total to eight, by spring 1988. Those six probably will be split between mall and tourist locations. The 2,000-square-foot Glendale store carries both licensed merchandise and items created exclusively for Disney's theme-park stores. Like Disneyland's premiere fifth store, the Main Street Emporium, The Disney Store stocks everything from $2.50 wind-up toys to $30 Mickey Mouse watches to a $2,700 registered porcelain scene from Cinderella. Three video screens behind the sales counter continuously play scenes from Disney movies.

Disney is also building a retail complex at Lake Buenavista, even though it has no prior experience with shopping centers. And, in what is perhaps the ultimate topper, the company is about to issue its own "Mickey money"—scrip good only on Disney premises. Not only does Disney lock in attendees with its own currency, but the company will earn money on the float until the unused portion is refunded.

Disney wants to develop a shopping and entertainment complex in Burbank, California, that could cost $150 million to $300 million. Sources familiar with Disney said the recreation and entertainment components of the center might be similar to the attractions under construction at Pleasure Island, a new 6-acre nighttime entertainment facility at Walt Disney World in Orlando, Florida. Pleasure Island will offer "contemporary entertainment," Disney has said, including such things as "high-tech dancing," jazz music, a comedy club, and rollerskating. The Disney center might have certain rides or attractions similar to those at Disneyland, the company's original

EXHIBIT 1 The Walt Disney Company and subsidiaries: Consolidated statement of income (in millions except per share data)

Year Ended September 30	*1986*	*1985*	*1984*
Revenues			
Theme parks and resorts	$1,523.9	$1,257.5	$1,097.4
Filmed entertainment	511.7	320.0	244.5
Community development	305.1	315.3	204.4
Consumer products	130.2	122.6	109.7
	2,470.9	**2,015.4**	**1,656.0**
Costs and Expenses			
Theme parks and resorts	1,120.2	1,001.8	911.7
Filmed entertainment	460.1	286.3	242.3
Community development	263.3	249.6	162.2
Consumer products	57.8	66.3	55.8
	1,901.4	**1,604.0**	**1,372.0**
Income before Corporate Expenses and Unusual Charges			
Theme parks and resorts	403.7	255.7	185.7
Filmed entertainment	51.6	33.7	2.2
Community development	41.8	65.7	42.2
Consumer products	72.4	56.3	53.9
	569.5	**411.4**	**284.0**

Year Ended September 30	*1986*	*1985*	*1984*
Corporate Expenses			
General and administrative	66.0	49.9	59.6
Interest-net	41.3	51.6	41.7
	107.3	**101.5**	**101.3**
Income before Unusual Charges, Income Taxes, and Accounting Change	462.2	309.9	182.7
Unusual charges			166.0
Income before income taxes and accounting change	462.2	309.9	16.7
Income taxes (benefit)	214.9	136.4	(5.0)
	247.3	**173.5**	**21.7**
Income before Accounting Change			
Cumulative effect of change in accounting for investment tax credits			76.1
Net Income	**$247.3**	**$173.5**	**$97.8**
Earnings per Share			
Income before accounting change	$1.82	$1.29	$0.15
Cumulative effect of change in accounting for investment tax credits			0.53
	$1.82	**$1.29**	**$0.68**
Average Number of Common and Common Equivalent Shares Outstanding	**135.8**	**134.8**	**143.4**

EXHIBIT 2 Consolidated balance sheet (in millions)

	September 30	
	1986	*1985*
Assets		
Cash	$ 70.0	$ 38.7
Accounts and notes receivable	318.3	240.8
Merchandise inventories	93.0	84.8
Film production costs	230.1	182.1
Real estate inventories	214.0	220.8
Entertainment attractions and other properties, at cost		
Attractions, buildings and equipment	2,727.9	2,531.2
Accumulated depreciation	(812.2)	(702.0)
	1,915.7	**1,829.2**
Projects in progress	106.1	144.2
Land	26.8	28.3
	2,048.6	**2,001.7**
Other assets	147.0	128.4
	$3,121.0	**$2,897.3**
Liabilities and Stockholders' Equity		
Accounts payable, payroll and other accrued liabilities	$ 339.8	$ 270.0
Income taxes payable	96.6	59.0
Borrowings	547.2	823.1
Unearned deposits and advances	201.0	171.9
Deferred income taxes	517.7	388.4
Commitments and contingencies		
Stockholders' equity		
Preferred shares, no par		
Authorized—5.0 shares, none issued		
Common shares, no par		
Authorized—300.0 shares		
Issued and outstanding—130.7 and 129.4 shares	283.2	255.7
Retained earnings	1,135.5	929.2
	1,418.7	1,184.9
	$3,121.0	**$2,897.3**

theme park in Anaheim, California. But Disney officials have stressed that they don't want to build a facility that would compete with Disneyland, which is about 35 miles southeast of Burbank.

Disney's strategic planners obviously have been hard at work formulating, implementing, and evaluating strategies. Which of Disney's strategies do you agree are best

EXHIBIT 3 (Dollars in millions)

	1986	*Change*	*1985*	*Change*	*1984*
Theme Parks and Resorts					
Revenues	$1,523.9	+21%	$1,257.5	+15%	$1,097.4
Operating income	403.7	+58%	255.7	+38%	185.7
Operating margin	26%		20%		17%
Filmed Entertainment					
Revenues	$ 511.7	+60%	$ 320.0	+31%	$ 244.5
Operating income	51.6	+53%	33.7		2.2
Operating margin	10%		11%		1%
Consumer Products					
Revenues	$ 130.2	+6%	$ 122.6	+12%	$ 109.7
Operating income	72.4	+29%	56.3	+5%	53.9
Operating margin	56%		46%		49%
	1986	*Change*	*1985*	*Change*	*(Nine Months)*
Community Development					
Revenues	$305.1	−3%	$315.3	+54%	$204.4
Operating income	41.8	−36%	65.7	+56%	42.2
Operating margin	14%		21%		21%

for the company? Which ones would you not recommend? How can Disney best finance its proposed strategies? Develop pro forma financial statements for 1987 and 1988 to reveal what impact your strategies will have on Disney's financial condition. Exhibits 1 and 2 contain Disney's consolidated income statement and balance sheet for 1985–1986.

Springfield Ballet Company, Inc.—1987

MARY K. COULTER
Southwest Missouri State University
RONALD L. COULTER
Southwest Missouri State University
ROBERT L. TREWATHA
Southwest Missouri State University

The house lights dimmed. The orchestra began the familiar strains of Tchaikovsky's *Waltz of the Flowers* as the curtain rose. Another performance by the Springfield Ballet Company (SBC) was underway. Joe Howard Fisk, outgoing board of directors president for the Springfield Ballet Company sat in the upper level of the partially filled theatre and said to a fellow board member, "I wonder how many more times the curtain will rise for SBC performances. Our uncertain future and the survival of the troupe are the pressing problems facing our new president."

Fisk realizes that a nonprofit arts organization must develop and implement strategic marketing and management skills, just as any profit-oriented enterprise must do. "Furthermore," he said, "it is our ability to formulate effective and appropriate short-run and long-run strategies that will determine if future performances by SBC will continue. However, I am not sure we will ever be able to achieve efficiently our objective of building a dedicated ballet company and expanding public awareness of the arts through dance."

HISTORY OF SPRINGFIELD BALLET COMPANY

A local Springfield, Missouri, businessman and his wife created SBC in August 1976 when one of the couple's children had expressed an interest in dance. They decided to create a place for their child to receive ballet instruction by hiring a married couple from a neighboring city to teach the first ballet classes in Springfield solely devoted to classical training. Later, a retired professional dancer was also employed as an instructor. The studio was developed in an old downtown section of Springfield.

Other parents who also had children interested in receiving ballet instruction were involved as officers in the original ballet organization. As a child would complete all of the instruction available, the parents of that child would leave the ballet company's board to be replaced by a new set of interested parents. Thus, the board was organized originally on a personal interest basis, and, as a consequence, the operations of the organization and the board were very loosely managed.

Early Operations—1976–1979

The early years generated enough interest in ballet that a satellite school at a small private college approximately 40 miles south of Springfield was opened. While the satellite school did well initially, declining interest eventually forced it to close. During this period, the organization began bringing to the community guest performances by touring professional ballet companies such as the Atlanta Ballet and Chicago City Ballet, a practice that continues today. Financing for the appearances of these guest companies was obtained through the receipt of local and state grants and also by sale of public tickets to the performances.

During 1976, the Springfield Ballet Company attempted to unite the various ballet instructors from the small local dance schools into a strong regional ballet dance company. The rationale for this proposal was that ballet students would benefit by having the best ballet instructors in the area available to them. Instructors' expenses were to be shared through tuition payments. This effort failed due to specific fears by some dance instructors of possibly losing students permanently to other dance instructors and a general fear of competition.

Ballet Guild

A noted success of the Springfield Ballet Company during 1976 was the creation of the Springfield Ballet Guild, a fundraising unit for the Ballet that is still active today. The Guild is composed of women in the local community who are interested in the social aspects of the ballet company. Overseeing fundraising events and managing the sale of ballet-related items (such as leotards, sweatshirts, and earrings) at performances are the main activities of the Guild. During its first year, the Guild started a satellite operation in Lebanon, Missouri (a city approximately 40 miles east of Springfield). Sales from tickets for garden parties held by the Guild raised approximately $3,000 during 1976. Throughout the years, however, the Guild has had a cyclical existence, involving formation, then disbandment, then re-formation.

The Ballet's early development and performances were reported in the Springfield newspaper. Coverage was initially frequent and extensive, reflecting an attitude of support and a desire to have a growing and prosperous ballet in the community. Today, newspaper coverage for the SBC as well as the other arts groups in Springfield has declined.

First Artistic Director Position

In 1979, the Springfield Ballet Company hired Ms. Polly Brandman as its artistic director. Ms. Brandman had previously been associated with the Dayton Ballet in Ohio. Her dance interests were modern and contemporary ballet styles. She was pleasant and a very competent artistic director for her style of ballet. To increase interest in ballet and to attract more students to the Springfield Ballet school, she conducted lecture demonstrations in the Springfield public schools. The Springfield Ballet Company board of directors, however, felt that Springfield audiences wanted more traditional ballet performances rather than Ms. Brandman's preferred modern and contemporary ballet. Since a philosophical agreement could not be worked out between the board and Ms. Brandman based on the objectives of the Springfield Ballet Company, she resigned her position as artistic director in 1980.

Time Period: 1980–1984

The period between 1980 and 1984 proved to be an interesting but difficult time for the Springfield Ballet Company. Its board voted to join the National Association of Regional Ballets in 1980. The association has its headquarters in New York City, and its role is to promote and help regional ballet companies. Certain standards of excellence must be maintained to be a member of the association. These standards relate to (1) having a certain number of dancers in various age categories who dance in the company and (2) maintaining a set level of professional proficiency. Yearly dues are paid to the association by the member ballet companies. Each spring, the association holds district meetings to help dancers and regional ballet organizations improve their operations and performances. Additionally, the director of the association is available to member organizations in an advisory capacity. The director's expertise includes fundraising, management consulting, and artistic training.

The financial picture for the Springfield Ballet Company was not strong by 1981, and financial support was essential to help keep the organization alive. The Springfield Ballet Company had incurred a deficit of nearly $21,000. A grant of $4,000 funded by the Springfield Junior League and a $6,000 fundraising event helped to trim part of the deficit. In 1983, further support came from a seminar presented by the leader of the national color analysis consultant group, "Color Me Beautiful" which generated $4,000 for the Ballet. In 1985, the Springfield Ballet Company received a $5,000 grant from the Missouri Arts Council. Unfortunately, the Springfield Ballet Company's financial problems still continued because revenues were insufficient to support the Springfield Ballet Company's expenses.

Time Period: 1985–Present

In 1985, the ballet board hired Joan Kunsch as its new artistic director. In addition to her regular duties as artistic director, she helped develop and stage a major ballet production, *The Nutcracker,* in December 1985 for the community. Following this production, Kunsch took a six-month study leave, which was approved by the board. After her return, another one-month leave was requested. This leave request was unacceptable to the board, and the board decided a change in artistic director was necessary. A new director, Kathleen Schwartz-Nolen, joined the ballet in August 1986. Her instruction emphasis—like that of her predecessor—was toward the more traditional ballet form.

THE COMMUNITY OF SPRINGFIELD, MISSOURI

Springfield is centrally located in the heart of the Ozark Mountain Country recreational region and is often called the Queen City of the Ozarks. For a city of approximately 150,000 residents, it has a reasonable variety of community arts organizations. In addition to the ballet, the community offers the Springfield Symphony, the Springfield Art Museum, the Springfield Regional Opera, the Chameleon Puppet Theatre, and the Springfield Little Theatre. Also, two of the five colleges located in Springfield provide various arts performances.

As a model organization to the ballet, Springfield Little Theatre has been very successful in recent years after facing several extremely tight financial years. By developing a patron's group whereby each patron donates established levels of funding each year, the Springfield Little Theatre was able to solidify its base of operations. Patrons are given complimentary season tickets for performances. Other community arts organizations (including the Springfield Ballet Company) have tried this format but have not had the success of Little Theatre. For one thing, the Little Theatre has received strong support from the community at large. For example, musicals have been especially popular in the community, and that popularity has been translated into financial success and support for the organization. Its schedule of productions for each season includes several popular musicals that have a wide general audience appeal. In addition, many of its actors, actresses, and stage hands are involved with one of the five local colleges and university. The Springfield Little Theatre is a benchmark of success for most of the other Springfield arts organizations.

Community Support

One way the Springfield community supports the performing arts is through the annual "Salute to the Performing Arts." Now in its fifth year, this fundraising event is held at the posh University Plaza hotel in Springfield and has become one of the premiere social events of the year. Tickets to a formal dinner/dance are sold in the community. For each ticket sold at a price ranging from $125 to $150, John Q. Hammons, a successful local businessman, matches the ticket price with a personal donation. The total amount generated is then equally distributed among four performing arts groups (the Symphony, Ballet, Opera, and Theatre) in the city. The event has generated from $12,000 to $15,000 for each of the organizations every year of its existence. Unfortunately, 1987 will be the final year for this event.

CURRENT OPERATIONS

The Springfield Ballet Company is a nonprofit organization governed by a board of directors and executive committee. The board is very alert to the survival of the Springfield Ballet Company and its ability to compete effectively in the local arts marketplace. The board is currently attempting, with limited resources, to correct several areas in which the organization is weak.

Marketing

Developing a comprehensive and effective marketing program has not been a primary goal of the Springfield Ballet Company in the past. As with other types of nonprofit organizations, artistic people often feel that marketing their "product" is neither necessary nor even valuable. Because competition for entertainment dollars exists in the local marketplace, the Springfield Ballet Company has begun to realize that its marketing efforts have to be more sophisticated than the competition's efforts.

During the spring of 1985, the president of the Springfield Ballet Company board asked a local university to conduct a marketing survey to determine the community's knowledge of and interest in the ballet. The survey questionnaire was designed to gather information on the five major arts organizations in Springfield (the Symphony, Little Theatre, Art Museum, Regional Opera, and Ballet Company). This approach disguised the Springfield Ballet Company's interest in the information and provided community perceptions of the other local arts organizations. Key findings from the survey were that the Springfield Ballet Company was perceived to have low visibility in the community, low prestige, limited variety of arts performances, and low performance quality. Another interesting finding was that respondents wanted to see elaborate costumes, scenery, and stage sets in the Springfield Ballet Company performances.

Services Provided (Product)

The Springfield Ballet Company offers dance to the community through two means: dance instruction at the ballet school and dance performances by the Springfield Ballet Company or by touring companies. A typical 9-month season includes two major touring performances, one to two major Springfield Ballet Company productions, and one to two smaller studio performances by the Springfield Ballet Company.

During some seasons, the Springfield Ballet Company has presented smaller-scale sample performances at selected public schools throughout the area and at shopping malls. Attendance at major performances varies according to the reputation of the visiting company and the type of dances being performed. The *Nutcracker* (described in detail later) has been one of the Springfield Ballet Company's very few successes.

The Springfield Ballet School provides instruction in classical ballet training (basic through professional), adult classes, pre-ballet, pointe, partnering, exercise (aerobics), and jazz and folk dance. Current levels of enrollment at the school have been extremely disappointing.

Price

Admission prices to the performances throughout a season vary. For example, a reknowned artist or dance group brought in could possibly command higher prices for a performance. The Springfield Ballet Company tries to encourage as many season ticket sales and patron contributions as possible. A 1986–87 season ticket good for five performances (two guest ballet companies, one *Nutcracker* performance, and two studio concerts) sold for $35. A breakdown of sales is shown in Exhibit 1. The 1987–1988 season ticket price is the same as for the previous season. Prices are kept competitive with other local arts organizations when possible.

Promotion

Past promotional efforts have been lackluster, particularly for the dance school. The market survey noted previously reflects low visibility of the Springfield Ballet Company's activities in this area.

For other activities, a mailing list of people interested in ballet is maintained, and this group receives flyers and brochures throughout the year. Other forms of promo-

EXHIBIT 1

Season Tickets/Membership Donations

1986–87 (Final)	*1987–88 (as of 17 July 87)*
33 adult × $35 = $ 1,155	338 adult × $35 = $11,830
37 s/s[1] × 30 = 1,110	103 s/s × 30 = 3,090
30 adult × 25 = 750	
5 s/s × 20 = 100	
77 memb tkts = 11,300	129 memb tkts = 5,704
	208 B & Co. × 35 = 7,280
182 Total Tickets = $14,623	**778 Total Tickets = $27,904**

Grants

1986–87 (Final)			*1987–88 (as of 17 July 87)*		
MAC[3]	$ 6,000[3]		MAC[2]	$ 8,000[5]	
M-AAA[4]	1,000	Chicago City B.	M-AAA[4]	3,690	Ballet Folklorico[6]
M-AAA	4,650	Tulsa B. Th.	M-AAA	4,060	Dayton Ballet
	$11,650			**$15,750**	

Notes: [1] s/s—Student/Senior Citizen

[2] Missouri Arts Council

[3] received only $5,740 due to reserved amount not released, $2000 spent on Chicago City B., $2000 spent on "Nutcracker" guest artist, $1,740 spent on management staff.

[4] Mid-America Artists Alliance

[5] The following amounts must be used as a minimum: $1,800 Ballet Folklorico, $1,980 Dayton Ballet; funds used for Springfield Ballet performances can be used only for guest artists.

[6] This funding is for the two-performance contract fee of $10,000.

tion have been radio and TV spots, newspapers, and posters located in various businesses throughout the area.

Place

Most Springfield Ballet Company performances take place at the Landers Theatre in downtown Springfield. The Landers is an old landmark theatre recently renovated to reflect its beautiful and impressive heritage. It is currently the home of Springfield Little Theatre, although other arts organizations use the stage at the Landers, working around scheduled rehearsals and performances of the Little Theatre. Ballet and dance instruction takes place at the Springfield Ballet Company offices in the Vandivort Center, a recently renovated building housing other local arts groups next door to the Landers Theatre. A complete description of the Springfield Ballet Company's facilities is included in the "Operations" section of this case.

Management

Actual management of the Springfield Ballet Company is a function of the working relationship between the Springfield Ballet Company employees and the board. "Very involved" would be an accurate description of the board's role in the operations of the Springfield Ballet Company.

Board of Directors

Much of the management of the Springfield Ballet Company—particularly in the area of setting goals, policies, and plans—has been a function of the board of directors. Board members are very active. They not only function as management of the organization, but they also help in soliciting funds, ushering at performances, and putting up posters in storefront windows. Board members reflect a cross-section of community individuals who bring a particular expertise to the group. Unfortunately, many Springfield Ballet Company board members know very little about ballet, its history, and its value as an art expression.

The board currently has twenty-eight members and is authorized to increase to thirty-five members if necessary. The Executive Committee composed of the ten board officers performs most of the comprehensive and detailed activities of the board. A weekly staff meeting between the board president, the artistic director, and ballet's general manager is held, if needed, to identify and resolve requests and problems. Several advisory committees of the board have been formed to assist the executive committee in decision making. One of the most active has been the Personnel Committee. The full board meets monthly to (1) hear reports from the committees, the artistic director, and the business manager and (2) vote on decisions that come before it. One step taken by the immediate past president of the board was to conduct a training session for new board members and interested current board members. This training session is considered by participants as extremely valuable in their orientation and preparation for serving on the board.

Organization Chart and Job Descriptions

An organization chart does not exist for the organization, which has only two regularly paid employees—the artistic director and the general (business) manager. Other personnel such as secretaries, additional dance instructors, and pianists are brought in and paid as needed. The artistic director is a full-time position, responsible for directing the Springfield Ballet Company's artistic activities including education and performances. A formal job description for this position is available, but the way it is written has led to conflicts between the board and the present director. As noted earlier, the tenure of artistic directors over the last few years has been relatively short. The general manager's position is a one-half time position. A job description for the general manager was recently prepared and presented to the board during its last meeting of 1987. The board did not accept or implement any action relative to the document. Part-time status for this position is viewed by the board as appropriate at the present time.

Mission and Long-Range Plan

Besides collecting marketing information, another purpose of the market survey described earlier was to help the Springfield Ballet Company define what it was and how it was perceived by the public. After extensive discussion of these findings, the board decided to develop a mission statement and long-range plan. The mission statement as presented in the long-range plan is as follows:

> Springfield Ballet, Inc. exists to EDUCATE students and the public in techniques of dance, to PERFORM at the highest level possible, and to PRESENT the finest dance available for southwest Missouri.

The long-range plan was the culmination of intense effort by the long-range planning committee over a 15-month period. The ad hoc long-range planning committee was composed of five members from the board. Included in the plan were twelve base-year goals and a series of more specific objectives for each category of goals. These objectives are specified for five years and are intended to be updated every year so that there is an ongoing 5-year plan. The introduction to the 5-year plan and the list of base-year goals (note the categories) are shown in Exhibits 2 and 3.

Operations and Facility

The Springfield Ballet Company brings dance to the community in two ways: education and performance.

Dance School

Springfield Ballet School has never fully realized its potential. Different types of dance instruction for various age groups are offered at the downtown studios in the Vandivort Center. During the 1986–1987 season, average enrollment at the school was sixty-nine. Predictions for 1987–1988 are for approximately the same number or lower. A very limited survey (sample size = 30) conducted recently on interest in the

EXHIBIT 2 Introduction

"And David danced before the Lord with all his might . . ."
2 Samuel 6:14

This five year plan is intended as a roadmap to achievement in dance education by Springfield Ballet, Inc. Beginning with twelve base year (1986–87) goals, the plan was developed by articulating very carefully what the long range planning committee, representing a wide variety of viewpoints, wanted to see projected by the end of the fifth year (1990–91). Working backwards from those fifth year projections, each of the remaining four years was developed in logical attainable increments of growth. That articulation amounted to considerable hours of thoughtful planning and projections, shrewd calculations and a wonderful foray into dreaming. This plan can only be workable if it is monitored and refined in each of the five years of its projection. Each year another year should be added so that there is an ongoing five year plan.

I should like to thank the members of my committee for their very generous gifts of spirit and of time in the development of this long range plan. As I leave the board of directors after a very happy six-year commitment, it is my sincere hope that this roadmap will augment a new plateau of achievement by an organization whose goals are worthy and laudable: To Educate, To Perform and To Present.

William Brandon Bowman

EXHIBIT 3 Mission statement

Springfield Ballet, Inc. exists to EDUCATE students and the public in techniques of dance, to PERFORM at the highest level possible, and to PRESENT the finest dance available for southwest Missouri.

1986–87 Base Year Goals

I. To maintain and build Springfield Ballet School. (School)

II. To build a Springfield Ballet Company. (Company)

III. To present company performances. (Company Performances)

IV. To present two guest dance companies in performance. (Guest Companies)

V. To continue producing "The Nutcracker" annually. (The Nutcracker)

VI. To support Springfield Ballet Guild and its projects. (Guild)

VII. To maintain artistic director, general manager, school secretary, and custodian. (Administration)

VIII. To establish financial stability for the improvement of the administration, company, school, day-to-day operations, and lease requirements. (Finances)

IX. To sustain and increase community support. (Community Support)

X. To collaborate with other arts groups within this area. (Collaboration with Arts Groups)

XI. To locate and establish a facility for future use of Springfield Ballet, Inc. (Facility)

XII. To establish a system of orientation and guidance for members of the Board of Directors which will be monitored and updated. (Board of Directors)

---

ballet school verifies the low visibility of the school. Results of the survey are shown in Exhibit 4.

Dance Company/Other Public Performances

One desired outcome by both the board and the artistic director of having a dance school is the opportunity to develop an ongoing, fully staffed dance company that could present dance performances throughout the year. As it is now, this goal remains unattainable. Low and fluctuating enrollments at the school have never afforded the Springfield Ballet Company the opportunity to build a viable and ongoing dance company. Public performances by the Springfield Ballet Company currently are staffed with school enrollees and supplemented with other dancers from the community. Public performances by touring dance troupes (such as the Tulsa Ballet, the Chicago City Ballet, and the Alvin Ailey Dance Theatre) are paid for and hosted by the Springfield Ballet Company. None of the performances by visiting ballet companies have ever broke even.

Facilities

The Springfield Ballet Company has been housed in its present facility in the Vandivort Center since September 1986. Exhibit 5 shows the layout of the facility and also compares size and cost between the previous and current locations. Equipment such as

EXHIBIT 4 Survey results (in percents)

Children Interested in Dance Classes	
Yes	66.7
No or no answer	33.3
Willingness to Send Children to Dance Classes	
Yes	82
No or no answer	18
Preference for School Location	
Northwest	4.3
Northeast	13.0
Southwest	43.5
Southeast	17.4
Downtown	4.3
Other	17.4
Type of Dance Classes Desired	
Modern dance	35
Jazz	24
Ballet	16
Tap dance	16
Other	9

the sound system, the piano, exercise barres, and mirrors are adequate, although improvements could be made if resources were available.

Exhibits 6, 7, and 8 provide information about the Vandivort Center and its new occupants. All the local arts groups are hoping for a synergistic effect from being housed in a common location, and all hope to reinforce each other's successes.

Financial

The financial position of the Springfield Ballet Company has been improving, although the company doesn't have clear sailing yet. A current balance sheet and statement of earnings are shown in Exhibits 9 and 10 respectively. In the statement of earnings, an operating surplus of $9,098 is shown. This surplus is deceiving, however, since the organization still has some outstanding liabilities including a personal loan to be repaid to one of the directors. Exhibit 1 (page 325) shows the breakdown of revenues from season ticket sales and membership donations for the years 1986–1987 and 1987–1988 (as of the writing of the case). One activity that has had a significant impact on changing the financial course and direction of the organization was the decision to stage and present the *Nutcracker* ballet.

EXHIBIT 5 Layout of new facility and cost comparisons with previous facility

AREA	400 South Ave.		301 E. Walnut	
large studio	26 × 60	1560 sq. ft	40 × 48	1920 sq. ft
small studio	20 × 25	500	19 × 30	570
reception area	18 × 20	360	L-shaped	210
office #1	12 × 16	192	10 × 10	100
office #2	12 × 26	390	12 × 15	180
W dressing rm	14 × 16	224	9 × 24	216
M dressing rm	none		9 × 16	144
storage	9 × 16	144	basement	1000

Rent/month	$1200/$900		$650 w/4.5% added 3rd, 4th, & 5th yrs of lease. (includes utilities)	

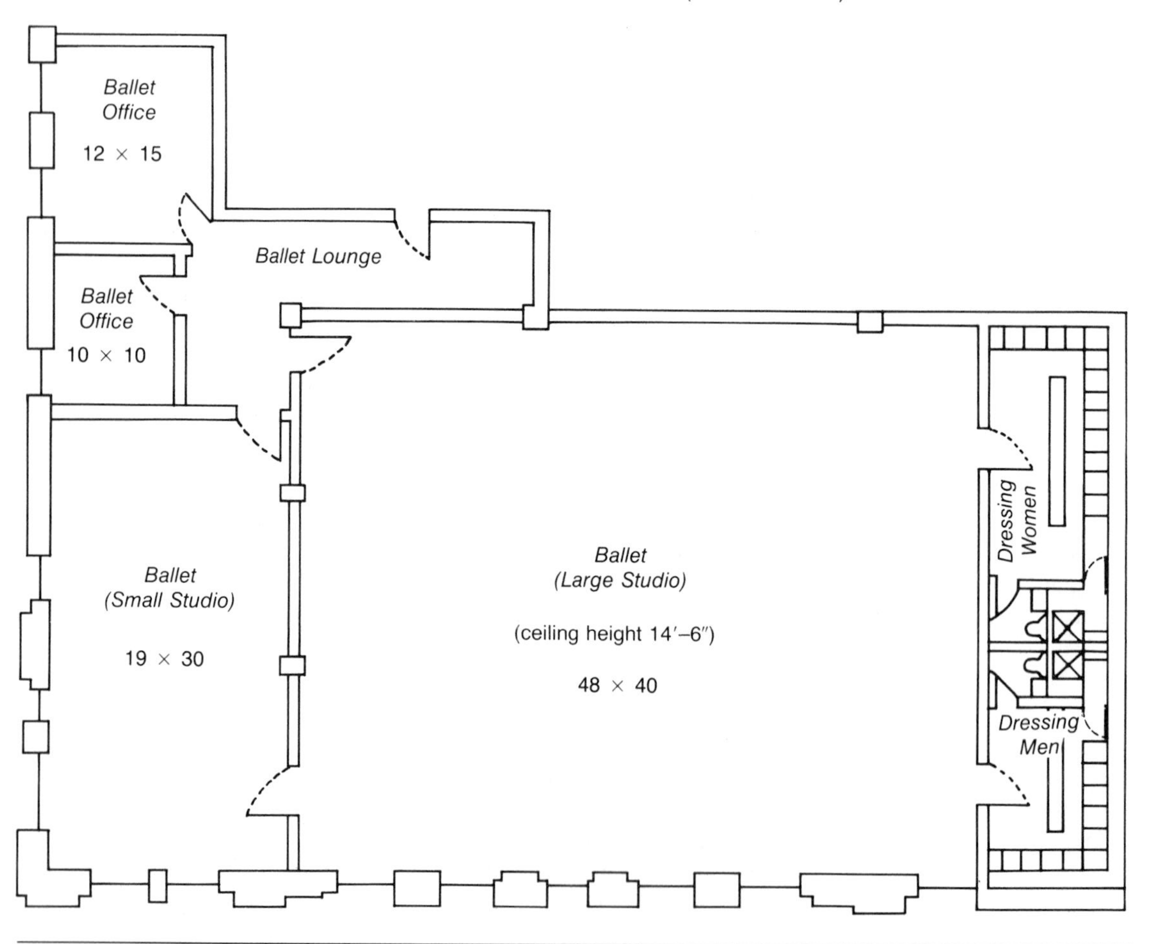

EXHIBIT 6 Newspaper information about the Vandivort Center

ARTS GROUPS SIGN LEASES FOR DOWNTOWN COMPLEX

By Peggy Soric
The Leader & Press

Four Springfield performing arts groups and the Springfield Area Arts Council announced today that they have signed leases for office, rehearsal and performance space in what will be Springfield's first arts complex, the Frances Vandivort Center at 301 E. Walnut St.

The third and fourth floors of the old Masonic Building will house offices and rehearsal space, as well as performance space for children's theater and puppet theater, for the Springfield Regional Opera, Springfield Ballet, Springfield Little Theatre, Chameleon Puppet Theater and the Springfield Area Arts Council.

Developer Jim Shirato, owner of the building adjacent to the Landers Theatre, said the projected date of completion of the renovation is August 1.

Shirato's firm, Manpower, will occupy one floor and office space on other floors has been leased to professional and service businesses, Shirato said.

At a news conference this morning at the center, Shirato said plans call for a ticket center in the lobby that will sell tickets for Springfield arts events as well as a variety of other functions.

"We're looking at future possibilities of catwalking from this building to the Boatmen's parking lot (Auto-Park)," he said. "That hasn't been agreed upon but will be considered when the need becomes greater."

Shirato said demolition of the Sedgwick Building, which he bought, is 35 percent completed. A parking lot will be created at that location to serve the theater patrons, patrons of events in the Frances Vandivort Center and employees.

Shirato said the lot will be "lighted, with a nice festive environment." He said he also has purchased the 14-space parking lot directly across from the Landers. "That will be used primarily during the day by tenants of the Frances Vandivort Center," he said, "and in the evening by patrons of the theater."

When renovation plans were announced in November 1985 Shirato said a first-floor restaurant with outdoor summer cafe service would be included, but those plans fell through. That space will be occupied instead by Architectural Designs Inc.

The building is on the city's list of historic sites and application for national historic site status has been made, Shirato said. He said his firm has located the company that manufactured and installed lights on 9-foot poles in the building in 1909 and purchased identical fixtures.

All interior and exterior lighting and security, elevators, heating and air conditioning will be computer-controlled. Shirato said, "The computers will act like day and night watchmen."

Shirato said he conceived of the idea of an arts complex downtown because he has long "been convinced the objectives of the performing arts groups would be enhanced if they could present a unified front."

"They were not going to be able to have that kind of administrative space available at the facility that is going to be built at SMS (Southwest Missouri State University)," he said.

The Springfield Symphony is the only major performing arts group in the city that will not locate offices in the downtown center. Shirato said he thinks the symphony made the best decision for its own purposes in choosing a location near their performance space at Evangel College. The symphony's offices will be located at 1536 E. Division St. in Smith Park.

"I can't take exception to their decision," Shirato said. "I congratulate them on a positive move."

Michael Murray, executive secretary of the SAAC, called the move a "coalition of arts groups." Murray said the complex has taken a high priority on the board agendas of arts groups

continued

EXHIBIT 6 continued

for the past six months. Completion of the center, he said, would be a significant moment in Springfield history.

Mick Denniston, artistic and business manager for Springfield Little Theatre, said theater administrators "envision a time in the not too distant future when the fourth floor theater will have performance events for young people every weekend of the year."

Springfield Ballet will make the move Sept. 1, said Louis H. Schaeffer, businesss manager and technical director for the group. "The space is wonderful," Schaeffer said of the two studios, two dressing rooms with showers and rest rooms, two office spaces and a lounge/reception room.

Dawin Emanuel, director of the opera company, said he thought the coalition of arts groups would be "a major solution to some problems of the past . . . not only greatly advantageous to these fine arts groups but will be a particularly convenient arrangement for arts audiences and participants."

Chameleon Puppet Theater executive director Nancy Spaeder said now that the company will have a resident theater in its home city after 10 years of touring, it will offer an advertised season from December until June with three original new puppet productions and 10 Saturday matinees.

Source: Springfield *Leader & Press,* May 27, 1986, p. 35. Reprinted with permission from Springfield Newspapers, Inc.

EXHIBIT 7 Additional newspaper coverage of the Vandivort Center

VANDIVORT CENTER EXCITES ARTS COMMUNITY

Stage Dell

By Peggy Soric

The big excitement in the performing arts community this week is the announcement that the Frances Vandivort Center will become a reality this summer.

Four major performing arts groups and the Springfield Area Arts Council have formed a coalition, coming together under one roof in a facility named for one of the arts community's most beloved figures, the late Frannie Vandivort.

The Springfield Little Theatre, Springfield Regional Opera, Springfield Ballet and Chameleon Puppet Theatre, as well as SAAC, will be office neighbors in the center and will share some rehearsal and performing space on the top two floors of the old Masonic Building, 310 E. Walnut. They'll also gain storage space in the basement.

Dawin Emanuel, director of the Springfield Regional Opera, said the basement space will be handy for SRO to store such equipment as portable light boards and cable.

Leaders of the groups say good use will be made of the fourth-floor theater, creating a space for children's theater and puppet theater as well as opera and ballet performances geared to children nearly every weekend of the year.

The opera company, Emanuel said, eventually will present programs there similar to the ones SRO took on tour through area schools.

Nancy Spaeder, executive director of the Chameleon Puppet Theatre, said she's thrilled to have a resident puppet theater in Springfield at last. Her company has been better known outside Springfield than in its home town for the past 8 years because most of that time the company has been in tour.

EXHIBIT 7 continued

In October Chameleon will begin holding classes in puppet making and acting with puppets for children in the new location and present three original puppet theater productions each season. The first at-home season will begin in December and continue through June.

Spaeder said Chameleon will also bring in guest puppet companies from around the U. S. and children's theater companies such as The Imaginary Theatre Company from St. Louis.

The Springfield Ballet Inc. will move into the center Aug. 1. Louis H. Schaeffer, business and technical manager for the ballet company, said he, board members and dancers are delighted with the prospect of working in two large dance studios (40-by-48 feet and 19-by-30 feet), two dressing rooms with showers and rest rooms, two office spaces and a lounge-reception area. Classes will begin Sept. 1.

Springfield Little Theatre will rent classroom and rehearsal space in the center, allowing for expansion of its ever-growing educational programs, directed by Philip Maguire. Rehearsal for seven LT mainstage productions will be held in the huge hall adajacent the 4th floor theater, and many, if not all, of the classes and workshops will move from the upper floors of the Landers to the center.

The new theater will seat 380, and LT hopes to use it for studio productions, opening night events and new programs for young people.

Mick Denniston, LT artistic and managing director, said he and others in LT management envision a time soon when the 4th floor theater in the center will be used every weekend of the year.

Denniston said the move to bring arts organizations into closer cooperation is significant. He's written an application for an Apple Community Foundation grant to provide a networking computer that would be shared by the opera, theater and ballet. The foundation gets many requests, but the Springfield arts community can hope.

Denniston said there's now a good bit of computer software that has specific applications to performing arts groups that would save staff time. For example, some programs could bring up seating charts at the touch of a computer command and tell reservationists immediately what's available on the requested night. The three groups would be able to use such a network for scheduling and creating common inventories of such things as costumes, for example. In a matter of seconds the computer could tell any member of the group where to find Spanish peasant costumes or Victorian costumes.

Incidentally, mark June 28, LT's sidewalk costume sale, on your calendar. "Lou (Louis Schaeffer) and I will go through and decide what we want to keep," Denniston said. The sale will be held in the parking lot directly across from the landers, 311 E. Walnut.

Denniston was very enthusiastic about the move to bring arts groups together next door to the theater. "Just to have that kind of focus on these two buildings as a joint center for the arts is not only good for the arts," he said, "but for the downtown area."

Source: Springfield *Leader & Press*, May 29, 1986, p. 50. Reprinted with permission from Springfield Newspapers, Inc.

THE NUTCRACKER

The *Nutcracker* ballet is a familiar, much-loved holiday tradition in many cities. Staging the *Nutcracker* ballet during the December holiday season has been the salvation of many struggling local ballet companies. It was with this thought in mind that the Springfield Ballet Company made a commitment to preparing and presenting public performances of the *Nutcracker*. Cynthia Cooper, board president during 1984–1985

EXHIBIT 8 More newspaper information about the Vandivort Center

HARMONY OF ARTS GROUPS BENEFITS THE OZARKS

Ours

Harmony. There's nothing like it. It's as good for relationships as it is for barbershop quartets.

That's why it's good to see what appears to be a new era of cooperation about to begin in the Springfield performing arts community.

The groups have worked together with greater frequency and enthusiasm in the last decade and that has been to everyone's benefit.

But in the next few months, four performing groups and the Springfield Area Arts Council will come together under one roof in the Frances Vandivort Center. It would seem likely that when creative artists combine efforts toward common goals the results will be exciting.

Plans call for an Aug. 1 move into the refurbished Masonic Building for the Springfield Ballet. Soon to follow will be the Springfield Regional Opera, the Chameleon Puppet Theatre and the arts council. Springfield Little Theatre, now located in the building next door, will be able to expand educational and studio theater programs in new work and performance space.

The children of Springfield may be the first to benefit. There will be live performances for children nearly every weekend of the year as soon as all the groups settle in and plan programs. When children benefit, the world becomes a better place.

But adult Springfield audiences have shown a growing appetite for the performing arts. They too will enjoy the benefits.

Beyond that, there's a bottom-line item. We know the importance of the quality-of-life issue to businesses and professionals when they search for a new community.

When a community has a performing arts coalition in an upward spiral gaining new advocates and audience growing and expanding, it gains points as a lure for the right kind of businesses the Ozarks would like to have.

While the Springfield Symphony is not included in this group, we have confidence that the creative fund raising the Symphony Guild has always done will continue and will keep that organization vital and strong.

And we join the groups that will become neighbors in the Frances Vandivort Center in their celebration of a new period in the arts for the Ozarks.

Source: Springfield *Daily News*, June 16, 1986. Reprinted with permission from Springfield Newspapers, Inc.

and a long-time supporter of the ballet, spearheaded the drive to make this a successful and financially sound event. She made the *Nutcracker* her personal cause to help change the direction and fortunes of the organization. Working closely with the director of the National Association of Regional Ballets, she developed a fundraising campaign directed to the *Nutcracker.* A series of parties called "Christmas in July" were held at three exclusive homes in Springfield. Prominent (and invariably wealthy) community residents were invited and were assured that if they donated at these parties, they would not be asked to donate to the Ballet for the next year. Significant cash donations as well as sponsorship of costumes and other scenery items needed for the performance were obtained. The sponsors' names appeared in program brochures and announcements. The parties were a huge success—a total of $30,000 was raised through private donations.

EXHIBIT 9 Springfield Ballet, Inc. balance sheet

	May 31 1987	*June 30 1987*	*Memo: June 30 1986*
	Assets		
Current Assets			
Cash on hand and in bank	9,358	23,460	11,729
Cash in savings	71,252	150,005	—
Prepaid expenses	2,164	51,810	2,391
Accounts receivable	707	520	216
Deposits	25	25	25
Total Current Assets	**83,506**	**225,820**	**14,361**
Property and Equipment			
Costumes & sets	14,217	14,217	12,814
Furniture, fixtures and equpment	14,739	14,739	14,369
Leasehold improvements	354	—	354
	29,310	**28,956**	**27,537**
Less accumulated depreciation	14,583	14,811	9,357
Net Property and Equipment	**14,727**	**14,145**	**18,180**
	98,233	**239,965**	**32,541**
	Liabilities and Fund Balance		
Current Liabilities			
Notes payable—current	16,000	16,000	18,306
Accounts payable	—	1,093	207
Payroll taxes payable	896	659	760
Accrued expenses	189	1,082	170
Advances for B. & Co. Concert	70,913	198,935	—
Total Current Liabilities	**87,998**	**217,769**	**19,443**
Notes Payable—long-term	**8,000**	**8,000**	**8,000**
Fund balance—beginning of year	5,098	5,098	5,098
Current surplus (deficit)	(2,863)	9,098	
Total fund balance	**2,235**	**14,196**	**5,098**
	98,233	**239,965**	**32,541**

The first *Nutcracker* was presented during one weekend (three performances) in December 1985. Although not a sellout, the presentation attracted a large crowd. Based upon the positive comments heard from the community, a commitment was made to present the *Nutcracker* over two December weekends in 1986. More funds were raised, and the Springfield Ballet Company was able to upgrade the scenery and

EXHIBIT 10 Springfield Ballet, Inc. Statement of Earnings, 12 months ended June 30, 1987.

	Current Year-to-Date	*Budgeted Year-to-Date*	*Prior Year-to-Date*
Donations	31,256	30,000	56,527
Grants	11,073	15,650	5,000
Admissions	35,096	44,000	26,985
Membership	28,881	12,500	5,090
Tuition	13,236	13,070	14,687
Other Income	10,070	5,700	6,915
Total Revenue	**129,612**	**120,920**	**115,204**
Production Expenses	50,197	52,500	22,588
Musicians	588	3,490	3,168
Artistic Director	18,678	18,360	18,325
General Manager	9,654	9,192	9,792
Instructors	3,365	4,596	2,879
Receptionist	1,698	0	45
Payroll Taxes	2,417	3,587	2,579
Rent	6,751	10,800	13,200
Telephone	1,951	1,980	1,801
Postage	3,326	1,290	919
Janitorial	1,567	1,200	978
Insurance	2,014	3,192	1,643
Supplies	2,653	1,230	935
Advertising	1,695	1,095	943
Dues and Sub.	126	258	651
Repairs and Maintenance	310	240	304
Miscellaneous	939	600	451
Depreciation	5,808	5,200	5,146
Interest Expense	2,020	2,160	2,651
Art. Dir. Select.	136	0	522
Moving Expenses	1,087	0	0
Audit	960	1,000	984
Bad Debt	125	0	0
Newsletter	2,449	0	2,036
Operating Expenses	**120,514**	**121,980**	**92,540**
***Operating Surplus* (Deficit)**	**9,098**	**−1060**	**22,664**

costumes. The 1986 season was almost a complete sellout. The Springfield Ballet Company hopes it has established a community tradition and is proceeding with plans to present the *Nutcracker* in December 1987. As each year passes, the Springfield Ballet Company is able to improve the quality of the presentation (such as scenery, sets, costumes, and paid dancers) because the company is no longer starting from scratch. Although the *Nutcracker* ballet has kept the Springfield Ballet Company afloat financially, problems still haunt the organization.

BACK TO THE PRESENT

A well-deserved round of applause for the dancers arouses Joe Howard Fisk from his thoughts. To his friend and fellow board member, he comments, "As the outgoing board president, what do I say to the new president and oncoming board members? What help and suggestions need to be given so that the Springfield Ballet Company survives and even prospers in the ever-competitive local arts marketplace? As you know, working with a small ballet company requires putting a lot of pieces of a complex puzzle into place. What should be our strategies and plans now?"

EPILOGUE

On June 3, 1987, a telephone call was received that could be instrumental in changing the course of the Springfield Ballet Company. The call was received at the Springfield Ballet Company offices; it stated that Mikhail Baryshnikov and Company was going on a nationwide tour, and the company representative wanted to know if Springfield was interested in hosting a performance. The only hurdle was that a financial commitment for $92,000 was needed within a week's time or the troupe would make plans to go elsewhere. The board immediately set about drumming up the support and, with no time to spare, accepted the Baryshnikov offer!

Currently, the Springfield Ballet Company is ecstatic, and the community is abuzz with excitement and anticipation. Tickets are priced at $50, $35, and $25 (in St. Louis and Tulsa—the only other two locations nearby that are hosting a performance—tickets are $100, $70, and $50). Tickets for the Springfield performance, which is to be played to a maximum of 4,000 persons, are sold out. Of the 4,000 available tickets, 1,000 are $50 seats, 1,000 are $35 seats, and 2,000 are $25 seats. Additional revenues can be generated from items sold at the concert, although Baryshnikov and Company receives 40 percent of the profits from these. Total costs for the concert (including such items as performance fees and advertising) are projected to be approximately $100,000. The board is already making plans to get out of debt and establish a small endowment with the profits from the concert. This concert may indeed be the "turning point" for the Springfield Ballet Company!

East Alabama Medical Center—1987

FRED DAVID
Auburn University
TOM DAVIDSON
Auburn University
DAVID MCBRIDE
Auburn University

"Nurse, may we have a bottle of A1 steak sauce and some more champagne, please?" This request may seem somewhat unusual to anyone who has spent much time in a hospital. However, a quiet, candle-lit steak and champagne (non-alcoholic) dinner for two is the customary night-before-checkout meal at East Alabama Medical Center's Maternity Ward. East Alabama Medical Center has a tradition of offering extra services to its patients and visitors and is actively seeking new ways to better serve the residents of Lee County and the surrounding areas.

BACKGROUND

The East Alabama Medical Center, which is owned and operated by the East Alabama Health Care Authority, was opened at its present site in the city of Opelika, Alabama, on February 16, 1952, as a public, non-profit, acute-care hospital with eighty beds. In order to keep pace with the growing health care needs of east central Alabama, the hospital has undergone several expansion and modernization programs. Facilities were expanded and modernized in 1963, 1967, 1970, 1971, 1980, and 1985. The 1985 expansion increased the hospital's licensed bed capacity to 334.

East Alabama Medical Center is presently a general, acute-care regional medical center operating 148 private beds, 166 semi-private beds, and twenty ward beds (all ward beds are located in the substance abuse wing). The East Alabama Medical Center is located on approximately 24 acres and consists of one major building, which contains 260,000 gross square feet, and three small support buildings. Parking for approximately 800 automobiles is provided on ground level adjacent to the main building.

The East Alabama Medical Center has been continuously accredited by the Joint Commission on Accreditation of Hospitals since February 1959 and is presently accredited through January 1988. It is licensed by the Alabama State Board of Health and is a member of the American Hospital Association, the Alabama Hospital Association, and the Southeastern Hospital Conference. The East Alabama Medical Center is certified for participation in the Medicare and Medicaid programs.

The primary service area for the East Alabama Medical Center is Lee County, Alabama, with 65 percent of its admissions originating from the county. The medical center is the only hospital within the primary service area. The secondary service area for the medical center is the five surrounding counties: Chambers, Macon, Randolph, Russell, and Tallapoosa. The remaining balance of East Alabama Medical Center admissions originated from Tallapoosa County (10%), Chambers County (9%), Macon

County (8%), Randolph County (2%), and other counties (6%). The population growth for these areas averaged 15 percent for the 1970s and is projected to be approximately 11 percent for the 1980s.

THE COMMUNITY

The East Alabama Medical Center is located about 100 miles southwest of Atlanta. Lee County is largely a rural area with the exception of the cities of Auburn and Opelika. Lee County has a total population of 90,000 people, approximately 50,000 of whom reside in the Auburn/Opelika area. The county population grew 24 percent in the 1970s, and the projected growth rate for the 1980s is approximately 19 percent.

Auburn University is the area's largest employer with more than 7,000 employees and 20,000 students. Other major area employers are Diversified Products, Uniroyal, and West-Point Pepperell. The East Alabama Medical Center has been deeply involved with the community over the past three decades, supporting many community service programs such as Lifeline—an emergency response unit, Rise & Shine Walking Club—a group that walks daily in a nearby mall and promotes fitness activities, Options in the 80s—an annual community fair, Adopt a School program, and groups that assist in overcoming chemical dependence and promoting community mental health.

INDUSTRY

Despite favorable long-term demographic trends and the nation's insistence on quality health care, the outlook for the hospital industry remained poor in 1986. A combination of negative factors, including declining utilization rates, increasing costs, and competition from alternate health care providers, continues to depress hospital earnings. High fixed and operating expenses and under-utilization of hospital facilities has severely penalized the industry. The earnings of leading hospital management chains generally declined in 1985 and 1986.

According to U.S. Department of Commerce estimates, hospital care accounted for about 39 percent of the nation's total $465 billion health care bill in 1986. That proportion has been declining since its peak of 44 percent in 1982, primarily reflecting sweeping reforms in Medicare reimbursement practices. Hospitals' share of health care costs is expected to remain below 40 percent in the years ahead. According to the Health Care Financing Administration, the nation's $167 billion hospital bill in 1985 was funded as follows:

- ☐ Federal sources (mostly Medicare) 43%
- ☐ Private health insurance 37%
- ☐ State and local funding 11%
- ☐ Direct private payments 9%

The industry was especially hard hit by sharp increases in contractual allowances—i.e., the difference between gross revenues or billed rates and amounts actually reimbursed by Medicare. Contractual allowances have risen markedly in recent years, reflecting the freezing of diagnostic-related group (DRG) rates and budget cuts under the Gramm-Rudman Act. Now completely phased in, the DRG system reimburses hospitals according to a fixed payment schedule for some 470 different kinds of illnesses. While hospital profitability fared relatively well during the initial DRG phase-in period, hospital margins have since deteriorated considerably. According to the American Hospital Association, net patient margins during the first nine months of 1986 fell 68 percent, to 0.6 percent from 1.09 percent in the earlier period.

After expanding at double-digit rates throughout the 1970s, expenditures for hospital services increased 8.5 percent in 1986, and similar growth is likely in 1987. Hospital costs rose at a compound annual rate of 13.2 percent in the 1974–1984 period but rose only 4.3 percent during the 1985–1987 period. This slowing reflected the imposition of Medicare's new DRG system, increased cost-consciousness on the part of third-party payers, and the creation of peer review organizations to oversee and audit procedures done on Medicare patients.

More Favorable Outlook

Admissions to psychiatric hospitals are not constrained by DRG limitations and have increased in recent years. Psychiatric service has increased due to a significant change in social attitudes toward this kind of medical care. According to the National Institute of Mental Health, approximately 29 million adult Americans suffer from mental illness; yet, fewer than one-fifth seek professional treatment. As public awareness of the problem increases, experts see a significant potential for expanded nationwide psychiatric service utilization in the years ahead. Supported by strong underlying demographic and reimbursement trends and a favorable supply/demand picture, the extended-care segment of the industry also remains a bright spot in the health care service market. Total spending for extended care rose at a 15.8 percent compounded annual rate in the twenty years through 1985, compared with a 12.8 percent rate for total health care outlays for that same period.

THE ORGANIZATION

The East Alabama Medical Center is headed by a nine-member board that oversees all operations. In 1983, National Healthcare, Inc., a firm specializing in hospital administration, was contracted to manage the East Alabama Medical Center. This type of arrangement has increased in popularity over the last few years. The hospital's administrator, Mr. Terry Andrus, reports directly to the board. Mr. Andrus, a graduate of Georgia Tech, has been at the East Alabama Medical Center since 1981.

The hospital administration staff is supported by an auxiliary staff of 210 adults and forty-eight youth volunteers. The auxiliary, largely supported by the United Way, is involved with various community projects and newsletters. Working with the board and hospital administration are seventy-three physicians, ranging from dermatologists to cardiologists.

Financial Services

The financial services function of the East Alabama Medical Center is headed by Ken Robinson and consists of five departments: PBX, Data Processing, Accounting, Materials Management, and the Business Office. These areas are primarily responsible for collecting and compiling financial information within the hospital. The information is used by management to prepare incremental budgets (quarterly and annual) for performance evaluations, for forecasting future monetary needs, and for conducting strategic planning. This information is gathered on a departmental basis so that each level of hospital operation can be examined separately.

Hospital Operations

Mr. Wayne Poe, senior vice-president, heads the operations function of the East Alabama Medical Center that includes Nursing Services, Operations, and Support Services. The Nursing Services Department is designed to respond to the needs of patients and employees. For patient care, the East Alabama Medical Center uses a "total care" approach with registered nurses (RNs) and licensed practical nurses (LPNs). The Educational Services Department provides nurses with many educational programs to assist them with re-certification and to enhance nursing care at the hospital. The Operations Department is responsible for providing patients with services such as radiology and anesthesia. Operations is also responsible for support functions such as housekeeping, laboratory services, social services, and pharmacy services.

COMPETING HOSPITALS

The EAMC is the only acute-care hospital in Lee County. The secondary service area contains seven competing hospitals, but none of these hospitals have the number of beds or range of services offered by the East Alabama Medical Center. Moreover, none of the competing hospitals are designated as referral centers. Rather, they refer complicated cases to other acute-care hospitals such as the East Alabama Medical Center.

Analysis of a hospital's market share in a service area is determined by comparing the patient origin of that hospital, along with the patient origin of all other hospitals that draw admissions from that service area. The state of Alabama conducts annual state-wide patient origin studies. These studies show discharges from each hospital in the state, with discharges grouped by the patient's county of residence. The East Alabama Medical Center's market share in the five-county service area is forecasted to remain stable at 33 percent.

SERVICE AREA UTILIZATION

Hospital utilization rate (use rate) is expressed in terms of admissions per 1,000 service area residents. For 1985, utilization rate was approximately eighty-five admissions per 1,000 persons residing in Lee County. For 1982, the East Alabama Medical Center's utilization rate was approximately eighty-five admissions per thousand. When admissions to all service area hospitals outside the service area are included, the 1985 estimated use rate for Lee County residents was 117 admissions per thousand, compared to 133 per thousand in 1982. The average use rate for both Alabama and the nation was 159 in 1985. The national use rate in 1982 was approximately 160 per thousand. The below-average inpatient use rate for Lee County may be due to the large number of college-age Auburn University students included in the county's population.

MEDICAL STAFF ANALYSIS

An important factor in the demand for hospital services at the East Alabama Medical Center is the continued growth, support, and viability of the medical staff. East Alabama Medical Center's staff has grown in number and increased in specialties offered over the past several years. Also, the single largest age group of physicians at the East Alabama Medical Center is the 35–44 age bracket. Assuming the absence of significant attrition among members of the medical staff, the high concentration of medical doctors in that age bracket should provide an adequate supply of admitting physicians.

Since July 1982, only one physician, an obstetrician/gynecologist, has left the active staff, while ten physicians—one anesthesiologist, one family practitioner, one surgeon, one psychiatrist, one pediatrician, one neurosurgeon, one emergency medicine physician, and three internal medicine physicians—have joined the staff. The resulting medical staff at year-end 1986 was composed of seventy-three members, fifty-four of whom are board-certified.

In addition to the active medical staff, the East Alabama Medical Center has an eight-physician dental staff and a courtesy staff of eight other physicians. Management of the East Alabama Medical Center intends to continue recruitment efforts for new physicians. Management anticipates that an additional cardiologist, an oncologist, and a cardiac surgeon will be added to the medical staff in the near future.

FINANCIAL HISTORY

A major source of East Alabama Medical Center revenues is outpatient services, such as emergency room visits, laboratory tests, outpatient surgery, radiology procedures, and various other services. The bulk of the East Alabama Medical Center's expenses are incurred as a direct result of the delivery of inpatient and outpatient services.

One of National Healthcare's initial activities in 1983 was to increase the East Alabama Medical Center's overall rate structure, which was well below that of comparable hospitals. This action, combined with the advent of Medicare prospective payment and the maintenance of a staffing ratio of 3.2 full-time equivalent per adjusted occupied bed, resulted in a significant increase in profitability in 1984. A major construction project at the East Alabama Medical Center was financed in February 1983 and completed in May 1985.

Fiscal 1985 represented a transition year for the East Alabama Medical Center. New facilities were brought on line that added to depreciation, interest, and personnel expenses without attendant increases in patient volume. Additionally, management implemented a new accounts receivable management process that improved cash flow significantly and resulted in a one-time adjustment to 1985 results. The East Alabama Medical Center experienced an operating loss for fiscal 1985.

For fiscal year 1986, the East Alabama Medical Center experienced significant increases in all key utilization indicators and generated an operating margin in excess of $1 million. The results reflect the successful completion of the expansion project as well as continued program development and close attention to operations.

FUTURE CONCERNS

In discussing the future of the East Alabama Medical Center, Mr. Terry Andrus cites several areas of special concern, such as decreasing population growth, increasing unemployment, emerging trends in third-party payments, offering of new services, and the rising cost of malpractice insurance. Sixty-five percent of the East Alabama Medical Center's admissions originate in Lee County; its population growth rate for the 1980s has declined to 19 percent from 24 percent in the 1970s. This five percent drop poses problems, especially if the trend continues into the 1990s. Reduced numbers of admissions and underutilization of inpatient and outpatient services could result. Reduction of present services and a loss of medical staff could also occur. In addition, declining population projections could curtail service expansion programs.

Both the primary and secondary service areas' economic forecasts predict an increase in unemployment. As unemployment increases, the general service area population will spend less on medical care. Typically, non-life-threatening surgery and treatment will be put off until more prosperous times. Some of the unemployed will become delinquent in payment on their accounts or discontinue payment altogether. This practice could place a financial strain on the hospital, especially when combined with the Medicaid DRG program.

Sound and timely strategic planning can enable the East Alabama Medical Center to better weather impending storms. Some possible strategies include use of self-insurance to decrease malpractice insurance costs, formation of an outpatient mental health program to help the unemployed cope with their situation, termination of unprofitable services, and termination of indigent care services.

Exhibits 1–18 provide related information about East Alabama Medical Center. In a formal statement of goals and objectives, the East Alabama Medical Center describes four key strategies for future growth and survival. What is your assessment of these strategies, and how could they best be implemented?

1. The East Alabama Medical Center must be committed to the continuing addition of new and improved services. In 1986, the cardiology service and the psychiatric substance abuse service were greatly expanded both from a facility and program standpoint. This type of progress must continue in 1987 and in the future. In 1987, some of the key services that will be added include oncology and cardiovascular surgery.

EXHIBIT 1 A picture of East Alabama Medical Center

2. The second key component for the continuous growth and survival of the East Alabama Medical Center is continuing good relationships with our physicians. The physicians on our medical staff are, along with our patients, our main customers. The physician admits patients to our facility for a variety of services and places his trust in the performance of our professional and service staff. A key for the East Alabama Medical Center is to continue to work with our physicians to provide them with the needed equipment, facilities, and professional and service staff to take care of their patients while at the East Alabama Medical Center. There may be new and different working relations with physicians in the future that have not occurred in the past. It will require the hospital to share potentially some of its power and potentially some of its revenue sources with physicians in order for the hospital and for the physicians to be successful.
3. The third component of the key strategy for the future is product segmentation. By product segmentation, we mean the creation of a product that sets the East Alabama Medical Center apart from your typical hospital. Much of this product segmentation will be intertwined into new services, but it is more than that. It includes the guest-related aspects of the hospital to create a friendly, personal atmosphere at our hospital.
4. The fourth component for the East Alabama Medical Center in the future is to maintain financial integrity. Our hospital must do well financially in order to continue to grow. We feel that there are three aspects of financial integrity that are vitally important. The first is profitability. The hospital has to be profitable year in and year out. The two components that management must address to maintain this profitability in 1987 are productivity, which relates to

EXHIBIT 2 East Alabama Medical Center Hospital Service Area

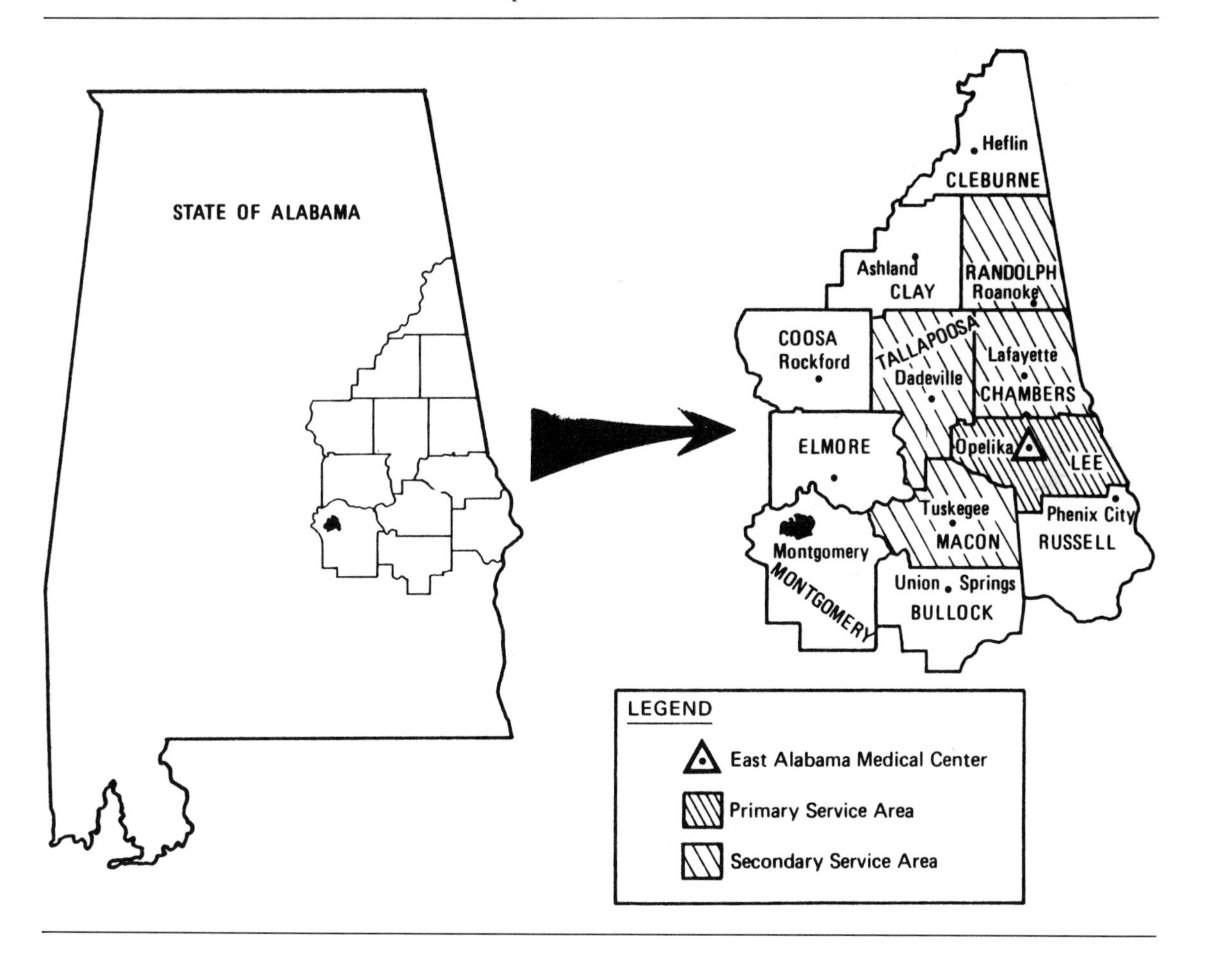

salary and people resources and non-salary operating expenses. The second factor that is important in financial integrity is cash accumulation. The East Alabama Medical Center has accumulated approximately five and a half million dollars worth of cash in the first several years, but that is just the beginning. In order for us to be positioned appropriately, we must accumulate cash. We are not in the same situation as some other institutions with large sums of money in the bank so that if the Medicare rules change, or if their census drops off, or if some other adverse occurrence happens that they cannot control, it does not create a crisis situation. The last aspect in regard to financial integrity is capital needs. The East Alabama Medical Center over the next several years needs to spend a great deal on capital needs, to renovate existing parts of the hospital, to create capital for some of the new services that we are adding and also capital for potential new services down the road.

EXHIBIT 3 East Alabama Medical Center Report for fiscal year ending September 1986

Patients admitted—adults and children				11,008
Total days of hospital care				78,464
Average length of hospital stay				6.44 Days
Available beds				334
Cost per day				
Semiprivate				$180.00
Private				$195.00
Progressive ICU				$350.00
Intensive Care				$475.00
Newborn deliveries				1,221
Room Costs—Normal Delivery				
ICU Nursery				$175.00
Nursery				$100.00
Semiprivate				$150.00
Labor-Delivery				$360.00
Minimum normal delivery cost				$1,950.00
Average cost per delivery				$2,300.00
Physicians on staff				76
Number of physicians board certified				60
Specialties offered and physicians				
Anesthesiologists	3	Orthopedists	6	
Cardiologists	3	Otorhinolaryngologists	1	
Dermatologists	2	Pathologists	2	
Emergency Services	4	Pediatricians	6	
Endoscopists*	2	Psychiatrists	2	
Family Practitioners	9	Radiologists	4	
Internists	10	Surgeons:	6	
Nephrologists	1	Plastic 1		
Neurologists	1	Vascular 1		
Neurosurgeons	2	Thoracic 1		
Obstetricians/Gynecologists	6	General 3		
Oncologists	1	Cardiovascular**		
Ophthalmologists	3	Urologists	2	
Oral Surgeons	1			
In-Patient surgical procedures performed				3,952
Out-Patient surgical procedures performed				2,277
Emergency Room patients				23,985
Licensed Practical Nurses				62
Registered Nurses				273
Average hospital daily operating cost				$85,630.00
Fiscal year hospital operating cost				$31,254,789.00

*Included in other specialties

**Expected in January 1988

EXHIBIT 4 Six physicians or physician groups with the highest number of admissions for the six months ended March 31, 1986

Rank	*Number of Physicians*	*Specialty*	*Percentage of Admissions*	*Age of Physician or Average Age of Members of Group*
1	11	Internal Medicine	24.2	41
2	7	Surgery	14.4	50
3	6	Obstetrics/Gynecology	13.3	46
4	9	Family Practice	11.1	47
5	3	Psychiatry	7.5	41
6	6	Orthopedics	7.4	41

Source: Medical Center.

EXHIBIT 5 Distribution of medical staff by age correlated to percentage of admissions for the twelve months ended March 31, 1986

Age Group	*Medical Staff as of March 31, 1986*		*Percentage of Admissions*
	Number	*Percentage*	
Under 35	8	11.0	9.0
35–44	33	45.0	41.0
45–59	27	37.0	47.0
60–64	3	4.0	2.0
65 and over	2	3.7	1.0
Total	**73**	**100.0**	**100.0**

Source: Medical Center.

EXHIBIT 6 Distribution of operating beds by service/accommodation type

	Beds in Service
Service	
Medical/surgical	150
Obstetric	32
Pediatric	11
Progressive care	21
Intensive care	16
Psychiatric	50
Total	**280**
Type of Accommodation	
Private	110
Semiprivate	132
Intensive care	16
Progressive care	22
Total	**280**

EXHIBIT 7 Historical inpatient utilization

Year	*Admissions*	*Average Length of Stay*	*Patient Days*	*Operating Beds*	*Occupancy Percentage*
1980	11,378	6.1	68,830	217	86.9
1981	11,178	6.4	71,802	217	90.1
1982	11,073	6.4	70,310	218	88.4
1983	10,909	6.4	70,033	218	88.0
1984	10,936	6.4	70,182	280	68.7
1985	10,550	6.7	71,099	280	69.6
1986*	6,602	6.7	43,922	280	73.9
1986**	10,900	6.7	73,000	280	71.4

*As of 4/30

**Projected

Source: Hospital Records.

EXHIBIT 8 Historical utilization

	Year Ended September 30			*Seven Months Ended April 30*	
	1983	*1984*	*1985*	*1985*	*1986*
Beds in service	218	280	280	280	280
Admissions	10,909	10,936	10,550	6,172	6,602
Patient days	70,033	70,182	71,099	41,171	43,922
Average length of stay (days)	6.4	6.4	6.7	6.8	6.7
Percent occupancy	88.0	68.7	69.6	69.4	74.0
Emergency room visits	24,317	23,506	25,938	14,646	13,991
Laboratory visits	111,787	127,753	134,177	77,807	90,255
Inpatient surgical cases	3,682	3,822	3,786	2,287	2,371
Outpatient surgical cases	1,248	1,683	1,874	1,132	1,267
Radiology procedures	25,845	30,601	30,939	17,808	19,859

Source: Hospital Records.

EXHIBIT 9 East Alabama Medical Center: Cash receipts (June, 1983–May, 1986)

Period	*Accounts Receivable*	*Bad Debt*	*PIP*	*Total*	*Percent Increase*
6/83–5/84	$16,960,926	$499,159	$5,781,000	$23,241,085	
6/84–5/85	$12,267,969	$563,637	$7,738,308	$24,569,914	5.72
6/85–5/86	$21,473,273	$829,231	$9,081,700	$31,384,204	27.73

EXHIBIT 10 Population

	Population				Percent Change 1970 to 1980	Percent Change 1980 to 1990
	Actual[1]		Projected[2]			
	1970	1980	1985	1990		
Primary Service Area						
Lee County	61,268	76,283	84,600	90,900	24.5%	19.2%
Secondary Service Area						
Chambers County	36,356	39,191	40,500	41,000	7.8	4.6
Tallapoosa	33,840	38,676	40,700	42,000	14.2	8.6
Macon	24,841	26,829	27,300	27,300	8.0	1.8
Randolph	18,331	20,075	21,100	21,700	9.5	8.1
	113,368	**124,771**	**129,600**	**132,000**	**10.1**	**5.8**
Total	**174,636**	**201,054**	**214,200**	**222,900**	**15.1%**	**11.1%**

Sources: [1] U.S. Bureau of the Census, 1980.
[2] Center for Economic and Business Research (CEBR), University of Alabama in Tuscaloosa, 1983.

EXHIBIT 11 Employment

Employer	Approximate Number of Employees
Auburn University (state educational institution)	7,000
Diversified Products Co. (athletic equipment manufacturer)	2,000
Uniroyal, Inc. (vehicular tires manufacturer)	1,500
Ampex, Inc. (magnetic tape manufacturer)	1,500
West Point-Pepperell, Inc. (textile manufacturer)	1,000
East Alabama Medical Center	800
Dexter Lock, Inc. (locks manufacturer)	450
Opelika Manufacturing Corp. (textile manufacturer)	250
A & E Data Technology (office equipment manufacturer)	250
Flowers Baking Company (commercial bakery)	250
Opelika Welding Machinery and Supply (welding)	150
Union-Camp Corp. (lumber finishing)	100
Vermont American Corp. (precision tools)	100

Sources: Chambers of Commerce of Auburn and Opelika. Medical Center.

EXHIBIT 12 Employment trends

	March, 1985		*March, 1986*	
	Number Employed	*Unemployment Rate*	*Number Employed*	*Unemployment Rate*
Lee County	35,210	6.2%	35,500	7.0%
State of Alabama	1,610,500	10.0	1,669,200	9.6
United States	105,769,000	7.5	107,642,000	7.5

Source: Alabama Department of Industrial Relations and U.S. Department of Labor, Bureau of Labor Statistics.

EXHIBIT 13 Inventory of competing service area hospitals

Hospital	*Approximate Miles From Opelika*	*Operating Beds*	*1985 Occupancy*	*Referral Center Status*
Lee County				
East Alabama Medical Center	—	280	69.6%	Yes
Secondary Service Area				
Randolph County Hospital	45	76	47.5	No
Wedowee Hospital	45	34	17.5	No
Russell Hospital	35	94	49.0	No
Lakeshore Community Hospital	30	46	51.8	No
Chambers County Hospital	20	38	37.5	No
George H. Lanier Hospital	25	117	66.0	No
John A. Andrew Community Hospital	30	51	28.4	No

Source: State Health Planning and Development Agency.

EXHIBIT 14 Admissions by county (twelve months ended March 31, 1986)

	Number	*Percent*
Primary Service Area		
Lee County	7,191	65%
Secondary Service Area		
Chambers County	996	9
Tallapoosa County	1,106	10
Macon County	885	8
Randolph County	221	2
	3,208	29
Other Service Area	664	6
Total	**11,063**	**100%**

Source: Medical Center.

EXHIBIT 15 East Alabama Medical Center: Key strategy elements

I. Additional Services
   A. Cardiovascular surgery
   B. Oncology services
   C. Cardiology services
   D. Mental health services
   E. Pediatric services

II. Hospital Physician Relationship
   A. Joint Ownership of Services
      1. Imaging Services
      2. Primary Care Centers
      3. Ambulatory Surgery
      4. Durable Medical Equipment

III. Segmentation of Product
   A. Guest relations program
   B. Patient representative program
   C. Patient services program
      1. Doorman
      2. Van
      3. Newspapers, juice, flower
   D. Womens' health care task force
   E. Primary care nursing

EXHIBIT 16 The East Alabama Health Care Authority Statement of revenues and expenses and changes in fund balance (eleven months ended August 31, 1986)

Patient service revenues	$44,436,062
Less provision for bad debts and contractual adjustments	14,309,788
Net patient service revenues	**30,126,274**
Other operating revenues	830,794
Total operating revenues	**30,957,068**
Operating expenses	
Service departments	10,320,999
Earning departments	14,351,131
Depreciation expense	2,148,221
Amortization expense	54,723
Interest expense	3,042,556
Total operating expenses	**29,917,630**
Excess of revenues over expenses from operations	1,039,438
Nonoperating revenues, net	713,738
Excess of revenues over expenses	**1,753,176**
Fund balance, beginning of period	**11,852,560**
Fund balance, end of period	**$13,605,736**

EXHIBIT 17 The East Alabama Health Care Authority: Balance sheet (August 31, 1986)

Assets	
Current Assets	$ 874,267
Cash and investments—Trustee held	1,328,286
Patient accounts receivable	10,051,946
Less allowance for uncollectibles and contractual adjustments	(3,132,609)
Contractual agencies—retroactive settlements	2,172,003
Other	128,031
Total Accounts Receivable	**9,219,371**
Inventories	970,220
Prepaid expenses	315,070
Total Current Assets	**12,707,214**
Board-designated investments	4,444,213
Trustee held funds	3,436,575
Accrued interest receivable on above funds	33,436
Property, Plant, and Equipment	
Land	60,409
Land improvements	805,516
Buildings	15,959,509
Fixed equipment	10,813,785
Major moveable equipment	12,586,976
Minor equipment	69,239
Construction in progress	490,561
	40,785,995
Less: accumulated depreciation	(12,523,268)
Net property, plant and equipment	**28,262,727**
Deferred financing costs, net of accumulated amortization	575,749
	$49,459,914

EXHIBIT 17 continued

Liabilities and Fund Balance	
Current Liabilities	
Bank overdraft	$ 921,212
Accounts payable	1,041,530
Accrued payroll and vacation compensation	721,798
Payroll taxes and employee withholdings	189,131
Accrued interest payable	1,510,009
Contractual agencies—retroactive settlements	167,716
Accrued pension costs	106,000
Current maturities of long-term debt	972,200
Total Current Liabilities	**5,629,596**
Long-term Debt	
Revenue-bonds, Series 1983, less unamortized discount of $773,956	25,226,044
Hospital Tax Anticipation Bonds, Series 1986	2,600,000
Hospital Tax Anticipation Bonds, Series 1967	14,000
Installment notes payable	2,557,577
	30,397,621
Less current maturities	(972,200)
	29,425,421
Contractual agencies—deferred reimbursement	799,161
Commitment	—
Fund Balance	**13,605,736**
	$49,459,914

EXHIBIT 18 East Alabama Medical Center organizational chart.

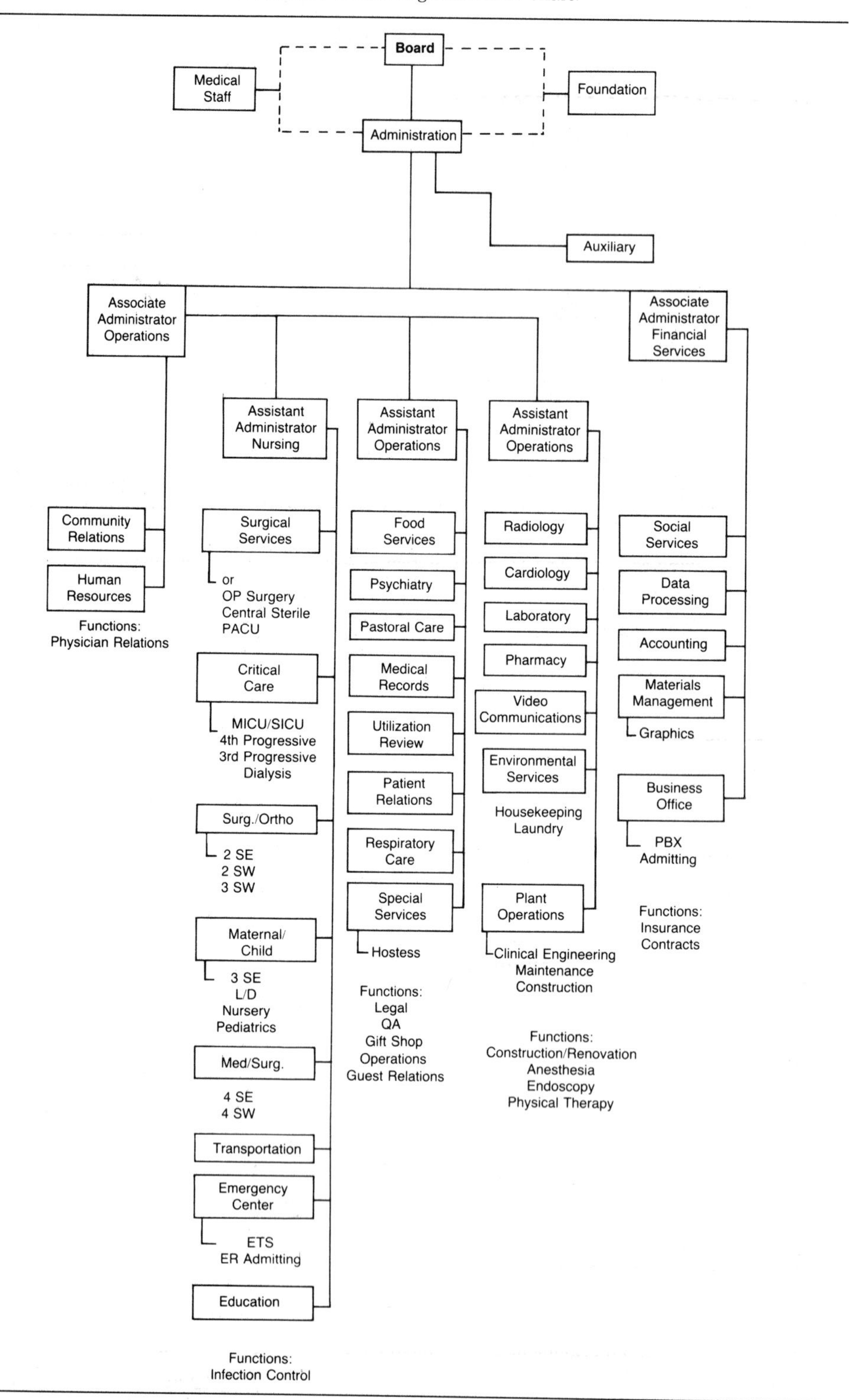

Source: East Alabama Medical Center records.

St. Francis Hospital—1987

DAVID M. RHYNE
University of Central Florida

Fiscal year 1987 had been a very active and progressive year thus far for St. Francis Hospital. Building a women's hospital was one of many projects and programs that had been developed and/or presented by St. Francis Hospital during the past year. Mr. Richard Neugent, the Hospital's president, intently read an article entitled, "Women's Hospital Battle Heats Up Again," in the October 18, 1987, issue of the *Greenville News*. Excerpts from the article included:

> Corporate officials from the Greenville Hospital System and St. Francis Hospital spent much of late last week huddling with their law firms in final preparation for a state health department hearing this week on St. Francis's proposed Eastside Women's Hospital. St. Francis Hospital maintains that it needs to offer obstetrical services to remain competitive with the Greenville Hospital System and that the obvious place to do that is on Greenville's growing eastside. The Hospital System ardently opposes the women's hospital, which it says the community does not need.

HISTORY

In 1932, the Franciscan Sisters of the Poor (a religious order devoted to nursing) bought struggling Emma Booth Memorial Hospital in Greenville from the Salvation Army. The Hospital soon needed additional capacity as the Sisters served diligently in caring for the sick. Plans for growth were finalized when an announcement was made on November 7, 1934, that four additional floors would be added to the top of the existing structure. This increase of space would double the bed capacity.

The Hospital received full accreditation in 1956. Sister M. Bernardine Kirchoff came to St. Francis in 1964 with plans for a new facility. The new Hospital opened in 1971 and was one of the first all-private-room facilities in the Southeast. St. Francis celebrated its Golden Anniversary in 1982. It continued to grow by expanding physically and technologically to meet the increasing medical needs of the community.

In 1985, St. Francis Hospital completed a $30 million expansion program that consisted of four floors being added atop the current patient tower and a major expansion behind the Hospital. Additional operating rooms and improvements to the laboratory, respiratory therapy, radiology, emergency, and outpatient services were made.

Acknowledgment: Several St. Francis Hospital reports and planning documents were used extensively and in close detail in preparing the case. The exactness of the case content could not have been provided without them. Deep appreciation is expressed to Ms. Nancy Furey, Director of Business Development for her kindness and willingness to share the relevant information. Special thanks go to Mr. Richard Neugent, the Hospital's president, for his approval and support of the case being written about the Hospital.

Today, St. Francis Hospital is Greenville's only private, not-for-profit hospital. With 252 private rooms and sixteen Intensive Care Unit rooms, the Hospital has more than $15 million worth of advanced medical equipment available to support a wide range of medical and surgical services on both inpatient and outpatient bases. A team of 350 physicians and 889 employees had the opportunity to demonstrate the Hospital's dedication to personalized, individual care to more than 10,000 patient admissions in 1986.

THE HOSPITAL CARE MARKET IN 1987

Major, earth-shattering changes are being experienced in the hospital industry. The planning horizon for hospitals has been drastically reduced, and the marketplace is highly unpredictable. In many ways, the health care industry should be at the top of the list of American industries experiencing rapid and fundamental changes. Four basic components of hospital operations are cited by Coddington and Moore (1987) as those experiencing significant change and causing new worries for hospitals. These changing components include the prospective payment system, capacity management, competition, and physician-patient-hospital relations.

Prospective Payment Systems

The concept of prospective payment systems, whereby hospitals are reimbursed for a fixed dollar amount for a specific medical treatment or surgical procedure, became reality on October 1, 1983. On this date, the U.S. Government began the fixed amount payment system for its Medicare claims. The prospective payment system has basically turned hospitals from a "cost-plus" way of doing business to a highly "cost-conscious" focus. The name of the game is now to keep treatment and care costs at a minimum. If patient costs are below the specified standard for a specific treatment, the hospital retains the differential as savings. Patient claims that exceed Medicare-specified maximums have to be absorbed by the hospital. A joint study produced by Arthur Andersen & Company and the American College of Hospital Administrators entitled "Health Care in the 1990's: Trends and Strategies" (referred to as the "Andersen Report") predicts prospective payment systems will continue into the 1990s. The use of such reimbursement systems will most likely be adopted by other payors along with the U. S. Government. Blue Cross and other commercial insurance companies are headed in this direction.

Capacity Management

Analysts estimate that U. S. hospitals have at least 25–30 percent too many beds. Joseph Califano is cited by Coddington and Moore (1987) for a claim he makes in his book, *America's Health Care Revolution: Who Lives? Who Dies? Who Pays?*. Califano predicts that the number of hospital beds may be reduced 30 percent by 1990 and another 20 percent by 1995.

In response to predictions that the average lengths of stay at acute-care hospitals will drop from the 1982 level of 7.6 days to 6.5 days by 1995, many hospitals will seriously need to consider the strategy of retrenchment. This reduction of capacity has already begun. In 1984, U. S. hospitals eliminated more than 10,000 staffed beds, or about 1 percent of the million beds now available as reported by Coddington and Moore. The ultimate downsizing decision, liquidation, will be experienced by at least 500 hospitals by 1990 as predicted by Averill and Kalism (1986).

Competition

Hospitals that formerly operated on a friendly basis are engaging in a variety of aggressively competitive actions. Coddington and Moore cite the recruitment of physicians from each others' staffs, claiming differences in quality of care through advertising campaigns, and engaging in price cutting as examples of the new thrust in competition among hospitals. Outpatient treatment, surgery, and birthing centers are also springing up rapidly as new competitors for hospitals. Some experts believe that by 1990, 40 to 50 percent of all surgery and as much as 40 percent of birth delivery will be performed away from the hospital. Health maintenance organizations (HMOs), preferred provider organizations (PPOs), and employer-hospital contracts will become very important factors in deciding where a patient will be hospitalized. As one panelist in the "Andersen Report" remarked regarding the new era of competition, "The important point is that consumers will have incentives to purchase care through new arrangements, and each hospital must determine how to position itself in this competitive market (p. 23)."

Physician-Patient-Hospital Relations

As a norm, physicians continue to control the level of hospital utilization. They accomplish this by admitting patients, prescribing treatment, and deciding when to discharge patients. As the pool of inpatient admissions declines, however, physicians are now competing more intensely with each other. It is predicted that physician specialists will be in oversupply by 1990, and, with reduced demand for their services, the stage is set for a new era. A large majority of physicians who participated in the "Andersen Report" study envision an unfavorable impact on health care quality due to increased competition. The newest trend in hospital-physician relationships is the "joint venture" of two parties in funding and supporting outpatient surgery centers; support service centers (e.g., laboratory and radiology); and the formation of partnerships to contract with HMOs and PPOs.

ST. FRANCIS' MARKET IN 1987

Patient Origin and Service Area

St. Francis Hospital's service area consists of Greenville, Anderson, and Pickens counties. A recent analysis indicates that these three counties account for more than 92 percent of the Hospital's discharges; Greenville County accounts for more than 80 percent of St. Francis's discharges. Population trends in the three-county service area are shown in Table 1.

TABLE 1 Historical estimated forecast

Total Population	*1980*	*1985*	*1990*	*1995*
Greenville County	287,913	304,500	319,700	331,500
Pickens County	79,292	84,400	88,800	93,000
Anderson County	133,235	142,000	151,200	159,600
Total	**500,400**	**530,900**	**559,700**	**584,100**

The population of this service area grew 6.1 percent between 1980 and 1985, and it is expected to grow 5.4 percent between 1985 and 1990. Use rates by county for all hospital service, based on discharges per 1,000 population, are listed in Table 2.

An analysis of Greenville County's demographic characteristics is provided in Table 3.

Market Demand

The projected utilization for all services at St. Francis Hospital for the period 1986 to 1992 is provided in Tables 4 and 5. These projections are based on the assumptions that the use rate for hospital services will decrease through 1989, and that the Hospital's market share will remain constant at levels approximately 8.9 percent higher than 1983 market shares, based on actual experience for the first five months of fiscal year 1986. As the Tables 4 and 5 indicate, St. Francis can anticipate a 7.3 percent decline in discharges between 1986 and 1989. During the period 1989 to 1992, the anticipated 2.5 percent growth in discharges without the women's hospital will be attributable to population growth.

Extensive research and planning have been conducted regarding the proposed women's hospital for St. Francis. A summary of the "moderate" market penetration scenario assumptions is given as follows:

1. The women's hospital will open on October 1, 1988 (fiscal year 1989).
2. St. Francis Hospital will capture the following shares of the three-county obstetrics market:

1989	*1990*	*1991*	*1992*
5.0%	10.0%	12.5%	15.0%

TABLE 2 Forecast of use rates

County	*1983*	*Percent Decline 1983–89*	*1986*	*1987*	*1988*	*1989–92*
Greenville	125.3	19	112.8	108.9	105.2	101.5
Pickens	141.4	19	127.3	122.9	118.6	114.6
Anderson	151.7	19	136.6	131.9	127.4	123.0

TABLE 3 Selected demographic characteristics for Greenville county zip codes

	ZIP Code Area	*Total Population* 1985	1990	Percent Change, 1985–90	1985 Median Household Income	*1990 Population* Percent 65 and over	Percent Females 15–44
	29601	13,065	12,543	−4.0	$12,555	18.6	39.5
P.O. Boxes	29602	23	23	—	20,000	13.0	41.7
P.O. Boxes	29604	113	109	−3.5	17,727	13.0	39.3
	29605	30,555	29,297	−4.1	12,024	12.7	43.3
P.O. Boxes	29606	73	78	+6.8	37,145	7.7	51.2
	29607	32,106	34,632	+7.9	24,821	10.6	50.8
P.O. Boxes	29608	67	72	+7.5	28,000	12.7	45.7
	29609	35,673	35,253	−1.2	20,459	14.6	45.8
P.O. Boxes	29610	49	51	+4.1	20,833	13.0	46.5
	29611	45,237	45,799	+1.2	17,741	13.0	45.3
Furman	29613	125	139	+11.2	23,333	6.5	65.2
Bob Jones	29614	149	145	−2.7	20,000	4.8	80.4
	29615	23,711	23,974	+1.1	33,364	11.1	47.9
	29635	778	846	+8.7	20,070	14.3	43.3
	29636	642	836	+30.2	20,000	9.7	45.2
Fountain Inn	29644	9,021	9,820	+8.9	22,843	12.3	45.7
Greer	29651	37,215	41,303	+11.0	24,289	13.2	43.3
	29661	5,076	5,533	+9.0	18,986	13.6	44.9
Mauldin	29662	7,955	8,611	+8.2	32,655	7.8	48.7
Piedmont	29673	16,505	18,239	+10.5	23,253	10.9	45.9
Simpsonville	29681	23,896	29,027	+21.5	29,507	8.3	47.3
	29683	432	478	+10.6	18,452	13.9	43.3
Taylors	29687	23,086	24,853	+7.7	29,456	9.7	46.9
	29688	450	449	—	23,000	12.5	47.3
Travelers Rest	29690	13,917	14,756	+6.0	24,065	11.7	45.8
Greenville County*		303,346	318,247*	+4.9	23,013	12.1	46.2

*Since several ZIP Code areas include portions of more than one county, the sum of the ZIP Code-specific data does not equal the figure for Greenville County.

Source: National Planning Data Corporation.

TABLE 4 Baseline forecast without the project

	For the Year Ending September 30,						
	1986	*1987*	*1988*	*1989*	*1990*	*1991*	*1992*
Discharges	9,406	9,172	8,944	8,721	8,808	8,875	8,942
Average length of stay	6.74	6.73	6.73	6.73	6.73	6.73	6.73
Patient days	63,354	61,770	60,225	58,718	59,301	59,750	60,202
Average daily census	173.6	169.2	165.0	160.9	162.5	163.7	164.9
Licensed beds	268	268	268	268	268	268	268
Occupancy (percent)	64.8	63.1	61.6	60.0	60.6	61.1	61.5

Assumptions:
1. Market shares remain constant at levels 8.9 percent higher than 1983.
   Greenville County 21.9%
   Pickens County 6.8%
   Anderson County 1.7%
2. Residents of other counties will represent approximately 7.9 percent of total discharges.

Note: Results are rounded.

Source: Amherst Associates.

3. St. Francis Hospital's market share for the four additional services proposed (breast surgery, gynecology surgery, plastic surgery, and treatment of genitourinary diseases) will increase from its baseline market share by the following amounts:

1989	*1990*	*1991*	*1992*
25%	30%	40%	50%

4. The women's hospital will provide all of the two-hospital system's obstetric services, and will account for the following percentage of the system's patient days in the other four services:

1989	*1990*	*1991*	*1992*
40%	50%	60%	60%

The impact of the women's hospital on the overall utilization of St. Francis Hospital is reflected in Table 6.

PRESENT OPERATIONS—1986

Organizational Structure

The organizational structure of St. Francis Hospital is represented in Exhibit 1. In 1986, the medical staff of St. Francis Hospital consisted of 366 physicians. A list of physicians by speciality is provided in Table 7. It is anticipated two additional anesthesiologists will be added to the staff to directly support the proposed women's hospi-

TABLE 5 1989 projections: base case, women's services

			St. Francis, 1989		
Service Category	*Service Area Discharges*	*St. Francis Share (%)*	*Service Area Discharges*	*% In-Migration*	*Total Discharges*
Obstetrics	6,915	0.5	33	3.1	35
Breast surgery	621	26.8	166	9.7	184
Gynecology surgery	2,682	32.0	858	4.2	896
Plastic surgery	290	64.2	187	14.7	219
Genitourinary diseases	1,022	10.7	110	8.1	119
Total	**11,529**	**11.7**	**1,354**	**7.3**	**1,452**
Excluding Obstetrics	4,614	28.6	1,320	7.4	1,418
Newborns	6,915	0.5	33	3.1	35

Note: Totals may not sum due to rounding.
Source: Amherst Associates.

tal. Otherwise, the new facility will be staffed by the members of the present medical staff at St. Francis Hospital.

Advertising/Marketing

To help respond to the highly competitive environment and to more effectively reach target markets for newly developed services, new modes of advertising/marketing were used in 1986. Television advertising by St. Francis was utilized for the first time.

TABLE 6 Average daily census and occupancy rates: Baseline forecast vs. moderate market penetration scenario

	Discharges		*Average Daily Census*		*Percent Occupancy*	
	Baseline	*Moderate Scenario*[1]	*Baseline*	*Moderate Scenario*	*Baseline*[2]	*Moderate Scenario*[3]
1989	8,721	9,319	160.9	168.2	60.0	62.8
1990	8,808	9,816	162.5	173.5	60.6	64.7
1991	8,875	10,182	163.7	178.1	61.1	66.5
1992	8,942	10,554	164.9	182.9	61.5	68.2

[1] Combined discharges for existing facility and women's hospital
[2] Based on licensed capacity of 268 beds
[3] Based on aggregate capacity of 268 beds: 218 at existing facility and 50 at women's hospital
Note: Results are rounded.
Source: Amherst Associates.

EXHIBIT 1 Organizational Structure of St. Francis Hospital

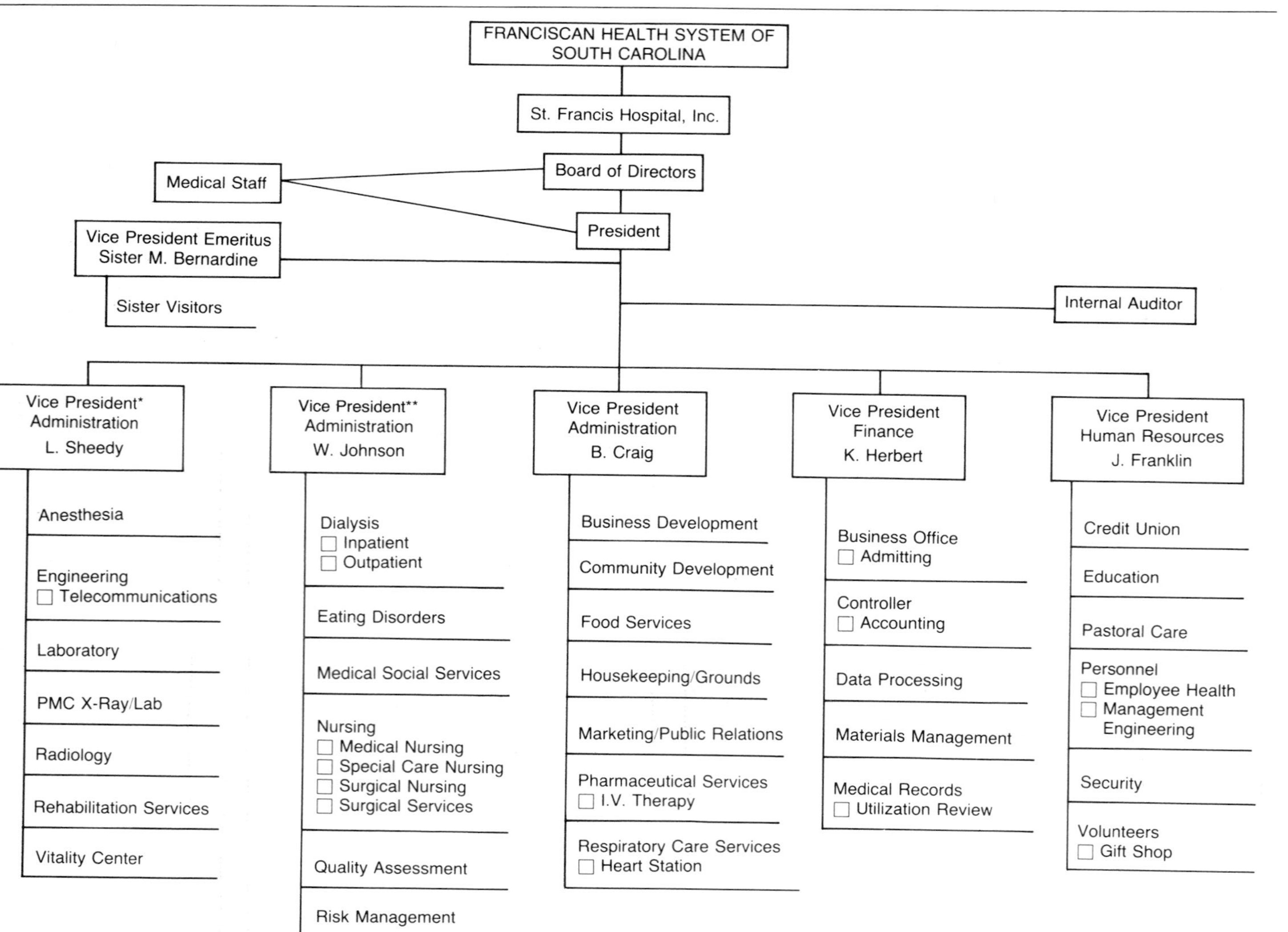

*In charge in the absence of the president. **In charge in the absence of both the president and vice president

TABLE 7 Medical staff membership by specialty

Anesthesiology	11
Family Practice	63
Pediatrics	11
Internal Medicine	48
Cardiology	11
Dermatology	6
Gastroenterology	10
Neurology	4
Psychiatry	11
Physical and Rehabilitative Medicine	3
Pulmonary Medicine	6
Pathology	9
Radiology	18
General Surgery	35
Neurosurgery	8
OB/GYN	31
Ophthalmology	16
Oral Surgery	5
Dentistry	3
Orthopedics	18
Podiatry	3
Otolaryngology and Head and Neck Surgery	10
Plastic and Reconstructive Surgery	5
Urology	14
Emergency Medicine	7
Total	**366**

Two commercials were produced depicting the caring environment, privacy of patient rooms, and personalized patient care. A third commercial portrayed the quality of emergency room care at St. Francis Hospital. It should be noted that emergency room visits increased by 35 percent in 1986. Brochure development, target market segmentation, and advertising campaigns were developed to market new services at St. Francis in 1986.

New Services and Programs

St. Francis Hospital maintains a keen sensitivity to the needs, perceptions, and requests of its target customers. A new Business Development Department was formed through reorganization in 1986. Functional areas such as Public Relations, Marketing,

Community Development, and Business Development will be included in the new area and will report to the same vice-president of administration. By acquiring the majority interest of Medical Personnel Pool of Greenville, St. Francis Hospital offers improved services for patients upon discharge. Home care can now be provided as an aid to the patient and can also reduce costs in the patient's hospitalization.

Physician-hospital relations were enhanced in 1986 by a series of Practice Management Seminars. These seminars were developed and presented with interest in improving the relationship between St. Francis Hospital and a physician's office staff. Four programs were conducted through the year for more than 340 physician office personnel. The feedback from the participants was highly positive.

Chemotherapy on an outpatient basis was initiated in October 1985. Through 1986, there were 235 patients utilizing this new service through 508 treatments. A Yag Laser was recently purchased for the operating room and Endoscopy lab. Since its purchase, forty-two procedures have been performed in the gastro-intestinal (GI) lab using the Yag Laser in addition to five procedures in the operating room. St. Francis Hospital is open-minded toward new technology (such as lasers) that improves patient care as well as cost effectiveness. Gastroenterology has been identified by the hospital president as a center of excellence at St. Francis Hospital. A 29 percent increase in endoscopy procedures over the previous year is an indicator of the emphasis on and quality of gastroenterology.

Diversification of Services

Ancillary departments of St. Francis Hospital are continually searching for ways to diversify their services and utilize equipment more efficiently. The Respiratory Therapy Department has been successful in this regard by obtaining contracts with three hospitals outside of Greenville County for providing pulmonary rehabilitation for those hospitals' patients.

The Nursing Department has enlarged its services by providing consultation in nursing homes for infection control programs. Also, the Food Services Department has implemented a computerized nutritional analysis program that will provide more complete patient care. A chef with culinary arts capabilities has been employed, and this resource may open the option of catering.

Hospital/Physician Relationships

Approximately twenty-six physicians have brought the Professional Medical Center at St. Francis to a 97 percent level of occupancy. The proximity of these physicians to the Hospital has improved the consistency of their admitting practices. Admissions from physicians who have not been on staff have increased too. In response to a wide range of topics and issues of a moral/ethical nature, the Medical Ethics Committee has been formed. Concerns related to living wills, euthanasia, and physician-patient-hospital relationships of a moral/ethical nature are addressed by the Committee.

Corporate Relationships

Numerous Greenville area businesses are developing a strong appreciation of health education programs for their employees. Companies are increasingly viewing such programs as a positive step toward reductions of absenteeism, major illness, and possibly health insurance costs. Through 1986, St. Francis Hospital's corporate health education program had been implemented in more than forty companies. The program, called "Vital," has a menu of health screening, evaluation, and more than thirty health-related training classes. Proponents of the program can work with a company's representative, such as a plant nurse, and develop a year-long health education program.

St. Francis Family

Planned, concerted efforts were made in 1986 to maintain and strengthen channels of communication among all levels of the St. Francis Hospital organization. Weekend retreats were held in November 1985 and April 1986 for board members and department directors, respectively. The administration staff met with both groups in developing and evaluating strategic plans.

Realizing that employees play the key role at St. Francis, a variety of programs have been utilized to improve communication, maintain the focus of the hospital, and insure a high level of morale. The St. Francis Touch Series, an example of these endeavors, was offered to keep employees highly sensitive to the urgency of good customer relations. Other activities, such as the Annual Awards Banquet and the Annual Picnic attended by 845 employees and their families, express appreciation for employee performance and loyalty. During the past year, a Pastoral Care program was begun, and a new director of Pastoral Care was hired to enhance the role of ministry by St. Francis Hospital. Through networking with local ministers, assistance and support are provided through the program for staff members who deal with dying patients.

Finally, a medical explorer post program was implemented in 1986 for high school students. The purpose of this outreach program is to build a growing relationship with healthcare schools. Sixty-five students are currently enrolled in the program.

COMPETITIVE ENVIRONMENT

Table 8 identifies hospitals in St. Francis Hospital's three-county service area. Of eleven hospitals in Greenville, Pickens, and Anderson counties, six facilities currently offer obstetric services. Only five of these hospitals have dedicated obstetric beds available for public admissions. Greenville Memorial Hospital has sixty-eight of the total 135 obstetric beds.

THE FUTURE

When Richard Neugent laid aside the newspaper article on the forthcoming women's hospital hearing, he was confident adequate preparation had been made by the St. Francis Hospital staff and their attorneys. However, he thought what-if St. Francis did not retain the state's approval to build. Exhibit 2 provides projections about St. Fran-

TABLE 8 Hospitals in three-county service area

Hospital	*Beds*	
	Total	*Obstetric*
Greenville County		
St. Francis Hospital	268	—
Greenville General Hospital	75	—
Greenville Memorial Hospital	662	68
North Greenville Hospital	5	—
Allen Bennett Memorial Hospital	86	8
Hillcrest Hospital	56	10
W. J. Barge Memorial Hospital	20	N/A[1]
Subtotal	**1,172**	**86**
Anderson County		
Anderson Memorial	522	29
Saluda Valley Hospital	28	—
Subtotal	**550**	**29**
Pickens County		
Easley Baptist	109	20
Cannon Memorial Hospital	56	—
Subtotal	**165**	**20**
Total Beds	**1,887**	**135**

[1] Not available for public admissions

cis Hospital's utilization with and without the women's hospital. A breakdown of the staffing levels that accompany the forecasted utilization is provided in Table 9.

Planned routine equipment acquisitions and replacements are given in Table 10. An annual 10 percent increase is anticipated for these items.

Per Diem Expenses

Total expense per patient day will experience an annual increase rate of 4.2 percent from an amount of $582.86 in 1986 to $746.46 in 1992. Patient service expense per discharge for the Hospital will increase from $3,263.42 in 1986 to $4,236.76 in 1992. Estimated average charges for inpatient and outpatient services per department applied to the forecasted departmental volumes provide a projection of patient service revenue. Based on a 6.0 percent annual increase for acute-care services, the average gross revenue per patient day will range from $785.99 in 1986 to $1,106.57 in 1992.

EXHIBIT 2 Summary of utilization

A. St. Francis Hospital—Baseline Forecast							
	1986	*1987*	*1988*	*1989*	*1990*	*1991*	*1992*
Discharges*	9,406	9,172	8,944	8,721	8,808	8,875	8,942
Average length of stay	6.7	6.7	6.7	6.7	6.7	6.7	6.7
Patient days	63,354	61,770	60,225	58,718	59,301	59,750	60,202
Average daily census	173.6	169.2	165.0	160.9	162.5	163.7	164.9
Licensed beds	268	268	268	268	268	268	268
Occupancy (%)	64.8	63.1	61.6	60.0	60.6	61.1	61.5
B. Women's Hospital—Moderate Market Penetration							
Discharges*	—	—	—	1,028	1,586	2,023	2,287
Average length of stay	—	—	—	4.9	4.6	4.6	4.5
Patient days	—	—	—	5,045	7,277	9,399	10,352
Average daily census	—	—	—	13.8	19.9	25.6	28.3
Licensed beds	—	—	—	50	50	50	50
Occupancy (%)	—	—	—	27.6	39.9	51.2	56.6
C. St. Francis Hospital—After Women's Hospital							
Discharges*	9,406	9,172	8,944	8,291	8,230	8,159	8,266
Average length of stay	6.7	6.7	6.7	6.8	6.8	6.8	6.8
Patient days	63,354	61,770	60,225	56,338	56,048	55,685	56,396
Average daily census	173.6	169.2	165.0	154.4	153.6	152.6	154.1
Licensed beds	268	268	268	218	218	218	218
Occupancy (%)	64.8	63.1	61.6	70.8	70.4	70.0	70.7
D. Existing Facility and Women's Hospital Combined							
Discharges*	9,406	9,172	8,944	9,319	9,816	10,182	10,554
Average length of stay	6.7	6.7	6.7	6.6	6.5	6.4	6.3
Patient days	63,354	61,770	60,225	61,383	63,324	65,024	66,748
Average daily census	173.6	169.2	165.0	168.2	173.5	178.1	182.9
Licensed beds	268	268	268	268	268	268	268
Occupancy (%)	64.8	63.1	61.6	62.8	64.7	66.5	68.2

*Excluding newborns.

TABLE 9 Forecast staffing levels

	For the Years Ending September 30,						
	1986	*1987*	*1988*	*1989*[1]	*1990*	*1991*	*1992*
Full-time Equivalents (FTEs)							
St. Francis Hospital—Baseline	811.6	791.3	769.4	752.2	759.6	765.4	763.3
Women's Hospital	—	—	—	60.5	83.8	96.2	105.0
St. Francis Hospital—After project	811.6	791.3	769.4	736.0	733.4	730.1	735.1
FTEs per Occupied Bed							
St. Francis Hospital—Baseline	4.68	4.68	4.66	4.68	4.67	4.68	4.63
Women's Hospital	—	—	—	4.38	4.20	3.76	3.70
St. Francis Hospital—After project	4.68	4.68	4.66	4.77	4.78	4.79	4.76

[1] Proposed women's hospital opens October 1, 1988

The anticipated patient revenue by payor class is given in Table 11. St. Francis Hospital's operating budgets and balance sheets for 1985 and 1986 are given in Exhibit 3 and Exhibit 4, respectively.

For Further Consideration

Given the situation of St. Francis Hospital and the anticipated future demands, consider the following alternative strategies:

1. If approval to build the women's hospital is not granted to St. Francis Hospital, would you recommend pursuit of the obstetrics and female surgery market segment? What strategies would be most effective in canvassing and obtaining this market?

TABLE 10 Capital additions

	St. Francis Hospital	*Proposed Women's Hospital*
1986	$1,500,000	—
1987	1,650,000	—
1988	1,815,000	—
1989	1,996,500	—
1990	2,196,150	$300,000
1991	2,415,765	330,000

TABLE 11 Patient revenue by payer class (in percents)

	Historical	*Forecast*					
	1985	*1986*	*1987*	*1988*	*1989*	*1990*	*1991*
A St. Francis Hospital							
Inpatient							
Medicare	53.1	53.1	53.1	53.1	53.1	53.1	53.1
Medicaid	0.7	0.7	0.7	0.7	0.7	0.7	0.7
Blue Cross	11.0	11.0	11.0	11.0	11.0	11.0	11.0
Commercial Insurance, Self Pay	35.2	35.2	35.2	35.2	35.2	35.2	35.2
Total	**100.0**	**100.0**	**100.0**	**100.0**	**100.0**	**100.0**	**100.0**
Outpatient							
Medicare	45.0	45.0	45.0	45.0	45.0	45.0	45.0
Medicaid	1.8	1.8	1.8	1.8	1.8	1.8	1.8
Blue Cross	11.5	11.5	11.5	11.5	11.5	11.5	11.5
Commercial Insurance, Self Pay	41.7	41.7	41.7	41.7	41.7	41.7	41.7
Total	**100.0**	**100.0**	**100.0**	**100.0**	**100.0**	**100.0**	**100.0**
B Women's Hospital							
Inpatient							
Medicare	—	—	—	—	10.0	10.0	10.0
Medicaid	—	—	—	—	0.5	0.5	0.5
Other	—	—	—	—	89.5	89.5	89.5
Total	—	—	—	—	**100.0**	**100.0**	**100.0**
Outpatient							
Medicare	—	—	—	—	10.0	10.0	10.0
Medicaid	—	—	—	—	1.0	1.0	1.0
Other	—	—	—	—	89.0	89.0	89.0
Total	—	—	—	—	**100.0**	**100.0**	**100.0**

2. If the women's hospital is approved, what strategies would you recommend? If the women's hospital building program is approved, St. Francis plans to "transfer" fifty beds from its current facility to the new facility. Since the capacity will actually still be available, what are some options to utilize the "vacated" bed spaces (e.g., day care for employees' children, long-term care for extended illnesses, or alcohol and drug abuse treatment).
3. How and in what areas should the Hospital continue to seek new ventures and thwart the competition? As alternate health care delivery systems (ADS) come into the market, what should be the position and strategy of St. Francis

EXHIBIT 3 1986 operating budget, St. Francis Hospital.

	1986 Budget	*1985 Budget*
Patient Service Revenue:		
Inpatients	39,756,212	33,058,981
Outpatients	7,012,650	4,618,129
Total Patient Service Revenue	46,768,862	37,677,114
Deductions from Patient Service Revenue		
Medicare and Medicaid	6,984,189	4,051,275
Hill-Burton	206,615	288,910
Provision for Doubtful Accounts	1,366,820	1,220,736
Outpatient Surgical Allowance	761,402	391,783
Other	123,003	110,167
Total Deductions from Patient Service Revenue	9,442,029	6,062,871
Net Patient Service Revenue	37,326,833	31,614,239
Other Operating Revenue	712,274	509,860
Total Operating Revenue	38,039,107	32,124,099
Operating Expenses:		
Wages	15,413,014	13,030,522
Fringe Benefits	3,129,510	2,535,781
Supplies and Other Expenses	11,509,248	10,122,024
Interest	3,099,766	3,262,624
Depreciation	2,999,856	2,219,840
Total Operating Expenses	36,151,394	31,170,791
Gain (Loss) from Operations	1,887,713	953,308
Nonoperating Revenues (Net)	827,367	807,213
Excess of Revenues over Expenses	2,715,080	1,760,521
Statistics:		
Patient Days Available	81,564	81,564
Patient Days	61,000	60,702

Hospital toward them? Ignore them? Compete aggressively? Establish joint ventures?

4. Based on your assessment of the strengths and weaknesses of St. Francis Hospital and the opportunities and threats in its environment, what strategies could best ensure the Hospital's survival and growth into the 1990s? How could those strategies be implemented?

EXHIBIT 4 Balance Sheets (September 30, 1986 and September 30, 1985).

	Assets	
	1986	*1985*
General Fund		
Current		
Cash and cash equivalents	$ 3,714,392	1,181,805
Patient accounts receivable (net of allowances for contractual adjustments and uncollectible accounts of $2,494,355 in 1986 and $2,577,915 in 1985)	7,023,269	6,316,526
Due from governmental agencies for settlement of cost reimbursements	303,265	878,962
Due from restricted fund	1,114,717	707,893
Accounts and note receivable—other	147,831	189,452
Inventories	670,358	679,331
Prepaid expenses	219,635	148,894
Total Current Assets	**13,193,467**	**10,102,863**
Board Designated		
Cash and cash equivalents	5,064,766	3,616,863
Accrued interest receivable	47,595	79,990
Total Board-Designated Assets	**5,112,361**	**3,696,853**
Funds held by Bond Trustee	5,119,048	4,003,656
Property, Plant and Equipment		
Land and land improvements	2,491,773	2,393,714
Buildings	20,829,816	20,522,497
Equipment	29,708,429	28,084,720
	53,030,018	**51,000,931**
Less accumulated depreciation	14,318,635	11,321,076
	38,711,383	**39,679,855**
Construction in progress	484,400	153,755
Net Property, Plant, and Equipment	**39,195,783**	**39,833,610**
Other assets, net	573,511	572,166
Total General Funds	**$63,194,170**	**58,209,148**

continued

EXHIBIT 4 Continued

	Assets	
	1986	1985
Restricted Fund		
Plant Replacement and Expansion Fund		
Cash and federal securities	2,615,597	1,909,739
Pledges receivable (net of allowance for uncollectibles of $125,833 in 1986 and 1985)	292,913	574,902
Accrued interest receivable	27,254	76,490
Total Restricted Fund	**$ 2,935,764**	**2,561,131**

	Liabilities and Fund Balances	
	1986	1985
General Fund		
Current		
Current installments of long-term debt	$ 1,208,018	1,095,734
Accounts payable	1,089,130	1,911,452
Accrued expenses	1,642,441	811,710
Employee compensation	1,260,981	1,054,240
Total Current Liabilities	**5,200,570**	**4,873,136**
Long-term Debt, Excluding Current Installments	31,055,472	28,340,839
Fund Balances	**26,938,128**	**24,995,173**
Total General Funds	**$63,194,170**	**58,209,148**
Restricted Fund		
Plant Replacement and Expansion Fund		
Due to general fund	1,114,717	707,893
Fund balance	1,821,047	1,853,238
Total Restricted Fund	**$ 2,935,764**	**2,561,131**

REFERENCES

Averill, Richard A. and Michael J. Kalism. "Present and Future Predictions for the Healthcare Industry." *Healthcare Financial Management*. March 1986, 50–57.

Coddington, Dean and Keith Moore. *Market-Driven Strategies in Health Care*. (San Francisco: Jose-Bass, 1987).

Health Care in the 1990s: Trends and Strategies. Arthur Andersen & Co. and the American College of Hospital Administrators, 1984.

Hershey Foods Corporation—1987

FRED DAVID
Auburn University

Which of the following types of candy are made by Hershey Foods Corporation: MR. GOODBAR, REESE'S, KIT KAT, BIG BLOCK, WHATCHAMACALLIT, ROLO, KRACKEL, SNICKERS, and GOOBERS. THE ANSWER: All of them are, except SNICKERS, made by Mars, and GOOBERS, made by Nestlé. Mars and Nestlé are Hershey Foods' two major competitors. SNICKERS is the best-selling candy bar in the world.

Where could you walk down Chocolate Avenue, see sidewalks lit with lights in the shape of HERSHEY'S KISSES chocolates, visit ZOOAMERICA zoological park, and see a tower in the shape of HERSHEY'S KISSES chocolate in HERSHEYPARK? THE ANSWER: Hershey Complex, Pennsylvania—the home of Hershey Foods Corporation. Since the turn of this century, Hershey Foods Corporation has grown from a one-product, one-plant operation, to a two-billion-dollar company with many U.S. and international plants providing an array of quality chocolate and confectionery products and services. Hershey Foods owns and operates a chain of 825 FRIENDLY Restaurants in the United States. Hershey Foods also manufactures and sells pasta under a variety of names, including AMERICAN BEAUTY and SAN GIORGIO.

HISTORY

Mr. Milton Hershey's love for candy-making began with a childhood apprenticeship under candy-maker Joe Royer of Lancaster, Pennsylvania. Milton Hershey was eager to have his own candy-making business. After numerous attempts and even bankruptcy, he finally gained success in the caramel business. Upon seeing the first chocolate-making equipment at the Chicago Exhibition in 1893, Mr. Hershey envisioned endless opportunities for the chocolate industry. He founded the Hershey Chocolate Company in 1893.

By 1901, the chocolate industry in America was growing rapidly. Hershey's sales reached $662,000 that year, creating a need for a new factory. Mr. Hershey moved his company to Derry Church, Pennsylvania, a town that was renamed Hershey in 1906. The new Hershey factory provided a means of mass producing a single chocolate product. In 1909, the Milton Hershey School for Orphans was founded. Mr. and Mrs. Hershey could not have children, so for years the Hershey Chocolate Company operated mainly to provide funds for the orphanage. Hershey sales reached $5 million in 1911.

In 1918, the entire Hershey business was donated to the Milton Hershey School for Orphans. In 1927, the Hershey Chocolate Company was incorporated under the laws of the State of Delaware. That same year, 20 percent of Hershey's stock was sold to the public, and the company became listed on the New York Stock Exchange.

Between 1930 and 1960, Hershey went through tremendous growth; the name "Hershey" became a household word. Mr. Milton Hershey died in 1945.

Hershey Chocolate Corporation acquired the H.B. Reese Candy Company in 1963 and San Giorgio Macaroni and Delmonico Foods, both pasta manufacturers, in 1966. In 1967, Hershey Chocolate Corporation acquired the Cory Corporation, a provider of coffee services to businesses in the United States and Canada. In 1968, Hershey Chocolate Corporation changed its name to Hershey Foods Corporation. Between 1976 and 1984, William Dearden served as Hershey Foods' chief executive officer. An orphan who grew up in the Milton Hershey School for Orphans, Mr. Dearden diversified the company to reduce its dependence on fluctuating cocoa and sugar prices.

In 1977, Hershey Foods acquired Y & S Candies Inc., a manufacturer of licorice-type products. In 1978, another pasta company, Procino-Rossi, was purchased, and in 1979, Skinner Macaroni Company and Friendly Ice Cream Corporation were acquired. Richard Zimmerman replaced William Dearden as chief executive officer of Hershey Foods in 1984. Mr. Zimmerman divested of Cory Food Services, Inc. in 1985. He acquired an additional interest in A.B. Marabou of Sweden that year. He purchased Marvin Franklin Enterprises, Inc. and The Dietrich Corporation, a candy manufacturer, in 1985 and 1986, respectively. On April 28, 1986, Mr. Dearden retired from Hershey Foods' board of directors after a lifetime association and 29-year career with the corporation.

HERSHEY FOODS TODAY

Organizational Culture

After an internal corporate values survey among Hershey Foods employees, four key values were determined to embody the Hershey Foods culture: 1) people orientation, 2) consumer- and quality-consciousness, 3) honesty and integrity, and 4) results orientation. Every Hershey Foods employee today carries a copy of these four values on a pocket-sized card. The strength of Hershey Foods' culture and value system is derived from Milton Hershey. A recent article in *Personnel* describes Mr. Hershey:

> Mr. Hershey gave his company values synonymous with his own life style: high moral and religious principles; truth, honesty, and integrity; thrift, economy, and industry; the golden "do unto others" rule; the value of education; very high quality standards; the rewards of doing good and benefiting others; and an emphasis on the family and the community (February 1987, page 47).

Hershey Foods' 1986 *Annual Report* describes the corporation's organizational culture:

> The Hershey tradition is based on the highest standards of quality, fairness, and integrity—a unique heritage which evolved from one man who, in his daily life, demonstrated a spirit of generosity and unselfishness rivaled by few others. Milton S. Hershey practiced these principles during his lifetime and set the example by which Hershey Foods Corporation has been guided. Although enormously successful in business, Mr. Hershey's contributions to the community and society were considerably more significant. The Corporation

perpetuates this legacy, making significant contributions to the communities in which it operates and to society in general. Hershey Foods remains committed to its founder's belief that businesses, like individuals, have a moral and ethical responsibility to society. Although Mr. Hershey's company has changed tremendously over the years, his beliefs have not been compromised. On the contrary, they have been reinforced (page 17).

Social Responsibility

Hershey Foods Corporation strives to be exceptionally socially responsible. The corporation annually sponsors the HERSHEY's National Track & Field Youth Program for more than 70,000 young boys and girls. Hershey Foods has a free film-lending program to inform students, teachers, and communities about chocolate manufacturing and business in general. Hershey Foods sponsors public television programming for young people. The corporation makes cash and product contributions to many national organizations such as the United Way and The Children's Miracle Network Telethon. Originally just for orphaned boys, but today for girls too, the Milton Hershey School still derives most of its revenue from the Hershey Foods business. Friendly Ice Cream Corporation, a subsidiary of Hershey Foods, donated a total of 17,321 books to sixty-four school libraries between 1983 and 1986. Nearly 300,000 books were read by children as part of the program. Hershey Foods' social responsibility efforts are aimed at making life for America's youth more rewarding and wholesome.

Research and Development

Hershey Foods engages in research and development activities to develop new products, improve the quality of existing products, and improve and modernize production processes. Corporation research and development expenditures increased from $9.9 million in 1984 to $11.2 million in 1985 and $13.2 million in 1986.

Organization

Hershey Foods is comprised of three strategic business units: (1) chocolate and confectionery, (2) restaurant operations, and (3) other food products. The chocolate and confectionery unit consists of three divisions: Hershey Chocolate Company, Hershey Canada Inc., and Hershey International Ltd. The restaurant unit consists of Friendly Ice Cream Corporation. The other food products unit consists of two pasta divisions: Hershey Pasta Group and Petybon Industrias Alimenticias, S.A. Hershey Foods Corporation's organizational chart as of March 1, 1987, is given in Exhibit 1.

CHOCOLATE AND CONFECTIONERY

The Chocolate and Confectionery unit of Hershey Foods Corporation enjoyed a net sales increase of 8 percent or $104 million in 1986 over 1985. This increase followed a percent increase the year before. Operating income in 1986 increased 10 percent or $22 million over 1985.

EXHIBIT 1 Hershey Foods' organizational chart

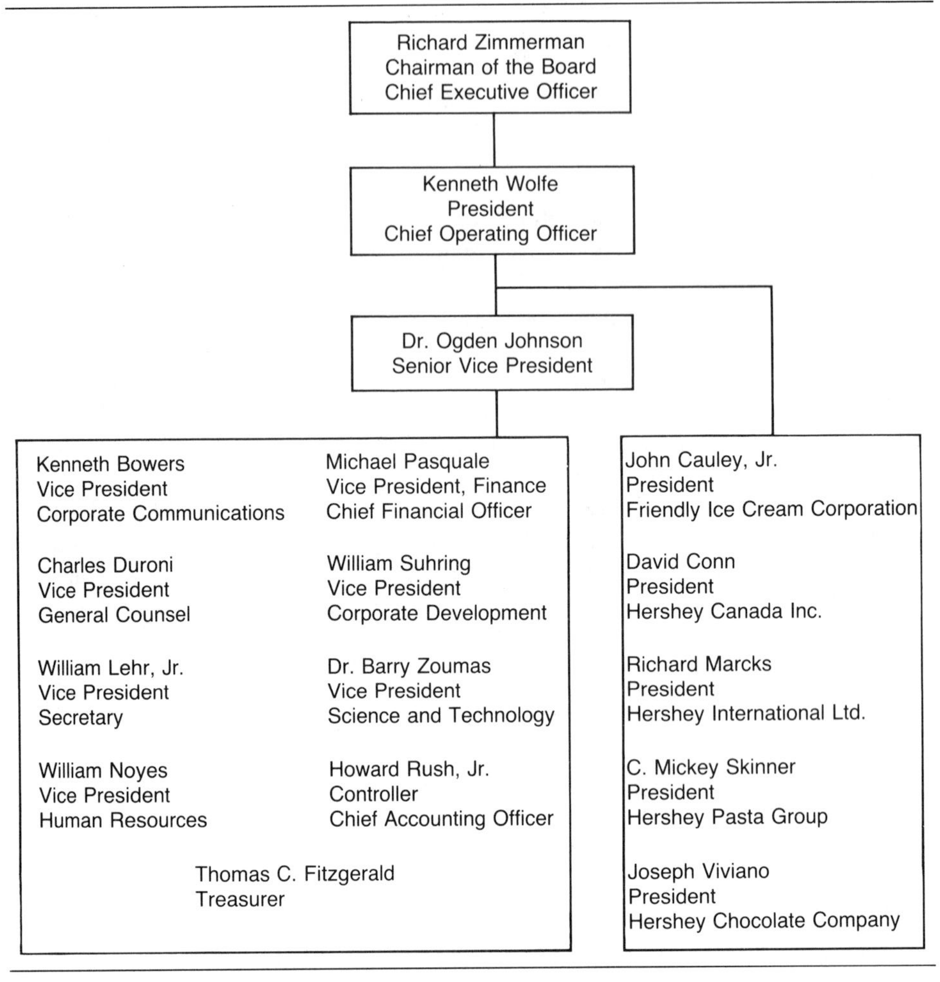

Source: Adapted from information in Hershey Food Corporation's 1986 *Annual Report,* p. 41.

Hershey Chocolate Company

Hershey Foods has chocolate and confectionery manufacturing operations in Hershey, Pennsylvania; Oakdale, California; Stuarts Draft, Virginia; Reading, Pennsylvania; Lancaster, Pennsylvania; Moline, Illinois; and Farmington, New Mexico. Hershey Chocolate Company's 1986 sales and operating income exceeded the record performance of the previous year. Hershey Chocolate Company produces an extensive line of chocolate and confectionery products, including bar candies, bagged candies, baking ingredients, chocolate drink mixes, and dessert toppings. These products are produced in numerous packaged forms, marketed under more than forty brand names, and sold in more than one million retail outlets in the United States.

Leading the sales growth in 1986 was REESE's peanut butter cups, along with HERSHEY's milk chocolate bar, and HERSHEY's milk chocolate bar with almonds. Other products showing strong sales increases were KIT KAT wafer bars, ROLO caramels, and Y & S candies. Most of Hershey Foods' standard candy bars increased in retail price from $.35 to $.40 in 1986 and increased in weight by 10 to 14 percent. Two new products were introduced: GRAND SLAM, a crisped rice, caramel, and peanut product enrobed in chocolate, and BAR NONE, a chocolate-coated, chocolate wafer product. HERSHEY'S NEW TRAIL granola snack continued to have trouble competing in the granola market. On October 27, 1986, Hershey Foods Corporation acquired The Dietrich Corporation, maker of LUDEN's cough drops, 5TH AVENUE candy bar, LUDEN's MELLOMINTS candies, and QUEEN ANN chocolate covered cherries. HERSHEY's chocolate milk is produced and distributed by about sixty independent dairies throughout the United States.

Hershey Canada Inc.

With manufacturing facilities in Smith Falls, Ontario, and Montreal, Quebec, Hershey Canada Inc. achieved record sales in 1986, but operating income was down. An important and disconcerting event in 1986 was the Canadian Government's decision to apply a 12 percent federal sales tax on all confectionery products, effective April 1986. A 7 percent price increase on HERSHEY candy bars at retail sites was implemented. Hershey Canada increased by 5 to 6 percent the retail price on selected licorice and grocery products. A decline in the cost of cocoa beans, almonds, and glucose helped spur strong sales growth in Hershey Canada's grocery items. A HERSHEY chocolate bar in Canada sells for $0.60 Cdn.

Sales growth in Hershey Canada's chocolate category was attributed mostly to the SKOR toffee candy bar and REESE's peanut butter cups. Growth was also achieved by the HERSHEY milk chocolate bar, the HERSHEY milk chocolate with almonds bar, and HERSHEY KISSES chocolates in 1986. A new Hershey Canada warehouse was opened in Montreal in 1986.

Hershey International, Ltd.

In 1986, export sale of Hershey Foods' products increased over the previous year, despite the negative impact of a strong U.S. dollar on export sales early in the year and difficult economic conditions experienced in Mexico, one of Hershey International Ltd.'s largest markets. Export sales of Hershey Foods' products decreased in the Middle East but increased in the Far East and Latin America. A licensing agreement with Hai-Tai Confectionery Company to distribute the HERSHEY milk chocolate bar, KRACKEL chocolate bar, and HERSHEY's Miniatures chocolate bars in Korea progressed well. A licensing venture with Fujiya Confectionery Co., Ltd. of Japan for producing HERSHEY's syrup was expanded in 1986. Additionally, Hershey Foods' Mexico and Philippine affiliates reported significantly improved results in comparison to the previous year. A.B. Marabou, Hershey Foods' 20-percent-owned affiliate in Sweden, reported increased sales in 1986 over 1985.

RESTAURANT OPERATIONS

Net sales for the Restaurant Operations unit of Hershey Foods Corporation grew 14 percent or $65 million in 1986 over 1985, while operating income increased 16 percent or $7 million.

Friendly Ice Cream Corporation

Based in Wilbraham, Massachusetts, Friendly Ice Cream acquired twelve restaurants on July 14, 1986, when it bought Idlenot Farm Restaurants Inc. Based in Vermont, Idlenot has restaurants in Vermont, New Hampshire, and New York. In December 1986, Friendly acquired Litchfield Farm Shops, Inc. of Waterbury, Connecticut, which operates twenty-three ice cream and sandwich restaurants in Connecticut. Friendly is converting seventeen Litchfield Farm Shops to FRIENDLY restaurants and is selling the other six. Friendly opened twelve restaurants in the Orlando area in 1986.

A total of forty-nine new FRIENDLY restaurants opened in 1986. Friendly also expanded its menu in 1986 to emphasize the "Lighter Side," composed of non-beef and non-fried items, and to increase its breakfast menu. Friendly closed ten restaurants in 1986.

Friendly was plagued in 1986 by high employee turnover and a shortage of restaurant workers in most operating areas. The declining number of teenagers in the population has made Friendly's employee problems more severe. Friendly's plans for 1987 include boosting efforts to attract working mothers, senior citizens, and non-teenage persons as employees. The company is also testing "Express Lunch" and "Drive-Thru" concepts. At year-end 1986, Friendly had more than 825 restaurants operating in sixteen states, mostly in the Northeast and Midwest United States and mostly in suburban areas. These restaurants specialize in ice cream and sandwiches.

OTHER FOOD PRODUCTS

The Other Food Products segment of Hershey Foods Corporation experienced a 2 percent or $4.3 million increase in net sales in 1986 over 1985, but operating income decreased 10 percent or $1.2 million.

Hershey Pasta Group

With pasta manufacturing facilities in Lebanon, Pennsylvania; Omaha, Nebraska; Louisville, Kentucky; Denver, Colorado; Kansas City, Kansas; and Fresno, California, the Hershey Pasta Group produces and markets six regional pasta brands: SAN GIORGIO, SKINNER, DELMONICO, P&R, AMERICAN BEAUTY, and LIGHT 'N FLUFFY. The pasta division achieved record sales in 1986 for the eighth consecutive year.

Hershey Foods realizes that the American pasta market is brand loyal. These preferences are usually regionally based, and Hershey Pasta Group has marketed its pasta line accordingly. In 1986, the Hershey Pasta Group maintained a national 17 percent share of supermarket pasta sales. In December 1986, Hershey Pasta Group acquired the G&R Pasta Company, Inc. of Philadelphia, a small specialty pasta manufacturer. Hershey Pasta Group's most successful brands in 1986 were AMERICAN BEAUTY and LIGHT 'N FLUFFY. SKINNER Lone Star Pasta did especially well too as a regional preference.

Petybon Industrias Alimenticias, S.A.

A producer of pasta, biscuits, and margarine products, Petybon is a 100 percent Hershey-owned subsidiary located in Brazil. In December 1986, Hershey Foods Corporation established a joint venture in Brazil with Bunge Born Group, one of the largest flour and fat suppliers in Brazil and a large distributor of consumer products. Petybon Industrias Alimenticias, S.A. did well in 1986 considering an uncertain Brazilian economic environment and a plant closing.

HERSHEY FOODS' MARKETING

Hershey Foods' advertising and promotion expenses increased from $176 million in 1984 to $193 million in 1985 and $218 million in 1986. Hershey Foods' advertising expenditures alone were $91 million in 1986, $83 million in 1985, and $78 million in 1984. The four media that Hershey Foods uses most for advertising are network television (about $40 million annually), spot television (about $20 million annually), magazines (about $15 million annually), and network radio (about $5 million annually). Hershey Foods has a nationwide distribution system that includes two regional centers and seventeen public warehouses. The corporation uses state-of-the-art computer systems to control inventories and process customer orders.

The year 1982 marked the first full year for national distribution of REESE'S PIECES candy. With E.T.'s support, it became one of America's most publicized candy products. The corporation negotiated an agreement with Universal Studios to secure the rights to continue promotion of REESE'S PIECES candy as E.T.'s favorite candy. This promotional action contributed significantly to increased sales of that product and brought to Hershey Foods a wealth of national publicity.

Halloween is an important season for the sale of confectionery products. Hershey Foods' shipments of Halloween candy to retail stores were at record levels in 1986 due to aggressive selling and marketing programs. Unfortunately, there were widespread reports of alleged confectionery products tampering, resulting in consumer apprehension and lower levels of "Trick or Treating" than in past years. Hershey is working with various industry associations to assure consumers that Halloween traditions can be enjoyed with confidence.

Hershey Foods introduced its line of NEW TRAIL granola bars to national distribution in 1983. After facing continued competition, Hershey Foods capitalized on a strong trend in the market and introduced three chocolate granola items in December 1985. NEW TRAIL granola bars were positioned to keep pace with current trends including a busy, fast-paced life style in America and an increased emphasis on health and fitness. The granola concept has been propagated by marketers who advertise the nutritional benefits and "energy boosts" of these products.

Under Hershey Foods, Friendly has become much more marketing and new-product oriented. It has tripled its promotional spending. Prime-time television advertising in major Friendly markets, in conjunction with product promotions, supports new Friendly menu introductions. Ice cream pies, successfully test marketed, were introduced on a chain-wide basis in a standard line of flavors.

The nation's $8.5 billion candy industry is moving upscale, with new, higher-priced products and advertising campaigns targeting adults. Hershey Foods is adding to its line of HERSHEY'S GOLDEN ALMOND bars that evolved from a premium box-candy product. Hershey Foods has begun the national rollout of its GRAND SLAM candy bar, a combination of caramel, peanuts, and crisp rice, targeted to 18–34-year-olds.

Hershey Foods recently changed its 15-year-old theme "HERSHEY'S, THE GREAT AMERICAN CHOCOLATE bar" to better appeal to adults. The new theme is "One of the all-time GREATS." A campaign for the new theme uses editing and animation to show a generation of stars from W.C. Fields to Elvis Presley eating HERSHEY chocolate bars. The spot ends with Joe Montana and an Apollo astronaut holding the bars. These campaigns attempt to maintain longtime baby-boom-age customers who grew up on HERSHEY candies.

HERSHEY FOODS' FINANCIAL CONDITION

Hershey Foods Corporation continued to show sales and profit growth in fiscal 1986. Sales grew to $2.2 billion, up 9 percent from 1985. Net income increased 18 percent to $132 million in 1986, up $20 million from 1985. Hershey Foods Corporation's income statement by strategic business unit is provided in Exhibit 2. The corporation's balance sheet is provided in Exhibit 3. Special notes to these financial statements are provided at the end of this case.

Hershey Foods had 74.9 million shares of common stock and 15.3 million shares of Class B common stock outstanding as of March 2, 1987. The average stock price continued to rise throughout 1985 and 1986. The dividend rate per share of stock increased 8 percent in 1986, representing the twelfth consecutive year of common stock dividend increases. A three-for-one stock split was instituted on September 15, 1986. Hershey Foods' New York Stock Exchange ticker symbol is "HSY." Hershey Trust Company owns 42 percent of Hershey Foods' common stock, but retains 77 percent voting control of the corporation through extensive holdings of Class B stock.

Hershey Foods' working capital decreased from $217 million in 1985 to $171 million in 1986. The corporation's long-term debt increased from $110 million in 1985 to $210 million in 1986. Hershey Foods' capitalization ratio increased from 14 percent in 1985 to 23 percent in 1986. Critics point to these factors as symptoms of Hershey Foods' weaknesses.

ENVIRONMENTAL ISSUES

The most important raw material used in production of Hershey Foods' products is cocoa beans. This commodity is imported from West Africa and South America. Cocoa beans have wide fluctuations in price and quality, due to: a) weather and other

EXHIBIT 2 Hershey Foods' income statements (in thousands of dollars)

For the years ended December 31,	1986	1985	1984
Net sales:[1]			
Chocolate and Confectionery	**$1,441,054**	$1,336,909	$1,287,100
Restaurant Operations	**536,461**	471,488	427,122
Other Food Products[2]	**192,099**	187,757	134,270
Total net sales	**$2,169,614**	$1,996,154	$1,848,492
Income from continuing operations before interest and income taxes:			
Chocolate and Confectionery	**$ 234,776**	$ 212,717	$ 195,810
Restaurant Operations	**50,435**	43,309	41,770
Other Food Products[2]	**9,869**	11,024	7,726
General corporate expenses	**(24,448)**	(22,208)	(22,464)
Income from continuing operations before interest and income taxes	**270,632**	244,842	222,842
Interest expense, net	**(9,799)**	(11,929)	(10,349)
Income from continuing operations before income taxes	**260,833**	232,913	212,493
Less: Provision for income taxes	**128,069**	112,264	102,058
Income from continuing operations	**$ 132,764**	$ 120,649	$ 110,435
Identifiable Assets at December 31:[3]			
Chocolate and Confectionery	**$ 820,950**	$ 611,425	$ 580,586
Restaurant Operations	**358,779**	310,955	273,356
Other Food Products	**110,418**	120,763	152,747
Corporate	**66,156**	154,289	115,878
Total assets	**$1,356,303**	$1,197,432	$1,122,567
Depreciation:			
Chocolate and Confectionery	**$ 22,484**	$ 20,171	$ 17,636
Restaurant Operations	**25,109**	21,616	18,874
Other Food Products[2]	**6,958**	6,761	3,733
Corporate	**1,436**	1,096	1,079
Total depreciation	**$ 55,987**	$ 49,644	$ 41,322
Capital additions:			
Chocolate and Confectionery	**$ 62,423**	$ 51,895	$ 37,508
Restaurant Operations	**61,496**	53,330	41,885
Other Food Products[2]	**7,966**	6,947	4,311
Corporate[4]	**3,943**	2,277	3,345
Total capital additions	**$ 135,828**	$ 114,449	$ 87,049

[1] No customer, government or other entity accounts for 10% or more of sales. Intersegment sales are not separately stated because such sales are not significant. Foreign sales and assets account for less than 10% of total sales and assets.
[2] Net sales, income from continuing operations, depreciation and capital additions for the Other Food Products segment for 1984 have been restated to reflect the sale of Cory Food Services, Inc. and Cory Canada Inc. (Cory) in November 1985.
[3] Identifiable assets are those assets that are used in the Corporation's operations in each segment. Corporate assets are principally cash and short-term investments, and corporate property and equipment.
[4] Corporate capital additions include capital additions of Cory through the date of disposition.

Source: Hershey Foods Corporation's 1986 *Annual Report,* p. 22.

conditions affecting crop size; b) consuming countries' demand requirements; c) producing countries' sales policies; d) speculative influences; and e) international economics and currency movements. Cocoa bean prices are determined by a provisional International Cocoa Agreement formed by certain producing and consuming countries. In July 1986, a fourth International Cocoa Agreement was negotiated among

EXHIBIT 3 Hershey Foods' balance sheet (in thousands of dollars)

December 31,	1986	1985
ASSETS		
Current Assets:		
Cash and short-term investments (Note 1)	$ 27,606	$ 110,636
Accounts receivable—trade (less allowances for doubtful accounts of $4,491 and $4,151)	77,382	76,617
Inventories (Note 1)	237,509	192,678
Prepaid expenses and other (Note 8)	50,923	32,359
Total current assets	393,420	412,290
Property, Plant and Equipment, at cost: (Note 1)		
Land	64,576	62,906
Buildings	251,075	221,901
Machinery and equipment	780,967	680,121
Capitalized leases	34,498	33,274
	1,131,116	998,202
Less—accumulated depreciation and amortization	337,792	296,435
	793,324	701,767
Intangibles Resulting from Business Acquisitions (Note 1)	149,025	66,240
Investments and Other Assets (Note 1)	20,534	17,135
	$1,356,303	$1,197,432

EXHIBIT 3 continued

December 31,	1986	1985
LIABILITIES AND STOCKHOLDERS' EQUITY		
Current Liabilities:		
Accounts payable (Note 4)	$ 102,959	$ 87,799
Accrued liabilities		
Payroll and other compensation costs	40,474	37,275
Advertising and promotional expenses	18,906	19,828
Other	34,414	31,544
	93,794	88,647
Accrued income taxes	16,990	9,253
Short-term debt and current portion of long-term debt (Notes 4 and 5)	8,400	9,623
Total current liabilities	222,143	195,322
Long-Term Debt (Notes 5 and 6)	210,792	110,169
Other Long-Term Liabilities	36,497	31,216
Deferred Income Taxes (Note 7)	158,930	132,826
Stockholders' Equity: (Note 2)		
Common Stock, $1 par value, outstanding shares: 74,886,450 in 1986; 26,235,710 on a pre-split basis in 1985	74,886	26,236
Class B Common Stock, $1 par value, outstanding shares: 15,299,886 in 1986; 5,101,402 on a pre-split basis in 1985	15,300	5,101
Additional paid-in capital	51,681	54,006
Cumulative foreign currency translation adjustments	(6,123)	(8,579)
Retained earnings	592,197	651,135
Total stockholders' equity	727,941	727,899
	$1,356,303	$1,197,432

Source: Hershey's 1986 *Annual Report*, p. 27.
Note: Special notes to these financial statements are provided on pp. 388–394.

cocoa bean producing and consuming countries. The intent was to stabilize prices. The United States was not a party to the Agreement.

To minimize the effects of cocoa bean price fluctuations, Hershey Foods purchases large inventories of cocoa beans and cocoa products. Hershey Foods also purchases and sells cocoa futures contracts. Hershey Foods maintains West African and Brazilian crop forecasting operations and continually monitors economic and political factors affecting market conditions. In 1985/1986, cocoa futures prices ranged from $0.82 per pound to $1.08 per pound. They hit a low of $0.65 in 1983 and a high of $1.23 in 1984.

Hershey Foods' second most important raw material is sugar. Sugar is subject to price supports under domestic farm legislation. Due to import quotas and duties, sugar prices paid by U.S. users are currently substantially higher than prices on the world market. The spot price for sugar as quoted by the *Journal of Commerce* on March 2, 1987, was $0.33 per pound.

Other raw materials that Hershey Foods Corporation purchases in substantial quantities include milk, peanuts, and almonds. The prices of milk and peanuts are affected by federal marketing orders and subsidy programs of the U.S. Department of Agriculture. Raising and lowering price supports on milk and peanuts greatly affects the cost of Hershey Foods' raw materials. Market prices of peanuts and almonds are generally determined in the latter months of each year, following the harvest of crops. Prices for both peanuts and almonds sharply increased in 1986, in part due to drought conditions in the Southeast United States.

Hershey Foods faces seasonal demand for its products. Chocolate and confectionery sales are holiday-related and typically highest during the third and fourth quarters of each year. Friendly's revenues are highest in warmer months, typically the second and third quarters. Domestic pasta sales are somewhat higher during cooler weather periods. The seasonality of sales has often caused Hershey Foods to borrow interim funds to compensate for excess working capital needs.

The 1986 Tax Reform Act directly affects Hershey Foods, as summarized by Mr. Zimmerman in Hershey Foods' 1986 *Annual Report* :

> As we move into 1987 and beyond, the lower maximum corporate income tax rate provided in the Tax Reform Act will more than offset the loss of investment tax credits, and our effective tax rate will be reduced accordingly. It is difficult, however, to predict how much the bottom line will benefit for a variety of reasons, including expenditures on programs to increase sales and enhance market share (page 2).

Industry analysts expect the candy industry to continue to grow through 1990. Americans will consume about 22 pounds of candy per person in 1987, up from 18.9 pounds per capita in 1984. The average per capita increase in U.S. candy consumption has been one pound annually in the 1980s. Chocolate accounts for about 54 percent of all candy consumed. There are other environmental trends that directly affect Hershey Foods. For example, consumers are becoming more and more weight conscious and health oriented. Numerous organizations and individuals discourage candy consumption and promote the need for exercise and nutrition.

COMPETITION

Mars

Six of the top-ten selling candies in the United States are manufactured by Mars. Analysts estimate that Mars has about 37 percent of the candy market, about the same as Hershey Foods. Forrest Mars, Jr. and his brother John, grandsons of the founder of Mars, control the company today. Mars is one of the world's largest private, closely held companies. Mars was the first candy company to persuade merchants to put candy displays near cash registers in 1979.

Industry analysts report that Mars failed to produce any new products from 1976 to 1985. Unlike Hershey Foods, Mars has historically relied heavily upon extensive marketing and advertising expenditures to gain market share, rather than product innovation. But that stance seems to be changing. Mars introduced Kudos Granola Bars in 1986 and is now testing Royal Chocolates. Mars spent more than $300 million on advertising in 1986, including about $90 million on network television, $40 million on spot television, $15 million on network cable, and $8 million on magazines.

Nestlé Enterprise

Like Mars, Nestlé is privately held. Based in Switzerland, Nestlé recently acquired Chicago-based Ward-Johnson Company, whose candy products include Oh Henry, Chunky, Bit-O-Honey, Goobers, and Raisinets. Nestlé spent $350 million on advertising in 1986, including about $80 million on network television, $60 million on spot television, $25 million on magazines, and $5 million on network radio.

Fall 1985 marked the first new campaign for Nestlé chocolate bars. The campaign was labeled "sweet dreams" and used soft rock music and dreamlike sequences to appeal to adults. The same theme is incorporated in advertising for Nestlé's new Alpine White Chocolate. Nestlé was the first of the top ten candy manufacturers to produce a premium product, Henri Nestlé, that targets the superpremium chocolate segment. This is a line of individually wrapped fine chocolates. Nestlé has been concentrating on relaunching old brands such as Oh Henry, Goobers, Raisinets, and Chunky.

HERSHEY FOODS' FUTURE

Hershey Foods Corporation is engaged in a small-scale cocoa growing project located in Belize, Central America. At the present time, Hershey Foods does not plan to expand its cocoa-growing activities, but the Belize operations represent a foothold toward gaining better control of raw materials through backward integration. There are several cocoa growing operations in Brazil and West Africa that Hershey Foods could acquire if needed.

Hershey Foods recently entered into several licensing agreements with toy and children's clothing manufacturers. Although not a significant revenue generator in

1986, licensing the HERSHEY name could be expanded in the future to promote the HERSHEY name.

Mr. Zimmerman says he is ready to increase Hershey Foods' debt as a percentage of capital to 40 percent for the right acquisitions. Mr. Zimmerman's strategy is to make acquisitions that will reduce Hershey Foods' vulnerability to cocoa price volatility, capitalize on Hershey Foods' candy expertise, and provide distribution or manufacturing efficiencies. For example, Quaker Oats Company currently has a 50 percent market share in the granola bar industry; General Mills has a 23 percent market share; Hershey Foods has only a 4 percent market share. Perhaps Hershey Foods should acquire the candy-making division of larger firms, such as Carnation, Kellogg, or Ralston Purina that also make granolas. Hershey Foods already plans to acquire RJR Nabisco's Canadian Candy and Nut Company for about $140 million in 1987.

Mr. John McMillin of Prudential-Bache says Hershey Foods should be divesting rather than acquiring. Specifically, he says the Friendly chain of restaurants should be sold because it owns extensive, undervalued, real estate assets in the Northeast United States. However, Mr. Zimmerman seems intent upon expanding Hershey Foods' Friendly operations throughout the United States by acquiring other restaurant chains.

In order to take advantage of the limited number of competitors in the pasta market, Mr. Zimmerman would like to further penetrate the pasta industry. Should Hershey Foods continue to increase advertising expenditures in order to attract customers and strengthen brand loyalty? Should Hershey Foods develop a new, elite product line, like Nestlé? These are a few of the important issues that concern Hershey Foods today. No organization can afford to pursue too many strategies, so Hershey Foods must make some major strategic decisions now. It would be sad for a company as socially responsible as Hershey Foods to falter. What recommendations would you offer to Mr. Zimmerman?

Hershey Foods Corporation, Notes to Consolidated Financial Statements

1. SUMMARY OF SIGNIFICANT ACCOUNTING POLICIES

Significant accounting policies employed by the Corporation are discussed below and in Notes 7 and 8. As described in Note 3, Cory Food Services, Inc. and Cory Canada Inc. were sold in November 1985. Accordingly, 1984 amounts have been restated to reflect discontinued operations.

Principles of Consolidation

The consolidated financial statements include the accounts of the Corporation and its subsidiaries after elimination of intercompany accounts and transactions.

Investments

Short-term investments are stated at the lower of cost or market. Investments in affiliated companies accounted for on the equity method are included in "Investments and Other Assets."

Commodities Futures Contracts

In connection with the procurement of major commodities, principally cocoa and sugar, the Corporation enters into commodities futures contracts as deemed appropriate to reduce its exposure to future price increases for anticipated manufacturing requirements. Gains and losses on such futures contracts are deferred and recognized in cost of sales when the related product is manufactured and sold.

Foreign Currency Translation

For foreign entities, assets and liabilities are translated to U.S. dollars using the exchange rates in effect at the balance sheet date. Results of operations are translated using the average exchange rates during the period. Resulting translation adjustments are recorded in a separate component of stockholders' equity, "Cumulative

Foreign Currency Translation Adjustments." For foreign entities operating in highly inflationary economies, non-monetary assets and liabilities are translated at historical exchange rates and related translation gains and losses are included in results of operations. Foreign exchange gains and losses included in the consolidated statements of income were not material.

Inventories

Substantially all of the Chocolate and Confectionery and certain Other Food Products inventories are valued under the last-in, first-out (LIFO) method at amounts that do not exceed realizable values. The remaining inventories are stated at the lower of first-in, first-out (FIFO) cost or market. The LIFO cost of inventories valued using the LIFO method was $172,685,000 in 1986 and $139,717,000 in 1985. Total year-end inventories were as follows:

December 31,	**1986**	1985
(in thousands of dollars)		
Raw materials	**$171,160**	$126,879
Goods in process	**30,575**	26,936
Finished goods	**131,673**	126,786
Inventories at FIFO	**333,408**	280,601
Adjustment to LIFO	**(95,899)**	(87,923)
Total inventories	**$237,509**	$192,678

Property, Plant and Equipment

Depreciation and amortization of buildings, machinery and equipment, and capitalized leases are computed using the straight-line method. Property, plant and equipment balances include construction in progress in the amount of $45,554,000 at December 31, 1986 and $27,756,000 at December 31, 1985.

Intangibles Resulting from Business Acquisitions

Intangible assets resulting from business acquisitions principally consist of the excess of the acquisition cost over the fair value of the net assets of businesses acquired (goodwill). Goodwill is amortized on a straight-line basis over periods not exceeding 40 years. The increase during 1986 was primarily the result of the acquisition of The Dietrich Corporation.

Other intangible assets are amortized on a straight-line basis over their estimated useful lives.

Promotion and Development Expenses

The costs of advertising and promotion ($218,148,000 in 1986, $193,036,000 in 1985 and $176,891,000 in 1984) and research and development ($13,225,000 in 1986, $11,181,000 in 1985 and $9,932,000 in 1984) are expensed in the year incurred.

Interest Expense

Interest expense, net consisted of the following:

For the years ended December 31,	**1986**	1985	1984
(in thousands of dollars)			
Long-term debt	**$10,303**	$ 9,883	$10,339
Capitalized leases	**3,046**	2,908	2,639
Short-term debt	**3,314**	8,277	3,573
Capitalized interest	**(3,642)**	(2,520)	(1,260)
	13,021	18,548	15,291
Interest income	**(3,222)**	(6,619)	(4,942)
	$ 9,799	$11,929	$10,349

2. CAPITAL STOCK

On November 14, 1986, Hershey Trust Company, as Trustee for Milton Hershey School (Hershey Trust), sold 5,175,000 shares of the Corporation's Common Stock in an underwritten secondary public offering. On the same date, the Corporation purchased from Hershey Trust 3,825,000 shares of Common Stock for $86,904,000 representing $22.72 per share, a price equal to the proceeds per share to Hershey Trust in the secondary public offering. Immediately thereafter, the shares acquired by the Corporation were retired and became authorized but unissued shares of Common Stock.

As of December 31, 1986 and 1985, the authorized number of shares of capital stock was 230,000,000. Of this amount, 150,000,000 shares were designated as Common Stock, 75,000,000 shares as Class B Common Stock (Class B Stock), and 5,000,000 shares as Preferred Stock, each class having a par value of one dollar per share.

In general terms, the Common Stock has greater dividend rights, but lesser voting power, than the Class B Stock. The Common Stock and the Class B Stock generally vote together without regard to class on matters submitted to stockholders, including the election of directors, with the Common Stock having one vote per share and the Class B Stock having 10 votes per share. However, the Common Stock, voting separately as a class, is entitled to elect one-sixth of the Board of Directors. With respect to dividend rights, the Common Stock is entitled to cash dividends 10% higher than those declared and paid on the Class B Stock.

Shares of the Class B Stock were issued in a one-time-only exchange offer to Common Stock holders on a share-for-share basis in late 1984. Class B Stock can be converted into Common Stock on a share-for-share basis at any time. During 1986, 4,320 shares of Class B stock were converted into Common Stock, and during 1985, 1,800 shares of Class B Stock were converted into Common Stock (number of shares adjusted for the three-for-one stock split effective September 15, 1986). At December 31, 1986, there was a combined total of 90,186,336 shares of both classes outstanding. No shares of the Preferred Stock were issued or outstanding. Hershey Trust Company, as Trustee for Milton Hershey School, as institutional fiduciary for estates and trusts unrelated to Milton Hershey School, and as direct owner of investment shares, held a total of 23,423,547 shares of

continued

the Common Stock, and, as trustee for Milton Hershey School, held 15,153,003 shares of the Class B Stock at December 31, 1986, and is entitled to cast approximately 77% of the total votes of both classes of the Corporation's common stock.

Net income per share has been computed based on the weighted average number of shares of the Common Stock and the Class B Stock outstanding during the year (93,508,322 in 1986, 94,011,336 in 1985 and 1984) as adjusted for the three-for-one stock split effective September 15, 1986 and the purchase of Common Stock shares on November 14, 1986. Dividends paid per share have also been adjusted for the three-for-one stock split.

3. ACQUISITIONS AND DIVESTITURES

On October 27, 1986, the Corporation acquired The Dietrich Corporation by the purchase of its outstanding shares of capital stock for approximately $100 million plus an amount equal to acquired cash and short-term investments. The acquired operations consist of Luden's, maker of LUDEN'S cough drops, 5TH AVENUE candy bar and LUDEN'S MELLOMINTS candies, and Queen Anne, a producer of chocolate covered cherries.

In 1986, the Corporation purchased the stock of Idlenot Farm Restaurants, Inc., a chain of 12 restaurants located in Vermont, New Hampshire and New York, and Litchfield Farm Shops, Inc., a chain of 23 restaurants in Connecticut. These acquisitions were made in July and December, respectively. In September 1985, the Corporation purchased the stock of Marvin Franklin Enterprises, Inc., a chain of 12 restaurants located in Pennsylvania.

In October 1986, the Corporation sold its 22½% interest in Chadler Industrial de Bahia S.A., a cocoa bean processor located in Salvador, Bahia, Brazil. The sales price approximated the Corporation's investment.

In December 1986, the Corporation formed a joint venture in Brazil with the Bunge Born Group. Under the joint venture agreement, a Brazilian pasta unit of the Bunge Born Group was combined with Petybon. Petybon, a producer of pasta, biscuit and margarine products, was a 100% owned subsidiary of the Corporation prior to the joint venture agreement. The Corporation retained a 45% equity interest in the joint venture. Accordingly, the Corporation adopted the equity method of accounting effective December 1986.

In November 1985, the Corporation sold the stock of Cory Food Services, Inc. and Cory Canada Inc., wholly-owned subsidiaries of the Corporation. The 1985 after-tax loss from discontinued operations of $8.4 million ($.09 per share) includes both 1985 operating losses and the loss on disposal. The 1984 after-tax loss from discontinued operations of $1.8 million ($.01 per share) represents operating losses. Per share amounts reflect the three-for-one stock split.

In November 1984, the Corporation purchased the inventory, buildings, land, machinery and equipment, trademarks and certain other intangible assets of American Beauty (a division of The Pillsbury Company) for approximately $56.0 million, and assumed certain liabilities.

In mid-1984, the Corporation purchased an additional interest in AB Marabou, a confectionery company in Sweden, thereby increasing the Corporation's ownership interest from 17% to 20%. Accordingly, the Corporation adopted the equity method of accounting for Marabou's results of operations during 1984.

The above acquisitions were accounted for as purchases, and accordingly, results subsequent to the dates of acquisition are included in the consolidated financial statements. Had the results of these acquisitions been included in consolidated results for the entire period 1984 through 1986, the effect would not have been material.

4. SHORT-TERM DEBT

The Corporation maintained lines of credit arrangements with commercial banks, under which it could borrow up to $100 million in 1986 and 1985 at the lending banks' prime commercial interest rates or lower. These lines of credit, which may be used to support commercial paper borrowings, may be terminated at the option of the banks or the Corporation. There were no borrowings under these lines of credit at December 31, 1986 or 1985.

Lines of credit are supported by commitment fee and/or compensating balance arrangements. The fees range up to ¼% per annum of the commitment. While there are no compensating balance agreements which legally restrict these funds, the Corporation generally maintains balances of up to 3¾% but not less than 2% of commitments under these lines of credit.

The average outstanding balance of short-term debt was $12,713,000 in 1986 and $5,901,000 in 1985. The 1986 average reflects foreign borrowings in Brazil and domestic borrowings under both lines of credit and commercial paper. Domestic borrowings were used to fund seasonal working capital requirements and provide interim financing for the acquisition of The Dietrich Corporation and purchase of 3,825,000 shares of the Corporation's Common Stock. The 1985 average balance related solely to borrowings in Brazil. Maximum short-term borrowings at any month-end were $109,710,000 and $10,182,000 in 1986 and 1985, respectively.

As a result of maintaining a consolidated cash management system, the Corporation maintains overdraft positions at certain banks. Such overdrafts, which are included in accounts payable, were $23,747,000 and $14,421,000 at December 31, 1986 and 1985, respectively.

5. LONG-TERM DEBT

Long-term debt and capitalized lease obligations at December 31, 1986 and 1985 consisted of the following:

(in thousands of dollars)	**1986**	1985
7.0% Notes due 1989	**$ 50,000**	$ —
8.7% Senior Notes due 1992	**12,000**	14,000
7.25% Sinking Fund Debentures due 1997	**1,023**	1,023
6.875% Industrial Revenue Bonds due 2000–2005	**4,000**	4,000
10.4% Industrial Revenue Bonds due 2002	**1,000**	1,000
9.5% Sinking Fund Debentures due 2009	**63,000**	63,000
10.625% Pollution Control Revenue Bonds due 2012	**2,100**	2,100
9.125% Sinking Fund Debentures due 2016	**50,000**	—
Other obligations, net	**8,696**	2,977
Capitalized lease obligations	**27,373**	26,877
	219,192	114,977
Less—current portion	**8,400**	4,808
Total long-term debt	**$210,792**	$110,169

On April 18, 1986, pursuant to Rule 415 of the Securities Act of 1933, as amended, the Corporation filed a registration statement with the Securities and Exchange Commission registering $200,000,000 aggregate principal amount of unsecured, unsubordinated Debt Securities. The Debt Securities may be offered from time to time. Terms are to be determined at the time the debt is offered.

On November 25, 1986, the Corporation issued $50,000,000 of 7% Notes due in 1989 and $50,000,000 of 9⅛% Sinking Fund Debentures due in 2016. The proceeds were used to substantially repay short-term borrowings incurred to finance the acquisition of The Dietrich Corporation and the purchase of 3,825,000 shares of the Corporation's Common Stock. After the issuance, $100,000,000 aggregate principal amount of Debt Securities remained available for issuance under the registration statement filed on April 18, 1986.

In 1985, the Corporation repurchased $14,427,000 of sinking fund debentures to be used to meet future minimum annual payments.

Aggregate annual maturities and sinking fund requirements, net of repurchased debentures and exclusive of capitalized lease obligations, are: 1987, $5,663,000; 1988, $2,578,000; 1989, $55,648,000; 1990, $5,700,000; 1991, $5,754,000.

6. LEASES

Total rent expense for all operating leases, which pertain principally to certain administrative buildings, distribution facilities, restaurants and transportation equipment, was $23,799,000 in 1986, $22,039,000 in 1985 and $19,637,000 in 1984.

Future minimum lease payments under noncancelable leases with an original term in excess of one year as of December 31, 1986 are shown in the following table.

(in thousands of dollars)	**Operating Leases**	**Capital Leases**
1987	$ 10,192	$ 5,989
1988	9,391	5,616
1989	10,889	4,322
1990	10,268	3,976
1991	9,537	3,871
1992 and beyond	172,367	26,264
Total minimum lease payments	$222,644	$ 50,038

The total minimum lease payments under capital leases include $22,665,000 of imputed interest. Capital leases primarily pertain to restaurant facilities and data processing equipment.

continued

7. INCOME TAXES

The provision for Federal and state income taxes is based on income from continuing operations before income taxes as reported in the financial statements. Income tax benefits relating to discontinued operations in 1985 and 1984 are included in the "Loss from Discontinued Operations" in the Consolidated Statements of Income. Investment and other tax credits are recognized as a reduction in the provision using the flow-through method. Investment tax credits for 1986 reflect the Tax Reform Act of 1986 (1986 Tax Act) which retroactively eliminated investment tax credits for capital investments initiated subsequent to December 31, 1985. The primary effect of the 1986 Tax Act was to eliminate approximately $3.6 million in investment tax credits for 1986. The resulting increase in the effective income tax rate was recorded in the fourth quarter of 1986 in accordance with the Financial Accounting Standards Board Technical Bulletin, "Accounting for Certain Effects of the Tax Reform Act of 1986."

Deferred income taxes are provided to reflect timing differences between reported results of operations for financial statement and income tax purposes. Timing differences relate primarily to accelerated depreciation, employee benefit plan contributions and deferred gains on sale and leaseback transactions. Such gains were taxable in a prior year but are amortized over lease terms for financial statement purposes. The provision for income taxes on income from continuing operations was as follows:

For the years ended December 31,	**1986**	1985	1984
(in thousands of dollars)			
Current	**$101,581**	$ 81,996	$ 79,604
Deferred	**26,488**	30,268	22,454
Provision for income taxes	**$128,069**	$112,264	$102,058

The following table reconciles the provision for income taxes with the amount computed by applying the Federal statutory rate:

For the years ended December 31,	**1986**		1985		1984	
(in thousands of dollars)	**Amount**	**%**	Amount	%	Amount	%
Income taxes computed at statutory rate	**$119,983**	**46.0**	$107,140	46.0	$ 97,747	46.0
Increase (reduction) resulting from:						
State income taxes, net of Federal income tax benefits	**11,522**	**4.4**	10,857	4.7	10,073	4.7
Investment tax credit	**(2,489)**	**(.9)**	(5,348)	(2.3)	(4,618)	(2.2)
Nondeductible acquisition costs	**1,835**	**.7**	1,718	.7	1,583	.7
Payroll tax credits and other	**(2,782)**	**(1.1)**	(2,103)	(.9)	(2,727)	(1.2)
Provision for income taxes	**$128,069**	**49.1**	$112,264	48.2	$102,058	48.0

8. RETIREMENT PLANS AND OTHER RETIREE BENEFITS

The Corporation and its subsidiaries sponsor a number of defined benefit retirement plans covering substantially all employees. Plans covering salaried employees provide retirement benefits based on career average or final pay compensation as defined within the provisions of the individual plans, while plans covering hourly employees generally provide benefits based on years of service. The Corporation's policy is to fund the normal cost plus amounts required to amortize actuarial gains and losses and prior service costs over periods ranging from 15 to 30 years. Plan assets are invested in a broadly diversified portfolio consisting primarily of domestic and international common stocks and fixed income securities. The Corporation also participates in several multiemployer retirement plans which provide defined benefits to employees covered under certain collective bargaining agreements.

In the fourth quarter of 1986, the Corporation adopted Statement of Financial Accounting Standards No. 87, "Employers' Accounting for Pensions" (FAS No. 87), for all domestic retirement plans, retroactive to January 1, 1986. Pension expense for the Canadian plan in 1986 and for all plans in 1985 and 1984 was determined using provisions of previous accounting principles. In accordance with the provisions of FAS No. 87, pension expense for 1985 and 1984 has not been restated. Pension expense for the first three quarters of 1986 was not restated as the effects would not have been material.

Pension expense for 1986 is not directly comparable with 1985 and 1984 because of the significant changes in accounting for pension expense under FAS No. 87. If FAS No. 87 had not been adopted for domestic plans in 1986, pension expense for 1986 would have been higher than 1985, primarily due to benefit improvements in certain salary and hourly plans. The pension expense decrease under FAS No. 87 reflects revised salary increase assumptions recognizing the outlook for lower inflation, updated discount rates and investment return rates based upon expectations of long-term rates of return.

The following is a summary of consolidated pension expense for the year ended December 31, 1986 (in thousands of dollars):

Corporate sponsored domestic pension plans, prior to application of FAS 87	$14,703
Effect of adopting FAS 87	(7,270)
Corporate sponsored domestic pension plans	7,433
Multiemployer plans	558
Canadian pension plan	221
Other	355
Total pension expense	$ 8,567

Pension expense for the years ended December 31, 1985 and 1984 was $13,810,000 and $13,542,000, respectively.

For the year ended December 31, 1986, pension expense for the domestic plans sponsored by the Corporation included the following components (in thousands of dollars):

Service cost (benefits earned during the period)	$ 9,758
Interest cost on projected benefit obligation	16,689
Investment return on plan assets	(31,514)
Net amortization and deferral	12,500
Corporate sponsored domestic pension plans	$ 7,433

The projected benefit obligation for the domestic plans was determined using an assumed discount rate of 8.5% and an assumed long-term compensation increase rate of principally 6%. The assumed long-term rate of return on plan assets was 9.5%.

The following table sets forth the funded status and amounts recognized in the consolidated balance sheet at December 31, 1986 for the domestic plans sponsored by the Corporation:

(in thousands of dollars)	**Assets Exceed Accumulated Benefits**	**Accumulated Benefits Exceed Assets**
Actuarial present value of:		
Vested benefit obligation	$162,521	$ 4,101
Accumulated benefit obligation	$173,498	$ 5,272
Projected benefit obligation	$210,123	$ 9,154
Plan assets at fair value	237,670	—
Plan assets greater than (less than) the projected benefit obligation	27,547	(9,154)
Unrecognized net (gain) loss at January 1, 1986	(6,862)	5,890
Unrecognized net (gain) loss during the year	(12,784)	(75)
Prepaid pension expense (pension liability) at December 31, 1986	$ 7,901	$(3,339)

The actuarial present value of consolidated accumulated benefits for the Corporate sponsored domestic pension plans at December 31, 1985 was $168,476,000 (of which $8,307,000 was nonvested), compared with market value of net assets available for benefits of $199,461,000. The assumed rate of return used in determining the actuarial present value of accumulated plan benefits was 8%.

Retirement benefits provided to employees in Canada are based on local practice and are administered through a separate plan. In accordance with transition provisions, the Corporation has not adopted FAS No. 87 for this plan. The actuarial present value of accumulated benefits for this plan at April 1, 1986 was $2,535,000 (of which $186,000 was nonvested), compared with net assets available for benefits of $4,661,000. The assumed average rate of return used in determining the actuarial present value of benefits was 7.5%.

The Corporation and its subsidiaries provide certain health care and life insurance benefits for retired employees. Substantially all of the Corporation's domestic employees become eligible for these benefits at normal retirement age. Retiree health care and life insurance premiums of $2,250,000, $2,027,000 and $1,760,000 were expensed as paid during 1986, 1985, and 1984, respectively.

continued

9. QUARTERLY DATA (Unaudited)

The following is a summary of quarterly data for the years 1986 and 1985. Per share data has been restated to reflect the three-for-one stock split effective September 15, 1986:

(in thousands of dollars except shares and per share amounts)

Year 1986	**First**	**Second**	**Third**	**Fourth**	**Year**
Net sales	$507,996	$450,201	$596,446	$614,971	$2,169,614
Gross profit	163,721	148,760	197,601	206,092	716,174
Net income	27,011	24,577	43,539	37,637	132,764
Net income per share	.29	.26	.46	.41	1.42

Year 1985	**First**	**Second**	**Third**	**Fourth**	**Year**
Net sales	$476,505	$431,074	$547,724	$540,851	$1,996,154
Gross profit	147,600	135,839	176,522	180,404	640,365
Income from continuing operations	22,962	22,578	39,532	35,577	120,649
(Loss) from discontinued operations	(224)	(504)	(7,694)	—	(8,422)
Net income	22,738	22,074	31,838	35,577	112,227
Income from continuing operations per share	.24	.25	.42	.37	1.28
Net income per share	.24	.24	.34	.37	1.19

The weighted average number of shares outstanding was 94,011,336 for all periods indicated except for the fourth quarter of 1986 and the year 1986 for which shares outstanding were 92,058,144 and 93,508,322, respectively.

10. INDUSTRY SEGMENT

Industry segment information is shown on pages 20 through 23.

SUGGESTED READINGS

Blank, S.J. "Hershey: A Company Driven by Values." *Personnel.* Vol. 64. February 1987, 46–51.

"Candy May Be Dandy, but Confectioners Want a Sweeter Bottom Line." *Business Week.* 6 October, 1986, 66–67.

"Chocolate Marketing No Longer Kids' Stuff." *Advertising Age.* 19 May, 1986, 22.

Dodds, L. S. "Sweetening Up the Bottomline." *Financial World.* 29 April, 1986, 14–15.

Hinckle, Samuel F. *Hershey.* (Princeton, N. J.: Princeton University Press, 1964.):8–14.

"It's Not Just Kid's Stuff." *Progressive Grocer.* Vol. 65. July 1986, 61.

Novack, Janet. "The High-Profit Candy Habit." *Forbes.* 29 June, 1987, 76.

"Top One Hundred Advertisers." *Advertising Age.* 4 September, 1986, 110, 124, 132.

"T.V. Campaign to Tout Mars' Rollout of Kudos Granola Bar." *Advertising Age.* 9 June, 1986, 3, 87.

"Why Lower Commodity Prices Are a Candy Lover's Dream." *Business Week.* 4 August, 1986, 16.

Seagram Changes Its Image—1987

BARBARA SPENCER
Mississippi State University
STEPHANIE WEIKERT
Clemson University

A drink is a drink is a drink. But no matter what you drink, drink responsibly.

This message concluded Seagram's proposed television advertisement, designed to inform the American public that 1.25 ounces of whiskey contain no more alcohol than a can of beer or a 5-ounce glass of wine. Announced in early 1985 by Edgar Bronfman Jr., president of Seagram's U.S. Liquor Division, the equivalency campaign was Seagram's attempt to change what it calls the public's misconceptions about alcohol. In an era in which the public is increasingly concerned about not only drunken driving, but also any harm alcohol might pose to physical health, affecting this change is no easy challenge.

The equivalency campaign represents a major shift in corporate strategy and philosophy for Seagram. For years, the world's largest distiller of spirits has avoided controversy and has fostered an image as a "sober corporate citizen." This image was created in part by Edgar Jr.'s grandfather, Samuel Bronfman, who founded Seagram in 1928. In those days, the elder Bronfman warned people not to drink too much of the company's product. Now family members who control the Montreal-based firm fear that this advice may have tarnished liquor's image by implying that beer and wine are safer.

THE CHANGING ENVIRONMENT

Social Trends

Shifting trends of the 1980s have brought about a phenomenon that one liquor industry executive has called the "sobering of America."[1] In 1978, per capita consumption of distilled spirits reached an all-time high of 3 gallons a year. Since that time however, consumption has declined steadily. In 1986 alone, consumption plunged 5.8 percent. One of the primary causes of this trend is the increasing concern for health and fitness. In a society where seemingly every other food or beverage is "light," "low calorie," or "diet," the strong taste and high caloric value of liquor is divergent. Ten years ago, it was not unusual for a business person to socialize over a lunch of beef and bourbon. Today, it is more common to squeeze in a light lunch of salad and Perrier after a game of racquetball or a jog around the track.

The current attitude toward moderation in drinking is indicative of this trend. At one time, it was acceptable, and even comical, for adults to drink until they lost all control. Now, Americans drink more conservatively. According to Ron Vilord, vice president of Houlihan's, a national restaurant chain, "It's almost stylish not to have too much to drink. It used to be no big deal if you got blind drunk. Now it's sort of

EXHIBIT 1 Distilled spirits growth rate by liquor type (in percents)

Category	*1975–1980*	*1980–1985*	*1985–1990**
Bourbon	−2.6%	−5.6%	−6.5%
Blends	−6.7%	−5.2%	−7.1%
Scotch	−3.6%	−3.2%	−2.5%
Canadian	0.9%	−0.9%	−2.0%
Total Brown Goods	**−2.9%**	**−3.7%**	**−4.2%**
Gin	−1.1%	−2.3%	−2.6%
Vodka	2.1%	—	−0.5%
Rum	10.2%	2.9%	—
Tequila	—	5.9%	—
Total White Goods	**2.9%**	**—**	**−0.5%**
Brandy	5.9%	2.7%	2.9%
Liqueurs	4.2%	4.6%	1.0%
Cocktails	14.9%	−5.6%	14.9%
Total Specialities	**5.9%**	**2.7%**	**2.9%**

*Estimate
Source: Impact Databank

disgusting."[2] Moreover, since liquor is generally perceived as having a higher alcohol content than beer or wine, this trend toward moderation will likely affect the distilled spirits industry with greatest severity. Exhibits 1 and 2 reveal specific growth rates of various alcoholic beverages.

Changes in consumer tastes have contributed to the turbulence in the distilled spirits industry in yet another way. Liquor can be divided into two categories: (1) the white goods or nonwhiskeys such as gin, rum, vodka, and tequila, and (2) the brown goods or whiskeys such as bourbon, blends, Scotch, Canadian, and Irish. Although

EXHIBIT 2 Recent performance: Alcoholic beverages

	Year (Percent Change)		
Type of Alcohol	*1983–1984*	*1984–1985*	*1985–1986*
Beer	−1.7	−0.4	0.1
Wine	−1.2	4.6	1.3
Liquor	−2.4	−3.0	−4.0

Source: U.S. Industrial Outlook 1986—Food

the market for distilled spirits is on an overall decline, the demand for some white goods such as rum and tequila in increasing. This trend is evidenced in Exhibit 3. The ever present consumer inclination toward lightness, or perceived lightness, is a major cause of this demand shift. The refreshing taste of specialty goods, such as Bailey's Irish Cream and Kahlua, has also captured consumer preference at an increasing rate.

Economic Factors

Economic instability of the eighties has also diminished liquor consumption. Throughout the early part of the decade, unemployment coupled with inflation severely decreased consumers' discretionary income. As a result, demand for goods typically purchased with discretionary income—such as liquor—slowed. However, premium liquor brands such as Chivas Regal or Johnnie Walker Black are usually unaffected by a changing economy. These prestige items are highly insensitive to price shifts. Demand may actually increase as price increases because the consumer places a higher value on them. In 1987, economic conditions have improved, but the alcoholic beverage industry has yet to recover. Conditions in this industry have a tendency to lag behind changes in the economy, and more time may still need to pass before complete recovery can be realized.

Indeed, there is some speculation that a full recovery may never occur. Total sales for the industry are expected to continue to decline through 1990. As a result of this shrinking market, most major spirits producers have now acquired and are operating unrelated businesses. Ideally, their distilling operations will provide a consistent stream of earnings while new operations supply growth.

EXHIBIT 3 Top ten liquor brands 1984–1986

			Rank			
Brand	*Marketer*	*Type*	*1986*	*1985*	*1984*	*Five-Year Growth Rate*
Bacardi	Bacardi	Rum	1	1	1	−2.1%
Smirnoff	Heublein	Vodka	2	2	2	1.6
7–Crown	Seagram	Blend	3	3	3	−6.2
Canadian Mist	Brown-Forman	Canadian	4	4	4	4.9
Popov	Heublein	Vodka	5	5	6	5.8
Jim Beam	Beam	Bourbon	6	6	5	0.2
Jack Daniels	Brown-Forman	Tennessee	7	7	6	−1.8
Seagram's	Seagram	Gin	7	8	9	3.1
Dekuyper Peachtree	National	Liqueur	9	23	NA	123.1
Windsor Supreme	National	Canadian	10	9	10	0.9

Brown-Forman, for example, which manufactures the popular Jack Daniels, Canadian Mist, and Southern Comfort brands, has acquired Lennox Inc., a manufacturer of fine china and crystal, Keepsake and Artcarved jewelry, and Hartmann luggage. The firm also owns California Cooler, the initiator of the wine cooler phenomenon. Hiram Walker, which markets Canadian Club whiskey, Tia Maria, and Courvoisier brandy, as well as its own line of Hiram Walker products, obtains about two-thirds of its earnings from natural resources and gas distribution.

A further sign of industry upheaval can be seen in the recent rash of divestitures and restructurings. For example, National Distillers and Chemical, which got its start in the liquor business, has recently sold its Almaden Vineyards subsidiary to Heublein Inc., and its spirits operations to Jim Beam. In turn, RJR Nabisco, the giant consumer products conglomerate, sold Heublein to Grand Metropolitan PLC for $1.2 billion. Glenmore Distilleries sold a substantial part of its assets, including the distribution rights to Amaretto di Saronno, a well-known liqueur. Hiram Walker formed a new division for the sole purpose of marketing low-alcohol beverages.

Political, Governmental, and Legal Factors

Few other industries are as highly regulated and restricted as the distilled spirits industry. The increasing number of drunk-driving-related fatalities has brought much attention to irresponsible drinking habits. With groups such as Mothers Against Drunk Driving (MADD), Students Against Drunk Driving (SADD), and The Center of Science in Public Interest pressuring authorities to take action, new laws, higher taxes, and stiffer penalties for drunk drivers have stunned the industry.

In this society, alcohol consumption is seen as something costly in terms of teenage deaths and forfeited work hours. Therefore, it is no surprise that legislators have targeted teenage alcohol abuse as a primary area for reform. In 1984, President Reagan signed the National Minimum Drinking Age Act granting the federal government the authority to withhold federal highway funds from states failing to raise their legal drinking age to 21 by 1986.

In further attempts to control alcohol abuse, the liquor industry has been subject to increasing local, state, and especially federal excise taxes. Graham Molitor, president of Public Policy Forecasting, states: "In all of the time that I have been tracking legislative and governmental policy worldwide, I have never seen anything that has been moving with the velocity, speed and comprehensiveness as alcohol and tobacco regulation."[3]

Evidence supports Molitor's statement. Recent legislation raised the federal excise tax on liquor from $10.50 per gallon to $12.00 per gallon. In fact, taxes now account for about 48 percent of the retail price of a bottle of liquor. Moreover, these taxes will be applied on a proof gallon basis. The effects of taxing higher proof brands at a greater rate than lower proof brands will be far reaching, since liquor will have a higher unit price than beer or wine. Evidence shows beer and wine sales have increased relative to liquor sales.

This neo-prohibitionist movement continues by hindering alcohol sales in public places such as bars and restaurants. For example, when an accident involves a drunk driver, a portion of the liability is more often being placed on the proprietor of the tavern or restaurant that served the excessively intoxicated driver. Fearing penalties, owners have taken action to protect themselves against lawsuits. They are closing earlier, giving free soft drinks or coffee to drunk customers, serving designated drivers free nonalcoholic beverages, and warning customers of the dangers of alcohol.

Another legislative proposal under consideration by lawmakers would require that every bottle of beer, wine, and spirits bear a warning label describing the dangers of excessive consumption. Distillers, and beer and wine makers are preparing to fight the bill by telling legislators that no evidence exists to prove that warning labels will prevent alcohol abuse. As one distiller comments, "People are not going to get their medical advice off a beer can."[4]

Finally, one of the most controversial areas of proposed legislation is the ongoing movement to restrict advertising of alcoholic beverages. Currently, the major television networks and some cable stations carry a plethora of beer and wine commercials, but these broadcasters maintain a voluntary ban on liquor advertisements. The Center for Science in Public Interest, a critic of beer and liquor promotional practices, is fighting to change this situation. This group has filed a petition with the Federal Trade Commission requesting that all alcohol-related television and radio advertisements be prohibited or that counter commercials be run to warn of the dangers of drinking. The petition also seeks to obstruct promotional activities directed primarily at young adults at locations such as rock concerts. Enough public criticism has been aimed at the industry-wide college promotional activities that it appears companies are phasing out their presence in this area.

Distillers Fight Back

Confronted by negative public opinion and increasing regulation, spirits producers are uniting to fight back. The Distilled Spirits Council of the United States, or DISCUS, has been formed to voice the industry viewpoint. The council responded to the federal excise tax on alcohol by pointing out that approximately 1,800 jobs would be lost, a variety of related industries would be harmed, and state and local liquor tax revenues would be decreased. Most recently, DISCUS has made an effort to improve the industry's image by redefining the role of beverage alcohol and illustrating ways in which moderate alcohol usage can bring social, economic, and health benefits to the public. The council especially wants to report the findings of a medical study that shows people who consistently use small amounts of alcohol to be in the lowest risk category for coronary heart disease and early mortality.

In addition to group efforts such as those by DISCUS, industry leaders are utilizing new product development to cope with the industry turmoil. Heublein, Inc., the leading American producer of vodka, is marketing Citronet, a light beverage consisting of 4 percent alcohol, fruit juice, and soda. Other spirits manufacturers have climbed aboard the low-alcohol bandwagon by offering such products as spirit- and malt-based coolers, as well as low-alcohol fruit-flavored drinks in cans. Jim Beam Distilleries, for example, is producing Jim Beam and Lemonade, as well as a product called Outback, an Australian rum mixed with cola. Seagram is test marketing Old Breed beer-flavored Schnapps, and Brown-Forman has introduced Jack Daniels Tennessee Cooler. Glenmore Distilleries recently launched its Hot Shot Tropical Fruit Flavored Schnapps through the use of a music video.

In keeping with this new emphasis, Heublein joined Seagram to request that the Federal Bureau of Alcohol, Tobacco and Firearms alter certain restrictions and thus make it easier to sell low-proof whiskey. Under current rules, products with alcohol content below a certain level must be labeled "diluted." However, Heublein and Seagram hoped to change this labeling of lower-strength spirits to a more pleasing and marketable description such as "mild" or "light." Unfortunately, this request was denied by the government.

The concerned citizen role is also being played by an increasing number of liquor firms. For example, the Alco Standard Corporation encourages customers not to drink too much by placing "Enjoy in Moderation" labels on its products. In addition, the company has conducted seminars to instruct restaurant and bar managers how to responsibly serve alcohol as well as to effectively market low-alcohol and alcohol-free products. Similarly, Glenmore Distilleries developed a television campaign strongly advising pregnant women to consult their doctors concerning alcohol or controlled substance usage. However, because the advertisement cited Glenmore as the sponsor, the campaign was refused by the primary networks.

Other efforts among industry members to raise faltering demand have focused on increased minority targeting. Brown-Forman is attempting to increase sales of its best-selling product, Canadian Mist, in the black market with an advertising campaign directed specifically to it. These advertisements utilize what Brown-Forman refers to as the "life style" approach. This approach is best exemplified by the "Misting" campaign, which features scenes of night life and black models dressed in fashionable, expensive clothing surrounded by a cool mist.

SEAGRAM'S INTERNAL ENVIRONMENT

Top Management

The Seagram Company today is still, in many ways, a family-run business. Edgar Bronfman, Sr. (57) serves as chairman of the board and chief executive officer. The eldest son of founder Samuel Bronfman, Edgar took control of the company in 1971. His brother, Charles (55), is the company's deputy chairman. Together, the two brothers own about 32 percent of the company's shares. Their sisters, Phyllis Lambert, a Montreal architect, and Minda de Ginzburg, a Paris socialite, together own approximately 8 percent, but they are not actively involved in the business. Indeed, Edgar maintains that an unwritten family tradition limits the number of family members who are active in the business to two per generation.[5] Currently, the third generation is represented by Edgar's two sons, Sam (33) and Edgar Jr. (31).

Sam Bronfman joined Seagram in 1979 after attending college and working in the advertising sales department at *Sports Illustrated.* He started with Seagram's California wine business, worked briefly in the spirits operation, and now is president of the Fine Wines Division.

In the meantime, Edgar Jr. refused to go to college, seeing it as a waste of time. Instead, he pursued a career in show business, financing and producing plays, movies, and television shows. When his father invited him to join the family business in 1982, Edgar advanced quickly. His first assignment, as special assistant to Philip Beekman, then Seagram's president, gave him a fast overview of all of Seagram's operations such as planning, marketing, and packaging, plus the opportunity to watch key committees in action. In just three months, the young Edgar convinced Beekman and his father that he was qualified to head European operations, a position he held for the next two years. He then lobbied to run the House of Seagram, the company's U.S. liquor subsidiary. In July 1984, at just 29 years of age, he accepted his current post as president of this, the company's premiere division.

Corporate Strategy and Operations

When Samuel Bronfman established the Seagram Company in the early 1900s, he had one goal: to be the undisputed industry leader. Bronfman's goal has been well-served in the past 58 years, as the company is presently the world's largest producer and marketer of distilled spirits and wines and has affiliates in twenty-seven countries. The company's financial statements are revealed in Exhibits 4, 5, and 6.

Today Seagram's 14,200 employees produce and market more than 190 brands of distilled spirits worldwide. Spirits produced by the company include such well-known brand names as Crown Royal, Seagram's V.O., Seagram's Five Star and Lord Calvert Canadian whiskeys; Chivas Regal 12-year-old scotch, Passport scotch, Glenlivit 12-year-old and Glen Grant single-malt scotch whiskeys; Seagram's Extra Dry and Boodles and Calvert gins; Seagram's Imported, Wolfschmidt, Crown Russe, and Nikolai vodkas; Myer's Dark Jamaican, Ronrico, and Captain Morgan rums, and the Leroux line of brandies and cordials. In addition, the company owns a 13.9 percent interest in the Irish Distillers Group, the producer of John Jameson and Old Bushmills Irish whiskeys, among others.

Since its inception, Seagram has followed a strategy of growth through acquisition; yet, the type of firms acquired has shifted over time. Whereas early additions to the corporation were primarily distillers, more recent acquisitions are from industries other than Seagram's core liquor business.

The company's first major venture into nonliquor areas was the acquisition of Texas Pacific Oil Company. This subsidiary was sold to Sun Company in 1980. Although Texas Pacific had rich potential in undeveloped reserves, Seagram wanted a subsidiary capable of yielding immediate profits in order to provide support for its capital-intensive distilleries.

In June 1981, funds from this sale were used to buy 27,882,575 common shares of Conoco, Inc., at a total cost of $2.6 billion. After losing a bidding war to E.I. DuPont de Nemours, however, the Conoco shares were exchanged for 20.2 percent ownership in that firm. Since that time, Seagram has increased its holding in DuPont to 22.5 percent but has signed a standstill agreement under which it agrees not to acquire more than 25 percent of DuPont stock through 1999. As part of this deal, Seagram now controls six seats on DuPont's 29-member board of directors, and three seats on the 11-member finance committee. Seagram's share of DuPont stock is worth about $6.5 billion. In 1986, dividends yielded $323.2 million of the liquor company's net income of $423.5 million.

The immense value of Seagram's DuPont holdings, while attractive, is seen by some as a strong incentive for a corporate takeover. To further exacerbate the situation, Minda de Ginzburg, the older sister of Edgar and Charles, recently sold about $40 million of her shares, thereby reducing the family control of the business to about 38 percent. With 95.5 million Seagram shares outstanding, experts believe that Seagram's stock is undervalued by $8 to $10 a share. As one analyst noted, if you subtract the value of Seagram's 22.5 percent stake in DuPont and its cash in the till, the rest of Seagram has been trading for only about $2 a share.

Seagram has already tried one protective tactic. In April 1985, the company asked shareholders to approve the creation of a new type of share that would carry ten votes instead of one. The Bronfmans intended to convert their holdings to the new shares, thereby increasing their voting rights by 86 percent without spending a penny on additional stock. Although this move would have ensured the family complete control of the company, the Bronfmans were forced to withdraw their proposal after shareholders vigorously objected to the plan. Although a takeover still remains a possibility, it is clear that the Bronfmans are prepared to fight if necessary.

Since 1981, a number of corporate moves have signalled changes in Seagram's strategic posture. In 1983, for example, Seagram acquired the Wine Spectrum from the Coca-Cola Company for $217 million. This purchase added several moderately priced brands, such as Taylor California Cellars, Taylor New York, and Great Western, to Seagram's wine products. Among the other brands produced by the company at that time were the moderately priced Paul Masson and Gold Seal Wines as well as the more expensive Sterling Vineyards and Monterey Vineyard labels. Numerous French, German, Italian, Australian, and Spanish wines were also produced.

Although the acquisition of the Wine Spectrum in 1983 moved Seagram to second place in U.S. wine sales with 8.3 percent of the market, number one, E. and J. Gallo, controls 26.1 percent of the market and are considered to have tremendous clout. As a privately owned firm, Gallo is able to wrest market share from competitors by settling for paper-thin margins and occasional losses that stockholders of publicly held companies will not tolerate for long. As a result, Seagram's returns in this area did not meet expectations. In 1986, firm managers were particularly disappointed with the performance of the company's moderately priced wines. For this reason, they agreed to sell several of their wine operations for about $200 million to Vintners International Company, a new concern founded by the wine unit's former president and other investors. Included in the sale were Taylor California Cellars, Taylor New York, Great Western, Paul Masson, and Gold Seal Wines. Presently, the one bright spot on the wine horizon appears to be wine coolers—the most rapidly growing segment of the beverage alcohol business. After Seagram signed T.V. and movie star Bruce Willis to do a series of Seagram Wine Cooler commercials, the brand moved to number two, again following the powerful Gallo, whose Bartles and Jaymes brand leads the field.

Seagram has also increased its stake in the lucrative U.S. mixer market by purchasing 30 percent of Premium Beverages, Inc., which produces and sells such products as club soda, tonic water, ginger ale, and seltzer. Premium was created in 1982 by Coca-Cola Bottling Company of New York, under a licensing agreement with Sea-

EXHIBIT 4 Consolidated statement of income (U.S. dollars in thousands, except per share amounts)

	Twelve Months Ended January 31,		
	1987	*1986*	*1985*
Sales and other income	$3,344,820	$2,970,669	$2,821,245
Cost of goods	2,189,628	1,940,993	1,834,233
Gross profit	1,155,192	1,029,676	987,012
Selling, general and administrative expenses	927,360	815,021	741,399
Restructuring costs[1]	35,000	—	—
Operating Income	192,832	214,655	245,613
Interest expense	84,294	82,013	88,054
Income before income taxes	108,538	132,642	157,559
Provision for income taxes	5,715	33,417	43,742
Income from spirits and wine operations	102,823	99,225	113,817
Interest expense related to share repurchase, after income taxes	(2,513)	(6,683)	(12,845)
Dividend income from E.I. du Pont de Nemours & Company, after taxes[2]	154,091	150,838	141,294
Equity in unremitted earnings of E.I. du Pont de Nemours & Company	169,057	75,694	141,352
Net Income	**$ 423,458**	**$ 319,074**	**$ 383,618**
Earnings per share data			
Income from operations and dividends	$2.67	$2.63	$2.67
Equity in unremitted earnings of E.I. du Pont de Nemours & Co.	1.78	.81	1.55
Net Income			
Primary	**$4.45**	**$3.44**	**$4.22**
Fully diluted	**$4.30**	**$3.34**	**$4.05**

[1]Notes: *Restructuring Costs.* During the quarter ended January 31, 1987, the company recorded a $35 million pretax provision for U.S. restructuring costs. This accrual reflects a loss on the sale of certain U.S. wine operations, including Paul Masson, Taylor California Cellars, Taylor New York, Great Western and Gold Seal wines, and the associated wineries and vineyards in California and New York. This provision also includes the estimated expenses associated with a reorganization of a U.S. marketing division.

[2]*Equity in DuPont.* In August 1981, the Company acquired 20.2 percent of the then outstanding shares of common stock of E.I. du Pont de Nemours and Company (Du Pont). With subsequent open-market purchases, the Company held at January 31, 1987, 54.3 million shares, or 22.6 percent of Du Pont's outstanding common stock.

The Company accounts for its interest in Du Pont using the equity method whereby its proportionate share of Du Pont's earnings is included in income. Cumulative unremitted Du Pont earnings of 567.7 million are included in consolidated retained earnings at January 31, 1987; no provision has been made for taxes in view of availability options for realization.

EXHIBIT 5 Consolidated balance sheet (U.S. dollars in thousands)

	Assets January 31,	
	1987	*1986*
Current Assets		
Cash and short-term investments at cost, which approximates market	$ 593,590	$ 386,466
Receivables	590,155	508,383
Inventories	1,250,029	1,250,165
Prepaid expenses	48,110	36,095
Wine company assets held for sale	220,000	—
Total Current Assets	**2,701,884**	**2,181,109**
Common Stock of E.I. du Pont de Nemours & Co.	3,329,727	3,150,611
Note Receivable from Sun Company, Inc.[1]	51,000	67,500
Property, Plant and Equipment, at Cost	842,593	917,551
Accumulated Depreciation	(343,634)	(346,023)
	498,959	**571,528**
Investments and Advances—Spirits and Wine Companies	76,686	49,330
Sundry Assets, Including Excess of Cost Over Net Assets of Companies Acquired	228,206	202,079
	$6,886,462	**$6,222,157**

gram, to test market Seagram's mixers. Premium, however, became so successful that Seagram decided to move into the business. The market for mixers is predicted to triple between 1985 and 1988; yet, the competition is intense with Canada Dry and Cadbury Schweppes currently controlling 50 percent of U.S. sales versus 4 percent for Seagram's line. Moreover, given the current anti-alcohol sentiments, some analysts speculate that Seagram's strategy of continuing to stress mixers as adjuncts to hard liquor rather than alternatives, could be short-sighted.

While company executives foresee the addition of other non-alcohol consumer products to complement current operations, Seagram's core business remains hard liquor. Seagram's principal operating subsidiary is the Joseph E. Seagram Company, commonly known as the House of Seagram, which manufactures and sells distilled spirits.

THE JOSEPH E. SEAGRAM COMPANY

The Seagram name has long been a symbol of quality in the spirits business. A bottle of Chivas Regal at a gathering conveys a clear message in today's status-conscious society. Yet, a careful look at Seagram's numerous product offerings reveals that its

EXHIBIT 5 continued

	Liabilities and Shareholders' Equity January 31,	
	1987	*1986*
Current Liabilities		
Short-term borrowings	$ 460,410	$ 233,838
United States excise taxes	61,047	86,370
Payables and accrued liabilities	450,780	404,283
Income and other taxes	57,637	77,040
Indebtedness payable within one year	72,420	141,952
Total Current Liabilities	**1,102,294**	**943,483**
Long-Term Indebtedness	911,764	803,601
Deferred Income Taxes and Other Credits	882,040	918,959
Minority Interest	34,804	34,133
Shareholders' Equity		
Shares without par value 1987–95,494,856 shares; 1986–95,145,420 shares	257,368	222,426
Share purchase warrants	27,679	27,691
Cumulative currency translation adjustments	(228,456)	(311,874)
Retained earnings	3,898,969	3,583,738
Total Shareholders' Equity	3,955,560	3,521,981
	$6,886,462	**$6,222,157**

[1]*Sun Note Receivable and Reversionary Interest.* In August 1980, the Company sold its U.S. oil, gas, and related properties to Sun Company, Inc. (Sun) for $2.3 billion. A gain of $1.2 billion, after provision for deferred income taxes of $616 million, was recorded.

Under the terms of the sale, the Company retains reversionary interests of 25% in producing properties which entitle the Company to participate if Sun achieves certain investment criteria. No value has been assigned to these reversionary interests for financial statement purposes. For tax purposes, a majority of the proceeds was treated as an installment sale and the remainder as a loan. The Company holds a $675 million note receivable on the sale which is due in 3 equal annual installments from August 31, 1987 through August 29, 1989.

strength is confined to brown liquors; indeed, the company has rarely excelled in products outside this specialty.

From the beginning, the company has relied on just five brands, four of them brown liquors, for 50 percent of its profits. Seagram's 7 Crown, a blended whiskey that for years was the best selling liquor in America, has now been far outpaced by Bacardi rum and Smirnoff Vodka. Its sales have declined more than 7 percent since 1981. Seagram's number two seller, V.O., lost its position to Brown-Forman's Canadian Mist. Only Crown Royal Canadian, Seagram's premium, high-margin Canadian whiskey, has shown a significant gain in the same period.

EXHIBIT 6 Consolidated statement of changes in financial position (U.S. dollars in thousands)

	Twelve Months Ended Jan. 31		
	1987	*1986*	*1985*
Operations			
Income from spirits & wine operations	$102,823	$ 99,225	$113,817
Interest expense related to share repurchase	(2,513)	(6,683)	(12,845)
Items not requiring the use of funds			
Depreciation	48,332	46,590	43,891
Deferred income taxes	(47,175)	(21,946)	35,742
Sundry	4,047	20,374	34,163
	105,514	**137,560**	**214,768**
Dividend income from E.I. du Pont de Nemours & Co., after income taxes	154,091	150,838	141,294
Funds Provided by Operations and Dividends	**259,605**	**288,398**	**356,062**
Wine company assets held for sale	(220,000)	—	—
Capital asset dispositions (expenditures)	38,581[1]	(74,516)	(78,532)
Receivables	(81,772)	(74,778)	(36,697)
Inventories	136[1]	(159,285)	75,559
Prepaid expenses	(12,015)	(1,105)	(5,716)
U.S. excise taxes, payables and accrued liabilities	21,174	52,990	(22,056)
Income and other taxes	(15,053)	50,529	79,445
Funds Invested in Operations—(Increase)/Decrease	**(268,949)**	**(206,165)[2]**	**12,003**
Net Funds Available from (Required by) Operations and Dividends	**(9,344)**	**82,233**	**368,065**
Dividends Paid	**(90,376)**	**(74,181)**	**(72,721)**

This lack of product diversity can be attributed to Samuel Bronfman's attitude toward white liquors. Because he believed such products would never sell, the company paid little attention to them. Seagram watched as more innovative competitors introduced such specialty products as Bailey's Irish Cream and Midori (a melon-flavored liquor). Says one competitor, "They've done a good job on a few products, but for the industry leader, they're not on the cutting edge."[6]

Seagram distributes its products through a worldwide network of company-owned affiliates and independent distributors. Samuel Bronfman long ago discovered that loyal distributors would be a key to success in this business. In fact, a number of Seagram distributors have been involved with Seagram from the beginning. Like Seagram, some of these affiliates are, themselves, family businesses now operated by second and third generation managers.

EXHIBIT 6 continued

	Twelve Months Ended Jan. 31		
	1987	*1986*	*1985*
Investments and Other			
Purchase of additional share of E.I. du Pont de Nemours & Co.	—	(25,588)	(130,005)
Sale of oil and gas properties	—	93,385	—
Change in cumulative currency translation adjustments	83,418	94,665	(90,521)
Acquisitions and other	(58,868)	(52,911)	6,455
Net Investment Activity	**24,550**	**109,551**	**(214,071)**
Financing Activities			
Issuance of shares for conversions of LYONs and debentures, exercise of warrants, and acquisition of Cemp Enterprises Ltd.	35,670	130,905	76,540
Repurchase and cancellation of 310,000 common shares	(18,579)	—	—
Issuance of long-term indebtedness	295,684	276,585	196,328
Repayment of long-term indebtedness	(187,521)	(299,003)	(176,318)
Short-term borrowings and indebtedness payable within one year—increase (decrease)	157,040	33,490	(140,028)
Net Financing Obtained (Repaid)	**282,294**	**141,977**[2]	**(43,478)**
Net Increase in Cash and Short-Term Investments	**$207,124**	**259,580**	**$37,795**

Notes

[1]Reflects reclassifications of wine company assets held for sale.

[2]Excludes the assets and liabilities of acquired companies, which for purposes of this statement are included in "Investments and Other."

The Seagram Family Association (SFA) was established in 1950 to ensure open communication among members of the growing network of distributors. SFA members meet annually to discuss new marketing programs, innovative financing approaches, and other key business issues and problems. Another program unique to the liquor industry, Seagram's Distributor Consulting Service provides support to distributors in such areas as inventory management, order processing, and warehouse design. About 250 distributors have used the consulting service since its beginning in 1961.

The distribution process for hard liquors is highly regulated, and every country has different laws and policies to which firms must adhere. For example, in the United States, liquor is sold to two classes of customers. In 32 states, the customers are wholesalers who resell the product to package stores and other outlets. But in 18 states, the government is involved in distribution. Here, liquor is sold to state and local liquor boards and commissions. In Canada, too, liquor is sold exclusively to provincial and territorial government liquor boards. As the company expands further into foreign markets, it must keep abreast of these requirements. Where possible, Seagram is integrating forward by distributing goods through its wholly owned affiliates and through joint venture agreements in such diverse locations as Thailand, Japan, and Venezuela. In other countries, all distribution is handled by independent organizations.

To appeal to the consumer, Seagram makes extensive use of radio and T.V. advertising, magazines, newspapers, and billboards. However, since 1980, Seagram has made deep cuts in its advertising budget in order to improve its bottom line.[7]

Organizational Structure

Presently, the Joseph E. Seagram Company has four operating divisions: Seagram Distillers Company, 375 Spirits Company, Perennial Sales Company, and Summit Sales Company. Both 375 Spirits and Perennial are new companies that replaced the old Calvert Distillers and General Wine and Spirits as part of a recent reorganization. The 375 Spirits Company was named after the company's corporate address at 375 Park Avenue.

Seagram's Distillers handles such high volume brands as V.O., Crown Royal, and Canadian Whiskey as well as Seagram's gin, vodka, rum, and its Leroux line of cordials.[8] All of these brands are capable of producing high profit margins, yet growth has slowed.

In contrast, the 375 Spirits Company carries premium and superpremium brands that are still considered to have high growth potential. Examples here include Chivas Regal, Glenlivit, and Myer's Dark Jamaican Rum.

The Perennial Company carries slowly growing brands that maintain strong brand loyalty in various areas of the country. Thus, this company will use targeted regional advertising as opposed to more expensive national ad campaigns. Both Wolfschmidt vodka and Passport scotch represent the type of brands assigned to this division since these brands are stronger on the East Coast than in other areas of the country.

Finally, the Summit Company handles only brands with small growth potential that do not merit additional investment. Some examples of these brands include Boodles and Calvert gins, and Eagle Rare Bourbon. The number of brands assigned to this company is expected to increase over time.

RECENT EVENTS AT SEAGRAM

In March 1986, Edgar Bronfman Sr. surprised family members and public observers by anointing Edgar Jr. as his successor to the chief executive slot at Seagram.[9] Despite the young Bronfman's lack of experience in the business, his father believes him to be better suited than his older brother to take the reigns of the giant corporation. This announcement, however, has led to some dispute within the company.

In an interview with the *Montreal Gazette* in April 1986, Charles Bronfman stated there had been no discussion by Seagram's executive committee, over which he presides, or by its board about who will succeed his brother as CEO. "Obviously both my brother and I realize that any succession is determined by the board. Not by Edgar and not by me, that's number 1."[10]

In this interview, Charles also disputed his brother's assertion that only a Bronfman would be a chief executive at Seagram, noting that the next CEO would be chosen on the basis of performance at the company over a long period of time. Secondly, he criticized Edgar's statement that only two Bronfmans of each generation would work at the company. Since Edgar Bronfman already has two sons at the company, that tradition would effectively eliminate Charles's two children and Edgar's five other children. Charles called the limit of two family members an "arbitrary" number that he never agreed to. He said: "I happen to have two children aged 22 and 17. I don't know whether they want to go into the company or they don't. If they do, God bless them."[11]

A second indication of possible conflict at the top was Philip Beekman's sudden resignation on June 27, 1986, less than three months after Edgar Sr.'s announcement. Although both Seagram and Beekman, himself, have publicly stated that the two events were not related, some former Seagram executives see Beekman's exit as just one more firing.

Beekman, who came to Seagram in 1977 from the presidency of Colgate-Palmolive Company, brought with him a reputation as a marketing expert. Yet after Edgar Jr. assumed presidency of the House of Seagram, Beekman had little say in Seagram's marketing direction. Also, he apparently disagreed with some of Edgar Jr.'s marketing decisions.[12]

In the wake of Beekman's resignation, David Sacks, 62, had been promoted to president. Sacks, a lawyer and financial expert, had been executive vice president of finance and administration at Seagram. He is expected to focus on corporate finances; he sits on the board of DuPont. Marketing responsibilities will be left to Edgar Jr. According to one analyst, "David Sacks is a financial man in a marketing company. I think it wasn't Edgar's time yet to take over the position (as president)."[13] Other analysts see Sacks' appointment as a sign that Seagram is interested in investments outside the distilled spirits industry. The Bronfmans aren't talking.

In a speech to the National Licensed Beverage Association in November 1986, Edgar Bronfman, Jr. announced that Seagram would end its efforts to support the alcohol equivalence campaign. Bronfman cited industry disunity as the major reason for this decision. Yet, his speech gave no firm commitment as to when the campaign would end, or how Seagram would act to restore unity among beer, wine, and spirits factions. As of January 1987, Bronfman had failed to respond to requests from Beer and Wine Institute leaders to clarify his intentions.

THE FUTURE FOR SEAGRAM

Although the Bronfman family expresses great optimism about Seagram, the company's future direction remains in question. The equivalency campaign received a negative response from T.V. networks, other beverage manufacturers, and consumer groups. An important question is how to replace this campaign in order to both appease warring factions in the beverage industry and convince the public that hard liquor is still a viable alternative to light beer and wine coolers.

In making this decision, a question that must be addressed by the company is whether the current anti-alcohol sentiment represents a permanent attitude shift or a short-term phenomenon. This trend has been described as "reminiscent of the Prohibitionist movement." Future moves at both the corporate and business levels hinge on the company's assessment of whether, like Prohibition, the current movement will come to an end.

A number of strategic alternatives must be considered. Should Seagram continue to expand into non-alcohol related businesses? If so, what types of businesses should be acquired? Does the present management team have the knowledge and skills to succeed in these areas? A related question is whether the company should reduce its emphasis on some or all types of alcoholic beverages. For example, should Seagram divest more of its remaining wine operations? At present, the firm's domestic holdings are focused on the high-priced segments of the market and on wine coolers. Do these investments make sense? Second, should Seagram divest part of its distilled spirits business? Although liquor is the firm's core business, can the company continue to increase liquor sales in today's hostile environment? If it does not choose to withdraw from these areas, then what steps can it take to stem its declining revenues?

NOTES

1. "How Seagram is Scrambling to Survive 'the Sobering of America.'" *Business Week.* 3 September, 1984, 94–95.
2. Kleinfield, N.R. "Decline in Drinking Changes Liquor Industry." *New York Times.* 17 September, 1984, A1 & D12.
3. Yovovich, B.G. "Regulations Chilling Hard Liquor Industry." *Advertising Age.* 26 July, 1984, 20, 22, 24.
4. Brody, M. "The Supreme Court Shakes the Ad Biz." *Fortune.* 4 August, 1986, 152.
5. Perry, N.J. "The Second Son is Heir at Seagram." *Fortune.* 17 March, 1986, 28–31.
6. "How Seagram is Scrambling to Survive 'the Sobering of America,'" 94.
7. Jervey, G. More targeted marketing aim of Seagram revamp, *Advertising Age,* Jan. 21, 1985, 4.
8. Edel, R. Ads pour new life into Canadian whiskeys. *Advertising Age,* July 26, 1984, 16–17, 20, 22, 24, 26, & 30.
9. Perry, N.J., 28.
10. Freeman, A. "Seagram Company Management Succession is Issue of Dispute between Bronfmans." *Wall Street Journal.* 16 April, 1986, 7.
11. Freeman, A., 7.
12. Winters, P. "Sacks Toes Bottom Line at Seagram." *Advertising Age.* 7 July, 1986, 2.
13. Winters, P., 2.

Winston Glass Company—1987*

JAMES BRUNNER
The University of Toledo

BACKGROUND

Pete Sudley, president of Winston Glass, a U.S glassware manufacturing company, is in a heated meeting with Vice-President of Marketing John Brickley, Production Manager Bob Caines, and Chief Engineer Steve Miller to discuss recent negotiations with Xia Xian. The negotiations concerned a potential joint venture with Xia Xian for manufacturing glassware in China (PRC). John Brickley, disheartened, commented at the end of the meeting, "I know the Chinese are just as interested in this joint venture as we are. Caines, Miller, and I were really encouraged by the great, positive interest the Chinese showed in our proposal. Mr. Tien, their president, thanked us profusely for our company's interest in China. We were thunderstruck when he politely informed us at our last meeting that the joint venture would not be possible at this time."

Alone in the conference room, Sudley reviewed the memorandum concerning the negotiations with Xia Xian. He knew Brickley was a shrewd, ambitious businessman, as well as a tough negotiator. Moreover, Sudley knew that the joint-venture enterprise was just as profitable to China as it would have been for Winston Glass, or else the minister of foreign trade would not have issued an invitation to his company to visit China. In the six months after the invitation was received, something had clearly gone drastically awry.

In February 1987, Winston Glass had sent their most efficient team consisting of three representatives to Qinhuangdao to negotiate with Chinese officials about a possible joint venture for the manufacture of glassware. The team consisted of Brickley, Caines, and Miller. An American-born Chinese interpreter was also included in the group.

Winston Glass produces glassware, including stemware, tumblers, table glasses, and plastic and glass prescription containers. Its worldwide sales in 1984 were $3.6 billion. The company has plants in Europe, Asia, and South America, and it has 44,000 employees. Its earnings have been flat for the past five years, and the management is seeking new avenues for growth. The plant being considered in China would produce all types of "Winston" glassware, the brand name used worldwide.

BACKGROUND OF QINHUANGDAO

Qinhuangdao is a major Chinese port city in northern China. Located on the Bohai Gulf, Qinhuangdao is only 277 kilometers (166 miles) southeast of Beijing and serves as the gateway to the capital due to its large, modern harbor.

Qinhuangdao has developed into an important economic center and is the glass capital of The People's Republic of China. The Great Wall starts at Qinhuangdao,

*It is suggested to read Appendix B at the end of this case, before analyzing this case.

and the city is adjacent to Beidaihe, the leading summer resort of China. Beidaihe is visited by leading government officials from Beijing who want to escape that city's summer heat. One of fourteen coastal cities open to the outside world, Qinhuangdao has a new economic and technical development zone. The area is rich in quartz, a major ingredient in the manufacturing of glass. Twenty-five glass factories in the area produce laminated glass, thermal glass, medical glassware, fiberglass, and heat-absorbing glass. Yan Shan University has 400 skilled technological graduates annually.

TRIP TO QINHUANGDAO

Arrangements

The Winston Glass representatives arrived safely in Qinhuangdao where they were greeted by their Chinese hosts. The Americans were escorted to the Jing Jiang Hotel expressly reserved for foreign guests. Left to settle in and unwind after their 23-hour journey, the Americans found to their surprise and pleasure that their lodgings were comparable to those of first-class hotels in the major cities of the United States.

The Chinese hosts had arranged for the Americans to be lodged in suites complete with comfortable beds and baths and a separate work area for business activities. Their rooms contained a television and a telephone and were fully carpeted and tastefully decorated. Room and wake-up services were available, and a dining room was available for meals, both Chinese and Western styles. Pleased by their surroundings and encouraged by the congeniality of their hosts, the Americans retired, confident that the negotiations scheduled for the next day would establish a beneficial working relationship with the Chinese.

The Tour

The next day, the Chinese contingency arrived promptly at 9 a.m. for scheduled negotiations at the hotel. Although provincial and special city level officials can engage in foreign trade negotiations, Qinhuangdao is one of four municipalities whose jurisdiction falls directly under the central government. Qinhuangdao also ultimately answers to the Bank of China for clearance of joint ventures. Therefore, the Chinese negotiating team was headed by a Chinese negotiator with significant negotiating power. The leader of the group, Mr. Tien, head of the Director's Office, introduced the others in his party as Mr. Mah, personal secretary and interpreter, and Mr. Pi, production manager. Tien was tall and thin; he stood erect and appeared very dignified and rigid in bearing. After formal, courteous introductions and an exchange of pleasantries, the group left the hotel for a tour of the Qinhuangdao manufacturing plant, Xia Xian Glass Works. Both parties relied on their interpreters for communication.

Arriving at the Xia Xian Glass Works, the group was greeted by Mr. Poh, the plant manager. Mr. Poh conducted the group tour of the plant.

The Americans were surprised at the scene that awaited them in the plant. Piles of parts waiting to be assembled lay scattered at random on the floor; piles of screws, tools, glasses, and crates of nuts and bolts were intermixed in disarray. Groups of employees were loitering, playing cards or conversing, while others were engaged in their employment activities. Surprised at the lack of activity in the plant, the Americans were told that the plant had met its quota for the year as set by the State Planning Commission, and there was a period of reduced production before a new quota was established and approved by the commission. Bob Caines, production manager for Winston Glass, inquired, "Wouldn't it be more profitable to manufacture more rather than shut down parts of production, or perhaps lay off some of the workers until the plant can operate at full capacity again?" Poh replied politely that the Premier knew best and that in their country, they did not profit at the expense of the workers.

The underutilized mechanical capacity of the plant also surprised the Winston Glass group. "They have more equipment than they can use for years," Miller commented to Brickley. "The best way for the joint venture to succeed would be to sell off its excess machinery to companies in the United States where there is a market for used machinery." As the tour progressed, Miller continued to be amazed by the advanced technological capacity of the plant. When Miller openly praised the equipment, Poh smiled broadly but said humbly to the surprise of the Americans, "Oh, our factory is very ill-equipped, with few modern machines unlike those you have in your country." Brickley, confused by Poh's statement since they had just viewed a great deal of modern machinery, quickly assured Poh that the plant was indeed impressive and very well equipped.

During the next few hours of the tour, the Americans fired questions at the Chinese concerning production and the general operation of the glass plant. The bottom line for the Americans was their interest in profits; whereas, the Chinese had their national pride and interest, political ideals (which do not recognize the profit motive), and state planning and bureaucratic allocations guiding them in their actions and response. In keeping face with these sensitive issues, Poh's answers were vague, although always modest and polite. (Face is the cooperative manner in which people behave toward one another in order to avoid loss of self-respect or prestige by either party to an exchange. Without the saving of face, the Chinese would most likely be justly offended and avoid dealing with the winner of the transaction—in this case Winston Glass—in the future.)

After the tour of the plant, the Chinese invited their guests to dine with them at a local restaurant. Name cards at place settings facilitated seating. The Americans were surprised to find that Tien took what they considered to be the foot of the table, the seat facing the wall opposite the door. To the right of Tien, Brickley, Mah, and Miller were seated. To the left of Tien were Pi, Caines, and Andy. When the first course arrived, the Chinese each served the American next to him a portion of the cold seafood.

After the first course had been cleared from the table, Tien rose and gave a speech welcoming the Americans to China and lauding Sino-American relations. No mention of the possible joint venture was made. Several toasts were offered during this speech. The Americans were unsure of the Mai Tai they had been served and toasted cautiously. After the third course, Brickley stood and toasted his hosts, giving a speech on Sino-American relations, but focusing on the proposed joint venture. Toasts continued to be offered by both parties, and the Chinese frequently urged their guests throughout the hearty nine course meal to eat, as they had at the beginning of the meal, saying "qing, qing" ("please, please").

During the meal, the conversation naturally turned to a discussion of the different cuisines of each region of China. Miller asked facetiously if it were true that the Chinese eat dog, snake, and monkey brains. Tien smiled broadly and replied affirmatively. Encouraged by Tien's grin, Miller began joking about some of the delicacies that had appeared on the menu, such as sea-snails. The Chinese seemed to enjoy this joking as they were grinning and nodding their heads in response. Encouraged, the Americans began to tell some of their popular Western jokes. The atmosphere was friendly and relaxed.

Brickley was encouraged by this atmosphere and decided that the time was right to again address the subject of the joint venture. Addressing himself to Tien, Brickley said, "With our technology and investment, Winston Glass could pull China from its backwardness and make it a world power." Tien replied, "Yes, yes, Winston Glass is a very strong company in a very powerful country. Qinhuangdao certainly could make use of a liaison with Winston Glass." Encouraged by Tien's reply, Brickley continued, expounding upon the mutual benefits which the joint venture would provide both parties. As Brickley spoke, tea and fruit were served. Tien listened politely to Brickley as he sipped his tea. After a third cup of tea, Tien stood and thanked the Americans for their company at dinner. The hosts then escorted the Americans back to the Jing Jiang Hotel and quickly departed.

Negotiations

The next day, the two groups met again. First on the agenda was discussion of the meaning of "joint venture." (See Appendix A.) Defined by the law of China, a joint venture is a "limited liability company. Each party to the joint venture is liable to the joint venture to the limit of the capital subscribed by it, and the joint venture shoulders the responsibility for its debt with the total capital of the venture." The Americans readily agreed to this definition of liability; Chinese law had defined the joint venture similarly to the American definition. Next, the Chinese pursued an initial agreement on very general principles without the clarification on the specific details. Mr. Tien presented Xia Xian's proposal as a total package: The Americans were to invest in the total capital invested in the joint venture in the form of cash, equipment, and training. The amount would be approximately $3 million.

The Americans were surprised at the Chinese proposal. The Americans were accustomed to focusing on specific details and avoiding discussions of generalities during the initial stages of the negotiations. The American team presented their proposal, one similar to that of the Chinese, using slides, photographs, statistics, and other supporting documents. Statistics, research, financial statements, and other documents were extensively discussed. The Chinese remained reserved, occasionally talking among themselves. The friendly dinner atmosphere from the previous evening had disappeared. It became apparent that the situation had become tense.

The negotiations continued the following day. Mr. Tien emphasized the need to reach an agreement on general principles. The American team showed some apprehension in agreeing to his plea. Mr. Tien commented that the two sides were friends and that the American team would be behaving dishonorably if they did not agree to the general terms. Feeling intimidated, Mr. Brickley agreed to the general principles.

Since the initial agreement, a week passed before the actual negotiations on specific details began. During this time, both sides felt a common bond of friendship. Elegant dinners were given by both sides, and spirits among the two teams remained high. But after a few weeks, the American team became perturbed because it was neither convenient nor economical to remain in China for nothing other than the sake of "being there." The American team became impatient. Brickley began using a high-pressure selling technique during the negotiations, stressing that the Americans had lots to offer a country like China and "with our help, we can make your country as strong and powerful as ours."

Finally, the Chinese were ready to discuss some of the specific details with the American team. Tien presented Xia Xian's new proposal. The Americans were to invest 35 percent of the total capital invested in the joint venture in the form of cash, equipment, and technology. The value of the equipment would be set at international market prices, while the value of the technology given was to be valued at a price mutually agreeable to both sides. The technology given was to be up-to-date, dependable, and practical for use in China. The Chinese were to provide 65 percent of the venture capital in the form of cash, buildings, property, and labor. The value of the property and buildings would be fixed by the People's Government of Qinhuangdao according to the relevant industry index and the location of the plant. Eighty percent of the goods produced from the joint venture were to be exported from China.

The Americans agreed to most of the Chinese proposal with the exception of the percentage of products that were to be exported. After negotiations, the parties agreed that 65 percent of the goods produced by the joint venture were to be exported from China, with the remainder being sold in the People's Republic of China. Tien was evasive when questioned about sales channels for the product, replying that sales would be handled through the sales department in Qinhuangdao, or by China's Foreign Trade Commerce Department. As the meeting progressed, the Chinese voiced little interest in or problems with the way the joint venture was to be organized or managed. However, they were keenly interested in the technology of the plant from theory to practice, and they showed a desire to learn about the machinery to be supplied by the Americans.

To relieve some of the tension, the American team avoided discussion of subjects upon which the two teams were in disagreement; again, the American team emphasized the great mutual benefits that would result from this venture in the future. The meeting ended well in the Americans' opinion. Some disagreements still remained, but much ground had been covered, and the remaining differences were not insurmountable.

The American team had good reason to feel confident in their negotiations since there were 2,000 foreign corporations operating in China by the end of 1986. Most of them were owned by overseas Chinese who have prospered throughout Asia. However, the total also included seventy U.S., sixty-seven Japanese, and forty-two British, West German, and French companies, most of which are bound in joint ventures with Chinese state enterprises. In 1986, more than 600 new joint ventures were entered into by Chinese and foreign firms. (See Appendix A for an example of a joint venture agreement.)

That evening, the Americans hosted the Chinese for dinner. The menu was simpler than those of the nights before because the Americans felt the meals had been too exotic for their tastes and digestion. Speeches were again given by Tien and Brickley; toasting continued as before. Miller again told some Western jokes, accompanied by friendly backslapping. The Americans tried to lighten the ongoing formal conversation by steering discussions to more familiar topics such as family, personal tastes and ideas, and sexual patterns in China. Due to their background, the Chinese are not comfortable with body contact such as handshaking or backslapping, nor do they discuss personal matters with others. However, they responded with much smiling and laughter although replies were vague.

Over the next week, the meetings and dinners continued. Brickley tried to assess the feasibility of the joint venture. He was encouraged by what he had seen and heard in China. Given the world's largest population and recently expanded marketing system, China provided a large and relatively unexploited market. Labor was inexpensive and abundant, without the problems of labor strikes. Supplies would also be less costly and easier to obtain than in other countries. A few concerns preoccupied Brickley as he evaluated the benefits.

JOINT VENTURE CONCERNS

Because China does not have an institutionalized legal system, his first concern was whether the Chinese whose culture has traditionally shunned legal considerations and rather stressed ethical and moral principles would honor the agreements made. Brickley knew that since the "open door" policy, the Chinese were developing a commercial code for joint ventures, but this fact wasn't very comforting for someone who normally operated in a legalistically oriented business environment. Brickley also considered that although firmly a socialist country, China suffers from political instability; China's recent "open door" policy is mostly the work of their former leader, Deng Xiaoping. The future of this policy is uncertain in the event of Deng's death because many diehard Maoists are still entrenched in the bureaucracy or established in the military. They have managed to resist and even reverse China's new direction.

In November 1983 Deng launched an attempt to put his mark—and a solid political mark—on China's new emerging economic policies. He began a three-year plan to purge the Communist party's forty million members of one million unregenerate leftists, most of them ill-educated Maoists. Deng has designed a rectification program of self-criticism and prescribed study and retirement to purge the party without creating chaos and fear.

Deng has done everything possible to clear the way for his proteges to rise to positions of power to insure continuation of his economic, political, and "open door" policies. He installed Hu Yaobang as chairman and Zhao Ziyang as premier. He chose not to accept positions for himself. Deng also had made certain that second- and third-level government officials who are younger, better educated, and philosophically aligned with his political and economic policies have been installed or moved up into positions of power which will help insure the continuation of his reforms and China's growth and development. But change is still slow, and other unknowns inherent in a foreign investment must be considered.

In October 1987, Zhao Ziyang became the party general secretary, succeeding Deng. However, Deng remained a paramount figure in the decision-making process. Zhao has proclaimed that socialism is in its primitive phase, and he is permitting some of the capitalistic methods to be adopted in China, such as using quotas, holding managers accountable for the profitability of their factories, and moving toward a market mechanism for setting prices.

RESULTS OF THE NEGOTIATIONS

In the end, the Americans were pleased with the arrangements resulting from the negotiations. The Americans had decided that the joint venture would be a good investment for the Winston Glass Company. They enjoyed meeting with their Chinese hosts and believed that they had initiated an excellent working and social relationship for future dealings. They were concerned that modern management techniques were not practiced, profits were not stressed, and marketing was almost nonexistent.

The Chinese too appeared pleased with the negotiations and were very careful to assure the Winston representatives that nothing had been left undecided. At the final scheduled meeting between the two parties, the atmosphere was light and friendly, anticipatory, Brickley thought, of the closing of concrete arrangements finalizing the joint venture.

Tien greeted everyone and proposed his customary toast to the Americans and to Sino-American relations. After all had been seated, Tien politely smiled and announced that the joint venture between China and Winston Glass would not be possible at that time, but he gave no explanation. The conversation during the balance of the dinner was very stilted, and the final conversations with the Chinese representatives were cool. The Chinese, while chilly, left the Americans with the impression that the Chinese still wanted to maintain their relationship.

APPENDIX A

The Law of the People's Republic of China on Joint Ventures Using Chinese and Foreign Investment Adopted on July 1, 1979, at the Second Session of the Fifth National People's Congress; Promulgated on July 8, 1979.

Article 1

With a view to expanding international economic cooperation and technological exchange, the People's Republic of China permits foreign companies, enterprises, other economic entities, or individuals (hereinafter referred to as foreign participants) to incorporate themselves, within the territory of the People's Republic of China, into joint ventures with Chinese companies, enterprises, or other economic entities (here inafter referred to as Chinese participants) on the principle of equality and mutual benefit and subject to authorization by the Chinese Government.

Article 2

The Chinese Government protects, by the legislation in force, the resources invested by a foreign participant in a joint venture and the profits due him pursuant to the agreements, contracts, and articles of association authorized by the Chinese Government as well as his other lawful rights and interests.

All the activities of a joint venture shall be governed by the laws, decrees, and pertinent rules and regulations of the People's Republic of China.

Article 3

A joint venture shall apply to the Foreign Investment Commission of the People's Republic of China for authorization of the agreements and contracts concluded between the parties to the venture and the articles of association of the venture formulated by them, and the commission shall authorize or reject these documents within three months. When authorized, the joint venture shall register with the General Administration for Industry and Commerce of the People's Republic of China and start operations under license.

Article 4

A joint venture shall take the form of a limited liability company.

In the registered capital of a joint venture, the proportion of the investment contributed by the foreign participant(s) shall in general not be less than 25 percent.

The profits, risks, and losses of a joint venture shall be shared by the parties to the venture in proportion to their contributions to the registered capital.

The transfer of one party's share in the registered capital shall be effected only with the consent of the other parties to the venture.

Article 5

Each party to a joint venture may contribute cash, capital goods, industrial property rights, etc., as its investment to the venture.

The technology or equipment contributed by any foreign participant as investment shall be truly advanced and appropriate to China's needs. In cases of losses caused by deception through the intentional provision of outdated equipment or technology, compensation shall be paid for the losses.

The investment contributed by a Chinese participant may include the right to the use of a site provided for the joint venture during the period of its operation. In case such a contribution does not constitute a part of the investment from the Chinese participant, the joint venture shall pay the Chinese Government for its use.

The various contributions referred to in the present article shall be specified in the contracts concerning the joint venture—or in its articles of association, and the value of each contribution (excluding that of the site) shall be ascertained by the parties to the venture through joint assessment.

Article 6

A joint venture shall have a board of directors with a composition stipulated in the contracts and the articles of association after consultation between the parties to the venture, and each director shall be appointed or removed by his own side. The board of directors shall have a chairman appointed by the Chinese participant (It is clear from the Chinese text that the chairman will be Chinese.) and one or two vice-chairmen appointed by the foreign participant(s). In handling an important problem, the board of directors shall reach decision through consultation by the participants on the principle of equality and mutual benefit.

The board of directors is empowered to discuss and take action on, pursuant to the provisions of the articles of association of the joint venture, all fundamental issues concerning the venture, namely, expansion projects; production and business programs; the budget; distribution of profits; plans concerning manpower and pay scales; the termination of business; and the appointment of hiring of the president, the vice-president(s), the chief engineer, the treasurer, and the auditors as well as their functions and powers and their renumeration, etc.

The president and vice-president(s) (or the general manager and assistant general manager(s) in a factory) shall be chosen from the various parties to the joint venture.

Procedures covering the employment and discharge of the workers and staff members of a joint venture shall be stipulated according to the law in the agreement or contract concluded between the parties to the venture.

Article 7

The net profit of a joint venture shall be distributed between the parties to the venture in proportion to their respective shares in the registered capital after the payment of a joint venture income tax on its gross profit pursuant to the tax laws of the People's Republic of China and after the deductions therefrom as stipulated in the articles of association of the venture for the reserve funds, the bonus and welfare funds for the workers and staff members, and the expansion funds of the venture.

A joint venture equipped with up-to-date technology by world standards may apply for a reduction of or exemption from income tax for the first two to three profit-making years.

A foreign participant who reinvests any part of his share of the net profit within Chinese territory may apply for the restitution of a part of the income taxes paid.

Article 8

A joint venture shall open an account with the Bank of China or a bank approved by the Bank of China.

A joint venture shall conduct its foreign exchange transactions in accordance with the Foreign Exchange Regulations of the People's Republic of China.

A joint venture may, in its business operations, obtain funds from foreign banks directly.

The insurances appropriate to a joint venture shall be furnished by Chinese insurance companies.

Article 9

The production and business programs of a joint venture shall be filed with the authorities concerned and shall be implemented through business contracts.

In its purchase of required raw and semi-processed materials, fuels, auxiliary equipment, etc., a joint venture should give first priority to Chinese sources, but may also acquire them directly from the world market with its own foreign exchange funds.

A joint venture is encouraged to market its products outside China. It may distribute its export products on foreign markets through direct channels or its associated agencies or China's foreign trade establishments. Its products may also be distributed on the Chinese market. Wherever necessary, a joint venture may set up affiliated agencies outside China.

Article 10

The net profit which a foreign participant receives as his share after executing his obligations under the pertinent laws and agreements and contracts, the funds he receives at the time when the joint venture terminates or winds up its operations, and his other funds may be remitted abroad through the Bank of China in accordance with the foreign exchange regulations and in the currency or currencies specified in the contracts concerning the joint venture. A foreign participant shall receive encouragements for depositing in the Bank of China any part of the foreign exchange which he is entitled to remit abroad.

Article 11

The wages, salaries or other legitimate income earned by a foreign worker or staff member of a joint venture, after payment of the personal income tax under the tax laws of the People's Republic of China, may be remitted abroad through the Bank of China in accordance with the foreign exchange regulations.

Article 12

The contract period of a joint venture may be agreed upon between the parties to the venture according to its particular line of business and circumstances. The period may be extended upon expiration through agreement between the parties, subject to authorization by the Foreign Investment Commission of the People's Republic of China. Any application for such extension shall be made six months before the expiration of the contract.

Article 13

In cases of heavy losses, the failure of any party to a joint venture to execute its obligations under the contracts or the articles of association of the venture, force majeure, etc., prior to the expiration of consultation and agreement between the parties and through authorization by the Foreign Investment Commission of the People's Republic of China and registration with the General Administration for Industry and Commerce. In cases of losses caused by breach of the contract(s) by a party to the venture, the financial responsibility shall be borne by the said party.

Article 14

Disputes arising between the parties to a joint venture which the board of directors fails to settle through consultation may be settled through conciliation or arbitration by an arbitral body of China or through arbitration by an arbitral body agreed upon by the parties.

Article 15

The present law comes into force on the day of its promulgation. The power of amendment is vested in the National People's Congress.

The China Investment Guide, 1984/1985. (Hong Kong: China International Economic Consultants, Inc., Longman Group Limited): 1984.

APPENDIX B

Chinese Versus American Culture

With the striking changes currently taking place in industry, agriculture, and enterprise in China, equally striking changes have come in the life styles, customs, and mores of the Chinese people. Shocking to some, somewhat surprising to all, these changes reflect a political and social atmosphere less restrictive and more encouraging of individuality than that of the recent past.

This paper does not suggest an abandonment by the Chinese of socialism and corresponding tenets of behavior, nor does it imply that traditional Chinese concerns with behavior have disappeared. Rather, the aim of this essay is to point out that a subtle yet pervasive adoption of Western culture has created a new blend in the behavior and culture of the Chinese. As a result, the culture, customs, and mores of the Chinese in the 1980s reflect a merger of thousands of years of tradition with the behaviors encouraged during the Cultural Revolution and the era of the Gang of Four and with the more individualistic and expressive atmosphere encouraged today by Deng Xiaoping through ties with the West.

China is a large country containing many regions, many different types of rural and urban populations, and many diverse ethnic groups. Customs and behavior have varied throughout history between regions and groups of people. The changes and conditions described in the following pages have been primarily in urban areas among urban people and are not presently as evident in more rural areas, unless noted.

Interpersonal Relations

Francis L.K. Hsu describes the social changes in China today as reflective of China's "human element": "China's forte, regardless of what else she is doing, is the way the people relate to each other and how that way of relating has been mobilized from the traditional to the new scheme of things."[1*] In adapting to modern, Westernized ways, the Chinese have retained the traditional focus upon the appropriate place and behavior of an individual among others and the ability to conform to reality by mobilizing thought and action toward that end.

Hsu contrasts these traits of the Chinese with the American tendency to focus upon the individual as apart from others, rather than among others, and the American tendency to strive to make reality fit the individual as opposed to the Chinese attempts to make the individual fit reality.[2] Not surprisingly, these fundamental differences in the way the Chinese and the American approach relationships with others have frequently been a source of difficulty and embarrassment when Americans visit or do business in China. Keeping the aforementioned distinctions in mind, the maxim, "When in Rome, do as the Romans do" can be of great benefit to relations "when in Peking." The Western guest in China need not fear that social differences are insurmountable. The Chinese have "opened the door" to the outside world, are eager for contacts with the West, and are friendly and accommodating to visitors.

*Footnotes are based on references provided in the case bibliography. For specific footnote information, contact the author.

Face

Paramount to an understanding of Chinese behavior in relationships with others is the understanding of the traditional concept of "face." Face is the cooperative manner in which people behave toward one another in order to avoid loss of self-respect or prestige by either party to an exchange.

While the concept of face is often a fiction in practice, it retains its importance in actual dealing. For example, given a situation where two people are bargaining with each other, one must "win," and the other must "lose." Each side expects that the other will consider face in the transaction. In reality, both sides know at the end who has won and who has lost, but the winner would make token concessions at this point to save the loser's face. This consideration is important because it allows the loser to "win;" i.e., he/she has been respected by the other, the winning party.

Without the saving of face, the loser will most likely be justly offended and avoid dealing with the winner of the transaction in the future. This avoidance reaction carries with it obvious consequences and hindrances to any potential ongoing business relationship.[3]

Another aspect of face is similar to the Western concept of "being a good sport," or "being a good winner." Modesty over one's own achievement and appreciation of the loser's skill and effort are central to saving face.[4] Face most often requires little effort but merely an attention to courtesy in relationships with others; yet, face will have a great positive effect upon the recipient. If lost, face will have a negative effect which, if shown by the loser, results in still further loss of face. With the exception of a show of controlled anger by a person in authority, such as by a policeman, loss of self-control, sulking, and displays of anger or frustration create further loss of face rather than drawing respect or conciliation.[5]

Once face has been lost, the loser will prefer to avoid the winner and ignore the "face-losing" incident as though it never occurred. In circumstances where the two parties must continue a relationship, the loser will return to formal and polite etiquette, pretending that the incident had not occurred. The other party should accommodate the loser's preference and not refer again to the incident.[6] Some of the traditional formality associated with face has lapsed in current times, but much has survived. The traditional concept of face continues to be an important aspect of human relationships in China today.

Smiling and Laughter: Laughter and smiling in Chinese culture represent the universal reaction to pleasure and humor. In addition, they are also a common response to negative occurrences, such as death and other misfortune. When embarrassed or in the wrong, the Chinese frequently respond with laughter or smiling, which will persist if another person continues to speak of an embarrassing topic or does not ignore the wrong. Westerners are often confused and shocked by this behavior, which is alien to them. It is important to remember that smiling and laughter in these situations are not exhibitions of glee; they are rather a part of the concept of "face" when used in response to a negative or unpleasant situation.[7]

Guanxi . . . the Value of An Ongoing Relationship. "Guanxi" describes the intricate, pervasive network of personal relations that every Chinese cultivates with energy, subtlety, and imagination. Guanxi is the currency of getting things done and getting ahead in Chinese society. Guanxi is a relationship between two people containing implicit mutual obligation, assurances, and intimacy. If an American firm were to employ a gradual approach to its Chinese business and use the resources necessary to learn the nature of their Chinese counterparts, the Chinese-American relationship is more likely to survive and prosper than with a swifter, though less-sure, approach.

The perceived value of an ongoing relationship and its future possibilities typically governs Chinese attitudes toward long-term business. If a relationship of trust and mutual benefits is developed, an excellent foundation will be built to future business with the Chinese.

Due to cultural differences and language barriers, visitors to China are not in a position to cultivate guanxi with the depth possible between two or more Chinese. Regardless, guanxi is an important aspect of interrelations in China and deserves attention so that good, friendly relations may be developed.

Formal and Informal Relations: At present, it is likely that the majority of social contacts Americans have with the Chinese are on a level more formal than informal. Formality in China relates not to social pretension or artifice, but to the concept of face discussed earlier. Great attention is paid to observance of formal, or "social," behavior and corresponding norms. The social level is the level of form and proper etiquette where face is far more important than fact.

It is considered both gauche and rude to allow one's personal feelings and opinions to surface here to the detriment of the social ambiance. It is much more important to compliment a person or to avoid an embarrassing or sensitive subject than it is to express an honest opinion if honesty is at the expense of another's feelings. Directness, honesty, and individualism that run counter to social conventions and basic considerations of politeness have no place on the social level; emotions and private relationships tend to be kept private in Chinese society.

In Chinese society, people who are colleagues, friends, or neighbors tend to show a great deal of courtesy toward each other. At times, the courtesy extends to such an extent that an outsider could become impatient with the endless disputes over each person wishing to give precedence to the other.

Chinese Etiquette for Social Functions: Ceremonies and rules of ceremony have traditionally held a place of great importance in Chinese culture. Confucianism perpetuated and strengthened these traditions by providing the public with an identity, mask, or persona with which a person is best equipped to deal with the world with a minimum of friction. Confucianism consists of broad rules of conduct evolved to aid and guide interpersonal relations. Confucius assembled all the details of etiquette practiced at the courts of the feudal lords during the period c. 551–479 B.C. These rules of etiquette are called the "li" and have long since become a complete way of life for the Chinese. The li may appear overly formalistic to Westerners at first glance. Upon closer inspection, it is apparent that the rules of etiquette play a very important role in regulating interpersonal relations. Some basic rules of behavior follow:

- ☐ A host always escorts a guest out to his car or other mode of transportation and watches until the guest is out of sight;

- ☐ Physical expression is minimal by Western standards. A handshake is polite, but backslapping and other enthusiastic grasping is a source of embarrassment;
- ☐ At cultural functions and other performances, audience approval of performers is often subdued by American standards. Although the accepted manner of expressing approval varies between functions and age groups, applause is often polite, rather than roaring and "bravo"-like cheers are not heard;
- ☐ Individuals keep their tempers;
- ☐ People avoid blunt, direct, or abrupt discussion, particularly when the subject is awkward; delicate hints are often used to broach such a topic;
- ☐ It is a sign of respect to allow another to take the seat of honor (left of host) or to be asked to proceed through a door first; before accepting either, one should protest and offer the honor to the other person;
- ☐ The serving of tea often signals the end or an interview or meeting. However, it is also served during extended meetings to quench the thirst of the negotiators.

When considered as a mode of conduct for harmonious living, Chinese etiquette is neither formidable nor difficult to learn. The majority of the rules just listed are either identical to or have counterparts in Western culture. As with other behavior, etiquette is often performed naturally and without thought once learned.

Marriage and Family: In China, the approach to love and romance in traditional society is less related to sexual expression, as is seen in modern Western cultures. Rather, the traditional approach is sentimental and delicate.[8] During the years of Mao and the Gang of Four, personal relations were not considered to be a major focus of life according to official guidelines. Emphasis was on the good and needs of the whole, rather than the individual. Today, romantic love has regained the attention of youth as a worthwhile pursuit, and courtship and marriage are discussed in detail in youth publications.[9]

Industrialization and growth of the urban areas in China has been accompanied by a shrinking in the size and structure of the family unit. National policy is encouraging the construction of large residential buildings with many small units for the "new" nuclear family. In traditional culture, the sons of a family would remain in the residence of the parents while the daughters would marry into other families and live with their in-laws and husbands. This extended family structure supported an agricultural society where many were needed to farm. Today, urban Chinese set up households apart from their parents at marriage.

The traditional family unit has decreased in size also due to the national "one child policy" now heavily promoted. Advertisements and publications report extensively on the glorious advantages of the one-child household. The perceptive guest in China will note that the "one child policy" is not accepted universally by the people. It would be best not to broach a discussion of this subject unless there has been clear indication that the subject is acceptable. The policy has wider acceptance in urban areas than rural; here, both parents most likely hold jobs outside of the home and child care is not easily obtained. In rural areas, it is economically beneficial to have large families, particularly in light of the recently instituted rural responsibility system, which links income with productivity. Fines imposed as penalty for having more than one child have lost effectiveness due to increases in income as a result of the rural responsibility system. To reconcile the two conflicting policies, a system of double contracting has been imposed which links production quotas to birth quotas.[10]

As in other cultures, the "only child" is apt to be spoiled by attention lavished upon him or her by doting parents. The Chinese press frequently reports upon the problem with advice to parents on child rearing.[11] Spoiled or not, the Chinese child is expected to behave with the same consideration toward others as that shown by adults. Rude or boisterous conduct that would interfere with the activity of others is not permitted. At a very young age, children are made aware of their part in a larger, communal society in which it is important to show consideration for others and where it is necessary to belong. Toward this end, children are praised for proper etiquette and social behavior and are encouraged to take part in communal games. Corporal punishment is discouraged, although not unheard of.[12]

Sex and Nudity: Questions of sex and displays of flesh remain likely to evoke embarrassment from the Chinese today, as in less modern periods. Chinese culture has never considered the nude human form as beauty or art. While symbolizing the superiority of humans in the natural order, clothing also symbolized status in traditional Chinese culture.[13] The Chinese have retained this tradition of modesty to a large extent. Urban areas are becoming more permissive of revealing clothing with the advent of Western imports such as shorts and skirts which show some "leg." Sex has been regarded in both traditional and modern Chinese society as functional, necessary to produce children and to gratify the body. The spiritual view of sex found in Hindu and European cultures where sex is an expression of love is notably absent.[14] In most recent years, the functional view of sex may be becoming more romanticized, particularly among younger age groups due to exposure to Western culture and the interest in love. Due to the embarrassing nature of the subject, this trend is difficult to quantify, though indicators would suggest this change.

Superstitions and Religion

Traditionally, superstition and semi-religious practitioners played an integral role in Chinese life. Symbols abounded, and even the hour of an undertaking was felt to be a major indicator of its potential success or failure. Strictly banned during the Cultural Revolution, superstition and semi-religious practitioners have openly returned to perform their function in Chinese life. Predominantly found in more rural areas, semi-religious practices have resurged to such an extent that numerous accounts of occurrences have appeared in the Chinese press. Formerly a forbidden subject, the press recounts incidences such as the consulting of geomancers prior to the construction of graves and buildings, the rebuilding of shrines to local tutelary gods and spirits, rituals to bring rain, and the renewed use of paper gods to bring various forms of good fortune to households and farms.[15] Officially, the People's Government carefully distinguishes between superstition and religion. Wen Fushan, vice-governor of the Fujian Provincial People's Government, is reported in the *Fujian Daily* as defining the difference:[16]

> The main differences are: first, normal religious activities must be patriotic and law-abiding and must support the Communist leadership and the socialist system; second, they must

> have a legitimate organization that is recognized by the government departments concerned and accepts their leadership; third, they must not affect production and the social order.

Although abhorred by the People's Government, superstitions and related practices have proved difficult to control. Reports appear in the press relating horror stories occurring in modern China, not infrequently resulting in death. One report told of a woman who "believed that she was immortal, that pigs were fairies and that her visions of green dragons were real." Upon the death of a relative with whom she did not get along, the woman became convinced that the ghost had come to haunt her and had taken over the body of her 13-year-old son. After paying a sorcerer to come almost daily for an entire year to exorcise the ghost, the woman and her husband beat the son to death.

Another report told of a man who claimed to be the Jade Emperor. He had traveled to many villages in his area performing the ancient rite of the emperor ascending the throne. Many people believed that he was the Jade Emperor and came to offer food, money, and services to him. At one such occasion, a woman came to him with two infant daughters. The two children began to cry. Enraged, the man cried out that they were "antimonarchist" and beat the two children to death, burning their bodies so that no evidence would remain.

Often the press report incidences resulting from the collision of superstition with modern technology. One story told of a group of people who became convinced that oil exploration was interfering with traditional water and wind spirits relied on in the practice of geomancy. The people attacked an oil rig destroying $300,000-worth of equipment.[17]

Newspaper accounts such as these and many others are reported with the hope that people will be discouraged from participation in superstitious practices. The current policy of freedom of religion in China has contributed to the resurgence in superstitions and semi-religious practices. Many people cannot distinguish between recognized religion and superstition, and the official guidelines (as reported previously by Wen Fushan) are frequently of little or no help. Even though governmental control has not been removed entirely from religion, and civil or criminal punishments are given for the exercise of superstitious and semi-religious practices, it appears that these practices persist.[18]

Attire

The blue or gray loosely fitted garb worn during Mao's time is no longer the sole attire of the Chinese people. Due to the availability of Western goods and a renewed interest in expressing individuality, clothing has become more varied both in style and color. Blue jeans and T-shirts are so popular that they are difficult to find in the marketplace. Shorter skirts and bright colors are typically reserved for young women and children, young men today find the color red particularly attractive.[19] It is especially important that clothing be fashionable where young people are concerned. An Zhiguo, the *Beijing Review's* political editor wrote in 1984 that "Over the last few years people have become increasingly fashion conscious. This should not be regarded as ideological contamination; rather, people should be encouraged to wear beautiful clothes and enliven their daily activities."[20]

With the general surge of interest in personal appearance has come the advent of hair salons, makeup, and perfumes. Currently allowed to operate as private enterprises, hair salons, which had previously only been allowed in hotels for foreign guests, have appeared all over the country. Permanent waves are popular, and customers will scan magazines with photographs of Western and Hong Kong models to decide on cuts and styles. Cosmetics are readily available in China, both imported and Chinese-made. Very popular with women are face creams and powders, lipstick, rouge, and nailpolish. Avon Products has been manufacturing their product lines in China for several years.

Perfumes have long been popular in China, though not readily accepted until recently. China first began producing its own brands of perfumes and then imported popular foreign brands. In May 1982, even the *People's Daily* declined to pass judgment on the question of the political correctness of wearing perfume. Rather, it pragmatically noted that goods such as perfume show "marketing promise, and produce quicker results with smaller investments, less energy consumption, and less pollution. They provide more jobs, bring in greater profits, and increase state revenues.[21] As for makeup, managements of stores are encouraging saleswomen to wear makeup as "an outward sign of respect for their customers."[22] No doubt, this use of makeup also helps to increase sales.

A visitor to China in the 1980s need not worry that Western attire, hairstyles, or makeup will offend the Chinese hosts. Attire and appearance has been Westernized to the extent that a Westerner's usual attire should be appropriate, with the exception of extremely faddish styles, such as "punk." For meetings and more formal occasions, a suit for men and a conservative-style dress for women would be acceptable.

Cuisine

Reknowned around the world for its excellence, Chinese cuisine consists of many styles and regional variations. Common to all styles of cooking, little salt or sugar is used, vegetables abound, and meals consist of many courses. Denigrated during the Cultural Revolution, the culinary arts and those who are skilled practitioners are once again held in high regard. Taste is only one element in culinary art. Texture and appearance are of primary importance. Foods are cut and arranged for serving in a way that is pleasing to the eye. Hors d'oeuvres and pastry chefs take special delight in creating dishes that resemble birds, flowers, and animals.[23]

Sichuan cuisine places much importance upon the use of seasonings. Often, more than twenty seasonings are blended in various manners to ensure that no two dishes taste alike.[24] Guangdong cuisine has strict criteria to be followed by its chefs. Dishes must be fresh, light in flavor, and either tender or crisp in texture. An unusually large number of ingredients go into the making of each dish.[25] Chefs of Shandong cuisine take pride in their ability to use the wok to cook food to even-coated perfection using a deft flipping technique known as "da fan shao" ("big flip with the wok").[26] Jiangsu-Zhejiang cuisine emphasizes light coloring and flavor. The Huaiyang school utilizes original food juices and flavors; the Suzhou style prefers a slightly sweet taste. Fish and shrimp are popular ingredients.[27] Two cuisines specialize in foods prepared for officials and emperors. The Qing dynasty produced dishes served at the Imperial Palace (Palace Cuisine) and developed cuisine served especially for Tan Zongjun and his family who were officials of the Qing dynasty (Official Mansion Cuisine).[28]

Initiates to Chinese cuisine should be forewarned that dishes are served at extremely high temperatures; caution should be used when beginning to dine. In addition, cuisine from the southern regions of China is apt to be very hot and spicy. When dining, wine is frequently served, especially at more formal occasions. Wine is used primarily to facilitate toasting, which is so frequent as to perhaps appear excessive to the foreigner. Wine should never be used to swallow food. Other alcoholic beverages are available in China. Most types of liquor can be found in stores. Beer is especially popular among visitors, since it is often recommended that guests to China not drink the water.[29]

Lodging

The Chinese have gone to great lengths to make certain that foreign guests will feel at home while visiting their country. Hotels have been built on a large scale and offer conveniences such as would be found in the best hotels in Paris or Dallas. Complete with full-scale lobbies (a luxury of space not found many places), the hotels for foreign guests feature room service, private telephones, suites, meeting rooms, and other conveniences to which Westerners have become accustomed. These hotels are primarily for foreign guests; visitors from other areas of China seek other accommodations.[30] Western food is also available in hotels and in cafes around major cities like Beijing (Peking). Popular "American style" foods served include pizza, hamburgers, white bread, and quiche.[31]

Entertainment

In addition to television and movie theaters, urban Chinese have diverse sources of entertainment from which to choose. Nightclubs are found in major cities; musicians, dancing, and refreshments are available.[32] Theater houses offer productions of plays; most popular in China are plays that include song and dance in the production, such as song opera (geju) and musical plays (yinyue Huaju).[33] Modern pop and rock music is extremely popular with Chinese youth. Western-style concerts are held in halls where hundreds in the audience sing along and show boisterous enthusiasm. Although this popularity of rock music with youth has caused concern among parents and conservative Party members, disco parties have been approved, and young people attend with enthusiasm.[34]

More traditional forms of music and entertainment are equally as popular with the young as well as the older generations. As observed by You Yuwen in a recent article, young people "see no reason why all sorts of artistic forms should not flourish. They think people should be left alone to judge for themselves." Accordingly, lines are long to purchase tickets for classical music as well, and people are willing to wait several hours for the opportunity to view all types of cultural events.[35] Traditional song and dance performances of the Han are being performed once again, after a period of banishment during the Cultural Revolution.

Minority art, such as that of the Uygur, is also supported by the Chinese. The Uygur are a Turkic people living primarily in the Xinjiang Uygur Autonomous Region, the most westerly and largest province in China. Heavily influenced by Islam, Uygur performing arts in traditional form are somewhat controversial. Emphasis is placed upon modern themes and praise of socialism, although love themes are again found in performances. Song is always accompanied by dance, and performances are elaborate and lengthy.[36]

Business and Advertising

Private enterprise is currently being heavily encouraged in China, and markets are flourishing. Special attention is being paid to upgrading the quality of Chinese products, and more consumer goods are being manufactured. Beijing's main department store requires that manufacturers and distributors conform to the opinions of consumers and produce quality items adapted to market trends. As a result, this department store has taken on the role of not only a seller, but also an exhibitor of goods for manufacturers and a supplier of consumer information.[37]

Customer opinion is particularly important in Chinese business and industry. Factories frequently send representatives to stores to poll customers and collect store buyers' opinions. These opinions are carefully heeded, and necessary changes are made in products and factories to conform to consumer expectations.[38] At present, demand currently exceeds production of quality consumer goods such as refrigerators and color television sets. Rather than raising prices to shift demand downward, China is approaching the situation from a socialist standpoint and is making efforts to increase production, while improving quality through inspection, customer service, and the introduction of new technology and equipment.[39]

Advertising and product names in China reflect the cultural affinity for flowers, birds, and animals. Billboards and posters typically show nature scenes with the product pictured or the political sentiment expressed therein. Products for men are given names such as "Red Horse," and products for women are given names such as "Bee and Flower". The most popular brand of Chinese-made perfume is named "Springtime Thunder."[40]

The Chinese people are enjoying the opportunity to earn higher incomes which allow for the purchase of a greater number of consumer items. Traditional skills and trades still flourish, particularly in rural areas, but modern Western products are eagerly sought. The Chinese have retained their historic self-confidence throughout the rapid political changes of recent times and have a healthy sense of national pride in their accomplishments, both past and present.[41] With this national pride comes a desire to show to others their culture, lives, and recent developments in industry, agriculture, and the arts. The Chinese are eager for exchange with other peoples and nations of the world. There is a growing interest in learning about the cultures and values of other societies. This interest and willingness to exchange has created an atmosphere extremely conducive to visits by foreigners. With attention to courtesy and a willingness to accept Chinese culture and customs, a visitor to China should experience a pleasant and rewarding stay in the People's Republic.

BIBLIOGRAPHY

Bonavia, David. *The Chinese.* (London: Allen Lane, Penguin Books, Ltd., 1980): 290.

Grub, Phillip D. "A Yen for Yuan: Trading and Investing in the China Market." *Business Horizons.* July–August 1987.

Hongfa, Liu. "Bringing Customers and Manufacturers Together." *China Reconstructs.* 33:12. December 1984, 13–14.

Hsu, Francis L.K. *Americans and Chinese: Passage to Difference,* 3rd ed. (Honolulu: University Press of Hawaii, 1981): 534.

Jiang, Dongmei. "Our Single-Child Family." *China Reconstructs.* 34:7. July 1985, 4–5.

Mackerras, Colin. "Uygur Performing Arts in Contemporary China," *The China Quarterly.* 101:3. March 1985, 58–76.

Manni, Tan. "Grand Review of Chinese Culinary Art." *China Encounters the West.* New York: Pantheon Books, 1980): 178.

________. *To Get Rich Is Glorious: China in the Eighties.* New York: Pantheon Books, 1984): 210.

Myers, Howard. "The China Business Puzzle." *Business Horizons.* July–August 1987.

Shao, Maria. "Zhao Gives China a Swift Kick Toward A Free Market." *Business Week.* 16 November, 1987.

Wickert, Erwin. *The Middle Kingdom: Inside China Today,* translated by Maxwell Brownjohn. (London: Howell Press, 1983): 379.

Wong, Sui-lun. "Consequences of China's New Population Policy." *The China Quarterly.* 98:6 (London: The Eastern Press, Ltd., June 1984): 220–40.

Yuwen, You. "What's On Young People's Minds." *China Reconstructs.* 34:6. June 1985, 6–8.

American Greetings—1988

DAN KOPP
Southwest Missouri State University
LOIS SHUFELDT
Southwest Missouri State University

"We're in touch" and the corporate rose logo identify the world's largest publicly owned manufacturer of greeting cards and related social-expression merchandise, American Greetings. In 1981, President Morry Weiss announced the formulation of a corporate growth objective to achieve $1 billion in annual sales by 1985, which would represent a 60 percent increase over 1982 sales of $623.6 million. The battle for market share dominance between the two industry leaders, Hallmark and American Greetings, had escalated and intensified. Previously, the two leading firms peacefully coexisted by having mutually exclusive niches. Hallmark offered higher-priced, quality cards in department stores and card shops, and American Greetings offered inexpensive cards in mass-merchandise outlets. However, in 1977 American Greetings formulated a growth strategy to attack the other industry leader and its niche.

THE GREETING CARD INDUSTRY

In 1985, Americans exchanged more than 7 billion cards—around thirty per person, marking the highest per capita card consumption ever. And with the average retail price per card of $1, that made "social expression" a $3.4 billion business. According to the Greeting Card Association, card senders gave 2.2 billion Christmas cards, 1.5 billion birthday cards, 850 million valentines, 180 million Easter cards, 140 million Mother's Day cards, 85 million Father's Day cards, 80 million graduation cards, 40 million Thanksgiving cards, 26 million Halloween cards, 16 million St. Patrick's Day cards, and about 10 million Grandparent's Day cards. Everyday, non-occasion cards

This case was prepared as a basis for class discussion rather than to illustrate either effective or ineffective administrative practices. The authors would like to acknowledge the cooperation and assistance of American Greetings. This case was presented at NACRA's November 9, 1987 meeting.

now account for more than half of all industry sales, and they're on the rise. People living in the northeast and north-central parts of the country buy more cards than average, and Southerners buy cards 30 percent fewer. People who buy the majority of tend to be between 35 and 54 years of age, come from large families, live in their own homes in the suburbs, and have an average household income of $30,000. Changes in society—demographic and social—are fueling the growth of alternative cards. These changes have included increases in the numbers of the following:

- blended families
- single-parent households
- working women
- divorces and remarriages,
- population segments which traditionally have included the heaviest greeting card users—35 to 65 year olds (baby boom generation approaching the peak card purchasing age)

Women purchase over 90 percent of all greeting cards. Women enjoy browsing and shopping for cards. In addition, a woman tends to purchase a card only if it is appropriate: when the card's verse and design combine to convey the sentiment she wishes to express. However, because an increasing number of women are working, these women are shopping less frequently and buying less impulse merchandise.

The growth rate for the industry has been 5 to 6 percent annually over the past several years. Sales of unorthodox cards aimed at 18–35-year-old baby boomers have grown 25 percent a year. However, sales of greeting cards for the past few quarters have been lackluster. The industry is mature; sales are stagnant at about 7 billion units. According to *Chain Store Age,* the channels of distribution have been moving away from speciality stores to mass merchants. Now, department stores are cutting back square footage and dropping cards altogether. Mass market appeal now has growth—one-stop shopping. Hallmark has been pushing its Ambassador line through mass merchants such as Wal-Mart and Target, in addition to diversifying into other areas.

American Greetings is concentrating on the social expressions business; it has launched a massive national television advertising campaign to firmly position itself in all aspects of the greeting card industry. On the other hand, Hallmark, whose recent acquisitions are unrelated to the social expressions industry, is shifting its emphasis. Irvine O. Hockaday, Hallmark's chief executive officer, said recently that he prefers outside businesses to contribute 40 percent of total Hallmark revenues, instead of the 10 percent now contributed. Cards accounted for 64 percent of American Greetings's 1985 sales. According to some industry experts, Hallmark is now playing follow the leader in card innovations and character licensing.

An overall slowdown in retail traffic has resulted in reduced sales. Generally, a soft retailing environment exists. The retailing industry is overstored and promotion oriented, which may result in retailers asking greeting card suppliers for lower prices to assist them in keeping their margins from shrinking. Retailers are losing their loyalty to manufacturers that supply a full line of products, including items such as cards and gift wrap, and are looking instead for the lowest cost supplier of each, according to Kidder, Peabody & Company. The competition in the industry has become and will continue to be intensified, especially in the areas of price, sales promotion, distribution, and selling.

More new cards have been introduced in 1986 than in any other previous year, according to the Greeting Card Association. More "feelings" cards, such as the In Touch line by American Greetings, have been introduced. Since men buy only 10 percent of all cards sold, they are the prime target for many of the new types of cards.

Hallmark and American Greetings are experimenting with different styles, fabricating novel reasons for people to buy their wares and using new technology that enables cards to play tunes or talk. According to *Time,* Hallmark offers 1200 varieties of cards for Mother's Day, while American Greetings boasts of 1300. The products range from a traditional card with a picture of flowers and syrupy poetry for $1 or less to a $7 electronic version which plays the tune, "You Are the Sunshine of My Life."

Hallmark has introduced several lines of personal-relationship-oriented cards, commemorating such milestones as the wedding anniversary of a parent and a stepparent. In 1984, Hallmark introduced its Honesty Collection, which has been discontinued, with messages that reflected the nature of modern day relationships. In May 1985, American Greetings's primary competitor brought out its Personal Touch line of cards, with intimate, conversational prose displayed on the front and with no message inside. The Greeting Card Association found that 83 percent of all card senders do something—add a snapshot or a newspaper clipping or jot a note—to personalize a card, and Hallmark has been quick to supply a vehicle to take advantage of this opportunity.

Forbes has reported there are more than 400 firms in the greeting card industry, but the two major ones, Hallmark and American Greetings, control approximately 75 percent of the market. Gibson Greetings is the third major firm in the industry. Approximate market shares for the three industry leaders have been:

Company	1985	1984	1977
Hallmark	40–45%	.45%	50%
American Greetings	30–35	33	24
Gibson	8–10	N/A	5

Analysts expect American Greetings to keep increasing its market share. Over the last five years, unit growth rate at American Greetings has been 4 to 5 percent a year, against an industry-wide growth rate of 1 to 2 percent. Industry expert. E. Gray Glass, III of Kidder, Peabody & Company, has indicated that American Greetings has been showing good growth at 15 percent or better annually. Furthermore, *Chain Store Age* has projected that American Greetings will continue to take some of Hallmark's market share but that it will take a long time for American Greetings to pass Hallmark.

The *New York Times* has reported that Hallmark has been successful in freestanding card shops, which account for about 40 percent of all greeting cards sold. The fastest growth area for American Greetings has been big drugstores and supermarket chains. Growth has been slower at variety stores, traditional department stores, and gift shops, which account for about 30 percent of American Greetings sales.

According to *Investor's Daily,* American Greetings and Hallmark have been increasing their market shares at the expense of smaller card companies, which have been forced out of the market due to the high costs of selling, distributing, and marketing, as well as the lack of extensive computerized inventory monitoring systems that only large companies can afford. Industry analysts, however, have predicted that small firms, with a focus niche and geographic area, will continue to enter the industry and can be profitable.

Richard H. Connor, American Greetings executive vice-president, stated that American Greetings has been gaining ground on Hallmark, although he wouldn't say by how much:

> If you compare the businesses that are similar with both companies, we are closing the gap. Between the both of us, we have 75 percent of the market, and some of our growth must be at their expense.

Both Hallmark and American Greetings are being challenged by Gibson, which is the fastest growing company in the industry. Gibson scored a coup with Walt Disney Productions when they secured the rights to use Mickey Mouse and his friends, who previously had been featured by Hallmark. Gibson also has licensed Garfield the Cat and Sesame Street characters, but Hallmark's line of Peanuts cards remains one of the industry's most successful.

HISTORY OF AMERICAN GREETINGS

The story of American Greetings is one of the "American Dream"—of an immigrant from Poland who came to the land of promised opportunity to seek his fortune. Jacob Sapirstein was born in 1884 in Wasosz, Poland, and because of the Russian-Japanese war of 1904, he was sent by his widowed mother, along with his seven brothers and one sister, to live in America.

Jacob, also known as J.S., began his one-man business buying postcards made in Germany from wholesalers and selling them to candy, novelty, and drug stores in Cleveland in 1906. From a horse-drawn card wagon, the small venture steadily flourished.

J.S. and his wife, Jennie, also a Polish immigrant, had three sons and a daughter; all three sons became active in their father's business. At the age of nine, Irving, the oldest, kept the family business afloat while J.S. was recovering from the flu during the great epidemic of 1918. The business had outgrown the family living room and was moved to a garage at this time.

J.S. had a basic philosophy: service to the retailer and a quality product for the consumer. He developed the first wire wall rack as well as rotating floor stands to make more attractive, convenient displays. In the 1930s, the Sapirstein Card Company began to print its own cards to ensure the quality of its product. The name of the company was changed to American Greeting Publishers to reflect the national stature and functioning of the company. Their first published line of cards under the American Greetings name, the Forget Me Not Line, went on sale in 1939 for a nickel. One card, which remains the company's all-time best seller, was designed by Irving.

The company saw great expansion throughout the 1940s, as loved ones found the need to communicate with World War II soldiers. The most significant trend of this time was the widespread use of greeting cards by the soldiers. In the past, cards had been primarily a product utilized by women; thus, the expansion to the male market was a significant breakthrough for the card industry.

The 1950s marked the first public offering of stock, and the company's name changed to American Greetings Corporation. Ground was broken for a new world headquarters, which lead the way for expansion to world markets. The company made connections with several foreign markets and acquired a Canadian plant.

In 1960, J.S. stepped down at the age of 76. His son Irving succeeded him as president. Under Irving's leadership and with the assistance of his brothers, Morris and Harry Stone (all three brothers had changed their name from Sapirstein, meaning sapphire, to Stone in 1940 for business reasons), the company has continued to expand into gift wrapping, party goods, calendars, stationery, candles, ceramics, and, perhaps most importantly, the creation of licensed characters.

Expansion into these related items has somewhat diminished American Greetings's recession-proof profits. Greeting card sales typically increase during recessions as people refrain from gift buying and instead remember others with a less-expensive card. The supplemental items now constitute one third of the company's sales. The amount of it is enough to greatly augment the company's sales during good economic times.

American Greetings's world expansion became a major pursuit throughout the 1960s and 1970s. Morry Weiss, a grandson-in-law of J.S., became the new president of American Greetings in 1978, with Irving continuing to act as the CEO and chairman of the board of directors. Morris Stone continues to serve as vice chairman of the Board, and Harry Stone remains as an active board member.

OBJECTIVES

In 1981, at the first national sales meeting ever held by American Greetings, President Morry Weiss announced the formulation of a major corporate objective: to achieve $1 billion in annual sales by 1985. During fiscal 1985, American Greetings strengthened its position as a leader in the industry; that year marked the seventy-ninth consecutive year of increased revenue: total revenue increased to $945.7 million, while net income increased to $74.4 million. This record of success represented a:

- ☐ 300% increase in total revenue during the past 10 years
- ☐ 613% increase in net income during the past 10 years
- ☐ 315% increase in dividends per share in the past 10 years, with two increases in fiscal 1985

According to Morry Weiss, president and chief operating officer:

> American Greetings today is positioning itself for transition from a greeting company to a total communications company. For years, American Greetings was thought of only as a greeting card maker. That narrow description no longer applies to the world's largest, publicly owned manufacturer of greeting cards and related social-expression merchandise. Today we are diversified into other major product lines, including gift wrap, candles, stationery, ceramics, party goods, and calendars. In addition, we lead the industry in licensing

characters, such as Holly Hobbie, Ziggy, Strawberry Shortcake, Care Bears, and Care Bear Cousins, which are featured on thousands of retail products and on television and in motion pictures.

Irving Stone, chairman of the board and chief executive officer added:

American Greetings is aggressively pursuing growth in their core business, concentrating specifically on increasing market share and unit volume, and continued margin. We'll grow through our retailers by providing the programs that will generate sales and make the greeting card department the most profitable area in their store. We'll grow through our consumers by understanding their needs and providing them with products they want and enjoy buying. We'll grow by constantly improving our operations and productivity through creativity, innovation, and technology.

He further added:

We expect growth and are planning for it throughout the corporation. In the past four years, we have invested heavily in increased capacity, plant expansion, new equipment, and new technology. Almost two years ago, we completed an equity offering that substantially strengthened our financial position; an additional offering is not expected in the near future. Today, we see no problem financing our growth while at the same time increasing our dividends.

A flurry of acquisitions occurred in the 1980s. A full list of subsidiaries, as well as American Greetings international operations is displayed in Exhibit 1.

MARKETING STRATEGIES

Product

American Greetings produces a wide product line including greeting cards, gift wrap, party goods, toys, and gift items. Greeting cards accounted for 66 percent of the company's 1986 fiscal sales. The breakdown of sales by major product categories is as follows:

☐ Everyday greeting cards	37%
☐ Holiday greeting cards	29
☐ Gift wrap and party goods	18
☐ Consumer products (toys, etc.)	7
☐ Stationery	9

American Greetings believes that one of the keys to increased sales is having a product line that offers a wide variety and selection of cards so that a consumer can always find the right card for that special person. Each year American Greetings offers more new products than ever before. The creative department produces more than 20,000 different designs to ensure the wide selection.

American Greetings's creative staff is one of largest assemblages of artistic talent in the world. The department has more than 400 designers, artists, and writers who are guided by the latest research data available from computer analysis, consumer test-

EXHIBIT 1 American Greetings's international and subsidiary operations

CARLTON AND SUBSIDIARY OPERATIONS

William L. Powell
Senior Vice President

David J. Gamble
Vice President
Carlton and Subsidiary Operations

Carlton Cards, Inc.
Dallas, Texas
Selwin Belofsky, President

Carlton Cards, Ltd.
Toronto, Ontario
James M. Semon, President

Plus Mark Canada
Toronto, Ontario
Richard L. Krelstein, General Manager

Rust Craft Canada, Inc.
Scarborough, Ontario
Mike Johnson, General Manager

The Summit Corporation
Berlin, Connecticut
William E. Condon, Chairman
Robert P. Chase, President

Summit Collection
Joy Sweeney, Vice President

LICENSING AND TOY OPERATIONS

Rubin Feldman
Chairman

AmToy, Inc.
Cleveland, Ohio
Those Characters From Cleveland, Inc.
Cleveland, Ohio
John S. Chojnacki, Co-President
Ralph E. Shaffer, Co-President

INTERNATIONAL AND SUBSIDIARY OPERATIONS

Al J. Stenger
Senior Vice President

Dale J. Beinker
Vice President
International

Plus Mark, Inc.
Greeneville, Tennessee
Ronald E. Clouse, President

P. A. Plymouth, Inc.
Bellmawr, N.J.
Robert C. Pappas, President

United Kingdom Operations
David M. Beards
Chairman

Andrew Valentine Holdings Ltd.
Dundee, Scotland
Rust Craft Greeting Cards (U.K.) Ltd.
Dewsbury, England
Alistair R.L. Mackay
Managing Director

Celebration Arts Group Ltd.
Corby, England
W. George Pomphrett
Managing Director

Denison Colour Ltd.
Guiseley, England
Brian Holliday, Managing Director

Continental European Operations
Richard J. Schulte
Director of Operations

Grako Oy
Helsinki, Finland
Risto Pitkanen, Managing Director

A/S Muva Grafiske Produkter
Oslo, Norway
Aage Dahl, Managing Director

Muva Greetings B.V.
Heerlen, The Netherlands
Muva Greetings S.A.
Zonhoven, Belgium
Huub Robroeks, Managing Director

Felicitaciones Nacionales S.A. de C.V.
Mexico City, Mexico
Antonio Felix G., President

Rust Craft International S.A.
Monte Carlo, Monaco
Michel Bourda, Managing Director

Source: American Greetings.

ing, and information from American Greetings's sales and merchandising departments. Careful monitoring of societal changes, fashion and color trends, and consumer preferences provides further guidance to product development. American Greetings also gives uncompromising adherence to quality—in papers, inks, and printing procedures.

American Greetings pioneered licensing and now dominates the character licensing industry. American Greetings's strategy has been to maximize the potential of its creative and marketing expertise. Holly Hobbie was American Greetings's first licensed character in 1968; Ziggy came along in 1971, and Strawberry Shortcake in 1980. When introduced, Strawberry Shortcake was the most popular new character in licensing history. Sales for Strawberry Shortcake will soon exceed $1 billion in retail sales, a revenue larger than that of any other character. In 1983, American Greetings introduced Care Bears and Herself the Elf. Care Bears was launched with General Mills and twenty three licensees, supported by an $8 million advertising and promotional campaign that included a half-hour animated television special. The Care Bears license identifies ten adorable cuddlies, each with a sentiment message on its tummy.

Another licensing creation, Popples, added a new dimension to a field crowded with look-alikes. Popples literally "pop out" from a plush ball to a lovable, furry, playmate; they also fold into their own pouch. Popples enable children to make arms, legs, and fluffy tail appear and disappear at will. Two new toys from AmToy are reaching another new and under-cultivated market: My Pet Monster and Madballs. They were the hits of 1986s Toy Fair show. These creatures are designed to delight the millions of young boys who prefer the bizarre to the cuddly. Forty companies initially signed up to manufacture other products such as clothing, knapsacks, and books featuring the characters. American Greetings and Mattel spent about $10 million promoting the characters, including a half hour Popples television special. The licensed product industry is $50 billion strong.

According to *Forbes,* all American Greetings licensed characters have not been successful. One flop, Herself the Elf, was perceived by retailers as being too much like Strawberry Shortcake; it also missed the Christmas season because of production problems. Another failure was Get Along Gang, which tried to appeal to both little girls and boys.

Distribution

American Greetings distributes its products through 90,000 retail outlets located throughout the free world. This figure has increased from 80,000 in 1983. Additionally, there has been growth in the channels of distribution where American Greetings is dominant. Consumers have been seeking greater convenience and one-stop shopping, channels in which American Greetings is strong—chain drugstores, chain supermarkets, and mass merchandise retailers. Thirty-nine percent of American Greetings sales went to drug stores, with the remaining sales (in order of rank) going to mass merchandisers, supermarkets, stationery and gift shops, variety stores, military post exchanges, combo stores (food, general merchandise, and gift items), and department stores. During the last five years, sales to drug, variety, and department stores as a percent of total revenue have declined, while sales to supermarkets, mass merchandisers, combo stores, and military post exchange units have increased, while stationery and gift shops have remained constant.

Promotion

In 1982, American Greetings became recognized nationwide, first through television commercials and then through a new corporate identity program. The new logo is now featured prominently at retail outlets; the updated corporate rose logo is now a standard and highly recognizable feature greeting American Greetings customers on all product packaging, store signage, point of purchase displays, and even American Greetings's truck fleet. The year-round advertising campaign occurred during daytime and prime-time programming and included the promotion of major card-sending holidays and non-seasonal occasions.

Other promotional material that supports marketing includes seasonal and special displays, special signs, sales catalogues, national televison advertising, media and trade journal exposure, televison programming, and special events featuring American Greetings's exclusive characters. Results can be seen in increased support for American Greetings's sales personnel, greater visibility within the financial community, and improved relations with employees and communities where plant facilities are operating.

The aim of American Greetings's national consumer advertising and public relations programs is to remind people to send cards; one of American Greetings's chief competitors is consumer forgetfulness. American Greetings is the only company in the industry to sponsor national consumer retail promotions. These consumer-directed programs serve to establish brand identity and generate retail store traffic.

In 1983, American Greetings employed 1600 full-time salespeople, in addition to 7,000 part-timers, all of whom have been directed through fifteen regional and sixty-six district sales offices in the United States, the United Kingdom, Canada, Mexico, and France. American Greetings employs a large force of retail store merchandisers who visit each department at regular intervals to ensure that every pocket in every display is kept filled with appropriate merchandise.

The American Greetings sales force is meeting the unique and challenging needs of its customers; no other company in the industry has sales and marketing personnel assigned to specific channels of distribution to give retailers the advantage of working with specialists who understand their markets, their customers, and their specific marketing needs.

The success of American Greetings's aggressive marketing programs is explained by William E. Schmitt, group vice president, marketing:

> First we have the creativity to develop the best products in the industry. Every year we prove this with new characters, new card lines, and other products and programs that attract consumers and increase sales for our customers and ourselves. Second, we have a close relationship with our customers. The retailer support programs we offer—including terms, display fixtures, advertising and merchandising programs, promotion support and inventory controls—are unsurpassed in the industry.

Programs are tailored for individual retailers to help plan their greeting card locations, department sizes, and displays. American Greetings shows the retailers how to merchandise innovative ideas and enhance visibility by means of proven promotional programs.

Computer technology is helping American Greetings's sales people to project retailers' needs better, which has resulted in improved sell-through of the product at retail. Management Information Systems (MIS), the data processing unit for American Greetings, is playing a vital role in increasing sales for American Greetings's products at the retail level. In 1984, American Greetings began implementing a computer-to-computer reordering system that allows retail accounts to control inventories and turnaround time by electronic transfer of data to American Greetings's headquarters data center.

Good retail presentation is a key to card sales; American Greetings has created a unique identification for the greeting cards department. It is called the Total Retail Environment, and it uses a completely planned and coordinated approach to integrate display cabinets, signage, lighting, product packaging, and even products to create a stunning new American Greetings look. The purposes of this new system are to establish greater consumer awareness of the American Greetings card department, to give a distinctive look and appeal, and to provide an attractive and enjoyable place to shop.

American Greetings also possesses the most favorable terms-of-sale program in the industry. To improve the retailer's return on inventory investment, American Greetings has successful merchandising plans, retail store merchandisers, and computerized inventory controls. American Greetings also sports a Direct Product Profitability (DPP) concept to evaluate productivity and space allocation for products in stores. DPP takes gross margin and return on inventory investment analysis a step further by reflecting revenue after allowances and discounts and subtracting all costs attributable to the product, including labor and freight. American Greetings's sales people can then demonstrate to retailers that their greeting card department returns a high rate of profit for the space allocated.

Richard H. Connor, American Greetings executive vice-president, recently announced:

> To increase market share, American Greetings revamped its sales force and created one sales department that specializes in independent retail accounts and another sales department that specializes in selling to retail chains. A third department will stock and service all types of accounts. This will give greater selling strength where it's needed and lowers our selling costs.

American Greetings has created a New Retail Communications Network (RCTN) which conducts research that will better enable American Greetings to identify for accounts the appropriate products to meet the needs of their customers. Data are compiled by monitoring product sales and space productivity from a chain of nationwide test stores that encompasses all demographic and geographic variables and represents all channels of distribution. The RCTN then interprets data as it would apply to an account's specifications, including type of store, size, location, and consumer profile. This total merchandising approach to achieving maximum sales and space potential is unique in the industry.

PRODUCTION STRATEGIES

American Greetings has forty nine plants and facilities in the United States, Canada, Continental Europe, Mexico, Monaco, and the United Kingdom.

American Greetings has been concerned with reducing production costs in order to remain the industry's lowest-cost producer through efficient manufacturing operations while maintaining quality and service to customers. According to Robert C. Swilik, group vice-president, manufacturing,

> Improved control of our manufacturing process through planning and scheduling enables us to improve productivity, reduce manufacturing costs, and reduce inventory. Increased productivity is the result of our growing sense of shared responsibility. The relationship between management and the work force is excellent.

Quality improvements have been consistently made. Some of the major improvements have been:

1. Upgraded die cutting and embossing capabilities with the purchase of nine high speed Bobst presses costing $1 million each.
2. Added capacity to the hot stamping and thermography operations.
3. Streamlined order filling in both everyday and seasonal operations.
4. Completed a 200,000-square-foot warehouse addition to the Osceola, Arkansas, plant and began operations on an addition to the Ripley, Tennessee, plant, which increased its capacity by 20 percent.
5. Installed a Scitex system that will dramatically improve product quality and increase productivity; new electronic pre-press system enables creative department to interact with manufacturing at the creatively crucial pre-press stage.
6. Installed additional high-speed and more powerful presses to further improve quality of die cutting and embossing at the Bardstown, Kentucky, plant; a 300,000 square-foot addition is also planned.
7. Installed new computer graphics system called Via Video for design and layout functions for a variety of in-house publications and brochures. (This system gives the artist freedom to create while quickly and inexpensively exploring options and alternatives, thus increasing productivity.)

PERSONNEL STRATEGIES

American Greetings currently employs more than 20,000 people in the United States, Canada, Mexico, and Europe.

According to Morry Weiss, American Greetings is deeply concerned about management succession:

> Our young executives are being developed to succeed retiring senior officers. Last year, more management movement occurred than in any of the preceding five years. The Stone family built and developed the company. However, managing this dynamic business today presents challenges beyond the capability of any one or two persons. Thus, over the past ten years, the management of American Greetings has been changing from a singular head

to a broad-based management group. We have broadened decision-making authority. Each business unit has been given stretch goals and responsibility for achieving those goals. Units are preparing strategic plans and are vying for corporate resources based upon projections of growth and profitability.

According to Robert C. Swilik, group vice-president:

The relationship between management and the work force is excellent. We have never had a strike in any of our plants, and we plan to work on keeping that harmonious spirit alive. We will expand an employee involvement program that brings all levels of employees into greater participation.

MANAGEMENT

In 1983, American Greetings underwent a major management restructuring to permit top officers of the company more time to concentrate on strategic planning. The company was reorganized from a centralized structure to a divisional profit center basis. Each division has its own budget committee, while an executive management committee comprised of five senior executives approves the strategic plans for all the divisions. Strategic plans are established in one-, three-, ten-, and twenty-year time frames. Corporate American Greetings maintains strict budgetary and accounting controls.

The basic domestic greeting card business was placed under the American Greetings Division. Foreign and U.S. subsidiaries and the licensing division have become a second unit, with corporate management a third. Restructuring has allowed corporate management to step back from day-to-day operations and focus on the growth of American Greetings beyond the $1 billion annual revenue.

According to Irving Stone:

The prime function of corporate management is to plan and manage the growth of the entire corporation, developing capable management and allocating corporate resources to those units offering the greatest potential return on investment. Greeting cards has been our basic business for 78 years and remains today our largest business unit; there are smaller business units which complement the greeting card business and are deserving of our attention.

American Greetings is composed of the following divisions.

- ☐ American Greetings Division: This division encompasses the core business of greeting cards and related products, including manufacturing, sales, merchandising, research, and administrative services. The division produces and distributes greeting cards and related products domestically. Some products are distributed throughout the world by international subsidiaries and licensees.
- ☐ Foreign and Domestic Subsidiares: Subsidiaries include two wholly owned companies in Canada, four in the United Kingdom, six in Continental Europe, and one in Mexico. Licensees use American Greetings designs and verses in almost every free country in the world. Sub-divisions include:

  Canadian Operations—Carlton Cards and Rust Craft are the two companies operated by American Greetings here.

United Kingdom Operations—The British are the largest per capita senders of greeting cards in the world. Three U.K. Americans Greetings companies include Rust Craft, Celebration Arts and Andrew Valentine.

Continental European Operations—American Greetings wholly owns five companies here.

Those Characters From Cleveland—This licensing division of American Greetings includes characters and the new television series, "The Get Along Gang."

Plus Mark—This division produces Christmas promotional products such as gift wrap, ribbon, bows, and boxed Christmas cards in an industry selling primarily to mass merchandisers.

AmToy—This division sells novelties, dolls, and plush toys.

American Greetings Industries—This division produces display cabinet fixtures in wood, metal, or plastic for all American Greetings retail accounts and a growing list of external clients.

Exhibit 2 provides a corporate directory of management personnel and their divisional assignments.

FINANCE STRATEGIES

Exhibits 3–5 contain relevant financial information of American Greetings. The financial condition of American Greetings has been exemplary over the years. However, American Greetings's financial performance in 1986 was disappointing, with revenue growth estimated to be at 7 percent and earnings to be similar to those of 1985. American Greetings revenue and earnings growth rate for the previous five years increased at compound annual rates of 17 percent and 29 percent, respectively. American Greetings's stock declined sharply after the disappointing financial report.

According to the research department of the Ohio Company, the reasons for the change in sales and revenues were attributed to:

1. Weak retail environment—decline in retail traffic.
2. Heavy investment in display fixtures—intense competition forced larger investment than anticipated.
3. Reduced licensing revenues—short life cycle of products and greater competitive pressures reduced licensing revenues.
4. Increased accounts receivables and inventory due to slower collections and weak ordering by retailers.
5. Increased interest expense due to increased accounts receivable and inventory levels.

Irving Stone remarked about the company's finances:

> In fiscal 1986, the retailing picture was a rapidly changing mosaic, featuring a generally poor environment marked by a substantial drop-off in store traffic. As a result, sales of many of our products, which are dependent upon store traffic and impulse buying, fell be-

EXHIBIT 2 Corporate directory for American Greetings

BOARD OF DIRECTORS

Jacob Sapirstein
Founder

Irving I. Stone [1]
Chairman
Chief Executive Officer

Morris S. Stone [1]
Vice Chairman

Morry Weiss [1]
President
Chief Operating Officer

Hugh Calkins [2]
Partner
Jones, Day, Reavis & Pogue
(attorneys-at-law)

Herbert H. Jacobs
(personal investments
and consultant)

Frank E. Joseph [2]
Attorney and Secretary
Kulas Foundation
(philanthropic foundation)

Millard B. Opper [2]
Retired Chairman of
Canadian Operations

Albert B. Ratner [2]
President
Forest City Enterprises, Inc.
(real estate, construction and
retail operations)

Harry H. Stone [2]
President
Courtland Management, Inc.
(personal investments)
Chairman
Barks Williams Oil

Milton A. Wolf
Former United States
Ambassador to Austria
(personal investments)

Morton Wyman [1]
Executive Vice President

1 Member of Executive Committee
2 Member of Audit Committee

CORPORATE OFFICERS

Irving I. Stone
Chairman
Chief Executive Officer

Morris S. Stone
Vice Chairman

Morry Weiss
President
Chief Operating Officer

Morton Wyman
Executive Vice President

Rubin Feldman
Senior Vice President

Henry Lowenthal
Senior Vice President
Chief Financial Officer

Packy Nespeca
Senior Vice President
Corporate Trade Development

William L. Powell
Senior Vice President

Al J. Stenger
Senior Vice President

Ralph L. White
Vice President
Chief Human Resource Officer

Allan J. Goodfellow
General Counsel & Secretary

John M. Klipfell
Controller

Eugene B. Scherry
Treasurer

AMERICAN GREETINGS DIVISION

Morton Wyman
Executive Vice President

James R. Van Arsdale
Group Vice President - Operations

H. David Bender
Vice President
Information Services

Edward F. Doherty
Vice President - Manufacturing
Everyday Division

James H. Edler
Vice President
Materials Management

John T. Fortner
Vice President
Manufacturing

Edward Fruchtenbaum
Vice President - Marketing

Gary E. Johnston
Vice President - Creative

Raymond P. Kenny
Vice President
Planning & Research

David R. Ledvina
Vice President
Computer Operations

William R. Mason
Vice President
General Sales Manager

William R. Parsons
Vice President - Zone II

Ronald J. Peer
Vice President - Zone I

Robert C. Swilik
Vice President - Manufacturing
Seasonal Division

Kenneth J. Valore
Vice President - Finance

George A. Wenz
Vice President - National Accounts

Acme Frame Products, Inc.
Chicago, Illinois
Robert E. Furer, President

A.G. Industries, Inc.
Cleveland, Ohio
Charles H. Nervig, President

Tower Products Company, Inc.
Chicago, Illinois
Melvin Mertz, President

Source: American Greetings.

EXHIBIT 3 Balance sheet for American Greetings

February 28, 1987 and 1986
Thousands of dollars

ASSETS

	1987	1986
Current Assets		
Cash and equivalents	$ 17,225	$ 26,853
Trade accounts receivable, less allowances for sales returns of $67,033 ($57,382 in 1986) and for doubtful accounts of $3,992 ($3,378 in 1986)	284,135	240,471
Inventories:		
Raw material	56,057	59,343
Work in process	69,668	60,179
Finished products	202,412	181,237
	328,137	300,759
Less LIFO reserve	75,392	76,552
	252,745	224,207
Display material and factory supplies	29,770	26,826
Total inventories	282,515	251,033
Refundable and deferred income taxes	26,593	36,669
Prepaid expenses and other	9,679	6,228
Total current assets	620,147	561,254
Other Assets	89,488	47,085
Property, Plant and Equipment		
Land	7,956	7,523
Buildings	183,481	165,241
Equipment and fixtures	269,644	222,718
	461,081	395,482
Less accumulated depreciation and amortization	148,097	130,519
Property, plant and equipment—net	312,984	264,963
	$1,022,619	$873,302

LIABILITIES AND SHAREHOLDERS' EQUITY

	1987	1986
Current Liabilities		
Notes payable	$ 25,092	$ 15,921
Accounts payable	69,175	66,685
Payrolls and payroll taxes	31,230	28,675
Retirement plans	10,966	11,697
State and local taxes	3,056	2,763
Dividends payable	5,343	5,317
Income taxes	—	18,988
Sales returns	29,964	23,889
Current maturities of long-term debt	10,894	4,786
Total current liabilities	185,720	178,721
Long-Term Debt	235,005	147,592
Deferred Income Taxes	77,451	64,025
Shareholders' Equity		
Common shares—par value $1:		
Class A	29,552	29,203
Class B	2,588	2,982
Capital in excess of par value	102,718	94,744
Treasury stock	(15,409)	(1,689)
Cumulative translation adjustment	(11,604)	(16,801)
Retained earnings	416,598	374,525
Total shareholders' equity	524,443	482,964
	$1,022,619	$873,302

Source: American Greetings.

low our expectations. Nevertheless, total revenue increased for the eightieth consecutive year, primarily due to increased greeting card sales. This is a proud record which few business enterprises can match. While this increase established a new corporate revenue milestone, it did not meet our performance goals, and earnings were flat for the first time in ten years.

THE FUTURE OF AMERICAN GREETINGS

Although American Greetings has had signficant growth in the past, events in its external environment are clouding the long-term picture.

Again, from Irving Stone:

We foresee opportunities to expand our business and profitability. Recent management restructuring provides key officers with the time necessary to concentrate on long-term strategic planning in order to identify specific opportunities, seize upon them, and transform them into bottom-line results. Much growth potential lies ahead in our basic greeting card

EXHIBIT 4 Income statement for American Greetings

Years ended February 28, 1987, 1986 and 1985
Thousands of dollars except per share amounts

	1987	1986	1985
Net sales	**$1,102,532**	$1,012,451	$919,371
Other income	**23,463**	23,200	26,287
Total Revenue	**1,125,995**	1,035,651	945,658
Costs and expenses:			
Material, labor and other production costs	**471,503**	416,322	377,755
Selling, distribution and marketing	**340,980**	308,745	274,095
Administrative and general	**145,012**	131,928	123,750
Depreciation and amortization	**29,059**	23,471	18,799
Interest	**24,875**	19,125	15,556
Divestiture loss	**12,371**	—	—
	1,023,800	899,591	809,955
Income Before Income Taxes	**102,195**	136,060	135,703
Income taxes	**38,834**	61,635	61,338
Net Income	**$ 63,361**	$ 74,425	$ 74,365
Net Income Per Share	**$1.97**	$2.32	$2.35

Source: American Greetings.

business, both domestically and internationally. We will strengthen our growing number of subsidiaries, improve efficiency, and increase productivity. Sales increases and expanded distribution in all channels of trade are key objectives. Licensing will continue to flourish, extending our horizons further and further.

Morry Weiss further added:

Our future growth plans: aggressively pursuing growth in our core business, concentrating specifically on increasing market share and unit volume, and continued margin improvement.

However, according to William Blair and Company, American Greetings's earnings growth will moderate significantly from the high earning growth rate over the past five years. This is due in part to cyclical factors in the economy, but also because of slowdowns in the expansion of market share, declining licensing revenues, and more intense competition. Furthermore, there are two conflicting trends for American Greetings's operating margins: gains should be made from increased productivity, but the increasing competitive nature of the industry with increased promotion might well erode such productivity increases.

EXHIBIT 5 Selected financial data for American Greetings

Years ended February 28 or 29
Thousands of dollars except per share amounts

SUMMARY OF OPERATIONS

	1987	1986	1985	1984	1983	1982	1981	1980	1979	1978	1977
Total revenue	**$1,125,995**	$1,035,651	$945,658	$839,914	$742,683	$623,604	$498,272	$427,469	$373,487	$315,644	$277,985
Material, labor and other production costs	**471,503**	416,322	377,755	339,988	310,022	276,071	222,993	190,135	161,654	131,769	118,252
Depreciation and amortization	**29,059**	23,471	18,799	15,507	13,890	12,752	10,863	10,070	8,453	7,544	6,982
Interest expense	**24,875**	19,125	15,556	16,135	24,086	21,647	13,548	9,716	5,911	3,935	5,423
Net income	**63,361**	74,425	74,365	59,658	44,582	32,843	26,515	25,638	22,911	19,926	16,787
Net income per share	**1.97**	2.32	2.35	1.91	1.54	1.20	.97	.94	.84	.73	.62
Cash dividends per share	**.66**	.62	.54	.40	.31	.27	.26	.25	.22	.19	.15
Fiscal year end market price per share	**28.75**	35.62	33.06	23.69	18.69	9.63	5.50	5.69	5.75	5.25	4.69
Average number of shares outstanding	**32,212,556**	32,059,851	31,629,418	31,240,455	28,967,092	27,352,342	27,314,594	27,302,686	27,293,376	27,292,036	27,292,484

FINANCIAL POSITION

	1987	1986	1985	1984	1983	1982	1981	1980	1979	1978	1977
Accounts receivable	**$ 284,135**	$ 240,471	$173,637	$146,896	$148,018	$131,996	$114,051	$ 76,629	$ 67,651	$ 54,634	$ 48,920
Inventories	**282,515**	251,033	214,449	180,019	177,459	159,623	133,836	112,279	98,075	71,581	53,741
Working capital	**434,427**	382,533	330,409	275,685	241,724	215,412	167,772	135,443	119,421	98,188	90,308
Total assets	**1,022,619**	873,302	747,897	685,894	580,675	491,854	433,204	344,395	305,746	256,297	247,503
Capital additions	**68,740**	61,799	43,575	46,418	33,967	26,720	22,768	34,516	25,205	20,586	7,630
Long-term debt	**235,005**	147,592	112,876	119,941	111,066	148,895	113,486	75,994	54,845	45,929	41,855
Shareholders' equity	**524,443**	482,964	425,748	365,496	316,368	227,784	205,550	186,043	167,168	150,242	135,370
Shareholders' equity per share	**16.32**	15.01	13.35	11.62	10.18	8.31	7.52	6.81	6.12	5.51	4. 96
Net return on average shareholders' equity	**12.7%**	16.5%	19.2%	17.8%	17.1%	15.4%	13.7%	14.6%	14.5%	14.0%	13.0%
Pre-tax return on total revenue	**9.1%**	13.1%	14.4%	13.0%	11.0%	9.2%	9.9%	11.2%	12.0%	13.3%	11.7%

Source: American Greetings.

Furthermore, according to industry expert, E. Gray Glass, III of Kidder, Peabody, & Company, there are some positives in the industry such as demographics and promising Christmas sales. However, major concerns exist, which include:

- ☐ aggressive price competition which was only modest in the past (mark up for greetings cards is 100 percent between factory and retail outlet).
- ☐ high account turnover as retailers look for most profitable lines and card companies fight intensely for large chain retail accounts (American Greetings recently acquired the Sears' account while Hallmark secured Penney's).
- ☐ increased cost pressures due to increasing advertising and distribution (racks, point of purchase, etc.) costs. Hallmark will spend in excess of $40 million in television and magazine ads for Hallmark merchandise and the benefits of sending cards. American Greetings will spend $33 million.
- ☐ market share gains at the expense of other firms which come at high cost to the winner.
- ☐ growth rate of past five years will not be matched over the next five years.
- ☐ new, viable, and growing competitors will emerge.
- ☐ investment decisions will have to be made more carefully.
- ☐ speculation exists that Hallmark may be formulating some counter-attack strategies.

Merrill Lynch recently reduced American Greetings's earnings estimates for fiscal 1987 and 1988 because of the above conditions as well as difficulties in production and shipment of the Christmas line to retailers, and higher-than-expected new business expenses. Needless to say, the Executive Committee of American Greetings is concerned about the future growth potential and is in the process of formulating long-term objectives and strategies.

REFERENCES

American Greetings. Corporate Reports. 1982–1986.

Chain Store Age. April 1985, 85–7.

Forbes, 16 December, 1985, 174–5.

Investor's Daily. 18 May, 1984, 19.

Kinder Peabody and Company. Research Reports on American Greetings and Greeting Card Industry prepared by E. Gray Glass, III. 16 May, 1986; 20 May, 1986; 11 December, 1986; 20 January, 1987.

Merrill Lynch. Research Report on American Greetings and Greeting Card Industry. September 1986; December 1986.

New York Times. 18 June, 1984.

Ohio Company. Research Report on American Greetings. 17 January, 1986.

Time. 13 May, 1985, 54.

William Blair & Company. Research Report on American Greetings. 27 March, 1986

Playboy Enterprises, Inc.—1988

FRED DAVID
Auburn University

Playboy Enterprises, Inc. was organized in 1953 to publish *PLAYBOY* magazine. (The term "company" means Playboy Enterprises, Inc., together with its subsidiaries). Since its inception, the company has expanded its publishing operations into other markets and has engaged in other businesses that relate to the life style which has been developed and promoted in *Playboy* magazine.

The company's businesses are classified into three industry segments: Publishing, Video, and Licensing & Merchandising. The company's trademarks are vital to the success and future growth of all of the company's businesses. The trademarks, which are renewable indefinitely, include the names of PLAYBOY and PLAYMATE and the Rabbit Head symbol. The company's recent financial statements are provided in Exhibits 1 through 5. The company's current offices and directors are named in Exhibit 6.

PUBLISHING

Playboy is the best-selling magazine in the world aimed at the adult male audience and is the major product of the Publishing segment. The magazine is sold principally in the United States by subscriptions delivered through the mail and on a single-copy basis at newsstands through distribution firms. Exhibit 1 shows the average net paid circulation per issue (single copy sales and subscriptions) for the first and second six months of each of the three calendar years through December 31, 1986, and for the first six months of 1987.

The net circulation revenues of *Playboy* for the three years ended June 30, 1987, 1986, and 1985 were $70,102,000, $75,789,000, and $77,164,000, respectively. Net circulation revenues are gross revenues less provisions for newsstand returns and unpaid subscriptions, and subscription agency commissions.

The company publishes *Playboy* in various geographical advertising editions, all of which contain the same editorial material but vary in advertising copy carried. The net advertising revenues of *Playboy* magazine for the three years ended June 30, 1987, 1986, and 1985 were $26,836,000, $40,488,000, and $41,991,000, respectively. Net advertising revenues are gross revenues less advertising agency commissions, frequency and cash discounts, and rebates.

In December 1986, the company completed the sale of *Games* magazine, a publication it acquired in 1978. The gain before income taxes recognized in fiscal 1987 on the sale was $2,390,000.

Note: The material in the case comes from Playboy Enterprises, Inc's 1987 Form 10K and *Annual Report.*

EXHIBIT 1

	Average Net Paid Circulation Per Month During		Approximate Percent of Circulation from	
Calendar Year	First Six Months	Second Six Months	Single Copy Sales	Subscriptions
1987	3,700,000		36%	64%
1986	3,900,000	3,500,000	30%	70%
1985	4,100,000	4,200,000	39%	61%
1984	4,200,000	4,200,000	44%	56%

Paper is the major raw material necessary to the publishing business. The company purchases paper from several suppliers and has not experienced any difficulty in obtaining adequate quantities for its publishing requirements.

Proceedings in which it has been contended that *Playboy* (or an issue thereof) is obscene and cannot be sold or otherwise distributed have been commenced from time to time in local jurisdictions within the United States. No obscenity ruling has ever been upheld against *Playboy* at a federal or state level; however, an adverse determination could have a negative impact on the company's revenues and profits depending upon the market involved and the nature of any such decision.

In February 1986, the Attorney General's Commission on Pornography ("the Commission") sent a threatening letter to several major convenience and drug store chains that sold *Playboy* and other adult titles. The company subsequently filed a lawsuit and won a preliminary court injunction ordering a retraction letter and forbidding the government from printing a "blacklist" of outlets that sell adult magazines or taking any other action that interferes with the distribution of constitutionally protected materials. The Commission's final report, issued in July 1986, clearly indicated *Playboy* was not a concern to them. Despite the outcome of the lawsuit and the commission's final report, the impact of the threatening letter caused the loss of nearly 20 percent of the approximately 110,000 retail outlets selling *Playboy* and prompted increased display restrictions in a number of stores which has adversely affected *Playboy's* newsstand sales. It is still uncertain in the near term the extent to which *Playboy* will be able to recapture additional lost outlets and display.

The magazine publishing field experiences intense competition for both readership and advertising revenues. Other major magazines of national and international circulation, particularly other publications aimed at men, are *Playboy*'s principal competitors. In addition, all other forms of advertising media, such as newspapers, radio, and television, compete with the magazine.

In fiscal 1987, the company continued to be affected by the industry trend of declining newsstand sales. As a result of this trend and the retail delistings stemming from the commission's letter, the company adjusted *Playboy*'s circulation rate base

EXHIBIT 2 Financial information relating to industry segments, Playboy Enterprises, Inc., and Subsidiaries, for the years ended June 30

(in thousands)	1987	1986	1985
Sales to Nonaffiliates (1)			
Publishing			
Playboy magazine	$ 98,359	$117,864	$120,721
Other	22,854	26,291	27,819
Total Publishing	121,213	144,155	148,540
Video	29,132	23,864	23,747
Licensing & Merchandising	10,462	12,642	16,381
Other businesses	960	978	1,147
Total	$161,767	$181,639	$189,815
Income (Loss) from Continuing Operations Before Income Taxes and Extraordinary Item			
Publishing	$ 12,216	$ 6,840	$ 8,125
Video	1,397	(7,170)	230
Licensing & Merchandising	2,643	4,841	8,070
Other businesses	32	(4)	(155)
Corporate administration and promotion	(16,030)	(16,518)	(16,684)
Interest, net	1,497	1,846	8,711
Other, net	9,321	289	305
Total	$ 11,076	$ (9,876)	$ 8,602
Identifiable Assets			
Publishing	$ 33,037	$ 37,042	$ 42,694
Video	19,541	24,243	33,371
Licensing & Merchandising	1,765	2,205	3,549
Other businesses	318	548	359
Corporate administration and promotion (2)	43,352	33,776	79,917
Total assets of continuing operations	98,013	97,814	159,890
Net assets of discontinued operations	–	–	3,696
Total	$ 98,013	$ 97,814	$163,586
Depreciation and Amortization of Property and Equipment			
Publishing	$ 607	$ 582	$ 583
Video	276	316	288
Licensing & Merchandising	108	150	191
Other businesses	17	14	19
Corporate administration and promotion	874	855	873
Total	$ 1,882	$ 1,917	$ 1,954
Capital Expenditures			
Publishing	$ 136	$ 750	$ 241
Video	36	112	195
Licensing & Merchandising	88	127	101
Other businesses	3	9	11
Corporate administration and promotion	336	835	388
Total	$ 599	$ 1,833	$ 936

The accompanying notes are an integral part of these tables.

Notes to Financial Information Relating to Industry Segments

(1) Sales to nonaffiliates include export sales of $21,242,000, $19,918,000 and $20,786,000 in fiscal 1987, 1986 and 1985, respectively.

(2) Corporate assets consist principally of cash and short-term cash investments and corporate property and equipment. Fiscal 1985 corporate assets also included receivables from the sale of the company's interest in the former Playboy Hotel/Casino in Atlantic City (see Note B of Notes to Consolidated Financial Statements).

Source: Playboy Enterprises, Inc. 1987 Annual Reports, p. 19.

EXHIBIT 3 Consolidated statements of operations, Playboy Enterprises, Inc., and Subsidiaries, for the years ended June 30

(in thousands except per share amounts)	1987	1986	1985
Net sales and revenues from continuing operations	$161,767	$181,639	$189,815
Costs and expenses:			
Cost of sales and operating expenses	(137,846)	(166,677)	(162,434)
Selling and administrative expenses	(23,663)	(26,973)	(27,795)
Total costs and expenses	(161,509)	(193,650)	(190,229)
Operating income (loss)	258	(12,011)	(414)
Nonoperating income (expense):			
Interest income	1,739	2,336	9,276
Interest expense	(242)	(490)	(565)
Gain on sale of *Games* magazine	2,390	–	–
Other, net	6,931	289	305
Total nonoperating income	10,818	2,135	9,016
Income (loss) from continuing operations before income taxes and extraordinary item	11,076	(9,876)	8,602
Income tax expense	(4,528)	(653)	(4,079)
Income (loss) from continuing operations before extraordinary item	6,548	(10,529)	4,523
Discontinued operations			
Loss from operations	–	(4,770)	(1,493)
Gain (loss) on disposal	389	(46,904)	1,213
Income (loss) from discontinued operations before extraordinary item	389	(51,674)	(280)
Income (loss) before extraordinary item	6,937	(62,203)	4,243
Extraordinary item–tax benefit resulting from utilization of loss carryforwards	4,180	–	2,456
Net income (loss)	$ 11,117	$ (62,203)	$ 6,699
Income (loss) per common share			
Income (loss) before extraordinary item:			
From continuing operations	$ .70	$ (1.12)	$ .48
From discontinued operations	.04	(5.49)	(.03)
Total	.74	(6.61)	.45
Extraordinary item applicable to:			
Continuing operations	.40	–	.36
Discontinued operations	.04	–	(.10)
Total	.44	–	.26
Net income (loss)	$ 1.18	$ (6.61)	$ .71

Source: Playboy Enterprises, Inc. 1987 *Annual Report,* p.23.

from 4.1 million to 3.4 million effective with the November 1986 issue. Exhibit 4 shows the position of *Playboy* in the ranking of the fifteen leading consumer magazines based upon *the American Broadcasting Company's* (ABC's) report of circulation for the first six months of calendar 1987.

The company also licenses thirteen foreign editions of *Playboy* in Argentina, Australia, Brazil, France, Germany, Greece, Hong Kong, Italy, Japan, Mexico, the Netherlands, Spain, and Turkey. These editions use translated U.S. editions. Originally, they created material in mixtures that permitted them to tailor their product to their

EXHIBIT 4

Magazine	Number of Copies Sold
1. *TV Guide*	17,300,000
2. *Reader's Digest*	16,800,000
3. *National Geographic*	10,500,000
4. *Better Homes and Gardens*	8,100,000
5. *Family Circle*	6,000,000
6. *McCall's*	5,300,000
7. *Woman's Day*	5,300,000
8. *Good Housekeeping*	5,200,000
9. *Ladies' Home Journal*	5,000,000
10. *Time*	4,700,000
11. *National Enquirer*	4,500,000
12. *Redbook*	3,900,000
13. *The Star*	3,700,000
14. *Playboy*	3,700,000
15. *Newsweek*	3,200,000

individual market needs while retaining the original style, look, and flavor of the U.S. edition of *Playboy*. The average monthly circulation of foreign editions in fiscal 1987, 1986, and 1985 was approximately 1.7 million, 1.6 million, and 1.4 million, respectively. In fiscal 1987, the three largest-selling editions, Germany, Brazil, and Japan, accounted for approximately 78 percent of the total royalty income from the sale of foreign editions.

The terms of the license agreements vary; however, in general, the licenses are for a term of at least five years and carry a guaranteed minimum royalty, as well as a formula for computing earned royalties in excess of the minimum. These royalty computations are generally based on both circulation and advertising revenues.

Through a subsidiary, Boarts International, Inc. ("Boarts"), the company is engaged in the international distribution of magazines and books (including the U.S. edition of Playboy.) In July 1987, Select Magazines, Inc., a national distributor of periodicals in the United States and Canada, appointed Boarts as its foreign distributor. Boarts currently distributes more than 200 titles for approximately eighty U.S. publishers. Boarts offers clients a full range of marketing and distribution services, including field sales, sales promotion, feasibility studies, product evaluation, general market research, traffic management and related services, management sales reports, and all billing and credit and collection activities. The distribution of Playboy publications accounted for approximately 33 percent, 41 percent, and 41 percent of Boarts' sales in fiscal 1987, 1986, and 1985, respectively.

EXHIBIT 5 Consolidated statements of financial position, Playboy Enterprises, Inc., and Subsidiaries, as of June 30

(in thousands, except share data)	1987	1986
Assets		
Cash and short-term cash investments	$ 31,300	$ 21,380
Receivables, less allowances of $3,478 and $2,548, respectively	15,159	13,854
Inventories	10,859	15,887
Film production costs	10,725	14,869
Other current assets	5,241	5,535
Total current assets	73,284	71,525
Property and equipment		
Land	472	472
Buildings and improvements	11,385	11,196
Furniture and equipment	15,644	15,686
Leasehold improvements	9,701	9,757
Total property and equipment	37,202	37,111
Accumulated depreciation	(26,596)	(25,011)
Property and equipment, net	10,606	12,100
Deferred subscription acquisition costs	8,714	8,377
Film production costs—noncurrent	1,840	2,071
Other assets	3,569	3,741
Total assets	$ 98,013	$ 97,814
Liabilities		
Current financing obligations	$ 3	$ 100
Accounts payable	13,600	14,986
Accrued salaries, wages and employee benefits	1,831	1,711
Net liabilities of and reserves for losses on disposals of discontinued businesses	2,128	6,131
Income taxes payable	628	764
Other liabilities and accrued expenses	5,199	5,788
Total current liabilities	23,389	29,480
Long-term financing obligations	1,321	1,205
Deferred revenue	33,849	39,154
Deferred gain on sale of partnership interest	2,217	2,608
Other noncurrent liabilities	5,889	5,136
Commitments and contingencies		
Shareholders' Equity		
Common stock, $1 par value, 15,000,000 shares authorized, 10,099,509 issued	10,100	10,100
Capital in excess of par value	14,903	14,903
Retained earnings	13,969	2,852
Cost of 693,826 shares in treasury	(7,624)	(7,624)
Total shareholders' equity	31,348	20,231
Total liabilities and shareholders' equity	$ 98,013	$ 97,814

Source: Playboy Enterprises, Inc. 1987 *Annual Report,* p.24.

The company is also engaged in the production and sale of newsstand specials and calendars. During fiscal 1987, 1986, and 1985, six newsstand specials were released. The specials are thematic presentations of photographs shot for the magazine; they provide a healthy flow of revenues and profits, with little additional investment. Due to the popularity of these specials, the company plans to increase the number of

EXHIBIT 6 Consolidated statements of changes in shareholders' equity, Playboy Enterprises, Inc., and Subsidiaries, for the years ended June 30, 1987,1986,and 1985

(in thousands)	Common Stock	Capital in Excess of Par Value	Retained Earnings	Treasury Stock
Balance at June 30, 1984	$ 10,100	$ 14,903	$ 58,356	$ (1,237)
Net income	–	–	6,699	–
Purchase of 515,961 common shares pursuant to tender offer	–	–	–	(6,387)
Balance at June 30, 1985	10,100	14,903	65,055	(7,624)
Net loss	–	–	(62,203)	–
Balance at June 30, 1986	10,100	14,903	2,852	(7,624)
Net income	–	–	11,117	–
Balance at June 30, 1987	$ 10,100	$ 14,903	$ 13,969	$ (7,624)

Source: Playboy Enterprises, Inc. 1987 *Annual Report,* p.25.

issues published from six to nine, in fiscal 1988. *Playboy* calendars, composed of readers' favorite Playmates, are sold in desk-top and wall-size versions.

VIDEO

The company is involved in the development, production, and distribution of programming principally for pay television (including monthly subscription pay cable, pay-per-view cables and hotel/motel distribution) and home video (video-cassettes). The programming is generally composed of short (30 or 60 minutes in length) original programming and longer (90 minutes or more) licensed, independently produced feature-length movies.

The majority of the original programming has been developed for the company's own cable television network, "The Playboy Channel" ("The Channel"), a ten-hour-per-day monthly subscription pay service, which is also offered to consumers in the United States in various pay-per-view cable packages by the Channel's local distributors. The Channel was launched in November 1982 with approximately 300,000 subscribing households. At June 30, 1987, The Channel had approximately 544,000 subscribing households. Net subscription revenues of The Channel for fiscal 1987 were approximately $22,381,000, compared to $19,692,000 and $20,380,000 in fiscal 1986 and 1985, respectively. Fiscal 1986 and 1985 subscription revenues were net of distribution fees of $5,219,000 and $7,573,000, respectively, related to the now-terminated distribution agreement with Rainbow Programming Services Company ("Rainbow").

The video segment's pay cable television business is largely dependent upon obtaining and maintaining distribution contracts with multiple system cable operators ("MSO's") to carry The Channel as a monthly service. Many MSO's control several cable systems which offer The Channel, and each cable system has a certain Playboy Channel subscriber base. At June 30, 1987, the Video segment's top three MSO's supplied Channel programming to 75 of the 561 cable systems on which The Channel is carried. Those cable systems supplied The Channel to approximately 151,000 of the 544,000 subscribers to The Channel.

In April 1986, the company and Rainbow agreed to terminate the October 1983 distribution agreement which had provided Rainbow with the exclusive rights of pro-

EXHIBIT 7 Consolidated statements of changes in financial position, Playboy Enterprises, Inc., and Subsidiaries, for the years ended June 30

(in thousands)	1987	1986*	1985*
Cash Flow from Continuing Operations			
Income (loss) from continuing operations before extraordinary item	$ 6,548	$ (10,529)	$ 4,523
Add (deduct) items not affecting cash:			
Depreciation of property and equipment	1,882	1,917	1,954
Loss related to video distribution agreement	–	2,295	–
Amortization and market value adjustment of film production costs	14,677	17,553	16,612
Gain on sale of *Games* magazine	(2,390)	–	–
Other, net	(137)	254	(1,165)
Additions to film production costs	(10,302)	(12,117)	(26,014)
Changes in working capital components:			
Accounts receivable	(1,131)	554	(1,348)
Inventories	4,729	6,744	(9,829)
Other current assets	194	919	(2,078)
Accounts payable	(1,383)	(2,737)	511
Income taxes payable	(136)	(1,051)	569
Other liabilities and accrued expenses	(993)	673	(1,953)
Decrease in deferred income, net of deferred subscription acquisition costs	(2,225)	(425)	(809)
Increase (decrease) in noncurrent liabilities	966	(617)	3,671
Other, net	(336)	686	(83)
Cash provided by (used for) continuing operations before extraordinary item and other sources of cash	9,963	4,119	(15,439)
Extraordinary item—tax benefit, not affecting cash	3,849	–	3,426
Collection of principal on note receivable	–	–	7,564
Cash provided by (used for) continuing operations before financing and investment activities	13,812	4,119	(4,449)
Financing and Investment Activities			
Additions to property and equipment	(599)	(1,833)	(936)
Sales of property and equipment	90	160	898
Net retirement of financing obligations	(100)	(123)	(162)
Payment of video distribution agreement obligation	–	(3,500)	–
Purchase of treasury stock	–	–	(6,387)
Cash used for financing and investment activities	(609)	(5,296)	(6,587)
Cash Flow from Discontinued Operations			
Income (loss) from discontinued operations before extraordinary item	389	(51,674)	(280)
Extraordinary item—tax benefit (charge), not affecting cash	331	–	(970)
Net proceeds from sales of discontinued businesses	–	1,702	1,642
Net (increase) decrease in net assets of discontinued operations	(4,003)	44,352	(7,890)
Cash used for discontinued operations	(3,283)	(5,620)	(7,498)
Increase (Decrease) in Cash and Short-Term Cash Investments	$ 9,920	$ (6,797)	$ (18,534)

*Certain reclassifications have been made to conform to the 1987 presentation.

Source: Playboy Enterprises, Inc. 1987 *Annual Report,* p.26.

motion, sales, marketing, and distribution of The Channel and certain other Playboy pay television products ("the service"). Effective April 1, 1986, Playboy assumed these marketing and distribution responsibilities, and the previous arrangement which entitled Rainbow to a distribution fee of 25 percent of gross subscription revenues was terminated.

The new arrangement allows the company to have total control over the television product from production through delivery to its various cable affiliates. In addi-

EXHIBIT 8 OFFICERS AND DIRECTORS, Playboy Enterprises, Inc.

Corporate Officers		Hugh M. Hefner	*Chairman of the Board and Chief Executive Officer*
		Christie Hefner	*Vice Chair, President and Chief Operating Officer*
		Richard S. Rosenzweig	*Executive Vice President, Office of the Chairman*
		James P. Radtke	*Senior Vice President, Chief Financial Officer*
		Howard Shapiro	*Senior Vice President, Law and Administration, and General Counsel*
		John A. Scott	*Senior Vice President and President, Publishing Group*
		A. William Stokkan	*Senior Vice President and President, Licensing & Merchandising Group*
		Dale C. Gordon	*Vice President, Secretary and Associate General Counsel*
		Russell A. Ringl	*Vice President, Human Resources*
		Thomas W. Aubin	*Corporate Controller and Chief Accounting Officer*
		Rebecca S. Maskey	*Treasurer*
Group Officers	*Publishing*	John A. Scott	*President*
		Arthur Kretchmer	*Senior Vice President, Editorial Director and Associate Publisher, Playboy*
		J. P. Dolman, Jr.	*Senior Vice President and Assistant Publisher, Playboy*
		Richard E. Smith	*Senior Vice President, Circulation Director, Playboy*
		Jack Bernstein	*Vice President, Circulation Promotion Director, Playboy*
		Michael T. Carr	*Vice President, Advertising Director, Playboy*
		Gary Cole	*Vice President, Photography Director, Playboy*
		Marilyn Grabowski	*Vice President, West Coast Photography Editor, Playboy*
		John B. Mastro	*Vice President, Production, Playboy*
		Tom Staebler	*Vice President, Executive Art Director, Playboy*
	Licensing & Merchandising	A. William Stokkan	*President*
		John J. Casey	*Vice President, Customer Service*
		Jack F. Friedman	*Vice President, Wholesale*
		Paul E. Jacquet	*Vice President, International Licensing*
		Robert E. Josephson	*Vice President, Direct Marketing*
		Mary E. Levenson	*Vice President, Licensing Services*
	Video	Richard V. Sowa	*President, Playboy Video Corporation, Inc.*
		Edward L. Rissien	*President, Playboy Programs, Inc.*
		Que Spaulding	*President, Playboy Programming Distribution Company of America, Inc.*
		Susan Eaton	*Vice President, Home Video*
		Michael K. Fleming	*Vice President, Sales and Affiliate Relations*
		Claudia Flintermann	*Vice President, Direct Broadcast Development*
		Michael Hale	*Vice President, Marketing and Product Development*
	Models	Valerie Cragin	*President*
Playboy Foundation		Cleo F. Wilson	*Executive Director*
		Burton Joseph	*Chairman, Board of Directors*
		Christie Hefner	*Director*
		Richard S. Rosenzweig	*Director*
		Howard Shapiro	*Director*
		James R. Petersen	*Director*
Directors		Hugh M. Hefner	*Chairman of the Board and Chief Executive Officer, Playboy Enterprises, Inc.*
		Christie Hefner	*Vice Chair, President and Chief Operating Officer, Playboy Enterprises, Inc.*
		Richard S. Rosenzweig	*Executive Vice President, Office of the Chairman, Playboy Enterprises, Inc.*
		William A. Emerson	*Adjunct Professor of Journalism, University of South Carolina*
		Mark H. McCormack	*Chairman and Chief Executive Officer, International Management Group*
		Sol Rosenthal	*Partner, Buchalter, Nemer, Fields & Younger*

Source: Playboy Enterprises, Inc. 1987 *Annual Report*, p.32.

tion, the company can now bring directly to cable television its special promotion and marketing expertise developed over the company's 35-year history. Under the termination agreement, Rainbow is to receive a monthly royalty of five percent of revenues received by the company for the service, subject to a minimum royalty based on the number of subscribers, as long as the service is in operation. This royalty is payable until April 30, 1991, if Rainbow has received payments by that date of $15,000,000, or April 30, 1996, if that level has been reached. The agreement provides for noncompetition in the distribution and production of an adult-oriented pay television service by Rainbow as long as royalty payments are being made.

While the principal focus of programming investments to date has been to serve the needs of The Channel, the programming is also utilized in other markets, including worldwide home video, the hotel/motel television market, and other U.S. pay television markets such as the pay-per markets. Revenues from these sources in fiscal 1987 were approximately $6,800,000, compared to $4,200,000, and $3,300,000 in fiscal 1986 and 1985, respectively.

The company's home video distribution agreement with Lorimar Home Video, Inc. ("Lorimar"), which provided for the distribution of Playboy original nontheatrical programming in the domestic and Canadian markets for video cassettes and discs, was scheduled to end in April 1988, unless extended by Lorimar for an additional year. The Lorimar agreement provided for the release of twelve videocassettes in each of the two years of the agreement, with minimum guaranteed advances and additional payments to the company of license fees based on sales to video wholesalers and retailers, as well as the development and marketing support of a separate Playboy Video line.

In September 1987, as part of an apparent desire to concentrate its distribution energies more in the theatrical area, Lorimar admittedly breached this agreement. The company has filed arbitration proceedings, in accordance with the contract, seeking therein damages, both compensatory and punitive. Third party discussions with candidates to replace Lorimar as the company's home video distributor have begun.

Prior to June 1985, the company had been operating under a now-expired agreement with CBS/Fox for the distribution of certain Playboy programming on videocassettes and discs. During the three years ended June 30, 1987, the company released a total of twenty–three videocassettes, of which six were distributed by CBS/Fox and sixteen were distributed by Lorimar. Six of the twenty–three videocassettes released have qualified for and/or been awarded "gold" (30,000 units sold or $1,200,000 in U.S. retail revenues) and/or "platinum" (60,000 units sold or U.S. retail revenues of $1,400,000) status by the Recording Industry Association of America.

In fiscal 1987, the company entered into agreements with Shochiku-Fuji Co. Ltd. and Palace Home Video to distribute twelve Playboy videocassettes in Japan and ten Playboy video cassettes in Australia, respectively. An agreement in principle has been reached with each such company to distribute an additional nine and ten videocassettes, respectively, through mid-1988.

Technological advancements in this highly competitive industry have increased the availability of Playboy programming via the pay-per packages mentioned previously. These packages are available on systems that offer subscribers two-way addressability or the capacity to "call up" specific programs on impulse. The technical hardware for such addressability is becoming more widespread, and The Channel's programming is currently available to more than 150,000 households on three cable systems. This expanded potential market represents an attractive method of distributing Playboy programming, and the company intends to market this service aggressively in the future. In addition, another market has emerged: providing The Channel via encrypted signal to home satellite dish viewers. The company plans to encrypt The Channel's signals by early calendar 1988. Households that previously had received their programs direct from The Channel's broadcast satellite without paying a fee will now have to subscribe to The Channel to view the programming.

While The Channel is not directly competitive with the principal mainstream pay cable movie services, such as Home Box Office, Cinemax, Showtime, and The Movie Channel, the company's pay television product competes for cable channel space and viewer dollars with such services. Competition among pay cable services, even those producing differentiated material, such as the Disney Channel and various sports services, involves such items as pricing, viewer perceived product value, and effectiveness of programming distribution.

Additionally, certain local governmental agencies and private individuals and organizations have sought to exclude The Channel from pay television distribution within their jurisdictions or locations because of the adult-oriented content of the programming. The nature and extent of the impact these factors will have on the company's future profitability cannot be accurately predicted at present.

LICENSING AND MERCHANDISING

The company, on a worldwide basis, licenses the manufacture, sale, and distribution of a significant number of consumer products. All these products carry some form of brand identification via one or more of the Playboy trademarks. The major product line consists of men's and women's apparel, including sportswear, activewear, nightwear, swimwear, footwear, accessories, jewelry, leather goods, glasses, and sunglasses. The items are sold through mass merchants, retail mail order catalogs, and other retail outlets. The sale and distribution of these products are accomplished through exclusive license agreements that include manufacturing as well as selling and distribution; however, the design and quality specifications are controlled by the company. Net sales and revenues from product licensing and merchandising, which are comprised principally of licensing royalties, catalog sales, and wholesale revenues, were $9,803,000, $8,751,000, and $8,476,000 in fiscal 1987, 1986, and 1985, respectively.

Licensing royalties were $5,700,000, $5,700,000, and $5,800,000 in fiscal 1987, 1986, and 1985, respectively. The royalties received under licensing agreements are based on a fixed or variable percentage of the licensee's total net sales against a guaranteed minimum. In fiscal 1987, approximately 56 percent of licensing royalties were derived from licensees in the United States, 28 percent from licensees in the Far East, with the remainder from Europe, Australia, and Canada.

Actively defending the company's trademarks and monitoring the marketplace for counterfeit products are vital to the success and the future growth of this business and all the company's other businesses. Consequently, the company is from time to time involved in legal proceedings resulting from unauthorized uses of the company's trademarks.

While the trademarks provide a level of product differentiation that cannot legally be duplicated, the products are in direct competition with other products, both branded and unbranded. The product categories, particularly apparel and jewelry, in which the company participates are intensely competitive and extremely sensitive to shifts in consumer buying habits and fashion trends.

The company also licenses the Playboy name and trademarks to individuals for use in the operation of nightclubs, which feature the sale of food and beverages served by Bunnies, and entertainment. Currently, there are nine licensed Playboy Clubs in operation. Domestically, clubs are located in Des Moines, Iowa; Lansing, Michigan; Omaha, Nebraska, and Wilkes-Barre, Pennsylvania. Internationally, clubs are located in Nagoya, Osaka, Sapporo and Tokyo, Japan, and in Manila, the Philippines. The company continues to pursue licensing expansion, primarily overseas. Competition in the food and beverage and leisure time industries is intense.

In September 1986, a new direct marketing membership program, Playboy Preferred was launched. Playboy Preferred is marketed to individuals principally through direct mail and advertisements in Playboy clubs. This new program makes available to members a discount on food and beverages served in the four domestic Playboy clubs, except where prohibited by law, as well as various Playboy products at reduced prices, including *Playboy,* videocassettes, and licensed fashions and accessories. In fiscal 1988, the company plans to expand the number of non-Playboy products and services it offers to members at good values and to expand the membership base.

PROMOTIONAL AND OTHER ACTIVITIES

The company believes that its sales of products and services are closely related to public recognition of its role in promoting a particular life style. To establish such public recognition, the company, among other activities, acquired in 1959 a property in Chicago known as the "Playboy Mansion" that has been used for charitable functions and a wide variety of promotional and other corporate activities. This property currently is leased to the School of the Art Institute of Chicago, an educational institution serving the public interest, through August 1989.

In 1971, the company acquired a mansion in Holmby Hills, California, which is utilized for various corporate activities, including serving as a valuable location for video production and magazine photography, business meetings, charitable functions, and a wide variety of promotional and marketing purposes. The California mansion generates substantial publicity for the company; this publicity increases public awareness and recognition of the company and its products and services. The total mansion operating expenses (including depreciation, taxes, and security) attributable to the above-mentioned activities were approximately $3,400,000, $3,500,000, and $3,500,000 for the years ended June 30, 1987, 1986, and 1985, respectively.

The Playboy Foundation, a department of the company, supports not-for-profit organizations and public interest projects that seek to foster and encourage freedom of speech and expression, as well as human rights, civil liberties, and social justice programs. In addition, the company encourages its employees to participate in not-for-profit organizations within their communities through its Neighborhood Relations Boards, and Employee Matching Gift and Time Match programs. The company from time to time also has contributed funds to the HMH Foundation, a tax-exempt charitable foundation, which donates funds to various community social service, cultural, medical, and community projects.

The company is also engaged in the operation of a model agency in Los Angeles. The company closed its Chicago model agency in October 1986.

EMPLOYEES

The company employs approximately 580 full-time employees; approximately 230 of them are engaged in the company's magazine publishing business, while approximately 350 are engaged in the company's other activities. While there are employment disputes occurring from time to time including actions before state and federal agencies, no material interruptions of services or activities have occurred due to any labor disagreements or individual employment disputes.

COMPETITION

During the 1980s, the number of magazines on newsstands has doubled. Magazines experience intense competition from radio, newspapers, and television for advertising revenues. In spite of *Playboy*'s newsstand sales decline, the magazine remains the world's best selling periodical for men. Major competitive magazines include *Penthouse*, *Hustler*, *Esquire*, and *Gentleman's Quarterly* (*GQ*).

Gentlemans Quarterly

Gentleman's Quarterly (GQ) magazine, founded in 1957, is headquartered in New York City. GQ is published by Conde Nast Publications and had a circulation of 662,801 copies in 1986, up from 645,348 in 1985. GQ is devoted to contemporary life style interests of urban men. Each issue explores current fashions, grooming, home decor, theater, film, food and drink, the arts, and sports.

Esquire

Esquire magazine, founded in 1933, is also headquartered in New York City. *Esquire*'s circulation of 702,512 copies in 1986 was down from 705,558 in 1985. *Esquire* deals with the real and rapidly changing world of the American man in today's society. Each issue delivers practical information on business, politics, health and fitness, sports, fashion, the arts, and the best in today's fiction from some of the world's best authors.

Esquire was recently purchased for $80 million by a group of investors led by the Hearst Corporation. Hearst has announced plans to continue to target older, affluent audiences. *Esquire* has recently boosted marketing efforts to increase subscription and newsstand sales.

Penthouse

Penthouse magazine was founded in 1969 by Bob Guccione. Its circulation in 1986 was 2,379,333 copies, down from 3,090,869 in 1985. *Penthouse* offers everything from outspoken contemporary commentaries to award-winning photo essays. *Penthouse* features leading authors, artists, cartoonists, graphic designers, and interviews with today's celebrities.

In 1988, Penthouse International expects to increase revenues to $230 million, mainly from *Penthouse* and *Omni* magazines, but the acquisitions of *Saturday Review* and other periodicals are expected to contribute to this total. Aimed at the young and affluent market, *Saturday Review* was acquired in early 1987 for an estimated $2.6 million. Guccione desires to acquire additional publications. He is working on package discount deals for companies advertising in several of his magazines.

Hustler

Hustler magazine is owned and published by Larry Flynt Publications (LFP). Although *Hustler*'s sales have been declining during the past few years, LFP's profits were up 50 percent in calendar 1986 on revenues of $32 million. This jump is in response to LFP's cost reduction program that led to employee layoffs and budget tightening measures. LFP has been for sale since 1985, but no one seems willing to pay the reported asking price of $25 million.

LFP has begun diversification into non-sexual titles, adding such magazines as *Men's Look,* a men's life style/fashion publication; *Rip,* a rock'n'roll monthly launched in October 1986; *Auto Technical*, an automotive magazine slated for a January 1988, start-up; *Running Times*, a magazine targeted to serious runners, and *Supercycle*, aimed at motorcycle enthusiasts. These magazines rely almost totally upon newsstand sales, and each appears to be building a solid following. *Men's Look* is aimed at a younger audience than either *GQ* or *Esquire* (20-to-30-year-olds) and currently has an annual circulation of 200,000. LFP plans to add two titles annually for the next several years. Many advertisers are hesitant about advertising in LFP publications due to the negative connotations associated with Flynt.

FUTURE CONCERNS

Looking ahead, the company is facing challenges and opportunities in each of its core business areas.

In the Publishing Group, paper and postage costs are expected to rise before the end of fiscal 1988. In response, the company plans to increase the charge per ad in *Playboy* magazine, and to review both the newsstand cover price and subscription price. Additionally, the firm has increased the number of magazine specials it publishes each year from six to nine. What do you think of these strategies? How high do you think the company can go with its cover price? Its subscription price? What types of test-marketing do you recommend the magazine does prior to making any product-pricing decision? Are there special challenges facing *Playboy* as a men's magazine in any of these areas? To whom should the company compare its advertising cost per page?

Playboy magazine reaches more young adult men than *Rolling Stone*, *Gentlemen's Quarterly*, and *Esquire* combined. How do you think they should "sell" this fact to potential advertisers? How do you feel the magazine can overcome bias against it by conservative companies who may like the audience reach but not the nude pictures?

The company does not consider other men's "sophisticate" magazines serious competition for ad pages since bias against *Penthouse*, *Hustler*, and others is so strong, advertising pages and revenues in these publications traditionally have been extremely low. Do you agree or disagree?

How do you think social issues like the AIDS epidemic will affect *Playboy* and other erotic publications and video products? What do you think the company should do about issues like this?

With more than $30 million in cash on their balance sheet, Playboy Enterprises, Inc. management has expressed an interest in making future acquisitions. Do you think the time is right for Playboy Enterprises, Inc. to acquire other publications? Do you think it should have acquired some of the CBS magazine group titles that were for sale? What kinds of magazines should Playboy Enterprises, Inc. be looking at? Are any acquisitions feasible, and how?

What problems do you foresee in the Licensing & Merchandising Group? What types of products do you think it makes sense for the company to further expand into? Geographically, where does it make the most sense for Playboy Enterprises, Inc. to market these products?

Recently, the company formed a wholly owned subsidiary called Licensing Unlimited, which gives the firm an opportunity to market and manage brands outside the Playboy name and trademarks. Do you think this is a logical expansion? Is it workable? Whom do you think would make logical acquisition candidates and why?

The company also currently produces catalogs of its products as part of its direct marketing operation. Recently, a catalog featuring Playmate fashions was sent to more than 400,000 subscribers of women's magazines and mail order purchasers from other women's catalogs. What do you think of this concept?

In the company's third strategic business unit, the Video Group, what steps do you feel should be taken to boost subscriber levels to the Playboy Channel? Do you think this a logical business for the firm to be involved with? What other options exist in the pay-television area that might be explored by Playboy Enterprise, Inc.? Should the company look to expand The Playboy Channel programming overseas? Is pay-per-view technology perhaps the most feasible option for this product?

While the firm's home videocassettes are selling extremely well in the United States, with most of the recent offerings having had a long stint on best-seller charts, do you think that an equally lucrative market for these products exists outside the United States? Specifically, what should the company's game plan be in terms of geographic expansion?

Do you see any "hidden" assets the company may have and be able to take advantage of? Does the firm have special expertise in certain areas that may be used to develop other core businesses or products?

What other strategies would you recommend to Christie Hefner, vice chair, president, and chief operating officer? What effects would these strategies have on the company's income statement and balance sheet?

Cessna Aircraft Corporation—1987

NANCY DANNER MARLOW
Eastern Illinois University

Man's dream of flying is as old as man himself; throughout history, man has attempted to bring that dream to reality. Man's earliest attempts to fly were with bird-like wings, a result of studying birds in flight. Balloons were his approximation of the airborne qualities of clouds. Leonardo da Vinci worked hard, long, and unsuccessfully to learn the mechanical principles of flight. In spite of his lack of success, da Vinci's work provided the basis for future development of the propeller, the fabric-covered airplane, and the parachute.

Most accounts of aviation's history begin on December 17, 1903, just outside Kitty Hawk, North Carolina, where Orville Wright was the first man to fly a heavier-than-air machine under its own power. His twelve-second flight went a distance of 120 feet. On that same day and in the same aircraft, Orville's brother Wilbur made a flight that lasted fifty-nine seconds and covered 852 feet. Many of history's heroes are also aviation's heroes. Edward Rickenbacker, Amelia Earhart, Charles Lindbergh, Richard Byrd, Ronald Amundsen, and Wiley Post are only a few of the well-known names associated with aviation. The list of heroes continues with the astronauts of the space program.

From its inception in 1927, Cessna Aircraft Corporation has grown from a one-man operation to a multimillion-dollar organization. For decades, Cessna was known as the major manufacturer of general aviation aircraft in the United States. Cessna's headquarters are located in Wichita, Kansas. Prior to 1981, Cessna enjoyed a history of outstanding success. However, between 1981 and 1985, sales and profits declined rapidly. The company lost more than $120 million in 1985 alone. Cessna was struggling to survive. This case focuses on Cessna Aircraft's problems and its sale to General Dynamics.

HISTORY

Cessna Aircraft Company was incorporated on September 7, 1927, but the company's actual beginnings can be traced to earlier events. On February 11, 1911, Clyde V. Cessna, an Enid, Oklahoma, car dealer, discovered his fascination with airplanes and flying at the Moisant International Aviation Air Circus in Oklahoma City. Clyde purchased and assembled a Bleriot airplane in which he installed his own water-cooled engine. Clyde Cessna taught himself to fly and began test flying the airplane. In June 1911, Mr. Cessna recorded his first successful flight and landing.

The years that followed were busy for Clyde Cessna. From 1912 through 1915, he spent the winters modifying airplanes. Each summer and fall, he performed aerial exhibitions in Kansas and Oklahoma. In the fall of 1916, an automobile manufacturer in Wichita let Clyde use his production facility in exchange for painting the name of the company's new car, the Jones-Six, on the bottom wing of Cessna's new plane.

The outbreak of World War I ended Clyde Cessna's flying until 1925, when he, Walter Beech, and Lloyd Stearman founded the Travel Air Manufacturing Company. Unfortunately, Mr. Beech and Mr. Cessna had different ideas regarding airplane designs. Beech preferred biplanes, and Cessna was convinced that monoplanes were the way of the future. These differences led to Cessna's resignation from Travel Air.

In a small shop in Wichita, Cessna designed a strutless monoplane. On September 8, 1927, he and Victor Roos organized the Cessna-Roos Company. Cessna's first factory, a 50-by 100-foot building, was constructed for $35,000 in December 1927, the same month that Roos left the company. When Roos departed, Cessna-Roos became known as the Cessna Aircraft Company.

As the United States approached World War II, Cessna Aircraft increased production to accommodate large military orders for training aircraft and troop/cargo gliders. In order to meet this increased demand, Cessna constructed another plant sixty miles northwest of Wichita. In its history, Cessna has won the Army-Navy "E" (for effort) Award five times.

With the end of World War II, Cessna returned to commercial production of two-seater light planes, in anticipation of a postwar boom in aviation. However, the anticipated boom was never realized, and the market for two-seater planes became saturated. Therefore, Cessna turned its production efforts to four- and-five-seat models.

The decades of the 1950s and 1960s were productive for Cessna. Cessna introduced the Skyhawk, the most popular airplane in history, and the Skylane, the most popular high-performance single-engine plane of the decade. During 1960, Cessna acquired a 49 percent interest in Reims Aviation, S.A. in France, and purchased McCauley Industrial Corporation, a manufacturer of propellers and other aircraft parts. Cessna's 50,000th plane was produced in 1963.

Cessna continued to lead the general aviation industry in the 1970s. During this decade, more than 1,100 Cessna Pilot Centers were opened across the nation. Cessna introduced its Citation, the world's leading business jet. The company was virtually unaffected by the recession of 1973–74.

The 1980s have not been so kind to Cessna. After achieving sales of more than $1 billion and a market share of 54 percent in 1980, the company began to experience declining sales and profits in 1981. Cessna ended fiscal year 1985 with a net loss of more than $120 million.

After two extensions and a delay, Cessna Aircraft Corporation was merged into a wholly owned subsidiary of General Dynamics on March 3, 1986. Exhibit 1 highlights Cessna's milestones from its first airplane through its merger with General Dynamics.

CESSNA'S PRODUCT LINE

Cessna specializes in the design and production of light commercial aircraft for business, personal, and military use, selling slightly more than 50 percent of the general aviation aircraft produced. The company also develops and produces a broad line of airborne navigation and communication equipment, including propellers, wheels, and brakes. To a lesser extent, Cessna manufactures hydraulic power systems for agricultural, construction, and light industrial uses; Cessna's market share for these products is estimated to be about 10 percent.

Cessna's most recent products include the Caravan I, the Caravan II, the Citation S/II, the Navy Citation, and the Citation III. The Caravan I, a utility aircraft, made its first flight in December 1982. It is a single-engine propjet with a 14-passenger load capacity. The Caravan I can be equipped with wheels, floats, or skis to allow effective operation on a variety of surfaces. Federal Express purchased thirty of these aircraft to go into service in December 1984 and ordered another seventy-nine in 1985.

The Caravan II, first introduced in Paris, is a twin-engine propjet utility aircraft. It is designed primarily for distribution in countries where aviation gasoline is scarce or expensive. The Caravan II's turbine engines use jet fuel.

Cessna's Citation business jets have been popular, accounting for 70 percent of Cessna's total aircraft sales. Citation II was introduced in 1978 and became a top-selling plane. The Citation S/II, a refinement of the Citation II, is designed to fly faster, go farther, and carry a larger load. Furthermore, Cessna guarantees lower operating costs for these planes than with turboprops. Cessna Chairman and Chief Executive Officer Russ Meyer and the Cessna Citation were chosen to receive the Collier Trophy in 1985.

The Navy Citation is also a refinement of the Citation II. In addition to improvements of the Citation S/II, the Navy Citation offers improved high-speed handling at low altitudes, plus better acceleration, climb rate, and speed. The Citation III is Cessna's newest and most advanced intercontinental business jet. The first Citation III was purchased by professional golfer Arnold Palmer.

In spite of its depressed sales, Cessna tried to follow a strategy of product development in the 1980s and allocated resources primarily to support this strategy. However, during 1984 Cessna halted production of more than ten models of aircraft, including Cutlas, Stationair, Skywagon, and agricultural aircraft. In 1985, Cessna stopped producing the Citation I.

COMPETITION

Cessna Aircraft Corporation has been the market leader in the general aviation industry, accounting for about 51 percent of the total output. The general aviation industry does not include military or commercial aircraft, but rather is comprised of personal and business planes. Cessna's major competitors are Piper Aircraft Corporation, Gates Learjet Corporation, and Beech Aircraft Corporation. Cessna, Piper, and Beech are the top three producers of general aviation aircraft in terms of volume. Until its merger with General Dynamics, Cessna was the only company among these top three not affiliated with a larger company.

Piper Aircraft Corporation is a subsidiary of Lear Siegler, a producer of electronic and automotive parts, farm equipment, and material-handling systems. Like Cessna, Piper has felt the impact of depressed sales. It has responded by consolidating its facilities and reorganizing its dealer structure.

Gates Learjet Corporation manufactures business jet aircraft, produces avionics equipment, and services its aircraft; almost 65 percent of Gates Learjet stock is owned

EXHIBIT 1 Cessna milestones

1911	Clyde Cessna builds and flies his first airplane.
1927	The Cessna Aircraft Company is formed on September 8.
1928	Cessna produces the first full-cantilever-wing light airplane to go into production in this country.
1936	For the third time, the Detroit News names the Airmaster the world's most efficient airplane, awarding the trophy to Cessna permanently.
1940	Production begins on the Bobcat, Cessna's first twin-engine plane.
1943	Cessna builds more than 750 gliders, capable of carrying thirteen troops plus equipment for the Army Air Force.
1944	Nearly 5400 Bobcat twins produced since introduction in 1940.
1946	Cessna returns to commercial production with the Models 120 and 140.
	Cessna's Fluid Power Division begins delivery of hydraulic power components to farm implement manufacturers.
1947	Production begins on the 5-place Models 190 and 195, Cessna's first all-metal airplanes.
1948	Cessna enters the 4-place airplane market with the Model 170.
1949	Cessna converts to metal-covered wings on the Models 120, 140, and 170.
1954	Introduction of the 310, Cessna's first business twin.
	Production of the T-37 Air Force jet trainer begins.
1956	Introduction of the Cessna Skyhawk, to become the most popular airplane in history.
	Introduction of the Cessna Skylane, to become the most popular high-performance single.
1959	Cessna purchases the Aircraft Radio Corporation as a wholly owned subsidiary
1960	Cessna affiliates with Reims Aviation, S.A., Reims, France.
	Cessna acquires McCauley, manufacturer of propellers and other aircraft components.
1963	Cessna produces its 50,000th airplane, a Skyhawk.
1965	Deliveries begin of the Model 411, Cessna's first cabin-class business airplne.
	Cessna announces the first turbocharged single-engine airplane, a Turbo Centurion.
	Cessna's new agricultural airplane, the Ag Wagon is introduced.
1967	The 75,000th Cessna airplane is delivered, a Skymaster.
	Cessna leads the industry in multiengine deliveries and total aircraft deliveries.
	Introduction of the Model 421 Golden Eagle, the first general aviation aircraft to combine cabin pressurization with a turbocharging system.
1968	The 1,00th T-37 jet trainer is delivered to the U.S. Air Force. Production of the new A-37B twin-jet attack aircraft begins.
1969	Introduction of the Aerobat adds a new dimension to flying through precision aerobatics.
	The Model 414 is introduced as Cessna's second pressurized business twin.

EXHIBIT 1 continued

1970	A nationwide network of Cessna SPilot Centers is inaugurated, featuring the exclusive Cessna Integrated Flight Training System.
1971	Introduction of the Cessna Citation, to become the world's leading business jet.
1972	The Model 340 is introduced to expand Cessna's pressurized twin market.
1975	Cessna delivers the 1,000th Golden Eagle.
	Cessna produces its 100,000th single-engine airplane.
1976	Deliveries begin on the all-new Titan, Cessna's largest piston-engine aircraft for business, commuter, and cargo use.
	Cessna announces initial design of the Citation III.
1977	Development begins of the Skylane RG, a retractable-gear version of the Skylane.
	Introduction of the Pressurized Centurion, the world's only pressurized single-engine piston airplane in production.
	First deliveries are made of the Conquest, Cessna's entry in the propjet market.
1978	First deliveries of the Citation II are made.
	Cessna leads the industry with the availability of weather radar on single-engine aircraft.
	The Ag Husky is introduced as the only turbocharged agricultural airplane in the world.
	Cessna refines and improves the most popular two-place training aircraft, and gives it a new name—the 152.
1979	The Turbo Centurion and Pressurized Centurion are certified for flight into icing, the only production singles to achieve this capability.
	Introduction of the Cutlass RG, to become the most popular retractable-gear airplane in its first year of production.
1980	Introduction of the Stationair 8—the only piston-powered 8-place single in production.
	Cessna sales top $1 billion for the first time.
	Cessna achieves an all-time high market share of 54 percent.
	Introduction of the Corsair propjet.
1981	First deliveries of the all-new Crusader twin.
1982	The 1,000th Citation is delivered.
	Introduction of the Citation III intercontinental business jet.
1984	Sale of ARC Avionics to Sperry-Rand.
	Introduction of improved P210.
1985	Introduction of Caravan I, single-engine turboprop with low operating costs.
	T47A begins operations as naval navigation trainer.
1986	Cessna Aircraft Company merges with General Dynamics.

Source: Company Reports.

by Gates Rubber Company. However, an agreement has been made for Gates to sell its share to a group led by Cobey Corporation for $6.50 per share. Gates Learjet is Cessna's closest competitor in terms of total general aviation dollar sales.

Beech Aircraft Corporation was founded in 1932 by Walter H. Beech, one-time partner of Clyde Cessna. Beech Aircraft is a wholly owned subsidiary of Raytheon Company. Raytheon, a *Fortune* 100 company, operates in five areas: electronics, aircraft products, major appliances, energy services, and other (which includes textbook publishing, field engineering, and construction). Beech has had to lay off 200 employees in an effort to alleviate the impact of depressed sales. Like Cessna, Beech Aircraft and Gates Learjet have home offices in Wichita.

THE MARKET

The market for general aviation planes has continued to decline during the first half of the 1980s in spite of favorable indications and projections. Unit volume in 1986 was only 8 percent of the peak of 17,811 aircraft in 1978. There are several reasons for the continued depression in general aviation. First, aircraft have a longer life. Second, the loss of the investment tax credit has hurt general aviation sales. Finally, product liability costs have become very high for these manufacturers. For example, Cessna faced more than $30 million in damage claims during 1984 because of design defects alleged to have caused two separate plane crashes. In 1986, Cessna was forced to lay off 900 employees (16 percent of its total work force) when it suspended the production of piston-engine airplanes for more than a year. According to Cessna's Chairman, Russell W. Meyer, Jr., the major factor in this decision was the large increases in product liability insurance premiums.

Furthermore, dealers are reluctant to stock new airplanes without retail contracts, due to previous losses, large inventories, and high interest rates. Dealers have been forced to reduce their sales staffs to offset high inventory costs. During 1984, Cessna went from 550 dealers and 700 dealer contracts to 190 dealers and 300 dealer contracts. In an effort to halt this decline in dealers, Cessna inaugurated a new dealer program to have fewer yet more financially secure dealers. Cessna established fifteen to twenty retail sales centers responsible for aircraft sales and eliminated wholesalers. The company also lowered the requirements for floor-planning aircraft.

During 1985, Cessna opened Hangar 10, aviation retail store prototypes, in Dallas and Minneapolis shopping centers. The purpose of these stores is to attract people into Cessna's flying lessons and eventually into Cessna's airplanes. These stores do not sell airplanes; they promote the idea of flying. Their merchandise includes aviation-oriented gifts, jewelry, videos, novelties, games and models, private label sportswear, pilot supplies, luggage, travel accessories, books and periodicals, photographs, and artwork. The focal point of each store is a flight module built around a Cessna Skyhawk airplane. Computerized video technology gives the consumers the sensation of flying. Cessna is also developing a Hangar 10 Club and a Hangar 10 credit card. The company plans to open 400 more Hangar 10 stores over the next five years.

Although financial experts do not forecast a sharp recovery for the general aviation industry, the last quarter of 1986 was better than expected, especially with exports.

SALES

Cessna Aircraft is considered the leader in the general aviation industry. However, Cessna's sales have continued to fall short of the $1.06 billion mark of 1981. During 1985, Cessna's total sales were $718 million, the highest they had been since 1982; unfortunately, Cessna's net loss was more than $120 million, or $6.20 per share. This was the greatest loss ever faced by the company. After its acquisition by General Dynamics, Cessna continued to record losses—more than $60 million for the first nine months of 1986.

During fiscal year 1985, Cessna increased sales of Citations and increased government business. Exhibit 2 reveals Cessna's sales by product type. Note that there has been a substantial decrease from 1981 to 1985 in sales of piston engine aircraft. Smaller decreases have been recorded in the sales of propjets and in fluid power sales. Propjet sales increased in 1985 over 1984 due to the introduction of the Caravan. The only long-range increases came in the sales of the Citation Fanjets and in government business.

Cessna's exports have also decreased during the early 1980s. In 1982, Cessna's export sales were 25 percent of total sales; whereas, in 1986, they were only 15 percent. According to Russell Roth, senior vice-president of finance, the reduction has been caused by restrictive import practices in many countries, a strong dollar, and a slow economic recovery in foreign countries. In addition, the process of licensing aircraft for use in foreign countries can be a slow, tedious process.

FINANCE

Selected financial data from Cessna's income statements and balance sheets for 1981 through 1985 are given in Exhibit 3. Cessna's net loss increased substantially in 1985. This net loss was primarily the result of management's establishment of several

EXHIBIT 2 Cessna's sales in millions of dollars by product type

	1981	*1982*	*1983*	*1984*	*1985*
Citation Fanjets	$364.4	$331.6	$211.5	$403.7	$420.3
Propjets	110.4	114.0	65.4	49.6	74.9
Piston Engine	431.1	234.4	135.0	104.7	85.2
Aircraft Parts	46.5	42.7	35.6	40.8	40.0
Government Business	4.2	4.5	5.2	4.2	13.3
Fluid Power	103.5	104.3	71.7	90.6	84.4

EXHIBIT 3 Selected financial data (in millions of dollars except for per share data)

	1981	*1982*	*1983*	*1984*	*1985*
Operating Results					
Sales	$1060.1	$831.5	$524.4	$693.6	$718.1
Earnings (loss) before tax	118.7	34.9	(37.4)	(31.7)	(146.9)
Net earnings (loss)	60.6	18.1	(18.8)	.9	(122.1)
Percent of sales	**5.7**	**2.2**	**(3.6)**	**.1**	**(17.0)**
Dividends paid	11.4	11.5	7.7	7.8	7.8
Expressed per share					
Net earnings (loss)	3.19	.94	(.98)	.05	(6.20)
Dividends	.60	.60	.40	.40	.40
Balance Sheet Data					
Current assets	412.9	329.3	391.1	354.6	336.3
Current liabilities	262.3	206.0	220.8	207.0	216.6
Working capital	150.6	123.3	170.4	147.7	119.7
Total assets	651.1	674.2	698.8	611.9	657.6
Fixed assets, net	90.8	99.0	92.9	82.7	80.8
Short-term borrowings	—	14.0	—	—	—
Long-term borrowings	35.7	33.9	129.5	125.2	123.3
Stockholders' equity	345.6	352.0	327.8	334.7	256.2
Equity per share	18.00	18.37	17.08	17.00	12.96

reserves, as shown in Exhibit 4. The establishment of these reserves also increased the liabilities. These reserves reflect changes that have occurred in market segments; they are provided to cover anticipated future expenses. The net loss was further affected by Cessna's inability to carry back all of its 1985 loss to previous years.

Working capital decreased by more than $40 million in 1985. More than 25 percent of this decrease resulted from the reclassification of certain current liabilities to noncurrent. The increase in cash by more than $50 million was the result of the sale of 3 million shares of preferred stock to General Dynamics.

ORGANIZATION

A list follows of the names and positions held by the executive officers of Cessna at the time of its acquisition by General Dynamics:

- ☐ Russell W. Meyer, Jr., Chairman of the board
- ☐ R. W. Van Sant, President
- ☐ Brian E. Barents, Senior vice-president, Marketing

EXHIBIT 4 Reserves established in 1985

Obsolete and inactive inventory	$28.7 million
T-47 program	25.0 million
Warranty expense	14.4 million
Product liability	13.2 million
Pollution control	8.4 million
Finance programs	7.5 million
Taxes	6.1 million

- Russell R. Roth, Senior vice-president, Finance
- John E. Moore, Senior vice-president, Personnel and Community Relations
- William A. Boettger, Senior vice-president, New Business Development
- Homer G. Nester, Vice-president and treasurer
- David R. Edwards, Secretary
- Thaine L. Woolsey, Vice-president and general manager, Fluid Power Division

Van Sant was elected president in 1983, at which time Meyer assumed sole responsibility as Cessna's chairman of the board. Van Sant joined Cessna after twenty-six years with John Deere Farm Equipment Company as vice-president of engineering and manufacturing services. Roth also assumed his position as senior vice-president of finance in 1983. Prior to that time, he was vice-president and controller of Allied Corporation's automotive group. Boettger assumed the position of senior vice-president of new business development in 1984. Before that, he had served seven years as the senior vice-president and general manager of the Pawnee Aircraft Division.

Cessna's principal manufacturing facilities are listed in Exhibit 5. In 1984 Cessna reorganized its Pawnee Road and Wallace aircraft manufacturing divisions into one division under single management. In addition to these facilities, Cessna leases facilities for service and maintenance operations at Houston, Texas; Orlando, Florida;

EXHIBIT 5 Cessna's principal manufacturing facilities

Location	*Product and Use*
Wichita, Kansas	
Pawnee Road Plant	Single-engine aircraft and executive offices
Wallace Plant	Turbine and twin-engine piston aircraft
Hutchinson, Kansas	Fluid power components and systems
Glenrothes, Scotland	Fluid power components and systems
Vandalia, Ohio	Aircraft propellers and accessories
Hampton, Iowa	Fluid power components and systems

Toledo, Ohio; Poughkeepsie, New York; and Sacramento, California. The company also leases space principally at airports for regional sales facilities.

RESEARCH AND DEVELOPMENT

Following a decrease of 13.6 percent in 1983, Cessna's research and development expenditures continued to decrease slightly. The long downturn in sales of general aviation aircraft hampered Cessna's efforts to fund research and development programs for the long term. In 1983, 1984, and 1985, respectively, Cessna spent $45 million, $57 million, and $41 million. The decrease in 1985 reflected substantial completion in the development of the Citation S/II, the T47A, and the Caravan I. In spite of these decreases, Cessna's expenditures for research and development in 1985 amounted to 5.7 percent of sales. This percentage is higher than those ratios for many competing companies.

In 1983, Cessna and General Dynamics Corporation entered into a joint technology program. General Dynamics, a leading United States defense contractor, produces military aircraft, Atlas and Centaur boosters, Tomahawk cruise missiles, and tactical missiles. Its marine division produces tankers, naval vessels, and Trident submarines. General Dynamics had long been interested in general aviation. In fact, the company had approached both Beech Aircraft and Gates Learjet about merger or acquisition possibilities. In exchange for $12.7 million, General Dynamics received 500,000 shares of Cessna's stock, which amounted to about 2.8 percent of the company's total shares at that time. In addition, David S. Lewis, then chairman of General Dynamics, became a member of Cessna's board of directors. The technology program included research and development in the areas of composite structures, aerodynamics, and flight control systems for high-performance aircraft. These new technologies were applied to Cessna's Citation, Conquest, and Caravan lines.

THE MERGER . . . AND BEYOND

At the time of the joint technology program in 1983, Meyer, Cessna's chairman, had stated that the program was not an indication of a merger between the two companies. However, on September 13, 1985, Cessna entered into an acquisition agreement with General Dynamics Corporation. General Dynamics contracted and agreed to buy those shares it did not already own for $30 per share or about $669 million. The offer was conditioned on the tendering of a minimum of 11,175,000 shares, which would give General Dynamics a minimum of 50.1 percent of Cessna's shares. Cessna and General Dynamics also entered into a preferred stock purchase agreement on that same date under which General Dynamics purchased three million shares of Cessna's series A preferred stock for $50 million. The merger cancelled and retired the preferred shares.

After two extensions of the merger agreement on the part of General Dynamics, the merger was indefinitely postponed on January 8, 1986, at which time General Dynamics owned 95 percent of Cessna's stock. This postponement followed a December 3, 1986, federal government ban on further contract awards to General Dynamics. This ban followed an investigation of General dynamics by a variety of government agencies and congressional committees for alleged overcharges and misuse of government funds, some amounting to hundreds of millions of dollars. General Dynamics feared that the ban could be applied to Cessna's government contracts as well. Cessna's T47A had begun operations in 1985 as a naval navigation trainer. In addition, Cessna had received an $18.9 million Navy contract for flight officer training in 1984. In 1986, the Air Force recommended during congressional hearings to extend the service of Cessna's T-37s used for initial pilot training.

On March 3, 1986, Cessna Aircraft Company was merged into a wholly owned subsidiary of General Dynamics with each outstanding common share converted to the right to receive $30 cash. With this acquisition, General Dynamics hoped to ease its heavy dependence on defense contracts, which amount to about 90 percent of its sales. The merger allows some diversification for General Dynamics and should benefit Cessna by giving it a parent company with more resources. Under the agreement, Meyer will continue to serve as chairman of the board and Van Sant will remain as president of Cessna. In addition, Meyer will be elected an executive vice-president of General Dynamics and appointed to its board of directors.

Unfortunately, the merger did not bring a sudden end to Cessna's troubles. In May 1986, General Dynamics laid off 2,500 Cessna employees and suspended piston engine airplane production. The continuing slump in the general aviation market led General Dynamics to write off $420 million during the fourth quarter of 1986. The first nine months of 1986 resulted in losses of about $60 million in its general aviation segment, which includes nearly all of Cessna. Analysts predict a modest loss for the Cessna division in 1987 and a potential advance in earnings through the last half of the 1980s.

Perhaps the major reason for Cessna's demise is the strong market for used planes. According to estimates by the Federal Aviation Administration, about 52,000 used planes will change hands in 1987, up from 46,000 in 1986. A 1978 Cessna 172, priced at $17,750 in 1982, commanded $33,000 in 1986. Cessna and its competitors will manufacture only 1,000 small planes this year, compared to 17,800 in 1978. Why is the demand for used single-engine and twin-engine planes surging? The answer is a major external threat—surging product liability costs:

> Manufacturers of small, piston-engine planes have suspended production in the face of escalating liability. One 1978 jury held Piper Aircraft liable for its design "defect" in using a carburetor rather than a fuel injection system. The engine was fully approved by the Federal Aviation Administration, and 90 percent of the other planes of that size used identical fuel systems. Beech continues to make a full line of planes but isn't making much money on them. Its product liability costs average $105,000 per plane. All this leaves the field to dangerous secondhand planes that were placed on the market at an earlier point in the liability system's spiral (*Forbes,* 13 July, 1987, p. 62).

ISSUES FOR CONSIDERATION

1. Was Cessna's decision to merge with General Dynamics a wise decision? What is your assessment of other alternative strategies that Cessna could have pursued at the time? Was the price tendered by General Dynamics ($30 per share) a "fair" price? Why or why not?

EXHIBIT 6 Summary financial information for General Dynamics, 1986 (in millions of dollars)

Net Sales	
Miliary aircraft	$ 2,671
Missiles, space, and electronic systems	2,329
Total Government Aerospace	**5,000**
Submarines	1,659
Land Systems	1,128
General Aviation	539
Material Service and Resources	476
Other	90
Total Net Sales	**$ 8,892**
Operating Earnings (Loss)	
Military aircraft	$ 335
Missiles, space and electronic systems	143
Total Government Aerospace	**478**
Submarines	175
Land systems	52
General aviation	(486)
Material service and resources	9
Other	1
Total Operating Earnings	**$ 229**
Earnings (loss) from continuing operations	(63)
Net earnings (loss)	(53)
Earnings (loss) per share from continuing operations	(1.46)
Net earnings (loss) per share	(1.23)
Capital expenditures	421
New business funds	308
At Year End, 1986	
Shareholders' equity	$ 1,264
Total assets	4,553
Outstanding shares of common stock	42,926,657
Number of employees	105,400

During the fourth quarter of 1986 General Dynamics wrote off $420 million of the purchase price of Cessna Aircraft; this reflected management's assessment of the general aviation, which had not recovered as anticipated. Without the effect of the company's charge to earnings for Cessna, net earnings were $367.7 million, or $8.61 per share for 1986.

2. What should Cessna do now? As the president of Cessna, prepare a strategic plan for presentation to the chief executive officer of General Dynamics. As chief executive officer of General Dynamics, prepare a strategic plan for presentation to the president of Cessna. What major differences exist between the two plans? How would you resolve the differences in deciding what Cessna should do? (Summary financial information for General Dynamics is given in Exhibit 6).

SUGGESTED READINGS

"Acquisition by General Dynamics Could Change Corporate Aircraft Business." *Flight International.* 28 September, 1985, 13.

"Cessna Aircraft Will Be Acquired by General Dynamics for $669 Million." *Wall Street Journal.* 16 September, 1985, 2; 17 September, 1985, 4; 23 September, 1985, 10; 3 October, 1985, 43.

"Cessna Aircraft Will Benefit from General Dynamics' Strength in Technology and Cash Position." *Flight International.* 12 October, 1985, 27.

"Cessna Banks on Retail Store for Plane Sales." *Sales and Marketing Management.* 3 February, 1986, 28–29.

"General Dynamics in the Dock." *Fortune.* 6 January, 1986, 8–9.

"General Dynamics Lands Cessna." *Fortune.* 14 October, 1985, 9–10.

"General Dynamics Under Fire." *Business Week.* 25 March, 1985, 70–76.

Gregory, W. H. "Diversification, Technical Gains Cited in Manufacturer Buyouts." *Aviation Week Space Technology.* 30 September, 1985, 18–19.

Huber, P. "Who Will Protect Us from Our Protectors?" *Forbes.* 13 July, 1987, 56–64.

Mayborn, M. and B. Pickett. *Cessna Guidebook.* (Dallas, Texas: Flying Enterprise Publications, 1973).

Winnebago Industries—1987

FRED R. DAVID
Auburn University

What has six feet of standup headroom, kitchen, dinette, shower, toilet, and closet, sleeps four, and gets 22 mpg on the highway? It's called LeSharo, a motor home made by Winnebago. Saving money is nice, but it isn't the real reason people travel in a motor home. Motor homing is just plain fun. Motor homers are an adventurous lot. They like to go, see, and do. Florida residents recently replaced Californians as the most active motor home campers. New Yorkers are third on the "most on the go" list. Recreational vehicle (RV) owners say they not only save money when camping, but they also "get the feel for where they are" by not having to stop for restaurants and bathrooms.

According to a recent study, motor home traveling is much less expensive than traveling by car or plane and staying in a motel. The average cost of eight nights in a motor home is $512, compared to $1,055 in a car/motel and $1,946 in a plane/motel.

Motor homers stop when there is really something to see and do. They often spend the summers where it is cool and the winters where it is warm.

Although once the undisputed leader in motor home sales, Winnebago Industries is now in second place between two major competitors: Fleetwood Enterprises and Coachmen Industries. Winnebago's motor home sales in 1986 were $346 million, down from $395 million in 1985 and $376 million in 1984. Comparatively, Coachmen's 1986 motor home sales were $300 million and Fleetwood's were an industry-leading $348 million. Based in Forest City, Iowa, Winnebago Industries' New York Stock Exchange symbol is WGO.

HISTORY

Early Motor Homing

Indians were the first Americans to engage in traveling with their home. American Indians did so for practical as well as recreational reasons. For them, survival was dependent upon staying close to sources of food, so as herds moved and weather changed, American Indians picked up their lightweight homes and traveled.

The first motor home was built in 1915 to take people from the Atlantic coast to San Francisco. The motor home had wood wheels and hard rubber tires. It was promoted as having all the comforts of an ocean cruiser. By the 1920s, the house car had become a fixture of America. A symbol of freedom, all kinds of house cars could be seen traveling all across America's dirt roads. They ranged from what looked like large moving cigars to two-story houses with porches on wheels. But these house cars had poor weight distribution, poor insulation, and poor economy. They gave way to the trailer in popularity from the 1930s to the 1950s.

In the mid 1950s, motor homes again emerged and were called motorized trailers. They were still overweight, underpowered, and poorly insulated, but they were vastly improved over the house cars of the 1920s. Then, in the 1960s, motor homing took off, largely due to the innovations of Winnebago. From Forest City, Winnebago set the pace for new developments in motor homes. The name "Winnebago" became synonymous with motor home. It became a household word in the 1960s.

Winnebago, 1958 to 1985

Founded in 1958 in Forest City, Iowa, Winnebago's phenomenal growth during the 1960s came to an end in 1970. That year was marked by a recession, and Winnebago's stock plunged nearly 60 percent before recovering. The OPEC oil embargo of 1973 and 1974 had disastrous effects on Winnebago because gas was either unavailable or unaffordable. The company's net income averaged less than one percent of sales between 1973 and 1978. From a sales level of $229 million in 1978, Winnebago's sales dropped to $92 million in 1979.

A troubled board of directors called John Hanson out of retirement in March 1979, re-electing him chairman of the board and president of Winnebago. Hanson had founded the company twenty-one years earlier. To resolve Winnebago's problems, Hanson reduced the number of Winnebago employees from 4,000 to 800 in less than nine months. He completely retired Winnebago's $18.5 million short-term debt within fourteen months. He initiated the development of propane conversion systems for motor homes. This system allows users to power their vehicles with less costly propane, eliminating worries about the supply and cost of gasoline. Hanson pioneered the development of a lightweight, fuel-efficient motor home powered by a revolutionary heavy-duty diesel engine. The following actions by Hanson helped reduce Winnebago's production capacity and retire debt:

1. selling the 131,000-square-foot plant in Riverside, California.
2. terminating the lease for the 66,000-square-foot van conversion plant in North Carolina.
3. closing the North Plant Complex in Forest City.
4. leasing to the 3M Company the 185,000-square-foot shipout building that comprised the South Plant Complex in Forest City.
5. consolidating all component assembly operations into one Main Production Plant.

Winnebago was nearly forced into bankruptcy in 1980 when net income was a negative $13.5 million. But conditions improved. Employment at Winnebago increased from 800 in 1980 to 1,400 by May 1981. The company introduced a fuel efficient, lightweight, aerodynamically designed line of motor homes. In 1982, Winnebago entered into an agreement with five manufacturers to allow use of the Winnebago name on products ranging from camping equipment to outdoor clothing. Winnebago declared its first cash dividend on common stock in October 1982, ten cents per share. In 1983, Winnebago introduced a new family of front wheel drive vehicles powered by Renault diesel engines. Sales of $239 million in 1983 set a company record, and the number of Winnebago employees was up to 2,200. On August 10, 1983, John Hanson was inducted into the Recreational Vehicle/Motor Home Hall of Fame in South Bend, Indiana. In 1984, Winnebago Industries won an award for the outstanding company turnaround in 1983.

In 1985, Winnebago's motor home sales were $395 million, up from $376 million in 1984. However, sales of other recreational vehicles and equipment, including van conversions and vans, declined to 19.3 million in 1985 from $21.2 million in 1984. Gross profit, as a percent of sales, decreased in 1985 to 13.7 percent from 15.9 the prior year. Winnebago Acceptance Corporation's (WAC) net income in 1985 was $456,000, down from $3.1 million in 1984. WAC provides financing for Winnebago dealers. Overall, Winnebago's net income declined to $18 million in 1985 from $27 million in 1984.

FISCAL YEAR 1986—WINNEBAGO'S INTERNAL OPERATIONS

Organization

Financial disappointments in fiscal 1985 led to a new management team being formed at Winnebago in 1986. Gerald Gilbert (age 53) was elected chief executive officer and president. Gilbert was previously president of a joint venture company between

Control Data Corporation and Honeywell, Inc. Clyde Church (age 39) was elected to a newly created position of vice president of product planning and engineering. Richard Berreth (age 50) was elected vice president of operations, and Bryan Hays (age 42) was elected vice president of sales and marketing. John Hanson (age 73) served as chairman of the board. Winnebago's current organizational chart is depicted in Exhibit 1.

Employees

As of September 1986, Winnebago had 2,520 employees, up from 2,130 employees in 1985. About 2,220 of these employees are involved in the shipping and manufacturing functions. Education programs initiated in 1985 were expanded in 1986 to involve more than 2,000 employees. These programs include approximately 21,000 hours of group instruction and 2,000 hours of computer instruction. Satellite transmission of computer programming classes from Iowa State University and the introduction of a chemical safety program for more than 1,700 employees are just two outstanding aspects of the education programs.

Winnebago has Task Force Teams and Action Teams designed to encourage employees at all levels to participate in decision-making. Task Force Teams consist of employees from Engineering, Concept Development, Marketing, Operations, Purchasing, and Materials. Action Teams are like quality circles. They encourage employees to find solutions to problems that affect productivity. Winnebago hopes these two programs will help its employees to work together as a team.

Winnebago also has a profit sharing plan and a stock bonus retirement plan for all eligible employees. For fiscal 1986, 1985, and 1984, Winnebago contributed $2.1 million, $3.6 million, and $2.4 million, respectively, to these two employee benefits.

Products

Winnebago manufactures three principal types of recreational vehicles: Type A motor homes, Type C motor homes, and van conversions. Type A motor homes are constructed on a chassis that already has the engine and drive components. Type A vehicles range in length from 22 to 37 feet. An example of the Type A motor home is the Elandan, which varies in length from 26 to 37 feet. The 31-foot Elandan offers a double-door refrigerator, water purification system, a four-burner range, water heater with electronic ignition, a powered range hood with deluxe monitor panel and digital clock, a shower, and rich carpet throughout. It can be purchased for approximately $60,000. Other Type A motor homes include the Chieftain, Windcruiser, and Itasca. Winnebago's newest Itasca Windcruiser model is 37 feet long and has a suggested retail price of $69,000.

Type C motor homes are constructed on a van chassis; their driver's compartment is accessible to the living area. Type C motor homes are compact and easy to drive. They range from 20 to 26 feet in range. The 20-foot LeSharo is an example of the Type C motor home. It can be purchased for approximately $33,000. The LeSharo has a two-liter diesel engine that gets 22 miles per gallon on the highway. This vehicle offers six-foot head room, a shower, a stove, a sink, a refrigerator, and two double

EXHIBIT 1 Winnebago's current organizational chart

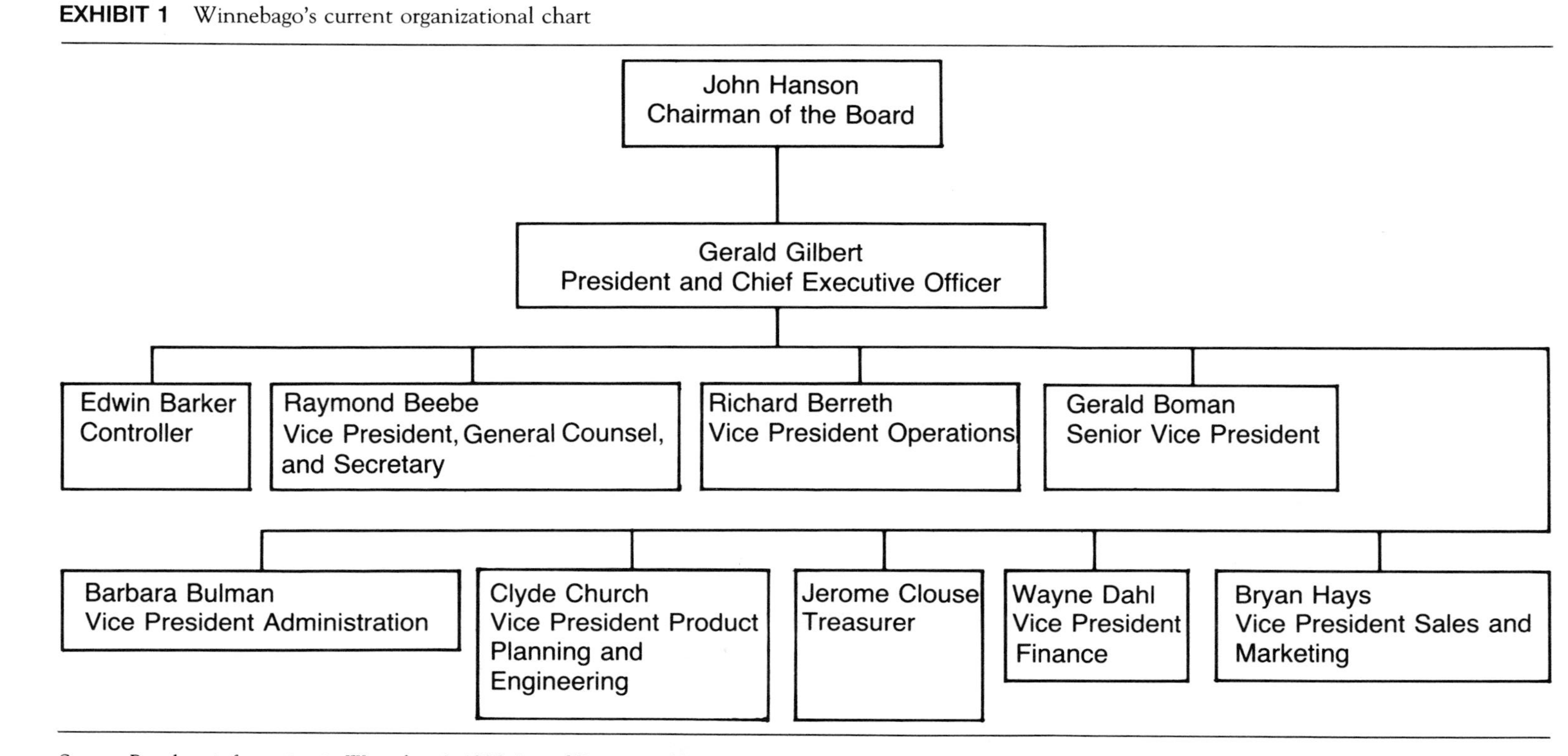

Source: Based on information in Winnebago's 1986 *Annual Report*, p. 29.

beds. The following passage discusses the popularity of the Minnie Winnie, one Type C motor home:

> There's a drive within all of us to forego the familiar and find new paths and places. Winnebago's Minnie Winnie is perfectly suited to meet this need. Minnie Winnie is the most popular Class C motor home in the country, because it has everything you need for life on the fly. It offers comfort, convenience, and performance at a very attractive price. With six models to chose from, there's a Minnie Winnie to meet your precise needs. And because it's built by Winnebago, you know that it will give you delightful, get-aways for years to come. Join the travelers who have discovered the way Minnie Winnie can turn any stretch of highway into a vacation spot (*Welcome Home*, 1986, p. 7).

The third type of recreational vehicle manufactured by Winnebago is van conversions. These vehicles are conventional vans manufactured by Ford, GMC, and Chrysler that are custom tailored by Winnebago with special interiors, exteriors, windows, and vents. An example is the 19-foot Centauri, the largest van conversion available. On a recent 3,000-mile test trip, the Centauri recently averaged 24.11 miles per gallon. In many American households, van conversions are replacing the family car as the vehicle of choice. Van conversions can change a long family trip from an ordeal to a pleasant adventure. Winnebago's unit sales of Type A and Type C motor homes and van conversions through 1986 are given in Exhibit 2.

In addition to recreational vehicles, Winnebago makes travel trailers that are pulled by car, pickup trucks, and vans. The company manufactures draperies, chairs, tables, metal stampings, aluminum products, and other plastic and fiberglass products for motor homes. The New Ventures Division of Winnebago has projects that include a vehicle for handicapped and elderly persons, and trams. A tram is a vehicle with a seating capacity of 274 persons that is designed for rapid loading and unloading. Universal Studios has ordered twenty-eight trams to be produced at a total cost of $9 million. Winnebago's net sales by major product line through 1986 are given in Exhibit 3.

EXHIBIT 2 Unit sales of Winnebago RV's

	Year Ended[1]				
	August 30, 1986	*August 31, 1985*	*August 25, 1984*	*August 27, 1983*	*August 28, 1982*
Motor Homes					
Type A	6,566	7,949	9,528	5,818	4,068
Type C	5,338	6,217	4,911	2,747	1,574
Total	**11,904**	**14,166**	**14,439**	**8,565**	**5,642**
Vans and Van Conversions	817	1,318	1,837	1,479	1,001

[1]The fiscal year ended August 31, 1985 contained 53 weeks; all other fiscal years in the table contained 52 weeks.

Source: Winnebago's 1986 *Annual Report*, page 10.

EXHIBIT 3 Winnebago's net sales by product class (dollars in thousands)

Year Ended (1)	**August 30, 1986**	August 31, 1985	August 25, 1984	August 27, 1983	August 28, 1982
Motor Homes	**$ 346,973**	$ 395,983	$ 376,733	$ 207,933	$ 129,578
	92.8%	93.3%	91.6%	86.9%	88.4%
Other Recreation Vehicle Sales (2)	**$ 16,901**	$ 19,369	$ 21,281	$ 18,077	$ 9,993
	4.5%	4.6%	5.2%	7.6%	6.8%
Total Recreation Vehicle Sales	**$ 363,874**	$ 415,352	$ 398,014	$ 226,010	$ 139,571
	97.3%	97.9%	96.8%	94.5%	95.2%
Non-Recreation Vehicle Sales (3)	**$ 9,945**	$ 8,821	$ 12,960	$ 13,255	$ 7,054
	2.7%	2.1%	3.2%	5.5%	4.8%
Total Sales	**$ 373,819**	$ 424,173	$ 410,974	$ 239,265	$ 146,625
	100.0%	100.0%	100.0%	100.0%	100.0%

(1) The fiscal year ended August 31, 1985 contained 53 weeks; all other fiscal years in the table contained 52 weeks.
(2) Primarily recreation vehicle related parts and service, van conversions and vans.
(3) Principally sales of extruded aluminum, commercial vehicles and component products for other manufacturers.

Source: Winnebago's 1986 *Annual Report*, p. 9.

Marketing

Type A and Type C motor homes are marketed under the Winnebago and Itasca brand names and are sold through a network of 371 dealers in the United States and Canada, down from 385 dealers in 1985. Less than 15 percent of the dealers account for more than 25 percent of Winnebago's motor home sales. Most Winnebago dealers also are dealers for automobiles and other motor home lines. Sales agreements with dealers are renewed on an annual or bi-annual basis. The locations of Winnebago's dealers are given in Exhibit 4. Notice that Florida, California, Texas, and Pennsylvania lead all states in the number of Winnebago dealers.

At the end of fiscal 1986, Winnebago had twenty-four field sales and service personnel to aid its dealers. Winnebago promotes its products through advertisements in national RV magazines and newspapers, on cable TV and radio and at trade shows. Almost all sales of motor homes to dealers are made on cash terms. Since 1984, Winnebago has offered a financing program to retail customers, providing ten-year terms at favorable rates. Winnebago Acceptance Corporation (WAC) provides "floor plan" financing for about eighty-five dealers in 1986, down from 100 dealers in 1985.

Numerous Winnebago caravans are arranged each year to travel across the United States, Mexico, and Canada. Customers can contact Winnebago International Travelers' (WIT's) home office at 515-582-6874 for information about nearby caravans. With more than 60,000 members since 1972, Winnebago International Traveler's

EXHIBIT 4 Winnebago's dealer locations at the end of fiscal 1986

State	*Number of Dealers*	*State*	*Number of Dealers*
Alabama	7	Nevada	6
Alaska	2	New Hampshire	3
Arizona	6	New Jersey	8
California	41	New Mexico	2
Colorado	8	New York	14
Connecticut	4	North Carolina	13
Delaware	2	North Dakota	3
Florida	25	Ohio	13
Georgia	5	Oklahoma	7
Idaho	5	Oregon	9
Illinois	10	Pennsylvania	24
Indiana	8	Rhode Island	1
Iowa	11	South Carolina	3
Kansas	6	South Dakota	3
Kentucky	4	Tennessee	5
Louisiana	6	Texas	19
Maine	3	Utah	3
Maryland	7	Vermont	1
Massachusetts	7	Virginia	6
Michigan	10	Washington	9
Minnesota	9	West Virginia	2
Mississippi	3	Wisconsin	9
Missouri	4	Wyoming	2
Montana	4	**Total**	**371**
Nebraska	6		

Club is one of the world's largest motor home associations. It organizes national, state, and local Winnebago rallies, has a monthly newspaper, and offer discounts at KOA campsites nationwide.

The Winnebago Logo

Eighty percent of all Americans recognize the Winnebago name. Nine licensees currently pay royalties to Winnebago for using the company's name on a range of products from camping equipment to clothing. Presently, 2,000 retail outlets carry at least one or more products bearing the Winnebago logo. Five major licensees of the Winnebago logo are given in Exhibit 5.

EXHIBIT 5 Some major licensees of the Winnebago logo

Licensee	*Products*
Outdoor Venture Corporation Steins, Kentucky	Cabin tents, screen rooms, dome tents, and sleeping bags.
Century Tool and Manufacturing Co. Cherry Valley, Illinois	Propane stoves, barbecues, and lanterns.
CSA, Inc. Foxboro, Massachusetts	Backpacks, sportsbags, and travel bags.
Taurus International, Inc. Wayne, New Jersey	Cotton rubberized air mattresses.
Oxford Industries, Inc. Atlanta, Georgia	Lines of men's rugged outdoor apparel: including shirts, sweaters, slacks, and jackets.

Although licensing of the Winnebago name began in fiscal 1982, revenues to date have not been significant. There are now Winnebago bass and fishing boats, marine flotation devices, backpacks, sport bags, travel bags, slacks, shorts, shirts, vests, jackets, gloves, socks, hats, stoves, lanterns, grills, sleeping bags, air mattresses, tents, screenhouses, and suitcases. Winnebago's Scout I sleeping bag, Chieftain IV tent, Double Diamond air mattress, and other products have been advertised in many magazines.

Production Facilities

Winnebago has major production facilities in Forest City, Iowa. These facilities encompass about 1.4 million square feet and contain the company's manufacturing, maintenance, and service operations. Winnebago has two leased fiberglass manufacturing facilities in Hampton, Iowa (69,300 and 74,000 square feet), and a sewing plant in Lorimor, Iowa (17,200 square feet). Winnebago has a parts distributor in Sparks, Nevada (28,000 square feet). The company also has 732,000 square feet of warehouse and executive office space in Forest City.

Winnebago manufactures most of the components used in its motor homes, but not the chassis, engines, auxiliary power units, or appliances. Winnebago uses computer technology to design all of its motor homes. A state-of-the-art, computer-aided-design/computer-aided-manufacturing system presently aids in producing low-cost sheet metal parts, new paint lines for steel and aluminum parts, and modifications in assembly equipment. The system was recently described in a *Winnebago Rolling Review* article:

> Under the computer-based system, a new design can take shape much more quickly than in the past. Working with the image of a motor home on a television-like monitor, designers can move the walls, alter the floorplan, make it longer or shorter, or change the entire styling. All that's necessary is a few quick sweeps of an electronic "pen" across a special template. The speed and flexibility afforded by computers allow Winnebago designers to explore new styles and experiment with more efficient, more economical motor homes (Vol. 11, No. 1, p. 8).

Winnebago has four, 1,000-foot assembly lines for producing its motor homes. As a motor home flows down the assembly line, quality control is carefully monitored. Units are randomly taken from the assembly line for a thorough examination. The performance of every RV is tested before it is delivered to a dealer's lot.

Winnebago performs a variety of tests on all of its products. The company makes sure all of its motor home components meet or exceed federal standards. Some of the tests routinely performed include lamination strength tests, appliance performance tests, chip resistance tests, vibration tests, drop tests, salt spray tests, and crash tests.

Financial Information

Winnebago's sales decreased 11.9 percent in fiscal 1986 compared to fiscal 1985. Unit volume of motor home shipments declined 16.0 percent. Selling and administrative expenses increased from 4.2 percent of sales in 1985 to 4.5 percent in 1986. General and administrative expenses also increased from 3.3 percent of sales in fiscal 1985 to 4.9 percent in fiscal 1986. Winnebago's 1984, 1985, and 1986 consolidated income statements and balance sheets are given in Exhibit 6 and Exhibit 7, respectively. A detailed inventory summary is given in Exhibit 8.

Winnebago's net earnings in 1986 totaled $19,665,000, or $.77 a share, up 9 percent over net earnings in 1985 of $18,089,000. However, net sales in 1986 declined to $373.8 million from $424.2 million the year before. Lower motor fuel prices, lower interest rates, and lower inflation rates were favorable to motor home sales growth, but uncertainty about tax legislation, energy resources, and agricultural conditions hurt Winnebago's sales. Winnebago made it's first appearance on the Fortune 500 list of the largest U.S. manufacturers in April 1986. It ranked as Number 500. In October 1986, Winnebago celebrated production of its 200,000th motor home in 20 years. The first Winnebago motor home was built in October 1966.

Winnebago's principal uses of cash during 1986 were to purchase capital assets ($9.6 million), to pay cash dividends ($5.1 million), and to make advances to Winnebago Acceptance Corporation ($30.0 million). The company's working capital on August 30, 1986, was $73.4 million, a decrease of $15.7 million from the same time in 1985. Winnebago has a revolving credit agreement with two banks for $35 million. Additional short-term credit totaled $15 million at the end of fiscal 1986.

Research and Development (R&D)

Winnebago's R&D expenses charged to operations for fiscal 1986, 1985, and 1984 were approximately $2.4 million, $1.8 million, and $1.9 million, respectively. Winnebago's R&D expenses include a major development program that was begun five years ago. The results of this program include:

1. Ninety percent of Winnebago's models did not exist five years ago.
2. The Elandan and Windcruiser that were introduced in 1984 are already setting sales records.
3. Winnebago now uses certain components that are unique in the industry.

EXHIBIT 6 Winnebago's consolidated income statements (dollars in thousands except per share data)

Year Ended	**August 30, 1986**	August 31, 1985	August 25, 1984
Net sales	**$ 373,819**	$ 424,173	$ 410,974
Cost of goods sold	**329,219**	365,979	345,685
Gross profit	**44,600**	58,194	65,289
Operating expenses:			
Selling and delivery expenses	**16,797**	17,663	15,182
General and administrative expenses	**18,172**	13,900	10,425
Total operating expenses	**34,969**	31,563	25,607
Operating income	**9,631**	26,631	39,682
Financial income, net	**17,944**	2,892	2,501
Income before income taxes and equity method income	**27,575**	29,523	42,183
Provision for income taxes	**9,186**	11,890	18,016
Income before equity method income	**18,389**	17,633	24,167
Equity in net income of unconsolidated subsidiaries	**1,276**	456	3,650
Net income	**$ 19,665**	$ 18,089	$ 27,817
Net income per common share	**$ .77**	$ .71	$ 1.10
Weighted average number of shares of common stock (in thousands)	**25,641**	25,509	25,397

Source: Winnebago's 1986 *Annual Report*, p. 14.

In 1986, Winnebago culminated R&D development and began operation of the most advanced modeling bridge used in the motor home industry. Used for development of new motor home designs, the modeling bridge has a digital electronic scanner that feeds data into Winnebago's computer drafting system.

WINNEBAGO'S EXTERNAL ENVIRONMENT

Economy

Since motor homes are primarily used for leisure travel and outdoor recreation, the peak retail selling seasons are concentrated in the spring and summer months. During fiscal years when interest rates are high, sales decline substantially. Industry sales of

EXHIBIT 7 Winnebago's consolidated balance sheets (dollars in thousands)

Assets	**August 30, 1986**	August 31, 1985
Current Assets		
Cash and marketable securities	**$ 52,257**	$ 29,944
Receivables, less allowance for doubtful accounts	**21,322**	21,162
Income tax refund receivable	**—**	3,500
Inventories	**54,991**	72,876
Prepaid expenses	**2,732**	3,087
Deferred income taxes	**5,531**	3,818
Total current assets	**136,833**	134,387
Investments		
Investments in and advances to unconsolidated subsidiary, at equity in net assets	**45,628**	15,397
Property and Equipment, at cost		
Land	**1,421**	1,315
Buildings	**32,129**	28,881
Machinery and equipment	**61,888**	57,600
Transportation equipment	**4,881**	4,692
	100,319	92,488
Less accumulated depreciation	**50,340**	42,134
Total property and equipment, net	**49,979**	50,354
Other Assets	**2,273**	2,403
Total Assets	**$ 234,713**	$ 202,541

recreational vehicles declined 6 percent in 1986 from 1985, due partly to rising interest rates. Increasing gas prices also have a negative effect on Winnebago sales. Whenever trouble erupts in the Persian Gulf area, gas prices tend to increase.

Winnebago motor homes are not just for the wealthy. Lower-priced Winnebago's sell for less than many automobiles. Some families rent motor-homes for vacation. You do not have to be overly affluent to enjoy the benefits of a motor home. However, as the number of two-income families increases and individuals have more disposable income, Winnebago sales generally increase.

The Tax Reform Act of 1986 allows for interest payments on motor homes to be deducted, just like interest on a second residence. This legislation could positively

EXHIBIT 7 continued

Liabilities and Stockholders' Equity	**August 30, 1986**	August 31, 1985
Current Liabilities		
Current maturities of long-term debt	**$ 1,050**	$ 1,171
Bank acceptances	—	3,363
Notes payable	**15,000**	—
Accounts payable, trade	**23,639**	19,905
Accrued expenses:		
Insurance	**3,058**	2,575
Profit sharing and bonus	**2,841**	3,495
Other	**6,511**	5,566
Income taxes payable	**5,823**	4,265
Liability on product warranties	**5,476**	4,825
Total current liabilities	**63,398**	45,165
Long-term Debt	**3,150**	4,200
Deferred Compensation	**1,607**	1,226
Deferred Income Taxes	**15,026**	15,465
Stockholders' Equity		
Capital stock, common, par value $.50; authorized 60,000,000 shares; issued 25,730,000 and 25,588,000 shares	**12,865**	12,794
Additional paid-in capital	**27,022**	26,203
Reinvested earnings	**112,603**	98,070
	152,490	137,067
Less treasury stock, at cost	**958**	582
Total Stockholders' Equity	**151,532**	136,485
Total Liabilities and Stockholders' Equity	**$ 234,713**	$ 202,541

Contingent Liabilities and Commitments (Notes 4 and 7)

Source: Winnebago's 1986 *Annual Report*, pp. 12 and 13.

EXHIBIT 8 A Winnebago inventory summary

Dollars in thousands	Aug. 30, 1986	Aug. 31, 1985
Finished goods	$ 22,970	$ 31,273
Work in process	10,542	10,363
Raw materials	31,959	39,781
	65,471	81,417
LIFO reserve	10,480	8,541
	$ 54,991	$ 72,876

Source: Winnebago's 1986 *Annual Report*, p. 18

affect Winnebago and other motor home manufacturers. Other aspects of the tax legislation however could hurt Winnebago sales, such as the investment tax credit provisions and the lengthening of depreciation schedules.

Motels and Restaurants versus Motor Homes

Motor home manufacturers such as Winnebago provide plentiful statistics to show that traveling and eating in a motor home is considerably less expensive than traveling via motels and restaurants. The motel industry and restaurant industry, however, are becoming more and more competitive, driving prices down and making that approach to traveling more affordable. Motor home sales increase whenever travel, tourism, and vacationing gain in popularity. Conversely, motor home sales decrease whenever leisure time activities decline.

Campgrounds

There are about 121,480 campsites in America's state parks. There are another 4,476 campgrounds in the U.S. Forest Service and 104 in our National Park system. In addition, the United States has more than 15,000 private campgrounds and more than 1,620 county parks. Winnebagos can access nearly all of these sites.

COMPETITORS

Winnebago's two major competitors in the motor home industry are Fleetwood Enterprises and Coachmen Industries. These two companies' sales in 1986 were $1,218 million and $348 million, respectively. Their net profit margins were 3.2 and 1.2, respectively, compared to Winnebago's 5.0.

Fleetwood

Fleetwood is headquartered in Riverside, California. The company has manufacturing plants in seventeen states and has approximately 10,000 employees. Fleetwood recreational vehicles include travel trailers and motor homes. The travel trailers are sold under the trade names Avion, Prowler, Terry, and Wilderness. The motor homes are sold under the names Bounder, Limited, Pace, Arrow, Southwind, Jamboree, and Tioga. The company's products are sold by 3,800 independent dealers. Retail prices range from $25,000 to more than $80,000. Fleetwood RV's are predominantly sold to 35-54-year-old individuals.

In 1986, Fleetwood introduced a new Bounder motor home that featured innovations not available in any competitive RV. The company also introduced a more affordable line of Type C motor homes. Motor home sales for fiscal 1986 were $438.1 million on unit shipments totaling 12,628, as described in Exhibit 9. Fleetwood's manufactured housing (mobile home) sales were $524.4 million on shipments of 40,000 homes; this figure is more than double that of Fleetwood's major competitor in the mobile home industry. Fleetwood believes that its future will be bright because of improving economic conditions, lower gasoline prices, lower interest rates, and higher levels of employment.

EXHIBIT 9 Fleetwood's financial summary

	Years ended April				
Dollars in Thousands	*1986*	*1985*	*1984*	*1983*	*1982*
Manufactured Housing					
Sales	**$524,168**	**$495,947**	**$517,792**	**$343,008**	**$232,026**
Units shipped					
Single-section	25,443	24,139	29,225	20,357	12,147
Multi-section	14,492	13,454	11,824	6,442	4,226
Total	**39,935**	**37,593**	**41,049**	**26,799**	**16,373**
Recreational Vehicles					
Sales					
Travel trailers	$252,772	$255,213	$294,918	$194,728	$167,596
Motor homes	438,144	521,748	604,487	319,083	180,696
Total	**$690,916**	**$776,961**	**$899,405**	**$513,811**	**$348,292**
Units shipped					
Travel trailers	25,573	27,026	33,297	22,779	20,784
Motor homes	12,628	17,289	20,511	11,206	7,144
Total	**38,201**	**44,315**	**53,808**	**33,985**	**27,928**

Source: Fleetwoods 1986 *Annual Report,* page 2.

Coachmen

Coachmen is headquartered in Elkhart, Indiana. Coachmen's net sales decreased from $356 million in 1985 to $348 million in 1986, a 2.1 percent decline. However, net income increased 14.7 percent from $3.8 million in 1985 to $4.3 million in 1986, as described in Exhibit 10. There were 3,195 Coachmen employees at the end of fiscal 1986, down from 3,294 the year before. Coachmen feels that because of the tax deductibility of interest on recreational vehicles as second homes, their sales will improve. For 1986, motor homes composed 53 percent of Coachmen's sales, travel trailers 16 percent, camping trailers 3 percent, truck campers 1 percent, parts and supplies 9 percent, ambulances 4 percent, and manufactured housing 14 percent. Coachmen has 1,100 dealers.

New developments at Coachmen in 1986 included the acquistion of 90 percent of the outstanding shares of common stock of Southern Ambulance Builders, Inc. Also in 1986, Coachmen sold the operations and assets of its Kenco Engineering Division. A new Royal Coachmen was introduced in 1986. This model incorporates all of Coachmen's most popular features. Coachmen RVs are manufactured and marketed through six companies, including Coachmen Van Conversions, Shasta Industries, Coachmen Recreational Vehicle Company, Sportscoach Corporation of America, Viking Recreational Vehicles, and Travelmaster Recreational Vehicles. The largest and oldest of Coachmen's RV companies, Coachmen Recreational Vehicle Company mar-

EXHIBIT 10 Coachmen's financial summary

	1986	*1985*	*1984*
Net Sales			
Recreational vehicle	$300,310,856	$319,143,207	$478,250,649
Manufactured housing	48,538,405	37,048,127	43,017,776
General corporate	—	—	—
Total	**$348,849,261**	**$356,191,334**	**$521,268,425**
Operating Income (Loss)			
Recreational vehicle	$ 7,689,979	$ 8,355,098	$ 31,770,832
Manufactured housing	112,815	(3,906,567)	(2,550,249)
General corporate	(6,602,321)	(7,102,067)	(7,061,884)
Total	**$ 1,200,473**	**$ (2,653,536)**	**$ 22,158,699**
Identifiable Assets			
Recreational vehicle	$ 85,464,986	$ 93,456,907	$ 90,865,930
Manufactured housing	8,536,612	8,480,256	9,773,167
General corporate	30,476,615	36,738,133	32,120,265
Total	**$124,478,213**	**$138,675,296**	**$132,759,362**

Source: Coachmen's 1986 *Annual Report,* p. 19.

kets and manufactures a complete line of Class A and Class C motor homes, travel trailers, mini motor homes, fifth wheel trailers, truck campers, and camping trailers.

FUTURE PLANS, PROBLEMS, AND CONCERNS

Many of the materials Winnebago uses to make motor homes are used to make mobile homes or manufactured houses. Winnebago's competitors derive a significant portion of their income from sales of manufactured housing. Although Winnebago currently does not manufacture mobile homes, diversification into this type of manufacturing could be a possibility for Winnebago in the future. Industry sales of manufactured homes declined 14.2 percent in 1986 as compared to 1985.

In October 1986, Winnebago acquired a majority interest in Cycle Video, Inc., a satellite courier business specializing in transmissions of commercials to TV stations. This acquisition was the first in Winnebago's history; it represents conglomerate diversification into the telecommunications industry. To build upon this initial foothold, Winnebago could pursue other acquisitions in the telecommunications industry.

In the future, it may become necessary for Winnebago to build regional production facilities to serve local markets. California, New York, and Florida, where most motor homers live, are a long way from Forest City, Iowa. Shipping costs alone to large dealers in these states is substantial.

Foreign markets are virtually untapped by producers of motor vehicles. Motor homing in foreign countries is not too popular at present, but this situation may change. No major motor home manufacturer has mounted a concerted effort to penetrate the international market.

Winnebago is experiencing some problems with its dealers' ability to service the new Renault engines. Many dealers are reluctant to carry the new, smaller RVs. This problem must be corrected by Winnebago in the future.

In Winnebago's 1986 *Annual Report,* John Hanson, chairman of the board, and Gerald Gilbert, president and chief executive officer, summarized their outlook for Winnebago as follows:

> Winnebago's new management team is developing strategies to best utilize the skills of our employees, the expanded capabilities of our equipment and facilities, and our leadership position in the motor home business. At the same time, the team is reviewing opportunities for growth in other areas. The ultimate objective of these plans is achievement of annual sales in excess of a billion dollars and net earnings of 10 percent of sales in the 1990s. For 1987, efforts are being directed specifically toward cost reductions by better equipment utilization, standardization, and just-in-time inventory systems. The widest range of vehicles ever produced by Winnebago is being offered in 1987 (p. 6).

Chrysler Corporation—1987

FRED DAVID
Auburn University
PHILLIPPE LINDSAY
Auburn University

> I didn't take $1 a year to be a martyr. . . . I did it for cold, pragmatic reasons. I wanted our employees and our suppliers to be thinking: 'I can follow a guy who sets that kind of example.'
>
> Lee A. Iacocca
> Chrysler Corporation chairman

No one would ever imagined that any top-level executive would except $1 for annual salary. But in 1987, everyone had noticed what a shrewd move Iacocca had made. By foregoing a salary in 1980 and taking stock options instead, Iacocca received $20.5 million in compensation in 1986 to lead all chief executive offices in America. Although this compensation could be called excessive, many people feel Iacocca earned every penny by turning around the nearly bankrupt Chrysler Corporation.

Since its inception in 1925, Chrysler has been riding a financial rollercoaster; record profits have usually been followed by record losses. Unsynchronized market strategies historically have led to Chrysler's reliance on good economic conditions for good economic health. Although at one time Chrysler was the United States' second largest automaker, it has slipped to third placed behind General Motors Corporation (GMC) and Ford Motor Company. Chrysler has recently completed the acquisition of American Motors Corporation (AMC) to prove its competitive position in world markets. But AMC has experienced a cumulative loss of $518 million during its 33-year lifetime, and plants are currently operating at only 49 percent capacity. The AMC acquisition pushes Chrysler's overall unfunded pension liability past $1.1 billion and raises its debt/equity ratio from 47 percent to 60 percent. This increase has occurred at a time when foreign automakers are building U.S. plants rapidly. Iacocca looked good in 1986, but 1990 may be a different story.

HISTORY

The Early 1900s

In 1922, Walter Chrysler assumed chairmanship of the ailing Maxwell Motor (MM) Company. He immediately persuaded creditors of Maxwell to extend new loans and to convert old debt to stock options. Following a major reorganization, MM built a new car centered around a high-compression engine. The car was called the Chrysler. It immediately became the company's best-selling model, and in 1925, Maxwell Motor Company changed its name to Chrysler Corporation.

By 1927, Chrysler was ranked fifth in the U.S. auto industry and was selling 192,000 cars annually. In order to expand production and avoid expenditures associated with construction of a new plant, Chrysler acquired the Dodge Brother's Car Company. With this acquisition, Chrysler became the nation's second-largest automaker overnight and received an excellent reputation for reliability and superior engineering that had made Dodge famous. However, following the acquisition of Dodge, Chrysler was saddled with enormous debt and did not become profitable again until 1934. During the late 1930's and early 1940's, Chrysler was financially sound and successful.

The death of Walter Chrysler and World War II signaled a change in Chrysler's fortunes. The company was slow in readying new models to meet post-war demand and operated at 75 percent capacity during the first half in 1948. *Fortune* noted that Chrysler "lacked some of that competitive fire and restless ambition that drove the company, under Walter Chrysler, to constant experimentation and innovation." Nevertheless, Chrysler's market share rose to 22 percent in 1951 due to an overall increase in industry demand. By 1953 however, Chrysler's market share had dropped to 12 percent. Chrysler's position continued to worsen until 1962 when its market share fell below 10 percent.

The appointment of Lynn Townsend as chairman and chief executive officer of Chrysler proved to be significant in Chrysler's history. He consolidated the Chrysler and Plymouth Divisions into a single operating unit, closed redundant plants, cut the white-collar work force by more than 25 percent, and computerized operations to eliminate 700 clerical employees. Townsend also implemented a 5-year/50,000-mile warranty (called the "gutsiest" warranty ever seen) and is credited for the creation of Chrysler's famous "Pentastar" symbol. A 30-year veteran of Chrysler recently recalled, "Townsend was probably the most creative and energetic leader Chrysler ever had, including Iacocca." Townsend rescued a company with just about "every problem in the book," including low market share, poor product quality, and a fading corporate image. Townsend believed that to serve shareholders' best interests, Chrysler had to become a multinational company. Townsend began Chrysler's most ambitious expansion program ever.

Chrysler diversified into several different industries in the 1960s. An auto leasing subsidiary was set up in 1962. Chrysler Realty was formed in 1967 to manage and market land for Chrysler dealerships. Chrysler Defense began production of the M-60 battle tank. Chrysler Chemical extended its product lines, and Chrysler Marine expanded into manufacturing boats and marine engines. Chrysler increased its holdings in France's second-largest automaker from 25 percent to 64 percent. Chrysler also acquired two-thirds of the stock in the Rootes Automotive Group, which eventually became known as Chrysler, U.K. By 1969, Chrysler had plants in eighteen countries.

The 1970s

By 1970, the American auto industry was showing signs of strain. The number of imports entering the United States was increasing dramatically. Chrysler chose not to enter the sub-compact market to compete with Ford's Pinto and GM's Vega. By 1973,

Chrysler fielded 30 percent fewer cars than it had in 1971. Chrysler President John J. Riccardo said, "Quite frankly, I think the day this company really turned around was the day we decided not to build that sub-compact. Chrysler no longer operates by knee-jerk reaction. It does not imitate everything that competitors do." Following this, Chrysler sunk $450 million into restyling all its large cars. In 1974, the Organization of Petroleum Exporting Countries (OPEC) declared an oil embargo on the United States. Overnight, the bottom dropped out of the large car market. The last quarter of 1974 saw Chrysler lose a record $74 million, a feat that would later be broken. In early 1975, the cover of *Business Week* featured a photograph of several acres of unsold 1975 Chryslers in storage (complete with rust) at the Michigan State fairgrounds.

The fall of 1975 saw the introduction of the Dodge Aspen and Plymouth Volare line of compact cars. Originally planned as a replacement for the popular Dodge Dart/ Plymouth Valiant, the Volare was instead introduced as a luxury compact to attract high-income customers. Chrysler's strategy seemed to be working. Consumers that were used to more luxurious automobiles, but worried about gas mileage, turned to Chrysler as the only maker of smaller deluxe cars.

Chrysler's position seemed solid once more by the fall of 1976. The Aspen/Volare line appeared to be a triumph (63 percent of Aspen/Volare buyers were new Chrysler customers) and temporarily restored Chrysler's dominance of the compact market. The year 1976 produced record profits, cost-cutting measures, and a 31 percent increase in sales (outdistancing the 22 percent industry-wide increase).

Beginning in 1977, Chrysler suffered a series of reversals that again placed the company's future in jeopardy. A mass modernization plan proposed in 1978 was met with tremendous scepticism. According to one commentary on Chrysler's modernization plan: "The attitude in the financial community and elsewhere seems to be: Here comes Chrysler again, hungry for capital, and peddling yet another one of those plans to save the company."

Following a record loss of $159 million in the third quarter of 1978, a proposed massive stock issue to fund the first stage of the $7.5 billion plan was announced. Two days after the approval of the stock issue, strategic plans involving major sell-offs of Australian, British, and other European operations were announced. This move increased public uncertainty about Chrysler's financial condition. At this point in time, Lee Iacocca was named Chrysler's president and CEO.

The Iacocca Years

During 1979, Chrysler teetered on the edge of bankruptcy. Expectations were for the company to fall short by more than $1 billion in its capital needs for 1979 and 1980. Chrysler was losing money at the rate of $1,000 a minute, and at any given moment, it had only 10 minutes of cash on hand. By the end of 1979, Chrysler had accumulated losses of $1.4 billion, an all-time American record.

In April 1980, Lee Iacocca went before the Chrysler Loan Guarantee Board requesting $1.2 billion in federally guaranteed loans. While persuading the government was the most conspicuous accomplishment by Iacocca, his carefully selected executive team orchestrated a wide range of financial, marketing, product planning, product engineering, and labor relations strategies.

Chrysler's comeback since 1980 has been unprecedented considering environmental conditions of the U.S. auto industry during the 1980s: the worst sales slump in thirty years, a national economy plagued by both recession and inflation, interest rates approaching 20 percent, fuel prices that precipitated unpredictable vehicle demand, and the strongest invasion of import cars ever encountered. The strategic management and ownership changes since Iacocca's appointment are summarized in Exhibit 1.

CHRYSLER TODAY

Chrysler and its subsidiaries manufacture, assemble, and sell Chrysler, Dodge, and Plymouth passenger cars, Dodge trucks, and related automotive parts and accessories. Chrysler also imports and distributes (under the Dodge and Plymouth trade names) small passenger cars and trucks manufactured in Japan by Mitsubishi Motors Corporation (MMC). Chrysler owns 24 percent of the capital stock of MMC. Chrysler and MMC have formed a 50/50 joint venture known as Diamond-Star Motors to manufacture small cars in the United States. The construction of an assembly/stamping plant, located in Bloomington-Normal, Illinois, began in 1986, and production begins the fall of 1988. The financial position of Chrysler is presented in the consolidated statement of earnings and balance sheet, in Exhibit 2 and Exhibit 3, respectively.

EXHIBIT 1 Chrysler's strategic ownership changes under Iacocca

August 1979	Chrysler sells its European subsidiary to Peugeot for $230 million and 12.5% equity in Peugot.
February 1979	GMC Purchases Chrysler assembly operations in Brazil and Venezuela.
April 1980	Volkswagen acquires Chrysler's equity in Chrysler Argentina.
May 1980	Mitsubishi purchases Chrysler's equity in Chrysler Australia.
December 1980	Volkswagen acquires Chrysler de Brazil.
April 1985	Chrysler increases holdings in Mitsubishi from 15% to 24%.
April 1985	Chrysler announces joint venture with Mitsubishi for 50/50 ownership in Diamond Stand Motors Plant to be built in Bloomington-Normal, Illinois.
April 1985	Chrysler announces joint venture with Maserati to build two-seat luxury coupe for sale in the U.S.
April 1986	Construction began on Diamond-Star Motors Plant in Bloomington-Normal Illinois.
June 1986	Chrysler sells its remaining equity in Peugot.
June 1986	Chrysler increases equity state in Maserati from 3.5% to 15.6%.
March 1987	Chrysler announces intention to acquire American Motors Corporation.
April 1987	Chrysler purchases 100% of Lamborghini.

EXHIBIT 2 Chrysler Corporation and Consolidated Subsidiaries consolidated statement of earnings.

	Year Ended December 31		
	1986	1985	1984
	(In millions of dollars)		
Net sales	$22,586.3	$21,255.5	$19,572.7
Equity in earnings of unconsolidated subsidiaries	298.6	255.9	126.1
Other income	120.7	41.7	18.4
	23,005.6	21,553.1	19,717.2
Costs, other than items below	18,635.2	17,467.7	15,528.2
Depreciation of plant and equipment (Note 4)	236.8	263.7	271.6
Amortization of special tools (Note 4)	306.8	212.6	282.8
Selling and administrative expenses	1,376.8	1,144.4	987.7
Pension plans (Note 11)	236.3	219.8	267.3
Interest (income) expense–net (Note 9)	32.7	(124.9)	(50.7)
Gain on sale of investment in Peugeot S.A. (Note 3)	(144.3)	—	—
	20,680.3	19,183.3	17,286.9
EARNINGS BEFORE TAXES AND EXTRAORDINARY ITEM	2,325.3	2,369.8	2,430.3
Taxes on income (Note 12)	921.7	734.6	934.2
EARNINGS BEFORE EXTRAORDINARY ITEM	1,403.6	1,635.2	1,496.1
Extraordinary item–effect of utilization of tax loss carryforwards (Note 12)	—	—	883.9
NET EARNINGS	$ 1,403.6	$ 1,635.2	$ 2,380.0
	(In dollars or shares)		
Per share data (restated to reflect stock splits–see Notes 8 and 15)			
Primary:			
Earnings before extraordinary item	$ 6.31	$ 6.25	$ 5.22
Net earnings	6.31	6.25	8.39
Average number of shares of common stock used in primary computation (in thousands)	222,324	261,426	278,643
Common stock dividends declared	$ 0.80	$ 0.44	$ 0.38

Source: Chrysler's 1986 *Annual Report*, p. 27.

Employees

At December 31, 1986, Chrysler and its subsidiaries had a total of 115,200 employees worldwide, including 87,800 in the United States. Wages and salaries paid by Chrysler totaled $3.7 billion in 1986. Chrysler's contract with the United Auto Workers (UAW) extends through September 14, 1988, one year beyond the expiration date of collective bargaining agreements at GMC and Ford.

EXHIBIT 3 Chrysler Corporation and Consolidated Subidiaries consolidated balance sheet.

ASSETS

	December 31	
	1986	1985
	(In millions of dollars)	
CURRENT ASSETS:		
Cash and time deposits	$ 285.1	$ 147.6
Marketable securities–at cost which approximates market (Note 13)	2,394.3	2,649.9
Accounts receivable (less allowance for doubtful accounts: 1986–$19.9 million; 1985–$17.3 million)	372.5	207.5
Inventories (Note 2)	1,699.6	1,862.7
Prepaid pension expense (Note 11)	348.9	260.0
Prepaid insurance, taxes and other expenses	263.6	185.8
TOTAL CURRENT ASSETS	5,364.0	5,313.5
INVESTMENTS AND OTHER ASSETS:		
Investments in associated companies (Note 3)	317.7	283.0
Investments in and advances to unconsolidated subsidiaries (Notes 3 and 13)	1,989.6	1,787.4
Other noncurrent assets	674.1	581.8
TOTAL INVESTMENTS AND OTHER ASSETS	2,981.4	2,652.2
PROPERTY, PLANT AND EQUIPMENT: (Note 4)		
Land, buildings, machinery and equipment	7,081.5	5,942.0
Less accumulated depreciation	2,767.5	2,664.8
	4,314.0	3,277.2
Unamortized special tools	1,803.8	1,362.4
NET PROPERTY, PLANT AND EQUIPMENT	6,117.8	4,639.6
TOTAL ASSETS	$14,463.2	$12,605.3

LIABILITIES AND SHAREHOLDERS' EQUITY

	December 31	
	1986	1985
	(In millions of dollars)	
CURRENT LIABILITIES:		
Accounts payable	$ 2,958.3	$ 2,504.5
Short-term debt	82.2	195.3
Payments due within one year on long-term debt	119.8	101.6
Accrued liabilities and expenses (Note 5)	1,960.7	1,927.8
TOTAL CURRENT LIABILITIES	5,121.0	4,729.2
ACCRUED EMPLOYEE BENEFITS (Note 11)	289.6	298.4
OTHER NONCURRENT LIABILITIES	661.3	604.5
DEFERRED TAXES ON INCOME (Note 12)	712.4	391.8
LONG-TERM DEBT (Note 6)	2,334.1	2,366.1
COMMITMENTS (Note 7)	—	—
SHAREHOLDERS' EQUITY (issued and treasury stock restated to reflect stock splits–see Notes 8 and 15):		
Common stock–$1 per share par value; authorized 300,000,000 shares; issued:		
229,802,603 shares	229.8	—
229,842,968 shares	—	153.2
Additional paid-in capital	1,866.6	1,943.2
Retained earnings	3,567.5	2,153.3
Treasury stock–Common stock, at cost:		
13,109,477 shares	(319.1)	—
2,039,661 shares	—	(34.4)
TOTAL SHAREHOLDERS' EQUITY	5,344.8	4,215.3
TOTAL LIABILITIES AND SHAREHOLDERS' EQUITY	$14,463.2	$12,605.3

Source: Chrysler's 1986 *Annual Report*, p. 28.

U.S. Properties

Approximately 50 percent of Chrysler's manufacturing and assembly operations are located in Detroit. Chrysler's other U.S. manufacturing plants are situated in Ohio and Indiana, except for a transmission plant in New York and an electronics plant in Alabama. Chrysler's U.S. car assembly plants are located in Detroit and Sterling Heights, Michigan; Belvidere, Illinois; Newark, Delaware; and Fenton, Missouri. Chrysler's U.S. truck assembly plant is located in Warren, Michigan.

Manufactured and Purchased Components

Chrysler uses more than 16,000 suppliers for services, supplies, equipment, materials, parts, and components. Chrysler purchases a larger portion of its materials, parts, and components from unaffiliated suppliers than do its principal competitors. Chrysler is the least integrated of American automakers, with only 30 percent of its parts coming from inside sources. Ford is 50 percent integrated, and General Motors Corporation (GMC) is 70 percent integrated.

Marketing

Chrysler had 4,026 franchised dealers in the United States on December 31, 1986, compared to 4,007 dealers in 1985. These dealers sold an average of 473 vehicles each in 1986, and 462 in 1985. In Canada, Chrysler had 563 and 555 dealers at the end of 1986 and 1985, respectively. Canadian dealers sold an average of 485 vehicles in 1986, and 443 in 1985. Chrysler has undertaken an extensive repositioning effort for its products. Advertising themes are as follows: Chrysler products stress luxury, Plymouth products stress value, and Dodge trucks stress performance.

Research and Development (R&D)

During 1986, 1985, and 1984, Chrysler spent $732 million, $609 million, and $452 million, respectively, for company-sponsored R&D activities. These activities relate to the development of new and existing products and services, as well as compliance with government standards.

Recent Innovations

Chrysler's retail car market share is increasing due to the successful introduction of new front-wheel-drive products, beginning with the Plymouth Reliant and Dodge Aries, followed by the Chrysler New Yorker and Dodge 600 six-passenger models, the Dodge Daytona sports car, the Chrysler LeBaron GTS and Dodge Lancer sedans, and, most recently, the Dodge Shadow and Plymouth Sundance. A listing of Chrysler's product offerings is presented in Exhibit 4. The improvement in Chrysler's retail truck market share from 8.7 percent in 1983 to 12.1 percent in 1986 is primarily attributable to the success of Chrysler's front-wheel-drive mini-vans, the Plymouth Voyager, the Dodge Caravan, and the Dodge Mini Ram Van.

CHRYSLER'S FOREIGN OPERATIONS

Canada

Chrysler Canada Ltd. operates assembly and manufacturing facilities in Canada. Chrysler Canada manufactures components and assembles rear-wheel-drive van/wagons and front-wheel-drive mini-van/wagons. In 1986, Chrysler Canada produced 404,789 vehicles and sold 356,859 of these vehicles in the United States. Factory unit sales by Chrysler Canada accounted for approximately 10.3 percent of the company's total car and truck sales in 1986 (compared to 11.5 percent in 1985). Chrysler Canada's retail market share was 14.8 percent of the total Canadian car market and 15.0 percent of the total Canadian truck market in 1986, compared to 16.0 and 16.2 percent, respectively, in 1985. Chrysler Canada was third in the industry in Canada in retail unit sales of both passenger cars and trucks in 1986.

Mexico

Chrysler de Mexico operates both assembly and manufacturing facilities in Mexico. It is the third-largest manufacturer of both passenger cars and light-duty trucks in Mexico, accounting for approximately 17.2 percent of the Mexican car market and approximately 19.5 percent of the truck market in 1986, compared to approximately 16.0 percent and 18.1 percent 1985. Chrysler de Mexico's 1986 domestic sales of 46,896 units were down 29 percent from 1985 unit sales of 65,871, while total industry unit sales in 1986 were down 34 percent from 1985.

In 1986, Chrysler de Mexico exported Plymouth Reliant and Dodge Aries passenger cars and Dodge Ramcharger sport utility vehicles to the United States. Chrysler de Mexico provides certain automobile components, including engines and air conditioner condensers, to Chrysler's U.S. operations. Chrysler de Mexico, in turn, depends upon Chrysler for approximately 36 percent of the material utilized in the assembly of vehicles sold in Mexico. Chrysler de Mexico's operations continue to be subject to substantial uncertainties in the Mexican economy and to various regulations imposed by the Mexican government.

Outside North America

Automotive sales outside the United States, Canada, and Mexico have grown significantly in recent years and now exceed the North American market. Most of the demand in these markets is met by vehicles produced in Western Europe and Japan. Chrysler no longer has significant sales in these areas as a result of divestiture of its European subsidiaries to Peugeot S.A. and the sale of substantially all of Chrysler's interests in South America, South Africa, and Australia. Ford and GMC have substantial overseas operations and are better positioned to participate in growth opportunities for profits outside the North American markets. Chrysler conducts sales activities on a small scale in markets outside North America and participates indirectly in foreign markets through MMC. Chrysler plans to establish a marketing network in Europe to distribute the new LeBaron J-coupe, its popular mini-van, and others of its

EXHIBIT 4 Domestically produced vehicles by American Automakers

		1986	*1985*
SubCompact			
Ford Erika (Escort)		219,000	210,000
GMC Nova		192,000	64,000
Chrysler L-Series (Omni)		168,000	140,000
AMC Alliance		46,000	74,000
Compact			
Ford Topaz (Tempo)		128,000	121,000
GMC J-Series (Cavalier)		134,000	154,000
Chrysler	K-Series (Reliant)	120,000	132,000
	P-Series (Sundance)	115,000	—
Sports Cars			
Ford Fox (Mustang)		178,000	188,000
GMC F-Series (Camaro)		139,000	214,000
Chrysler G-Series (Daytona)		33,000	48,000
Intermediates			
Ford	Taurus (Taurus)	232,000	—
	S-Series (T-Bird)	117,000	150,000
GMC	G-Series (Monte Carlo)	93,000	171,000
	A-Series (Celebrity)	214,000	232,000
	L-Series (Corsica)	170,000	—
	N-Series (Grand Am)	155,000	140,000
Chrysler	H-Series (Lebaron GTS)	59,000	80,000
	E-Series (Caravelle)	58,000	60,000
	J-Series (Lebaron Coupe)	140,000	—
Standard			
Ford—*No entry*		—	—
GMC	B-Series (Caprice)	123,000	165,000
	H-Series (Bonneville)	156,000	—
Chrysler	M-Series (Gran Fury)	28,000	23,000

best-selling vehicles. Officials estimate that Chrysler will sell 25,000 vehicles annually outside North America by 1990.

During 1986, Chrysler purchased approximately 15.6 percent of the outstanding ordinary stock of Maserati. Chrysler has options exercisable in 1989 and 1995 to purchase additional shares of Maserati that would amount to 48 percent and 51 percent

EXHIBIT 4 continued

		1986	*1985*
Luxury			
Ford	LS (Continental)	23,000	22,000
	Panther (Town Car)	137,000	120,000
GMC	C-Series (Deville)	126,000	152,000
	E-Series (Toronado)	24,000	43,000
	K-Series (Seville)	22,000	29,000
Chrysler	M-Series (5th Ave)	122,000	106,000
Mini Van			
Ford Aerostar		150,000	—
GMC Astro		148,000	106,000
Chrysler Voyager		225,000	219,000
Small Sport Utility			
Jeep		207,000	181,000
Ford		152,000	156,000
GMC (Chevy)		269,000	296,000
GMC (GMC)		106,000	112,000
Full Size Pickups			
Ford		545,000	562,507
Chevrolet		443,000	476,048
Chrysler		106,000	160,000

ownership. In early 1987, Chrysler purchased Lamborghini Motors, a small Italian manufacturer of high-performance vehicles produced entirely by hand.

THE AMC ACQUISITION

On March 5, 1987, Chrysler announced plans of a merger with American Motors Corporation (AMC) contingent upon shareholder approval. In June 1987, an offer to purchase 46.1 percent of AMC stock from Renault was accepted by the French automaker. The deal is expected to be completed by October 1, 1987, costing Chrysler between $1.75 and $2.30 billion. A summary of the ramifications of the acquisition is presented in Exhibit 5. Comparative financial information for AMC and Chrysler is given in Exhibits 6 and 7.

The AMC acquisition will add four manufacturing plants to Chrysler's operations and boost truck capacity by 34 percent. In addition, the Jeep Division gives Chrysler an instant entry into the booming four-wheel-drive truck market and completes

EXHIBIT 5 Ramifications of the AMC acquisition

1. The purchase price is between $1.1–$1.6 billion (plus $707 million assumption of AMC debt).
2. The acquisition requires only $60 million upfront. In addition, there will be $60 million in previous losses that Chrysler can carry-over in fiscal 1987.
3. The acquisition will increase Chrysler's debt/equity ratio from 47 percent to 60 percent.
4. The deal will complete the Chrysler-Plymouth product line less expensively than development of their own line.
5. Chrysler acquires AMC's new assembly plant in Bramalea, Ontario (world's most technologically advanced).
6. The acquisition gives Chrysler distribution rights of the Renault Medallion and Premier.
7. The deal increase Chrysler's market share to 15 percent of the car market and 20 percent of the truck market.
8. The deal gives Chrysler rights to the Jeep name, one of the most widely recognized brand names in the world today.
9. The acquisition expands Chrysler's operations to include facilities in Egypt, China, and Venezuela.

EXHIBIT 6 Chrysler Corporation and consolidated subsidiaries pro forma statement of earnings for the year ended December 31, 1986 (unaudited) (in millions of dollars)

	Historical		*Pro Forma*	
	Chrysler	*AMC*	*Adjustments*	*Combined*
Net sales	$22,586.3	$3,462.5	$ —	$26,048.8
Equity in earnings (loss) of unconsolidated subsidiaries	298.6	(1.5)	3.4(A)	300.5
Other income (expense)	120.7	14.4	—	135.1
	23,005.6	**3,475.4**	**3.4**	**26,484.4**
Costs, other than items below	18,635.2	2,858.3	—	21,493.5
Depreciation of plant and equipment	236.8	50.7	—	287.5
Amortization of special tools	306.8	104.4	—	411.2
Selling and administrative expenses	1,376.8	418.0	14.2 (B)	1,809.0
Pension plans	236.3	62.1	(25.6)(C)	272.8
Net interest expense	32.7	73.2	0.5)(D)	105.4
Gain on sale of investment in Peugeot S.A.	(144.3)	—	—	(144.3)
	20,680.3	**3,566.7**	**(11.9)**	**24,235.1**
Earnings (Loss) Before Taxes	2,325.3	(91.3)	15.3	2,249.3
Taxes on income	921.7	—	(17.6)(E)	904.1
Net Earnings (Loss)	1,403.6	(91.3)	32.9	1,345.2
Dividends earned on preferred stocks	—	18.2	(18.2)(G)	—
Earnings (Loss) Applicable to Common Stock	**$ 1,403.6**	**$ (109.5)**	**$ 51.1**	**$ 1,345.2**

Source: American Motors Corporation, *Special Report to Stockholders,* July 2, 1987, p. 34.

Chrysler's line of trucks that previously was limited to only the mini-van/wagon and light-duty truck segments. The AMC acquisition will increase Chrysler's total production capacity to 2.9 million vehicles annually.

AMC's new Ontario plant is the newest and most technologically advance automobile manufacturing plant in the world. The Renault Premier is scheduled for production at this plant. The association with Renault gives Chrysler a potential overseas distribution partner. Plans have been announced to incorporate AMC/Jeep into a Chrysler operating division, called the Jeep/Eagle Division. A list of the facilities Chrysler is purchasing from AMC is provided in Exhibit 8.

EXHIBIT 7 Chrysler Corporation and consolidated subsidiaries pro forma balance sheet March 31, 1987 (unaudited) (in millions of dollars)

	Historical		*Pro Forma*	
	Chrysler	*AMC*	*Adjustments*	*Combined*
Current Assets				
Cash and time deposits	$ 546.9	$(13.4)	$(37.1)(A) (6.7)(A)	$ 489.7
Marketable securities	2,355.7	145.8	—	2,501.5
Accounts receivable	464.6	290.2	29.2(A)	784.0
Inventories	1,796.4	424.0	—	2,220.4
Prepaid expenses	578.5	48.8	—	627.3
Total Current Assets	**5,742.1**	**895.4**	**(14.6)**	**6,622.9**
Investments and Other Assets				
Investments in associated companies	300.2	18.6	—	318.8
Investments in and advances to unconsolidated subsidiaries	2,049.9	133.6	37.1 (A)	2,220.6
Other noncurrent assets	660.3	42.9	567.8 (A)	1,271.0
Total Investments and Other Assets	**3,010.4**	**195.1**	**604.9**	**3,810.4**
Property, Plant and Equipment				
Land, buildings, machinery and equipment	7,315.1	1,259.3	—	8,574.4
Less accumulated depreciation	2,851.3	423.0	—	3,274.3
	4,463.8	**836.3**	—	**5,300.1**
Unamortized special tools	1,879.9	460.9	—	2,340.8
Net Property, Plant and Equipment	**6,343.7**	**1,297.2**	—	**7,640.9**
Total Assets	**$15,096.2**	**$2,387.7**	**$590.3**	**$18,074.2**

Source: American Motors Corporation, *Special Report to Stockholders,* July 2, 1987, p. 31.

continued

EXHIBIT 7 continued

	Historical		*Pro Forma*	
	Chrysler	*AMC*	*Adjustments*	*Combined*
Current Liabilities				
Accounts payable	$ 3,248.7	$ 408.5	$ —	$ 3,657.2
Short-term debt	81.6	7.3	—	88.9
Payments due within one year on long-term debt	57.7	88.9	—	146.6
Accrued liabilities and expenses	2,166.7	334.3	20.0(A)	2,521.0
Total Current Liabilities	**5,554.7**	**839.0**	**20.0**	**6,413.7**
Accrued employee benefits	300.2	28.3	384.2(A)	712.7
Other noncurrent liabilities	652.0	220.9	—	872.9
Deferred taxes on income	765.2	—	—	765.2
Long-term debt	2,340.9	897.9	(200.0)(C) 200.0 (A)	3,238.8
Shareholders' Equity				
Chrysler				
☐ Common Stock—$1 per share par value; authorized 300,000,000 shares; issued 229,773,664 shares	229.8	—	16.6(A)	246.4
☐ Additional paid-in capital	1,867.9	—	571.1(A)	2,439.0
☐ Retained earnings	3,779.3	—	—	3,779.3
☐ Treasury stock—common stock at cost; 15,122,432 shares	(393.8)	—	—	(393.8)
AMC				
☐ Convertible Preferred Stock—$0.01 per share par value; authorized 20,000,000 shares; outstanding 6,470,126 shares	—	0.1	(0.1)(B)	—
☐ Junior Convertible Preferred Stock—$0.01 per share par value; authorized 6,696,428 shares; outstanding 6,078,281 shares	—	0.1	(0.1)(B)	—
☐ Common Stock—$0.01 per share par value; authorized 350,000,000 shares; outstanding 130,402,136 shares	—	1.3	(1.3)(B)	—
☐ Additional paid-in capital	—	998.7	(998.7)(B)	—
☐ Accumulated deficit	—	(598.6)	598.6 (B)	—
Total Shareholders' Equity	**5,483.2**	**401.6**	**186.1**	**6,070.9**
Total Liabilities and Shareholders' Equity	**$15,096.2**	**$2,387.7**	**$590.3**	**$18,074.2**

Source: American Motors Corporation, *Special Report to Stockholders,* July 2, 1987, p. 32.

EXHIBIT 8 Properties acquired from AMC (Assembly/Stamping Plants)

1. Bramalea, Canada (Ontario)
   Date Built: 1986
   Capacity: 200,000
   Value: $400 million
   Vehicles: Premier
2. Brampton, Canada (Ontario)
   Date Built: 1986
   Capacity: 80,000
   Value: $21 million
   Vehicles: AMC Eagle; Jeep Wrangler
3. Kenosha Assembly/Stamping (Wisconsin)
   Date Built: 1900
   Capacity: 250,000
   Value: $431.41 million
4. Beijing Jeep Corporation (China)
   Date Built: 1950s
   Capacity: 27,000
   Value: Joint venture with Chinese government; Chrysler currently has 31% equity with options to increase share to 49%.
   Vehicles: Jeep Cherokee, BJ212 Utility Vehicle
5. Valencia Assembly (Venezuela)
   Date Built: 1962
   Capacity: 10,500
6. Toledo Jeep Assembly/Stamping (Ohio)
   Date Built: 1906
   Capacity: 250,000
   Value: $10.5 million
   Chrysler also has $250,000 in property in Lucas County.
7. Arab American Vehicle (Egypt)
   Date Built: 1979
   Capacity: 9,600
   Note: Chrysler owns 49% share
   Vehicles: Jeep CJ & One Fiat Model
8. Milwaukee Manufacturing (Wisconsin)
   Date Built: 1920
   Products: Metal stamping and small subassemblies.
   Value: $6.94 million

COMPETITION

The U.S. automotive industry is composed of three principal domestic passenger car and truck manufacturers—General Motors, Ford Motor, and Chrysler Motors—as well as a number of foreign manufacturers that distribute automobiles and trucks assembled both overseas and domestically. The 1986 market share of U.S. car and truck manufacturers is presented in Exhibits 9 and 10, respectively. Many of Chrysler's competitors have larger sales volumes and greater financial resources. Chrysler is particularly dependent on economic conditions in the United States, Canada, and Mexico. Chrysler lags behind other American manufacturers in the number of joint ventures and equity agreements with other car companies, as shown in Exhibit 11. In addition, Chrysler's ability to increase vehicle prices is significantly affected by the pricing actions of principal competitors. Chrysler produced more cars per plant on average than did Ford or GMC in 1986. Chrysler reduced inventories from a 1979 level of $2.1 billion to $1.4 billion in 1986.

Ford

Although Ford's product quality is rated the best among American automakers, Chrysler has been making significant inroads and is rapidly closing the gap. The Sable/Taurus line has proved to be the most significant introduction since the Mustang was introduced by Ford in the 1960s (ironically created by Iacocca). However, Ford's market share has continued to erode from its 1978 level of 26.5 percent to its current position of 21.2 percent. Ford is expected to be able to increase its market share by

EXHIBIT 9 United States car market share* year ended December 31

	(Percent of Total Industry)					
	1986	*1985*	*1984*	*1983*	*1982*	*1981*
United States Manufacturers (Including Imports)						
General Motors	41.2%	42.7%	44.6%	44.3%	44.2%	44.6%
Ford	18.2	18.9	19.2	17.2	16.9	16.6
Chrysler Motors	11.5	11.4	10.4	10.3	10.0	9.9
AMC	0.6	1.2	2.0	2.5	1.9	2.0
Total United States Manufacturers	**71.5**	**74.2**	**76.2**	**74.3**	**73.0**	**73.1**
Imports by Foreign Companies**						
Honda	6.1	5.0	4.9	4.4	4.6	4.4
Toyota	5.4	5.3	5.0	5.9	6.6	6.7
Nissan	4.7	5.2	4.7	5.7	5.9	5.5
Mazda	2.0	1.9	1.6	1.9	2.1	2.0
All Other	10.3	8.4	7.6	7.8	7.8	8.3
Total Imports by Foreign Companies	**28.5**	**25.8**	**23.8**	**25.7**	**27.0**	**26.9**
Total United States New Car Retail Sales	**100.0%**	**100.0%**	**100.0%**	**100.0%**	**100.0%**	**100.0%**
	(In Thousands)					
	1986	*1985*	*1984*	*1983*	*1982*	*1981*
United States Car Retail Deliveries						
Total Industry	11,401	10,980	10,324	9,147	7,955	8,514
Chrysler Motors	1,309	1,245	1,079	945	794	841

*All United States retail sales data are based on publicly available information on manufacturers from the Motor Vehicle Manufacturers Association, and data on foreign company imports from Ward's Automotive Reports, a trade publication.

**"Imports by Foreign Companies" include cars manufactured and sold in the United States.

Source: Chrysler Corporation, 1986 Form 10-K Report, p. 43.

three points in the next few years with the success of its Taurus/Sable line and with the Mexican-built Tracer, the Korean Festiva, and a redesigned Mustang. A financial summary of Ford Motor Company is provided in Exhibit 12.

General Motors

General Motors' market share declined from a 1978 level of 47.3 percent to 38.4 percent today. With the recent acquisition of Electronic Data Systems, GMC's quality, productivity, and efficiency rates were expected to increase substantially, but this im-

EXHIBIT 10 United States truck market share* year ended December 31

	(Percent of Total Industry)					
	1986	*1985*	*1984*	*1983*	*1982*	*1981*
United States Manufacturers (Including Imports)						
General Motors	32.4%	34.8%	34.5%	39.5%	40.2%	37.2%
Ford	28.1	26.8	28.1	31.4	30.7	31.5
Chrysler Motors	12.1	12.8	12.6	8.7	9.5	8.2
AMC	4.2	3.8	3.7	2.6	2.5	2.8
Navistar	1.4	1.5	1.7	1.7	1.9	3.0
All Other	1.7	1.9	1.8	1.3	1.4	2.4
Total United States Manufacturers	**79.9**	**81.6**	**82.4**	**85.2**	**86.2**	**85.1**
Imports by Foreign Companies**						
Toyota	8.5	7.9	7.4	5.8	5.7	6.1
Nissan	4.6	5.4	4.9	4.3	4.2	5.3
Mazda	3.2	2.4	2.9	2.4	1.6	0.7
Isuzu	1.8	1.6	1.1	0.8	0.7	0.4
All Other	2.0	1.1	1.3	1.5	1.6	2.4
Total Imports by Foreign Companies	**20.1**	**18.4**	**17.6**	**14.8**	**13.8**	**14.9**
Total United States New Truck Retail Sales	**100.0%**	**100.0%**	**100.0%**	**100.0%**	**100.0%**	**100.0%**

	(In Thousands)					
	1986	*1985*	*1984*	*1983*	*1982*	*1981*
United States Truck Retail Deliveries						
Total Industry	4,919	4,745	4,160	3,163	2,582	2,279
Chrysler Motors	596	606	526	274	246	187

*All United States retail sales data are based on publicly available information on manufacturers from the Motor Vehicle Manufacturers Association, and data on foreign company imports from Ward's Automotive Reports, a trade publication.

**"Imports by Foreign Companies" include trucks manufactured and sold in the United States.

Source: Chrysler Corporation, 1986 Form 10-K Report, p. 44.

provement has not been realized. GMC is placing great hopes in its new Corsica/ Beretta, GM T400, and GM 10 lines currently being introduced over a period of three years. A financial summary of General Motors is provided in Exhibit 13.

A comparison of U.S. retail outlets among domestic car manufacturers is given in Exhibit 14. An overall rating of domestic car manufacturers is provided in Exhibit 15.

EXHIBIT 11 Domestic automakers' joint ventures and equity stakes in other car companies

Chrysler

49% of Arab American Vehicles, Egypt

31.4% of Beijing Automobile Works, China

50% of Diamond-Star Motors, Bloomington-Normal, Illinois

24% of Mitsubishi Motors, Japan

15.6% of Maserati S.P.A., Italy

100% of Lamborghini Motors, Italy

Ford

70% of Ford Motor Company of Taiwan

25% of Mazda Motor, Japan

48% of Ineco-Ford Truck, Great Britain

10% of Kia Motors, South Korea

49% of Autolatina, Brazil (pending)

42% of South African Motor Corporation

30% of AMIN Holdings, Malaysia

30% of Ottomobile Sanayii Anomin Sirketi, Turkey

General Motors

50% of Daewoo Motors, South Korea

38.6% of Isuzu Motors, Japan

24% of Volvo-GM Heavy Truck Corporation, Greensboro, N.C.

5.3% of Suzuki Motors, Japan

50% of New United Motors, Fremont, California

49% of General Motors Kenya

49% of Constructora Venezolana de Vehiclos, Venezuela

45.9% of Autos Y Mawuinas del Ecuador

31% of General Motors Egypt

22% of Omnibus BB Transportes, Ecuador

20% of Industries Mechaniques Maghrebines, Tunisia

Source: Adapted from *Automotive News,* 1987 Market Data Book.

Foreign Competition

Competition from foreign manufacturers has increased sharply in recent years. The market share for foreign passenger cars sold in the United States increased from 21.0 percent in 1979 to 28.5 percent in 1986. Approximately 77.8 percent of the passenger cars imported to the United States during the period 1979–1986 were of Japanese origin. Japanese producers still have a significant cost advantage over domestic manu-

EXHIBIT 12 Ford Motor Company financial summary

	1986	*1985*
Sales and revenues (in millions)	$ 62,716	$ 52,774
Net income (in millions)	$ 3,285	$ 2,515
Earnings per share	$ 12.32	$ 9.09
Long-term debt (in millions)	$ 2,137	$ 2,157
Average number of employees	382,274	369,314
Average labor cost per hourly employee	$ 27.12	$ 26.45
Current ratio	1.18	1.10
Debt/Equity ratio	0.23	0.28
Total Assets (in millions)	$ 37,933	$ 31,603

Source: Ford Motor's 1986 *Form 10–K.*

EXHIBIT 13 General Motors Corporation financial summary

	1986	*1985*
Sales and revenues (in millions)	$102,813.7	$ 96,371.7
Net income (in millions)	$ 2,944.7	$ 3,999.0
Earnings per share	$ 3.21	$ 5.34
Long-term debt (in millions)	$ 4,007	$ 2,500
Average number of employees	$876,000	$811,000
Average cost per hourly employee	$ 24.000	$ 23.40
Current ratio	1.17	1.09
Debt/equity ratio	0.13	0.08
Total Assets (in millions)	$ 72,593	$ 63,832

Source: General Motors' 1986 *Form 10–K.*

facturers, as a result of differences in labor practices, wage rates, and tax policies, although recent changes in the value of the yen relative to the dollar have reduced the magnitude of Japanese cost advantages. Further changes in the yen-dollar relationship will continue to affect this cost advantage. Restraints for the period April 1, 1987 through March 31, 1988 limit Japanese exports to 2.3 million units. When these restraints are lifted, Iacocca believes the unrestrained importation of cars manufactured in Japan will seriously affect the sales and profitability of domestic automakers. Chrysler has entered into a distribution agreement with MMC to attempt to lessen the effects of this threat.

EXHIBIT 14 Number of retail outlets of American-made passenger cars in 1987 versus 1986

	January 1, 1987		*January 1, 1986*	
	Total Number of Dealers	*Net Number of Dealers*	*Total Number of Dealers*	*Net Number of Dealers*
American Motors/Renault	**2,567**	**1,249**	**2,686**	**1,421**
AMC	1,309		1,368	
Renault	1,258		1,318	
Chrysler Corporation	**9,057**	**4,023**	**8,985**	**4,003**
Chrysler	3,064		3,049	
Dodge	2,960		2,927	
Plymouth	3,033		3,009	
Ford Motor Company	**8,984**	**5,460**	**9,027**	**5,517**
Ford	4,616		4,682	
Lincoln	1,617		1,598	
Mercury	2,751		2,747	
General Motors Company	**15,690**	**9,680**	**15,795**	**9,830**
Buick	2,950		2,960	
Cadillac	1,615		1,615	
Chevrolet	4,975		5,050	
Oldsmobile	3,175		3,190	
Pontiac	2,975		2,980	
Volkswagen	**878**	**878**	**877**	**877**
TOTALS	**37,176**	**21,390**	**37,370**	**21,648**

MISUBISHI MOTORS CORPORATION (MMC)

In 1986, Chrysler sold 219,002 MMC-manufactured vehicles in the United States (of which 135,528 were cars), representing 11.5 percent of Chrysler's U.S. retail vehicle sales. For the fiscal year ending March 31, 1987, MMC's passenger car shipments to the United States were approximately 195,000 units. During the period of voluntary restraints currently in effect, MMC has agreed to allocate to Chrysler 71.4 percent of the passenger cars that MMC may export in the 1987 and 1988 model years.

In 1987, Chrysler has the exclusive right to distribute the Colt Vista. The Colt three-door, Colt four-door, Dodge Raider, Chrysler Conquest, Dodge Ram 50 and Power Ram 50 models are marketed under separate name plates by both Chrysler and MMC. Similar agreements are in effect covering the Canadian Market, but in practice, Chrysler Canada acts as sole distributor of MMC products and is allocated all

EXHIBIT 15 Making the grade

Category	*1973*	*1978*	*1984*	*1985*	*1986*	*Grade*
Chrysler						
Quality	—	—	90.3	77.3	69.6	A
Profit/Unit	$131	($129)	$1210	$1080	$1057	A−
US Market Share	15.6%	11.2%	11.9%	11.8%	11.7%	B−
Return On Sales	2.1%	(1.5%)	12.1%	7.7%	6.2%	C
Productivity	13.0	13.0	18.1	17.0	19.8	A+
Inventory Turns	5.6	6.3	14.5	18.8	22.1	A+
Overall Grade—B+						
Ford						
Quality	—	—	113.6	95.3	104.5	A
Profit/Unit	$273	$424	$755	$644	$847	A+
US Market Share	29.8%	26.5%	22.7%	20.3%	21.2%	A+
Return On Sales	3.9%	3.7%	5.5%	4.7%	5.3%	C
Productivity	13.7	13.7	15.6	16.4	16.8	B
Inventory Turns	5.3	6.5	14.5	14.8	13.8	D
Overall Grade—B						
General Motors						
Quality	—	—	91.2	92.6	92.4	C
Profit/Unit	$481	$667	$666	$466	$157	F
US Market Share	51.5%	47.3%	39.1%	40.3%	38.4%	F
Return On Sales	6.7%	5.5%	5.4%	4.1	2.9%	F
Productivity	11.4	12.0	11.5	12.7	12.2	C
Inventory Turns	5.4	6.7	10.3	11.9	11.7	C
Overall Grade—D						
American Motors						
Quality	—	—	51.5	65.0	86	A+
Profit/Unit	$147	$101	$35	($320)	($317)	F
US Market Share	3.5%	2.3%	2.8%	1.9%	1.7%	D
Return On Sales	4.3%	1.4%	.36%	(3.1%)	(2.6%)	D−
Productivity	18.2	17.1	18.1	14.7	13.3	F
Inventory Turns	7.2	6.4	15.5	15.6	15.3	C
Overall Grade—D						

Source: *Automotive Industries*, March 1987, p. 40–43.

MMC vehicles allowed to be imported. In addition to vehicles, Chrysler purchases from MMC 2.6-liter, V-4 engines as well as 3.0-liter, V-6 engines for use in production of the Dodge Caravan, Plymouth Voyager, and other vehicles. Chrysler intends to buy approximately 123,000 2.6-liter engines and 161,000 3.0-liter engines during the 1987 model year.

CHRYSLER SUBSIDIARIES

Chrysler Financial Corporation

Chrysler Financial Corporation (CFC) provides diversified financing and related insurance services through its major operating subsidiaries: (1) Chrysler Credit Corporation provides automotive financing, (2) Chrysler First provides financing to manufacturers, distributors, and dealers, (3) Chrysler Capital Corporation provides commercial leasing and lending, (4) Chrysler Insurance Company and (5) Chrysler Life Insurance Company provide finance-related insurance, and (6) Chrysler Realty Corporation provides automotive dealership facility development. The automotive financing operations of CFC are conducted through 115 branches in the United States, Canada, and Mexico. Chrysler First conducts consumer and financing operations through 274 offices in the United States. Chrysler Realty Corporation owns and leases 242 automobile dealerships in the United States.

Gulfstream Aerospace Corporation

On August 16, 1985, Chrysler Corporation acquired 100 percent of the outstanding shares of Gulfstream Aerospace for $641.8 million. Gulfstream is engaged in the design, development, production, and sale of general aviation aircraft. Gulfstream markets its products and services through seven sales offices located in the United States, including its headquarters in Savannah, Georgia, and one distributor in Saudi Arabia. Gulfstream has an excellent reputation, and its products have been referred to as "the world's most desired jets." Gulfstream currently has more than a one-year backlog of orders.

Electrospace Systems, Inc.

In June 1987, Chrysler agreed to acquire Electrospace for approximately $367 million, to be followed by a merger with Gulfstream Aerospace. Electrospace is primarily engaged in the design, manufacture, and installation of command, control, and communication systems, aircraft modifications, and technical services, principally for the U.S. Department of Defense. Electrospace also manufactures commercial telecommunications equipment. For the 1985 and 1986 fiscal years, Electrospace reported revenues of approximately $145 million and $191 million, respectively, and net income of approximately $13 million and $10 million, respectively. Electrospace had total assets of approximately $111 million in December 1986.

FUTURE ISSUES AND CONCERNS

The Energy Tax Act of 1978 imposes a graduated "Gas Guzzler" tax on automobiles with a fuel economy rating below specified levels. Chrysler will pay a fine of $500 for each of its M-body rear-wheel-drive passenger cars that is sold in model year 1987 and beyond, pursuant to this law. In 1988, Chrysler plans to introduce a new front-wheel-drive, full-sized luxury car. Chrysler is also planning to introduce a luxury, two-seat sport convertible in 1988 that is being developed jointly with Maserati. Also in 1988, a new line of small cars will be produced by Diamond-Star Motors Corporation. The success of Chrysler's products will depend on a number of factors, including the economy, consumer confidence, the degree of competition from foreign and domestic manufacturers, fuel price levels, consumer preferences, the effects of government regulation, and the strength of Chrysler's marketing network. Chrysler is substantially committed to the types of vehicles currently in production and could be adversely affected by developments requiring a major shift in design.

An immediate concern for Chrysler is the huge debt obtained in the acquisition of AMC. In order to control the effects of the acquisition, Chrysler must consolidate and streamline operations. Industry analysts remain skeptical about Iacocca's ability to perform the same type of turnaround with AMC that was experienced at Chrysler. Iacocca presently faces eroding market share, perceived quality differences between domestic and foreign cars, increasing labor costs, and strained relations with the UAW due to the recent success of Ford. The UAW is not likely to be as generous during negotiations in 1988 as they were with Chrysler in recent years. Labor costs must be kept at a minimum due to low-cost automobile production operations emerging in Malaysia, Korea, and Yugoslavia.

Perhaps the greatest threat to Chrysler today is the proliferation of U.S. plants being built by foreign auto companies. As a result, many analysts expect U.S. automobile supply to far exceed U.S. automobile demand by 1990. In addition, many analysts expect the U.S. economy in 1987 to worsen, thus resulting in individuals delaying the purchase of new cars and trucks. These trends could require massive layoffs and plant closings at Chrysler.

Do you think the strategies formulated by Iacocca are best for Chrysler in the long run? What recommendations would you offer to Iacocca?

Software Publishing Company—1987

WILLIAM C. HOUSE
University of Arkansas
ROBERT D. HAY
University of Arkansas

Fred Gibbons, Janelle Bedke, and John D. Page started Software Publishing Company in 1980. All are former employees of Hewlett Packard's marketing division and have been strongly influenced by the Hewlett Packard environment. Gibbons is president and chairman, Bedke is vice-president/general manager, and Page is vice-president for research and development. Initially, the company followed a strategy similar to that of many packaged good distributors: striving to develop a complete family of brand name software products that could be advertised wisely and sold through retail channels.

The first program produced by Software Publishing Company was developed for the Apple computer system in the early 1980s and was called Personal Filing System, or PFS. In addition to the file management system, additional programs were added to perform word processing, graphing, communications, proofreading, and spreadsheet functions. All programs in the series have a common interface and command structure, which facilitates learning how to operate them and makes it easy to transfer data from one program to another.

After the initial success with programs designed to run on Apple computers, the PFS series was adapted for use on IBM and IBM-compatible machines in the mid-eighties. Gibbons remarked there was a general feeling that expansion was occurring much more rapidly in the IBM software sector than in the Apple area, but development efforts and energies had been so concentrated on Apple products that the company failed to take advantage of the obvious transition.

PFS programs are inexpensive, easy to use, and compatible with each other, but they have fewer capabilities than programs marketed by major competitors such as Microsoft, Lotus, and Ashton Tate. Until 1986, Software Publishing had no single program that would perform an integrated series of spreadsheet, word processing, and file management functions on the order of Lotus's 1-2-3 or Ashton Tate's Framework. Although the company had been increasing profits and sales during the fourth quarter for every year since 1980, sales volume declined significantly during the last quarter of 1985 due to increasing competition from other software companies and a slowdown in the demand for personal computers.

In December 1985, while on the ski slopes at Squaw Valley in Nevada, Fred Gibbons suffered a stroke which left him paralyzed on one side. Janelle Bedke took over many of Gibbons' functions temporarily, but within one month, the hard-charging Gibbons was back in his office with only a slight limp to show for the experience.

Note: The research and written case information was prepared by W. C. House and R. D. Hay, University of Arkansas. The information was presented at the Case Research Symposium (New Orleans, 1987) and was evaluated by the Case Research Association's editorial board. Distributed by Case Research Association

PRODUCT LINES: BREADTH, DEPTH, AND PRICING STRATEGIES

Gibbons' initial strategy was to develop a broadly based, widely recognized family of programs that were easy to learn to use and that would fall within the price range of the average home computer or office computer user. Programs developed initially for the Apple computers were converted to IBM versions, and both versions were sold through retail channels. IBM made arrangements with the company to sell the entire PFS line under the IBM assistant series label, further enhancing the company's sales prospects.

While other companies concentrated on larger, more complex programs with greater functionality and carrying prices ranging from $300 to $600, Software Publishing sold its programs for prices ranging from $125 to $140. Several of the more successful software companies (e.g., Lotus and Ashton Tate) obtain the bulk of their revenues from a single product. Software Publishing Company, in contrast, receives no more than one third of its revenues from any single product.

As of the end of 1985, Software Publishing had sold more programs than any other software developer (i.e., about two million units compared to about 1.6 million for Lotus), but the gross profit per package was about $60 compared to approximately $200 for more sophisticated programs. Many retailers claim that PFS profit margins were too narrow and program capabilities were too limited to justify full-scale promotion of the PFS line. In addition, the demand for easy-to-use, limited-function programs was decreasing while demand was increasing for more powerful programs with expanded capabilities that could take full advantage of faster operating speeds and larger memories of newer computer hardware. The number of first-time computer users appeared to have tapered off during the past two years.

Software Publishing was also experiencing competition from unexpected quarters. Apple Computer had switched from being a user of PFS programs to becoming a powerful competitor. Appleworks, a file manager which sold for about $250, competed aggressively with PFS series for the same customers, resulting in lost sales to the company. Symantec, a software company formed by industry veterans several years ago, had introduced a new program called Q&A which was the equivalent of three combined and upgraded PFS programs. Although not as successful as Dbase and LOTUS, Q&A at a price level of about $300 had obtained a number of sales that otherwise might have gone to the PFS family.

Gibbons ruefully conceded that the company spread itself too thin during the mid-80s, trying to develop programs for the MacIntosh, Apple, IBM private label, and IBM PC compatible audiences. Despite clear-cut indications that the IBM compatible programs were going to have the greatest future growth potential, the company waited almost two years to start phasing out the Apple programs.

Software Publishing company markets the PFS line through distributors, independent sales representatives, and in-house salespersons to more than 3,500 retailers. Sales are also made directly to corporations, although PFS products are not on the approved list of many corporations and many organizations consider the PFS series as designed for home rather than business or office use. Retail sales have typically been highest in the fourth quarter and lowest in the first quarter.

EXHIBIT 1 Distribution of sales revenues

	1986	*1985*	*1984*
Retail Sales	72%	61%	80%
OEMS/IBM Royalties	20%	30%	16%
Direct Consumer Sales	8%	9%	4%

In order to beef up its marketing efforts, Software Publishing Company has hired four brand managers from packaged goods companies (e.g., Procter & Gamble, Clorox). This augmented sales staff is trying out a number of new marketing ploys to increase revenues and profits. Free trial diskettes are offered to potential customers. Information on software products is being sent out via direct mail to targeted personnel, and advertisements are frequently placed in personal computer magazines. Selected corporate managers are being sent free copies of some software packages in order to help increase organizational awareness of the PFS family.

Exhibit 1 shows the changing distribution of sales revenues for the company.

NEW PRODUCT DEVELOPMENT AND PRODUCT LINE ACQUISITION

Two new product lines were announced by Software Publishing Company in 1986. File management, report generation, spreadsheet, word processing, and communication capabilities formerly provided by separate programs in the PFS series were combined in a single program called First Choice. This integrated program was designed for novices and first-time users. Software Publishing believed the moderately priced and highly touted First Choice would prove attractive to a new wave of first-time users. Although officially priced at $195 through normal retail channels, the program could be obtained from discount mail order houses for slightly less than $100. The individual PFS programs were also available from the same sources for less than $90 each.

The previous PFS program family did not allow users to upgrade to more sophisticated programs, and many industry observers felt the product development process took too long to complete. The PFS professional Write, File, and Plan packages were developed to provide expanded word processing, file processing, and spreadsheet capabilities to experienced users. These updated, expanded versions of the stand-alone PFS programs were designed to appeal to a growing number of veteran users with a price tag of about $150 per program.

A major disadvantage of the high-end programs is that they faced stiff competition from the more sophisticated software programs offered by other major software suppliers. Many prospective purchasers might think the more expensive programs with greater capabilities such as LOTUS 1-2-3, Dbase III, RBASE V, or Q&A were better buys than a medium-price-range version of the PFS series.

The Professional Word Processing program has expanded mail merge capabilities while the Professional Plan spreadsheet can read data and formulas from other worksheets such as Lotus. The professional programs, while menu-based like the simpler and earlier PFS programs, have added pull-down menu structures, macros, and quick-entry keys to appeal to more experienced users. On-line help facilities have been expanded and manuals upgraded. These programs stress ease of use, but they provide more powerful capabilities than available previously. The company has slowly moved away from its image of providing programs for beginners only. One drawback is that the change of image and modifications in the familiar user interface might cause confusion among dealers and users alike as to the level at which the programs are aimed.

Many of the new product decisions were made by employee committees rather than by a few top-level executives. A major decision was to change the familiar user interface, and other product line changes were made on the assumption that a large number of buyers would be purchasing low-price PC clones. The product line modifications apparently did not consider the effect that the introduction of the new PC-2 personal computer would have on application software sales. The PC-2 offered faster, larger capacity, and multi-user capabilities along with 3 and 1/2 inch disks. The company has stated it will continue to sell Apple versions of the PFS series but its primary emphasis in future years would be on its IBM-compatible lines.

Software Products acquired Harvard Software in 1986 as another means of expanding its existing product lines. This acquisition gave the company access to Harvard Project Manager and Harvard Presentation Graphics programs, which were higher priced and more complex than the PFS series. Shortly after, Software Products introduced the Harvard Professional Publisher Desktop publishing program for the IBM PC's. This program was developed by an outside software developer to be marketed exclusively by Software Publishing Company. The Clickart Personal Publishing line of desktop publishing programs was also acquired from T-Maker to give the company desktop publishing capabilities in the low-end market.

SOFTWARE ECONOMICS AND COMPETITION

Software packages developed for large mainframe or mini-computer systems normally have long product life cycles, high user-assumed maintenance costs, and small unit-volume sales. In contrast, software packages for smaller systems tend to have shorter life cycles, larger unit sales, and lower maintenance costs. At least one microcomputer software developer, Lotus Development, had announced its intention to develop and market a mini-computer and mainframe version of its popular spreadsheet package, 1-2-3. It is generally uncommon for a given company to try to establish a position in all three market areas: microcomputers, minicomputers, and mainframe computers.

According to Ashton Tate spokesmen, the major competitive factors in microcomputer software sales are package price/performance, marketing efforts/expenditures, ease of maintenance and use, documentation and training, vendor size/reputation, and product line integration. (*Industry Surveys,* 6 November, 1986). Brand recognition and new product acquisition or introduction is also becoming more important in the current marketing environment. The software industry is similar in many ways to the book publishing industry where a company could be successful if it could develop and market one or two best sellers.

Site licensing and quantity discounts have become increasingly important as sales to corporate buyers increase. Site licensing allows unlimited copying of products and availability of multiple copies on a much lower per-unit basis than otherwise possible. Software Publishing permitted site licenses to be purchased for a one-time fee of $75,000 for the PFS series and $100,000 for the Harvard series. The site licensing included rights to duplicate disks and manuals, technical notes, technical support for one year, and sizable discounts on upgrades. Unlimited multiple hard disk installations were also permitted in contrast to previous policies.

Barriers to entry exist in the microcomputer software industry, and it is quite possible than only a few of the present leaders will survive without further product line acquisitions or mergers. Extensive research and development outlays by existing companies, the ability to market products through multiple distribution channels, and required adaptation of existing software to take advantage of technological improvements in computer hardware are likely to inhibit the successful entry of additional software development companies.

Microcomputer software package sales were estimated to be more than $3 billion in 1986. Sales for 1986 increased 26 percent over 1985, compared to more than 50 percent annual increases in 1984 and 1983. Software sales have tended to closely follow sales of microcomputer hardware. While sales of spreadsheet, word processing, and file management/data base systems seem to be stabilizing, sales of project management, CAD/CAM, and graphics programs are expected to increase much faster in the next several years than sales of other types of application software. Personal computer sales in units and dollars and microcomputer sales for the six largest microcomputer software companies for 1983 to 1986 are shown in Exhibit 2.

Research and Development efforts and expenditures are likely to assume increasing importance in the last half of the 1980s. R&D outlays as a percentage of sales revenues for the major microcomputer firms are given in Exhibit 3.

FINANCIAL AND SALES ANALYSIS

After increasing from $4 million in 1982 to $37.2 million in 1985, Software Publishing's revenues declined to $23.7 million in 1986. In addition, net income declined to $700,000 in 1986, as compared to $5.8 million in 1985. Exhibit 4 presents the sales revenues and market shares for Software Publishing and five of its major competitors for 1983 through 1986.

Exhibit 5 shows net incomes in millions of dollars and net income as a percentage of sales for the six largest microcomputer software companies for the years 1983 to 1986.

Software Publishing's net income as a percent of sales declined from 15.7 percent in 1985 to 2.95 percent in 1986, and return on assets decreased from 35.7 percent in 1982 to 24.0 percent in 1985. Return on equity declined from a high of 132.0 percent in 1982 to 32.3 percent in 1985. The company has no long-term debt, and its current ratio increased from 2.8 in 1983 to 7.2 in 1985. Earnings per share have

EXHIBIT 2 Personal computer sales and microcomputer software sales for years 1983 to 1986

	1983	*1984*	*1985*	*1986*
Personal Computer Sales				
Units (millions)	6.2	7.7	6.4	7.1
Dollars (billions)	8.6	14.3	16.2	16.8
Microcomputer Software Sales				
in millions for six largest microcomputer software companies	177.0	400.0	555.0	808.00

Source: Dataquest in *USA Today* (May 1987 U.S. Industrial Outlook).

EXHIBIT 3 R & D Expenditures as a percentage of sales revenues

Company	*1984*	*1985*
Ashton Tate	6.0	9.3
Lotus Development	9.4	9.4
Micropro	14.5	19.6
Microsoft	12.2	10.4
Software Publishing	12.3	16.1

EXHIBIT 4 Sales revenues (in millions of dollars) and Market Shares (percentages of sales) for the six largest microcomputer software companies, 1983–1986

Company	*1983*		*1984*		*1985*		*1986*	
Lotus	$53	29.9%	$157	39.3%	$226	40.7%	$283	35.0%
Ashton Tate	18	10.2	43	10.8	82	14.8	211	26.1
Microsoft	50	28.2	97	24.3	140	25.2	198	24.5
Micropro	45	25.4	67	16.8	43	7.7	52	6.4
Sw Publ.	10	5.7	24	6.0	37	6.7	24	3.0
Borland	1.0	0.6	12	3.0	27	4.9	41	5.0

ranged from 0.13 in 1982 to 0.83 in 1985. Per share earnings for the 1985–1986 fiscal year were 0.10. The price earnings ratio of Software Publishing's stock varied from 9–1 to 20–1 in 1984 and 1985, respectively.

On November 15, 1984, the Company sold 1,840,000 shares of common stock at $7.00 per share in its initial public offering. Company officers and directors hold about 30 percent of the shares outstanding. The stock price ranged from $4.75 to $8.50

EXHIBIT 5 Net income in millions of dollars and net income as a percentage of sales for the six largest microcomputer companies for years 1983 to 1986

Company	*1983*		*1984*		*1985*		*1986*	
Lotus	$13.7	25.9%	$36.0	23.0%	$38.2	16.9%	$48.3	17.1%
Ashton Tate	1.1	5.9	5.3	12.3	6.5	7.9	16.6	13.6
Microsoft	6.5	13.0	15.9	16.3	24.1	17.2	39.3	19.9
Micropro	4.3	9.5	5.8	8.7	0.2	0.5	0.3*	0.6
Sw Publ.	1.4	14.0	3.6	15.4	5.8	15.7	0.7*	3.0
Borland	0.1	10.6	1.5	13.0	5.2	19.2	8.4**	20.6

Notes:
*Preliminary figures for 1986
**Based on fiscal year ending March 31, 1986

during 1986. The company has not paid any dividends so far and does not plan any dividend declarations at present, believing that company earnings should be plowed back into company operations.

QUESTIONS

1. The director of planning has asked you to develop a series of sales revenues forecasts for Software Publishing Company and the microcomputer software industry (limited to the six largest microcomputer software companies), using common statistical forecasting methods, including time series, simple linear regression, and multiple linear regression. Relevant company, industry, and national economic series are to be included (see Exhibit 2 and Appendix A). The projections produced by the various methods should cover five years and should be compared in terms of accuracy or forecasting error. You are to recommend a method for forecasting, stating your reasons for selection of the chosen method.

APPENDIX A National economic indicators for years 1983 to 1986 (in billions of dollars)

	1983	*1984*	*1985*	*1986*
Personal consumption expenditures	2,234.5	2,428.2	2,600.5	2,762.5
Durable goods expenditures	289.1	331.2	359.3	388.1
Nondurable goods expenditures	816.7	870.1	905.1	932.7
Expenditures for services	1,128.7	1,227.0	1,336.1	1,441.7
Corporate profits	196.7	230.2	222.6	244.1
New plant/equipment outlays	304.8	354.4	379.3	390.8
Business equipment expenditures	115.4	134.2	139.6	138.6

Source: Department of Commerce, Bureau of Economic Analysis

APPENDIX B Unit shipments for 1985 for Software Publishing

PFS: Access	9,800
PFS: File	286,600
PFS: Graph	90,200
PFS: Plan	80,300
PFS: Proof	15,100
PFS: Report	189,500
PFS: Write	337,300
Harvard Project Manager	26,100

Source: Software Publishing's 1985 Annual Report.

APPENDIX C Comparative Financial Statements ($000)

	Microsoft	*Lotus*	*Ashton Tate*	*Software Publishing Company*
	Income Statement			
Net Revenues	**197,514**	**225,526**	**121,571**	**37,181**
Cost of revenues	40,862	42,893	20,729	5,901
Research and development	20,523	21,192	11,303	5,969
Sales and marketing	57,668	73,046	12,821	12,589
General and administrative expenses	17,555	27,464	46,827	3,708
Income from operations	60,906	60,931	29,891	9,014
Other income (loss)	5,078	6,472	—	1,874
Income before taxes	65,984	67,403	29,891	10,888
Taxes	26,730	29,253	14,112	5,045
Net income	**39,254**	**38,150**	**15,779**	**5,843**
	Balance Sheet			
Current assets	147,980	139,049	53,684	25,253
Net fixed assets	19,544	38,203	12,611	1,403
Other assets	3,215	8,551	22,103	748
Total assets	**170,739**	**185,803**	**88,398**	**27,404**
Current liabilities	29,528	45,428	29,481	3,497
Long-term liabilities	1,879	1,833	5,389	191
Stockholders' equity	139,332	138,542	53,528	23,716
Total Liabilities and Equity	**170,739**	**185,803**	**88,398**	**27,404**

Source: Various Annual Reports for Fiscal Years Ending June 30, 1986, January 31, 1986, December 31, 1985, and September 30, 1985.

The Planning Director is also interested in knowing if company profits can be forecasted in the same manner as sales revenues. He has expressed an interest in determining what factors may affect profit. In addition, he would like to know whether Software Publishing Company's revenues are likely to grow at the same rate as industry sales and what impact this growth rate might have on company profits and the company's ability to generate the cash needed to develop and market its products.

2. Software Publishing Company has a diverse product line, including a word processing program, an electronic spreadsheet, a graphics program, a communication program, project management programs, desktop publishing programs, and an integrated software package incorporating word processing, file management/reporting, and spreadsheet capabilities. The planning director has asked you to evaluate the growth possibilities for each type of software and to recommend what types of software the company should concentrate its efforts on during the next five years, considering such factors as market growth, competition, profit margins, and marketing resources needed.
3. The company controller has asked you to evaluate the financial performance of Software Publishing Company in relation to its major competitors using common liquidity, leverage, activity, and profitability ratios as well as such measures as market share and average sales growth. You are to prepare a report pointing out the company strengths and weaknesses in the performance areas measured.

Springfield Remanufacturing Corporation—1987

CHARLES BOYD
Southwest Missouri State University
KEITH DENTON
Southwest Missouri State University

Salespeople desperately tried to generate new orders. Company President John Stack stated that he had enough work for the remaining employees through August, but that he needed a "big play" by September. Stack considered whether to lay off employees or to avoid the layoff and risk the financial stability of the corporation (Springfield Remanufacturing Corporation [SRC] had never had a layoff). As indicated in Exhibits 1 through 4, SRC's profit margin and general financial condition worsened in 1986 compared to 1985.

This case was prepared by Professors Charles Boyd and D. Keith Denton of Southwest Missouri State University as a basis for class discussion and not as an illustration of effective or ineffective handling of an administrative situation.

EXHIBIT 1 Springfield Remanufacturing Company, sales and profits by cylinder

Cylinder	*Sales/profits (000 omitted)* 1985	1986
Automobiles	$10,980/ $549	$19,003/ $950
Trucks	800/ 311	9,855/ 355
Construction equipment	7,016/ 290	4,961/ 150
Agricultural equipment	4,200/ 210	4,884/ 150
Total	**$30,196/$1,360**	**$38,703/$1,605**

FORMATION OF THE COMPANY

On February 1, 1983, after nearly three years of rumors and frustration, the financially troubled International Harvester (IH) sold one of its last remaining diesel engine and engine component remanufacturing operations as part of its turnaround strategy. IH needed to do something because of its $4 billion debt load and $1.6 billion in operating losses. During a depressed truck and farm economy, the corporation was seeking answers to its troubles. Therefore, it decided to sell the Springfield plant and four other parts-remanufacturing centers. IH's sale of their Springfield, Missouri, facility marked the end of IH's remanufacturing activities but not the end of its troubles. IH later sold its Farm Division in order to save its Truck Division, and the firm later reorganized as NAVISTAR.

The Springfield Remanufacturing facility employed 171 workers at the time of the sale. It was originally meant to be sold to Dresser Industries, a major customer of the plant despite the fact that SRC's employees had had a bid on the table to purchase the company. When negotiations with Dresser broke down in December 1982, employees of the firm began to consider forming their own company. Springfield Remanufacturing Corporation (SRC) was the result of these discussions when two months later employees obtained financing from the Bank of America in San Francisco. The company and the 68,000-square-foot plant was bought from IH by a group of thirteen employees for approximately $7 million at three percentage points above the prime rate. The plant's assets provided enough collateral so that the employees did not have to give the lender any of the equity in the firm.

Twelve of these new owners were former employees and managers of IH at the plant. The thirteenth was Don McCoy, the controller of the IH Division of which the Springfield plant was part. President of the new corporation was John P. (Jack) Stack who had previously been plant manager. Stack and the other twelve owners decided to broaden the ownership of the new corporation through an employee stock ownership program. As former employees were rehired, the owners decided to set aside each year a portion of the corporate earnings to buy some of the company's unissued stock. This stock would then go into a trust fund for workers. The employee stock ownership plan (ESOP) was greeted with enthusiasm. Foreman Joe Loeber noted, "It adds a little incentive to know you're working for your own future and not

EXHIBIT 2 Springfield Remanufacturing Corporation and subsidiary consolidated balance sheets

	January 25, 1987	*January 26, 1986*	*January 27, 1985*	*January 29, 1984*
		Assets		
Current Assets				
Cash	$ 50,082	$ 13,584	20,597	316,688
Trade accounts receivable, less allowances for doubtful accounts	2,237,471	3,184,409	2,098,321	2,547,771
Inventories	9,230,828	10,451,968	8,055,556	9,514,189
Prepaid income taxes	—	—	—	298,200
Prepaid expenses and other current assets	32,637	37,875	39,826	48,645
Total Current Assets	**11,551,018**	**13,687,836**	**10,214,300**	**12,725,493**
Property, Buildings and Equipment	2,244,519	1,905,348	669,177	291,043
	$13,795,537	**$15,593,184**	**$10,883,477**	**$13,016,536**
		Liabilities and Stockholders' Equity		
Current Liabilities				
Notes payable	$ 383,658	$ 2,677,195	$ 2,526,557	7,141,616
Accounts payable	3,867,352	5,825,521	2,661,636	1,907,233
Accrued contribution to employee stock ownership trust	—	521,011	413,510	—
Income taxes payable	363,340	47,000	—	—
Other current liabilities	1,211,717	900,450	771,721	727,954
Current portion of long-term debt	358,533	309,002	297,280	10,006
Total Current Liabilities	**6,184,600**	**10,280,179**	**6,670,704**	**9,786,809**
Excess of Net Assets Acquired over Cost	786,710	1,573,420	2,360,129	3,146,838
Long-Term Debt	2,537,847	1,317,522	1,126,922	43,377
Deferred Income Taxes	10,000	34,000	—	—
	9,519,184	**13,205,121**	**10,157,755**	**12,977,024**
Stockholders' Equity				
Class A Common Stock, voting, par value $.10 per share, 1,500,000 and 500,000 shares authorized, 1,140,000 and 500,000 issued and outstanding	114,000	50,000	50,000	50,000
Class B Common Stock, nonvoting, par value $.10 per share, 10,000,000 and 1,000,000 shares authorized, 1,984,500 and 541,500 shares issued and outstanding	198,450	54,150	51,000	50,000
Additional paid-in capital	603,300	124,365	5,100	—
Retained earnings	3,688,114	2,159,548	619,622	(60,488)
Treasury stock, at cost	(327,511)	—	—	—
	4,276,353	2,388,063	725,722	39,512
	$13,795,537	**$15,593,184**	**$10,883,477**	**$13,016,536**

EXHIBIT 3 Springfield Remanufacturing Corporation and subsidiary consolidated statements of earnings

	January 25, 1987	*January 26, 1986*	*January 27, 1985*	*January 29, 1984*
Net sales	$37,937,498	$27,818,322	$23,976,808	$16,347,600
Cost of goods sold	30,864,793	23,766,826	20,696,029	13,420,229
	7,072,705	**4,051,496**	**3,280,779**	**2,927,371**
Gain (loss) on disposal of inventory	(2,229,765)	115,138	—	—
	4,842,940	**4,166,634**	**3,280,779**	**2,927,371**
Operating Expenses				
Selling, general and administrative	2,850,189	2,570,828	2,158,463	2,826,165
Contribution to employee stock ownership trust	706,216	521,011	419,610	—
Interest	442,039	597,462	798,305	948,403
	3,998,444	3,689,301	3,376,378	3,774,568
	844,496	**477,333**	**(95,599)**	**(847,197)**
Nonoperating Income				
Amortization of excess of net assets acquired over cost	786,710	786,709	786,709	786,709
Other, net	331,295	351,884	—	—
	1,118,005	**1,138,593**	**786,709**	**786,709**
Earnings (Or Loss) Before Income Taxes	1,962,501	1,615,926	692,110	(60,488)
Income taxes	350,000	76,000	103,000	—
Earnings (or Loss) Before Extraordinary Item	**1,612,501**	**1,539,926**	**588,110**	**(60,488)**
Extraordinary item—tax benefit from utilization of loss carryforward	—	—	92,000	—
Net Earnings (or Loss)	**$ 1,612,501**	**$ 1,539,926**	**$ 680,110**	**($ 60,488)**

just the other guy's. Everybody's excited." The managers owned shares of stock and signed an agreement that the corporation would issue shares of stock directly into the ESOP. Thus, the ESOP became the vehicle for employee ownership of the firm.

Stack and other management realized the plant's future lay outside of IH. He noted, "We were really different. IH employees were normally represented by United Auto Workers, and the Springfield plant wasn't." As early as two years before the actual sale, local management at the Springfield plant submitted a bid for the plant that was not given serious consideration by IH. A year later, a more detailed plan was submitted but again was rejected. In 1983, they closed the deal in five weeks.

The day after the sale, SRC brought back thirty of its former IH employees. The company increased the number of employees by thirty a day until most of the original

EXHIBIT 4 Springfield Remanufacturing Corporation and subsidiary consolidated statements of changes in financial position

	January 25, 1987	*January 26, 1986*	*January 27, 1985*	*January 29, 1984*
Source of Funds				
Operations				
Earnings (loss) before extraordinary item	$1,612,501	$1,539,926	$ 588,110	($ 60,488)
Charges (credits) to operations, not requiring outlay of working capital				
Amortization of excess net assets acquired over cost	(786,710)	(786,709)	(786,709)	(786,709)
Depreciation	499,901	247,408	97,057	30,349
Increase (decrease) in deferred income taxes	(24,000)	34,000	—	—
Funds provided by (used in) operations	1,301,692	1,034,625	(101,542)	816,848
Additions to long-term debt	2,688,500	489,500	1,500,000	60,275
Extraordinary item—tax benefit from utilization of loss carryforward	—	—	92,000	—
Contribution of common stock to employee stock ownership trust	706,216	121,500	6,100	—
Excess of net assets acquired over cost	—	—	—	3,933,547
Sale of treasury stock	258,073	—	—	—
Disposals of property, buildings and equipment	—	51,495	—	—
Proceeds from sale of common stock	—	915	—	100,000
Decrease in working capital	—	135,939	—	
	$4,954,481	**$1,833,974**	**$1,496,558**	**$4,093,822**

employees were back. When SRC started business, it had signed up 60 percent of its old customers. Before the sale it had $10 million in sales of parts for construction equipment, another $7 million for farm equipment, and $3 million for trucks.

On February 1, 1983, Jack Stack, president of SRC, issued a news release stating that the new firm would remain in Springfield and would continue to be a major rebuilder of diesel engines, injection pumps, water pumps, and other engine components. The news release noted that SRC would be a supplier of remanufactured engines and engine components to IH's agricultural equipment and truck dealers.

The news release, like the news about the IH sale of the Springfield facility, did not tell the whole story about this unique situation. It was no secret that many of IH's manufacturing facilities had suffered from abrasive employee-management relations. When Jack Stack arrived at the facility four years before the eventual sale, the employees were on the verge of forming a union, and the company was running behind production schedule. Stack was sent from IH headquarters and given six months to straighten out the problem at the plant or close it.

EXHIBIT 4 continued

	January 25, 1987	*January 26, 1986*	*January 27, 1985*	*January 29, 1984*
Application of Funds				
Reduction and current maturities of long-term debt	$1,468,148	$ 298,900	$ 416,455	16,898
Additions to property, buildings and equipment	839,072	1,535,074	475,191	321,392
Purchase of treasury stock	688,500	—	—	
Increase in working capital	1,958,761	—	604,912	2,938,684
	$4,954,481	**$1,833,974**	**$1,496,558**	**$3,276,974**
Analysis of Working Capital Changes				
Increase (decrease) in current assets				
Cash	$ 36,498	($ 7,013)	($ 296,091)	$ 316,688
Trade accounts receivable	(946,938)	1,086,088	(449,450)	2,547,771
Inventories	(1,221,140)	2,396,412	(1,458,633)	9,514,189
Prepaid income taxes	—	—	(298,200)	298,200
Prepaid expenses and other current assets	(5,238)	(1,951)	(8,819)	48,645
	(2,136,818)	**3,473,536**	**(2,511,193)**	**12,725,493**
Increase (decrease) in current liabilities				
Notes payable	(2,293,537)	150,638	(4,615,059)	7,141,616
Accounts payable	(1,958,169)	3,163,885	754,403	1,907,233
Accrued contribution to employee stock ownership trust	(521,011)	107,501	413,510	—
Income taxes payable	316,340	36,000	—	—
Other current liabilities	311,267	139,729	43,767	727,954
Current portion of long-term debt	49,531	11,722	287,274	10,006
	(4,095,579)	**3,609,475**	**(3,116,105)**	**9,786,809**
Increase (Decrease) in Working Capital	**$1,958,761**	**($ 135,939)**	**$ 604,912**	**$2,938,684**

Stack called a meeting with all employees and "begged" them to give him and his team a chance to change things. He promised to listen, and he promised change. The employees agreed to give him a chance. The union election was scheduled for March 10; this time frame gave Stack two months to win over the employees. Stack won the election; more than 75 percent of the employees voted in favor of management over the union.

Management's relations with employees began to change. There were better human relations, better communications, and better cooperation. Three topics were emphasized to the employees: safety, housekeeping, and quality. Statistical measures for these three activities were developed by management and taught to the employees. Eventually, the employees were taught about costs and profits. Data were graphed, kept updated, and posted in prominent places within the plant. As a result, employees became very goal-oriented. Stack commented:

> You've got to have an enemy to have a team. If you can set that enemy outside your organization and declare what that enemy is, that's the unifying factor behind the whole organization.

So such things as safety problems and quality rejects became the enemy, and improving performance in these areas became the employees' goals. As a result, the organization's efficiency and effectiveness improved dramatically.

One year later, production was up 30 percent. By June 1984, the facility had become the "best" of the outside firms performing remanufacturing work for IH. SRC had remained profitable during the time that similar facilities had been losing money.

Several programs that Stack and others started during this time were given credit for helping turn things around. One of these is the Quality of Work Life (QWL) program in which employees analyze and propose solutions to organizational problems. The work force had also formed small employee groups, known as quality circles, that were used to make the plant more efficient and productive. Innovative approaches were also used. For example, when IH imposed a wage freeze, the QWL group decided to go to a flex-time, four, 10-hour/day week. This schedule saved employees money on transportation and lunches and reduced absenteeism by giving workers a day off so they could take care of personal business.

METEORIC RISE

The rise of SRC from the ashes of IH was almost immediate and profound. The company's success did not go unnoticed by the news media. Several articles on its success were written, and the firm was featured in an issue of *INC* magazine. A television documentary by PBS aired during the fall of 1987.

During 1984, SRC increased sales by 20 percent to $15.5 million. A year later, business increased by 40 percent to $23 million in sales, and 100 employees were added to the payroll to bring total employment to 225.

In one year, SRC remanufactured 2,500 engines, and in two years of operation, the firm had warranty returns averaging less than 1 percent. SRC's customers included Ingersol-Rand, J.I. Case, Dresser Industries, and International Harvester.

A red-letter day for SRC came in April 1985, two years after its formation, when SRC announced that it had received a contract from General Motors (GM) to remanufacture 15,400 5.7-liter V-8 diesel engines for GM's Oldsmobile Division. There are about 1.5 million GM cars in service powered by the 5.7 liter engine. GM decided to subcontract the remanufacturing of these engines because daily demand had stabilized at a level which GM management no longer considered justifying the plant space it had devoted to the remanufacturing. GM ceased production of the 5.7-liter diesel engine a week prior to signing the contract with SRC. The volume of SRC's work was expected to slowly decrease as the cars powered by the 5.7 are taken out of service over time.

Lee Shroyer, marketing manager, said the contract could mean forty new jobs in Springfield and sixty new jobs at a satellite operation in the nearby community of

Willow Springs. With this contract, SRC became the first company to be named as an authorized engine rebuilder for GM. The three-year contract was expected to be worth $40 million to SRC. An SRC manager stated, "We should continue to work with GM as long as we can maintain their quality and safety requirements, and I don't see any problem with that." With this new business, 1985 sales were expected to exceed $30 million.

Due to this new business, additional fixtures, tooling, jet sprays, and new arrangements were made in the Springfield plant to improve the flow of materials. To accommodate increased business, SRC needed a new building. In May 1985, it secured an additional building in Willow Springs, a small town 70 miles away. Stack expected to be turning out five engines per day by mid-May and 125 per day by November. By November, SRC expected to employ seventy-five persons and eventually employ 150 after two years.

REASONS FOR SUCCESS

SRC's 40 percent growth rate did not come by accident. The company would not have received the GM contract if it did not turn out extremely high-quality products. Stack noted that a remanufacturing or recycled assembly is 30 to 40 percent the price of a new one, which means lower inventory carrying cost for the original equipment manufacturer (OEM) customer. SRC warranties are as good or better than those of a new product. Less than 1 percent of its products are returned for any reason—the industry average is 6 percent. Some of its products are guaranteed to be delivered within 48 hours. Within the industry, SRC has some of the best warranties, lowest costs, and highest reliability. During recent years, SRC experienced almost a 400 percent growth in business, and a 5 percent decrease in overhead cost. This growth occurred despite the depressed agriculture and construction industries.

SRC's success is built on at least four ingredients: Jack Stack, the charismatic and thoughtful president; a very capable management team; a positive philosophy toward employees; and employee ownership. Stack is the visionary who keeps the company focused on its objectives and clearly believes in his management style. Stack is complemented by those around him. Mike Carrigan, vice-president of production, is a self-confessed "pack rat" who totally understands the production process. He is always looking to improve methods of operation and reduce waste. He would much rather fix what he has rather than buy something new. He seems ideally suited to this recycling work. Gary Brown, the human resources manager, likewise knows the personnel function and knows what kind of people SRC is looking for. Both Brown and Carrigan say there are two types of people—competitive and noncompetitive ones. They look for the competitive, "hungry" ones: the ones who like to win, who like to compete, and who are interested in self improvement.

SRC tries to maximize its people. The company spends a great deal of time trying to cultivate an air of trust and openness between people. Stack noted, "There's not a financial number our employees don't know or don't have access to." SRC conducts weekly meetings with employees where the business is discussed, including financial statements, operating income, profits, losses, assets, liabilities, and other financial figures. All employees may not know or understand all the financial figures, but they know the figures are available. They do know what each department contributes and costs the company. Stack has been quoted as saying, "We teach them about finance and accounting before we teach them how to turn a wrench."

Management at SRC also tries to make work "fun". They are constantly setting standards for direct and indirect labor and then trying to make "games" out of achieving results. These games are set up so employees understand what is needed; incentives and rewards are given. A popular phrase around SRC is STP-GUTR (Stop The Praise—Give Us the Raise). SRC pays employees a sizable bonus if quarterly financial goals are met. Winning at the "game" is based on an employee's ability to save labor and/or material cost. Some employees at the plant receive as much as 12 percent of their salary in bonus money. Employees also receive cash payments for suggestions that save the company money. When safety goals were met, insurance money refunded to SRC was used to purchase gifts of appreciation.

SRC also practices a decentralized-participative style of management where it tries to push decision-making down to the lowest level. Employees and first-line supervisors are encouraged to take on new tasks. For example, most supervisors "adopt" an area outside their supervisory area. One supervisor may be in charge of controlling chemical costs ranging from solvents to "white out" correction fluid. Another supervisor may be in charge of all plant abrasives. Management at SRC believes it teaches everyone the value of cooperation and makes them better at communicating and persuading since they must convince others outside their area to control costs in their "adopted" area. Of course all of these programs are enhanced because of ESOP. It is not someone else's business—it's theirs.

MARKETING CONCEPT

SRC fills a market niche with the OEM being the customer. The marketing concept is simple and straightforward. Diesel engines are usually employed in trucks, earth-moving equipment, and other types of "workhorse" applications in which these engines labor daily under heavy strain. Due to this heavy usage, vital engine parts eventually break down, and the user must either purchase an entirely new piece of equipment, have the engine repaired, or have the engine or its major components rebuilt. The first option is so often passed up due to the very high expense of purchasing an entirely new piece of equipment. Each of the other two options requires the services of a firm which either builds or repairs engine components. This business segment is known as the aftermarket.

Most firms in the engine or automotive aftermarket compete against the OEM company that originally built a particular engine component by offering their own repair service or replacement part. As a result, the OEM loses market share in the aftermarket. The distinctive difference of SRC is that the company seeks to restore a portion of this lost market share to the OEM by serving as the OEM's contracted provider of aftermarket engine components by providing the OEM with a replacement engine or engine component. As a result, the OEM is spared the tremendous costs of real estate, plant, and equipment investment that would be necessary to do their own remanufacturing work. SRC incurs these expenses for the OEM and sells a quality remanufactured product built to exacting specifications that will cost the OEM customer less than if it produced its own new component. In addition, new engines or components are available when needed because they are produced in quantity rather than individually prepared upon demand. With this availability, the end user can get a failed piece of equipment up and running again much quicker and at a lower cost than might otherwise be possible.

An example will help illustrate the advantages SRC can offer an OEM customer. Suppose a truck operated by a commercial carrier is put out of commission by the failure of the fuel injection pump. The trucking company will likely inquire to the OEM regarding the problem. The OEM may be able to offer a new replacement pump for $580. The trucking company may instead buy a new or rebuilt pump at a lower price from a competing company in the aftermarket. Another alternative would be to have the failed pump repaired, but this option would entail more downtime for the truck and thus lost revenue to the trucking company. If the OEM had a contract with SRC, however, the OEM would have a high-quality remanufactured fuel injection pump that had the same warranty as a new pump to sell to the trucking company for $300.

As a result of its remanufacturing operations, SRC is able to add value to its OEM customers in a number of ways:

1. Preserving part of the OEM's market share in the automotive aftermarket.
2. Providing the OEM more total profitability over the entire life of the engine.
3. Preventing costly investment in plant and equipment for remanufacturing operations (these operations cannot be performed on an OEM's existing production lines). These savings become even more important when the OEM must continue to supply components for an engine that has gone out of production.
4. Providing cost savings to the OEM. Since SRC uses an efficient job shop operation, it is able to sell its products to its OEM customers at a relatively low price, which saves the OEM customer money and lowers its inventory carrying cost.

SRC sales personnel visit OEM engine and equipment builders around the country and try to explain to their management teams how SRC can add value to their operations in the previously listed ways. The SRC sales personnel try to make them aware of all the costs they must still incur *after* they have sold their products. These costs include warranties, return parts, labor, and inventory carrying costs. The representatives try to explain how SRC can minimize these costs and increase the OEM's total profitability and share of the aftermarket.

SHORT-TERM FORECASTS FOR THE AUTOMOTIVE AFTERMARKET[1]

The success of automotive aftermarket companies is highly dependent upon the rate of new car sales and the number of older vehicles in service. The size of the "pipeline" of new-to-aging cars represents the size of their market.

TABLE 1

Average age of American produced cars and trucks (years)		
Year	*Passenger Cars*	*Motor Trucks*
1985	7.6	8.1
1984	7.5	8.2
1983	7.4	8.1
1982	7.2	7.8
1981	6.9	7.5
1980	6.6	7.1
1979	6.4	6.9
1978	6.3	6.9
1977	6.2	6.9

The 1987 outlook for the U.S. automobile industry has been summarized as follows:

> For 1987, U.S. car and truck output is projected to decline about 5 percent from the 11.5 million units estimated for 1986, even if no lengthy strikes occur when UAW contracts expire next fall. Following an estimated 12 percent decline in 1986, profits for 1987 may recede another 20 percent or so, despite efficiency gains. This relatively unfavorable outlook reflects lower unit volume, mounting competition, a less favorable sales mix, costly sales incentive programs, and plant closing costs.

While 1987 sales are projected to be 5 percent lower than 1986 sales, it should be remembered that 1984–1986 sales were well above the long-term U.S. sales trend for this industry.

The average age of vehicles on the road is particularly important to SRC and other firms in the automotive aftermarket since their business comes from the wearout of vehicle parts and components. Table 1 reveals that the average age of American-produced cars and trucks in use has increased during recent years.

Major replacement parts supplier Federal-Mogul Corporation estimates that sales of automotive aftermarket parts will grow approximately 2.6 percent in real terms over the next few years. GM estimates a 2.5–3.0 percent real growth rate. The Motor and Equipment manufacturers Association (MEMA) estimates a 3.3 percent average compound growth rate in the number of vehicles in operation through 1990.

A TURNING POINT

Four years after its initial formation, SRC was enjoying its success. The firm was by now sufficiently diversified into the industry's market niches, which Stack referred to as the "four cylinders":

1. Construction equipment
2. Agricultural equipment
3. Trucks
4. Automobiles

Customers had been added rapidly to each "cylinder" during the 4-year period. Exhibit 1 shows SRC's sales to its dominant customer in each "cylinder" for 1985 and 1986. Stack decided it was time to consolidate the company's gains. The 1987 financial plan was prepared in August 1986, completed in October, and approved in November. The strategy for 1987 would be to seek no new customers. Instead, the sales and marketing operation would be reorganized and would concentrate on enhancing service to SRC's present customers. There had not seemed to be time to do that during the four previous years of rapid growth; this year, the company would take the time.

But during the period from November 1986 to February 1987, several significant things occurred at General Motors (GM): the $700 million payoff to Ross Perot, a huge stock buyback, and continued competitive problems in the automobile market. And what happened to GM was important to SRC, since 50 percent of SRC's business was with GM during 1986. In April 1987, GM notified SRC that they would need 5,000 fewer engines from the firm during 1987 than previously planned. To SRC, this reduction translates into 50,000 manhours, or 25 percent of its 1987 business.

Fortunately, SRC moved six months ago from remanufacturing diesel engines exclusively to also remanufacturing gasoline engines. The firm began remanufacturing thirty gasoline engines per day for Chrysler in February 1987, and later began remanufacturing them for GM too. This new business helps cushion the blow from the loss of GM's diesels, but not nearly enough. It is clear that SRC will have to work hard for new business during 1987; it cannot be the year of concentrating on customer enhancement as Stack had hoped it would be.

By early June 1987, Springfield Remanufacturing Company (SRC) had responded to the situation with an increased attrition rate from its 400-person work force. During the past six months, forty-three employees had been terminated: twenty for performance reasons, the rest voluntarily. Still no layoff program has been instituted, but time is running out. Stack's "big play" has to come soon. He wonders what options are available and what will be the effect of his actions.

ENDNOTES

1. The data reported in this subsection of the case were obtained from Standard & Poor's *Industry Surveys*, April 1987, pp. 75, 80, and 85.

Morton Thiokol, Inc.—1987

JYOTI N. PRASAD
Western Illinois University

On May 7, 1987, the *Wall Street Journal* reported what Morton Thiokol had been dreadfully apprehensive of. The report said that Jane Smith, widow of Challenger co-pilot Michael Smith, had filed a $1.5 billion lawsuit against the U.S. government, Morton Thiokol, Inc., and former space agency engineer Lawrence Mulloy, who supervised the shuttle-booster rocket program at the time of the January 28, 1986, disaster that caused a massive dent in the U.S. space program. All seven space shuttle crew members, including teacher Christa McAuliffe, were killed in the accident.

The suit, filed in U.S. District Court in Orlando, Florida, sought $500 million in damages jointly from the three defendants, accusing them of negligence in the shuttle accident. The suit asked for an additional $1 billion in punitive damages from Morton Thiokol, manufacturer of the shuttle's booster rockets. The complaint alleged that Morton Thiokol's behavior was "willful, wanton, malicious" and showed a "reckless disregard for human life." The suit also demanded to bar Morton Thiokol from further shuttle work. It asserted that Morton Thiokol was wrong in telling NASA that the rocket defect could be fixed. "The fact is," the complaint said, "that these joints are so fundamentally and basically unsound that it is impossible for them to be fixed."

While the families of four astronauts reached a settlement with the Justice Department and Morton Thiokol late in 1986, giving up the right to file future claims in return for at least $750,000 each, survivors of another astronaut, Ronald McNair, filed a suit against Morton Thiokol. In addition, Roger Boisjoly, a Morton Thiokol engineer who argued against the shuttle launch, had filed two suits against his former employer.

In its 1986 *Annual Report,* Morton Thiokol reported that:

> Along with other business enterprises, the Company has experienced, effective April 1, 1986, substantial increases in insurance premiums and substantial decreases in the risks covered. With respect to the Company's aircraft products liability insurance, the policy limits remain the same, but the extent of the coverage has been reduced to exclude certain property damage, most significantly property damage to or losses (including loss of use) of satellites or space launch vehicles or their cargoes. This creates an exposure to the Company for satellite placement motors previously delivered but unflown or under contract for delivery to customers. In both cases, the Company has warned its customers of the situation and is seeking to negotiate an appropriate allocation of risk exposure, limiting the Company's exposure to an acceptable dollar amount such as the replacement cost of the particular motor involved in any accident. If such negotiations are not successful, if there is a loss, and if the Company's liability were determined by a court in a particular situation not to be so limited, the resultant damages could have a material adverse effect on the financial condition of the Company. (Morton Thiokol, 1986 *Annual Report,* p. 27.)

BUSINESS AND PRODUCTS

Morton Thiokol operates in three business segments: Aerospace, Specialty Chemicals, and Salt Manufacturing, and markets a wide range of products for industrial, government, and consumer use, both in the United States and internationally.

Aerospace

The Aerospace segment consists of propulsion and ordnance products and services performed principally under contracts and subcontracts with various U.S. government agencies and aerospace prime contractors.

Propulsion includes research, development, and production of solid rocket motor systems which are used for space vehicles such as the Space Shuttle, to position satellites in orbit, for strategic missiles such as the Trident (submarine-launched), and for tactical missiles such as the Maverick, Sidewinder, and MX missiles. This propulsion technology has been applied by Morton Thiokol in the manufacturing of gas generators for use in automobiles' passive restraint systems.

Development and production of gas generations for automobile airbag inflation systems dramatically increased; the 100,000th production unit was recently delivered to Mercedes Benz. Additionally, Morton Thiokol was selected by Chrysler late in fiscal '86 to be its airbag production source. Both domestic and foreign auto manufacturers are investigating airbag installation resulting from the Mercedes initiative and the Department of Transportation ruling to require passive restraint systems for 10 percent of all model cars sold in the United States.

Services of the aerospace segment include the launch and recovery operations for the Space Shuttle. The loss of the Challenger shuttle flight resulted in the suspension of production of Space Shuttle solid rocket motors and the redirection of resources to the failure investigation and redesign of the field and nozzle joints of the motors. Approval of the motor redesign will be followed by requalification and certification of the motors, which will lead to resumption of motor production for shuttle flights. Shuttle flights are currently scheduled to recommence in fiscal 1988.

Morton Thiokol has numerous patents in the aerospace field, most of which relate to solid propulsion. These patents demonstrate the technical inventiveness of the aerospace segment's staff and are useful in furthering the company's business relationship with its customers. The U.S. government has a royalty-free license under each patent for an invention developed at its expense. Since the government provides, directly and indirectly, the majority of this segment's business, the loss of all such business would have a materially adverse effect on Morton Thiokol's operations.

The aerospace segment had 1986 fiscal sales of $933 million, an increase of 8 percent over fiscal 1985. Profits also rose 6 percent to $96 million. Morton Thiokol is the largest producer of solid rocket propulsion systems for the U.S. market, representing approximately 40 percent thereof. Principal competitive factors are technical performance, quality, reliability, price, depth, capabilities of personnel, and adequacy of facilities. Space sales, which account for 18 percent of Morton Thiokol's total sales, were down 7 percent in 1986 from 1985, largely stemming from the stand down of shuttle flights.

The solid propulsion facilities are located at Elkton, Maryland; Huntsville, Alabama; Carson City, Nevada; and near Brigham City, Utah. The Elkton and Carson City land and buildings are owned by the company. Those facilities in Huntsville are substantially owned by the U.S. government, and those in Utah are partly company-owned, partly government-owned, and partly leased.

Specialty Chemicals

Morton Thiokol manufactures high technology chemical products for a wide variety of customer applications. The largest product group consists of laminating adhesives and coatings designed primarily for use in the manufacturing of food packaging materials from paper, film, and foil. The second largest group consists of chemicals for the electronics market, including principally dry film photoresists and curable screen resists used as part of a process to imprint circuit patterns onto printed circuit boards and semiconductors (silicon chips).

Morton Thiokol also manufactures customized performance coatings principally for use on plastic substrates in the automotive, consumer electronics, appliance, and business machines markets, and liquid dyes to color petroleum products for identification purposes. Other dyes and coloring products are used in printing and writing inks, plastics, foods, drugs, and cosmetics. Specialty chemical products are marketed throughout the world directly to customers and indirectly through distributors and agents.

Morton Thiokol considers it important to acquire domestic and foreign patent protection for the numerous proprietary products and processes of the specialty chemicals segment deemed valuable to the business. Accordingly, such protection is usually obtained whenever possible. Patent protection currently extends for various periods up to the year 2004. Patents in the electronic chemicals, packaging, adhesives and coatings, biocides, and heat stabilizer product lines are considered to contribute to the company's market position.

The majority of this segment's business, including the two largest product groups, is highly competitive. There is substantial competition from a variety of alternative materials. The company has more than 90 percent of world capacity to produce sodium borhydride (used principally as a bleaching chemical in paper manufacturing), and it has a majority share of the markets for biocides to incorporate into plastics, inorganic research chemicals, hydride chemicals, and specialty metal powders. Principal methods of competition include technical service for specialized customer requirements, price, and quality.

The specialty chemical group achieved 1986 fiscal year sales of $652 million, a gain of 6 percent over the prior year. Operating profit, however, showed a decline of 3 percent to $87 million.

The worldwide electronics industry recession affected Morton Thiokol in the second half of fiscal 1985 and worsened throughout fiscal 1986. Considered by many to be the most severe ever experienced by the industry, this recession detracted significantly from the specialty chemical group's sales growth and was responsible for the operating profit decrease.

Specialty chemical products are manufactured at twenty-five locations in the United States (some of which are operated through divisions or wholly owned subsidiaries); by wholly owned subsidiaries in Canada, Mexico, France, the United Kingdom, Italy, the Netherlands, Singapore, and West Germany; and by three joint venture corporations in Japan.

Salt Manufacturing

Morton Thiokol produces and sells salt principally in the United States and Canada for human and animal consumption, water conditioning, and highway ice melting, as well as for industrial and chemical uses. Sales of "Morton" brand table salt in the United States are approximately equal to the aggregate of all other table salt sales. Salt for water conditioning is sold principally for residential use mostly in packages. Salt for industrial and chemical use is sold in bulk and in packages, and is used for food and meat processing and in a wide variety of chemical applications. Salt for ice melting on streets and highways is sold mostly in bulk form to government agencies; some ice melting salt is sold in packages under the "Safe-t-Salt" brand.

Sales of salt are made through the company sales forces, as well as through independent distributors, agents, and brokers. Regional sales offices and customer service facilities are maintained throughout the United States.

Total salt production by Morton Thiokol aggregated about 9.8 million tons in fiscal 1986. Rock salt brine well reserves have sufficient reserves to satisfy anticipated production requirements for the foreseeable future. Sales of highway ice control salt are quite seasonal, and vary with winter weather conditions in areas of use. Ice control salt is stockpiled by both the company and by its customers.

All areas in which the salt segment operates are highly competitive. Its market share varies widely depending on the geographic area and the type of product involved. This segment uses price, service, product performance, and technical, advertising, and promotional support as its principal methods of competition.

Sales for this segment increased 4 percent to $365 million, and earnings were at $74 million in 1986, compared to 1985. However, new product national introductions for Morton Seasoned Salt and Morton garlic salt brands offset the increase in this business segment.

ACQUISITIONS

Four years ago, Morton-Norwich was searching for an acquisition that would help it expand in specialty chemicals. It was fresh from selling its pharmaceutical division to Proctor and Gamble and was willing to pay $540 million to acquire 49.5 percent of Thiokol common stock. This acquisition boosted Morton-Norwich's stake in the fast growing chemical market as well as put the company into the space and defense business. Morton-Norwich's plan was to nurture the specialties area with funds from its

EXHIBIT 1 Morton Thiokol, Inc., Consolidated balance sheets (in millions of dollars as of June 30)

	1986	*1985*	*1984*	*1983*	*1982*	*1981*
		Assets				
Current Assets						
Cash and short-term investments	46.1	93.5	92.8	15.8	307.1	47.2
Receivables	316.6	275.3	282.4	222.7	101.9	142.6
Inventories	221.5	200.9	187.6	195.4	86.2	126.0
Prepaid expenses	12.4	13.1	11.4	14.0	20.6	18.1
Total Current Assets	$ 596.6	582.8	574.2	447.9	515.8	333.9
Other Assets						
Cost in excess of net assets of acquisitions, less amortization	192.0	194.3	146.8	148.5	4.9	6.7
Non-current assets of discontinued operations	—	—	—	—	—	33.5
Miscellaneous	34.5	30.4	51.1	32.0	19.4	44.3
Property, Plant & Equipment:	890.1	798.8	756.3	718.4	367.1	472.8
Less allowances for depreciation	296.2	238.1	229.6	195.5	160.3	194.7
Net property, plant & equipment	593.9	560.7	526.7	522.9	206.8	278.1
Total Assets	**$1,417.0**	**1,368.2**	**1,298.8**	**1,151.3**	**746.9**	**696.5**

"cash cow," Morton salt. Morton-Norwich felt the marriage with Thiokol would offset some revenue loss suffered in the sale of its pharmaceutical division.

Morton Thiokol is far from finished in the acquisition game. However, the company does not want to dilute earnings with costly acquisitions just for the sake of expanding. It has about $95.5 million in cash and short-term investments with a low debt-to-equity ratio to use in expansion. Morton Thiokol continued an aggressive expansion in late 1985 when an agreement was finalized for the purchase of the powder coatings assets and business of Polymer Corporation, a subsidiary of Cheeseborough-Ponds Inc. This acquisition will further Morton Thiokol's growth in the specialty chemical area and improve its business portfolio. Exhibits 1 through 3 provide Morton Thiokol's financial statements for recent years. A historical summary of Morton Thiokol's history is given in Appendix A.

POISON PILL ANTI-TAKEOVER PLAN

Morton Thiokol has adopted a "poison pill" and anti-takeover measure which is designed to make a hostile takeover very costly. This measure is in light of the perceived takeover attempt by Dow Chemical in November 1984. Dow had held 8 per-

EXHIBIT 1 continued

	1986	1985	1984	1983	1982	1981
	Liabilities and Stockholders' Equity					
Current Liabilities						
Notes payable and current portion of long-term debt	$ 26.5	15.7	12.4	13.0	12.8	32.7
Accounts payable	128.9	131.0	144.5	108.3	46.8	67.2
Accrued salaries and other expenses	140.6	140.8	134.3	134.6	77.7	44.6
Income taxes	57.0	29.5	94.5	70.9	99.9	20.1
Total Current Liabilities	$ 353.0	317.0	385.7	326.8	237.2	164.6
Non-Current Liabilities						
Long-term debt, less current portion	31.7	152.7	149.5	149.9	69.1	98.9
Deferred income taxes	161.7	139.5	83.2	78.8	35.8	45.5
Other non-current liabilities	48.7	54.2	44.1	45.8	20.9	5.3
Stockholders' Equity						
Common stock	51.1	51.1	16.9	16.8	13.7	13.7
Additional paid-in capital	75.8	76.1	70.6	59.8	59.2	59.3
Retained earnings	799.3	698.7	565.5	484.6	429.7	313.8
Foreign currency translation adjustments	(7.9)	(22.0)	(16.7)	(10.7)	(9.5)	—
Less cost of common stock in Treasury	(96.4)	(99.1)	—	—	(9.5)	—
Net Stockholders' Equity	821.9	704.8	636.3	550.5	383.9	382.2
Total Liabilities and Stockholders' Equity	**$1,417.0**	**1,368.2**	**1,298.8**	**1,151.3**	**746.9**	**696.5**

Sources: *Moody's Industrial Manual*, 1986, pp. 3288–95, and Morton Thiokol, Inc., *Annual Report*, 1986.

cent of Morton Thiokol's common stock and was seeking to increase it to as much as 15 percent, stating that its only interest in Morton was as an investment. To stop the takeover, Morton Thiokol agreed to sell its Texize division to Dow for $131 million in cash; in return, Morton Thiokol got back 1.4 million of its shares that Dow held. Morton Thiokol also received an agreement from Dow not to buy any additional shares for the next decade. Giving up Texize provided cash without a negative impact on earnings and gave Morton Thiokol a chance to retire some of its stock. The Texize business accounted for about 13 percent of Morton Thiokol's sales and about 12 percent of its earnings.

EXHIBIT 2 Morton Thiokol, Inc., Consolidated statements of income and retained earnings (in millions, except per share data, year ended June 30)

	1986	*1985*	*1984*	*1983*	*1982*	*1981*
Net sales	$1,949.9	1,832.3	1,735.0	1,270.4	534.7	486.0
Interest, royalties, and sundry income	16.2	14.9	10.2	17.4	17.5	11.3
	1,966.1	**1,847.2**	**1,745.2**	**1,287.8**	**552.2**	**497.3**
Deductions from income						
Cost of products sold	1,476.0	1,398.3	1,334.9	976.7	383.6	351.0
Selling, administrative and general expense	203.6	186.0	192.8	158.7	95.8	88.6
Research and development expense	37.7	33.7	28.0	20.9	6.6	6.0
Interest expense	23.6	24.1	22.3	24.3	16.4	13.2
Total deductions from income	**1,740.9**	**1,642.1**	**1,578.0**	**1,180.6**	**502.4**	**458.8**
Income from continuing operations before income taxes	225.2	205.1	167.2	107.2	49.8	38.5
Income taxes	92.3	85.6	70.1	42.0	14.9	11.9
Income from continuing operations	**132.9**	**119.5**	**97.1**	**65.2**	**34.9**	**26.6**
Income from discontinued operations	—	3.3	12.7	13.3	21.8	26.4
Gain on disposition of discontinued operations		75.1			79.8	
Net Income	**132.9**	**197.9**	**109.8**	**78.5**	**136.5**	**53.0**

EFFECTS OF THE SHUTTLE DISASTER

The orbiter Challenger was destroyed and its seven crew members killed in an explosion 73 seconds after liftoff January 28, 1986. Investigation of the disaster was focused on the O-rings—produced by Morton Thiokol and used to seal the booster segments—as the cause of the failure. The immediate effects of the disaster on Morton Thiokol were the layoff of about 200 workers and the placement of 1,400 others on a 4-day week. The company's aerospace unit also instituted overhead cost restraints in all areas of its organization. The layoffs were the first in twenty years at the Morton Thiokol facility.

The company experienced other related problems as well. Although the company's aerospace program was a big money maker during the early 1980's, its growth in

EXHIBIT 2 continued

	1986	*1985*	*1984*	*1983*	*1982*	*1981*
Retained earnings at beginning of year	698.7	565.5	484.6	429.7	373.8	280.9
	831.6	**763.4**	**594.4**	**508.2**	**510.3**	**333.9**
Less						
Cash dividends paid	32.3	30.7	28.9	23.6	20.6	20.1
Common stock split effected in a dividend		34.0				
Retained earnings at end of year	**$ 799.3**	**698.7**	**565.5**	**484.6**	**429.7**	**313.8**
		Share Data				
Income Per Common and Equivalent Share						
Income from continuing operations	$ 2.80	2.44	1.92	1.43	.86	.65
Income from discontinued operations	—	.06	.25	.29	.54	.65
Gain on disposal of discontinued operations		1.51			1.98	
Net income	**$ 2.80**	**$ 4.01**	**$ 2.17**	**$ 1.72**	**$ 1.40**	**$ 1.30**
Cash dividends per share	$ .685	.627	.574	.527	.507	.497

Sources: *Moody's Industrial Manual,* 1986, pp. 3288–95, and Morton Thiokol, Inc., *Annual Report,* 1986.

that sector had begun to mature even before the explosion. The whole business grew at 50 percent in sales, but slower development is expected for the second half of the 1980s because the aerospace program simply could not continue at the same rate. The total loss of the shuttle business would be a large negative, but the major growth there has already occurred—growth had started to slow before the disaster. The company had $1.83 billion in sales for the fiscal year ending June 1985, and the Space Shuttle program accounts for about 15 percent of its profit from continuing operations. Each launch brings the company between $10 and $20 million. Morton Thiokol is currently under contract with NASA for thirty-five launches, and so far there have been twenty-five.

Morton Thiokol faced heavy criticism after the disaster occurred. Although Morton Thiokol recommended that the launch be postponed during a telephone conference between company representatives in Utah and NASA and company representatives at Kennedy Space Center January 27, four Morton Thiokol managers reversed the decision later the same day because, they said, the data on which the engineers based their fears was uncertain and inconclusive. Company engineers continued to

EXHIBIT 3 Morton Thiokol, Inc., Operations in different businesses

	Sales[1]			*Profit*[2]		
Sales And Profit	*1986*	*1985*	*1984*	*1986*	*1985*	*1984*
Aerospace	$ 933.1	864.5	733.8	96.3	91.2	71.5
Specialty chemicals	651.8	615.8	646.2	87.4	89.7	82.9
Salt	365.0	352.0	355.0	74.3	57.6	50.7
Business Totals	**$1,949.9**	**1,832.3**	**1,735.0**	**258.0**	**238.5**	**205.1**
General Corporate Expense—Net				(32.8)	(33.4)	(37.9)
Consolidated Net Sales and Pretax Income	**$1,949.9**	**1,832.3**	**1,735.0**	**252.2**	**205.1**	**167.2**

Notes: [1] Aerospace Group sales encompass propulsion and ordnance products and services performed principally under contracts and subcontract with various United States Government agencies and aerospace prime contractors. Net sales under United States Government contracts and subcontracts amounted to $888, $835, and $702 million for 1986, 1985, and 1984, respectively, or 46%, 46% and 40%, respectively, of the Company's net sales; export sales from the United States were less than 10% of sales to unaffiliated customers; and intersegment and intergeographic area sales and transfers were insignificant.

[2] Business segment profit is before income taxes, interest income, interest expense, and allocation of certain corporate administrative expenses, but includes foreign exchange gains (and losses) of $3.8, ($.3) and ($.5) million in 1986, 1985, and 1984, respectively.

Sources: Moody's *Industrial Manual,* 1986, pp. 3288–95, and Morton Thiokol, Inc., *Annual Report,* 1986, pp. 22–23.

protest that the launch was unsafe. Morton Thiokol managers were criticized as being worried more about the company's pocketbook than flight safety. The month before the January 28 launch, NASA had taken the first step toward finding a second supplier for the booster rockets.

Morton Thiokol has been the space agency's only supplier since 1973, when it was chosen over three competitors to develop and produce the booster rockets. In the past two years, four companies—Hercules Inc., United Technologies Corp.'s Chemical System Division, Aerojet Strategic Propulsion Co., and Atlantic Research Corp.—have expressed strong interest in making booster rockets for NASA. NASA also said that it plans to purchase at least 50 percent of its rockets from Morton Thiokol and to require a second supplier to buy the nozzles for the rockets from Morton Thiokol, which would drive down the cost and enhance national security. However, NASA does not believe it can afford to spend $100 million or so in certification costs for a rocket produced by a new supplier. Potential suppliers also are reluctant to spend the money. In addition, one industry source says that NASA clearly wants to keep Morton Thiokol's skilled corps of engineers from being broken up and that Morton Thiokol is still the best supplier of solid-fuel rockets.

The investigation commission report stated that Morton Thiokol management changed its position to go ahead with the launch to accommodate a "major customer." One senator contended the managers who overrode their engineers to give the go-ahead for the Challenger launch were saying, "Let's get our pocketbook and forget about safety."

Two Morton Thiokol engineers publicly testified that they argued against the ill-fated launch but were overruled by Morton Thiokol superiors under pressure from NASA. Morton Thiokol was accused of taking punitive steps against the engineers after they testified that they opposed the launch. Morton Thiokol denied the charges, saying that both men's job responsibilities had changed progressively in the accident's aftermath, owing to the shift from production to investigative work and redesign studies.

The report did stress that top NASA officials who gave the final approval for the Challenger launch did not realize the seriousness of the joint problem and did not know that Morton Thiokol had initially advised against launching. But the commission report also found that a briefing at NASA headquarters last August provided enough evidence to warrant "corrective action" before subsequent shuttle flights.

OUTLOOK

Specialty chemicals will probably contribute about 40 percent of Morton Thiokol's operating profits in fiscal 1987. This segment is now the company's top profit center, helped by recent redeployment of assets. Meanwhile, we expect Morton Thiokol's electronic chemicals business to improve in coming months, aided by a modest rebound in the depressed electronics industry. The weaker dollar is also helping with exports and the currency translations of foreign earnings.

Until the Shuttle launches resume, Morton Thiokol's shuttle work will consist primarily of redesign and testing of the booster rockets. Morton Thiokol is expected to continue to be the best supplier of solid rocket fuels into the 1990s and will probably remain a key space shuttle contractor for the next several years because of its agreements with NASA and its expertise in advanced booster rocket technology. However, space division revenues may fall about 10 percent, with profits falling by a greater percentage.

Looking further ahead, Morton Thiokol's specialty chemical business will probably become even stronger with the help of additional small acquisitions. These gains will more than offset declines in space shuttle and salt businesses.

At the present time, Morton Thiokol may select one or more of the following alternatives to help it cope with difficulties resulting from the shuttle disaster:

1. Attempt to obtain out-of-court settlements for the suits filed by the survivors of Michael Smith and William McNair, and also by their former employee Boisjoly. However, the company should evaluate the possibilities of negative publicity as a result of its settlement efforts.
2. Increase insurance coverage by negotiating with several companies in the United States and abroad.
3. Continue the R & D efforts to improve the design of the booster rockets and conduct full-scale testing of the same to convince NASA and the people of the United States that the booster rockets have a defect-free motor.
4. Improve communication within the company, reorganize the decision-making process involving shuttle missions, and conduct press conferences to inform the taxpayers.
5. Seek new opportunities to diversify into other areas of business operations to stabilize its financial position, particularly if it is held accountable for damages.

APPENDIX A Morton Thiokol, Inc., Company history

1969	
April 25	Title of Morton-Norwich adopted and plan of merger with Morton International.
September 2	Incorporated in Delaware.
November 30	Merged with Morton International.
1971	
	Morton International, Norwich Pharmaceutical, and Texize Chemical, Inc., merged and became operating divisions thereof.
1982	
June	Company sold Norwich-Eaton Pharmaceuticals Division to Proctor & Gamble for $371,000,000.
August	Acquired assets of Specialty Chemicals Group of Phillip Morris Industries, Inc.
September	Merged with Thiokol Corporation and corporate name changed to Morton Thiokol.
1984	
	Sold Southwest Chemical Services, Inc.
1985	
	Sold Texize Division to Dow Chemical Co. for $131,000,000 cash and 1.4 million shares of company stock.
1986	
January 28	Space Shuttle tragedy occurred and seven astronauts were killed. Failure of booster rockets designed and manufactured by Morton Thiokol were blamed for the tragedy.
1987	
May 7	A $1.5 billion suit was filed against Thiokol by the widow of one of the astronauts who perished in the Challenger disaster.
May 28	Thiokol successfully staged a full-scale test of a redesigned and improved booster rocket. NASA set the next shuttle flight for June 1988.

REFERENCES

Chemical and Engineering News. "Merger Would Be Big in Electronics Chemicals." 26 July, 1982, 7.

Chemical and Engineering News. "Dow Increases Holding of Morton Thiokol." 16 April, 1984, 47.

Chemical Week. "A Merger to Create a Huge Specialties Firm." 28 July, 1982, 12.

Chemical Week. "A Fast Takeoff for Morton Thiokol." 7 December, 1983, 41.

Chemical Week. "Greenmail Gambit?" 21 November, 1984, 14.

Investment News and Views. "Explosive Growth." 11 January, 1984, 47–51.

James, Frank E. "Analysts See No Severe Impact on Morton if Rocket is Faulted in Shuttle Disaster." *Wall Street Journal.* 4 February, 1986, 2.

Kolcum, Edward H. "Morton Thiokol Engineers Testify NASA Rejected Warnings on Launch." *Aviation Week & Space Technology.* 3 March, 1986, 18–19.

Levin, Doron P. "Dow Chemical Will Buy Unit From Thiokol." *Wall Street Journal.* 16 November, 1984, 8.

McGinley, Laura. "NASA to Probe Transfers of Engineers at Thiokol After Damaging Testimony." *Wall Street Journal.* 14 May, 1986, 5.

Mills, David. "Morton Thiokol, Inc. Wants to Increase Its Acquisitions in a Drive for Growth." *Wall Street Journal.* 20 May, 1985, 12.

Moody's Industrial Manual. "Morton Thiokol, Inc." 1986, 3288–95.

Stevenson, Gelvin. "Morton Thiokol Heads Dow Off at the Pass." *Business Week.* 3 December, 1984, 37.

Treehitt, Jeffery. "Morton Thiokol: A Fit in Specialty Chemicals." *Chemical Week.* 20 October, 1985, 27.

Value Line. "Morton Thiokol." 17 July, 1987, 514.

Wall Street Journal. "Dow Chemical Agrees to Stop Buying Shares In Thiokol for 10 Years." 19 November, 1984, 20.

Wall Street Journal. "Morton Thiokol, Inc. Adopts a Poison Pill Anti-Takeover Plan." 29 March, 1985, 48.

Wall Street Journal. "U.S., Thiokol Sued by Widow of a Pilot on Challenger." 7 May, 1987, 6.

Wall Street Journal. "Morton Thiokol Successfully Staged a Full-Scale Test of a Space Shuttle Booster Rocket. . . ." 28 May, 1987, 1.

Weyerhaeuser Company—1987

LUCRETIA ZIENERT
Auburn University

On June 28, 1986, the Weyerhaeuser Company planted a small Douglas fir seedling in the shadow of Mount St. Helens. Planting this tree completed the reforestation of Weyerhaeuser's tree farm devastated by the 1980 volcano blast. This seedling marked the two billionth tree that Weyerhaeuser had planted in the twenty years since the company implemented High Yield Forestry, a scientific forest management program. High Yield Forestry was designed to produce more timber while at the same time protecting the environment for fish and wildlife. To realize how impressive planting two billion seedlings in twenty years is, consider that it represents planting more than 800 trees per minute or 400,000 trees every day for twenty years.

The Weyerhaeuser Company (Weyco) is committed to environmental excellence. In addition to its extensive reforestation program, the company is a leader in forest genetics and silviculture, continually searching out new methods for improving the quality and yield of forest lands. Scientific growing techniques have yielded remarkable results, achieving growth rates of two-to-one over natural stands.

Although Weyco is the largest private owner of standing timber in the world, the business is not limited to forestry. Weyerhaeuser is one of North America's largest single-family home developers, one of the largest mortgage bankers in the United States, and an active commercial real estate developer.

EXHIBIT 1 The top ten forest products companies

	Sales		*Profits*		*Assets*	
	Twelve Months 1986 $ Millions	*Change from 1985 %*	*Twelve Months 1986 $ Millions*	*Change from 1985 %*	*Twelve Months 1986 $ Millions*	*Change from 1985 %*
1. Weyerhaeuser	5652	9	276.7	38	6558	9
2. Georgia-Pacific	7223	8	296.0	43	5114	5
3. International Paper	5500	22	305.0	133	7848	30
4. Kimberly-Clark	4303	6	269.4	1	3676	5
5. Ford Howard Paper	1549	14	146.4	−7	2096	36
6. Champion International	4388	−24	200.8	23	6028	−2
7. Union Camp	2045	10	129.9	37	2751	3
8. James River Corp. of Virginia	3982	56	147.1	38	4040	115
9. Scott Paper	3437	13	186.5	−7	3939	12
10. Great Northern Nekoosa	2039	5	85.3	85	2077	6

Source: Adapted from *Business Week*, April 17, 1987, page 140.

In addition to owning six million acres of United States timberland, Weyerhaeuser owns the harvest rights to another 7.8 million acres of forest land in Canada. As shown in Exhibit 1, Weyerhaeuser was second in sales in the forest products industry in 1986. The company's two closest competitors, Georgia-Pacific and International Paper, both produced higher profits than Weyco did in 1986. Also included in Exhibit 1, the 1986 profit figures for Georgia-Pacific and International Paper were $296 million and $305 billion, respectively, compared to Weyco's $276 million.

HISTORY

For more than 130 years, the name "Weyerhaeuser" has been associated with forest products. The company began in the 1850s when a young German immigrant named Frederick Weyerhaeuser acquired a lumber yard and sawmill in western Illinois. In 1900, he organized a group of Midwestern investors to buy timberlands in the Pacific Northwest. Then 65 years old, Weyerhaeuser could scarcely have dreamed of his enterprise becoming a giant in American industry. The investor group named the company for Weyerhaeuser and opened the first office in Tacoma, Washington—the headquarters for Weyco today. In addition to acquiring a sawmill, buying timber, and selling wood products, the new company's owners decided to keep harvested lands for reforestation, leading to development of the High Yield Forestry Program. Exhibit 2 chronicles Weyerhaeuser's history from 1900 to 1986.

EXHIBIT 2 Weyerhaeuser's history, 1900–1986

1900	Weyerhaeuser Company incorporated by group of investors led by Frederick Weyerhaeuser, a 65-year-old Midwest lumberman. Offices opened in Tacoma, Washington.
1902	First Douglas fir sawmill acquired in Everett, Washington.
1919	Weyerhaeuser Sales Company formed in St. Paul, Minnesota.
1941	Established nation's first tree farm (The Clemons) at Grays Harbor, Washington.
1942	Development department opened in Longview, Washington; formalized corporate forestry research and development began.
1947	First bark-processing plant began operations. First major plywood plant began operating in Longview, Washington.
1956	Acquired Mississippi and Alabama timberlands.
1957	Company entered packaging business: Kieckhefer Container Company and the Eddy Paper Corporation merged into Weyerhaeuser; acquired North Carolina-Virginia timberlands.
1958	Weyerhaeuser International S.A. formed; first foreign investments.
1959	Weyerhaeuser Sales Company merged into Weyerhaeuser Company.
1961	Entered fine paper field by acquiring Hamilton Paper Company of Miquon, Pennsylvania.
1963	Listed stock on New York and Pacific Coast Stock Exchanges. Tokyo, Japan, sales office opened.
1964	Opened sales office in Paris, France.
1965	First Southern Pine plywood mill at Plymouth, N.C.
1966	$150 million debenture offering; first major long-term borrowing. Acquired timber rights, sawmills, and veneer capacity in Malaysia, the Phillippines and Hong Kong.
1967	Acquired A. DeWeese Lumber Company in Philadelphia, Mississippi, adding 345,000 acres to Mississippi-Alabama holdings as well as a pine plywood plant and sawmill, hardwood dimension plant, charcoal production and wood-treating plant. Launched the High Yield Forest program.
1968	First real estate expansion outside areas of historical timber ownership with participation in Rinconada Hills, California housing development. Sales exceeded $1 billion for the first time.
1969	Established investment evaluation department to analyze new business opportunities, mergers, acquisitions, etc.
1970	Formed Weyerhaeuser Far East Limited under Weyerhaeuser International to manage holdings in Southeast Asia. Began construction on disposable diaper manufacturing plants at Harmony, Pennsylvania and La Puente, California.
1971	Made largest overseas investment with acquisition of majority interest in International Timber Corporation, Indonesia, with cutting rights on 1.5 million acres on Borneo. Kamloops Pulp & Paper became Weyerhaeuser Canada.
1972	President George H. Weyerhaeuser announced company reorganization plans on the basis of eleven geographic regions, five business groups, and the land and timber resource group, each headed by a vice-president.

continued

EXHIBIT 2 continued

1973	Began construction on shipping container plants at Jackson, Mississippi and Tampa, Florida.
	Acquired Rothschild, Wisconsin, fine paper mill from American Can Company.
	President George Weyerhaeuser announced a three-year $2 billion expansion plan, nationwide, to build new and replacement facilities. Modernization and new technology to fully utilize the harvest on company lands were the emphasis. Sales exceeded $2 billion for the first time.
1974	Sales were a record $2.5 billion.
1975	Far East Region headquarters established in Hong Kong.
	Aquaculture set up as a pilot business under New Business Development. Included Homestead, Florida shrimp rearing facility and Oregon Aqua Foods, Newport, Oregon, a salmon rearing firm acquired by Weyerhaeuser.
1978	Company completed $40 million 450,000-square-foot technology center near Corporate Headquarters; houses about 800 research, development and technical employees; contains 100 laboratory areas and a two-acre, two-story developmental area for pilotscale testing of manufacturing processes.
1980	The eruption of Mount St. Helens on May 18 affected some 68,000 acres of the company's St. Helens Tree Farm. The company launched a raw materials salvage, utilization and reforestation program unique in American forest history.
	Company's fiber business observed its 50th anniversary.
1981	Observed the 40th anniversary of Weyerhaeuser's dedication of America's first tree farm, The Clemons, in Southwestern Washington.
1982	Columbus, Mississippi paper mill produced its first paper in August.
1986	Weyerhaeuser planted its two billionth seedling on domestic forestland through its High Yield Program.
	Weyerhaeuser changed to a divisional organizational structure by dividing its major businesses, forest products, paper, and real estate, into separate companies.

COMPETITION

Georgia-Pacific (GP)

Georgia-Pacific is a major manufacturer and distributor of building products, pulp and paper products, packaging materials, and related chemicals. While Weyerhaeuser ranks first in market share, GP has consistently outperformed industry rivals in sales. The company has realized steady, remarkable growth in its sixty years of business. As seen in Exhibit 3, GP's sales increased 8 percent in 1986, while profits increased 43 percent.

GP's success is due in part to its strong vertical integration and an ongoing strategy to focus on the forest products business. For example, GP recently acquired Superwood Incorporated, a hardwood producer with plants at Duluth and Bemidji, Minnesota. The company also purchased Challenge Lumber Products and Klamath Moulding Mill Incorporated to increase its fir and pine moulding production.

EXHIBIT 3 Georgia-Pacific financial highlights

(Dollar amounts, except per share, and shares are in millions)	*1986*	*1985*	*Percent Change*
Net sales	$7,223	$6,716	8
Income from continuing operations before extraordinary item	296	207	43
Net income	296	187	58
Per common share—fully diluted			
Income from continuing operations before extraordinary item	2.64	1.80	47
Net income	2.64	1.61	64
Depreciation and depletion	339	310	9
Cash provided by continuing operations	575	771	(25)
Cash dividends paid	97	94	3
Total assets at year end	5,114	4,866	5
Return on capital employed	10.4%	8.7%	
Return on common equity	13.8%	10.2%	
Total debt-to-capital	26.3%	32.0%	
Cash dividends declared per share of common stock	$ .85	$ .80	6
Shares of common stock outstanding at year end	107	103	4
Number of common shareholders of record	66,000	74,000	(11)
Number of employees	39,000	39,000	—

Source: Georgia-Pacific 1986 *Annual Report*, p. 1.

Another move that will improve GP's position in the wood products market is the purchase of United States Plywood Corporation for approximately $215 million. Already the largest national wholesale building products distributor, GP will add six manufacturing plants and forty-four distribution centers with this acquisition.

GP's dedication to the wood products business is also evidenced by its sales mix. The company is selling more lumber and plywood than ever, and its nationwide building products distribution network gives GP an edge in the "do-it-yourself" market. The company's pulp and paper sector is also strong, comprising about 44 percent of capital expenditures in 1986. Sales by industry segment show that GP is concentrating on the wood products market, as seen in Exhibit 4. Sales from other operations have been less than 2 percent of GP's total sales for the last three years.

GP controls 25,000 acres of timber through ownership, leases, and long-term contracts. The bulk of this timberland is in the southern, northeastern, and northwestern United States. Florida, Mississippi, and Arkansas house the highest concentration of GP timber in the South. Maine is GP's northeast stronghold, and in the Pacific Northwest, Washington and Oregon have large tracts of timberland belonging to GP. The company's mineral ownership includes gypsum mines, coal reserves, and oil and gas fields. The gypsum mines, quarries, and reserves are scattered throughout the United States. The coal reserves, containing more than 220 million tons of coal,

EXHIBIT 4 Georgia-Pacific selected industry segment data

	Year ended December 31		
	1986	*1985*	*1984*
Trade sales			
Building products	$4,853	$4,470	$4,452
Pulp and paper	2,281	2,134	2,111
Other operations	89	112	119
	$7,223	$6,716	$6,682
Operating profits			
Building products	$ 500	$ 391	$ 379
Pulp and paper	146	29	202
Other operations	35	35	20
	681	455	601
General corporate	(91)	(33)	(68)
Interest expense	(138)	(132)	(156)
Unusual items	33	19	19
Income taxes	(189)	(102)	(143)
Income from continuing operations	$ 296	$ 207	$ 253

Source: Georgia-Pacific 1986 *Annual Report,* p. 27.

are located in Virginia, West Virginia, and Kentucky. The majority of GP's oil and gas fields are in West Virginia, Mississippi, and Louisiana.

GP's leadership in building products is supported by a 141-branch Distribution Division. Although concentrated in the eastern United States, this network extends nationwide. Almost all of GP's wood products plants and paper mills are in the East, with a few located in Washington, Oregon, and California. The gypsum and roofing plants are scattered across the country in proximity to gypsum reserves. Because the distribution centers are so widely dispersed and accessible to manufacturing operations, the company's plants and mills can run at or near capacity.

International Paper (IP)

International Paper Company is the world's largest paper company. Through its majority ownership of IP Timberlands, Ltd, International Paper controls approximately 7 million acres of timberlands. The company manufactures pulp, paper, and paperboard. In addition, IP is involved in oil and gas exploration and real estate activities, and it manufactures and sells specialty chemicals and nonwoven textiles. As shown in Exhibit 5, however, paper products are the company's major source of earnings, comprising 75 percent of overall sales.

Although sales dipped in 1985, IP's sales have otherwise consistently increased. The company's financial summary for 1984 through 1986 appears in Exhibit 6. Sales increased 22 percent during fiscal 1986, while profits for IP soared 133 percent that year.

EXHIBIT 5 International Paper sales by product

Product	*Percentage of Sales*
White papers	21%
Coated papers	5%
Containerboard	22%
Bleached packaging	15%
Industrial papers	6%
Envelopes	6%
Pulp	8%
Land and timber	4%
Wood products	9%
Other products	4%

Source: International Paper *Annual Report,* pp. 21–29.

IP acquired Hammermill Paper Company for $1.1 billion in late 1986. Hammermill, now a wholly owned subsidiary, is one of the largest producers of commercial and specialty papers in the United States. The acquisition is consistent with IP's recent strategy of focusing on its core paper products business. Since 1979, the company has been committed to one of the largest capital spending programs in the forest products industry. At that time, IP launched a $5 billion program to modernize paper mills and began to shift into higher margin products such as those produced by Hammermill.

Excluding this acquisition, capital spending declined in 1986. The company plans to continue its modernization program but to do little expansion in 1987. Therefore, IP's management projects capital spending will decrease further in 1987, as shown in Exhibit 7. The decrease is possibly in response to a total debt-to-capital ratio in 1986 exceeding 35 percent, the industry average.

Foreign Competitors

Since Weyerhaeuser has a strong export business, no discussion of the forest products industry would be complete without including major international competitors. Two countries that have major wood export businesses are Canada and Sweden. Labor unrest in British Columbia coupled with the 15 percent export tax to the United States have effectively neutralized Canada's competitive position for the moment.

Sweden, however, has great influence on the forest products industry worldwide. The forests that carpet half of Sweden's land are productive and regulated to ensure prompt regeneration and cultivated growth. Sweden exports half of its production, and Swedish companies lead the industry worldwide in both size and efficiency. In the early and mid-1980s, the United States was swamped with imports of key printing and writing grades of paper from Sweden and other Scandinavian countries.

EXHIBIT 6 International Paper financial summary

In millions of dollars — except per-share amounts	1986	1985	1984
Summary of Earnings			
Revenue			
Net sales	$5,500	$4,502	$4,716
Other income, net	53	42	60
	5,553	4,544	4,776
Costs and Expenses			
Cost of products sold	3,991	3,477	3,582
Distribution expenses	302	253	262
Selling and administrative expenses	355	298	303
Depreciation	326	267	249
Taxes other than payroll and income taxes	69	71	65
	5,043	4,366	4,461
Earnings Before Interest, Income Taxes and Other Items	510	178	315
Interest income	32	45	65
Interest expense	121	91	81
Gains on offerings of IPT Class A Units	33	56	
Provision for early retirement program		29	
Provision for adjustments to facilities and investments			155
Earnings Before Income Taxes, Cumulative Effect of Accounting Change and Extraordinary Item	454	159	144
Provision (benefit) for income taxes	149	28	24
Earnings Before Cumulative Effect of Accounting Change and Extraordinary Item	305	131	120
Cumulative effect of change in COTH method, less applicable income taxes		2	
Extraordinary item, less applicable income taxes			
Net Earnings	305	133	120

Source: International Paper 1986 *Annual Report*, p. 47.

Pulp and paper prices are extremely sensitive to changes in the exchange rate. The decline of the U.S. dollar in 1986 aided American forest products companies by making their pulp and paper prices more attractive on the world market. Additionally, the drop in the dollar versus Scandinavian currencies cut back imports from Sweden.

THE ECONOMY

The forest products industry is very cyclical, prospering when the economy strengthens and suffering as the economic cycle bottoms. Housing starts, a key determinant of demand for wood products, plunged during 1980 in response to high fixed mortgage rates. Housing starts in mid-1981 were the lowest in two decades, resulting largely from exorbitant mortgage rates.

EXHIBIT 7 International Paper capital expenditures

In millions	1987(Est.)	1986	1985
Pulp, Paper & Packaging Facilities:			
Modernization	$375	$215	$270
Expansion	35	210	246
Woods Equipment & Wood Products Facilities	40	40	22
Timberlands & Leases	50	35	38
Other (including capitalized interest)	50	76	218
Total	$550	$576	$794

Source: International Paper 1986 *Annual Report*, p. 33.

In the early 1980s, the strong American dollar made wood imports, especially Canadian wood, very attractive to U.S. builders. Even as housing starts began to rise, imports displaced U.S. wood and depressed prices in the industry. The resulting overcapacity created prolonged decreases in lumber prices. The continued influx of Canadian imports kept prices down through 1986, despite heavy domestic softwood lumber consumption. The National Forest Products Association reports U.S. softwood consumption in 1986 was a record 46.8 billion board feet, compared to 44.2 billion board feet in 1985. In 1982, during the housing slump, consumption was a disappointing 31.2 billion board feet. Nonetheless, prices have shown little improvement over the depressed levels of recent years, and they are far below those recorded during the golden years of the late 1970s.

In 1986, U.S. lumber producers rebounded with strong earnings and a promising future. Several factors contributed to this resurgence. First, the value of the dollar dropped sharply and stimulated export sales of logs, pulp, linerboard, and certain papers. An agreement between the governments of Canada and the United States to levy a 15 percent export tax on Canada's softwood lumber shipments across the border raised the price of Canadian imports. This allowed U.S. producers to raise domestic prices. Additionally, the Canadian dollar strengthened against the American dollar, making Canadian lumber even more expensive.

Housing Starts

One reason for the upswing in lumber prices in 1986 was high demand due to the number of housing starts, especially single-family units. These dwellings use a higher proportion of lumber per unit than do duplexes and project housing. Although residential construction decreased during the year, December's housing starts pushed the 1986 total to the highest level since 1978. Housing starts in 1986 totaled 1,806,600 units, a gain of 3.7 percent over 1985. The single-family total was 1,179,400 units, 10 percent above 1985, while multi-family units totaled 627,300 units, a 6.3 percent drop from 1985.

The National Association of Home Builders predicts a decline to 1.6 million housing starts in 1987. Housing starts began slipping in February, partly in connection with the jump in fixed rate mortgages from 9 percent to 10.7 percent. Higher interest rates typically result in lower construction rates. The current rise in interest rates may not hit housing as hard as it did in the past because adjustable-rate loans are more available today for home buyers.

International Markets

Wood product exports increased 8 percent in 1986 and are expected to increase 10 percent more in 1987. The strong recovery in European markets helped increase soft plywood exports. In fact, in early 1987, the European community increased its quota for duty-free softwood plywood imports. At the same time, Japan reduced its duty on softwood plywood from 15 percent to 12.5 percent. Japan will decrease its duty even further to 10 percent in 1987.

Although Japan is the largest U.S. export market, a slack economy and housing recession caused wood consumption in Japan to decrease from 1981 to 1985. The 1986 increase is due primarily to the yen gaining value against the dollar. Japan is also responding to pressure from the United States to reduce trade restrictions. Another factor for the coming years is Japan's efforts to stimulate its economy. There should be a significant increase in housing starts, which will increase demand for U.S. wood products. Of Japan's forecasted 1.27 million housing starts in 1986, 45 percent were wood frame.

Other potential export markets include Australia, Korea, Taiwan, China, and other Pacific Rim countries. Two Pacific Rim nations, Taiwan and the Republic of Korea, are reducing tariffs on wood products. West Germany, Italy, and the Netherlands have decreased demand for wood products due to poor economic conditions; however, these countries also represent export potential.

Tax Reform

Changes in the U.S. tax laws in 1987 offer few benefits to wood products companies. The new law discourages capital expenditures for plant and equipment since the investment tax credit formerly associated with these projects has been eliminated. Lowered construction will of course have an unfavorable impact on lumber demand. A bill passed by Congress in December 1985 limits applying the lower capital gains tax rate on the sale of timber. It also repeals a 10 percent credit on reforestation costs and requires slower write-offs of some production expenses and depreciation schedules. These factors will hurt the now reviving forest products industry.

Tax reform has also crimped multi-family construction activity. The legislation eliminated, among other tax shelters, fast write-offs of rental properties. Many large apartment projects were started during 1985 and 1986 in anticipation of this change, which is another reason that multi-family starts will be down.

INDUSTRY OUTLOOK

The outlook for 1987 seems favorable for the forest products industry. Since there will be fewer people in the family-forming age group through the end of the century, housing demand cannot continue to rise indefinitely. However, single-family housing starts are expected to increase for the next decade. Growth in the repair and remodeling market will continue to be steady.

The American paper industry's long-term future will be closely tied to developing export markets, especially in the Third World where paper consumption is increasing. Since the United States has the greatest fiber growing capacity in the world, it was assumed that American companies would pick up the lion's share of these markets. However, the eucalyptus tree poses a threat to traditional pulp sources. It is an extremely fast-growing and inexpensive fiber source and provides a high-quality pulp. Brazil is the leader in eucalyptus production, followed by Portugal and Spain.

The takeover and merger trend established in 1986 should continue in 1987. Building new pulp and paper mills is less economical than buying an existing plant. In addition, the repeal of the investment tax credit makes purchasing more attractive than building capacity.

Competitive pricing will continue to be a problem in the lumber and plywood markets. Products here are subject to a "buyer's market" due to excess capacity. Therefore, paper companies are moving away from being vertically integrated forest products companies. Most major paper producers are selling or closing sawmills and plywood facilities. The trend for paper companies is to concentrate on papermaking. Nonetheless, the overcapacity problem continues for the wood products industry as a whole. Despite low lumber prices, the forest products industry overall shows good promise for continued growth.

GLOBAL DEFORESTATION

A final topic of environmental concern to the forest products industry is the destruction of huge tracts of forests the world over. Deforestation has created barren hillsides, creeping sand dunes, and malarial swamps. Soil erosion, flooding of rivers, and silting of canals, harbors, and reservoirs are other environmental effects. The destruction of the tropical rain forests is creating unfavorable changes in climate, wildlife, and quality of human life.

In the last 5,000 years, humans have reduced the Earth's forests from 50 percent of the surface to 20 percent, and the devastation is accelerating. To put that into a U.S. perspective, when Europeans first explored this continent, the eastern third of the country was blanketed with dense forests from the Atlantic Ocean to the central Great Plains. It has been said that the cover was so thick that a squirrel could travel in the treetops from the Atlantic Coast to the Mississippi River and never have to touch ground.

Weyerhaeuser and other large forest products companies need to be concerned about the problems of deforestation. Paper products use a quarter of the world's commercial wood harvest, and this proportion is expected to increase. The strategies for reforestation and selective cutting should be shared with Third World countries who have been lured by the industrialized world's hunger for hardwood. Companies like Weyerhaeuser should be aware of the problem and lead the campaign to save these forests. Otherwise, the countries may overexploit their forests to the point of exhaustion.

WEYERHAEUSER INTERNAL OPERATIONS

Employee Strike

On June 16, 1986, thirty-two Weyerhaeuser mills in Oregon and Washington were shut down by 7,500 striking woodworkers and loggers. Labor and management could not agree on labor contracts which expired on June 1. The strike ended with the signing of a contract containing basic wage and benefit reductions. According to management, decreasing the hourly wage rate by $2.90 to $9.60 became necessary in order to remain competitive with small nonunion operations in the region.

Organizational Structure

In 1985, Weyerhaeuser reorganized its major businesses into three operating organizations: (1) the Forest Products Company, (2) the Paper Company, and (3) Real Estate, Diversified, and Specialty Businesses. Each business unit has a separate strategic management team. Exhibit 8 lists the names and positions of these management teams as well as the corporate staff, headed by George Weyerhaeuser.

FOREST PRODUCTS COMPANY

Weyerhaeuser's Forest Products business produces the industry's most comprehensive mix of wood-based building and industrial materials and is a leading supplier of logs and chips. Some of the products made are softwood veneer and plywood, particle board, fiber board, gypsum wallboard, and panelling. The Forest Products Group also manages 6 million acres of timberland. The business consists of four self-contained, geographic divisions: Washington, Oregon, the South, and Weyerhaeuser Canada.

The Southern Division is the largest of the four, with 3.1 million acres of commercial timberland. The Washington Division is second with 1.7 million acres of land, followed by the Oregon Division with 1.3 million acres. Through licensing arrangements, Weyerhaeuser Canada has access to 12 million acres of Canadian timberland. Exhibit 9 depicts these ownership figures.

Washington Division

The Washington Division is the best suited to serve export markets, especially Japan and other Pacific Rim countries. This division supplies logs to Japan, China, and Korea. As a result of dealing with Far East customers, Washington has developed new products such as a hemlock veneer currently being marketed in Japan. The Washington Division also sends lumber and plywood to Europe and the southwest United States.

The Washington Division rose to the challenge of restoring 45,000 acres of timberland devastated by the eruption of Mount St. Helens in 1980. Within a month after the blast, foresters ran tree-planting tests. By early 1981, the division had begun full-scale replanting. The enormous task of reforestation of the area was completed on June 28, 1986.

EXHIBIT 8 The Weyerhaeuser management team

SENIOR OFFICERS

George H. Weyerhaeuser
President and chief executive officer
Charles W. Bingham
Executive vice president
John W. Creighton, Jr.
Executive vice president
Robert L. Schuyler
Executive vice president and chief financial officer
Fred R. Fosmire
Senior vice president, human resources, technology and engineering

CORPORATE STAFF

Frank K. Guthrie
Vice president, information systems
Mary J. Hall
Vice president
Corporate contributions and Weyerhaeuser Company Foundation
Steven R. Hill
Vice president, employee relations
Walter C. Howe, Jr.
Vice president, government relations
Norman E. Johnson
Vice president, research and development
John G. Kauffman
Vice president, transportation and materials management
Robert C. Lane
Vice president and general counsel
John S. Larsen
Vice president, energy and environmental and regulatory affairs
William H. Oliver
Vice president, corporate communications
Kenneth J. Stancato
Vice president and controller
William C. Stivers
Vice president and treasurer
Alan P. Vandevert
Secretary
Neil P. Wissing
Vice president and director of taxes

U.S. NATIONAL AFFAIRS OFFICE

Fred S. Benson
Vice president, federal relations, Washington, D.C.

FOREST PRODUCTS (1)

Lynn E. Endicott
Vice president, building products group
John P. McMahon
Vice president, timberlands
G. C. Meyer
Vice president, southern division
John N. Purcell
Vice president, Oregon division
Donald E. Rush
Vice president, Washington division
John H. Wilkinson
Vice president

WEYERHAEUSER CANADA LTD. (1)

D. L. McInnes
President and chief executive officer, Weyerhaeuser Canada Ltd.

WEYERHAEUSER FAR EAST, LTD. (1)

W. E. Franklin
President, Weyerhaeuser Far East, Ltd.

WESTWOOD SHIPPING LINES (1)

Tom Luthy
President

PAPER (2)

John H. Waechter
President, Weyerhaeuser Paper Company
- **Peter G. Belluschi**
  Vice president, newsprint
- **Hans A. Brune**
  Vice president, pulp and secondary fiber
- **James B. Collett**
  Vice president, packaging
- **Michael J. Cordry**
  Vice president, quality
- **R. L. Erickson**
  Vice president, manufacturing and technology
- **Carl W. Geist, Jr.**
  Vice president, containerboard and bleached paperboard
- **Robert F. Meyer**
  Vice president, paper

WEYERHAEUSER REAL ESTATE COMPANIES (3)

C. Stephen Lewis
Senior vice president, Weyerhaeuser Real Estate Company
- **The Babcock Company**
- **Centennial Homes, Inc.**
- **Cornerstone Columbia Development Co. (50%)**
- **Pardee Construction Co.**
- **The Quadrant Corp.**
- **Scarborough Corporation**
- **Scarborough Constructors**
- **Trendmaker Homes, Inc.**
- **Westminster Company**
- **Winchester Homes, Inc.**
- **Weyerhaeuser Venture Co.**

WEYERHAEUSER FINANCIAL SERVICES COMPANIES (3)

GNA Corporation
Republic Federal Savings and Loan Association
Weyerhaeuser Mortgage Company

DIVERSIFIED (3)

Robert J. Gemmell
Vice president, Weyerhaeuser diversified business group
L. J. Osterhage
Vice president, independent wood products and specialty building materials

(1) Reports to Mr. Bingham
(2) Reports to Mr. Schuyler
(3) Reports to Mr. Creighton

Source: Weyerhaeuser 1986 *Annual Report*, p. 32.

EXHIBIT 9 Weyerhaeuser timberland ownership

Division	*Location*	*Acreage*
Washington	Twin Harbors	657,000
	Longview	452,000
	Cascade	551,000
Oregon	Klamath Falls	654,000
	Springfield	404,000
	Coos Bay	214,000
Southern	N. Carolina	589,000
	Mississippi/Alabama	576,000
	Oklahoma/Arkansas	1,807,000

Canadian License Arrangements:
British Columbia—3,590,000 acres
Saskatchewan—8,474,000 acres

Source: Weyerhaeuser Company Statistical Information, p. 9.

Oregon Division

This division has four manufacturing locations and 1.3 million acres of timberland to utilize in making its products. Operating in Oregon offers several natural advantages, including the availability of deep-water ports and the proximity to Pacific Rim markets. This division ships products throughout the United States.

Oregon is very concerned with reforestation. The division has set new records for efficiency in fertilization, planting, thinning and other silvicultural activities. Another area of concern for Oregon is transportation. The Springfield mill has begun piggybacking vans loaded with high-value products on rail cars, rather than shipping by conventional box-car or truck. With this method, customers receive orders more quickly, and shipping costs are reduced.

Southern Division

This is the largest of all Weyerhaeuser's divisions with 3.1 million acres of commercial timberland, more than half of the company's U.S. ownership. This division stretches over 1,200 miles and includes five states. The South's primary markets include the Eastern Seaboard, the Sun Belt, the Midwest, and Texas.

The Southern Division makes a variety of pine and hardwood products, and it trades in land, timber, logs, pulpwood, and minerals. Southern pine is uniquely suited to pressure-treating with chemical preservatives. The Southern Division is working to develop new treated pine products that will give it a better market share.

Weyerhaeuser Canada

Operating six sawmills in southern British Columbia, Weyerhaeuser Canada relies heavily on government-owned timber. The division has its own sales and distribution group that operates in Kamloops, and has established markets in Europe, Japan, and Australia in addition to those in North America.

Weyerhaeuser Canada's mills are located in an area that has extremes of terrain and weather. The land varies from near-desert to steep mountain ranges. The weather varies from 100 degrees plus in the summer to 40 degrees below zero in the winter. Logging roads are rendered impassable at most locations for two months each year. However, each of the six mills is equipped with the best of modern technology.

Exhibit 10 shows the manufacturing and production facilities for Weyerhaeuser Forest Products Company. The exhibit demonstrates that the company still revolves around the Pacific Northwest, where the majority of Weyco's lumber mills are located. Sales in 1986 were $2.66 billion, up less than 1 percent from 1985. Net earnings, however, increased 44.7 percent over 1985 levels.

PAPER COMPANY

Weyerhaeuser Paper Company markets six product lines: pulp and secondary fiber, newsprint, paper, containerboard, shipping containers, and bleached paperboard. The heart of the Paper Company is four fine-paper mills located in Longview, Washington; Rothschild, Wisconsin; Plymouth, North Carolina; and Columbus, Mississippi.

The marketing activities of the Paper Division are centered in Plymouth Meeting, Pennsylvania. Four strategically located zone offices provide sales coverage for all parts

EXHIBIT 10 Manufacturing and production facilities for Weyerhaeuser Forest Products Company

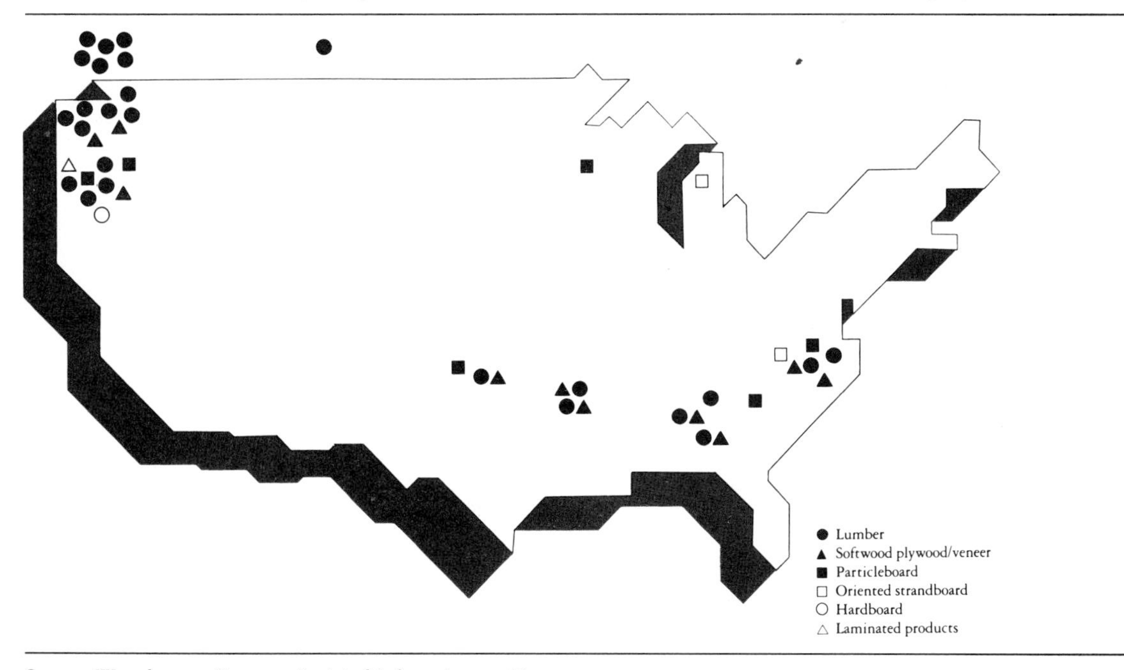

Source: *Weyerhaeuser Company Statistical Information*, p. 11.

of the United States. Plymouth Meeting is the home for the Atlantic zone. The Southern zone is based in Atlanta, Georgia. The Midwest zone is serviced from Chicago, Illinois, while the West Coast zone is based in Los Angeles, California. Exhibit 11 shows the facility locations for Weyerhaeuser Paper Company. Sales in 1986 were $2.39 billion, up 10.6 percent from 1985 levels. Net earnings for 1986 were $95.6 million, nearly double the earnings in 1985.

REAL ESTATE, DIVERSIFIED, AND SPECIALTY BUSINESSES

Real Estate

Weyerhaeuser Real Estate Company (WRECO) serves as a holding company for ten regional real estate development and building companies. It is also the parent of Weyerhaeuser Mortgage Company and of Republic Federal Savings and Loan. WRECO also has a land-development department and insurance subsidiaries. Exhibit 12 lists the businesses and locations for WRECO.

In 1986, WRECO had its fourth consecutive record year. Weyerhaeuser Mortgage Company's loan servicing portfolio grew to $11.2 billion, with loan originations of 2.75 billion. Sales were up less than 1 percent in 1986 to $784 million, and net earnings were $91 million, a 23.7 percent increase over 1985 earnings.

EXHIBIT 11 Facility locations for Weyerhaeuser Paper Company

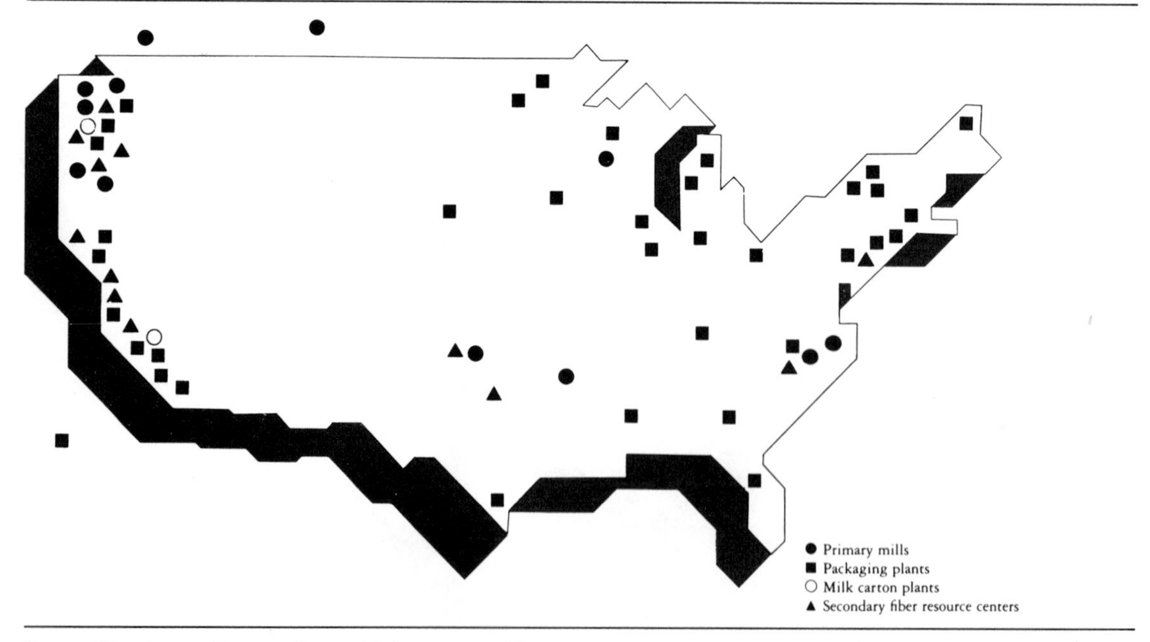

Source: *Weyerhaeuser Company Statistical Information*, p. 16.

EXHIBIT 12 Weyerhaeuser real estate and financial services subsidiaries

		Products					
Building Companies	*Primary States of Operations*	*Single-family*	*Multi-family*	*Residential lots*	*Commercial lots*	*Acreage*	*Commercial projects*
The Babcock Company	Florida	X	X	X	X	X	X
Centennial Homes, Inc.	Texas	X		X		X	
Cornerstone Columbia Development Co. (50% Ownership)	Oregon, Washington	X			X		X
Land Management	Alabama, Arkansas, Mississippi, North Carolina, Oklahoma, Oregon, Virginia, Washington	X		X	X	X	
Pardee Construction Co.	California, Nevada	X	X	X			X
The Quadrant Corp.	Oregon, Washington	X		X	X		X
Scarborough Building Co.	New Jersey, Virginia	X		X			
Scarborough Constructors	Florida			X			
Trendmaker Homes, Inc.	Texas	X		X	X		X
Westminster Company	North Carolina, South Carolina	X	X	X	X	X	X
Winchester Homes, Inc.	Maryland, Virginia	X	X	X			X
Weyerhaeuser Real Estate Co. (Parent Company)	Washington						

continued

EXHIBIT 12 continued

Financial Service Companies	*Primary States of Operations*	*Financial Products*						
		Mortgage lending	*Mortgage servicing*	*Savings deposits*	*Venture capital*	*Insurance*	*Investment sales and service*	*Mortgage securities*
Republic Federal Savings and Loan Association	California	X	X	X			X	
Weyerhaeuser Insurance Services	California, Nevada, Washington					X		
Weyerhaeuser Mortgage Co.	Branches in 13 states with major concentrations Arizona, California, Nevada, Texas	X	X				X	
Weyerhaeuser Venture Co.	Alaska, Arizona, California, Colorado, Florida, Nevada, Oregon, Washington				X			
Mortgage Securities Companies	California, Washington							X
GNA Corporation	Licensed in 42 states and the District of Columbia with major concentrations California, Illinois, Louisiana, Oregon, Texas, Washington					X	X	

Source: *Weyerhaeuser Company Statistical Information,* p. 24.

Diversified and Specialty Business Groups

The Diversified Business Group produces personal care products, markets nursery supplies nationwide and in Europe, markets a line of chemicals, and operates a food products business. Through the Diversified Business Group, Weyerhaeuser is the largest supplier of disposable diapers to the private label market. The group's wholesale nursery supply distribution business is also the nation's largest.

In 1986, the personal care products business realized heavy competition with new super-absorbent disposable diapers. Facility locations for the Diversified Business Group appear in Exhibit 13.

The Specialty Business Group manufactures and markets architectural doors, gypsum wallboard, hardwood veneer, paneling, and wood-fiber-based specialty products. Weyerhaeuser is the world's leading supplier of high quality doors. As anticipated, commercial door orders weakened toward the end of 1986. This drop reflects a decline in commercial building construction due to the 1986 tax reform. Another factor is excess construction of apartment buildings in recent years. Sales for the Diversified and Specialty Business Groups were up 25 percent in 1986 to $714.8 million; however, before tax earnings decreased 23 percent to $46.4 million. Exhibit 14 depicts the facility locations for the Specialty Business Group.

EXHIBIT 13 Weyerhaeuser Diversified Business Group facility locations

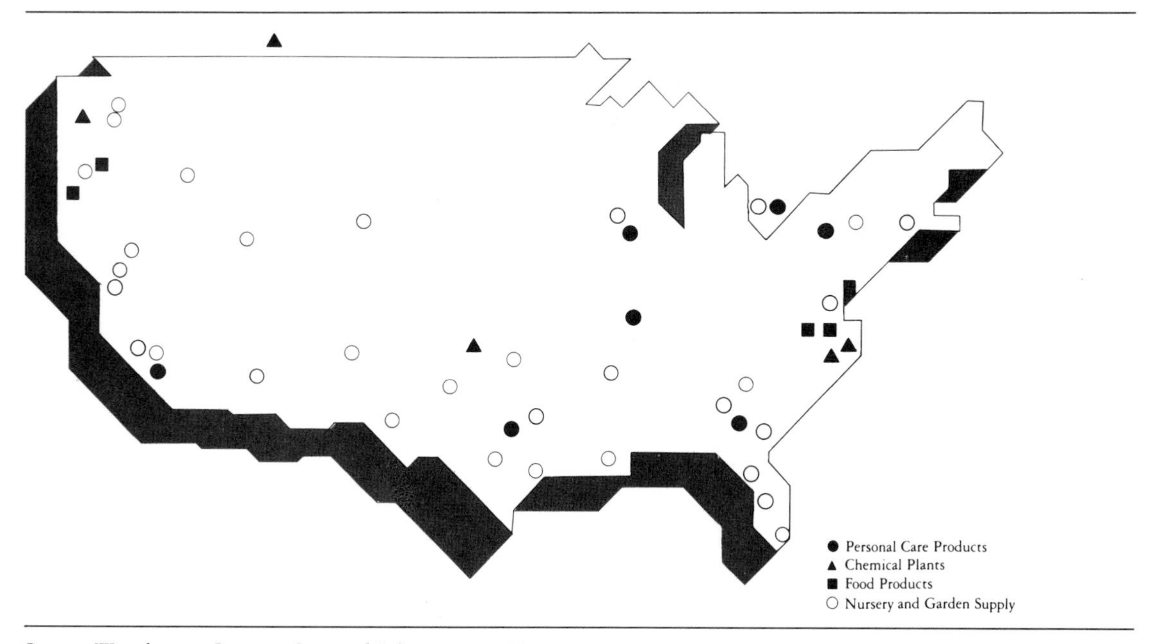

Source: *Weyerhaeuser Company Statistical Information*, p. 20.

EXHIBIT 14 Weyerhaeuser Specialty Business Group facility locations

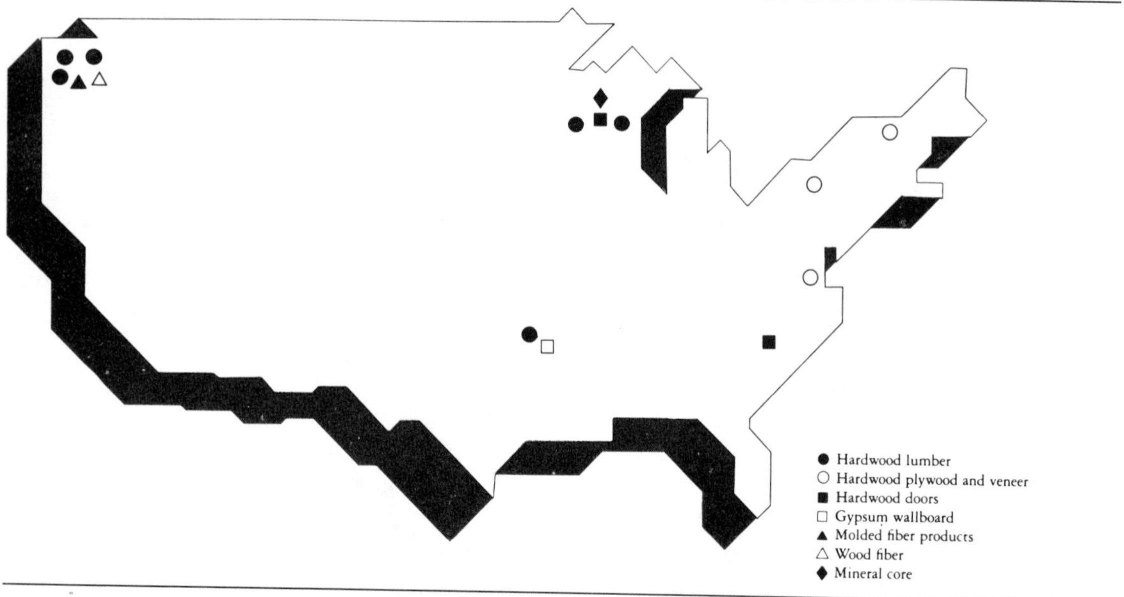

Source: *Weyerhaeuser Company Statistical Information,* p. 21.

FINANCIAL PERFORMANCE

Weyerhaeuser achieved record sales of $5.7 billion in 1986, up 9 percent from 1985. Earnings per common share were $1.91, a 45 percent jump from 1985. Sales figures are summarized by segment for the past two years in Exhibit 15. Exhibits 16 and 17 contain the consolidated earnings statement and consolidated balance sheet, respectively, for Weyerhaeuser.

Weyerhaeuser's strong financial position in 1986 resulted in a $678 million cash flow from operations. Cash was generated as well from maturing investments in short-term financial assets and the issuance of commercial paper and debt securities. Capital expenditures for 1986 were $605 million, which included fixed assets from the acquisition of Prince Albert Pulp Company. Capital expenditures for the past five years are summarized in Exhibit 18. The company paid cash dividends totalling $198 million and redeemed $170 million of preferred shares. Long-term debt to capital neared the industry average of 35 percent as Weyerhaeuser increased its ratio of long-term debt to capitalization from 25 percent in 1985 to 34 percent in 1986.

COMPANY STRATEGIES

One of Weyerhaeuser's main concerns is decreasing the cost of production. The largest single expense incurred by the forest products operations is cost of labor, accounting for 40 percent of final product costs. Weyco reduced wages and benefits after last

EXHIBIT 15 Weyerhaeuser Company, financial data by segment

Year ended December 28, 1986 *Dollar amounts in millions except per share figures*	*Operations* *Forest Products*	*Paper*	*Diversified and Specialty*	*Real Estate and Financial Services*[1]	*Corporate and Other*	*Eliminations*	*Total*
Revenues							
Trade sales	$2,434.2	$2,339.5	$ 714.8	$ —	$ 163.5	$ —	$5,652.0
Intersegment sales	197.6	51.8	74.6	—	19.3	(343.3)	—
Other income, net	29.4	.6	1.3	128.8	(10.0)	—	150.1
	2,661.2	2,391.9	790.7	128.8	172.8	(343.3)	5,802.1
Operating costs	2,248.4	2,002.6	654.1	—	182.4	(343.3)	4,744.2
Selling, general and administrative expenses	169.1	167.9	90.2	—	80.8	—	508.0
Earnings before interest and taxes	$ 243.7	$ 221.4	$ 46.4	$ 128.8	$ (90.4)	$ —	549.9
Interest expense, net of capitalized interest							129.3
Earnings before income taxes							420.6
Income taxes							143.9
Net income							$276.7
Earnings per common share							$1.91

Year ended December 29, 1985 *Dollar amounts in millions except per share figures*	*Operations* *Forest Products*	*Paper*	*Diversified and Specialty*	*Real Estate and Financial Services*[1]	*Corporate and Other*	*Eliminations*	*Total*
Revenues							
Trade sales	$2,357.0	$2,120.5	$ 569.3	$ —	$ 158.8	$ —	$5,205.6
Intersegment sales	284.3	41.8	77.6	—	44.7	(448.4)	—
Other income, net	9.5	3.7	(7.3)	111.9	24.5	—	142.3
	2,650.8	2,166.0	639.6	111.9	228.0	(448.4)	5,347.9
Operating costs	2,318.1	1,875.8	505.9	—	207.0	(448.4)	4,458.4
Selling, general and administrative expenses	169.8	166.2	73.4	—	66.2	—	475.6
Earnings before interest and taxes	$ 162.9	$ 124.0	$ 60.3	$ 111.9	$ (45.2)	$ —	413.9
Interest expense, net of capitalized interest							110.2
Earnings before income taxes							303.7
Income taxes							103.6
Net income							$200.1
Earnings per common share							$1.32

Source: *Weyerhaeuser Company Statistical Information*, p. 6.

EXHIBIT 16 Weyerhaeuser's income statements

For the three years ended December 28, 1986 *Dollar amounts in thousands except per share figures*	*1986*	*1985*	*1984*
Net sales	$5,652,029	$5,205,579	$5,549,738
Real estate and financial services subsidiaries earnings	128,838	111,914	86,935
Other income, net	21,215	30,419	(61,864)
	5,802,082	5,347,912	5,574,809
Operating costs	4,744,233	4,458,356	4,658,969
Selling, general and administrative expenses	477,298	431,480	426,918
Research and development expenses	30,680	44,141	45,648
Interest expense incurred	138,277	116,453	124,603
Less interest capitalized	8,991	6,234	2,716
	5,381,497	5,044,196	5,253,422
Earnings before income taxes	420,585	303,716	321,387
Income taxes	143,900	103,600	95,200
Net earnings	$ 276,685	$ 200,116	$ 226,187
Per common share			
Net earnings	$ 1.91	$ 1.32	$ 1.52
Dividends paid	$ 1.30	$ 1.30	$ 1.30

Source: *Weyerhaeuser Company Statistical Information*, pp. 1–4.

summer's strike, but the company added individual unit productivity and profit-sharing incentives. Management plans to establish profit-based wage restoration plans and pay-for-production systems. Salaried employees have already gone through layoffs and salary freezes. In the past five years, 11,000 Weyco employees have been released, and salaries have been frozen twice. This trend will probably continue until the cost of labor is reduced enough for Weyerhaeuser to remain competitive.

Weyerhaeuser recently sold three of its major businesses, its unbleached draft paper mill, and its multiwall log plant assets in Pine Bluff, Arkansas, in February 1986. In May 1986, Weyerhaeuser agreed to sell its salmon ocean ranching subsidiary, Oregon Aqua-Foods.

In November 1985, Weyerhaeuser signed an agreement to acquire the assets of Tri-Wall, Inc. of Woodbury, New York. This action marks the company's entry into the triple-wall corrugated market. In April 1986, Weyerhaeuser's board of directors approved the acquisition of the Prince Albert Pulp Company and related timber licenses from the Saskatchewan government by Weyerhaeuser Canada. Weyerhaeuser is presently constructing its second oriented strandboard plant at Elkin, North Carolina. Construction of a plant to produce microboard, a new, high-quality wood panel, is underway at Moncure, North Carolina.

These acquisitions and expansions, along with its present product lines, will give Weyerhaeuser Company the needed product mix to serve today's and tomorrow's markets. The additions also help the company gain breadth and stability and give it an

EXHIBIT 17 Weyerhaeuser Company consolidated balance sheet for three years ended December 28, 1986 (dollar amounts in millions)

	1986	*1985*	*1984*
Assets			
Cash and short-term investments	$ 38	$ 40	$ 173
Receivables	597	520	512
Inventories	600	547	559
Prepaid expenses	109	93	95
Total Current Assets	**1,344**	**1,200**	**1,339**
Investment in real estate and financial services subsidiaries, including advances	669	509	318
Property and equipment, at cost	6,494	6,097	6,000
Less allowance for depreciation and amortization	2,994	2,785	2,663
	3,500	**3,312**	**3,337**
Construction in progress	177	121	107
timber and timberlands, net	649	646	633
Other assets	219	217	224
Total Assets	**$6,558**	**$6,005**	**$5,958**
Liabilities and shareholders' interest			
Notes payable	6	8	9
Current maturities of senior long-term debt	155	8	226
Current maturities of capital lease obligations	14	17	15
Accrued income taxes	46	36	36
Accounts payable and accrued liabilities	641	640	605
Total Current Liabilities	**862**	**709**	**891**
Senior long-term debt	1,412	1,156	1,067
Limited recourse income debenture	172	—	—
Deferred income taxes	513	464	445
Minority interest in subsidiaries	32	30	30
Other long-term liabilities	299	307	322
Redeemable preference shares	15	15	15
Shareholders' interest	3,253	3,324	3,188
Total Liabilities and Shareholders' Interest	**$6,558**	**$6,005**	**$5,958**

Source: Weyerhaeuser 1986 *Annual Report*, pp. 16–17.

EXHIBIT 18 Weyerhaeuser Company and subsidiaries capital expenditures by segment

Dollar amounts in millions	*Business*				
	Forest Products	*Paper*	*Diversified and Specialty*	*Corporate*	*Total*
Timber and timberlands					
1986	$ 49	$ 5	$ 1	$ —	$ 55
1985	64	2	1	—	67
1984	62	8	1	—	71
1983	56	8	—	—	64
1982	54	5	—	—	59
	285	28	3	—	316
Property and equipment					
1986	142	346	47	15	550
1985	114	163	35	17	329
1984	108	150	27	27	312
1983	100	105	23	20	248
1982	111	339	24	15	489
	575	1,103	156	94	1,928
Combined total					
1986	191	351	48	15	605
1985	178	165	36	17	396
1984	170	158	28	27	383
1983	156	113	23	20	312
1982	165	344	24	15	548
	$ 860	$1,131	$ 159	$ 94	$2,244

Source: Weyerhaeuser Statistical Summary, p. 7.

avenue for earnings and growth. Weyerhaeuser has a good financial position and is in the right business to become a growth firm in the future.

WEYERHAEUSER'S OUTLOOK

What is in store for the forest products giant? CEO George Weyerhaeuser predicts more engineered wood in Weyco's future, similar to the gypsum wallboard produced currently. Mr. Weyerhaeuser forecasts that in the next decade, his company will manufacture a new set of basic wood products representing mixtures of natural species and synthetic fibers.

China is viewed as the big market of the future. Having overcut forests for centuries, China cannot hope to increase its internal lumber production for decades. As the Chinese move toward a market economy, they will inevitably need more wood products. This need could prove to be an immense opportunity. Weyco currently receives nearly one-half of its total revenue from exports. The company can ship goods at lower transportation costs to Japan than it can to Chicago.

To increase its market share, Weyco could seek to acquire other forest products companies such as Great Northern Nekoosa or Union Camp. Or, Weyco could acquire large distributors of paper products, such as Scott Paper or Fort Howard Paper. Consolidation in the forest products industry is being spurred by the high cost of building new plants and the advantages of economies of scale.

In the company's 1986 *Annual Report,* Mr. Weyerhaeuser says:

> We will increase investment in our two traditional groupings, but that investment will be in newer, engineered products with higher value-added potential. And, we will pursue opportunities to broaden our product mix and improve our geographic marketing reach through acquisition, as we did in the case of Prince Albert Pulp Company's assets in 1986. (p. 3)

Should Weyco experience financial troubles in the future, the company could become a takeover target. Effective strategies must be formulated and successfully implemented to assure Weyco's competitiveness and survival in the 21st century. Resource constraints limit the number of strategies that Weyco could pursue, so major decisions need to be made now.

Stone Container Corporation—1987

M. RAY GRUBBS
Millsaps College
GLYNN RAWSON
Millsaps College

"It's simply up to us to constructively manage our vast opportunities in the forest products industry. If we do, then we can clearly feel free to rewrite Charles Dickens and state that, 'It was the worst of times, it is the best of times!' " These were the words of Roger Stone, chairman of the board and chief executive officer of Stone Container Corporation, in a speech before the annual meeting of the Fibre Box Association, May 2, 1984.

The speech was built from the framework of an industry that was experiencing its first real growth in five years (see Exhibits 1, 2, and 3). The year 1984 proved to be a transition year in which the corrugated industry, as well as the entire paper industry, realized healthy growth and profitability. During this year the growth-through-acquisition trend also continued in the paper industry; this trend was the means by which Stone Container eventually claimed the number one position as the world's largest producer of products in its three main business segments.

THE CORRUGATED INDUSTRY

Corrugated paper material (of which pasteboard boxes are made) was first patented in 1856 in England by Edward Healey and Edward Allen. In its initial form, the fluted material was used for sweatbands in hats. As a packing material, it was patented in

EXHIBIT 1

Corrugated price index by area (1967 = 100)			
	1984	*1985*	*1986*
Area One—Northeastern			
1st Quarter	224.0	246.3	221.0
2nd Quarter	234.5	238.0	221.0
3rd Quarter	236.2	228.0	225.5
4th Quarter	248.7	222.6	231.4
Year	**235.8**	**233.7**	**224.7**
Area Two—Southeastern			
1st Quarter	231.6	254.1	223.3
2nd Quarter	245.3	246.1	225.4
3rd Quarter	243.5	228.0	227.2
4th Quarter	259.3	226.1	237.4
Year	**244.8**	**238.5**	**228.4**
Area Three—East Central			
1st Quarter	224.3	251.3	223.5
2nd Quarter	236.3	241.6	222.5
3rd Quarter	237.0	227.4	225.8
4th Quarter	250.2	223.9	230.3
Year	**236.7**	**235.9**	**225.5**
Area Four—North Central			
1st Quarter	232.0	257.2	230.5
2nd Quarter	245.1	247.4	230.6
3rd Quarter	244.3	232.6	233.8
4th Quarter	257.0	231.2	242.7
Year	**244.4**	**241.9**	**234.5**

the United States in 1871 by Albert Jones, whose patent covered a fluted (corrugated) material for protecting vials and bottles.

Initially, corrugated materials were largely used as cushioning and wrappers for bottled goods, then as light parcel post and express boxes. The uses for corrugated material grew measurably in the ensuing years. Today, there are few items of commerce, large and small, that are not packed in corrugated boxes.

The growth of corrugated material was greatly influenced by the Interstate Commerce Commission's Pridham decision in 1914 that ended discrimination against corrugated containers. Up to the time of this decision, freight rates for corrugated con-

EXHIBIT 1 continued

Corrugated price index by area (1967 = 100)	*1984*	*1985*	*1986*
Area Five—South Central			
1st Quarter	222.0	243.0	213.9
2nd Quarter	230.8	235.1	214.2
3rd Quarter	230.2	217.4	217.4
4th Quarter	242.6	214.5	225.5
Year	**230.8**	**227.4**	**217.7**
Area Six—Western			
1st Quarter	255.9	280.1	246.9
2nd Quarter	271.9	279.6	254.9
3rd Quarter	273.0	264.6	256.9
4th Quarter	275.4	253.8	257.8
Year	**269.2**	**269.5**	**254.4**

Corrugated Price and Producer Price Index (1967 = 100)

Year	*1st Qtr.*	*2nd Qtr.*	*3rd Qtr.*	*4th Qtr.*	*Year*	*BLS PPI*
1980	209.7	214.3	212.9	214.4	212.8	268.8
1981	222.8	232.5	232.4	232.6	230.0	293.4
1982	229.4	229.6	223.2	221.3	225.9	299.4
1983	217.3	218.6	217.2	224.8	219.5	303.1
1984	230.0	242.6	242.6	254.1	242.3	310.3
1985	254.0	246.5	231.5	227.2	239.7	308.8
1986	225.1	226.6	229.6	236.0	229.4	299.8

Source: Adapted from Fibre Box Association 1986 *Annual Report.*

tainers were much greater than those for wood boxes. This rate discrepancy greatly impaired the utilization of corrugated shipping containers. With the favorable ruling by the ICC to lower corrugated packaging freight rates, corrugated materials saw phenomenal growth in the years to come.

The range of sizes and capabilities of corrugated boxes grew in the years after World War II to fit the array of new products developed by American industry. As refrigerators replaced ice boxes and as radios and televisions entered the American home along with food freezers, air conditioners, and home computers, corrugated box manufacturers found a growing demand for their products.

The use of corrugated containers in the shipment of produce expanded to the point where most types of fruits and vegetables are now packaged in corrugated mate-

EXHIBIT 2 Industry value of shipments

Year	*Total*	*Corrugated*	*Solid Fibre*	*Year to Year Growth*
1980	9,075,381,800	9,010,411,600	64,970,200	+7.9
1981	10,019,521,200	9,956,771,000	64,750,200	+10.4
1982	9,343,619,900	9,278,989,700	64,630,200	−6.7
1983	9,845,258,200	9,778,198,700	67,059,500	+5.4
1984	11,567,050,900	11,491,431,700	75,619,200	+17.5
1985	11,486,830,500	11,431,175,600	73,654,900	−0.7
1986	11,753,044,200	11,673,330,200	79,714,000	+2.3

Source: Adapted from Fibre Box Association 1986 *Annual Report.*

rials. With the advent of wax coating on corrugated material, new uses in packaging fresh meat and poultry in ice were also opened.

The versatility of pasteboard has been enhanced to such a degree that now a growing practice is to accumulate consumer packages into units and form the shipping container around the product rather than insert the product into the preferred box.

MANUFACTURING PROCESS

A corrugated box is made from two or more sheets of linerboard and one or more fluted sheets of corrugating medium. In the United States, almost all of the linerboard used in corrugated boxes is Kraft, a type of paperboard made predominantly from virgin softwood fibres. Most of the corrugating medium used in boxes is made by a semi-chemical pulping process that utilizes mostly virgin hardwood fibre. Approximately one-third of all corrugating medium used is made from recycled corrugated box plant waste.

EXHIBIT 3 Industry shipments

Year	*Total*	*Corrugated*	*Solid Fibre*	*Year to Year Growth*
1980	214.377*	240.490	.887	−3.7
1981	246.152	245.331	.821	+2.0
1982	235.185	234.306	.879	−4.5
1983	252.539	251.618	.921	+7.4
1984	267.547	266.565	.982	+5.9
1985	267.453	266.490	.963	−.04
1986	283.921	282.852	1.069	+6.2

Note: *Billions of Square Feet

Source: Adapted from Fibre Box Association 1986 *Annual Report.*

The *Fibre Box Handbook* describes the Kraft process of producing linerboard as follows: "Chemicals and heat are used to dissolve the material which holds the wood fibres together in the sawdust and chips. This cementing material, called lignin, must be removed in sufficient amounts to allow separation of the fibres. The solid wood is fed, together with the required amount of chemicals, into a large pressure vessel and cooked at a high temperature and pressure for up to three hours. After cooking and refining to separate the fibres, they are put in a water suspension of one part fibre and ninety-nine parts water. This mixture is poured on a screen more than 30 feet wide, moving at a speed in excess of 20 miles per hour. A portion of the water is removed by suction, and the resulting sheet is passed through a series of presses which drop the moisture content. From this point, the sheets are dried by heating and reeled into rolls for shipment to the corrugator plant."

The linerboard and corrugating medium are joined together on the corrugator, a large assembly of several machinery sections, by means of an adhesive combined with a series of heat plates. The corrugated sheet can take the form of a single wall, whereby two liners and one corrugating medium are used, or double walls, whereby three liners and two mediums are used. For additional strength and durability, some corrugators are equipped to produce triple wall board. Before the liners and medium are joined, the medium is run between two meshed rolls that fit together like huge gears. This process causes the medium to become fluted, thus giving the board much added strength.

The board, which now consists of two facings and a fluted corrugated medium between them, passes between sets of movable knife-edged wheels. Some, designed to cut completely throughout the board, are used to trim the outside edges to the desired width. Other wheels simply press a scoreline (crease) into the board in the places where it will eventually be folded when made into boxes.

Finally, a revolving knife blade chops the continuous web of corrugated board into sheets of length ordered by the customer. The sheets are then either stacked for later processing or conveyed directly to the next machine in the box-making sequence or shipped to a sheet plant for conversion into boxes.

The corrugating machine is roughly the length of a football field. Machines run at varying speeds; the more modern ones run at 800 feet per minute at top speed and 300 feet per minute during order changes. Various pieces of converting equipment are used in the box plant for functions such as folding, glueing, and printing to the customer's specification. Most plants have some combination of printer slotters, die cutters, and folder gluers with printing capabilities as well as a number of specialized pieces of equipment.

The converting end of the integrated corrugated industry consists of two types of manufacturing facilities. The corrugator plant is equipped with a series of corrugating machines that take rolls of container board, liner, and medium, and produce sheets of board to be converted into boxes or sold as sheets to what are called "sheet plants." These plants do not have corrugating capabilities and must obtain sheets of board from either a corrugator plant within their company or in the marketplace. Sheet plants, often times independents, do not generally compete with the larger corrugator plants because sheet plant converting equipment is usually geared toward smaller, short-run business.

For each corrugated plant in an area, you might expect to see three or four sheet plants. Most areas of the country have more than one corrugator plant in close proximity, and in most populated areas, there are a number of competing firms. This situation makes for an extremely competitive environment, with much price cutting and low margins.

A medium-size corrugator plant will generally sell 10 percent to 20 percent or more of its finished board to smooth out the cyclical conditions experienced in the market. The modern purchasing agent in charge of box purchases is knowledgeable about corrugated material and often insists on sealed bids, from which the lowest bidder is rewarded with a 6- to 12-month contract.

COMPETITIVE ENVIRONMENT

Even with the great number of acquisitions that have taken place within the industry, there still remain a number of competitors with a fair share of the market. The Fibre Box Association, the corrugated industry's association, discontinued its practice of publishing key market share numbers of individual firms several years ago; therefore, market share breakdown by company cannot be determined with any degree of certainty. It is agreed that the following such breakdown closely approximates the actual numbers: Stone Container, 14 percent; Jefferson Smurfit, 9 percent; International Paper, 6 percent; Weyerhaeuser, 6 percent; and Georgia-Pacific, less than 6 percent (See Exhibit 4). As can be seen of the top five corrugated companies, the two smaller corporations (Stone and Jefferson Smurfit) have the lead and are less diversified.

A look at total shipments of corrugated material within the industry over the past twenty-five years reveals that the health of the overall economy tends to influence the success of the industry. The demand for corrugated containers is a derived demand; its demand is dependent on the demand for goods to be shipped in the containers. Negative growth trends in the industry occur in those years when the economy is experiencing recession or some other economic phenomenon such as the oil crisis and high inflation.

Several of the more important competitors in the corrugated industry are diversified companies with interest in a wide array of businesses. For example, during the first half of the 1980s, much of Weyerhaeuser's growth, and a significant portion of its earnings, came from non-traditional businesses such as real estate development, financial services, and specialty businesses. These operations, oriented almost entirely to U.S. markets, were to a large degree insulated from the declining competitiveness of the United States in world markets.

Weyerhaeuser, like International Paper Company, carries a great deal of timberland on its balance sheet. With the decreasing value of timberland over the past few years, companies of this type have suffered from the devaluation of this asset.

Weyerhaeuser manages 6 million acres of commercial forestland in the United States and operates fifty-eight wholesale distribution units for its building materials line. The company operates thirty-six container plants with 4.7 million tons of production capacity.

EXHIBIT 4 Selected data for industry leaders

1984	*Georgia Pacific*	*Weyerhaeuser*	*Int'l Paper*	*Champion Int'l*	*Boise Cascade*	*Jefferson Smurfit*	*Stone Container*
Sales (in thousands of dollars)	7,120,000	5,549,738	4,715,600	5,121,089	3,816,150	678,112	1,244,395
Net income	119,000	226,187	120,000	(5,968)	69,610	24,504	33,657
Net income as % of sales	1.7	4.1	2.6	—	1.8	3.6	2.7
Net income as % of equity	5.2	7.0	3.6	—	4.9	21.5	11.4
Return to investors	3.84	(9.85)	(4.62)	(21.56)	(2.8)	(22.30)	(20.13)
1985							
Sales (in thousands of dollars)	6,716,000	3,083,000	4,502,000	5,769,759	3,737,220	630,425	1,229,148
Net income	187,000	(26,800)	133,000	163,139	104,290	16,826	3,778
Net income as % of sales	2.8	—	3.0	2.8	2.8	2.7	0.3
Net income as % of equity	8.2	—	3.4	6.3	7.2	13.4	1.1
Return to investors	7.84	23.97	(2.64)	13.39	19.32	47.07	21.99
1986							
Sales (in thousands of dollars)	7,223,000	5,652,029	5,501,000	4,387,623	3,739,970	1,044,313	2,032,325
Net income	296,000	276,685	305,000	200,832	101,540	28,003	35,415
Net income as % of sales	4.1	4.9	5.5	4.6	2.7	2.7	1.7
Net income as % of equity	11.8	8.5	8.1	7.8	6.5	19.7	7.4
Return to investors	43.07	27.22	53.43	26.17	31.76	187.07	54.96

International Paper is a worldwide forest products company. It is principally engaged in the manufacture and sale of pulp, paper packaging, lumber, and plywood products and is involved in the development of mineral properties, oil and gas drilling, and agricultural operations. Currently, International Paper owns some 6.7 million acres of timberland in the United States. In 1985, International Paper produced 1.8 million tons of containerboard.

Jefferson Smurfit Corporation is a major integrated manufacturer of paper products, operating more than ninety paperboard mills, converting facilities, and other plants in the United States. Jefferson Smurfit is a producer of both paperboard and packaging products. Sales are generally concentrated in the Midwest, Southeast and Southwest.

Georgia-Pacific was founded in 1927 as a wholesaler of hardwood lumber and has expanded to become a major manufacturer and wholesale distributor of building products, pulp paper, packaging, and related chemicals. Today, Georgia-Pacific operates 366 plants, mills, and distribution centers and employs 38,000 persons. Its entrance into the pulp and paper business in the 1950s was on a regional operator basis. The company now owns or has cutting rights on 52 million acres of timberland in North America plus substantial reserves of gypsum, coal, oil, and natural gas.

Georgia-Pacific's building products distribution system is the industry's most extensive, with more than 140 branches serving every major metropolitan area in the United States. The company's presence in the corrugated and linerboard industry occurred rapidly within a five-year time frame. Georgia-Pacific currently operates more than thirty corrugated container facilities nationwide (first quarter, 1987).

Fortune magazine lists the 500 largest U.S. industrial corporations annually. Thirty-two companies on the list for 1987 were from the paper industry, second only to the food industry in total number of corporations within an industry on the list.

STONE CONTAINER CORPORATION

Stone Container Corporation operates principally in one industry segment—the vertically integrated production and conversion of unbleached containerboard and Kraft paper. Within this industry segment, the company participates in three major product categories. The company's mills produce linerboard, corrugating medium, and Kraft paper. The containerboard (liner and medium) is converted at the company's corrugated container plants into corrugated boxes. Kraft paper is converted at the company's bag plants into sacks and bags.

Stone Container was founded in Chicago as J. H. Stone and Company by Joseph H. Stone and his sons, Norman H. Stone and Marvin N. Stone. Initially, the company was a jobber of paper, twine, and shipping room supplies. Jerome H. Stone joined his father and brothers a few years later, and the company name was changed to J. H. Stone and Sons.

In 1933, the company purchased some equipment from an existing corrugated sheet plant and became a container manufacturer. In 1936, the first corrugator was installed, and in 1939, Stone built a new corrugated container manufacturing facility. The company was incorporated in Illinois as Stone Container Corporation in 1945.

During the ensuing years, Stone purchased or built several additional corrugator plants and paper mills. In 1961, the corporate headquarters was moved to North Michigan Avenue, Chicago, and the building's name was changed to the Stone Container Building. In 1962, Stone Container's common stock was admitted for trading on the New York Stock Exchange under the symbol MSTO.

In the first twenty years of operation, the company obtained through acquisition and construction only three manufacturing facilities. Rapid growth then took place, and between the years 1956 and 1987, there were only three years in which the company failed to build or acquire a manufacturing facility. Although these individual additions added greatly to the manufacturing capacity and market share, it was two major acquisitions in the 1980s that brought the company to the forefront as a leader in the production of containerboard, boxes, and paper bags.

In 1983, Stone purchased from Continental Group three containerboard and Kraft paper mills, fifteen corrugated container plants, and five bag converting plants. With this acquisition, Stone became the nation's largest producer and converter of unbleached container board and Kraft paper. The purchase price of this acquisition was approximately $550 million and was considered a bargain purchase by paper analysts, who claimed that the cost to construct one world-class paper mill would amount to more than $500 million.

"Stone's timing was perfect," applauded William Laimbeer, group vice-president for forest products at Owens-Illinois, Inc., "the industry is poised for a surge," he continued. *Business Week* wrote that Stone was able to purchase the entire deal for about a third of the replacement value of the mills alone.

To close the Continental deal, Stone Container arranged to borrow $600 million. This loan boosted Stone's debt to a hefty 79 percent of capitalization from 39 percent, but the company prepared by raising $37.5 million through its first equity offering since going public in 1947 (see Exhibit 5). This offering changed the family's holdings from 57 percent to 49 percent and resulted in the hiring of the company's first president from outside the family, James Frew, former group vice-president of Georgia-Pacific Corporation. Roger Stone assumed the role of chairman of the board and chief executive officer in 1980. Thomas Clephane, a paper analyst with Morgan Stanley and Company, said that recruiting Frew, "took Stone Container beyond a family partnership."

Barron's Weekly, in its "Investment News and Views," compared Stone's acquisition of Continental to trying to swallow an elephant, as Stone was acquiring a business larger than itself. Barrons further contended, however, that although the purchase price was well above Stone's total assets, the move made sense, timing-wise, since the paperboard industry was moving into a strong upward cycle.

In late 1985, Stone officials announced that a definitive agreement had been reached with Champion International to acquire most of Champion's Forest Product Division. With this acquisition, Stone obtained twenty-five corrugated plants, fifteen sheet plants, three mills, and eleven bag plants. This acquisition allowed Stone Container to claim the position of industry leader in all three product segments. The cash portion of the purchase of assets was $404 million. The agreement also required the issuance of 1.6 million shares of Stone common stock.

Business Week warned that, "this carton maker may be boxing itself in," in an article shortly after the announced purchase of Champion assets. The article voiced concern that the industry heavyweight, Stone Container, was, "writing an acquisition script as full of risks and potential rewards as any Wall Street takeover battle. In an attempt to pick up valuable assets cheaply in a depressed market, Chicago-based Stone, already one of the most highly leveraged United State paper companies . . . will see its debt soar to about 70 percent of capitalization after the purchase, but management is betting that rising prices could almost quadruple earnings within five years."

"If Roger Stone pulls this one off, he'll be a hero, but he's definitely taking a gamble," said William Laimbeer, executive vice-president of Owens-Illinois, Inc."

The results for 1986, with the ten months of the Champion acquisition reflected in the financial statements, proved the acquisition to be well worthwhile. Stone

EXHIBIT 5 Selected financial data

	1986[b]	*1985*	*1984*	*1983(b)*	*1982*
Summary of Operations					
Net sales	$2,032,325	$1,229,148	$1,244,395	$655,847	$426,639
Cost of products sold	1,564,619	944,142	924,879	525,988	328,701
Selling, administrative and general expenses	241,178	156,995	147,643	83,444	57,036
Depreciation and amortization	92,309	67,807	64,375	34,213	21,551
Interest expense	85,336	63,313	59,277	24,858	12,849
Income (loss) before income taxes	59,729	1,493	55,328	(8,282)	21,485
Provision (credit) for income taxes	24,314	(2,285)	21,671	(5,360)	7,300
Income (loss) before extraordinary charge and cumulative effect of accounting changes	35,415	3,778	33,657	(2,922)	14,185
Net income (loss)	35,415	3,778	33,657	(2,922)	14,185
Per Share of Common Stock[a]					
Income (loss) before extraordinary charge and cumulative effect of accounting changes	$ 1.95	$ .24	$ 2.39	$ (.31)	$ 1.46
Net income (loss)	1.95	.24	2.39	(.31)	1.46
Dividends and distributions paid on common shares	.60	.60	.60	.60	.60
Price range of common stock—N.Y.S.E.:					
High	60.00	39.50	43.25	45.00	24.25
Low	34.13	24.00	25.75	20.25	12.50
Average common shares outstanding (in thousands)	15,939	13,844	14,088	11,047	9,735
Financial Position at End of Year					
Current assets	$ 530,459	$ 320,177	$ 323,254	$252,042	$103,984
Current liabilities	203,410	165,130	164,379	104,054	50,243
Working capital	327,049	155,047	158,875	147,988	53,741
Property, plant and equipment—net	924,362	642,558	657,658	689,151	255,718
Total assets	1,523,600	1,010,321	1,006,661	968,249	381,063
Long-term debt	766,991	493,252	482,830	548,243	138,631
Deferred taxes	69,895	49,206	55,804	38,033	42,621
Redeemable preferred stock	1,500	8,000	8,500	7,608	7,400
Shareholders' equity	481,804	294,733	295,148	270,311	142,168

EXHIBIT 5 continued

	1986[b]	1985	1984	1983(b)	1982
Other Information					
Paperboard and paper (thousand tons)					
Produced	3,154	2,168	2,236	1,194	880
Converted	2,461	1,495	1,409	767	467
Corrugated shipments (billion square feet)	25.53	14.63	14.04	8.25	6.35
Paper bag and sack shipments (thousand tons)	585	418	382	182	21
Employees (end of year)	15,500	9,375	8,950	8,900	3,625
Capital expenditures	$ 63,254	$ 47,090	$ 41,917	$ 21,028	$ 63,101
Funds provided by operations	$ 149,604	$ 68,412	$ 116,920	$ 26,508	$ 42,812
Working capital ratio	2.6/1	1.9/1	2.0/1	2.4/1	2.1/1
Percent long-term debt/total capitalization	61.3%	62.0%	61.4%	66.4%	48.1%
Pre-tax margin	2.9%	.1%	4.4%	(1.3%)	5.0%
Effective tax rate	40.7%	nm	39.2%	(64.7%)	34.0%
After-tax margin	1.7%	.3%	2.7%	(.4%)	3.3%

(a) Amounts per share and number of shares have been adjusted for a 5-for-4 stock split in 1982 and 3-for-2 stock splits in 1981 and 1976, refer to the Stock Split footnote for pro forma net income per common share amounts reflecting the 2-for-1 stock split declared March 2, 1987.

(b) The Company made major acquisitions in 1986 and 1983. Further information regarding the 1986 acquisition may be found in the Acquisitions, Investments and Divestitures footnote.

nm–not meaningful

achieved record net income on record sales for the fourth quarter and full year of 1986. A major factor in the significant increase in sales was the inclusion of results of the operation acquired from Champion. "Our February 1986 acquisition, like an earlier acquisition made in 1983, was accomplished during an industry downtown," said Roger Stone. "Thus, we were ready, when conditions improved, to utilize the dedicated workforce and the excellent assets acquired to demonstrate the earnings potential of our expanded company." In addition to record earnings, Stone was able to vastly improve its cash flow, resulting in the company being able to reduce the outstanding borrowings under its basic credit agreements by $62 million during the fourth quarter.

Perhaps the greatest vote of confidence in Stone's major acquisitions by the financial community is its stock valuation. At the time of the Continental acquisition announcement, Stone's stock was trading on the New York Stock Exchange at around $26 per share. In early 1987, Stone's stock was trading briskly at $94 per share. Stone recently announced a 2 for 1 stock split for all common shares.

These major acquisitions follow the basic philosophy of Stone Container Chairman Roger Stone. In the 1985 annual report, Stone said, "the anticipated shortage of growth in new capacity is indicative of the risk/reward ratio for new mill investment. It is our belief that because of this, as well as other economic factors, the industry will continue to see more consolidations and restructuring. Companies will increasingly be interested in buying facilities at a fraction of their replacement value. It is far less costly to buy good capacity in place than to build it. We believe that the result of industry restructuring will be capacity redistribution, rather than capacity increase."

Further revealing his strategy, Stone said, "the implication of the growth in demand, without a comparable growth in supply, is that there will be product shortages. Given the basic law of supply and demand in a free market, price increases will be implemented until a fair return on investment is achieved. Until that time, those producers with low cost capacity in place will have significant upside earnings potential."

In a move that lends further credence to his strategy, Roger Stone announced in late 1986 that an agreement had been reached with Southwest Forest Industries for Stone to acquire the assets of Southwest through a cash purchase transaction. With this acquisition, Stone was to receive nine corrugator plants, ten sheet plants, two mills, a number of wood-related manufacturing facilities, and 334,000 acres of timberland. The cash price was approximately $400 million, and Stone was to assume $162 million in debt. At the time of this writing, both companies' boards of directors had approved the transaction and were awaiting final governmental approval.

The basic corporation objectives of Stone Container, as defined in the company's *Corporate Handbook,* are as follows:

- ☐ to achieve an annual standard of profitability not less than 15 percent return after taxes on shareholders equity.
- ☐ to reach a sales target reflecting a minimum real growth rate of 1 ½ times the growth rate of gross national product.
- ☐ to produce innovative, quality products backed by excellent service.
- ☐ to enhance opportunities for individual fulfillment by helping employees achieve their goals.

Stone Container Corporation is market oriented as opposed to production oriented. Roger Stone was quoted as saying, "we do not view our box plants as volume outlets for mill production. Instead, we view our mills as dependable sources of supply for our container division's basic raw material, containerboard." Stone has said that the company's philosophy is to be a net seller of containerboard. He would like to convert 60 to 75 percent of the company's own containerboard internally, and he plans to sell the rest, half domestically and half in the export market.

In 1981, Stone Container launched its IQS program company-wide. The IQS (Innovation, Quality, and Service) program was the nucleus around which a major advertising campaign was initiated. The ads depicting Stone as a company truly interested in innovation, quality, and service appeared in many of the leading business publications such as *Business Week, Fortune,* and *Forbes.*

With the IQS program, each manufacturing location is required to keep performance records on the quality standards of its product as well as the service delivered to the customer. After five years on the program, IQS is recognized throughout the industry as Stone's commitment to its corporate philosophy.

Stone Container operates (not including the Southwest purchase) seventy-three corrugated container plants, nineteen bag plants, and nine containerboard and paper mills in thirty-four states with concentration in the South, Midwest, and Northeast (see Exhibit 6). The Southwest acquisition will add to its presence in the Southwest.

EXHIBIT 6 Stone Container facilities.

Most of the company's manufacturing facilities are unionized. The predominant union in the paper industry is the United Paperworkers Union. The company is segmented organizationally into three major operating divisions with senior vice presidents serving as general managers of each division. Reporting to the senior vice presidents are a number of vice presidents-regional managers. These regional managers are located geographically throughout the company and are responsible for a given number of manufacturing facilities. For example, within the corrugated division, one regional manager is responsible for seven to ten plants, depending on plant size and geographical proximity. (See Exhibit 7: organizational chart.)

The management team at a Stone plant or mill generally consists of a general manager, production manager, sales manager and controller. Stone Containers' plants and mills have a great deal of autonomy with operational decisions being made by local management. The accounting, personnel, and data processing operations, for example, are decentralized at the plant/mill level.

While the selling function is in the hands of the local sales force, the corporate sales department lends assistance with national account sales. National account representatives work out of different areas of the United States and are assigned to specific national accounts.

The majority of paper consumed by the corrugated plants comes from Stone's paper mills; however, occasionally, the plants will purchase some of their rollstock from an outside supplier. Stone has a containerboard marketing department that is charged with the responsibility of coordinating all rollstock needs between the plants and mills. The normal inventory level of rollstock throughout the industry for a corrugated plant is a 6-week supply. For a medium-size corrugated plant, that figure would equate to between 4,000 and 5,000 tons of inventory.

Containerboard is shipped to the corrugator plants by both rail and truck, with railcars being the most predominant means of transportation. Finished boxes are shipped by company trucks as well as by common carrier. Due to the cost of freight involved in a very competitive environment, long-haul deliveries in the corrugated industry are uncommon. The average one-way delivery for the average plant is less an 100 miles.

THE FUTURE

Acquisition and other forms of consolidations have played an important role in the corrugated industry in recent years; mergers have always been a characteristic of the industry. One of the first sizable mergers in the industry was in 1926 with the formation of Container Corporation of America. This firm was a consolidation of five smaller companies who joined forces to form what one article called, "a big fish in the box pond." In 1986, CCA was acquired by Jefferson Smurfit and Morgan Stanley. An article appearing in the March 1987, issue of *Boxboard Containers* asked the question, "are the big getting too big, the few getting too few?"

Shortly after the acquisition of Southwest Forest Industries, Roger Stone, chairman and chief executive officer of Stone Container, was asked by *Boxboard Containers* if his company had intentions of further major acquisition. Stone's reply: "as always, if things make sense to us and are to our advantage, we will pursue them."

EXHIBIT 7 Stone Container Corporation organizational chart of operating units

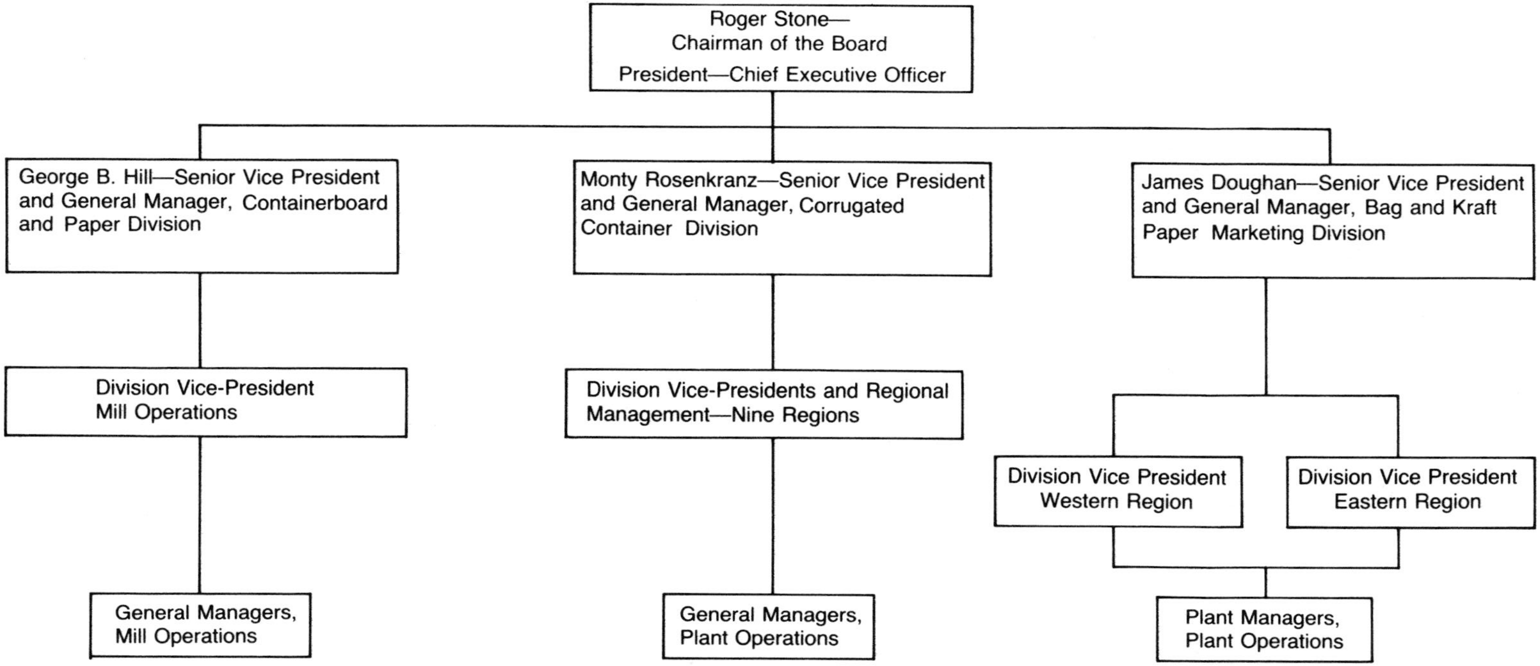

Brenton S. Halsey, CEO of James River Corporation, a company with several major acquisitions in the past few years, says the obvious result of acquisitions for his company has been expanded markets. Halsey said, "We are trying to get bigger shares of the market and create more efficient operations."

Analysts generally agree that the main reason for the increase in consolidation activity in the boxboard industry is the high cost of building new plants, as well as strong demand for U.S.-made paper products.

According to *Boxboard Containers,* an informal poll of several top boxmaking executives and their suppliers showed a general approval of the industry's mergers and consolidations. "Consolidations in the box business are good to the degree that available cash is being spent to buy other facilities instead of building new ones and adding excess capacity," said R. D. Cartledge, CEO of Union Camp Corporation. Roger Stone believes that consolidations give a company a bigger stake in the box business so that boxmaking "is not a sideline to these companies, but a major activity. They are dedicated and committed to it. Therefore, it will create the need for a reasonable return in this business all the time, instead of some of the time."

Bringing the matter into broad perspective is Marvin Pomerantz, chairman, Gaylord Container: "We think there is a precedent for what is going on in the brown-paper segment of the paper industry . . . indeed, the entire paper industry. For a long period of time, these industries have been splintered and have had small market shares. If you review the history of mature industries, you will see they have consolidated, and stronger and fewer have emerged. Essentially, that is what is going on in the paper industry."

Roger Stone said, "This is the most fragmented basic industry in the country, and perhaps in the world, and it certainly makes good sense for companies to consolidate, particularly with the difference between the cost of acquiring capacity via consolidation versus building new capacity and the time lag involved."

While consolidations can certainly be justified for the major players in the industry, what about the hundreds of small independents operating in the country and generally dependent on the majors for their containerboard supplies? Bradley Curry, president, Rock-Tenn Company, said, "On the whole, consolidations tend to be good. The folding carton industry is highly diversified, and there's still plenty of room for independents like us, and for single-unit plants that focus on geographical service or products."

"I don't think there will be a Mead, Georgia-Pacific, or PCA around in the future," said Richard Troll, executive director of AICC. "They may be swallowed up by another, integrated, or merged." It is interesting to note that many in the industry who feel that there will continue to be consolidations do not feel that there will be a problem with antitrust. Mr. Halsey of James River Corporation, said, "the market shares held by any one company, including Stone, are still too small."

Subject Index

Name Index

Company Index

About the Author

Dr. Fred R. David received his B.S. and M.B.A. from Wake Forest University and his Ph.D in Business Administration from the University of South Carolina. Dr. David has written more than seventy articles, cases, and professional papers, including publications in the *Academy of Management Review, Journal of Management Case Studies, Long Range Planning, Managerial Planning, Journal of Small Business Management, Journal of Business Strategies,* and *Journal of Systems Management.* He is active in the Academy of Management and the Southern Management Association.

Dr. David has taught business policy and strategic management for nearly a decade. He is currently an Associate Professor of Management at Auburn University where he teaches business policy at both the undergraduate and graduate levels. He was previously on the management faculties at Mississippi State University, East Carolina University, and the University of North Carolina at Pembroke. He is also a strategy consultant for many businesses and government agencies.